CADOGAN

South Africa
Swaziland & Lesotho

Cadogan Guides
27–29 Berwick Street, London W1V 3RF
guides@cadogan.demon.co.uk

The Globe Pequot Press
6 Business Park Road, PO Box 833, Old Saybrook,
Connecticut 06475–0833

Copyright © Rupert Isaacson 1995, November 1998

Book and cover design by Animage
Cover photographs © South African Tourism Board
Illustrations © Polly Loxton 1995
Wildlife chapter designed by Kicca Tommasi
Maps © Cadogan Guides, drawn by Map Creation Ltd

Series Editor: Rachel Fielding

Editing: Catherine Charles
Updating: Rupert Isaacson and Mark Igoe
Proofreading: Linda McQueen and Vicki Harris
Indexing: Isobel McLean
Production: Book Production Services

A catalogue record for this book is available from the British Library

Printed in Great Britain by Cambridge University Press

The author and publishers have made every effort to ensure the accuracy of the
information in this book at the time of going to press. However, they cannot accept
any responsibility for any loss, injury or inconvenience resulting from the use of
information contained in this guide.

Please Help Us Keep This Guide Up to Date

We have done our best to ensure that the information in this guide is correct at
the time of going to press. But places and facilities are constantly changing, and
standards and prices fluctuate. We would be delighted to receive any comments
concerning existing entries or omissions. Authors of the best letters will receive
a copy of the Cadogan Guide of their choice.

About the Author

Rupert Isaacson is of southern African parentage and has trekked and travelled around South Africa on horseback, hitching and driving. He has also travelled extensively throughout Europe, the USA and Canada, Africa and Eastern Europe as a freelance journalist for wildlife and conservation magazines. He lives in Colorado and is currently writing *The Healing Land*, about the Bushmen and his family in Africa.

The illustrations for this guide have been provided by Rupert's mother, South African-born artist and sculptor Polly Loxton.

About the Updater

Mark Igoe has been researching and writing about travel, history and sport in southern Africa for twenty years, and wrote the first guide book to Zimbabwe. He has also been involved in TV and video production in the region for British and US companies.

Acknowledgments

I cannot thank Aart Bijl enough for lending me the laptop computer and for being so understanding about its theft. Of the many people who helped me on my travels particular thanks go to Wendy Pickstone for renting me the excellent vehicle; to Deborah, Loshini and Billie, Claudine and James for initiating me into Cape Town, and to Bruce for fixing my computer; to the Metelekamps for putting up with me in Knysna; to Nikki and Co. for the 'Maritzburg stay; to the Durban policemen who took me fishing in Kosi Bay; to his excellency Tutor Ndamase for helping me in Transkei as well as Kirk and Ben in Port St. Johns; to Johnny at Semonkong—thanks for the stay and the good horses; also to Rod de Vletter at Phopanyane in Swaziland, and Darron for organizing the stay at Mkhaya; to Russel Suchet at Sani Lodge—a mine of information—and Penny in 'Maritzburg.

Special thanks also to Mark Igoe for his excellent updating, to my publisher, Rachel Fielding, at Cadogan, and to Catherine Charles for her diligent editing. Finally, to my wife, Kristin—for her support.

Contents

Northern Province 575–602

Northwest Province 603–18

Language 619–24

Chronology 625–30

Further Reading 631–37

Index 638–51

Wildlife Index 652–653

Maps

To my parents, Polly and Laurence

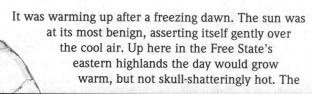

It was warming up after a freezing dawn. The sun was at its most benign, asserting itself gently over the cool air. Up here in the Free State's eastern highlands the day would grow warm, but not skull-shatteringly hot. The

Introduction

night's frost was melting off the grasslands which were slowly turning from summer green to autumn gold—for in South Africa it is the grass that changes colour in autumn, not the leaves of the trees. The road, a thin ribbon of yellow ochre, stretched away to the great flat-topped mountain with the sheer sides, on whose cliffs and ledges lived eagles and baboons.

A group of schoolchildren, tiny against the unbounded landscape, were walking barefoot on the road. Girls in gymslips and neat white shirts, boys in shorts, their thin brown legs dark against the yellow road, walking in a halo of fine golden dust in the fresh and waking morning. As they approached, so too did the sound of their singing. They clapped a rhythm, over which one small girl carried the main, high tune and the others backed her with instinctive harmonies. Singing like adults. You could get drunk on this highveld air, pure as spring water, cleansing the brain. The singing was the morning's only sound.

South Africa is known to most Westerners only through clichés of fear and disgust, the legacy of 20 years' media coverage of the worst aspects of white rule, officially known as apartheid. Brutality, violence, the injustice of white privilege and black suffering—all these were true, but were only a part of the story.

The wide emptinesses of its impossibly beautiful landscapes, the gaiety of day-to-day life, the deep forest hush and the chattering of colourful birds, the twitching, fidgeting herds of antelope forever on the watch for predators, the peace of the empty coasts—these were also true, and remain so.

Few travellers are prepared for the country's immense diversity. There is a dramatic sense of scale—those mountains over there go on for hundreds of kilometres, not mere scores. That man walking by the side of the road may be walking for two days to reach his destination.

Climates range from sub-alpine to sub-tropical, from desert to year-round rainfall. The flora, which incorporates the Cape Floral Kingdom—one of only six such zones on the planet—has over 5000 plant species found nowhere else in the world. Mammals include lion, leopard, elephant, buffalo, both kinds of African rhino, zebra, giraffe, wildebeest, and antelope as big as a horse or as tiny as a small dog. Several hundred species of bird, including some of the world's most spectacular raptors, inhabit the forests and plains, and the catalogue of reptiles and invertebrates has still not been fully documented.

There is indigenous architecture, from graceful 18th-century Cape Dutch mansions to traditional rondavels, and even houses built from tin cans or Coke bottles in the squatter camps on the outskirts of the cities. As a clue to the complexity of South Africa's human mosaic, the country has eight official languages, and local culture embraces the strong rural traditions of spirit diviners and traditional healers as well as the high-tech computerized world of Johannesburg business. In short, South Africa is a place of exceptional human and natural energy.

To travel here is to step continually from one world into another. Yet there is nothing frenetic or traumatic about this, even though the transitions in landscape and human or animal life can be startlingly abrupt. Underlying the country's well-documented strife and conflicts there is a slower pace, a greater appreciation of natural beauty and community life, than the endless pictures of violence shown in the Western media would suggest.

This may seem paradoxical, but that is just the point: South Africa is a place where the paradox is king, where conflict can exist side-by-side with a deep, almost hedonistic languor, or, more importantly, where the medieval oppression of a police state can produce an emergent enlightened democracy in the face of overwhelming odds to the contrary.

Yet despite its surface Westernization, South Africa is still deeply rural, with vast stretches of wild country that have barely changed in a millennium. To savour the place, the traveller must change down a gear or two and move more slowly, notice the smell of earth, dung and wood smoke, enjoy the transition from subtle morning to hard midday and to soft evening light, not get fussed by cattle on the highway, sit and wait in the wild places for the game to come down to drink. For this is Africa, and it will not be rushed.

Landscapes

Once, when asking directions from a Free State farmer, I asked, 'Is the route beautiful?' He looked at me, shrugged, and said 'The whole place is beautiful. Have you seen any ugly land since you came here?'

South Africa is a land of intense physical beauty; one of the few things that all South Africans have in common is a shared love for the silence, winds and endless wide spaces of their country. Space and room to breathe: in the red and black, blasted hills and semi-desert

plains; in the wide, green farmland valleys; in the high splendour of its ancient mountains, whose peaks, long since levelled to flat plateaux, rise vast and aloof, to hang suspended in mid-sky; in the dense, cathedral forests; in the singing, sub-tropical thickets of the bushveld; in the smooth golden grasslands of the highveld plateaux; in the endless beaches of white sand—space, and colours sharpened by the intense southern sun, the whole landscape radiating a presence born of heat and harsh light. Ancient and independent of man, even in the stillest midday hour South Africa's landscape feels deeply alive: raw, remote and beyond understanding.

Mountains

In the Cedarberg we climbed to a great cliff whose face was split with fissures that widened to smooth corridors, and gave on to a circle of level grass encircled by a rampart of savagely eroded rock through which the wind whistled and sang like flutes. In the greener heights of the Hottentots' Holland, we spent the night cowering in our tent as a male baboon descended from the wooded kloof above and challenged our scent with barks and shouts.

On horseback in the high Malutis of Lesotho, our pack mule bolted down a mountainside so steep that he seemed certain to tumble into the river gorge below. Yet with a skip and a buck he dumped our provisions on the brink and cantered back up to us, arching his neck and snorting to show how clever he was. In the Bankberg of the eastern Karoo we sheltered in a cave as the heavens opened and rain that had been two years in coming transformed the dry mountains into giant, sodden mud-slides. Intent on shelter, a family of mountain zebras skittered by, their thick black stripe doubled now with stripes of running water.

Semi-Deserts

Our first night in the Karoo, awed to silence by the level plain whose distant hills turned blue and mauve and disappeared into a night of stars so bright and close and numberless that you imagined they were singing. Next day, in the fearsome heat of Christmas Eve, we panted in the shade of thorn trees and traced patterns with a stick around the paw-print of a lynx impressed in sand too hot to touch, the air drowsing to the cooing of doves.

Coasts

Night-time with the moon at Cape Columbine, the dry veld inland awash with spring flowers. The rough Atlantic exploded on to the rocks where we sat swaying with tequila sipped from limpet shells and glimpsed the silvered backs of playing seals breaking surface to greet the moon. Further north, with the moon waxing, we walked a wild beach and came upon a young seal beached and heaving with exhaustion; through the long night we sat with it until we realized that it should be left to die alone with the proper, secret dignity of a wild thing.

At Noordehoek in the icy, sapphire waters, a mother whale and calf rolled, lazy, in the swell just off the beach, and a lone male splashed his enormous tail far out in the bay. On a moonless night as black as pitch, we cast the round, weighted net into the warm Keiskamma estuary and filled the buckets with writhing prawns. Again by night, on the Wild Coast, walking a forest path above the sighing breakers, we were halted by a delicate scent as pretty as a song—a creeper covered in secret night-flowers, white like ghosts that open only when the last rays have fully gone and await the great grey moths that come to take their pollen.

On the wide lagoon at Kosi Bay the silver milkfish took the line and made its run for the open sea, bending the rod double, sending the reel into rattling hysterics and causing the fisherman to leap from the boat into the waist-deep shallows, heedless of the crocodiles and his sarong, which dropped from his body and left him bare to the sunlight, water and the laughter of his friends.

Forests

In the Outeniquas, a woodland green as England under an un-African drizzle— except that the trees soar to a canopy too high for anything but the vervet monkeys that occasionally distract the eye with branches left swinging, dropped twigs and leaping, shadowed forms. Rustlings and crashings in the thickets as animals escape the eye; giant ferns, twice as high as you, create a forest within a forest; above all there is a great calm disturbed only by the knowledge that, somewhere in the woods, elephant are walking, perhaps watching you now.

Atop the Soutpansberg, another drizzle falls on tall, sub-tropical trees that disappear halfway down the mountain, revealing brown bushveld hundreds of metres below, where rain will not fall for another six months; on the sodden forest floor, porcupine quills wet with blood mark a leopard's lost night-time battle; across the track flies a blurred arrow of russet, as a red duiker—shy forest antelope—crosses quicker then the eye can follow.

In the dense, impenetrable sand forests of Tsongaland, lithe spotted cattle and their herd-boys follow elephant tracks to hidden clearings whose pasture they share with the forests' great beasts. At Hogsback, above the tree-line, we stumble on a herd of aggressive, half-wild cattle by night and have to creep beneath a huge bramble bush, shivering at the thought of giant spiders down the back, as the great horns swish and we quiver, half terrified, half embarrassed until they move on and only the owls remain.

Bushveld

In the dry and golden morning an impala ewe stepped from cover on to the warm dirt road. Such a common sight, an impala, but so beautiful that you must stop and wonder how so elegantly perfect a form should be no more than protein for half the predators of Africa. Another morning, after sleep disturbed by the distant sound of lions—their heaving cough waking us immediately, a primeval memory of danger as clear as yesterday, jutting rudely into our modern psyche, despite the millennia since our ancestors worried about such things as lions—another morning, but this time the yellow bushveld grasses wet with dew and the thorn trees hung with summer green. An incessant chatter of birds, who swing and flit between the thorns in little darts of colour. A hundred yards in front of the tent stands the massive bulk of a rhino, who only snorts and carries on feeding when we get up and light the fire for coffee.

Kalahari

No surface water for hundreds of miles, yet reserves of water below the ground give life to the great camel-thorn trees and shimmering grasses that march between the miles of blood-red dunes. Atop one, using the sandy rim as shade, sprawl a pair of lions, lazy with daylight, drowsing away the hours of heat until night-time and the hunt. Knowing this, the antelope—dainty, liquid-eyed springbok on fragile legs, and great, sturdy gemsbok with horns like lances—stand quietly about, despite the proximity of their persecutors. Taking their cue, we stop around a sand-dune corner from the lions, switch off the engine and listen to the silence. Despite the life around us, nothing stirs. Below the road is a dry river-bed. Breaking all the safety rules, we leave the car and cross the fossil river into Botswana, tense with knowing that the great cats are close, and dance a silent polka under the wide and sunlit heavens.

Guide to the Guide

Since the democratic elections of April 1994, South Africa's regional boundaries have been redrawn, erasing both the arbitrary land-partitioning of the colonial surveyors, and the racial boundaries laid out by apartheid—in particular the artificial 'tribal homelands', which no longer exist.

The chapter headings of this guide follow the new provinces, beginning in Cape Town, at the southwest corner of the lush Western Cape Province, heading north to the vast, arid Northern Cape Province, east to the mountainous Eastern Cape Province and KwaZulu-Natal, then up to the highveld of the Free State (whose boundaries have not changed), on to the independent countries of Lesotho and Swaziland and finally into the recently partitioned provinces of the old Transvaal—Gauteng (PWV: Johannesburg, Pretoria and surrounds), the game-rich bushveld and mountain country of Mpumalanga and Northern Province, and the dry expanse of the Northwest Province.

Within the chapters, the guide follows the more traditional regional names by which South Africans know their country: for example, the Western Cape is divided into Cape Town and Peninsula, the Winelands, Overberg, West Coast, and Garden Route/Little Karoo. Similarly, the Northern Cape is divided into the Great Karoo, Namaqualand, Bushmanland and West Griqualand, and within KwaZulu-Natal the areas are still referred to as Natal and Zululand. The Transvaal has been kept as a historical or cultural reference to the old Transvaal, particularly when the area referred to over-runs the new provincial boundaries.

Travel

By Air

Most visitors travel to South Africa by air, and international connections are excellent. **Direct flights** from London are traditionally the cheapest (there are approximately 40 flights a week), but the choice now is so great that it pays to shop around—and seasonal offers are always worth looking for. Bucket-shop deals are certainly the cheapest way to go, as long as you do not mind the inevitable restrictions that apply to such deals. London reputedly has the best-value bucket-shop tickets. **Flight times** from the UK are between 12 and 13 hours, and from the USA about 14 hours.

Some good deals, especially returning, can be had by flying via other African destinations such as Harare, Windhoek or Lusaka. Prices vary dramatically with seasonal and currency changes. At the time of writing, an open economy fare between London and Jo'burg can cost between £400 (US$630) and £1200 (US$1870), with dozens of options in between.

From the UK

main carriers

British Airways, ✆ (0345) 222 747, from Gatwick to Jo'burg, Cape Town, and Durban.

Virgin Atlantic Airways, ✆ (01293) 562 345, from Heathrow to Jo'burg, and onward connections through Sun Air.

South African Airways (SAA), ✆ (0171) 312 5000, from Heathrow to Jo'burg, Cape Town and Durban.

charter flights

Scour the pages of *Time Out* and *TNT* magazine for the latest deals. Try **Trailfinders**, ✆ (0171) 938 3366, or ✆ (0171) 938 3939, and **STA**, ✆ (0171) 361 6161 (and other branches). Caledonian, Monarch and Britannia are the main UK operators that they use.

From Mainland Europe

SAA fly from Amsterdam, Frankfurt, Paris and Zurich several times a week, as do the national airlines:

Amsterdam: SAA, ✆ (20) 604 1457, **KLM**, ✆ (20) 474 7747.

Frankfurt: SAA, ✆ (69) 6902 2531, **Lufthansa**, ✆ (69) 255 255.

Paris: SAA, ✆ (01) 42 61 57 87, **Air France**, ✆ (01) 43 17 22 00.

Zurich: SAA, ✆ (01) 215 1111, **Swiss Air**, ✆ (01) 812 1212.

From the USA

American Airlines fly to Jo'burg out of New York's JFK airport 7 times a week, and out of Miami 5 times a week (the service is operated by SAA):

American Airlines, USA, ✆ (800) 433 7300; UK, ✆ (0345) 789 789.

From Australia and New Zealand

SAA and Qantas fly from Sydney (7 flights a week) and Perth (4 flights a week) to Jo'burg. The current open-return economy fare between Sydney and Jo'burg is between Aus$2000 and Aus$3200.

SAA, ✆ (02) 9223 4402 (Sydney), ✆ (09) 309 9132 (Auckland).

Qantas, ✆ (02) 957 0111 (Sydney), ✆ (034511) 747 767 (UK).

transport to and from the airports

South Africa's three international airports, Johannesburg, Cape Town and Durban all run half-hourly bus services to and from their respective city centres. Services run from 5am until 10pm. Taxis can be picked up from the drop-off points.

By Road

A more interesting way to go, however, for those with the money and the time, is by over-land truck across Africa, or with a self-drive safari from southern Africa.

Encounter Overland, ✆ (0171) 370 6951, *adventure@encounter.co.uk* organizes truck journeys from London down through the Western Sahara, through west and east Africa and finally to Cape Town over about 26 weeks at a cost of about £4500. Alternatively, you can fly to Nairobi in Kenya and travel by truck to Cape Town over 10 weeks at a cost of about £2300.

Truck Africa, ✆ (0171) 731 6142, *truckafrica@zambezi1.demon.co.uk* offer a cheaper deal—a 5–7-month trip down through Africa (via Kenya and Zimbabwe) to Cape Town from £2500.

Economic Expeditions, ✆ (0181) 995 7707, *ecoexped@mcmail.com* offer a 22-week London–Nairobi trip for £1280 which can connect with a Nairobi–Jo'burg one at £380.

Safari Drive, ✆ (01488) 681 611, *Safari_Drive@compuserve.com* will hire out fully equipped 4x4 vehicles from the neighbouring countries of South Africa (bases at Victoria Falls in Zimbabwe, Maun in Botswana and Windhoek in Namibia) at a cost of about £410 per person per week. These vehicles may be taken into South Africa which means that you can travel by the most remote, wild routes away from main roads. This highly experienced company will set out an itinerary, provide a driver, book accommodation or make any other arrangements, just as you wish.

Entry Formalities

Travellers from most western countries (e.g. the EU, USA, Switzerland, Japan, etc.) do not require **visas** to enter South Africa for holiday or business travel. Most other countries are subject to various time restrictions, so if in doubt check with a South African diplomatic mission (UK, ✆ (0171) 930 4488). Visas can be obtained free-of-charge from a South African embassy or high commission. Allow several weeks for it to process. Do not try to obtain a visa upon arrival as you will become involved in a long wrangle and may be turned back. (The South African bureaucracy is fearsome and not to be trifled with.)

You need a valid **passport** for travelling within South Africa, partly for ID, partly because you need to produce a passport to enter Lesotho and Swaziland.

South Africa's **customs** allowance is 400 cigarettes, 250g of tobacco and 50 cigars per person. You may bring in 1 litre of spirits, 2 litres of wine, 50ml of perfume and 250ml of *eau de toilette*. This is meagre, but prices for booze and smokes in South Africa are so low, and the quality so good, that there is no need to import. An airport arrival tax of R61 is charged if coming long haul (R40 for regional and R19 for domestic flights), although this is usually included in the price of the ticket.

Self-catering and Special-interest Holidays

In the UK

Cazenove & Lloyd Safaris, 3 Alice Court, 116 Putney Bridge Road, London SW15 2NQ, ✆ (0181) 875 9666, ✉ (0181) 875 9444, *c&l@cazloyd.demon.co.uk* offer tailor-made trips (guided or self-drive) featuring anything from flowers to wine, wildlife to Cape cuisine, usually for small groups.

Guerba Expeditions, Wessex House, 40 Station Road, Westbury, Wilts BA13 3JN, ✆ (01373) 826 611, ✉ (01373) 858 351, *info@guerba.demon.co.uk* organize tours by truck and minibus with hotel accommodation or camping, including trips which continue into Zimbabwe and Namibia.

Naturetrek, The Cadcam Centre, Bighton, Alresford, Hants SO24 9RE, ✆ (01962) 733 051, ✉ (01962) 736 426, *sales@naturetrek.co.uk* offer bird-watching, botany and general wildlife tours for groups of 6–16 people.

Temple World, 13 The Avenue, Kew, Richmond, Surrey TW9 2AL, ✆ (0181) 940 4114, ✉ (0181) 332 2456, *safari@templeworld.demon.co.uk* offer a variety of holidays which include game-viewing, the Cape Floral Kingdom in August, and tours of Zulu war sites and Early Man sites.

Worldwide Journeys and Expeditions, 8 Comeragh Road, London W14 9HP, ✆ (0171) 381 8638, ✉ (0171) 381 0836, *wwj@wjournex.demon.co.uk* organize tailor-made fly-drive holidays for independent travellers on any budget, staying in B&Bs, guest houses and private game reserves.

In the USA

New Horizons Safari Specialists, P.O. Box 5700, Glendale Heights, IL 60139-5700, ✆ (630) 893 2545, ✉ (630) 529 9769, *www.africa-nh.com* arrange trips with a strong emphasis on education, studying flora and fauna, and history and culture.

Park East Tours, 1841 Broadway, New York, NY 100223, ✆ (212) 765 4870, or ✆ (800) 223 6078 (toll free), *www.parkeast.com* offer eco-friendly, tailor-made itineraries.

Rothschild Travel Consultants, 900 West End Avenue, New York, NY 10025, ✆ (212) 865 3772, ✉ (212) 749 6172, *www.divesafaris.com* specialize in scuba-diving, shark-diving and safaris for all budgets.

Safari Consultants, 1253 Paddock Court, Aurora, IL 60504, ✆ (630) 761 2991, or ✆ (800) 762 4027, (toll free), *safcon@ix.netcom.com* is a small company run by Bonnie Fogg, who organizes custom-designed holidays for independent travellers or groups whatever the budget.

Getting Around

Travelling with an organized tour takes care of the hassle of organizing flights and accommodation. The only problem is that you are also organized during your stay in South Africa—this is both frustrating and unnecessary—the country is suited to independent travel and, unless you are on a special interest tour, it is more rewarding to float around freely.

By Air
internal flights

Flying within South Africa is expensive and rather defeats the object of going—to see the country. However, if you are in a hurry, the internal air service is very good. Travellers intending to fly internally can buy an African Explorer ticket which offers discounts of between 6% and 30% for travellers originating outside the country. These can be booked from the UK by calling SAA, ✆ (0171) 312 5001. Other internal airlines are SA Airlink and SA Express (part of SAA), Comair (associated with British Airways), Metavia Airways and Nationwide (associated with Sabena).

Internal Flight Routes

Johannesburg–	Bloemfontein–	Cape Town–	Durban–	East London–
Bloemfontein	Cape Town	Alexander Bay	Cape Town	Bloemfontein
Cape Town	Durban	Bloemfontein	East London	Cape Town
Durban	East London	Durban	George	Durban
East London	George	East London	Jo'burg	George
George	Jo'burg	George	Nelspruit	Jo'burg
Hoedspruit	Kimberley	Kimberley	Port Elizabeth	Port Elizabeth
Kimberley	Port Elizabeth	Jo'burg	Richard's Bay	Umtata
Mmbabatho	Upington	Kleinzee	Umtata	
Nelspruit		Port Elizabeth		
Phalaborwa		Springbok		**Port Elizabeth–**
Pietermaritzburg		Upington		Bloemfontein
Pietersburg		Walvis Bay		Cape Town
Port Elizabeth				Durban
Richard's Bay				East London
Skukuza (Kruger)				George
Sun City				Jo'burg
Tzaneen				Umtata
Umtata				
Upington				

For more information call the airports direct:

Port Elizabeth Airport, ✆ (041) 507 7319.

East London Airport, ✆ (0431) 46 1400.

Cape Town International Airport, ✆ (021) 934 0407.

Johannesburg International Airport (domestic), ✆ (011) 921 6668/91 111; **Lanseria Domestic Airport,** ✆ (011) 659 2750.

Durban International Airport, ✆ (031) 426 145.

Bloemfontein Airport, ✆ (051) 33 2901.

By Car

Travelling by car is by far the best way to get around South Africa, which has always been geared towards the independent traveller—whether travelling by ox-wagon, horse or cart. Car hire is comparatively cheap if you avoid the main companies and seek out local companies, including **Europcar,** ✆ (021) 439 9696, and **Budget,** ✆ (011) 392 3900, which are listed in the individual 'Getting Around' sections of this guide. In Jo'burg, Cape Town or Durban, the following companies offer the cheapest deal:

Johannesburg

U-Drive, ✆ (011) 392 5852, **Tempest,** ✆ (011) 402 7100, or the slightly more expensive **Imperial,** ✆ (0800) 2131 000, after hours ✆ (0800) 118 898.

Cape Town

Peninsula Car Hire, ✆ (021) 591 0155, or **Adelphi,** ✆ (021) 439 6144.

Durban

Forest Drive Rent-a-Car, ✆ (031) 562 8433 (✆ (031) 423 547 after hours), **Windemere,** ✆ (031) 230 339, or **Maharani Car Hire,** ✆ (031) 370 211.

By Train

South Africa's railways are not what they once were. Many of the smaller regional tracks have been closed or converted to goods services only. However, the mainline routes are still efficient and good value; first and second class carriages have fold-down bunks and third class is strictly no frills.

Spoornet is the official name for South Africa's railways. The passenger services central information line is ✆ (011) 773 2944.

steam trains

Union Line, ✆ (011) 773 9238, offer a number of routes through different areas of the country, taking up to 2 weeks and making side trips into Zimbabwe and Namibia.

Outeniqua Tchoe-Choo, ✆ (0441) 738 202, runs in the Garden Route.

Neerail Line, ✆ (0551) 41 362, runs in the Eastern Cape Drakensberg.

Shamwari Express, ✆ (041) 31 1127, runs from Pretoria to Shamwari Game Reserve.

Banana Express, ✆ (03931) 76 443/22 322, runs in Southern Natal.

Umgeni Steam Train, ✆ (031) 764 5313, runs once a month from Durban to Botha's Hill.

Magaliesberg Express, ✆ (011) 888 1154, runs once a month from Johannesburg to Magaliesberg.

Ostrich Express, ✆ (0443) 223 540, runs at weekends between Oudtshoorn and Calitzdorp.

Midmar Steam Railway, ✆ (0332) 305 390, runs at weekends between Pietermaritzburg and Midmar Historic Village near Howick.

The luxury **Blue Train**, ✆ (011) 773 9194, runs from Cape Town to Jo'burg/Pretoria, and offers 5-star VIP trips (including to the Victoria Falls) for those who can afford it.

Rovos/Pride of Africa, ✆ (012) 323 6052/3/4, runs from Pretoria to Cape Town and Mpumalanga, right up to Dar-es-Salaam in Tanzania, as well as offering VIP trips.

For further information on these lines, *see* the 'Activities' sections of the relevant chapters.

A Note About Rail Fares

Train travel is more expensive than bus. At the time of writing a first class return fare Jo'burg–Cape Town costs approximately R340 per person and a second-class return approximately R230 per person. A couple sharing a two-person compartment (known as a coupe) for the same return fare cost R596 first class, proving to be the best value fare. Tourists get a 25% discount on first class fares. A Jo'burg–Durban return ticket costs approximately R283 per person first class, R279 return second class, and again the best value deal was a two-person coupe (for couples only) which cost R164 per person. The coupe deal applies to all long-distance journeys.

Train Timetable

Destination	Frequency	Journey Time (hrs/mins)	Service
Johannesburg–Cape Town	Daily	26:15	**Trans Karoo** express
Cape Town–Johannesburg	Daily	23:10	
Johannesburg–Durban	Daily	13:30	**Trans-Natal** express
Durban–Johannesburg	Daily	13:14	
Cape Town–Durban	Mon	36.25	**Trans-Orange** express
Durban–Cape Town	Thurs	36:45	
Johannesburg–East London	Daily	20:45	**Amatola** express
East London–Johannesburg	Daily	21:00	
Johannesburg–Port Elizabeth	Tues/Thurs/Sun	20:25	**Algoa** express
Port Elizabeth–Johannesburg	Mon/Wed/Fri	20:30	
Johannesburg–Mossel Bay	Thurs	27:41	
Mossel Bay–Johannesburg	Sat	26:53	
Johannesburg–Komatipoort	Daily	12:29	**Komati** express
Komatipoort–Johannesburg	Daily	12:09	
Kimberley–Pretoria	Daily exc Sat	11:24	
Pretoria–Kimberley	Daily exc Sat	11:25	
Johannesburg–Bulawayo	Tues	24:50	
Bulawayo–Johannesburg	Thurs	24:05	

There is also the daily Marula Express which runs between Jo'burg and Louis Trichardt (and back) via Potgietersrus and Pietersburg.

By Bus

Buses are by far the most efficient means of affordable public transport in South Africa. But remember: *always book your ticket 24 hours in advance*. The bus companies insist on this, and jumping on at the last minute, or buying a ticket on the day, is, irritatingly, not allowed. Listed below are the main national services and their operators. Local office and telephone numbers are listed in this guide with the bus stations in the main cities.

There are six main bus companies offering a long distance service between all major South African towns and points in between. These range from the relatively luxurious **Trans-Lux**, **Greyhound** and **InterCape Mainliner & Trans Zambezi** companies, to the more basic, but cheaper, **Transtate**. All have offices in the bus stations of South Africa's cities (except for Transtate, *see* below). Central information numbers are listed here. Another large bus company runs between the Western and Eastern Cape and KwaZulu-Natal, **Garden Route InterCity** (*see* below).

Transtate, Jo'burg, ✆ (011) 774 7449, Cape Town, ✆ (021) 405 2582, Durban, ✆ (031) 361 7789, Bloemfontein, ✆ (051) 408 2262, and Port Elizabeth, ✆ (041) 552 585, operates the densest and cheapest network of bus services. You may safely assume that most small regional towns may be reached by Transtate.

The company used to be for blacks only, and because of black reliance on public transport offers a more comprehensive service than the other bus companies, running services into the former 'homelands', and into Lesotho and Swaziland as well as into the more remote areas of South Africa.

Be aware that for this reason, in most big towns, Transtate bus stops are usually at a slightly different location from the main bus stations, but you can get directions for the Transtate bus stops from the main bus stations.

InterCape Mainliner, Cape Town, ✆ (021) 386 4400, Gauteng, ✆ (012) 654 4114, Bloemfontein, ✆ (051) 447 1448, and Port Elizabeth, ✆ (041) 586 0055, links the main towns of the Western, Northern and Eastern Cape with those of the Free State and Northern and Northwest Provinces, Mpumalanga and Durban. Services also run between Cape Town and Windhoek in Namibia.

Greyhound, ✆ (011) 830 1301, links the country's cities (Cape Town, Port Elizabeth, Grahamstown, East London, Durban, Pietermaritzburg, Bloemfontein, Kimberley, Upington, Jo'burg and Pretoria) along the main highways, with stops at main towns in between.

TransLux, ✆ (011) 774 333, is part of the same company as Transtate, but is, as the name suggests more luxurious, and runs only between the main cities. Services are also provided up to Harare in Zimbabwe and Windhoek in Namibia.

Garden Route Intercity, ✆ (0441) 707 993, links Cape Town and Port Elizabeth via the N2 with stops at all large towns along the route.

The Baz Bus, ✆ (021) 439 2323, is a new bus service for the budget traveller, providing cheap door-to-door transport between the backpacker hostels of Cape Town, the Garden Route, Eastern Cape, Natal, Swaziland and Jo'burg. At the time of writing a sample fare Cape Town–Durban would be R495.

By Black Taxi

Black taxis (which are not black) are minibuses that ply within towns and on long-haul journeys. Almost every town in the country, no matter how small, can be reached by black taxi, and they are cheaper (and sometimes faster) than buses.

However, there are three potential problems in using this mode of transport: a high accident rate, mugging at the taxi ranks in towns (and where they stop in townships) and over-crowding. It would be irresponsible for this guide to recommend that anyone travel by black taxi except on well-known routes within towns. Female travellers using them for long-haul journeys may well get into trouble. They are for the adventurous only. If you want to be assured of safety, leave them alone.

For those who do want to travel by black taxi, within towns they ply the municipal bus routes (i.e. along the main roads, stopping at bus stops), while each town has a taxi rank from which long-haul journeys leave. Ask at the local publicity association for directions. If you are determined to travel long distance, it is better to take a bus or train out of the city first, so as to avoid the first leg of the journey through the townships. The same goes for arriving in a city—better to get off at an outlying town and catch a train or bus in. At the time of writing fares were roughly R10 per 100km.

Hitch-hiking

Hitch-hiking is also risky, but many travellers do it. As with black taxis, it is better to get beyond the township zone if hitching out of cities. On main routes lifts can be a long time coming, as people drive fast and, on the whole, have become a little scared of hitchers. Display your backpack and always carry a sign and you should get a lift eventually.

In between small towns, your chances of getting lifts are much higher, especially from local farm traffic. The only problem is that this traffic *is* local, so travelling a long distance can only be done in fits and starts. However, for getting from small towns into nature reserves and state forests, hitching can be the best way to go, if you have no transport.

A way around having to hitch for local lifts is to visit the local Publicity Association. Especially in the smaller towns, the people working there will tend to know many farmers, game rangers, foresters and other such useful people in the region. It is always worth asking if a lift can be arranged, even if you have to wait a little. South Africans are generally friendly and happy to help, and such requests usually meet with a sympathetic response.

Tour Groups

For those who cannot afford a car, getting into game reserves and remote areas can be a problem, as even the Transtate buses and black taxis limit you to towns. A way round this is to book a trip through a tour group. For game reserves this will mean sitting in the vehicle and being driven around by the guide, which can be annoying, but better than not going in at all. However, many tour groups offer packages for guided hiking, riding, canoeing and other activities that get you out into the bush, and generally involve seeing game—in some places even big game (*see* **Practical A–Z**, 'Sports and Activities', p.26, and the 'Getting Around' and 'Activities' sections of the regional chapters).

Any company listed with a major town phone number will organize your transport into and out of the area you wish to visit, while companies listed with local numbers require you to reach them independently. If you ask for a pick-up from the nearest town reachable by public transport, they are often happy to oblige.

Practical A–Z

Beaches

South Africa has thousands of kilometres of coastline, most of which meet the sea in long, sandy beaches. Those on the West Coast have cold water, from the South Atlantic's Benguela Current which drifts up from the Antarctic. Those on the south and east coasts front the warm Indian Ocean, whose sub-tropical Aghulas Current supports a brightly coloured universe of marine life. In winter (April–Sept), the West Coast beaches and the Indian Ocean beaches near Cape Town are too cold for swimming, but during the blistering summer months they provide blessed relief from the heat. From the Eastern Cape up to northern Natal, the beaches are warm enough for swimming all year.

Choosing where to go can be a problem—some stretches of coastline have been heavily developed, others have hardly been touched since the first Europeans sailed by in the late 15th century. Here is a pick of where to go and where to avoid.

Undeveloped coastline with good swimming and vehicle access can be found at: the West Coast, especially in the West Coast National Park and Eland's Bay; Smitswinkelbaai, Noordehoek, Rooi Els and Gordon's Bay near Cape Town; Arniston, De Mond and De Hoop in the Overberg; Buffalo Bay, Nature's Valley and Oyster Bay in the Garden Route; Kenton-on-Sea, Kariega and Morgan's Bay in the Eastern Cape; Hamburg in the former Ciskei; the Wild Coast in the Western Cape (former Transkei); and Umlalazi, St Lucia, Sodwana Bay and Kosi Bay in Natal. Avoid the developed resort beaches of Port Elizabeth, East London and the KwaZulu-Natal coast from Port Edward up to Stanger. For slightly developed but still unspoilt beaches try: Camp's Bay and Boulders near Cape Town; Hermanus and Arniston in the Overberg; Still bay, Wilderness and Plettenberg Bay in the Garden Route; Port Alfred and Kidd's Beach in the Eastern Cape; Port St John's in former Transkei; and Sheffield Beach, Ginigindlovu and Mtunzini in KwaZulu-Natal.

Any developed beach will have public toilets, usually a shower, and places to eat and drink. A few in the undeveloped category will have facilities nearby, but on the whole you should bring your own supplies. Hazards when swimming away from main resorts are bad currents and sometimes sharks. Currents are worst on the West Coast and there are sharks in the Indian Ocean. These only become a danger if you swim far out, although there have been recent attacks on swimmers. Avoid swimming near river-mouths when the tide is changing.

For fishing, diving, windsurfing and other watersports, see under 'Sports' below.

Cafés That Aren't

An irritating aspect of travelling in South Africa is the apparent profusion of cafés in small towns. After a long, hot journey your eye will continually be caught by the word 'CAFE' printed in large letters on the side of a building, and you will think 'Ah yes, just what I need'. But a café in South Africa is almost never a café—it is a small supermarket or general store where you can get anything but a cup of coffee and a bite to eat (unless you buy instant coffee and a loaf of bread). Equally confusing and frustrating is being directed to a 'café' when you want to buy groceries.

One word of warning, however; in smart Cape Town and Johannesburg shopping malls a café *does* mean somewhere to sit down and have a cup of coffee. So do not go to these places to buy groceries.

South Africa has nearly 300 shows, festival exhibitions and sports meetings yearly, ranging from the Mushroom Festival in Gauteng in September to the International Pretoria Show in August. Here is a selection.

The Cape Minstrel Carnival better known as the **Coon Carnival**: Despite its politically incorrect alias, this New Year's parade of music and street partying is staged by Cape Town's 'coloureds' for themselves, and can be riotous fun. The floats start from the Gardens area and end up at Green Point stadium. Contact Mr Hendicks, ✆ (021) 397 6429, for more details.

The Standard Bank National Arts Festival, otherwise the **Grahamstown Festival**: South Africa's answer to the Edinburgh Festival—theatre, art, cabaret, performance art and music and a festively cultured atmosphere for two weeks every July at Grahamstown in the Eastern Cape. Contact the Grahamstown Foundation, ✆ (0461) 2 7115, for this year's dates.

Ncwala Festival and Umhlanga Dance: The Ncwala is Swaziland's sacred festival to the harvest and the monarchy—a moveable feast which usually occurs at the end of December or beginning of January. The Umhlanga is the annual dance of the Swazi unmarried maidens which takes place every August/September. (*See* also 'Swazi Culture', p.483). Contact Swaziland Tourism for details, ✆ (09268) 42531.

Manzini Trade Fair: Also in Swaziland, an agricultural fair held every August/September and worth visiting for the exhilarating *sibhaca* team dancing (*see* 'Swazi Culture').

Domba Dance: The dance in honour of the Python God held every year between September and December in the Venda country of the Northern Province (*see* 'Venda Culture' p.596). Contact Venda Tourism, ✆ (0159) 41577 for details.

Mampoer Festival: A great event in the Boer culture of the Northwest Province—celebrating the devastating home-made peach brandy made by the local farmers. Expect some serious drunkenness and bonhomie. Held in the town of Zeerust in the Northwest Province near the border with Bostwana. Contact William Prinsloo Agricultural Museum for this year's dates, ✆ (01213) 44171.

Splashy Fen and Rustler's Valley Music Festivals: These two Woodstockian events held every April/May provide a showcase for the best of South Africa's incredibly diverse musical talent, ranging from township jive to hard rock, and all points in between. Splashy Fen is held on a farm just outside Underberg in the Natal Midlands, near the Drakensberg foothills. Rustler's Valley is held at the Rustler's Valley farm in the Witteberg mountains in the eastern highlands of the Free State. Both locations are stunningly beautiful. Ring Bart (Splashy Fen), ✆ (031) 23 9812, and Frik (Rustlers Valley), ✆ (05193) 33939, for exact dates.

Stellenbosch combined Spring Festival, better known as the **Wine Festival**: Famous booze-up for the Cape's smart society, Stellenbosch's students and serious connoisseurs, held every October/November in the elegant Winelands town of Stellenbosch. Contact Stellenbosch Tourism and Information for this year's dates, ✆ (021) 883 3584, *eikestad@iafrica.com*

Roughly speaking, South Africa can be divided into two climatic zones—of winter rains (from the Garden Route west to the Atlantic) and of summer rains (from the Garden Route east). In general, the countryside everywhere is at its prettiest and the climate at its most temperate just after the wet season. In the west this will be from September to December, and in the east from March to June. Highlights of the post-rainy season in the west are the coastal and desert wildflowers of the West Coast and Namaqualand, and the fynbos flowers of the mountain heaths. In the east after the rains, the Mpumalanga lowveld and Zululand game reserves are full of animals with their young.

Winters in the west can be cold. Around Cape Town, you will need a jacket and jumper during the day, although in the Great Karoo a T-shirt is sufficient. However both areas experience bitter nights, and snowfalls are not uncommon on the highest ground. Winters in the east are much milder, and characterized more by dryness than by cold. Here the coasts are still warm enough for swimming. The exception to this is the highveld, where winter days can be chilly and nights frosty. Again, mountains are colder with snow on the highest tops.

Summers everywhere are baking—dry in the west and on the highveld, but progressively more humid through the Eastern Cape, lowland KwaZulu-Natal and the Mpumalanga lowveld. Avoid Durban, Zululand and the Mpumalanga in high summer. If hiking, riding or trekking in any region through the summer, remember always to wear a hat and to carry at least two litres of water per person. Mean temperatures are listed in the table below, but remember this is only an average—heatwaves can send temperature soaring way above what is officially listed.

Long-term travellers to South Africa can avoid the extremes of climate by making an anti-clockwise circle over about six months, west–east, beginning at Cape Town in September and travelling through the hotter east until December, then heading into the highveld for the hottest months. Finally it is worth avoiding the school holidays (particularly December and January) when everywhere is packed.

Average maximum temperatures in degrees Celsius

	Jan	Feb	Mar	Apr	May	June	July	Aug	Sep	Oct	Nov	Dec
Cape Town	26.5	27.1	25.8	23.0	19.9	18.5	17.2	18.1	19.1	21.5	24.0	25.5
Pretoria	28.8	28.1	26.8	25.1	22.5	20.2	19.1	22.7	25.7	28.3	28.1	28.7
Jo'burg	26.3	25.6	24.3	22.1	19.1	16.5	16.4	19.8	22.8	25.0	25.3	26.1
Port E'beth	25.4	25.5	24.6	22.8	21.9	20.1	19.5	19.9	20.1	20.9	22.4	24.0
E. London	25.2	25.6	24.7	23.5	22.6	20.9	21.0	21.3	21.4	21.6	22.8	24.0
Durban	27.2	275	26.9	25.6	24.1	22.5	22.0	22.4	22.9	23.6	24.9	26.2
Bloem'ein	29.8	28.3	26.3	22.8	19.0	16.6	16.4	19.6	22.8	25.8	27.5	29.2
Kimberley	32.5	31.0	28.4	25.3	21.2	18.6	18.5	21.8	24.6	28.3	29.9	31.7
Kruger	31.4	30.6	30.1	28.6	27.0	25.0	25.0	26.0	28.5	29.0	30.0	30.0

Dagga

Dagga (marijuana) is so widely available in South Africa that the traveller is almost bound to come across it at some point. Although its use is better tolerated here than in the west, it is an illegal substance and the tolerance does not extend to high-profile use (i.e. smoking openly in public, or taking it across international borders).

If you do try it, remember that African marijuana tends to be much stronger than the western variety and first-timers should exercise some restraint, especially if the dagga comes from Swaziland or the Eastern Cape (former Transkei). Certainly you should not drive after smoking it, nor go anywhere where you need your wits about you (bus stations, taxi ranks, city centres, etc.).

Independent travellers, especially backpackers, who go into the Eastern Cape (former Transkei), Lesotho or Swaziland, will generally be offered dagga for sale, rather than just by other users. Be careful—the police in these areas and the South African regions surrounding them look out for hippy types who may be going in to buy.

Also, be aware that many people regard whites who smoke as drop-outs worthy of little respect. Finally, if anyone offers you 'buttons' or mandrax, refuse. This is a plant extract from India that some smokers mix with dagga to produce a sledgehammer effect. It is extremely bad for the health and reduces most people to a numb, twitching wreck within seconds.

Disabled Travellers

Information for disabled travellers planning a trip to South Africa can be obtained from the following organizations:

in South Africa

Disabled Adventure Tours, PO Box 60554, Flamingo Square, 7441, ✆/✉ (021) 557 4496, in Cape Town.

in the UK

RADAR (Royal Association For Disability and Rehabilitation), Unit 12, City Forum, 250 City Road, London EC1V 8AF, ✆(0171) 250 3222, publish 'Holidays and Travel Abroad: A Guide For Disabled People'.

Mobility International, 228 Borough High Street, London SE1 1JX, ✆ (0171) 403 5688.

in the USA

Mobility International USA, PO Box 3551, Eugene, Oregon 97403, ✆ (503) 343 1284.

SATH (Society for the Advancement of Travel for the Handicapped), 347 Fifth Avenue, Suite 610, New York 10016, ✆ (212) 447 7284.

Electricity

The voltage in South Africa is 220/230 volts AC, except for in Pretoria, where it is 230 volts AC and Port Elizabeth where it is 200–250v. Buy a three-point round-pin adapter for any electrical appliances you may bring.

Embassies and Consulates

Australia	Pretoria, ✆ (012) 342 3740.
Botswana	Pretoria, ✆ (012) 342 4760/4.
Canada	Pretoria, ✆ (012) 342 6923.
European Union	Pretoria, ✆ (012) 464 319.
Lesotho	Pretoria, ✆ (012) 322 6090/1/2.
Namibia	Pretoria, ✆ (012) 342 3520.
New Zealand	Harare (Zimbabwe), ✆ (026) 347 5922.
Republic of Ireland	Pretoria, ✆ (012) 342 5062; Cape Town, ✆ (021) 457 050.
Singapore	Pretoria, ✆ (012) 343 4371/4.
Swaziland	Pretoria, ✆ (012) 342 5782/4; Jo'burg, ✆ (011) 336 9776.
UK	Pretoria, ✆ (012) 343 3121; Jo'burg, ✆ (011) 337 8940/4; Cape Town, ✆ (021) 253 670; Durban, ✆ (031) 305 3041; Port Elizabeth, ✆ (041) 55 2423; East London, ✆ (0431) 55 2423.
USA	Pretoria, ✆ (012) 342 1048; Jo'burg, ✆ (011) 331 1681/3; Cape Town, ✆ (021) 214 280; Durban, ✆ (031) 304 4737.
Zimbabwe	Pretoria, ✆ (012) 342 5125; Jo'burg, ✆ (011) 838 2156/7; Cape Town, ✆ (021) 461 4710.

Food and Drink

Food

Cape cuisine

Unbeknownst to most people, South Africa has its own cuisine, known as Cape cooking. A mixture of Malay, Dutch, French and German influence, the cuisine has evolved over the last 300 years and focuses on spicy variations of European dishes (*see* p.109.)

seafood

Seafood is cheap and plentiful in South Africa, and the country is a paradise for seafood addicts. Both shellfish and line fish are easy to get hold of, whether fresh off the boat (if you are on the coast), or in restaurants. Although most shellfish are common, South African specialities are crayfish (clawless lobster) and perlamon, or abalone (mother of pearl). For distinctively South African line fish, try kingclip, snoek, red roman, cob or snapper.

venison and game

Ostrich meat is served in almost every Cape and Little Karoo restaurant, as are guinea-fowl (a much tastier bird than chicken). For venison, try the smaller antelope, whose meat is tender and aromatic from browsing on veld herbs: springbok, duiker and reedbuck are the best. Some of the larger antelope provide good meat if hung: kudu and gemsbok steaks in a wild mushroom or fruit sauce are often on restaurant menus during the winter months. Fresh trout is common in KwaZulu-Natal and Mpumalanga. Delicacies such as crocodile tail (delicious—like a more delicate version of lobster), giraffe (very lean) and occasionally even fried marula grubs can be found at the more expensive city restaurants.

red meat: braais, *Karoo mutton and* poitjies

Beef and mutton are the staples of most white South African diet;, many visitors are taken aback by the level of red meat consumption. The *braaivleis,* shortened to *braii,* is a weekly ritual among many white South Africans—a barbecue in which quantities of meat, sausage and beer are consumed, along with a few token vegetables like baked squash and aubergine.

While you may not want to eat as much red meat as those around you, do not leave South Africa without having tried the superb Karoo mutton, whose distinct flavour comes from the succulent semi-desert plants and herbs on which the sheep feed. Karoo mutton has very little fat and is more tender then European lamb. A variation on the *braaivleis* is the *poitjiekos* (pronounced poikykos), a Boer traditional feast in which meat, beans, squash and whatever else the cook wants are layered in a black cast-iron cooking pot (the *poitjie*), covered in water, and left to cook over several hours until the water has boiled away and all the levels have been cooked. The concentration of flavours is mouth-watering and, as usual, the meal is accompanied religiously by beer drinking.

biltong *and* boerevors

South Africa's wind-dried meats, or *biltong,* look highly inedible, coming in blackened strips that resemble an odd hybrid of leather and wood (unless you buy it ready-shredded in a supermarket). But the tough outside usually belies a moist, often still red inside that remains juicy for months. *Biltong* can be made from most meats, but the best is undoubtedly from game, especially kudu and springbok. Your best bet is to ask at small-town butchers for their current varieties. The only problem with *biltong* is that it can be expensive—a tragedy, as the stuff is supremely moreish. If you can find any cured with black peppercorns, buy large amounts, or you will run out and suffer withdrawal.

Less universally loved is the long, coiled *boerevors* sausage. The quality of this general-purpose protein can vary from the sublime to the inedible. Again, buy from small-town butchers, many of whom stuff the meat with African veld herbs. Some *boerevors* is made with a thin strip of cheese running through the centre, which melts with cooking and adds a richer quality to the meat.

cheeses

South Africa is strangely lacking in good local cheeses—strange for a country with a thriving dairy industry. Most cheese tends to be mass-produced and overpriced. However, this is slowly changing, and many local farms now sell their own cheese. The countryside around Stellenbosch, Franschoek and Paarl in the Cape Winelands now produces some very good cow's and goat's milk cheeses. Ask at the local publicity offices for directions to the farms. Otherwise, it is worth asking around when you are in a farming district—there will generally be somebody making cheese in an on-site dairy, and you may discover something wonderful.

fruit and vegetables

Fruit and vegetables are often ignored by the meat-mad South Africans, but the country is one of the world's major producers of citrus and soft fruit as well as exotic vegetables. The orchards of the Cape produce vast quantities of peaches, nectarines, apricots, eating grapes, apples, oranges and pears, all of which can be bought cheaply from the many farm stalls on the country roads. From the Eastern Cape through KwaZulu-Natal and lowveld Mpumalanga and Northern Province, sub-tropical fruits like guava, mango, pawpaw, banana and avocado grow wild and are offered (very cheaply) for sale by women and children at most roadsides. A delicacy of the usually arid Karoo is the fruit of the prickly pear, which tastes somewhere between pineapple and pomegranate, but is sweet and does not desiccate the mouth. Ask in small town stores in the Karoo during the summer months. Watermelon and honeydews are available everywhere. Fruit preserves—jams, chutneys and bottled slices—can be bought at most craft shops and farm stalls all over the country. Around the Cape, these tend to be spicy, with a sweet and sour edge. Devotees claim that the best preserves come from the Breede River Valley in the Cape Winelands.

South Africa is one of the few countries where fresh asparagus can be grown year-round and, again, farm stalls (mostly in KwaZulu-Natal and the Free State) often sell it beside the road. Butternut squash (delicious when cooked with butter and cinnamon), small star squash, courgettes, marrows and, of course, the omnipresent *mealie* (maize) form the staple vegetables of the South African diet. A vegetarian dish popular among blacks, but almost universally snubbed by whites, is *samp*, a tasty mish-mash of maize and beans that can keep you going for weeks. This can be bought from street stalls in most towns (often near the taxi ranks) for very little money. Mushrooms are always expensive, and do not thrive in South Africa's dry soils and climate; apart from a few wild species in the temperate hardwood forests (*see* below), they generally have to be artificially raised.

veldkos

An Afrikaans word meaning, literally, 'field cooking', *veldkos* stands for all edible produce of the wild African veld. For the initiated, this represents a universe of edible delicacies, such as Kalahari desert melons, desert truffles and a vast array of wild fruits. But for the novice the obvious choices are few: easy to identify are monkey oranges—large round fruits in a hard skin that grow on trees in KwaZulu-Natal and the lowveld. It is best to get a field guide to edible plants (*see* **Further Reading**).

breads, pastries and puddings

These are another Boer speciality. Around the Cape, the home-baked breads are among the best baked anywhere. Try the poppyseed and sesame-seed sprinkled wagon wheels—large, round white loaves usually sold hot from the oven—or the dense, almost oily wholemeal loaves with sunflower seeds. Almost anywhere in the country you can buy Boer pastries. The most common is the *koeksister*, a very sweet small cake rolled in a spiral shape. Fruit tarts, cheesecakes and *melktaart* are standard desserts and, in general, are of very high quality. Home-made biscuits can usually be bought from the little craft shops found in country towns.

foreign cuisine

The massive influx of Indians to South Africa from the 1860s to the 1920s brought a wealth of Indian cuisine—usually southern Indian and Sri Lankan. Durban's better Indian restaurants are rated as among the best in the world, while Cape Town and Johannesburg also have some superb Indian eateries. Less good is South Africa's Chinese food, which tends to be very bland to suit the Western palate. South Africa's many Portuguese restaurants, mostly owned by refugees from Mozambique and Angola, are much better. Specialities are deep-fried calamari steaks and chicken *peri-peri* (fried chicken in a hot, hot sauce).

Apart from these, most European cuisine is represented in South African towns. Good Greek and Italian restaurants are always easy to find in the larger towns, while in the cities you can find superb French *cordon bleu* cooking. *See* 'Eating Out' sections for details.

cheap and fast food

Despite its huge choice of indigenous food, South Africa can be a hard place to find a good meal when you do not have time for a full sit-down affair in a restaurant. Most light meals are catered for by take-away shops, which can generally be found in even the smallest of towns, and which invariably serve deep-fried food or toasted sandwiches (for some reason, usually billed as 'toasted treats'). However, look for Indian-owned take-aways, and you will generally find good *bhajees* and *samosas*. In KwaZulu-Natal, the general Indian influence has spread to all fast-food joints, resulting in a peculiarly South African phenomenon, the Bunny Chow. These are quarter, half or three-quarter (depending on the price) loaves of bread, hollowed out and filled with vegetable curry, making a meal that is its own plate. Bunny Chows are normally filling, tasty, very cheap and prevent the budget traveller from overdosing on fried food. For the cheapest eating out (i.e. not cooking for yourself), try the many take-aways you will find in even the smallest town, many of which cater mainly to black Africans, and where you can generally fill up for around R10 or less.

Prices

expensive	over R100 per head with wine.
moderate	R75–R100 per head with wine, though if you choose wisely many restaurants in this category will feed you for less.
cheap	under R75 per head with wine. Many cheap restaurants charge close to R50 per head with wine

Drink

wine

One of the world's major producers of red, white and fortified wines, South Africa is heaven to the traveller who likes to drink well for little money. A history, guide to the varieties and suggestions on wine-buying are included in the Cape Winelands chapter (*see* p.161). Suffice it to say here that South Africa's staple red is the good old Cabernet Sauvignon, while for the white, Chardonnay is the most widely successful. Table wines are produced in the Winelands region north and east of Cape Town, along the Orange River in the Northern Cape, and in some parts of the Little Karoo. Ports and sherries are mainly produced in the Breede River Valley and Little Karoo. *See* pp.162-3 for more information on Cape Wine.

beer

Most South African beer is of the lager type, produced by the conglomerate South African Breweries, who apart from their well known Lion and Castle lines produce a number of foreign brands under licence. Some local lager is made with maize, which is not to everybody's taste, but there are plenty of imported beers available in the middle-market bars and retail outlets. SAB makes its own milk stout and Guinness is locally brewed, although addicts to English bitter may have a problem. The exception to this, however, Bosuns Bitter, is brewed in the Garden Route town of Knysna. Many Cape pubs, and some in the main cities, serve Bosuns on tap. African home-produced beer is worth drinking, but usually agreed to be an acquired taste. Often made from maize or sorghum, it is generally sold at country road stores in the Northern Province and Zululand. However, strains vary with the locality and you should (discreetly) ask where to buy the best at local bars.

spirits

The best Cape brandies command high prices the world over, but the cheap stuff can easily double as a sweet paint-stripper. Top of the cheap brands is Klipdift which, served with Coke, is an Afrikaner staple at *braais*. Anyone attending such an evening will be sure to know the full effects of a hot-sun hangover next day, usually after waking where they fell. A home-made spirit common on farms is *witblitz* or 'white lightning', which can be made from anything and takes your head off in true home-brew style. Another hard-hitting Afrikaner speciality is *mampoer*, a clear peach brandy or schnapps that is famed for its debilitating qualities. Those interested should attend the annual *mampoer* festival in Zeerust in the Marico district of the Northern Province.

fruit juices and soft drinks

Far more healthy, and just as good as South Africa's alcohols, are its fruit juices. South Africa has two main brands, Liquifruit and Ceres—both produced in the valley of Ceres in the Cape Winelands. Exotic juices such as apricot, mango, banana, strawberry, peach, and guava vie with the more traditional citrus varieties.

Home-made soft drinks are Afrikaner specialities, most easily found in small stores in small Karoo towns. Home-made ginger beer, lemonade and prickly pear fruit juice make the long, hot driving rewarding.

tea

While South Africa produces Indian teas on plantations in the Northern Province, the KwaZulu-Natal Midlands and the Western Cape, the country has two indigenous bush 'teas' that lack both tannin and caffeine, yet are more robust and tastier than most herb teas. The best-known of these is *rooibos* (meaning 'red bush' tea), which comes from a Cape mountain shrub. The town of Clanwilliam in the Cedarberg region of the Western Cape is famous for producing *rooibos*, and teabags of it can be bought in almost any shop. According to taste, *rooibos* can be served with milk, black with sugar, or with sweet fortified wine. Slightly sweeter is honeybush tea, also made from a Cape shrub. Not as dark as *rooibos*, honeybush should be brewed strong and taken black with sugar.

coffee

South Africa produces some coffee, but mostly imports it. It is not hard to find good coffee in shops and the better city cafés, however in small towns, and often in people's houses, good coffee is harder to track down. For some reason, many South Africans prefer cheap chicory coffee (or a mixture of the two) to the real thing, and take it very milky and weak with plenty of sugar. In small coffee shops, be sure to ask for your coffee brewed strong. Having said this, there are some decent instant coffees, such as Nescafé, on sale.

Geography

South Africa rises from a low-lying coast to a high central plateau via a series of mountain ranges. In general, the land gets drier as it rises, with the coastal mountains being forested and the inland plateaux turning to dry bushveld or grassland—the exception to this is the arid Cape West Coast. The series of main mountain ranges dividing the inland from the coastal zones is known as the **Great Escarpment**, and can be traced on a map as a giant U-shape from the far northwest down to the temperate southern Cape coast, eastward through the arid Great Karoo to the greener Eastern Cape and KwaZulu-Natal and finally northeast up into Swaziland and the Northern Province. The Great Escarpment is divided into several different ranges connected by high passes, and behind the highest section, the Natal Drakensberg, lies the remote Kingdom of Lesotho, where rise most of South Africa's perennial rivers. East of the Great Escarpment falls the **lowveld**, a sub-tropical bushveld and forest zone that continues into Mozambique via the low Lebombo Mountains. West and north of the Northern Province section of the Great Escarpment lies the **highveld**, an upland plateau of wide grasslands, extending west towards the Kalahari region of the Northern Cape, through the drier grasslands of the Free State into the arid Great Karoo.

Health and Insurance

Health

South Africa has a remarkably antiseptic climate, owing to the high elevation and dry air of much of the country. Only in the foetid, sub-tropical lowveld and on the KwaZulu-Natal coast do the more typically African health problems occur. Both areas are highly **malarial**, and should not be visited without a course of tablets started at least four days before going in. **Bilharzia**—a debilitating parasite that punctures its way around the intestines—is also a problem in the rivers and lakes of these regions. The disease does not usually manifest itself until a few weeks after the parasite has entered, and symptoms are a general torpor and loss of energy with, eventually, blood in the urine. However, bilharzia is easily cured with a course of pills available from chemists in South Africa and in the West. Another parasitic problem can be **tick-bite fever**, which is like a more intense but shorter-lived version of glandular fever. This can be avoided by checking yourself for ticks after a foray into the bush and removing any you find—if you do contract it, you simply have to rest until it works its way out of your system. More serious problems are **hepatitis**, which can be avoided by vaccination and washing fruit or vegetables before eating, and **HIV/AIDS**. Although South Africa has a far lower incidence of the latter two diseases than most African countries, the risks are still clear, and appropriate precautions should be taken.

As for **vaccinations**, doctors recommend that you get shots against polio, tetanus, hepatitis, typhoid, cholera and yellow fever, though the latter three are only necessary if you intend travelling further up into Africa, or if spending time in the poorest squatter camps (for example as a voluntary or health worker). **Tap water** is safe everywhere.

Other dangers to avoid are **sun-stroke** and **dehydration** when hiking (always wear a hat and carry at least two litres of water per person), and **fatigue** from long-distance driving (the drives are always longer than you think). Danger from animals is minimal—you will seldom be close enough to big game for it to chomp you, and snakes tend to avoid people. Exceptions are the highly toxic puff and berg adders, which sometimes sun themselves on roadsides and walking trails. Spitting cobras may also sometimes sit on a trail. There are more toxic snakes but, unless you find and deliberately disturb one, it is rare to be bitten. Keep a look out and, if you see one, back off and give it a wide berth. Always hike in pairs, so that if someone does get bitten, another may run for help. There is usually a grace period of a few hours during which you can find serum without terminal damage to tissue.

Insurance

One of the best deals in the UK is through **Endsleigh Insurance**, ✆ (0171) 436 4451/930 8343, which offers specialized South African cover of up to a year, including travel within other southern African countries. It is worth insuring your baggage as certain areas, notably Johannesburg, the Transkei and any of the larger cities, are known for theft. Other comprehensive cover can be found through **Trailfinders** in the UK, ✆ (0171) 938 3939, and Australia, ✆ (02) 92 47 7666, and **American Express** in the UK, ✆ (0444) 239 900, and the USA, ✆ (212) 493 6500. If you plan to do any specialized sports, such as scuba diving, white-water rafting, microlighting or parascending, it is worth checking whether or not you need additional cover. If going on an organized tour or safari that includes insurance, it is still as well to have your own cover for any time you spend in the country away from the tour company.

Money and Banks

Currency and Exhange Rates

The South African currency is the *rand*: 100 cents = 1 *rand*.

The great thing about South Africa for most western travellers is the exchange rate. Although not cheap by African standards, the country nonetheless offers you a chance to multiply by four or five times the amount of sterling you bring in (make the appropriate adjustment for dollars or deutschmarks), as a rand buys in South Africa only a little less than what a pound buys in Britain, and the exchange rate is generally around eight and a half *rand* to the pound, four to five rand for a US dollar and deutschmark. When exchanging, always keep your receipts, which must be produced if you change your last rands on departure.

The favourable exchange rates make available a wide range of possibilities for more specialized travel, sports and safaris, even for budget travellers. If you have an enthusiasm, such as scuba-diving, riding or simply staying in good hotels and eating well, you will be able to afford it in South Africa. Changing money on the black market is not really an option in South Africa, and does not exist as in neighbouring Zimbabwe and Mozambique. However, you may be asked to exchange money privately by people you stay with. This is illegal, but the choice is yours.

Banks

Foreign currency can only be (officially) exchanged at banks, and the opening hours are archaic—between 9 and 3.30 only, with an hour off for lunch in the small town branches. Only in large towns will you find a branch open on Saturdays (usually from 8–11). Opening a bank account is a hassle too, as no South African bank will allow someone with a foreign address to have a cheque book or cashpoint card. Worse, they will insist that you queue at the enquiries desk and fill out several forms before you can draw from a teller. Irritating, but useful if you want to budget yourself, as the prospect of a trip to the bank to get more money after a blow-out does not appeal when you know you will have to queue for at least an hour.

The obvious way around this is using traveller's cheques (which can be exchanged at any bank and at some hotels and travel agents) and credit (and debit) cards. However as regards the latter be warned: most petrol stations, many smaller places to stay and some of the accommodation in nature reserves do not accept plastic, and you should always have at least R200 in cash on you to cover emergencies. If travelling outside South Africa, US dollars are accepted in many hotels in Zimbabwe and Zambia, while *deutschmarks* are accepted in some hotels and guest farms in Namibia. The most widely accepted credit cards are Visa, American Express, Diners Club and Mastercard.

National Parks, Nature Reserves and State Forests

South Africa's conserved areas are mostly governed by three state bodies: the National Parks Board, the Provincial Parks Board and the Ministry of Agriculture and Forestry. All charge an entrance fee, but the rules regarding each are slightly different, and it is helpful to have an idea of the bureaucracy before going in.

The **National Parks Board** administers 12 parks with tourist facilities, and is busy establishing several others. Compared to the provincial nature reserves and game reserves, prices for entrance fees, accommodation, camping and facilities such as hiking or riding trails tend to be slightly more expensive. Trails must also be booked in advance, either by telephoning the park direct (local numbers are listed where appropriate in this guide) or by telephoning the National Parks Board in Pretoria, ✆ (012) 343 1991. Some trails, like the 5-day, guided big game hikes in the Kruger, are very popular and must be booked several months in advance. Others, like the Springbok Trail in the Karoo National Park, can be booked with only a few days' notice.

All national parks have a shop where you can buy (overpriced) supplies—though do not rely on being able to find non-essentials such as camera film—and most have a restaurant. The Kruger even has village-sized camps with bank machines, post offices, supermarkets and several restaurants. Most national parks have petrol stations, but always fill up before you go in. Entrance gates shut at sunset and open at dawn.

The **Provincial Parks** and **Nature Reserves** have a head office in each province. These reserves are often larger than the national parks (except for the vast Kruger National Park) and in some cases cover entire mountain ranges (these are usually called Conservation Areas or Wilderness Areas). Some, like the reserves of Zululand and the Northern Province, harbour big game. Others, like those of the Western Cape, are better known for their flora and landscape, yet still support significant wildlife populations. Entrance fees, accommodation and hiking/riding facilities are cheaper than in the national parks, and in general do not need to be booked more than a week in advance (accommodation and camping in the smaller, or more remote reserves can usually be had just by showing up). The exceptions are the reserves of Zululand, whose facilities get booked up in holiday periods (December/January). To book accommodation or other facilities, telephone the reserve direct (numbers listed in 'Activities' or 'Where to Stay' in each section). Most reserves close their gates at sunset, so arrive before 6pm. Larger reserves have shops and sometimes petrol, but you cannot always rely on this. Accommodation is always self-catering.

State Forests are usually in mountain areas and offer hiking trails with refuge huts or camp sites. Other accommodation, petrol and supply stores are not offered. Trails sometimes have to be booked in advance (telephone numbers of state forests with hiking trails are listed in this guide), but often you can simply show up, as state forest trails are seldom fully booked. Fees for hiking and overnight huts/camping are cheaper.

National/Public Holidays

January 1	New Year's Day
March 21	Human Rights Day
Good Friday	
Easter Monday	Family Day
April 27	Freedom Day
May 1	Workers' Day
June 16	Youth Day
August 9	National Women's Day
December 16	Day of Conciliation
December 25	Christmas Day
December 26	Day of Goodwill

Opening Hours

Government office hours: Mon–Fri 8.30–4.30, often closed 1–2 and at weekends. To be safe, always plan to track down tourist information on a weekday.

Liquor stores (known as 'bottle stores'): Mon–Fri 9–6 (so always remember to stock up before the evening), Sat mornings only (usually), closed Sun. You can usually buy wine at supermarkets on Saturday afternoons, but not beer or spirits, and you can buy booze on Sundays in bars.

Museums: These generally stick to business hours (8 or 9–4 or 5), but there are usually variations of half an hour to an hour for each museum. Also, all but the largest close for lunch, usually between 1 and 2 (again with minor variations), so always plan to go mid-morning or mid-afternoon. Most museums have a small entry charge of R2–R5.

Pubs: 10am–2am daily.

Safety

Cities and Townships

Despite the high level of political violence, it is mainly confined to the townships of the larger cities, and the traveller will not encounter it. Crime, however, is high. Break-ins to houses are often bloody affairs, so if staying with friends make sure you double-lock all doors and windows. Mugging is a problem in downtown Johannesburg by day (by night you should avoid it altogether), the former Transkei and to a lesser extent Cape Town by night. Stay out of the townships altogether unless on a guided tour or with local residents—poverty and racial hatred make the townships a bad place to be a stranger and alone.

Hitch-hiking and Black Taxis

Many people will tell you never to hitch or take a black taxi. While there have been horror stories about both (attacks with hitching, high-speed crashes with black taxis), it is only fair to point out that many people continue to use both forms of transport. The risks are there, but with hitching the number of violent incidents tends to go up and down according to the local political situation, so ask young people and youth hostel keepers for the latest information before setting out. Mugging can be a problem at the taxi-ranks for black taxis in large towns—and anyone using them for a long-haul journey should not pick them up or ask to be dropped off until outside the city, as they pass through the townships on their way in and out. As for the crashes, these are real enough at any time. Drink-driving and drivers falling asleep are the usual causes. The choice is yours.

Shopping

Although conspicuous consumption of Western goods is very much a part of life for the wealthy South Africans, tourist shopping is most rewarding if confined to things African.

VAT

Travellers can reclaim Value Added Tax on any purchase of over R250 when leaving the country by presenting the goods and receipts to the airport customs upon departure.

African crafts

There is a large range of exquisite South African crafts for sale—notably South Sotho woollen rugs woven with geometric designs, Zulu bead jewellery, Xhosa woodwork and basket-weaving and Venda totemic carving. These are by no means the only crafts on offer, and there is a certain amount of overlap between regions, but these can serve as a pointer.

Widely available from curio shops in most cities, most African crafts are best bought from markets and workshops in the indigenous region (listed where appropriate throughout the guide). If you cannot get into the back-country, try the Operation Hunger shops in Cape Town and Johannesburg, the craft shop at the Cape Town National Art Gallery or the flea-markets in Durban and Johannesburg.

Crafts such as leatherwork, printed textiles and silver and goldsmithing can be bought from independent craftspeople at any of the larger city flea markets such as Greenmarket Square in Cape Town and Bruma Lake in Johannesburg, as well as smaller markets in tourist towns like Knysna on the the Cape south coast (which is also known for furniture-making from the local hardwoods) and Grahamstown in the Eastern Cape.

precious and semi-precious stones

Semi-precious stones such as tiger's eye, amethyst, agates, malachite and a host of others are cheap in South Africa, and some very good jewellery can be found in Johannesburg's Smal

Street Mall and Market Square flea market, Cape Town's Waterfront shopping arcades and the better city curio shops. Gold and diamonds are also cheaper in South Africa than just about anywhere else, and addicts of costly baubles should trawl Johannesburg's jewellery shops for bargains.

traditional curios

Traditional curios such as animal skins (worked and plain), antelope horn products, stuffed animals and the like are sold at curio shops in all the big cities, as well as at the shops attached to the National Parks. Some of these, such as spotted cat skins (from culled animals), may not be exported, and all skins require a veterinary stamp for legal exporting. Make sure the curio-seller knows you are intending to take the product out of the country, so that you will not buy something that will later be confiscated.

Sports and Activities

South Africa has an outdoor climate and a largely unspoiled landscape. Sports of all kinds are popular and widely practised.

Hiking

There are few countries with better facilities for wilderness hiking. Most of South Africa's national parks, nature reserves, state forests and conservation areas have marked hiking trails of one to several days in length, with overnight huts provided containing a toilet, fresh water, firewood and (usually) cooking implements. Hikes are always booked in advance by telephone. Most are described area by area in the guide, but for general orientation here is a list of what is on offer.

coastal hiking

The best areas are: the Otter Trail of the Garden Route's Tsitsikamma National Park, the Eastern Cape's Wild Coast Trail, and the hiking trails of St Lucia Nature Reserve and Cape Vidal State Forest in KwaZulu-Natal.

forest hiking

South Africa's unique hardwood forests can be explored by marked trails in the Diepwalle State Forest and the Tsitsikamma National Park in the Garden Route, in the Hogsback, Katberg and Pirie forests of the former Ciskei, in the Kosi Bay nature reserve of northern KwaZulu-Natal and in the Soutpansberg mountains of the Northern Province.

hiking with game

Guided hikes through 'Big Five' country with an armed game ranger are offered in the Kruger National Park and adjacent private game reserves in Mpumalanga, and Umfolozi Game Reserve and Phinda Private Game Reserve in Natal. Guided hikes with large, but less dangerous game (including white rhino) can be organized at Mkuzi and Itala Game Reserves in Kwazulu-Natal, Tsolwana and Double Drift Reserves in the former Ciskei, the Lapalala Wilderness Area in the Northern Province and Tuissen die Rivieren Game Farm in the south-west Free State. Although you won't see big game, there are hiking trails in Eastern Karoo's Mountain Zebra National Park and Western Karoo's Karoo National Park offer close encounters with antelope and zebra. Both trails close during the hot summer.

The best areas are: KwaZulu-Natal, Eastern Cape and Mpumalanga Drakensberg, the south-western Cape ranges near Cape Town, the Cedarberg of the West Coast, the Swartberg and Baviaanskloofberg of the Little Karoo, the Tsitsikamma mountains of the Garden Route, the Amatola Mountains of the Eastern Cape, the Belelesberg of northwest KwaZulu-Natal, western Swaziland and the Soutpansberg of the Northern Transvaal.

Riding

South Africa offers some really spectacular long-distance trails on good horses. There are private riding stables near most towns, and the larger country hotels also generally offer riding. Details are listed with the appropriate region, but here is a rough guide at a glance:

Equus Horse Trails, ✆ (011) 788 3923, in the Lapalala Wilderness Area of the Northern Province, guide riders for several days through bushveld, with sightings of large game. **Benghoil Horse Trails**, ✆ (04562) 2203, lead trail-rides deep into the mountains near Cathcart in the Eastern Cape. **Giant's Castle** and **Rugged Glen Nature Reserve**, ✆ (0331) 471 961, in the Natal Drakensberg, both offer rides of up to several days into the mountains, while **Jacana Country House & Trails**, based in Pretoria, ✆ (012) 2499, offer trips into the mountains of Zululand around the town of Melmoth. Lesotho's **Government Pony Project**, **Malealea Lodge** and **Semonkong Lodge** will guide you and a pack mule into the remote valleys of Lesotho where machines cannot go, and where villages resemble those of the medieval Scottish Highlands (*see* **Lesotho**). Bokpoort, ✆ (058) 256 1181, and **Rustler's Valley Guest Farm**, ✆ (05193) 33 939, in the Eastern Highlands of the Free State offer day-trails into the Witteberg on well-schooled horses. **Horse Trail Safaris**, based in Cape Town, ✆ (021) 734 396), offer trips of up to five days into the forests near Knysna, into the Cedarberg north of Cape Town, and up the beaches of the barren West Coast.

Many smaller guest farms can arrange riding, and those interested should always ask at the local hotel or publicity office, where something can generally be arranged. Always look in the 'Activities' sections of this guide, where individual riding schools will be listed.

Drag-hunting can be arranged near Cape Town through the Cape Hunt Club, and near Johannesburg through the Rand Hunt Club (contact Captour and the Johannesburg Publicity Association for details). The hunt season is from May to September.

Polo is also popular, particularly among the farmers of KwaZulu-Natal and the Free State. Also, in Afrikaans-speaking areas, a form of Dutch high-school dressage riding called *Boereperd* ('farmer's horse') still thrives. Horses are trained to five gaits and individual farmer/trainers will often allow competent visitors to ride their beautifully schooled beasts. Ask at the local hotel or publicity association if you are interested.

Other Sports

balloooning

Balloon safaris over the veld can be arranged through Lindbergh Lodge in the Northwest Province, ✆ (018) 22041, an upmarket hotel and private game reserve near Wolmaranstad, west of Johannesburg (*see* p.613). You can also go ballooning in the Winelands of the Western Cape near Paarl. Contact the Paarl Publicity Association (*see* p.174) for details.

bungee-jumping

You have to be completely mad to do this, but if you are one of the many people out there who appear to be just that, head for the bridge at Gouritsmond (*see* p.244).

camel safaris

Journeys by camel into the back-wilderness of the Orange River country in Bushmanland in the Northern Cape are offered by **Camel Runners**, © (011) 403 2512, a branch of River Runners in Cape Town. Clients have the option of breaking the jouney into different sections by horse or canoe (*see* p.303).

canoeing and white-water rafting

Long canoe trips along the Orange River through Bushmanland and the Richtersveld can be arranged through **River Runners**, © (021) 762 2350, and **Felix Unite**, © (021) 762 6935; both have offices in Cape Town and Johannesburg (*see* p.287). Trips down the Breede River northeast of Cape Town are aranged by **Breede River Adventures** in Cape Town, © (021) 762 5602 (*see* p.194). Canoeing in Mpumalanga's rapid waters is organized by several guest lodges and hotels, (*see* respective 'Activities' for details). In Natal, white-water rafting through the thunderous Tugela Gorge is arranged via **Kwa-Zukela** in Johannesburg, **Sunwal** and **Felix Unite** in Durban (*see* p.439).

caving

South Africa's mountains are riddled with caves but there are few that are generally known about and those can only be safely explored with the proper equipment and with experienced party leaders. Those interested should contact the caving clubs at the universities of Cape Town, Gauteng (Johannesburg), and KwaZulu-Natal (Pietermaritzburg). Less problematic to visit are the **Kalk Bay Caves**, just above the fishing village of Kalk Bay on the eastern side of the Cape Peninsula, south of Cape Town. There are no lights to mark the way, but the local publicity office (at Muizenberg) can arrange for a guide with torches.

More publicly accessible cave systems with guided tours are the **Cango Caves** of the Little Karoo, the **Sudwala** and **Echo** of the Mpumalanga and the **Sterkfontein Caves** in the Northwest Province. The Cango Echo and Sudwala systems are famous for their stalactite/stalagmite formations, and the Sterkfontein caves for their pre-human fossil and early remains (*see* respective chapters for details).

climbing

The Cape Mountains, and KwaZulu-Natal and Mpumalanga Drakensberg are famous the world over for their climbing routes. Contact the mountaineering clubs at the universities of Cape Town, Gauteng and KwaZulu-Natal to join an expedition.

fishing

Sea fishing off South Africa's coasts is very rewarding. A range of line and game fish can be hooked from beach and rock promontory. Much sought-after by anglers are the large, hard-fighting snoek, kingclip and kob of the Cape coasts, the large sharks, fierce barracuda and elusive milk-fish of the KwaZulu-Natal Coast, and the deep-sea game species such as marlin and dorado which can be caught anywhere off the Indian Ocean coast. Tackle-hire and boat operators can be contacted through the publicity associations of the larger coastal towns.

Fresh-water fishing: fly-fishing for trout is popular in the the mountains near Cape Town and in the Eastern Cape, KwaZulu-Natal, Lesotho and Mpumalanga. The Orange and Vaal rivers offer indigenous coarse fish such as yellowfish and barbel (a South African catfish), while most dams, lakes and some streams harbour bass. Check the 'Activities' sections of all regions for details.

kloofing

If you have had your fill of bungee-jumping, try kloofing—make your way along a mountain watercourse, leap off waterfalls and let the rapids do the work for you (see p.151).

mountain biking

For those who have not brought their own, bikes and guided tours for the Mpumalanga mountains and/or recommended independent itineraries can be had via **Excitement Seekers Cycle Tours**, in Johannesburg, ✆ (011) 792 7109.

paragliding

In Cape Town, on the hill called Lion's Head, a paragliding school offers ascents, leaving you hovering high over the Eastern Cape Peninsula. Contact **Captour**, in Cape Town, ✆ (021) 418 5214, to arrange a trip, or **Paragliding Africa**, in Johannesburg, ✆ (011) 880 9229.

scuba diving

The KwaZulu-Natal coast is reknowned for its coral reefs. **Sodwana Bay** has a permanent school with courses for beginners and diving safaris for the experienced. Contact **Tourism Durban**, (031) 3044 934, for the latest prices at Sodwana and the other Natal locations. There are also scuba courses and guided wreck and reef dives around Cape Town.

shark diving

Shark diving is a relatively new attraction in Cape Town (open to total diving novices), where you are kitted out with wetsuits and aqualungs and sent down, in cages, among the great white sharks of False Bay (see p.150).

skiing

South Africa is the only African country where regular (if poor quality) skiing can be had. Three places have permanent ski-lifts: above the Hex River Pass in the Western Cape, on Ben Macdhui near Rhodes in the Eastern Cape Drakensberg and at Oxbow in the Maluti Mountains of northern Lesotho. Snow deep enough for skiing is by no means to be counted on, but the 'season' is usually in June and July. To arrange skiing at Hex River, contact **Captour**, in Cape Town, ✆ (021) 418 5202 (see p.126); for skiing at Rhodes contact the **Rhodes Hotel**, ✆ (04542) 21(see p.3337); for skiing at Oxbow contact **Oxbow Lodge** in Lesotho (see p.457).

watersports

Windsurfer and jet-ski hire can be arranged at most coastal resorts. Ask for details at the local publicity association.

Telephones

Public phones are cheap and easy to use. You insert your coin (a minimum of 20c) and dial. You also get several minutes of chat for your coin, and longer-distance calls are comparatively cheap. Card phones are also wide-spread and more reliable. The number for the free call operator in the UK (reverse charge and BT charge cards) is (0800) 990 044.

Telephone booths are usually blue (if public) or free-standing with an orange soundproof shell if outside a post office where queues are often long. In big towns, avoid trying to make calls at lunchtime or at knocking-off time in the late afternoon, when it can take an hour for a phone to come free.

As the national telephone network is expanded the local dialling codes in South Africa are changing. As far as we are aware, the telephone numbers in the guide are correct at the time of going to press, but if you have problems reaching a number we suggest contacting a nearby tourist office or international directory enquiries for the latest information.

Time

South Africa is two hours ahead of GMT, one hour ahead of Europe and seven hours ahead of eastern US standard time. There are no different time zones within South Africa.

Tourist Offices

South Africa's tourist offices are divided into a confusing number of semi-independent groups for each town. These are usually called **publicity associations**, but sometimes go by other names such as visitor's bureau, publicity office and, very occasionally, tourist information. Annoying as this may be, when asking for the local tourist office, just use the words 'tourist information' and most people will know what you mean.

Very small towns, such as those in the Karoo, will have tourist information in the town clerk's office, usually referred to as the 'Municipality'. To make matters worse, all tourist offices keep strictly to weekday office hours, usually close between 1 and 2pm for lunch and are seldom open at weekends. So bear in mind that you cannot rely on them at odd times of day or in an emergency.

You can greatly simplify the tourist office problem in the Cape by visiting **Captour**, © (021) 418 5202, ✆ (021) 418 5202, *captour@iafrica.com* a tourist office on Adderley Street in Cape Town that deals with everything. Visitors arriving in Johannesburg can get information for the whole country by visiting the **Satour Office**, © (011) 970 1669 in the arrivals hall at Johannesburg International Airport. Durban's main tourist information centre, **Tourism Durban**, © (031) 304 4934, ✆ (031) 304 6196, is at 160 Pine Street.

It is as well to do a bit of research before you go—particularly if you are a budget traveller looking for cheap safari outfitters and for specialist tour-operators. Satour, the South African Tourist Board, has several offices abroad:

UK, Ireland & Scandinavia, 6 Alt Grove, Wimbledon, London SW19 4DZ, © (0181) 944 8080/6646, ✆ (0181) 944 6705.

USA, 500 Fifth Avenue 20th Floor, Suite 2040, New York, NY 10110, © (212) 730 2929, © (800) 822 5368, ✆ (212) 764 1980 and 9841 Airport Boulevard, Suite 1524, Los Angeles, CA 90045, © (310) 641 8444.

Australia & New Zealand, Level 6, 285 Clarence Street, Sydney, NSW 2000, © (02) 261 3424.

Canada, Suite 2, 4117 Lawrence Avenue East, Scarborough, Ontario M1E 2S2, ✆ (416) 283 0563, 🖷 (416) 283 5465.

Zimbabwe, Offices 9 & 10, Mon Repos Building, Newlands Shopping Centre, Harare, ✆ (4) 707 766 & ✆ 786 487/8, 🖷 (4) 786 489.

Where to Stay

Over the past 15 years, most South Africans have been cut off from the rest of the world by sanctions and a weak currency. The result has been a massive development of internal tourist facilities, including places to stay.

Traditionally, this has been through **chain hotels** aimed at the upper end of the market (South Africans love the word 'upmarket'), but with the recent influx of foreign travellers the market has changed to suit people used to less institutionalized travelling and those looking for bargains. The result has been a growing number of B&Bs and guest farms in the moderate price range, and of youth hostels and budget accommodation in the cheap price range. South Africa is now open to travellers on any budget, even in the remote places.

The best of the top-end, but still personally run accommodation, is found through the **private game reserves** of the Northern Province and KwaZulu-Natal, and through the old lodges and country hotels (though seldom town hotels, which tend to be scruffy) in the Cape, Free State, Swaziland and Lesotho. All are listed in this guide. Some of the game lodges will also be able to provide accommodation for moderate and cheap budget travellers in separate facilities.

Town and country B&Bs and the chalets and rondavels found in the national parks and nature reserves provide very comfortable accommodation (which is generally self-catering) for travellers in the moderate price range. This type of accommodation can be brought into the cheap price range if shared between more than two people. All such accommodation usually comes with its own bathroom.

Backpackers' and youth hostels have sprung up everywhere in the last few years, reflecting the increased number of backpackers visiting the country, often as part of a general Africa tour. These are generally very well-run and offer a choice between dormitory accommodation and double rooms. Bedding is sometimes an extra, however, and you will inevitably share bathrooms.

The owners of backpackers' hostels are generally good sources of local information, and will sometimes arrange tours and other activities, as well as pick-ups for people with no transport.

Recently, some of the guest farms of the Drakensberg, Lesotho and the spectacular eastern highlands of the Free State have begun to offer facilities for budget travellers, as have some near the game reserves of Mpumalanga. All are listed in the guide.

Camp sites can generally be found in every town and nature reserve—almost always with ablution facilities. Alternatively you can often camp on farms, with permission from the owner, if you are far from anywhere and need to stop for the night.

Prices

This guide divides places to stay into four price categories as follows:

luxury–very expensive   over R500 per person per night.
In some cases, such as in the Mpumalanga private game reserves, prices may be up to R2000 per person per night.

expensive   between R400 and R500 per person per night. The guide will generally state if a place is at the bottom or top end of this scale.

moderate   between R150 and R300 per person per night. Again, the guide usually states which end of the scale applies.

cheap   under R150 per night, but hotel prices vary seasonally. Accomodation in Cape Town at Christmas will cost twice as much as the same thing in Durban in June. In the case of backpackers' dormitory accommodation and parks' board camp sites, expect to pay around R20 per person per night, self-catering, going up to R80 for a double room and up to R50 for a single when available. In the case of hiking huts in state forests or nature reserves, expect to pay under R20 per person per night self-catering. Those with cars can usually camp for free in the *veld* with prior permission from the local farmer/village headman.

Women Travellers

Unless hitching, or walking around bus/train stations and dark streets late at night, women travellers will generally experience no more hassle for simply being female than in any Western country. However, one tip for lesbian women is important—most outward displays of homosexual affection are taboo with both white and black South Africans. Nude bathing is also not a good idea, unless in a large, mixed party and/or away from the public eye.

History

Prehistory to Colonial Times

Anthropologists often refer to Africa as the 'cradle of mankind', a claim based largely on the discovery of the world's earliest fossil hominid remains by Dr M. D. Leakey in northeast Africa during the 1950s. Although it seems unlikely that the entire human race sprang from under the rocks of Kenya, Tanzania and Ethiopia, equally early finds from South Africa seem to support the idea of man developing his present form on the African continent. Earlier this century, the fossilized skulls of pre-human primates known as *Australopithecus africanus* had been identified at two cave sites—at Sterkfontein in the Northwest Province and at Taung in the Northern Cape—dating back an estimated 1 to 3 million years.

These finds were followed by the discovery of skulls of the more advanced *Homo erectus* in two other Northwest Province cave systems—Makapansgat and Swartkrans—near modern Potgietersrus and Krugersdorp respectively. Thought to have lived 80,000–1 million years ago, *Homo erectus* was a hunter-gatherer who used co-operative hunting techniques, such as driving game into ambush, and was probably the first hominid to use fire. He was not confined to Africa, but seems to have spread all over Europe and Asia, which indicates a northward drift from 'mankind's cradle'. This may account for the lack of early *Homo sapiens* finds in South Africa; few sites have been dated to earlier than 20,000 years ago, and these remains bear similarities to the San (bushman) hunter-gatherers who inhabited much of southern Africa when the first whites arrived in the 15th century, and who still cling on in scattered communities in Botswana and Namibia today.

Archaeologists speculate that between 80,000 and 20,000 years ago people drifted north from southern Africa up to the Sahara, then green and lush. Very early rock paintings, similar to those of the South African San, found in the mountain ranges of the central Sahara support this view. Others claim that South Africa was populated from 100,000 years ago by the ancestors of the modern San, on the evidence of a few isolated engravings in South Africa and Namibia. What seems likely is that some *Homo sapiens* stayed on in South Africa while others forayed north, only to migrate slowly southward again around 30,000 years ago when archaeologists speculate that the Sahara began to dry out.

Certainly, most of South Africa's late-Stone Age finds date from around this period. Scattered across the country are caves painted in San style and strewn with the San's customized tools, such as ostrich-egg water containers. The San lived in small family groups of hunter-gatherers, moving with the timeless cycles of game migration, rain and drought; a lifestyle unchallenged until as late as about 2500 years ago, when the first groups came into contact with black pastoralists migrating down from the north, and acquired livestock.

These groups were initially confined to the lush grazing country of northern Botswana, but the practice seems to have drifted south into the Cape within a few centuries, and from this point there is a recognizable division between the livestock-owning San and those who remained hunter-gatherers.

The herders began calling themselves Khoi, which is thought to mean simply 'real men'. A certain amount of inter-breeding between the northern groups and black pastoralists and farmers, combined with a milk diet, seems to have increased the stature of the Khoi and given them an appearance slightly distinct from the San, but generally the difference between Khoi and San was merely one of lifestyle.

To confuse matters, South Africa's coastal caves are known to have been inhabited as early as 40,000 years ago by *strandlopers*, non-hunting KhoiSan who lived off shellfish, seabirds and fruits from the coastal bush. When the pastoral Khoi reached the Cape coast about 2000 years ago, some abandoned or lost their stock and joined the *strandlopers*, others kept their livestock and established themselves on the good grazing lands of the coasts, while the San hunter-gatherers retreated to the wilder mountain areas.

Meanwhile, black pastoralists and farmers had also migrated south, but on an easterly path to the modern Transvaal. These small groups had iron-working skills and practised rudimentary agriculture, and their slow southeastward drift became a mass migration 1000 years later (historians set the date between AD 1 and 300). Bantu-speaking people (Bantu is a general term for southern Africa's black languages) began to fill the Northern and Western Transvaal. Skilled smiths, with a sophisticated technology of pottery, weaving and house-building, their complex religious and ritual life was based around ancestor-worship, animism and, above all, cattle. Any San hunters in the way of the new invaders were either killed or absorbed into the dominant black peoples. By about AD 500 the steady trickle had reached the Eastern Cape. And by the end of what we call the Middle Ages, modern Transvaal, Natal except for the Drakensberg, Swaziland, Free State and parts of the Eastern Cape were densely settled with various Bantu-speaking clans, while the Western and Northern Cape was still the range of the San hunters, Khoi herders and, on the beaches, *strandlopers*.

Such was the picture when the first Portuguese ship rounded the Cape in 1488. Why the Portuguese deemed it necessary to brave the unknown southern Atlantic at a time when it was still thought possible to sail off the edge of the world requires explanation. The search for a sea route to the Indies was not in itself enough reason, as there were existing overland trade routes east via the Mediterranean. The answer lay in Portugal's vulnerable position with the Spanish House of Castile, which had come to dominate the Iberian Peninsula during the 14th century. From 1383 to 1411 the Portuguese fought to keep the Castilians out of their little country, and by the end of the war it became clear that only a powerful trading economy could secure Portugal the necessary foreign support to check Castile. It fell to the Portuguese King Jao (John) I to act.

A great fleet was prepared to attack the Moorish city of Ceuta, on the north coast of Africa, which had grown rich on the gold trade north across the Sahara from West Africa. The gamble paid off—Ceuta fell in 1415 and turned out to be far richer than the Portuguese could have hoped. Portugal suddenly found herself more than just the owner of a new trading port: she was mistress of the trans-Saharan gold route from Guinea and the Congo— a wealth of gold that gave credence to an old European legend of a Christian king, called Prester John, who was supposed to live somewhere down in Africa in a kingdom incomparably rich in gold. The legend was partly substantiated when Portuguese explorers reached Christian Ethiopia much later in the century—though there was no sign of any Prester John—and from the 1430s, Portuguese ships searching for both this mythical king and, more practically, for a trade route round to the East, began sailing ever southward along Africa's west coast. In 1488 the explorer Bartolomeu Dias sailed around the Cape of Good Hope and put ashore at modern Mossel Bay, where he attempted to bargain with the local Khoi for cattle. However, the Europeans and the Khoi misunderstood each other's intentions and fighting broke out.

It was not until 1498 that the Portuguese sailed that way again, this time under Vasco da Gama, who also put in at Mossel Bay. He stayed two weeks but, after successfully bartering for cattle, his sailors also fell foul of the locals and, after a brief skirmish, da Gama fired a cannon and broke up the party. From then on, the Portuguese traders regarded the South African coast, with its bad currents, frequent storms, and dangerous locals, as not worth the trouble of settling. The Cape's only importance lay in its marking the halfway point from Europe to the East Indies.

During the 16th century other Europeans learned of the route to the Indies and, from around 1580, Dutch, English and French captains began rounding the Cape on a regular basis. Some stopped to barter with the Khoi; cattle and sheep were acquired for metals, particularly copper wire, which the Khoi fashioned into fine jewellery. The Khoi/European relationship became friendly and familiar. The white men never stayed, but they brought trade, while the bartered livestock and fresh water came as blessed relief to the mariners who had already been at sea for months.

In 1608, to impress the South African natives with European splendour (and no doubt to impress the Europeans with a genuine 'savage'), a Dutch captain took a Khoi man to London and Holland, then returned him to his home on the Cape Peninsula with instructions to set up a regular cattle-supply for Dutch ships at Table Bay. And again, in 1631, the Dutch took a Khoi chief (whom they dubbed Harry) to Java, where the newly formed Dutch East India Company was setting up trading stations, and trained him in Dutch and English. Harry was also returned to the Cape, and was persuaded to act as interpreter, post-master and cattle-supplier for the Dutch and the English. Other shipping captains began to use large trees and boulders along the Cape coast, as 'post offices' where messages for colleagues could be left.

But in 1647 the *Haarlem*, a Dutch ship, was wrecked off Table Bay. The survivors built a makeshift fort and waited for rescue. A timely coincidence—the Dutch East India Company now had an established East Indies trade and was looking for a permanent supply stop for its ships. In 1650 it sent a commission to look into the possibilities of Table Bay. The leader, Jan Van Riebeeck—the ship's doctor on the rescue team that succoured the *Haarlem* survivors— saw a chance to advance his career. Despite the Cape's frequent storms and cross-currents, Van Riebeeck waxed enthusiastic about the area's potential. By 1652 he had persuaded his employers to take the same view, and was sent to Table Bay with about 100 men and women to set up the supply station. A strong fort was erected and Cape Town was born.

The Dutch Colonial Era

The Dutch East India Company was formed from a syndicate of powerful merchants from Holland's major towns. They acted with the sanction of their government, but were expected to fund their own adventures. Modelled on the medieval trading oligarchies of the Mediterranean, the Dutch East India Company's success inspired several other northern European powers, especially Britain, to form similar companies, two of which (the London Company of Adventurers, later the Hudson Bay Company, and Britain's East India Company) were to attain unprecedented commercial power in the northern hemisphere. Commerce, rather than conquest, was their motto. Although such companies all eventually became masters of huge foreign territories, empire-building was never the original idea, for conquest was expensive. The Dutch Cape Colony was thus never meant to extend into the interior.

To this end, the first colonists were expressly forbidden to enslave the locals, trade with them on anything other than Company business, or settle outside the confines of the fort. However, cattle-buying expeditions into Namaqualand in the northwest and the Hottentots' Holland (today's Winelands, *see* p.181) gave the colonists a glimpse of the great sub-continent's potential, and from the 1670s settlers began to mark out farms around the Cape Peninsula. At first the Company protested, then it capitulated, and from 1679 onwards began granting farms to its colonists. In the 1680s the adventurous governor Simon Van der Stel sent mineral prospecting and cattle-buying expeditions up the West Coast into Namaqualand, and beyond the Hottentots' Holland Mountains, where he founded the colony's second town, Stellenbosch. The same decade saw the arrival of settlers from France (Huguenot refugees) and Germany, who set up extensive European-style wine and dairy farms, and the Dutch Cape Colony was officially extended over the entire Western Cape. Individual trade with the Khoi was finally allowed and land was bought cheaply from the Khoi for iron, brass and copper.

Many traditional histories assert that the Khoi were easily persuaded to work for the Europeans and that they became an underclass by default of a natural fecklessness. But this was not the case. Resistance was often fierce. Many Khoi resented the white men's steady expansion into the hinterland, while others took to raiding both the settlers and the neighbouring Khoi who had grown rich from the cattle trade. From the 1670s the Company found itself having to send troops on regular seasonal campaigns against hostile Cape Khoi. Having committed itself to the colony, the Company was now obliged to uphold it, spending money on a series of inconclusive wars that resulted in a gradual northward and eastward extension of the colony's border—dragging the Company into a reluctant but steady cycle of conquest of the interior. At the same time, the Company began to lose control over its own settlers. Many adopted the Khoi's pastoral lifestyle and set off with wagons and flocks to live as they pleased. This new class of settler became known as *trekboer* (meaning literally, 'travelling farmer')—a freebooting, independent bunch who grazed their sheep, hunted game and subjugated the local Khoi and San as they wished. By 1700 the *trekboers* had pushed to the north and east, as far away from European authority as they could.

Smallpox, brought ashore in soiled linen at Cape Town, erupted among the Cape Khoi in 1713. Thereafter, regular epidemics ruled out concerted resistance to the Dutch and, while wars flared between Khoi and settlers until the 1750s, the Khoi rapidly lost their territories.

Still technically forbidden to own Khoi slaves, the *trekboers* began to force them into servitude. The Company had brought out slaves from Batavia—Djakarta—and West Africa from the early 1650s to pre-empt the colonists' obvious temptation to enslave the Khoi, but the plan had never really worked. Buying slaves was beyond the means of most colonists and their care involved cost. To the *trekboers*, far from Company authority, the Khoi seemed a gift from nature; scattered into already feuding tribes, they presented no united front against white settlement and could be subdued with firearms. South Africa's 18th-century *trekboers* began to use the Khoi as slaves in all but name, treating them with a careless brutality that became legendary among liberals back in Europe, and setting a precedent for violence from employer to hired hand that persisted to modern times.

By the 1760s the Dutch East India Company could no longer finance its huge and expanding trading empire. Despite several attempts to regularize the colony's frontiers through the establishment of *landdrosts* (magistracies) there simply was not the money to administer the interior. The *trekboers* pushed east to the Fish River in the Eastern Cape, flagrantly flouting the Company's orders to the contrary. But there they drew up short. They had encountered the Xhosa—a mighty black African nation whose territory extended east from the good grazing lands around the Fish River. At first relations between the Xhosa and *trekboers* were peaceable enough, but as more and more settlers drifted in, competition for grazing became inevitable. Three centuries of white/black conflict for the land were to follow.

Enter the British: the Frontier Wars

While Holland's maritime fortunes floundered, Britain's were on the rise. The latest of the European powers to pursue territory in the east, by the 1790s Britain required its own refreshment point for ships rounding the Cape. On top of this, she was at war with Revolutionary France, whose powerful navy was anxious to cut Britain off from India— control of the Cape meant control of the shipping route east and Britain could not afford to let the French get there first. In 1795 a British force took Cape Town from the Dutch (at the request of Holland's exiled House of Orange) and annexed the colony. In 1803, thinking the French defeated in Europe, Britain restored the Cape to Holland, but in 1806, seeing that Bonaparte meant to resume hostilities, Britain retook it.

Immediately, the new masters of South Africa found themselves embroiled in war on the eastern frontier between *trekboers*, Khoi and Xhosa. With no experience of Africa, the British dispatched troops to sort out this three-way struggle and embarked on a series of nine Frontier Wars that were to last almost 100 years, until 1879 (*see* p.312). First the Boers rebelled against the British, then the Khoi against the Boers, then the Khoi against the British, while the Xhosa periodically invaded the Cape Colony. No sooner had the Boers and Khoi been settled than the British went to war against the Xhosa in earnest. By the mid-1830s the British government was desperate. If the Dutch had found South Africa costly, the British found it ruinous. Not only were the Frontier Wars draining the treasury, but the frontier was not even secure; despite the influx of thousands of English settlers and the constant annexation of more Xhosa land, the eastern and northern frontiers remained dangerously unstable. From 1834 disgruntled Cape Boers began to trek away from British rule into the great interior, hoping to found their own republics there. In 1836 a huge number of Eastern Cape Boers, tired of both the British and the continued Xhosa threat, organized themselves into three parties of several thousand, got into their wagons and headed north and east away from European rule, just as their *trekboer* forebears had done.

The Great Trek and *Mfecane*

This mass movement to colonize the northeast differed from the *trekboers'* in its organization and fixed objective. While the *trekboer* had travelled with just his family and servants, in search of a spot far from anyone else, the Boers of the Great Trek (or 'Voortrekkers' as they became known) set out en masse to conquer a new country for themselves. Pastoral nomadism was no longer a Boer ambition. Under Louis Trichardt, Andries Potgieter and Hans van Rensburg, the first parties crossed the Orange River, the Cape Colony's official northern boundary, into the great unknown. Colonial histories often assert that this great territory was largely empty, owing to a series of massive tribal upheavals caused by the rise of the Zulu empire in modern-day Natal through the 1820s and '30s.

The traditional line is that the Zulus caused a domino effect over thousands of miles—that they forced clans to flee into each other's territories, fighting, moving and gradually depopulating the interior. However, this process, usually referred to as the *Mfecane* (Zulu for 'crushing'), has more recently been refuted as grossly inaccurate. Instead, the violent rise of the Zulu empire is regarded as part of a much wider process of warfare and political upheaval taking place between Natal and the Transvaal and across to the Orange Free State—various ethnic groups, competing for local control of the expanding ivory- and slave-trade routes to the Cape and to Delagoa Bay, subjugated their weak neighbours and went to war with their competitors. In the early 1800s the expanse of country north of the Orange River (today's far Northern Cape, Free State and Transvaal) had been explored and settled by missionaries such as John Campbell, Robert Moffat and, later, David Livingstone ('I presume')—who arrived in 1841. They had encountered a violent, semi-desert world where rival groups of Tswana, Griqua (mixed Khoi and white) and, latterly, Ndebele (a renegade regiment of the Zulu army) competed for control of the trade routes and raided each other mercilessly.

The Ndebele had invaded TransOrangia (as the highveld was then called) in the early 1830s, and the Voortrekkers ran into immediate resistance from them as soon as they entered the 'empty' north. Gathering Tswana and Griqua allies, the Voortrekkers pushed eastwards over the Vaal River, driving the Ndebele before them and causing them to overrun countless other clans. Contemporary accounts of this chaotic time describe how the Voortrekkers, arriving after the Ndebele, found villages abandoned and the surrounding *veld* strewn with bone shards. On the strength of this, later colonial historians claimed that these areas had been depopulated through genocidal warfare, and that the Voortrekkers' conquest of the north was peaceful. But the truth is that such 'empty' areas had only been abandoned for safer sites in more defensible positions, and the Voortrekker advance was a violent affair made slow by continual resistance from local chiefs.

The Boers experienced a major setback when a group of about 2000 Voortrekkers, under Gert Maritz and Piet Retief, broke away from the highveld parties in 1837 and set off across the Drakensberg into Natal—the southern extent of the Zulu empire, then ruled by Dingane, half-brother of the legendary chief Shaka. Dingane was quick to realize that the arrival of the Voortrekkers could only mean disaster for his independent kingdom. The following year he invited the leaders to negotiate a land grant, had them killed once they were in his court, then sent warriors to massacre two large Voortrekker parties near the Tugela River. It took the Boers some months to retaliate, but eventually they drove Dingane north where he was killed—probably by the Swazis, whose territory he had consistently raided during his reign. The Boers then put Dingane's brother Mpande on the Zulu throne, and declared their own republic in Natal (*see* 'Zululand: History', p.428).

It was to last only five years. The British were close on their heels and annexed Natal in 1842. Through the 1850s the Boer settlers abandoned the territory and trekked north again to join their fellows in the new republics of the Orange Free State and the Transvaal.

While the British began to colonize Natal in earnest, and continued to make war on the Xhosa of the neighbouring Eastern Cape, the Voortrekker statelets in the north sank into their own series of wars with the Swazi, Pedi, Sotho and Venda. The Boers managed to hold on to an extensive territory, but were unable to dislodge these established African nations from their best land.

Diamonds, Gold and War between the Whites

In 1870 the British, Griquas and the *burghers* of the Orange Free State came into conflict over Colesberg Kopjie, a small rocky hill west of the Vaal River. The land belonged to the Griquas, but the British took it anyway and paid off the Free Staters to keep the Griqua quiet. The hill in question was full of diamond-bearing rock. Diggers and prospectors were already active in the area and the hill soon became a hole, with hundreds of small claims worked by Tswana from the Orange Free State and Western Transvaal.

Within a few years the hole was surrounded by the booming mine town of Kimberley. The small claims were steadily bought up by larger companies, the biggest of which, De Beers (named after the farmer on whose land the town was built), was run by a charismatic young Englishman called Cecil Rhodes. Britain was overjoyed—it seemed that her costly South African colonies would finally be made to pay. The Free Staters felt robbed by the hated British, and both they and the Transvaalers resented the drift of black labour away from their farms. Caring little for the Boers' laments, the British secured their northern boundary by annexing the South African Republic (SAR) in 1877.

In the late 1870s gold was found near Barberton, in the Transvaal Drakensberg, but, under British rule, the local farmers had to sit by and grind their teeth while the revenues from the Barberton rush went into the hands of foreigners. Eventually, in 1881, a small Boer force under General Joubert managed to eject the British troops from the SAR after a battle at Majuba Hill on the Natal border (an incident that later became known as the First Anglo-Boer War) and, embarrassed, but lacking the means to retaliate effectively, the British ratified the SAR's independence in 1884. However, the republic remained grindingly poor until a new, massive gold strike was made in 1886 along the 500km Witwatersrand, just south of Pretoria. Excited, the SAR Boers, under their fiercely anti-British president Paul Kruger, realized that this new mineral resource could both enrich their country and buy enough arms to keep the British out forever.

But the SAR government also lacked the money to mine the gold on a large scale. Not without misgiving, they invited De Beers and the other Kimberley mining companies to the Witwatersrand and let them provide the necessary machinery and labour, while levying a tax on mining revenue. This plan worked insofar as the first mines near the new village of Johannesburg were operational by 1887. Black migrant labourers drifted in from all over the country, and revenue filled the Transvaal's coffers. However, the mining magnates and businessmen of the new Johannesburg were mostly English-speaking and their loyalties lay with Britain. Cecil Rhodes, in particular, was outspokenly jingoistic and active in Cape politics. Knowing this, President Paul Kruger sought to prevent the magnates threatening his republic by denying the vote to all foreigners, meanwhile using the mining revenues to stockpile weapons from Germany.

By 1890, the mining companies had transformed their financial power into political power—albeit outside the SAR—after Cecil Rhodes, now the richest man in South Africa, became Prime Minister of the Cape. Johannesburg was now the territory's largest town, stuffed with foreign businessmen who chafed at being denied the franchise. Rhodes began to stir up the Cape and Johannesburg press against Kruger's government, and the British government, eager to grab the gold mines and to redress their 1881 embarrassment at Majuba, expressed support. In 1895 Rhodes decided to force the issue by financing a *coup d'état* against Kruger's government in Pretoria. Under one Dr Jameson, an associate of Rhodes, a force of mounted adventurers crossed into the Transvaal from the new protectorate of Bechuanaland—now Botswana—under cover of dark and rode towards Pretoria. The Jameson Raid, as the affair became known, was hopelessly bungled; the invaders were picked up by a Boer *Kommando* and jailed in Pretoria. Rhodes, highly embarrassed, resigned as Cape Prime Minister. The British government, although it had not openly supported the raid, came under heavy fire from the European press, whose sympathies lay with the Boers. War was inevitable. The British gave Kruger an ultimatum over the foreigners' franchise, but he remained defiant, and, in 1899, the Second Anglo-Boer War broke out.

The war lasted three years, costing both sides dear. At first the Boers made use of their newly bought artillery and rifles to hold the British invasion force at bay for almost a year at the Tugela River in Natal, while also besieging the existing British garrisons in Ladysmith, Mafeking and Kimberley. But, once the British had broken the Tugela line and invaded the Orange Free State (with the loss of thousands of soldiers), and thrust into the Transvaal from Kimberley, the Boers broke up into small war parties—*Kommandos*—using guerrilla tactics against the lumbering British columns. By 1902, 450,000 British soldiers had been sent to South Africa, and General Kitchener began burning Boer farms and interning the women and children in concentration camps (where over 20,000 died). The *Kommandos* finally surrendered, leaving the gold fields in British hands. But Britain had lost over 25,000 men (mostly to disease), dipped alarmingly deep into the national treasury, and etched the already existing hatred for the British deeper in the Boer mind.

Following the surrender at Vereeniging, in the Transvaal, the Boer generals—Louis Botha and Jan Smuts—decided to work with the British, and negotiated the share of power while keeping South Africa as a British dominion. In 1910 the Union of South Africa was declared, with Botha as Prime Minister. But the Boer struggle was far from over. In 1914 a renegade Boer group formed a new political wing—the National Party in Bloemfontein—whose objectives were to win back South Africa for the Afrikaners and enforce white rule, which they saw as threatened by British tolerance of the growing black labour movements in the mines and political movements in the Eastern Cape.

A Three-Way Split: Blacks, Brits and Boers: 1879–1948

To understand this rise in black political consciousness, we must look back to the late 1870s, when the military might of the Xhosa, Zulu and Pedi nations had finally been crushed by the British, after the Ninth Frontier War, the Zulu War and the Pedi Campaign (all 1879). Despite their defeats, the Xhosa and Zulu people bounced back during the 1880s and '90s and began to make money from wool, maize and vegetables—to the point where many black communities in the Eastern Cape and Natal were making more than white farmers. Under British colonial law, blacks who owned land had voting rights, and the thought of an economically strong black majority alarmed the Cape government into passing the Glen Grey Act in 1894, which restricted the amount of land that black individuals could own.

Despite this, the rising tide of black fortune extended outside the Cape and Natal—from 1870, the Tswana, Pedi, Swazi, Venda, Sotho and other black nations of the Boer republics began offering themselves for contract work, first in the sugar-cane fields of Natal, then in the mines of Kimberley and Johannesburg. Under Boer rule, these blacks had been denied the right even to own land, let alone vote, and had suffered repeated Boer raids against their villages to kidnap children to work on farms. But, with the advent of migrant work, many black families gained breadwinners who earned hard cash, and who were often given a firearm as part of their pay-off. In the 1880s and '90s, the Pedi, Sotho, Venda and other Transvaal peoples rebelled against the Boers, while the Swazi and BaSotho maintained their independence. During the Second Anglo-Boer War, many Tswana fought for the British. By 1900 South Africa's blacks, despite being generally dispossessed, were beginning to exercise political power.

A small middle class of mission-educated blacks was also emerging, especially in the Eastern Cape and Natal, where the previous generation had suffered crushing military defeats. These men realized that they could best protect their societies through the white man's methods. Men like Alan Soga and J. T. Jabavu, Pixley Seme, Alfred Mangena, George Monstsioa, John Dube and Sol T. Plaatje entered the professions, becoming lawyers and journalists, and began to garner support for black grievances through the publication of native language newspapers and through parliamentary lobbying.

These men were by no means always in agreement. Soga, Seme, Plaatje, Dube and others favoured aggressive (by the standards of the day) politics, and in 1912 founded the South African Native National Congress (SANNC), later to become the ANC. Jabavu and his followers favoured more subtlety and began raising funds to create a black university that could compete on equal terms with any white institution. It took some years, but Jabavu eventually garnered enough philanthropic support at home and abroad to inaugurate the University of Fort Hare in 1916, at Alice in the Eastern Cape. Still active today, the university provided a launch-pad for the political careers of many future black freedom fighters. Graduates include Nelson Mandela, Walter Sisulu, the late Oliver Tambo and the President of Zimbabwe, Robert Mugabe.

Parallel with the efforts of the new black middle class, the Indians of Natal and the Transvaal also began forming political cells under the leadership of a young Indian-born lawyer called Gandhi, who had become committed to fighting racism since his first week in South Africa when he was thrown off a train at Pietermaritzburg for refusing to leave a carriage full of whites. Gandhi aimed at elevating Indians to the middle classes through commerce, starting a self-help scheme in 1906 at Phoenix, just north of Durban, with finance from prominent Indian businessmen. Preaching passive resistance to acts of government racism, such as the Pass Laws of 1913, Gandhi put Indians on the political map, masterminding strategies such as a protest march from Newcastle to the Transvaal—which, though broken up by baton-wielding police, made it plain that Indians would push for equal rights, no matter how summarily the government dealt with them.

Although black and Indian politics were still far removed from each other, by 1914 concerted political resistance to white rule was well established. This was just as well; if the new British/Boer government was anything but liberal, the emerging Boer Nationalists, under Barry Hertzog, were busy establishing an even more right-wing opposition, and lobbied government to extend the 1913 Pass Laws into an almost total ban on non-white ownership of land—whites were to own 87 per cent of the land space, blacks a mere 13 per cent, all inside set 'reserves', the forerunners of the later 'homelands'.

Hertzog's predominantly rural nationalists found unexpected support among the skilled white workers of the Rand gold fields. The mining magnates had long wanted to break the colour bar between skilled and unskilled labour, knowing that it could reduce costs by putting blacks in skilled jobs. At the same time the companies could solve what had become a chronic labour shortage, as blacks, lacking the incentive of more senior jobs to make them stay on, drifted away from the mines once their contracts were up. But white workers had no intention of competing for jobs with an overwhelming black majority.

Immediately before the First World War mass strikes, involving tens of thousands of white workers, broke out across the Witwatersrand, protesting at the mining companies' attempts to break the job/colour bar. But, with conscription, most of these white workers went into the army, and black miners, inspired by the success of white strikes in securing wage increases, also staged mass strikes. Distracted by its war effort and the need for increased production, the government and mining companies gave in to a few of the demands (though making a show of force in putting the strikes down).

When the white workers returned from the war and found their jobs once again under threat from cheap black labour, their anger knew no bounds. From 1918 white mine workers staged a series of violent strikes and riots, which culminated in a General Strike of whites in all industries in 1922. Prime Minister Jan Smuts only restored order to the gold fields after sending in the combined army and air force, but capitulated to the white workers and made the job/colour bar law.

This is one of the sad ironies of South African history. With so much in common, a united front by white and black workers might have brought an early racial equality, and saved the country tens of thousands of deaths throughout the rest of the 20th century. But with working class whites and blacks competing for jobs, a united front could never happen. From the 1920s the country became increasingly racially divided, and the fear felt by working class whites towards blacks provided the grass-roots support for the later apartheid governments.

The far right opposition was quick to exploit this. In 1918 an organization known as the Afrikaner *broederbond* ('brotherhood') had been set up, with the objective of infiltrating industry and government with educated Afrikaners of Nationalist persuasion.

At the same time, the growing black resistance became increasingly political. In 1923 the SANNC changed its name to the African National Congress (ANC)—now a household name throughout the world—and in 1928 began working with the South African Communist Party (SACP) to build a white/black workers' movement. Hertzog's Nationalists countered this by forcing the government to make racial segregation compulsory in urban areas, and took advantage of the general world economic depression to foment more fear among white workers at losing their jobs to blacks. By 1930 even the more moderate whites were moving to the right, and in 1934 Hertzog and Smuts formed the United South African National Party—the iron fist of racism inside a velvet glove—a joint prime-ministership with Smuts as the soft-talking front man pushed ever further to the right by Hertzog and his followers.

In defiance, the ANC and SACP united to urge a general burning of pass books, but the government retaliated by summarily taking away the Cape's black franchise, leaving South Africa's blacks with no vote at all. However, the whites were still not united, and the Smuts/Hertzog union began to suffer internal splits. In 1939 Hertzog resigned over South

Africa's joining the British war effort. The Nationalists reverted to their isolationist, anti-British stance and prepared for a mass attack on the colonial government as South Africa went to war against Germany again. The furthest right wing even formed a Hitlerist society called the *Ossewabrandweg* (ox-wagon sentinels—referring to the Great Trek) who dodged the draft and beat up South Africans seen in uniform. English and Afrikaner whites were as divided as they had been since the British annexation 150 years before.

Not so the blacks. With the eyes of government for the second time diverted by a World War, the ANC and black trade unions capitalized on their successes of the 1930s. From 1940 a series of bus boycotts brought down the cost of public transport for black workers in Johannesburg's townships. Blacks waiting to be allotted housing rebelled, and began erecting huge squatter camps. The African Mineworkers' Union (AMU) was founded in 1941 and the ANC Youth League in 1943. The same year saw the SACP and ANC unite over anti-Pass Law protests, and in 1946 the AMU went out on mass strike over segregation and low pay. But with the Second World War over, the government could once again concentrate on home affairs. The strike was crushed by paramilitary police units. In 1948 a general election was called, amidst white alarm at the rising strength of black politics, and the Afrikaners, burying their many differences, came together and voted in the ultra-right-wing Nationalists, under Prime Minister D. F. Malan.

Apartheid and the Rise of Violence: 1948–90

With the arrival of the Nationalist government any pretence at positive race relations went out of the window. Between 1949 and 1960 mixed marriage, squatting, 'riotous assemblies' (i.e. black demonstrations), even mixed education, were all banned. The Cape 'coloureds' were disenfranchised (despite a national outcry from white liberals), the residents of Johannesburg's lively Sophiatown, the centre of black counter-culture, were forcibly removed to the new township of Soweto, Sophiatown itself was razed and the SACP and ANC suppressed.

Of course, there was resistance—in 1952 rioting broke out over the loss of the 'coloured' vote, and in 1953, after the Bantu Education Act which denied blacks entry to white universities. A short-lived 'Defiance Campaign' led by the ANC's Youth League under a young lawyer, Nelson Mandela, attempted to thwart racist government policies. But to many blacks the ANC seemed powerless, especially after the publication of their Freedom Charter in 1955 only led to a huge government crackdown on left-wing political organizations—even on marginal movements such as the liberal white women's organization, the Black Sash, who had protested at the ban on the Cape 'coloured' franchise (but these were confined to warnings). Members of the ANC and Communist Party leaders (black and white) were dealt with more harshly—being arrested and tried for treason.

The Treason Trials lasted four years, severely hobbling the liberation struggle. In 1959 militants from the ANC expressed their frustration by forming a new anti-white organization, the Pan African Congress (PAC), under the charismatic Robert Sobukwe. In 1960 the PAC called on all Johannesburg's blacks to burn their pass books, deliberately provoking a mass arrest of the entire black workforce—bringing industry to a halt and overloading the police. The plan was welcomed, but at Sharpeville, south of Johannesburg, a vast crowd of demonstrators milling around a police station were fired on and, in the panic, the police killed over 200 people. With typical over-reaction the Prime Minister Hendrik Verwoerd, a Dutch-born super-racist, declared a brief State of Emergency. Sobukwe was arrested, and both the ANC and PAC banned. Oliver Tambo, who was one of the ANC's most senior leaders until his death in 1993, went to London to carry on the liberation struggle from abroad.

The government resisted foreign pressure to tone down its racist stance, withdrawing from the Commonwealth in 1961. South Africa's leaders were no longer answerable to the British Crown, but were heads of state who could do as they pleased. But the struggle had advanced too far to be given up so easily and both organizations went underground, forming military wings. *Umkhonto we Sizwe* (the Spear of the Nation——MK for short) was the ANC wing determined to target government installations and public services, but *Poqo*, the PAC wing, favoured terrorism, and several white civilians were killed at locations around the country. To avoid arrest, the MK and *Poqo* based their operations in Communist-backed countries such as Algeria, Angola, Tanzania, Mozambique, and also Ethiopia.

In 1962 Nelson Mandela, chairman of the MK, returned from Ethiopia and met with other MK members at their headquarters on a farm in Rivonia, near Johannesburg. He was picked up in the small town of Cedara and initially sentenced to five years for 'inciting African workers to strike, and leaving the country without valid travel documents'. But a year later the security forces got wind of the Rivonia meetings, tracked down the farm, found draft documents outlining plans of guerrilla warfare, and managed to arrest other MK leaders, including Walter Sisulu—today one of the most prominent members of the ANC government. Together with Mandela, they were charged with sabotage, and sentenced to life. The ten years following the Rivonia Trial are referred to as the 'silent decade'. Those ANC and PAC leaders who escaped arrest were forced into exile, and the liberation struggle was effectively on ice, as the resistance leaders struggled to organize operations from abroad.

The government took advantage of the lull to enforce apartheid to a greater extent. It began the 'homelands' policy of creating separate states (or 'bantustans') for blacks, stripping them of South African citizenship, and giving them poor, overcrowded, but nominally independent reserves within the country that would still supply the labour market. Between 1960 and 1981 ten of these 'bantustans' were created, complete with repressive puppet regimes that would act under Pretoria's directives.

The one voice of open dissent in the early 1970s came from a young black medical student called Steve Biko, who was studying in Durban. One of the few multi-racial organizations left in South Africa was the university-based NUSAS, or National Union of South African Students. Biko, despite being isolated on a black campus, became a prominent figure in the organization. He began to publish in its journal criticisms of South Africa's white liberals, whom he accused of complacency. His writings were distributed on white and black campuses alike, and his philosophy, which he called Black Consciousness, widely accepted. The basic idea behind the movement was simple enough: blacks should not feel undermined by white supremacy, and should take a conscious pride in their black identity. Whites and blacks should be prepared to share democratic power, wrote Biko, but South Africa was wasting a vast talent pool by denying blacks equality and by fearing a black political majority. Furthermore, he pointed out that the running of apartheid was too expensive to be sustainable for more than a generation, and that all South Africans, white and black, would ultimately suffer the continual drain on the economy.

The Black Consciousness movement sparked a series of demonstrations. Biko was arrested in 1974 and accused of inciting terrorism. Yet he argued his own case so eloquently in court that he won over many of his jurors and inspired a wave of support in the international press. By far the most sophisticated politician of his time, Biko inspired a deep fear in the government. Taking heart from Biko's stand, the black working class began to find a voice again from 1973, with the Labour Movement. Strikes in Durban spread through the country, protesting not at working conditions or pay, but at apartheid, pure and simple. By 1974/5, the ANC and PAC leaders who had been jailed for 10 years after the Rivonia Trial completed their terms. On their release they began gathering support from both the Black Consciousness and Labour movements. Neither movement involved violence (except on the part of the police); but this was soon to change.

In 1976 the liberation struggle exploded into action again, and in the last place the government would have expected—among Soweto's schoolchildren. There was no central organization, just a few demonstrations against the compulsory learning of certain subjects in Afrikaans. Riot police called into Soweto were stoned and attacked, and hundreds of schoolchildren were shot or jailed. For black youth to act independently of parental authority was unprecedented; traditional South African society is severely hierarchical, and the Soweto rising pointed as much to a breakdown of the traditional black societies under ghetto life as to a precocious political awareness among Soweto's adolescents. Those who escaped arrest fled to ANC camps abroad, and the organization gained much new blood to take the freedom struggle into the next decade.

But for the moment the strength of the government's crackdown on the new rise of black protest was harsher than ever. Police violence against detainees became murderous. The most famous victim was Steve Biko, who died while in police custody in Port Elizabeth in 1977. Tragically his death did not unite the new generation of freedom fighters—far from it. Soweto schoolchildren supporting his Black Consciousness democratic movement, and those supporting the more anti-white, hardline PAC policy, began to fall out, and sporadic but lethal fighting broke out between the factions.

Meanwhile, the ANC was looking for allies abroad. In 1979 the late Oliver Tambo met with one Mangosotho Buthelezi, a young Zulu nobleman who was head of a Natal-based black organization called Inkhatha. Although formed back in the 1920s, Inkhatha had languished in obscurity until taken up by the charismatic young Buthelezi, who had wide Zulu support. The ANC saw Buthelezi and Inkhatha as an opportunity to form an above-ground wing in Natal that could play a vital role in upholding the freedom struggle in Natal. But Buthelezi was not content to be a tool of the ANC. He and Tambo could not reach an agreement—a split that was to have violent consequences later on. In the early 1980s Buthelezi re-organized Inkhatha into the militant pro-Zulu Inkhatha Freedom Party (IFP), and began to campaign for his own place in the national political arena.

The same period saw a marked increase in general violence in South Africa. Existing ethnic tensions were eagerly promoted by the South African government in the mines, the townships, and even in the surrounding countries, as South African troops were deployed to support rebel factions fighting the new communist governments in Angola and Mozambique. Troops were also deployed in Namibia (then governed by South Africa) to put down anti-South African terrorism there. This divide-and-rule policy, honed over the centuries of white colonial rule, caused intense fighting in the Witwatersrand miners' hostels—between Zulu, Xhosa and other 'tribal' groups, advancing the government's claim that only it could control the violence inherent in the African soul. But today it is widely believed that the government security forces (generally referred to as the 'Third Force') were behind much of this fighting, which claimed thousands of lives through the 1980s and early 1990s. This claim seems likely, given the billions of dollars the government spent on its military projects abroad.

By 1986 world condemnation of apartheid was made concrete in the form of international sanctions against the country. Gold prices plummeted and massive disinvestment by foreign companies threatened the financial future of apartheid. The government realized that it would have to make concessions, yet still it clung to the hope that outward reform would be sufficient. Under president P. W. Botha, the more obviously right-wing members of the National Party were expelled, and a small number of Indians and 'coloureds' were allowed back into Parliament. The exiled ANC began to court white liberals (mostly academics) from abroad, and set up the United Democratic Front (UDF) to campaign for the release of political prisoners.

However, by now the political violence in the townships had reached fever pitch. From 1986 to 1990, the disputes between Soweto schoolchildren supporting Biko's Black Consciousness and those favouring a hardline anti-white policy caused an adolescent death-toll that mounted into the thousands. IFP and ANC fighting in Natal townships claimed even more lives. Many black shopkeepers and businessmen claimed that local PAC, IFP and ANC leaders were demanding money from them for their campaigns, threatening those who did not pay, and that businesses forced to support one group were burned out by another. A 'them-and-us' mentality arose, in which anyone publicly denounced as a government informer or sympathizer was liable to be killed by a mob, often by 'necklacing'—a form of public murder in which the victim had a petrol-filled tyre put around his or her neck and was then set alight.

The government took advantage of the black-to-black fighting, and its attendant atrocities, to declare a State of Emergency (i.e. martial law) and send troops into the townships. Detention without trial, even of white academics supporting the UDF, became common. Many people suspected that the extreme violence in the townships was being fomented by the security forces, and P. W. Botha's 'reforms' were seen to be a sham. However, the extent to which black factional fighting had run out of control was tellingly revealed when Winnie Mandela was implicated in a murder trial in 1989.

The body of a 14-year-old boy named Stompie Mokhetse was found at her house, and subsequent investigations alleged that Mrs Mandela was at the centre of a series of beatings and kidnappings, even murders, of Soweto youths opposed to the ANC. Mrs Mandela was charged with hiring thugs, who posed as a 'football club' for boys from broken homes, to carry out the crimes. Graffiti appeared on walls all over South Africa announcing 'Winnie's in the Pooh'—the lighter side of what turned out to be a sinister web of intimidation and violence. She was brought to trial, amid much national and international media shock, having been much fêted through the preceding years for standing by her husband and for helping to make him an international symbol of the wrongs of South Africa. Although Winnie Mandela's case was hardly representative of the ANC's ethics, it severely damaged the party's credibility, and exposed cracks in the morality of South Africa's liberation struggle.

Although found guilty, Mrs Mandela was not charged—the political climate was too tense. The ANC was quick to distance itself from her, and she has moved to the political sidelines.

In 1989 tightened sanctions and a badly failing economy finally prompted the white government to begin the dismantling of apartheid. P. W. Botha was voted out in favour of President F. W. de Klerk and real reforms followed. While the far right of the National Party broke away to form the Conservative Party, and the neo-Nazi AWB (Afrikaner Weerstandsbeweging—Afrikaner Resistance Movement) gained popularity among many Afrikaans-speaking whites, de Klerk set about repealing some of the apartheid laws, such as segregation, and the ban on mixed marriage and education. By 1990, nursing South Africa's crippled economy, de Klerk persuaded the foreign powers to lift sanctions against his country by withdrawing the army from Angola and Namibia, unbanning the ANC and PAC, and releasing Nelson Mandela from jail. The eyes of the world were on de Klerk as he pledged to work towards a multi-racial society in which the black majority would gain power through democratic election.

Into the Great Unknown

This is a time to heal the old wounds and build a new South Africa.

Nelson Mandela

Mandela's release did not stop the violence. Conflict between the IFP and ANC continued to rage in the Rand and Natal. From 1992 unemployment became acute as the mines, suffering under the ever-dropping gold price, laid off tens of thousands of workers. Violent crime rose accordingly, as did terrorism. For example, during 1993 APLA (formerly *Poqo*), the armed wing of the PAC, launched a series of attacks on white civilians across the country, and yet more rioting followed the assassination of the South African Communist Party president Chris Hani by a right-wing fanatic. Political violence finally spilled from the townships into the white city centres and a general fear polarized the racial communities until it seemed that the long-awaited election, set for April 1994, would plunge the country into civil war. This was compounded by Buthelezi and the IFP's refusal to aid the peace talks between the National Party, the ANC and the other political parties.

But to everyone's surprise, and great relief, the elections went off with almost no violence at all. It was as if the country had sated itself during the bloody lead-up to the ballot day. The ANC polled 62.6 per cent of the national vote, a percentage which qualified them to hold 252 of the 400 seats in the national assembly, but not quite the two-thirds of the vote which would have allowed them to write a constitution without input from other parties. On 10 May 1994 Nelson Mandela was inaugurated as South Africa's first black president, with a dream to bind the wounds of the country and unite all South Africans.

So what of the future? Does 'the New South Africa' exist, and if so, where is it going? For many whites the first problem is that of Affirmative Action. White-collar jobs have traditionally been reserved for white necks in South Africa, but this is changing fast. Not only are black students suddenly filling the universities, but many companies are adopting a positive discrimination policy for new recruits—though many businessmen feel that this influx of unqualified staff at every level, combined with growing government and corporate corruption, will be the ruin of the country. The economy has still not recovered from the economic downturn caused by the international sanctions and foreign disinvestment of the final apartheid years. The gold price is at an all-time low, and, to cut costs, mines are laying off workers: unemployment is getting worse and crime rising. People are scrambling for local government jobs—a tempting security in the present economic climate—and there is a danger that government itself may become silted up in the process.

The accession of the ANC has brought its attendant problems. Many South Africans fear that there is too great a gulf between the party's senior leaders and the increasingly disaffected black youth—especially as the change in government has not automatically produced economic benefits for the poor. An ideological split in the younger leadership of the ANC—a divide between socialism and communism fostered in different ANC training camps abroad —may also threaten the future of the party. An effective opposition has already established itself in KwaZulu-Natal in the form of the IFP, which now promises to challenge the government on a national level.

However, the prospects are by no means all gloomy. Considering that, for an African police state, a relatively bloodless change from repressive to democratic government is unprecedented, one should not underestimate the enormous will of the South African people as a whole to make their new country work. This is evident, for example, in the retention of many former white, Afrikaans-speaking Nationalist Party MPs as regional directors of agriculture—the whites had taken the land in the past, but had also learned sustainable techniques of food production, so their expertise is not being thrown away. At the same time, improved education will mean an inevitable alleviation of problems such as overpopulation, erosion through bad farming and environmental destruction, especially in the former 'homelands', where education and all public services have long been neglected. Foreign investors are trickling back to South Africa, and tourism is booming.

Even changes within the army have not caused serious upheaval; for example, following the absorption of the MK into the regular South African army in April 1994, a group of former MK members, dissatisfied with army life, assaulted their commanding officer and marched on the government buildings in Pretoria. President Mandela—himself a founder member of the MK—met them personally, and defused the situation. Unlike most other African countries, South Africa is not threatened by its armed forces.

Most South Africans feel great relief at having made the change at long last—though the burgeoning crime rate causes many, both black and white, to sigh for the law and order that was apartheid's one positive feature. Travellers who have visited the country more than once report that the fear of political violence that built up before the elections has dissipated. South Africans finally have access to one another's cultures. South African sport is back on the international circuit and its rugby and cricket teams have stolen some world titles over the past few years. Soccer, traditionally the sport of South Africa's black communities, has finally entered international competition—and its league teams rival the best in Africa.

South Africa is on the brink of coming of age as a society. Nationalism and racism will continue to flare, but Lesotho and Swaziland, the two independent countries within South Africa's borders, have already demonstrated that a multi-racial society can work, despite the conflicts suffered for 300 years. A democratic government has finally come to power, there is a Bill of Rights, and a reconstruction and development programme that avoids the settling of old racial scores and concentrates on simply re-organizing the country along more just lines.

Perhaps the best omen for this is contained within the new national anthem, *Nkosi Sikelel' iAfrica* (God Bless Africa), whose meaning is purely religious, and leaves politics aside.

However, whether this relative stability can last is an open question. In 1999 President Mandela steps down. Can Thabo Mbeki, his immediate successor, keep the country united? Will the Zulus again become a destabilizing force? Will the far right-wing Afrikaners take up arms again—after all, they have never given up their dream of an all-white homeland. Winnie Mandela, having once again evaded conviction, may well stir up the township youth, whose criminal underclass has been holding Johannesburg to ransom throughout the nineties. Once again, South Africa's future is uncertain, but it has come through darker days than this. South Africa is a powerful country. Above all, its people love the land they were born to, and there is a common desire, at all levels, to see it work.

Wildlife and Conservation

Xkhoagu, Hunting star,
blind with your light the springbok's eyes.

San hunting song

Conservation

Since primeval times, South African conservation and the hunting of its wildlife have gone hand-in-hand. But the instinctive conservation of the San and Khoi hunters, who left animals alone in certain seasons and never killed more than they needed, meant that neither they nor the pit-traps and spear-hunts of the black cattle-herders made much impression on the vast numbers of game that then lived in the country. It was only when gun-bearing Europeans began to penetrate the interior during the 18th and early 19th centuries that mass wildlife slaughter came to South Africa. Although the eastern areas, settled later, remained game-rich, the Cape and Free State were all but stripped of their game in under 100 years.

To give an idea of the original numbers involved, early travellers in the Karoo reported antelope migrations, particularly of springbok, which could take two days to pass a farm. The trekking antelope numbered millions. One Gordon Cumming, travelling the Karoo during the 1840s, reported 'the plains and hillsides, which stretched away on every side, thickly covered, not with herds, but with one vast mass of springboks, as far as the eye could strain, the landscape was alive with them, until they softened down to a dim mass of moving creatures' (quote from *Plains of the Camdeboo*, Eve Palmer, Collins Cape Town, 1966). Along with the springbok came a host of other species and, trailing them, great numbers of predators.

With such an apparent infinitude of wildlife it was small wonder that the early settlers and travellers orgied in killing, whether for sport or to clear the veld for their livestock. But the muskets killed faster than the game could reproduce. By 1850 three species, the Cape lion, the quagga (a kind of zebra) and the bluebuck,' had vanished, and by the 1870s the Cape interior was all but empty of game. As settlement penetrated Natal and the Transvaal, the game there began to disappear too. It was only at the end of the century that a few far-sighted individuals began pressing the colonial governments to begin conservation of game.

In 1895 President Paul Kruger of the South African Republic (Transvaal) was persuaded to proclaim an area of what later became the Kruger National Park. Around the same time, the British in Natal preserved Umfolozi, the old royal hunting ground of the Zulu kings, and in the 1900s the Pongola Game Reserve (now known as Itala) was set up. These provided a starting point for South Africa's conservation ethic, and began to attract the first non-hunting, wildlife-spotting tourists. Poaching remained rife as local farmers asserted their right to hunt, but the efforts of men like James Stevenson-Hamilton, head ranger of the Kruger National Park for over 40 years, began to persuade the government that wildlife preserves could both bring in money through tourism, and also make attractive show-pieces for the country's public image.

The conservation movement had begun: between the 1930s and '60s serious attempts were made to rehabil-itate South Africa's wildlife. Species like the bontebok, Cape mountain zebra and Eastern Cape elephants, which had been on the brink of extinction, were given their own reserves. Several national parks and hundreds of new nature reserves were proclaimed across the country, even in the Karoo, where restocking programmes brought back most of the non-dangerous game with unexpected speed.

What is surprising is that most of this positive conser-vation happened during the most repressive era of apartheid: while the South African government spent millions on restocking the old game ranges and on setting up well co-ordinated armed patrols to prevent the poaching of elephant, rhino and spotted cat, South African soldiers abroad in Namibia, Mozambique and Angola attacked the game in those countries with a will, and the scandal of South African army officers trafficking in illegal ivory from those countries has now been thoroughly documented.

However, at home, through the 1970s and '80s, things got progressively better for game as even the hunter began to work for conservation. Many farmers in the lowveld districts of the Northern and Eastern Trans-vaal began to look to raising game, after trying for years to raise livestock in the feverish, drought-ridden country. By restocking their farms with game species, many of these farmers found that they could produce meat without veterinary bills, without having to irrigate, and without the veld becoming overgrazed. On top of selling the meat, they could actually charge hunters money to come in and slaughter the meat for them. At long last the gun was working in favour of wildlife—admittedly only because it paid—and through the late 1980s many farmers in the Eastern Cape and the Karoo also restocked their huge farms with wild game. Even tradi-tional livestock farmers have become far more accepting of game on their land in recent years, and many are beginning to restock with antelope for purely aesthetic purposes.

Today, the proclamation of new nature reserves and national parks continues. New national parks have been laid out at Vaalbos, near Kimberley in the Northern Cape, in the Tankwa Karoo area of the Northern Cape (south of Calvinia), in the semi-desert Richtersveld (also in the Northern Cape) and at several other locations. Of these, the Richtersveld and Vaalbos are open to visitors, and major restocking programmes are under way in the others, and the National Parks Board intends to let the vegetation recover (these are old farming areas) before setting up tourist facilities.

Meanwhile, a massive new nature reserve in the Northwest Province (part of the former 'homeland' of Bophuthatswana) called Madikwe has been restocked with the 'Big Five', and lion have been re-introduced to the Eastern Cape and Shamwari Private Game Reserve near Grahamstown, as well as extending their present range in Zululand with re-introduction to the new Phinda Game Reserve. Plans are afoot to extend the vast Kruger National Park into neighbouring Mozam-bique, and to establish similar vast reserves around Weenen in Natal (at present overgrazed farmland) and in Tsongaland.

The number of game reserves, nature reserves, national parks, wilderness areas, conservation areas and state forest—all of them subject to strict anti-poaching laws—now exceeds 350, and if you add to this a similar number of game farms—many of which extend to tens of thousands of hectares—a very healthy conservation picture, easily the healthiest on the African continent, begins to emerge. Meanwhile, within these reserves work is being carried out to re-establish all the indige-nous vegetation and take out all exotics. So successful has South Africa's conservation policy been that today it is one of the few countries in Africa where even rare game species such as elephant, leopard, lion and white rhino are actually expanding, while endangered species such as black rhino and cheetah are stable.

With tourism on the increase in South Africa since the elections, the new government has pledged to keep ploughing money into its wildlife. On top of this, some of the reserves are beginning to pay for their own conservation, either through selling hunting licences to take out game marked for culling (the money from which pays for the special breeds programmes such a rhino and cheetah), or by selling live game to game reserves elsewhere in Africa which have become depleted. For example, the Kruger National Park now has too many elephant and, rather than cull them, has sold and translocated hundreds to reserves in Kenya, Namibia and Zimbabwe. Even black rhino, now breeding a small surplus in the Kruger National Park, have been sold to restock areas of Namibia, and, if this trend continues, South Africa's wildlife can look to a secure future.

To see dense concentrations of game, your best bet is to head for the bushveld country of the Eastern Cape, Natal, Mpumalanga, and the Northern Province, or into the Kalahari.

Mountain ranges tend to be more limited in the amount of game you can see, but large herds of eland,

Mammals

The Big Five (or Six)

South Africa is home to the 'Big Five' (in reality the Big Six): elephant, buffalo, lion, leopard, and white and black rhino. The reserves where all these can be seen together are confined to Mpumalanga and Zululand. However, apart from lion, the 'Big Five' can be found at game reserves throughout the country. Indeed the leopard (the shyest but most common big cat) lives in almost all the South African mountain ranges, even if it is not actively conserved there. A pair is even reputed to breed on Table Mountain above Cape Town. As for elephant and rhino, while populations elsewhere across the continent continue to decline under the heavy toll of poaching, in South Africa the species are well protected and are actually on the increase.

blesbok, mountain reedbuck, zebra and grey rhebok will still be seen, plus baboons, and leopard or caracal if you are lucky. The lush indigenous forests that flourish in some of the coastal mountain ranges support the least game, usually only bushbuck, duiker, genet, vervet monkey and baboon, with lynx and leopard as predators. However, the forests above Knysna, in the Western Cape, still support a few shy elephant, survivors of uncontrolled ivory-hunting that wiped out a population of thousands between 1860 and 1920.

Even in the dry Karoo, the nature reserves are surprisingly rich in game, and it is worth looking out at night for the rare aardwolf (an insect-eating relative of the hyena) and for the elusive brown hyena, smaller than its spotted cousin, which feeds on the night rodents and birds of the semi-desert.

Lion

The lion is an incredible creature. Its beauty, massive physical strength and swiftness; its seeming indifference to the world around, knowing that it is top predator; the way it looks at you, appraising you as potential food; hearing it cough and roar in the night, making you sit bolt upright from the soundest sleep: all stir a memory of primordial fears, long-buried beneath the comforts of modern life.

For all this, lion kill a negligible number of people in Africa, compared to the number killed by, say, hippo, elephant or buffalo. They would rather have nothing to do with you and will generally only attack if you get too close. Even when encountered on foot during a walking safari, your guide will generally tell you to back off slowly while holding the creature's gaze.

Mammals 53

Lion are highly adaptable, inhabiting just about every eco-system, including desert fringe. They will take on dangerous game, despite the risk of injury and death. Prides will often leave a hunt after more 'easy' game such as zebra, in order to turn on a buffalo. Nobody has yet worked out why.

Despite their athletic ability and strength, most prides only kill during about 30 per cent of their hunts. The hunts and kills require a huge investment of energy; the animal has to be suffocated or have its neck broken by the lion wrapping its forelegs around the neck and fastening its teeth on the windpipe. It's a slow process; large animals can resist for up to an hour. Then the kill has to be defended against hyena and other predators. Small wonder then that when you come across lions by day they are usually flaked out, exhausted after the labours of the previous night.

▶ Best places to see them: Mpumalanga, N. Province, Natal, the Kalahari, Shamwari Reserve in E. Cape.

Leopard

Although leopard are much more numerous than lion, you are much less likely to see one. They have an uncanny ability to live close to man (most farms have a couple of resident leopard) without being seen. This secretive nature has allowed them to survive in areas where other big cats were exterminated decades ago.

If you are lucky enough to see a leopard, the encounter will be unforgettable. These sleek spotted cats are almost always solitary, and superbly beautiful:

found in just about every habitat. They are not dependent on a plentiful supply of large and mid-sized game, but can subsist on dassies (rock hyrax), rodents, baboons and other small prey.

▶ Found in all regions.

White Rhinoceros

The term white rhino is a contraction of 'wide-lipped rhino'. While the black rhino is a browser, and has a pointed upper lip useful for grabbing sweet bits off branches, the white rhino is a grazer and its wide, straight upper lip is designed to stay out of the way when it's got its head down. However, the white rhino does also happen to be lighter in colour than its black cousin, which is why the name has stuck. It is also more massive (though not always taller), with a larger head and, in general, a more placid nature.

Again, poaching has pretty much done for all but a few relict populations of white rhino, except for in South Africa, where the conservation has been more effective and the species is actually expanding its range. Like the black rhino it can go some days without drinking, and will dig for water during droughts. But, unlike the black rhino, white rhino females are sociable. Small herds of five or six cows are commonly seen in daylight hours, which move back to their own ranges at evening. Females will also go in pairs.

White rhino prefer open woodland and grassy plains with reasonable water supplies, which limits their natural range to southeast Africa.

Leopard   Black Rhinoceros   White Rhinoceros

lithe, graceful, self-contained. They are incredibly strong —able to pull a mid-sized antelope up into a tree or crag away from other predators.

Leopard hunt almost exclusively at night. In some remote mountain areas you will hear them 'coughing', a kind of grunting roar that warns other leopards not to stray into their hunting territory. Male and female ranges may overlap, but same-sex territories seldom do, if ever. Fights do occur between rivals if they meet on the hunt. Leopard are even more adaptable than lions and are

Although white rhino do not mate for quite the same extended periods as black rhino, they still manage an impressive half-hour or so.

▶ Best places to see them: all regions except W. Cape.

Black Rhinoceros

This used to be one of the more numerous and dangerous large browsers of southern Africa, charging out of the bush angrily if it heard or smelled something unusual. No longer. Despite the shoot-to-kill policies (for poachers, not rhinos) employed by southern African nature conservation departments, the black rhino has been all but poached out, the incredibly high price of rhino horn having made hunting it worth risking life for. The surviving black rhino are now very, very shy and rarely come out of heavy cover.

Black rhino, when left alone, are highly adaptable animals, able to live in both very lush and very arid zones. In semi-deserts they can get most of the moisture they need by chewing succulent plants such as euphorbias and sanseverias. However, they must get to permanent water at least once a week, and where water is available they drink every day. If there has been no rain they will dig for water in dry riverbeds.

Black rhino are solitary, with few territorial fights between accustomed neighbours, although newcomers will be fiercely challenged. What is interesting, however, is the time spent mating. While most mammals tend to get it over with fairly quickly, black rhino go on for hours. There's even a form of foreplay, with the male mounting without erection. Once firmly aboard, the mating itself takes the better part of an hour.

▶ Best places to see them: All regions except for Western Cape.

Buffalo

This aggressive, cunning and massive bovid occurs just about everywhere outside the desert and higher mountain areas. It tends to be shot out of everywhere except reserves, however, owing to its dangerous nature and its tendency to carry cattle diseases such as rinderpest and foot and mouth.

It would be very unwise to walk alone and unguided through bush, savannah or woodland where buffalo are prolific. They are second only to hippo and elephant in their danger to humans, but it does tend to be only lone, bad-tempered old bulls pushed out of their herds, or mothers with young, that will charge. Large groups tend to be more peaceful, as they feel less threatened.

Buffalo tend not to stray too far from permanent water sites and only herd in hundreds on river flood plains or around big lakes and marshes. Otherwise they tend to run in small groups of males or females, with the odd lone, embittered bull, wanting to take out his ire at losing his harem on the rest of the world.

Strangely for an animal so ready to use aggression, buffalo are not territorial. Herds come together freely during the rainy season and although breeding bulls tend to be dominant over cows, that's about the end of the social pecking order. Young bulls will routinely challenge breeding bulls but don't stand much of a chance until the old men pass their prime.

Another surprising aspect of the buffalo is its vulnerability to predators. Although it can take a pride of lion a long time to pull down an adult buffalo, with the accompanying risk of serious injury and even death, some prides seem deliberately to choose buffalo as their favoured prey.

▶ Best places to see them: all regions except for Western and Northern Cape.

Elephant

The largest of the world's land mammals has had a happier recent history than the rhino. Despite large-scale poaching, a world moratorium on ivory has gone a long way towards making poaching unprofitable. Indeed, many southern African reserves now have to cull elephant as the species begins to expand its range again. Even so, the wildlife departments of all the countries have, until now, honoured the ivory ban, which has now been lifted; how this will affect southern Africa's burgeoning elephant populations remains to be seen.

Elephant cannot go for long without water, yet they can inhabit very dry regions, browsing between the few available springs and staying in shaded dry riverbeds during the day. But if they are restricted by the need for water, they can eat just about anything, including the pulpy inner wood of baobab trees. Mineral earth, tree bark and other young woods can also be consumed, though foliage and grasses are more easily digestible. Because of their huge size, elephants spend up to 16 or 17 hours a day just feeding.

Cows and bulls tend to live separately, with female herds numbering up to 30, and bachelor herds usually fewer than 10. Lone bulls are common, and should be given a wide berth. In the height of the dry season elephants group together in much larger numbers by forested rivers. But the herds, whilst associating, do not mix, and break up into their smaller original groupings again once the rains come.

Oddly enough, elephant are not territorial. Bulls will fight for females or just for the hell of it, but they do not compete for range. In fact, elephant herds can be remarkably co-operative in sharing resources. Although some bloody-minded old bulls will hog a waterhole, most elephants will form an orderly ring, each take a turn, then let the others in, regardless of tribe.

Elephants have affected the landscape of Africa quite as much as man. Chances are the road you're driving on was once an elephant trail, particularly if it winds over hills or mountains: almost all African roads follow old elephant migration routes. Savannah woodland is often created by elephants pushing down and clearing trees, allowing grazing animals to expand their ranges and smaller browsers to benefit from fallen branches.

Like man, the elephant's effect on the landscape tends to be beneficial if there is no overpopulation, and disastrous if the balance is tipped, at which point areas can be devastated by the hunt for food. Hence the need for intensive culling, as human populations increase outside the reserves and elephant populations increase inside. Some farmers—generally cattle-farmers—will in fact tolerate elephants. But small subsistence farmers, the bulk of Africa's rural population, will not or cannot.

▶ Best places to see them: Mpumalanga, N. Province, Natal, Swaziland, E. Cape and W. Cape.

Cheetah

The cheetah's exceptional high-speed sprints (up to 70mph) are matched by an exceptionally gentle nature: unlike lion and leopard, cheetah are easily domesticated, and several guest farms keep them in the house as pets.

Unlike lion and leopard, wild cheetah specifically need open grassland and savannah to course their prey. They have a higher success rate of kills than other predators; small to mid-sized antelope are the usual prey, taken after a fast chase with the prey's hindquarters slapped sideways so that the creature falls. It is then suffocated by a death grip of canine teeth on the windpipe. However, cheetah have a foolish tendency to hunt domestic animals in broad daylight, which inevitably brings them into contact with livestock herders. In general this cat is on the decline—it does not help that lion sometimes kill cheetah, that most predators routinely steal their kills, or that cubs are hunted by big cats, wild dogs and hyena and the larger raptors.

▶ Best places to see them: Natal, Mpumalanga, N. Province, N. Cape, some E. Cape reserves.

Cheetah

Giraffe

Southern Africa's giraffe species have lighter spots than those of eastern and northeastern Africa. They are just as big however—up to 18ft at the head—and inhabit a similarly wide range of habitat: although they are tree-browsers, giraffe will inhabit even semi-desert mopane areas, bending low to eat from the tops of the stunted trees, just as readily as they will inhabit lusher open woodland and bushveld. Contrary to many popular folk-tales, giraffe do lie down to sleep at night, though this is rarely seen. What you are likely to see though—and it's an unforgettable sight—is giraffe running. Because of their great length of leg, they appear to run in slow motion, even though the top speed is around 40mph. The animals hardly seem to be moving until you notice how the ground is eaten up under their apparently slothful stride. Most predators can't keep up for long.

Giraffe can eat even the thorniest acacia leaves, having a long, sensitive and flexible tongue that wraps itself around the thorns without being pierced by them. Another interesting adaptation is that, unlike most other ruminants, they are not territorial. Individuals form loosely connected herds that continually break up and re-form. There are no dominant herd leaders and both sexes mingle without much ritual. This may be because the giraffe's size makes it less vulnerable to predators than the smaller ruminants, so there is less need for a highly structured herd bound together for mutual security. Nevertheless, males still compete for females. Older, heavier bulls tend to get the pick of the females, but younger males will challenge them. Bulls fight by bashing heads and horns, but the older guys tend to win owing to the knobbly bosses that develop on their nasal bones as they mature. But it is rare to see fights; challenges are not continual and the strongest male usually has access to the females once he has proved himself. Only when he becomes old and frail will he be supplanted.

Lion will take adult giraffe from time to time, if they can catch them lying down; some prides even make a speciality of it. Generally, though, it's only the calves that are at risk—from lion and spotted hyena. Mothers will vigorously defend their young, and predators have been seen to be killed by kicking and trampling.

▶ Best places to see them: Natal, Mpumalanga, N. Province, E. Cape, Swaziland.

Hippopotamus

A huge mammal—adults outweigh even white rhino—hippos occur wherever there is water enough and where they have not been shot out. By far the most dangerous of African animals, hippos kill more people than any other animal on the continent. Most attacks

result from feeling threatened; if you come between a hippo and the water they are likely to charge to remove you as an obstacle. Male hippo can get territorial in water and routinely attack fishing boats and tourists' canoes, which they can bite through. Look out for the yawning display, which is designed to show predators the fearsome incisors. Hippos do have some reason to be afraid: crocodiles take babies, as do land predators and angry farmers. However, one can't help wondering if they are not a little paranoid, especially as females will sometimes mob fighting males in order to calm them and stop them frightening—or stepping on—the children. Males can seriously injure each other in fights.

Hippos generally live in small herds of around three to seven cows with one or two bulls who tend to stay a little apart, looking for trouble. Canoeists should look out for him and avoid him. The occasional solitary hippo does occur, though usually in areas that have been extensively shot out.

For such huge animals, hippos are remarkably delicate. Their tough-looking skin is quite thin and they suffer greatly if they cannot submerge adequately to keep it out of the worst of the African sun. They are also more agile than one would think, and capable of almost 20mph during a dash for water. They can sleep underwater, and will resurface to breathe without waking.

▶ Best places to see them: Eastern Cape, Natal, Mpumalanga and N. Province.

Burchell's Zebra

Although you quickly get used to seeing zebra, it's as well to remember your first sighting and how impressed you were with the symmetry, the beauty, the sheer boldness of the zebra's colouring. There's nothing in the northern hemisphere to match it—well, perhaps the tiger. Bear this in mind when you start taking zebra for granted in the bush.

Burchell's (or plains) zebra are more elegant than their cousins, the Cape mountain zebra. Like blue wildebeest (which zebra often associate with during migrations) they are seen in small family groups, occasionally singly (old stallions kicked out of their herds or young ones just setting out from a family herd), or in concentrations numbering hundreds or even thousands. In dry grasslands large-scale migrations of tens of thousands of zebra occur, the giant herds made up of many smaller harems with dominant stallions and small groups of bachelor colts. Whenever a filly comes into season, bachelor colts will challenge the dominant harem stallion in a bid to abduct her. Sometimes one of the youngsters will win and this is how, gradually, he will build himself his own harem. However, if she fails to calve, she will go off with the next stallion to fight for her when she again comes into season. This may seem fickle, but mares, once inseminated by a stallion, will not then leave his herd unless he is killed by predators,

an unlikely event as strong stallions will take on most predators with great ferocity. Most zebras taken by lion, wild dog and hyena are very young or old, sick or have been cut off from their herd.

Open woodland and bushveld make good habitat for zebra, though they prefer to graze in large meadows where the stallions can keep a watch for predators.

▶ Best places to see them: E. Cape, Natal, Free State, Mpumalanga, N. Province, Swaziland.

Burchell's Zebra

Cape Mountain Zebra

Unique to South Africa, the Cape mountain zebra can be identified from the Burchell's zebra by its slightly ass-like ears, which are larger than those of the Burchell's zebra. Once hunted almost to extinction, populations are now stable.

▶ Best places to see them: mountain ranges in the Western Cape and the Great Karoo.

Caracal (Lynx)

Like the leopard, this smaller solitary cat is found just about everywhere, including farmland, but its secretive, nocturnal nature has ensured its survival. And, as with leopard, you will be lucky to see a caracal in the wild unless you know a lair and are willing to sit up at dawn and dusk for days.

Caracal are beautiful creatures, reddish-grey in colour with the distinctive tufted ears of the lynx. The tail is short and blunt. They are adept bird-catchers and rodent-hunters, but small antelope, dassies, mongoose, monkeys and other small animals also make up a large proportion of their diet. Birds are crunched up feathers and all, while furred animals tend to be eaten with some effort to separate the skin from the meat.

▶ Found in all regions.

Serval

The serval is a similar size to a caracal but has a spotted coat, no tufts on the ears and a longer tail. Habitats tend more to Kalahari thornveld, bushveld and savannah, and prey tends to be mostly rodents, with some reptile, bird and antelope young where available.

These solitary cats are less secretive than caracal and, were they not so small, would probably be seen more often. However, they make good use of cover and tall grasses, so sightings are uncommon.

▶ Best places to see them: Natal, Mpumalanga, N. Province, Kalahari.

Spotted Hyena

Despite their dog-like appearance, these ecologically successful predators are not wild dogs, but form, along with brown and striped hyena (only brown hyena occur in southern Africa), their own zoological group—*Hyaenida*—which is more closely related to civets and genets than to dogs. Spotted hyena can be found just about anywhere apart from desert and mountains; they prefer the Kalahari thornveld, bushveld and savannah.

This much-maligned animal is not the low-down dirty scavenger that it is often made out to be. Spotted hyena not only hunt (at night), but will take on prides of lion, drive leopard from their kills, even hunt cheetah. Highly adaptable, they can hunt in small groups, large groups or alone, and if there are enough of them they will take on big, dangerous prey. Their social system is highly developed, with females dominant and pack members competing as much as co-operating (unlike wild dog), despite the fact that they raise their cubs in communal dens. The females are the larger and there is a definite pecking order. Females tend to stay with the clans they are born into, while males disperse on reaching maturity and join up with whoever will have them, sometimes living alone for a time.

Hyena are fierce hunters, but they tend to back off if humans put up a fight, although small children and sick or injured people are sometimes taken. Rival clans may fight—as do competing cubs—often to the death.

At night listen out for the low, rising whoop that sounds sinister but is in fact merely a contact call. A cackling laugh denotes excitement: the nearness of carrion, a kill, or danger.

▶ Best places to see them: Natal, Mpumalanga, Northern Province, Kalahari.

Cape Mountain Zebra

Caracal

Spotted Hyena

Brown Hyena

This, the southern version of the striped hyena, also occurs in northern Africa, the Middle East and Asia. A shy, usually nocturnal scavenger and insectivore, the brown hyena will not go near humans if it can avoid them. Normally foraging in pairs, brown hyenas are not territorially aggressive, tending rather to spread out from their clan den by mutual consent. However, several will converge on a big kill, the latecomers waiting their turn rather than challenging those who got there first.

Insects, reptiles, wild fruits and vegetables make up the bulk of the diet. Brown hyena are able to survive in some of the least hospitable areas of southern Africa.

Unlike spotted hyenas, brown hyena cubs do not compete and the females will suckle any young that asks for milk. Adults never compete with other predators for meat, but will scavenge from large kills once the bigger predator has moved away. However, the occasional account of brown hyena driving a leopard or cheetah off its kill has been recorded.

▶ Found in all regions, but most common in the Northern Cape.

Black-Backed Jackal

Also known as the silver-backed jackal, for the grey streaks that stand out against the black, this handsome,

Jackal pairs mark their boundaries together. If one of the pair dies, others pick up the sudden lack of a scent and will invade, sometimes resulting in a fight to the death and almost invariably with the newly single jackal being driven off. However, singletons do not tend to stay single for long, and territories are small enough for new ones to be carved out.

Black-backed jackals prey on small mammals, but will eat just about anything, even wild berries and insects. Adult jackals are themselves taken by leopard, and the young by raptors.

▶ Best places to see them: all regions; densest in Mpumalanga, Northern Province, Natal and Kalahari reserves.

Cape Hunting Dog or Wild Dog

This distinctive tri-coloured (black, brown and yellow) dog is recovering from having been severely persecuted by white farmers, and is re-establishing ranges in areas from which it was formerly shot out. A remarkably co-operative and effective hunter, the wild dog has been extensively studied, owing to its complex social interaction. They tend to run in packs of twenty (sometimes more), though smaller packs and even individuals may be seen in areas that are being recolonized. Co-operative upbringing of young is key to their social

Cape Hunting Dogs

fleet scavenger and omnivore occurs just about everywhere (except mountains). Despite their small size, jackals usually manage to dart in and grab a piece of everyone else's kill. Quickly tamed, jackals will live close to humans if possible.

A fraction larger than a European red fox, these small dogs run singly, in pairs or in small groups. Small wild mammals and domestic beasts up to the size of full-grown sheep may be taken. Jackals may be seen day or night, but are most likely to be spotted at dusk. Pairs mate for life and almost always hunt together unless the female is nursing. At night, jackals will howl to establish territorial boundaries, sounding like a chorus of reed-voiced children.

system, with mothers suckling the young of other mothers. Either males or females may be dominant among breeding pairs. Females tend to leave their natal pack at around two years old and join other packs, while males tend to stay where they were born. Unlike spotted hyenas, fights within the packs are rare, as is the killing of cubs by rival adults. The greeting ceremonies of wild dogs are protracted, complicated and frequent; members of the same pack will even go through the ceremony if they have been separated during a hunt. Meat from a kill is disgorged and given to cubs, any cub, and not just the offspring of a particular parent. Cubs continue to beg and be given food until they are about a year old.

A savannah, grassland and woodland hunter, the wild dog can take prey many times larger and fiercer than itself, using carefully planned systems of decoy and surprise attack to tear at the flanks of the prey until the beast is exhausted and the whole pack can close in on throat, belly and anus, often tearing the entrails from the still-kicking quarry—the same method as that used by spotted hyena packs. Humans are never threatened.

Although wild dog do not run particularly fast, and cannot bring down an antelope or other animal in a straight sprint, they are tireless runners and can generally run their prey into the ground. During a well-planned hunt different members of a pack hunt in relays, keeping the prey on the move but taking time out to rest while other dogs keep up the chase. The dominant pack members will chase into a herd, scattering the animals and looking out for any that look slow or weak. Then they will retire for a 'pow-wow' before launching a systematic attack on the chosen victim.

Stand-offs and even fights between spotted hyena and wild dog packs are frequent. Large groups of spotted hyena will generally drive wild dogs off their kill.

▶ Best places to see them: Kruger, Umfolozi and Kalahari Gemsbok Parks; Natal, Mpumalanga, Northern Province and Northern Cape.

African Civet

A large raccoon-like creature, this nocturnal hunter is a handsome fellow, with a striped robber's mask and black and white marbled coat. It eats insects, rodents, reptiles, birds and berries. It tends to be seen alone, in the woodland and more temperate grassland zones, avoiding dry grasslands like the Kalahari, though it may be seen in the mopane woodland of the Kalahari fringe.

▶ Found in all regions with suitable habitat.

Bat-Eared Fox

This beautiful but strange-looking fox, with outsize ears, occurs more or less anywhere on the Kalahari fringe or in the Kalahari itself. The huge ears, dark face and grey body make this animal unmistakable. It tends

to be active by night and lie up during the day. If disturbed it will usually run a short distance then turn and face you before running on or taking cover, thus allowing you to get a good look at it.

The bat-eared fox feeds mostly on termites, but will take most creepy-crawlies and some wild fruits. However, ground-nesting birds, eggs, reptiles and amphibians, and any small rodent that comes within pouncing range, will also be eaten.

▶ Found in all regions.

Aardwolf

This insectivorous member of the hyena family is seldom, if ever, seen, and has suffered much at the hands of farmers, who erroneously believe it to be a stealer of livestock.

Almost entirely nocturnal, aardwolf resemble a striped hyena without the long, shaggy coat. Aardwolf are found in very dry, inhospitable places and will break into termite mounds wherever possible. Pairs mate for life and males take some share of the infant care, taking turns with the mother to go foraging. Cubs tend to disperse to new territories at about one year old. Once the cubs have grown, the father and mother also tend to go off alone, though they will come together to mate and bring up the young cubs when the female next comes into season. Clan dens have been reported, but most aardwolves occupy single dens. Burrows dug by aardvark are often used as dens, and a single aardwolf may move between several of these.

▶ Best places to see them: Karoo, N. Cape, Free State.

Genet

A smaller, tree-dwelling member of the civet family, the genet is more lightly built than the civet and lacks the bandit's facial stripe. It has a similar marbled coat, but the tail is longer, giving it greater balance when tree-climbing. They are opportunists and will eat whatever comes their way—small animals, insects and wild fruits. Southern Africa has two species of genet: the large spotted genet, which lives in woodland regions, and the

Black-Backed Jackal

Bat-Eared Fox

feline genet, which can be found in the drier regions wherever there is sufficient cover to allow it to hunt. Like civet, genet cats are usually seen at night, alone.

▶ Found in all regions.

Yellow Mongoose

The most common of South Africa's mongoose species. Like all mongoose species these are fearless hunters. Either singly or in pairs they routinely take on the most poisonous snakes and have lightning reflexes to avoid the strike. However, mongooses will eat insects and wild fruits as well as eggs, ground-nesting birds and any small rodents they can catch. Larger predators will catch and eat mongooses.

▶ Found in all regions.

Meerkat or Suricate

Of all the mongoose species, only the suricate is immediately identifiable to the layman. Considerably smaller than other mongooses, meerkats live in colonies in holes in the ground. Being small and vulnerable to raptors, they mount one or two sentries on top of a termite-mound, making sure that no tell-tale winged silhouette swoops low without warning. They will stand up on their hind legs for better vision. Other distinctive traits are the almost elfin features—huge eyes, sharp tapering nose—and the stripes along the upper body. Meerkats also tame easily.

▶ Best places to see them: all arid regions; most common in N. Cape.

Ground Squirrel

Alert, quick-moving creatures, ground squirrels often catch the eye with their mad chasing games.

▶ Best places to see them: N. Cape, Free State, Northern Province.

Ratel or Honey Badger

This tough, surly, lone hunter and forager is larger than the European badger. Its black body, with a long white stripe running along the sides, may be small, but larger carnivores think twice before messing with a honey badger: the thick hide is resistant to all but the most committed of bites and the creature's own bite, once locked on, is almost impossible to dislodge.

Honey badgers are opportunistic omnivores and will eat insects, fruits, small animals, eggs, birds, snakes and amphibians. Most African peoples have a place in their folklore for the ratel because of its habit of seeking out wild honey with the help of its feathered ally, the honeyguide, which, having located a hive, will seek out a ratel and then lead it to the bees, hopping from branch to branch and twittering to make sure that the ratel does not lose it in the thick bush. The ratel, being almost impervious to stings, will simply dive into the hive, tearing out the combs and eating them, wax and all, while the bird waits its turn before going in to feast

on the larvae. It is found in all habitats except mountains, but prefers bushveld.

▶ Best places to see them: all regions, but rare in Western Cape.

Aardvark

Ultra-shy, nocturnal and virtually hairless, these pig-like insectivores are common in all habitats, but almost never seen, even on night drives. Their digging ability is awesome, as many will testify who have broken their axle in an aardvark (or antbear) hole. The depressions left by their nightly diggings are used by many other animals as convenient lairs: warthog, aardwolf, porcupine and ratel all use them. Many African peoples will attempt to smoke aardvarks out of their burrows, as they make very good eating. Very little is known about the social behaviour of these solitary creatures. If cornered the aardvark will put up a dangerous fight, armed with its enormous, clawed shovels of forelegs.

▶ Found in all regions.

Porcupine

The African porcupine is larger than its European and North American counterparts, and lives in all habitats. They tend to patrol set territories during their nightly rambles and their progress is clear from the tell-tale bleached-white urine markings on rocks along a trail. The porcupine is almost always left alone by other predators as its quills are sharper than skewers and have a nasty habit of breaking off in a wound. Like aardvark, porcupines dig for termites but will also eat fruits and other invertebrates where they can.

▶ Found in all regions.

Pangolin

To spot a pangolin is extremely rare. Another nocturnal insectivore, it is a very basic mammal, a throwback to the early days of armoured scales rather than fur. The long body, anteater's snout, and reptilian scales of horn-like cells make it unlike any animal you are likely to have seen before. Related to American armadillos, relatively little is known about the social and mating patterns of these creatures.

▶ Found in all regions.

Hyrax (Dassie)

By a surreal twist of the evolutionary chain the hyrax is related to the elephant. Generally called by their Afrikaans name of dassie, hyraxes form the staple diet for a number of mammalian and airborne predators. They live in colonies in the driest of rocky uplands; even the driest old grass will do for food. Males tend to be territorial, making young male dassies vulnerable to predators as they wander in search of a *kopje* lacking a dominant male. As a result there is a high ratio of females to males, good news for those males who do eventually get their own *kopje*.

The most commonly seen hyrax is the rock hyrax. However, in some sub-tropical forests, there occurs a smaller, tree-dwelling hyrax, although still technically a hoofed animal! Though relatively rare, once heard they are never forgotten: the tree hyrax's night scream chills the blood of even the hardest men. Listen out for it during the dry season when the moon is full. It's only a territorial advertisement, but it sounds like something from the gates of hell.

▶ Found in all regions.

Primates

Baboon

Every hiker in southern Africa has been startled by what they thought were shouts from across the hillside, only to realize that a male baboon was 'barking' at them. Baboons are found just about everywhere. They are highly adaptable and can live in forest or in desert.

Social groupings tend to be large troops of females dominated by one or two mature males, who regularly fight with the juvenile and lower-status males to retain breeding rights.

Baboons are extremely intelligent and, if they lose their fear of man, positively dangerous. They are opportunistic omnivores: young antelope, insects, wild fruit, young vervet monkeys will all be eaten if the chance arises. It's quite a sight to see a baboon eat a scorpion, grabbing it without fear of being stung, tearing off the poisonous bit and stuffing the now prawn-like creature into its mouth like a gourmand in a seafood restaurant. National park and reserve camp sites are fair game, and baboons are not above clawing their way into an empty tent if they smell food. Rubbish scattered from ransacked bins is a typical sign of baboon raiding.

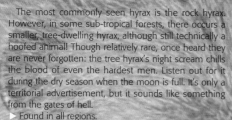
Hyrax

Meerkats

Although they are powerful creatures, most inter-male baboon fights are more ritual than serious, and dominant males tend to step down after a certain time, as if conscious of the need to expand the gene pool. Most of the time, baboons are peace-loving creatures intent on feeding and staying out of the way of predators such as leopard, who will be mobbed if caught stalking one of the troop.

▶ Found in all regions.

Vervet Monkey

This energetic and social tree-dweller is recognizable by its smallish grey body, long tail and alert black face. Vervet monkeys throng camp sites in national parks and reserves, where they will appropriate stray food and bright or interesting objects the instant an unwary camper's back is turned.

Vervets can be savage with each other. I have actually witnessed the mobbing of a female vervet by a group of others. It was unclear what had started the fight, but it soon became bloody, with great gashes being torn in the lone female's sides. Surprisingly she turned and fought angrily rather than fleeing, which only earned her more wounds. Finally the noise and blood became so insupportable that the campers broke up the fight by flinging stones and mud into the trees. Annoyed at being deprived of their victim, the mob growled and spat at the campers from the trees before dispersing.

Vervets are remarkably adaptable, and can live in open woodland, dry savannah and thick forest. Bands of vervets consist of a core of females defended by a smaller group of 'warrior' males. As shown above, fights between rival groups (and sometimes within groups) are common. Among females there is a definite hierarchy, those higher up the ladder being 'served' (groomed) by lower-status females. Females stay with their natal clan, but males tend to be pushed out by the dominant males, enlisting as 'warriors' in other clans where they will try to work their way up to dominant status, with access to the females. The entry process into a new clan is not smooth, however, and a newcomer will have to fight, and at the same time avoid being mobbed. Nepotism can help; males tend to go for clans already occupied by older relatives.

▶ Found in all regions which are even partially wooded.

Bushbaby

Like tree dassies (*see* above), bushbabies utter blood-curdling night-time screams but are rarely seen; this is a shame as there can be few cuter creatures. But these large-eyed bundles of fur have to stay hidden, or they would be eaten by every passing predator.

Bushbabies are relatively primitive primates, very small in size. But they can catch insects on the wing in pitch dark and rotate their heads 180 degrees. They tend to live in small female groups with adult males going it alone.

Of the several species of bushbaby in southern Africa the largest is the greater bushbaby, which reaches a size of almost 2ft from head to tail. Fruit and insect eaters, they occupy territorial ranges of small areas of woodland canopy. Unlike the smaller bushbabies it does not jump from branch to branch, but tends to walk along branches, making small leaps only when necessary. Thick forest is the preferred habitat.

Lesser bushbabies are about 7in long and inhabit open woodland, often in fairly dry regions, but can also live in upland forests if the temperatures do not get too cold. In bushveld and open woodland areas, acacia gum is a staple food. Twins are born twice a year, and can start jumping biggish gaps between branches after about two months.

Bushbabies tend not to have a problem with predation while in the trees, but if they venture on to the ground anything can get them.

▶ Best places to see them: Mpumalanga, N. Natal, Swaziland lowveld.

NB 'Seeing' will mean, at best, picking up eyes in a torch beam if you hear a loud scream from a nearby tree.

Vervet Monkeys

Bushpig

Pigs

Warthog

These tusked pigs are fearsome, with facial knobbles and strange foreshortened bodies, but actually they are shy and vulnerable and will fly at the first sign of alarm.

Warthogs are found more or less everywhere except dune desert and thick forest. They can locate and dig up most forms of edible root, including water-bearing ones in times of drought. Great breeders, they tend to drop piglets at the beginning of the rains. They mate for life and bring up the kids together.

Although many predators enjoy warthog meat, an adult, if it has a hole or other defensible place to run to, can be a powerful adversary. Diurnal animals, warthogs tend to stay in safe burrows at night when most big predators are hunting. However, some clever carnivores will ambush warthogs when they emerge at dawn.

▶ Best places to see them: all regions except W. Cape.

Reptiles and Insects

Reptiles abound. From the dozens of harmless lizard species (one of which, the leguaan or rock monitor, grows to over a metre) to the most venomous of snakes, the *veld* literally crawls with the creatures. The only problem (for the enthusiast) is that they tend to hear people coming and hide.

This is particularly true of snakes. While the bush around you may harbour a huge number of them, you are unlikely to see them except by chance, and even then they will tend to speed off as quickly as possible. The exception is the sluggish puff adder, which sometimes suns itself on mountain paths, and delivers a nasty bite if you tread on it. Be careful climbing trees in the sub-tropical regions: poisonous green mamba and boomslang often hunt birds in the lower branches. Other common poisonous snakes are the deadly black mamba, the Cape cobra and the spitting cobra, or

Warthog

Bushpig

This forest pig is more like a European wild boar than the warthog, with smaller tusks and a taller, heavy-shouldered build. Where warthog inhabit open areas, bushpig like forest and thick bush. Where warthog are diurnal, bushpig forage at night. Where warthog are essentially peaceable, bushpig are much more ornery, though seldom encountered owing to their nocturnal habits and natural shyness.

Bushpig have relatively few predators, but leopard will take them and they are hunted by man because they cause havoc on planted land and can get through even the strongest fences with prolonged effort.

▶Best places to see them: all forested regions.

rhinkals. However, it can never be asserted enough that the traveller has little to fear from snakes and is unlikely even to see one.

This is not true of creepy-crawlies. Outsize insects and arachnids are a feature of southern Africa, and the traveller will have to get used to living with large spiders, beetles, crickets, locusts and sometimes scorpions around. The only really hair-raising invertebrates are the yellow baboon-spider (related to the tarantula and as big as your hand), the back-hunting spider (a bit smaller), the scorpion (usually dun-coloured), and the sun-spider or solugifid, which looks like a giant cross between a spider and a scorpion minus the sting and the claws. Of these, the first three are venomous, but not enough to induce more than a fever, while the sun-spider is harmless.

In any case, encounters with these big nasties are rare, and can be avoided by shaking out shoes and sleeping bags, zipping up tents, and not carelessly putting your hand under stones or logs.

On a more positive note, the landscape also abounds with colourful butterflies and beetles, which are encountered far more often than the scary stuff, and it is worth buying a field guide if you want to identify them (see Further Reading).

Nile Crocodile

Once endemic to all but the coldest rivers, crocodiles are now confined to certain reserves. Very dangerous to man, they can grow to over 3m.

▶ Best places to see them: Mpumalanga, N. Province, Natal, some reserves in E. Cape.

Antelope

Antelope are common everywhere—large species in the nature reserves and hunting ranches; small species in even the most settled farmland.

Eland

These are the largest antelope in the world, reaching the size of large horses. Sacred to the San for their bounteous flesh, their ability to live in arid, almost waterless regions and their gentle nature (they have even been domesticated on farms in Russia), eland are massive, ponderous creatures. Notwithstanding that, they are agile and athletic and can jump a 7ft fence from a standstill. The spiral horns do not twist like those of a kudu (see below), but extend straight back from the head at about a 70° angle. Although the horns look fearsome there are almost no records of these animals attacking humans, as some of the smaller antelope do when cornered. Eland tend to be shy, and will keep their distance. They are seen singly (usually old bulls), in pairs, in small family groups or in herds scores strong, and inhabit just about every southern African habitat barring true desert or thick forest. They may often be seen on montane grasslands. Both males and females have horns.

▶ Found in all regions.

Greater Kudu

Second in size only to the eland, the greater kudu is similarly adaptable in terms of habitat and social grouping. Incredibly handsome creatures, they vary from dark brown to almost grey-brown, with white stripes along the flanks. The males have distinctive spiralled horns and can grow almost as large as a bull eland, sometimes appearing to be taller owing to the greater proportion of leg to body. Like eland, kudu are shy and will run from humans. Males will fight hard for females however and, while they seldom injure each other, it is not unknown for fighting bulls to lock horns inseparably and eventually to die from starvation or thirst, being unable to graze or to agree on a direction. They are also very vulnerable to predators in this state.

Males and females tend to run in separate herds, except in the middle of the dry season when they will come together to rut, the calves being born at the end of the rains in February or March. Like eland, kudu are adept at jumping, and inhabit fenced farmed areas as readily as nature reserves. However, when living close to man, the usually diurnal kudu will tend to feed at night and lie up during the day. Only males have horns.

▶ Best places to see them: All regions except W. Cape and around Cape Town.

Bushbuck

Bushbuck are spiral-horned antelope common to most forest and woodland areas. Although a lightly built, athletic antelope, its horns are more like those of the eland than the kudu or nyala. Only males have horns. Look for the distinctive spinal mane on males and spots along the flanks of the reddish-brown coats of both males and females. Bushbuck may be found at high altitudes as well as in lowland areas with good cover. Unlike its larger cousins, this smaller spiral-horned antelope is dangerous: many sportsmen have been gored by a sudden charge from the thicket after wounding a bushbuck. However, like kudu, bushbuck are adept at living near man and become nocturnal in farmed areas.

Gemsbok

▶ Best places to see bushbuck: W. and E. Cape, Natal, Mpumalanga, N. Province, Swaziland.

Gemsbok (Oryx)

This large desert antelope is common to the dry country of the Kalahari and the bushveld territories around the deserts.

Kudu

Specifically adapted to arid zones, gemsbok can go over 100 days without water, gathering what they need from desert fruits like the *tsamma* melon, and roots, for which they dig. Yet, if water is available, gemsbok will drink as often as any other antelope.

Gemsbok can be dangerous. Hunters tell tales of being charged with the spear-like horns of both bulls and cows, and many hunters have been seriously injured this way. Gemsbok are also aggressive towards predators; lions and spotted hyenas will hesitate before taking them on in open desert areas (though not in bushveld, where gemsbok frequently fall prey). Bulls will challenge each other at waterholes. However, hikers can pass close to gemsbok without any display of threat provided they are not approached deliberately.

You will usually see gemsbok in groups of up to ten in desert regions, and in much larger herds in bushveld areas, but you may equally see old bulls wandering on their own.

▷ Found in all regions except mountains.

Reedbuck

Common in southern Africa, the reedbuck is another marsh-dweller. However, the larger, mountain reedbuck has adapted to steep, rugged uplands, where it runs in herds of up to 20, as opposed to the smaller family groups of the marsh-dwelling reedbuck. Mountain reedbuck do not rely on marsh grazing in the same way that lowland reedbuck do. Both sub-species may be seen singly or in pairs as well as in groups.

Reedbuck are light ochre in colour, and the males have forward-curving horns. Lowland reedbuck tend to

Eland

mate for life and go in pairs; small groups will be allied pairs, or a pair with almost-grown young. Mountain reedbuck tend to run in female herds, sometimes with a dominant male, or in bachelor groups, or as lone males. Just about everything preys on both types, their main defence being very swift flight.

▷ Found in all regions.

Red Haartebeest

This relative of the wildebeest is another strange looker, with a long, narrow face, reddish body, and crumpled-looking, forward-pointing horns. Like blue wildebeest this is a grassland and bushveld grazer that thrives in the Kalahari regions. They tend to run in small male or female groups or pairs and will graze close to cover. Like blue wildebeest, red hartebeest that inhabit the drier Kalahari grasslands will migrate long distances following the rains. They can survive long periods without drinking, by eating *tsamma* melons and digging for water-bearing roots and tubers during droughts.

Red hartebeest are highly territorial and males will fight if they meet, usually after a ritualized rubbing of shoulders. The victor chases after the loser, who holds his mouth open, perhaps as a gesture of submission.

Females drop calves at any time of the year, though most births seem to occur in the middle of the dry season. Small family groups usually consist of a few allied mothers and up to three calves of varying stages of maturity. Both males and females have horns.

▷ Best places to see them: E. and N. Cape, Natal, Mpumalanga, N. Province, Free State, Swaziland.

Sable Antelope

A spectacular large antelope with sweeping scimitar horns, chocolate-brown to black body, a neck mane, and a distinctive black and white striped face, this is one of Africa's most beautiful. A woodland and bushveld creature, it tends to run in small herds of around 10 with a dominant male, although bachelor herds and lone bulls may also be encountered.

Bulls tend to be blacker and taller than the females. Both sexes have horns. Watch out if you're on foot; the sable is aggressive, and predators tend to give adult sables a wide berth. Because of its popularity as a trophy, sables were all but shot out of many areas earlier this century. Now, however, many white farmers will tolerate resident sable herds for their aesthetic and sporting value.

▶ Best places to see them: Natal, Mpumalanga, N. Province, Swaziland.

Roan Antelope

Closely related to the sable and almost as handsome, the roan is a light chestnut colour and stands taller than the sable, but has less spectacular horns. Like sable, roan antelope were hunted almost to extinction in southern Africa and have only been brought back from the brink by expensive conservation and re-introduction programmes. A good thing too; though roan breed year-round they seem to be erratic procreators, and have never been very common.

Roan antelope favour forest over savannah, and like to live close to water. Like sable, adults will attack predators wherever possible and therefore tend to be left alone. Calves, however, are vulnerable and frequently taken.

Females and males tend to run in separate herds, though alpha bulls will move with their own harems. You will sometimes see them crossing forest roads in late afternoon. Both males and females have horns.

▶ Best places to see them: Natal, Mpumalanga, N. Province, Swaziland.

Waterbuck

This common large antelope favours marshy areas, and is easily recognizable by a white circular strip on the rear. Only the males have horns, which are long and widely arched. Coats tend to be shaggy. Males and females may feed together but tend to run in separate groups at other times, though a young dominant male may have his own harem.

Despite their large size and big horns, waterbuck are not aggressive towards predators and tend to dash for cover or water if attacked. Calves are dropped during the rains and kept close to water, which helps them keep away from cat and dog predators but can make them vulnerable to crocodiles.

Waterbuck are mostly diurnal and tend to lie up in cover at night. Despite this, they are a regular food source for just about every predator. However, their high breeding rates greatly exceed predation levels.

▶ Best places to see them: Natal, Mpumalanga, N. Province, E. Cape, Swaziland.

Topi or Tsessebe

Related to the red hartebeest, this tall-shouldered antelope is dark brown in colour, with black legs and a more lyre-shaped horn than the hartebeest. Both males and females have horns.

Tsessebe usually run in herds of up to 30. They are fast sprinters and, if two herds meet to share grazing, the males will do a lot of ritual displaying, cantering and galloping up and down in what seem like races.

Interestingly, tsessebe can go for long periods without drinking when grass is young and green, but have to drink every day in the dry season. They will migrate long distances after the rains, often with herds coming together to form larger herds of several hundred. However, fights between males break out whenever there is a halt in the march. Calves tend to be dropped at the beginning of the rains (October/November).

▶ Best places to see them: Natal, Mpumalanga, N. Province, Swaziland.

Impala

Roan

Impala

Although these reddish-coloured antelope are not part of the gazelle family, they have gazelle-like beauty, grace and leaping ability. Watch any herd of impala and you will see leaps of astounding height and length. This is put to great effect when a predator rushes in; the herd explodes in all directions, confusing the eye, with some impala jumping to heights of 8ft.

Impala run in female herds, bachelor herds and harem herds. Bucks may also be seen singly. Dominant males with harems will tolerate immature males up to the age of about 18 months before driving them out to join a bachelor herd.

During times of drought a female impala can withhold giving birth to her young for several weeks, waiting for the rains to break. If the drought continues she will re-absorb the foetus into her body, a kind of self-imposed abortion which retains the vital fluids that might be lost during birth, and re-ingests the minerals given over to the embryo.

Impala breed prolifically in good years, but this numeric success is countered by heavy losses to every predator in Africa, including raptors, the largest of which routinely carry off fawns.

▶ Best places to see them: Mpumalanga, N. Province, E. Cape, Natal, Swaziland.

Grey Duiker

Common in most areas, even farmland, duikers are small, stockily built antelope with short horns (on male and female) and a distinctive grey-brown coat. If startled they run, dodging and swerving to evade pursuit. Duiker are found just about everywhere except deserts, and, although primarily nocturnal, daytime sightings are not uncommon. Duikers will eat lizards and insects as well as vegetation and have even been known to eat the resin of certain trees. It has two sub-species, the red and blue duiker.

Expect to see duiker singly or in pairs. They are highly territorial, and both males and females will drive out newcomers. This helps spread the range, as newly mature duiker are always searching for new territories.

Everything eats duiker, including man. Despite their mall size, duiker will defend themselves and their young vehemently. If a small predator tries to snatch a fawn lying in the grass, its distress bleat can bring the mother in a groin-high explosion from the thicket, horns pointed where it hurts.

▶ Found in all regions.

Cape Grysbok

Tiny, shy, greyish-brown with miniature horns (on the males), grysbok are hard to tell from steenbok. The bottom line is—if you spot it, it's probably a steenbok: grysbok are so shy that they are almost never seen. If you do see one, it will probably be alone, but grysbok are monogamous and usually run in pairs within sharply defined territories of under 100 acres, which they will defend against incomers. Although they inhabit arid scrub, grysbok are dependent on having either water or succulent plants from which to gain moisture.

▶ Best place to see them: Western Cape.

Bontebok

Some zoologists dispute whether the bontebok is in fact its own species—there is a trend of opinion that says they are merely a sub-species of blesbok. There are certainly differences in appearance and range, though not in behaviour. Bontebok are distinguished from blesbok by having one continuous white blaze on the front of the face, while blesbok have a sort of heart shape between the horns, then a brown gap between that and the main blaze. Bontebok are also slightly lighter in build. Hunted almost to extinction, they were only saved when a farmer in the Overbeg region decided, in 1931, to conserve the last known remaining population. This farm is now the Bontebok National Park, near Swellendam. Since the 1930s the species has recovered to viable breeding numbers.

▶ Found in the grasslands of the Western Cape.

Waterbuck

Sable

Nyala

Blesbok

Springbok

Nyala

Almost as large as a kudu, the nyala is another spiral-horned antelope that favours thick cover. The males have a less curved horn and a distinctive shaggy neck ruff. They also tend to be dark grey-brown in colour, with pale stripes along the flanks, while the cows are chestnut with very discernible stripes. Although kudu and nyala ranges overlap, nyala tend to prefer woodland and forest to thickets and bushveld, and cannot stray far from water. They are less adept at colonizing farmed areas than kudu. Only the males have horns and, like kudu, males and females almost always run in separate herds, the males gradually becoming more solitary. Look for nyala browsing in cover around early to mid-morning, and during early evening.

▶ Best places to see them: Natal, Mpumalanga, N. Province, Swaziland.

Springbok

Southern Africa's only representative of the gazelle family, this lyre-horned antelope (males and females have horns) is immediately distinguishable by its chestnut and ochre-coloured upper body separated by a strip from its white belly. The face is mostly white, with two dark brown stripes running between eyes and nose.

These grassland and desert-dwelling antelope have a formidable jumping ability. Yet, while impala tend to reserve this for flight from predators, a springbok will leap high into the air (erecting its white tail and dorsal hair) seemingly without provocation. This 'pronking' is a display of high spirits, performed by male and female, young and old alike. Of course, 'pronking' is especially useful when under attack from a predator.

Springbok live singly, in pairs, in small family groups, in herds of females with a dominant male, in bachelor herds, or in large herds of several hundred individuals (even thousands have been recorded). This adaptable nature is reflected in its range of habitats: springbok can survive in the driest regions of the Kalahari, but can exist equally well in more regularly watered zones.

▶ Found in all regions.

Oribi

Klipspringer

Steenbok

Often mistaken for a duiker, this small reddish-coloured antelope inhabits both dry grasslands and woodland edge.

Sacred to the San, who still hunt it in most areas, yet revere it, this is a most elegant creature, slender and fluid in movement where duikers are stocky and jerky. Although they can thrive in dry areas, they require sufficient surface water to be able to drink daily. They have been known to survive by digging up water-bearing roots and tubers.

Steenbok are usually seen by day, either singly or in pairs, and are fiercely territorial. If you startle a steenbok it will stare right at you for a time then suddenly explode into action, running and leaping like a miniature impala or springbok.

Unlike the duikers, only male steenbok have horns, and fawns can be dropped at any time of year.

▶ Best places to see them: all regions, but rare in Western Cape.

Oribi

Another small, ochre/red-coloured antelope, this is a grassland and bushveld dweller. The male has longish horns standing straight up from his head.

Oribi tend to mate for life and run in pairs over small territories. However, the females are not faithful and will mate with itinerant males who happen to drift through the territory. This manipulation of the gene pool does not result in a large range, the reason seeming to be that the oribi is not well adapted to drought conditions, a necessary quality for any widespread animal in southern Africa.

Oribi are browsers and grazers and will usually stay within their territories of 100–200 acres.

▶ Best places to see them: Natal, Mpumalanga, N. Province, Swaziland.

Klipspringer

This stocky, ochre-coloured antelope, both sexes of which have straight-up horns, appears larger than it really is owing to its bulky build. The klipspringer—in Afrikaans, 'rock jumper'—has a truly awesome ability to leap up, down and along boulders of whatever gradient or incline without losing balance, footing or aim. Because it browses on succulent plants, the klipspringer does not have to drink water. You generally see klipspringers in pairs, but occasionally you will see groups gathered together.

Extremely vigilant for predators in cliffs, behind boulders and in the sky (large eagles will sometimes go for a klipspringer), one of a pair will usually stand guard while the other browses. If danger is heard, smelled or sighted, the look-out will whistle a high-pitched alarm call, a sound you become used to when hiking in dry, rocky areas.

▶ Found in upland areas of all regions.

Blesbok

This handsome, white-faced antelope will often attract your attention before you notice him—snorting at you and stamping his front hoof to tell you you are near his territory. Once he's sure you're looking, he will then canter in a tight circle, still snorting, to tell you where his exact boundaries are. All this is bluff—should you actually approach, the blesbok will generally move off. A grazer, this antelope is a common sight in grassland. Calving season tends to be late November and gestation lasts eight months.

▶ Best places to see them: Free State, parts of the Drakensberg and Natal Midlands.

Blue Wildebeest

The blue wildebeest has one of the strongest populations of any species on the continent, and moves in herds of up to many thousands. Also called the gnu, the blue wildebeest do not look like antelopes at all; their horse-like gait, cow-like head, horns and tail, and antelope's body make them something of a mish-mash to the eye, an effect that is only heightened by their light-coloured beard and neck ruff. Both males and females have horns.

Steenbok

Blue Wildebeest

Common everywhere but the desert and thick bushveld regions, blue wildebeest favour grasslands and meadows in bushveld and forest zones. They are a favorite prey of many, including lion, spotted hyena and wild dog. They seldom put up much of a fight, instead relying on speed to get away. However, some hunters, having wounded a wildebeest, have been charged from long grass.

At first glance, a wildebeest herd may seem to number hundreds of individuals, but on closer inspection it becomes clear that these large groupings are made up of scores of smaller herds, whose males continually challenge each other by cantering in circles and snorting before suddenly falling to their knees (keeping their bums in the air) and locking horns. It's a comic sight and the fighting, though spirited, is more ritualized than fierce. When one male has had enough he will abruptly disengage and canter off, pursued for a short distance by the victor who then breaks off for a victory lap before rejoining his harem.

▶ Best places to see them: all regions except for Western Cape.

Black Wildebeest

Found only in South Africa, the black, or white-tailed, wildebeest is very handsome and horse-like. They usually occur in small groups, or as a lone male.

▶ Best places to see them: Free State, Natal Drakensberg, Western, Northern, and Eastern Cape.

Rhebok

An occasional sight, this slender creature can look insubstantial, almost ghostlike, especially when glimpsed through a mountain mist. However, this antelope, whose males have distinctive short vertical horns, is a tough beast, able to go completely without water if necessary.

They are diurnal, usually go in small groups, and are vulnerable to most small predators. Perhaps for this reason, they can be aggressive (though not towards humans). Accounts exist of male rhebok chasing down big male baboons intent on snatching a fawn.

▶ Best places to see them: in the mountains of the Western Cape, and (less commonly) in Natal and Mpumalanga.

Suni

A tropical forest-dweller, South Africa's smallest antelope is not only tiny, but also very shy—unlike the dik dik, an antelope of a similar size that lives up further north in Namibia. Because of this, little is known about suni behaviour. All that is certain is that it is highly territorial, and keeps to the densest undergrowth—out of the necessity of avoiding even small predators such as jackal.

▶ Best places to see them: KwaZulu-Natal, parts of Mpumalanga and N. Province lowveld.

Birds

Southern Africa is one of the best places in the world for seeing birds. The range of climates, and the migratory patterns from northern hemisphere to southern hemisphere, make for a constant procession of colourful, exotic and rare species that thrive in these open, non-industrial countries.

In all areas of South Africa the bird life is profuse and colourful. Of the hundreds of indigenous species, many, like the green lourie, the long-tailed sugarbird and the hadeda ibis (whose harsh call has almost made it an emblem of the country), are unique. Spectacular birds of prey, such as fish eagles, black eagles and crowned eagles, goshawks, secretary birds and a host of others, are commonly seen. Strangely, though, vultures, despite their scavenging lifestyle, have been largely shot out and thrive only in the bushveld game reserves and in a few isolated mountain locations.

Anyone at all interested in birds should pick up a copy of Gordon Maclean's *Roberts' Birds of Southern Africa* upon arrival. *Roberts'* is an institution in southern Africa. It is updated every year and as an information source it is hard to beat. However, it is a big tome and not really suitable as a field guide; *Newman's Birds of Southern Africa* is a useful and portable substitute.

Jackass Penguins

Cape Gannets

Coast

Jackass Penguin

A small, slender penguin about 2ft high, found in colonies on rock promontories and in coves. The name derives from its harsh cry.

▶ Best place to see them: Western Cape coast.

Cape Gannet

Found in similar locations to the jackass penguin, this larger counterpart of northern gannets lives in large colonies on promontories and islands. Be warned—the smell as you approach a colony may bring you to your knees. It's not just guano; gannets nest on top of the corpses of their dead ancestors and relatives, some just a few days old.

▶ Best place to see them: Western Cape coast.

Lesser Flamingo

Lesser flamingos are migrant from the north, usually appearing in small family groups, but with larger flocks at the West Coast National Park. After good summer rains, flamingos will fly far inland to feed off the freshwater shrimp that hatch out of the salt pan mud every few years.

▶ Best places to see them: all regions, but most common on W. Coast.

Lesser Flamingos

Bataleur Eagle

Sacred Ibis

Kori

Southern Africa's largest land bird after the ostrich—though some cranes almost match his height of around 5ft at the wedge-shaped head. When they take flight the wingspan is truly awesome.

▶ Best places to see them: Cape, N.W. Province.

Cape Vulture

The Cape vulture is a big bird, almost white all over. It has been shot out of most areas except nature reserves. However, farmers, realizing their 'clean-up' value, are persecuting them less, and numbers are rising.

▶ Best places to see them: Eastern Cape, Natal, Mpumalanga, N. Province, Swaziland; isolated colonies in Free State, Western Cape.

Lammergeier

A rare vulture, which drops bones on to rocks in order to extract the marrow.

▶ Best places to see them: Eastern Cape, Natal, Mpumalanga Drakensberg.

Bataleur Eagle

Ornithologists have differed on the question of whether the bataleur is an eagle or in fact its own

Fish Eagle

Cape Eagle Owl

Saddlebill Stork

species, something akin to the gymogene. It is spectacular in colour—you can recognize the bataleur eagle by its black head, vivid red beak, black and tan body and square tail in flight. It is easy to spot as it flies low over bush. Can take prey up to small antelope calves.

▶ Best places to see them: Mpumalanga, N. Province, Bushmanland.

Secretary Bird

The strangest of Africa's raptors, this long-legged hawk is usually seen walking in search of its favoured prey, snakes. Secretary birds stand about three and a half feet high, with white bodies, long tails and heads that are

crested when alarmed or angry. It inhabits bushveld, grassland and savannah.
▶ Best places to see them: all regions except for Western Cape.

Pale Chanting Goshawk

Often seen atop telephone posts along dirt roads, these pale grey birds with angry red eyes are agile predators of small birds, rodents or reptiles. Their appearance in flight—their straight wings, slender body and a tail that looks rather too long in proportion to the rest of its body—is very distinctive and makes them easy to identify.
▶ Best places to see them: Mpumalanga, N. Province, Natal, Bushmanland.

Cape Eagle Owl

Cape eagle owls live in rocks, cliffs and forests. Their main prey is spring hare.
▶ Found in all areas; most common in eastern regions.

Wetlands

Fish Eagle

Fish eagles can be found in the shore foliage of most watery areas. Their piercing cry is one of the distinctive

Sacred Ibis

One of many ibis species resident in southern Africa, sacred ibis gather in large flocks near most marshes and rivers. They sometimes fly far afield to feed. They can be recognized by their black bills, heads, neck and tail feathers, with white bodies.
▶ Best places to see them: all regions except for Northern Cape.

Cattle Egret

Rather unspectacularly named, considering its beauty, the cattle egret is a sub-species of heron, and may often be seen in farmlands hunting for grubs near livestock—hence its name.
▶ Found in all regions.

Egyptian Goose

Egyptian geese have brown bodies, are relatively small, and have eyes that seem to have been made up with light eye shadow and mascara. They usually occur in pairs or small flocks.
▶ Found in all regions.

Hammerkop

A strange, dwarf stork with dull brown plumage and a blunt bill, the hammerkop can be recognized by its

Cattle Egret

Hornbill

sounds of the southern African river or lake, and the sight of one swooping to the water to take a fish is unforgettable. Identification is easy—white head and chestnut-brown body.
▶ Found in all regions.

Saddlebill Stork

Not a common bird but an unmistakable one, with its glossy black body and flashy yellow and red bill. These are shy birds which, once seen, are never forgotten.
▶ Best places to see them: Mpumalanga, N. Province, Zululand; most common in St Lucia Nature Reserve and Kruger.

head, which seems to extend backward as much as it does forward. Many folk tales are told about this enigmatic-looking solitary wader.
▶ Found in all regions.

Darter

This freshwater cormorant spears fish on its long, dagger-like beak, then tosses them into the air before catching and swallowing them. Darters are very elegant birds with snake-like necks that seem almost able to coil around corners. Look out for them sitting in trees with wings outstretched, drying out after a dive.
▶ Found in all wetland regions.

Malachite Kingfisher

The smallest of South Africa's kingfishers, Malachite kingfishers look very much like the small, jewel-like European kingfisher, only possibly brighter in colour. They dive for their prey and can be seen sitting in dead trees by the banks of permanent rivers.

▶ Found in all regions.

Malachite Kingfisher

Bushveld and Lowland Forest

The great variety of vegetation and the relative reliability of a good rainy season make bushveld areas great for bird life. Low-lying forest areas generally border the bushveld zones, and thus most local species can thrive in both habitats.

Martial Eagle

Biggest of the southern African eagles, these are usually seen soaring at such a height that it can be hard to identify them from any other large raptor. Come across one sitting over a kill, however, and there's no doubt. The bird is simply huge. Also rather shy, it may be seen flapping into the air as you approach a thicket. Again the sheer awesome size, as well as the speckled plumage, gives the bird away.

▶ Best places to see them: Mpumalanga, N. Province, Natal, E. Cape, Swaziland.

Martial Eagle

Whydah

The whydah belongs to the finch family. In summer the males sport long, long tails—about four times the length of their bodies—and can be seen hovering like dark, elongated handkerchiefs above the grass as they display for their females. The weight of the tail only allows for a few seconds of hovering before the bird has to grab a twig or strong bit of grass and get its breath back. So much effort is taken up by this hovering flight that presumably the males are displaying their strength as well as their physical beauty. They can often be spotted on telegraph wires.

▶ Best places to see them: Natal, Mpumalanga, N. Province, Swaziland.

Whydah

Crested Hoepoe

A summer visitor, this bird will be familiar to anyone who has travelled in the Mediterranean, from where it migrates to southern Africa during the European winter. Some places seem to attract them in great numbers. Look out for them walking along the ground, inflating their round head-crest whenever a choice invertebrate scuttles within reach of their long bills.

▶ Found in all regions.

Paradise Flycatcher

Another spectacular long-tailed bird, the paradise flycatcher is common in riverine forest in bushveld

Crested Hoepoe

areas. The distinctive, rolling flight as it chases flying insects usually catches the eye first. Follow this and you may be rewarded with a sight of the bird resting on a branch in all its long-tailed crested glory, before it hurls itself at another passing fly.

▶ Best places to see them: Mpumalanga, Natal, Swaziland.

White Stork

Every summer great flocks of white storks fly down from Europe to southern Africa. They are commonly seen in areas where bushveld and grassland meet, the forest edge teeming with the small creatures on which these beautiful migrants rely for food.

▶ Best places to see them: Western and Eastern Cape, summers only.

Orange-breasted Sunbird

Most spectacular of the sunbirds, southern Africa's answer to the humming-bird, these jewel-like, metallic-feathered nectar-sippers do not hover, but perch to feed. They are larger than most humming-birds, though with a similar long, thin curved bill, and they are seldom still for long.

They usually only spotted as an iridescent flash between two flowering shrubs. However, many suburban gardens support resident sunbirds and you may well be lucky enough to see one sunning itself in the early morning on a branch before it begins the day's rather feverish activities.

▶ Best places to see them: Western and Eastern Cape, Natal Drakensberg.

Crowned Crane

One of the most quintessentially 'African' of birds, these elegant cranes with their yellow afros are generally seen in marshy areas of the bushveld zones, or where the bushveld meets the grasslands, especially during times of good rains. They tend to go in pairs and are not generally seen near other crane or stork species. They are known for their beautiful courtship dance.

▶ Found in all regions, but most common in the east.

Blue Crane

South Africa's national bird, the blue crane turns up everywhere, but never for too long. A nomadic migrant, it congregates by lakes and dams.

▶ Found in all regions.

Wattled Crane

One of South Africa's rarest (and largest) birds, the wattled crane is confined to the wetlands of a few

Crowned Crane   Bishop Bird

lowveld reserves.

▶ Best places to see them: Northern Province, Mpumalanga.

Bishop Bird

Look for these flitting between stands of reeds in wetlands, marshes and riverbanks of bushveld zones. There are two main varieties, red and black and yellow and black, usually seen together.

Bishop birds are not particularly shy and it's wonderful to see them busy in the reeds at morning and evening, their peak activity times. They live in colonies and are highly territorial.

▶ Found in wetlands in all regions.

Crimson Shrike

One of the many representatives of the shrike family to be found in southern Africa, this is the most spectacular, with a bright spot on its chest as red as blood, appropriate for a bird also known as the butcher bird, because shrikes catch small reptiles and large insects and impale them on thorns or barbed-wire fences—sometimes still wriggling—to be snacked on later.

▶ Best places to see them: Mpumalanga, N. Province, Natal, Swaziland.

Grey Lourie

The 'go-away bird'—so called for its distinctive cry—is an inquisitive, vocal regular at any bushveld camp site. They tend to gather in large, loosely associated flocks wherever food is good, filling the air with their eccentric call, somewhere between a nasal human voice in mid-whine and an electronic alarm clock.

▶ Best places to see them: Northern Province, Mpumalanga.

Yellow Hornbill

Only one of several hornbill species on the sub-continent, the yellow-billed variety is the most common. Bushveld areas, some forests and Kalahari grasslands all harbour small groups of yellow-bills. Spectacular at the first sighting, the hornbill soon becomes routine. It has a swooping flight.

▶ Best places to see them: E. Cape, Natal, Mpumalanga, N. Province, Swaziland.

Lilac-Breasted Roller

Like a giant kingfisher, only with a shorter bill and a more mauve colouring on its breast, this is a colourful roadside sentinel. Look out for them on the tops of telephone poles or twisting in the air just above the road as they try to snatch flying insects. As with kingfishers, what catches your eye first is a flash of bright, sapphire blue.

▶ Best places to see them: Mpumalanga, N. Province, Swaziland.

Little Bee-Eater

The beautiful bright green and yellow little bee-eater is one of the most commonly seen of the many varieties of bee-eater in South Africa. It is usually found near water, where you can see the myriad nests it makes in holes in sandy riverbanks. Despite its name it will eat almost any insect.

▶ Best places to see them: Mpumalanga, N. Province, Natal, Swaziland.

Mountains and Uplands

The mountains comprise a specific climate, and hence harbour vegetation, bird and animal life peculiar to the area.

Crowned Eagle

Whereas black eagles favour the open, rocky areas of hills and mountains, this spectacular, but rare, crested raptor hunts the forest canopy. The favoured prey is samango monkey, but most other things will do, including snakes. If you spot what you think is a large crested eagle, chances are it's a crowned eagle.

▶ Best places to see them: Eastern Cape, Natal, Mpumalanga, Northern Province.

Black Eagle

A great soarer found in all upland areas, the black eagle is the dassie's main predator. Immediately recognizable by its great size and thin white stripes on the underside of the wings, black eagles are an impressive, frequent sight. Less well vegetated uplands have smaller populations.

▶ Found in all regions, but most common in all areas of the Cape. (Also found in the Fish River Canyon, in Namibia, just over the border from the Richtersveld National Park.)

Lilac-Breasted Roller   Little Bee-Eater   Grey Lourie

Marine Life

Southern Right Whale

This inquisitive and highly approachable whale is only found in the southern hemisphere. In the past it suffered from over-exploitation for its valuable oil, meat and whalebone—hence its name: it was the 'right' whale to hunt. Recognizable by its large head covered in calluses, broad finless back, large paddle-shaped flippers, and the irregular white patches on its belly, it is a slow but highly acrobatic swimmer—southern right whales have been known to perform 'head-stands' (waving the flukes high in the air) for up to 2 minutes.

▶ Best places to see them: Walker Bay and De Hoop Nature Reserve on the Overberg Coast.

Cape Fur Seal

Also known as the South African fur seal, these social animals are the largest of the species. The males can reach up to 7.5ft (2.3m) long and weigh up to 660lb (300kg), with seemingly coarse, black-grey fur. Females are smaller and lighter. They live on the southwest and south coast of Africa, along as far as Port Elizabeth, due to the cold, oxygen-rich Benguela current which comes up along the coast from the south and forces food-rich water near to the surface where the seals hunt. In October adult bulls stake out (and will fiercely defend) their territories on land, with up to 50 cows (but 28 on average) within their 'harems'.

▶ Best places to see them: Mossel Bay, Cape Town, Paternoster, and Cape Columbine Nature Reserve.

Cape Fur Seal

Southern Right Whale

Great White Shark

The most aggressive and ferocious shark, the great white's reputation as a man-eater is widely spread, as is its habit of consuming its prey whole. It has extremely sharp, saw-edged teeth, and its body is light grey with a white belly. Usually found in the open sea, it sometimes comes closer to shore, and is almost always seen on its own. Often about 20ft (6.5m) long (but sometimes up to 30ft), its progress through the water is remarkably swift and controlled in spite of a body weight of about 3000lb (1350kg).

▶ Best places to see them: Gansbaai, Western Cape.

Tiger Shark

So-called because of the stripes on the body of young sharks (adults become a more uniform greyish colour with only the faintest trace of the stripes), tiger sharks can be recognized by their short snout and sharply

dangerous). They have also been found in river waters several hundred kilometres inland from the coast. Hippos won't tolerate them—they kill them if they can.

▶ Best places to see them: Kei River mouth and Zululand coast.

Dolphins

There are many species of dolphin living off the coasts of South Africa, the most common of which is the unimaginatively named Common Dolphin—distinctive for the yellowish patch on its sides and its dark back, stretching to a V shape under the fins. It is highly active, appearing to spend as much time above the water as beneath the surface, and is happy living out at sea, or closer to the shore. The much rarer Southern Rightwhale Dolphin is recognizable (like its namesake) for its lack of dorsal fin. It lives out at sea or in deep water nearer land, and often accompanies the

Great White Shark

pointed tail. They can be dangerous to man, and have very sharp, very efficient serrated teeth. Known for their indiscriminate appetite, they will eat almost anything, from fish and crustaceans to smaller sharks and dolphins. They are usually about 18ft (6m) long (but sometimes up to 30ft), and, unlike the great white, are often seen in schools.

▶ Best place to see them: off the Durban Coast.

Bull Shark

Bull sharks live in the river mouths of the KwaZulu-Natal coast, roughly from the Kei River north into Zululand (and have been known to attack man—they average about 10ft long which makes the river mouth crossings on the Wild Coast Hiking Trail potentially

Dusky Dolphins which also live on Africa's southwest-ernmost tip. These are the most acrobatic of dolphins, known for their high leaps and graceful somersaults. They live in large groups during the summer, and are recognizable for the contrast between their dark upper and light lower body, their short, thick beak, and mostly white face, with a small dark patch around the eyes.

▶ Best place to see them: anywhere on the Indian Ocean coast.

Flora

South Africa boasts a wealth of fauna, but even this is easily surpassed by its spectacular flora. The world has six known Floral Kingdoms and most of them cover several continents; but one, the Cape Floral Kingdom, is entirely contained within South Africa. The country has over 20,000 plant species—about 10 per cent of the world total—of which several thousand occur in South Africa alone.

The Cape Floral Kingdom is mainly composed of a heathland vegetation locally known as fynbos (which is Afrikaans for 'fine bush'), many species of which, such as ericas and strelitzias, flower profusely in the spring. The most famous are the weird, prehistoric-looking protea flowers, some of which grow to become huge. Whole forests of protea trees flourish in the Cape and Drakensberg Mountains.

them. Readers of the Victorian adventure writer H. Rider Haggard will remember that in his book *She*, about the mythical Rain Queen of southern Africa, a weird forest is described as surrounding her homeland. This was inspired by the real cycad forest in Lebowa, in Mpumalanga—the only such forest in South Africa—which is sacred to the Pedi nation and is home to a real Rain Queen who sometimes grants an audience to those who ask. The cycad forest is now a nature reserve and can be visited by anyone (*see* Mpumalanga).

What the oak, ash and cypress tree are to Europe, the thorn tree is to South Africa.

So wrote the South African novelist Charles Bosman in the 1930s. And he was right: the richest areas of flora do not support the most game. It is in the less spectacular bushveld that most animals live, where the densely packed acacia thorn trees provide a dense thicket of cover within which the game thrives. The bushveld

King Protea

Along the Garden Route coast, and in some parts of Natal, Mpumalanga, and the Northern Province, grow dense temperate rainforests that appear almost European but for the giant ferns, taller than a man, which sprout beneath them, and the weird shapes of some of the trees, most of which, again, are unique to South Africa. Strangest of all are the knobthorn trees whose trunks are covered with formidable wooden spikes. Some species, like the yellow-wood, mature to become giants of over 30m, and can live for over 1000 years.

A throwback to prehistoric times is the cycad, a giant fern that lives on high downland. Found in the Eastern Cape, Natal, Swaziland and Mpumalanga, these plants were so sought-after by gardeners that they began to disappear from the wild, and it is now illegal to disturb

regions of the Eastern Cape, Natal, and the Swaziland and Transvaal lowveld most closely resemble the picture of 'Africa' many travellers have in their minds: an endless plain of flat-topped thorn trees under which animals graze.

Far less spectacular than the other floral regions of South Africa, the bushveld still holds some surprises. Giant wild fig trees, sometimes the size of buildings, grow in the dry riverbeds, while the even larger, bulbous-trunked baobab trees stand like the frozen children of Daleks and Michelin men on the acacia plains of the Northern Province. In the wetter bushveld areas, the smooth, white-trunked fever tree (named for its association with malaria) grows in dense copses. At night the trunks shine faintly and appear as ghosts.

Finally, there is the arid zone of Namaqualand and the Kalahari. The strange *halfmens* tree, a giant desert succulent (water-holding plant) named for its human-like form, clings to the heat-blasted, shale hillsides of Namaqualand, occasionally sharing space with the giant aloe tree known as the *kokerboom* or quiver tree—the name a throwback to the days when the San (bushmen) still hunted the dry country, and used the tough bark to make quivers for their arrows. In the Kala-hari, golden grass fed by meagre annual rains shimmers between the widely spaced giant camel-thorn trees, creating a natural parkland where antelope graze.

It is the dry region that in fact steals the floral show in South Africa. Every September, just after the winter rains, the Namaqualand and western Karoo desert-floor erupt into bloom. A carpet of wild daisies, orange, white, yellow and pink, stretches over the veld and smiles in the warm sun. The flowers stay for one glorious month, then shrivel and the land returns to drought.

South Africa can be visited for flora alone, and the traveller cannot help but be enchanted by the constant diversity. A wealth of literature that almost equals the number of plant species has been written on the subject—it is a good idea to pick up some of the widely available handbooks so as to be able to identify what you see (*see* Further Reading).

People and Culture

Most Westerners are familiar with the word *apartheid*, having read about its injustice and racial oppression in their home media. But racial segregation and rule by force exist to a lesser or greater extent in many countries of the world. What attracted Western media attention to South Africa in particular was that its ruling white society resembled the Western model so closely that Western commentators felt a profound discomfort and not a little guilt when looking at South Africa. This was no bad thing: the Western media's incessant condemnation of apartheid did much to push their own governments to impose economic sanctions on South Africa and so hasten the system's demise. But, as many foreign onlookers are now becoming aware, the Western picture of South Africa was over-simplified—the most obvious interpretation of a more complicated web of ethnic and racial tensions permeating all levels of South African society.

Apartheid was inspired by deep fear, felt over a century and a half by the Afrikaans-speaking descendants of the Voortrekkers for those they had conquered by means of horse and gun. At the back of the Boer mind lay the very real fear that one day the conquered, who vastly outnumbered the conquerers, would rise. The only way to prevent this, it seemed, was to keep the conquered under an iron heel from the beginning. In his superb, painful book *My Traitor's Heart* (Bodley Head, 1990), the white South African writer Rian Malan illustrates just how deliberate was this philosphy of oppression:

> *Soon, many Afrikaners were calling themselves Doppers, after the little metal caps with which they snuffed out their candles. They called themselves Doppers because they were deliberately and consciously extinguishing the light of the Enlightenment, so that they could do what they had to do in darkness...There are many truths about Afrikaners, but none so powerful and reverberent as this wilful self-blinding.*

This 19th-century fear is easy to understand. Less easy is the confidence of the 20th-century architects of apartheid, who seemed so sure that they could uphold their system indefinitely, despite the overwhelming numbers and the ever-growing resentment of the oppressed. Alan Paton, in his novel *Cry the Beloved Country* (Charles Scribner, 1948), written in the year of the first apartheid government's accession, sheds some light on this:

> *...We shall live from day to day, and put more locks on the doors, and get a fine fierce dog when the fine fierce bitch next door has pups, and hold our handbags more tenaciously... We shall be careful, and knock this off our lives, and that off our lives, and hedge ourselves about with safety and precaution. And our lives will shrink, but they shall be the lives of superior beings... And the conscience will be thrust down....put under a bushel...for a generation that will live by it again, in some day not yet come; and how it will come, and when ...we shall not think about at all.*

So much for apartheid, which for all its police and soldiers and gold lasted no more than a generation. By no means all South African whites supported the system, and many suffered at its hands, particularly during the repressive State of Emergency of the 1980s, when anyone suspected of having ANC contacts could be detained without trial. However, barring certain individual incidents, white suffering was a drop in the ocean compared to that of South Africa's more than 20 million blacks.

So why did the blacks not rise and smash apartheid with one strike of their collective fist? Many Western journalists could never come to terms with the oppressed majority's apparent inability to offer concerted resistance to apartheid. But the problem was that these journalists, with their Western eyes, were making judgements that, though well-intentioned, were in some ways just as racist as those of apartheid. For referring to 'the blacks' in South Africa is like looking at the West before the Second World War and referring to the different nations collectively as 'the whites'.

Many of South Africa's black nations were and are as culturally removed from each other as, say, the English from the Hungarians. Some had, and still have, histories of warfare and conflict. Some, like the Zulus, suffer from endemic inter-clan fighting within their own nation. Even in the gold mines, where black trade union and labour movements have been active since the First World War, fighting between different groups in the workers' hostels consistently hampered the labour leaders' attempts at industrial action. The mine bosses knew this all too well, and encouraged ethnic conflict from the start by dividing the workers' hostels by 'tribe', knowing that the periodic fighting would keep the workers mistrustful of each other and sabotage any possibility of unity.

The colonial administrators and after them the apartheid leaders applied the same divide-and-rule policy to devastating effect, and tragically many of these ethnic conflicts exacerbated by white rulers continue today—though with the exception of Zulu inter-clan fighting in KwaZulu-Natal's townships ethnic strife has fallen off dramatically since the 1994 elections, and the present ANC leadership is the first to represent South Africa on a pan-ethnic level. However, it will be a long time before South Africa can be said to be one nation.

The racial question does not end with mere black and white—what is the future for South Africa's 6 million 'coloureds', a racially mixed people descended from the Cape's original Khoi inhabitants, Mozambiquan and Malaysian slaves and European settlers (*see* **History**)? A predominantly Afrikaans-speaking people, they also suffered terrible repression under apartheid, yet, not being officially 'black', they are now caught between cultures. And then there are South Africa's more than 1 million Indians, who were similiarly repressed under apartheid, yet who are also caught between cultures. Apartheid may have ended, but racism remains on all sides, and these people in particular may well suffer from alienation and discrimination in the new South Africa, albeit not by law, unless the national psyche can relax sufficiently to bid a final farewell to the whole issue of race and colour. Perhaps in a generation or two.

Complicating the situation still further is the matter of creed. The Afrikaners, in an attempt to justify their oppressive rule, adopted a stern Calvinist brand of Christianity (the Dutch Reformed Church), which successfully rolled their political and religious creeds into one: South Africa was their promised land, or so their *predikants* (pastors) preached; and by this premise the subjugation of blacks was perceived as a necessary part of the divine scheme for bringing Christianity and 'civilization' to the unenlightened. The fact that the 'enlighten-mentees' would be denied the benefits of this 'civilization', and would merely be its drawers of water and hewers of wood, was firmly ignored.

The Voortrekkers claimed that God had demonstrated his sympathy for their cause by granting them victory over the mighty Zulu empire in 1838 at the Battle of Blood River, when the Boers, installed behind their *laager* (or circle of wagons), poured volleys of lead at the charging Zulu *impis* and mowed them down without losing a single man. The day of Blood River was subsequently called the Day of the Vow, after the supposed pact with God that had given the Boers their victory, and was made a day for Afrikaner celebration. Under apartheid it became a public holiday, complete with a thanksgiving service in the massive Voortrekker Monument in Pretoria. It says much for the new government's will to forgive that the public holiday has been kept but the name has now been changed to the Day of Conciliation.

Fortunately for South Africa it was only the Afrikaners who complicated their political creed with an aggressive God. Many blacks under apartheid used religion more positively, holding fast to Christian faith to alleviate their suffering, whether under the apolitical Zionist Church or the more active Anglican and evangelical orders. Some black church leaders did much to advance the freedom struggle, notably Desmond Tutu, Cape Town's first black archbishop, who organized peace marches from Cape Town's cathedral through the 1980s and preached passionately for black unity and an end to violence. In fact, religion has proved to be South Africa's one point of general tolerance. For example, there is almost no religious tension between South Africa's Muslims (there are over a million, both Malay ('coloured') and Indian), Christians and Hindus, and religion has never been an issue even with the white governments. This bodes well. Religious hatreds never die, but racial hatreds can and do diffuse over time.

A recent development in South Africa is a movement among Afrikaans-speaking, educated, liberals—both whites and 'coloureds'—to call themselves 'Afrikaansers'. Whether this will spread remains to be seen, but its existence is a welcome acknowledgement of the culture they share.

First World or Third World?

Many visitors to South Africa find the juxtaposition of Western and traditional life confusing. Most of us like being able to classify things and put them into boxes, and South Africa, maddeningly, presents so many different faces that this is impossible. The large cities, with their high-rises, shopping malls, freeways and wealthy suburbs, belie the appalling living conditions of the surrounding shanties and squatter camps.

At the same time, the centuries-old traditions of some of the older residential quarters and villages, such as the 18th-century Malay Quarter (or Bo-Kaap) of central Cape Town, and the Moravian mission stations of the Western Cape, present a picture of Cape life that seems hardly to have changed since the early 1800s.

The contrasts become more abrupt as you penetrate the interior— for example the medieval world of the Lesotho Highlands, whose people get about almost entirely on horseback, sits just above the rich, westernized farms of the Natal Midlands. In the former 'homelands', you might be confronted with traditional life only marginally removed from the way it was when the first settlers arrived, yet five minutes later drive into a modern, pre-fabricated city complete with industrial areas, government offices and all the regular South African chain stores. Wild bushveld country whose primeval, game-rich landscape has never been touched by man might sit next to a sophisticated mining operation whose administrators will live in neat little bungalows with garages, and the workers in traditional huts in the bush.

Driving the endless, empty roads of the Northern Cape, you will pass donkey carts and horse-drawn wagons moving across the hot landscape at a fast trot or people simply walking. Stop and offer the person a lift and you will often find that they are making journeys of up to 100km on foot in the hot sun, thinking little of the distance, the time or the hardship.

Even in the cities you will glimpse horse wagons, roadside butcheries and people in traditional dress from the highways that speed over the townships and squatter camps to the city centres. Downtown, the markets are alive with the traditional life of the country—stalls and shops selling animal skins, organs and herbs for *muti* (magic and traditional medicine) and sometimes even *inyangas* and *sangomas* (diviners and faith healers) walking the main streets in their costume of office—complete with inflated goat's bladders affixed to the head—amid the besuited hurry of the commuter crowds.

The mix is confusing, but enthralling. Time and again you think you have the measure of the country, only to be shocked or surprised into a total change of view. The South Africans have a way around the problem. They term their country 'Second World'—poised midway between the traditional and the modern, both of which exert an equally strong influence on the people.

The pictures of modern South Africa are multitudinous and unforgettable—cattle and goats unhurriedly crossing a busy highway, ancient tribal rituals attended by office workers, beds in township houses raised on bricks to allow spirits to pass underneath, baboon skulls and hi-fi equipment for sale side-by-side on the same stall, boys daubed with the white clay of initiation into manhood standing in a queue at a take-away, white farmers consulting a diviner.

People, Culture and Language

While most visitors to South Africa are more than aware of the country's ethnic conflicts (*see* p.84), few are aware of just how many different cultures there are, and from which areas they come. The following is intended as a brief outline.

KhoiSan

These were the Cape's original inhabitants (*see* also **History**, p.34). By the time the first European settlers showed up in the 17th century, the KhoiSan had divided into three distinct cultures: the cattle-owning Khoi pastoralists, the San hunter-gatherers, and the *strandlopers* (beachcombers) of the the coast, who were non-cattle-owning Khoi reduced to living off shellfish and seabirds.

The Khoi were nicknamed 'Hottentots' by the white settlers after the linguistic clicks of their language, and after the songs of their regular moon-worshipping ceremonies, which early travellers describe as revolving around a regular chant that sounded like 'hottentot' to the Western ear. The Khoi were gradually stripped of their land by conquest, weakened by smallpox, alcohol and venereal disease, and gradually absorbed into a mixed-blood labouring class, known as 'coloured', that today provides the bulk of the poor classes in the Western and Northern Cape.

Some of these mixed Khoi/Europeans went north in the 18th century and established free bands of raiders and cattle-herders, known as Bastaards or Griqua and established large territories near the Orange River in the Northern Cape, even trekking into Natal. However, these too were eventually dispossessed—this time by the British—and under the racial obsessiveness of apartheid were redefined as 'coloureds'—bogus 'ethnologists' classified 11 different degrees of 'coloured' to make sure that none slipped through the 'white' net, however white they might appear. The original Khoi language exists only in poems written down by early missionaries (*see* 'Literature').

As for the San, they were called 'Bushmen' by the Dutch and English, and had every hand in the country—white and black—turned against them during the 19th century. Dutch farmers hunted them for sport, while the Xhosa, Sotho and Zulu peoples also killed the San where they found them. By the 1850s the San had been driven into the remoter Cape and Natal mountain ranges, and then north into the dry Kalahari. The San people still exist, but no longer in South Africa—their few remaining nomad bands now wander the remote wastes of eastern Namibia and western Botswana. The language and culture has survived, but their numbers are few and their future uncertain.

Cape Coloured and Malay

These are the Cape's four million 'coloureds', or descendants of mixed Khoi/European, and in some cases Malay slave blood. Although there is great variation in ancestry and thus outward appearance, the 'coloureds' (a name made up by white racists in the 19th century, but still unfortunately in general use today) are united in language, being predominantly Afrikaans-speakers.

The urban culture of Cape Town's 'coloureds' is jazzy and vibrant, a world away from the farm-labourers of the Winelands and Garden Route, or the desert shepherds of the Northern Cape. But despite this, the shared experience of racism and language has forged the Cape 'coloured' culture into a recognizable whole, and one that is uniquely South African in that it is made up purely of a blend of all the cultures and peoples who have come to the country since 1652.

The Malay culture is specific to Cape Town. Although designated 'coloureds' under apartheid, Cape Malays trace their ancestry to the highly skilled Javanese and Indonesian slaves brought over from Dutch Indonesia in the 18th century. A few Malay princes, such as the Sultan of Macassar, were also exiled to the Cape after rebelling against the Dutch, and their tombs, at False Bay, are now Muslim pilgrimage sites.

Following the abolition of slavery in the 1830s, many Malays bought properties in an old residential quarter on Signal Hill, just above the city centre—known as the Bo-Kaap, and still a Malay quarter today. Others were forcibly removed to the township of Mitchell's Plain in 1966. But the culture has survived: Muslim mysticism is even practised by some of the *mullahs* and young men who perform a dance called the *Khalifa* that involves the ritual piercing of flesh with blades and walking on hot coals while in trance.

Xhosa

The Eastern Cape province is the heartland of the Xhosa people, who speak a language classified as part of the Nguni group of southern Africa. The Xhosa fought the longest and hardest fight of all against white rule, resisting every inch of settlement and invasion between 1799 and 1879 (the Frontier Wars). These wars of resistance ultimately left them landless and had a devastating effect on national morale, resulting in a strange mass destruction of most of the nation's cattle and grain in a collective act of despair during the 1850s.

However, the Xhosa bounced back during the 1870s, and were the first black people to begin effectively fighting the white man at his own game by sending the sons of their nobility through mission schools and British universities at the end of the 19th century. By 1916 a group of Xhosa professionals founded the country's first black university at Fort Hare, near Alice in the Eastern Cape, whose graduates have produced some of South Africa's best-known black freedom fighters, including Nelson Mandela.

Traditional life is still strong in the countryside and the traditional red clay facial cosmetic is still seen among rural women, as are long smoking pipes. Traditional costume has all but disappeared, but adolescent initiation rituals and belief in the occult are still strong in the countryside. Numerically, the Xhosa are the largest ethnic group after the Zulu. For a more detailed look at Xhosa culture, *see* p.340.

Zulu

Also part of the Nguni language group, Zulu is spoken by most blacks in KwaZulu-Natal, and the Zulu nation, which now incorporates other groups in the region, such as the Hlubi and the KwaZulu-Natal Tsonga, is the largest in the country, and there has been talk of KwaZulu-Natal seceding from the union to form its own country.

Famed for their martial culture, the Zulus have long fascinated military and social historians, both for the rise of their early 19th-century empire under Shaka, the first Zulu king, and for Shaka's grandson Cetshwayo's massive defeat of the British at the Battle of Isandlwana in 1879.

Unfortunately, this warrior culture has its nihilistic side, and the townships and farmlands of KwaZulu-Natal's 'tribal' areas are riven by bloody inter-clan wars whose obscure origins of past grievances defy the comprehension of anyone not born into the Zulu way of life. Having said this, Zulu culture is highly creative. Zulu crafts such as basket-weaving and bead-work jewellery are sold in shops all over the country and are renowned for their beauty and exquisite detail. For a more detailed look at the Zulu nation, *see* p.427.

Swazi

Another Nguni-speaking group are the Swazis, some of whom live within South Africa, but most of whom live in the small independent kingdom of Swaziland and whose language, Seswati, is very similar to both Zulu and Xhosa. Although several of southern Africa's black nations have kings, perhaps no nation reveres its monarchy so much as the Swazis, whose king has absolute state power within Swaziland. Except for those who now live within South Africa, the Swazi were never ruled directly by whites, nor did they suffer the injustices of apartheid. As a result, white/black relations in Swaziland are noticeably unstrained. Although Swaziland is relatively westernized, rural life is still ruled by tradition, and, more than the Xhosa, the rural Swazi have a reputation for belief in witchcraft and the occult. For a more detailed look at Swazi culture, *see* p.483.

Pedi

The Pedi are a North Sotho-speaking group who live mostly in Mpumalanga, north of Swaziland. Traditional rivals of the Swazi until the 1830s, the Pedi then turned their military attention to the Voortrekkers, after repeated incursions into their territory forced them to war. The Pedi put up a spirited resistance to white settlement and beat off several Boer attacks until the British finally put them down in 1879 having annexed the Boers' South African Republic.

However, the Pedi were among the first of South Africa's black peoples to see an opportunity for independence in the diamond and gold mines of the Northern Cape and Johannesburg, signing up as contract labourers for fixed periods after which they received a cash payout and a firearm. These they used to great effect in armed insurrection against the Boers in the 1880s and '90s. Since then, the Pedi have remained a largely rural people, from 1972 to 1994 forcibly confined to the 'homeland' of Lebowa.

Ndebele

The Ndebele were originally an offshoot of the Zulus who, under the leadership of the opportunist general Mzilikazi, broke away from Zululand and invaded the highveld in the 1830s, establishing themselves as the dominant military force there.

However, their power was challenged by the Voortrekkers who arrived in the highveld in 1836 and immediately went to war against Mzilikazi, pushing him gradually north, and finally forcing his people accross the Limpopo into modern Zimbabwe.

South Africa's remaining Ndebele live, for the most part, in modern Gauteng. With a rich material culture, the Ndebele are justly famous for the superb, brightly coloured geometric designs with which they paint their houses, and whose bold primary colours make startling contrasts with the brown highveld grasslands. Traditionally, Ndebele women used to wear their wealth on their bodies, in the form of huge necklaces and arm-rings of beads wrapped around the arms, legs and torso and elongating the neck. Incredibly uncomfortable as this must have been in a hot climate, the practice was widely seen until a few years ago, and even now Ndebele women in a few areas continue the tradition. For a more detailed look at Ndebele culture, *see* p.542.

Tsonga

Also known as the Shangaan, the Tsonga speak their own *bantu* language and inhabit two main areas of South Africa: northern KwaZulu-Natal and Mpumalanga's former homeland of Gazankulu. Part of a much larger nation in Mozambique, the Tsonga maintain a slight cultural distance from the other South African black cultures.

Those of northern Zululand have been governed by the KwaZulu administration for over 20 years, but still maintain their language and take no part in Zululand's inter-clan wrangling. The Tsonga of Mpumalanga originally came over the Lebombo Mountains from Mozambique to escape the widespread tribal wars that flared in that country during the mid 19th century, but were forcibly resettled by the apartheid government in the fragmented 'homeland' of Gazankulu. For more information about the Gazankulu Tsonga, *see* p.589, and for a look at the Tsongaland territory in northern KwaZulu-Natal, *see* p.437.

Venda

Another group whose language is distinct from the other black language groups of South Africa are the Venda of the Northern Province. Although they represent the smallest black nation within South Africa (approx 550,000 people), the Venda were never conquered by either Boer or Brit, and have lived in their remote country since at least the 12th century.

Builders and settlers rather than pastoralists, by the 16th century the Venda had built permanent stone fortresses and towns similar to those of Great Zimbabwe north of the Limpopo River. Protected by the wide river to the north, by the Lebombo Mountains to the east and the Soutpansberg to the south, the Venda were able to beat off numerous attacks, both from the neighbouring Pedi and Swazi, as well as Zulu and Ndebele forays and the inevitable attacks by white settlers.

The Venda also have a strong mystic and occult tradition, stronger even than those of the Xhosa and Swazi, and the lakes and rivers of their well-watered forested country all have sacred significance. Totemic wood carving is widely practised, and propitiation ceremonies common—the most spectacular being the annual *Domba* snake dance of the unmarried maidens, who dance to win the favour of the Python God, the deity who controls both the rains and the fertility of the people.

Less picturesque is the territory's reputation for *muti* murders, or ritual killings to obtain body parts for magical use. While this goes on, to a greater or lesser extent, in all rural areas of South Africa, it has apparently reached something approaching epidemic proportions in

Venda over the past 15 years. This does not affect tourists, however, and is contained in secret within the community. For a more detailed look at Venda culture, *see* p.596.

Tswana

Like the Pedi, the Tswana people are a North Sotho-speaking conglomeration of several large clans. Spread over a very wide area, the Tswana are the third largest ethnic group in South Africa, living mostly in the Northwest Province and Northern Cape, although there are also other communities scattered throughout the highveld. The Tswana are thought to have the longest direct chronology of any black nation in South Africa—historians claim to be able to trace them back about 1000 years.

When the apartheid government forced the Tswana people to move into the 'homeland' of Bophuthatswana in the 1970s, the new Tswana government promptly took advantage of their 'separate' status to open casinos—at the time forbidden in South Africa. Sun City, the first large hotel/casino complex, was such a success that it inspired all the other 'homeland' governments, as well as those of Lesotho and Swaziland, to open similar enterprises.

The Tswana have also, to a large extent, kept out of the political violence that has dominated South African life over the last 20 years —with the exception of one attempted *coup d'état* of the Bophuthatswana government by the 'homeland's' army in the mid 1980s, and the early 1994 shooting of three AWB men by a Bophuthatswana policeman—and it may well be that, at last unfettered by the restrictions of white rule, the Tswana may become one of the country's dominant economic communities. For a more detailed look at the Tswana people, *see* p.614.

South Sotho

Usually known as the BaSotho, or simply Sotho, the South Sotho language speakers live mostly in and around the kingdom of Lesotho and the Free State. Keepers of cattle, sheep and angora goats, the Sotho are known for their superb wool-weaving, for their houses decorated with painted geometric patterns (similar to those of the Ndebele, but with more muted colours) and, in Lesotho itself, for their hardy, well-trained BaSotho ponies.

As a nation, the BaSotho have not existed for very long, being the offspring of various groups of refugees who fled into the area from the 1830s to the 1850s to escape the warfare and raiding in Natal and the highveld and flocked to the mountain fortress of the charismatic South Sotho-speaking chieftain Moshoeshoe. Moshoeshoe forged a nation out of his ever-growing numbers of subjects and fought off continual attacks from the Griqua, Tswana, Ndebele, Boers and Brits. The BaSotho were never conquered and those living in Lesotho itself escaped the apartheid yoke.

However, their most fertile territories were annexed by the Orange Free State in the 19th century, and the independent BaSotho retreated to a narrow arable plain east of the Caledon River and the high mountain country behind. Thus the South Sotho speakers today are culurally divided between those living in the Lesotho and Free State lowlands, and the fiercely independent highlanders, whose horse culture is famed throughout southern Africa, and whose world, though beautiful, suffers one of the harshest climates on the continent. For a more detailed look at BaSotho culture, *see* p.449.

Xhomani

The Xhomani Bushmen were the last group still living traditionally in South Africa in the 1930s, when the Kalahari Gemsbok
National Park was created to protect them. Under apartheid they
were moved out of the park, and they now have a human rights
lawyer working to restore to them a large area of land, as well
as some of their basic rights. Current opposition to their
cause comes mainly from local farmers who themselves only make a meagre living and are concerned
that they will not be sufficiently compensated for any
redistribution of land.

Indian

The areas around Durban have a huge Indian population—both Hindu and Muslim—which, combined
with smaller populations in and around Johannesburg
and Cape Town, numbers an estimated million, of
mostly Tamil- or Gujarati-speakers. Durban city centre has a very Indian feel, with its
huge mosque, bazaars and restaurants (the Indian food in Durban is superb). The Hindu
temples are mostly in the old Indian townships some distance from the city centre—one in
the Durban suburb of Westville and another in Pretoria's city centre allow tourist visits.
South Africa's Indians almost all trace their ancestry to poor, low-caste labourers brought over
from southern India in the 1860s to cut the sugar-cane fields of Natal. Paid criminally low
wages, these labourers had nonetheless begun to climb out of pauperdom by the 1900s,
having obtained traders' licences. Some went north to Johannesburg, but most stayed in
Natal. It was here that the Indians began their long freedom struggle, under the leadership of
one Mohandas Gandhi, an Indian-born lawyer who went to South Africa on business in 1893
and stayed until 1914.

After being ejected from a train for refusing to leave a whites-only carriage, Gandhi began to
weld South Africa's Indians into a political force, founding a self-help business scheme at
Phoenix, north of Durban, in the late 1890s, an Indian Red Cross during the Boer War of
1899–1902 and a newspaper called *Indian Opinion* in 1903. In 1913, when all non-whites
were ordered to carry passes, Gandhi organized a peace march from Newcastle to the
Transvaal, which despite being met with police violence, was ultimately successful in having
Indians removed from the 'native register'.

Under apartheid, Indians were again made to carry pass books, were disenfranchised and
made to live in 'townships'. Although by then many were successful businessesmen, they
were subjected to racism on two fronts: whites regarded them as inferior, blacks regarded
them as alien. Much of this racism survives today, yet the Indian freedom struggle has never
resorted to violence, trusting instead to patience and parliamentary lobbying.

Afrikaner

Of all the white people living in South Africa, only the Afrikaners are truly African, in that
many can trace 10 generations of Dutch, German and Huguenot French ancestors in the

sub-continent and whose Afrikaans language, though evolved from European Germanic roots, has developed entirely in Africa.

In order to understand the nuances of Afrikaner culture, the meaning of the words 'Afrikaner' and 'Boer', respectively 'African' and 'farmer', need a little clarification. Both have wider implications: 'Afrikaner', while occasionally used as a collective expression referring to all Afrikaans-speakers, usually refers to those of the Cape, while 'Boer' generally refers to those of the Free State and Transvaal. 'Afrikaner' often implies a certain liberalism, while 'Boer' implies reaction and racial intolerance.

There are reasons for this: the Cape has always had a more liberal tradition than the rest of the country, perhaps because it was never threatened by black military power during the 19th century, and because life there was comparatively prosperous: the great manorial wine-growing estates, Cape Dutch architecture, furniture-making, music and literature and the Afrikaans language all evolved in the Cape—albeit on the back of Khoi and 'coloured' virtual slave labour. The elegance of the Western Cape's Afrikaner lifestyle was enviously noted by that inveterate social commentator Anthony Trollope who, after visiting the Cape in the 1870s, wrote,

> ...the visitor is tempted to repine because fate did not make him a wine-growing, orange-planting, ostrich-feeding Dutch farmer.

The Boer heritage also has its roots in the Western Cape, but has been culturally distinct since the mid 19th century. The word derives from the term '*trekboer*', meaning 'travelling farmer', and describes the first white pioneers to wander into the interior with their livestock during the 18th century. These people represented the poorer side of Cape Afrikaner culture, those who had no land and who stood to inherit nothing. They followed the rains and the grazing, hunted the plentiful game, traded a little with the indigenous people and, eventually, carved out extensive farms around permanent water sites.

In the Northern Cape, the *trekboers* hunted out and annihilated the San hunters who killed their sheep and cattle in retaliation for the white depredation of game stocks, but in the east they encountered a power that was stronger than their own—the Xhosa nation. At first, they shared grazing land with the Xhosa, but increasing numbers of *trekboer* settlers soon led to competition and conflict—the Frontier Wars into which the British were drawn from 1799, following their annexation of the Cape. During this period, a vehement racism began to creep into the Boers' (as they were now known) relations with both Khoi and Xhosa—inspired by fear and the need to hate one's adversary.

The Eastern Cape Boers decided to leave the eastern frontier to the British and the Xhosa during the Great Trek of 1836 and headed for the interior, solidifying their racism through incessant wars with the nations of the interior—in which the Boers, or 'Voortrekkers' (meaning 'forward travellers'), did not always come off best, despite their superior weaponry. Added to this, only a few Boers really prospered in the new territories—life for most was an incessant struggle against parasites, fever, wild animals, justifiably hostile locals and sometimes British troops.

When gold was found in the Transvaal in the 1870s and '80s, few Boers benefited from the mining—most of which was controlled by English-speaking companies from the Cape. A few years later, Britain invaded the Boer republics of the Transvaal and Orange Free State, and in the course of this, the second Anglo-Boer War (1899–1902), many Boers lost their farms and families. In the years of reconstruction, most Boers remained poor, and only gradually managed to penetrate the professional and governmental world, being obstructed all the way by English snobbery and condescension.

Given all this, it becomes easier to understand the ferocious racism and xenophobia that characterized the Boers' 20th-century rise to supremacy via the brutal workings of apartheid. However, their brand of tough survivalism and attendant racism is capable of change—as has been demonstrated by the lack of right-wing reprisals in reaction to the accession of the new ANC government. Hopefully, the Boer/Afrikaner energy and desire to succeed will, in future, be harnessed for the whole country's benefit.

British

There are few areas of South Africa where English is the dominant language. Sizeable English-speaking communities exist in Cape Town, the Garden Route, Johannesburg and Mpumalanga, Swaziland, and over a wide area in KwaZulu-Natal. But in all these places English is still only one language among many. However, since it was a British colony from 1806 to 1910, and a British dominion from 1910 to 1948, the *lingua franca* of South Africa's administration was solidly English until the rise of apartheid, and even that aggressively Afrikaans system did not eradicate it from official use. Added to this, the mining companies have always been run by English-speakers.

British South Africans have traditionally presented themselves as liberal and non-racist, and, while this has often been true in spirit, inevitably it is by no means a generally accurate picture. It was the British who systematically destroyed the Xhosa nation during the Frontier Wars of 1799–1879, who smashed the Zulu and Pedi kingdoms, and who acted as arbitrary brokers of the independent kingdoms of Swaziland and Lesotho until their independence in the 1960s.

The British brought in, and then ostracized, the Indians of Natal, and most of the later British missionaries harangued and condemned the African cultures they had been sent to evangelize. Britain exploited South Africa's human and mineral resources for her own benefit, and used South Africa as a testing-ground for experiments in total war, such as Lord Kitchener's concentration camps, which were responsible for the deaths of tens of thousands of Boer and African women and children between 1900 and 1902.

However, under apartheid, English-speakers often found themselves at odds with the new order. Though they remained the most economically privileged group, their old racism began to fray and most of the country's whites who campaigned for black rights through the 1970s and '80s were English-speaking.

This did nothing to improve the old enmity between them and the Afrikaners and Boers, whose slang names for Brits included *soutpiels* (which translates to 'salt dicks', meaning that they had one foot in Britain, the other in South Africa, and their genitals hanging in the sea), and *rooinek*, meaning 'red neck', referring to the British inability to withstand the African sun (and therefore its hard life). Fortunately, in recent years this Boer/Brit division has eased a little and while the communities still lead largely separate social lives, the old hatreds have softened to rivalry.

Towards a Composite Society

Finally, it must be said that although it is worth understanding the complexity of South Africa's ethnic scene, it is easy to overemphasize the differences between the cultures. Perhaps for the first time in the country's history, there is now a conscious movement among South Africans of all races finally to lay down the burden of mutual hostility and misunderstanding and to work towards something new—the chance of becoming a composite society.

That such a deliberate movement should be taking place after so many centuries of conflict is exceptional—we are far more used to seeing the negative side of humanity whenever the problems of nationalism, racial difference and intolerance arise—and South Africa more than anywhere else has come to be seen as a symbol of this negativity.

But what the traveller will notice is an almost unbelievable will to forgive and forget among most South Africans that would have been unimaginable even five years ago. Today's South Africans are doing their best to become what they have never really been—South Africans. Nobody expects the transition to be smooth but, as Steve Biko wrote in his last book before his death in police custody in 1977:

> *We are looking forward to a just and egalatarian society in which colour, creed and race will form no point of reference.*

Art and Architecture

Architecture

South Africa's indigenous architecture goes back to the early Middle Ages, when the ancestors of today's Venda people migrated south from Zimbabwe into the Northern Transvaal, bringing with them the Zimbabwean tradition of building walled villages and towns of stone. The practice was abandoned after the 17th century, when the Venda monarchy collapsed and the society reverted to a series of chiefdoms, but the ruins of the old capital, Dzata, can still be viewed, and the workmanship, though simple, is beautiful, with the bases of rounded towers and the rough-dressed masonry of the main walls still standing, despite the ruins having been reclaimed by the surrounding forest (*see* **Northern Province**, 'Venda', p.594).

However, South Africa's most famous architecture is known as Cape Dutch, a simple elegant building style that began in Cape Town in the 17th century and continued through the whole of the old Cape Province into the early 19th century. Its most elegant period was from 1790 to 1810, led by the architect Louis Thibault and the sculptor Anton Anreith, who built the best-known Cape Dutch structures, Groot Constantia and the Lutheran Church (*see* 'Cape Town, Architecture', p.121).

Cape Dutch style is immediately recognizable by its distinctive curved roof gables, sitting atop simple white-washed fronts, with well-proportioned mullioned windows and dark roofs of slate (in the towns) and thatch (in the country). Most houses spread over one storey, and only the very late buildings (or very grand) rise higher. In general, the gable is the only purely decorative feature, and is thought to have been inspired by the Renaissance gables of Florence, adopted and gothicized. But the Cape gables are often curved in a way that is not seen in Holland or the Low Countries, and this is ascribed to a

Batavian (Indonesian-Malay) influence, the Dutch having colonized the East Indies some years before the Cape of Good Hope. Though more deliberate decorations are lacking, the calm and proportion of Cape Dutch style relies on this simplicity. The earliest surviving houses (from around 1710) are usually built in a T-shape, the long part of the letter extending back from the gabled front. From about 1750 a grander H-shape appears, whose gables are sometimes adorned with mouldings or, occasionally, a pediment. At the apex of Cape Dutch style (roughly 1790–1820), a more complex U-shaped house appears, with the space formed by the U generally occupied by a courtyard, sometimes with pillars supporting a railed balcony.

Cape Town and the Cape Peninsula, the Winelands regions and the Overberg have the highest densities of Cape Dutch architecture, the best examples being the Constantia home-steads, the towns of Stellenbosch and Paarl (and surrounding countryside), Tulbagh, Greyton and McGregor. However, the Northern Cape has some fine set-piece towns, notably Graaff-Reinet in the Eastern Karoo (built 1781) and Colesberg (1814–30).

Side by side with this later, aristocratic Cape Dutch building came some beautiful, if very simple, vernacular cottages. Many old wine estates' workers' cottages survive from this period, but from a traveller's point of view the best places to see whole surviving villages is the Bo-Kaap (Malay Quarter) of Cape Town, and in the Moravian mission stations of the Western Cape countryside. At the same time, in the Northern Cape, the earliest Boer settlers of the 1800s built beehive huts of layered stone (known as corbelled houses), similar in form to the ancient Celtic brochs of Scotland, Ireland and Brittany, and a number survive around the Western Karoo towns of Williston and Carnarvon.

The early British occupation saw some elegant Georgian building, particularly in the settler country of the Eastern Cape. Though not as elegant as the Cape Dutch style, the British Georgian period nonetheless produced some superb buildings whose look will be familiar to British travellers. Some whole towns survive, notably Grahamstown, Salem and Bathurst, between Port Elizabeth and the Fish River. During the Victorian era many buildings of the solid imperial school went up in all of South Africa's larger towns. But in general this period, though handsome, is not exciting, and is all too familiar to Western travellers.

However, in one town, Pietermaritzburg, the Victorian building achieved a harmony and simplicity of design unusual for the colonial architects of the time, who generally built large edifices designed to impress. Pietermaritzburg's residential neighbourhoods, in particular, have some superb houses—almost all in fine red brick, one to three storeys high, with fili-greed verandas of white-painted wrought-iron extending up the fronts.

This ironwork became a mainstay of Edwardian design and until the 1960s almost all South African towns boasted handsome arcades. But unfortunately the early apartheid govern-ments, with their economic boom and aggressive adoption of the Western industrial aesthetic, tore down many of these arcades and replaced them with ghastly concrete-and-glass lumps. Some good examples do still survive—notably upper Adderley Street and Long Street in Cape Town, and Diagonal Street in Johannesburg.

The Edwardian era also produced South Africa's most innovative architect, Sir Herbert Baker. Mostly active in Cape Town, he contrived an ingenious mix of the Cape Dutch with the English vernacular. Baker's most famous work was Groot Schuur in Rondebosch, Cape

Town, commissioned by the mining magnate and empire-builder Cecil Rhodes. Now the Cape Town residence of the South African presidents, Groot Schuur was followed in 1910 by the Union Buildings in Pretoria, a terracotta design of Classical style. But after this Baker left South Africa to collaborate with Lutyens on the building of New Delhi in India, and the Union Buildings represent the last distinctively South African Western design to appear in the country—although some handsome Art Deco buildings went up in Cape Town and Johannesburg in the 1930s (take a walk around St George's Mall and Greenmarket Square in Cape Town, or on Jeppe and Eloff Streets in central Johannesburg). Since the Edwardian period little has appeared that is not merely imitative of Western post-war industrial design.

However, this is to forget that the most distinctive form of South African architecture does not appear in the cities or centres of white culture. Just as South Africa's architecture begins with the black tradition, so does it end. Throughout all the periods listed above, the most common style of building has been the rondavel, or thatched round hut (though many are far larger than mere 'huts'), found in almost all rural areas. For simplicity of design and harmony of form, there is nothing to touch the rondavel. It blends with and complements the landscape, rather than attempting to dominate or influence it. Not all black rural housing conforms to the round pattern (tradition has it that the lack of corners is to give malevolent spirits no place inside the house to hide)—the Ndebele, South Sotho and Xhosa often build oblong buildings, painted with complex, exact geometric designs (*see* 'People and Culture' above). But almost all black rural architecture uses an adobe or mud/dung mix, cool in the heat, yet holding the warmth of a fire when it is cold outside.

In Zululand, the traditional form of building is a large, round grass hut with a low entrance door, densely woven from reeds so as to be both watertight and windproof. In the Lesotho Highlands, rondavels are often constructed from dry stone with an inner and outer plaster of mud and dung which can withstand the harsh climate for an indefinite period. As yet, the rondavel has not been incorporated into civic architecture. But now that South Africa is finally being ruled by the majority it may be that vernacular forms of architecture may finally start to appear in the cities and transform the towns' overall feel to something more genuinely African.

Art

South Africa's earliest rock engravings (mostly found near the Vaal River in Northwest Province) have been traced back approximately 1000 years, and much of the San (bushman) rock painting (found at sites all over the country) is around 30,000 years old. Bearing great resemblance to the prehistoric rock paintings of the Ahaggar Mountains of the central Sahara, San art, with its animal and spirit-world motifs, varies from the highly stylized to the incredibly lifelike—especially in its depiction of animals. The San tradition of rock art continued until about 1850, when the last known artist was shot by a farmer (the San were hunted like game from the late 18th century—*see* **Northwest Province**, 'History') in the Drakensberg Mountains, the unfortunate man's corpse being found to have a quiver of pigments strapped around the waist.

The later San paintings often depict white men on horses with guns and ox-wagons and sometimes even show running fights between San and white men, or San and Bantu warriors, who also ruthlessly persecuted the hunter-gatherers. That both black and white South Africans combined to exterminate the San, who raided their livestock as game was steadily denuded through the 19th century, was a crime that will never be atoned for, and which has deprived the country of one of its oldest, most peaceful and, many would argue, richest cultures.

In the early 19th century, white South Africans began to celebrate the landscape, and in some cases the people and wildlife, of what was then regarded as a savage land. However, a few artists portrayed the indigenous people without caricature; some of the early watercolours and drawings by Samuel Daniell (an English artist who visited the Cape between 1801 and 1803) are superbly beautiful, though the landscapes he sets them in are more an ideal of classical Europe than an accurate portrayal of South Africa. Daniell also painted some famous pictures of *trekboer* life. His best paintings are in the Rust-En-Vreugd collection, in Cape Town.

Another Englishman, Andrew Smith, who travelled into the highveld in the early 1830s, painted an amateurish but highly valuable record of life among the Tswana, KhoiSan, Ndebele and BaSotho before white settlement. These are housed in the Museum Africa collection in Newtown, Johannesburg. Other commentary-style artists of the period include Thomas Baines (particularly good for the Frontier Wars), W. J. Burchell (mainly pictures of the Khoi), Eugene Carsalis and C. D. Bell (again, pictures of life in the highveld and Karoo), also in the Museum Africa collection.

The later 19th century saw a rise of epic landscape painting in oils, the most notable exponent of which was Pierneef, whose bold colours and slightly stylized outlines resemble the real landscapes of South Africa far more than those of the earlier illustrative painters. Pierneef has a museum dedicated to him in Pretoria, though most of his landscapes were of the Cape and Namibia, rather than the Transvaal. Even more stylized was the Cape Town artist Irma Stern, who studied with the German Expressionists in Berlin from 1913 until the First World War. Her work, featuring African landscapes and people, though not well received in conservative South Africa, remained popular in Europe until the 1950s. She made painting expeditions to Swaziland, the Transkei and Zululand, and further up into German Central Africa (Cameroon) and Tanzania. Her house, in Rondebosch, Cape Town, is now a museum, and has a good collection of her work.

More populist in her approach (she used to sell sculptures to sailors docking at Cape Town) was the nun, Sister Helen Vorster, who created an incredibly lifelike collection of scupltural portraits of San, Khoi and Tswana people in the Northern Cape during the 1930s and '40s. Most belong to private collections, but some of her family groups, showing village and family life, are now in the National Cultural History Museum in Pretoria (*see* p.533), and serve as a precious record of a now-vanished culture, the KhoiSan of the region having moved north or been absorbed into the general Cape 'coloured' population soon afterwards, while many of the Tswana were forcibly resettled in reserves by the apartheid government in the 1960s and '70s, resulting in an erosion of much of the original culture.

Helen Martins, another woman artist active from the 1940s to the 1960s, hardly sold or exhibited any of her work, yet is considered by many to be South Africa's most original white artist. A recluse, Martins lived in the tiny Eastern Karoo village of Nieu Bethesda, north of Graaff-Reinet. Many rumours have been circulated about her private life, from suggestions that she worked as a prostitute (unlikely in the lonely Karoo) to ascribing her an almost saintly status. Certainly her work—almost all sculpture, and almost all contained in the back garden of her small house—is often biblical or occult in subject, with prayers to the moon, and, above all, owls, all crafted in, of all media, concrete; they crowd into the small outdoor space, creating an atmosphere that is impossible to define. The Owl House, as Martins' home became known, is now open to the public (*see* **Northern Cape**, p.277).

With the exception of some sculptors, such as Eric Skotnes, there is little contemporary white South African art to compare with the work of the past. However, in the past 25 years black artists have emerged to lead the art world in South Africa. Township art, as it is known, became a recognized movement in the late 1930s, but did not achieve outside recognition until the 1960s, just as apartheid was coming into its own. The early artists, like Gerard Sekoto, George Pemba, Selby Mvusi and others, painted and sculpted in a *naïf* style that was a blend of traditional craft motifs and depictions of street life—a meeting of the traditional rural and emerging urban black cultures of the time. Their work was mainly realistic, but this gradually changed, with ritual and superstitious subjects being brought in by artists like Eric Ngcobo and Gladys Mgudlandlu in the 1940s and '50s.

Despite the rise of apartheid, growing interest in township artists caused several unofficial art schools to open up—the best-known being on Polly Street in Sophiatown, Johannesburg (which later moved to Soweto after Sophiatown was razed), and in the Lutheran Church at Rorke's Drift in Zululand. A plethora of work emerged from these schools, much of it reflecting the suffering and hardship of black life, and combining urban, mythical, Christian and animal motifs to express a variety of strong emotions.

Of note within this movement are Julian Motau, Welcome Koboka, David Mbele, David Mgalo and a host of others. Although some of the work is brutally realistic, much is heavily stylized in its attempt to put across the extreme nature of black South African life in the late 20th century. Sculptors such as Sydney Kumalo, Ezrom Legae, Aubrey Nxumalo and Lucky Sithole have been particularly effective. Painters in great demand include Louis Maquela (famous for his use of mythological themes) and Winston Saoli. Commercial galleries, especially those of the smart Rosebank and Sandton suburbs of northern Johannesburg, now ask very high prices for township art. Public collections can be viewed at the Johannesburg, Pretoria and Cape Town art galleries, but the largest and most comprehensive collection is at the University of Fort Hare, near Alice in the former Ciskei (now part of the Eastern Cape).

Literature

European-style poetry and prose have thrived here for only 200 years, but the indigenous traditions of KhoiSan and Bantu oral poetry have their roots in prehistory, and their preoccupation with suffering, survival and the surrounding natural beauty has affected all subsequent South African literature, whether black, English or Afrikaans, almost every work containing a similar atmosphere of profound if unspoken melancholy, combined with passionate love of the landscape and the wild creatures that live there.

South African Poetry: From the San Era to the Present

San and Khoi poetry, transcribed by a handful of 19th-century missionaries and linguists, unveils a picture of South Africa before the primeval order was upset by colonial adventure. In many, the poems are simple, beautiful appeals to the animal spirits to grant success to the hunter. But occasionally there is room for something more abstract. For example, in one San poem, the wind is perceived as a man coming out of his hut and travelling freely with the birds, scattering grasses over the land. A shaman watches their passage and is noticed by a bird, who speaks, saying, '*I am he who arouses the wind.*' How better could one convey the limitless space and power of the South African wild?

Khoi poems use the animal world as an allegory for human life. In one song from the 18th century, a hyena mother laughingly asks her children, as they clamour for food, how she can possibly satisfy them, when every man's hand is set against her? Humour, hardship and the life of a scavenging predator—the Khoi poet might have been singing of his own life on the arid *veld*.

In another Khoi poem, about a zebra stallion, the poet declaims, '*You dappled fly, you of the shadow and light.*' The hunter salutes his prey: for its beauty, for its skill in using its stripes for camouflage—the '*shadow and light*' of its hide merging with that of the bush—and for the swiftness of its flight from danger, dodging the thrown missile, eluding its clumsy hunters who must watch its escape through the dappled shadows of the bushveld.

The Bantu oral tradition concerns itself with ancestor-worship in the form of epic praise poems to their warrior kings. However, allusions to the natural world are again the main themes of these long anthems. In one such, recording the birth of King Moshoeshoe, the leader who forged the BaSotho nation in the early 19th century (*see* **Lesotho**, 'History'), the poet talks of the birth pangs echoing through the caves of the surrounding mountains, the antelope taking fright and stampeding on the *veld* as the young king emerges from the womb, shield in hand. '*Halala you Zulus!*' cries the poet, challenging the BaSotho's hereditary rivals, '*We too have a chief today!*'

The Zulus themselves have probably produced more praise poems than any other South African nation, echoing their succession of legendary 19th-century warrior kings. Shaka, the first and fiercest of these, is the object of most such poems. Again, the natural world is brought in to provide similes. Shaka is compared to the slippery pebbles on the riverbed of a ford his enemies are trying to cross, to a leopard stalking his prey in the day, to a buffalo turning on the attacking hyena pack and driving them off with his horns.

Not all poetry from the black tradition is taken up with war, and there is a wealth of more reflective work. Among the most beautiful is a poem by Makholotso Makhomo, a Sotho woman poet who began publishing her work in the 1950s. In one long poem called 'When He Spoke to Me of Love' she becomes a young bride fearing that her new-found bliss may slip away: her voice is burned by a fire in her throat. Despite her pride, she cries, silently, for fear that the groom might change his mind and leave, that the village dogs will drive off the cattle of her bride-price. She goes to him as if in prayer. Only when he speaks is she reassured, and finds words: '*my tongue, unstrung, confessed to him*'.

Most of the more recent black poets deal, inevitably, with the sufferings of their people under apartheid. 'Black Mamba Rising', an anthology of worker poets published in 1986, is a good example of the bitterness and anger the system inspired.

More considered are the works of Dennis Brutus, a 'coloured' writer born in Zimbabwe in 1924, who spent many years teaching in South Africa before joining the freedom struggle. Brutus was shot by police, and survived, but was imprisoned on Robben Island. He is still writing today (though he now lives in the USA), and his poems rank among the most emotive of the apartheid era. In one poem, 'Pray', written while imprisoned on Robben Island, he looks at his ideals which have been broken by white rule, crying that he and his people '*have splintered our hearts on their marble whiteness*'.

The necessity of moving to the cities for work, and the breakdown of traditional culture, became a theme of black poetry from the late 19th century which continues today, and here the allegories of the natural world begin to disappear.

In the poem, 'The Dispossessed', by Modikwe Dibode, the hero leaves wives, children and cattle to go and work in the mines in order to pay the hut taxes and poll taxes imposed by the British. The family hold back their tears as their man leaves: '*The custom allows no crying.*' He describes the seeming efficiency of the white man: '*He is awake earlier than you, murmuring, "Blooming Kaffir",*' but the hero is worked to the bone under the ground. When he returns home he finds more taxes that cannot be paid, and in his absence, one wife has disappeared, and his son has left for the mines and

> *Nothing is left. Take another contract.*

Finally, the frustration and sense of futility suffered by blacks merely trying to live from day to day under apartheid is summed up in Jabulani Sibaya's peom 'What Do you Want Me to Do?'. As he points out,

> *You arrest me when I complain. You kick me like a dog when I do not complain. What do you want me to do?*

Equally rich is Afrikaans poetry. The earliest 18th-century poems tend to eulogize the natural beauty of the land. Many 19th-century poets, such as Jakob Du Toit (known as 'Totius', a famous campaigner for Afrikaans as an official language), deal with tedious religious themes, but some delve into a strange fatalistic look at suffering—from the elements, from the British, and from themselves—coupled with a fierce love of place.

Much of the early 20th-century poetry develops this theme, often beautifully. In 'The Gods Are Mighty' N. P. van Wyk Louw considers the guilt of his people, and his own place among them: '*I know the final dream of my breed,*' he says, aware of but not condoning his people's lust to conquer and rule the land; to him that is the way of things, '*but blood is manifest, and words are vain*'.

More lyrical is C. Louis Leipoldt (also a doctor, traveller and famous gourmet—*see* 'Cape Cuisine'), who sees the whole country as beautiful, but inextricably caught in bloody conflict. In his poem 'The Banded Cobra' the snake emerges from its hole to find that the long-awaited rains have come. But the other animals, gathering around, point out that the ground is not wet with water but with human blood, and the bushes of the countryside are feeding on it. In the late 1940s Alan Paton, who is better known as a novelist, summed up the extension of this fatalism towards his people's instigation of the apartheid system:

We are going to set you apart for ever.
We mean nothing evil towards you.

Some of the most recent Afrikaans work harks back nostalgically to the natural world of the KhoiSan, before it was broken and dipsersed by the ancestors of the writers themselves, before the land became tainted with the conflicts and injustices of its colonial and recent history. Michael Picardie, a contemporary South African poet, mourns the vanished KhoiSan, becoming for a moment the San hunter struggling in the face of white settlement; '*He hunts me*', sings the San of the farmer; '*I am become his animal.*' Then he prophesies the evil that will follow the annihilation of his people: '*My death is the death of the world.*'

English-language poets have taken this nostalgic line right from the beginning. One work from 1812, written by one George Marshall, an early settler at the Cape, eulogizes the Khoi lifestyle (although part of the poem expresses disgust for their physical appearance), and allows that they may hold the key to some ancient wisdom that the white man has forgotten:

He knows no wants but those which instinct gives...
He pities us in search of wealth who roam.

Much of the 19th-century poetry then breaks with any such attempts at understanding the country and its people and deals with adventure, but continues to laud the wild—subduing wild animals and wilder men, digging for gold, fighting and winning—the usual 'Boy's Own' subjects of Victorian imperial verse make the English poetry from this period amusing, but not particularly interesting.

However, this changes in the early 20th century. A good example is Guy Butler who described the colonial scene with more ambiguity. In his poem 'Surveyor', he becomes the white government man, in starched khaki, trying to fulfil his contract of cutting a road through the bush. He has reached an impasse, as the local chiefs try to block him—

I called an indaba of headmen and foremen,
and sat like Solomon in my canvas chair between them,

knowing himself to represent '*The invaders, the roadmakers, the breakers of custom.*' He sits as the chiefs wrangle, thinking of girls and malaria and booze until he admits defeat, at which point the chiefs suddenly withdraw their objections, and the road goes through. The surveyor makes no pretence at understanding this, nor the people that surround him. His last comment on the road is, '*The Commies are using it now.*'

Like the contemporary Afrikaans poetry, much of the recent English-language work concerns itself with despair at the modern South Africa and a futile desire for the pure, prehistoric past. Mark Swift writes about a trip to the Natural History Museum in Cape Town, in which there is a life-size display of San life, using realistic models to create a tableau of the country before white men. Here, the themes of suffering and love of the natural world come together clearly. Swift sees the model of the bushman (San) '*taut behind glass*', and '*stripped to the bone*', exposed for the education and curiosity of modern tourists, his freehold of the land gone, his world collapsed, and his people and the game dispersed and vanished.

South African Prose

South African prose, particularly fiction, is comparatively recent. The earliest work is related literature written by explorers, such as the Portuguese mariner Vasco da Gama (*c.*1469–1524), and the much later English-speaking visitors of the early 1800s—Lady Anne Barnard, who wrote entertainingly of life at the Cape, Thomas Baines, who travelled the Eastern Cape, and Andrew Smith, one of the first explorers to travel the highveld in the 1830s (just before the Voortrekkers) and who met with the region's warlords—men like Moshoeshoe and Mzilikazi—and saw their world before the Boer conquest. However, South Africa's best novels are 20th-century.

The works of Eugene Marais, an early 20th-century Afrikaans author (also widely regarded as a fine poet), bridge the gap between the early commentaries and fiction, being mostly fanciful but perceptive studies of the natural world. His two most famous, *The Soul of the Ape* and *The Soul of the White Ant*, deal with those eminently South African but hardly eulogized creatures, baboons and termites.

He finds all of human life displayed in the behaviour of wild creatures. In this extract, from *The Soul of the White Ant*, Marais talks of the lifelong attachment between the king and queen ants of a termite colony—despite the female's gradually growing far larger than the male. Even if the mound is broken open,

> he [the termite king] clings to her gigantic body and tries to defend it, and
> if the ruthless attacker so wills, he dies at her side. What a wonderful
> example of married love and fidelity, which can survive this terrible change
> of his beloved to a loathsome mass of fat.

It seems as if there is irony here. However, the most ironical writer of them all has to be Herman Charles Bosman, another Afrikaans writer, active in the 1930s, whose short stories deal with every aspect of South African life from racism, through war and the occult, to simple love stories and the eternal bickering between Boer families. Again, there is a great love of place, even though the Marico Bushveld of the Northwest Province, where the stories are set, is one of the driest and least spectacular areas of the country (*see* **Northwest Province,** 'Groot Marico'), and no visitor to South Africa should go without reading Bosman's set of short stories, *Mafeking Road*.

By contrast, the works of Olive Schreiner, though from the same period, lack any irony at all. Her short novel *The Story of an African Farm*, about life in the arid Great Karoo, is a simple romantic tragedy, with some painful passages of religious torment and guilt, but it has somehow won the position of being South Africa's most widely read novel. It is worth reading some of Schreiner's short stories, contained in most anthologies of the country, which deal, again, with hardship—this time for the early Transvaal Boers. Schreiner's grave, near the town of Cradock in the Eastern Karoo, is a mecca for many Afrikaans devotees of early South African fiction.

A far different perspective on the dry regions is offered by Laurens van der Post, who published *The Lost World of the Kalahari* in the 1950s. Rather than write about the white struggle to survive, van der Post was concerned with the fate of the country's original inhabitants, the San, and describes a journey into the Kalahari desert of Botswana to find the few groups of San who still survived with their traditional culture intact, looking at what the white man has destroyed.

South African prose came into its own under apartheid. Many writers from this period are now international names, and there is a clear difference between the work of the established white authors and the emerging black writers of the time. The period's best-known novelist is probably Nadine Gordimer, who won the Nobel prize for literature in 1991. Her anti-apartheid novels are famous, particularly *Burger's Daughter*, in which a young woman, born into an established white family, awakens to the injustices of her people's way of life.

J. M. Coetzee, a Cape Town author, has also achieved international fame with his stylized novels which act as effective metaphors for apartheid. *Waiting For the Barbarians*, his best-known work, is set in an imaginary country where the governor of an imperial outpost awaits the inevitable destruction of his world and the retribution of those he governs.

André Brink's novel *A Dry White Season* is more direct—a young Afrikaner befriends a black man, only to learn of his death while in police custody. In his attempt to find out what really happened, the young Afrikaner enters Soweto for the first time, and learns something about that other side to his city—an alien world on his doorstep.

Johannesburg's black areas are also the setting for Alan Paton's superb story *Cry the Beloved Country*, written in 1948, the very year that the first apartheid government came to power. A Zulu pastor from Natal comes to Johannesburg to find his lost son, who has vanished after going to work on the mines. The world of destroyed African values, of broken culture that the priest encounters illustrates clearly the hugely negative impact of white colonial society on South Africa's traditional world, and the confused, amoral vacuum it left in its wake.

However, undoubtedly the most powerful book about the apartheid era by a white author is *My Traitor's Heart* by Rian Malan. Although the book is not fiction, the sheer power of its delivery—as Malan reconstructs his family history and their place in creating the system, and recounts his experiences of white/black, black/black and white/white violence and atrocity—is almost too much to bear, exactly because the reader knows that none of it is imaginary. Malan's final admission of his own culpability as a white Afrikaner is moving and real. Anyone who wishes to gain a greater understanding of the violent, apparently direction-less hatred and violence that consumed the country through the climactic years of apartheid should read this book.

The best-known black writer of the apartheid years was probably Steve Biko. Again, though not a novelist, Biko's writings were so much to the point, so powerfully accurate in their crit-icisms of both white complacency and black internecine conflict, and moving in their appeals for simple justice and democracy, that they warrant mention at the head of a list of black literature. His best-known work, *I Write What I Like*, shows just how far Biko was prepared to go to put his case. One passage describes the brutalities of police interrogation (of which he had experience)—the internee, beaten and exhausted, is told by the policeman that he will be killed. His only response is '*How long will it take you?*' Biko's bravery was exem-plary. He himself was killed in police custody in Port Elizabeth in 1977.

A welcome note of humour (albeit morbid) appears in Lewis Nkosi's work, especially his story *The Prisoner*, in which a white man falls in lust with his black maid, seduces her, and is then blackmailed—mixed sexual intercourse was banned under apartheid. The white man is jailed, and subjected to the routine beatings and tortures usually reserved for black prisoners, and the narrator speaks dispassionately, and with humorous asides, of the victim's surprise and shock at suddenly being on the other side of the fence.

Less vindictive are the works of Daniel Kunene. In his collection of short stories *From the Pit of Hell to the Spring of Life* Kunene deals with the dilemma of being black and middle class, of hesitating to commit to the dangers of the freedom struggle:

A young black worker deliberates whether to join a strike or try to keep his head down and survive. A black man and wife revisit the black Johannesburg neighbourhood of Sophiatown, razed by bulldozers in the 1950s and its inhabitants forcibly removed to Soweto, with two friends who are a white couple.

The problems of mixed-race friendships under apartheid are beautifully underplayed amid the ruins as the four try to reconstruct in their minds the bustling life that has been reduced to mere blocks of rubble.

The apartheid years produced few 'coloured' novelists compared to black. However, Alex La Guma—a Cape Town 'coloured' who became a leading light in the South African Communist Party (SACP) in the 1950s and '60s, and who, after being jailed in 1964, went into exile in England—has emerged as one of South Africa's best novelists. Cape Town's ghettos provide the scene for *A Walk in the Night*, in which the squalor and poverty is vividly portrayed:

> the massed smells of stagnant water, cooking, rotting vegetables, oil, fish, damp plaster and timber, unwashed curtains, bodies…cheap perfume and incense, spices and half-washed kitchenware, urine, animals and dusty corners became one vast, anonymous odour.

Amid this world, a young 'coloured' man finds a murdered white man in a back alley, and wonders what to do, knowing that he could be implicated, fearing any brush with the brutush white authority.

More recently, Zoe Wicomb, another 'coloured' writer, published *You Can't Get Lost in Cape Town*, the sad story of a young, unattractive 'coloured' woman who leaves her poor family farm in Namaqualand for a scholarship in Cape Town, where she falls in love with, and is made pregnant by, a white student. Again, the daily humiliations of being a second-class citizen are made apparent, while at the same time the author brings alive the fierce gaiety of Cape 'coloured' life.

Last Days in Cloud Cuckooland by Graham Boynton (Random House, 1997) is worth reading for its insights into the recent upheaval in the lives of white South Africans. Boynton, who spent his childhood in what was then Rhodesia, describes in journalistic vignettes their transition from the top of the social tree downwards, towards a more uncertain future.

The authors featured here represent only a fraction of those who make up South African literature, both poetry and prose, and unfortunately there is no room here to go into further depth. However, it is worth speculating for a moment on what changes can be expected from the new era of flux that this complex country has just entered, and how writers will confront the new set of problems which are now presenting themselves.

Muti and Traditional Medicine

Muti, meaning magic, is a word that travellers in South Africa will hear continually. Magic in South Africa carries a different meaning from in Europe, where it is confined to the fantastic and the mythical. Magic or *muti*, as it is understood in South Africa, is better described as folk medicine and divining. About 80 per cent of the population regularly consult traditional healers and herbalists (generally referred to as 'witch doctors'), and many Western-trained doctors in the country speak of their knowledge of the curative powers of indigenous roots and herbs with high regard.

The word 'witch doctor', though widely used, is misleading. The correct appelations are, for a diviner, *inyanga*, and for a herbalist and healer, *sangoma*. *Inyangas* are usually men, whose services are psychic and spiritual—called in to deal with possession, where bad spirits must be exorcised and bad influences diverted, to look into the future and to talk with ancestor spirits to ask advice.

Sangomas are usually women and their job is more practical—to treat the sick. Both offices take some years to learn and there are recognized schools that teach the initiates (usually chosen by one already in office) in most eastern parts of the country. Most do not allow outsiders to observe any part of the training process, but there is an exception—the Swazi government *Inyanga* and *Sangoma* Training College at Siteki, where visitors are allowed in by prior arrangement (*see* **Swaziland**, 'Siteki', p.495).

So strong are these traditions that they have been one of the few aspects of black culture to survive fully the shift from rural to urban life. Holders of both offices can be seen even on the busiest streets of the big cities, where their services are required more than ever by the rapidly growing black populations.

Muti shops, where the requisite animal skins, roots, herbs and charms are sold, can be found in almost any town, and to enter one is to step back immediately into old Africa. Some of the items on sale can be gruesome, including the dried organs of animals, dried snakes and lizards and the like, while others are beautiful—spotted genet cat or ochre-coloured lynx skins—and some, like the myriad dried roots or crosses in bottles filled with holy water, frankly baffling. However, the owners of *muti* shops are generally friendly and willing to explain the use of most things on sale, and a visit and chat reveals much about South Africa that you cannot learn from books.

Until the 1960s such willingness to talk about *muti* was largely unknown, and even now the mysteries surrounding the real practice of *inyanga* and *sangoma* rituals are kept secret. However, in 1966 a Zulu *inyanga* called Credo Mutwa decided to break the silence and publish the entire Zulu mythology (which is very similar to that of the Xhosa and Swazi) in a great work (still in print) called *Indaba My Children*. Although this met with much opposition from his colleagues, Mutwa defended his decision, explaining that in his opinion the roots of white oppression of the blacks lay in the whites' total misundertanding of black culture. He sought to try and rectify this by publishing the oral mythologies, followed by several other works of oral history and, finally, novels.

Mutwa had good reason to do this, having lost his fiancée to a police bullet during the Sharpeville shootings in 1960. He pointed out that, from the beginning of colonial history, the white man's ignorance of some fundamental points of belief had brought unnecessary conflict—for example, in *My People*, his book of oral history, he asserts that an undocumented reason for the unceasing resistance of the Xhosas to white settlement during the Frontier Wars of 1799 to 1879 was the whites' unthinking and endless slaughter of the Eastern Karoo's great springbok herds, which were sacred to the Xhosa people. Such assertions are impossible to verify, but his point was valid, and his books did much to open white eyes to the wealth of culture that lay in the country they had settled. More importantly, they also prompted genuine white interest in *muti* itself, and today there are several white *inyangas* and *sangomas* practising in Natal, with numbers steadily growing.

There is a darker side to *muti*, however. Human sacrifice, or ritual murder to obtain body parts, is still fairly widespread all over southern Africa. In the Venda country of the Northern Province it reached such a pitch a few years ago that an official investigation was called, which cost the jobs of several people in local government (*see* p.597). Human parts are generally needed for rituals designed to intercede with the spirit world for matters of material fortune or warfare.

Therefore, areas undergoing rapid urbanization and business development, such as the new cities of the former 'homelands', have been hard hit by *muti* killings in recent years, as have those areas, like Zululand and the townships of the Natal Midlands, where large-scale clanfighting still continues. Victims are generally children, and are often chosen with the community's (even the parents') consent, and the matter is generally kept quiet and not investigated by the police unless—as in Venda—it gets out of hand.

This seems a sad development of traditional culture, but it clearly illustrates how disrupted and eroded traditional life has become over the course of this century. However, it must be stressed that this is only one side of *muti*, which in no way involves the modern traveller.

Animism and spirituality has formed a strong part of South African life from prehistoric times—the surviving San hunting songs are full of reverence for the spirits of the natural world—and any visitor to the country will not fail to be impressed by the landscape's almost palpable charge. Occult, or at least inexplicable, experiences come to most people who spend any time there.

These can be everyday in nature: for example when the author was in Swaziland, his highly westernized hostess came down one morning, visibly upset. She had dreamed that night of snakes, and while vacuuming her room had tripped and fallen. When asked why that should be so distressing, she said both were bad omens, not personally, but for someone close. Some hours later, she had a phone call informing her that her niece had been run down by a car.

They can also verge on the fantastic: for example, in the 1930s the doctor, poet and gourmet C. Louis Leipoldt records being told of an old labourer on a farm in the Lowveld, who could speak with the dead. Leipoldt was known for his incisive, almost cold intellectual objectivity, and at the time held the position of health inspector of schools in the Eastern Transvaal. It was on one of his rounds in that region that he was introduced to the man, who was almost a derelict, and decided to put him to the test, though the man in question was unwilling and claimed he was too old. Rather flippantly, Leipoldt asked him to raise the Renaissance German alchemist Theophrastus von Hohenheim (also known as Paracelsus), widely regarded as the father of medical chemistry. To Leipoldt's astonishment, after achieving trance, the old man began to talk in high German, described by Leipoldt as 'clear and lucid'. Coming out of his trance, the old man begged not to be made to confront the spirit again, as he had been too terrifying, and asked for some alcohol to drink.

Magic and its usage exists not only in the traditionally black areas of South Africa, but even in Cape Town, among the devoutly Muslim Cape Malays, who have retained certain practices of Indonesian animism, locally known as *paljas*, for predicting the future. Trance and spiritual ecstasy is also very much a part of Cape Malay life—manifest in the form of the *Khalifa* dance, where initiates pierce their bodies with knives and skewers and walk over hot coals, displays of which are sometimes put on for the public.

Medicine

Orthodox Western medicine has a strong, if more recent, place in South African culture, and it is a common saying there that the country's best export is its doctors. The demand for them abroad testifies to the excellence of the medical schools. At the same time, many young European doctors opt to do their internships in South Africa because, in the words of one such internee the author met in Cape Town, 'you get more trauma on one Saturday night in a South African town than in three months in Europe—gunshot wounds, knives, everything. We even get to do chest drains here, which we'd have to wait years to do at home.'

However, such meatball surgery is not the only foundation for South Africa's medical reputation. South African researchers near Tzaneen in the Eastern Transvaal in the 1920s and '30s discovered effective prophylactics against malaria; South African medical research also provided the basis for the finding of a cure for bilharzia, the debilitating sleeping sickness caused by water parasites; the world's first heart transplant operation was performed in Groot Schuur hospital in Cape Town in 1967 by Dr Christiaan Barnard; South Africa can even claim to have launched the career—albeit a secret one—of Western medicine's first woman doctor—Dr 'James' Barrie (*see* p.146).

Cape Cuisine

Cape cooking, evolved over 250 years from various imported cuisines, has been in existence long enough to qualify as truly 'indigenous', the original blend of late medieval Dutch, German, French and 18th-century Malay styles having combined to produce a wealth of dishes that are truly South African in both ingredients and flavours. At its simplest, Cape cuisine can be described as spiced, curried and often sweetened variations on European fish, meat, game and dessert recipes, but this belies both the range of dishes and the art that goes into preparing them.

Although the first cookery books of Cape cuisine only appeared about 100 years ago, printed recipes in Dutch, English and Afrikaans had been in existence for some time before, and many of the recipes they included were written about and applauded by 18th-century travellers to the Cape.

At the core of Cape cooking is the *bredie*, or **pot-roast** of spiced meat and vegetables, cooked in a cast-iron pot over several hours. The result is succulent and highly flavoured.

There are several kinds of *bredie*, whose names are usually determined by the main vegetable—for example, potato *bredie* or tomato *bredie*, spinach *bredie* or quince *bredie* (there are several others)—while the meat is generally the same—a thick rib of good Karoo mutton, itself flavoured with the wild herbs browsed by the sheep before slaughter (though at a pinch any meat will do). Seasonings include coriander, crushed chilli, rosemary and white wine.

Soesaties (meat grilled on wooden skewers) are popular for pork and mutton. After sitting for up to two days in a spiced marinade (curry, dried fruit, ginger, almond and tamarind are recommended), the skewers are grilled and served with rice and cooked fruit. More commonly found in Cape restaurants is *bobotie*, which is said to have been brought to Europe by the Crusaders, and to Africa by both the Dutch and the Malays. Again served with rice, *bobotie* is made from minced meat, plenty of turmeric, garlic, cumin, pepper, herbs and sometimes lemon.

Fish and shellfish form a large part of Cape cuisine. Grilling, steaming, stewing, currying, kedgerees and even pounding the flesh into fish cakes are all common, and different fish are recommended for different ways of cooking. The *snoek*, probably the commonest large eating fish caught off the Cape, is usually simply grilled or fried either fresh or dried, with lemon, garlic and butter, or curried, as is *kabeljou* (cod).

The *galjoen*, a fish with strange marbled flesh, is harder to find, but worth trying if baked, while *roman*, another comparative rarity, is usually steamed in wine. The large *kingklip*, sought-after by sea-anglers for its tremendous fighting ability, is served in most ways and is superb if fresh that day. A number of dishes involve crayfish (rock lobster), either served the usual way, baked, or even curried. Shellfish, such as the fleshy *perlemoen* (mother-of-pearl), as well as mussels, oyster and even giant limpets, are steamed, stewed or grilled (though straight frying in breadcrumbs is common in non-Cape seafood restaurants).

Perhaps the most exciting Cape dishes involve **game**. The doctor, poet, writer and gourmet Louis Leipoldt (died 1947), whose book *Leipoldt's Cape Cookery* is widely regarded as the best and most entertaining recipe book on the subject, has some incredible (though not inedible) dishes: stuffed breast of flamingo served with chilli and lemon is, he says, the king of all game-bird dishes—though flamingos are now protected by law and your chances of eating one slim; porcupine crackling, roast leguaan (monitor lizard), python, tortoise in jelly and even lion (apparently good as a marinated steak or even as biltong) appear on his recipe list.

However, Cape game dishes usually consist of venison and game birds. For venison, the smaller antelope such as springbok, steenbok and duiker are prized for their tender, aromatic meat, while for game birds the succulent, flavoursome guinea-fowl and francolin make a popular roast. In Cape country restaurants, venison is usually filleted and cooked in wine and served with a rich gravy or stewed fruit preserve. If staying in somebody's house, however, you might be lucky enough to be served a haunch of bushbuck, kudu or eland, usually well-hung and faintly high, but tasting of the wild.

For those travelling by themselves, and who wish to try out some Cape cooking, *Leipoldt's Cape Cookery* is the bible—though do not expect weights and measures, but 'handfuls', 'sprigs' and other intuitive vagaries with which you must take your own chances.

Bobotie

Ingredients

2 onions
1 kg minced meat (preferably lamb, beef or game)
1 cup milk
1 tablespoon curry powder
½ teaspoon pepper
2 teaspoons salt
½ tablespoon turmeric
1½ tablespoons sugar
a generous wodge of butter
a bit of olive oil for glazing
1 slice of good white bread
2 eggs
1 lemon
½ cup of raisins (or dried apricots)
3 tablespoons chutney
4 bay leaves
6 almonds, cut into quarters

Method

Pre-heat your oven to 350°F.

Peel and thinly slice the onions and sauté them lightly in butter and oil for half an hour.

Add the minced meat and fry until slightly cooked.

Soak the bread in the milk, then squeeze out the milk, and mash the bread.

Pop all the ingredients (except the milk, one egg and bay leaves) into a bowl and mix them up, then put the lot into a greased dish.

Put the bay leaves into the meat mixture and bake for an hour.

Meanwhile, beat the egg into the remaining milk and pour over the meat after half an hour.

Serve on yellow rice with a piquant chutney and as big a salad as you can make. (This is particularly good with watercress and nasturtium flowers).

Where to Taste the Best Cape Cuisine

If the prospect of cooking your own *bobotie* is too much effort, the following restaurants serve superb Cape cuisine (details listed in the relevant sections of the guide).

Cape Town

Kaapse Tafel, Queen Victoria Street

Rozenhof, Kloof Street

The Winelands

Ralph's, Die Kelder, Le Pommier and **Doornbosch**, Stellenbosch

The **McGregor Haus** and **Old Mill Lodge**, McGregor

The Overberg

Wildenkrantz Country House, near Grabouw

Huis De Villiers, Greyton

The West Coast

Plaaskombuis Guest House, near Eland's Bay

Van Meerhof Lodge, Piekenaars Pass, south of Citrusdal

Reinhold's, Clanwilliam

Garden Route and Little Karoo

Portland Manor, Plettenburg Bay

Welgevonden Guest House, near Calitzdorp

Great Karoo

De Rust Gasthuis, Williston

Johannesburg

Gramadoela's, by the Market Theatre, Newtown

Leipoldt's (named after the man himself), Braamfontein.

Western Cape

Table Bay

...the most stately thing, the fairest Cape we saw in the whole circumference of the earth...

> Sir Francis Drake, after rounding the Cape of Good Hope in 1580

If the wind is in the north, the flat top of Table Mountain is hidden by a great cloth of white cloud, giving the impression of a giant locomotive frozen in headlong rush to the sea. If the wind is in the west, the clouds pour over the landward slopes in a thick cotton-wool waterfall, a leviathan duvet 10 miles long. One of several legends has it that the cloud is smoke from the pipes of the Devil and St Peter, who sit playing cards on the mountain, their hands deciding the fate of the great vibrant city that sprawls below, spilling out across the plain of the Cape Flats towards the far-off wall of the Hottentots' Holland.

The Cape Peninsula, a narrow spine of forest and mountain, runs 75km out into the ocean off Africa's extreme southwest corner, neatly dividing the warmer and cooler ocean currents. Table Mountain and Cape Town form the boundary between the Peninsula and the continent behind. The Cape of Good Hope marks the Peninsula's southernmost point, terminating at Cape Point in a white-topped swirl of shifting waters.

On the east side, the Agulhas current creates warm water beaches overlooking the wide miles of False Bay, along whose distant further shore marches the southern end of the Hottentots' Holland Mountains. The west side's beaches are chilled by the Benguela current, up from the Antarctic.

On both sides, small resort and fishing towns cling to the narrow coastal strip between mountain and beach. The Cape of Good Hope itself is now a nature reserve, while the Peninsula's mountains, also divided into several reserves and national forests, culminate in a high massif on the north end of the Peninsula—Devil's Peak and Table Mountain—whose wooded slopes lead down to Cape Town's handsome city centre and the harbour of Table Bay. A smaller upland—the Lion's Head and Rump (the Rump is also known as Signal Hill)—also rises out of the city, joined to the north side of Table Mountain by the Tamboerskloof Pass. Below this lie the wealthy beachside suburbs of Sea Point, Clifton and Camp's Bay.

Inland from Table Mountain, between False Bay and Table Bay, stretch the Cape Flats, a marshy, sandy plain some 60 to 70km across. Cape Town spills into them first as white suburb—the residential areas of Bellville and Parow around the low Tygerberg hills—then as industrial suburb and township, or 'locations' in the old language of apartheid. These vary from the relatively prosperous 'coloured' townships of Athlone and Mitchell's Plain to the poorer, predominantly black townships of Langa, Guguletu,

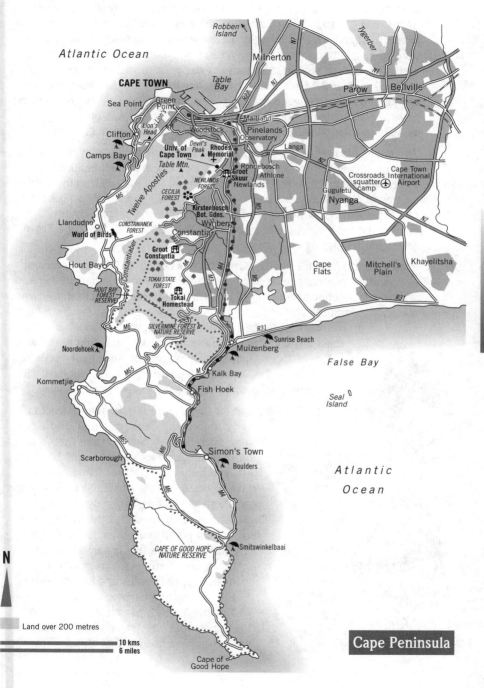

Atlantic Ocean

Robben Island

Milnerton

CAPE TOWN

Table Bay

Parow   Bellville

Sea Point   Green Point

Maitland

Clifton   Lion's Head

Woodstock   Pinelands

Observatory

Camps Bay   Devil's Peak   Rhodes Memorial   Langa

Univ. of Cape Town   Table Mtn.

Twelve Apostles   NEWLANDS FOREST   Groot Skuur   Rondebosch   Athlone

CECILIA FOREST   Newlands   Cape Town International Airport

Crossroads squatter camp

Llandudno   World of Birds   Kirstenbosch Bot. Gdns.   Guguletu   Nyanga

CONSTANIANEK FOREST   Wynberg

Constantia

Hout Bay   Groot Constantia

Cape Flats   Mitchell's Plain   Khayelitsha

HOUT BAY FOREST RESERVE   TOKAI STATE FOREST

Tokai Homestead

SILVERMINE FOREST & NATURE RESERVE   R31

Sunrise Beach

Noordehoek   Muizenberg

False Bay

Kommetjie   Kalk Bay

Fish Hoek

Seal Island

Scarborough   Simon's Town

Boulders

Atlantic

Ocean

N

CAPE OF GOOD HOPE NATURE RESERVE   Smitswinkelbaai

Land over 200 metres

10 kms
6 miles

Cape of Good Hope

Cape Peninsula

115

Monwabisi and Khayelitsha. There are desperately impoverished shanty towns, like Crossroads, and many squatter camps, which are now creeping from the Cape Flats to the Peninsula mountains. Townships used to be divided by law into more-or-less exclusively 'coloured' and 'black' areas, and, even though apartheid no longer exists, the townships have mostly retained their racial boundaries. Lately, however, there has been greater ethnic movement between the townships, and those who have the money have begun moving into Cape Town proper. Certain areas of the city, such as Maitland and Woodstock, are now at least half 'integrated'.

The north and east of the Cape Flats are still farmed, mostly as market gardens, giving way to vineyards. In the far eastern stretch behind False Bay, some 40km from the city proper, racehorse studs and training stables sit among pine plantations below the slopes of Sir Lowry's Pass. The N1 and N2 highways, which connect Cape Town with the great country beyond the mountains, both cross the Flats, the N2 servicing Cape Town International Airport as it goes.

Possessed of a tangible vitality, Cape Town's collage of human, floral and geographical contrasts seduces most visitors. Capetonians themselves, at whatever economic level, tend to love their city fiercely, regarding it as a place apart from the rest of South Africa. From the busy Art Deco streets and wrought-iron arcades of the old colonial town, you can look up at the deep forest and giant buttresses of rock that cling to the wild face of Table Mountain. Lynx, baboon and small buck still live up there, and even leopard have been reported. The blue ocean is never more than a few minutes away.

At the core of Cape Town life are two distinct but related cultures, the Cape 'coloured' and 'Malay' Islamic, both derived from three centuries' mix of the Cape's original KhoiSan, Dutch settler, Malaysian and West African slave blood. Afrikaans and English culture are equally strong among Cape Town's whites. Black African influences (mostly Xhosa) and a small Indian population add spice, giving the city an atmosphere that is part Asian, part African, part European. Street markets, musicians, prostitutes and beggars throng the old city and harbour areas. Neighbourhoods have distinct flavours. Alternate *joie de vivre* and languorous *ennui* best describe the feel of Cape Town.

Climate

Cape Town and the Peninsula are blessed with a 'Mediterranean' climate; a green winter of heavy rains and chill northwest winds, and a largely cloudless, baking summer (though the odd shower does occur). Wind is the love and bane of Capetonians. Winter sea-winds bring coughs and colds. Summer brings the southeasters—violent blustery annoyances that can blow for days at a time. Locals call them the 'Cape Doctor' for their supposedly cleansing property: they blow the smog away and take the edge off a potentially foetid summer.

Flora

Cape Town and the Peninsula are part of the unique Cape Floral Kingdom (one of the world's six Floral Kingdoms). Over 3000 species of fynbos (heath) plants and flowering protea shrubs cover the mountains where exotic tree species have not been planted, with some species specific to the area. The most spectacular of these are the silver trees—largest of the protea family at up to 10m high—whole shimmering woodlands of which grow on Table Mountain and Lion's Head. In spring and early summer look out for clumps of purple erica, similar to heather; tall watsonias, like a wild iris, in scarlet and rose; fiery flowering aloes, called red-hot pokers; micranthus, whose tiny blue flowers are tinged with red; the bright orange 'flames' flower (endemic to the southern Peninsula); white, blue and purple wood orchids; dry-petalled everlasting flowers; and a host of others, all colourful.

The dense forests which extend along eastern Table Mountain, brushing the edges of many residential neighbourhoods, are almost all composed of introduced pine, oak and gum. Most noticeable from the city are the tall, flat-topped Mediterranean umbrella pines, groves of which dot the slopes around the University of Cape Town campus, and under which eland, wildebeest and zebra graze safely behind a game fence.

Cape Town's wet winter is cheered by tall white arum lilies that grow wherever there is grass. In summer the city riots with myriad exotic flowers. Most common are bougainvillaea (whole trees of it), purple jacaranda, luxuriant hibiscus, red flowering gum, and clematis—many of the world's most colourful flowers are found in Cape Town's parks and gardens.

History

The Cape's original inhabitants were the San and Khoi peoples (respectively the 'bushman' and 'Hottentot' of colonial language). Both were yellow-skinned, athletic people, but with distinct cultures: the San were hunter-gatherers and the Khoi pastoral nomads, herding sheep and cattle. Historians dispute the exact date of the arrival of animal husbandry to the Cape, but current estimates put the Khoi's move to pastoralism early in the first millennium AD, following contact with black African pastoralists moving down to central and eastern southern Africa from Cameroon and the Sahel. By the time the first Portuguese mariners rounded the Cape in the 1480s, Khoi culture seems to have become dominant on the good grazing lands near the coast. Living off a milk diet, the Khoi had grown taller and stronger than the San and had pushed them further into the interior where the grazing was less good. A sub-culture of Khoi clans who had lost, or never possessed, cattle existed on the Cape beaches, and were christened *strandlopers* (meaning 'beachcombers') by the Dutch. They gleaned their living from the tides and were held in low esteem by livestock-owning Khoi. As with pastoralist cultures elsewhere in Africa, livestock, and in particular cattle, were at the centre of social and ritual life. The Khoi trained their cattle for riding and even, by a series of whistles and shouts, trained them to surround, trample and stampede through the enemy in times of war.

The first documented contact (though there was almost certainly contact before this) between Khoi and Europeans at Table Bay was violent and portentous. Contemporary Portuguese chroniclers recorded that in 1510, the Viceroy of India was on his way back to Lisbon to retire and receive due honour from the King. He ordered the ships to put in for water at the Cape and to barter for cattle with the local Khoi. The Portuguese took more beasts than were agreed, and the Khoi became aggressive. The outraged Europeans went back to the ships for reinforcements, landed again with about 100 men, drove off more cattle and snatched some children. The Khoi whistled to their cattle to surround the invaders, who had come ashore without armour or guns, thinking the Khoi not worth the trouble. In the ensuing skirmish, most of the Portuguese, including 12 captains and the Viceroy himself, were killed. As Noel Mostert wrote in his superb history book *Frontiers* (Pimlico Press, 1992), they had *'fallen at the hands of those they considered the least of men...victims of their own contempt'*.

Over the following 150 years, Europeans and Khoi continued to trade, and sometimes fought, but both peoples seem to have become accustomed to each other. Portuguese, Dutch, English and French ships began stopping for fresh water and food at Table Bay before rounding the Cape and plying the dangerous currents of the south coast towards the Indies, but no European power claimed the Cape for its own until the mid 17th century, when Holland's maritime economy, having survived the chaos of the European religious wars that had collapsed both the Portuguese and Spanish overseas empires, became suddenly dominant. The Dutch had acquired prosperous new colonies in Batavia (modern Djakarta), but their fleet had no permanent stopping point for taking on water and supplies during the long voyages to and from the East Indies.

Dutch ships had traditionally used Lisbon to service their East Indies shipping, but the wars had put paid to that, and the Dutch East India Company was looking for a new servicing point further towards the East. The Cape was not their immediate choice; its storms and cross-winds could prevent ships from making landfall for weeks. However, in 1650, a Dutch East India ship was stranded there for some months and the crew survived well, trading with the Khoi and hunting the plentiful game. They managed to get word of their plight back to Europe and, in 1651, a relief force was sent to fetch them home. One of the rescue party was a ship's doctor called Jan Van Riebeeck who had, in fact, been dismissed from the Company for dishonesty, and was trying to get re-hired. While at the Cape he made a tentative survey of its resources. Back in Holland he urged the East India Company directors to opt for Table Bay, and suggested himself as a possible governor.

In April 1652 Van Riebeeck returned to the Cape with about a hundred settlers, whose initial enthusiasm very soon waned; elephant, lion and the local inhabitants made walking around dangerous, and limited farming to what could be raised inside a bank-and-ditch barricade. The settlers were under strict orders not to invite trouble by infringing on Khoi land with the plough. Nor were they to enslave the Khoi for labour. Instead, slaves were imported from Batavia (Djakarta) and from West Africa. Many of these died in the cold winters or tried to escape. The surrounding Khoi did brisk trade capturing runaways and returning them for a fee, but the settlers, lacking a vigorous labour-force and unwilling to labour themselves, immediately began to stagnate.

A certain mutual contempt between Khoi and settler had been present from the beginning. The Khoi seem to have regarded the Dutch as weak, for their inability to prosper in the surrounding plenty. For their part, the Calvinist Dutch found many Khoi customs repugnant. For example, the Khoi used to cover their bodies in animal fat, both for adornment and to keep the flies from biting; this stank, and there are many accounts of settlers retching while doing business with the locals. On top of this, the Khois' nudity and polygamy inflamed both the religious outrage and libidos of the frustrated settlers.

A dislike of the Khoi seems to have been the early colonists' only point of agreement. Behind the colony's earthern ramparts resentment smouldered: the Company forced its settlers to service the visiting ships for their livelihoods, but only as Company employees shifting Company merchandise—they were forbidden to trade their own goods. Fortunes were not being made. Morale among settlers and garrison was low, and the Company's officers only kept discipline via a regime of brutal floggings and hangings. After five or six years the pressure of settlers trying to evade the authority of the mud and brick fort from which Van Riebeeck governed finally forced the Company to abandon its initial caution and approve 'Free Burgher' farms outside the colony boundary. Morale improved, but the first land conflict between white settler and native South African had begun.

Once the Dutch moved outside the fort, the Khoi immediately around Cape Town began to become dependent on the settlers—as farm employees and suppliers of cattle—despite a series of wars in which the Dutch did not always come off best. Disease, alcohol and firearms were powerful weapons for the Dutch, and the Khoi tribes around Cape Town lost land and herds and, in the space of about 30 years, became dependent on the settlers for food.

Through the 18th century towns sprang up on the Peninsula and in the immediate interior, while Cape Town saw a steady immigration from both Christian Europe and the Muslim East (modern Indonesia and Malaysia). These Asians, brought in as slaves, were often skilled craftsmen. A few aristocratic Indonesians, such as the Rajah of Tambora and Sheik Yussuf of Macassar, who had rebelled against the Dutch East India Company in Indonesia, were exiled in the Cape, but the majority were brought in as skilled slaves (mostly craftsmen) and became the ancestors of today's Cape Malay population.

By the 1780s the Dutch East India Company was foundering, but the Cape itself was finally prospering, and the 'coloured' and Malay cultures were well established, giving Cape Town a cosmopolitan flavour that surprised many travellers of the time. The white settlers too, now several generations in, were evolving their own Cape Dutch society, used to acting without governmental control. But their independence was about to be curtailed.

Confident after a century of sporadic but victorious wars with the Dutch, and worried at the rise of Napoleon's navy, the British East India Company found itself in the same position as the Dutch had been 150 years before. Valuable new possessions in the Indies necessitated control of the trade route east. In 1795 Cape Town was taken from the Dutch following the Battle of Muizenberg off the Cape Peninsula, given back for a few years, then annexed again in 1806 after the Battle of Blaauwberg.

The Cape's British governors tore their hair out trying to keep the Cape Afrikaners under British rule. The most prosperous burghers had little difficulty adapting to the tighter regime, but many poorer Afrikaners simply boarded their wagons and headed even deeper into the interior, involving the British in a series of expensive native wars. Meanwhile, Cape Town's port, servicing all of Europe's cargo and troop-carrying ships to and from the Indies, was thriving, and acquired its name 'Tavern of the Seas'.

Through the 19th century, Cape Town became the centre of sporadic British attempts to unite the rest of the fragmented country under the Union Jack. But, despite the inevitable stuffiness of British rule, Cape Town had by now evolved its own atmosphere—a mix of narrow but educated liberalism among the old Cape Dutch and English, and a unique brand of anarchic, hedonistic survivalism among the Cape's down-trodden 'coloureds'. After the Boer War (1899–1902), the Cape parliament was re-organized along Westminster lines. Blacks had a qualified vote, while 'coloureds' had full male franchise. Cape Town's English colonialism, though racist, could not actively stifle 'coloured' culture.

The Second World War saw the apex of Cape Town's importance as a port—the Suez Canal was closed, and all British troop and merchant shipping had to round the Cape. Simon's Town, on the Peninsula, became a prime British navy base. Many 'coloureds' joined the Cape Corps, as they had in the Frontier Wars, Boer War and the First World War (*see* **History**) and fought with distinction overseas.

Even following the accession of the Afrikaner Nationalist Party in 1948, geographic and cultural distance from Pretoria meant that Cape Town and its enfranchised 'coloureds' continued their lively isolationist culture for two more decades as apartheid slowly closed in. The 'coloureds' finally lost their vote in the late 1950s, following the Separate Areas Act of 1950. But it was another 16 years before Cape Town's 'coloureds' were subjected to the full, humiliating demonstration of their newly official status as second-class citizens.

In 1966 District Six, the vibrant 18th- and 19th-century residential and commercial centre of Cape Town's 'coloured' culture, was declared a 'white' area. Often described as 'the soul of Cape Town', District Six suffered the expulsion of most of its 55,000-odd inhabitants to a new township called Mitchell's Plain, out on the Cape Flats. Government blustered that the area had become a health hazard, and was to be the figurehead of a benign urban re-planning. Bulldozers razed the quarter. Though the land was prime real estate, developers did not buy it, and the empty patches of grass remain today, green scars between the city centre and the Southern Suburbs. Plans are now afoot to redevelop the site for housing, but so far nothing has happened.

But through the 1970s and '80s, Cape Town still retained its (much debated) reputation as South Africa's most liberal city. Archbishop Desmond Tutu, Cape Town's first black archbishop, began his long campaign of conscience from St George's Cathedral (which continues today in his appeals to end the factional violence). The University of Cape Town was known as a hotbed of anti-apartheid activity through the 'State of Emergency'. Students and academics were routinely arrested and detained.

Since the dismantling of apartheid began in 1990, Cape Town has changed drastically. More politically violent than before, the city has also seen, over the past 15 years, a huge acceleration in the influx of Xhosa people from the former Transkei and Ciskei 'homelands' to vast squatter camps on the city fringes, which have introduced all the problems of Third World urban poverty. But today's city of 2 million and rising is still one of the most culturally viva-cious and geographically beautiful in the world, and a distinct world apart from the rest of South Africa.

Architecture

The Cape has a rich architectural history. The earliest buildings, of which many still survive (both humble and grand), were constructed in a style now commonly known as Cape Dutch. Their principal feature is a curved gable, which evolved from the Florentine-influenced medieval buildings of Holland, the colony's 'motherland', and from the Asiatic styles seen by the Dutch East Indian settlers in Batavia (Djakarta) and designed and built at the Cape by Indonesian slaves. Walls are usually whitewashed with a tough lime produced from sea-shells. In country areas, the roofs were traditionally thatched, but those in the city were built with flat, slate roofs to guard against fire. Half-doors, like those of a stable, are common, and windows are generally mullioned.

Cape Dutch interiors were also distinctive, with an emphasis on indigenous South African hardwoods. Yellowwood, which casts an airy, golden light, was generally used for ceilings, beamed across with dark, reddish stinkwood. Cape furniture makers also used yellowwood and stinkwood in their work, creating simple, well-proportioned pieces of great beauty often with simple but pleasing inlaid patterns, but also creating such a demand for the woods that whole forests were cut down. Today yellowwood and stinkwood are rare and expensive. For a more detailed look at the various forms of Cape Dutch architecture and how they devel-oped, *see* **People and Culture**, 'Art and Architecture'.

During the late 18th and early 19th centuries, Cape Dutch architecture flowered in the work of two European artists, Anton Anreith and Louis Thibault—sculptor and architect respec-tively—who settled in the Cape at the end of the 18th century and blended their styles with great success. Born in Germany in 1754, Anreith came to South Africa as a soldier in 1777, but switched to sculpting and remained in the Cape until his death in 1822. His wood or plaster sculptures in high baroque style can be seen on many of the city's pediments and church pulpits. Louis Thibault, born near Amiens in 1750, studied architecture and military engineering in Paris, and also came to the Cape as a soldier (1783), his regiment having been hired by the Dutch East India Company. He turned architect before the British invaded in 1795. The pair's best-known works are the Lutheran Church, on Strand Street, and the wine-cellar at Groot Constantia, the Cape's oldest and most opulent wine estate.

More modest, but no less beautiful, is the Bo-Kaap, an area of 18th-century artisans' cottages on the Lion's Head, just above the city centre, which were taken over by Malay ex-slave craftsmen in the 1830s, after Britain abolished slavery in her colonies. The area has a strong Eastern flavour, the houses painted in bright colours, and the minarets of small mosques peeping above the cottages.

Under the Victorians, Cape Town acquired solid neoclassical and Gothic public buildings, such as the Houses of Parliament and St George's Cathedral, and whole streets of elegant townhouses with distinctive wrought-iron balconies, good examples of which still survive in Long Street, Upper Adderley Street and in the Southern Suburbs. The Edwardian era saw some superb work by the architect Sir Herbert Baker, who built Groot Schuur manor house in Rondebosch for the billionaire mining magnate Cecil Rhodes—a building that has since become the Cape Town residence of the South African heads of state. Baker went on to design the Union Buildings in Pretoria, before heading off to India to work on the New Delhi project with Sir Edward Lutyens.

In the 1930s (British Imperial prosperity at its height), there was a flurry of building in the Art Deco style—Cape Town's St George's Mall and Greenmarket Square are pure Art Deco.

After the Second World War, Cape Town suffered, as did everywhere, from lumpish modern building; the Foreshore and the Business District below Strand Street are unhappy testaments to this, as is the Golden Acre Shopping Mall on Adderley Street, by the train station. However, most of the concrete and glass was concentrated in the compact little business district below Strand Street. If you stay in the upper city centre, you hardly need look at any ugly buildings.

Cape Town

Cape Town ✆ (021–)

Getting There

by air

International and domestic flights arrive at Cape Town International Airport, 20km from the city centre, on the Cape Flats along the N2 highway. **Car hire** can be arranged at the airport, and a **bus service** to Cape Town's bus station (run by Inter-Cape) leaves every half hour from outside the international terminal. Passenger services and general information, ✆ 934 0444.

by car

The main highway connections to Cape Town (Kaapstad) are the N1 northeast to Pretoria, Jo'burg and Bloemfontein via the Winelands and the Great Karoo; the N2 east to Durban via the Garden Route and Eastern Cape; the N7 north to Windhoek in Namibia via Springbok.

by bus

Bus services along main highways are run by **InterCity Greyhound**, ✆ 418 4310/4312, **Inter-Cape**, ✆ 386 4400, and **TransLux**, ✆ 405 6209/3333. All mainline buses leave from the central bus station on Adderley Street. The **Baz Bus**, ✆ 439 2323, offers a better alternative—door-to-door transport between the backpacker hostels of Cape Town, the Garden Route, Eastern Cape, Natal, Swaziland and Jo'burg. It's cheap, convenient and safe. Ring them to discuss where you need to go.

by taxi

Black taxis, cheap, fast but more dangerous, run along all the main highways and connect Cape Town with even the smallest towns along them. These also pick up and set down at the Adderley Street bus station.

by rail

Cape Town is linked to most of South Africa's (and southern Africa's) larger towns by rail. Trains are often slow, but are still the best way to see the landscape. Particularly scenic is the Cape Town–Jo'burg train—24 hours through the Winelands, the Cape mountains and the Great Karoo. All services depart from and arrive at the central train station on Adderley Street once daily. Information, ✆ (0800) 112 568, and reservations, ✆ 405 3871. The luxury Blue Train and the 'Pride of Africa', ✆ 218 2672, also leave from Cape Town (*see* **Travel**, 'By Train').

Cape Town ✆ *(021–)*   ***Getting Around***

For the compact city centre, walking is best. It is hard to get lost in Cape Town with Table Mountain as a landmark. In the city centre, if the mountain is behind you, you are facing east; if it is to your right, you are facing south; to your left, north, and facing west gives you a full-on view of the mountain.

by bus

Buses to the suburbs and residential neighbourhoods leave from Adderley Street and the terminus just behind it. The stop immediately outside the OK Bazaar supermarket services the Gardens, Tamboerskloof, the cable-car station, and the western side of the Peninsula to Hout Bay. The stop opposite, on the other side of Adderley, services Green Point, Clifton and Camps Bay. The main bus terminus, in the Parade, the great open area behind the Golden Acre shopping mall, services the Southern Suburbs and east side of the Peninsula as far as Simon's Town. Turn south on Strand Street where it joins Adderley and the station is half a block on the right.

by train

Trains servicing the Southern Suburbs, and the eastern Peninsula as far as Simon's Town, leave every half hour from the main train station on lower Adderley Street. Trains running eastwards into the suburbs of the Cape Flats, servicing Maitland, Bellville and Durbanville, also leave every half hour from the main station.

by taxi

Black taxis follow the main bus routes and pick up and set down at regular bus stops. They are marginally more expensive than buses, but much quicker. However, they do have a reputation for cowboy driving (crashing). Hail them as they pass bus-stops, as the 'conductor' leans out and shouts the destination and stopping points en route.

Rikki's, ✆ 786 2136, is a new, safe (but slow) minibus taxi operating in both directions between Simon's Town Station (the end of the little railway) and Cape Point. They also run some services in Cape Town itself. Sometimes you can hail them on the street. Otherwise ring ✆ 234 888.

Ordinary taxis are expensive and should only be used when there is no other option. There are three official taxi ranks, two on Adderley Street and one in Plein Street, just behind the main post office building, or find a number in the *Yellow Pages*, or try **Star Taxis**, ✆ 419 7777, **Unicab**, ✆ 448 1720 or **Marine**, ✆ 434 0434. You can't just hail a taxi on the street.

by car

Avoid the city centre in a car unless you want to sit in idle frustration between short traffic-light hops and in one-way systems. For the rest of the city, two main highways service the residential neighbourhoods and Peninsula: the M5 runs from Sea Point

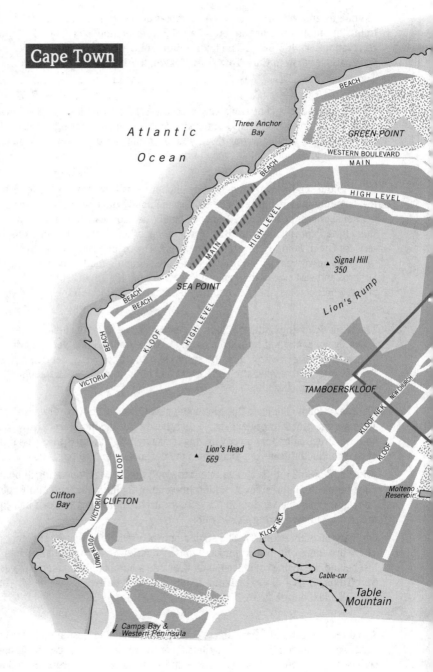

Cape Town

Atlantic

Ocean

Three Anchor Bay

BEACH

GREEN POINT

WESTERN BOULEVARD

MAIN

HIGH LEVEL

BEACH

HIGH LEVEL

▲ Signal Hill 350

MAIN

HIGH LEVEL

SEA POINT

BEACH

BEACH

Lion's Rump

HIGH LEVEL

KLOOF

TAMBOERSKLOOF

VICTORIA

KLOOF NEK

NEW CHURCH

KLOOF

Lion's Head 669

KLOOF

Molteno Reservoir

Clifton Bay

CLIFTON

VICTORIA

LOWER KLOOF

KLOOF NEK

Cable-car

Table Mountain

Camps Bay & Western Peninsula

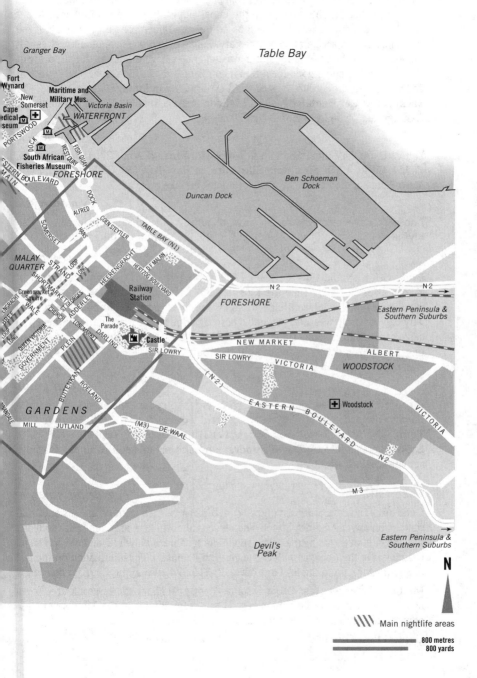

Granger Bay

Table Bay

Fort Wynard

Maritime and Military Mus.

New Somerset

Cape Medical seum

PORTSWOOD

Victoria Basin

WATERFRONT

DOCK

South African Fisheries Museum

EASTERN BOULEVARD MAIN

FORESHORE

Duncan Dock

Ben Schoeman Dock

ALFRED

DOCK

SOMERSET

HANS

COEN STEYTLER

TABLE BAY (N1)

N2

N2

MALAY QUARTER

STRAND

LOOP

LONG

HEERENGRACHT

HERTZOG BOULEVARD

Railway Station

FORESHORE

Eastern Peninsula & Southern Suburbs

SHORTMARKET

Greenmarket Square

BREE

LOOP

LONG

QUEEN VICTORIA

GOVERNMENT

PLEIN

GEORGES

DALE

CHURCH

ADDERLEY

LONGMARKET

DARLING

The Parade

Castle

SIR LOWRY

NEW MARKET

SIR LOWRY

VICTORIA

ALBERT

WOODSTOCK

BUITENKANT

ROELAND

(N 2)

EASTERN   BOULEVARD

VICTORIA

GARDENS

MILL

JUTLAND

(M3)

DE WAAL

Woodstock

N2

Devil's Peak

M 3

Eastern Peninsula & Southern Suburbs

N

\\\\ Main nightlife areas

800 metres
800 yards

125

through the city centre towards Muizenberg, along the border of the mountain and the Cape Flats; the M3 runs along the upper slopes, in the same direction. Avoid both highways during rush-hour and be careful at all times: one is often fed into the fast lane, so quick acceleration is necessary. Cape Town drivers are often careless and aggressive. All the international **car hire** agencies have offices at the airport, but Cape Town has some good local rental companies that are cheaper, and who will deliver cars to the airport, bus or train stations if you arrange it in advance. Try **Backpacker Car Rentals**, ✆ 448 124, **Econocar**, ✆ ✆ 689 7217, or **All People's Car Rentals**, ✆ 683 8770 or ✆ 615 797.

by bicycle

You can hire a mountain bike from **Mike Hopkins**, ✆ 232 527, **Day Trippers**, ✆ 461 4599, or **Tilt Mountain Bike Hire**, in Hout Bay, ✆ (cellphone) (083) 448 4606. Some of the hostels are also starting to run bike rentals.

by motorcycle

Another convenient way to get around quickly, and cheaper than a car. Call **FlyBike**, 5 Somerset Road, Green Point, ✆ 21 328, or **Buffalo Bikes**, ✆ 450 718.

by cable car

Every visitor should ride the Table Mountain cable car to the summit just once, ✆ 245 148/248 409. Take the Kloofnek bus from outside the OK Bazaar supermarket on Adderley Street. Expect long queues in summer, and no service at all in very bad or windy weather, when it is best to phone before making the journey. The cable car runs from 8am–10pm Dec–April, and 8.30–6 May–Nov, weather permitting. Pre-booked tickets are available at the Tourist Rendezvous, ✆ 418 5214, a good way to avoid queueing.

by tour group

If you'd like a guided look at the city, in order to get your bearings, there are a number of good tour groups to try: **Legend Tours**, ✆ 697 4056, **Mother City Tours**, ✆ 551 7281 or ✆ 562 580, or **Far Hills Discovery Tours**, ✆ 919 9548. Backpackers should try **Day Trippers**, who also organize all sorts of adventure activities, ✆ 461 4599.

Cape Town ✆ *(021–)*   **Tourist Information**

CapTour: The central tourist office, ✆ 418 5214/5, is in front of the bus and train stations on lower Adderley Street. The office is almost like a museum it has so many displays, and even has a little coffee shop. The staff are very helpful and can advise on most areas of the Cape, as well as the city and Peninsula. For information on the rest of South Africa, go to the **SATour** office, ✆ 216 274, also in the CapTour building.

Medical Emergencies: Groot Schuur, ✆ 404 9111, is the largest Cape Town hospital and the best in emergencies. This vast building is in the Mowbray neighbourhood, on Main Road. For ambulances call ✆ 101 77.

Central Post Office: On the corner of Plein and Adderley Streets.

Police: ✆ 418 2852 or ✆ 10 111.

Internet: The Connection Internet Café, on Heerengracht, ✆ 419 6180, opposite the US Embassy.

National Park Reservations: Office on Long Street, ✆ 222 810.

Safety

Despite its easy-going atmosphere, Cape Town's high unemployment and poverty levels make for one of the highest violent crime rates in the world. Admittedly, much of this is confined to the townships, but it does spill into the city and the suburbs too.

Cape Town centre at night can be dangerous, especially near the harbour area (though you are more likely to see drunks fighting than be mugged yourself) and around St George's Mall, which gets deserted after dark. However, in a group you should be fine if you treat Cape Town as you would any large city where the poverty level is high. Do not go into the townships unless with a local or a tour. Women should not walk alone in the centre at night, nor on the mountain—though attacks are relatively rare, they do happen.

Cape Town City Centre

Laid out along an easy-to-follow grid, central Cape Town is small and can be crossed in half an hour of fast walking. However, so much is packed into the centre that at least a couple of days are needed to explore it. Adderley Street runs down the middle from the sea to the Old Company Gardens. Where Strand Street crosses Adderley marks an invisible division of the city centre into two areas: upper and lower.

The lower centre (downhill from Strand) and upper centre have distinct characters. Together, the two halves of Cape Town's centre, dominated at all times by the mountain, make up a pleasant mix of 17th-, 18th- and 19th-century Dutch and English colonial styles, and Art Deco (especially the upper centre), marred only by the inevitable concrete and glass.

Unlike many colonial towns, Cape Town's old buildings are often still in use. Only a few are museums, so there is no museum feeling to the place. Bustling and infectious, the hotch-potch culture that created the city still prevails.

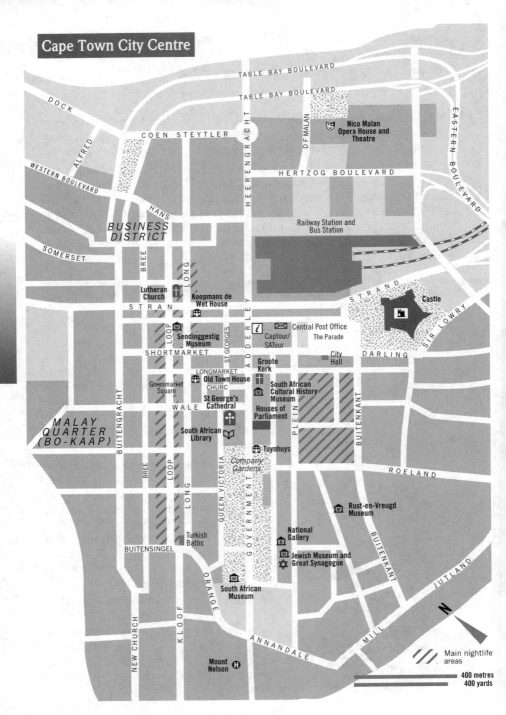

Cape Town City Centre

TABLE BAY BOULEVARD

TABLE BAY BOULEVARD

DOCK

COEN STEYTLER

ALFRED

WESTERN BOULEVARD

HANS

BUSINESS DISTRICT

SOMERSET

BREE

LONG

HEERENGRACHT

D F MALAN

Nico Malan Opera House and Theatre

EASTERN BOULEVARD

HERTZOG BOULEVARD

Railway Station and Bus Station

STRAND

Castle

SIR LOWRY

Lutheran Church

Koopmans de Wet House

STRAND

Sendinggestig Museum

LOOP

ST GEORGES

ADDERLEY

Central Post Office

Captour/ SATour

The Parade

DARLING

SHORTMARKET

LONGMARKET

Greenmarket Square

Old Town House

CHURC

St George's Cathedral

Groote Kerk

City Hall

South African Cultural History Museum

BUITENGRACHT

MALAY QUARTER (BO-KAAP)

WALE

South African Library

Houses of Parliament

PLEIN

BUITENKANT

BREE

LOOP

Tuynhuys

Company Gardens

ROELAND

LONG

QUEEN VICTORIA

GOVERNMENT

Rust-en-Vreugd Museum

Turkish Baths

BUITENSINGEL

National Gallery

Jewish Museum and Great Synagogue

BUITENKANT

ORANGE

South African Museum

JUTLAND

NEW CHURCH

KLOOF

ANNANDALE

MILL

N

Mount Nelson

Main nightlife areas

400 metres
400 yards

The Castle of Good Hope

Open daily 10–5, 15 Jan–30 Mar, guided tours every half hour; rest of the year 9–4, tours every hour, and last tour 3pm. Closed Christmas and New Year's Day.

The Castle of Good Hope, on Darling Street and facing the south side of the Parade, is where colonial South Africa began. The original earth-walled fort of 1652 was expanded in the 1660s to the present massive pentagon. The Castle has never lost its military function; it has been the headquarters of the South African Defence Force's Western Cape Command since the 1920s, and houses the Maritime and Military Museum, in what was the old Cape Governor's House. The museum exhibits artefacts from the early days of the colony. The entrance has a beautifully ornate 18th-century pediment, called the Kat balcony, designed by Anreith (*see* 'Architecture').

The official tour of this, South Africa's oldest existing building (begun 1665), is more fun then you would expect, and the only way into the Castle's interior. A soldier in ceremonial dress leads you from outside the reception/guard room, through the second courtyard, to the Dolphin Court—a fountain pool where Lady Anne Barnard, the spirited and highly intelligent wife of the Cape's Secretary to the British Empire, was supposedly spotted bathing nude by sentries and had to be reproved by the Governor. Lady Barnard went to the Cape soon after the first invading force of 1795. Her journals, letters and watercolours provide some of the most vivid, and most irreverent, accounts of early Cape Town (and interior) life. It is worth picking up a copy of her letters (available from any Cape bookshop) which are often hilarious in their descriptions of the pompous colonial characters of the time. While staying here at the Castle, Lady Barnard witnessed the coming of the Cape Town burghers to swear their allegiance to Britain after annexation. Fresh from England, and unaware of the already deep-seated independent spirit of the Cape Dutch, she glibly wrote: '*I think many of them seemed very sulky and ill-affected. Their manner seemed to say, "There is no help for it. We must swear, for they are the strongest".*'

Once inside the castle the tour takes you past whipping chambers and cells where people were put to die. In one of these there are deep scratches on the wall, which the guide claims were made by the exposed finger-bones of one of the inmates.

The soldiers' cells—used for less lethal punishment—have two centuries of graffiti carved into the oak doors, including a swastika left by the crew of a German U-Boat that was captured off the Cape coast—the city's only direct involvement in the Second World War. The tour then takes in one of the bastions before ending in an archaeological display of the earliest colonial artefacts found during restoration work. The castle also houses three museums: a military museum detailing the history of the Cape, the Castle and local regiments; the William Fehr Art Collection, spanning 400 years of pictorial history—Western, Eastern and African; and the Good Hope collection on Company life during the Dutch and British periods.

Around Buitenkant Street

The area around Buitenkant Street has been known for producing clothing for almost 200 years. Indeed the street itself is known as **Old Slave Walk**, after the Malay slaves who worked the textile factories here before the abolition of slavery in the 1830s.

If approaching Buitenkant Street from the Castle, the first two blocks are taken up (on the left) with 19th-century factories, many of them still functioning and now mostly owned, as well as staffed, by the descendants of Cape Malays. There are many good take-away shops on the ground floors, serving spicy curries, samosas and fried fish. Halfway up the first block is the **Old Granary**, a very handsome Cape Dutch 18th-century building with an Anreith lion and unicorn added to the front after the British Cape annexation in 1806. Now the Ministry of Works, one can only admire the front. On the right side of the street are the backs of Cape Town's red-brick late-Victorian government offices, still in use today.

At the junction of Roeland and Buitenkant Streets, the large late-Victorian building with an upstairs veranda on the right-hand side is the **Kimberley Hotel**. Even if you don't have a drink, take a peek at the public bar. The building is held in trust by the man who owns the liquor store across the road. One of the conditions of inheritance is that nothing, not even the plumbing, can be changed. The result is a gem of an original bar, with nothing kitsch or modern added because nothing but straight repairs have been done to it. The walls are tiled, the ceiling sculpted in plaster, the bar is luxuriant hardwood, all solid and still in use. The place is a hang-out for 'coloureds' and the less racist working class Afrikaners. If you have time, it's worth getting into conversation with the regulars who can reveal something of 'coloured' life to the non-Afrikaans speaker.

Rust-en-Vreugd Museum

Open weekdays 9–4, admission free with the ticket from the Castle guided tour.

Another minute's walk uphill on Buitenkant's north side, a large white wall with a wrought-iron gate conceals a herb garden, behind which stands an 18th-century mansion, now a museum housing a huge collection of historical Cape lithographs, engravings and water-colours (late 18th- to mid 19th-century). Many of the period illustrations in South African history books come from pictures in this collection. The best is upstairs—especially the grotesque George Cruikshank cartoons, from the early 19th century, of the first British settlers in the Cape being tricked into ideas of a land of plenty, then being devoured upon arrival by grinning savages. Oddities of colonial life, such as pictures of British cavalry officers fox-hunting through Xhosa villages, and heavily stylized paintings of wildlife, hang next to pictures of the now-vanished Khoi tribes who inhabited the Cape when the Europeans first arrived. As a pictorial record of colonial expansion from the Cape colony to the interior, the collection has no equal.

Last stop on Buitenkant Street, at no.83, is the **Perseverance Tavern**, Cape Town's oldest pub (the present building dates from 1836, but occupies an earlier site). It claims to have the country's oldest grape vine in the courtyard. The Perseverance used to be the first stop for wagoneers entering Cape Town from the rough mountains beyond and the last stop for those leaving town. Its cellar-like interior is a good place to drink and rest before heading back down Buitenkant to **Plein Street**, which runs along the west side of the Parade.

Along here is the old **City Hall**, a pompous building dating from 1905 that is now a concert hall and occasionally used for ceremonial purposes, including Nelson Mandela's first speech to the nation on 9 May 1994. One block further, Plein Street crosses Darling. On the east corner is the huge Art Deco **Central Post Office**, a 1920s edifice. Inside are huge murals romanticizing early Cape colonial life; rather beautiful, if politically unsound.

Around Adderley Street

From Plein, a left turn takes you into upper Adderley Street, a mish-mash of Edwardian colonial and older buildings, in the middle of which is the **Groote Kerk**. This suitably austere building was the first Dutch Reformed church built in South Africa. Begun in 1678, consecrated in 1704, the original building was burned down in the early 19th century. Only the steeple remains, sadly dwarfed by the squat, ugly main church, rebuilt in 1841. The carved pulpit (an Anreith) was saved from the fire, and adds the only graceful note to an otherwise lumpish landmark.

Further up Adderley on the same side is the far more attractive **Old Slave Lodge**, which now houses the **South African Cultural History Museum** (*open Mon–Sat 9.30–4.30*). The building started life in the late 17th century as an unofficial brothel (the Dutch East India Company was practical, if discreet, about such matters) using Asian and West African women. The British changed that, turning it (with unconscious irony) into the city's Supreme Court. As with the Old Granary on Buitenkant Street, a lion and unicorn pediment sculpted by Anreith was tacked on to the building's back pediment (on Church Square, which runs behind and parallel to Adderley Street) after the British annexation in 1806.

Today's museum is eclectic and rather eccentric. The first few rooms are not South African at all, but devoted to Egypt, Greece, Rome, India, China and Japan, no doubt for the education of Cape Town's schoolchildren. South Africa only begins upstairs. Highlights include a room devoted to the 'Post Office Stones' under which the Dutch, Portuguese and English sea captains rounding the Cape from the 15th to the 17th centuries left messages for each other. A room devoted to the Frontier Wars between the British and the Xhosa (*see* **Eastern Cape**, 'History') lacks actual artefacts, but gives a concise (if settler-orientated) chronology of this confused and tragic 100-year conflict. Other curiosities include the flag of a Confederate ship from the American Civil War, sunk off Table Bay in the 1860s by a passing Union frigate, and the cobbled courtyard, shaded by oaks, where sits a replica of the tombstone of Jan Van Riebeeck and his wife.

The museum lacks any display of 'indigenous' culture (i.e. San, Khoi, or black African)—there is an excellent exhibition of these cultures at the South African Museum (*see* below).

After the museum, Adderley Street swings right towards Signal Hill, becoming Wale Street. Continuing in the same direction as Adderley is **Government Avenue**, a shaded pedestrian walk that marks the beginning of the **Company Gardens**. **St George's Cathedral** sits at the entrance to the Gardens. A fine piece of neo-Gothic (designed by Sir Herbert Baker in 1848), the timbered ceiling in the choir is particularly lovely. The cathedral came to prominence in the 1980s, following the appointment of Archbishop Desmond Tutu. A beautiful Mass is sung here on the last Sunday of every month.

The Company Gardens

Behind the cathedral are the Company Gardens. Part botanical collection, part park, they started life as the first colony's vegetable patch (1652), when the surrounding country was still off-limits to the settlers, and too full of Khoi livestock and wild game to allow crop-rearing. Once the colony was allowed to expand beyond the original earth rampart, the Company Gardens became ornamental. A pavilion was built in the 1680s (now called the

Tuynhuys, and used by the State President as a downtown residence). Rare plants were introduced from Asia, and the gardens extended. Today massive exotic trees shade the walks. Look out for an old pump embedded in an oak tree, having been wrenched from the ground as the tree grew. There is a Victorian Aviary and Tea Garden (and 17th-century slave-bell) at the centre, near a statue of the De Beers founder and tireless empire builder Cecil Rhodes (*see* **History**) giving what appears to be a Nazi salute.

Government Avenue

South of the Gardens, on Government Avenue, are the Victorian neoclassical **Houses of Parliament** (built 1884, expanded 1910). The buildings are not heavy or ponderous, but genuinely handsome. Take a guided tour when Parliament is not sitting (July–Jan/Feb), or buy a ticket for the public gallery when it is.

Inside, the **Library of Parliament** houses the Mendelssohn Collection: 50,000 reference books on Africa, mainly of interest to academics. The rather uninspiring **Parliamentary Museum** exhibits portraits of South Africa's past statesmen and ceremonial paraphernalia, and houses important historical records.

On up Government Avenue to the **Tuynhuys** and its wide lawn, called the Stal Plein. The mounted statue in the centre is of General Louis Botha—first prime minister after the Union in 1910, and one of the last generals to surrender in the Anglo-Boer War. The avenue then opens into a wide piazza. On the left is the **South African National Gallery** (*open Mon 1–5, Tues–Sun 10–5*), a must-see. The gallery is small, but has some very fine modern paintings and sculpture, alongside some indifferent 18th- and 19th-century British paintings. Of particular note is the life-size sculpture 'The Butcher Boys', by Jane Alexander, depicting three youths seated on a bench, horns sprouting from their heads, spines bursting from their backs. The gallery shop sells some of the best examples of indigenous arts and crafts you can buy outside the townships and former 'homelands'.

Next door, the **Great Synagogue** (dating from 1905) stands next to the smaller **Jewish Museum** (*open Tues 2–5, Thur and Sun 10–12.30*), in fact South Africa's oldest synagogue, founded in 1862. From here, the avenue continues uphill from the piazza. On the corner of the two is the **South African Museum** (*open daily 10–5*). The ground floor has a comprehensive display of ethnic South Africa in chronological order, from bushman through to the present black African societies. There are life-size models cast from real people, a little eerie in their lifelikeness, and technically correct in dress. More importantly, histories, beliefs and mythologies, ethics and material culture are clearly explained. This display is somewhat out of place here: the South African Museum is supposed to be devoted to natural history but, under apartheid, African ethnicity was confined to these zoological, rather than cultural, premises. Today's curators are trying to have the display moved to the South African Cultural History Museum.

Upstairs, whales hang from the ceiling as you mount a series of ramps to cases of stuffed animals: South American deer, North American bears, rooms of South African reptiles and fish, and natural curiosities such as the sea bean, a giant palm nut that looks like a leviathan coffee-bean and which occasionally floats from Mozambique to the South African coast. The bean used to be much prized by witch doctors. The history of printing is displayed next to a large, unlit case of unidentified birds. South African mammals occupy another gallery, while yet another is devoted entirely to Table Mountain's flora and fauna. In short the museum is educational, but exhausting.

Along the last stretch of Government Avenue runs a high, white wall. A gate marked 'Bertram House' leads into a collection of old buildings that is now the University of Cape Town's downtown campus. **Bertram House** itself (*open Tues–Sat 9.30–4.30*) is a museum of furniture and ornaments from the 18th century. Behind this is the **Egyptian Building** (1839), now the Sculpture Department of the University of Cape Town's Fine Art faculty. Wander in and look at the students' work.

From here, the shaded walk of Government Avenue brings one blinking on to the busy rush of Orange Street. A right turn one block into Queen Victoria Street (which runs parallel with Government Avenue down the north side of the Company Gardens) leads to a cheerless, narrow street with just one point of interest—the **South African Library** (built in 1818) (*open Mon–Fri 9–6, Sat 9–1*). The library contains two famous collections of early Africana: the Grey Collection of rare books and the Von Dessin Collection (dating from 1761). For researching African history and natural history there are few better libraries. It is pleasant just to sniff the scent of old books and take in the high classical interiors. Admission is free and anyone can use the reference books.

Long Street

Long Street, which runs one block north of and parallel to Queen Victoria Street, is one of the city's best walks, having an attractive mixture of colonial wrought-iron arcades, second-hand bookshops, antiques, restaurants and general browsing. Start at the top, at the junction with Orange Street, and stroll slowly downhill towards the harbour. Here are the city's old **Turkish Baths** (*open daily 9.30–8*)—still a pleasant place to steam among the Victorian tiles on a gusty, wet winter day. Then stop for a drink or sandwich in **McGawley's Pub**, an old Cape Town institution complete with dusty hunting trophies and pool tables. Across the road is the **Junk Shop**, behind a beautiful colonial wrought-iron front, selling anything from coins to pinball machines.

The rest of the street is a jumble of second-hand bookshops (from collectors' first editions to torn paperbacks), old clothes shops, restaurants, pawnbrokers and antique shops. There are also two elegant little mosques dating from the early 19th century. At the lower end of Long Street, near the junction with Castle Street, is the head office of the **National Parks Board** (*open weekdays 8–4.45*), useful for booking trails or accommodation in advance, and the **Sendinggestig Museum** (1804) (*open weekdays 9–4*), the first mission church to be built by South Africans. This simple but elegant old church has a yellowwood gallery held up by pillars made from ships' masts. It lost its 'coloured' congregation after the Group Areas Act removed everyone who wasn't white from the city centre (*see* **Cape Town**, 'History').

The junction at Castle Street, the next one, is the end of the upper city centre. From here down, Long Street enters first the dull (and tiny) finance district (concrete buildings), and then the red-light sleaze (after dark) of the wind-blown Foreshore. Avoid that part at night.

But that is not quite all. Double back up Long Street to **Shortmarket Street**, and into **Greenmarket Square**. This wide cobbled space is home to a permanent craft market selling clothes, shoes, jewellery and antiques, bounded on three sides by some of Cape Town's grander Art Deco buildings, some of which have terraced cafés. The northwest corner has a heavy, late-Victorian Methodist church, but on the fourth (west) side is the **Old Town House** (*open daily 10–5, adm free*), a mid 18th-century Dutch building of singular beauty. Once the seat of the old Burgher Senate, it now houses the Michaelis Art Collection of works by Dutch and Flemish Masters, including some Van Dyck portraits. The paintings, on the whole, are not first-rate, but some of the drawings on display on the ground floor (depicting 17th-century agricultural life in the Netherlands and the Cape) are very fine. The building is worth visiting just for itself though. Look out for the Dutch tiles painted with 17th-century soldiers around the walls and ornamental brick fireplaces of the side-rooms, the night sky painted above the grand staircase, and the dark wood and white plaster ceiling of the upstairs gallery. A wide balcony gives out from here on to the square.

St George's Mall leads down towards the harbour from near Greenmarket Square. An extension of the craft market, it is a pedestrian street, which also contains some fine Art Deco office buildings (the *Cape Argus* newspaper building is one example). These peter out into concrete as the road connects with Strand Street and the lower city centre. **Church Street**, which runs between Queen Victoria and Long Streets, is known for its antique shops and open-air stalls, which sell both South African and European antiques.

Loop Street runs parallel to Long Street (one block north), and has some elegant Cape Dutch buildings still in use as offices. The area is best known for nightclubs (*see* 'Nightlife'). These vary from student rock 'n' roll and techno dance clubs to good live music venues and 'Korean' clubs, discos aimed specifically at sailors, many of whom come from the Far East, hence the name. Many prostitutes—female, male and transvestite—walk the street at night.

The Bo-Kaap

Arguably the most interesting residential area in the city is the Bo-Kaap (meaning 'above-Cape'), a small neighbourhood on the lower slopes of Signal Hill. The heart of Muslim Cape Town runs roughly parallel with Long Street, beginning four blocks to the north. Composed of brightly painted 18th-century artisan cottages bought by Cape Malay (Dutch Indonesian) slaves freed in the 1830s, the area has been solidly Islamic ever since. There are many small mosques, and a little **museum**, at 71 Wale Street (*open Tues–Sat 9.30–4.30*), which shows how Cape Malay home interiors would have looked in the early 19th century. Cape Town's Muslim culture keeps itself to itself, and you are unlikely to get a look inside the present houses unless accompanied by a guide. But Cape Islamic culture, though often hidden, is rich, and has some extreme practices. For example, behind the colourful but locked doors of the neighbourhood, young men practise a dance called *Khalifa*, in which they pierce their flesh with knives while in ecstatic trances. The dance is occasionally performed at festivals which outsiders can attend. Generally, though, the outward atmosphere in the Bo-Kaap is rather sleepy. The narrow streets make for pleasant strolling, and there is a superb Cape Malay restaurant, called Biesmiellah, near the museum on Wale Street (*see* 'Eating Out').

The Lower City Centre

This generally refers to everything downhill from the line made by Strand Street where it crosses Adderley, and includes the **Waterfront** harbour complex and the reclaimed land of the **Foreshore**. The **Golden Acre Mall**, where Adderley and Strand meet, supposedly stands on the site of Jan Van Riebeeck's original fort, built in 1652, and the remains of a 17th-century reservoir is on view behind glass on the basement floor.

Downhill on Adderley from Strand Street, the entire block on the right is occupied by the **Central Train and Bus Station**. On display in the station hall is South Africa's first steam train (imported from Scotland in 1859). In front of the station is a permanent **flea market**, selling mostly clothes and imported goods (watches, stereos, etc.), as well as fruit and vegetables. It makes for a lively scene. Next to the train and bus station, at the east end of the block, is the **CapTour Tourist Office**. After the stations, Adderley widens into a large traffic circle, in the middle of which are fountains and a statue of Jan Van Riebeeck and his wife. This is the beginning of the Foreshore. A right turn at the traffic circle takes you on to Hertzog Boulevard and towards the **Nico Malan Theatre Complex** (*see* 'Entertainment').

Strand Street, north of Adderley, has two national monuments, the **Koopmans-De Wet House**, built in 1701 (*open Tues–Sat 9.30–4.30*), and the **Lutheran Church** (*open Mon–Fri 8.30–1 and 1.30–4.30*). The former, a townhouse, was home to one of the 19th century's principal campaigners for recognition of the Afrikaans language, Maria Koopmans-De Wet. The front of the house is well known for its combination of Anreith's carving and Louis Thibault's design. Inside are early Cape furniture, Chinese porcelain, and European ornaments from the 17th and 18th centuries. The Lutheran church and its neighbouring parsonage, both recently restored, are on the opposite side of Strand Street, uphill from the Koopmans-De Wet House. The church is simple inside but the carved pulpit is ornate Anreith, as is the design of the parsonage, behind which is a quiet walled garden where you can escape the rush of the city for a while.

Cape Town's small financial district lies on the opposite side of Strand Street. Mostly an uninteresting collection of tower blocks, this area can be bypassed. Better to walk back to Adderley and the CapTour Office, outside which there is a bus that runs every 15 minutes to the **Waterfront Harbour Complex**.

A lot of media hype surrounded the opening of the 'finished' Waterfront development, in 1992. The area centres around the original docks, the Victoria and Alfred (not Albert) basins. A mixture of kitsch and history, with restaurants, bars, cinemas, a flea market and shops, shops, shops, the Waterfront still harbours many of Cape Town's small trawlers. Seals dive off the inlet called Bertie's Landing. The Robinson Graving dock still operates for light cargo ships, and most of the handsome old warehouses still stand. Amongst all this thrives a consumer maelstrom. Love it or hate it, you should at least have a look at the Waterfront.

The bus sets you down by the entrance to both the flea market and the Waterfront proper. The flea market (to the right of the entrance) sells some of the best of Cape Town's local crafts. In the Waterfront you can relax, in the summer months, to live outdoor jazz in a small amphitheatre in the main concourse. The **Marpro Fish Market** is a covered hall where one can wander among aisles of Atlantic and Indian Ocean fish. On the dockside, opposite the market, is **Quay Four**, a gigantic bar, always teeming with drinkers. **The South African Fisheries Museum** (*open Tues–Sun 10–4*) has a computerized marine encyclopaedia that can tell you what a jib-sheet is, or how to catch a snoek. Other attractions are a small aquarium, and old fishing and naval artefacts, including three museum-ships, docked in the wharf below.

There are several good (but expensive) seafood restaurants around the Waterfront (*see* 'Eating Out'), including Bertie's Landing, reached by the 'Penny Ferry', a rowing boat costing R1 per person. After wandering the shops (which sell everything from South African wine and curios to Scottish terriers cast in pewter), take one of the various **boat trips** out into Table Bay. A cruise to the aptly named **Seal Island** can be made for R5 per person (takes an hour). Cruises to the notorious ex-prison, **Robben Island**, cost R70 per person (three hours, price includes cold drinks and snacks). A ride in a catamaran can be had for R30 per person (takes an hour). All boats leave from the dock outside the Victoria and Alfred Hotel.

The Waterfront has two live **jazz bars** (*see* 'Nightlife'), and makes a good place to spend at least one evening. However, unless you have a car, you will have to pick up a taxi home. Make sure you agree the price before you get in.

Table Mountain

In Cape Town, you are constantly aware of Table Mountain. It dominates the city, a massive chunk of wild nature rearing above the crowded streets. Whenever you look up, there it is; cliff, forest, mountainside and cloud.

Table Mountain is not a single entity, but the northern extremity of the Peninsula Mountain chain, joined to them via Devil's Peak, a sharp promontory that dominates the residential neighbourhoods known as the Southern Suburbs. In the city itself Table Mountain is joined by a saddle pass (Tamboerskloof) to the Lion's Head and Signal Hill.

There are many walks, climbs and trails on Table Mountain's 1086m sandstone bulk—some gentle, some very strenuous. CapTour issues a map of all trails, both on the city side of the mountain and in the state forests on the slopes behind Devil's Peak (*see* 'Southern Suburbs').

The traditional way to the summit is by cablecar from the cable station on Kloof Street, a five-minute ride (*see* 'Getting Around'). The flat plateau at the top of the mountain, if not obscured by cloud, provides an awesome view clear down the Peninsula to Cape Point, foreshortening the 70-odd-kilometre distance to what seems only a few hundred metres. There is a little restaurant, and a prosperous colony of dassies (rock hyraxes) who eat what the tourists drop.

About 350 paths wind from various access points to the summit. More interesting for the tourist, and less strenuous, are the two **Contour Paths** connecting Table Mountain with Constantia, 20km to the south. It is a climb to reach the paths, but once on them it's level walking, and there are hop-off points from the Contour Paths every few kilometres.

Table Mountain has a wilder climate than the city below it. Don't go walking on the upper slopes without a waterproof, good boots and a map. Even on a fine day, the weather can change very quickly and there are fatalities every year from falls and hypothermia, so don't try anything too ambitious unless with someone who knows the mountain.

The Cape Floral Kingdom is well in evidence on the mountain (roughly 3000 species of wilflower and fynbos). There is wildlife too. Rhebok is the largest antelope; more common are the smaller duiker and grysbok. Baboons are common, as are caracal, though you would be lucky to see one. There are even one or two leopard in the kloofs and inaccessible gullies, whose territorial radii have been marked as far as 100km inland from the mountain. Walkers often spot the exotic Himalayan tahr (an Asian mountain goat), colonies of which have established themselves on the mountain since their escape from the Groot Schuur Paddocks (a fenced nature reserve on the southern part of the mountain) in the 1930s.

Exotic trees are everywhere, mainly bluegum, oak and various pine species. The gum trees are in the process of being slowly removed (killed by having rings cut from their bark), as they have been found to dry out the thin topsoil.

Devil's Peak (also over 1000m) is the sharp point that divides Table Mountain from the rest of the Peninsula chain. You can walk up it from access points in Rondebosch and Newlands Forest (*see* 'Southern Suburbs') or from the Contour Paths. On the lower slopes are the **King's** and **Queen's** blockhouses, small ruined stone forts built after the first British occupation in the early 1800s.

The **Lion's Head** and '**Rump**', officially known as **Signal Hill**, comprise the long upland with a conical peak that rises from the city opposite Table Mountain—to which it is joined by the Tamboeskloof. The walk up the Lion's Head (through shining woods of silver trees), ends with a strenuous pull up the final steep slope with chains bolted into the rock. The Lion's Head is used by Capetonians as a weather-vane. If there is a little ring of cloud just around the tip of the Head, bad weather is coming.

For practical information on hiking and rock-climbing on Table Mountain and the Peninsula chain, *see* 'Activities'.

The Central Residential Neighbourhoods

The **Gardens District** is a residential neighbourhood to the west (uphill) of the Company Gardens (with which it should not be confused) and extending south in a curving arm. This is an eclectic area, part 'coloured', part Cape Malay, part white yuppie. Entertainment is plentiful. The interestingly named **Labia Cinema** (*see* 'Entertainment') shows good repertory films. The **Fringe Nightclub** (*see* 'Nightlife') also screens films and plays music from township sounds to funk to thrash. Gardens also has several of the city's best restaurants, particularly Cape Malay and Cape country (*see* 'Eating Out'). Cape Town's most luxurious hotel, the **Mount Nelson**, offers superb teas with tiered cake-dishes of cream cakes and pastries (*see* 'Cafés and Bars').

The Southern Suburbs

The Southern Suburbs are a series of 19th- and early 20th-century neighbourhoods extending from the city centre south to the eastern side of the Peninsula, running along the centrally connecting Main Road and joined by rail to Cape Town's central station. The first, **Woodstock**, has traditionally been an area of working class 'coloureds' living in elegant, but run-down, 19th-century houses. The part of Woodstock furthest from town is being gentrified by white yuppies.

Closest to town is the 'coloured' district, which includes the semi-industrial region, **Salt River**. This is lively by day and night. One of Cape Town's most notorious nightclubs (for gangsters and their molls) is **Odyssey,** on Main Road (*see* 'Nightlife').

Further along is **Observatory**, a hippie neighbourhood favoured by university students. The street which runs parallel to and downhill from Main Road, **Lower Main Road**, has some handsome colonial arcades with good live music bars, cheap restaurants (*see* 'Nightlife' and 'Eating Out'), and general evening fun. Some of Cape Town's best youth hostels are here (*see* 'Accommodation').

Observatory's eastern boundary is formed by the Liesbeeck Parkway (part of the M5 highway), which runs along the **Liesbeeck River**. Despite the rushing traffic, you can walk the riverbank and see kingfishers, darters (river cormorants) and other waterfowl. Just off the Parkway is **Valkenberg Manor** (*open Mon–Fri 9–5*), a large Dutch homestead, built in 1770, that used to farm the area.

On the far side of the river (where Station Road crosses the Parkway) is the **Observatory** that gives the neighbourhood its name. This opens to the public, free of charge, on the first Saturday of every month at 8pm and offers views of the night sky through the large telescope. Ask to be shown the rings of Saturn.

Mowbray, just south of Observatory, is another student area, notable mainly for the massive **Groot Schuur Hospital**. **Rosebank**, the next south, is worth visiting for the **Irma Stern Museum**, on Cecil Road (*open Tues–Sun 10–1 and 2–5*). Irma Stern was a Cape artist active in the early part of the 20th century. The museum comprises her house, studio and a small collection of her work (*see* **People and Culture**, 'Art and Architecture').

Rondebosch is home to the **University of Cape Town**, a beautifully laid-out campus of late 19th-century neoclassical buildings on the mountainside above Main Road and the M3 highway (connected with Main Road by a pedestrian tunnel and stairway). **Mostert's Mill** (*open weekdays 10–5*), built in 1796, sits just below the campus, as does Cecil Rhodes' old house, **Groot Schuur**, a 17th-century barn that was converted into an opulent mansion in the 1890s for the jingoist billionaire by the architect Sir Herbert Baker. What was good enough for Cecil Rhodes is now good enough for South Africa's state presidents—Groot Schuur has been their main Cape Town residence since Rhodes' death in the 1900s. Behind the house are two smaller residences, the state guest house **Westbrooke**, and the **Woolsack** (now a campus residence), where Rudyard Kipling used to stay as Rhodes' guest when visiting the city.

Next to the university campus, on the city-ward side, is the **Rhodes Memorial** (in the style of a Greek temple) and **Tea Garden**, which give a panoramic view of the city. Around both Memorial and Tea Garden are the **Groot Schuur Paddocks**, shaded by umbrella pines, where fallow deer graze and sensual, white arum lilies grow. One can follow a track uphill from here to the King's Blockhouse and the mountain's Lower Contour Path.

On Main Road, below the university campus, is the **Baxter Theatre and Cinema**, showing repertory drama and films seven days a week (*see* 'Entertainment'). Below Main Road, academics and the wealthier students live next to each other in large houses set in larger gardens.

Newlands, a suburb for the rich (it always has been—Lady Anne Barnard lived here in what is now the Vineyard Hotel), has two museums that warrant a visit, both in the same building.

Josephine's Water Mill (*open weekdays 10–2*), next to the **International Rugby Stadium**, was built in 1840 and named after the then Queen of Sweden. Unlike Mostert's Mill in Rondebosch, this mill works. The **Newlands Rugby Museum** (*open weekdays 10–4*) occupies the mill's ground floor. A clue to just how much of a religion rugby is among white South Africans, the museum has a varied selection of exhibits from the late 19th century to the present day, many of which have the status of holy relics.

Best of all, though, is the magnificent **Newlands Forest**. The entrance (and car park) is a little tricky to reach; you have to cross the M3 highway, but there is a footbridge near the University, on the border with Rondebosch. The world under the pines is deep green. Trails lead up to the Contour Paths between crowding oaks, silver trees (a species of giant protea) and more pines. Hanging above, through the breaks in the trees, are the towering cliffs of Devil's Peak. Above the treeline, if you follow the trail to the Upper Contour Path, is a steep series of steps cut into the mountainside, leading up to a pass over Devil's Peak. A few hours in Newlands Forest clears the mind and refreshes the spirit.

Claremont, the next suburb south, is unremarkable except for a lovely Victorian park, the **Ardene Gardens** (on Main Road), and the **Cavendish Square Complex**, which is another shopping mall that houses a multi-screen cinema (also on Main Road, south of the gardens).

Wynberg, further south along Main Road, has a large public park, behind which is an area of pretty, white-washed 19th-century houses called **Little Chelsea**, home to some good antique shops, and Cape Town's best Indian restaurant, Ramola's (at least, in the author's opinion) (*see* 'Eating Out'). There is also a good craft shop, the **Operation Hunger Showroom**, in the Coates Building, on Maynard Road. This is a non-profit organization and the African crafts it sells are first-rate, more authentic than what one sees in the many curio shops around Cape Town.

South from Wynberg, at the foot of the mountain, is **Kenilworth**, whose **Racecourse** is on the M5 road to Muizenberg, and **Plumstead**, a residential neighbourhood. Then comes **Retreat**, also residential, and named after the Dutch army's rout following the Battle of Muizenberg (1795), when the British chased them through this area back to the Castle.

Constantia and the Wine Estates

Constantia, uphill from and south of the Southern Suburbs, is a gracious area of mansions set in forest, vineyards, horse paddocks and mountain. Some of the Cape's most famous Dutch homesteads are to be found here.

The area takes its name from South Africa's oldest and most famous wine estate, **Groot Constantia**, © 794 5178. Founded by Simon Van der Stel, Cape Governor in 1685, and run by Huguenot settlers, Groot Constantia's wines were in demand even in Europe throughout the 18th century. The estate has changed hands many times, but has always been the leading one in the colony. Lady Anne Barnard was brought here in 1798, and was treated to the sight of Hottentot (Khoi) slaves treading wine. Ignoring the gracious buildings around her, she instead wrote of the slaves, 'what struck me most was the beautiful, antique forms, perpetually graceful, of the three figures, half naked, dancing in the wine press'.

Now state-owned, Groot Constantia is still operational, though not through slavery. Noted for red wine, its vineyards spread away up the hillsides to the forested **Constantiaberg** (part of the transition between Table Mountain and the rugged spine of the Cape Peninsula). The homestead is one of the most handsome (and largest) examples of early Cape Dutch gabled architecture in the country. Inside is a museum (*open weekdays 10–5*), exhibiting Simon Van der Stel's fine furniture, some exquisite antique porcelain, and a history of the estate. In the old stables behind the main house is a second museum (*open weekdays 10–5*), of wagons, carts and carriages. A craft and wine shop in the courtyard in front of the homestead offers free wine-tastings. The two-storey wine cellar was designed by 18th-century French architect Louis Thibault, its pediment frieze carved by Anreith (*open by guided tour, on the hour from 10–6*). The vineyards and forest fringes can be wandered at will. Two restaurants—the Tavern (buffet food), and Jonkershuis (Cape cuisine lunches and teas)—adjoin the main homestead. If you have the time and energy, the best way to reach Groot Constantia is on foot along the Lower Contour Path on the mountain. Otherwise, take the M3 highway to the Constantia exit and follow the signs.

The neighbouring estate of **Klein Constantia** (1796) is privately owned, but also open to the public (*open for tastings weekdays 9–5, Sat 9–1*). Renowned for its white wines, this fine homestead is smaller than Groot Constantia's, but less crowded with visitors.

Next door is a third estate, **Buitenverwachting**, a new winery with a well-known restaurant. Its wines have won many awards, and are worth bringing home as they are hard to find outside South Africa.

Alphen, another fine Cape Dutch manor, and now a hotel and restaurant, is an 18th-century estate (also with its own vineyards) that used to belong to a Captain De Waal, a senior officer in the Dutch Company army. Louis Thibault, a military man as well as an architect, witnessed Captain De Waal commanding his troops during the Battle of Muizenberg, and was not impressed. Thibault wrote, 'He was too prudent to expose himself, and kept his distance half-a-mile back from the line of combat, so as to have a good view of the whole adventure.' Whatever its first owners' shortcomings, the estate and homestead are fine, and worth visiting for their own sake—they are on the M42 between Kirstenbosch and Hout Bay. (*See* 'Where to Stay and Eating Out'.)

Kirstenbosch Botanical Gardens (*open daily 9am–sundown*), just off the M3 between the city and Groot Constantia, display an incredible variety of South African plants: 9000 of the country's 18,000 species, with thousands more exotic. One of the southern boundary points of the original Cape Colony, part of the defensive hedge and earthwork erected by Jan Van Riebeeck's men still runs through Kirstenbosch. The formal gardens and lawns stretch expansively (the total area is 560ha, over 1000 acres) below a steep, wild section of mountain forest cut through with signposted paths. Picnicking in Kirstenbosch is a Cape Town tradition, the manicured beds of exotic flowers and small copses of trees affording a measure of privacy in which to enjoy the peace, the colours and the songbirds that flock to the gardens in great number. Watch particularly for the iridescent sheen of sunbirds (brightly coloured relatives of the humming-bird), which suck nectar from the blooms. Landmarks within the Kirstenbosch are **Lady Anne Barnard's Bath**, a natural spring that (according to local historians) was never actually used by Lady Barnard (but never mind) and the **Compton Herbarium**. Kirstenbosch has a unique disabled facility—a **Braille Walk** that leads along a route of plants selected for their perfumes. Please note that it is almost impossible to get to the gardens by public transport. If you don't have a car, take a taxi.

Table Mountain's Forests

Cecilia State Forest, one of Table Mountain's four state forests (named after Cecil Rhodes), has its entrance on the winding mountain road that continues on uphill from Kirstenbosch and Groot Constantia towards Constantia Nek and Hout Bay. The forest's many trails are clearly marked on the CapTour Table Mountain map. For the fit, a steep uphill path from the forest entrance leads to a small waterfall, with wide views over the Cape Flats and False Bay. The same path leads into **Constantia Nek Forest**, which can also be reached by car along the Hout Bay road on from Cecilia Forest. Predominantly pine, the forest gives way to fynbos as it climbs the mountainside. Baboons and lynx are common here, though the lynx are too shy for any but the very lucky to spot, and the baboons tend to leave hikers alone (you might hear them, though). After a few hours under the trees, cross the road from the forest entrance to the **Constantia Nek Inn**, which has an open-air terrace for teas, and serves meals. Folk bands often play in the evenings (*see* 'Eating Out' and 'Nightlife').

Tokai, the forest suburb south of Constantia, also centres around an old wine estate, **Tokai Homestead** (1795), named after a wine-producing region of Hungary. Attributed to Thibault, Tokai is smaller than Groot Constantia, but of great proportional beauty. Take the M3 to the Tokai exit and follow the signs to the homestead, either driving or walking past (you can't go in).

Tokai State Forest begins 500m left of Tokai Homestead. The lower section, on the Cape Flats, is not very interesting—serried ranks of commercial pine plantation. But as the forest climbs the mountainside, it becomes mixed with various deciduous exotics—oaks, chestnuts, maples and flowering gums, as well as indigenous species, all planted at the turn of the century as part of an experiment to see which species would be hardy enough for commercial growing in South Africa. Many Capetonians call the upper section of Tokai Forest the 'enchanted woods', and certainly, among the kloofs and frequent mists, you could be forgiven for fairy-tale imaginings. There is a cave (the Elephant's Eye) and a network of trails (marked on the CapTour Table Mountain map).

Newlands Forest is the closest forest to the city centre, beginning on the mountain slopes above Newlands (*see* 'Southern Suburbs'). A network of trails lead up to both Contour paths, or up a steep series of steps to Devil's Peak.

Cape Peninsula

Getting Around

By car is the easiest. However, trains run out along the east side of the Peninsula as far as Simon's Town from the central station in Cape Town. This is worth taking just for the view, especially the last few kilometres, where the railway runs along the actual sea-shore, and the waves crash directly below the train windows.

Black taxis go as far as Muizenberg in the east and Camps Bay in the west. Buses leave the terminus in Cape Town Parade every hour, going around both sides of the Peninsula, though not to Cape Point. Tour buses to the Cape of Good Hope Nature Reserve and Cape Point can be arranged through the CapTour office.

Many people hitch around the Peninsula; there is always a steady stream of traffic, even to the further points like Noordehoek, and picking up hitch-hikers is a fairly well-accepted tradition in Cape Town. Best is to get as far as Muizenberg or Camps Bay by train, bus or taxi, then try your luck from these points. Do be aware that some people have been assaulted and worse this way. Girls should never hitch alone, and even hitching in a pair can be risky.

Eastern Peninsula

Muizenberg

Continuing south from Tokai and Retreat, the M3 splits—left to **Muizenberg** and right over the Silvermine Pass to the western Peninsula. The train through the Southern Suburbs also stops in Muizenberg. At the turn of the century, this was Cape Town's seaside resort for the wealthy. The town was beloved of Cecil Rhodes (who built a seaside house there: Rhodes Cottage) and Rudyard Kipling (who eulogized the 'white sands of Muizenberg' in a poem). Today, though many of the old villas still stand, the town has become rather glitzy and, on weekends and hot days, crowded with thousands of holidaymakers from the city.

The beach is still white sand, but can be over-full. Better is to walk south along the promenade to **St James Beach** or eastwards around Muizenberg beach, for about a kilometre, as it curves into the warm waters of False Bay and becomes **Sunrise Beach** (*see* p.148).

Muizenberg has some interesting sights. **Rhodes Cottage** (*open Tues–Sun 10–1 and 2–5*), on Main Road at the end of town furthest from Cape Town, is a small museum of Cecil Rhodes' personal effects from the last days of his life, following the Anglo-Boer War of 1899–1902 (*see* **History**). On the slope behind Rhodes Cottage is **Rust-En-Vrede** (Afrikaans for 'rest in peace'), a brick mansion designed for Rhodes by Sir Herbert Baker and Sir Abe Bailey (two prominent English Edwardian architects). The name was perhaps a little fateful, for Rhodes died before the mansion was completed.

The somewhat spectacularly named **Natale Labia Museum**, a satellite museum of the National Gallery, is on Main Road, in the centre of town (*open Tues–Sun 10–5, but closed during August*). It is named after the Italian Prince Labia (an ambassador to South Africa who married a mining magnate's daughter, and after whom the Labia Cinema in the Gardens area of Cape Town is also named), who lived here in the early 20th century. Patrons of the arts, their collection of furniture and paintings is on display.

The Edwardian **Muizenberg Railway Station** on Main Road has been converted into a seafood restaurant and craft market (*market open Sun and public holidays only*).

Kalk Bay

Kalk Bay is the next village south of Muizenberg, along the Peninsula by Main Road and the railway. Not a resort, but a pretty, working fishing village of white-washed cottages and houses crowding down to a small harbour. The word 'kalk' is Afrikaans for lime; in the 19th century the village made a living burning sea-shells to produce lime for whitewash. But fishing has always been the main activity. In the early afternoon, when the boats come in from False Bay, you can buy fresh fish on the small concrete jetty in the harbour. There is a cabaret theatre, the **Eauvre the Top Café**, and the **Brass Bell**, one of the Cape's most fun restaurant/live music venues, overlooks the sea at Kalk Bay; you should indulge in one of the Brass Bell's obscenely large seafood platters.

Behind Kalk Bay are a line of steep hills, hollowed out underneath by a series of **caves**, often interconnected. These are blessedly undeveloped, no guides, no entry fee, no artificial lights. One can explore them (safest in a group as it is easy to get lost) by torchlight. The **Fish Hoek Publicity Association**, ☎ 782 1162, on Main Road, supplies maps of the caves and can arrange a guide.

Fish Hoek

Fish Hoek is the next town south on the Peninsula, founded by the British Cape Governor, Lord Charles Somerset, in 1818. Predominantly a retirement and holiday-home town centred around a beach, Fish Hoek has little for the tourist. However, it does have the dubious distinction of being the only 'dry' town in South Africa. No alcohol may be bought or sold here at all, an irritating leftover clause from the town's original title deed. At the time of Fish Hoek's founding a British naval base had just been established at Simon's Town, a few kilometres south, and the Cape Governor decreed the no-liquor clause to prevent Fish Hoek from becoming a sailor's roistering spot. Since then no one has seen fit to overturn it. Fish Hoek is reached by the Main Road and by train.

Simon's Town and Around

Simon's Town was founded in 1810 by Lord Charles Somerset as a naval base, taking his cue from the Dutch, who had long been using it as a wintering spot for the fleet, preferring False Bay's calmer waters to the unpredictable squalls of Table Bay. During the Second World War, Simon's Town became Britain's crucial naval base for the southern hemisphere. The South African Navy is still based here. Even now, there are signs forbidding you to take photos of the base, not that one would want to snap the dull concrete docks behind high wire fences. However, the town itself is very attractive; the Main Street has a grand 19th-century colonial front, complete with wrought-iron balconies and arcades. This is the end of the line for the Peninsula railway.

Simon's Town's Georgian and Victorian **Main Street** (known locally as the Historical Mile), is lined with antique shops, restaurants and tea shops (see 'Eating Out'). **Runciman's Buildings** (1785), on St George's Street, are particularly fine, and have now been converted into a coffee shop and tea garden, set around with the obligatory curio and gift shops and, unfortunately, twee art galleries.

The **Stempastorie**, on Church Street (*open Mon–Sat 9.30–4.30*), originally a Dutch Reform Church parsonage, carries an eccentric display, the story of South Africa's national emblems (its flags, songs, regimental and sporting team devices and so on). This was where the Afrikaans national anthem, 'Die Stem', was written.

The **Simon's Town Museum**, on Court Road (*open Tues–Fri 9–4, Sat 10–1*), is, not surprisingly, dedicated mostly to the Dutch, English and South African navies. The building itself, built in 1777, is stolidly handsome, being the old slave quarters, or less politely, the town's original brothel.

The **Martello Tower** (*open Mon–Fri 10–3.45*), displaying the history of the modern South African navy, is in the Naval Dockyard. The British built it on arrival in 1796, after the Battle of Muizenberg, and it claims to be the oldest surviving British building in the country. Also in the Naval Dockyard is the **South African Naval Museum** (*open Mon–Fri 9–4, Sun 10–1*).

A lighter-hearted contrast is the **Warrior Toy Museum** (*open daily 10–4*), on St George's Street, a permanent exhibition of vintage toys, particularly original Dinky Toy cars, boats and trains. Semi-precious stones are processed at a nearby factory called **Topstones**, on Dido Valley Road. Their 'scratch-patch' (or reject dump) is a good place to pick up malachite, amethyst, tiger's eye, rose quartz and other beautiful stones at no cost. Many of Cape Town's flea market jewellery-makers get their gems from here.

A 2km walk or drive south leads to **Boulders**, one of the most charming swimming spots in the Cape. A tiny cove with a miniature beach, sheltered by giant rocks, Boulders is both a place to swim and a nature reserve for a resident colony of **jackass penguins**, who gaze at you quizzically from the rocks and will sometimes swim to within a few feet of you, or come and join you on the beach. Neither particularly shy nor forward (they do not come for food), the penguins give the impression of generously sharing their territory with the human visitor. The result is one of the real treasures of the Peninsula. However, you should avoid Boulders at weekends, when it can get a bit crowded, and the penguins retreat to the caves and sea fringes. Another swimming place (with a good restaurant) is **Miller's Point** (*see* 'Eating Out'). Below the restaurant is a pool with only a low wall separating it from the sea, so that the tides wash clean water in and out. Fish and anemones live in the pool.

From Simon's Town, the Main Road becomes a coastal drive along cliffs, climbing gradually to the top of the Peninsula. The cliffs drop dizzyingly away from the road on the seaward side, giving an uninterrupted view of the Hottentots' Holland Mountains, 60km away on the other side of False Bay. There are no more towns between here and Cape Point; instead, fynbos and purple-flowering erica (like heather) cling to the slopes on the landward side.

About 7km south of Simon's Town, the road bends around a large cliff buttress to a viewpoint where you can park and look out over the ocean. A small footpath leads down the cliffside from here to **Smitswinkel Bay**, another small cove and sheltered swimming spot. The steep walk down the cliff is not for the vertiginous, but the cove is worth reaching for its isolation. On weekends there are usually a few people there. On weekdays, seldom anyone.

The Peninsula road continues along the cliff sides for another few kilometres, steadily climbing until it reaches the plateau in the middle of the Peninsula. Here the road forks; west to the other side of the Peninsula, or south (straight on) to **The Cape of Good Hope Nature Reserve**, © (021) 780 9100, and **Cape Point**.

As it enters the reserve, the road swings inland to the windswept fynbos heath of the Peninsula's end. There is a gate, open sunrise to sunset, that takes your money (R5 per car plus R3 per person) and then you are on the road to Cape Point. Ostriches are a common sight here, but the rest of the reserve's considerable list of fauna (Cape mountain zebra, red hartebeest, white-faced bontebok, rhebok, grysbok, eland and duiker) tend to keep away from the road. It is better to walk one of the reserve trails (marked on the map they give you at the gate) if you want to see game.

What you will certainly see is baboons. They hang around the car park below the hill that climbs up to Cape Point, wanting food. Don't feed them. Several people get bitten every year by baboons. The man who owns the ice-cream cart outside the car park's refreshment kiosk carries a long metal stick to keep them at bay.

It is a steep climb to Cape Point, but worth it (alternatively there is a bus from the car park that goes most of the way up). In front of the balustrade, the ground becomes cliff and plunges about 100m into the ocean. Contrary to traditional belief, the Indian and Atlantic Oceans don't actually meet here, but you do see part of the massive meeting of their two currents, the warm Agulhas (Indian Ocean) and cold Benguela (Atlantic). Look out for gulls and cormorants flying to their cliffside nests. The wind picks them up as they approach the wall of rock, accelerating them to what seems certain oblivion. At the last minute they swing back and, miraculously, brake in mid-air, landing on their narrow ledges with ease.

According to legend, a ship called the *Flying Dutchman* has sailed the turbulent ocean around Cape Point since the 17th century. A Dutch East Indiaman captain, Hendrik Van der Decken, frustrated by the notorious cross-winds of the Cape, swore to round the Point even if it took forever. It is still sailing. Many people have claimed to have seen the phantom ship, including King George V, who visited Cape Point while serving in the Royal Navy.

The reserve has about 40km of wild coastline, including some deserted beaches, excellent for walking. Expect to see some interesting bird life, for example concave-beaked avocets (a much-coveted sight for British bird watchers) and black oystercatchers. From the Reserve the M5 continues over to the western side of the Peninsula.

The Cape Flats

Most visitors are so busy with Cape Town's centre that they do not see the Cape Flats, where the townships are, except at a distance. However, a whole side of Cape Town culture exists in the townships. In the past there was fairly free social movement between city and township, though a certain risk, legal or otherwise, was always present. But times have changed. In the current tense political climate and rapidly rising crime rate, most townships have become very dangerous, even for those who live there. Unless you know someone in a township, contact **Otherside Tours**, ✆ 637 5763, for a knowledgeable guide.

Western Peninsula

Facing the cold Atlantic, the Cape Peninsula's western side begins in the city centre at Green Point, near the Waterfront, and continues around to Cape Point via Sea Point, Camps Bay, Llandudno and Hout Bay. South of Hout Bay, the western Peninsula is wilder than the eastern and its lonely beaches such as Noordehoek—reckoned by many to be Cape Town's loveliest—are worth making a special trip for.

Green Point

Green Point, the area between Signal Hill and the Waterfront, is best known for its old lighthouse (1824) and sports stadium (on Main Road). The stadium is the end point of the **Coon Carnival New Year Parade**, a procession of floats accompanied by a drunken street party (*see* 'Festivals'). Green Point is mainly passed over by people on their way to the beaches of the Western Peninsula. At night, it is a red-light district.

Green Point has three museums. The **Cape Medical Museum** (*open Mon–Fri 9–4, adm free*), inside the New Somerset Hospital, on the corner of Beach and Portswood, is the best of the three. Cape Town's doctors have long been one of South Africa's most popular unofficial exports to the rest of the world, and the displays of medical innovation in the museum help you to see why. Most interesting of all, though, is the story of Dr James Barrie, a diminutive and charismatic Scot who came to the Cape in the early 1800s (and performed the colony's first Caesarean operation in 1818). A confidant of the then Cape Governor, Lord Charles Somerset, the time they spent together and the doctor's effeminate figure led to rumours of a homosexual affair. After the doctor's death it was discovered that Dr Barrie was, in fact, a woman, who had disguised herself through medical school in Edinburgh and through her years in the male-dominated Cape Colony.

Sea Point

The next suburb along, Sea Point, is a neighbourhood somewhat distinct from the rest of Cape Town. Its stretch of Main Road is one of the liveliest in the city, with flagrant displays of glamour from the young suburbanites who live in the houses on the hill above Main Road, and much pleasure-seeking from everybody else. The cafés, bars, clubs and restaurants pulsate with life, especially through the summer (*see* 'Nightlife' and 'Eating Out'). There are few places in Cape Town as good as Sea Point's Main Road for people-watching. However, Sea Point's rocky beach front has been heavily built up, and is unpleasant for swimming.

Clifton, however, the neighbouring suburb, has a fine beach packed with young narcissists strutting their magnificent bodies up and down the sand. This is entertaining for a while, but not for long; there is little humour in the place, and the atmosphere is rather forced.

Camps Bay

The beach at Camps Bay is wider, and there is a healthier mix of the beautiful people and others just there to swim. You can watch the surfers out in the bay, and there is a good selection of cafés and restaurants with outdoor terraces fronting the beach. These are mostly chain pizza and burger joints, but the location gives them atmosphere. Camps Bay also has a couple of fine restaurants set back from the beach front, and a good youth hostel set in a Victorian house (*see* 'Eating Out' and 'Where to Stay'). Behind the beach the Cape Peninsula mountains rise in twelve peaks known as the Twelve Apostles. As the beach faces west, Camps Bay is one of the favoured spots for 'sundowners', a Cape Town tradition of taking a bottle (or bottles) of something and watching the sun set over the ocean. Look out for dassies (rock hyraxes) among the rocks on either side of the bay.

Llandudno is separated from Camps Bay by 15km of mountain road with the standard spectacular Peninsula views. The town itself is far downhill from the Main Road, clustered around a small bay. Picturesque from a distance (though most of the buildings are modern beach-mansions), and a good surfing spot, Llandudno is of little interest as a town. Better to take the road on the left as you turn off the main road to Llandudno, signposted to **Sandy Bay**. This winds for about a kilometre among houses and ends at a little car park. From here, a leisurely 2km stroll through fynbos and tunnels of wind-blown trees leads to Sandy Bay. Do not be shocked if a naked man or woman comes walking up the path towards you: Sandy Bay is one of South Africa's few legal nudist beaches. For all that, about half the people wear swimming costumes, and there is no tension between those that wear and those that don't. Sandy Bay itself is entirely undeveloped, a lovely place to spend an afternoon.

Hout Bay

From Llandudno another drive along the precipitous cliffs leads to Hout Bay. 'Hout' means wood in Dutch; the early sailors and colonists felled timber here, and the slopes around the town are still densely forested.

Hout Bay is a worthy destination in itself. It has a working fishing fleet, and freshly caught fish can be bought from the little harbour. On Main Road is an old Dutch homestead, **Kronendal** (1800), now a museum and restaurant (*see* 'Eating Out'). Unfortunately the harbour has been developed for tourism, but not enough to take the soul out of the place. Mariner's Wharf is a kind of mall full of curio shops, with a good but expensive seafood restaurant (*see* 'Eating Out'). It is pleasant simply to wander around the small harbour, or walk behind it, to Andrews Road, and the **Hout Bay Museum** (*open Tues–Sat 10–12.30 and 2–4.30*), which has some good exhibits of the area's early *strandloper* (beachcomber) cultures, settlement sites of which have been found in caves near Hout Bay, the Cape of Good Hope Nature Reserve, and round the Peninsula at Fish Hoek. Fishing and fishermen, naturally, takes up most of the rest of museum.

Just outside Hout Bay is the **World of Birds**, ✆ (021) 790 2730 (*open daily 8.30–6*). It sounds kitsch (and it certainly is a major tourist draw) but the bird park is actually fascinating. Giant aviaries house hundreds of South African birds living naturally in landscaped habitats. An hour in the World of Birds is as informative as a day spent looking at a bird book (though only 450 of the thousand-odd South African species are represented; not all the country's birds can survive in the Cape climate).

From here yet another spectacular cliff-side drive leads on round the Peninsula. Officially known as **Chapman's Peak Drive**, this 10km of cliff-sides and look-out points is a riot of wild flowers in spring. But whatever the season, the drive is always breathtaking: wide views of the ocean and sudden, sharp bends.

Noordehoek lies at the end of Chapman's Peak Drive. Many Capetonians say this long, long beach is the most beautiful on the Peninsula. It stretches for over 10km of white sand, with seldom more than a few people dotting its wide expanse. The water is cold, and the distance from Cape Town far (about 40km), which helps to keep the crowds away. Neither is there any beach-front town. In the mornings and evenings, riders bring their horses down for exercise on the packed sand at the water's edge. Visitors can rent horses from a nearby stable (*see* 'Activities').

Kommetjie and **Scarborough** are the two small resort villages between Noordehoek and Cape Point. Both are known surfing spots, with a cluster of holiday houses clinging round the small beach. At Scarborough watch out for 'dumper' waves at the north end of the beach. These are waves in a cross-current that dump you on the sea-floor rather than taking you to the shore. From Scarborough, the road winds up between wind-battered farms, along the boundary of the Cape of Good Hope Nature Reserve, until it meets the M5 and drops down to Simon's Town on the east side.

The Peninsula's Central Spine

Much of the Peninsula's central mountain chain is inaccessible by road. However, the **Old Cape Road** does traverse part of it, through **Silvermine Forest Nature Reserve**, ✆ (021) 753 040, which begins south of Tokai and runs over the central mountains above Muizenberg and Kalk Bay. The road goes through the reserve and comes out at Noordehoek. There is an official parking area from where you can walk one of the many trails, easy or strenuous, to viewpoints over Hout Bay, False Bay, Cape Town and Constantia. To get there, take the M3 highway out of Cape Town towards Muizenberg, take the Muizenberg exit, but turn right at the Stop sign, instead of left into Muizenberg. At the next junction, turn left up a steeply climbing road, which takes you to Silvermine. If you have no car, take the train to Kalk Bay and enter via the steep hillside walk called **Jacob's Ladder** (ask for directions at the station).

Alternatively, you can take a guided three-day hike along the whole chain from Table Mountain to Cape Point (*see* 'Activities').

False Bay

Though not a part of Cape Town proper, the waters of False Bay lap the coastline of the eastern Peninsula, the Cape Flats and the southern Hottentots' Holland Mountains. Known for whale sightings in early summer (November and December), False Bay's beaches are less developed than many others in the Cape Town area. To get there, take the M5 (car or taxi) to Muizenberg, but at the traffic circle before Muizenberg, turn left to **Sunrise Beach**. This was designated a 'coloured' beach under apartheid, and this, coupled with its proximity to the townships of Mitchell's Plain and Khayelitsha, has kept it relatively free from crowds, though locals and shrimp fishermen use it regularly. False Bay, because of its warm current, can be prone to tides of jellyfish called **bluebottles**, usually after high winds (and Sunrise Beach can be *very* windy). These have a very painful sting. Before going in the water, check the tide-line. If a lot of bluebottles have been washed up, take care in the surf. If you see none, then swim with impunity. Fishermen net from the shore on the Muizenberg end of Sunrise Beach and, if you go at about two, you should catch them trawling in—a good time to buy fresh fish.

Following the R310 (Baden Powell Road) around the beach eventually takes one past Strandfontein (a small resort on an extension of Sunrise Beach, with a reptile park and pavilion) to a junction with the N2 highway. Continue through two sets of traffic lights and turn right to Gordon's Bay, a holiday village made up simply of cottages and a beach. Gordon's Bay and Rooi Els (an even smaller village just south) are considered among the best swimming-spots in the Cape. This road follows the coastal feet of the Hottentots' Holland Mountains, all the way around to Cape Hangklip, their southern extension and the eastern-most point of False Bay.

Table Bay

Much of the bay is taken up by the docks, but the northern side is worth visiting. You get there via the R27 through the suburb of **Milnerton**. The main street is quite lively with junk shops and family-run stores, but that's about the extent of it. The next suburbs are Table View and Blauberg. These are uninteresting, but the long cold-water beach that runs in front of them, **Blaubergstrand**, is truly lovely, looking across at Table Mountain on the other side of the bay: a good spot for a photograph, and the one used for most postcards of Table Mountain seen from afar. The annual South African surfing championships are held here in the summer.

Robben Island, the infamous prison where three centuries of African political prisoners were held—from the first Khoi chiefs to fall foul of the Dutch, to the Xhosa kings that fought the British (*see* **Eastern Cape**, 'History') and Nelson Mandela—lies about 30km out in the bay. The prison is now unused and has been opened to visitors. Boats charter out to it from the Victoria and Alfred Dock at the Waterfront (*see* p.136). It is rumoured that plans are afoot to develop Robben Island for tourists, but as yet there is no confirmation. The island's austere, arid face seems ill-suited for such frivolity. The boat trips to Robben Island are good for seeing Cape fur seals and large seabirds (skua and albatross), but the island is nonetheless very bleak, and carries an unmistakable aura of despair.

Festivals

Cape Town is, to some extent, in a permanent state of festivity. The biggest orga-nized festival is the **Coon Carnival New Year Parade**, in the first week of January. This mainly 'coloured' celebration involves a procession of floats which starts in what used to be District Six and proceeds down Main Road to Green Point, where they enter the stadium to be judged.

The Carnival is controversial; the word 'coon' is provocative, and whites have tradi-tionally ignored it either for this reason or from a desire to distance themselves from 'coloured' culture, depending on their political orientation. Ironically, the word 'coon' was adopted by the 'coloureds' themselves as a piece of self-mockery and a subtle jibe at white South Africa. The result is an event that tends to embarrass white Capetonians, but provides entertainment for those who participate in the Carnival.

Shopping

Crafts, particularly jewellery, clothing and shoes, are something of an institution in Cape Town. The range is wide but usually reflects a blend of African and European styles. The two permanent **craft markets** in Greenmarket Square (and St George's Mall) and the Waterfront sell some of the best, although prices are jacked up for tourists. Rondebosch Library hosts a covered market (on St Andrews Road) on Wednesdays, Fridays and Saturdays. There are monthly craft markets in Constantia and Hout Bay, usually advertised in the back pages of the *Cape Argus*. Prices here are lower, but the quality is as good. A word of warning; if buying a pair of the soft leather boots or shoes that are a speciality of these markets, stick to ones with solid soles; the others are often only glued together and tend to split. More unusual are the Herb Market, on St Andrews Road, Rondebosch, every Thursday, and the Botanical Society Market at Kirstenbosch, Constantia, which sells plants and flowers on the second Saturday of every month.

For **African crafts**—jewellery, wall hangings, wire cars and bicycles, and cloths— the craft shop in the National Gallery sells some of the best in the country. Also try the **Operation Hunger Showroom,** on Maynard Road in Wynberg. Alternatively, you can go out to Khayelitsha Township's **African Craft Market**, where prices are lower and you are sure of getting the real thing. They can arrange safe transport and escorts, ✆ 542 963 or ✆ 361 5246. More upmarket, and selling the same stuff at higher prices, is the **Red Shed** on the Waterfront, Victoria Wharf.

Although **antiques** may be difficult to transport home, they are worth looking for. Cape Town's 300-year history and colonial culture brought a lot of valuable objects into the country, both indigenous and imported. The weekend open-air antique stalls on Church Street are worth a look, as are the smarter shops on Long Street. Long Street's **bookshops** are well known for selling first editions cheaper than in the West, and South Africa has many excellent private libraries to stock such shops.

Activities

The mountain and the ocean are irresistible forces in Cape Town, and the city has a strongly outdoor culture, whether it's paddling on a beach, strolling in a forest, or doing the hardcore stuff like rock-climbing, surfing, paragliding, kloofing, diving with sharks, abseiling or scuba diving.

Action and Adventure Activities

boat trips, sailing and sea kayaking

Trips from Hout Bay to Duiker Island, a smelly but interesting Cape fur seal colony, give non-anglers the chance to see the Peninsula coast from the sea. **Drumbeat Charters,** ✆ 438 7208/✆ 790 4859, charge under R20 for an hour. Also *see* p.136. Sailing courses and boat charter can be arranged through **Le Tigre Catamarans** on the Waterfront, ✆ 419 7746. Learn to sea kayak, or take a guided trip—either a day's paddle or a longer expedition along the Peninsula or up the West Coast—with **Real Cape Adventures,** ✆ 706 5611.

climbing and abseiling

This is an institution on Table Mountain and the Lion's Head. Ring **Abseil Africa,** ✆ 254 332.

diving and snorkelling

For scuba courses and guided wreck and reef dives ring **Table Bay Divers,** ✆ 419 8822, **Ocean Divers,** ✆ 438 9317, or **Aqua Vision,** ✆ 929 819. To dive, in cages, down among the great whites of False Bay (scary, but it's worth it), ring **White Shark Ecoventures,** ✆ 419 8205. **African Adrenaline,** ✆ 254 332, can arrange for you to **snorkel** with seals.

kloofing, mountain biking, sky diving, bungee-jumping

African Adrenaline, ✆ 254 332, can organize all of the above. Kloofing is the completely mad art of following a mountain watercourse—which means leaping off waterfalls and letting the rapids take you. Not for those with vertigo. Day trips are also organized by **Dream Days,** ✆ 964 4553, and **Footprints,** ✆ 461 1999.

paragliding

There are a number of schools offering courses and taster days to see if you like it before committing yourself to a full-on course. Try **Dream Days,** ✆ 964 553, **African Adrenaline,** ✆ 254 332, or **Tandem Paragliding,** ✆ 231 646.

riding

Experienced riders can rent horses for guided exploratory one-day rides into the Peninsula Mountains and along the beaches (including Noordehoek) from John Foster at **Horse Trail Safaris,** ✆ 734 396. Beginners should try the **Downs Riding Centre,** ✆ 621 414.

On Sundays from May to October there is a drag-hunt based in Cape Town with whom you can ride to hounds in the nearby countryside after a pre-laid scent (there is no live quarry). Call the secretary, ✆ 963 968, about hiring a horse for the day.

sand boarding

Going very, very fast down the dunes—you don't get hurt when you fall though, just a mouthful of sand. Ring **Downhill Adventures,** ✆ 251 056 or ✆ 254 332.

sea angling

The Cape Peninsula, like most of South Africa's coastline, offers excellent fishing in largely unpolluted waters which, because of the two ocean currents, are heavy with cold- and warm-water species. Tackle can be hired from most tackle shops in the Peninsula towns. No permit is required for fish or shellfish, and you can cut mussels from the rocks of many beaches at low tide. Oysters, crayfish and abalone can also be taken, but are subject to strict catch quotas (CapTour supplies a leaflet with full details). Everywhere on the coast except Table Bay Harbour is open for fishing.

Big-game fish abound in the further waters. Marlin (black and blue), three species of tuna, swordfish, doredo and other monster species can be sought via several big-game charter companies: **Big Game Fishing Safaris,** ✆ 643 837, **Wild Thing,** ✆ 438 8270, **Hout Bay Boat Yard,** ✆ 790 3619; **Bluefin Charters,** ✆ 831 756, **African Fishing Safaris,** ✆ 721 272, **Condor Charters,** ✆ 470 741, and **Neptune,** ✆ 782 3889. **Sunfish Safaris,** ✆ (083) 261 7542, can also take you diving for crayfish.

surfing and wind surfing

Unless you have several months to spare there is not much point in trying to learn to surf—it's a bit like trying to learn a musical instrument in an afternoon. Body-surfing, though, is great fun and can be done by beginners (though you should always stay close to those who know where rocks and currents are). Camps Bay, Llandudno and Muizenberg are good spots. Call CapTour, ✆ 418 5214/5, for details of hire companies for both body surf-boards and wind-surfers, as companies tend to come and go by the season.Cape Town also has a surf school, with guided trips for the experienced. Ring **Surfari**, ✆ 510 2026.

Other Activities

beaches

You can escape the city's summer heat by plunging into sparkling ocean within half an hour of any point in town. Bear in mind that beaches on the east side of the Peninsula have warm water, while beaches on the west side are cold. The best of those close to the city are **Camps Bay**, which is busy and friendly, with cold water, white sand and safe swimming, and **Sunrise Beach**, on False Bay, between Plumstead and Muizenberg, which is often all but deserted. White sand, warm water, no bad currents, but look out for bluebottle jellyfish. On the eastern Peninsula **Boulders** beach, at Simon's Town, is a tiny warm-water cove sheltered by huge rocks and inhabited by jackass penguins that you can swim next to. **Noordehoek** beach, in the western Peninsula, is long, lonely and fabulously beautiful, with white sand and water so cold you gasp.

bird-watching

Table Mountain and the Peninsula reserves offer birding as good as any up-country, with over 300 species recorded. The best spots are Kirstenbosch, Rondevlei Reserve (a small wetland reserve on the Cape Flats near the township of Mitchell's Plain), Rietvlei reserve, on the coast north of Milnerton and outside Cape Town's official limits (an important breeding place for wildfowl and seabirds), the Liesbeeck River in Observatory (sadly marred by the roar of traffic), and the Cape of Good Hope Nature Reserve. Call the **Cape Bird Club**, ✆ 686 6393, for a guide.

languages

If you'd rather stay in and learn Afrikaans, Xhosa or Zulu, call ✆ 439 3101.

township tours

To organize a tour into the townships, contact Mike Sombre, ✆ 237 3850.

walking

Table Mountain, Devil's Peak and the State Forests: For those who would rather not hike up Table Mountain on their own, **John Macdonnel**, ✆ 452 503, or Peter of **Peter's Walks**, ✆ 438 7206, will collect you, guide you along the strenuous first-recorded route up to the summit, and bring you down again by cable car. Alternatively, and for free, join a party of walkers. There are various hiking and walking clubs in Cape Town. The **Mountain Club**, ✆ 453 412, organizes easy or killer excursions into the mountains around Constantia and Kirstenbosch Gardens.

In the Peninsula: The hiker can roam at will in the Cape of Good Hope Nature Reserve, and has a good chance of seeing large game, usually red hartebeest, Cape

Mountain zebra and bontebok. Guided day-walks in Silvermine Nature Reserve and Table Mountain Reserve (over the Twelve Apostles) are offered by **Wanderlust Walks**, ✆ 438 1948. Or do it yourself using the CapTour map of the Table Mountain Reserve, or the map of Silvermine's trails, available from the reserve office.

Hout Bay: There is some beautiful walking in Hout Bay, both strenuous and easy. The Hout Bay Publicity Association, in the Trading Post on Main Road, ✆ 790 4053, has a map of the trails. Breeding leopard have been reported near here. You won't see them, but it's nice to know they're around.

A hard, three-day hiking trail from Table Mountain to Cape Point is open through the **National Hiking Way Board**, 7th Floor, Foretrust Building, Hammerschlag Way, Foreshore, ✆ 402 3093.

Cape Town ✆ *(021–)*   ***Where to Stay***

City Centre

luxury

The **Mount Nelson Hotel**, on De Waal Drive, just opposite Government Avenue, ✆ 231 000, is British colonial Africa flaunted unashamed. From the high wrought-iron gates, the drive leads through landscaped parkland to the handsome classical pile that is the hotel. Famous for its formality, luxurious suites and cream teas (though not its restaurant), there is really nowhere else to stay in Cape Town, if you can afford it. White-liveried waiters and footmen will attempt to fulfil your every whim. However, in healthy competition for both age and status, the **President**, on the beach front at Sea Point, ✆ 434 0809, is another handsome relic from colonial days, with its renowned restaurant, Finch's.

The other five-star hotels in the town centre are rather dull modern chain hotels, including no less than three of Sol Kerzner's Southern Sun chain. They are: the **Capetonian Protea**, on Heerengracht, ✆ 211 150, **Cape Sun**, on the corner of Strand Street and St George's Mall, ✆ 238 844, the **De Waal Sun**, on De Waal Drive, ✆ 451 311, and **Newlands Sun**, on Main Road, Newlands, ✆ 611 105.

expensive

St George's, in St George's Mall, ✆ 419 7010, is big, modern and rather dull. More interesting is the **Tulbagh Hotel**, ✆ 215 140, in an early 19th-century town house in Tulbagh Square, in the upper city centre. Very quiet, even though it's at the heart of things. In Greenmarket Square, one of Cape Town's most atmospheric quarters, is the **Inn on the Square**, ✆ 232 040. You pay more for the location than for the quality of the rooms, which are clean, neat and comfortable, but not especially charming. However, you can sit on the terrace and sip coffee while the busy square goes about its business. The **Metropole**, on Long Street, ✆ 236 363, is comfortingly small and handy for second-hand bookshops. It has a family-run feel, the service is attentive and the rooms very comfortable. The **Underberg Guest House**, 6 Tamboerskloof Road, ✆ 262 262, in Tamboerskloof, above gardens with lovely views out over the bay, is only moderately expensive.

There is little moderately priced accommodation in Cape Town's centre. In Green Point's Norman Road, the Norman Guest House, ✆ 434 7055, is convenient for the Waterfront. B&B is offered at **7 Hof Street**, ✆ 244 984, a family-run house in the Gardens neighbourhood. Very straightforward and unpretentious, the nicely proportioned rooms are comfortably furnished. The **Room with a View**, 51 Upper Cambridge St, ✆ 472 820, is similar. If you don't mind self-catering, then the **Waterkant Cottages**, on Waterkant Street, ✆ 418 6081, offer central accommodation in converted 18th-century cottages. Back up in the Gardens is **Saasveld Lodge**, 73 Kloof Street, ✆ 246 169.

For low-budget accommodation in central Cape Town, you are spoilt for choice. Most places are youth-hostelish (sharing rooms or dormitories), but some offer very cheap single and double rooms as well. Most central is the **Amblers Backpackers**, 57 Strand Street, ✆ 242 292, but the heaviest concentration of lodges is on Long Street. **Long Street Backpackers**, ✆ 230 615, is the oldest, though some travellers have reported a slip in standards here. More popular alternatives are **Cat & Moose**, at no.305, ✆ 237 638, **Travellers Inn**, at no.208, ✆ 249 272, the **Overseas Visitors Club**, at no.230, ✆ 239 832, **One World**, at no. 309, ✆ 230 777, and the **Lion's Den**, at no.255, ✆ 239 003.

If you want something quieter, still within walking distance of the city centre, try the lodges in the Gardens neighbourhood, uphill from Long Street. The **Backpackers**, 15 Faure Street, ✆ 235 485, is a current leader. **Shanti Lodge**, 11 Hof Street, ✆ 238 721, offers dorm accommodation only, with a free pick-up from the city centre. On New Church Street, at the mountain end of Buitengracht Street, is the **Zebra Crossing**, ✆ 221 265, offering dorms, singles or doubles, bedding and 24-hour check-in.

Southern Suburbs

The Cellars, on Hohenhort Avenue, Constantia, ✆ 794 2137, though ungraded, qualifies as a luxury hotel. A 19th-century homestead with sumptuously furnished suites, it is not as interesting as the Constantia homestead hotels in the cheaper 'expensive' range (*see* below). **La Provence**, ✆ 762 8124, is a handsome Victorian place on the Constantia/Kirstenbosch border.

By far the best of the expensive range is the **Vineyard Hotel**, on Main Street, Newlands, ✆ 683 3044. Built at the end of the 18th century, and famous for being where Lady Anne Barnard stayed, it is decorated in early Cape style, with stinkwood and yellowwood furniture, crystal and silver. Similar in style is the **Alphen**, in Constantia, ✆ 794 5011. Another 18th-century Cape Dutch homestead, set under tall oaks and with its own vineyards, the Alphen is opulent, quiet and beautifully furnished. Its superb restaurant specializes in Cape cuisine.

Stanmar B&B, 48 Williams Street in Observatory, ✆ 448 2014, offers clean comfort. **Rodenburg**, 8 Myrtle Road, Rondebosch, ✆ 689 4852, a large, handsome turn-of-the-century house, offers B&B (or meals by request) in spacious, comfortable rooms. The place is family-run, and guests can relax in the huge living-room (which has a very large record collection) and enjoy the garden.

Sea Point also has a number of B&Bs and guest houses. Recommended are: **El Hann Guest House**, 5 Scholtz Road, ✆ 434 0968, **London Lodge**, 126 Main Road, ✆ 434 3040, **The Olive Branch**, 9 Richmond Road, ✆ 434 9198, and **Verona Lodge**, 11 Richmond Road, ✆ 434 9477.

If none of these are available, try **Rous House B&B**, ✆ 797 7211, out in Kenilworth, which has the bonus of a pool, or **Koornhoop Manor**, ✆ 448 0585.

Observatory has several budget places. **Rolling Stones Youth Hostel** is on the upper floor of one of the colonial arcades on Lower Main Road, opposite Pancho's Mexican Restaurant, ✆ 474 834. The front rooms have verandahs. Dormitories and double rooms at R20 per person per night. Residents get 15 per cent off meals at Pancho's, and at Moghul's Indian restaurant, also on Lower Main Road. The **Green Elephant**, 57 Milton Road, ✆ 448 6359, has become very popular lately. Newer on the Observatory scene are these backpacker lodges: **Crazy-S-Cape**, 4 Lynton Road, ✆ 479 393, and **Riverview Lodge**, on Anson Road, ✆ 479 056.

At Green Point, the **Hip-Hop Traveller's Stop**, ✆ 439 2104, can be found at 11 Vesperdene Road. The Waterfront is close by, you can check in 24 hours a day and they will arrange a pick-up from the bus and train station in town. An extra attraction is a large swimming pool.

As on Long Street and in Observatory, Green Point and Sea Point have both seen a recent rise in the number of backpackers' lodges: **The Bunker**, 15 Graham Road, Sea Point, ✆ 434 0549, the **TransAtlantic**, on the corner of King and Regent Roads, Sea Point, ✆ 439 6281, **St John's Waterfront Lodge**, 4 & 6 Braeside Road, Green Point, ✆ 439 1404, the **Sunflower Stop**, 179 Main Road, Green Point, ✆ 434 6535, **El Hana Guest House**, 5 Scholtz Road, Sea Point, ✆ 434 0968, **Veronda Lodge**, 11 Richmond Road, Sea Point, ✆ 434 9477. **Globe Trotters**, 17 Queen's Road, ✆ 434 1539, is situated where Sea Point merges with Clifton beach front.

Peninsula

On the M42 road between Kirstenbosch and Hout Bay, **Hout Bay Manor**, ✆ 790 5960, is a National Monument, another gracious white homestead set under large oaks, facing a fountain-court and over-shadowed by Chapman's Peak. Surprisingly priced on the moderate end of the expensive range, it is a good place from which to explore the Peninsula. In Simon's Town, the self-catering suites in the Victorian set-piece **British Hotel**, 90 St George's Road, ✆ 790 4930, sneak into the bottom end of this category, as does the **Lord Nelson Inn**, ✆ 786 1386, on the same road.

moderate

If you have a car, why not stay in the Peninsula? On the east side, **Boulders Beach Guest House**, ✆ 786 1758, is convenient for Simon's Town and the penguin colony. At Kalk Bay, there is the **Chartfield Guest House**, ✆ 788 3793. In Hout Bay, on the west side, there is an abundance of good, moderate self-catering accommodation. Try **Silwerberg**, ✆ 790 6926, **Black Rock Cottages**, ✆ 790 5985, **Kutali Mountain Lodge**, ✆ 790 0738 or **Red Mountain Cabins**, ✆ 790 4809.

Further down the west side of the Peninsula, at Noordehoek Beach, are the self-catering **Noordehoek Cottages**, ✆ 789 2811. For B&B try **Montrose Cottage**, on Chapman's Peak Drive, ✆ 785 3730, and **Goose Green Lodge**, ✆ 789 2933.

In the northern suburbs, at Blauberg, which has the best view of Table Mountain anywhere in the area, try **Jade Castle B&B**, ✆ 561 139. Up the road in Milnerton is **Le Rendezvous**, ✆ 551 7188.

cheap

If you fancy staying on the Peninsula, try the **Backstop**, a backpackers' at 16 Melrose Road, ✆ 788 4184, in Muizenberg, **Boulder's Beach Backpackers**, ✆ 786 1758, near Simon's Town (handy for the penguins and they can organise watersports), or the **Kalk Bay Backpackers**, ✆ 788 2943.

In Scarborough, way down the Peninsula by the Cape Point Nature Reserve, is **Scarborough Backpackers**, ✆ 780 1154.

On the other side of the Pensinsula, hang out with the beautiful people at Camps Bay, staying at **Anamasz Lodge**, 73 Camp's Bay Drive, ✆ 438 9294.

The Cape View Hostel, in Bloubergstrand on Table Bay, ✆ 562 127, is some way from Cape Town, but has a superb view out over the bay. The hostel runs a free shuttle service from the city centre, and can arrange water-skiing.

Cape Town ✆ (021–)   **Eating Out**

Cape Town and the Winelands evolved a distinct cuisine through the 18th century, mixing French, Dutch and Malay cooking. Game, lamb and fish feature strongly. Spicy, but not overly hot, Cape cuisine uses fruits and curries to create original versions of European food. Some dishes are very simple, like *bobotie* (a kind of curried moussaka). More elaborate are spiced game dishes, using guinea fowl and venison. For more about Cape cuisine *see* p.109–12.

City Centre

expensive

If you like Cape food (or want to try it), head straight for the **Kaapse Tafel**, 90 Victoria Street, ✆ 231 651. For *sausaties*, *bobotie* and other Cape delights you could do no better.

The **Aubergine**, Barnett St, Gardens, ✆ 454 909, in an elegant early 19th-century building, serves continental dishes among a wider menu. Try the springbok in cocoa butter. If you like Greek food, then **Greek Boyz**, in Kloof Street, ✆ 242 282, is probably the best in town. Prices are almost in the moderate category. **Rozenhof**, on Kloof St in the Gardens area, ✆ 424 1968, is a formal place, serving a mixture of Cape, French and house dishes. The service is excellent, and the food very tasty, but the place does feel a bit impersonal.

The Mussel Cracker, in the Victoria and Alfred Basin on the Waterfront, ✆ 419 4300, is a well-known and lively seafood restaurant. Apart from traditional shellfish and line-fish (all fresh that day), there are some good Portuguese seafood dishes. Ask for the specials or go for the excellent buffet.

Le Med, in Camp's Bay, ✆ 438 7193/2320, is a deceptively casual place. Set under tall trees in The Glen (just behind the beach front), this place serves extremely good Mediterranean dishes. It is also a great place to people-watch.

moderate

Biesmiellah, on Wale St in the Bo-Kaap, ✆ 423 0850, occupies two small front rooms of a cottage dating from the early 1800s. The food is good value, beautifully prepared, very hot and eaten with fingers. No alcohol is allowed.

Crammed into a small, very beautiful 18th-century house in one of the Gardens' most handsome squares, **Maria's**, on Barnett Street, ✆ 465 2096, is very informal and serves some of the best Greek food on offer anywhere—try the salad. Very popular, so booking is advisable.

Also in the Gardens is **African Flame**, 12 Mill Street, ✆ 465 5846. Good ethnic African dishes abound. Up the mountain a little, in Tamboerskloof, try **Fields**, ✆ 423 9587, a health food restaurant open for lunch only—handy if you've just come off the cable car.

Downtown, Long Street has a great variety of good restaurants. **Christo's**, ✆ 249 250, with a beautiful Art Nouveau front and a simple, spacious interior, serves a mixture of good pasta and fish dishes. Also good for pasta is **Serendipity**, ✆ 248 796, or try **Mama Africa**, serving everything from Cape cuisine to Ethiopian food.

Nino's, on Greenmarket Square, ✆ 24 766, serves great pizza and pasta, but can get crowded. If so try **De Roode Kat,** at 10 Spin Street, which offers good pub food.

cheap

Sooz Baguette Bar, on Long Street, is hard to beat if you want cheap good food fast. For inexpensive African cuisinne, try **Ethio Africa**, 29 Jamiston Road.

If you don't mind a loud TV, catch some of the cheap, excellent seafood at the **Vasco de Gama Tavern**, 3 Alfred Street. This is run by Mozambiquan Portuguese, *for* Mozambiquan Portuguese. No pretension, just fantastic food.

Mykonos Souvlaki ✆ 439 2106, on Main Road, Sea Point, serves very good value Greek and Lebanese food. The falafels are really good. Cheerful, crowded and cheap. On the same road is **Backpacker Bob's**, serving hearty meat and two veg. Take your own wine. It can get loud later in the evening.

Southern Suburbs

expensive

Parks, on Constantia Road, Wynberg, ✆ 797 8202, is an unpretentious restaurant with a simply furnished interior that has quite a following in the Cape for the excellence of its food. Traditional Cape, seafood and French dishes are served in an informal atmosphere. Ask about the day's specials. Alphen, Buitenverwachting and the Jonkershuis are three showpiece restaurants in 18th-century manors on old Constantia estates. All are period furnished, formal and very beautiful.

Alphen, on the M42 between Kirstenbosch and Hout Bay, ✆ 794 5011, is set in forest; **Buitenverwachting**, signposted from the M5, ✆ 794 3522, is the homestead next to Klein Constantia; **Jonkershuis**, also signposted from the M5, ✆ 794 6255, is on the Groot Constantia estate.

moderate and cheap

The Palace, on Albert Road, Woodstock, ✆ 479 540, serves an original menu of Cape Malay dishes in cheerful surroundings. The cooking is of the highest quality, and the restaurant is justifiably popular. Booking is advised.

Ever good for value, Observatory's Lower Main Road offers the **Obz Café**—really good wines and try the springbok prosciutto, or the **Africa Café**, at no.213, ✆ 479 553, to my mind Cape Town's best African cuisine, or **Pancho's**, ✆ 74 854, a Mexican restaurant with a really beautiful late 19th-century, two-floor interior. Try to get a table upstairs in the covered balcony. The food isn't terrific, but the helpings are big and the prices very reasonable.

Ramola's, 13 Wolfe Street, ✆ 797 0019, in the area of Wynberg known as 'Little Chelsea', is perhaps Cape Town's finest Indian restaurant. Mostly open for lunches, the restaurant serves dinner on varying nights of the week—check by phone. The kitchen is open, so you watch the food being prepared. The dining room is simple but pleasant. Incredibly good value.

Eastern Peninsula

expensive

The Brass Bell, in Kalk Bay, ✆ 788 5455, has a great seafood restaurant overlooking the ocean. At the moderate end of expensive, their seafood platter is a challenge even to those with huge appetites. Informal and relaxed, with the ocean breaking on a sea wall about 50m from the windows.

moderate

The Harbourside, in Kalk Bay, does superb seafood at reasonable prices. **Restaurant Don Pepe**, on Main Road, Muizenberg, ✆ 888 459, serves really good Portuguese food. Take your own wine.

Black Marlin, on Main Road, Simon's Town, ✆ 786 1621, serves set menus, with an emphasis on seafood fresh that day, in the front room of a Victorian house. Very friendly. Booking is advised.

Western Peninsula

moderate

The Mariner's Wharf Grill, in Hout Bay, ✆ 790 1100, does great seafood at the upper end of this price scale. Cheaper are **The Laughing Lobster** and **Snoekies**, both down in the harbour.

Bars and Cafés

The Purple Turtle, on Long Street, just round the corner from Greenmarket Square, is where the backpackers hang out. Funkier are **Lola's**, 238 Long Street, and **Shackleton's**, a sort of techno-cum-World-War-One-Air-Aces bar (you'll see what I mean) at the top of Long Street next to **McGawley's Pub**, and the **Kimberley Hotel**, on the corner of Buitenkant and Roeland Streets (it can get a little rough at night), which have colonial atmosphere and pool tables.

The **Perseverance Tavern**, on Buitenkant Street, is interesting for its history (*see* 'City Centre'), but is a little conservative, as is the **Stag's Head** on Hope Street (parallel to Buitenkant, one block north), where fights are not uncommon. **Doo-Me**, on Lower Long Street, near Waterkant, is a bar catering to a mixed crowd of young pleasure-seekers. The Waterfront has several bars: **Quay 4** is the busiest (usually packed to capacity), but you can sit outside by the dock. (*See* 'Live Music' for other bars here.)

In the Southern Suburbs, Observatory's Lower Main Road has several relaxed bars; **Ruby in the Dust** (also a live music venue) has a hippie and racially mixed crowd of musicians and students, as does its sister bar, **Ruby 2**, on Victoria Road, Salt River. **Heidelberg**, also on Lower Main Road, is more hearty—long benches and loud drinkers. **Barrister's**, on Main Street, Newlands, is quiet and civilized. On the eastern Peninsula, the **Brass Bell**, at Kalk Bay (also a restaurant and live music spot), is friendly, provides complimentary fish 'n' chips (usually Tues and Thurs about 7pm) in the bar and has the ocean outside the window. On the western side, **Barrister's** in Hout Bay (same owner as Barrister's bar in Newlands) has jazz on Sundays.

Cafés are harder to find. Despite Cape Town's sunny climate, there is a distinct lack of outdoor terraces on which to sit and have a coffee. However, lower **St George's Mall** has outdoor tables in the middle of the thoroughfare. Sit down at one and a waiter will find you. On the same street is **Square's**, which serves light meals as well, but is rather expensive. **Greenmarket Square** has several cafés.

The **Tea Garden**, by the aviary in the Company Gardens, is a peaceful break in the city's rush; sit inside or out. The **Mount Nelson Hotel**, on De Waal Drive, serves teas of splendour in the most gracious surroundings for surprisingly little. In the Southern Suburbs, Observatory has **Fiddlewoods** (also excellent for breakfasts and light meals), on Trill Road, just off Lower Main Road. The **Rhodes Memorial Tea Garden**, off the M5, is a shaded place of great beauty whose outside terrace over-looks the Cape Flats and False Bay. The cheesecake is fabulous. After a walk in the state forests above Constantia, wander into the **Constantia Nek Restaurant**, which operates as a café in the afternoons.

theatres

The **Nico Malan**, on Hertzog Boulevard, Foreshore, ✆ 217 695, has an opera house and two theatres and its own permanent opera, ballet and drama companies. The Cape Town Symphony Orchestra regularly give classical concerts here.

The **Baxter**, on Main Road, Rondebosch, ✆ 685 7880, is more avant-garde. Fringe theatres include **Café Mozart**, on Church Street, ✆ 243 774, with only 25 seats, the **Little Theatre**, in Orange Street in the Company Gardens, ✆ 242 340, the **Dock Road Theatre**, at the Waterfront, ✆ 419 5522, the **Herschel**, on Main Road in Claremont, the **Masque**, on Main Road, Muizenberg, ✆ 750 141, the **Eauvre the Top**, in Kalk Bay, ✆ 788 3746 (specializing in cabaret), and the **Theatre on the Bay**, in Camps Bay, ✆ 438 3300.

classical music

The **Cape Town Symphony Orchestra** plays at the **Nico Malan** and at the **City Hall**, ✆ 461 7084, on the Parade (usually Thurs and Sun, though the orchestra takes a holiday mid-Dec–mid-Jan, June and half of July).

The **Baxter** theatre, ✆ 438 9007, usually has concerts once a month. The **Old Town House** in Greenmarket Square, ✆ 246 367, has a chamber orchestra. Concerts are irregular, but worth finding out about for the setting alone.

cinema

The best for non-Hollywood movies are the **Labia**, ✆ 245 927, on Orange Street, and the **Baxter**, in Rondebosch (downstairs from the theatre).

Nightlife

live music

Try **Ruby in the Dust**, Lower Main Road, Observatory, or **Ruby 2**, on Victoria Road, Salt River, for township music, funk and original rock bands. Also in Observatory are the **River Club**, down by the Liesbeeck River—you need a taxi to get there—where indie and rock are the mainstays, and **The Planet**, on Station Road, featuring all sorts of acts. Also try the **Blue Rock** on Sea Point's Main Road.

The **Constantia Nek Restaurant**, opposite the entrance to Constantia Nek State Forest, has live folk bands on Saturday nights. The **Brass Bell**, in Kalk Bay (behind the station on Main Road), has blues and rock 'n' roll. In the Waterfront, **Bertie's Landing** has live bar bands playing American rock covers for yuppies to get drunk to, as do **Quay 4** and the **Hardrock**.

Good jazz is played at the **Blue Note**, College Road, Rylands, **Green Dolphin**, and **Rosie's**, at the Waterfront, at the **Fire Escape**, on Buitengracht Street, at **Jean's Jazz Gallery**, Lloyd Street, Bellville, the **Dizzy Jazz Café**, on The Drive, Camp's Bay, at **Mannenberg's**, at Church and Adderley Streets, downtown, and at **Tattler's**, in the Don Hotel, Main Road, Sea Point.

Cape Town's nightlife is notoriously fickle; clubs open and close almost by the month, and the scene is constantly changing. The clubs listed below were active at the time of publishing, but it is possible that some of the venues may have changed by the time you check them out. Ask in local bars for the latest lowdown.

D-Life, 31 Loop Street, **Funktion**, at the corner of Loop and Shortmarket, **Club Vibe**, 88 Shortmarket Street, **The Fringe**, on Canterbury Street, and **The Loft** and **The Magnet**, on Bree Street, all play funky dance grooves. More eclectic is **Quench**, on Long Street—you never quite know what you're going to get. The same applies to **The Shack**, on De Villiers Street, in District Six.

More House-oriented is **Springfields**, at Sport Pienaar Road, in Newlands, and the **G-Spot**, **Elusions** and **D-Lite**, downtown on Loop Street. If it's drum'n'bass and more underground stuff you want, try **The Gallery**, on Glynn Street, in the Gardens, uphill from Long Street.

Around Green Point there are also a bunch of clubs for the rich kids of Sea Point, Clifton and Camps Bay. Try **Rush** or **Angels**, on Somerset Road, or **Fat Boys**, 9 Alfred Road (though it's more drinking than dancing here).

If you want a **rave**, massive techno parties are put on by the organizations **Pharcyde**, ✆ 24 617, **Vortex**, ✆ 790 4736, **Madame Freak**, ✆ 788 5084, **DJ Syndicate**, ✆ 452 532, **Rise Up Parties**, ✆ (082) 570 8559, and **6th Circle**, ✆ (082) 577 7736. These might be in Cape Town, out in the Winelands or up in the deserts of the Karoo.

The Winelands

This is our Holland, the Hottentots' Holland

The Khoi chiefs of the Winelands to the first Dutch land speculators in the 1650s

On either side of the Hottentots' Holland Mountains, some 60km north and east of Cape Town, stretch the Cape Winelands, a region of vineyards and orchards sheltered by tall mountains and watered by cold, fast-flowing rivers. In the wide valleys stand white-washed 18th-century mansions, serene beneath groves of great oaks. The juxtaposition of cultivated charm and rugged mountain wilderness delights the eye, and is reminiscent of the idealized landscapes of old Europe in fairy-tale books.

The Winelands (or Boland, meaning 'upland'), are the home of Cape Dutch architecture (*see* pp.96–8), of well-proportioned manor houses whose distinctive roof-gables owe a little to the medieval Low Countries and a little to Indonesia (the Dutch having colonized the East before South Africa). Cape Dutch interiors are light and airy, fitted with bright yellowwood ceilings, rich, red stinkwood floors and simple, handsome furniture. Dating from the 1680s, the oldest Winelands towns, such as Tulbagh, Stellenbosch and Franschoek, are still largely Cape Dutch, while most others have sizeable sections of old buildings. Almost every wine estate has its big Cape Dutch homestead (and small workers' cottages in the same style), many of which are open to tourists.

History

Jan Van Riebeeck's first Cape-grown wine was poured in 1659, seven years after the Cape Colony's founding. Of all the European plants he coaxed from the sandy soil of the Company Gardens outside the colony's fort, the vine was the one that Van Riebeeck wanted most to thrive. 'Praise Be The Lord', he wrote in his diary the day the first bottle of wine was brought to him. Unwittingly, he had found the formula that would make the southwest Cape rich.

Then came the Huguenot settlers in 1688. Their early Cape vineyards pre-date even those near Bordeaux in France, and were laid out when elephant and lion still lived around Table Bay. In the mid 1700s Governor Simon Van Der Stel harnessed the Huguenots' knowledge to found Groot Constantia, the first Cape wine estate to export wine to Europe. He is thought to have used sweet Muscat grapes from Alexandria, known in South Africa as hanepoort (a name derived from the word '*hanekloot*', which is Dutch for 'testicles'). However, the pious burghers of the Cape quietly neutered the name, changing it to hanepoort, which doesn't mean anything, and by which name the grape is still known. Hanepoort grapes can be red or white, but these days are generally grown only for eating.

The Cape vineyards developed as settlers established estates out in the valleys of the present Winelands region during the early 19th century, importing the hardy red Cabernet Sauvignon grape which gradually began to dominate the Cape vineyards. This grape is still reckoned to be the best for withstanding the Cape's wet winters and searingly hot summers, producing a full-bodied, mellow claret said to need about seven years' ageing to reach its prime. Many purists still believe that the Bordeaux-like Cabernet Sauvignon is the Cape's 'true' wine, and certainly it is the most successful grape grown near the coast. But these days, it is the Pinotage, a uniquely South African hybrid of Pinot Noir and Cabernet Sauvignon grapes, that is regarded as the Cape's best wine.

Since the mid 1970s greater experimentation has taken place and South Africa now produces and exports over 100 varieties of wine. Recent successes include Merlot (a Bordeaux-like claret), Chardonnay (a white Burgundy grape, said to produce South Africa's finest dry white wine), Sauvignon Blanc (from which some Cape estates have produced vintages that have been compared to the best white wines of the Loire) and Chenin Blanc (a versatile white that can be fruity, sweet or dry depending on the estate).

Also popular in the Winelands are the German Gewurztraminer (a sweetish, spicy white wine), and Weisser Reisling (off-dry to sweet, depending on the age), the French Gamay (a successful Beaujolais now exported from the Cape to California and France) and the smoky, purple Shiraz wines. In the drier, arid regions bordering the Karoo, Muscadels and fortified wines have been winning international awards since the early 1980s.

At harvest time (February and March) the Winelands resemble an Old Master painting: a wide, green landscape peopled by armies of ragged labourers hand-picking the grapes under tall windbreaks of oak and pine, the ever-present Cape mountains looming behind.

Small estates still flourish, partly due to the availability of cheap labour. This means that the corporate producers (such as KWV, the Cape's largest exporter) and the Anglo-American owned estates (such as Boschendal, the largest estate in the Franschoek region) are in no danger of dominating and thus dulling the market. In fact, the opposite has been true: the smaller estates' continued success has encouraged the larger producers to follow their example, importing oak barrels from France and ageing their wine for even longer to improve the quality.

Buying Cape Wine

Until recently, South Africa's bottling system followed uniform guidelines denoting quality. A blue band on the neck meant a wine of origin (i.e. grapes from a single area), but whose grapes might be from different vineyards and years. A red band confirmed that the year printed on the bottle was the year of harvest. A green band meant that the wine contained at least 75 per cent of the grape variety printed on the label. A red, white and green band was an indication of high quality, and this was reflected in the price. The highest grading a bottle could have was a gold seal, which meant that the wine had been judged superior by a team of experts and could be very expensive. Although bottles are still sold with these bands on the neck, this system is being phased out, as the corporate producers, such as KWV, complained that the market was being prejudiced against good blended wines.

Price is no longer a sure gauge of quality; many of the smaller estates now sell their own wines, often bottled on the premises, and of good years, for as little as R10–15. The best way to find the wine you like is to ask around, or to explore one or more of the Wine Routes (outlined further on in the chapter) and taste the wines for yourself.

The Different Wineland Regions

The Winelands are divided into several separate regions. The lush, populated **Hottentots' Holland region**, close to Cape Town, includes the graceful Drakenstein Valley and the old towns of Stellenbosch, Franschoek, Paarl and Somerset West. The **Breede River Valley** is a drier, emptier region north of the Hottentots' Holland reached by the N1 highway or the

The Winelands

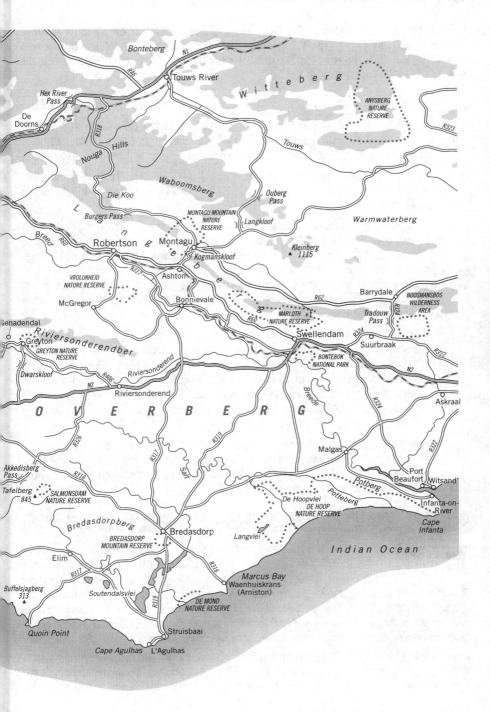

train via two spectacular passes, Du Toit's Kloof and Bain's Kloof. **Ceres** and its environs (the most outlying part of the Winelands) is divided into two, the **Warm Bokkeveld** (lowlands) and **Cold Bokkeveld** (uplands). Finally, the **Hex River Valley** connects the Breede River Valley with the arid Karoo.

Cape Town ✆ (021–)   ***Getting Around the Winelands***

By train: Stellenbosch and Paarl can be reached by rail from Cape Town, with services running several times per day. Call Paarl's Publicity Office, ✆ 872 3829, or Stellenbosch Station, ✆ 808 1111, for train times.

By bus: Translux run services Cape Town–Paarl and Cape Town–Stellenbosch. Boland Passenger Transport, ✆ 872 2114, run Paarl–Franschoek (via Groot Drakenstein).

Otherwise, several tour companies offer bus trips into the Winelands, although usually only to the Hottentots' Holland region. These are mostly day trips from Cape Town, but some companies offer longer tours. **Springbok Atlas**, ✆ 654 5448, offers a day-trip around Stellenbosch, Paarl and Franschoek, with a visit to two estates, as well as longer tours into the Breede River Valley and to the beautiful town of Tulbagh. If Springbok Atlas is booked up, call CapTour, ✆ 418 5202, for details of other tour companies operating.

By car: The best way round the Winelands is by car, allowing independent movement around the side-roads and access to the many B&Bs and farms for camping. Good, cheap car hire is available in Cape Town (*see* **Cape Town**, 'Getting Around'). Beware, however: following a Wine Route can obviously involve downing several glasses of wine, and although nobody seems to mind tourists driving from estate to estate in a mildly sozzled state, some of the precarious mountain roads can catch you out. And drinking and driving is still an offence.

Hitch-hiking: Hitching is fairly easy in the Winelands themselves, but thumbing a lift out of Cape Town can be dangerous, as the N1 highway passes through the Cape Flats and their townships. Better to take a train out to Stellenbosch and hitch from there. The same applies to taking black taxis.

Stellenbosch

 Stellenbosch is the heart of the Winelands. Its fine Cape Dutch buildings and oak-lined streets nestle in a natural bowl beneath jagged, forested mountains, which form part of the vast Hottentots' Holland Nature Reserve. Stellenbosch is known for its restaurants, museums, and as the beginning of the Stellenbosch Wine Route, the most extensive of the Cape's wine routes. It is impossible to wander the beautiful old town and surrounding countryside without catching a sense of the gracious living cultivated here by the Afrikaans wine-growers since the early 18th century.

Despite being a solidly conservative town, Stellenbosch has an Afrikaans university which has traditionally been regarded as the centre of Afrikaner liberalism. Some free-thinkers have certainly been produced, but it must be said that Stellenbosch University also produced almost all the National Party prime ministers of the apartheid era, and few Stellenbosch academics were outspoken in their criticism of the government.

History

Stellenbosch's name betrays its history. The word can be translated as 'Stel's Bush', after Simon Van der Stel who was Cape Governor through the 1670s and who founded Groot Constantia, the country's first wine estate, in the Cape Peninsula. He visited the Stellenbosch area in 1679 and made a semi-permanent camp where the town now stands. In 1680 the first settlers planted oak trees here, and built white lime-washed cottages with thatched roofs which were later expanded into the grander town houses you see today.

It is hard to imagine quiet, gracious Stellenbosch as the frontier town it was through the 1680s. Beyond the encircling mountains stretched Africa. Hunters, adventurers and a few settlers trickled over the mountain passes, returning to Stellenbosch for the annual fair that Van der Stel inaugurated and attended each year. At that time big game roamed where today there are vineyards, orchards and timber plantations.

Tourist Information

Stellenbosch Publicity Association, 36 Market Street, ✆ (021) 883 3584/9633.

Stellenbosch Town

The first thing to do is to visit the **Village Museum** (*open Mon–Sat 9.30–5, Sun 2–5*), four early 18th- to mid 19th-century houses on Rynveld Street, set under spreading oaks in the old town centre. The museum gives a good idea of the gradual rise of this wealthy town. Lovingly restored and furnished in the original style (even the gardens are planted with what would have been grown at the time, according to the little guide booklet), the houses range from the humble Schroederhuis (1709), a small pioneer cottage, supposedly the oldest in town, to the magnificent Grosvenor house (dating from 1800, round the corner on Drostdy Street), with two later, Victorian houses showing the contrast between Cape Dutch and British colonial architecture. Allow at least a couple of hours to get around the four houses, which are all within a block of each other. A map and explanatory booklet are supplied at the museum entrance in the Schroederhuis.

The **Eban Dondes Gallery**, on Rynveld Street (*open Mon–Fri 9–4, Sat 9–5, Sun 2–5*), displays work by Maggie Loubscher, a Cape artist whose use of vibrant colours sets her apart from the usual restrained style of Cape landscape painters.

The **Kruithuis** (*open Mon–Sat 9.30–5, Sun 2–5, closed June and July*), the old Dutch East India Company powder magazine (1777) on Bloem Street, houses a small military museum. After the indigenous KhoiSan tribes were pushed out of the area in favour of the vine, bands of dispossessed Khoi bandits and army deserters haunted the local mountains until the mid 19th century, and the museum charts both early colonial history and some of the later campaigns against the freebooters (*see* p.37).

Bird Street and **Dorp Street** run through the oldest quarter of the town. Bird Street leads past handsome terraces of old Cape Dutch town houses to **Die Braak**, a green on which there used to be military parades. Around Die Braak are some important old buildings, including the beautiful **Rhenish Mission and Parsonage**, a fine Cape Dutch church and small, thatched manor, set amid oaks, with a miniature formal garden dating from the 1700s. **The Burgher House** (*open weekdays 8.30–4.30*), also overlooking Die Braak, is a good example of later Cape Dutch style and is now a museum devoted to the history of the Dutch East India Company. Built in 1797, it mixes the simple Dutch gabling with modest classical forms. The English colonial days are represented by the **Anglican church** (St Mary's), dating from 1852—a young building by Stellenbosch standards. The **Dorp Street Gallery**, 176 Dorp Street (*open Mon–Fri 10–5, Sat 10–1*), shows work by local Cape artists. Exhibitions change every month, and works are for sale, so it is worth popping in to see what is on display.

The old **Krige Homestead**, on Dorp Street, is the house where Isie Smuts, wife of former Prime Minister Jan Smuts, was born. This is a private home, but a few doors down is the fine **Libertas Parva** (*open Mon–Fri 9.30–12.45 and 2–5*). Built in 1783, this H-shaped manor house contains the small **Rembrandt Van Rhyn Gallery,** showing works by some of the better-known South African artists, including some excellent paintings by Irma Stern. Another small art gallery belonging to Stellenbosch University occupies the old **Lutheran Mission**, built in 1851. One of the mission homesteads, **La Gratitude**, has the eye of God sculpted on its gable, to ensure that you are paying proper attention to the town's architectural details. Lastly, there is the craft shop, **Oom Samie Se Winkel** (meaning 'Uncle Sammy's Shop'), an old trading store that is now a national monument. Among other things, it sells kitsch pioneer memorabilia and rather good biscuits and fruit preserves. A coffee shop attached to the store serves light lunches. (*Both are open daily until about 6pm.*)

The Oude Libertas Centre (on the R310, just south of town) is an open-air amphitheatre used for plays, concerts, dance and the like. On Sunday afternoons in the summer, this place is full of people picnicking and drinking wine. The Publicity Association has concert listings.

Slightly out of the town centre, next to the railway station, is the **Bergkelder** ('Mountain Cellar'), a series of cellars hollowed out of the sides of 'Parrot Mountain', one of the massifs that rise above Stellenbosch town. Wine is stored here in huge vats. *Tours (including wine tastings) Mon–Sat 9–5.*

The Stellenbosch Wine Route

Stellenbosch's countryside has the Cape's oldest wine estates (after Groot Constantia near Cape Town) and some of the province's loveliest mountain walking.

Cape tourist offices tend to overplay the Wine Route, which in fact does not follow a logical 'route' at all, but incorporates a collection of estates lying around Stellenbosch. Unless you have days to spare, or have come to the Cape specifically to taste wine, don't try and see all the estates, and, unless you take a tour bus from Cape Town (*see* 'Activities'), you will need a vehicle to reach them. Each estate offers free wine tastings, and most let you wander the vineyards and, in some cases, look around the homesteads and their gardens. Watch out though: the tastings often come in full glasses, and you can be drink-driving before you know it. An afternoon spent at one or two estates is enough to get a feel for them without trying to take in too much, as, despite their beauty, most of the estates are very similar. The list that follows should not be considered a comprehensive guide to the Wine Route, but the pick of the bunch (in the author's opinion). A detailed map of the Wine Route is available from Stellenbosch Publicity Association, or call Wine Route Information, ✆ (021) 886 4310.

Rustenberg estate is over 300 years old, with a beautiful Cape Dutch manor and one of the most famous Cape wine labels. Although it has only produced wines since the 1880s, the estate is known for its reds, particularly its Cabernet Rustenberg Gold and Cinsault-Merlot, both deep, rich clarets. The Pinot Noir 1988 was described by experts as 'lively and fruity', and the dry, white Chardonnay has been called 'charming'.

Libertas is the area's largest producer, and has a fine homestead set in lawns, just 1km out of town on the Cape Town road. The Stellenbosch Farmer's Winery (a co-operative) has its cellar here. The Libertas Pinotage, a wine blended from Pinot Noir and Cinsault grapes, and unique to South Africa, is highly rated by wine critics.

Delheim, a mountain estate on the Simonsberg (one of the mountains that tower above Stellenbosch), is also a famous label. You can get lunch here, exclaim over the superb views, and try the very good Cabernet Sauvignon, which is considered one of the Cape's best-value quality Bordeaux. The Merlot/Cabernet blend is also considered good, as are the Sauvignon Blanc and Chardonnay. Delheim produces a variety of other grapes, including sweet German whites such as Gewurtztraminer, as well as Shiraz and Pinotage reds.

Delaire, at the head of the Helshoogte Pass (on the road to Franschoek), has breathtaking views out over the Berg River Valley and the tall Wemmershoek and Simonsberg Mountains. Delaire is known for white wines, especially a full-flavoured Chardonnay blend called Barrique, and a light, dry Rhine Reisling.

Spier, on the Cape Town road, has two superb Cape country and continental restaurants, where you can end the day with more wine and some food to absorb it. The Pinotage is considered the estate's best wine.

Avontuur, a young estate (since 1987) on the Somerset West road, is a thoroughbred stud as well as a winery. The reds are best: Avon Rouge is a good, gentle Cabernet. Their full-bodied Merlot has also had good reviews.

Simonsig is famous, and has been in the Malan family for several generations. A large range of reds and whites are grown. The red (Cabernet and Merlot) vintages from 1984–1991 are generally regarded as excellent, as are the Chardonnays made between 1988 and 1991. The estate also produces popular dessert wines.

Blauwklippen ('blue rocks') has one of the area's best Cape Dutch homesteads (1789) and sells preserves as well as serving lunches. Like Simonsig, this estate scored high with its 1980s reds, especially its Cabernet Reserve. Zinfandel, a red wine hardly grown in South Africa, has done well here, and is worth trying for its rarity alone.

Scenic Drives

The Wine Route covers most of the countryside around Stellenbosch, but if you just want to drift a little try the **Devon Valley** (off the R310 to Cape Town), a meander among gentle farmlands. Along the way is the **Protea Heights Nature Reserve**, a few kilometres from Stellenbosch, on the northern slopes of the Papegaaiberg. Alternatively, the road to Franschoek takes you through **Helshoogte Pass**, which has scenery you would normally only see when hiking through the Hottentots' Holland: fynbos uplands, waterfalls and wild-flowers. Many of the local farms have roadside stalls, selling most kinds of fruit very cheaply.

There are several interesting stopping points on these drives. The **Van Rhyn Brandy Cellar**, signposted from the R310 to Cape Town, is South Africa's largest brandy distillery. Concerts are sometimes given in the cellars, and tours of the distillery itself are available. The **Jean Craig Pottery** is off the R310, along the Devon Valley Road. Set amid woods and fields, the pottery also offers tours and sells its wares from a small shop. The crockery is good, but the ornaments rather twee.

Activities

The Stellenbosch Brandy Route: If wine is too sissy for you, hit the hard stuff with this potentially lethal tour of the region's brandy cellars. Make sure you designate a driver. To book call ✆ (021) 511 7537.

Walking in the Wine Route: The Vineyard Hiking Trail (24km over one or two days) is a way to explore the estates on foot. There are no steep hills, just a long, pleasant wander amid orchard and vine. The trail starts at Oude Libertas. Permits are available from the the Publicity Association in Stellenbosch.

Walking in the Hottentots' Holland Mountains: The mountains visible from Stellenbosch are mostly part of the huge Hottentots' Holland Nature Reserve, whose closest access point to the town is Jonkershoek State Forest, on the Franschoek road. Marked trails lead from the Forest Station through timber plantations and across great sweeps of bare hillside.

The Boland Hiking Trail, a two-day hike from the Forest Station, crosses the wild heart of the Hottentots' Holland Mountains, with refuge huts every 20km or so. The required permits are available from the Forestry Department at Jonkershoek. There is some small game: duiker, grysbok, grey rhebok and baboons are most common, while dassies and birds of prey are also in evidence. At night, genet cats and porcu-pines snuffle about. There are lynx and leopard, but you are unlikely to see them.

Plants and their associated birdlife are abundant. The mountains are covered with fynbos, which flowers in spring. Proteas and wildflowers are particularly good in the nearby Assegaibosch Nature Reserve, which also has marked walking trails. To get to Assegaibosch, take the road to Jonkershoek State Forest and follow the signs.

Easy day walks in the mountains are: the Banhoek Trail (11km) and Panorama Trail (17km), and the Swartbod Trail (19km), ✆ 886 5858. Alternatively the straighfor-wardly named 'The Trail' has three routes of 7, 15 and 24km (overnight hut if necessary), ✆ 883 9633.

Riding: There is no better way to explore the vineyards and mountains than on horseback. **Vineyard Horse Trails**, ✆ (021) 981 2480 and ask for Michele, supply good horses for full- and half-day rides on local estates. They also lead more expen-sive overnight trails up into the mountains, and moonlight rides and evening rides with a bottle of champagne at the end. **Amoi Horse Trails**, ✆ 887 1623, also has good horses.

Accommodation in town is somewhat limited and most of it is expensive. Cheaper accommodation tends to be out of town.

Stellenbosch Town

expensive

The Lanzerac Hotel, on Jonkershoek Rd, ✆ 887 1132, is a late 18th-century manor, beautifully furnished with Cape Dutch yellowwood, saffronwood and stinkwood period furniture, with polished yellowwood ceilings and stinkwood floors. There are 32 en suite rooms and a private suite. It also has one of Stellenbosch's best restaurants (*see* 'Eating Out').

Bonne Esperance, 17 Van Riebeeck St, ✆ 887 0225/6, is a large Victorian bungalow built in high colonial style, with a wrought-iron verandah, corrugated-iron roof and a small tower. The 16 rooms are furnished in period, and are all en suite. The dining room is large and airy, and lit by chandeliers.

D'Ouwe Werf ('the old farmyard'), 30 Church St, ✆ 887 1608, a simple, elegant Georgian house (1802) furnished with antiques, has 25 large rooms, with polished brass bedsteads, armchairs and fireplaces. Its vine-shaded courtyard restaurant is open to non-residents (*see* 'Eating Out'). **110 Dorp Street**, ✆ 883 3555, is a Georgian town house restored to include a sauna, steambath and jacuzzi. There are three luxurious suites furnished in Victorian style. The **Fynbos Guest House**, on Neethling St, ✆ 883 8670/1/2, is a Victorian house with seven en suite rooms done up in expensive chintz, complete with hangings above the beds, a pool and garden.

moderate

Hakuna Matata, 100 Dorp Street, ✆ 887 8841, is a very reasonably priced B&B right in the centre of town. Also in the town centre is **De Oude Meul**, ✆ 887 7085. Out of town, **Natte Valleij**, ✆ 875 5171, is a B&B dating back to 1715 that also arranges self-catering cottages in and around Stellenbosch, or try **Villa Jonde**, 27 Noordewaal West, ✆ 883 3568.

cheap

Stellenbosch has two good backpacker lodges, the **Stumble Inn**, 12 Market Street, ✆ 887 4049, and the **Hillbillies' Haven**, 24 Dennesig Street, ✆ 887 8475. Both have dorms and limited double rooms, as well as cheap camping. They will also help arrange winelands tours, hiking etc.

Stellenbosch Wine Route

expensive

L'Auberge Rozendal, near Jonkershoek, ✆ 887 6854, is a wine farm a few kilometres south of town, that produces a red Bordeaux. The 19th-century house serves as dining room and lounge, while guests stay in a terrace of Victorian single-storey cottages, each with a wrought-iron verandah. There are large oaks in the garden, and views over the vineyards to the surrounding mountains. All 16 rooms are en suite.

Nassau Guest Farm, Vlottenburg, ✆ 881 3818, about 5km from Stellenbosch on the R310, has old thatched cottages shaded by big oaks. Each cottage has brass bedsteads and a self-contained kitchen. Alternatively, there is a suite in the old farm-house. Guests can wander the paddocks and vineyards, and the owner also has an impressive collection of vintage cars—it is worth asking for a ride.

moderate

Wedge Farm B&B, in Ida's Valley, ✆ 883 2826, is an old farmhouse with a solid teak front door, a rose garden and views over the farming valley and forest. After about 5km from Stellenbosch on the Franschoek road, turn left into Lelie St which leads to the farm. **Oak Cottage**, also on the Franschoek Rd, 10 minutes' drive up the Helshoogte Pass from Stellenbosch, ✆ 855 1818, has three bedrooms (sleeps five) on, of all things, a protea farm. Self-catering accommodation only, with moun-tain walks and a swimming pool.

cheap

Joostenberg Guest Farm, on the R304, Malmsbury Road, north of Stellenbosch, ✆ 884 4425, offers very good B&B in an old cottage, but prices are at the top end of the range. **Gasthuis Die Eike**, a farm about 20km down the Kuilsrivier road (M12), ✆ 903 1203, offers bed and hearty breakfast for R66 per person. The owners will organize riding and hiking in the area. This place is well known to budget travellers.

Stellenbosch ✆ (021–)   ### Eating Out

expensive

Ralph's, on Andriga St, off Drostdy St, ✆ 883 3532, serves Cape country cuisine and game, with variations on the traditional menus, all cooked by Ralph, the proprietor and chef. Try the thinly sliced kudu meat as a starter, and the springbok with cranberry sauce or the tender ostrich steak to follow. You can drink their wine or take your own. Ralph's has a relaxed formality; the seating is in padded armchairs so comfortable that one could gladly stay all night (people often do). It is better to book.

The restaurant at the **Lanzerac Hotel** incorporates a small art gallery and one of the most renowned wine cellars in the country. Despite the formality of the interior, with its dark, polished wooden ceiling and floor, starched linen table-cloths and subdued lighting, the atmosphere is less severe than one would expect, and the waiters will happily help you through the vast wine list. Cape seafood fresh from the Peninsula is a speciality.

Die Kelder ('The Cellar') is on Dorp Street, ✆ 883 3797, in an old house (1790). It is a little snootier than the previous two, but serves some very good Cape country cooking (particularly the succulent Karoo mutton), complemented by fresh home-made breads. **Doornbosch** (the 'Thorn Bush'), on Old Strand Road, ✆ 886 6163, is more cordon bleu than Cape country, despite the Afrikaans name. It is very popular with Capetonians, and, like Ralph's restaurant, is comfortable and relaxed. Try any of the poultry dishes and finish with some of the local fruits.

Le Pommier, on New Helshoogte Rd, ✆ 885 1269, serves traditional Cape country cuisine in chintzy surroundings. They do an excellent, spicy *bobotie*, and the home-made vegetable soups are good to start with. **Cortina**, on Bird Street, ✆ 886 474, is an Italian restaurant which serves home-made pasta in a cosy dining room with a big fireplace. There are also separate rooms if you are a large party.

Die Volkskombuis ('The People's Kitchen', though the word 'Volk' implies Afrikaner farming folk, rather than everyone in general), is on Old Strand Rd, ✆ 887 2121. Yet more Cape country cuisine. Try the *bredies*, slightly sweetened mutton and vegetable stews seasoned with unusual spices such as aniseed and cinnamon. **D'Ouwe Werf** has an outside courtyard shaded by a mature vine trellis, making it an idyllic place to eat in summer. An inside dining room with a log fire serves in winter. Again, there are traditional Cape country dishes, mixed with seafood (always fresh) and some French cuisine.

cheap

Decameron, on Plein St, ✆ 883 3331, serves pasta and pizza with no frills. The sauces are thick and garlicky, and the seafood antipasti as fresh as anything from the Mediterranean. **Oom Samie Se Kaffiekammer** is the eatery attached to Oom Samie Se Winkel on Dorp St, ✆ 887 0797. Unfortunately it only does lunches, but good Cape country ones. Try the Vleis Pasties, spicy meat pies with vegetables. **Mama Roma**, off Merriman Ave, ✆ 886 6064, in the modern and none-too-attractive Pick 'n' Pay centre, makes up for what it lacks in period atmosphere with good, inexpensive pasta.

Nightlife

Being a university town, Stellenbosch has some lively bars, all of which stay open until about 3am. **Die Akker** ('the acorn'), on Dorp Street, plays good rock music and has a less conservative atmosphere than is normal for Stellenbosch. Those students that pretend to hippiedom drink here, as well as the more general pleasure-seekers. **Die Kelder**, on Dorp Street, has a cellar pub decorated in Cape Dutch style, that attracts a more mature crowd. **Legends**, on Dorp Street, has irritating mass-produced posters of old Hollywood stars on the walls, but there is a pleasant bar under the rafters of the upper floor, and you can sit outside.

Paarl

On the north bank of the Berg River, in the Drakenstein Valley, about 30km northeast of Stellenbosch, is Paarl, the second town of the Winelands. Paarl translates to 'Pearl', after the dome-shaped rock on the mountain summit that dominates the town, on which stands the Taal Monument to the Afrikaans language. The old section (through which runs the R45 road, which becomes Main Street) is similar to Stellenbosch, with many Cape Dutch build-ings and, in some places, vineyards reaching right down into Main Street from the slopes of Paarl Mountain. **KWV**, the best-known of South African wine labels abroad, has its head-quarters on Main Street, in the grand, pedimented building called La Concorde. Across the river from town are the Klein Drakenstein Mountains, a hiking and mountain-driving paradise. Oaks and jacarandas line Main Street, the long road (7km) along which the old town straggles. At the northern end is a small, shabby industrial area, which contrasts sharply with the serenity of the old town.

History

The Berg River Valley was first charted by an explorer, Abraham Gabbema, in 1657, while hunting for game to bring back to Cape Town. Settlers drifted in during the 1680s, displacing the local Khoi and laying out farms, but Paarl itself is a latecomer by Winelands standards. Founded by the Dutch East India Company in 1720, as a base from which people could cross the mountains into the interior, it became the 18th-century centre of Cape wagon-making. The local craftsmen used indigenous hardwoods to build wagons strong enough to survive the rugged treks through the Cape mountains and into the stony semi-deserts beyond.

The fertile Berg River Valley also provided Paarl with a local farming community. Orchards and vineyards were planted, and grand homesteads built, and today the area around Paarl has wine estates to rival those of Stellenbosch. While along the Groot Drakenstein Valley (which follows the Berg River towards Franschoek) grow peach, pear and apricot orchards. However, despite its gentle surroundings, Paarl was one of the fiercest hotbeds of emergent Afrikaner nationalism during the late 19th century, and it was from here that the movement to have Afrikaans recognized as an official language enjoyed its first successes.

Paarl and the Afrikaans Language

The Winelands have always been staunchly Afrikaner, under both Dutch colonial and British rule. In 1875 Arnoldus Pannevis, a Dutch schoolteacher working in Paarl, became intrigued by the richness of shared culture and language in the Cape: white Afrikaners, Cape Malays, and Khoi people were all speaking a language evolved in the Cape. Pannevis decided to regularize the Afrikaans language. He and some friends formed the Institute of True Afrikaners, and set down a standard grammar and vocabulary. In 1876, they published an Afrikaans newspaper (*The Afrikaans Patriot*) from the house of Gideon Malherbe, an Institute member. The house is now a museum (*see* below).

From then the movement grew until, in 1925, Afrikaans replaced Dutch as the country's second official language after English, and after 1948 it became the major language of politics and business (though English remained as the joint official language) and a compulsory part of black education—a highly controversial rule that sparked the famous Soweto schoolchildren's risings of 1976 (*see* **Gauteng**, pp.508–9). However, this last aspect has been done away with since the 1994 elections, and there are now 11 official languages in South Africa.

In 1975 the rather ugly Taal Monument to the Afrikaans language was unveiled on the mountain above Paarl. Abstract, lumpy shapes symbolize the African and Malay influence, while more elegant arches give thanks to the European for making it all possible. A fountain represents the language's growth, and a soaring pillar represents hope that Afrikaans will continue to develop.

Tourist Information

Paarl Publicity Association, 251 Main St, ✆ (021) 868 2468, or ✆ 872 3829.

Main Street

Most of the sights worth seeing are along Main Street, which comprises most of the old town. **La Concorde**, the headquarters of KWV, South Africa's biggest exporter of wine, is worth seeing for the imposing classical front. Inside are offices, but round the corner on Kohler Street are the actual **KWV Cellars** (*open for tours and tastings Mon–Fri 9.30–5*). KWV also run **Laborie**, ✆ 631 001, an estate at the foot of Paarl Mountain, whose vineyards come down to Main Street. Laborie's cellar is open by appointment only, although its restaurant can be visited anytime.

Further down Main Street is **Die Oude Pastorie & Strooidakkerk** ('the old parsonage and the thatched church'). The Parsonage, next door to the Tower Church on Main Street, now houses a collection of Cape Dutch furniture, silver and assorted Afrikaner and Huguenot antiques. The building dates from 1786. Built on the site of an earlier church, the Strooidakkerk, further down Main Street, is a later Thibault design dating from 1805 (*see* 'Architecture') and is still used for services. A coffee shop serving light meals is attached to the church. *Open Mon–Fri 9–5, Sat 11–4, Sun 2–4.*

Off Main Street, on Pastorie Avenue, is the **Gideon Malherbe House** (*open weekdays 9–5*). The museum occupies the house where the Institute for True Afrikaners used to meet during the 1870s and '80s. The museum is interesting more for its cultural significance than for the exhibits themselves, an example of which is the printing press on which *The Afrikaner Patriot* was produced.

Around Paarl

Paarl Mountain Nature Reserve and the **Taal Monument** sit just below the pearl-shaped summit of the mountain that gave the town its name. In fact, the summit comprises three separate dome-shaped peaks: Brittania Rock (the biggest), Gordon Rock and Paarl Rock. The first two names seem oddly British for a town and mountain dedicated to Afrikaans and Afrikanerdom, an unwitting monument to the cultural jumble that makes up South Africa. On the lower slopes stands the Taal Monument, while on the rest of the mountain nature takes over in a huge sweep of fynbos, protea, hardwood copses and aloes. There is plenty of bird life. Look out for sugarbirds and black eagles. There are marked trails and good views. To reach the monument and nature reserve, follow the signs from Main Street past the **Mill Stream Wild Flower Garden**, a wash of colour in springtime.

Other hiking trails—including some for the disabled—can be found at **Kagga Kama**, ✆ (021) 863 8355 (not to be confused with the 'human zoo' bushman reserve of the same name up in the Ceres Karoo (*see* p.188), and **Limietberg Nature Reserve**, ✆ (021) 886 5858, which has day and overnight trails, as well as access to the tougher 2-day Boland Trail (*see* p.179). **Groot Baviaanskloof**, ✆ (021) 611 535, also has day trails, but no disabled facilities. For spring wildflower walks, call **Meulwater Reserve**, ✆ (021) 872 3658.

Bonheur Crocodile Farm, on the Franschoek Road just south of town (follow the signs), is a strange thing to find here in the un-African atmosphere of the Winelands. Still, if you have never seen a croc, crocs are here, more than a thousand of them waiting to become handbags, shoes and exotic items on restaurant menus (crocodile tail has a wild flavour, a little like chewy crayfish). Belts and bags are sold in the farm shop.

The **Nederberg Wine Estate**, about 10km north of Paarl, off the Wellington Rd (R303), is one of the best-known vineyards in the Cape, with one of the best-preserved original home-steads, an H-shaped gabled mansion built in 1792. Nederberg produces around 50 wines, mostly reds. Just about all of them are good, and the reds did especially well in the 1980s. The estate has a wine auction every April, which becomes a Cape society booze-up lasting a couple of days. For some reason, Nederburg does not want to be included in the official Paarl Wine Route, but there is nothing to stop the traveller from including it in his or her itinerary.

The Paarl Wine Route

Like the Stellenbosch route, Paarl's Wine Route follows no logical sequence, but includes estates in all directions from the town, although far fewer than the Stellenbosch route. For a comprehensive map and guide booklet, visit the Paarl Publicity Association. In the mean-time, here is the pick of the bunch.

The **Paarl Rock Brandy Cellar** is in town on Dromadis Street. Watch brandy being made from grape to spirit, then try some. **Fairview**, south of town on the slopes of Paarl Mountain, offers tastings of its own, very good, estate-produced goats' cheese, as well as wines. Fairview's reds (Cabernet, Merlot and Pinotage) did well from 1987–91, as did the dry, white Chardonnays from 1991–3. The estate's full range is wider than this, however, and it is worth asking the staff in the tasting cellar for their recommendations.

Backsberg estate, on the Stellenbosch road, has won a lot of prizes for both reds and whites. Its Bordeaux blend, Klein Babylonstoren, has been reviewed as 'delicious'. Backsberg has a small wine museum as well as a cellar.

Rhebokskloof ('Reedbuck Gorge'), just north of Paarl Mountain, offers a guided tour in a Land-Cruiser. The range of wines is small, and most of the estate's success has come from its Cabernets. Rhebokskloof has a Cape country restaurant. South of town, **De Leuwen Jagcht** ('the lion hunt') has a very handsome Cape Dutch homestead, but the wines have not been particularly celebrated.

Villiera (on the R101 parallel with the N1 highway towards Cape Town), on the other hand, produces popular white wines, dry and sweet, and has a terraced restaurant serving lunch under great, spreading trees. The Sauvignon Blanc and Rhine Reisling are recom-mended by wine guides, and the Merlots from the late 1980s and early '90s were described as 'exceptional'.

Paarl © (021)   **Where to Stay and Eating Out**

expensive

Pontac Estate, 16 Zion Street, © 872 0445, is a restored Victorian mansion, convenient for the town centre. A little less expensive is **Rodeberg Lodge B&B**, © 863 3202, a pretty late-Victorian guest house near town, or **Villa Tusca**, 8 Stirling Street, © 872 8222.

If you want to stay further out of town, try **Mountain Shadows**, © 862 3192, a beautifully preserved old mansion dating from 1823. Baasie Maartens, the owner, is also a mine of local information. Springbok and other small game roam the estate.

Roggeland, in the Dal Josaphat Valley, ✆ 868 2501, is an old homestead, also at the expensive end of things. The kitchen has a good reputation. You could also try **Bosman's**, ✆ 632 727, another expensive restaurant set in a handsome old homestead, that has won several awards for both its gourmet fare and its wine. With less of a Cape menu than a continental one, Bosman's is worth visiting in summer, when you can dine outside on its terrace.

moderate

More moderately priced accommodation in the country near town is to be found at **Kleinplass Guest House**, ✆ 458 8284, and **Berghof Wine and Guest Farm**, ✆ 871 1099, both on Paarl Mountain. Nearby is **Even-Haezer Country House**, ✆ 862 7420. **Acorn Lodge**, ✆ 863 1366, and **Goedemond**, ✆ 871 1020, a family-run B&B on Cecilia St, are both in the town centre.

Troubadour, ✆ 633 556, a French restaurant with a good reputation, is in town on Church Street. Book in advance as it is generally full. **Rhebokskloof Estate**, ✆ 638 606, has a good country restaurant. Take the road about 4km to the village of Agter Paarl. The gates are on the north side of the road.

cheap

Winelands Backpackers Lodge, 91 Main Road, ✆ 863 1378.

Franschoek and the Drakenstein Valley

Tourist Information

Franschoek Tourism Bureau, Main Road, ✆ (021) 876 3062/3

This is the loveliest part of the Winelands. As you travel the 20km up the Drakenstein Valley to Franschoek, following the swift Berg River, the mountains crowd closer and the cultivated lands become narrower. Orchard and vineyard give way to pasture and pine forest, from which rocky outcrops jut like turrets. The village of Franschoek sits at the head of the valley, before the road climbs up into the Hottentots' Holland proper, and disappears into the mist, over the Franschoek Pass.

Franschoek itself ('French Corner') was settled in 1688 by Huguenot rather than Dutch settlers. The site was, in fact, given to the Huguenot refugees as a land grant. Perhaps as a result, Franschoek, though very small, is one of the loveliest villages in the country, a few streets of white-washed buildings, with thatched and slated roofs, while the wine estates around the town are perhaps the most graceful in the region.

Despite its small size, the Main Street has plenty for the tourist. Of particular note are **La Patisserie Bakery** (which sells good Boer breads as well as light pastries), the **Pippin Farm Stall**, selling fruit, preserves, honey, dried fruit, cakes and other wholesome goodies, and the **Oude Stallen**, a little period enclave of shops and eateries around a vine-shaded court near the **Huguenot Monument and Museum** (*open Mon–Fri 9–5, Sat 9–1 and 2–5, Sun 2–5*) on Lambrecht Street, the road leading up to the Franschoek Pass. A history of the Huguenots in early colonial South Africa is housed in a very grand Cape Dutch homestead, called Saasveld, which was translocated from Cape Town in the 1960s.

The Franschoek Wine Route

A detailed map and booklet are available from the Publicity Office at **La Provence Estate**, on the R45 just west of town, or at the **Vignerons Office** on Main Street, ✆ (02212) 3287.

Boschendal estate is in the Drakenstein Valley between Paarl and Franschoek, set under the flatiron wall of the Groot Drakenstein Mountain. The estate is owned by the huge corporation Anglo-American as, indeed, is most of the valley (and sizeable sections of the whole country). These orchards and vineyards were originally aquired by Cecil Rhodes in the 1890s, and bought by the huge corporation after his death. Boschendal is one of the most prestigious wine estates in South Africa. It dates from 1685, though the present manor is 18th-century, and is open to the public. Estate tours run Mon–Sat, with tastings in the Taphuis—try the Chardonnay. There are also two restaurants open for lunch.

L'Ormarins homestead was built in 1811, although the original estate dates from 1694. It produces a wide selection of wines—any red from 1984–89, or Chardonnay from 1988–91, is likely to be very good. The Sauvignon Blanc, aged in oak, has been praised for its light, lemony quality.

Bellingham is another estate high on the prestige list. Founded in 1693, it produced South Africa's first Shiraz, rosé and Premier Grand Cru wines. Recently, however, none of Bellingham's wines seem to have caught the critics' attention, but this does not stop the wines selling.

The nearby **La Motte** estate dates from 1709, the manor and cellar from 1752. Hidden in the Wemmershoek mountains on the north side of the Berg River, La Motte has attracted a lot of praise lately. The reds from 1986–91 were described as 'intensely flavoured'.

La Couronne is a stud, breeding showjumpers and dressage horses, as well as a wine estate, and a look around the stables and paddocks is fun. The wines have received no particular attention recently, but it is a beautiful estate to visit.

Nearby is **La Bri**, which dates from 1694. A classic H-shaped homestead, it was granted by Cape Governor Simon Van der Stel to one Jaques De Villiers, a Huguenot who founded one of the longest-running family dynasties in South Africa. The current owners (no longer De Villiers) have won various awards for their white wines and are involved in developing Britain's largest vineyard: 100 hectares in Surrey. La Bri's tasting room is a small art gallery showing work by local landscape artists.

Haute Provence sells a wine called Larmes des Anges ('Angel's Tears'), based on a legend wherein angels descended on a French village, tasted the wine, and wept for joy because it was so good.

Activities

Walking: The Franschoek, Wemmershoek and Groot Drakenstein Mountains (all part of the Hottentots' Holland chain) loom above Franschoek village and valley. One can disappear into them on foot for hours or days. Most of the trails require permits and map, both available from the Huguenot Museum.

The **Franschoek Pass Trail** starts at the head of the Pass in the **Mont Rochelle Nature Reserve**, about three kilometres above the village. You are supposed to buy a permit first from the office at the Huguenot Museum, but there is nobody up there to check. The trail winds up through high kloofs, crossing clear, drinkable streams, to reach a small pass with a spectacular view over to the Wemmershoek Mountains, whose almost sheer cliffs form a deep valley around the blue Wemmershoek Dam. Look out for dassies, baboons, black eagles and klipspringer. You do need to buy a permit for **Wemmershoek Dam**, as there is a man to check at the gate. The dam fills a valley that used to be farmed by a family called Wemmer. It is worth walking the trail around the shore, listening to mountain silence broken only by the occasional barking of baboons on the cliffs. Take a picnic. There are wonderful wild flowers in spring.

The Boland Trail, part of the same two-day trail that begins at Jonkershoek State Forest near Stellenbosch and crosses the Hottentots' Holland to Somerset West, runs through the mountains near Franschoek. Get a map and permit from the Huguenot Museum. There are overnight huts on the trail.

The **Catspad** (11km) and **Perdekop** (5km) are easier day hikes, ✆ 876 2055.

Franschoek ✆ (021–)   **Where to Stay**

expensive

L'Auberge du Quartier Français, on Huguenot St, at the corner of Wilhelmina and Berg Streets, ✆ 876 2151/2248, is worth the money. Simple, elegant and not chintzy (as many South African country hotels can be), it was voted best country hotel in the Cape in 1992. It has 14 double en suite rooms with fireplaces and period furniture. There is also a courtyard, garden and a pool. (*See* 'Eating Out'.)

Le Ballon Rouge, On Dirkie Uys Street (one up from and parallel to Huguenot Street), ✆ 876 2071, is another restored Victorian villa, but more intimate than the Auberge. Bed and hearty breakfast. **Auberge Bligny**, 28 Van Wijk Street, ✆ 876 3767, again a restored period house, furnished with antiques, offers luxury with a guest house feel.

moderate

By far the most beautiful place to stay in the Winelands is **Lekkerwijn**, ✆ 874 1122, in Groot Drakenstein, a few miles back down the valley from Franschoek towards Paarl, opposite the Boschendal wine estate. An early 18th-century thatched and pillared mansion around a central courtyard, surrounded by its own small estate, this is a magical place and worth staying for several days—though if you only have one night you could do no better. The owner, Wendy Pickstone, now runs the place as a very intimate B&B along with her maid, Dahlia—who takes a percentage of the profits, thus breaking with the old feudal tradition.

Franschoek Guest House, ✆ 876 3366, in the town centre on Huguenot Road, just before Louis Botha Street, ✆ 876 2081, is a convivial pub that locals frequent, with good B&B in pleasant, simple rooms. (Also *see* 'Eating Out'.) **La Merci**, on the lovely Bellingham Wine estate, ✆ 874 1011, offers B&B in en suite rooms. Down the R45 (over the Berg River bridge) towards Paarl. **Vermers Cottage**, on the La Terra de Lucqe Farm (R45 just west of town), ✆ 876 2493, has B&B in a tiny cottage. **La Provence**, ✆ 876 2163, offers another opportunity for B&B on one of the old wine estates, on the R45 just west of town. This one is in the Jonkerhuis cottage (meaning the house for the eldest son), dating from the 1700s. **Bo La Motte Cottages**, ✆ 876 3067, converted workers' cottages on a wine estate, are also worth staying at.

The area around Franschoek has a lot of moderately priced self-catering accommodation in farm cottages, offered on a formal or informal basis. **Paradise Cottage**, on Robertsvlei Farm, a right turn on Lemabrecht Street away from the Pass, ✆ 876 2160, has access to marked walking trails and horses for hire, and you can even fish for bass in the dam. **Chamonix Wine Estate**, above town (follow La Cotte Street uphill from Huguenot Street), ✆ 876 2498, has two five-bedroomed guest houses. You need several people to bring the cost down, but the estate is lovely, being higher up the valley than most of the others.

Reeden Lodge, ✆ 876 3174, a farm cottage overlooking a dam, with trout fishing, sleeps four. **Dassenburg**, ✆ 876 2107, is another farm cottage with mountain and river walks. **La Bri Holiday Farm**, ✆ 876 2593, has budget dormitory accommodation in pleasant surroundings. Follow Lambrecht Rd to the right, away from the Pass. The cheapest option is **Franschoek Backpackers**, 6 Kruger Street, ✆ 876 2619.

Franschoek ✆ (021–)   ***Eating Out***

For such a small place, Franschoek and the Drakenstein Valley have a surprising wealth of choice, albeit mostly of French cusine.

expensive

L'Auberge Du Quartier Français has made a big noise in South African travel and gourmet magazines, and the place is lovely: an old Victorian hotel with tin roof, white walls and wrought-iron pillars on the verandah. It has two restaurants: **Le Quartier**, very French and voted one of the best in South Africa, and the more informal **Café Français**, where you can have lunch outside and drop jaws over the towering mountains.

Le Ballon Rouge, on Dirkie Uys St (the block before Berg Street), ✆ 876 2651, is in Franschoek, so it must be French. The chef grows his own vegetables and herbs.

Chez Michel, ✆ 762 671, is the oldest restaurant in the village. Its informal, bistro-type atmosphere is more fun than the rather self-consciously good French restaurants nearby. **La Maison de Chamonix**, on Main Road (opposite the corner of Uitkyk Street), ✆ 867 2393/2498, does yet more cordon bleu, in case you are missing French cuisine. But to be fair, this restaurant does some superb Cape country cooking too. For lunch you can picnic in the garden with one of their buffets. Wonderful views over vineyards.

Boschendal Restaurant, ✆ 874 1031 or ✆ 847 1252, in an old homestead on the Boschendal Estate, 15km towards Paarl, is formal and rather grand. Very tasty, very large helpings of Cape Huguenot cuisine, which is much the same as Cape country—spicy variations on European dishes. Only open for lunch. It also has a more relaxed, cheaper outdoor lunch place, annoyingly called **Le Pique-Nique**, where you can sit outside by ponds and pines.

moderate

Gideon's Pancake House, on Huguenot Road between De La Rey and Bordeaux Streets, ✆ 2227, is very reasonably priced, and serves imaginatively filled pancakes in an informal atmosphere

La Vie, on Main Road, just after La Cotte Street, ✆ 876 2101, is French again, but a more Mediterranean version this time, in atmosphere as well as menu. Tables outside or in. *Closed Mon.* **Dominics**, on the corner of Huguenot and Kruger Streets, ✆ 876 2255, is better for lunch than dinner as the helpings are not enormous. Some good spicy food, though. **Lanternhof** (in **La Cotte Inn**) is connected to the bar where many of the locals drink, and is a good place to meet people. Hearty fare and reasonable prices.

Polyfyntjies, ✆ 876 2493 ('souvenirs' in Afrikaans), is in **La Terra De Luc**, a restored farmhouse just west of town on the R45, with log fires in winter and garden tables in summer. *Closed Mon.* **La Petite Ferme**, ✆ 876 3016, is an out-of-town inn, high up the road to the Pass, with magnificent views which merit a visit for lunch or tea even if you are not staying there. The smoked trout is a speciality. Beware: the drive back to town has sharp bends that challenge wine-addled brains.

Somerset West

Tourist Information

Somerset West Publicity Bureau, 11 Victoria Street, ✆ (021) 851 4022.

Last of the 'oldest towns of the Winelands', Somerset West sits on the southern slopes of the Hottentots' Holland, just inland from False Bay and Strand, about 25km from Stellenbosch and Franschoek. Cape Town is only 45km away along the N2 highway.

Somerset West is where the name of the region, 'Hottentots' Holland', was born. The first Dutch adventurers visiting the area found a prosperous tribe of Hottentots (Khoi) flourishing amid well-watered pastures; several mountain rivers meet at this point on their way to the nearby sea. During 'negotiations' with the Dutchmen, the Khoi compared their love of their land with the Dutchmen's love for Holland. However, despite the Khoi's attachment to the region, the beloved land was traded piecemeal with settlers for cattle, beads and iron. The colonists then called the area the 'Hottentots' Holland', reflecting their nostalgia for Europe (remember that in 1657 the Cape Colony was only five years old, and was not flourishing).

Somerset West remained a loose-knit farming community until the British decided to make it a magistracy and named it after Lord Charles Somerset, the then Governor, in 1820. Through the 19th and 20th centuries, Somerset West existed quietly, prospering as a wine town. However, over the last 20 years, the improved road to Cape Town has caused the town to grow into something of a commuter suburb, and the handsome old centre is now surrounded by development.

The countryside towards the mountains is as lovely as anything in the Winelands, and the old town centre has some fine buildings, in particular an **Old Dutch Reformed Church**, on Victoria Street, whose parsonage operates as a small restaurant and coffee shop, and serves light meals. Follow Victoria Street down to the Lord Charles Hotel, turn right at the traffic light, drive for about 2km and take the signpost for **Vergelegen Winery** (*open daily 9.30–4*), a superb H-shaped Cape Dutch manor house and wine estate whose homestead sits under two huge camphor trees. Visitors can wander the house, which has a very good library and a collection of Cape Dutch furniture; the old slave quarters behind are also open. Vergelegen has a small restaurant that serves lunch outside under the trees.

Helderberg Nature Reserve, ☎ 855 4308, climbs the mountain behind town and looks out over the sea. The reserve is approximately 400ha, with walks through the fynbos, and is particularly good for proteas and birds. You may spot grey rhebok and duiker, and there is also a small forest of yellowwood, hard pear, stinkwood and various other hardwood trees.

Another good place for a day walk is at **Taiibos**, ☎ 554 308. It's tough, despite being only 11km, and there's an overnight hut for those who need it.

Gordon's Bay

Somerset West is only about 8km inland from the sea and the large commuter beach-town of **Strand** lies just to the south. Better to visit is **Gordon's Bay**, on the R44, where the road turns away from the N2 (which climbs up into the Hottentots' Holland via the spectacular **Sir Lowry's Pass**). Gordon's Bay is a fishing village and weekend resort (rapidly becoming more resort than village), with good beaches running along the foot of the mountains.

Somerset West ☎ *(021–)*   ***Where to Stay and Eating Out***

expensive

Die Ou Pastorie, 41 Lourens Street, ☎ 852 2120, has eight large en suite rooms furnished in mock-Victorian style, with a verandah, tin roof, and communal sitting room with log fires in winter. Its small restaurant serves Cape country cuisine. *Open Mon–Sat for dinner, Tues–Fri for lunch.* **The Lord Charles Hotel**, on Victoria Street, ☎ 512 970, has a good restaurant (fresh seafood) on the terrace overlooking the garden.

Willowbrook, ☎ 851 3759, a few kilometres from town, is a Victorian country house with bedrooms that look out on to a parkland garden, through which a fast-flowing river tumbles down from the surrounding mountains. There are 12 en suite rooms and one suite, a beautiful sitting room with french windows looking on to the garden, and a conservatory. Turn up Lourensford Road from Main Road and then up Morgenster Ave.

Thornberry Guest Lodge, 12 Mayfair Avenue, ☎ 855 2623, and **Albourne Guest House**, ☎ 852 2184, down in Strand, are comfortable, and convenient for shops. Out of town, towards Stellenbosch and Paarl, is **Stellendal Guest House**, ☎ 851 2599, an early 19th-century B&B at the moderate end of expensive. **Chez Michel**, on Victoria Street, ☎ 516 069 (not to be confused with the one in Franschoek), is very pleasant and relaxed, with more fresh seafood.

Arksey Guest House, 200 Main Road, ✆ (517) 853 200, offers B&B (with dinner by request) at the expensive end of moderate. Accommodation is in an Edwardian bungalow with 12 en suite bedrooms, a log fire in the sitting room, a large garden, a pleasant, family-run atmosphere, and a small pub attached.

Keerweder Farm, up the R44 towards Stellenbosch, ✆ (02231) 90 053, offers B&B in an old farmhouse at the foot of the mountains, with some good hill walks and a pool. **Dove's Den Garden Cottage,** ✆ 552 623, offers B&B or self-catering accommodation on a farm in a small one-bedroomed cottage (with fireplace, large garden and pool).

Winelands Backpackers, 63 Caledon Street, ✆ 851 5175.

The Northwest Winelands

Follow the R44 north from Paarl towards Wellington, and the land flattens out to the left, into the vast wheat- and vine-growing plain of the Swartland. The western edge of the Great Escarpment, of which all the Cape mountains form a part, masses to the right. Far behind the mountains, which retreat, chain after chain, to the north and east, lies the great, dry Cape interior. Along their fringe, as the R44 travels north, cling the last valleys of the Boland.

Wellington

Wellington is a prosperous farming and wine town lying below the Slanghoekberg ('snake's corner mountains') and Limietberg ('farthest mountains'). The first 17th-century settlers called this area the Limiet Valley ('farthest valley'), as it was about as far as 'civilization' reached. The valley gradually established itself as a fruit-growing region through the 18th and 19th centuries, and even enjoyed a brief boom as a wagon-building town when the Kimberley diamond rush began in the 1870s. Before that, however, Wellington (so named by Cape Governor Sir George Napier in 1840, after the Duke of Wellington) had produced its own 'great man': Piet Retief, who moved from Wellington to the Eastern Cape in the 1820s, and became one of the great heroes of Afrikaner history. The man who emerged as one of the main leaders of the Great Trek of the 1830s (*see* 'Zululand, History'), Retief was eventually killed in Natal by the Zulu king Dingane, while negotiating land grants for the trekboers. Dingane's act of deliberate treachery helped to stave off white encroachment into Zululand for another generation, and ensured Retief his status as an Afrikaner martyr.

Wellington was garrisoned during the Anglo-Boer War, after Boer *Kommandos* (mobile fighting units) began campaigning in the Cape. The British (under Lord Kitchener) built 8000 blockhouse forts across the country to help intercept the *Kommandos*. One is just north of Wellington and is open to visitors.

Apart from **Twistniet,** an old homestead on Main Street (the farmhouse of the farm called 'Champagne', on which the original town was laid out), there is little in the town to interest the traveller. Not as beautiful as the southern Winelands towns, Wellington is generally used by tourists as a petrol and food stop on the way to Tulbagh and the Ceres Valley. But north of town, signposted off the R44, stands the **Boer War Blockhouse** (*open weekdays 9–4.30*), now a national monument.

A handsome Cape Dutch wine estate called **Onverwacht**, ✆ (02211) 34 315, sits on Addy Road in the outskirts of town, offering tastings and tours. The estate's manor house is a particularly fine example of 18th-century Cape Dutch. (*Open Mon–Fri 9–5.*)

The Phantom and the Blanket

Wellington also has a famous ghost story, from around 1880. At Brakwater, a farm not far from town, the owner died, leaving a widow and a daughter. The widow's brother took over, but made life hard for the women, especially for the daughter, who was courting a young man from Wellington. One night, the suitor rode to the farm and met the ghost of the old farmer, who bade him tell the brother-in-law to treat the women better, or he would burn the man alive.

He then told the gaping young man to wrap a blanket round his fist. The youth did as he was instructed. The ghost grasped the covered fist, his phantom hands scorching the blanket, and then disappeared. The terrified young man told the brother-in-law what had happened, showing him the blanket and repeating the ghost's words. This was evidence enough for the brother-in-law, who promptly vacated the property. Convenient for the young man and the daughter, perhaps.

Where to Stay

Fisantekuil Guest Farm, ✆ (02211) 641 184, is a fruit and wine farm that offers mountain walks and fishing in the dam (bring your own tackle) and secluded cottages, just off the Paarl–Wellington road, about 5km south of town. It is moderately priced, but you must bring your own food. Walking trails wind off towards the nearby mountains.

Also try **Bloublommetjieskloof Farm** ('little blue flower valley farm'), on Olyvenbosch Road, ✆ (021) 873 3696, a moderately priced guest farm which also has a cheap **backpackers' dorm**.

Bain's Kloof and the Limietberg Mountains

Bain's Kloof is a spectacular pass which runs east to west through the Limietberg, east of Wellington (R303), into the Breede River Valley. Built in the 1840s by Andrew Geddes Bain (son of the engineer Thomas Bain, who built most of the Cape pass roads), using convict labour, it runs through some of the loveliest Cape mountain scenery accessible by road.

At Tweede Tol **camp site**, in the Hawequas State Forest, halfway along Bain's Kloof, is the start of a two-day hiking trail over the mountains (with overnight hut) to Du Toit's Kloof. Permits and maps are sold at Tweede Tol. For the less ambitious there is a three-hour circular walk along a watercourse, with good birdlife, small antelope, dassies and fynbos vegetation. For information on maps, trailheads and overnight huts, ring the Hawequas Forest Station, ✆ (021) 887 0111.

Tulbagh

Following the R44 about 40km north along the escarpment of the Elandskloofberg, the road climbs up into the tortuous Nuwekloof Pass, then drops down into a bright green, narrow valley between tall mountains (the Witsenberg, Winterhoekberg and Saronsberg), where sits the town of Tulbagh, a backwater that has remained almost unchanged in outward appearance since the 18th century—a jewel in the mountains.

History

Early in the 18th century a few settlers pulled their wagons over the Nuwekloof Pass and discovered this valley, where the Klein-Berg River (main tributary of the Berg River) has its source. The Khoi and San people both used the valley as a hunting ground. The familiar pattern repeated itself: the indigenous people were hunted out, vineyards planted, homesteads built, and a town sprang up.

Tulbagh has always been a tranquil spot, though it produced the militant Afrikaner Boer War hero, Daniel Theron, who led a team of English-speaking scouts in and out of the British lines when the British invaded the Orange Free State in 1900. Theron's end came later that year while single-handedly holding off a British attack on the hill where his small force was camping. Theron sniped at the British while his own men evacuated safely. The British finally stormed the hill, showering it with rifle-fire, but were perplexed to find only one body when they reached the top. It was Theron. His men had escaped without harm.

Tulbagh drifted through the 20th century without much incident, until 1969, when a freak earthquake killed nine people and destroyed much of the old town. As the 32 buildings on Church Street constituted the largest concentration of old buildings in South Africa, a massive restoration programme got under way, and today you would never know there had been any damage.

Tourist Information

Tulbagh Publicity Office, the Old Church, Church Street, ✆ (0236) 301 348.

The Town

Tulbagh has two main thoroughfares: the R46 is lined with shops and fairly modern buildings (i.e. up to 1950); behind and parallel to the R46 runs **Church Street**, which has barely changed since the 18th century. Two of the houses here are museums, **The Pioneer Museum**, dedicated to early Cape life (including a detailed display of herbs and their medicinal uses), and the **Tulbagh Museum**, 4 Church Street, which gives a brief history of colonial Tulbagh, and a photographic record of the restoration that followed the earthquake. (*Both open Mon–Fri 9–4.30, Sat 10–4, Sun 11–4.*)

At the eastern end of Church Street is the **Old Church Museum**. Built in 1743, it is a splendid thatched affair with a gallery, now housing a collection of particularly fine Cape Dutch furniture and period curiosities, including six original paintings by Thomas Bain, the famous pass-builder. Also on Church Street is **The Victorian House**, home to more antiques. (*Both open Mon–Fri 9–4.30, Sat 10–4, Sun 11–4.*)

Tulbagh has a very good vineyard, the **Paddagang Estate**, the gates to which are off Church Street, about a block west of the Old Church. Paddagang has a Cape country restaurant and produces what the author and his travelling companions thought was one of the best red wines of the Cape. The Paddagang labels are distinctive, always depicting a frog.

About 3km from town, along the Winterhoek road, is the **Old Drostdy**, ✆ (0236) 301 086 (*open Mon–Sat 10–1 and 2–4, Sun 2.30–5*), a beautiful building designed in 1804 by the famous Cape Dutch architect Louis Thibault. Sherry from the Tulbagh wineries can be tasted here, and the building houses a collection of Cape Dutch furniture. Also on the premises is Tulbagh's old jail. Visitors can sit in the cells. Next door (about 1km further north) is the **Tulbagh Wine Cellar**, ✆ (0236) 301 001, which also offers tastings and tours (*open Mon–Sat 9–5*).

The Mountains Around Tulbagh

The ranges circling this valley are very wild. To the north, the **Groot Winterhoekberg** sweeps off to an area of jagged wilderness, accessible to fit hikers via the **Groot Winterhoek Forest Station** (take the R44 north of town to Porterville, then take the dirt road east over the Daskup Pass). Choose between three long trails of three to four days each, with abandoned farmhouses to sleep in along the way. Maps and permits are available from the Forest Station. Particularly rewarding is the hike into Die Hel, a deep, wild gorge and waterfall that drops into a large, cold pool surrounded by cliffs. Black eagles, klipspringers, sunbirds and dassies will be your companions, and you may be watched from afar by leopard and lynx.

Tulbagh ✆ (0236–)   ***Where to Stay and Eating Out***

moderate

Schalkenbosch, ✆ 300 654, lies under the Witsenberg Mountains, 8km north of Tulbagh. The road ends at the farm, which offers self-catering accommodation in luxurious cottages dating from 1792. Spend a night in this peaceful valley if you can. **Kloofzicht Wine Estate**, ✆ 300 658, has a lovely self-contained cottage. Other homesteads offering accommodation are: **De Oude Herberg**, ✆ 300 260, **Hunter's Retreat**, ✆ 300 582, **Waterval Country Lodge**, ✆ 300 807, and the **Wild Olive Farm**, ✆ 301 160, which offers self-catering cottages. Of these, the first two have *à la carte* restaurants serving country cuisine and good local wines.

In the town itself, there's the rather charming **30 Church Street B&B**, ✆ 301 448, or the rather bland **Tulbagh Hotel**, ✆ 300 071. (Though this does contain the **Kirzenlicht Resturant**, which has a reasonably priced continental menu for breakfast, lunch and dinner.) Or there's the **Paddaagang Estate**, just off Church Street, ✆ 300 242, which offers moderately priced lunches in its Cape Dutch dining room.

Michell's Pass

To reach the Bokkeveld from Tulbagh, drive over the 2031m **Michell's Pass**, which saw its first wagon in 1760. Andrew Geddes Bain built the existing road, naming it after Charles Michell, Surveyor-General of the Cape in 1846. For 30 years, until the building of the Hex River Pass near Worcester (where the N1 highway now goes), Michell's Pass carried most of the country's northward traffic. The transport riders, who took the inland cargoes north by ox-wagon, are commemorated in a museum in Ceres. The **Old Toll House**, where they paid before descending into the town, is now a national monument, craft shop and tea room.

Ceres

Ceres lies east of Tulbagh over the Hex River Mountains, flush against the Witsenberg Mountains, and facing the vast Bokkeveld Valley. The tree-lined Dwars River snakes through town. The town lies in a warm bowl which is blindingly hot in summer and warm in winter, even when the surrounding mountains are covered in snow.

Ceres is synonymous with fruit and fruit juice: the LiquiFruit and Ceres fruit juices sold all over the country are produced here. A latecomer by Cape standards, it was founded in 1854 to process the fruits of the Bokkeveld Valley, and was named after Ceres, the Roman goddess of fruit.

The town is not beautiful, having been much 'improved' during the 1950s and '60s. However, the **New Belmont Hotel** is a relic of the Victorian age, and has a 7ha **Bird Park** (home to over 200 species) in the grounds. Huge walk-in cages afford the opportunity of being splatted on from above by brilliant-feathered exotics. The hotel grounds run along the Dwars River and make good strolling after a long time in the car. Sundry other animals, such as goats and donkeys, provide distraction.

The **Transport Riders Museum** (*open Mon–Fri 9.30–11 and 1–5, Sat 9–12*) celebrates the era of ox-wagons straining over the Cape passes to the Kimberley diamond mines and Rand gold fields. Some very good old photographs show just how tough this was.

The Mountain Fynbos Reserve, ✆ (0233) 2177, lies just between town and the Witsenberg Mountains (the entrance is at the end of town, just as the road curves uphill to Michell's Pass). The reserve is full of flowers in spring; there are a number of walking trails and an indigenous nature garden. Take water in summer and avoid walking at midday.

The Warm Bokkeveld

The Warm Bokkeveld is the farming area of the valley around Ceres. Some of the Warm Bokkeveld fruit farms can be visited via the **Fruit Route** (map and guide booklet from Ceres Publicity Association). There are only so many fruit farms and processing plants that one can look at. The biggest, **CFG** (Ceres Fruit Growers), has its packing sheds just outside town, where Ceres, LiquiFruit and Fruitree juices are parcelled up. If the thought of industrial-scale fruit-juice packing doesn't appeal, try the **Du Toit Fruit Farm**, further down the R46. You can tour around the military-order farm and watch boxes of fruit travel about on water canals to avoid bruising.

Klondyke Cherry Farm (*open Mon–Sat 9–5*) is more fun. This 'pick-your-own' is along the Lakenvlei road, over the low Swaarmond Pass and 18km beyond. Watch out for baboons on the road. Pay R2.50 entry, pick as many cherries as you can, then pay R7 per kilo for them on the way out. They get annoyed if you climb the trees for the good cherries, so wander as deep into the orchard as possible. Be wary of snakes in summer.

The Cold Bokkeveld

The Cold Bokkeveld is a beautiful mountain area alongside the Skurweberg mountains, on the R303 towards Citrusdal. Before climbing, the R303 passes through the unremarkable village of Prince Alfred Hamlet. However, the Prince Alfred Hotel is owned by Jos Kahn, chairman of the local Publicity Association, so stopping in for a drink or coffee often yields good local information. After Prince Alfred Hamlet the road rises steeply over the Gydo Pass, with fabulous views back over the Ceres Basin.

Along the road beyond the pass is **Houdenbeck** farm (*see* 'Where to Stay'), scene of a slave revolt in 1825 when the owner and some guests were killed. At **Morester-Houdenbeck** farm, next door, you can pick onions or potatoes, or just walk around and breathe the clean, cold air. The neighbouring farm, **Sandrivier**, has an old homestead that offers accommodation (*see* 'Where to Stay'), and which has trails for day-hikes in the silent mountains around.

The Ceres Karoo

East of the Cold Bokkeveld Mountains is an empty upland plateau, where begins the southwestern section of the Great Karoo. This area is semi-desert, quite rich in game, and a sharp contrast to the lush scenery of the Winelands. Follow the R303 north until a dirt road turns off east, marked with a brown sign that says **Kagga Kama**. This is one of two private game reserves (the other one is **Sadawa**) in the vast emptiness of the Ceres Karoo. Both reserves offer accommodation (*see* 'Where to Stay').

Kagga Kama has a bizarre tourist attraction: a resettled bushman (San) family lives on it, although the Ceres Karoo's last original San inhabitants were hunted out in the 1820s. Apparently the owner of the vast reserve (37,000ha) made a deal a few years ago with some bushmen who were struggling to survive in the Kalahari: they are supposed to be able to hunt and live for free, provided they put on dances for the tourists and look picturesque. But in reality they just act for the tourists and sit and drink most of the rest of the time, and the brochure for Kagga Kama is full of photographs of young San girls with bare breasts. However one feels about the morality of this, it is certainly an interesting phenomenon.

Ceres ℗ (0233–)   ***Where to Stay***

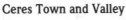

Ceres Town and Valley

expensive

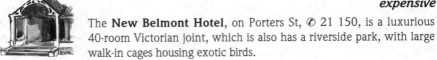

The **New Belmont Hotel**, on Porters St, ℗ 21 150, is a luxurious 40-room Victorian joint, which is also has a riverside park, with large walk-in cages housing exotic birds.

The **Herberg Guest House**, on Voortrekker St, ✆ 22 325, provides B&B in 20 rooms (some en suite) and seven self-catering chalets. Lunch and dinner are optional. **The Mill and Oaks**, a country inn on the R43 at the foot of Michell's Pass, ✆ (0236) 310 860, is comfortable and friendly, with a pub-restaurant frequented by locals. **Prinshof Farm**, a 19th-century farmstead 9km from town on the R46, ✆ 22 298, has accommodation by arrangement only.

cheap

Pine Forest Holiday Resort, squeezed between Ceres and the Skurweberg Mountains (at the north end of town), ✆ 21 170, has chalets, caravan and camping sites, a pool, and access to the Mountain Fynbos Reserve. Last check-in at 10pm.

Cold Bokkeveld & Ceres Karoo

expensive

Kagga Kama Private Game Reserve, ✆ (02211) 638 355, has luxurious thatched huts with fireplaces, a wide variety of game, many hiking trails, rock formations, bushman paintings and real bushmen, specially imported from the Kalahari. Take the R303 north and then the signposted dirt road east for about an hour. **Sadawa**, ✆ 22483/22512, is another private game reserve in the Ceres Karoo, 65km north of town, on the Sutherland road (follow R46 east from town to Hottentotskloof, then northeast on the R356 dirt road). Most plains antelope live in the hills of this vast private reserve (160,000ha). Day and night trails offer good bird watching, including eagles, owls, bustards and waterfowl. There are also bushman paintings.

cheap

Houdenbeck Guest Farm ✆ 70748/70636, offers moderately priced B&B in its old farmhouse; full board is offered at slightly higher prices. Farm walks, and pick-your-own vegetables are also offered.

Sandrivier Guest Farm, ✆ 70757/70748, in the Cold Bokkeveld uplands, on the R303 towards Citrusdal, is very good value. Choose between bed only, B&B, or full board. Hiking trails and bass fishing are offered, and there is snow in winter.

The Breede River Valley

North of the Hottentots' Holland, dividing the lush southwest Cape from the Karoo, runs the broad valley of the Breede. The valley runs west to east, its main centres being Worcester, Montagu, Robertson and McGregor, all handsome towns with much surviving Cape Dutch architecture. Vineyards, orchards and pastures cling to the river. Roadside farm stalls sell fresh fruit, preserves and other goodies. A wild mountain hinterland rises behind, much of which is accessible to the rambler or hiker through various nature reserves (listed below) rich in small game, bird life and fynbos.

Passage into the valley from the south is limited to two mountain passes, **Du Toit's Kloof** (through which runs the N1 highway) in the Klein Drakenstein Mountains north of Paarl, or Bain's Kloof in the Limietberg east of Wellington. Both are spectacular drives, and provide

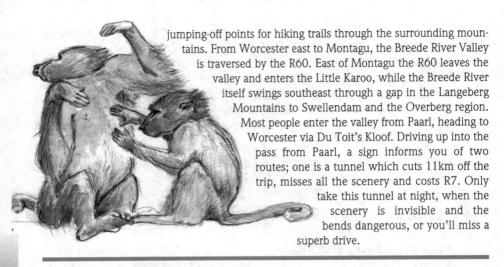

jumping-off points for hiking trails through the surrounding mountains. From Worcester east to Montagu, the Breede River Valley is traversed by the R60. East of Montagu the R60 leaves the valley and enters the Little Karoo, while the Breede River itself swings southeast through a gap in the Langeberg Mountains to Swellendam and the Overberg region. Most people enter the valley from Paarl, heading to Worcester via Du Toit's Kloof. Driving up into the pass from Paarl, a sign informs you of two routes; one is a tunnel which cuts 11km off the trip, misses all the scenery and costs R7. Only take this tunnel at night, when the scenery is invisible and the bends dangerous, or you'll miss a superb drive.

The Ghosts of Du Toit's Kloof

Two ghosts are supposed to haunt Du Toit's Kloof. One is a large black car that sometimes appears at night, driving on the wrong side of the road, straight at the oncoming traffic. Several people have reported encounters with this phantom car, shutting their eyes in expectation of the impact, and then finding that the car has disappeared. Apparently the police even chased it once, while looking for a car that matched its description, only to be treated to the same experience. The second ghost is more lethal: a girl hitch-hiker said to cause fatal accidents to those who pick her up. While looking out for her, be careful not to run over baboons, which are very real and sometimes sit in the middle of the road, playing chicken with the traffic.

A hiking trail runs from Du Toit's Kloof to Bain's Kloof, with an overnight hut halfway. Hikers can start from either end, but most people start from Bain's Kloof, as the trail-head is better marked from there (see p.184).

Worcester

After Du Toit's Kloof the N1 leads to Worcester, the largest town in the valley, with a wine route to equal that of Stellenbosch. The town centre, built around a huge, bare square, is not so attractive (more 1950s and '60s 'improvements') but a stroll into the residential streets reveals some very handsome early 19th-century houses.

Tourist Information

Publicity Office, 75 Church Street, Worcester, ✆ (0231) 71408.

Worcester was founded in 1818, and named after the Marquis of Worcester, elder brother of the then Cape Governor, Lord Charles Somerset. Its function has hardly changed since: half wine and agricultural town, half stopping and servicing point for those on the road north.

Worcester has four museums, the largest and best of which is the **Kleinplasie Open Air Museum** (*open Mon–Sat 9–4.30, Sun 10.30–4.30*), on the main road at the east end of town. A museum of old farm life, occupying the site of two of the smallholdings sold as part of the original town layout, it has replicas of farm buildings, a restaurant and a cellar of local wines. Various traditional activities include Witblitz-making (White Lightning distillation), tobacco-rolling and corn-threshing using horses. The activities change from week to week.

The **Stofberghuis** (*open Mon–Sat 9–4.30, Sun 10.30–4.30*), built in 1920, houses a history of Worcester. The **Hugo Naudenhuis** (*same hours*), on Russell Street, was the home of Hugo Naude, a landscape-painter active in the late 19th century. This rather grand house, built by him in 1900, is now a gallery of his paintings, and those of his contemporaries, and includes a sculpture garden. The **Beckhuis**, on Baring Street (*open Mon–Fri 9–1 and 2–5, Sat 8.30–4.30, Sun 2–5*), was built in 1841 and is named after Cornelius Beck, who owned a lot of property in the town during the first half of the 19th century. The museum is furnished as a Victorian town house.

The **Karoo Botanical Gardens** make lovely walking. Take the N1 north and follow the signs for about 3km. The garden is large—154ha—and full of flowers through winter and spring. (*Open daily sunrise to sunset.*)

The **Pioneer School**, in Church Street, is a craft shop selling carving, leatherwork and jewellery made by the blind.

The Worcester Wine Route

The Worcester Wine Route consists of 26 wineries dotted along the Breede River Valley. A map and guide booklet can be had from the Publicity Office or from the display wine cellar at the Kleinplasie Open Air Museum.

The Worcester estates are not as historically interesting as those of the Hottentots' Holland, but there is plenty here for wine buffs. The cellars are mainly co-operatives producing white, dessert and fortified wines—on account of the Breede River Valley's more arid soil and drier climate—though a few reds are produced. Most prestigious is the **Nuy Estate**, which hugs the foothills of the Hex River Mountains, a few kilometres east of town. Nuy has won awards for dessert wines, fortified muscadels and for a well-regarded Cape Colombard, a sharp table white that should be drunk soon after bottling.

Botha Wine Estate, ℗ (0234) 740, is 20km from Worcester on the Ceres Road. An elegant Cape Dutch homestead, it offers tastings, but tours by appointment only. Also handsome are **Groot Eiland**, ℗ (0231) 91 140, 16km from Worcester towards Rawsonville, which offers regular tours and tastings through the week of dry and semi-sweet white wines, a few reds and sweet hanepoort juice, and **Slanghoek**, 30km from town, which also produces dry and semi-sweet whites.

Other Worcester estates worth visiting include **De Doorns** and **Louwshoek**. While they are estates of great scenic beauty, they lack the graceful manors and homesteads of the other estates and are pretty well limited to fortified wines and the odd white table wine. For a greater range, you have to travel further east along the Breede River Valley to the town of Roberston (*see* below).

The Hex River Mountains and Valley

Before heading east down the rest of the Breede River Valley, it is worth making a trip north as far as the Hex River Pass, which is the main road and rail route north. The pass is as spectacular as one would expect, but, as is usual with mountains, it is better to get out and walk. Hikers can explore the Hex River Mountains most easily by taking the **Jan Du Toit's Kloof Trail** (not to be confused with Du Toit's Kloof in the Klein Drakenstein Mountains). The trail starts at **Kluitjieskraal** (pronounced 'Klykieskraal') **Forest Station**, ✆ (0232) 2327, near the small town of Wolsely (west of Worcester on the R43). Maps and permits are sold at the forest station. The Hex River Mountains are skiied in winter (one of three regular ski points in South Africa). The ski-club hut is on the Hex River Pass. Trips can be arranged through the Worcester Publicity Office.

Robertson

The next town east of Worcester along the Breede Valley is Robertson. Though not a particularly attractive town, Robertson's surrounding countryside is lovely. The vineyards specialize in fortified wines from muscadel grapes, producing sherry, brandy and jeropico as well as some very fine whites. There are fifteen wineries around the town. There is also a lot of thoroughbred breeding in the area, fourteen studs in all, and it's worth taking a detour or two on some of the country roads off the main R60 to enjoy the scenery, particularly along the road to McGregor.

The Robertson Museum, on Paul Kruger Street (*open Mon–Fri 9–4.30*), houses the obligatory collection of local Victoriana.

The Local Wineries

One can visit most of the surrounding farms and estates by arrangement through the Publicity Association in the Municipal Buildings on Main Street, ✆ (02351) 4437. Meanwhile, here are a few pointers: **Bon Courage** is a superb 18th-century Cape Dutch estate producing well-received dessert wines and a good Chardonnay. **De Wetshof** had success with Chardonnays from 1987–91, as well as producing dessert wines. The **Graham Beck Winery** makes very dry white wines, while **Van Loveren** specializes in South African rarities such as the Spanish Fernao Pires and the Hungarian Harlesvlu, both whites. **Welvevrede** is a new estate, trying its first few Chardonnays and fortified wines, and **Zandvliet** is one of several wineries producing reds in the Breede River Valley. Its Shiraz is reckoned to be one of the best in the country.

McGregor

To reach McGregor, detour 26km south from the R60 through the Vrolijkheid Nature Reserve to where the little town lies at the foot of the Riversonderend Mountains.

McGregor has been described as the best-preserved 19th-century town in Cape Province, and many travellers recommend it as the place to stay while exploring the Breede River Valley. It is an almost completely intact late-Georgian village of whitewashed cottages clustered round a mill stream, and is certainly the prettiest town in the valley. What was once a backwater for farmers and wine-growers is increasingly becoming a holiday-home village, because of the pretty white buildings, shading oaks and surrounding mountains. There is an old mill to stay in, from which you can explore the great stretch of wild mountain rising to the south, and there are almost no 20th-century buildings in sight.

The **McGregor Winery** is about 300m north of town on the main road. **Greengables Restaurant and Coffee Shop**, on Voortrekker Street, and the **Pottery**, on Breede Street, are all within a few blocks of each other.

Vrolijkheid Nature Reserve, ✆ (02351) 4437, north of town, is the trail-head of a two-day hike into the southern mountains called the **Boesmanskloof Trail** which winds south over the Riviersonderend Mountains to the small town of Greyton (*see* p.206). Vrolijkheid (pronounced 'frolick height') is known for bird-watching.

Montagu

Montagu is the last town of the Breede River Valley winelands before the river turns south east into the Overberg region. The approach is dramatic: a spur of the Langeberg Mountains juts abruptly across the valley, causing the road to twist suddenly through the Kogmanskloof canyon, whose walls of folded strata rear 1500m towards the sky. The town is surrounded by the large Montagu Mountain Nature Reserve, of which the encircling mountains form a part. About 3km west of town the R60 passes under a natural rock arch overlooking a large bend in the Breede River: atop the arch is the ruin of an old fort built by the British during the Boer War.

Montagu is a singularly pleasant, peaceful place, with many surviving late-Cape Dutch buildings. There are two hot springs north of town; one is sadly over-developed, the other quiet, and only used by local farmers. The usual juxtaposition of orchard, vineyard, pasture and wild mountain provides the backdrop.

Long Street has a wealth of Cape Dutch houses, barns and cottages, some 14 of which are national monuments. The **Montagu Museum** (*open weekdays 9–4.30*), also on Long Street, concentrates more on the Little Karoo region than on the Breede River Valley (Montagu is roughly the border point between the two). The museum occupies several buildings, one of which is Joubert House, the oldest house in town. The Montagu Museum collects and supplies (by mail or for sale on the premises) fresh herbs, both African and European, and provides information on their nutritional and medicinal uses.

The Something Special Coffee Shop, on Bad Street ('bath street', the road to the hot springs), does fabulous cheesecake and sells local crafts.

Around Montagu

Montagu Hot Springs Spa is 4km north of town, in a deep valley between the Langeberg and the excellently named Waboomsberg ('Wagon-tree mountains', rather than mountains that go WA-BOOM!). Although the back of the spa looks on to a canyon where black eagles, dassies and klipspringers live, the place itself is a monument to 1970s bad taste, complete with concrete mini-golf course, large hotel and all.

Fortunately, there is another hot spring about 4km further north, on a farm called **Baden** (on the right off the R318, about 2km down a dirt road; look out for springbok on the hillside by the road). This spring flows into a small man-made pool. Visitors can only bathe on Sundays, presumably to stop the place from being overrun.

Montagu Mountain Nature Reserve, 2km west of town, is very lovely. There is a hiking hut in a ravine (where live hundreds of dassies), giving access to two long day-walks (one 12km, one 15km) that lead up into the wild kloofs of the Langeberg. The 15km trail is tough but beautiful, climbing almost 1500m through high valleys that resemble miniature gardens. Several waterfalls are encountered on its homeward stretch. There is also a 7km hike along a river to the Hot Springs Spa. The river is full of fish, some of which are unique to the area. Hikers should see klipspringers, baboons, sunbirds, sugarbirds, black eagles, many dassies and several types of protea. To book the trail, call ✆ (0234) 42471.

North of Montagu

Follow the R318 north past the hot springs and the road leads first to **Die Koo**, a fertile valley on the north side of the Langeberg where most of South Africa's fruit and vegetables for canning are grown. From there, the road winds through the wild Nouga Hills into the Hex River Valley and the Karoo; an interesting drive if you are heading north to the N1.

Activities

Hiking in the mountains: The Breede River Valley and its surrounding mountains have excellent hiking trails, details of which are included with the town entries in this section.

Canoeing: The Breede River itself is made accessible through **Breede River Adventures**, 104 Upper Maynard Street, Cape Town, ✆ (021) 762 5602. Trips run from two to seven days.

4x4 trails: The Waboomsberg 4x4 Trail offers 80km of rugged mountain off-road driving with camping facilities. Trail starts in Montagu, ✆ (0234) 42 209.

Where to Stay and Eating Out

Worcester ✆ (0231–)

moderate

The **Kerkstraat Herberg Country Lodge**, 27 Church Street, ✆ 25 194 (along the R60 for about 10km from Worcester, then turn north on a dirt road about 2km to Nuy), occupies some old workers' cottages, and is rather luxurious. The owners let you prepare your own breakfast basket. **Oude Schuur Country Cottage**, ✆ 21 275, in the Nuy Valley is a self-contained old thatched cottage that takes up to six people. Bass fishing and good walking are available at the farm, and you can check out the farm dairy where they make feta cheese. **Nooitgedacht Farm**, ✆ 21 284 (8km down the R60), offers B&B, farm walks, fireplaces and breakfast in bed.

Kleinplasie Farm Museum Restaurant, ✆ 2225/6, is a country restaurant specializing in Cape dishes and Breede River wines. At lunchtime there are old-time farm displays, such as corn-threshing with horses on a round stone floor. Also good is **Fairburn's**, on Fairburn St, ✆ 24 479, which offers good value, filling but unimaginative food. The **Barlinka**, on Stockenstroom St, ✆ 72 641, is slightly more expensive, and has a continental menu.

Robertson ✆ (02351–)

moderate–cheap

Excellent accommodation is offered by the **Pat Busch Private Nature Reserve**, in the Langeberg about 10km north of town, ✆ 2033, in self-catering chalets, from where you can go hiking along streams and through fynbos where small buck and birds live.

The **Breede Valley Lodge**, 29 Loop Street, ✆ 62 296, is in town, or there's the **Weltevrede Guest Farm**, ✆ 2073, just outside town.

The **Braenewynsdraai Winehouse**, on Kromhout Street, ✆ 3202, serves classic Cape Dutch dishes and a wide range of local wines. You could also try the **Oude Fontein**, on Reitz Street, ✆ 6141, which offers a slightly cheaper, more standard continental menu, or the **Loer-in Koffiekroeg**, on Church Street, ✆ 2346, a coffee shop serving light lunches, teas and cakes.

In the neighbouring village of Ashton is the **Normandy**, ✆ (0234) 51 590, serving very good French dishes at the expensive end of moderate.

McGregor ✆ (02353–)

expensive

McGregor has the best expensive accomodation in the Breede River Valley. The **Old Mill Lodge**, on Mill St, ✆ 841, offers luxury and pampering in an old mill, with waterwheel and all. Victorian furnishings and large, comfortable beds with the sound of the mill stream tumbling by at night make this a tranquil place to stay. It also has a good country restaurant, serving Cape dishes, such as *denningvleis* (diced, braised mutton sharpened with vinegar and tamarinds) and *sosaties* (grilled, marinaded meat on a skewer).

The **McGregor Haus**, at the south end of Mill St (on the corner of Hoff and Voortrekker Streets), ✆ 925, is an old Victorian town house with seven double rooms. It also has a good Cape restaurant specializing in Karoo mutton, home-made breads and local fruits, and a pub.

McGregor Country Cottages, ✆ 816, offer en suite accommodation in a group of self-contained old thatched workers' cottages.

The **Greengables Restuaurant**, on Voortrekker St, ✆ 626, does delicious lunches, such as *vleis* pasties or trout.

Bonnievale ✆ (02346–)

moderate

Bonnievale has some good B&Bs and guest farms, such as **Bonnie's**, ✆ 2251, **Merwenstein Country House**, ✆ 2806, or **Wolvendrift**, ✆ 2837.

Die Rietdak, ✆ 3236, is a good traditional Cape country restaurant.

cheap

Bonnievale also has a backpackers' lodge, **Die Houthut**, ✆ 2738.

Montagu ✆ (0234–)

expensive

The **Montagu Country Inn**, ✆ 614 3125, ✆ 419 05, is a period piece offering the full treatment.

moderate

Montagu has a bunch of good B&Bs: **Murphy's B&B**, 27 Kohler St, ✆ 41 513, **Montagu Guest House**, 19 Kohler St, ✆ 42 681, **Down the Lane**, 6 Bad St, ✆ 41 455, and **Aasvoelkrans**, ✆ 41 228, who also have cheaper, hostel accommodation.

cheap

Hostel accommodation can also be had at **De Bos Farm**, ✆ 42 532.

The Something Special Coffee Shop, on Bad St, does special things for lunch (especially cheesecake).

The Overberg

> *South Africa is so far off that I cannot hope to be able to excite English readers to visit the Cape colony for the sake of the scenery—though...*
> *I cannot imagine that any trip should be more pleasant and serviceable.*
>
> *Travels in South Africa Volume I*, Anthony Trollope

South and east of the Hottentots' Holland lies the Overberg, a coastal land of sheep pasture and wheat fields bounded by high, wild mountains. To the west, the high Riviersonderendberg falls to a narrrow coastal plain whose old resort towns give way to wilder and emptier beaches as you travel east. The Overberg coastline is famous for whales and from June to November mothers and calves can be seen rolling in the swell just a few hundred metres offshore. Inland, the farmlands stretch away north to the handsome 18th-century town of Swellendam, behind which the sheer walls of the Langeberg mark the beginning of the great interior.

The Overberg has some fabulous nature reserves, the best being the **Harold Porter Botanical Reserve** and **Kogelberg Nature Reserve**, which protect a large chunk of coastal mountain behind Betty's Bay, **De Hoop Nature Reserve**, a sweep of wild coastline in the east, **Marloth Nature Reserve** and **Boosmansbos Wilderness Area** in the towering Langeberg to the north, and **Bontebok National Park** near Swellendam. Lapped by the warm Agulhas current, the Overberg's coast is popular among Capetonians, who escape to the crowded, elegant 19th-century resort town of **Hermanus**, or to the emptier beaches at **Gansbaai, Arniston** and **Port Beaufort**. Africa's southernmost point, **Cape Agulhas** (unfortunately a rather ugly resort town), lies on the Overberg Coast, 20km below the town of Bredasdorp.

History

The Overberg was one of the first 'interior' regions to be affected by white expansion outside the original Cape colony. At the end of the 17th century, by following the elephant herds that trekked seasonally from the coast to the interior, ivory-hunters and explorers had discovered the mountain passes leading from the Cape to the Overberg, whose temperate climate and rich grazing attracted settlers seeking to live outside the control of the Dutch East India Company. By the 1720s trekboers (nomadic farmers who had adopted the Khoi's pastoral lifestyle) were pouring in with their vast sheep herds, much to the dismay of the indigenous Khoi and San people. By the 1740s, there were so many settlers in the region that the San had gone, and almost all of the Khoi were reduced to working on farms that had once been grazing land for their own flocks. In 1743 the Dutch East India Company decided to regularize the Overberg (i.e. make it taxable), created a town and *landdrost* (magistracy) at Swellendam, and the region became part of the Cape Colony.

As Swellendam's administration became more effective through the 18th century, many of the Overberg's more independent-minded settlers trekked east to the present-day Garden Route and Eastern Cape. In fact, the area became something of a corridor for the Cape's more lawless types to pass through on their way to the wild interior. In the Overberg's mountain ranges, deserters from the Dutch East India Company garrisons, dispossessed Khoi and runaway slaves formed bandit gangs, raiding farms and travellers as the opportunity arose. By the late 18th century, their depredations were forcing many farmers to abandon their properties, and the Dutch Governor-General tried to induce trekboers to settle permanently by offering 200 rix-dollars to any burgher who converted 50ha into freehold property.

In the decades following the Cape Colony's extension to the Fish River in the Eastern Cape (1780), the Overberg began to settle into its present farming landscape. The local garrisons swelled, and the mountain freebooters and bandits drifted to the new lawlessness of the eastern frontier. Although Xhosa warriors from the Eastern Cape raided into the Overberg a couple of times during the early 19th-century Frontier Wars, the region bowed out of South Africa's political theatre and became a prosperous agricultural hinterland for Cape Town. Swellendam evolved into a wealthy regional capital whose burghers serviced both the local farming population and the steady stream of settlers, traders and hunters journeying to and from the Eastern Cape and, after 1840, Natal.

By 1850 the Overberg's Khoi had virtually ceased to exist as an identifiable group, following the inevitable sexual exploitation of their women by farmers and townsfolk alike. As with

Cape Town and the Winelands, the Overberg's indigenous people had therefore been absorbed into both the white economy (as labourers and servants) and population, yet were still referred to as 'Hottentots' or 'coloureds' and treated as an underclass. A few managed to trek north to the (as yet) barely settled reaches of the vast Karoo to merge with the free Griqua (mixed Khoi/Boer) groups living around the Orange River, but most lacked the means to do so and stayed on the farms.

Today, little has changed. The Overberg has remained a quiet, predominantly Afrikaans-speaking rural backwater, remote from the turbulent events of South Africa's late 19th- and 20th-century history. Apart from the tourism on the coast, most of the economy still relies on sheep and grain, and the wild mountain reaches, once the haunt of bandits, are now a hiker's paradise of uninhabited fynbos and forested kloofs. Most travellers still only pass through the Overberg on their way east–west, so its quiet pleasures are known only to the few that take time to explore.

Getting There

By car: There are three ways into the Overberg from Cape Town: over **Sir Lowry's Pass** through the southern end of the Hottentots' Holland Nature Reserve to Grabouw; via the northern Hottentots' Holland from Franschoek in the Winelands via the spectacular **Franschoek Pass**; or along the coast, following the east side of False Bay along the foot of the southernmost Hottentots' Holland Mountains where they jut into the sea at **Cape Hangklip**, around to Betty's Bay (R44). The first and last of these routes are the most beautiful, and, if making an excursion into the Overberg from Cape Town, it is worth going in by one route and out by the other.

From the north, the R60 from the Wineland town of Montagu (via the Kogmanskloof Pass), or the R324 from Barrydale in the western Little Karoo (via the Tradouw Pass), provide spectacular drives over the Langeberg. From the east, the N2 from the Garden Route towns of Knysna, George and Mossel Bay runs between the Langeberg and the coast.

By bus: InterCape, **Greyhound** and **TransLux** all travel east–west along the N2, and stop at the main towns en route. From here local transport to nature reserves and/or the coast can usually be arranged by contacting the Publicity Association of the town nearest your destination. Alternatively, the Baz Bus, ✆ (021) 439 2323, stops in Hermanus.

By rail: Trains run from Cape Town to Swellendam via Worcester, taking in the beautiful Hex River Mountains and running along the foot of the Langeberg. From the east, trains from Port Elizabeth to Cape Town take in Swellendam and the other main towns. Again, for local transport, telephone the Publicity Association of the town closest to your final destination.

The Overberg Coast

The R44 road south from the N2 (just west of Sir Lowry's Pass), between the Hottentots' Holland and False Bay, enters the Overberg via Cape Hangklip, a small peak falling into the sea at the southern extremity of the Hottentots' Holland range.

Cape Hangklip was a bandit stronghold (*see* **South African History**) during the late 18th century, but today its **Hangklip Hotel** is a haunt of fishermen, both amateur and professional. It's worth spending an evening in the bar hearing coastal yarns. The clientele can get a little rough, although this tends to be with each other, rather than with strangers.

Betty's Bay, a small settlement of holiday houses strung out along the coast, with a single store, has a couple of small, safe swimming beaches, but the real attraction is the **Harold Porter Botanical Reserve**, © (02827) 29 311, set just into the coastal mountains rising behind the bay, and clearly signposted from the R44. The reserve's walking trail follows a deep kloof up a series of waterfalls. In spring the profuse wildflowers are a feast for the eye. Duiker, grysbok, baboon and dassies (as well as the usual invisible leopards) live here, and over 60 bird species are recorded. There is no accommodation.

The mountain country behind the Harold Porter Reserve is protected by the 18,000ha **Kogelberg Conservation Area**, © (0225) 4301. The entrance is along the R44 from Betty's Bay, about 2km before the town of Kleinmond. Kogelberg is a typical stretch of wild western Cape mountain fynbos with forest kloofs. Grey rhebok, klipspringer and baboon are common. Leopard are the main predators. Day hiking only is permitted, with one particularly beautiful trail along the course of the Palmiet River, and there is no accommodation within the conservation area.

From Betty's Bay the road wanders on beneath the mountains to Kleinmond. Another small resort of Capetonian holiday homes, Kleinmond sits on a small lagoon at the mouth of the Palmiet River. There are several camp sites, with safe swimming in the lagoon (though not on the beach, which has a cross-current). **Kleinmond Nature Reserve**, west and north of town, incorporates sea-shore, coastal fynbos and montane fynbos. Five short walking trails cimb into the mountains behind. The entrance is signposted from the R44 west of the village. Kleinmond is a popular fishing spot, but for private anglers only. There are no tackle-hire shops until Hermanus.

Between Kleinmond and Hermanus is **Onrus** ('restless'—after the pounding surf). One of the quieter holiday villages, Onrus also has a small lagoon, safe beach and camp site. Sand Bay is another safe beach a few kilometres further east.

Hermanus and Around

Tourist Information

Tourist Information Office, Marine Drive, © (0283) 22 629.

Hermanus is the largest town on the Overberg Coast, named after one Hermanus Pieters, a trekboer who, in the mid 1830s, settled with his flock at a spring near the shore here. His peaceful life as fisherman and grazier became more disturbed each year, as the tiny natural harbour, rich grazing and vast fish-shoals off-shore attracted more and more settlers. By the end of the 19th century, Hermanus had been discovered by Capetonians. Hotels sprang up around the little town of white lime and thatch cottages. Larger mansions for the wealthy followed. Hermanus has been a resort ever since.

Although the small harbour has been restored as an open-air fishing museum, and despite the town's bustle and life, Hermanus is no longer as attractive as the quieter places further east along the coast that it once resembled. However the mountains and the beaches are worth exploring, and in summer, Hermanus is a good place to spot whales.

The **Old Harbour Museum**, on Marine Drive (*open Mon–Sat 9–1 and 2–4*), displays old fishing boats and an old fisherman's cottage, with old photographs of the days when the fishing harbour was active. **Lemm's Corner Craft Market** (*open Sat am only*), just off Marine Drive, is a good place to pick up crafts, preserves, biscuits and other goodies.

Walker Bay, just east of town, is where Hermanus' famous beaches begin, and is the best vantage point for whale-watching; **Grotto Beach** and **Voelklip Beach** stretch for some miles along the bay. Both have safe swimming and beautiful walking.

A hiking trail runs along **Hermanus Cliffs**, west of town, giving spectacular views out over the Indian Ocean. Where Marine Drive meets the foot of the cliffs, is the **Mermaid's Tidal Pool**, in fact a set of clear freshwater pools. Nearby is a monument of four wagon wheels commemorating the first Overberg ox-wagon to creak north over the mountains to join the Great Trek in 1836 (*see* **South African History**). About 3km east of town is **De Mond Lagoon**, a small resort (signposted from the R44) where you can hire canoes, windsurfers, fishing tackle, snorkels etc. There is also good, calm swimming, bird-watching and fishing.

Fernkloof Nature Reserve is in the mountains just north of Hermanus. Like most of the southwestern Cape reserves, it comprises a wild stretch of montane fynbos, with indigenous forest lining the kloofs. Hikers may see grey rhebok, duiker, grysbok and klipspringer on the network of walking trails. To reach the reserve, take the 'Mountain Drive' road signposted from the R44 just west of Hermanus.

Under the mountains at the eastern end of Walker Bay are **Die Kelders**, a set of magical undergound pools whose farmer-owner sometimes allows the public in to swim. Ask at the Tourist Information Office in Hermanus.

However, Hermanus is probably best known nowadays for **whale-watching**. It even employs a special **whale crier**—actually a blower—who sounds a horn whenever one is sighted within easy reach of the town centre. If you've always wanted to see a whale—and some of them pass just 100m or so from shore—then Hermanus is your place.

Gansbaai

Gansbaai ('Goose Bay'), the next town east of Hermanus, is less of a resort than a fishing village, known by local anglers as one of the best spots for shore fishing. Whale-watching from here can also be rewarding, and the village is still fairly unspoilt, with some handsome old lime and thatch cottages among the newer buildings. Get down there around 2pm, when the boats are coming in, to buy fresh fish straight from the fishermen (they put in and out from the old harbour at the end of the main road into the village).

'Women and Children First!'

On the promontory south of Gansbaai is **Danger Point**, marked by a lighthouse, and scene of a famous shipwreck. In 1852, the HMS *Birkenhead* was carrying about 500 soldiers from Cape Town to the Eastern Cape, to fight in the eighth Frontier War (*see* **Eastern Cape**, 'History'). Also on the ship were about 20 women and children. A storm washed the ship on to the rocks at

Danger Point. As it foundered, the crew found that only three of the lifeboats were in working order. Lt. Col. Seton, the officer commanding, called the troops up on deck, drew his sabre and threatened with death any man who crowded the boats where the women and children were gathering. Even as the horses were being put overboard to swim for it, the troops stayed in line, and when the ship went down almost all were drowned or eaten by sharks. The incident was much celebrated in Victorian England as a noble tragedy and tradition has it that the maxim 'women and children first' originated here (though this seems far-fetched, as the soldiers were presumably obeying the maxim when they went to their deaths). There is a memorial to the dead at Danger Point.

Elim

From Gansbaai the coast becomes wilder and less populated. Rough grazing farms come down to the sea. About 8km east of Gansbaai the road forks: one road continues along the coast to **Pearly Beach**, a lonely stretch of pale sand bordered by huge dunes, with safe swimming and good walking; the other, a dirt road, heads inland to the old Moravian Mission station of Elim.

Like Wuppertal in the Cedarberg, Elim (built in 1824) is a jewel of early 19th-century architecture, left untouched owing to its status as a 'coloured' community—the village was never modernized. The road enters Elim via some common grazing land (watch out for loose horses) to a village that might serve as a film set for a Thomas Hardy novel. The old white-wash and thatch cottages of the village's three streets have suffered no alterations, only loving care or dismal neglect depending on the circumstances of their occupants. Chickens scratch in the street. Kids play. There seem not to be any vehicles. At the top of the main street is the large white **Moravian Church** and its **Old Mill**, now restored and a national monument, but seldom open to the public. Very few of the 'public' ever get to Elim. In no way has the place been altered to accommodate tourism.

Around Cape Agulhas

Whether you have followed the coast road, or headed inland to Elim, the next 20km of coastline has no road, and to explore the Overberg Coast further you must swing north to the town of Bredasdorp (*see* p.208) and then south again, across the marshy plain of Africa's southern tip, to **Cape Agulhas**, the continent's southernmost point. Here, unfortunately, Africa ends unobtrusively, with none of the drama of Cape Point. Worse, man has made it ugly. The holiday resort villages at Struisbaai and Cape Agulhas (the two run into each other) are dull to say the least, with no centre and few permanent residents. There is a lighthouse to look around, but otherwise the only reason to go is to be able to say that you have seen Africa's southernmost point. 'Agulhas' means 'needles' in Portuguese, either in warning of the sharp rocks waiting to bite into the bellies of unwary ships, or from the fact that at this point, the needle of a compass points due north—which is the only way out of Agulhas: back to Bredasdorp (20km). However, from here you can make some more rewarding trips.

De Mond Nature Reserve, ✆ (0284) 4217 (not to be confused with De Mond resort near Hermanus), is reached from the Bredasdorp–Arniston road (look out for the signpost 11km south of Bredasdorp). This is a hidden stretch of milkwood forest and coastal dunes fronting a wild beach where a small river (safe for swimming) flows into the sea. The birdwatching is superb, especially for pelicans and terns, and there are small buck in the woods. There is no accommodation—a good thing, as this quiet corner would soon be spoilt by too much human presence.

Arniston and Around

Another there-and-back route to the coast is to **Arniston** (also known as Waenhuiskrans—'wagon house cliff'). Arniston today offers the tranquility and romance that Hermanus must have offered many years ago. The old fishermen's cottages still stand: two-roomed, single-storeyed thatched buildings that are cool in summer and warm in winter. People do holiday here but it seldom gets crowded. There are miles of white sandy beach, with some enormous caverns eroded into the low seaward cliffs behind.

The largest is **Waenhuiskrans Cave**, into part of which flows the sea, but which stays sufficiently dry to overnight in, something people have been doing for millennia. Small stone mounds on the beach nearby are the remains of prehistoric fish-traps and shell-middens made by the *strandlopers* (beach-dwellers) who originally inhabited the caves.

Much newer, from the 19th to the mid 20th centuries, is the **Fishermen's Graveyard** at Arniston. Worth a visit, it has many crudely cut headstones fashioned by the fisher folk themselves, who had no stone-masons to do the job professionally. Most are the graves of 'coloured' fishermen lost at sea, who, because of their traditionally low status, have not been honoured except by their own community. Today, the old fishing village is mostly owned by Capetonians, though a few fishermen still inhabit the farther-flung cottages. Arniston has a camp site, and cottages for rent (*see* 'Where to Stay').

From Arniston, you again have to back-track to Bredasdorp to go further east, but it's worth it, for the road (R319 north, then after 8km take the dirt road east) leads to **De Hoop Nature Reserve**, ✆ (02922) 700, one of the wildest accessible spots on the Western Cape's south coast.

The reserve, which includes an offshore area, is vast (over 60,000ha) with about 40km of wild beach. Inland is a huge fynbos heathland, a range of hills and a large lake. The reserve supports large mammals, including the rare Cape mountain zebra, eland, bontebok and grey rhebok, as well as smaller antelope and mammals. The Salt River, which flows into the lake, is a good place to spot otters (if you're very quiet and still). Whales are often seen offshore, and the reserve harbours 228 recorded bird species. Of the many indigenous fynbos plants, 50 are known to exist only within the reserve.

De Hoop has several groups of rondavels and camp sites, so accommodation is not a problem, and it is worth spending a few days here walking the trails or just beach-combing in the wind and silence.

At the far-eastern end of De Hoop Nature Reserve, at **Cape Infanta**, the Breede River flows into the sea. A small resort (again, just a few holiday homes) on the east side of the estuary, Cape Infanta marks the border between the Overberg Coast and the Garden Route.

Activities

Walking and hiking: All of the reserves listed above have good day trails through beach and upland fynbos country. De Hoop Nature Reserve is the only place offering overnight hikes.

Fishing: The Overberg Coast is known for its superb sea fishing, both from the shoreline and in the deeps of the warm Agulhas current offshore, where big game fish can be caught. Tackle and boat hire for both kinds of fishing can be arranged through Hermanus' Tourist Information Office.

Whale-watching: The Overberg Coast is also known for the large numbers of southern right whales that cruise offshore. Between September and March every year several hundred drift past its beaches in ones and twos, while, in September and November, mothers calve in the waters of Walker Bay. Some swim to within a few hundred metres of the beaches, and can be clearly watched for hours as they roll in the swell. The beaches at Walker Bay, near Hermanus, and De Hoop Nature Reserve are the best sighting spots, though almost any beach or promontory will do. Call their **whale hotline**, ✆ (0283) 22 629.

Shark diving: The **Great White Backpackers Lodge**, at Gansbaai, ✆ (02384) 41 380, arranges day trips to the Overberg Coast's great white feeding grounds. They lower you down in a cage with an aqualung and wetsuit (as well as metal bars to keep you alive).

Bungee-jumping: **Kiwi Extreme**, ✆ (021) 726 420, will arrange for you to leap off the high bridge at Gouritsmond, and lose your lunch.

Where to Stay

expensive

Stanford House, 20 Victoria Street, ✆ (0283) 300, in the small village of Stanford (10km east of Hermanus on the R44 around Walker Bay), is a 19th-century manor house set just below the mountains. The rooms are done up in colonial style, but without being overblown. The **Marine Hotel**, on Marine Drive, Hermanus, ✆ (0283) 701 000, ✉ 701 009, is the town's best-known hotel, dating from 1902. Very pricey, but beautifully furnished, it has views out over Walker Bay and serves superb seafood.

moderate

Mountain Drive Guest House, 66 Mountain Drive, Hermanus, ✆ (0283) 24 452, is a short walk from the old harbour and the bay. Good value, friendly and informal B&B (with reductions for kids). Also very good value is **Zoete Inval**, 23 Main Road, in the town centre, ✆ (0283) 21242, which offers clean and comfy B&B.

Arniston Seaside Cottages, ✆ (02847) 59 772, must be booked at least a day in advance. This will secure an old lime and thatch fisherman's cottage, allowing you to explore the beaches and caverns on the empty coast. Very romantic. Take your own food. **The Arniston Hotel**, ✆ (02847) 59 000, is a good bet if you cannot get a cottage. Not as beautiful as the other buildings of Arniston, but a small, friendly place with 23 en suite rooms. **Potbergerhuis Guest House**, ✆ (02922) 665 976, is the author's recommendation: a farmhouse under the Potberg Mountain, just outside the eastern edge of De Hoop Nature Reserve, with ostriches as well as sheep grazing the surrounding fields, horses to ride, endless walking, and the great wild coastline of the nature reserve to explore. Set in the classic high, rolling Overberg landscape, the house is simply but comfortably furnished (sleeps up to six) and has log fires. You can either bring your own food, arrange B&B, or ask the farmer's wife to cook three meals a day, just as you wish.

cheap

The best value roofed accommodation is at **De Hoop Nature Reserve**, ✆ (028) 542 1126, which has seven sets of rondavels in quiet seclusion, with comfortable beds and a communal kitchen. Those by the De Hoopvlei lake have excellent bird-watching. These are often booked up in holiday season, but mid-week is usually safe. Phone first. There's also the **Hermanus Youth Hostel**, ✆ (0283) 21 772, on Church Street, and the **Hermanus Travellers Lodge**, on Tweefontein Farm in the Hemel en Aarde Valley, just outside town, ✆ (0283) 22 829, offering a choice of backpacker-style hostel dorms or double rooms and B&B. The **Great White Backpackers Lodge** is at Gansbaai (*see* 'Activities').

The Diedre Gasthuis, 38 Du Toit Street, Bredasdorp, is poised inland between Cape Agulhas, Arniston and De Hoop Nature Reserve. It offers simple, straightforward B&B in a family house.

Eating Out

Should you tire of buying fish direct from the fisherman, almost all the Overberg's coastal restaurants serve seafood. Menus vary little, though the quality is always very high, and what you eat is always fresh from the sea.

expensive

The **Marine Hotel**, Hermanus, ✆ (0283) 701 000, is well known for seafood of all kinds. The dining room is a little impersonal, but a good place to eat the more exotic big-game and deep-sea fish, as well as the usual seafood repertoire.

moderate

The **Beach House Hotel**, Kleinmond, ✆ (02823) 3130, is smart but not too pricey, and has a nice Edwardian feel. More seafood. The **Arniston Hotel** serves good fish and is a good place to meet people, normally Capetonians with cottages in Arniston.

cheap

The **Cape Hangklip Hotel**, Betty's Bay, serves the fish 'n' chips end of seafood cuisine, and is very good, everything being freshly caught. The bar is a regular hangout for local fishermen. If you get talking, good stories usually follow.

Inland from the Overberg

To enter the Overberg interior from Cape Town, take the spectacular Franschoek Pass (R45) through the northern edge of the Hottentots' Holland Nature Reserve. The winding road drops from the mountains to the Overberg's rolling plain, coming out on the shores of the huge **Theewaterskloof Dam,** where the little town of **Villiersdorp** hugs the foot of the wild Riviersonderend Mountains.

Villiersdorp's ugly Main Street hides the pretty houses and gardens behind. Here, a community of artists, exiled from Cape Town, have collaborated to form the **Akkedis Art Route,** a tour covering seven studios around the little town, which you visit to see the artists at work. It makes a pleasant, easy walk after time in a car. The map is available from the **Dagbreek Museum and Restaurant.** The house is late Cape Dutch, decorated in Victorian style. Light meals and coffee are served on the porch, overlooking the garden. The **Overberg Protea Nursery,** on Van Riebeeck Street, displays just about every weird sub-species of this extraordinary flower. Some of the open, fleshy forms are almost obscene.

The R43 north of Villiersdorp leads over the Riversonderend range towards Worcester. On the **Elandskloof Pass** is **Bo Radyn,** a farmstead built in 1777. You can look around the farm, or hike from the **Villiersdorp Nature Reserve.** Two circular overnight trails, the **Ratelberg** and **Spitskop,** begin from here. There is also a cultivated wildflower garden and a caravan/camp site. South of Villiersdorp is the orchard town of **Grabouw.** Named by its German founder after a town in his native land, this is the centre of South Africa's apple-growing region. Naturally, Grabouw has an Apple Museum, on Main Road, with a display of old implements from local farms. More interesting are the area's mountain passes, and their views. **Sir Lowry's Pass,** on the N2, 20km west of town, looks on to the whole sweep of False Bay, and in the 18th century was a hot-spot for bandit attacks; the viewpoint is still notorious for robberies and you should beware if stopping here. **Houw Hoek Pass,** 20km further east on the N2, winds over fynbos heathland to the Houw Hoek Inn, which claims to be South Africa's oldest. **Viljoen's Pass,** on the R321 to Franschoek, is quieter, and forested at the summit, from where the road takes a deep plunge down to the Palmiet River.

Caledon, a market and spa town about 40km east of Grabouw along the N2, is one of the Overberg's larger towns. Once handsome, the centre has suffered 'improvement' 1950s-style, although a few things have survived. Donkin Square still has some Georgian houses. The Holy Trinity Church, on Trinity Street, is solidly neo-Gothic, having been designed by Sophia Grey, the energetic wife of Cape Town's Archbishop Grey who, in the 1850s, designed and built Anglican churches throughout the colony. The Caledon Museum, on Krige Street, has a collection of Victoriana. The Old Mill Art Gallery sells work by local artists, sometimes very good, sometimes not, but worth a look.

Caledon Hot Springs pour into a pool built in the last century. Around it has been built a small, rather smart resort, **De Overberger,** surrounded by forest and mountain and offering tennis and riding, weights and aromatherapy.

For quiet strolling, a wander in the **Caledon Nature Reserve and Wildflower Garden** is hard to beat. A flower show is held here every spring, when the reserve erupts in colour. Either walk in the cultivated garden or wander on to the slopes of the Swartberg Mountains and check out the views. About 30km north of Caledon, under the Riversonderend Mountains (passing the 1089m Swartberg peak), are two gems, Genandendal and Greyton.

Genadendal is a Moravian Mission station dating from the 1830s. Lime and thatch cottages line the narrow street and cluster around the old church. The Cape's surviving Moravian

Mission stations (there are others at Elim, Wuppertal, Zoar, Mamre and Stilbaai, set up by Protestant missionaries from Moravia, now part of the Czech Republic) are set pieces of 19th-century living, untouched because they are home to 'coloured' families, so no bungalows, or even tarred roads, have appeared in these little villages. Genadendal is no exception. All of the Cape's mountain villages must have looked like this 100 years ago.

Greyton, 6km east, is equally pretty, but wealthier and less poignant than Genadendal. Also mostly composed of 19th-century white buildings, it is a peaceful farming village. A two-day hiking trail, the **Boesmanskloof Trail**, leads from the **Greyton Nature Reserve** over the Riviersonderend Mountains north to McGregor in the Breede River Valley (*see* p.192). The trail winds through uplands where dassies, duiker, baboon, klipspringer and grey rhebok live. Like so many wild areas of the Western Cape, the mountains blaze with flowers in the spring. East of Greyton the R406 (a gravel road) follows the Riviersonderend massif for about 30km, before joining the main N2 highway for a last 60km through the sheep and wheat farmlands to **Swellendam**.

Swellendam

Before Swellendam was founded in 1743, the Overberg was a chaotic world of wandering trekboers, Khoi tribes, and freebooting raiding bands composed of deserters from the Company's garrisons, escaped Malay and West African slaves and dispossessed Khoi.

All were gradually drifting east, extending the range of 'settled' land outside the sphere of Company control. The region's few settled farmers were beginning to demand protection. The Company laid out their new town, complete with grand government buildings, at the foot of the Langeberg, on the banks of the Koornlands River.

The Overberg soon settled down as the lawless element drifted east to the Fish River frontier, and by the early 19th century, Swellendam had become the quiet administrative and agricultural town that it is today. The old town has been lovingly preserved, though today it is a tourist and farming centre, and there is little to suggest its old function as an outpost of European colonial adventure.

Tourist Information

Publicity Association, The Oefeninghuis, Voortrek Street, ✆ (0291) 42 770.

The Old Town

The **Drostdy Museum** (*open Mon–Fri 9–5, Sat and Sun 9–4*) is housed in seven old buildings on Swellengrebel Street (map available from the Publicity Association). This is a modest piece of classic Cape Dutch civic building, the white walls topped with thatch to take the edge off the grandeur. Built in 1747, it now houses the standard collection of fine Cape Dutch furniture and crafts. Some interesting details are the early paper money minted by the Dutch East India Company during the 18th century, and the original watermill, still grinding corn. The flour and bread are sold at a stall in the museum gardens.

The late 19th-century **Dutch Reformed Church**, on Voortrek Street, while of less historical importance, dominates the small town's skyline. Far more ornate than is usual for the Calvinist austerity of most of South Africa's Dutch Reformed churches, this one has a bit of everything—Baroque, classical, Gothic. Much simpler in style is the **Oefeninghuis**, which now houses the publicity association. Built in 1838 as a Sunday School (Oefening translates roughly to 'religious exercise') and later used as a school for educating freed slaves, the building also has a semi-permanent exhibition of local art.

Around Swellendam

Immediately north of town rise the **Langeberg Mountains**, a great dark wall scored deep with tangled forest kloofs of yellowwood and milkwood trees. The stretch of the mountains visible from town are part of the huge **Marloth Nature Reserve**, ✆ (0291) 41410. The 5-day **Swellendam Hiking Trail** runs over these heights, with huts at the end of each section. This trail should not be attempted unless you are reasonably fit: summer temperatures can soar on the Langeberg slopes and the gradients can be really punishing. There are several day trails in the reserve though, which, while still steep, are comparatively short. However, it is worth overnighting at one of the Swellendam Trail huts; at night the kloofs are a-dance with fireflies and, in the exhilarating mountain air, you might be tempted to dance with them. Look out for black eagles. There are plenty of pools to swim in and to drink from. The way to the reserve from town is along Andrew White Street, following the signposts to Swellendam State Forest. The office there will issue permits for the walks you choose to do.

There are two scenic drives drive north over the Langeberg into the western end of the Little Karoo. Either follow the R60 for 50km west to Ashton, before driving over the **Kogmanskloof Pass** to Montagu, or head 11km east on the N2 until the junction with the R324. After 14km, turn north over the breathtaking **Tradouw Pass** to Barrydale. The English author Anthony Trollope crossed this pass in the 1870s while making a tour of South Africa. When the axle on his Cape cart gave way, a young Boer farmer offered to take Trollope's party to the next town. The writer's offer of half a crown for the trouble raised a smile and the comment, 'I might as well take it, but you'd have had the cart all the same without it.' Trollope was continuously impressed by the open-handedness of the Afrikaners. He was also impressed by Tradouw Pass, which he claimed 'beats in sublimity all other South African passes that I saw. I have never seen rocks of a finer colour or twisted about into grander forms...'

On the road to Tradouw Pass is a tiny settlement, **Suurbrak**, originally a mission station founded by the London Mission Society in the mid 19th century. It is still known for its furniture workshops, which produce a kind of chair that is considered unique. Visitors can watch the furniture-makers at work, and buy from the workshops at cost price.

Follow the R322 past the turn-off for Tradouw Pass and Barrydale, for about 10km towards Heidelberg, and you reach a signpost for the vast, wild **Boosmansbos Wilderness Area**, ✆ (02934) 22 412, part of the even larger **Groot Vadersbosch Nature Reserve**, an area of the Langeberg that very few people visit (or even hear of). This is one of the wildest accessible areas in the Western Cape. Larger even than Marloth Reserve, Boosmansbos is a huge expanse of steep montane fynbos, rising to tall peaks. Yellowwood, stinkwood and the rare mountain cypress (one of Southern Africa's few indigenous conifers) thrive in the kloofs, home to a lot of game, albeit shy. Bushbuck, grey rhebok, duiker, klipspringer and grysbok live on the slopes; black and martial eagles are common; there are lynx and leopard. It can rain at any time of year here, so it is as well to carry a waterproof whatever the sky looks like.

Permits for a two-day hiking trail with overnight huts, and various day trails, are available from the Forest Station as you drive in.

South of Swellendam is South Africa's smallest national park, the **Bontebok National Park**, ✆ (0291) 42 735, founded in the 1960s to protect this large antelope species, which was then almost extinct. The bontebok are curious-looking animals—a handsome chocolate brown with white bellies and legs and a broad white blaze down the face. They look almost identical to the blesbok, which occurs widely through northern and eastern South Africa. In fact, there is much controversy among zoologists as to whether these two antelope are not, in fact, sub-species of one species, rather than separate cousins. Who knows? They canter in circles and snort and look at you with bovine confidence, exposing their flanks to full view so that it is small wonder that they were shot almost to extinction. However, the park has been very successful, and from the 80-odd individuals left when the Park was founded, there are now thousands scattered through reserves all over the Cape. The park also has grey rhebok (rarely seen anywhere, so grab the chance), zebra, and red haartebeest. Lynx are the only large predators. There is a camp site and self-catering accommodation. Apart from two short walking trails, one of them along the Breede River, visitors are confined to their cars.

Bredasdorp

Bredasdorp sits at the head of two there-and-back roads to the coast, one to Cape Agulhas, and one to Arniston. If heading for either coastal spot it is as well to stop in Bredasdorp for supplies, as they are cheaper here than in the little coastal villages. Founded in 1838, Bredasdorp serves both the coast and the sheep-farming downland hereabouts. A small town, it has a fascinating **Shipwreck Museum** (*open Mon–Thurs 9–4.45, Fri 9–3.45, Sat 9–1, Sun 11–12.30*). So many ships have foundered on this treacherous coastline that it is hard to keep track of them. Some, like the HMS *Birkenhead* (*see* 'Overberg Coast'), are famous, but most are only known to enthusiasts. The museum charts all the recorded wrecks, a catalogue of human tragedy and vulnerability. Stirring stuff for such a quiet town.

East of the Breede River

The dirt road east of town leads beyond De Hoop Nature Reserve (*see* p.202), past the **Potberg Mountain**, to the Breede River, where it becomes estuarine on its way to the ocean. Clinging to the banks is **Malgas**, a collection of smallholdings with a trading store, unchanged since the 1930s, and a large church. You cross the river here by a **pontoon bridge**, hand-operated by two men and the last of its kind still working in South Africa. It is very cheap, so tips are appreciated. Follow the dirt road along the western bank of the Breede for 32km towards the coast and you come to **Infanta-on-River**, one of the quietest hidden beaches on the Overberg Coast, with great wild camping and beach walking.

The R324 gravel road along the eastern bank of the Breede leads to two more quiet coastal gems: **Port Beaufort** and **Witsand**. Port Beaufort, now a sleepy village, was once a port of some importance: the Breede River is navigable for about 32km upstream from its mouth, and a lot of cargo traffic used the port in the last century. But the only remaining evidence of this is a huge church (the 'Barry Church') where the port's merchants and seamen used to worship. Today Port Beaufort is a tranquil haven much favoured by fishermen. A chat with the locals could secure a fishing trip or water-skiing outing. Witsand is the beach a few kilometres down from Port Beaufort. A bit busier than Port Beaufort (i.e. not very), Witsand has safe beaches. Again, there is camping and good beach walking.

Activities

Walking and hiking: All of the above nature reserves offer good day-hikes. Longer overnight mountain trails are the 5-day **Swellendam Trail**, in Marloth Nature Reserve, ✆ (0291) 41410, the 2-day **Boosmansbos Trail**, in the Boosmansbos Wilderness Area, between Swellendam and Heidelberg, ✆ (02962) 1812, and 2-day **Boesmanskloof Trail**, ✆ (02353) 621/671, between Greyton and Robertson.

Riding, mountain biking, gliding and fuffi-sliding: Ring Swellendam Outdoors, ✆ (0291) 42 628.

Where to Stay

expensive

Wildenkranz Country House, near Elgin, in the Grabouw area, ✆ (02824) 49 042, is an elegant Cape Dutch building built in 1820, set in pear orchards, with luxurious rooms furnished in period. **The Houw-Hoek Inn**, Grabouw, ✆ (02824) 49 646, is supposedly the oldest licensed inn in South Africa. A charming 2-storey white building c.1834, it sits on the Houw-Hoek Pass (N2) east of Grabouw.

De Overberger, ✆ (0281) 41 271, is a small, late 19th-century resort surrounding Caledon's hot mineral springs. Set in forest, the mountains towering behind, it is a bit institutional, though luxuriously so. The **Swellengrebel Hotel**, Swellendam, ✆ (0291) 42 493, is large, modern, expensive and dull, with TVs in every room.

Walkabout, ✆ (021) 262 520, is a bush camp set among milkwood forest on the banks of the Breede River south of Malgas (continue past Malgas on the Malgas/Buffeljags dirt road and look out for the signpost on the left). Beautifully landscaped, the camp has wooden cabins on stilts or stone-and-thatch cottages, and offers excellent river-rafting in inflatable canoes to ride the local rapids. Forest hikes, bird-watching and fishing are also offered, as well as excursions to Swellendam and local nature reserves. Self-catering only.

moderate

Huis De Villiers, 13 Victoria St, Villiersdorp, ✆ (0225) 31 386, is particularly nice in winter, with fires, gluwein and a view of the snowy peaks that dominate the town. There are five en suite bedrooms.

The **Post House**, Main Road, Greyton, ✆ (028) 229 995 (built 1860), used to be the village post office. The house is beautiful, with splendid yellowwood ceilings, although the 14 en suite rooms are a bit chintzy. Locals drink at the attached bar. Also in Greyton is **Greyton Lodge**, 46 Main Street, ✆ (028) 254 787, a set of renovated 19th-century cottages set round a charming garden.

Swellendam has some good moderate accommodation. Try the self-catering **Kadie Cottages**, in the town centre, ✆ (0291) 43 053, or the **Waenhuis B&B**, outside town (*see* below).

Swellendam has two backpacker lodges: **Swellendam Backpackers**, 5 Lichtenstein Street, in the town centre, ☎ (0291) 42 648, who are on the Baz Bus Route and arrange all sorts of local tours and activities; and **Waenhuis B&B and Backpackers**, ☎ (0291) 42 281, on a farm outside town. Ring for a free pick-up.

Camp sites: Villiersdorp Nature Reserve; Bontebok National Park.
Wild camping: Infanta-on-River.

All the establishments listed above have good restaurants in the same price bracket. Particularly recommended are **Wildenkrantz Country House**, which serves succulent Karoo lamb and game in season, and the **Houw-Hoek Inn**, which specializes in Cape country cooking, in particular an excellent spicy *bobotie*. **Huis De Villiers**, in Villiersdorp, and **The Post House**, Greyton, have a more intimate feel, with log fires, small dining rooms and carefully prepared Cape and French dishes and home-made breads.

There is little that is both good and cheap, with the exception of the **Dagbreek Museum restaurant**, a small Victorian house on the corner of Graaf Street and Union Avenue in Villiersdorp, now a museum. Good food is served on the verandah and there are seldom more than one or two other people, but unfortunately the restaurant is only open for lunch.

The West Coast

Fronting the chill Benguela current, Africa's lonely Atlantic coast stretches north of Cape Town in an almost unbroken beach. The west coast is barren and eerie: the ocean roars incessantly against empty beaches shrouded with mist at morning and evening, and the currents, even close to shore, can be treacherous. Apart from a small area around **Saldanha Bay** and a few fish-processing towns to the north, the coastline itself is largely uninhabited, and accessible via a few villages and nature reserves, the best being the **West Coast National Park**, south of Saldanha, and **Cape Columbine Nature Reserve**, just to the north, which support game species and large populations of seabirds. In spring, the coastward scrub is covered with yellow, orange and purple wild flowers. Summers are dry and parched, winters stormy with a brief season of heavy rain. Inland, the country is empty but for scattered farms and hamlets. The few larger towns are generally rather ugly, but are made up for by the romance of the smaller fishing villages of 19th-century thatched cottages, where poor 'coloured' fishermen still live as they have for over a hundred years, netting their living from the harsh Atlantic.

For the first couple of hundred kilometres north of Cape Town, the inland area is a patch-work of coastal fynbos and scrubby farmland. To the east, the land becomes more fertile, stretching in a vast, wheat-growing plain called the **Swartland** to a wall of high mountains—first the Perdeberg and Kasteelberg, then the wild, jagged **Cedarberg**—the western edge of South Africa's Great Escarpment. Running north–south, parallel with the Cedarberg, is the **Oliphants River Valley**, which winds north through progressively drier wine and orchard country until the river turns to the sea and the Cedarberg merges with the lower Bokkeveld escarpment, some 400km north of Cape Town.

Getting to the West Coast

As always in South Africa, a car is most convenient, although the West Coast can be reached by public transport. **InterCape Mainliners** run a bus service to the main town of Saldanha from Cape Town's bus station. From there, black taxis to other towns and villages are generally safe, if recklessly driven. Access to the reserves is more difficult, but this can be overcome by hitching. Otherwise ask at the town's Publicity Office if a lift can be arranged with a ranger or a local going that way.

Cape Town to the Oliphants River Mouth

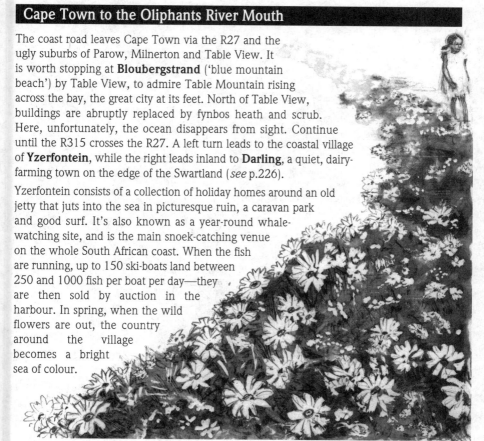

The coast road leaves Cape Town via the R27 and the ugly suburbs of Parow, Milnerton and Table View. It is worth stopping at **Bloubergstrand** ('blue mountain beach') by Table View, to admire Table Mountain rising across the bay, the great city at its feet. North of Table View, buildings are abruptly replaced by fynbos heath and scrub. Here, unfortunately, the ocean disappears from sight. Continue until the R315 crosses the R27. A left turn leads to the coastal village of **Yzerfontein**, while the right leads inland to **Darling**, a quiet, dairy-farming town on the edge of the Swartland (*see* p.226).

Yzerfontein consists of a collection of holiday homes around an old jetty that juts into the sea in picturesque ruin, a caravan park and good surf. It's also known as a year-round whale-watching site, and is the main snoek-catching venue on the whole South African coast. When the fish are running, up to 150 ski-boats land between 250 and 1000 fish per boat per day—they are then sold by auction in the harbour. In spring, when the wild flowers are out, the country around the village becomes a bright sea of colour.

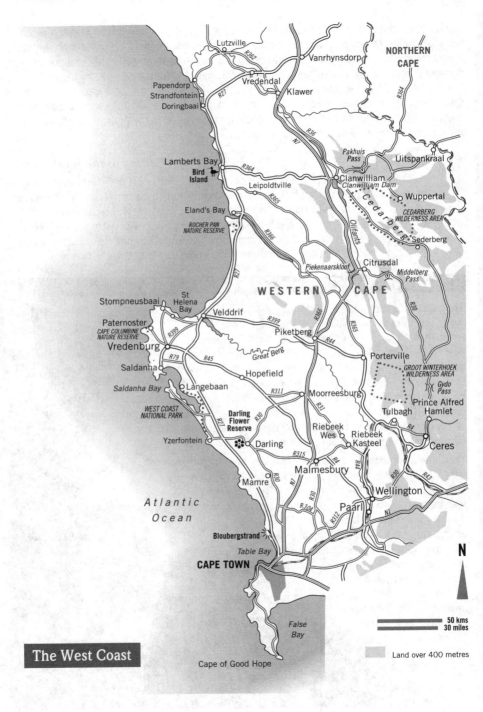

The West Coast

Yzerfontein is within spitting distance of the southernmost tip of the **West Coast National Park**, but to gain access to the park you have to drive about 40km north to **Langebaan**, on the eastern shore of the lovely **Saldanha Bay**, a vast expanse of calm water dotted with rocky islands colonized by nesting seabirds (*see* below).

Langebaan is another example of ugly man-made structures rising out of glorious natural beauty, a theme repeated all over South Africa. Perhaps ugly is too strong a word, but it is not an attractive town. Langebaan lies at the mouth of a lagoon (in fact a large inlet of the bay). A resort town of temporary-looking holiday homes frequented mostly by Afrikaans-speaking Capetonians, it has three caravan and camp sites, two bungalow parks and a brand-new, expensive self-contained resort called Club Mykonos, apparently modelled on a Greek village. Watersports go on loudly in the lagoon.

West Coast National Park

Follow the signs from Langebaan to the **West Coast National Park**, ✆ (02287) 22 144, at the south end of town. Near the park entrance is **Langebaan Lodge**, which doubles as park reception and visitors' accommodation. From here, tours set out for the three bird-colony islands in the Bay, which was part of the park and home to Cape gannets, cormorants, jackass penguins and southern black-backed gulls. The park also includes Langebaan Lagoon, and part of Saldanha Bay's west shore, covering 20,000ha in all. An old Cape Dutch thatched homestead, **Geelbeck**, about 5km along the park road from the entrance, is a coffee shop and education centre, and the starting point of several **walking trails**, though these are only open in spring, when the flowers are out, and must be walked with a guide.

As the park road swings up along the west shore of the bay, extensive mud flats come into view. When exposed at low tide, these are covered with wading birds. A superb swimming spot can be reached from the road by a wooden walk-way. Underfoot, the mud changes to sand and the water stays shallow for hundreds of metres out into the bay. About a kilometre on from here, the road is blocked by a gate. Passing through, the visitor is in the peninsula end of the national park (actually a separate reserve managed by the national park), where the park's large antelope live.

Eland, zebra, bontebok, black wildebeest and gemsbok, as well as smaller game (the author saw an African wildcat here), thrive on the peninsula. There are also thousands of tortoises and you are likely to see snakes on the road. Eventually you have to turn and come back the way you came, as the park ends abruptly at a fence declaring itself to be the boundary of Defence Force land. Oh, well. There are the grazing antelope to look at, as well as a double sea view to admire (of the open Atlantic to the west and the calmer Saldanha Bay to the east) before heading back out of the national park.

Saldanha

Larger, but no less ugly, than Langebaan, Saldanha is also the gateway to an area of intense natural beauty, the **St Helena Peninsula**. Saldanha does have an interesting history though. The name Saldanha was originally given by the Portuguese to today's Table Bay to commemorate the visit, in 1503, of Admiral Antonio de Saldanha, who anchored his fleet there on the way round to the Indies. When the Dutch began taking an interest in the Cape, during the following century, they transferred the name to present-day Saldanha, even though the admiral of that name had never anchored there.

In the early 17th century, before Holland colonized the Cape, French sailors visited Saldanha Bay regularly, hunting the colonies of seals and seabirds (both of which have, thankfully, survived to this day). Later, merchant traders began collecting the rich guano from the colonies and shipping it back for sale to farmers in Europe. Such was the demand for this excellent fertilizer that fortunes were made, and the collecting parties sometimes fought each other for possession of the pungent prize; local legend has it that the preserved body of a French victim of a guano skirmish was dug out of the muck on one of the three main bird colonies in the bay during one of the last collecting sprees in the late 19th century. It was shipped back to Europe as a curiosity.

Saldanha Bay was also a pirate refuge during the 18th century, when lawless bands operated from here almost unchallenged: the bay's sea bed is littered with the wrecks of ships that they plundered and sank. Treasure has been recovered from some, one wreck alone yielding about half a million rands' worth of gold. Divers still try their luck under the sheltered bay's calm waters.

Today, the town has little to suggest such a romantic past. There is a permanent whiff from the fish-processing factory, and a general industrial feel. However, the coast north of Saldanha is heavenly, and dotted with guest farms that offer riding, canoeing and bird-watching (*see* 'Activities' and 'Where to Stay').

St Helena Bay, Paternoster and Cape Columbine Nature Reserve

Take the R399 north of Saldanha to Vredenburg, a largish farming town, where the road forks: the west fork, a gravel road, leads directly to Paternoster and the Cape Columbine reserve; the R399 continues, bearing east and north, until a westward turn-off on to another gravel road, signposted to **St Helena Bay**. This eventually leads back around the coast to Paternoster and Cape Columbine. More interesting than the direct route from Vredenburg, it leads between dusty ploughed fields at the centre of which stand groups of oddly shaped boulders, heaped together by the area's first farmers. These resemble megaliths, which seem somehow in keeping with the brown emptiness of the coastal fields around them.

Then the road hits the coast. At St Helena Bay, you pass groups of old, white thatched fishermen's cottages and newer, small fish-processing sheds. Out in the bay swim huge shoals of anchovy and pilchard, netted by small trawlers crewed by 'coloured' fishermen. The beaches, unlike those in the sheltered lagoon in the West Coast National Park, are too cold for swimming. The road goes on to **Stompneusbaai**, a slightly larger settlement than any of the hamlets strung along St Helena Bay, and then turns back inland for about 8km before forking west again to the coast at **Paternoster**.

Paternoster is almost untouched, a period piece from the 19th century. 'Coloured' fishermen and their families peer from the open doors of square, lime-washed cottages, living in much the same conditions as their forefathers did. The village is lively—people will be anxious to chat and sell you seafood. However, unless you speak Afrikaans, talking will be problematic and, as for the seafood, never buy crayfish on the street, however tempting the price, as it is strictly illegal and can be a set-up for a spot fine.

However, it is well worth walking around (in the day—at night the locals can be a little rough). It is generally acceptable to take photos, though you should ask first.

On around the coast, the road passes the last manned lighthouse to be built on the South African coast (in 1936) at Teities Bay, and then enters **Cape Columbine Nature Reserve**. A small ranger's booth spans the road, selling entry and camping permits. Inside, the ocean crashes against weird volcanic rocks that seem to have been moulded by giants from massive chunks of Plasticine. This is a wonderful place to watch seals playing offshore. You can hike a 13km trail along the lonely beaches and rock promontories, go fishing or gather shellfish (*see* 'Activities'). The author camped here one memorable night under the moon, and found that the giant limpet shells that litter the beaches, if filled with guava juice and tequila, make a superb natural marguerita.

Farther North: Velddrif, Eland's Bay

The Great Berg River meets the sea at **Velddrif**, a town about 15km east of St Helena Bay. The town is nothing much, though the last few years has seen it develop as a tourist spot for South Africans. The countryside inland, where the river is estuarine, is worth exploring by car, if only for the flocks of flamingos and pelicans that live on the water.

North of Velddrif the country gets ever drier on the way to Eland's Bay. The ocean retreats again behind a range of low hills and the R27 changes to gravel. At this point, there is a small lagoon to the west of the road, **Rocher Pan Nature Reserve**, © (02625) 727, clearly signposted from the road. Although it is not possible to camp here, there are some short walking trails around the lagoon, where wading birds and waterfowl congregate in large numbers. There are also small antelope: springbok, duiker and steenbok. Look out for mongooses hunting along the paths.

The road to Eland's Bay passes through a farmyard and runs alongside another freshwater lagoon, or lake, the 25km-long **Verlorenvlei**. Watch out for loose livestock. Again, there is often good bird life to be seen here, though to see it you have to get out on to the lake in a boat, which can be arranged at **Verlorenvlei Guest Farm**, a 150-year-old homestead, 5km along the lake from Eland's Bay (*see* 'Activities' and 'Where to Stay'). The town itself, so long awaited, is little more than a village, much frequented by surfers ('tube' waves, similar to those off Hawaii, break here) and crayfish divers in summertime. In winter it is rather dead, but it is still rewarding to explore the countryside around Verlorenvlei. North of Eland's Bay, the countryside seems even more deserted. The road passes old ruined farms shaded by tall gum trees, their thatched roofs falling in. It seems unlikely that another town should lie this way, but there is one, in fact the West Coast's largest.

Lambert's Bay and Beyond

Lambert's Bay announces itself in its own tourist literature as 'the Star of the West Coast'. Whatever that means, it is an interesting and quietly eccentric little town. The crayfish-canning capital of South Africa, it also has an extraordinary colony of Cape gannets, jackass penguins and southern black-backed gulls called **Bird Island**, reached by a causeway leading out from the small harbour.

Bird Island is incredible, a churning, squawking morass of seabirds, constantly shifting and shuffling shoulder-to-shoulder as those flying come in to land, and those sitting launch into flight. Don't go near the place with a hangover; the stench brings you to your knees. A concentrated guano reek staggers the brain, augmented by a stomach-turning under-stench of decay; a closer look (handkerchief over mouth and nose) reveals that these sociable birds live atop the corpses of their dead relatives. For the brave, there is a fenced-off walk-way leading to a bird-watching tower, giving intimate eye and nose access to the colony. Expect the smell to linger in your hair for a day.

Lambert's Bay has an entertaining **Publicity Office**, ✆ (027) 42088/58, on D.F. Malan Street, behind the old harbour. The man in charge will dress you in a white coat and hat and march you off to the crayfish-canning factory. Delights of the tour include the 'spare parts department' where bits of broken crayfish are cobbled together into a collective whole, packed and sold to Japan at vast profit.

More ordinary attractions include the **Sandveld Museum** (*open Mon–Fri 9–12 and 2–4, Sat 9–12*), one of South Africa's many museums of spartan pioneer farm life. The prize exhibit is a Bible printed in high Dutch and reckoned to be 300 years old. There is also an old horse-driven mill.

Lambert's Bay was also distinguished (when the author visited) by having one of the last bottle stores to practise apartheid, with one side for 'coloureds' and another for whites. The author wandered into the 'wrong' side and was not served until he went into the side for whites. Such throwbacks to the bad old days are now sufficiently rare as to warrant inclusion as curiosities.

North of Lambert's Bay, the country gets even drier and emptier than before. Trees disappear completely. Low sandveld scrub spreads on either side of the road. Amazingly, there are two small resort villages up here, **Doringbaai** and **Strandfontein**. The beach at Strandfontein is good for swimming, and is often all but deserted. Only swim in the section facing the town, as the cross-currents further up the beach are dangerous. One of the best wild camping spots on the West Coast is accessible by car from here. Follow the dirt road running north along the low sandstone cliffs parallel with the beach for about 3km. It becomes quite bumpy and sandy, so go slow. Eventually you will come out by a large salt pan on the right and dunes on the left. The dunes give excellent shelter. By night, the long beach is pure magic. Don't risk more than a paddle though, as, again, the cross-currents are strong.

Just north of Strandfontein the R27 turns inland to follow the Oliphants River back south, under the wall of the high Cedarberg, while a dirt road turns west to the mouth of the river at a cluster of houses called **Papendorp**. Before heading back inland, it is worth having a look at the Oliphants River's sluggish entry to the sea: north of here, there isn't another perennial river flowing into the Atlantic until the Orange River, more than 500km away.

Walking: The best time to walk is between August and early October when the countryside is ablaze with spring flowers. Marked hiking trails can be found at West Coast National Park (guided walks only). Cape Columbine Nature Reserve, ✆ (02281) 32 216, north of Saldanha, has a 13km hike along the rocky shore. There are usually seals playing in the water and interesting shells to collect. Rocher Pan Nature Reserve has short trails along the lagoon, where flamingos, pelicans and other waterfowl congregate. You may also see small buck. All the above reserve trails require a permit, issued at the reception offices.

Riding: The open beaches and wide fynbos scrub inland make the West Coast good riding country. **K'Taaibos Adventures**, near Saldanha, ✆ (02281) 44 094, offers day rides or 2–5 day treks (beach and inland riding). All levels of ability are catered for. **Horse Trail Safaris**, near Lambert's Bay, ✆ (021) 734 936, offer day rides along the beach or trips of several days into the Cedarberg Mountains. **Orangevlei Guest Farm**, also near Saldanha, ✆ (02281) 42261, offers 1–3 day rides at all levels. **Oliphantskop Guest Farm**, near Langebaan, ✆ (02287) 22 326, offers day rides.

Whale-watching: The whole West Coast is good for whale-watching (from the shore) from October to about January. Contact the West Coast Regional Tourism Association, P O Box 139, Saldhana 7395, ✆ (02281) 42058/88, 🖷 44 240.

Swimming: Any of the beaches fronting the resort towns of Yzerfontein, Langebaan, Eland's Bay, Doringbaai and Strandfontein are safe. Otherwise do not swim unless guided to a safe spot by a local, as the West Coast cross-currents are dangerous.

Watersports: Langebaan lagoon is a sheltered spot for windsurfing, which can be arranged through Langebaan Lodge, in the West Coast National Park. Boat trips out to the bird colony islands of Saldanha Bay are also arranged from here.

Canoeing trips: These are sometimes available from Verlorenvlei Guest Farm, near Eland's Bay. The bird-watching is good—for waterfowl, including pelicans and flamingos—and if you trawl a line, you may catch your supper.

Surfing: Whether you want to learn or are already a surfer, **Surfari**, ✆ (021) 510 2026, offer a 3-day surfing trip up the West Coast from Cape Town.

Where to Stay and Eating Out

Although there are various holiday camps and hotels dotted around the West Coast towns, the area's guest farms offer the most attractive settings, the best food, and often the most reasonable prices.

expensive

Orangevlei, near Saldanha, ✆ (02281) 42 169, a large farmstead dating from 1832, specializes in riding (beach rides or treks of up to five days into the interior), but also has tennis courts and a pool. Offering similar facilities, **Oliphantskop**, near Langebaan, ✆ (02287) 22 326, is more modern, has horses for day rides, and offers out-of-season rates. Both places provide either B&B or full board and offer Cape country cuisine, and seafood of the highest standard (to guests and non-guests). Try the kingclip, if it is in, or any of the shellfish. **The Farmhouse**, by the Langebaan Lagoon, ✆ (02287) 22 062, offers similar period (1860s) style.

The **Marine Protea**, on Voortrekker Street, Lambert's Bay, ✆ (027) 432 1240, will do if neither of the above guest farms have space. It offers the usual bland luxury of the expensive Protea chain, but its restaurant serves very good seafood, including a well-buttered and garlicky crayfish thermidor that leaves you sated and gasping.

Langebaan Lodge, run by the West Coast National Park, is over-priced and has horrid orange curtains in the five bedrooms, but does overlook the sea and has access to swimming in the lagoon and a pool.

The **Kreefhuis**, on Strand Street, Lambert's Bay (just behind the old harbour), ✆ (027) 432 2335, also serves seafood fresh that day, with crayfish the speciality.

moderate

Verlorenvlei Guest House, ✆ (0265) 724, built in 1842 and 5km inland from Eland's Bay, faces the Verlorenvlei lake. Waterfowl by the thousand live on the lake margins. The homestead has five double en suite rooms. At the expensive end of moderate, Verlorenvlei offers B&B or full board by request. Nearby is **Redeluiguys Manor**, ✆ (0263), offering much the same.

Plaaskombuis Guest Farm, near Lambert's Bay, ✆ (0276) 732 326, is a restored, thatched 19th-century farmhouse on Steenbokfontein Farm, 9km south of Lambert's Bay on the R27. The owners are a good source of local information, and can help organize permits and equipment for more complicated activities, such as diving for crayfish or sea fishing. There is good bird life on the farm, and its kitchen is open to non-guests. Seafood *braais* are the speciality.

Cashel Bed and Breakfast, ✆ (02245) 475, a Spanish-style house overlooking the tiny old harbour at Yzerfontein, has two double rooms and a self-contained flat that sleeps 6. The beach is right there, all 20km of it, and you can arrange fishing trips with the owners. The **Paternoster Hotel**, ✆ (022) 817 2703, overlooks the beach near the small fishing village of Paternoster. A little run-down, what recommends it is its location near the old fishing village. Local fishermen drink here, making it a good place to hear tales of the sea.

In Saldanha, a modern but period-style B&B called **The Moorings**, ✆ (02281) 44 087, overlooks the bay. They don't allow kids.

All the guest farms listed above provide Cape country cooking of the highest order for their guests.

The **Strandkombuis**, at 16-Mile Beach, Yzerfontein, ✆ (02245) 206, has some of the best seafood in South Africa. Bring your own booze. The **Strandloper,** on the beach at Langebaan, does seafood *braais* (shellfish, plus the catch of the day) in the open air. Bring your own wine and gorge yourself as the waves break on the night-time beach.

Bosduifklip Farm, 4km along the R364 between Lambert's Bay and Clanwilliam, ✆ (026732) 661, *braais* seafood, beef, lamb and game (in season) in the open air.

Oddly out of place on the barren West Coast is the **Villa Romano**, on Voortrekker Street, Lambert's Bay. This Italian restaurant is surprisingly good, especially the seafood antipasti. No need to book.

cheap

The only cheap accommodation to be found is camping; however the West Coast has some beautiful camping spots. **Kliphoek Guest Farm** and **Verlorenvlei Guest Farm** both have water-side camp sites with ablution blocks and good bird life.

You can also camp at the **Cape Columbine Nature Reserve**, ✆ (022) 752 1718, at Tieties Bay, with the ocean roar only metres away. There's an ablution block.

The Oliphants River Valley and Cedarberg Mountains

The Oliphants River Valley, if followed north to south, winds from dry country to lush. Though by no means South Africa's largest river, the Oliphants is known to support more species of indigenous fish than any other south of the Zambezi. To the north, near its mouth, the river supports a narrow belt of orchard and vineyard, which makes a ribbon of vivid green against a dusty backdrop of brown and ochre hills. The Bokkeveld, part of the Great Escarpment, runs along the eastern horizon. The R27, which has led so faithfully up the coast, follows the river only as far as the small town of Lutzville, then breaks away east to the Great Karoo. To keep along the river, follow the R363 south to Vredendal, amid the narrow farms and irrigation channels of this semi-arid region until it joins the N7 highway at **Klawer**. The N7 then heads south, through a landscape gradually quickening with vegetation, until the ridge of the Bokkeveldberg retreats further east to become the higher, more jagged Cedarberg range. An interesting parallel route runs on the east side of the river. About 10km south of Klawer, take the sign marked 'Oliphants River Irrigation Scheme'; this is a dirt road, and not for those in a hurry. Both roads follow the river for 52km south to Clanwilliam.

Clanwilliam

Clanwilliam, the gateway to the Cedarberg, has existed since about 1732, though its 'official' status as a magistracy was only granted in 1808. The town, which had been predominantly Dutch in population, was deliberately settled with English during the 1820s, which accounts for the town's name—after the Earl of Clanwilliam, the then Cape Governor. Only six of the English settlers persevered in this staunchly Afrikaans region, but the name remained. Today, Clanwilliam is a handsome little town, dominated by the conical peaks of the Cedarberg to the east (unusual in this country of flat-topped mountains) and the massive Clanwilliam Dam to the west.

The **Old Prison** (1808), at the eastern end of Main Street, is now the **Publicity Office**, ✆ (027) 482 2024, and houses a small museum of early pioneer life in the Cedarberg (*open Aug–Sept, Mon–Fri 8–4.30, Sat–Sun 9–1*). **Visser Street**, which runs behind and parallel with Main Street, has some fine old buildings, including the **Old Magistrate's Court** (also built in 1808), and an old **Dutch Reformed Church** (1864), closely rivalled by an **Anglican Church** (1866).

Far more picturesque is the early 19th-century **'coloured' location**, behind the Old Prison. This small quarter is composed almost entirely of old thatched cottages in various states of repair. This is by far the liveliest part of the small town and wandering here is generally fine by day (after dark is less advisable, and out of the question for a woman alone). But for the jeans and T-shirts, the scene could be a century ago: ragged children playing in the dusty street between the old thatched cottages, dogs and chickens.

Most of the cottagers work at the **rooibos tea factory** on Main Road, about 100m up from the fork by the Old Prison. The factory was built in 1831, which entitles Clanwilliam to the position of 'the home of rooibos tea' (in the words of its own tourist literature).

The Cedarberg and its rural life have inspired a lot of South African artists. Some of the better local attempts to capture it are for sale in the **Clanwilliam Art Gallery**, on Main Road, which advertises itself as 'the only gallery between Paarl and Windhoek' (in Namibia). Be this true or no, it is worth looking in, as some of the work is very good.

Around Clanwilliam

Before entering the high passes of the Cedarberg proper, there are some places to explore in the foothills.

Clanwilliam Dam is a very large expanse of water just southwest of town, the haunt of windsurf and powerboat enthusiasts. There is good angling and bird-watching too, though the latter is better further into the hills. If you follow Main Road south towards the dam, you will pass the **Clanwilliam Wildflower Garden**. The flowers are named and labelled, making it easier to recognize them when in the veld.

Also dedicated to flora is the **Ramskop Nature Reserve**, to the southeast of town and well signposted. The small (54ha) reserve has a mixture of sandveld and fynbos plants, representative of the two vegetation zones that meet around Clanwilliam. A wildflower garden from each vegetation type has been set aside.

Pakhuis Pass, north of town, is a rugged, twisting, beautiful drive (via the R364, a good gravel road) through the northern foothills of the Cedarberg. The road leads over an upland of red boulders, fynbos and lone, weathered trees, including oaks and a few surviving examples of the Cape cedar, the tree that gave the surrounding mountains their name. From the picnic spot halfway up the pass wind some marked walking trails, but you can also wander at will, drinking in the clean air and the wide views. The poet Louis Leipoldt (also a famous gourmet, see **People and Culture**, 'Cape Cuisine' and 'Literature') loved this pass so much that he asked to buried here. His grave is marked by an inscribed stone under a rock overhang on the north side of the pass. Pakhuis was also the involuntary grave of an English soldier killed in a skirmish during General Smuts' raid into the Cape during the Anglo-Boer War (1899–1902).

To the north, the pass descends into the wide Doring River Valley before climbing away via the Botterkloof Pass towards the town of Calvinia in the endless Karoo. Turning back into the Cedarberg foothills, take the turning on the south side of Pakhuis Pass for **Wuppertal**. If Clanwilliam's 'coloured' quarter is reminiscent of the 19th century, Wuppertal has never left it. A Moravian mission station dating from the 1830s, Wuppertal is a jewel barely touched by the technological age, a tiny village of thatched cottages, often snowed up in winter, and subject to all the savage vagaries of the Cape mountains' climate. The villagers produce superb leatherwork, especially shoes (and have done since the 1800s), which can be bought if you show up on a weekday. Wuppertal is on a dead-end road. Unless you plan to continue into the mountains on foot or horse, retrace your tyre tracks to Clanwilliam where you can pick up a road into the main range.

The Cedarberg Wilderness Area

Rising to over 2000m at Sneeuberg, the highest point, the Cedarberg is spectacularly beautiful. Formed from conical and jagged peaks, rather than the more usual flat-topped massifs so typical of South Africa's mountain ranges, the Cedarberg is full of what appear to be natural rock sculptures: various elemental assaults on the natural sandstone have formed galleries of strange rock shapes on the mountains' higher points.

The entire Cedarberg range is protected as a reserve. A good thing too, as within its 80,000ha are some species of vegetation found nowhere else, including the Cape cedar, one of Africa's few indigenous conifers. The trees, like small, gnarled Scots pines, used to be common here, but the early settlers' axes and fires destroyed all but a few. More modern timber plantations now cloak many of the valleys, but these are not unsightly. The only road into the Cedarberg from Clanwilliam (via Algeria Forest Station) passes through several mature plantations before penetrating the wilder recesses of the range.

Algeria Forest Station, **Kromrivier Farm** and **Dwarsrivier Farm** are the usual jumping-off points for hiking in the Cedarberg, whether for day-trails or hikes of several days (*see* 'Activities'). All issue maps, but overnight hiking permits can only be bought from Algeria.

Dwarsrivier, in particular, is the trail-head of some superb walks. Marked one-day trails lead to spectacular sculpted rock formations such as the **Maltese Cross**, the **Wolfberg Cracks** (which involves a steep scramble up and down) and the **Wolfberg Rock Arch**. For the first two trails, allow four to five hours, but for the Wolfberg Arch, a full day. There is also a shorter trail along the Driehoeks River. This is pure heaven in summer: the river falls over a series of steps, forming still, deep swimming pools accessible from the trail. Hikers should see klipspringer, grey rhebok, mountain reedbuck, duiker, baboon and dassies by the score. Black eagles and sugarbirds are frequently spotted along the trail. Leopard and caracal lynx are quite common, but seldom seen.

South of the Cedarberg and Clanwilliam, the Oliphants River runs broad between banks of white sand to the town of **Citrusdal**, a tiny, sleepy place nestled between the Cedarberg and Citrusdalberg. Citrusdal was founded as recently as 1916 as a fruit-packing station for the local citrus farmers. It is unremarkable, except for its **hot springs**, which are 15km south of town down a dirt road following the Oliphants River.

The hot springs (temperature about 42°C), are some of the least developed in South Africa. They rise on a farm called, unsurprisingly, 'The Baths'. There is a central pool, looking much the same as it did in the 1920s, a set of jacuzzis fed by the spring, well hidden in a wooden shed, and a handsome Victorian stone house (*see* 'Where to Stay'). Several walking trails head off from the farm into the surrounding hills. There are bushman paintings on some of them. Ask for a map at the office.

The Citrusdal valley is a fruit-growing area, and the town itself is mainly concerned with servicing the farms, but there are one or two points of interest, if you have the time. South Africa's oldest orange tree grows on one of the farms, **Hexrivier**. The tree is about 200 years old and still bearing fruit. It is pleasant just to wander around the orchards. The local **Museum**, on Church Street (*open Mon–Fri 9–4.30*), has exhibits of early settler life in the valley. The **Marmalade Pot Craft Shop** is housed in the same building.

Around Citrusdal, you'll also notice car registration plates with 'CAR' as the first three letters. This is Citrusdal's registration, and a useful reminder if you cannot remember what the machine is called.

There are two ways to drive south out of Citrusdal, both over spectacular mountain passes. The tamer one (tamer in that it's tarred) is **Piekenaarskloof Pass**, the route taken by the N7 highway. Piekenaar means 'pikeman', recalling the 18th-century garrison that guarded the pass against Khoi raiders. A new holiday resort has been built on the crest of the pass. Not too glitzy, it consists of thatched stone cottages built around a large pond where geese cruise to and fro. The central lodge has a 'farm shop' selling local foods and preserves, and a Cape country restaurant (*see* 'Eating Out').

The other mountain route south of Citrusdal is the **Middelberg Pass**, towards Ceres (the R303), which becomes a dirt road shortly after leaving town. Be careful on the sharp bends, corrugations and worn patches where wheels can slip. Stay in low gear and do not attempt the pass if towing a trailer. In spring the mountainsides are covered with orange daisies, and in winter it is sometimes snowed up. Small, white-washed farmsteads pop up from time to time. Eventually, the road levels on to a high plateau, a green, lonely drive between two sets of matching peaks leading 100km into the Cold Bokkeveld and to the town of Ceres.

Activities

Walking and hiking: The Cedarberg is among the best hiking ranges in South Africa. Trails of 2 hours to 5 days snake through the passes and over the lower peaks, taking in bushman paintings, impressive rock formations and wide views out over the range or north to the Karoo. There is abundant wildlife and a great sense of space. Call the main offices of the **Cederberg Wilderness Area**, ✆ (027) 482 2812, for more details.

Algeria Forest Station, ✆ (022) 682 3440, **Dwarsrivier Farm**, ✆ (027) 482 2825, and **Kromrivier Farm**, ✆ (027) 482 2807, are the best places to hike from. Algeria has a system of marked trails and refuge huts for hikes of more than one day, while Dwarsrivier and Kromrivier have day-hikes to the better-known rock formations. **Baths Farm**, at the hot springs, ✆ (022) 921 3609, has one-day trails to bushman paintings. **Van Meerhoff Lodge** has trails into the Citrusdal Mountains.

Guided hiking trips are a good idea if you are worried about getting lost up in these wild vastnesses. Ring **Maltese Mountain Walks**, ✆ (021) 593 2494.

Riding: The most exciting riding is with **Horse Trail Safaris**, ✆ (021) 73 496, a Cape Town-based company that offers a 4-day ride into the Cedarberg. The trail covers some tough terrain, and includes visits to bushman paintings, and camping out with the horses, which are schooled and do not just follow the leader. Booking is essential. **Van Meerhoff Lodge** has horse trails too.

Canoeing: 4-day trips down the Oliphants River are offered by **Felix Unite** of Cape Town, ✆ (021) 461 0033. The route leads through a mixture of wild and farmed country, and you camp on the white sand banks by the river.

Where to Stay and Eating Out

Clanwilliam

expensive

The moderately expensive **Clanwilliam Hotel,** ✆ (027) 482 1101, a rather tasteless 1930s imitation Cape Dutch building in the town centre, has 17 en suite bedrooms, a pool and an outside tea garden. It has a very good Cape country restaurant, as well as a cheap bar menu, and is best used as a journey-breaker before going into the Cedarberg proper.

moderate

Recommended B&Bs in Clanwilliam itself are at **8 Visser Street,** ✆ (027) 482 2212, **30 Freesia Avenue,** ✆ (027) 482 2249, and **13 Skoolstraat,** ✆ (027) 482 1522.

Reinhold's, opposite the hotel on Main Street, Clanwilliam, ✆ (027) 482 1101, is a relaxed restaurant set in an old Cape Dutch house with polished yellowwood beams and a dark oak floor. There are outside tables in the garden in summer and a Cape country menu interspersed with fresh seafood from Lambert's Bay. Try the succulent Karoo lamb, or springbok (in season).

Around Clanwilliam

About 13km north of Clanwilliam, on the Pakhuis Pass, is **Krakatouw,** ✆ (027) 682 1222, a farm with two moderately priced, self-contained thatched cottages. The hikes and walks in the Cedarberg foothills are spectacular.

The Cedarberg

expensive

The Baths, ✆ (022) 921 3609, is the farm where the Citrusdal Hot Springs rise. Accommodation is in a large Victorian stone-built lodge with views out over the Oliphants River Valley to the Cedarberg.

Van Meerhoff Lodge, 7km south of Citrusdal on the N7, ✆ (022) 921 2231, has chalets, a pool and superb mountain views. Its fairly new restaurant, with old-style stone walls, thatched roof and beams, serves Cape cooking at its best. Try the *bobotie*, springbok (in season) and the *waterblommetjie* (a stew seasoned with watercress flowers and fried onions).

moderate

Nuwerust Guest Farm, ✆ (027) 482 2813, is a handsome old farm lying in a green, lonely valley on the Cedarberg's southernmost tip. Getting there involves a

Cedarberg: Where to Stay **223**

spectacular drive: take the road from Clanwilliam to Algeria Forest Station and, ignoring the turn-offs for Sandrif, Kromrivier and Dwarsrivier, follow the signs for Ceres across the Matjies River. At the sign for Ceres and Wuppertal turn right and continue for about 8km, then look out for the sign to Nuwerust. The farm offers self-catering accommodation (except for breakfast, which is provided), so take your own food and bedding. There are three cottages. The farm is old-fashioned and barely mechanized; a stay here is a step back into old Cape life.

In the same area is **Kunje Guesthouse**, ✆ (022) 921 3536, which offers B&B and walking trails, climbing and kloofing. Fun if you're into outdoor adventure.

The Baths has self-catering chalets, a cheaper alternative to the expensive accommodation at the Citrusdal Hot Springs. These are clean, comfortable stone chalets with cooking and bathroom facilities.

cheap

Algeria Forest Station, ✆ (027) 682 3440, has a camp site and trails leading up to spartan refuge huts (only firewood and water provided), several hours' hike into the mountains. Bear in mind that fires are not allowed so you must take a cooking stove.

If Algeria is booked up, a few kilometres further on is **Dwarsrivier Farm**, ✆ (027) 482 2825 (turn left at the fork after Algeria), and, beyond that, **Kromrivier Farm**, ✆ (027) 482 2807. Both farms have been in the Niewoudt family for over 100 years. In fact, almost all the farms in the Cedarberg are owned by this once pioneering family—look out for the name on farm signs. Kromrivier and Dwarsrivier each have self-catering chalets (cheap if shared between 2 or 3 people), and a camp site with ablution block.

The Baths also has isolated camp sites, set under trees near the hot springs.

The Swartland

Once over the Piekenaar Pass, south of Citrusdal, the mountains fall abruptly to the great wheat-growing plain of the Swartland ('black land'). Some sheep- and wine-farming goes on, but in general, the Swartland is known as the bread-basket of the Cape.

There are two theories as to how the region got its name: the first that it refers to the rich, dark soil, the second that it is named after the rhenoster bush which once covered the plain and which apparently turned black in summer. Whichever is correct, the first sight of the Swartland from the north is breathtaking, a vast flat plain seeming to stretch into infinity. Once on the plain, however, there is little drama for the eye. The farms are large and widely spaced between great, open wheat fields. The landscape soon becomes rather monotonous, though still impressive for its sheer scale. In winter the plain is green with winter-wheat, in summer a sea of shimmering gold.

Piketberg, nestled under the mountains, gets its name from the Dutch word 'piket', meaning guard, after the soldiers posted on the mountains above in the 18th century to defend the valley from bands of raiders made up of Khoi and deserters from the Cape garrisons. However, the settlers themselves were no saints, and often brought trouble down on their own heads by raiding the Khoi.

The Piketberg Uprising

In 1739 a party of Swartland burghers went raiding into Namaqualand, driving cattle away from the Khoi living up there and snatching San (bushman) children for slaves. The burghers had taken their own Khoi servants along to do the fighting, promising them a share in the stolen livestock, but, when they returned to Piketberg, the burghers kept the cattle, distributing only a few head to their neighbours. The Khoi servants got nothing. They complained to the Dutch East India Company at Cape Town, which officially disapproved of cattle-rustling, and was always wary of rebellion among the Khoi. The Company ordered cattle to be given to the servants. The burghers refused, threatening their own rebellion, and the Company backed down. This outraged the Khoi. Farms all over the region were suddenly attacked. The Company, now seriously alarmed, reversed their tactics, and offered pardon to the burghers who had taken part in the Namaqualand raid, if they would form a *Kommando* against the rebellious Khoi servants.

The rebels were cornered in a mountain cave near Citrusdal, but repulsed the burghers with poisoned arrows. The revolt spread. Farms all over the Swartland and Oliphants River Valley were attacked, and their stock driven off to the mountains. Regular troops were then sent over the Piekenaar's Pass, and indiscriminately attacked Khoi kraals wherever they found them, killing whoever they found, men, women and children. The rebel leaders were finally shot during a skirmish, but sporadic revolts came again in the 1750s and 1770s.

After this, gangs of Khoi and European bandits began using the mountains above Piketberg as a permanent refuge for seasonal raids on the Swartland, which were not finally put down until the early 1800s. Today, Piketberg's only relic of the frontier days is one rusty cannon mounted by the High School.

Moorreesburg is now the principal town of the northern Swartland. A prosperous place, mostly built in solid early 20th-century colonial style, with ugly 1950s 'improvements', Moorreesburg nonetheless has a fine (if small) **Art Gallery**, in the Dirkie Uys High School, with good landscapes by well-known painters such as Pierneef, whose paintings capture the melancholy mood of the Cape Mountains. On Main Street is the **Wheat Museum** (*open Mon–Fri 8–12 and 2–5*), a good example of South African eccentricity. The history of wheat is charted from its untamed beginnings as a wild grass to the present docile varieties.

Head reeling from the drama of wheat-growing, follow the R311 side-road to **Riebeek West**. Before reaching the village, there is a sign for **Jan Smuts' Birthplace** (*open daily 9–5*), a modest old white-washed Cape farmhouse. The statesman's chronology is well documented around the walls. Further along the same road is another ex-prime minister's birthplace, that of D. F. Malan—on **Allesveloren Farm**. Malan's premiership is not generally remembered with quite such nostalgia as that of Smuts. Visits are by appointment only. Call Mr S. F. Malan, ✆ (02246) 320.

Riebeek West itself is a quiet little farming town that seems to have changed little since the 1930s. There are two eccentric monuments here, the **Pieter Cruyhoff Monument**, which commemorates the first white man to set foot in the area, in 1661, and the **Rooi Os Monument**, which was raised in memory of a red ox who acquitted himself particularly well during the Great Trek. Only in South Africa.

In **Riebeek Kasteel**, the next town on, is the **Swartland Wine-growers' Co-operative**, on Station Road (*open for tastings and sales Mon–Fri 8–12.30 and 1.30–5.30*).

From here, the R311 loops back to the N7 at **Malmesbury**, the largest town in the Swartland. It is also the dullest. Another victim of 1950s 'improvements', Malmesbury exists to supply the region's farmers and to process their grain. The **Communion Well**, on Piet Retief Street, is a hangover from the days when farmers used to drive their horses in from distant farms every Sunday for church. It was here that they watered their 'spans' (teams). The old **Dutch Reformed Church**, on Church Street, is, unusually for such churches, neo-Gothic. The beamed ceiling is very fine.

Just outside town, on the Riebeeksrivier Road, is **Spesbona Farm**, which boasts the biggest oak tree in South Africa (that anyone has bothered to record, that is). It is a monster, and the farmer is happy to show it off.

From Malmesbury either continue the last hour or so south to Cape Town or, if it is spring and time is not too pressing, take a detour west, past the **Mamre Road Wine Cellar** (*open for tastings Mon–Fri 9–5, Sat 9–12*).

Further along is the small dairy-farming town of **Darling**. The town's setting lives up to its lovely name; its green pasture is irrigated all year and becomes a joyous frenzy of colour in the spring wildflower season. The name's origin is not so charming, being called after Charles Darling, Lieut. Governor of the Cape in 1851.

Being a dairy town, Darling naturally has a **Butter Museum** (*open Mon–Sat 9–12*), on Parsonage Street, which, equally naturally, contains a variety of butter-making utensils. Fascinating stuff. The annual **Darling Flower Show** is more spectacular, albeit in a quiet way. It happens in the third week of September, when the surrounding wild flowers are at their peak. The **Darling Flower Reserve**, ✆ (02241) 3361, 13km west of town on the road to Yzerfontein, is a wilder show of flowers in season, particularly the large, orange Namaqualand daisy.

On the Burgerspan road, 5km out of town, is the **Hildebrandt Monument**, commemorating the southernmost skirmish of the Anglo-Boer War. The Boers involved were Jan Smuts' famous *Kommandos* that dodged around the Cape for a year, avoiding British columns, unfriendly farmers and facing the threat of hanging if caught. By the end of their campaign the local farmers were so terrified of the consequences of helping them that the Boers were, on several occasions, reduced to eating their boots. The *Kommandos* finally surrendered in 1902, when called in by the other Boer generals at the end of the war.

South of Darling, heading back to Cape Town on the R307, is **Mamre** (*open daily sunrise to sunset*), a Moravian mission station dating from the 1820s, and built in the lime-wash and thatch style of the time. The gabled church is austerely classical, while the thatched mission cottages cluster round it like hens. Shaded by tall oaks, the mission has been made a national monument. It still has a working water mill. There is also a small nature reserve—good for wild flowers in the spring, **Mamre Sandveld Reserve**, ✆ (0226) 61 073.

expensive–moderate

Carollanns, on the corner of Voortrekker and Long Streets, in Riebeek West, ✆ (02246) 245, offers very friendly accommodation (with en suite bathrooms) in five rooms of a Victorian house. Its restaurant serves very good Cape country dishes—big servings and good value. In the same village, but much more expensive, is **The Lodge**, on Denerhoff Street, ✆ (02246) 211, which occupies a renovated 19th-century building originally designed as a municipal conservatoire.

In Malmesbury, the **Swartland Tuishuis** is another 19th-century building now renovated and offering clean, comfortable rooms at the top end of the expensive scale. **Kontreispens**, on Piet Retief Street, ✆ (0224) 21 456, serves reasonably priced Cape country cooking.

If it's summer, ring **Die Lapa** (in the countryside near Malmesbury), ✆ (0224) 77 040, to see if they are running their good value open-air fish and poultry *braais*.

The slightly run-down, moderately priced **Nederberg Hotel**, in Piketberg, ✆ (0261) 314 645, offers a relaxed, old-fashioned atmosphere and a pub much frequented by locals. About 3km out of Piketberg, up the Versfeldt Pass road, is **Noupoort Guest Farm**, ✆ (0261) 5754, which offers about the best value in the immediate area, and has some superb mountain walks.

In Darling, try the **Darling Guest House**, ✆ (02241) 2385, or the **Old Buffers B&B**, ✆ (02241) 3008.

Also moderate is **Die Herberg** guest house, in Porterville, ✆ (02623) 2416.

cheap

Malmesbury, ✆ (0224) 23266, and Piketberg, ✆ (0262) 31674/31126, both have municipal **camp sites** with ablution blocks.

The Garden Route

The inhabitants of this country are tawny coloured. Their food is confined to the flesh of seals, whales and gazelles, and the roots of herbs. They are dressed in skins, and wear sheaths of olive wood over their virile members. They are armed with poles of olive wood to which a horn, browned in the fire, is attached. Their numerous dogs resemble those of Portugal, and bark like them.

Vasco da Gama, on landing on the Garden Route coast, 1498.

Between Stilbaai and Port Elizabeth, a distance of about 500km, runs the coastal strip known as the Garden Route, a temperate zone of tangled hardwood forest, green pasture, beach town and lagoon, separated from the interior by a continuous chain of high mountains. Down on the coast, the daytime temperature seldom drops below 15°C, and seldom gets higher than 30°C. Rain falls year-round all along the Garden Route, supporting the largest indigenous forests in southern Africa on the seaward slopes of the mountains. The result is the lushest temperate landscape in the country—a patchwork of green pastures and greener woodlands that look almost European at first glance, and give the region its name.

Although the Garden Route towns have been on the tourist map for a long time, its mountain country and nature reserves are still very remote. Nature-lovers flock here, whether for the incredibly diverse bird life (a mixture of forest species, such as louries and wood hoepoes, and waterfowl), for the splendour of the forests, most of whose trees only occur in South Africa, or for the unspoilt, rugged coastline.

History

Unlike many other areas of the Cape, this region did not develop as a single unit, but sporadically, town by town. This was largely owing to the dense forest that, until the mid 19th century, covered most of the area except for a narrow strip along the coast. As a result there was little inland infrastructure until quite recently, and settlements were reliant on the sea for communication.

This said, the rich coast has been inhabited for many thousands of years. In the caves of the Robberg Peninsula archaeologists have found evidence of *strandloper* (beachcomber) culture, probably of KhoiSan origin, dating back to the 7th century BC. That there was habitation before this is likely, but the only material culture left behind by the *strandlopers* was

The Garden Route

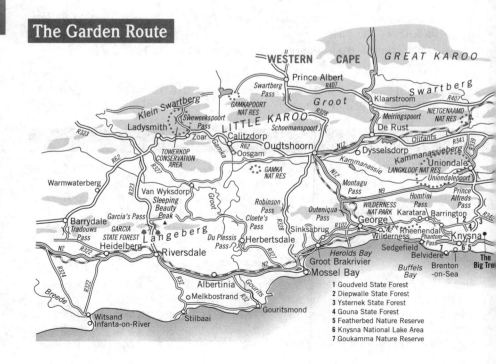

1 Goudveld State Forest
2 Diepwalle State Forest
3 Ysternek State Forest
4 Gouna State Forest
5 Featherbed Nature Reserve
6 Knysna National Lake Area
7 Goukamma Nature Reserve

shell middens (refuse heaps), which rot and leave no trace after a certain time. Some historians maintain that Khoi cattle- and sheep-herders were grazing their stock on the rich coastal strip as early as 1 AD. The forested mountain country behind was left largely uninhabited, except along certain trails beaten by large game migrating over the mountains from the north. Usually made by elephants, these natural roads were later developed into the modern road passes between the Garden Route and the Little Karoo.

The first Portuguese to round the Cape—under Bartolemeu Dias—stopped along the Garden Route to take in water and to barter for the cattle and sheep they saw from their ships. Dias' party landed at modern-day Mossel Bay, but could not communicate effectively with the Khoi, and the encounter ended in violence. Vasco da Gama also stopped at Mossel Bay but, after some initial success, also ended up firing a cannon at the Khoi.

However, as the route around the Cape to the Indies opened up to general European trade, both Mossel Bay and Formosa Bay (later Plettenberg Bay) became regular stopping points for ships from all maritime nations, and the Khoi and the Europeans quickly established a trading relationship, once it became clear that the intruders were no threat. Iron, brass and copper seem to have been the most valued trade items. By the mid 16th century this trade had created a secure enough environment for ships' captains to leave messages for each other on 'post-office' stones and trees and, by the 1650s, when the Dutch set up their Cape Town colony, the Khoi and the Europeans were on largely friendly terms.

This changed abruptly when the first permanent Dutch settlers began trickling into the region from the 1680s. As with the Khoi near Cape Town, Namaqualand and the Winelands (*see* **History**), those of the Garden Route were clear in not wanting strangers settling in their midst. But by 1730, Stilbaai, Mossel Bay and Formosa Bay all had permanent Dutch settlements, and the local Houteniqua, Gouriqua and Attaqua Khoi were reduced to a virtual slave caste, subdued by firearms and imported diseases such as smallpox.

Today, the names of the region's rivers and mountain ranges are the only intact relics of Khoi culture. The people themselves, exploited sexually by the European masters, gradually lost their distinct ethnicity, and by the mid 19th century had become the 'coloured' labouring class, an Afrikaans-speaking majority in most of the Western and Northern Cape.

Because of the forested terrain, European settlement of the coast continued slowly. In the late 18th and early 19th centuries the British developed the town of George from small Afrikaner farming hamlets, and ports were established at Mossel Bay and Knysna. Timber from the interior began to be cut at a furious rate, and this, combined with a short-lived gold rush at Millwood, near Knysna, in 1880, denuded most of the wild interior of its cover, and by the 20th century the landscape had been dramatically transformed. At the same time, the forests' large elephant herds were wiped out and the land opened up to settlement.

However, even with the forests gone, the rugged nature of the hinterland confined most settlement to the coast, and, by the 1950s, much of the forest had recovered—with both indigenous growth and imported eucalyptus and pine.

Under apartheid, and in the build-up to the 1994 changeover, the Garden Route, like many areas of the Western Cape, remained largely aloof from political strife. Although bad things certainly happened (in 1986, while visiting Knysna, the author was informed of a man being 'helicoptered'—hung upside down and beaten so that he spun—in the local police station), most of the political campaigning was confined to ritualized jousting between Afrikaner Nationalists and English-speaking liberals.

Today, the region retains its old tranquillity. However, over the past 10 years, large numbers of Xhosa people from the poverty-stricken Transkei and Ciskei former 'homelands' seeking work have drifted into the area en route to Cape Town, and large squatter camps have appeared in the countryside near George and Knysna. With such a wealthy white population nearby, the unemployed, often desperate incomers sometimes resort to crime. However, despite gloomy speculation by local residents, there has as yet been no evidence of this getting out of control, and the Garden Route remains one of the safest, as well as one of the most beautiful regions of South Africa.

Getting There

By road: The beaten track through the Garden Route is along the N2, whether from the west via Swellendam and Heidelberg, or from the east via Port Elizabeth. The N2 is fast and passes through all the major centres, but it is worth bearing in mind that, in terms of scenery, most of the best of the Garden Route lies away from the main road, on the coast and in the mountains. The exception is the town of Knysna, which should not be missed (though again, the best of Knysna's scenery lies in its coastline and montane forest).

By bus: Knysna and George and the other towns along the N2 can be reached by the Cape Town–Durban buses, run every day by **InterCape** and **TransLux**, but none of the towns have bus stations, only central bus-stops. The local tourist information office will give directions, bus times and fares. Buses between George and Jo'burg are run by **Garden Route Express** three days a week, and **TransCity** (a cheaper branch of TransLux) run services between Kimberley and Plettenberg Bay, via Knysna and George.

The **Baz Bus**, ✆ (021) 439 2323, also services the backpacker lodges of the Garden Route—Mossel Bay, Wilderness, Knysna, Plettenberg Bay, Nature's Valley and Jeffreys Bay—en route to the Eastern Cape, Natal, Swaziland and the Transvaal.

By train: The only long-distance service is between Jo'burg and George, via Bloemfontein, Colesberg and Graaff-Reinet. At the time of writing, services are weekly only. Call George railway station, ✆ (0441) 773 8202, for details. Otherwise, the only Garden Route train service is the Outenqua Choo-Tjoe, a steam train that runs daily across the lagoons between Knysna and George (*see* 'Activities').

Riversdale and the Langeberg Mountains

If entering the Garden Route from the Overberg, in the west, follow the N2 to the small town of **Riversdale**. The small town itself is uninteresting, except for the **Julius Gordon Africana Museum** (*open Mon–Fri 10–12 only*), which has some superb Cape landscape paintings by two of the better South African artists, Bowler and Volschenk. North of town, in the towering Langeberg Mountains, are **Garcia's Pass** and **Sleeping Beauty Peak**, reached via the R323 north. Garcia's Pass is easy to drive and very beautiful, winding through forest to a series of small plateaux whose fynbos heathlands are cut with wooded kloofs and fast-flowing streams. This is a good place to observe the abrupt climatic switch from temperate to semi-arid that occurs between the the Garden Route and the Little Karoo. From the old tollhouse (now a hiking hut) on the east side of Garcia's Pass, several good hiking trails snake away across the mountainsides.

Stilbaai and the Kafferkuils Estuary

South of Riversdale, the R323 twists for 30km along the Kafferkuils River to the small coastal resort of **Stilbaai**. Except at peak holiday times, Stilbaai is usually all but empty. Mostly composed of newish holiday homes, the village has one or two old buildings. One, the **Palinggat Residence and Fountain** (built in 1809), is an old Cape Dutch manor that now houses Stilbaai's **Publicity Association,** ✆ (02934) 42 602. The house has a small museum (*open Mon–Fri 8.30–12.30 and 2–4.30, Sat 9–12*), mostly devoted to the natural history of the local sea and shore. The fountain has some extraordinary residents—a population of tame eels (one over a metre long) which will come and take food from your hand. The former owners of the Palinggat Residence first started feeding the eels about 50 years ago, and the tradition has remained to this day. The eels sometimes leave the fountain and glide over land down to the sea to mate. However, there are always some left, and occasionally the fountain fills up with the creatures. Visitors too sqeamish to dangle fishing bait in the water for the great black slitherers can watch them being fed at 11 o'clock every morning from Monday to Saturday.

There are two small nature reserves on the Kafferkuils estuary, just north of the village: the **Pauline Bohmen Nature Reserve** and the **Krantzfontein Reserve**. Both require a permit from Stilbaai Publicity Association. In the mouth of the estuary are the remains of some prehistoric fish traps, ingenious leftovers from early *strandloper* culture, constructed from boulders to create small dams between the high- and low-water marks. Again, contact Stilbaai Publicity to arrange a boat and guide.

An interesting contrast to prosperous Stilbaai is the 'coloured' fishing village of **Melkbostrand**, reached by a dirt road not marked on the map, but signposted about 1.5km north of Stilbaai. Melkbostrand is another of the early 19th-century Moravian mission stations that dot the Cape, none of which have changed outwardly over the last 100 years. Most of the men who live here fish and sell their catch in Stilbaai.

After Melkbostrand, the dirt road leads past **Gouritsmond**, a tiny farming, fishing, and holiday house hamlet at the mouth of the wide Gourits River. There is safe bathing in the bay, and an under-used beach. The reeds that grow along the estuary are in great demand for thatching Cape Dutch houses, and reed-gatherers can often be seen slashing away at the fringes of the marshy water margins.

Mossel Bay

Northeast of Gouritsmond is Mossel Bay, an unattractive town with a positively ugly industrial fringe. Unless you absolutely want to see its large museum, Mossel Bay should be avoided. However, the South African Tourist Board promotes the place because of its size and historical significance, as the site of the first two recorded Portuguese landings in South Africa in 1488 and 1510, after which it became a regular stopping point for European ships on their way to the East Indies (*see* 'Garden Route History'). The site was never developed as a port, and remained a fishing and whaling backwater until its discovery as a holiday resort in the 1930s. Today, Mossel Bay retains a beautiful beach, but the town itself has been sadly industrialized, mainly as the site of **Mossgas**, a large petrol refinery, visible from the N2, and set up by the South African government during the years of sanctions against apartheid, when no oil could be bought from abroad.

The **Bartolomeu Dias Museum Complex**, on Market Street (*open Mon–Fri 9–5, Sat 10–1*), is the town's only point of interest. This comprises most of the surviving old buildings, including the remains of the original Post Office Tree, a large milkwood on which passing captains left messages for each other during the late 16th and early 17th centuries. You can still post a letter from here in a small postbox next to the tree. There is a maritime museum, which includes a replica of a Portuguese galleon, and an arts and crafts shop.

Mossel Bay has a pleasant beach (though there are better, wilder ones elsewhere on the Garden Route coast) looking out towards **Seal Island**, a large Cape fur seal colony, cruises to which leave from the harbour. Times and prices can be found at the museum.

Inland from Mossel Bay is some lovely mountain country, which can be seen from the R328 north towards Robinson Pass, a good scenic drive. It is worth detouring east off the R328 on the dirt road about 2km after Ruitersbos. Drive slowly: there are precipitous drops away down to the Brak River, and a fair amount of loose rock. The road descends and ascends through 20km of forested gorges, crossing the river several times and passing isolated old farmsteads, until finally joining the R102 at Groot Brakrivier. The R102 goes west, back to Mossel Bay, or east, parallel with the N2, to George.

George

The largest town on the Garden Route is another ugly, if bustling, town, much 'improved' during the 1950s and '60s, again with beautiful country all around. The **Outeniqua Mountains** (which get their name from the Khoi tribe living there in the 18th century) begin just north of here. Signposted from the R29, which winds up over the truly spectacular **Outeniqua Pass**, connecting George with Outsdhoorn in the Little Karoo, is the Forestry Station from where begins the five-day **Outeniqua Hiking Trail**, one of the classic South African trails (*see* 'Activities').

The town itself is only worth visiting for the **Dutch Reformed Church**, built in 1842, with elegant yellowwood pillars, ceiling and dome, and red stinkwood pulpit, and the **George Museum**, in the Old Drostdy (*open Mon–Fri 9–4.30, Sat 9–12.30*), built in 1813. This museum houses a remarkable collection of gifts given to ex-President P. W. Botha by various foreign heads of state. None of the gifts appear to have any economic value, prompting speculation as to the whereabouts of the gifts that did. A bust of the man, himself a resident of George, adorns the entrance hall.

Around George

About 15km east of George is the small resort of **Wilderness**, best known for its superb, if sometimes crowded, beach and the fabulously beautiful **Wilderness National Park** © (0441) 877 1197, an enchanting series of forest-fringed freshwater lagoons dotted with wooded islands and connected by great stretches of marsh, home to otters and waterfowl.

The N2 runs along the southern boundary of the park, but the best route in is via the tarred turn-off from the north side, marked 'Hoekvil'. The next dirt road east winds through the lagoons, finally looping back to the N2 just west of Sedgefield, on the Knysna road. The lagoons are home to a vast array of birds; there are fish eagles, and most of the South African waders. There are day-hikes, along which you can expect to encounter bontebok, bushbuck and duiker. In summer the area abounds with ticks, so wear long trousers. Maps of the trails and bird-watching hides, and information on the wildlife, are available at the park's **Ebb and Flow Camp** (telephone the park's main number), off the N2, 3km east of town.

Along the N2, at the eastern edge of the park, is **Sedgefield**, a small and unsightly holiday village. However, just east of here is the incomparable **Goukamma Nature Reserve**, ✆ (04455) 31 316. A huge freshwater lagoon, Groenvlei, the lower estuarine Goukamma River, and the sand dunes and rock-strewn coast, can be explored on foot or by boat. Fynbos and marsh alternate with large stands of milkwood trees. Again, expect to see fish eagles, green louries, bontebok, bushbuck, vervet monkey and, if you are lucky, bushpig. The coastline is not safe for swimming, and puff adders are common in summer, so be careful when hiking. There is no accommodation.

Knysna

A peaceful contrast to George, Knysna lies at the head of a large saltwater lagoon at the foot of hills that sweep away to the great hardwood forests of the Outeniqua Mountains. For the last 150 years a furniture-making industry has flourished here, using the fine local hardwoods. **Knysna Lagoon** is almost entirely separated from the sea by a spit of cliffs, broken in the middle, through which narrow channel the lagoon is connected with the ocean beyond. These twin spits of land are known as the **Knysna Heads**. The Western Head is mostly covered by the privately owned **Featherbed Nature Reserve** (*see* p.236), which can only be reached by boat from the old harbour.

Architecturally, Knysna is a mixture of Cape Dutch, 19th-century English and 20th-century jumble, all of which somehow combines to an attractive whole. The town is known for its tranquillity and racial tolerance. A community of artists and craftspeople have settled here, giving the town a youthful, lively feel—hence the many good bars, restaurants and cheap accommodation. It also has the country's only decent brewery. The lagoon and surrounding forest are administered by the National Parks Board to prevent over-development.

History

Knysna started life in the early 18th century as a settlement of Afrikaner farms, largely cut off from the rest of the coast by deep forests and the difficult gradients of the few roads through them. In 1803 the largest of these farms was bought by a wealthy and eccentric Englishman called **George Rex**, whose name, opulent hospitality and flouting of social rules (he had two common-law wives, though not at the same time) generated a rumour, that quickly became legend, that he was the illegitimate son of King George III of England.

George Rex never made any such claims himself, but neither did he deny them outright, no doubt enjoying the cachet. In fact, although his English origins *were* obscure, he had come out to the Cape in the 1790s with the British occupation, as a secretary to the Admiralty.

Rex managed to accrue an immense fortune while working as a civil servant, which the purchase of the farm at Knysna only served to increase. He was the first of many to exploit the seemingly endless hardwood forests of the area. The local tree species included the giant yellowwood and stinkwood, the former of which could grow to 40m and live 2000 years (a few such specimens survive today). He encouraged ships to call in at the sheltered lagoon and buy wood, building a harbour there and sometimes piloting the ships through the tricky channel himself. By the time of Rex's death, in 1839, Knysna had grown up around the harbour and his homestead.

Meanwhile a community of Afrikaner woodsmen had grown up deep in the forest, itinerants who had mostly been attracted into the area to work for Rex, then set up on their own, with their own teams of workmen and oxen. Living deep in the forest, these men seldom came into Knysna itself, which grew ever more English. Younger sons of the English aristocracy, attracted by Rex's social status, the distance from the authority of the Cape, and the richness of the land, began building great homesteads nearby. But the forest Afrikaners, cut off from the town's society, retreated into their own superstitious world, haunted by Khoi nature spirits and the more real threat of death from the elephant herds that roamed the forest.

Originally, the foresters had done well, felling the timber and hauling it out over the difficult terrain. However, by the mid 19th century, agents had set up in town, buying the wood from the foresters and selling it either to the furniture factories further afield or as cargo for house-building and wagons. The agents kept the price of timber down and gradually forced the foresters to fell at a feverish rate. When they could no longer survive from the timber alone, the woodsmen turned to intensive ivory-hunting, but this also soon became an artificially depressed market. By the 1870s, so much of the forest had disappeared that the Cape government appointed conservation officers to control the felling. But they misundertood the root of the problem and attacked the foresters rather than the agents, so that the rape continued unabated.

In the 1880s, gold was discovered deep in the Knysna Forest, and a short rush followed. Overnight, a mining town was established at Millwood, about 40km into the forest from Knysna. Within a few years Millwood had six hotels, two newspapers, and several brothels. But most of the gold turned out to be alluvial. Only one or two real seams were found, and these quickly dried up. Although a few fortunes were made, most of the prospectors went bust or left for the richer Transvaal gold reefs. The activity had caused even more of the forest to be felled, and the once deep primeval Knysna Forest was reduced to patches of remnant woodland in the deeper kloofs. By the 1900s most of the woodsmen were gone, and most of the elephants with them.

However, since then, stringent conservation measures have been applied and the great Knysna Forest has reclaimed much of its range, and, although only a few of the giant trees remain, the mountains north of town are once again cloaked with mature growth. The elephant have not recovered so well, and a mere three now survive in the forest.

Meanwhile, Knysna steadily lost its importance as a commercial centre. By the late 1920s the port had ceased operations, and today only the traditional industries of forestry, furniture-making, dairy- and hop-farming still flourish. In recent years, Knysna has seen something of a tourist boom, coupled with an influx of young arts and crafts people, but, despite the liveliness and youth of many of its inhabitants, the town's calm is still one of its chief attractions.

Knysna Publicity Association, Main Road (look out for the big plate-glass window with the elephant skeleton in it), ✆ (0445) 825 510.

The Town

Knysna has some good, small museums. The Old Gaol, a Victorian building on Queen Street, houses the **Angling Museum, Maritime Museum** and **Knysna Art Gallery** (*all open Mon–Sat 8.30–5*). Of these, the Angling Museum is the most interesting—apart from its history of non-commercial fishing, the museum has a display devoted to the coelacanth, a surviving prehistoric fish species that lives off South Africa's Indian Ocean coast. Discovered back in the 1960s by one Professor J. L. B. Smith, the fish is famous among zoologists for providing a 'missing link' between land and sea creatures—the coelacanth's fins are apparently midway along the evolutionary scale between fins and limbs. Smith called the fish 'Old Four Legs' and wrote a book about it using the nickname as a title. So popular was the book that Smith used its proceeds to buy Knysna's Western Head, which is now the Featherbed Nature Reserve, and is run by his son. A preserved coelacanth is on display, but alas, not so the professor, who is only represented in photographs.

The Maritime Museum has a brief, concise history of Knysna's old port, while the Art Gallery houses displays by local artists and photographers that change each month. Some of the work, especially local landscape paintings, is very good, and it is always worth having a look at the latest exhibition.

Millwood House Museum, also on Queen Street (*open Mon–Fri 10–12 only*), was one of the only surviving buildings from the gold-rush town of Millwood. This cottage was brought down to Knysna in the 1960s after Millwood fell into ruin and was reclaimed by the forest. It houses a collection of George Rex's belongings and a history of the pilots that used to guide the large boats through the Heads to the harbour. Should you wish to pay homage to the great man, George Rex's grave lies in a stone enclosure a kilometre down a footpath off the N2 east of town, just before the turn-off to the Heads. Two tall pines sway over the grave.

Opposite the church on Main Road is a permanent **flea market** of local crafts, where it is fun to browse and chat with the stallholders. At around 5pm they will start to drift down towards the old harbour, where, in one of the old warehouses, is a bar and grill, **Tapas**, which doubles as a local for the bohemian set (*see* 'Eating Out' and 'Nightlife'). Always lively, the place is often riotous by closing time, which is whenever the last person leaves.

Between Main Road and the Lagoon are several craft shops set up by creative incomers: **Mackintosh's Weaving and Country Store, Bitou Crafts**, and the **Carver's Gallery** (*see* 'Shopping'). Across the lagoon, on the Western Head, is **Featherbed Nature Reserve**, ✆ (0445) 2693, home to the tiny, elusive blue duiker, as well as a host of birds.

The Knysna Forest

The Knysna Forest is a general term describing all the woodland, indigenous and planted, that stretches from behind the town into the southern slopes of the Outeniqua Mountains. There are four nature reserves via which the public can gain access to the forest—Gouna

State Forest, Goudveld State Forest, Diepwalle State Forest and Ysternek State Forest—in the mountains about 25km north of Knysna.

The forest itself is magical. A permanent hush rules under the great trees, between whose trunks grow giant (up to 10ft) prehistoric ferns. In some places the trees have been labelled, and their names, like ironwood, assegai, hardpear and saffronwood, somehow add to the romance. There are a lot of mature stinkwoods and—in some places—some surviving yellowwood giants. The largest of these, known as King Edward's Tree, is 46m high and is reckoned to have been a sapling some time before the Norman conquest. The Knysna Forest's three surviving elephant (now possibly four; a calf has been spotted) live in and around Diepwalle, but you stand no chance of seeing them. Pastured next to the Forestry Station is a herd of grey Percheron draught horses, used for dragging the indigenous timber still harvested for sale out of the woods, causing less damage than machines. You can lose yourself in the forest for days, among the waterfalls and hidden streams, watching bright birds flash suddenly across the path and bushbuck leap from the trees as you turn a corner.

Gouna State Forest and **Diepwalle State Forest** are two extensive tracts of indigenous forest that are home to the forest's last surviving elephant, and are reached via the N2 as it passes through the western end of Knysna. From here a signposted dirt road winds tortuously into the mountainous forest. Neither reserve has accommodation, except for the hiking huts of the **Outeniqua Hiking Trail**, which must be booked in advance (*see* 'Activities'). **Goudveld State Forest** is reached from the N2 about 5km west of town via the signposted turn-off north to Rheenendal, a village at the forest's edge. Hidden away here is the now overgrown site of Millwood mining town. One or two of the ex-streets have been signposted by the Forestry people; it's eerie to walk them. Eerier still is the cemetery, complete with the headstones of unfortunates from all over Europe, now the home territory of a troop of baboons. A few kilometres into the forest is a lonely rock pool deep enough to swim in. Again, part of the Outeniqua Trail passes through Goudveld and there is a hiking hut at Millwood that can be booked in advance.

Ysternek State Forest is at the northern extent of the forest (reached via the R339, a rough road), where it meets the fynbos heath of the higher slopes. Here there are leopards (as well as at Diepwalle), bushpig and bushbuck. For those who want to drive rather than walk, the R338 leads up through some of the densest forest before crawling up over the steep, ruggedly beautiful Prince Alfred's Pass into the Little Karoo. Make sure you have a full tank of petrol and a good spare tyre for this road.

The Passes Road, the old main road between Knysna and George, was laid by Thomas Bains, the Victorian road engineer who opened up most of the Cape's major pass roads in the 1850s and '60s. This is a fascinating ride along the southern foothills of the Outeniquas, through alternate forest, fynbos, pasture, and over several steep passes, including Kaimans Pass, which was worn to a deep chute by oxen hooves before the present road was built.

In those days it took two weeks to make the journey, presuming, of course, that your team could manage the gradients. Today it takes about three hours if you do not rush. The road is not numbered, but is marked in red on the road map, leaving the N2 west of Knysna via Phantom's Pass (named after a species of moth, rather than a ghost) and the small village of Barrington.

The Coast Around Knysna

Buffalo Bay (or Buffelsbaai), 22km west of Knysna, has a long, often deserted swimming beach. The road is signposted south off the N2 about 15km west of town, and passes **Buffalo Bay Game Farm**, home to a variety of indigenous antelope as well as zebra and wildebeest. A look around the farm involves a 3km drive or a half-hour walking trail.

East of Knysna, also signposted south off the N2, are **Noetzie**, and **Brackenhill Falls**, a series of falls plunging steeply towards the sea, surrounded by dense forest. A hiking trail runs alongside them. Noetzie is a small, rather exclusive resort of holiday homes which fronts the beach at the end of the road that leads on south of the falls. It is remarkable only because of a fashion in the late 1920s, when this resort went up, to build houses that looked like castles. Otherwise Noetzie is not very interesting, although, if you're there, note that the beach is good for swimming.

Around the other side of the lagoon are **Belvidere** and **Brenton-on-Sea**, reached via the N2 west (about 5km), and signposted off south just after the road crosses an inlet of the lagoon. Belvidere's 19th-century church, built in neo-Norman style, has a rose window fitted with shards from the great windows of Coventry Cathedral (in England) after it was bombed during the Second World War. Brenton-on-Sea is the closest swimming beach to Knysna (12km). The village is tiny and has a pleasantly isolated feel.

Plettenberg Bay

Known to most South Africans as 'Plett', this small, rather exclusive resort is crowded in summer, with wealthy holidaymakers, yet for all its fashionable status, Plett has nothing on Knysna. Its three beaches are very good for swimming, but the coastline has been marred by the building of a multi-storey hotel on one of the promontories between the beaches. The town has one, very modern, main street, with shops, restaurants and bars.

History

Evidence of early *strandloper* culture dating from around 700 BC to the 17th century has been found in caves by Plettenberg Bay's beaches. A KhoiSan settlement flourished here from about the first century AD, and these people were still herding their flocks here when a Portuguese ship, the *Sao Ganzalo*, ran aground in 1630 (the site of the shipwreck is marked on the peninsula).

Once ashore, the Portuguese sailors did their best to survive, salvaging what they could from their ship, and seeking the help of *strandloper* seal-hunters living on the long peninsula, west of the present town (later named the Robberg Peninsula by the Dutch—'rob' is Dutch for seal). Archaeologists have excavated the Portuguese settlement and found fragments of Ming pottery, brought with them from the East to the wild shores of Africa. By the time they were rescued, they had christened the sheltered inlet Formosa Bay.

By the early 18th century, the modern Garden Route region was busy with trekboers on their way east, heading away from the Dutch East India Company's authority to the lush coastland of the Eastern Cape, and Formosa Bay became a small Dutch settlement. But officialdom followed, if slowly. The rough village became a magistracy in 1770, and was renamed Plettenberg Bay after the Cape Governor of the time. After the British annexation of the Cape in the early 1800s, Plett then grew into a small fishing, whaling and agricultural town, until its second 'discovery' as a resort town in the 1930s.

Tourist Information

Publicity Association, the Municipal Buildings, just off Main St, ✆ (04457) 34 065.

Around the Town

There isn't much in Plett itself besides the main street of shops. Around town, however, there is plenty. The **Robberg Nature Reserve**, on the Robberg Peninsula on the west side of the bay, used to be a colony of thousands of Cape fur seals (*see* above), but most were killed or driven away as the town became settled. Still, the bird-watching is tremendous— especially on the promontory's northern cliffs. Great numbers of southern black-backed gulls, black oystercatchers and white-breasted cormorants breed here. The **Nelson Bay cave** (reached by a footpath) still has Stone-Age *strandloper* shell middens around its entrance.

Keurbooms Nature Reserve and **Keurbooms State Forest** are along the N2 east of Plett (turn left on the R340 just before the N2 crosses the wide Keurbooms River mouth). Look out for bushbuck, dassies, baboons and vervet monkeys. Rare Caspian terns breed on a sandbar near the river mouth.

The old **Plettenberg Whaling Station** (1831) is on Beacon Island, just offshore. Plett's small whaling industry only closed down in 1916 and the slipway and blubber cauldron can still be seen. The island gets its name from a stinkwood sailing beacon put up there in 1771, later replaced with one of stone. Trips out can be arranged via the Publicity Association.

Waddrift Nature Reserve is a half-wild private farm in the small Bitou Valley, signposted on the northern side of the N2 east of town. The **Old Nick Trading Store**, on the N2 just east of town, dates from 1880 and now sells teas and crafts.

East of Plett, settlements become fewer and further apart, and the forest and mountains begin to crowd closer to the N2. A worthwhile detour, 25km east of Plett, is to **Forest Hall**, a stone manor house surrounded by a large estate of pasture and forest and overlooking its own stretch of coast. Forest Hall was built for Henry Newdigate, one of the younger sons of the English aristocracy, attracted to the area in the early 19th century by the legendary George Rex. Like the manor houses near Knysna, Forest Hall is superbly isolated. The present owner (descended from the Newdigates) breeds Arab horses which can be hired for rides into the milkwood bush. You can walk in the nature reserve, which has bushbuck, duiker, bushpig, vervet monkey and louries. Less energetic fun is tea on the wide veranda (*see* 'Where to Stay').

Nature's Valley

East of Forest Hall there is only one more town before the Garden Route coast becomes wild. This is **Nature's Valley**, on the eastern edge of the **Tsitsikamma National Park** in the **De Vasselot Nature Reserve**.

Nature's Valley is incredibly beautiful. The road signposted to it from the N2 descends through mature yellowwood forest (the coastal forests from here eastwards were too remote to be exploited like those around Knysna and it was not until the 1860s that woodcutters began to appear). Having seen the rape of the Knysna forests, the Cape Governor appointed conservators for the Tsitsikamma region as early as 1880. The last of these, the Comte Henri de Vasselot, lived at Nature's Valley, and gives the surrounding reserve his name. Fortunately, by the time of his appointment, the momentum of forest clearance had slowed and today the great trees survive from the Tsitsikamma Mountains to the sea.

Nature's Valley is now a very small resort town surrounded by milkwood bush and undeveloped beaches. Visitors must check in to the office of the De Vasselot Nature Reserve to get maps of the coast and forest walks around the small town. One of these follows the beach, and then winds over rocks back into the bush and over a steep hill to a deserted, forested bay where the trees have been sculpted into weird, dancing shapes by the wind.

De Vasselot Reserve is also the start of two long hiking trails into the Tsitsikamma National Park, the **Otter Trail** along the coast and the **Tsitsikamma Trail** into the mountains.

If you haven't time to explore the Tsitsikamma coast and mountains by foot, the N2 runs between the two. Take the turn-off to **Storms River Mouth** for a half-hour stroll along a short section of the Otter Trail to the mouth itself, a spectacular, roaring flow of fresh water coming down between cliffs and into the open sea. A hanging bridge across the mouth allows you to photograph the head-on collision of waters. Storms River Mouth, as the one point in the wild coastline accessible by car, has been rather developed by the Parks Board, but that detracts little from the sheer natural force of the place.

At the Paul Sauer Bridge, a few kilometres along the N2 east of the Storms River Mouth turn-off, is the **Tsitsikamma State Forest Reserve**, a publically accessible point of the great forest. The Tsitiskamma Trail runs through here, as does a short, circular hike. Look out for a forest giant, a yellowwood over 36m high, and the usual forest wildlife, though this tends to be shy, owing to the number of visitors. The narina trogon, a rare, brightly coloured bird similar to a lourie, may be seen here, but only if you sit quietly for some time in a forest clearing. East of here, the N2 and the parallel, smaller R102 head straight through empty country between mountain and sea to **Cape St Francis**, which roughly marks the geographical end of the Garden Route, and the meeting of the official districts of the Western and Eastern Capes.

Cape St Francis is reached via Humansdorp. Now a large resort, Cape St Francis is attractive enough with its mock Cape Dutch white-wash-and-thatch timeshare holiday homes, but unspectacular. The beaches of the bay are good for swimming and surfing.

If you have time, take the dirt road turn-off to **Oyster Bay**, about 8km north of Cape St Francis. This leads for about 25km across the cape to a small, seldom-used beach with a store and gas station. Big waves, but safe for swimming.

Jeffrey's Bay, 20km east of Humansdorp on the R102, is another resort, a bit glitzier than Cape St Francis, and packed with surfers during summer. A good place to make friends or learn to surf, but otherwise, it has little to interest the traveller.

Between Jeffrey's Bay and the sprawling, ugly town of Port Elizabeth are several small nature reserves: the **Van Stadens Wild Flower Reserve** (signposted from the N2) covers about 500ha of coastal fynbos and forest. The fynbos flowers bloom between April and September, and there are walking trails, but no accommodation.

Maitland Nature Reserve, on the Seaview Road south of the N2, covers 127ha at the mouth of the Maitland River. A large stand of coastal forest and milkwood bush, with a hiking trail and camp site, it is known for bird-watching.

Cape Recife Nature Reserve covers 336ha of shoreline and dunes. Marine birds predominate, including great numbers of waders in summer. There are paths and bird-watching hides, but no accommodation.

The **Island Conservation Area** is a stretch of coastal forest reached via the Seaview Road from Humansdorp. Bushbuck, vervet monkey, bushpig and duiker are sometimes spotted from the reserve's 16km hiking trail. There is no accommodation.

Shopping

Knysna is the centre of the Garden Route's crafts tradition, and most craftspeople from the area sell their wares here.

The **Flea Market** happens every day on the south side of Main Road, opposite the church, selling good-quality jewellery, hand-made shoes and clothes. For carvings and utensils in the beautiful local hardwoods, try the **Carver's Gallery**, 18a Main Street.

For hand-woven hangings, rugs, sweaters etc. try **Bitou Crafts** or **Mackintosh's Weaving**, both in Thesen House, 6 Long Street, a large Edwardian trading warehouse. They also sell pottery, herbal products (locally produced) and work by local artists. New shops and galleries open and shut from year to year in Knysna, so it is worth exploring the small shopping centre behind the flea market to discover the latest galleries.

Hiking: Few areas of South Africa offer so much variety of scenery in such a comparatively small space. Almost all the Garden Route's nature reserves have walks and hikes ranging in length from half an hour to several hours, most of which can be broken into smaller sections. Trails of several days can usually be broken up into sections. The Garden Route is very popular with hikers, and the overnight huts have limited space, so it is always advisable to phone in advance. A mattress, bunk and water are always provided at the huts. Firewood and cooking pots are generally provided too, but this should be checked.

The Garden Route has several marked long-distance trails. The **Otter Trail**, ✆ (021) 222 810, runs for 48km (5 days) from the Storms River mouth to the Grootrivier mouth. Arguably the most popular trail in South Africa, it is usually booked up months in advance, but cancellations are common. Unfortunately this trail cannot be broken into shorter sections. Huts are provided. Maps and permits from De Vasselot Reserve, Nature's Valley. If you are unable to get on the Otter Trail try the **Tsitsikamma Trail**, ✆ (0423) 51 180, five days in the mountains and forests of the Tsitsikamma range, with wide views out over the ocean. The trail eventually climbs out on to the fynbos high ground, skirting deep kloofs of cliffside forest where many hikers have seen leopard. The trail can be broken into shorter sections. Maps and permits are available from De Vasselot Reserve, Nature's Valley.

The **Outeniqua Trail**, ✆ (0445) 23 037, is five days in the mountains and forests of the Outeniqua range. The trail climbs and drops for about 100km across high fynbos to the great forests behind Knysna, passing through Millwood ghost town and the range of the few remaining southern Cape elephant. Maps and permits from Southern Cape Forest Region Office, Main Road, Knysna.

Garcia's Pass, north of Riversdale, is the starting point for two overnight trails (with huts) and two short hikes. These trails are under-used, and your only companions are likely to be wind and silence. Maps and permits from Garcia State Forest office on the R323 north of Riversdale, ✆ (02933) 32 558. **Sleeping Beauty Trails**, ✆ (02933) 32 418, offer trails of 1–5 days through some of the loneliest, loveliest country in the Langeberg. All trails can be broken into shorter sections. Maps and permits are obtainable from Garcia State Forest office. **Keurbooms Nature Reserve** has lovely walks along the steep, forested banks of the Keurbooms River and good, cheap accommodation. For the energetic there is a 2-day hiking trail into the neigh-bouring Keurbooms State Forest. The **Keurbooms River Trail**, east of Plettenberg Bay, ✆ (04457) 9309, winds through fynbos and forest. It too can be broken into shorter sections. Maps and permits from the reserve office.

On the Kafferkuils estuary, the **Pauline Bohmen Nature Reserve** has some nature walks, and the **Krantzfontein Reserve** has longer trails.

Gouna State Forest has a 1-day hike, the **Terblans Nature Trail**. Further along, **Diepwalle State Forest** has an overnight hut (part of the 5-day Outeniqua Trail), and three walks ranging from 1–5 hours.

The one hiking trail in **Ysternek State Forest** is very short, but leads through some incredibly dense stands of timber and giant fern, with breathtaking views out over the bare fynbos to the highest peaks of the Outeniquas.

Two tour companies lead organized hikes and provide all equipment plus permits and transport: **Oxygen Tours**, in Knysna, ✆ (0445) 826 234, offers 1- to 5-day hikes in the Knysna Forest and Outeniqua Mountains, while **Judith Hopley's Forest Walks**, ✆ (0445) 871 133, offer day-walks guided by Judith Hopley herself—a well-known amateur botanist, and author of *The Garden Route on Foot*.

Riding: Equi-Trailing, ✆ (04457) 9718, offers guided rides for beginners and the experienced through forest, fynbos and along the beach. Day, half-day, hourly and moonlight rides leave from the stables in Wittedrift village, 10km north of Plettenberg Bay. **Forest Hall**, ✆ (04457) 8869, 15km east of Plettenberg Bay, offers hourly rides on Arab horses. **Eight Bells Mountain Inn** offers hourly riding through local forest. Also near Mossel Bay is **Coastal Riding**, ✆ (0444) 981 269, who offer beach and fynbos rides with the chance to swim your horse into the sea. The **Sleeping Beauty Guest House** also has a riding stable. In Sedgefield, between George and Knysna, is **Cherie's Riding School**, ✆ (04455) 31 575.

Canoeing: Knysna Adventures, ✆ (0445) 871 133, offers guided trips of around 4 hours for beginners (longer for the experienced) through the freshwater lagoons of Wilderness National Park. **Krantzfontein Reserve**, on the Kafferkuils estuary, hires out canoes, as does the **Keurbooms Nature Reserve**, for the Keurbooms River.

Eden Adventures, ✆ (083) 628 8547, also run canoe trails along the Garden Route, as well as **abseiling, kloofing** and **mountain biking**.

Freshwater fishing: Superb angling for springer can be had in the **Wilderness National Park** (permits available at the park office, which also hires boats and tackle) and at **Hunter's Country House**, ✆ (04457) 7818, east of Plettenberg Bay, where you can fish for black bass.

Sea fishing: At present, the largest operator is **Knysna Fishing Charters**, in Knysna ✆ (0445) 21 548, who can offer line and big game trips, as can **South Cape Charters**, ✆ (0445) 825 590. Or, if you have your own tackle, hire a boat from **Hire Away**, ✆ (0445) 825 702. Otherwise apply to the tourist offices for information (*see* above). Recommended spots are: Knysna Lagoon, Nature's Valley beach, Storms River Mouth, Oyster Bay and Cape St Francis.

The Knysna Oyster Company, ✆ (0445) 22 168, on Tuissen's Island in the Knysna Lagoon, offers tours and tastings in its oyster beds.

Scuba diving: Diving and snorkelling in Knysna Lagoon is particularly rewarding as there are some unique fish species, such as the Knysna seahorse (larger than its ocean cousin). Trips are arranged via **Waterfront Scuba**, in Knysna, ✆ (0445) 22 938.

Steam trains: Aficionados of steam will delight in the Garden Route. The **Outeniqua Choo-Tjoe**, an old steam train offering a 3-hour trip on raised tracks over the coastal lagoons, runs daily between George and Knysna. Tickets from George railway station.

Mitchell's Brewery Tours: At the Knysna brewery in the old harbour, ✆ (0445) 24 685, you can look around the place where the only decent beer in South Africa is produced. The brewery is quite liberal in its tastings, and you can expect a jolly time. Tours leave at 10.30 from reception, Mon–Fri.

Bungee-jumping: Jump off the bridge spanning the Gouritz River, near Stilbaai, or the Bloukrans Bridge, between Plett and Nature's Valley (organized from Cape Town, ✆ (021) 725 839).

Surfing: The Cape Town-based company **Surfari**, ✆ (021) 510 2026, offers surfing trips along the Garden Route for beginners and experienced surfers alike.

Paragliding: Courses, as well as 'taster days' for beginners, are offered by **Cloud Base Paragliding**, a Wilderness-based outfit, ✆ (044) 877 1414.

Mountain biking: For biking around Knysna, ring **Outeniqua Biking Trails**, ✆ (0445) 77 644.

Kloofing: **Storm's River Adventures**, ✆ (042) 541 1609, at Storms River Village (not the river mouth), offers trips in the coastal cliffs east of Plett.

Where to Stay

With the exception of the budget range, the amount of accommodation to be found on the Garden Route is staggering. Listed below are the author's recommendations. Should these be full, any Garden Route tourist office will supply alternatives.

Similarly, national parks and nature reserves usually have accommodation (always self-catering), from luxurious to basic, and most have camp sites. It is advisable to book. For telephone numbers of national parks and nature reserves, see individual listings above.

expensive

Forest Hall, ✆ (04457) 8869 (*see* p.240), has one of the most beautiful interiors in South Africa, complete with original Cape Dutch furniture, a galleried hall, and ancestral portraits. The hospitality is friendly, not at all stuffy.

In town, there's **The Plettenberg**, ✆ (04457) 32 074, a 19th-century mansion which offers nature trails, whale- and dolphin-watching, tennis and fishing.

Hunters Country House, ✆ (04457) 7818, 10km east of Plettenberg Bay along the N2 between the Tsitsikamma Mountains and the sea, comprises a set of thatched white cottages furnished with antiques, including four-poster beds. There are forest trails, a river with bass fishing for guests and swimming holes, and a good library.

Also near Plett (signposted from the N2 16km east of town) is **Hog's Hollow Country House**, ✆ (04457) 8879, popular amongst bird-watchers for its location on the edge of dense forest, and with gourmets for its award-winning chef. Guests stay in individual cottages, each of which has its own wooden deck. Walking trails wind off into the trees.

Portland Manor, ✆ (0445) 4804, 🖷 4863, just north of Knysna on the road to Rheenendal, built by another aristocratic settler, Henry Barrington, in 1864, is also still in the family. Its interior is more 'done-up' than Forest Hall and somehow less intimate. However, there is game wandering in the park (including hippo in the home lake). Bass fishing is available for guests. **Yellowwood Lodge,** ✆ (0445) 825 906, a country house built in 1897, overlooks Knysna Lagoon but is only a short walk from the town centre. There are curtained beds and much expensive, lacy chintzerie in the suites (there are no single rooms). Strictly no smoking.

Stilbaai River Lodge, ✆ (02934) 41 317, is a very lovely white thatched house overlooking the estuary at Stilbaai. Set in its own estate, the place has tidal sea-fishing, small game-spotting and good bird life. The rooms are comfortable, but not ornate. Deep leather chairs in the bar and dinner by candlelight. The **Eight Bells Country Inn,** on the south side of Robinson's Pass (R328), ✆ (0444) 951 544, is modern, but not unpleasantly so. This is a collection of white rondavels and log cabins set in woodland. There is good access to both the Garden Route and Little Karoo, as well as horses to ride and trails to walk.

Hoogtekraal, ✆ (0441) 277/8, was built between the 1760s and 1820s. A particularly good Cape Dutch edifice. Its suites (no rooms) are period furnished. There is a working farm to wander in and the house borders the small resort of Glentana (midway between Mossel Bay and George) which has 20km of white sandy beach. Glentana is signposted from the N2. **Sleeping Beauty Guest House,** ✆ (02933) 31651, a handsome late-Victorian house in Riversdale, has seven comfortable and unpretentious rooms, a 9-hole golf course and riding stables.

moderate

If you have to stay the night in Mossel Bay, the **Old Post Office Tree Guest House,** ✆ (0444) 913738, offers clean and comfy B&B.

Ganzvlei Cottage, ✆ (0445) 830 063, is the author's choice; a secluded, very comfortable old farmstead set on the Ganzvlei Farm, 15km west of Knysna and overlooking the Goukamma River, with its back to milkwood forest. There are fish eagles, jackal buzzards, louries, bushbuck and perfect peace. Reached by rowing across the narrow Goukamma River, Ganzvlei cottage is self-catering only. There is a second cottage, equally old, but closer to the main farm, which is worth staying in if the river cottage is booked.

Hunter's Moon Guest House, ✆ (0445) 830 063, 3km from Knysna, offers B&B in comfortable en suite rooms overlooking the lagoon. There is a swimming pool and *braai* facilities.

Knysna Manor, ✆ (0445) 243 891 or 825 440, in Knysna itself, offers good value, comfortable B&B.

Oak Tree Cottage, ✆ (0445) 21877, offers B&B for six in a timber cottage with a garden overlooking the lagoon. **Lud's Island,** ✆ (04457) 7818/7858, is a 30ha private island in the Keurbooms Estuary, 3km east of Plettenberg Bay. Bird-watching, antelope-spotting, canoeing, fishing and swimming are offered, as well as B&B in modern cottages, and optional evening fish *braais* in the summer.

At the bottom end of the moderate price scale is **Mike's Guest House,** ✆ (0445) 21 728, on Knysna's Main St, which offers superb value rooms with en suite bathrooms and a big English breakfast. Mike, the owner, is a mine of local information and can sometimes arrange transportation for guests needing to get into the mountains and forest. Also very good value is **The Caboose**, ✆ (0445) 825 850, on Knysna's Grey Street, a timber building constructed around a courtyard with a small pool. The tiny rooms are built to resemble old railway carriage interiors. B&B is offered.

If you'd rather stay in calm, serene Sedgefield, the **Sedgefield Arms**, ✆ (04455) 31 417, offers B&B in farm cottages, with a country pub to add cheer. Nearby is the **Milkwood House B&B**, ✆ (04455) 31 730, secluded and out of the way in a surrounding forest.

In George there's also a good, moderate B&B called **Haus am Berg**, 35 Witfontein Road, ✆ (0441) 708 337.

Plettenberg Bay has a whole host of B&Bs on the outskirts of town and in the surrounding countryside. Choose from the following: **Bay Robberg B&B**, ✆ (04457) 34 107, **Bay View**, ✆ 32 019, **Beachy Head House**, ✆ 33 242, **August Hill**, ✆ 31 788, **Arbury**, ✆ 32 193, **Bill's Inn**, ✆ 31 190, **Bright Water** ✆ 30 467, **Cottage Pie**, ✆ 30 369, **Dolphin**, ✆ 33 607, **Edenderry**, ✆ 7838, **Ham House**, ✆ 31 912, and **La Provencale**, ✆ 32 397.

Further down the coast, for B&B in Nature's Valley, try **390 St George's Road**, ✆ (04457) 6834, and the **Heidehof Guest House**, ✆ (04457) 48 751. In Tsitsikamma, near the Storm's River mouth, the **Greenside B&B**, ✆ (042) 750 3681, has seclusion and hikes in the forest.

cheap

The **Hiker's Home**, 17 Tide St, Knysna, ✆ (0445) 24 362, offers self-catering budget accommodation in shared dorms in the lower town near the lagoon, and is popular with backpackers. **Knysna Backpackers' Hostel**, 42 Queen St, Knysna, ✆ (0445) 21 877, offers much the same accommodation, in a converted Victorian house. Self-catering only. Newer is the **Peregrine Backpackers**, ✆ (0445) 23 747.

George Backpackers' Hostel, on York St, ✆ (0441) 747 807, makes a convenient stopover along the Garden Route, though George is not a very attractive town. Dorm accommodation only. **Mossel Bay Backpackers**, 1 Marsh St, ✆ (0444) 913 182, is in the town centre, and has double rooms or dorms. On the same street is **Dolphin House**, ✆ (0444) 4317, while not far away is **Santos Express**, ✆ (0444) 911 995.

Wilderness also has two backpackers': **Wilderness Backpackers**, on Beacon Street, in the town centre, ✆ (0441) 877 0493, and **Fairy Knowe**, ✆ (0441) 877 1285, nearer the national park.

More tranquil than any of the above are the **Hiker's Haven**, on St Patrick's Street, Nature's Valley, ✆ (04457) 6805, which has the advantage of excellent hikes more or less from the front door, and **Kurland Bakpackers Farm**, ✆ (04457) 48 666, which has a private stretch of river, horses, a swimming hole and lots and lots of monkeys. Also at Nature's Valley—or rather, on a private island between there and Plett—is **Backpacker's Island**, ✆ (04457) 9442, a place you could easily while away a whole week, swimming, fishing, canoeing, partying and watching the waves.

Plettenberg Bay now has the **Otter Trail Backpackers**, ✆ (04457) 48 657, at The Crags, just outside town. In the town centre are **Nothando Backpackers**, 5 Wilder Street, ✆ (04457) 30 220, and **Albergo Backpackers**, ✆ (04457) 34 434.

Further down the coast, at Oyster Bay, there's another newcomer: **Ichubu Backpackers**, ✆ (0423) 970 081.

Finally, there's **Jeffrey's Bay Backpackers**, 12 Jeffrey Street, ✆ (0423) 931 739, the place to stay if you want to hang out with surfers. Dormitory accommodation and double rooms are available. Self-catering only.

Eating Out

expensive

Portland Manor's restaurant, ✆ (0445) 4804, is open to non-residents. The game, seafood and French cuisine are good, the vegetables and herbs grown on the estate.

Eight Bells Mountain Inn serves mostly Cape country cuisine. Game and seafood from the coast are specialities. The dining room is unpretentious and many locals eat here. The **Lake Pleasant Hotel**, in Groenvlei, near Sedgefield, ✆ (04455) 31 313, occupies a large country house. It is best to arrive early so as to enjoy the views over Groenvlei Lake and its surrounding forest. The restaurant serves a good mixture of dishes, from traditional Cape, like *bobotie*, to French cuisine and the pick of the morning's catch.

Hog's Hollow Country House has an award-winning chef whose Cape country recipes have been featured in magazines and newspapers all over the country. **Hunter's Country House** has an elegant candle-lit dining room and serves a fantastic roast guinea fowl.

O'Pescador, in the forest 6km west of Knysna, ✆ (0445) 871 386, is an excellent, moderately priced and informal Mozambiquan Portuguese seafood restaurant. Traditional shellfish and line-fish, with hot food such as chicken peri-peri, are specialities. Log fires in winter. In Knysna itself are two nouvelle cuisine restaurants in the same price range: **La Lourie**, on Main Street, ✆ (0445) 825 401, and **Melville's**, in the Knysna Lodge Hotel, also on Main Street, ✆ (0445) 21 616.

moderate

The Pink Umbrella, on the Knysna lagoon's Leisure Island, ✆ (0445) 22 409, has become famous among gourmets all over the country. The restaurant serves fairly expensive lunches and teas only, and is strictly vegetarian. This does not sound promising, but the food is really superb and imaginatively presented. **Crab's Creek**, ✆ (0445) 871 043, is a pub overlooking Knysna lagoon, about 8km west of town. The restaurant section does a lot of seafood, but there are also some pleasant surprises, such as Cumberland sausage with herbs. Knysna's excellent home-brewed beer, Bosuns Bitter, is served on tap. Long wooden tables and benches.

Jetty Tapas, ✆ (0445) 21 927, is another pub/restaurant set at the far end of the old jetty in Knysna's small harbour. Make up your own dish from the spiced Portuguese seafood on display behind a counter. Tapas is Knysna's (and much of the Garden Route's) principle meeting spot, and is always noisy and lively. A good place to meet locals. No need to book. The **Pelican Restaurant**, on Woodmill Lane in central Knysna, ✆ (0445) 85711/3, is mainly an oyster bar, but also serves seafood and some devastating cocktails. Very popular with locals, so booking is advised.

The Islander, ✆ (04457) 7776, 8km west of Plettenberg Bay, serves fish, poultry and pork dishes, with herbs and vegetables grown in the restaurant's organic garden. Smoked fish and ham and home-made soups are specialities. Service is buffet-style. Simple, unpretentious and very tasty food.

cheap

The **Duck Inn**, on Plettenberg Bay's Main Street, is the only cheap restaurant with any atmosphere in Plett. This friendly, diner-style place serves soups, toasted sandwiches, *boerwors* and beer, and is much frequented by young holidaymakers. Garish wall murals. No need to book.

Nightlife

There are no nightclubs on the Garden Route. Pubs and hotel bars are used as meeting places by locals who tend to party later on, either at each other's houses or, in summer, on the beaches. Most Knysna partiers kick off the evening at Jetty Tapas, as do a lot of people from George and Plett. Young South African travellers passing through tend to drink there, as the place has a reputation for fun.

The Little Karoo

Here the wild bees make their honey and the white, wild geese have their home.

The Little Karoo, Pauline Smith (1925)

North of the Garden Route's coastal mountains begins the Little Karoo. Divided into two valleys—the Little Karoo proper and the Langkloof ('long valley')—the region marks the transitional point between the Cape's temperate and arid climatic zones. Higher and drier than the lush Garden Route, but not as bone-bleachingly dry as the Great Karoo, the Little Karoo is a strange, contrasting world of green river meadows, dry, aloe-covered scrublands, high mountains, and level, stony pastures grazed by flocks of ostrich.

In the east, the Little Karoo rises to a wild massif that falls into the Eastern Cape province. To the west, it merges with the Breede River Valley. To the north and south tower dramatic, jagged ranges that seal off the Little Karoo from the rest of the country; with mountains on almost all sides, entering and leaving the region is always spectacular. Nestled under these protecting ramparts the countryside, away from the region's one large town—Oudtshoorn— has a peculiar, quiet charm, born of long isolation from the rest of the country.

History

This quiet farming country, enclosed by its surrounding mountains, has never had a front seat in South African history. San hunters and Kammannassie and Inqua Khoi (winter pastoralists from the Garden Route coast) shared the region and its plentiful game before the first trekboers hauled their wagons over the western mountains in the early 1700s. Settling around the Gamka River, where a perennial water supply could keep their livestock alive through the arid summer, the trekboers laid out permanent farms, and, as was the custom, went vigorously about annihilating the local San and enslaving the Khoi.

Some of these back farming areas, often hidden away in remote mountain kloofs, have remained isolated even to this day; for example, Die Hel, a deep gorge cut by the Gamka River in the northern Swartberg Mountains (*see* p.255), was only reachable by foot or horse until the 1960s, and still receives few visitors.

However, down on the Little Karoo's central plain, larger towns had established themselves by the 1850s—the largest being Oudtshoorn, on the Kammannassie River. A quiet farming town until 1870, Oudtshoorn and its surrounding farmlands suddenly became one of the richest areas in South Africa after the local farmers began raising ostriches to supply first Cape Town, then the European fashion industry, with feathers. Until the 1930s, when the fashion for ostrich feathers declined, the Little Karoo experienced something of a boom.

In the past 10 years, the ostrich farms that still characterize the region have experienced a revival of their fortunes as ostrich meat has suddenly become very 'in demand' in the USA, as well as within South Africa. Costing next to nothing to raise (ostrich can thrive in the driest, most barren regions), the profits from their flesh are great. Wine-farming has also taken off recently—especially in the richly alluvial area around Calitzdorp, west of Oudtshoorn, where award-winning fortified wines are produced.

Despite South Africa's dense and turbulent recent history, the Little Karoo has little to report from the apartheid years and the violent run-up to the government change-over. Too rural, too sparsely populated and too remote from the rest of the country, the Little Karoo continues with its quiet, prosperous farming life as uneventfully today as it has done since its first European settlement.

Getting There

By road: The N10 and R328 traverse the Little Karoo from north to south via Oudtshoorn, while the R62, R341 and N9 traverse it from east to west.

By bus: TransLux run a connecting service between Cape Town and Port Elizabeth via the Little Karoo every day. Regular services are also run by **Transtate**, between

Cape Town and Oudtshoorn via the Breede River Valley. Call the Oudtshoorn Visitor's Bureau, ✆ (0443) 222 221/8, for details.

By train: A service from Mossel Bay to Jo'burg via Oudtshoorn runs every week; call the Oudtshoorn Visitor's Bureau for details.

Across the Little Karoo

It is west of Oudtshoorn, where the R62 enters the Little Karoo from the town of Montagu in the Breede River Valley, that most travellers enter, at the little town of **Barrydale**. Set in a narrow valley of orchards under aloe-covered red mountains, the town is not geared for tourism, but it is worth stopping at the signposted **Annie Roux Flower Garden**, where Little Karoo wild flowers are displayed and labelled.

About 20km east of Barrydale on the R62 is the **Warmwaterberg Hot Spring**. If you are in need of refreshment after a long drive, the mineral pool (40°C) will reduce you to a relaxed lump of sleepy bliss. Close your eyes and soak. The R62 then winds over 60km through an ever-drier landscape of flowering aloes, sheep farms and mountains, with the Witteberg to the north and the Langeberg to the south. Occasionally the eye is surprised by lush green pastures and lucerne fields flanking a willow-fringed river.

Ladismith, the next town along the R62, sits under the massive wall of the Little Karoo's second-highest range, the Klein Swartberg, which rise to over 6000ft (2000m). Like Barrydale, Ladismith is more a village than a town. Many of the houses have beautiful Victorian wrought-iron verandahs and balconies, and the surrounding countryside is a green jewel of pasture, orchard and perennial streams. The Little Karoo's ostrich farming country begins here, and it is strange to see, rather than four-footed livestock, these giant, awkward, wild-looking birds grazing as contentedly as sheep.

The R62 follows the southern wall of the Klein Swartberg through some of the most spectacular mountain scenery accessible by tar road. About 25km after the Moravian mission station of **Zoar,** (set 3km south of the main road), whose lime-wash and thatch cottages have changed little since the last century, the R62 leads into the breathtaking sheer red cliffs of the **Huisrivier Pass**. Drive slowly, so as to take in the views while negotiating the bends, as the road leads through fold after fold of soaring flatiron mountain wall.

If you are feeling adventurous, and are not in a hurry, head back up the pass to Zoar and take the dirt road north to the **Sweweekspoort Pass**, past the sleepy village of **Amlienstein**, an all but untouched relic of 19th-century Cape Dutch life. The Sweweekspoort Peak (2325m) rears up over the pass as the road follows the twisting course of the Sweweekspoort River, crossing it twice by low bridges. Both are safe swimming spots. The pass is known for its beauty and remoteness, but also for a particular kind of protea flower, the *protea aristata*, a brilliant red variety that grows only in this area.

The **Towerkop Conservation Area**, ✆ (028) 551 1077, is accessible from the Sweweekspoort road, and covers a dramatic chunk of the Klein Swartberg range, including several peaks of over 6000ft. You can hike from anywhere along the pass road or follow a marked trail near Ladismith (*see* 'Activities'). Two hiking huts allow for overnight stays. Look out for black, martial, and booted eagles on the mountain slopes, as well as sunbirds and sugarbirds among the fynbos flowers. Klipspringer, grey rhebok and baboon are common, and leopard hunt the kloofs. Take your own water.

Once over the Sweweekspoort Pass, you are in the Great Karoo. To re-enter the Little Karoo either head back over the pass, or head west 55km to where the dirt road joins the R327 and drive south through the furrow separating the Witteberg and Klein Swartberg ranges for about 70km until it rejoins the R62.

At **Calitzdorp**, 24km east of the Huisrivier and Sweweekspoort Passes, the Little Karoo broadens out to a wide and well-irrigated plain. The town is surrounded by greenery—lucerne, ostrich pastures, wheatfields, orchards and vineyards, watered by the Gamka River that flows down from the Groot Swartberg. Another victim of 1950s 'improvement', Calitzdorp is famous for producing port, and has a small **wine route** leading off into the back roads of the surrounding plain, taking in several vineyards, and more attractive to explore than the town itself. Maps are available from the Town Clerk, Voortrekker Street.

Calitzdorp Spa, about 20km east of town, was also developed in the 1950s into an ugly, over-priced resort. However, another 15km or so beyond is a small dirt road heading north between ostrich fields towards **Kruisrivier**. After about ten minutes' drive you will see a set of massive red, rocky hills rising about a kilometre west of the road. These are worth climbing, especially at sunset. Head through one of the ostrich farm gates into the scrub (the ostrich fields give out at this point). The red hills are full of little holes that harbour birds of all kinds; you might find an owl staring at you at face-level. From the top is a sweeping view of the green valley below. At sunset, the hadeda ibises come winging across the plain, shrieking their distinctive call. The only other sound in the silence will be the weird booming of male ostriches in the pastures below.

Gamka Nature Reserve, set up to protect the Cape mountain zebra, is a beautiful place to walk. About 46km east of Calitzdorp along the R62, double back west for 18km on the old Calitzdorp–Oudtshoorn road, then head 7km south on a signposted dirt track. There are six one-day trails of varying length, and a two-day guided hike (you must book in advance) leading through an isolated plateau and surrounding deep ravines in the northern slopes of the Outeniqua Mountains. As well as zebra, there are grysbok, grey rhebok, klipspringer, duiker and steenbok. You might see leopard if you are very lucky. Black eagles are often spotted, as are their favourite prey, dassies.

Oudtshoorn

Oudtshoorn, about 60km east of Calitzdorp, is the economic centre of the Little Karoo, the heart of the ostrich-farming industry and largest tourist draw. In the late 19th century, owing to the demand for ostrich feathers, many of the local farmers became fabulously wealthy, building grand mansions on their estates—nicknamed 'feather palaces'—and maintaining substantial town houses for the weekends, when they came to Oudtshoorn to attend church and to meet their neighbours. However, when Anthony Trollope passed through here in the 1870s, he described it as 'an uninteresting village, about two miles long'. This still applies today but there is much to see around Oudtshoorn, and it has good, cheap accommodation, as well as some interesting old houses in its residential quarters.

By road: Oudtshoorn can be reached via the spectular Outeniqua Pass from George in the south, by the R29 road. The R328 runs north–south, connecting the town with two more spectacular passes—the Swartberg Pass north into the Great Karoo, and the Robinson Pass down to the Garden Route at Mossel Bay.

By bus: **InterCape** and **Greyhound** connect Outdshoorn with George in the south and Beaufort West in the north, via the R29. The **Baz Bus**, ✆ (021) 439 2323, also services the backpacker hostels of Oudtshoorn.

By train: A railway runs south to George through the Outeniquas, but services are poor. Better to go by bus.

Tourist Information

The Visitor's Bureau, corner of Voortrekker and Van Reede Sts, ✆ (044) 279 2532.

The Town

The **C. P. Nel Museum**, on the corner of High Street and Baron Van Reede Street (*open Mon–Sat 8.30–1 and 2–5*), gives the history of the ostrich boom in an eccentric display that includes the preserved bodies of chicks born with four legs and biblical quotations referring to ostriches. The museum also has the preserved interior of a synagogue, and a brief history of the town's Jewish community (now largely gone), as well as the usual Victoriana. In the main hall, old photographs of hunting parties in the area give an idea of how wild the Little Karoo was even up to the 1930s. You may encounter a particularly ardent female museum attendant who gets upset if you fail to follow the museum via the recommended route.

The **Tuinhuis Museum**, 146 High Street (*open Mon–Fri 8–1 and 2–5*) is a well-preserved weekend town house belonging to one of the leading Edwardian ostrich-farming families, furnished in oppressively ornate style. The **Arbeidsgenot Museum**, on Jan Van Riebeeck Road (*open Mon–Fri 9–12.30 and 2–5, Sat 9–12.30*), was the home of the Afrikaans poet and author C. J. Langenhoven, who was part of the early 20th-century movement to gain official status for the Afrikaans language. However, his best-known work was much more light-hearted, a children's story called *Herrie op die Ou Tremspoor* ('Harry on the Old Tramcar', published 1925), in which a man takes home an elephant and, his wife not wanting it in the house, teaches it to pull a tram. Langenhoven's house has a large carving of Harry as well as the more usual author's memorabilia.

Die Oude Pastorie, on Baron Van Reede Street, is an arts and crafts shop selling a mixture of twee pottery, good leatherwork (particularly shoes) and Boer biscuits and preserves. In the town centre, look out for small brass plaques on the pavement that say 'No Spitting'.

Around Oudtshoorn

The countryside around Oudtshoorn is probably the lushest of the Little Karoo. Three local ostrich farms and their old feather palaces are open to the public, as are three wine estates.

Safari Ostrich Show Farm (*open daily 8–4*), ✆ (0443) 227 311, offers 2-hour guided tours. Safari's homestead, Welgeluk, is one of the largest of the feather palaces, complete with marble floors, dazzling wrought-iron and general overblown Edwardian splendour. Visitors can ride an ostrich (worth it for the weird, rubbery bounciness of their surprisingly fast gait, though you are bound to fall) or watch the farmworkers (skilled jockeys) race them. **Highgate** (*open daily 8–4*), ✆ (0443) 227 115, is similar to Safari and offers tours, rides, races and a feather palace, as does **Cango Ostrich Farm** (*open daily 9.30–6*), ✆ (0443) 224 623. Maps and directions to the ostrich farms are distributed free at the Visitor's Bureau.

The **Klein Karoo Wine Trust** offers tastings and tours of the local wineries, most of which grow grapes for ports and muscadels in the deep alluvial soils of the local river banks. **Domain Doornkraal**, ✆ (04439) 2556, where the Wine Trust has its office, is in the village of De Rust, east of town at the meeting of the R341 and the R29 (*see* below).

Cango Crocodile Ranch and Cheetahland (*open Mon–Sat 8.30–5, tours leave at half past the hour*), ✆ (0443) 22 593, just north of town on the R328, is as kitsch as the name suggests but, for all that, it is an interesting place. There is something compelling about watching the big, reeking reptiles catch lumps of sheep tossed to them by the guide, and the Cheetahland part of the ranch is definitely worth seeing; visitors walk along a raised wooden walkway between cages of various big cats from around the world. At the cheetahs' enclosure they spring on you that—for an extra R20—you can get in and cuddle them. Amazingly tame, they will lie there while you scratch behind their ears, or rub their bellies, purring loud as a motor. Children are not allowed in. The ranch breeds cheetahs for re-release in the wild, so the extra charge is not a rip-off. Ask if you can see the cheetah cubs being fed: they make a chirruping noise like a loud chick. Few things can be so heart-stoppingly cute as a chirruping cheetah cub.

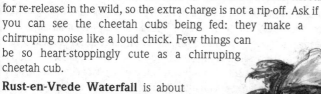

Rust-en-Vrede Waterfall is about 15km further north on the R328. Take the dirt road turn-off east, marked Raubenheimer Dam. Worthy of its name ('rest and peace'), the slender waterfall is set, unusually for the Little Karoo, in a wooded hillside. Trees fringe the wide pool, where you can swim. The falls are reached from the small dirt car park via a short path.

The Cango Caves

Tours leave on the hour, 9am–4pm low season, 8am–5pm high season (Jan, Feb and April) daily, except Christmas Day.

Under the massive Swartberg Mountains, about another 25km north along the R328, lies a massive cave system. Not all of it is open to the public, but what is open is definitely worth seeing, despite the development of the site as a first-class tourist trap. After exploring some way into the system in the 1870s, Trollope wrote: 'the wonderful forms and vagaries of the stalactites are infinitely finer than anything I have seen elsewhere.' Trollope went on to say that certain of the formations reminded him of organ-pipes, a demonic orchestra conductor, and 'some wondrous animal of hideous form'. Unfortunately, the developers have taken such comparisons a stage further. For your amusement there is a sad little tableau, just inside the caves' entrance, of near-life-sized plastic bushmen, attempting to depict those who lived in the caves until they were driven out in the early 19th century. The guide then leads you, en masse, down into a massive, illuminated chamber, hundreds of feet long, about 100ft wide and almost the same high.

When the author went there, the tour was kitsch to say the least. The lights went out and a taped voice-over told us what each stalactite formation is supposed to resemble—mostly biblical analogies—as they were lit up one by one with garish coloured lights. The magic of the place immediately evaporated. However, I am told that the dubbed tour with the coloured lights is no longer happening, and that tours now go with a mere human guide, which is much better. Apparently there are now three tours to choose from, the last of which involves a wriggle, crawl and climb through a series of narrow pipes and tunnels through almost total darkness, before being led back to the light.

The Swartberg Pass

This superb scenic drive is the continuation of the R328, as it turns to good dirt road north of the caves and climbs up and over the Swartberg, to the Great Karoo on the other side. The Swartberg Pass is one of the most famous drives in South Africa. The seemingly endless series of sweeping curves leading up and up for several thousand feet is one of Thomas Bains' masterpieces of engineering, dating from 1888. On the way up, the views back over the agricultural patchwork of the Little Karoo are spectacular. As the road rises the temperature drops until, at the top, you can be seriously chilled in the high winds that buffet the Swartberg's summits. The trip down must be taken slowly; the gradients and bends will not forgive a wide skid. The descent leads into much drier country. Red rock faces, gorges and ravines soar or drop away on every side, as the road twists down to the vast, unguessable distances of the dry Great Karoo.

The mountains are protected by the **Swartberg Conservation Area**, which has marked out some one-day hikes from the top of the pass. The range can be explored in more detail via the 5-day **Swartberg Hiking Trail** (*see* 'Activities').

From the north side of the pass you can either continue on into the Karoo, via Prince Albert, or turn east along the Swartberg wall (R407) to re-enter the Little Karoo through a lower pass via the R29 to De Rust, 35km east of Oudtshoorn. An alternative, parallel, route to the R29 is a good dirt road which leads south through a hidden farming valley along the very foot of the Swartberg. (If you take the R407 east from the bottom of Swartberg Pass for about 3km, the dirt road turns south in front of a Cape Dutch farmstead.) The road leads for about 30km through several old pioneer farmyards, where ostriches and donkeys sometimes stray across the road, until it comes out on the R29. Drive slowly into any dips and riverbeds.

Meiringspoort Pass, a canyon formed by the Groot River, is where the R29 turns back into the Little Karoo. Much lower and quicker to drive than the Swartberg Pass, Meiringspoort is no less beautiful and should be travelled slowly to take in properly the towering, crimson cliff faces. At the southern end is the small village of **De Rust** ('the resting place'), an untouched Victorian gem. Stop for tea at the Blue Elephant café, on the east side of Main Street. Ten kilometres from De Rust is **Meiringspoort Waterfall**, reached by a footpath from the small car park. The falls are 60m high, and surrounded by a deep hush.

Nature Reserves and Hell

Gamkapoort Nature Reserve, ✆ (0443) 291 739/829, is about 35km west of the north end of the Swartberg Pass, along a signposted dirt road. An isolated reserve on the northern slopes of the Swartberg, Gamkapoort has no accommodation, but a walking trail leads to views out over the lonely Gamkapoort Dam, which sits at the confluence of the Gamka and Dwyka Rivers. Below the dam, the trail drops into a deep, lonely gorge. A mixture of dry fynbos, aloes, succulents and thorn trees, the reserve is inhabited by kudu, rhebok, springbok, klipspringer, steenbok, duiker and dassies. Expect to see antelope if you walk quietly. Look out for black eagles. There are leopard and caracal in the kloofs.

Gamkaskloof, ✆ (0443) 733 367, which used to be known as 'Die Hel' ('the hell'), is a remote farming valley cut deep into the northern Swartberg. This utterly remote country was a stronghold of Khoi and San until they were pushed out by trekboers in the early 19th century. The farmers remained cut off from the rest of the world until the 1920s, when a school was built. But there was no driveable road until the 1960s. Even now, the farmers, who farm for prosperous subsistence rather than commerce, are an aloof lot. The kloof got its name from the intense heat that builds up in its deep cleft during summer. However, it is fertile, wooded and very, very, beautiful, and well worth the trip if you have time.

Nietgenaamd Nature Reserve is 65km east of De Rust along the R341 towards Willowmore, then north for 16km along a gravel road. This is a gem: hot springs with no attendant resort, and walking trails through the aloe- and thorn-covered mountainsides, which turn to fynbos on the high ridges. A few cottages and a camp site make up the accommodation. Springbok, duiker, steenbok and klipspringer are often spotted on the trails.

In the Kammannassieberg, further east along the R62, is the **Langkloof Nature Reserve**, a 25,000ha expanse of wild mountain that is home to the Cape mountain zebra, grey rhebok, klipspringer and baboon. The hardwood forest and fynbos on the southern slopes change to a drier landscape to the north. Hiking is allowed, but visitors follow their own routes and take all their own provisions.

The Eastern Little Karoo's Wild Massif

The R62 through the Langkloof and the R341 from De Rust meet about 60km east of De Rust, north of the towns of Uniondale and Avontuur. East of here the land rises to a rumpled mass of mountains that run for about 150km, forming the boundary between the Little Karoo and the Eastern Cape. To the south run the mountains of the Garden Route. Few travellers explore these eastern Little Karoo ranges, but they are accessible by both road and foot. They comprise perhaps the wildest corner of the southern Cape and were one of the last strongholds of the Cape's free Khoi and San.

Uniondale, on their western fringe, is a small fruit-farming village. The **Old Water Mill** dates from the mid 1800s and has, oddly enough, the largest water-wheel in the country. There is also a **Boer War Fort**, built by the British to keep the Boers out of the Cape. A drive south through the **Uniondalepoort Pass** leads to **Avontuur**, an even smaller and rather uninteresting fruit-farming village in the Langkloof. Continue south and the road rises steeply over the almost conical **Prince Alfred's Pass**, through the gap between the Outeniqua and Tsitsikamma Mountains, to Knysna and the Garden Route.

The Eastern Massif's Conservation Areas

There are two ways through the wild Baviaanskloof and Kougaberg massif. East of Uniondale and Willowmore, turn from the R57 on to the R332 (a good dirt road) to the **Baviaanskloof Conservation Area**. Covering 70,000ha, the range contains a variety of different habitats, from montane forest and fynbos to bushveld and karoo scrub. Set hiking trails are being laid out, but visitors can hike and camp anywhere.

Large animals such as eland and the Cape mountain zebra thrive here, along with the usual klipspringer, grey rhebok and baboon. Leopard and caracal are common. The conservation area's literature warns visitors to fill their petrol tanks before entering the Baviaanskloofberg, and to avoid the winter rainy season, when the dirt road in can be flooded.

Further east is the **Cockscomb Conservation Area**, which runs into part of the Groot Winterhoekberg, on the R332. The reserve begins beyond the hamlet of Andrieskraal. Cockscomb, even larger than the Baviaanskloof area, covers a similar transitional vegetation zone, and supports kudu, eland, Cape mountain zebra, bushbuck, grey rhebok, duiker and klipspringer. Again, leopard and caracal are common, and the well-watered kloofs are hunted by fish eagles. Hikers can wander at will. Two equipped camp sites can be found along the R332 (with ablutions block), but otherwise visitors must camp in the wild.

To the south, where the Kougaberg falls into the Langkloof, is the **Formosa Conservation Area**. This vast (70,550ha) swathe of mountain is accessible from Joubertina, in the Langkloof, via a signposted dirt road. Again, hikers must choose their own routes, and the reserve's literature advises carrying water. Fires are forbidden. Mountain reedbuck and grey rhebok are the largest antelope in the ranges, otherwise the fauna is the same as for Cockscomb and Baviaanskloof. Formosa has a very basic camp site at its entrance, which does not have an ablution block.

The remoteness of these mountains is summed up by one hiker's experience of hearing leopard cough next to his camp every night of his foray into the Baviaanskloofberg: while leopard are present throughout the Cape ranges (even in the well-populated Cape peninsula mountains), they have learned to steer well clear of humans. That a leopard should follow a hiker from curiosity shows how very few people ever penetrate these eastern ranges.

The Killing of Jan Prinsloo

Most hikers who have explored these mountains comment on their mysterious feel, and it comes as no surprise that there is a gruesome ghost story attached to the area. The full version is well told in several story books, the best being Alice Miller's beautifully illustrated *Myths and Legends of Southern Africa* (T. V. Bulpin Books, 1979), but here is the jist of the story.

Jan Prinsloo's Kloof lies in the northern foothills of the Kougaberg, overlooking the Baviaanskloof. In 1860 the one farm in the kloof was bought by a young Englishman. Despite its isolation, the farm had good grazing and commanded a great swathe of mountain, but the Englishman acquired the property for an unusually low price.

On the young settler's first night, under a waxing moon, screams were heard from the horse kraal. He rushed from his bed to investigate, and found the animals huddled together in a corner of the stone pen, plainly terrified. But whatever had disturbed them had vanished. Next morning, he questioned the farm's old Khoi foreman, but received only a shrug in reply. Determined to find out what had disturbed his horses, the Englishman sat up with his musket for several nights until he heard the scream again, saw the rush of frightened horses, and glimpsed a large shadow slinking away. Squinting in the moonlight, the Englishman fired, but the figure slipped away.

Again he questioned the old farmhand, but to no avail. However, late the next afternoon, the old man asked could he sleep in the house that night. Guessing that he might learn something about the mysterious goings-on, the young man agreed, and asked no further questions. Around midnight, the young man woke to another piercing scream, jumped from his bed, and saw the old Khoi farmhand standing at the front door, looking out.

In the moonlit kraal the horses were again quivering with fright in a corner. Small wonder—a huge figure with a gun was running around, chased by five smaller men waving spears and knives. Grabbing his musket, the young man ran towards the intruders, but stopped dead when he saw empty eye sockets and livid flesh where their faces should have been. The big figure stumbled and the others fell on him, hacking out his entrails and dancing round the kraal. The moon passed behind a cloud, and when it reappeared, the figures had gone. The young foreman fainted.

Next day the old Khoi foreman finally told the story. He had been born on the farm, he said, which was then owned by the Jan Prinsloo after which the kloof was named. A cruel freebooter, Prinsloo, after the manner of the time, tortured, bullied and flogged his Khoi farmhands according to his whim. One day he whipped to death the husbands of two women who had left the farm to visit relatives without permission. Then he shot the women and retired to the house with a bottle of brandy. That night all his Khoi left the farm and Prinsloo woke to find himself alone. Feeling that the silence boded ill, he saddled up, but halfway down the kloof was ambushed by six of his ex-workers. He galloped back to the farm, took position in the horse kraal, and downed one man with his musket. But the others stormed the wall and the rest happened as the Englishman had seen. By a strange twist of fate, said the old man, the avengers were killed during an insurrection that same year, and since then the horrid drama had repeated itself every year on the night of the killing. The farm was sold again, and it is said that the new owner died on the way to claim it. And, according to the story, it has stood empty ever since.

East of the Baviaanskloof and Kougaberg

At the far east of these great massifs rises the **Groendal Wilderness Area**, in the Groot Winterhoekberg, which is reached via the R329, R332, or N2 to Uitenhage, then Caledon Street, Gibbon Street and the Groendal road to the Forest Station.

The wilderness has a network of marked overnight trails of up to several days (you will need to get a permit and maps, available from the Forest Station) and most hikers carry tents. There are no huts on the trails, but caves are used as overnight spots, and many of them have bushman paintings. Like the Baviaanskloof area further to the west, so few hikers actually make the trip that one stands a better chance of seeing the shy leopard or caracal here than in most of the Cape mountain ranges. The vegetation is mostly fynbos with densely wooded kloofs. For the traveller who really wants to see the Cape wilds, there can be few better places to explore.

Activities

Hiking: Apart from the trails in the Gamkapoort, Gamka, Nietgenaamd and Groendal Nature Reserves already listed, the Little Karoo's only marked hikes are the 3-day **Swartberg Hiking Trail**, ✆ (044) 270 1736, which can be broken up into 15 different shorter trails ranging from 4km to 21km, and the trails of the **Groendal Wilderness Area**, ✆ (041) 992 5418. Booking is essential for both.

Wilder hiking can be undertaken in the **Baviaanskloof**, ✆ (04232) 30 270, **Cockscomb**, ✆ (04232) 30 270, **Formosa Conservation Area**, ✆ (04427) 31 530, and the **Langkloof Nature Reserve**, ✆ (04462) 110, with tents and maps. Again, booking is essential—you want the mountain rescue people to know that you are in there.

Mountain Biking: Joyrides, ✆ (044) 279 1163, rent out bikes for both self-guided and guided trips (vehicle support if necessary). Their most challenging route is up and over the Swartberg Pass.

Wine Tasting: The Little Karoo has established a route that takes in nine wineries, beginning at Barrydale and ending east of Oudtshoorn. The region is best-known for fortified wines, especially port, although everything from *méthode champenoise* sparkling wines to brandy are produced.

The flagship estate is **BoPlaas,** out of Calitzdorp, on Saayman Street, which makes a port that has won 25 medals in the last 15 years. For beauty, the **Domain Doornkraal** estate between Oudtshoorn and De Rust is king, sitting at the foot of the huge Rooi Krans ('red cliff') and producing muscadels and fortified wines. The other wineries centre around Calitzdorp and Ladismith. Maps of the route can be found at the Klein Karoo Marketing Association on Voortrekker Street, Oudtshoorn, ✆ (0443) 226 643, from the Oudtshoorn Visitor's Bureau, ✆ (044) 279 2532, from the Calitzdorp Town Clerk on Voortrekker Street, Calitzdorp, ✆ (04437) 33 312, or the Town Clerk, Church Street, Ladismith, ✆ (02942) 20.

Where to Stay and Eating Out

The Little Karoo lacks independent restaurants other than the burger and chips variety. Most hotels double as restaurants.

expensive

Rosenhof Country House, ✆ (0443) 222 232/262, is a large 19th-century farmstead on the road north of Oudtshoorn, with yellowwood ceilings and antiques throughout. The place is small, with only four en suite rooms, built around a courtyard and large pool. The restaurant serves Cape country cuisine with some very good Cape wines. There is a rose and herb garden, and there are log fires in winter.

moderate–expensive

Oue Werf, ✆ (0443) 228 712, is a beautiful Cape Dutch farm in the village of Schoemanshoek, 15km north of Oudtshoorn on the Cango Caves road (R328). This is one of the green valleys of the Little Karoo. B&B in two self-contained cottages. Swimming is allowed in the pool and farm dam. No restaurant and no credit cards.

moderate

Welgevonden Guest House, near Calitzdorp, ✆ (04437) 33 642, offers B&B (and homecooking in the evenings if you want), with excellent traditional Cape country cuisine: game, *boerwors,* home-made breads and home-grown fruits. There are four en suite rooms. In the centre of Oudtshoorn is the **Bed Stop B&B,** ✆ (044) 272 4746, on Van der Riet Street, which is quiet, comfortable and hard to beat for convenience. Just outside Oudtshoorn is **The Feather Inn,** ✆ (0443) 291 727, while at **Eagle Falls,** ✆ (044) 745 1122, midway between Oudtshoorn and Unionville, is a self-catering guest house on a farm, offering hiking trails, horses, and the chance to see white-crested eagles. On the other side of town, in the red mountain country about 20km from Oudtshoorn, is a group of 19th-century cottages on an ostrich farm, ✆ (044) 272 2121. Closer to town, the **Goegekloof** ostrich farm, ✆ (0443) 227 213, has a choice of self-catering or B&B.

Barrydale also has some pleasant guest farms and B&Bs: **Green Gables,** ✆ (028) 572 1137, the **Barrydale Country Inn,** ✆ (028) 572 1226, **Kannaland Holiday Farm,** ✆ 029720 and ask for 1404, and the **Tradouw Guest House,** ✆ (028) 572 1434, with superb hiking within easy reach of the front door.

The **Traveller's Oasis**, 3 Church Street, Oudtshoorn, ✆ (044) 279 1163, offers single and double rooms, as well as dormitory accommodation, at very low prices. Clean and friendly, you can check in 24 hours a day. There is a pool, kitchen, *braai*, and a free pick-up from anywhere in Oudtshoorn for new arrivals. Most rooms have their own shower.

There's also a new backpackers' in town, the **Backpacker's Paradise**, 148 Baron Van Reede St, ✆ (044) 272 0725, which has a pool and bike hire.

Camp sites with ablution blocks can be found at **Nietgenaamd Nature Reserve** and **Cockscomb Conservation Area** (*see* 'Activities' for telephone numbers), and wild camping without facilities is permitted in the other conservation areas.

Northern Cape

The full African moon poured down its light from the blue sky into the wide, lonely plain. The dry, sandy earth, with its coating of stunted 'karoo' bushes a few inches high, the low hills that skirted the plain, the milk-bushes with their long, finger-like leaves, all were touched by a weird and almost oppressive beauty as they lay in the white light.

Story of an African Farm, Olive Schreiner

The Great Karoo appears as a great emptiness on the map. Tourist offices offer little information on the area and consequently few people ever explore it. Its few towns are connected mostly by dirt roads that seem to pass through hundreds of miles of nothing, and most visitors to South Africa never visit the region—at best they hurry across it on the way to somewhere else. When the author first asked a representative of SaTour what the Karoo comprised, he was told 'Miles and miles of bugger-all!'

Nothing could be further from the truth. Blessedly free from dense human settlement the Karoo certainly is, but the vast thirstland (which is what its name means in the Khoi and San languages) is wide, silent and serenely beautiful. High mountains jut and fold along its western and southern spaces. The central pans stretch and shimmer to undiscernible horizons. A hot landscape of red, ochre, brown and black blisters in the flat light of midday. By night the skies are so clear, the stars so close and bright, that it seems you could reach up and gather them in handfuls.

Some parts of the Karoo are well vegetated, others dry as a bleached skull. Occasionally you come upon a green, willow-fringed dam, whose tell-tale lone metal windmill marks the point of an underground spring. For the Karoo is well watered. Under its dry, rocky surface lies enough water to support the thousands of sheep that browse the region's impossibly huge farms. And the Karoo's soil is very rich, having once been the floor of a vast lake system some millions of years ago. As a result, provided crops can be irrigated, almost anything can be grown, and the rare patches of Karoo alfalfa (clover) are among the richest in the world.

When it rains, the effect is almost mystical. The heavens open with thunder, and sheets of water pour down. Tough Karoo farmers—who may have been waiting up to ten years for their dams to be replenished—fall to their knees in gratitude and cry and pray.

It is impossible not to react emotionally to the Great Karoo, its heat, its distances, its endless sun and thirst, its remote beauty. Even just driving across it, intent on the next horizon, the road running straight as a ribbon to the haze, you find yourself one moment oppressed by the desolation and silence, the next hugely liberated by the vast, unfettered space.

Climate

Somewhere around an invisible line between the towns of Beaufort West and Graaff-Reinet, the Great Karoo crosses the climactic zone between summer and winter rainfall. The western Karoo, from the Hex River Mountains to Beaufort West, is the winter rainfall area. East of Beaufort West, rain falls in summer. In general the west is drier. The mountain ranges of both regions become very cold on winter nights and in the Sneeuberg, in the far eastern Karoo, snowfalls are common on the highest peaks. Summers in both regions are very hot, with temperatures often exceeding 40°C, but it is a dry heat and easy to bear, provided you do not over-exert yourself in the middle of the day.

Flora and Fauna

In places the Karoo is still surprisingly rich in wildlife, particularly in the protected reserves, though this is a shadow of the former numbers—until the mid 19th-century, migrating herds of springbok in excess of two million animals used to cross the Karoo. Today, kudu, gemsbok, Cape mountain zebra, mountain reedbuck, black wildebeest, klipspringer, duiker and springbok (still to be found in large herds in places) are the most common species. A few reserves harbour white rhino, the occasional cheetah (in the Bo-Karoo), eland, hartebeest and blesbok, while leopard and caracal are present through most of the mountain ranges, whether conserved or not.

Recently many Karoo farmers, concerned at the desertification of their land by sheep, have begun replacing their sheep farms with hunting ranches. While game ranching is by no means widespread, the trend may well result in a general increase in Karoo game populations in the next few years.

Birdlife includes large raptors such as black eagle and secretary birds in the mountain areas, and blue and crowned cranes by the dams and vleis (they often stop for water on their long, migratory flights). Ostrich are common, and there is a host of smaller species, including rarities like sand grouse and white-faced owl.

Look out for some of the more spectacular invertebrate life, like baboon spiders (a kind of tarantula), scorpions and solugifids, or 'sun spiders', fearsome-looking arachnids that hunt lizards and have the most powerful jaws in the invertebrate world.

Plant life is specially adapted to the Karoo's low rainfall; aloes, euphorbias and other water-retaining species (collectively known as 'succulents') have to survive the extreme heat of summer (up to 45°C) and sub-zero winter nights of hard frost. The Karoo's present super-arid appearance is largely due to overgrazing by sheep. A visit to one of the nature reserves or hunting ranches reveals a very different landscape of dry grasses—the Karoo can support a large number of indigenous grazers without becoming overgrazed.

Cultivated land is very uncommon, owing to the low rainfall, but where there is sufficient underground water you will see small fields of alfalfa in the middle of the semi-desert.

The Western Karoo (Hantams Region)

The Western Karoo begins north of the Cape mountain ranges that form the northern extent of the Winelands and Little Karoo. To the west, it ends at the great Cedarberg Mountains that run parallel to the West Coast, eventually merging into Namaqualand in the northwest,

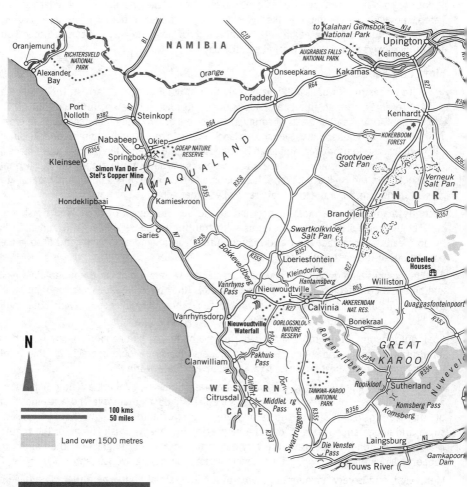

The Great Karoo

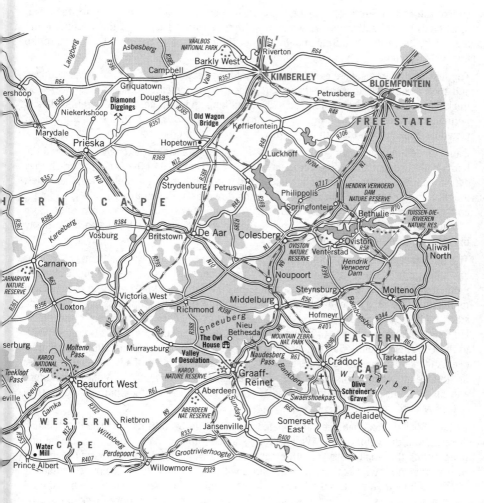

near the border with Namibia. The region gets its name from the Hantams Mountains around the small farming town of Calvinia, roughly the Western Karoo's central point. One of the most sparsely populated areas of South Africa, the region is full of solitude and space.

History

Unlike the rest of South Africa, the Western Karoo's past is relatively easy to trace. San (bushmen) hunter-gatherers and wandering Khoi pastoralists followed the seasonal game migrations in search of hunting and grazing for thousands of years before the arrival of the first white hunters.

The first white settlers were generally trekking further east, towards the Fish River country, and took a route via the Karoo because the coastal routes east from the Cape were too thickly forested for easy travelling. Some stopped here and built homesteads around sites of permanent water, which brought them into immediate conflict with the Khoi and San, generally dispossessing the former and driving the latter into the mountains.

Game tended to congregate around these watering points and the *trekboers* slaughtered the herds both for meat and to protect their sheep herds. Deprived of the game on which they depended, the San began raiding farm stock and, through the 18th and early 19th centuries, fought a running war with the settlers, coming down from the mountains at night to raid, and vanishing back into the kloofs by day. In some places, like the eastern Sneeuberg Mountains (*see* 'Eastern Karoo History'), they were sufficiently effective to force many burghers to abandon their farms.

The settlers retaliated with counter-raids. At first these were simply expeditions to recover lost stock, but by the 1750s the Boers and their Khoi servants were snatching San men, women and children to work on their farms. But the San would only work until their new masters became used to them, then simply escape into the great emptiness. Meanwhile the stock raiding continued and the Boers began to turn their raids into murdering sprees. Hunting the bushmen seems to have become something of a sport; accounts from the 1790s to the 1850s even tell of the 'bag' accounted for at the end of a trip. The 18th-century traveller Anders Sparman wrote, 'Does a colonist at any time get sight of a Boshieman, he takes fire immediately and spirits up his horses and dogs, in order to hunt him with more ardour and fury than he would a wild beast.' The Boers spared the young children, whom they trained as farmworkers.

By the 1860s the San had been annihilated or pushed north towards the unsettled Kalahari Desert. From this point on, the Western Karoo lapsed into a kind of rural, apolitical vacuum. Even during the Anglo-Boer War little happened, barring a brief occupation of Calvinia by Boer *Kommandos* who skirmished a few times with the British columns before surrendering in 1902. Since then neither the Western Karoo farmers, nor their workers, seems to have taken much interest in politics, though this was probably more a matter of lack of opportunity than desire.

Even through the intensely violent years building up to the 1994 elections, the Western Karoo remained somehow remote, both in culture and by geographical distance. Today, as ever, the region pursues its timeless course and makes a peaceful change from the hustle and energy of the country's more populated regions.

By car: The main route is via the N1. From the south this includes a spectacular climb up through the Winelands to Worcester and on over the Hex River mountains to **Touws River**. Most of the main Karoo roads, many of which are dirt or gravel, lead due north from the N1 into the Hantams. The other way in is over the Swartberg Pass from the Little Karoo to Beaufort West, the region's only large town, through which the N1 also runs.

By bus: Beaufort West is on the N1 Highway between Jo'burg and Cape Town, so all the buses—InterCape, TransLux and Greyhound—stop here. Then you can take a minibus taxi out to the Karoo National Park or, if you want to access the deeper Karoo, take plenty of water and stick your thumb out. Some of the Eastern Karoo towns—Cradock, Graaff-Reinet and Colesberg—have good bus services with minibus taxi connections to surrounding towns and reserves. *See* p.275 for details.

The Southern Fringe

Before heading in to the Hantams proper, it is worth detouring east along the N1 to **Matjiesfontein** (pronounced 'Mikeysfontein'), which is, like many Karoo towns, a Victorian set-piece. Founded in the 1880s as a health spa (the dry air being good for chest complaints), Matjiesfontein attracted a fashionable international crowd for a few years. Centrepiece of the town's high-Victorian architecture is the **Lord Milner Hotel**, a museum piece that was used as a military hospital during the Anglo-Boer War and still takes guests. The story of the hotel, and of the few Victorian celebrities that came here for their health, is told in the nearby jumbled and eccentric **Matjiesfontein Museum**.

The R354 heads due north from Matjiesfontein, over the tall buttresses of the **Komsberg Mountains**, to the small town of **Sutherland**, famous for some of the coldest winter temperatures in South Africa, and for the clarity of its night skies (there is a small observatory in the town).

An alternative route north is via **Hottentotskloof** (west from the N1 on the R46 southwest of Touws River, then north on the R355). This long, lonely road leads to Calvinia, running along the western edge of the **Roggeveldberg Mountains** and passing one of the Karoo's more interesting guest farms, **Elandsvlei**, site of one of the Cape's few Anglo-Boer War skirmishes. The antelope that gave the farm its name have long since gone, but smaller game can be spotted on the farm's walking and riding trails (*see* 'Where to Stay').

Some 70km further north, the emptiness flows up to the **Hantamsberg**, under which huddles **Calvinia**, which, though quiet, is a large town by Karoo standards. Calvinia is one of the few towns in the Western Karoo to have played any direct part in South African history. During the Anglo-Boer War, the town's 'coloured' population, having long suffered at the hands of their Afrikaner 'employers', became open supporters of the British. One Abraham Esau, a leading light of Calvinia's 'coloured' community, tried to organize a small defence force to be on hand in the event of a Boer attack, but was refused by the local British magistrate, who feared it might excite rebellion among the district's Afrikaner farmers. In early 1901 a Boer *Kommando* did enter the town, unopposed except for a force raised by Esau, which attacked with whatever was to hand. They were quickly beaten off, and the Boers, perhaps alarmed by this unexpected 'native' resistance, began a reign of terror, flogging and incarcerating 'coloureds' on flimsy charges. Many local farmers relished the chance to take the 'coloureds' down a peg, especially Esau, who was regarded as a 'cheeky Hottentot'. They kidnapped him and handed him over to Nieuwoudt, the Boer commandant. Over a period of about a week, Esau was publicly flogged and beaten, then finally dragged by his heels from a horse and shot. Ironically (and tragically), the Boer occupation only lasted another week, when the *Kommando* left town in front of an approaching British column.

Today, Calvinia is one of the Karoo's main sheep-breeding centres, although it has none of the bustle one would normally associate with a prosperous market town. There are some handsome buildings on the wide, dusty streets, including the **Hantam Huis** on Main Street (*open Mon–Fri 9.30–1 and 2–4.30*), a museum of Victorian life (with ex-fashion boutique mannequins dressed in bonnets and shawls to add an inauthentic note), and a small restaurant and craft shop selling the usual pottery, wooden spoons, *veldskoens* and Boer preserves.

The **Calvinia Museum** (*open Mon–Fri 9–1 and 2–5*) ranks as one of the most eccentric in the country. Housed in the roomy Old Synagogue (the town's Jewish population drifted to the cities long ago), the museum includes such gems as a biscuit tin struck by lightning inside a local farm kitchen, which hurled the farmer's wife across the floor, and a stuffed sheep with wool so long that it trails the ground—a farm escapee that lived wild on the Hantamsberg for some 15 years, dodging leopard, lynx and all attempts to catch it. It finally died peacefully on the mountain.

Akkerendam Nature Reserve, 4km north of town, takes in part of the Hantamsberg, the southern slopes of which form an amphitheatre of red rock. From here two walking trails overlook the brown and red Calvinia flats, in which the Akkerendam itself makes an inviting circle of blue. Gravel roads bisect the reserve. Expect to see springbok and perhaps mountain reedbuck and duiker. Migrating waterfowl stop at the dam and, though fenced off, it also makes a welcome swimming hole after a hot walk on the mountain. The reserve does not have any accommodation.

There is no road north from Calvinia. The R355 (gravel) and R27 (tar) go west 100 lonely kilometres to the towns of Nieuwoudtville and Loeriesfontein in Namaqualand. East of town, the tarred R27 bears north into country that becomes flat and desolate, opening into vast white salt pans north of the little town of **Brandvlei** (meaning 'burnt lake'). The town—a few baking hot streets of ugly buildings—does not warrant a visit, except perhaps as an example of somewhere you would not want to live, and as a pit-stop for drinks and petrol. The R27 then runs straight as an arrow 150km across the **salt pans** to Kenhardt, in Bushmanland. The largest pan, named Grootvloer, was the scene of Sir Malcolm Campbell's tragic 1929 attempt to break the land speed record in his car, the *Bluebird*, which tipped over, killing him. This incredibly barren area was also the unlikely scene of one of the Anglo-Boer War's lesser-known campaigns when, in 1902, General 'Mannie' Maritz led his *Kommando* into the region in an attempt to forge a supply-line into South West Africa (Namibia). In order to stay one step ahead of the British, Maritz stayed in the Karoo, somehow finding enough water and food in the waterless, scorched landscape, until the Boer surrender at Vereeniging allowed him and his exhausted troops to come in from the veld. Maritz was unhappy with the surrender and later joined the Boers' last, ill-fated revolt against British rule in 1914 (*see* **History**, p.41).

Just over 100km due east of Calvinia the tiny, quiet town of **Williston** is built around a huge sandstone church that used to attract up to 400 farmers every Sunday, who would drive a horse and cart as far as 90km to attend the service and chat with their 'neighbours'. Today, most 'coloured' farm-workers still use horse and donkey carts to travel these distances; the carts you pass on the roads may be making journeys of several days. The church still attracts a good 100 or so locals, demonstrating the continuing power of the Bible in this biblical landscape. Williston is very old-fashioned; one or two of the older Boer women still wear Victorian sun-bonnets. Horses and carts are more common on the streets than cars, largely because the 'coloured' population greatly exceeds the white. There is a small open-air **swimming pool** where you can float in cool water under the red hills. Swifts and swallows swoop to drink as you revel in the water after a dry, dusty drive.

The farms around Williston are known for their many surviving **corbelled houses**. These, the first permanent structures put up by the *trekboers* that settled the area in the early to mid-1800s, resemble Celtic brochs in construction; flat stones piled one atop the other in a conical beehive shape. The one-roomed dwellings, which would have housed the entire family and servants, have hard floors of beaten dung. **Arbeidsfontein**, a farm 30km east of town, has the most easily accessible corbelled house, now a national monument. The owners, the Esterhuizens, have farmed Arbeidsfontein for over a hundred years, and their ancestors used to inhabit the sparsely furnished corbelled house. By arrangement, they occasionally allow visitors to stay the night (*see* 'Where to Stay').

From Williston you can either head east 140km to Carnarvon, a small town set among high mesas rising from a flat plain, or southeast on the R353 to **Fraserburg**, a well-known fossil site. The **Fraserburg Museum** on Main Street (which also doubles as the local tourist information office; *open Mon–Fri 8–12 and 2–5, closed Wed pm*), has displays of fossilized skulls and eggs of very early (pre-Triassic) dinosaurs found on local farms. The museum issues a map of where to see **dinosaur footprints** on a farm 1km north of town on the Williston road, and the woman at the tourist office can also arrange visits to farms in the **Nuweveldberg Mountains** south of town, on which there are hidden waterfalls and herds of game, despite the apparent dryness.

The R353 south of Fraserburg leads through the Nuweveldberg back to the N1. If you have time, take the dirt road west to **Merweville**, another tiny town about 70km south of Fraserburg. About 40km through the low hill country east of Merweville is **Nova Vita**, a farm offering **walking trails** through the wild hills around.

Once back on the N1 highway, one can either head west back to Cape Town or east to the Western Karoo's largest town, **Beaufort West**. Beaufort West itself is a traditional pit-stop for drivers travelling from the Cape to Johannesburg, and as such the main street is quite busy. There are some handsome 19th-century buildings, including the **Museum Complex** on Donkin Street (*open Mon–Fri 9–5*) which has pioneer displays. The complex also doubles as the Tourist Information Office.

The **Karoo National Park** covers much of the Nuweveldberg mountain country north and west of town. It is interesting to note the difference in vegetation between the park and the farms on the other side of the game fence. The park is covered in grass, while the surrounding farms only support low Karoo-scrub—a direct result of over-grazing, and an illustration of how the Karoo might have looked at a time when it was only game that wandered its expanses.

The park supports a lot of game. Cape mountain zebra, red haartebeest, mountain reedbuck, gemsbok, springbok (including the larger sub-species of Kalahari springbok), grey rhebok, steenbok, duiker, klipspringer, kudu and ostrich are common. Leopard and lynx stalk the kloofs and dry river beds. Bat-eared fox and jackal come out at dusk. The rare blue crane (South Africa's national bird) often uses the park as a foraging spot.

Leaving Beaufort West for the north, the **Molteno Pass**, on the R381 north towards the town of Loxton, is surprisingly well vegetated. Great boulders jut from grass-covered hillsides and here and there are even small planted woodlands. The northern entrance to the Karoo National Park is on the left, about 5km after the head of the pass. To the right stretches a vast private game farm, so you can expect to see antelope on either side of the road, especially in the evening.

Prince Albert, about 140km south of Beaufort West, is the last town in the Great Karoo before the mighty Swartberg mountains. Another well-preserved 19th-century town, its **Fransie Pienaar Musuem** (*open Mon–Fri 9.30–1 and 2–5*) is a gem; an intimate history of the town, it includes children's exercise books from the turn of the century until the 1930s, badly stuffed local reptiles, weapons and other memorabilia. There is an old **watermill** just north of town on a tributary of the Gamka River, which flows down from the Swartberg, whose dark wall rises behind the town. The mill and stream contrast oddly with the dry country stretching north of town.

Activities

Hiking: Akkerendam Nature Reserve has two hiking trails—one gentle (4km), one quite demanding (10km)—through the low Karoo scrub.

The Karoo National Park, ✆ (0201) 52 828, has several walking and hiking trails; the **Fossil Trail** and **Bossie Trail** are very short, paved strolls with labelled fossils and Karoo plants on view. There is also an 11km hike up into the first dry kloofs and river beds near the camp, a 7km hike on the highlands (reached by another entrance to the park on the R381 north of town), and the 3-day **Springbok Trail**, complete with overnight huts, though this is not open during the blistering summer months.

Riding: Riding is offered at Elandsvlei Farm, *see* 'Where to Stay'.

expensive

The **Lord Milner Hotel**, Matjiesfontein, ✆ (023) 551 3011, ✉ 551 3020, is a set-piece of late Victoriana in a town that is a living museum of the period. Built in the early 1900s as a spa hotel—for clean, dry air, rather than mineral baths—the original interior has been carefully preserved, even down to the bath taps. The **Prince Albert Protea**, ✆ (04436) 332, is an old Victorian hotel south of Prince Albert with only 20 rooms. A little bland inside, like all hotels in this chain, the rooms are clean and comfortable rather than luxurious. There is good access to the Swartberg Mountains and Little Karoo, and a swimming pool. Also try **Sunnyside Guest Farm**, ✆ (0201) 3327, an 18th-century place just outside Beaufort West—excellent Cape cuisine, hikng trails and wildlife.

moderate

Karoo National Park, ✆ (0201) 52 828/9, has self-catering thatched chalets built in Cape Dutch style around a swimming pool, under the Nuweveldberg Mountains. The park entrance is about 10km west of Beaufort West on the N1. Also near Beaufort West is **Lemoenfontein Game Lodge**, ✆ (0201) 52 847, which offers B&B, home-cooking, hikes, 4x4 trails and some game viewing. Other good guest farms in the area are: **Donkin House**, ✆ (0201) 4287, **Christie's Guest House**, ✆ (0201) 51 682, and **Clyde House**, ✆ (0201) 4083.

If you want to overnight in the town itself, **Ye Olde Thatch**, 155 Donkin Street, ✆ (0201) 2209, has nice rooms and a good restaurant serving Karoo country dishes.

In Prince Albert, the rather long-windedly named **Prince Albert of Saxe-Coburg Guesthouse**, ✆ (04436) 267, offers clean and comfy B&B along with detailed info about all the Swartberg hiking trails.

Elandsvlei Guest Farm, ✆ (0273) 411 712, about 60km south of Calvinia on the dirt R355, has riding, walking trails, game and a house built into a cave for visitors. Self-catering or farm cooking. The **Dorphuis** on Main St in Calvinia, ✆ (0273) 411 606/059, is a small Victorian townhouse still furnished in period style, with big brass beds, lithographs and polished wooden floors. Self-catering or farm cooking.

De Rust Gasthuis, ✆ (02052) 2104, is a small, 4-bedroomed farmhouse 11km along the Sutherland road from Williston. Its small restaurant is possibly one of the most authentic for Cape country cooking in South Africa (*see* 'Eating Out').

BrakRivier Guest House, ✆ (02052) 2104, 70km from Calvinia on the R364 towards Clanwilliam, is another lonely guest farm surrounded by the wide, hot emptiness. There are good walks on the farm, and, of all things, a tennis court. **Meltonwold Guest Farm**, ✆ (02042) and ask for 1430, just outside Victoria West, has very good value accommodation in the middle bracket of the moderate scale. You can walk on the farm, ride the horses, swim or play tennis.

Finally, if you're driving to Jo'burg and you just want to stop for the night on the N1 as it crosses the Karoo, the **Travalia Guest Farm**, ✆ (053) 621 0809, is just 1km off the N1 highway near the Three Sisters UltraCity petrol station and truck stop.

cheap

Matoppo Inn, 23 Meintjies St, Beaufort West, ✆ (0201) 51 055, is useful for breaking a trans-Karoo journey. There are no frills, but the dormitory and double rooms are clean and comfortable.

Otherwise the **Beaufort West Caravan Park**, ✆ (0201) 2800, has caravans for hire, or you can camp.

Arbeidsfontein, a farm 30km east of Williston, has a corbelled house whose owners occasionally allow visitors to sleep there if asked politely, and may even provide water and firewood. There is an old brass bed covered with a kaross (skin blanket), a beaten earth floor and a candle for light. The owners normally refuse payment, but a donation is polite. There is no telephone.

All the above towns have **camp sites**, as does the Karoo National Park. More interesting is to camp on farms in the veld, but always ask first. Often you will end up being given a beautiful spot for free, and maybe even supper with the family.

Eating Out

The Western Karoo has few restaurants, except for those attached to hotels, and take-away places. All the accommodation listed above provides food, except for Arbeidsfontein. Make sure you try the Karoo mutton, which is sweet with the flavours of the wild herbs and Karoo-scrub upon which the local sheep graze. Justly famed throughout South Africa, Karoo mutton is as organic as farmed meat can be, has very little fat, but is tender as a good steak.

The **De Rust Gasthuis** serves some of the best Karoo mutton specialities, such as sheep's tails in mustard sauce, sheep's head and *spitbraaid* sheep, as well as the Boer breads and cakes such as *vetkoek* and *roosterbread*. The **Matjiesfontein Museum Coffee Shop**, next to the museum, is little changed inside since the 1900s, and a good place for a drink and a light meal before ploughing on into the interior.

The Eastern Karoo

And like other deserts and semi-deserts, ours is a country of life. The squat, fat, angled plants; the hunting spiders that flicker between them; the ground squirrels upright beside their burrows; the vultures; the pale gladioli; the cobras, the scorpions; the mantis coloured like a flower; the black beetles rolling balls of dung. Here moves a steenbok, a duiker, a springbok, a lark clapping its wings above us; here are the tracks of an antbear (aardvark) in the soil; red dust and a mottled egg upon it; arrowheads; the smell of rain; Karoo bush, wild asparagus, mountains and hills floating in a mirage of water; a white hot sky; the sound of cicadas and wings and wind.

Plains of the Camdeboo, Eve Palmer

With a higher rainfall than the Western Karoo, this landscape is better vegetated and richer in game. The towns are larger and the farms more prosperous. The Nuweveldberg, Bankberg and Sneeuberg mountains are higher than those in the west, one range crumpling into another towards the distant Drakensberg, whose foothills, the Bamboesberg, fall into the northeastern corner of the Great Karoo, beyond the town of Cradock. However, the Karoo's wide emptiness still prevails.

Between the Sneeuberg mountains and the Orange River is an area known as the **Bo-Karoo**, meaning Upper Karoo, forming a triangle between the towns of Prieska, Colesberg and Victoria West. Until recently, the Bo-Karoo ranked as one of South Africa's least known regions, a vast back-country of semi-desert farms.

History

As in the Western Karoo, the Khoi and San were masters of the region until late 18th-century *trekboers* on their way to the Eastern Cape frontier stopped and laid out farms by the springs and permanent water sites. Many *trekboers* settled the mountain slopes of the Nuweveldberg, Sneeuberg and Bankberg, fighting, enslaving and gradually absorbing the Khoi into their farms and annihilating the San, who raided their cattle.

The Dutch East India Company, ever desirous of bringing the *trekboers* back under colonial control, founded a magistracy at Graaff-Reinet in 1786 and appointed a *landdrost*. By then *trekboers* had already settled far beyond, in the Xhosa country of the Eastern Cape, and were busy trading, raiding and hunting there. The little village of Graaff-Reinet had to administer the whole Eastern Karoo and much of the Eastern Cape coast, a vast, anarchic region of Khoi, San, Xhosa and *trekboer*, all jostling to keep their semi-nomadic lifestyles intact.

The frontier *trekboers* were a rough bunch. Their cruelty to their Khoi servants (who less than a generation before had been freeholders of the land) became legendary. By the mid 1790s, increasing frustration with their inability to crush the San caused them to drift eastward at the same time as the Xhosa, drifting west, were entering the Eastern Karoo.

The frontier Boers forced the first Graaff-Reinet *landdrost* to form official *Kommandos* to attack the Xhosa. However, *landdrost* Maynier (the second Graaff-Reinet *landdrost*) was a liberal product of the enlightenment. Known to have sympathy for the Khoi, he enforced the Company's edicts that farmers guilty of ill-treating their Khoi servants should be punished. The resentful Boers, under Adriaan Van Jaarsveld, Marthinius Prinsloo and Conraad De Buys, rebelled against the Company and expelled Maynier in 1795.

The Company retaliated by cutting off all supplies of powder and shot to Graaff-Reinet. When Britain first occupied the Cape Colony, in 1796, the Boers allied with them against the Company. The British demanded unconditional surrender from the Boers, which they got in 1797. Van Jaasveld and Prinsloo were imprisoned but De Buys escaped and went to live among the Xhosa, where he became a principal courtier to the frontier chief Ngqika, before finally heading north into the Transvaal, where he settled in the Soutpansberg mountains.

In 1799 and again in 1813 the Graaff-Reinet Boers rebelled against the British, even attempting to get support from the western Xhosa. But they failed; after a short campaign the new British-appointed *landdrost* captured the ringleaders. Their trial took three years, but they were hanged in 1816 on a ridge called Slagters Nek, an event that engendered early hatred between Boers and the British government (*see* **Eastern Cape** 'History').

Meanwhile, during the 1799 rebellion, many Khoi saw their opportunity in the chaos to run away from their brutal 'employers'. They formed their own rebel army and joined the Xhosa in the Zuurveld, near present-day Port Elizabeth. The British, already using Khoi in their own colonial forces at Graaff-Reinet (a cavalry regiment called the Cape Corps), were suddenly caught in a confused position as referee to the Boer, Khoi and Xhosa power struggle.

After a hard but inconclusive campaign many rebel Khoi were persuaded by the British to return to the Eastern Karoo. But they feared retribution and mostly converged on Graaff-Reinet, so as to be under the protection of *landdrost* Maynier, whom the British had re-appointed. The Boers foresaw renewed attacks. Armed burghers from all over the region rode to Graaff-Reinet and demanded that the Cape Corps and the great mass of ex-rebels be dispersed. Maynier managed to placate them but the continued plunder of the Eastern Karoo farms by isolated bands of rebel Khoi caused the Boers to besiege Graaff-Reinet in 1801.

The British again put this down, but Khoi bandits remained on the loose. Events became even more confused when the British handed the Cape back to the Dutch. In 1803 the Boer *Kommandos* failed to quell a resurgence of Khoi rebellion, which renewed panic among the settlers and caused abandonment of many farms. The new Dutch governor subdued the rebels by granting their leaders land on the colony's frontier. However, much of the abandoned farmland had been occupied by roving Xhosa bands. When the British returned to the Cape and to Graaff-Reinet in 1806, and expelled the Xhosa by force, they became locked into a series of Frontier Wars with the Xhosa that were to last into the 1870s. However, the scene of the fighting soon shifted east to the country around the Fish River, and after the 1820s Graaff-Reinet and the Eastern Karoo ceased to be so strategically important.

Graaff-Reinet settled into its modern existence as a prosperous agricultural centre. The Eastern Karoo Boers continued their warring with the San in the Sneeuberg mountains, finally annihilating them by attrition in the 1860s and '70s. Many of the Khoi drifted north, away from the Boers, to the free country around the Orange River, and their place on the farms was gradually taken by Xhosa, who continued to drift west despite, or sometimes because of, the continuing Frontier Wars. By the turn of the century the Eastern Karoo was as much Xhosa as Afrikaner, though small pockets of Khoi (by now much mixed with white blood and generally referred to as 'coloured') remained—and still do remain—in the smaller farming settlements.

Today, the Eastern Karoo is something of a peaceful backwater, but its largest towns—Graaff-Reinet and Cradock—have a great support for the ANC among the farmworkers. Whether this will eventually result in a white/black sharing of land in the Karoo, or whether the tradition of white farmer and black labourer will continue, is open to speculation. Certainly it is hard to imagine the wide, empty spaces as the scene of political strife.

Getting There

By road: Three main roads cut across the Eastern Karoo; the N1 between Beaufort West and Colesberg, the N9 between Colesberg and Aberdeen (along which route lies Graaff-Reinet, the region's centre) and the N10 between Middleburg and Cradock. The Bo-Karoo is bisected by the N12 between the Orange River (at Hopetown) and Victoria West.

By bus: Graaff-Reinet and Cradock (on the TranLux route) can be reached direct by bus from Jo'burg or Port Elizabeth, and Colesberg and Beaufort West can be reached from Jo'burg and Cape Town via TransLux, Greyhound or InterCape. Local transport by black taxi can be risky, and travellers should either hire a car in Graaff-Reinet or Colesberg or try to arrange local lifts through the tourist information offices.

By rail: Beaufort West can be reached by train from Jo'burg or Cape Town, with a bus connection through to Graaff-Reinet.

Graaff-Reinet

The late 18th-century frontier town and original administrative capital for the Eastern Cape is now a quiet farming town and tourist draw. Huddled around the Sundays River, one of the few perennial rivers in the Karoo (though it is often little more than a trickle), Graaff-Reinet has little in its present atmosphere to suggest the town's turbulent early history.

Early Graaff-Reinet was described by one British officer as a 'miserable collection of dusty cottages'. It did not prosper until the 1800s, two decades after its founding, when the colony's eastern frontier had moved deep into the present Eastern Cape, and the town's oldest buildings date from this time. Many of the old buildings survive, making Graaff-Reinet one of the most architecturally attractive towns in South Africa. White-washed cottages and houses, some humble, some grand, make up the central streets, while the surrounding residential neighbourhoods are late 19th- and early 20th-century. The only modern buildings are on the edges of town.

The high hills that rise on three sides of the town are conserved as wild country by the large Karoo Nature Reserve, which includes the Valley of Desolation west of town. To the south stretch the hot, dusty plains of Camdeboo.

Parsonage Street, in the very centre of town, has been declared a national monument. A perfectly preserved early 19th-century Cape Dutch street, the buildings are all still in use.

Reinet House, on Parsonage Street, (*open daily 9–5*), was built in 1812. A splendidly proportioned mansion with (unusually for Cape Dutch manors) a grand ornamental staircase leading to the front door, the interior, with its yellowwood ceilings, stinkwood floors and period furniture, is now a museum. More interesting is the cobbled yard at the back, which has (reputedly) the world's largest grapevine (and it is huge), and a pioneer farming museum in the outbuildings.

The **Residency** (*open Mon–Fri 9–5*), another manor house from the same period, contains a museum of early 19th-century life, including a collection of hunting rifles. Of note are the unwieldy large-bore muskets that the early ivory-hunters used in their semi-legal forays into Xhosa country. Given the intelligence and agility of the great animals, and the inefficiency of the guns, it is easy to see why early big-game hunters had such short life expectancy.

The **Drostdy**, on Church Street, was the first residence of the *landdrost* (though the present building, built on the original site, only dates from 1806) and is now a hotel. The building is simple, gracious and well-proportioned—typical of its designer, Thibault (*see* 'Cape Town History'). **Stretch's Court**, behind the main building, is a small street of elegant early 19th-century cottages that are now self-contained suites of the hotel. The **Reinet Museum** (*open*

Mon–Fri 9–12 and 2–5) is on the corner of Church Street and Somerset Street. Its most interesting exhibits are the fossils and early dinosaur bones collected from the area, ranging from small molluscs to large skulls and semi-intact skeletons, and an explanation of the formation of the Karoo-shale strata from which the fossils come. Around the walls of the main room are enlarged reproductions of some of the finest San art currently known.

The **Hester Rupert Art Museum**, a few doors down from the Reinet Museum (*open Mon–Fri 9–1 and 2–5*), houses a mediocre collection of South African paintings, mostly by white artists imitating European styles. However, there are some emotive Karoo landscapes, an unusual subject in traditional South African landscape paintings, where Cape and Drakensberg scenes are more the norm. The **Jan Rupert Centre**, on Middle Street, is a craft workshop producing woven goods from the local Merino sheep wool, using dyes produced from Karoo plants. The project was started about 10 years ago as unemployment relief for the local Xhosa and it seems to have been commercially successful. There is also some pottery and woodwork.

The Karoo Nature Reserve and the Valley of Desolation

The Karoo Nature Reserve comprises all the land immediately north, west and east of the town, over 30,000ha. High, aloe-covered hills predominate, though there is a grass-covered plain north of town, past the Graaff-Reinet dam and camp site. Inside the reserve kudu, bontebok, black wildebeest, springbok, reedbuck, duiker and steenbok are the most common game species. Less numerous are eland and red hartebeest. Look out for bat-eared fox and secretary birds.

The reserve is divided into three parts: the western section includes the high Spandau Kop and Valley of Desolation; the middle section comprises the central plain and game-viewing roads; the eastern section includes Hangklip Mountain and an overnight hiking trail with a sleeping hut. The **Valley of Desolation**, a deep, narrow gorge in the mountains above Graaff-Reinet, is what most people come to see. Walk or drive up a steep mountain road about 2km northwest of town to reach the look-out point, from which great, sweeping views stretch away to the south over the Camdeboo. Immediately below the look-out point runs the deep gash of the Valley of Desolation. A hiking trail leads down through it, while the shorter **Cape Crag trail**, named after a lizard species only found here, winds along the ridge from the look-out point. Hikers are likely to see game if they are quiet. Look out for vervet monkeys and dassies.

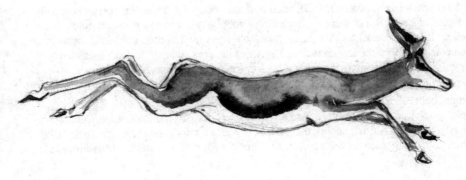

Nieu Bethesda and the Sneeuberg Mountains

About 60km north of Graaff-Reinet, at the foot of the great Sneeuberg range, is a fertile, isolated valley watered by a tributary of the Sundays River. The village is divided in two: the old white section has a population of just 23, whereas 400 live in the 'coloured' location on the hillside above. There is a great feeling of peace in Nieu Bethesda, perhaps because of the green valley, a relief to the eye after the endless browns, ochres and reds of the Karoo, or perhaps because of the high, encircling mountains and the resulting quiet.

The Owl House

Nieu Bethesda has no tarred road, but the tiny place is famous in South Africa for having been the home of **Helen Martins**, a reclusive sculptor whose house in the village, known as the Owl House, has become a strange monument to her half-biblical, half-occult view of the world. When Martins came to live at Nieu Bethesda in the 1950s she began to transform her garden into an outdoor studio, working in concrete to produce naïve figures. Some have an obvious biblical origin, such as her Three Wise Men and their camels. Others are moon-worshippers, and are constructed around poems written in letters cut from metal and hung on griddle frames. Everywhere there are owl sculptures, inside the house and out.

Martins and her eccentric life have been the object of much scrutiny. One play about her suggests that she supported herself through quiet prostitution to local burghers. Other sources deny this, suggesting that she and her 'coloured' servant (in fact her friend and helper) were having an affair. Others again say this was nonsense. However, her work attracted enough attention during her life to ensure its loving conservation and, after initial rejection by those seeking to conserve the house, Martins' 'coloured' friend, who in her arthritic old age became her hands for the last sculptures, now helps to maintain the Owl House.

Nieu Bethesda gets a steady trickle of pilgrims to the Owl House every year, and some similarly artistic recluses have settled in the village or on the farms outside. At the full moon every January there is a festival of music and dance, loosely organized and informally run, to which young hippies, musicians, New Agers and generally interested people come. But there has been no development around the Martins myth and on an average day in Nieu Bethesda there will be very few people. The village remains remote, jewel-like in its greenery, and isolated behind its hills and bad roads.

The **Sneeuberg Mountains** rising to the north of the village were for over 100 years a bastion against northern colonial expansion. The San used it as an impregnable natural fortress in their incessant raiding wars with the Boer settlers, who gave up trying to penetrate the country beyond the range between the 1700s and the 1870s. The name means 'snow mountains', and indeed, despite the dry Karoo climate, these mountains see snow most winters. Their highest peak, the **Compassberg**, rises close to Nieu Bethesda, while the main massif rolls away wild for almost 100km beyond. The Sneeuberg have some perennial springs, and hence good game populations. Hiking and riding trails into the Sneeuberg have been organized by the local farmers (*see* 'Activities' and 'Where to Stay').

The Bo-Karoo

The Bo-Karoo is hardly geared for even the most basic of tourism. However, the very small town of **Orania**, on the banks of the Orange River near Hopetown, is of interest to those fascinated by the more eccentric political vagaries of the country. Orania was the subject of a well-known Channel 4 television documentary (produced in England in 1990) about life among radical right-wing Afrikaners. It is also the proposed capital of the Boer Homeland that many right-wing groups are demanding. A word of warning: Orania is a working town that has been beset by visitors since the less-than-flattering documentary. Avoid gawping at people. More important still, avoid making political statements, which will at best be met with indifference. Afrikaner tempers can be short.

Colesberg, founded in 1829, is just off the N1 at the southeast end of the Bo-Karoo, a good place to break your journey between Cape Town and the Transvaal. Perhaps more than Graaff-Reinet, this town evokes the isolated feel of the early Karoo towns, and many of the buildings are national monuments. It was founded by the British in an attempt to pacify the once anarchic and violent frontier region of TransOrangia (the country around and north of the Orange River), which at the time was populated partly by wandering bands of 'Bastaards', groups of free half-white, half-Khoi people who could find no place in colonial society. They were later renamed 'Griqua' by missionaries who found 'Bastaard' distasteful. The rest of the sparse population was made up of free Khoi fleeing their cruel Boer masters, Boers fleeing the British, and errant bands of Xhosa and Tswana warriors. Raid and counter-raid of the different groups' herds, pastured on the fertile islands in the middle of the river, gave the area an almost mythical reputation for lawlessness (*see* 'Bushmanland' and 'West Griqualand History').

Unlike Graaff-Reinet, Colesberg never expanded beyond its original size, even once the area had settled down in the mid-19th century. Its bright, white-washed buildings reflecting the harsh sunlight are reminiscent of the Mediterranean.

Doornkloof and **Rolfontein Nature Reserves** are two large, seldom-visited reserves set close to each other on the west bank of the P. K. le Roux Dam on the Orange River (reached by the R369 north of Colesberg). Doornkloof—which covers more than 10,000ha—is remarkable for having woodland in some of its sharp riverside kloofs; woodland is almost unheard of in the Karoo. The reserve supports kudu, reedbuck and small antelope such as duiker. Baboons and vervet monkeys are also common. Waterfowl live in the reedbanks and trees along the dam's shore, and look out for fish eagles. There is no accommodation. Rolfontein, about 20km north of Doornkloof, is half the size of its neighbour, but supports more game, including big animals such as white rhino, zebra, eland, kudu and blesbok. There are also a few shy cheetah still living here. Like Doornkloof, Rolfontein has some kloof and riverine woodland.

Oviston Nature Reserve lies on the south shore of another Orange River dam, the Hendrik Vervwoerd Dam, reached by the R58 from Colesberg. Oviston follows the dam's entire southern coastline, but only a limited area is open to visitors. There are herds of black wildebeest, springbok, blesbok and hartebeest. Ground squirrels are common, and their frenetic bursts of play (a very fast tag with tails held stiffly erect) are fun to watch. The reserve has a small, ugly town, **Oviston**, in the middle, with shops and a swimming pool that is blessed relief on a hot day. At the eastern end of the Hendrik Verwoerd Dam is another, larger reserve, **Tuissen Die Rivieren** (meaning 'meeting of rivers') where the Orange and Caledon rivers converge. This reserve is densely populated by game and has very good walking but is officially in the Free State (*see* **Free State**). **Victoria West**, at the southern end of the Bo-Karoo, straddles the N12. Although the town is unattractive, the **Victoria West Nature Reserve**, just to the south, makes a good place to stretch the legs if you are passing through. The reserve is home to Burchell's zebra, springbok, eland, black wildebeest, gemsbok and blesbok. There is no accommodation.

Cradock and the Mountain Zebra National Park

Cradock is another 19th-century set-piece, though with more modern building on its outskirts than Colesberg or Graaff-Reinet. Large by Karoo standards but small by any other, Cradock (named after Sir John Cradock, one of the first British Governors of the Cape) lies at the easternmost extent of the Eastern Karoo, just north of the unpopulated massifs of the Bankberg and Winterberg mountains on the N10 highway. Cradock is a very handsome town, but less quiet than others in the Karoo.

A very large black—mainly Xhosa—'location', lies just south of town along the N10. Unemployment here is high, and the poverty is obvious. By the roadside, children make and sell exquisitely constructed wire windmills based on the kind that pump water above ground in the Karoo. These are unusual in South African township art, where wire bicycles and vehicles are the norm, and this will probably be your only chance to buy one.

The **Mountain Zebra National Park**, in the Bankberg Mountains about 30km west of town, is one of the loneliest and most beautiful of South Africa's national parks. The Bankberg sweep away for over 100km of upland emptiness to Graaff-Reinet. Although the usual reds and ochres prevail, the park is far better vegetated than is normal for the region. Trees, grass-covered hillsides and Karoo-scrub make for a distinctive landscape.

The wild country is inhabited by kudu, mountain reedbuck, eland, red hartebeest, black wildebeest, springbok, blesbok, klipspringer and, of course, the Cape mountain zebra that the park was formed to protect. Birds of prey are much in evidence, particularly black eagle (who feed on the dassies), booted and martial eagles and eagle owls. Leopard and caracal are common, and there is a small research station into the hunting behaviour of these cats.

The village of **Aberdeen** is 55km southwest of Graaff-Reinet, where the R57 crosses the vast, flat, hot plains of Camdeboo en route for the Little Karoo. Popular among enthusiasts of late Victorian colonial architecture, the village's verandahed houses present an eclectic mix of styles with little turrets and half-timbered houses among the more orthodox Cape gables and tin roofs. Just west of town is **Aberdeen Nature Reserve**, under whose sweet thorn trees and Karoo-scrub graze springbok, kudu, gemsbok, red hartebeest and black wildebeest.

Activities

Hiking: The **Karoo Nature Reserve**, ✆ (0491) 23 453, has a 3-day trail to the east of town. Overnight huts, water and firewood are provided, but must be booked in advance. **Sneeuberg Farm Trails**, ✆ (04923) 749, run a network of guided and non-guided hiking and climbing routes. The 12 co-operating farmers are familiar with the mountains and their wildlife, San history and geology. The individual farms provide information about local bushmen paintings. **Trails of the Camdeboo,** ✆ (0491) 910 546, is a similar set-up in hill-country east of Graaff-Reinet, offering hiking and good opportunities for wildlife photography. **Aberdeen Nature Reserve**, just west of Aberdeen, has a short trail. **Doornkloof Nature Reserve,** ✆ (051752) 1304, or (051) 753 0043, has good trails, including a 5-day trail to Rolfontein reserve. **Rolfontein Nature Reserve,** ✆ (05782) 160, has a guided 2-day trail and some shorter self-guided day walks. **Oviston Nature Reserve,** (0553) 50 000, has a 2-day trail, and various day walks. There are short walking trails through the Karoo-scrub of the **Victoria West Nature Reserve**. The **Mountain Zebra National Park,** ✆ (012) 343 1991, has a 3-day hiking trail. For those who don't want to hike (and the going is tough), there is a network of game-viewing roads and one-day trails.

Riding: Sneeuberg Farm Trails, and **Trails of the Camdeboo,** offer riding trails of between half a day and several days (guided). The **Mountain Zebra National Park,** ✆ (012) 343 1991, also has horses for hire.

Motorcycle scrambling: Van Zylsvlei Scrambler Trails, ✆ (051) 753 0589, offer trails along the Orange and Seekoei River and into various mountain farms.

Where to Stay

expensive

Thibault's **Drostdy**, on Church St, Graaff-Reinet, ✆ (0491) 22 161, 📠 24 582, also has a street of early 19th-century cottages behind it (Stretch's Court), which have been incorporated as self-contained suites. Guests can sit in a formal garden around a fountain, and there are two restaurants (*see* 'Eating Out'). Colesberg has a lovely guest farm, **Eenboom Country Manor,** ✆/📠 (051) 753 1418, which offers great Karoo cuisine, riding, hiking and accommodation in period rooms.

moderate

Cradock Tuinhuise, ✆ (0481) 5098, is a terrace of old artisans' cottages in the centre of Cradock, where you have the feeling that they are staying inside an old pioneer museum. They principally provide B&B, but evening meals can be included by prior arrangement; the owners cook a good leg of mutton, Karoo-style, with herbs and garlic.

Graaff-Reinet has some good B&Bs, including **Caledonia B&B,** 61 Somerset Street, ✆ (0491) 23 156, **Cypress Cottage B&B,** 80 Donkin Street, ✆ (0491) 23 965, and **Die Pophuis Cottages,** 104 Somerset Street, ✆ (0491) 910 404.

Sneeuberg Farm Trails, north of Nieu Bethesda, offer accommodation on several farms, either self-catering or with home-cooking: **Gordonville,** ✆ (04923) 727/720, the closest to Graaff-Reinet, has a library of 2000 books, many of African interest, game on the farm, and riding. In the outbuildings is a wool-spinning workshop. It has been in the same family since 1903. Further into the Sneeuberg, **Groenvlei Gasthuis,** ✆ (04925) 627, has tennis. Also try **Weltervreden,** ✆ (04923) 740, a guest farm 13km north of Nieu Bethesda.

Trails of the Camdeboo offer similar facilities on farms in the hills east of Graaff-Reinet. **Camdeboo Safaris**, ✆ (0491) 23 038, 50km east of Graaff-Reinet at Sondagsrivierhoek, is the largest guest farm on the list, offering good B&B or full board in chalets. **Pardjiesberg Farm**, ✆ (0491) 23 050, is an old farmhouse that sleeps 7 and offers hiking, climbing, horses and hunting. At **Langfontein Farm**, ✆ (0491) 910 906, you can hike, swim and, in winter, relax in front of a log fire.

The only accommodation in the **Rolfontein Nature Reserve** is in the overnight hiking hut, which has water and firewood.

Fountains, ✆ (0424) 61492, is on Cranemere Farm, near Pearston, 75km east of Graaff-Reinet. A 4-bedroomed farmhouse, Fountains offers self catering accommodation (cook available), with walking trails, good bird-watching and game-spotting.

South of Graaff-Reinet, 170km down the Knysna road, is **Honingkrantz**, ✆ (0491) 910 814, a guest farm which has riding, swimming and good country cooking.

Mountain Zebra National Park, ✆ (012) 343 1991 (call 9–4.45), has self-catering cottages for 4 or 6 in its rest camp, with very comfortable bedrooms set under the wild Bankberg mountains. With the exchange rate, these work out to a moderate price for two. The rest camp also has a pool and restaurant, and guest chalets.

West of Colesberg (7km along the Tzamenkomst road, then turn right at the red tractor and continue for 28km to the farm signpost) is **De Poort Guest Farm**, ✆ (051) 753 1323, an old farmstead offering excellent value B&B, farm walks, donkey-cart rides and other such delights, as well as the requisite space and silence you would expect from a Karoo farm.

The **Oviston Nature Reserve**, has untempting chalet accommodation or an overnight hut. However, Parks Board cottages can be found about 33km east, over the Free State's border at the eastern end of the dam, at **Tuissen Die Rivieren Nature Reserve** (*see* **Free State**, 'Southwest'). If shared between a group, these self-contained cottages fall into the cheap category.

Colesberg has a variety of moderately priced, early 19th-century B&Bs to choose from: **Die Tuinhuis**, on Bell Street, ✆ (051) 753 0582, **Nanna Rous' Townhouse**, ✆ (051) 753 0025, and **De Oude Werf**, 11 Hospital Street, ✆ (051) 753 0360. Outside town are the following guest farms: **Crane Cottage**, ✆ (051) 654 0337— offering B&B or self-catering; **Seekoeirivier Farm**, ✆ (051) 753 1378, which offers the same choice plus riding and hiking, **De Poort Farm**, ✆ (051) 753 1323, offering the same, and **Halfway House B&B**, ✆ (051) 753 1391, about 30km north of town on the way to Bloemfontein, which has swimming.

There are some excellent guest houses in Nieu Bethesda: **Stokkiesdraai**, ✆ (04923) 711; **Nieu Bethesda Cottage**, ✆ (04923) 758, or **On the Edge**, ✆ (04923) 740, which operates lets on several self-catering cottages in and round town.

cheap

There is no budget accommodation as such, although all the towns and most of the nature reserves listed have **camp sites** with facilities, and there is always free camping on farms (with permission) if you have your own equipment.

As with the Western Karoo, there are no listed restaurants other than fast food and take-away joints except in hotels, which usually have an *à la carte* restaurant serving tolerably good food.

The **Drostdy Restaurants**, Graaff-Reinet, ✆ (0491) 22 161 (expensive–moderate), warrant a mention. They have long, spacious rooms with polished wooden floors and ceilings and are furnished in period. Karoo mutton is the house speciality. The atmosphere is friendly but formal.

A good, very cheap eatery in Graaff-Reinet is the **Trail Inn**, on Caledon St, which though unlicensed serves as a meeting point for most of the town's youth and the many backpackers passing through. Pizzas are good value here, and the atmosphere is more that of a fun bar than a restaurant.

Nieu Bethesda has a **Coffee House and Restaurant,** in one of the village houses, which serves very cheap and very good home-made breads and holistic meals.

Namaqualand and the Richtersveld

Father ... says, 'Ja-nee' with the sense of the equivocal born out of watching rainclouds gather over the earth and then disperse. 'Ja-nee', he repeats, 'that's a place now, hey!' and with a whistling extraction of marrow from the neck of the goat, he laughs the satisfied laugh of one who has come to see the hidden blessings of drought.

You Can't Get Lost in Cape Town, Zoe Wicomb

South Africa's far northwest is a semi-desert area with low winter rainfall, barely vegetated shale hills, giant aloe trees and bare rock. Namaqualand (named after the Nama, the Khoi tribe that originally inhabited this region and now lives in the south of Namibia) is vast, with merino and dorper sheep farms that stretch over scores of kilometres to a desert coast on the cold Atlantic Ocean.

For most of the year, people breeze through Namaqualand as fast as possible on the straight-as-straight-can-be N7 that connects Cape Town with Windhoek in Namibia. But, for a few weeks in spring, tourists flock to Namaqualand to watch the desert burst into flower.

This it literally does. Once the July and August rains have fallen, specks of bright colour begin to dot the brown surface of the veld. In the first week of September, the flowers come out en masse, a scarcely credible carpet of yellows, oranges, pinks and blues covering almost every inch of ground. Some flowers, like the orange and white Namaqualand daisy, are easy to identify. Others, like the delicate purple *Lapeirousia silenoides*, and the *Cheridopsis pillansi*, a pink and white flowering succulent whose leaves look like living stones, require a local guide to identify them (*see* 'Activities'). The flowers stay until October, then die back and the land returns to its parched state for another year.

History

Namaqualand was not colonized until the 18th century, until when its dry land was sparsely inhabited by nomadic KhoiSan, who followed the grazing down to the hot plains during the winter rains and retreated to the cooler Bokkeveld and Cedarberg mountains during the long summer droughts. The region was first explored by Europeans in the 1680s when the Cape Governor Simon Van Der Stel, who had heard from Khoi tribesmen that copper could be found in the region, took a prospecting party north and successfully sank shafts into a mountain a few kilometres east of the present-day town of Springbok. The largest shaft—now a national monument on the dirt road to Carolusberg—bears the faint impression of Van Der Stel's carved initials. But no harbour could be found on the Namaqualand coast suitable for getting the ore out of the region, and the venture was abandoned, not to be resumed until 1852, when several mines around Springbok, such as Nababeep and Okiep, were opened up, and small harbours constructed at Port Nolloth and Alexander Bay.

Trekboers from the Cape colony began to establish themselves in Namaqualand from the end of the 18th century and, by the 1850s, small farming villages were emerging wherever there was accessible underground water. The farmers hunted out the San, pushing them north into the Kalahari, and forced the local Nama Khoi to work on their farms. The young Khoi women were generally pressed into the farmers' beds and, as happened throughout the Cape colony, the Khoi developed into the 'coloured' population of today's Cape Province—a largely landless, Afrikaans-speaking people who have traditionally been exploited by the whites as cheap labour.

In the 1860s diamonds were discovered on the Namaqualand coast, and the towns of Port Nolloth and Alexander Bay experienced a brief boom. Today small-scale diamond-mining still goes on but, despite this, Namaqualand is not a wealthy region. The huge farms suffer from acute seasonal drought, and the main economy remains agricultural, at a level not all that far above subsistence.

Inland Namaqualand

Getting There

By car: Namaqualand's main towns of Springbok, Kamieskroon and Vanrhynsdorp, sit astride the main N7 highway between Cape Town and Namibia. Springbok is also a 4–5-hour drive from Upington on the Orange River.

By bus: InterCape run every day up and down the N7 between Cape Town and Windhoek in Namibia. They stop in the main towns en route. There's also a smaller bus service, called **Namaqualand Busdiens**, ✆ (0251) 22 061, which plies the same route.

Springbok is the principal town of the region (Tourism Office ✆ (0251) 22 011). The nearby **Goeap Nature Reserve** (formerly the Hester Malan Nature Reserve), ✆ (0251) 21 880, is one of the best places to see spring flowers. The large reserve (15,000ha) is made up of flat plains between domed granite outcrops, hiking trails and gravel roads. Weird desert succulents, such as the halfmens (a humanoid water-holding 'tree' the name of which means 'half man') and kokerboom (giant aloe) grow on the dry hillsides. The reserve is excellent for photographing flowers, particularly at Hartmann's Mountain where zebra, eland, gemsbok, springbok and klipspringer graze amongst them. The reserve has no accommodation.

Kamieskroon, about 70km south of Springbok, is where connoisseurs of the flower season head. Guided hikes of up to three days into the flowered veld are led by local experts who can identify all the flora and know which farms to head for at which particular time. People in the know come from all over the world to Kamieskroon, a tiny, one-street dorp, and stay at the Kamieskroon Hotel (*see* 'Where to Stay') before going out into the veld. The hotel organizes hikes with local guides which must be booked in advance (*see* 'Activities'). While waiting for a tour it is worth taking the dirt road 8km north of Kamieskroon to **Bowesdorp**, the original site of the village, now a ghost town.

South of Kamieskroon the land flattens to a dry plain, with the only greenery lying on the sandy river beds running along the western wall of the **Bokkeveld** escarpment. At **Vanrhynsdorp** (about 200km south of Kamieskroon, past the village of Garies), the R27 crosses the straight N7. Vanrhynsdorp itself is not much to look at—the first thing you see is a 24-hour truck-stop and petrol station—but east of town the R27 heads straight for the Bokkeveld escarpment, which it climbs via the **Vanrhyns Pass**. The look-out point at the top gives views back over the dry, blasted landscape stretching to the coast, while to the east, on the plateau, the scene changes suddenly and dramatically. A landscape of irrigated pastures and pine trees, reminiscent of the countryside around Cape Town, makes a sharp contrast with the unremitting dryness of the region below. It is hard not to feel a lift of the heart at the sudden greenery, after the hours of parched driving.

The village of **Nieuwoudtville** is roughly 10km east of the pass. At its eastern end is the **Nieuwoudtville Flower Reserve**, a 120ha stretch of grassland that explodes into colour in the spring. **Oorlogskloof Nature Reserve**, ✆ (02726) 81010, a few kilometres south of Nieuwoudtville, is larger and wilder. To get there, follow the dirt road southwest from Nieuwoudtville towards Clanwilliam. The road is signposted but, if you have trouble finding it, ask at the garage at the west end of the Main Street. Follow the dirt road for about 7km, then turn right on to a smaller dirt road, signposted to Oorlogskloof. The reserve lies in a spectacularly deep-cut kloof formed by the Oorlogs River (one of the few perennial rivers in the region) as it falls through the Bokkeveld plateau and over the escarpment into the dry flats below via a beautiful water-fall, active most of the year except in high summer. Leopard and caracal hunt in the kloof's vegeta-tion. Klipspringer, grey rhebok, duiker, grysbok, baboon and dassie are common and the rare aardwolf is a nocturnal resident, as are smaller cats and foxes. The bird life includes Cape eagle owls, black eagles, booted eagles, and lanner and peregrine falcons which nest on the cliffs. The reserve has hiking trails and swimming holes in pools of the Oorlogs River. Accommodation is in permanent tents.

As you travel east of Nieuwoudtville, you soon realize how narrow is the vegetated belt surrounding the village. Before long the road enters the arid Karoo, meeting the R357 to **Loeriesfontein** at its western edge, before heading back into the parched landscape and vast horizons of Namaqualand. After Nieuwoudtville, about 20km along on the right, is a signpost for the **Kokerboom Forest**. This, the southernmost large collection of these giant aloes in South Africa, lies on a range of low but steep shale hills, about 5km down the sign-posted farm track. There are several gates and some steep humps in the road to take the driver by surprise. Be careful. Loeriesfontein itself has few houses, but its Spar supermarket supplies all the surrounding farmers. The owners stock everything from food to televisions, guns and coffins; everything that an isolated Namaqualand farm could need.

From Loeriesfontein, the R357 and R355 east lead back into the Karoo, while the R355 west heads straight along the Bokkeveld escarpment, a lonely drive with views over some of the Bokkeveld's higher peaks, before dropping back to the lowlands at the junction with the R358 (which leads northeast to Pofadder or west to the N7).

Far Inland Namaqualand

The R64 from Springbok to **Pofadder**, the region's only inland centre, passes through a land-scape so apparently devoid of life that it is hard to understand how it was ever settled. However, in spring the veld is carpeted with flowers, even at Pofadder (150km inland), and beyond to the Orange River at Kakamas (*see* 'Bushmanland'). The perennial springs around Pofadder provided hide-outs for various Griqua chiefs and cattle rustlers who operated in the area during the mid-19th century. Today, Pofadder is a true 'dorp'—a desolate, forgotten interior town where there is little to do but pass through on the way to the Orange River and the national parks further north. However, 'dorps' such as Pofadder are central to the South African (and particularly the Cape's) culture. It does no harm to visit one, to take in the stoic, patient atmosphere of such places which somehow survive, despite the pull of the cities and the difficulty of eking a living from the unforgiving land.

The Namaqualand Coast

Like the West Coast, of which the Namaqualand coast is the northern extension, this is a barren, sandy coastline of cold Atlantic beaches and treacherous currents. Wilder than the West Coast, most of the coastline is privately owned, although there are some points of access which make interesting side-trips.

Port Nolloth, about 150km northwest of Springbok, was founded in 1854 as a port for ship-ping copper from the Namaqualand mines. The discovery of loose diamonds in the surrounding sandveld let to a brief diamond rush in the 1860s, which survives today in the form of a rough crew of seasonal prospectors who use underground hoses to suck the sea-floor sand into boats for sifting, and dive offshore for the elusive stones. The town itself is windy, dusty and temporary looking, its corrugated iron houses painted bright colours to alleviate the monotony of the surrounding browns. The town's few bars are lively at night.

The road to Port Nolloth from the N7 (R382) passes through some of Namaqualand's loveliest scenery. It crosses the Buffels River at the village of Steinkopf, then winds over the folded hills that comprise the **Ananous Pass**. On the west side of the hills wheat fields (the last thing you would expect to see in Namaqualand) stretch to the further hills. From here, though, the land becomes steadily drier until you hit the coastal sandveld.

An alternative route back to the N7 from Port Nolloth is via the dirt road south from the N382 (about 20km east of Port Nolloth) to **Kleinsee**, a tiny coastal settlement at the mouth of the Buffels River. The R355 then takes you east back to Springbok along the river, which is usually flowing—a welcome glimpse of water in the dry landscape. The road climbs up another pass with attendant spectacular views (the appropriately named **Spektakel Pass**) before turning back to tar for the home run to Springbok.

Hondeklip Bay, roughly 170km southwest of Springbok (via the Messelpad and Wildeperdehoek Passes), is a coastal village where little seems to have changed since the 19th century. Whereas Port Nolloth is small but lively, Hondeklip Bay is tiny and almost inert. 'Coloured' fishermen's cottages cluster round the little windswept bay and small harbour. Crayfishing, trawling from small boats and seasonal trade keeps the town alive. Hondeklip Bay is a good place to spend a few days and forget about the rest of the world, though most people spend no more than an afternoon here before driving back to the N7 and Kamieskroon via the Grootvlei Pass.

The Richtersveld

This huge tract of empty, mountainous desert in the far north of Namaqualand has recently been proclaimed the **Richtersveld National Park**. It occupies the stretch of territory between Alexander Bay (a closed diamond mining town north of Port Nolloth) and the Orange River border with Namibia. The land is savagely desolate, its beauty intimidating. Even by African standards this is an untamed territory. However, it should be said too that the Nama and 'coloured' graziers of the wild area resisted the formation of the park, and it is worth asking what moves have been made to accommodate these people, now that the park is 'official'.

Access is via the N7 from Springbok to Steinkopf. From there take the R382 to Port Nolloth, then the restricted road north to Alexander Bay at the Orange River Mouth. From Alexander Bay follow the signs to **Sendelingsdrift**. The total distance from Springbok is 326km. The last section of road has sharp bends and bad gravel patches which can make a car spin, so drive slowly. The Parks Board office for the Richtersveld is at Sendelingsdrift. The Richtersveld has not yet been developed for tourism in the same way as the more established national parks and there are no fuel stations or grocery shops after Alexander Bay, so stock up there. The Parks Board do not allow traffic on the Richtersveld's few gravel roads by night, when broken-down vehicles cannot be located, so make sure you arrive at the office with plenty of daylight to spare.

The office provides a map of the existing roads with specific overnight camping spots marked. Remember to take your own food and water. The reason for the controlled camping is to protect the areas wide variety of fragile plant life, which thrives despite the Richtersveld's barren appearance. The rocks in fact support small lichens and succulents, as well as the larger, more distinctive kokerboom and halfmens trees. However, walking is freely permitted, as is swimming in the Orange River, although bathers are warned not to swim out too far, as there are treacherous currents in the centre. You can buy fishing permits for the camp site along the Orange River at the office.

Summer temperatures can shoot up above 50°C so it is worth getting up at dawn to enjoy the morning, having a siesta through the heat of the day, and getting up again for the evening cool, when you should spot the gemsbok and springbok herds that somehow manage to thrive here. As always in deserts, nights are much colder, so take a good sleeping bag.

Activities

Wildflower viewing: Apart from the reserves listed above, Colla Swart at the **Kamieskroon Hotel** offers trails of 3–5 days into the deep valleys and hills of private farms around Kamieskroon. There is also a **Steam Train for Viewing Wildflowers**, ✆ (021) 405 4395—a luxury service from Cape Town that takes a week (31 August–7 September) to chug up from Cape Town to Namaqualand and back. It's called the 'Golden Flower'.

Hiking: Trails can be found in the **Goeap Nature Reserve**, the **Nieuwoudtville Flower Reserve**, the **Oorlogskloof Nature Reserve** (near Nieuwoudtville) and in the **Richtersveld National Park** , ✆ (0256) 831 1506 (free walking in the veld around the camping spots).

Canoeing: Trips of 3–5 days down the Orange River in the Richtersveld are offered by these Cape Town-based companies: **Felix Unite**, ✆ (021) 762 6935, **River Runners**, ✆ (021) 762 2350, and **Rivers Unlimited**, ✆ (021) 790 4821.

Riding: It is possible to hire horses for guided forays into the Richtersveld. Details can be had from the National Park office at Sendelingsdrift.

Fishing: Permits for fishing in the Richtersveld can be obtained in person also from the National Park office at Sendelingsdrift.

4x4 Trails: Richtersveld 4x4 (Port Nolloth Adventures, ✆ (0255) 8041), offers tough trails of 1–5 days through the back country near the Orange River. Other trails exist on farms in the region. For more details ring Springbok's tourism office. Good deals on 4x4 hire can be had from **Upington 4x4**, ✆ (054) 25 441.

Where to Stay

expensive

The **Narries Guest Farm**, ✆ (0251) 22 462, near Springbok, offers full board with superb home-cooking (the lamb and venison raised on the local veld is succulent) in 4 comfortable rooms. Further south, the family-run **Kamieskroon Hotel**, ✆ (027) 672 1614, offers clean, comfortable accommodation at the moderate end of the expensive scale. As the centre from which most flower-spotters organize their hikes, the hotel's atmosphere is less provincial than is usual for a small Northern Cape town, and some interesting folk pass through.

moderate

At Port Nolloth, on the coast, is the excellent **Bedrock Lodge Guest House**, ✆ (0255) 8865, a small family house owned by one of the local diamond divers. In Springbok, the owner of the **Springbok Lodge**, ✆ (0251) 21 321, is a mine of local information, and the place is popular with the younger crowd visiting for the flower season. Outside Kamieskroon is **Pedroskloof Farm**, ✆ (0257) 666, a guest farm B&B that is great in flower season.

Around Vanrhynsdorp, there is a good selection of guest farms and town houses: **Gifberg Holiday Farm**, ✆ (02727) 91 555, is below the Bokkeveld escarpment; in town, the **Van Rhyn Guest House**, ✆ (02727) 91 429, an old house on Voortrekker St, offers traditional B&B; if the guest house is closed, try the **Van Rhijn Inn**, ✆ (02727) 91 003, which has more rooms but is slightly less personal.

Port Nolloth Adventures also organize comfortable B&B in and around the town.

cheap

Oorlogskloof Nature Reserve, ✆ (02726) 81 010, has a permanent tented camp, but this is often booked up and you should ring beforehand. Otherwise there is a lack of cheap accommodation in Namaqualand. However, all the larger towns have camp sites with ablution facilities, and camping can usually be had on farms by permission.

Bushmanland and West Griqualand

I was born near the great river, in the heart of what for thousands of years had been great Bushman country. The Bushman himself...had already gone, but I was surrounded by so many fragments of his race and culture, that he seemed extraordinarily near.

Lost World of the Kalahari, Laurens Van Der Post

Bushmanland and West Griqualand form the top section of the Northern Cape, between the Karoo in the south, the Free State and Transvaal to the east, the Botswana border in the north and the Namibia/Namaqualand border in the west. The Orange River forms both an eastern boundary for the two regions, and a central focus, cutting through them on its way to the Atlantic.

Bushmanland, the more northern and western section, is a mixture of arid semi-desert in the south (except for the fertile floodplain around the Orange River) and Kalahari camel-thorn savannah mixed with red sand dune country in the north. Most of the population lives alongside the great river, where the wine farms and large towns, such as Keimoes and Upington, give the impression of a prosperous, peopled land, belying the great tracts of dry emptiness behind. In the northwest, forming a jutting tongue between Namibia and Botswana, is the huge Kalahari Gemsbok National Park, home to great herds of game and their predators. Squatting in the dunes just outside are South Africa's last Bushmen, the *Xhomani*, who were kicked out of the park back in the early 1970s. They are now fighting a land claim to be allowed hunting and gathering access back into their ancestral land.

West Griqualand also has a narrow strip of fertile country along its stretch of the Orange River, with dry, under-populated country beyond, a great chunk of which—the former Bophuthatswana—belongs to the Tswana people. Kimberley, the town that grew up around the diamond diggings that made South Africa's fortune, sits at the extreme east of the region, hard by the border with the Free State.

History

Bushmanland and West Griqualand take their names from the people that occupied them until the late 19th century. The San (bushmen) retreated north into the Namibia and Botswana Kalahari during the late 1800s, but the Griqua of West Griqualand remain, and in a few places have even kept their patrimony, despite colonial expansion and apartheid.

'Griqua' was the name given by English missionaries to the people of mixed Khoi and European (mainly Afrikaans) blood who trekked up to this barren region in the early 19th century, in an attempt to distance themselves from the encroaching white man. The missionaries were offended by the people's own name for themselves—Bastaards. Griqua was the name of one of the first Bastaard leaders that the missionaries came into contact with, and first the preachers, then the Bastaards themselves, began to use the name.

At that time the general area around the Orange River was known as TransOrangia, a vague, undefined territory into which people who wished to escape the confines of colonial society had been drifting since the 1770s. The Griqua were among the first to do so, having no place in either white or Khoi society. Nomadic herders of sheep and cattle, they became the first *trekboers* to open up the northern routes and establish their own nation in a country where no colour lines existed. Using horses, wagons and guns they soon established mastery over the indigenous KhoiSan groups, and raided the Tswana villages and cattle-herds to the north. Some even trekked into northern Namibia to escape the society that had both created them and cast them aside.

By the 1790s TransOrangia was peopled by various bands of Griqua, free Khoi, escaped Khoi bondsmen, European army deserters, renegade Boers, Tswana and some Xhosa, while the great emptiness on either side was hunted by the San. There was plentiful game in the desert and sufficient water and pasture along the river and on its islands to support cattle.

Most groups along the river lived by plunder, using the river islands as fortresses or stationary pirate ships, preying indiscriminately on other people's herds. Most of these groups were made up of any number of different race and colours. Only the Bastaards (Griqua) and the Tswana remained ethnically distinct, being sufficiently numerous both to protect and preserve their own cultures.

Although various government officials and explorers passed through TransOrangia in the late 1700s and early 1800s, there was no permanent colonial activity until the Griqua began to

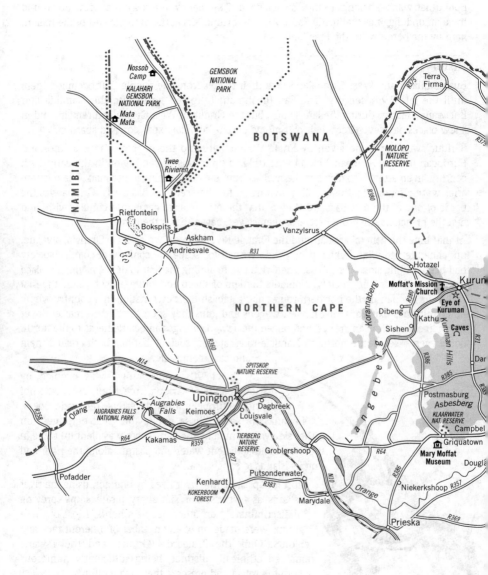

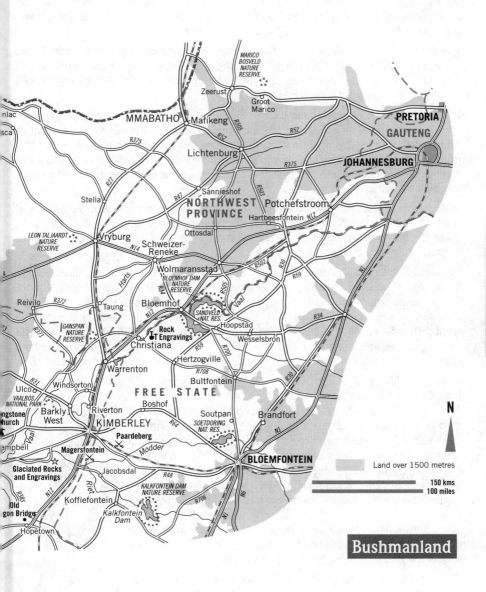

Bushmanland

Land over 1500 metres

150 kms
100 miles

invite missionaries to come and live among them. The first, John Campbell (who arrived from London in 1814),was followed in 1820 by Robert Moffat and his wife, Mary. By encouraging the nomadic Griqua and Tswana to settle around permanent waterholes, it was these missionaries who were to establish the region's first towns.

The arrival of missionaries attracted the attention of Government House in Cape Town, where there was worry that the general instability of the TransOrangia region would attract Afrikaners wishing to flee British rule and involve the government in costly native wars, such as were already being fought in the Eastern Cape.

Governor Cradock also wanted to harness the TransOrangia raiding peoples as a pool for raising army conscripts and asked the missionary Campbell and his assistant, William Anderson, to enforce this. Both missionaries warned that such demands would only bring trouble. The few Boers who had already settled in the region warned the Griqua that this was just the beginning of a process which would eventually end in annexation of their territory by the English.

Sure enough, in the 1820s British soldiers and government agents arrived in TransOrangia, and a fierce anti-colonial reaction followed. But the missionaries, who helped the Griqua to dodge the draft and took no sides in the light skirmishing that followed, remained popular, and the British gave up the project as too expensive.

Meanwhile at Lattakoo, north of modern Kuruman in northwest Bushmanland, Robert Moffat had established another mission among the Tswana, and colonial expansion into TransOrangia began, with neither troops nor government officers to enforce it. Although Christian converts were pitifully few (Moffat achieved no more than eight in the years he spent there), the missionaries built on the trust they had achieved with all the TransOrangia peoples, managing to stay on friendly terms with the Griqua, Tswana Koranna (mixed Griqua/Tswana) and the Ndebele, despite these groups' continual raiding of one another.

During the 1830s large groups of Sotho and Tswana, displaced by the general warring on the highveld (see **History**, p.39), and followed by the Boers of the Great Trek, began to settle around the Orange River. Still the Griqua held their territory, cleverly allying with different groups and relying on their military expertise and horsemanship, and knowledge of the country. They were again helped by the missionaries, who did everything they could to keep the Boers from taking the permanent water sites around Kuruman, Griquatown and Lattakoo, and began calling on the British Government to make the area a protectorate. However, some of the Griqua were pushed out by Boers—one group, under Adam Kok, trekked as far east as Natal (see 'Natal History'). Meanwhile the San, alarmed at the rapid disappearance of the game, retreated north to the Kalahari.

The combined missionary/ Tswana/Griqua attempt to keep the Boers out was largely successful, and most trekked east to found the Orange Free State under President Brand in the 1850s. Griqualand was then recognized as a separate territory by the Boers and the British, both of whom signed treaties with Nicolaas Waterboer, the

Griquas' most influential leader. However, wrangling over the exact borders became a problem as each group vied for the narrow strips of fertile land amid the great dryness. A measure of how established the Griqua had become is the fact that Nicolaas Waterboer had a Scottish South African land agent, David Arnot, operating on his behalf.

In the 1860s diamonds were found in the Kimberley area, on territory disputed between the three groups. The Orange Free State asked the Cape authorities to mediate in their dispute with the Griqua, with a view to making a later deal with the British, once the troublesome Griqua were dealt with. But Arnot managed to persuade the British Cape Governor that this was Griqua land (the extent of the diamond deposits were not yet known), which was placed under protection as nominal British territory.

The Orange Free State did not give up, forcing several new surveys of the boundary in question, but the British kept asserting their right. Finally the Free State's President Brand went to London to present his claim to Parliament, but to no avail. The British Government paid the Free State £90,000 and bought off Brand with private land grants and pensions.

For the Griqua this was the end of independence. With the diamond-boom of the 1870s, diamond diggings erupted around the hastily constructed town of Kimberley. The mission centre of Kuruman lost its importance, Moffat returned to England, and British occupation became complete. The Griqua, like the Tswana and Sotho who had moved to the area, were gradually stripped of their seasonal grazing lands, and absorbed into employment by the overwhelming number of diamond-diggers moving in.

Through the 20th century they lost their recognized status, were classified as 'coloured' under the laws of apartheid, and stripped of most of their civil rights. During the 1970s large areas of the far north were designated part of the former tribal 'homeland' of Bophuthatswana (now re-absorbed into the union of South Africa), and most of the region's Tswana were forcibly removed there after 1973, mostly to live in dire poverty with insufficient water and grazing.

However, quietly and unobtrusively, many descendants of the Griqua have managed to hang on to property and even to prosper, particularly around the town of Keimoes on the Orange River in central Bushmanland, where many 'coloured' wine farms survived both apartheid and the political upheavals of the years since its abolition.

Kimberley

This large, unattractive town on the border of West Griqualand and the Free State was where South Africa's commercial boom began. The diamond rush (and the later gold rush in the Transvaal) transformed South Africa from a collection of economically stagnant states to a land where extreme wealth could be found, and laid the foundation for the country's great prosperity through much of the 20th century.

History

There are many stories of how the diamond-digging began. The most popular is that the first main diamond find in the area was made by a 16-year-old Afrikaner boy near Hopetown, on the banks of the Orange River, in 1866. He gave it to a farmer, who in turn passed it on to a doctor in Grahamstown. The stone—named the 'Eureka' diamond—weighed 21¼ carats. The same farmer, one Schalk Van Niekerk, was given another stone of 83½ carats in 1869 by a Griqua in exchange for 10 oxen, a portent of what the diamonds were to mean for the Griqua. This diamond, the famous 'Star of Africa', precipitated a rush of prospectors to the Vaal and Orange Rivers around present-day Barkly West.

Then, in 1870, several veins of kimberlite (diamond-bearing rock) were found in the low hills on the farm of two Afrikaner brothers named De Beer. One of these hills, Colesberg Kopjie, was tapped in 1871. The haul it produced was staggering. The farm was sold and, by 1872, a tent-town of over 50,000 inhabitants was centred around the kopjie, which had been divided into over 3500 claims, one next to the other. The kopjie soon began to look more like a hole. A confusing network of ropes and pulleys allowed each claim to be worked, but in reality there was chaos.

At first, the free-for-all was surprisingly democratic; anyone, including blacks, was allowed to make a claim, and many hundreds of local Tswana took advantage of the opportunity. However, the white diggers soon banded together to disallow black claims, and the resident Tswana were forced to seek work for white prospectors. Still, for some years Kimberley's mining was controlled by no central company, only a host of small operations jostling for space, and thousands of black migrant labourers from all over South Africa drifted to the diggings, seeking work, swelling the town's population.

In the 1880s Cecil Rhodes, a young English immigrant who had arrived in Kimberley in 1872 from a failed farming attempt in the Eastern Cape, began buying up the smaller syndicates using borrowed money and cash made from his own prospecting. He concentrated on those held by a company named after the original farming brothers, De Beers. Rhodes' business momentum was phenomenal. After buying out De Beers in 1887 he raised funds from the European De Rothschild family to buy the largest operation, the Kimberley Mine, owned by Barney Barnato, a Jew from the East End of London known for his opulent style, love of sport—especially boxing—and success at the diggings. After a year's wrangle Rhodes incorporated the mine into De Beers at a cost of over £5 million, an incredible sum for those times. De Beers gradually secured control of the mining, and the town began to settle into more established life. Three lasting South African phenomena had been established: the status of the De Beers Company (which later secured much of the Transvaal gold fields—see p.505), the importance of mining to South Africa's economy, and the drift of black people away from their rural homelands to, and subsequent reliance on, the cities that grew up around the mines.

Although its boom days are long past Kimberley has steadily continued to make money since the original diggings opened, apart from a period of siege during the Anglo-Boer war in which many of the town's black workers were press-ganged into military service and killed, while at the same time being starved, as most food was requisitioned for whites. Four diamond mines still operate in the area, though not at Colesberg Kopjie, which is now a huge water-filled depression known as the 'Big Hole'—and it is big.

Getting There

By car: Kimberley lies at the centre of several main routes and is easily accessible by main road from Gauteng, Bloemfontein, Cape Town and Upington.

By bus: Greyhound connect Kimberley with Jo'burg; TransLux with Jo'burg, Cape Town and Knysna; InterCape use Kimberley as a stop between Cape Town and Gauteng. All stop at the Shell UltraCity on the N12 Highway just outside town. For booking details ring © (0531) 811 062.

By train: Kimberley is a main stop on the Spoornet Jo'burg–Cape Town run. Services also run to Bloemfontein and Durban. To book ring © (0531) 882 100.

The Town

Modern Kimberley is ugly, having been much 'improved' in the 1950s and '60s, but around the Big Hole is the **Kimberley Mine Museum**, at the west end of town, on Tucker Street (*open daily 9–5*), a large open-air museum incorporating 50 of the original buildings, still laid out in street form. The best way to get there from town is on the **Kimberley Tram** which runs from the City Hall to the Big Hole (*daily roughly every hour from 9–4, more at weekends*). The cottages, churches, shops, offices, surgeries and pubs used by the mining community have been well preserved, including the cottage originally inhabited by the De Beers brothers when it was just a farm. It takes at least an hour to get around what really is a fascinating and intimate (if rather romanticized) look at late Victorian and Edwardian colonial life. A tea room and restaurant break up the concentration of exhibits.

The **Star of Kimberley pub**, another preserved relic of the frontier town, is located in the main town, just outside the Mine Museum. Follow Tucker Street and turn right on North Circular Road: the pub occupies half a block on the left. Still serving drinks, the pub has an untouched Edwardian interior.

There are several smaller museums in town. The **McGregor Museum**, on Atlas Street (*open Mon–Fri 9–5, Sat 9–1, Sun 2–5*), is housed in a hotel and health spa built by Rhodes in the 1870s and where he lived during the Boer's siege of Kimberley (1900). The displays are mostly of local natural history. An eccentricity is the Hall of Religions, an educational summary of several of the world's better-known belief systems which, for some reason, has been placed here. The **Alexander McGregor Memorial Museum**, round the corner on Chapel Street (*open Mon–Fri 9–5, Sat 9–1, Sun 2–5*) is another Edwardian building housing a colonial history of the Northern Cape and a collection of rocks and minerals.

The **William Humphreys Art Gallery**, in the Civic Centre, off Jan Smuts Boulevard (*open Mon–Sat 10–1, 2–5, Sun 2–5*), houses a collection of South African painting and sculpture by the better-known artists like Pierneef and Irma Stern, with some reasonable Dutch and Flemish landscapes and portraits. There is a furniture collection, mainly Cape Dutch. The more interesting **Duggan Cronin Gallery**, on Egerton Road (*open Mon–Fri 9–5, Sat 9–1 and 2–5, Sun 2–5*) is an ethnographic museum of black South African life at the turn of the century, albeit from a colonial and very general point of view. The most valuable exhibits are the photographs taken by Cronin of Griqua, Tswana and Sotho (as well as settlers), whose cultures in the area were eroded and squashed by the success of the mines.

Kimberley has several Victorian houses open to the public among the more assertive modern buildings. The interiors are still furnished in period, but there are no specific displays. These include: **Dunluce**, 10 Lodge Road (built 1897); the **Kimberley Club** on Du Toitspan Road, where the mining magnates used to meet; **Rudd House**, 5–7 Loch Road, a large colonial bungalow; and **7 Lodge Road**, the house where Harry Oppenheimer was born and lived before the family moved to Johannesburg in 1915. This last house can only be viewed from the outside. The others are viewed inside by appointment only, but generally you can turn up during office hours and ask to be shown around.

Around Kimberley

Magersfontein battlefield is 32km south of town, with a small museum displaying weaponry and a brief history of the long battle fought here in 1899 during the early period of the Anglo-Boer War, when Britain was getting the worst of the fighting. At Magersfontein, Boer general Koos de la Rey's *Kommandos* dug into position and surprised a large British column under the command of Lord Methuen. Precision sniping from the Boers' Mauser rifles brought the column to a complete halt. Magersfontein was one of the first recorded effective uses of trench warfare to hold a geographical line.

Barkly West, about 40km northwest of Kimberley, is where the area's diamond-diggings were initially centred. The miners, in an attempt to secure the diggings for themselves, declared their own republic in 1870, but it fell apart within the year. People still prospect in the gravel along the Vaal in summer, and finds are common enough for several diamond-dealers to operate in the town. The town, which fronts the Vaal River, has a stone bridge dating from 1884; the first bridge over the Vaal, it is still in use. More interesting is **Canteen Kopjie**, a nature reserve and open-air archaeological and geological museum. Miners in the area have turned up a lot of early Stone Age tools and bones, as well as fossils which are displayed here and at the small **Mining Commissioner's Museum** in town.

The newly created **Vaalbos National Park**, ✆ (053) 561 0088, a huge area of wild veld west of Barkly West, is watered by the Vaal River and marks the meeting point of Karoo and Kalahari vegetation. Rhino and buffalo have been re-introduced, and the area also supports plains game such as kudu, springbok, giraffe and eland. This is an interesting area ecologically, as three biological zones come together here: Karoo semi-desert, grassveld (as in the Free State and ??Transvaal), and the beginnings of the Kalahari duneveld. There are chalets and some walking trails. To get there take the R31 about 65km northwest from Kimberley.

Stellaland is a huge tract of Kalahari grassland stretching north of Barkly West, in which are two large chunks of what was Bophuthatswana, centred around the town of **Vryburg**. This area proclaimed itself a republic in 1882, but it lasted less than a year and today is almost entirely given over to cattle ranching. However, about 5km north of Vryburg on the R378 is the **Leon Taljaardt Nature Reserve**. Although not large, the reserve has white rhino, buffalo, both kinds of wildebeest, gemsbok, hartebeest and several large antelope species. A much larger stretch of wild country, the 24,000ha **Molopo Nature Reserve**, ✆ (0020) and ask for 1322, sits in Stellaland's far northwest, south of the tiny dorp of **Voorstershoop**. Molopo's thornveld is watered from under ground—the Molopo river, which forms its western boundary (and the border with Botswana) flows only once every 50 years on average. However, game concentrations are fairly dense, with gemsbok, red hartebeest, kudu and springbok predominating. Leopard and cheetah are the main predators, though brown hyena are common. Large raptors, including bateleur eagles and white-backed vultures, are often seen. Visitors can hike in the large reserve, but *must* carry a plentiful water supply, and arrange their route with the reserve's office before setting off. There are no chalets or camp sites at Molopo—you are really on your own.

Bushmanland

For the purposes of this guide, Bushmanland, west of Griqualand, is divided in two: the green, fertile strip along the Orange River, and the semi-desert Kalahari to the north.

Getting There

By air: Several daily SAA flights connect Upington with Cape Town and Jo'burg, for access to Bushmanland.

By car: Upington is on the main N10 Highway.

By bus: InterCape use Upington as a stopover for the journey between Jo'burg and Cape Town and between Jo'burg and Windhoek in Namibia. The office is on Lutz Street, ✆ (054) 332 6091.

Orange River

This bright corridor of startling green is reached by three main routes: the N10 from the south, the R54 from Kimberley via Griquatown, and the R27 from Vryburg and the Transvaal via Kuruman. The N10 runs along a 120km section of the Orange River, whose alluvial banks from Groblershoop to Upington are given over to small, intensive wine and fruit farms with dry rocky hills stretching away on either side.

West of Upington, the R359 continues along the river through similar country to the **Augrabies Falls National Park**, where the river plunges suddenly into a deep, narrow gorge, creating an angry churning wall of water whose roar is deafening against the surrounding silence. West of Augrabies, you can continue down river by raft or canoe (*see* 'Activities') or by road (R64), into the empty spaces of Namaqualand.

To the south, near the town of Groblershoop and 120km south of Upington on the R32, is **Witsand**, a weird white 'island' of sand dunes known as the **Roaring Sands**. During the summer months the 100m-high dunes make a sound like a human moan if disturbed. You can usually rely on the wind to do this for you, but even kicking at the white sand can produce the sound, the origin of which lies in its loose composition, through which air moves continuously. There is a hutted camp at the foot of the dunes for those wanting to break their journey here.

Upington, Bushmanland's main centre, is another town that was ruined by 'improvement' in the 1950s and '60s. An important wine-growing centre, it has a **Wine Route** that follows the N10 east towards Groblershoop. Originally a mission station (like most of the towns in the area), there is little to see in Upington itself, despite its river frontage and the beauty of the surrounding fruit farms and vineyards. The **Kalahari Oranje Museum**, (054) 26 911, is housed in the church of the old mission station (built in 1875). The usual pioneer life exhibits are displayed. More fun is the Donkey Monument, a bronze statue paying just tribute to the Southern Africa desert regions' principal worker. The **Hortentia Windmill** (1879), by the bridge on the Groblershoop Road, can only be viewed from the outside.

Spitskop Nature Reserve, 13km north of town on the R360, lies amid the rocky, barren landscape north of the Orange River. As a testament to just how much game the landscape can support, the reserve boasts zebra, gemsbok, hartebeest, eland, steenbok and many, many springbok. There is no accommodation, but there is a short walking trail.

Keimoes, 40km southwest of Upington along the river, was founded by a Griqua band known as the 'Koranna River People', pirates and brigands that had two punitive raids sent against them during the 1860s. The village was named Keimoes, which means 'mouse's nest', after the colonies of tree mice discovered in the vegetation fronting the river. Keimoes is remarkable in that it is one of the few places where the Griqua managed to hang on to prosperous land through the fiercely racial policies of the late 19th and 20th centuries. Many of the farms around are still owned by 'coloureds' descended from the Griquas who originally moved here to escape white domination of the Cape. The town has a waterwheel (still in use) on Main Road, and the original mission church (also on Main Road).

Outside town is the **Orange River Wine Cellars Co-operative**, offering wine-tastings and tours of the cellars. 4kms west of town is **Tierberg Nature Reserve**, a very small reserve teeming with springbok and noted for its tall aloes, some of which flower a spectacular red in winter. There is a walking trail to the summit of the hill that gives the reserve its name, a perfect place from which to observe the green river valley set against the harsh reds and browns of the hills around. **Kakamas**, another fruit and wine village a further 40km west, has several operational wooden waterwheels (through which run several irrigation canals) and a series of water tunnels bored from farm to farm in the alluvial lands around the village. Kakamas was also one of the few sites of skirmishing between German Southwest African troops and South African soldiers during the First World War. Just west of town is a monument to the several Germans killed.

Augrabies Falls National Park centres around the spectacular 300ft-deep gorge into which the broad, peaceful Orange River plunges, kicking up spray into the bone-dry air. A bridge spans the ravine, creating the opportunity to take fantastic photographs. The accessible part of the park covers about 10,000ha, but a vast 70,000ha hinterland also falls under park protection. Black rhinoceros are currently breeding in this back-veld. The park is now open to the public and forays can be arranged into the conservation areas and beyond. Away from the river banks, dry thorn bush predominates, supporting springbok, steenbok and klipspringer. Baboons and vervet monkeys, ground squirrels, jackal and bat-eared fox are also likely to be seen. The resident leopard and caracal remain hidden. Black and martial eagles are often sighted. The best thing about the park is its 3-day **Klipspringer hiking trail** (*see* 'Activities').

To the west of Augrabies begins Namaqualand, a great arid borderland between South Africa and Namibia that lies along the Orange River (*see* 'Namaqualand'). The wild emptiness between Bushmanland and Namaqualand has few roads, but can be penetrated either by **canoe or camel safari** for guided trips of about a week (*see* 'Activities').

On the R27, south of Keimoes, lie the great white salt pans of the upper Western Karoo. At the edge of these, 85km south of Keimoes into the bleached dry country, is the small, remote town of **Kenhardt**. Its perennial springs and desert location made the place a haven for Griqua, Boer and Tswana cattle-rustlers during the early 19th century, but in the 1860s the British decided to curb the activities of the raiders, sending in a magistrate and some police who set up camp under a camel-thorn tree. The town developed around the tree, which still stands, despite being over 500 years old. 8kms south of town is the **Kokerboom Forest**, one of the southernmost points where these strange giant aloes are found. There is a marked 4km trail through the 'forest', which consists of about 5000 giant aloes, each of which grows taller than a man.

The Kalahari

Bushmanland's northern reaches form a transitional zone between the Karoo scrub typical of most of the northern Cape, and the game-rich Kalahari. Red and grey dunes of fine sand alternate with camel-thorn trees so tall and wide that they resemble a man-made parkland. In between stretch dry grasslands the colour of spun gold.

The best way in is via the N14 to **Kuruman**, hard by the westernmost section of the former Bophuthatswana. (If you don't have a car, the town is on the InterCape Route between Jo'burg and Windhoek in Namibia, which also stops at Upington.) Kuruman, one of Bushmanland's only well-watered spots, was taken from the San (bushmen) by the Koranna (a Griqua band who lived by raid and conquest) in the late 18th century, and in the early 1800s became the site of the first mission to penetrate the region, under John Campbell of the London Missionary Society. It was taken over, around 1816, by the energetic and influential missionary Robert Moffat (*see* p.292), whose daughter later married the legendary David Livingstone (who also spent some time preaching here before heading north).

In a park on the Main Road in Kuruman, water gushes up from the ground through a crack in a tall rock known as the **Eye of Kuruman** into a deep, clear pool in which live large shoals of freshwater fish. Over 20 million litres of water pour out every day.

The **Kuruman Moffat Mission** was begun just after the Napoleonic Wars and completed around 1840. For a long time there was no larger building in the Northern Cape. Moffat, the missionary in charge, designed it to seat 800, even though he only had 8 converts from the local Tswana and Khoi. However, after his daughter married David Livingstone (in the Mission church), the Mission's status was assured. Moffat retired in 1870, just before the Kimberley diamond boom caused Kuruman to lose its importance in the area and slip into its present-day regional obscurity. Today the mission is a national monument, and occasional services are still held there. Interestingly Kuruman has recently become of interest to other heavenly seekers—though these are **paragliders**, rather than missionaries. The warm, still air around the Kuruman district creates thermals that allow for unusually high flying. Records are regularly set here, both for height and distance (*see* 'Activities', p.303).

In the hills 84km south of Kuruman are a set of caves known as the **Wonderwerk Grotte**. Some of South Africa's best-preserved bushman art is etched on to the rock wall of the main cave (though some has been desecrated with graffiti). Beautifully detailed animals and hunting scenes are scattered across the stone. The cave can be viewed by permission of the farmer at Wonderwerk Farm, signposted from the R31.

Just outside **Danielskuil**, a tiny dorp 60km further south, is a dolomite sinkhole into which the local Griqua raiders reputedly cast their prisoners. Snake-ridden and waterless, the thought sends a shiver through anyone standing at the lip. So far, no one has excavated the hole for human remains, and the legend remains unconfirmed. Danielskuil also has a ruined British fort on a hill overlooking the town, built during the Anglo-Boer War.

However, it is north of Kuruman that most people head, to the vast Kalahari Gemsbok National Park. The road there, the R31, leads for 61 lonely kilometres through dry country, the distant, jagged outline of the uninhabited Korannaberg Mountains (named after the Koranna people) forming the western horizon. At the tiny, excellently named mining town of Hotazel (meaning exactly what it sounds like), the R31 becomes a sandy dirt road, which leads to the tiny town of **Vanzylsrus**. Drive carefully, as cars can spin very easily on this section of road.

At Vanzylsrus, the character of the landscape changes from thorn scrub to a gracious natural parkland of giant camel-thorn trees, which continues all the way to the Kalahari Gemsbok National Park. Vanzylsrus is a good place to stop the night before travelling the next 200-odd kilometres on bad dirt roads to the turn-off for the park. It has an old hotel, a camp site under the trees, a post office and precious little else. Despite the amount of travellers who pass through on their way to the park, Vanzylsrus has never grown beyond its few buildings. After a long, dusty drive, a cool drink on the hotel verandah is recommended, watching the sun set over the tall camel-thorn trees.

Accessible from both Hotazel and Vanzylsrus is a new private game reserve: **Tswalu**. In the early 1990s a self-made English multi-millionaire called Stephen Boler bought up a staggering 300,000 acres of arid, overgrazed farmland in the Kalahari region and put it back under game. The result is the third-largest stretch of conserved land in South Africa—after the Kruger and Kalahari Gemsbok National Parks.

Tswalu runs a breeding programme for endangered species, including roan and sable antelope and black rhino. You can also see lions here. However, owing to the size of the reserve and the harshness of the country, visitors should not expect to see concentrations of game, but treat Tswalu as a true wilderness experience. As a side note, British visitors might find it interesting to know that Stephen Boler's money was made through the Kwik-Fit car exhaust and Kitchens Direct chains. Anyone who has ever spent money on either product can get a kick out of knowing where the profits have gone.

Tswalu operates low-density tourism, with some controlled hunting, as well as game-rearing for profit. If you're interested in staying there, ring the office, ✆ (0537) 819 211, or Kuruman Publicity, ✆ (05373) 21 095.

The R31 from Vanzylsrus to the turn-off for the national park at Andriesvale should be driven in daylight only. Varying in condition from deep sand to bald corrugations, this is a dangerous road. Make sure you have a full tank—the deep sections make the car use more fuel than usual, and the first petrol station is not until the tiny settlement of Askham, just 20km from the turn-off.

From here there are another 61km of dirt road, with occasional dangerous bends, before the camp entrance. The parkland gives way to the dry river bed of the Nossob, which runs parallel with the road. The first red sand dunes appear, some of them with little tin-shack farms owned by Nama people (the only Khoi group that managed to retain some land in South Africa, though most now live in Namibia) standing hot and bright against the sand. These farms are a far cry from the rich alluvial domains along the Orange River. The Kalahari's Nama farmers scratch a living from the sand and dry grasses, keeping cattle, sheep and goats. Few have motor transport.

The **Kalahari Gemsbok National Park** is entered at Twee Rivieren, where there is a rest camp (beautifully built from local stone and thatch), restaurant, shop (which does not sell camera film) and camp site. The two other camps, at Nossob on the Botswana border, and Mata Mata on the Namibian border, are both about 120km north of Twee Rivieren. Bear in mind that it takes around 3–4 hours' driving to reach them.

The Kalahari Gemsbok park is enormous, and adjoins an even larger protected area in Botswana. Game is plentiful, despite the lack of ground water. Huge herds of springbok, blue wildebeest, and gemsbok predominate. Eland and red hartebeest also occur. Lion, cheetah and spotted hyena are common, and the visitor can expect to see them from the park's three roads even in broad daylight. By night, leopard, brown hyena, jackal and bat-eared fox wander the veld.

One drawback of the park is that there are no walking trails and you are confined to your vehicle. But the rich, golden landscape, interspersed with red dunes and camel-thorn park-land, and the density of game and bird life (kori bustards, secretary birds and bataleur eagles are common) make it all worthwhile. The park has very little rainfall, and herbivores derive most of their moisture from succulent plants and desert fruits, such as the Kalahari melon, which grow on the veld floor, while predators get their water from the bodies of their prey. However, the park authorities have recently installed water troughs and pumps as well, and these make good points for photographing large concentrations of game.

Look out for the huge, unmistakable nests of the sociable weaver birds, colonies of up to 200 of which build communal nests the size of small houses in the camel-thorn tree tops. Avoid the park in summer, when the temperatures usually exceed 40°C. In winter, take a good sleeping bag, as the night time temperature often falls below freezing.

For all its wild beauty, the park has a dark side. When it was declared, back in the 1930s, it was designed to protect the **Xhomani Bushmen**, the last group still living traditionally in South Africa at that time. However, when apartheid reached its height in the early 1970s the government decided that, as non-whites, the Xhomani could no longer occupy a white-use area (as the national parks were then defined).

So they were moved out, to squat in the dunes by the side of the road and make their living as best they could.

Today, there is a possibility that this may change—the Xhomani have a human rights lawyer working on a land claim that would restore to them a large area of dune veld adjacent to the park, as well as the right to hunt, gather and lead tourists into the park. South Africa's land minister, Derek Hanekom, has pledged to carry the claim through, and even Nelson Mandela demonstrated support for the Xhomani—inviting Dawid Kruiper, the leader, to have tea with him.

There is a problem, however. The local farmers of the Mier Community—hardbitten, fiercely independent 'Coloureds'—do not want to give up land to the Bushmen. Many of the Mier do not have title to their landholdings, which are leased from the government, and they do not trust that they will be sufficiently compensated. The Mier are not fat-cats, many of them farm at subsistence level only, so their cause is of equal concern to that of the Bushmen. One can only hope that a settlement will be reached in the coming years.

In the meantime stop at the small Bushman huts you will see on the road into the park and buy a few crafts—it's all the income they get. If you want to organize a visit to their main village over the dunes, contact Andrew Hockley (see 'Activities'), an Upington-based operator trusted by Dawid Kruiper and the other Xhomani.

The only way out of the park is the way you came in, via the R31. At the junction with the R360 at Andriesvale you can either head south to Upington, east to Vanzylsrus and Kuruman or west into Namibia via the border post at Rietfontein (70km).

The route to Namibia is a spectacular and lonely journey. Again, make sure you have a full tank (fill up at Askam, Twee Rivieren or Rietvlei) before penetrating into Namibia as there is no petrol station until Aroab, 40km on the other side. The R31 leads abruptly out of the camel-thorn country into a wide salt pan that stretches off to cliff-edges on the horizon that glow with an almost electric red, like the rings on a stove seen through haze.

Rietfontein, when you finally reach it, is one of the most desolate of all South African towns: a string of shacks with a trading store and petrol station in a wide, blasted emptiness of dry veld. To the west are distant mountains and eroded hills with exposed rocky spines like the fossilized vertebrae of dinosaurs. Into that western Namibian landscape the road stretches like a ribbon to the horizon for 200km, until the town of Keetmanshoop.

Activities

Hiking: In West Griqualand, day trails can be found at **Vaalbos National Park**, **Canteen Kopjie Reserve**, **Klaarwater Reserve** near Griquatown, and on the private guest farms listed below.

Wild hiking at **Molopo Game Reserve** is allowed, but there are no marked trails, and hikers must carry a good water supply with them.

Around the Orange River day trails can be found at **Spitskop Nature Reserve**, **Tierberg Reserve**, and **Augrabies Falls National Park**, © (012) 343 1991. Hikers should look out for the brightly coloured Cape flat lizard, which often basks on the trail, waiting until the last moment before moving. Overnight huts with firewood, cooking pots and water are provided. There are also some shorter walks into the veld and along the gorge. The national park has chalets and a camp site.

In the Kalahari, **Kuruman Nature Reserve** has short walking trails in flat, rocky terrain among Karoo thorn bush with chances of viewing antelope.

Camel and horse safaris: Camel Runners, ✆ (011) 839 4105 or ✆ 830 0878, organize camel trips of 5 days, as well as horse and canoe trips, into the Orange River wilderness west of Augrabies.

Canoeing: A number of canoe companies offer 1–5-day trips on the river near Augrabies: **Rivers Unlimited,** ✆ (021) 790 4821, ✆ 762 7916; **Walkers Augrabies Canoe Trails,** ✆ (021) 788 1715 (who also offer rafting); **Augrabies Canoe Trails,** ✆ (054) 451 0177.

Paragliding: Two outfitters, based in Jo'burg, run courses for beginners and experienced alike from Kuruman—fast becoming one of the sport's prime sites in the world: **Fly Cross Country,** ✆ (011) 883 5017, or **Fly Africa,** ✆ (011) 434 918.

Bushman art: Very detailed rock etchings can be seen in the Wonderwerk Caves on Wonderwerk Farm.

General adventure packages: Egerton Game Ranch, ✆ (0531) 812 659, has 10km of river frontage, and offers rafting up to Grade IV, 4x4 routes, game viewing, hiking trails, horse trails, abseiling and climbing, fishing, mountain biking and a foefie slide. You need about 2–3 days here if you decide to visit.

Visiting with the Bushmen: To drop in at the Xhomani village of Welkom, near the Kalahari Gemsbok National Park, or to organize longer bush forays with these fascinating people, contact Andrew Hockley in Upington, ✆ (054) 451 0177.

Where to Stay

West Griqualand ✆ (0531–)

expensive

The **Halfway House Hotel** in Kimberley, ✆ 25 151, is a survivor of the Edwardian age. Its 12 en suite rooms are still decorated in Edwardian style, with much use of heavy reds and maroons for wallpaper and curtains. The bar has a strange quirk; a drive-in section where people can drink without getting out of their cars, a left-over from mining days when people could drink without getting out of the saddle.

moderate

De Beer's Gasthuis, 28 Pickering Ave, Kimberley, ✆ 612 192, is a colonial bungalow in the quiet suburb of Lindene, west of downtown. Meals are available by request, and the house is clean and friendly. Closer to the town centre are **Farwardene Lodge,** 18 Rhodes Avenue, ✆ 861 2482, and **Pembury Lodge,** 11 Currey St, ✆ 24 317, another Edwardian survivor, with 5 en suite bedrooms and B&B. Dinner by arrangement. Also in the suburbs (Belgravia) is **Elsmere Lodge,**

℗ 33 101. About 10 minutes outside town is **Marrick Guest Farm**, ℗ 861 1530, where you can choose between B&B and self-catering, and eat home-killed game.

cheap

Kimberley Youth Hostel, on Bloemfontein Rd, ℗ 28 577, has both dorms and private rooms, as well as a cheap restaurant serving good, simple food. Also try the **Gum Tree Lodge Backpackers**, ℗ 828 577.

Bushmanland: Orange River ℗ (054–)

expensive

The **Upington Oasis Protea Hotel**, ℗ 311 125, which fronts the river, lacks much atmosphere, but offers good service, good food and is a convenient place to break a journey west.

The **Waterwiel Protea**, ℗ (011) 431 0838, about 80km further on in the town of Kakamas, occupies a more tranquil setting. Also by the river, the hotel is near the village's old wooden water-wheel. Slightly more luxurious (and pricier) than the Upington Protea, the Waterwiel offers the usual efficient service and good food with mediocre decor verging on the quietly tasteless.

moderate

Yebo Guest Lodge, in Upington, ℗ 24 226, has comfy double rooms (self-catering, though), at the cheap end of the moderate price scale. Also recommended is **Le Must Manor**, ℗ 332 4015, a mock-Georgian affair in a lovely garden over-looking the river, decorated with early Cape furniture. There's a fantastic restaurant bearing the same name a short walk away at 11 Schroder Street.

Otherwise, try the **Travellers Inn Guest House**, ℗ 311 753, also in Upington, or the **Chateau Guesthouse**, ℗ 27 504.

About 40 minutes west of Upington, in the town of Kakamas, is a truly lovely place, the **Ebenaesar Guest House**, ℗ 431 1024, which has a private cottage in vine-yards on the bank of the Orange River.

Closer to the Kalahari Gemsbok National Park, **Molopo Lodge**, ℗ 902 and ask for Askham on 916 213, has just changed hands, and the owner is planning to run safaris with the Xhoman Bushmen, offering them a profit share.

The **Augrabies Falls National Park**, ℗ 451 0050, has a number of self-contained cottages and huts, which sleep 4, all at moderate prices. There is a shop and restaurant at the rest camp. The national park, with its spectacular falls, big game-viewing and wild landscape, is almost certainly the best place to stay in Bushmanland's Orange River region.

cheap

In Upington, the **Yebo Guest Lodge**, ℗ 24 226, also offers backpacker accommodation. Apart from this you either have to share a Parks Board cottage or chalet at Augrabies, or **camp**. All towns have a municipal site, as does Augrabies Falls National Park and the Kalahari Gemsbok National Park.

moderate

Vanzylsrus is the best place to break the journey between Kuruman and the Kalahari Gemsbok National Park.

In Kuruman, try the **Riverfield Guest House**, ✆ (05373) 30 003, in the town suburbs, or **Red Sands Country Lodge**, ✆ (05373) 30 269, a private game reserve outside town that offers riding out to see plains game. Also just outside is **Kamdebo B&B**, ✆ (05373) 21 450.

The **Vanzylsrus Hotel** is old and a bit run down. Few rooms have bathrooms. But it has a shabby charm, not having been altered much for the last 30 years, and a verandah to sit out on while the sun sets over the camel-thorn trees out front. Alternatively there are various guest farms in the vicinity, but as roads are bad, it is advisable to call first to check availability and road conditions.

Korannaberg Estate, ✆ (01475) 215, at the foot of the Koranna Mountains, is a game farm on a 19th-century farmstead, with opportunities for walking and game-viewing (plains game only). **Avontuur Guest Farm**, ✆ (01475) 416, and **Caledonia Guest Farm**, ✆ (01475) 442, are on the road to the national park.

Kalahari Gemsbok National Park, ✆ (054) 561 0021, has cottages and chalets at its 3 rest camps. All are self-catering, but there is a restaurant at Twee Rivieren camp at the park entrance, plus a shop and petrol pump.

cheap

The self-catering accommodation at **Gariep Lodge**, ✆ (054) 902 and ask for 91 982, comes into the cheap category, otherwise budget accommodation exists as **camping** at the municipal town sites, in the Kalahari Gemsbok National Park, or on farms (by permission).

Eating Out

expensive

The **Halfway House Hotel** in Kimberley, ✆ (0531) 31791, has an *à la carte* restaurant in the Edwardian dining room, which is informal but expensive. The speciality is spiced, aromatic Karoo mutton, with some French cuisine and game.

Tiffany's at the Savoy Hotel, Kimberley, ✆ (0531) 26211, is more pretentious, though not as tempting; French cuisine dishes alternate with meat and two veg on the menu. The restaurant also pipes irritating muzak at you. Otherwise try the **Diamond Protea Lodge**, ✆ (0531) 811281, who serve decent *à la carte*, with occasional game.

moderate

Kimberley has the usual South African chain restaurants (Spur, Mike's Kitchen, etc.) as does Upington. Most of the regular town hotels do food (toasted sandwiches, burgers etc.) at reasonable prices.

In Upington there are various chain eateries offering palatable fare. But in a class of its own is **Le Must**, 11 Schroder Street, which has an unusually good and varied menu for the Northern Cape.

The **Kalahari Gemsbok** and **Augrabies Falls** National Parks both have moderately priced restaurants at their rest camps that specialize in game culled from the parks themselves. Particularly good is gemsbok in a creamy pepper sauce. Game is culled all year, so there is no set season.

cheap

The region's towns have take-away joints serving sandwiches, burgers and salads.

The Eastern Cape

The land is beautiful, like a young girl

The Eastern Cape, Ciskei and Transkei comprise a borderland in every sense, a gradual transition between South Africa's temperate and sub-tropical climatic zones, between the arid Karoo plateau and the Drakensberg, between the predominantly 'coloured' west and the predominantly black east.

In few other parts of southern Africa can you find so many natural contrasts crammed into one region. Rich grasslands fall to the coast; dense thorn bush fills the game-rich river valleys; the Amatola Mountains, covered in majestic hardwood forest, rise just inland, giving way to the higher Winterberg, Bamboesberg, Stormberg, Witteberg and Drakensberg ranges in the north; dry vegetation reminiscent of the Karoo contrasts with areas so lush that they resemble Europe or the tropics rather than southern Africa; along the coast of Transkei, empty white sand beaches stretch for hundreds of kilometres; there is big game in the reserves.

The diverse terrain and sheer size of this mountainous territory make the Eastern Cape one of South Africa's most rewarding areas for walking, hiking and riding. The bush and mountain trails often take you to within a few yards of the plains game and sometimes even to larger animals such as rhino. Try to allow time to explore the Amatola Forests, the Cape Drakensberg to the north, and the Transkei Wild Coast.

Climate

As elsewhere in South Africa, the Eastern Cape's climate changes with altitude; the higher, the more temperate, the lower, the more humid. Summers are blindingly hot, but winter snowfalls on the higher ranges are common. Summer is the rainy season, winter the dry. Despite the region's lush vegetation and perennial rivers, localized drought strikes about once every five years, turning the surrounding country into a dust-bowl, and radically altering each landscape's appearance from year to year.

Fauna and Flora

Here, the fynbos heath of the Cape Floral Kingdom gives way to the thorn vegetation more typical of the rest of Africa. Thick, green acacia and euphorbia bush blankets the river valleys near the coast (if they have not been cleared for cattle). Prehistoric plants such as giant cycads and giant aloes grow on the hills. In the eastern reaches, wild banana mixed with hardwood forest gives the landscape a semi-tropical look.

South Africa's southernmost viable elephant population (as opposed to the few Knysna Forest elephants of the Garden Route, who are considered 'non-viable', or of insufficient number to ensure future survival) inhabits the dense thorn bush of Addo Elephant National Park, north of Port Elizabeth. Rhino, both black and white, are found in many reserves through the region, as are the larger plains game such as buffalo, kudu, eland, zebra, wildebeest, hartebeest, blesbok and impala. Leopard and occasional hyena make up the region's large predators, except at Shamwari Game Reserve, near Port Elizabeth, where lion have recently been re-introduced.

A regional oddity is the tree dassie of the coastal forests, similar in looks to the more common rock dassie, but known for its spine-chilling night-time scream.

Bird species include most of those found in the temperate southwestern Cape, plus some from the hotter east. The woods are alive with the chattering of wood hoopoes, or the growling boom of louries. Hornbills are a common sight, while large raptors thrive in the mountain ranges.

History

The Eastern Cape's 200-year colonial history has been one of continual war and struggle. Many of South Africa's black freedom fighters, including Steve Biko, Nelson Mandela and Walter Sisulu, were born in this troubled area, and the region's bitter past offers many clues to South Africa's turbulent recent history. The best telling of the tragic, complicated saga is in Noel Mostert's superb book *Frontiers* (Pimlico, 1991). However, for those without the time to read the 1300-odd-page book, the following will have to do.

Until the 18th century, the Eastern Cape was populated by Khoi in the west (around Port Elizabeth and the eastern Karoo), San (bushmen) in the mountains to the north, and several large clans of Xhosa people from east of Port Elizabeth to the eastern Transkei. Apart from a few shipwrecked sailors who had been succoured by the Transkei Xhosa in the 17th century, no white man had yet settled in the Eastern Cape. The region's Khoi were still freeholders of their own land west of the Fish River, and shared the grazing of the Zuurveld, the grassland area immediately west of the Fish, with seasonal Xhosa herders from across the river.

The Xhosa nation is known to have been riven by endless warring between the clans. All Xhosa owed nominal allegiance to the paramount **Gcaleka** clan in the Transkei, with the next most powerful being the **Rharabe**, east of the Fish River, and the **Gqunkwebe**, who seasonally pastured cattle west of the Fish. However, individual chiefs of sub-clans acted independently when it came to local politics, carefully shifting allegiance as each situation demanded. The many petty wars resulting from this were of a contained nature, involving neither mass butchery, nor the the killing of women and children, an ethic that continued through most of the later Frontier Wars, despite no such restraint on the colonists' part.

During the 1750s and '60s, large numbers of *trekboers*, intent on escaping the authority of the Dutch East India Company, began settling west of the Fish River, near modern Ciskei. For the next 20 years, they busily enslaved and dispossessed the Khoi, but treated the Xhosa (who outnumbered them) with a healthy respect. Some Boers, like the legendary Conraad de Buys (*see* p.273), even lived at the courts of Xhosa chiefs as client subjects and councillors.

By 1780 so many Boers had settled in the Eastern Cape that the Dutch East India Company feared it might lose control of its colony, and extended its frontier to the Fish River. But not until 1786 did it found a *landdrost* (magistracy) and garrison town from which to control the vast swathe of country. Even then the new administrative town, Graaff-Reinet, was in reality unable to govern the *trekboers*, being built in the eastern Karoo, about 300km from the Fish River, too far from the frontier to contain its settlement. A land conflict between the growing numbers of *trekboers* and the Xhosa was inevitable.

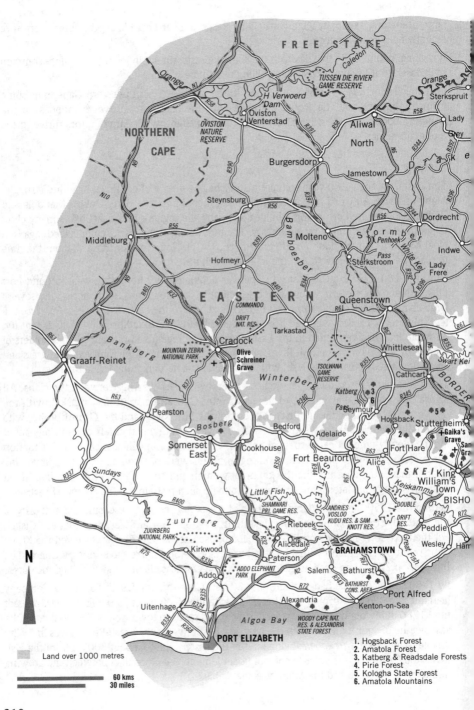

1. Hogsback Forest
2. Amatola Forest
3. Katberg & Readsdale Forests
4. Pirie Forest
5. Kologha State Forest
6. Amatola Mountains

Land over 1000 metres

60 kms
30 miles

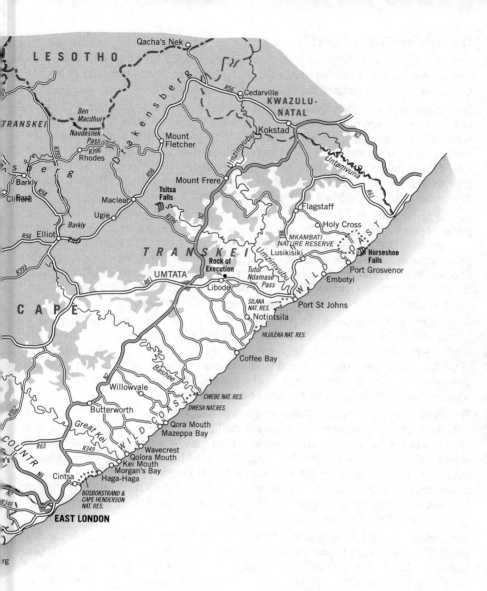

The Frontier Wars (1780–1878)

Confused, unjust, and sharpened by race-hatred, the Eastern Cape's nine Frontier Wars between Boer, Briton, Xhosa and Khoi lasted almost 100 years, destroyed the Cape's last free Khoi tribes and brought tragedy and humiliation to the Xhosa.

The earliest wars were fought over the good grazing country of the Zuurveld, west of the Fish River near modern Port Elizabeth. In 1781 the Dutch East India Company ordered several Xhosa clans in the Zuurveld to move east of the Fish River. More numerous than the settlers, the clans ignored the order. With cynical expedience, the Zuurveld Boers formed their own *Kommando*, invited the Xhosa chiefs to parley, and opened fire on them unexpectedly. From there it was a simple matter to fall on the unsuspecting villagers and drive them west of the Fish. Such was the **First Frontier War**.

But the Xhosa nation was expanding, and the number of settlers growing, and it was only a matter of time before conflict came again. In 1789 the large Gqunkwebe clan migrated into the Zuurveld. Outnumbered, the Zuurveld Boers pragmatically allied with the Rharabe Xhosa (who, under their chief, Ndlambe, were old rivals of the Gqunkwebe), and opened the **Second Frontier War** late in 1789. But after some initial victories, civil war broke out in the Rharabe's home country east of the Fish and the warriors left to go and fight at home. The Boers lost their allies and the Gqunkwebe, now hostile, stayed put.

Disgruntled, the frontier Boers turned on the Dutch East India Company, whom they saw as unable or unwilling to keep the Xhosa at bay. In 1795 they abandoned the Zuurveld and rebelled—first against the Dutch, and then against the British (1799) after their annexation of the Cape. Both rebellions failed, and the second was put down by the British with Khoi cavalry raised near Cape Town, making the frontier Boers fearful that their own Khoi servants, having seen a Boer defeat, would be inspired to revolt.

This fear was confirmed late in 1799 when the British sent an army to clear the Gqunkwebe from the Zuurveld. As soon as the redcoats arrived, Khoi farmhands from all over the Eastern Cape abandoned their cruel masters to join the British army, which happily absorbed them as guides and sharpshooters. The joint force began the **Third Frontier War** in 1799, and soon forced the Gqunkwebe east of the Fish. But the British then returned to the Cape, unwittingly abandoning their Khoi allies to certain Boer retaliation for having left the farms. The Khoi had little choice but to throw in their lot with the Gqunkwebe, and in 1800 the two forces re-invaded the Zuurveld.

In the middle of this confusion, Britain handed the Cape Colony back to Holland. The new Dutch Governor, seeking a quick end to the tiresome wars, granted the Khoi rebels land near present-day Port Elizabeth, founded Uitenhage, a new military town, at the western edge of the Zuurveld, and with this assurance of military protection, persuaded the Boers to resettle the Zuurveld and share it with the Gqunkwebe, who were also sick of war.

However, the Rharabe's civil war east of the Fish had caused the clan to split in two—the Ndlambe (under the chief of that name), and the Ngqika, under Ndlambe's nephew. In 1809, following a drought, the 20,000 strong Ndlambe clan crossed the Fish in search of new pasture, and spread across the entire settled region. With such a large Xhosa presence, the raiding of settler herds was inevitable. Boers began abandoning their farms again, calling on Britain (who had re-annexed the Cape in 1806) to eject the Xhosa by force.

The British took three years to respond, but finally did so with alarming ferocity. In 1812, Colonel John Graham's large army, supplemented with Khoi and Boer auxiliaries, began the **Fourth Frontier War**. The idea was to push the Ndlambe east as quickly as possible, and the army killed indiscriminately, massacring uncounted Xhosa women and children, and enlarging the military post, Grahamstown (built three years before), in the Fish River Valley. The Ndlambe, deeply shocked, were driven east inside a year, and the brutal war established a kind of peace, despite a short-lived Boer rebellion over being forced to pay their Khoi workers a minimum wage (*see* Slagter's Nek, p.332). Over the next few years, Xhosa and Boer still crossed the Fish to raid cattle, but there were no open hostilities.

It was the British, so confident of their ability to govern, who were to destroy the hard-won peace. In 1814 they sent a dangerously autocratic new governor, Lord Charles Somerset, to the Cape Colony. Determined to make his mark by bringing proper law and order to the frontier, Somerset launched an ill-advised scheme to stop Xhosa cattle-raiding, creating a system of cavalry patrols who were to track stolen cattle east of the Fish and demand restitution from the first Xhosa village they came to, regardless of its innocence or guilt. He then sought out the most powerful of the frontier chiefs—Ngqika—and, overestimating the extent of the chief's authority, ordered him to take responsibility for all Xhosa cattle raids. Ngqika had no control over the other clans, but was intimidated into accepting.

Somerset's raiding patrols could not fail to provoke trouble, and in 1818, the **Fifth Frontier War** erupted when the Ndlambe clan, who had lost thousands of cattle to the patrols in just four years, lost patience and (unsuccessfully) attacked Grahamstown with 6000 warriors. This gave Somerset an excuse to meddle even further. As part of a grand experiment to 'whiten' the frontier, he confiscated a large tract of prime grazing land *east* of the Fish from Chief Ngqika as 'punishment' for not having prevented the invasion, even though Ngqika had had no control over it. Somerset christened the area Albany and brought out 5000 English colonists to populate it. But the 1820 Settlers, as these new colonists became known, proved unfit for frontier life. Youths from Ngqika's clan raided the settlers' herds. This, combined with the harsh climate and wild animals, forced most to abandon their farms and drift to Grahamstown and Port Elizabeth. By 1825 most of Albany lay empty, but the Ngqika were still denied grazing rights to the territory.

Somerset seems to have wanted war; in 1829, he provoked Ngqika again, this time by expelling Maqoma, Ngqika's warlike brother, from land near the Kat River, also east of the Fish, to make way for a self-governing Khoi settlement. The Khoi were proven bush fighters and, by settling them on the frontier, Somerset thought to redress the failure of his Albany colony, and secure the frontier against invasion. But it could never work on land stolen from the Xhosa. In 1834 Maqoma declared the **Sixth Frontier War**, stating that he would fight only until the confiscated lands had been returned. Taking refuge in the high forest of the Amatola Mountains, Maqoma successfully kept the new British general, the firebrand Sir Harry Smith, at bay. Frustrated, Smith took his soldiers far to the east across the Kei River into Gcaleka territory, where no whites had yet settled. Without any orders from Cape Town, he captured Hintsa, paramount chief of all the Xhosa, thinking to hold him hostage until the Ngqika surrendered. But the plan went wrong and Hintsa was shot while trying to escape. Smith then illegally claimed part of the Gcaleka territory as British, setting up military bases at King William's Town and East London.

For the Xhosa, the murder of Hintsa was an act of outrage greater even than John Graham's killing of women and children. In even the smallest clan, a chief and his property were inviolate. By murdering the Xhosa's paramount chief, Smith (and by extension the British) had irreparably insulted the whole Xhosa nation. Britain had unwittingly committed herself to a war to the death. Meanwhile, the Amatola campaign degenerated into exhausted stalemate and Maqoma, prepared to bide his time, offered peace, but without surrender. The war was emptying the treasury so the British government forced Smith to accept, and appointed a man called Stockenstroom (an ex-*landdrost* of Graaff-Reinet) to draw up the treaty. Somerset and Smith were both recalled to England, and Stockenstroom, a rare Boer humanitarian, put a long-overdue end to Somerset's provocative cattle patrols. In the teeth of opposition from the Grahamstown settlers, who wanted a full and final crushing of the Xhosa, he then restored to the Gcaleka the land around King William's Town and East London. But to Stockenstroom's immense frustration, Britain retained part of the land that Smith had stolen and stirred further resentment by offering it to the Mfengu people, refugees from Zulu raids (*see* **Natal**, 'History'), who had been succoured by the Gcaleka in Transkei, but treated as subordinates. The Mfengu jumped at the chance of having their own country under British protection, and swore to fight in any subsequent wars against the Xhosa.

Through the 1830s, Stockenstroom's live-and-let-live policy enraged the frontier whites; many Boers abandoned the Eastern Cape to join the Great Trek in 1836 and the British settlers called continuously for his resignation. But he kept the peace until 1842, when yet another bad drought re-started the cycle of Xhosa cattle raids. Tension mounted. In 1844, the **Seventh Frontier War** (known as the War of the Axe) broke out between Maqoma, Sandile (Ngqika's son) and the British, after one of Sandile's subjects was imprisoned for stealing a cheap hatchet from a shop in the new garrison town of Fort Beaufort. Some friends broke him out of jail and when the British demanded his return, Sandile refused. A British column sent into the Amatolas to find Sandile was attacked, and his clan, backed by thousands of Gcaleka warriors, invaded the Cape Colony, raiding and burning as far as Port Elizabeth. The insult to Hintsa had not been forgotten.

The advance was only checked when a cavalry regiment chanced on 500 Ngqika warriors near Peddie and cut them down. The Gcaleka retaliated by burning the grass around the British columns, starving their oxen and horses. Pressing their advantage, Maqoma and Sandile offered peace if their confiscated lands (Kat River and Albany) were returned. But Cape Town and Britain could not allow such a reversal. Harry Smith, who had been distinguishing himself in India against the Sikhs, was recalled to the Cape, this time as Governor, and told to bring the Xhosa to heel.

Smith promptly re-occupied the land around King William's Town, called in the local chiefs, forced them to kneel to him, and humiliated them in front of their people. He supported the Grahamstown settlers' view that the Khoi's Kat River settlement was too good for non-whites, and, in 1850, sent troops to evict hundreds of people accused of being squatters. But Smith went too far and deposed Sandile from the Ngqika chieftaincy. Late in 1850 a military column crossing the Amatolas was cut to pieces by Sandile's warriors, who poured into the colony once more. Smith, besieged in King William's Town, ordered the Kat River Khoi to mobilize, despite his recent persecution of them. Disgusted, the Khoi levies promptly took the field with the Xhosa, who rose en masse, with all but two of the clans joining the war.

This, the **Eighth Frontier War**, lasted three years, claimed far more lives (British, Xhosa and Khoi) than any before, and the expense cost Smith his military career. But by 1852 the Xhosa had lost all their territory except the Transkei, and the Kat River Khoi were evicted and forced to seek work with the contemptuous whites who now occupied the settlement. Maqoma was captured and sent to Robben Island, where he died. The insults to the Xhosa chiefs were unavenged and the best of the land had been lost. Contemporary accounts talk of a despair coming over the nation.

Many historians link this catastrophic defeat with the Xhosa's great, irrational, national near-suicide four years later, when a millenarian prophetess of the Gcaleka people in Transkei declared that if all Xhosa clans destroyed their cattle and crops, their ancestors would rise and sweep the British into the sea. Tragically, Sarili, son of the murdered Hintsa and paramount chief of the Xhosa, became a convert and ordered this done. A few clans held on to their stock, but tens of thousands starved (*see* 'Transkei History').

In a single year the Xhosa had lost their independence. Transkei was opened up to settlement and most of the chiefs (except for Sandile and Sarili, who fled), imprisoned. Yet this was not quite the end. Over the next 20 years the Xhosa population gradually recovered. Sandile and a few other chiefs were 'forgiven' and appointed magistrates, and put on the British payroll. But there was to be one last campaign. In 1877 Sandile and some Gcaleka chiefs attended a Mfengu wedding. The Mfengu had fought for the British in the last three wars and were now hated by the Xhosa. There was a brawl, and some Mfengu were killed. The government, bound by treaty to protect the Mfengu, sent troops to arrest Sandile, who took his followers back to the Amatolas (in the Pirie Forest, near King William's Town), where he fought until he was killed in 1878, ending the **Ninth** and last **Frontier War**.

Recent History

Throughout the Frontier War period, English, German and American missionaries had been active among the Xhosa clans. Although late 19th-century prejudices had made most of these mission stations priggish affairs, their schools gave the Xhosa a peaceful means of resisting white oppression. The last decades of the 19th century saw many alumni of these mission schools go on to universities abroad, and several Xhosa (such as the future politician Alan Soga) later graduated from Edinburgh, entering the professional world on their return. John Jabavu became a journalist, and in 1884 published a newspaper called *Imvo Zabantsudu* ('Native Opinion') from King William's Town. The journal became a forum for black political thought and, after Jabavu's death, it continued under his son, Davidson, until the 1930s. In 1908, Jabavu and his circle fought successfully for a black franchise in the Cape, and, in 1916, formed a black college near Alice in the former Ciskei, later to become the University of Fort Hare, whose subsequent graduates include Robert Sobukwe, founder of the PAC, and Nelson Mandela. Despite his political influence, Jabavu was not in favour of blacks forming their own political parties, and was opposed by Alan Soga who published another newspaper, *Izwi Labantu* ('The People's Voice'), to espouse the cause of active black power. Soga and his supporters had formed the South African Native National Congress in 1898, and this gradually gathered support, eventually becoming the African National Congress in 1923.

Military action against blacks in the Eastern Cape had not abated by the early 20th century. For example, in 1920, police fired on blacks gathering to organize better wages in Port Elizabeth, killing about 25 people. In 1921, members of a black Christian cult called the

Israelites gathered at Bulhoek, near Queenstown, apparently to await the end of the world. About 800 police were sent to move them, and in an ensuing skirmish killed almost 200 of the unfortunate Israelites.

However, the ANC and other black political groups from the Eastern Cape moved into the national political arena during the 1930s and '40s—especially in the Transvaal, where increasing numbers of Xhosa (and other nations) now worked on the mines. Following the arrival of apartheid in 1948, black political groups began to organize direct action, but in the 1960s and '70s, following the famous Rivonia Trial (*see* **Gauteng**, 'History'), most were forced underground. During this time large chunks of the region were designated tribal 'homelands' (Ciskei and Transkei), and it was these parts of Eastern Cape that produced most of the freedom fighters: many political commentators claim that, while the ANC and PAC have never been specifically Xhosa organizations, the core of their leadership and support has always been found in the Eastern Cape. The early 1990s saw sporadic strife, with faction fighting between the ANC and PAC, and attacks on whites, threatening always to upset the balance so painstakingly sought by South Africa's main political leaders, and it remains to be seen whether the new government can settle the conflicts which have shaped the province's bitter history. However, since April 1994 the region, like much of South Africa, has been remarkably quiet, and a long-awaited peace seems to have settled on the beautiful, troubled, Eastern Cape.

Port Elizabeth

Port Elizabeth marks the coastal transition point between the Garden Route and the Eastern Cape. The third largest port in South Africa, Port Elizabeth is, it must be said, one of the country's least attractive towns. Except for a small collection of period buildings in the very centre of town, car assembly plants, freeways and ugly concrete buildings predominate. You should spend as little time here as possible.

However, the country around Port Elizabeth is beautiful indeed, with a sub-tropical, forested coastline and a hinterland of game reserves harbouring big game. Port Elizabeth is therefore convenient as a jumping-off point for the area around it, and you may find yourself having to spend a day or two in the city en route.

History

Port Elizabeth was founded in 1820, on the site of the British Fort Frederick (1799), just south of the Dutch military town of Uitenhage, to receive the 5000 English settlers sent out to populate the country between Algoa Bay and the Fish River (then known as the Zuurveld), from which several Xhosa clans had been forcibly evicted (*see* 'Frontier Wars'). This was Britain's first serious attempt to regularize the Eastern Frontier, after inheriting an endless cycle of Boer, Xhosa, Khoi and English settler raiding that the Dutch had found insoluble. Port Elizabeth was named by Sir Rufane Donkin (the acting Cape Governor sent to welcome the 1820 settlers), after his wife, who had died in India.

The town remained a small village and military post for some years, until the failure of many British settlers to make a living from the fickle Eastern Cape *veld* forced them to abandon their plots and come into the settlement for work. Like Grahamstown further east, Port

Elizabeth soon began to thrive on the commercial opportunities opened up by the escalating warfare between the British and the Xhosa. Increasing numbers of troops passing to and from the Cape and the frontier gradually augmented trade, and the town became rich. By the 1850s, grand public buildings were being erected. Few Boers lived in this British imperial atmosphere, but one, the famous Piet Retief, leader of the 1836 Great Trek from Eastern Cape to Natal, lived here during the 1820s.

Port Elizabeth began its transition to a major port city in the late 19th century, when farming in the frontier region became sufficiently established to create a regular supply of meat, maize and wool for export to Cape Town and beyond. In particular, Angora wool (still a mainstay of the eastern Karoo farmers, both black and white) helped establish the town's fortune. In 1920 Port Elizabeth entered big-time commerce when Ford Motors opened a plant there. The city grew quickly, attracting more factories and a massive population drift of Xhosa labourers from the Ciskei and Transkei. Today's population is around 800,000.

Port Elizabeth saw much political unrest through the 1980s, causing many commercial companies to leave the city. This, coupled with South Africa's recent recession, has caused a downturn of the city's fortunes, and unemployment is rife. But for all that, the city centre is generally safe to wander by day and is well policed by night.

Port Elizabeth ✆ (041–) **Getting There and Around**

by bus

Buses to and from Port Elizabeth Airport (about 4km from the city centre) every half hour *c.* 6am–10pm. Call the **Supercab Shuttle**, ✆ 523 720, for details.

Port Elizabeth is on the N2 highway linking the Garden Route with the Eastern Cape, Transkei and Natal. Buses follow this route from Cape Town, Durban, Grahamstown, Umtata and East London, stopping at all large towns in between. The **bus station**, ✆ 558 751, is below Main Street between Donkin Road and Whites Road, just east of the Market Square. The big bus companies operate to and from other major cities: **TransLux**, ✆, 507 3333, **InterCape**, ✆ 560 055, and **Greyhound**, ✆ 564 879. More local companies are: **Whippet Express** (Port Elizabeth–Graaff-Reinet), **Copper Rose** (Port Elizabeth–East London), **Leopard Express** (Port Elizabeth–Grahamstown). Two tour companies make excursions out to the game reserves of the Port Elizabeth hinterland—**Springbok Atlas**, ✆ 351 038, and **Algoa Tours**, ✆ 558 751.

Port Elizabeth is also on the Baz Bus Route (*see* **Travel**, p.9), which runs door-to-door between the backpackers' of Cape Town, the Garden Route, KwaZulu-Natal, Swaziland, Mpumalanga and Gauteng. The **Hopper**, ✆ 554 000, is another backpacker service linking Port Elizabeth with Mossel Bay, then a shuttle to Cape Town.

Port Elizabeth's compact city centre and old town can be crossed in about 15 minutes. Buses for the beaches and suburbs leave roughly every half hour until about 10pm from platform 5 of the bus station.

by car

Apart from the main east–west route along the N2, Port Elizabeth is connected to the north via the R75 along the Sundays River to Graaff-Reinet, or the R32 via

Cradock and Middelburg to the Free State and Transvaal (the N2/R32 junction is 70km east of town). More interesting ways to enter the Eastern Cape are via the R75 and R329 along the dry north wall of the Baviaanskloof Mountains, via the R332 through the wild, lonely Baviaanskloof itself, or via the R62 through the fruit-growing Langkloof behind the Garden Route.

Car hire: Apart from the large chain car rental agencies, Port Elizabeth lacks really cheap car hire. However, **Dolphin Car Rentals,** ✆ 513 8878, offers slightly cheaper rates than the mainstream companies. Also try **Economic Car Hire,** ✆ 515 826, and **Key Car Rental,** ✆ 514 455. Otherwise, it's **Avis,** ✆ 511 3306.

by rail

Port Elizabeth is connected with all major centres via the **Rovos** railway, ✆ (021) 214 020, and **Spoornet,** ✆ 507 2400, as are the larger towns in the region. Steam enthusiasts will delight in two narrow-gauge steam lines that leave from the main station. One chuffs along the Langkloof; the other goes east for a short distance along the coast (*see* 'Activities').

by taxi

For getting around Port Elizabeth safely at night, ring **Unicab,** ✆ 553 0030, **Hunters,** ✆ 557 344, or **City Taxi,** ✆ 342 212. There are no taxi ranks.

Port Elizabeth ✆ *(041–)*   **Tourist Information**

Publicity Association: Donkin Park, between Belmont Street and Western Street, ✆ 585 8884.

Main Post Office: 259 Main Street. *Open Mon–Fri 8–4.30, Sat 8.30–12.30.*

Emergency Numbers: Ambulance, ✆ 10 177; Police, ✆ 10 111; Provincial Hospital, ✆ 392 3911; St George's Hospital, ✆ 392 6111.

Old Port Elizabeth

Fort Frederick (*open Mon–Fri 8–5*), the original fort at the mouth of the Baakens River, where the 1820 Settlers had their tented camp, is on modern Port Elizabeth's Belmont Terrace. A large, square, stone fortification, it was one of the few British forts in the Eastern Cape never to be attacked. The **Campanile** (*open Mon–Fri 9.30–5, Sat 9.30–12.30*) is next to the fort at the entrance to the docks on Strand Street. Built in the 1920s as a monument to the 1820 Settlers, it has a very long spiral stair leading to a high platform with good views of the city and bay.

The **City Hall** and **Market Square** form the most handsome part of town, a collection of solid mid-Victorian buildings all recently done up and cleaned. An **Open Air Market** operates on the square every day. **Fleming Square,** a smaller square off the Market Square, has the **Prester John Monument**, a tribute to the mythical Christian African king and his land of gold that lured so many medieval adventurers south (*see* **History,** p.35). Various national monuments are still in use around the two squares, including the **Feather Market Hall** (1885), a large stone building originally used for auctioning luxury goods, such as ostrich feathers and game skins, and now a concert hall. The **Opera House** on Whites Road (just uphill from Market Square) is still an opera house today.

Uphill, behind Market Square, is **Donkin Park,** an open area designated as 'a perpetual open space' by Acting Cape Governor Donkin in 1820. **Donkin Street,** which leads from the town centre to the park, has a well-preserved terrace of handsome colonial houses built between 1860 and 1870. Behind Donkin Park are a few blocks of period houses, and then the modern, ugly city takes over again.

The Sea Front

Port Elizabeth is known for high winds. Consequently, its beaches and coast, while popular with windsurfers, yachtsmen and the like, can be uncomfortably blowy. There are four main beaches (*see* 'Activities'), but in general the seafront is better visited for its **Museum Complex,** by Humewood Beach.

The **Port Elizabeth Museum** (*open Mon–Sat 9–1 and 2–3*) presents a history of the town and the 1820 Settlers, and has a maritime hall dedicated to shipwrecks and their treasure. Fossil bones and Early Man tools found in the Eastern Cape are also on display, along with the usual natural history and Victoriana.

The **Oceanarium** (*open Mon–Sat 8–4.30; dolphin shows between 9 and 1*), next to the museum building, is part of the same complex, but requires a separate ticket. Trained dolphins, seals and penguins are the main attraction, but there are also sharks, turtles and most local sea fish in the aquarium. The **Snake Park and Tropical House** (*open Mon–Sat 8–4.30*) also require a separate ticket. The Snake Park has the usual spine-shivering poisonous snake-handling shows. Also on view are crocodiles, giant tortoises and other reptiles. The Tropical House connects the main museum with the Snake Park; brightly coloured tropical birds flit amongst the luxurious plants.

Happy Valley, along the beach front road between the town centre and the Museum Complex (by Humewood Beach), is a strange piece of high kitsch, and worth visiting, especially in the evening. This pleasure garden (signposted from the road) was designed in the 1950s as a kind of suburban family theme park. The lawns are divided by footpaths, ponds, a river and a giant, open-air chessboard. At night it's illuminated with fairy lights. Oddly enough, Happy Valley does achieve a kind of plastic romance after dark which, despite oneself, it is hard not to enjoy.

Settler's Park, at the north end of town, is an area of fynbos heath, hardwood coastal forest, and grassland, that follows the Baakens River along a series of small cliffs. Bushbuck still thrive here, even though the park is bordered on all sides by the city; the quiet walker may well be rewarded with a sighting.

St George's Park is more formal, housing South Africa's first cricket club among its orchids, indigenous flowers and wide-spaced, mature trees. The **George VI Gallery** (*open Mon–Sat 8–4, Sun 11–2.30*) is housed in a building called the Cenotaph, inside the park. Its permanent collection of indifferent 19th- and early 20th-century English painting includes some good South African landscapes and some oriental miniatures. The monthly art market, **Art in the Park,** is held on the first Sunday of every month, ✆ 561 356/7. Apart from the usual arts and crafts, some very good township artists sometimes sell their work here.

The **Historical Museum,** 7 Castle Hill, parallel with and one block west of Whites Road (*open Mon–Fri 8–4*), is a Victorian house furnished in period. Nearby, at the junction of

Russell and Cape Streets, the **South African Horse Monument** is a rather touching statue of a trooper watering his horse. Erected in honour of the horses that died in the Anglo-Boer War, it's worth reflecting on the anonymous 19th-century poem:

> *Look back at our struggle for freedom*
> *Trace our present-day strength to its source*
> *And you find that man's pathway to glory*
> *Is strewn with the bones of a horse.*

Activities

Beaches: Port Elizabeth has four main beaches, just west of town along Marine Drive via the Museum Complex. The most developed and the safest for swimming, **King's Beach**, is also the closest to town, and offers mini-golf, fast-food outlets, water-slides and a miniature train. **Humewood Beach**, next along, is the most popular with swimmers. Its waves are good for body-surfing, and it's a little more sheltered than Port Elizabeth's other windy beaches. **Hobie Beach** is rougher and mainly used by surfers, windsurfers and Hobie-cat sailors. **Pollock Beach**, the furthest along, can be really rough and isn't much fun for swimming.

Watersports: Windsurfers, bodyboards and Hobie-cats can be hired (though the latter should only be handled by an expert) through the Publicity Association, or the **Boardsailing Association**, ✆ 554 3384. To arrange to go scuba diving, ring **Scubadventures SA**, ✆ 515 3328; for surfing, ring **Frontchaser Surfing Guides and Tours**, ✆ 375 9093.

Walking: Settler's Park, on Valley Road, has some lovely trails through natural woodland where bushbuck can often be spotted.

Steam railways: The **Apple Express**, ✆ (041) 507 2333, runs from Port Elizabeth along the Langkloof to the town of Loerie. It includes a spectacular chuff along the Van Stadens Gorge, views of the Winterberg Mountains and the gentle Loerie Valley.

The **Dias Express** is a much shorter ride, from the station to the Campanile and a small rail museum where you can watch the locomotives being maintained. The Dias Express must be reserved: call ✆ 520 2260.

Township tours: ring **Fundani Township Tours**, ✆ 631 4471, or **Gqebera Walmer Township Tours**, ✆ 512 5572.

Shopping

General crafts and jewellery, as well as some good township art, are sold at **Art in the Park**, held on the first Sunday of every month in St George's Park.

Port Elizabeth ✆ *(041–)*

Where to Stay

expensive

Port Elizabeth has the usual expensive chain hotels, but the clear choice within this price range is the independent **Edward Hotel**, on Belmont Terrace, ✆ 562 056. Within walking distance of the city centre, it is a charming survivor from the late 1920s, a combination of Art Deco, mock Tudor and mock Cape Dutch. It is large, with 126 rooms, mostly en suite, overlooking the ocean. There is also an inner courtyard, and the restaurant serves fresh seafood. The **Walmer Gardens Hotel**, ✆ 414 322, in the suburb of Walmer Gardens, 12km from the city centre, is also independent. Built in a 1930s hacienda style (South Africa has the climate for such buildings not to look out of place), there are 27 rooms, all en suite, with a courtyard and pool, and an outdoor grill. The restaurant also does good seafood, and some French dishes. The **Humewood Hotel**, 33 Beach Road, ✆ 558 961, a 1930s building, fronts the popular Humewood Beach. Its 64 rooms are all en suite. The Museum, Oceanarium and Snake Park are behind; the beach with its mini-golf and water-slides in front.

moderate

Langerry, 31 Beach Rd, ✆ 552 654, is next to the Humewood and has all the surrounding facilities at less expense. It is clean and comfortable. Self-catering only. In the town centre, **Trocadero Lodge**, 2 Parliament Street, ✆ 522 651, is a large guest house offering B&B or self-catering. It's not fancy, but it is comfortable. Also try **Caboose Sleepers**, ✆ 560 088/9, at the cheap end of moderate.

Pine Lodge, on Marine Drive, ✆ 534 004, has a choice of chalets, caravans or self-contained apartments. There are outside braai facilities and the beaches are within reach by bus. **Rema Apartments** are also in the city centre, at 45 Western Road, ✆ 521 772. These self-contained flatlets have their own bathrooms and fridges. B&B is optional.

If these places are full the following suburban B&Bs should yield some joy: **Bishop's Lodge**, ✆ 533 869; **Brighton Lodge**, ✆ 534 579; **City Lodge**, ✆ 563 322; **First Avenue Lodge**, ✆ 534 030; **The Lazy Leopard**, ✆ 513 616; **Lemon Tree Lane**, ✆ 334 103; **Park Place**, ✆ 555 062.

cheap

Port Elizabeth Backpackers, 7 Prospect Hill, ✆ 586 0697, near the centre of town, is a friendly, well-run place with dormitory accommodation. On the same street, at no.17, is **Protea Lodge**, ✆ 551 7212/4. Also good, and aimed at the budget market, are **Jikeleza Lodge**, 44 Cuyler Street, ✆ 586 3721, and **King's Beach Backpackers**, 41 Windermere Road, ✆ 585 8113, just behind the beach.

Port Elizabeth ✆ (041–)   **Eating Out**

expensive

Aviemore, 67 Parliament Street, ✆ 555 1125, is probably central Port Elizabeth's best restaurant, serving game and seafood cooked in the Cape style. **De Kelder**, on Marine Drive, Summerstrand, ✆ 532 750, offers similarly excellent fare.

moderate

Up the Khyber, on Western Road, ✆ 522 200, isn't run by the *Carry On* team, but serves good traditional Indian food. **Blackbeard's Seafood Tavern and Pier**, on Western Road, ✆ 555 567/341 424, serves fresh seafood amid the standard fishing-net and lobster-pot decor. The adjoining bar gives the place an informal feel.

Sebastian's, on Cape Road, ☎ 339 293, also serves great seafood. **Don Carlos**, 153 Russell Road, ☎ 555 2828, should not be missed. It's a tiny little Spanish place run by an old Catalonian couple. Bring your own wine. **Le Med**, 70 Parliament Street, ☎ 555 8711, is a pan-Mediterranean place, with everything from pasta to some Middle Eastern dishes. Lots of good seafood. Excellent calamari, and a fillet in garlic sauce are specialities of the **Coachman**, on Lawrence Street in the town centre, ☎ 522 511. **Zorba's**, also on Parliament Street, sounds like a standard Greek place, but it isn't. They do have Greek dishes, but also things that are purely southern African. Ask for the specials. **Nattie's**, Clyde Street, in the city centre, ☎ 554 301, is an excellent Thai place.

cheap

The Casbah Roadhouse, on Marine Drive, is a good, cheap diner. **The Stage Door**, on Chapel Street, offers good-value pub food. Good Chinese food can be had at the **Little Swallow**, in the Cape View Centre on Cape Road, just out of the town centre, ☎ 307 382. **Rio Hamburger Hut and Game Centre**, on Russell St, ☎ 522 440, is handy for the backpackers' hostel, and serves American and spicy Indian fast food, burgers and bunny-chows (curry served inside a hollowed loaf of bread). *Open till 2am.* Also try **The Blinking Owl**, 306 Cape Road, out in the suburb of Newtown Park, and **Rome Pizzeria**, 63 Campbell Street, in the centre of town.

Nightlife

The **Red Lion Hotel**, on the eastern end of Main Street, is a little rough, but often has local live acts, ranging from dull cover bands to some really good rock and township sounds. Live bands also play at the **Clarendon Hotel**, on Leutman Street. Check in *Splash Magazine* for listings.

Most backpackers drink at **Cadillac Jack's**, 7 The Boardwalk, on Marine Drive, Hobie Beach, in the suburb of Summerstrand, before going out to dance at **Lush**, 95 Parliament Street, in the city centre, ☎ 354 4675.

Around Port Elizabeth

The charm of the countryside and coastline near Port Elizabeth make up for the ugliness of the city. Here you can explore orchard country, coastal forest, thick thorn bush and montane forest and grassland, dotted with nature reserves and national parks preserving some of the larger fauna. The **Addo Elephant National Park**, ☎ (0426) 400 556, in the thorn bush country about 50km north of town on the R335, is home to Africa's southernmost viable wild elephant herd, along with buffalo and black rhino. In 1931, when the park was proclaimed, the local elephant were down to just 11, having been mercilessly shot out by the local fruit and potato farmers, whose activities the elephant naturally interfered with from time to time. Now protected, today's elephant population has recovered to over 100.

The Addo bush is dense and high, so game-viewing can be difficult. Elephant are usually at the water holes, and sometimes buffalo, but the rhino are shy and tend to stay out of sight. Other game includes kudu, eland, red hartebeest, and bushbuck, and the usual wide variety of bird life. In summer, look out for groups of white storks. There are hides near the office,

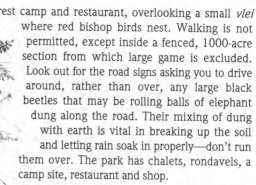

rest camp and restaurant, overlooking a small *vlei* where red bishop birds nest. Walking is not permitted, except inside a fenced, 1000-acre section from which large game is excluded. Look out for the road signs asking you to drive around, rather than over, any large black beetles that may be rolling balls of elephant dung along the road. Their mixing of dung with earth is vital in breaking up the soil and letting rain soak in properly—don't run them over. The park has chalets, rondavels, a camp site, restaurant and shop.

Zuurberg National Park, now amalgamated with the Addo Elephant National Park, is reached via the R335 dirt road, and spreads over the entire range of low, grass-covered mountains to the north of Addo. The park covers a vast area of steep, deeply wooded kloofs and high, rolling downs which provide cool relief from the baking hot plain below. Among a number of day-hikes are several leading to remote waterfalls. Horses can be rented by the hour and ridden wherever you like. The rare cycad, a prehistoric tree-fern, grows on the Zuurberg's higher reaches. Cape mountain zebra, kudu, baboon, grey rhebok, duiker, bushbuck, grysbok, caracal and leopard are to be found. The deep milkwood forest in the kloof is home to ticks, so, in summer, remember to check yourself every few hours. At present, Addo's big game cannot roam freely into the Zuurberg, but the Parks Board is constructing a game fence around the hills, so that in the near future the downs and forests will again be home to elephant, buffalo and rhino. The park has no accommodation.

Addo Village, the small settlement where most people stock up before going into the national parks, has an interesting shop called **Elsa's Little People**. Despite the twee name, it sells good African crafts, as well as exquisite small ceramic figures of Xhosa, Sotho, Venda, Tswana, Tsonga, and other South African people, in traditional dress, all hand-made by Elsa, the shop's owner.

Where to Stay and Eating Out

moderate–cheap

The old **Zuurberg Inn**, ✆ (042) 233 0583, a moderately priced, charming old hotel by the entrance to the Zuurberg National Park, offers the only accommodation in the area. It has been a resting place on the road north for over 100 years. The rooms and self-contained rondavels are clean and comfortable, and there is a lively bar, with resident parrots and assorted dogs. Cheap camping can be negotiated, and riding and hiking in the Zuurberg can be arranged from here. Apart from the Zuurberg, the only place to eat out in the area is in the restaurant in the Addo Elephant National Park.

Algoa Bay and Inland between Port Elizabeth and Grahamstown

Algoa Bay, named after the needle-shaped rocks off Port Elizabeth (*algoa* means 'needles' in old Portuguese), runs east of the city for 100km. **Sardinia Bay**, an inlet from the main bay, 18km east of Port Elizabeth, has a nature reserve of coastal forest and dune, with safe swimming and a walking trail (the Sacramento Trail) known for wild flowers in spring. **Woody Cape Nature Reserve and Alexandria State Forest**, ✆ (04652) 1103, are at the further end of Algoa Bay, beginning at the mouth of the Sundays River, about 50km east of Port Elizabeth, and running a further 50km east along a wild coastline of white dunes, coastal bush, and forest. Bushbuck and duiker are often spotted, as are a variety of birds. The two-day **Alexandria Hiking Trail**, with an overnight hut, runs through the reserve, but needs booking through the Eastern Cape Forest Region, Forestry Branch, Dept of Environmental Affairs, ✆ (041) 390 2126, or ✆ (0433) 23 445.

Shamwari Private Game Reserve, ✆ (042) 851 1196, midway between Addo and Grahamstown, covers a huge area along the Bushman's River and is the only reserve in the Eastern Cape where all of the **Big Five** are found. Follow the signs from the N2 to Paterson, then to Alicedale, and from there to the reserve. Here you can also see most of the large antelope, as well as hyena, warthog and bushpig. Fish eagles hunt the river, which is also the haunt of hippo and croc. The reserve offers guided day-hikes, with accommodation in comfortably appointed 1820 Settler cottages. Recently, a luxury steam line has opened connecting the reserve with Johannesburg via Port Elizabeth, ✆ (041) 311 1127. Reserve accommodation is fairly expensive.

Settler Country

> *...their chief object is to oppose and render odious all authority and to sow the seeds of discontent wherever their baneful influence can extend*

Cape Governor Lord Charles Somerset to Colonial Secretary, Lord Bathurst in 1825

The Settler Country takes its name from the 5000 settlers brought out by the British government in 1820 to populate the land from the Fish to the Keiskamma Rivers (christened 'Albany' by the Cape government), from which the resident Xhosa clans had been forcibly ejected in 1812. One of the most fought-over stretches of country during the Frontier Wars, today's Settler Country is a quiet rural patchwork of farm, forest and wild bushveld, at whose centre lies the Settler capital of Grahamstown and its satellite villages of Bathurst, Salem and Fort Beaufort.

History

During the mid 18th century the resident Khoi tribes and seasonal Xhosa graziers had been joined by an increasing number of Dutch *trekboers*. At this time, the region was known as the Zuurveld, after its coastal grassland which could turn sour and ungrazable in certain seasons. Much of the inland area was, and still is, covered by thick acacia bush, especially around the Fish River itself. During the various raiding wars between Boer, Xhosa, Khoi and Briton that flared across the Zuurveld from the end of the 18th century, the Xhosa used the bush as a fortress from which to raid and into which to drive cattle.

In 1809, three years after the British annexed the Cape for the second time, a garrison village was built at Grahamstown, in the eastern Zuurveld, 60km west of the Fish River. In 1812, during one of the frontier's interminable wars, the Ndlambe and Gqunkwebe clans of the Zuurveld were driven east of the Fish River in a scorched-earth campaign of indiscriminate slaughter. In order to stop the Xhosa clans from cattle-raiding once they had been forced east of the Fish, a system of patrols and *Kommandos* was set up from Grahamstown by Henry Somerset, the local military governor, and arrogant son of the Cape Governor, Lord Charles Somerset. Whenever a farmer reported a loss, the cavalry would ride into the Fish River bush, following the tracks of the stolen beasts, and demand payment from the first Xhosa homestead they came to. This unfair system provoked the Ndlambe, under the leadership of a millenarian prophet, Nxele, to re-enter the Zuurveld in 1819, attack Grahamstown and lay waste the entire countryside (*see* p.313).

In 1820, Lord Charles Somerset attempted to turn the region into a working British colony overnight, renaming it Albany and persuading Britain to use £50,000 of the public treasury to send 5000 English settlers to the region. But the harsh climate and fickle rainfall (alternate floods and drought), wild animals and continued Xhosa raids (the land had been summarily appropriated from the Ngqika clan) were too much for most of the settlers, who, with a few exceptions, gradually abandoned their farms and drifted to Grahamstown. As the British continued to invade east of the Fish River and penetrate further into the heart of Xhosa country, the town prospered. Troops had to be supplied and fortunes were made.

From the 1830s Grahamstown grew to become the Cape Colony's second town, and a centre of anti-Xhosa feeling during the later Frontier Wars. Indeed, the surrounding country was invaded three times by various Xhosa clans between 1842 and and 1853, each time with increasing ferocity. However, many of the wealthier Grahamstown settlers, such as Robert Godlonton, who published anti-Xhosa propaganda in his influential *Grahamstown Journal*, had a vested interest in continued warfare—land occupied by the British after each war could be bought up cheaply by Grahamstown speculators and sold later at great profit. The newspaper actively supported Henry Somerset's legalized cattle-raiding, and stirred up hostility to the residents of the Kat River settlement—an area of prime land east of the Fish River given to the local Khoi in the late 1820s. The Kat River Khoi were continually accused of treachery and thieving, were racially snubbed by the settlers, and were only protected by liberal administrators such as Andries Stockenstroom, who himself became the object of derision in Grahamstown's colonial society.

Naturally, the reactionary Grahamstown residents eventually got their way, seeing the full annexation of all the Xhosa land west of the Kei River and the confiscation of the Kat River settlement after the Eighth Frontier War (1852). By the end of the Ninth (and last) Frontier War in 1878, Grahamstown was a solidly English outpost in a British-dominated part of South Africa; the local Xhosa and Khoi were reduced to farm labourers. Centred around its neo-Gothic cathedral, Grahamstown became the country's second city, until the discovery of the Transvaal gold reefs caused Pretoria and Johannesburg to mushroom in the 1890s.

Today Grahamstown is much quieter. Rhodes University (one of South Africa's most prestigious) was founded in the 1900s, and Grahamstown is now principally a university town of some 20,000 people. Most of the old buildings, fine examples of late Georgian architecture, still stand, giving the town a period air. In term time, the huge number of students make Grahamstown lively, but it lapses into torpor during the holidays. Every July the Grahamstown Arts Festival causes the city to overflow with visitors for a fortnight. One of the least troubled towns of the often violent Eastern Cape, Grahamstown and the surrounding bush country are a pleasure to visit and a relief from the tense atmosphere of the larger Eastern Cape towns.

Grahamstown

Getting There

By car: Grahamstown lies on the N2 highway midway between Port Elizabeth and the Fish River.

By bus: Greyhound, InterCape, TransLux, Transtate (*see* Port Elizabeth for their numbers), **Copper Rose** and **Leopard Express**, ✆ (046) 622 4589, connect Grahamstown with Cape Town, Durban, Umtata and East London along the N2, stopping at all large towns in between. The Baz Bus (*see* **Travel**, p.9), connects the backpackers' in and around Grahamstown with Port Elizabeth, the Garden Route and Cape Town, as well as Natal, the Transvaal and Swaziland.

To get down to Port Alfred, take the **Bee Bus**, ✆ (082) 651 6466.

By train: Grahamstown is linked to Cape Town, Port Elizabeth, East London and Durban by the coastal railway line.

Tourist Information

Grahamstown Publicity Association, Church Square, ✆ (046) 622 3241.

Festivals

For two weeks every July, Grahamstown goes mad. The Grahamstown Arts Festival is South Africa's most prestigious arts festival with theatre, music, cabaret and performance artists from all over Africa. Like the Edinburgh Festival in Britain, it distributes itself around various locations through the town. Finding accommodation can be very hard. For more information, contact the Grahamstown Publicity Association.

Grahamstown has so many old and attractive buildings that simply wandering the streets around the huge central cathedral is satisfying. The **High Street** is the central thoroughfare, running east–west, with Rhodes University campus at the west end and the cathedral at the east. Still largely Georgian, the street is a working one, with grocers, bookshops and general stores. At the west end is the **Yellow House**, Grahamstown's oldest building, and originally a prison, now a public hall. The **Village Market**, now a bazaar and coffee shop, is also on the High Street, and has one of the loveliest 19th-century yellowwood ceilings in the country. The nearby **Grand Hotel**, a fine piece of high Victoriana, is still in use.

Somerset Street, which runs north–south at the far end of High Street, along the eastern end of the campus, has most of the town's museums. The **Albany Museum** (*open Mon–Fri 9.30–1 and 2–5, Sat and Sun 2–5*), founded in 1885, has a fairly detailed history of the 1820 Settlers, although the information cards fail to say that many of the Settlers were drifters and ne'er-do-wells pushed into emigrating to South Africa by their families and communities, that most lied about their agricultural experience (the colony was to be one of farmers, re-creating an English rural society) and that those who prospered either adapted to the Boer way of life or exploited the many Frontier Wars against the Khoi and Xhosa. The wars themselves are also depicted from the standard colonial viewpoint.

Next door, the **National History Museum** (*open Mon–Fri 9.30–1 and 2–5, Sat 2–5*) is mostly devoted to displays of early man in South Africa, and the early San, Khoi and black African cultures. The nearby **Institute of Ichthyology** (*open Mon–Fri 8.30–1 and 2–5*), also on Somerset Street, is an eccentric museum dedicated to South African fish, in particular the coelacanth, a prehistoric survivor discovered off South African coasts in the 1960s. The **Provost's House** (*open Mon–Fri 10–1 and 2–5, Sat 2–5*), on Lucas Avenue, west of Somerset Street, is another early prison, built around a small tower, and houses a permanent craft shop. The **Botanical Gardens** on Lucas Avenue, next to the Provost's House, have a wide variety of South African plants and trees and spacious lawns. A flea market is held here at weekends; Grahamstown attracts craftspeople, and some of the jewellery and clothing is of very good quality.

The **Observatory Museum**, on Bathurst Street (*open Mon–Fri 9.30–1 and 2–5, Sat 9–1*) is a stunning piece of Victorian colonial architecture, with a three-storey veranda of wrought-iron running up the back of the building. It was here that the Eureka Stone, the first big diamond to be found in the Kimberley area, was identified in 1867. Apart from the early astronomical equipment on display, the museum has a lovely, fragrant herb garden. **Fort Selwyn** (1836), on the evocatively named Gunfire Hill above the university, was one of a series of forts built by the British from the 1830s throughout the Amatolas and the country between the Fish and Keiskamma Rivers—an attempt to partition and control Xhosa territories there. It was abandoned in 1870, but visitors can still see the heavy cannons with which the British pounded the Fish River bush in their clumsy attempts to drive the Xhosa from cover during the later Frontier Wars (*see* 'History', p.313). The **Settlers' Wildflower Reserve**, also on Gunfire Hill, covers 61ha. Cycads, ponds, proteas, aloes and other wild flowers make it a pleasant place to wander. The **Settlers' Monument** sits atop Gunfire Hill—a huge, ugly brick building, complete with gift shop, pub, restaurant and fountain, its main function is as a theatre.

Grahamstown ✆ (046–)

Where to Stay

expensive

The **Cock House** (built in 1820), 10 Market Street, ✆ 636 311 287, has 4 en suite rooms in one of the town's most handsome period houses. **Oatlands**, in Caroline Close, off Florence Street, ✆ 622 3058, is a large manor, once surrounded by the estate belonging to Henry Somerset, who lived here until 1852. B&B is provided in rooms furnished in high Cape Dutch style. The **Cathcart Arms**, on Market Square, ✆ 622 7111, has been a hotel since 1825. Again, its 14 rooms are decorated in period. There is an *à la carte* restaurant, a bar and a garden with a swimming pool. The new **St Aidan's Court Hotel**, on Milner Court, ✆ 636 311 188, occupies what used to be the old Jesuits' College. It is the town's most expensive hotel, with 24 luxurious rooms, all en suite.

moderate

The **Guest House**, 16 Jacobus Van Uys Way, ✆ 622 3393, offers B&B in a late 19th-century cottage with a quiet garden overlooking the town. **Longleat**, 9 Mount Street, ✆ 622 6163, is a larger 19th-century house, offering B&B in old rooms with new, but not jarring furniture. No smoking. **Suffield House**, 21 Oatlands Road, ✆ 622 6033, also offers B&B, and you will be brought tea or coffee in bed. Another pleasant 19th-century building with garden.

Also try **Oak Lodge**, 95 Bathurst St, ✆ 622 2324, a small B&B, the **De Geel Kafee Guest House**, 62 Beaufort St, ✆ 622 5907, or **Atherfold's B&B**, ✆ 622 3393.

cheap

The **Backpackers Barn** is at 4 Trollope Street, ✆ 622 9720.

Grahamstown ✆ (046–)

Eating Out

expensive

Grahamstown's best restaurants are both attached to hotels. The restaurant at the **Cock House** is decorated in late-Georgian style, and serves good Cape cuisine, game (in season) and cordon bleu. The food is very good, and the atmosphere relaxed. At St Aidan's Court Hotel, **Il Tinello**, despite the name, serves not only Italian food, but also some French, seafood and Cape dishes.

moderate

The **Copper Kettle**, 7 Bathurst Street, ✆ 622 4358, serves light suppers in a small Georgian cottage. **Peacocks** is a health food/wholefood restaurant on the corner of High and Hill Streets (by the Church Square), serving a young crowd in a scrubbed pine atmosphere. Very good, filling food. No need to book. You *do* need to book for **La Galleria**, 28 New Street. The **Monkey-Puzzle Bistro**, in the Botanical Gardens, ✆ 622 5318, specializes in game. The ostrich and kudu dishes are recommended. Also try the **Monument Restaurant**, on Lucas Avenue, ✆ 622 4656.

cheap

The **Rat & Parrot**, on New Street, ✆ 622 5002, serves pub food to a largely student crowd. **Gino's Pizza and Steak House**, on Hill Street, ✆ 622 7208, serves exactly what it says. Apart from these, there are few cheap restaurants in Grahamstown, but there is no shortage of fast food and take-away places on Market and High Streets. Try the **Curry Den**.

cafés

Grahamstown has some good cafés. The **Copper Kettle** serves coffee, waffles, pastries and light meals on an outside terrace. The **Village Market**, on the High Street, also has a coffee shop, though the decor is a bit twee. The **Cock House** serves excellent coffee on the veranda.

South and east of Grahamstown the rolling farmland around the old Settler villages of Bathurst and Salem gives way to dense milkwood and euphorbia forest near the coast and wild thorn bush in the Fish River Valley. Large nature reserves and state forests have conserved sizeable stretches of wild land and, despite its proximity to 'civilization', this area offers some of the Eastern Cape's best opportunities for 'going bush'.

Tourist Information

Port Alfred Publicity Association, 29 Sports Road, ✆ (0464) 644 1235.

Salem, Bathurst and the Farmlands

Salem and Bathurst lie south of Grahamstown, near the sea. They and their surrounding farms are considered the heart of Settler Country. **Salem**, 15km south of Grahamstown, is a well-preserved early Georgian village. It came under siege twice during the Frontier Wars, when its larger houses and church doubled as forts.

North of town is the **Thomas Baines Nature Reserve**, a stretch of bush country on either side of the Palmiet River that harbours white rhino, buffalo, eland, bontebok, black wildebeest, reedbuck and impala. The reserve is named after the settler artist Thomas Baines, whose ink and gouache landscapes, scenes from settler and Khoi/Xhosa life, and wildlife portraits are one of the best records of the mid 19th-century frontier. Many have been used to illustrate South African history books, and a collection of his work is housed in the Rust-En-Vreugd Museum in Cape Town. The nature reserve has game-viewing roads, and guided walks can be organized (*see* 'Activities'). There is only hostel accommodation. **Bathurst** is larger than Salem, a town of late-Georgian houses shaded by large fig trees. The **Pig and Whistle Hotel and Pub** is the reason why most people come to Bathurst. It has been open since 1831 and served as a fort during the Frontier Wars. Bathurst has various historical buildings, including a powder magazine on Bird Street, a double-pulpited church (which also served as a fort on occasion) on Donkin Street, and an **Agricultural Museum** on Trappes Street (*open Mon–Fri 9–4.30*). A short walk from town (2.4km from the Pig and Whistle) is **Bradshaw's Mill** (1822), which claims to be the first place in South Africa where cloth was woven from wool. The wooden water-wheel still works. The countryside immediately around Bathurst is known for its pineapples.

The Bathurst Conservation Area protects a huge sweep of euphorbia and milkwood bush between Bathurst and the coast, mostly following the west bank of the Kowie River. The conservation area includes the small **Horseshoe Bend Nature Reserve**, 7km west of Bathurst, which follows a stretch of the beautiful Kowie River, along whose wooded banks graze small herds of antelope. There are walks, but no accommodation. Also part of the conservation area is the much larger **Waters Meeting Nature Reserve**, which follows the Kowie River north of the Horseshoe Bend Reserve. There are walking trails through the dense vegetation, from which an occasional bushbuck or duiker may spring, and an overnight canoe trail (canoes hired from the reserve office) up to Horseshoe Bend and back. At night, tree dassies scream, and if you are very quiet and patient, you might spot otters in the early morning. There is a camp site for tents only, and an overnight hut for canoers.

Kowie Nature Reserve, a stretch of dense aloe, euphorbia and milkwood bush, is only 199ha in extent, but follows a particularly lovely stretch of the Bloukrans River, a tributary of the Kowie. Bushbuck, vervet and samango monkey, and otter are common. Walking trails have been laid out but there is no accommodation. The reserve is along the R67 to Port Alfred, about 15km south of Grahamstown.

The Settler Coast

Port Alfred, at the mouth of the Kowie River, is a small resort town with safe swimming beaches. If you don't have a car you can get here from Grahamstown via the **Bee Bus**, ✆ (082) 651 6646. The town itself is not of particular interest, but the Kowie can be canoed (a two-day paddle) and in **Kowie Nature Reserve**, just outside town, an 8km hiking trail leads through tranquil wetlands haunted by fish eagles. The town's harbour was never actually finished and Port Alfred was never a port. **Kenton-on-Sea**, west of Port Alfred, is an even smaller resort (also with safe swimming beaches) where the Portuguese explorer Bartolomeu Dias (*see* **History**) erected one of his stone crosses in 1481. A replica still stands, reached by a 2km trudge across the dunes.

The Fish River Valley

The Fish River was designated the official eastern boundary of the Cape Colony in the 1760s in a futile attempt to halt the eastward advance of the *trekboers* and ivory-hunters. For the next 100 years it remained the official boundary. Apart from the towns that grew up around the British forts, there is little in today's Fish River bush country to recall the 100 years of continual warfare that the region suffered. The landscape, with its tall acacias and yellow grasses, looks more East than South African, and much of it was never settled—today large areas have been set aside as nature reserves.

Ecca Nature Reserve is the first reserve of the bush country, just 16km northeast of Grahamstown on the R67. This small reserve (120ha) has a marked trail through the bush, with information boards on rock and vegetation types. It is famous for fossils: very early dinosaur bones have been found here. Kudu, bushbuck, duiker and steenbok are common. There is no accommodation. The **Andries Vosloo Kudu Reserve and Sam Knott Reserve** form a huge sweep of over 45,000ha on the west bank of the Fish River. On the opposite bank is the large Double Drift Game Reserve (*see* p.341), in the former Ciskei, making this a vast area over which game can move, hunt and browse at will, including black rhino, buffalo, eland, impala, kudu, bushbuck, duiker, springbok and steenbok, as well as bushpig, warthog, baboon and vervet monkey. Leopard and caracal hunt the reserve. There are game-viewing roads, walking trails (booked in advance) and bird-watching hides (*see* 'Activities'). Accommodation is in chalets or a permanent tented camp.

The **Great Fish River Wetland Reserve**, at the mouth of the Great Fish River, just off the N2 on the former Ciskei border, is a haven for waterfowl, waders and seabirds. There is a gorgeous, unspoilt beach, safe if you stay in the shallows, and a camp site hidden among the dunes (with an ablution block).

The Settler Country and Fish River Valley are best known for their reserves and walking/hiking trails from which to spot game.

Day hikes: Kowie Nature Reserve, Waters Meeting Nature Reserve and **Thomas Baines Nature Reserve** offer trails south of Grahamstown near Salem, Bathurst and Port Alfred, as do the **Andries Vosloo** and **Sam Knott Nature Reserves** in the Fish River Valley.

Overnight hikes: The **Andries Vosloo** and **Sam Knott Nature Reserves**, ✆ (0461) 27 909, have a connecting overnight trail (with hut) that must be booked. **Woody Cape Nature Reserve**, ✆ (04652) 1103, has a beautiful 2-day hike through coastal forest. Access is from Alexandria Village, south of Salem.

Riding: Horses are available from Glenthorpe Farm, 10km west of Grahamstown, ✆ (0461) 28 868. Near Port Alfred, try the **3 Sisters Trails**, ✆ (046) 675 1269, with beach and forest rides overnighting in a rustic treehouse. These trails can also be done on foot.

Canoeing: The **Kowie Canoe Trail**, ✆ (0464) 42 230, is a very cheap, overnight trip up one of South Africa's least-known, most secluded rivers. Look out for otters.

Diving: Port Alfred's **Kowie Dive School**, ✆ (0464) 42 213, will get you qualified, or take you out on guided dives to the reefs offshore.

Where to Stay

expensive

Kariega Park, on the R343 between Kenton-on-Sea and Salem, ✆ (0461) 311 049, is a private reserve with self-contained log cabins tucked away in the bush. There are walking trails through the riverine forest. Giraffe, zebra and bushbuck are common, as are most antelope species. Look out for martial eagles.

moderate

The well-known Georgian **Pig and Whistle Hotel**, Bathurst, ✆ (0464) 250 673, has been an inn since 1831. The dining room and pub are period-furnished, but the rooms are more modern. **Glenthorpe Farm**, ✆ (0461) 28 868, sits in an oak-shaded valley, signposted from the N2, 10km west of Grahamstown. It offers B&B, and meals by request. There is a swimming pool, and they have horses to ride.

Fort Beaufort has the **Yellowwoods Hotel**, ✆ (046) 684 0708, a small affair with just six rooms, as well as the larger **Savoy**, ✆ (04634) 31 146.

Port Alfred's **Coral Guest Cottages**, ✆ (0464) 42 849, offer privacy and comfort. If you get no joy there, also try **Molly Robinson's B&B**, ✆ (0464) 43 465, **Quetu Country Home**, ✆ (0464) 71 070, **Albany Guest Farm**, ✆ (0464) 71 170, or the **Ferryman's Hotel**, ✆ (0464) 41 122.

The Fish River Valley nature reserves also have moderately priced accommodation.

There are backpackers' in Port Alfred, ☎ (0464) 644 1235, and Fort Beaufort, **Talking Drum**, ☎ (0461) 413 107.

Near Grahamstown, the **Top House Guest House**, on Bucklands Farm, ☎ (0461) 26 055, on the road to Fort Beaufort, is handy for the Fish River Valley reserves. Clean and simple, it is self-catering only. There are camp sites at **Waters Meeting Nature Reserve** (tents only) and at the **Great Fish River Wetland Reserve**.

North of Settler Country: The Karoo Fringe

Getting There

There are two main routes into the northern reaches of the Eastern Cape. The most interesting is via the R335, over the Zuurberg Mountains, on a good dirt road that winds for a spectacular hour through the forest and open grassland to Somerset East, roughly 80km north. The second, quicker, way is via the R32 to Cradock, and then up the R390 to Burgersdorp, Aliwal North, Lady Grey and the Drakensberg Region.

Somerset East is more or less the point at which the Karoo meets the grass veld. Depending on the season, the surrounding country can be parched or green. Behind the town rises the **Bosberg**, a range of low mountains cloaked in yellowwood and milkwood forest, cut by streams and waterfalls that make a dramatic contrast to the dry country below (there is an overnight hiking trail through here). As you enter Somerset East, a sign invites you to 'Stop Awhile, You'll Like It Here'. However, though the town has some attractive Georgian and Edwardian buildings, there is little of interest save the **Somerset East Museum**, dedicated to church history, with the usual collection of pioneer tools, clothes and other artefacts, and the **Walter Batiss Art Gallery**, displaying work of a landscape artist who was well-known in South Africa earlier this century, and who was born in the town.

Adelaide and **Bedford** are east of Somerset East. Adelaide is a large, pretty village set below the Winterberg Mountains. It's worth driving a short way north into the foothills to see the arcadian **Mankazana Valley**, whose green, well-watered farms front a winding, tree-fringed river. Thomas Pringle, a Scot who came over in 1822 and made a mark as an espouser of the early missionary cause to 'enlighten', rather than directly enslave, the local Khoi and Xhosa, farmed this valley for a while. An enemy of the reactionary Grahamstown settlers, Pringle moved to Cape Town and published a liberal newspaper called *The South African Journal* during the 1820s and '30s, which called for better treatment of the Khoi, and indirect rule of the Xhosa through their existing chiefs. He also attacked the British Governor Lord Charles Somerset's tyrannical policies, and eventually had the pleasure of seeing Somerset recalled after the costly, inconclusive sixth Frontier War (1834). However, Pringle didn't much like Africa, and went home after a few years to work for the Anti-Slavery Society and lobby Parliament to reform colonial mismanagement of the Cape.

Bedford is famous for nearby **Slagter's Nek**, the ridge where the first British execution of Boer rebels took place in 1815, after one Fanie Bezuidenhout led an ill-fated rebellion against British restriction of movement across the Fish River and the ill-treatment of the Boers' Khoi servants. Interestingly, the Boers tried to enlist Xhosa support for the venture, but failed. Bezuidenhout and four others were executed in 1816 at Slagter's Nek, and the event subsequently went down as a landmark date of Anglo-Boer hatred. Certainly, the execution itself was a cruel farce: the condemned were too heavy for their ropes, which broke on the first attempt. Although they pleaded for their lives, they were marched back to the scaffold for a second, successful hanging. Andries Stockenstroom, *landdrost* of Graaff-Reinet in the early 19th century, and a man who shaped many of the events in the history of the Eastern Frontier, farmed nearby when he retired from public life (*see* 'History', p.314).

Fort Beaufort, on the Kat River, is the next town east. A small Georgian town surrounded by citrus farms, it began life as a garrison fort in 1823. The original officer's mess on Durban Street is now the **Fort Beaufort Museum** (*open Mon–Sat 9–5*), with a small collection of Victoriana and local natural history and some paintings by Thomas Baines, an early settler who recorded what he saw in watercolour. Fort Beaufort was attacked in 1851, during the long Eighth Frontier War, but today is a quiet country town, except on Friday and Saturday nights, when the local citrus workers come in to spend their wages. Nearby is the **Lovedale Mission Station**, open to visitors, founded in 1841. Several alumni, like the famous Alan Soga, went on to become the first black South African university graduates, being sent by the London Missionary Society to Edinburgh University in the late 19th century.

In the high uplands north of Fort Beaufort is the **Fort Fordyce Conservation Area**, an expanse of montane hardwood forest and wild pasture inhabited by bushbuck, baboon, klip-springer and duiker. A hiker's paradise, the protected mountains are criss-crossed with marked trails. However, these forests were not always such a joy to foreign walkers—much of the fighting of the Eighth Frontier War (1850–3) between Sandile and Maqoma and Sir Harry Smith took place here (*see* p.314), with the British columns lumbering through the impenetrable forest after the fleet and silent Xhosa. The horror of hand-to-hand fights in the half-dark under the great trees, and the constant struggle of the over-equipped British troops with the terrain, earned the uplands the title of **'Mount Misery'**. Lieut. Col. Fordyce, after whom the hills are named, was one of many British soldiers to die in the fierce campaign.

North to the Drakensberg

North of the Winterberg, Afrikaans signs re-appear on the farm gates. To the west and north stretches the dry Karoo. To the east and northeast rise the first tiers of the Bamboesberg and Stormberg, the foothills of the high Cape Drakensberg itself.

Leaving the R32 at Cradock (*see* 'Eastern Karoo', p.279) and taking the R390 north, head for the mountains via the small town of **Hofmeyr**, which has hardly changed in outward aspect since the mid 19th century. The general store sells delicious home-made ginger beer, lemonade, Boer breads and biscuits. Alternatively, you can head north over the Witteberg to **Tarkastad** (R344), a small town surrounded by vast game farms. Some of these offer accommodation, with marked hiking and riding trails leading through the game-rich hills.

You come out on the R56, in country that is part Karoo, part grassland, at the foot of the Bamboesberg and Stormberg. From the Hofmeyr route, go north along the R391 and R58 to Burgersdorp and Aliwal North, or east via Molteno (R56) to the N6 highway, which also goes north to Aliwal North. If coming over the Winterberg either head east to Dordrecht, on the R56, which skirts the southern wall of the Cape Drakensberg and the northern edge of former Transkei, or go up the N6 to Aliwal North, and enter the Drakensberg from here.

Aliwal North is a strange town, and staunchly Afrikaans, despite its name, which celebrates Sir Harry Smith's victory over the Sikhs at Aliwal in India, before he came out to the Cape as Governor in the 1840s. The town sits on the Orange River, on the border between the Cape and the Free State. There is a **Hot Springs Resort** on the eastern edge of town, unfortunately housed in a grey concrete building, and the town has an ugly Main Street, but a pleasant, old residential district behind. A gem is the **Old Library Museum**, now a museum of local history. When the author visited, the old library books, many of them first editions from the 1930s and '40s, as well as a large collection of Victorian editions, were being sold in the museum for R1 each. There are some treasures to be picked up here and, as few people visit the town, it will take a long time before the collection is seriously diminished.

The last farm on the right as you leave town towards the Drakensberg belongs to Martin Vogel, a farmer and horse-trainer known as 'Oom Martin' (Uncle Martin). Mr Vogel trains horses in the traditional *boerperd* fashion that harks back to the classical riding traditions of 17th-century Holland. If asked, he may show you the horses being put through their paces.

Lady Grey, a charming village set in the high foothills of the Cape Drakensberg, is again, despite the name, a primarily Afrikaans settlement of wrought-iron and sandstone Victorian houses clustered round a large church. On the Main Street is a small **museum** (*open Mon–Fri 9–2*) which displays a Victorian hearse designed to be drawn by people rather than horses. So steep are the hills surrounding Lady Grey that a **narrow-gauge railway**, constructed in 1911 from Aliwal North to Barkly East via Lady Grey, was constructed as a series of reverses, the only one of its kind in the world. The high, lonely train ride is worth taking for the scenery alone. For hikers, the **Lammergeier Trail** winds for two days through the mountains above the town, with accommodation in a refuge hut (*see* 'Activities', p.336).

The Cape Drakensberg

All kinds of monsters, cannibals, even the legendary unicorn, were rumoured to roam those heights

Stormberg, Johannes Meintjies

East of Lady Grey begins the Drakensberg proper. The range, South Africa's highest, stretches all the way through northern Transkei, Natal and Mpumalanga. Most tourists only visit the latter two regions: the Cape Drakensberg, towering and silent, remains largely unexplored. Hiking and riding trails abound, through vast uplands scattered with sandstone outcrops, boulders, overhangs and caves, often painted with bushman (San) art—the Cape Drakensberg was one of the last strongholds of the San in the 19th century, until combined white, Xhosa and Sotho migration into the area in the 1840s and '50s caused their demise.

Unlike the Natal and Mpumalanga Drakensberg, the Cape Drakensberg has no big hotel complexes, golf courses or camp sites, and only a few tarred roads. Visitors tend to be hikers, climbers, trout fishermen, riding enthusiasts and skiers (there is a ski-lift at the village of Rhodes). Still, there is no shortage of moderately priced guest farms and small hotels in the villages, and camping can always be had by permission on the huge mountain sheep farms.

Despite the largely Afrikaans farming population of the region, the names of the mountains are mostly borrowed from Scotland (for example the 3000m Ben Macdhui, rising above

Rhodes) which the Cape Drakensberg resembles in its higher reaches, especially in summer, when the hillsides are green from the summer rains, and during the winter snowfalls. The highest driveable mountain pass in South Africa, the **Naudesnek Pass**, connects Rhodes and Maclear in the east of the region. Worth driving just for the scenery and solitude, the pass gives views over Transkei and Lesotho.

A word of warning: the small, triangular section of the former Transkei 'homeland' between Lady Grey and Lesotho is known for being dangerous for white drivers.

Barkly East is a small town on the R58, with little for the traveller except a hotel that arranges trout fishing on streams owned by surrounding farms, but it is also the start of a two-day wild hike, the **Ben Macdhui Trail**, which climbs over the mountains to the remote village of Rhodes. About 20km further along the R58 is a farm called **Denorben**. Just behind the farmhouse is a sandstone overhang that shelters the longest set of bushman paintings in South Africa. The paintings are mostly of animals and hunters, but there is one half-man, half-animal, representing a shaman in trance communicating with animal spirits. The cave in which the present farmer keeps his sheep was used by the San to hide cattle rustled from the lowland farmers. The stronghold was discovered by settlers in the 1850s, and the San raiders were massacred in the cave; the soot from their fires still blackens the cavern's ceiling. About 10km beyond Denorben is the magnificent **Barkly Pass**, which connects the mountains with the lowland town of Elliot. Falling thousands of metres, the road passes vast outcrops of sandstone that resemble misshapen giants. Long-tailed whydah birds hover low on the mountain pastures. Driving the pass is spectacular, but it is better to get out and walk: the **Ekowa Hiking Trail** winds through the mountains.

Rhodes is the gem of the region. A perfectly conserved, tiny Victorian village, it has a white population of 23, and a Sotho/Xhosa village just outside, of about 200. Sotho horsemen frequently cross the mountain wall north of the town, where Ben Macdhui rises. Rhodes has a beautiful small hotel, a Victorian wood-and-corrugated-iron set piece, furnished in period, whose pub (still serving beer) used to be a rest spot for 19th-century brandy-, cattle- and gun-smugglers between the Cape Colony and Lesotho. Horses can be hired from the hotel, there are some marked hiking and riding trails, and shooting (for francolin and mountain reedbuck) is available in autumn. There is even a small ski-lift on Ben Macdhui that is open through June and July. Despite the range of activities, there is no modern development to the town and hotel and Rhodes is one of the most tranquil spots in the country.

The **Naudesnek Pass**, connecting Rhodes with Maclear, is South Africa's highest road pass (2027m). The views are breathtaking, but the condition of the road deteriorates in summer when the rains turn parts of it into a mud-slide, and in winter when the pass sometimes snows up. However, if the weather is reasonable, it is worth driving the 80km pass for the scenery and solitude: you are unlikely to pass another vehicle on the way over. Don't hurry, it can take two days to get over the pass in an ordinary car, so be prepared for a long haul and to camp if need be. Look out for red-hot poker flowers in summer and beware of rock-falls. The hotel at Rhodes can usually give up-to-date information on the state of the pass road: if they tell you it's safe, then it's safe.

Maclear lies at the eastern end of the Naudesnek Pass. Although small, it seems a hive of activity after the loneliness of the preceding drive. In fact, the town is pretty lively, being the only trading post for miles around for the local Sotho, Xhosa and white farmers. Maclear's surrounding mountains have several good hiking trails, including the **Tsitsa Falls** (a half-day hike) and the **Woodcliffe Trails** (hikes of several days with accommodation in huts set in caves, with donkeys available to carry packs and pots). Early dinosaur tracks can be seen on the Pot River near town (*see* 'Activities'). **Ugie**, the next village on from Maclear (back on the tarred road), nestles in the Prentjiesberg, a foothill chain jutting out from the main Drakensberg, and known for its forests of rare protea trees. **The Prentjiesberg Hiking Trail** leads two days through the mountain country (*see* 'Activities').

Elliot, next town along the R56, lies at the foot of the magnificent Barkly Pass. Apart from this, there is not much to recommend the town, which serves as a small banking and shopping centre for local farmers, and houses some of the offices of the Mondi Forestry company, whose vast plantations cover the mountains northwest of town.

Further west, **Dordrecht** is handsome and Victorian, with the reputation for being South Africa's coldest town in winter (although many Karoo towns make the same claim). The **Anderson Museum**, on Grey Street, houses the usual pioneer stuff, plus a more interesting photographic collection of some of the best examples of the Cape Drakensberg's bushman rock paintings. Just north of town, the lovely **Dordrecht's Kloof** has gentle walking trails. A harder hike is the **Kranskop Trail**, on the Gelegenfontein farm, where hikers can overnight in a huge cave, climb to some remote waterfalls, then stagger back to Gelegenfontein via a series of narrow, beautiful kloofs (*see* 'Activities'). East of Dordrecht the R56 crosses the N6 highway, from where you can head north to Aliwal North and the Free State, or south through the Stormberg Mountains to Queenstown and the Settler Country.

Activities

Hiking: The following trails all offer overnight accommodation in huts with firewood, water, cooking pots and sheepskins to sleep on. The **Woodcliffe Cave Trail**, ✆ (045322) 1222, a 5-day trail through the Drakensberg near Maclear, can be divided into sections of one or more days. The **Kranskop Trail**, ✆ (045312) 6330, runs for 3 days through the mountains near Dordrecht. The **Ekowa Hiking Trail**, ✆ (045312) 11, winds for 3 days through the mountains and protea forests above the Barkly Pass. The **Lammergeier Trail**, ✆ (0423) 19, named after the rare, bearded lammergeier vulture found nearby, is a 2-day walk above Lady Grey. The tough **Ben Macdhui Trail**, ✆ (04542) 7021, is a 2-day trail in the beautifully remote mountains above Rhodes, on the Lesotho border. The 2-day **Prentjiesberg Hiking Trail**, ✆ (045332) 42/44, in the mountains above Ugie, has some good bushman paintings and game-spotting.

Riding: The Rhodes Hotel hires horses by the hour or day. Simply show up at the hotel to book.

Skiing: Rhodes is one of the few places in South Africa that has sufficiently reliable snow to warrant a ski-lift. All arrangements, including hire of gear, are made through the Rhodes Hotel.

Steam railway: This area is famous among train-spotters for having a unique series of railway reverses, necessary to get the narrow-gauge steam trains up the steep gradients. Enthusiasts come from all over the world to ride this slow train through the spectacular Cape Drakensberg, past stations that service only hill farms and miles and miles of uninhabited upland scenery. To book, phone the Mountain View Hotel at Lady Grey, ✆ (05552) 112.

Trout fishing: This is some of the best in the southern hemisphere. To book an all-in, luxury trip in the mountains near Ugie and Maclear, call ✆ (044) 870 7200. More down-to-earth are the fishing packages offered by **Franschoek Guest Farm**, near Barkly East, ✆ (04542) and ask for 1722. There are also great walking, mountain biking and 4x4 routes. Self-catering or B&B.

Where to Stay and Eating Out

expensive

The **Rhodes Hotel**, ✆ (04542) 21, is moderately expensive, and well worth the price. This undeveloped 19th-century hotel in the undeveloped 19th-century village of Rhodes is beautiful, furnished with period pieces throughout. The bar used to be popular with brandy-smugglers and cattle-rustlers in the last century, and was the scene of more than one shoot-out. The Cape food served in the small restaurant is exquisite, as is the choice of wine. If it were not so isolated, it would command far higher prices.

moderate

The **Mountain View Hotel**, Lady Grey, ✆ (05552) 112, is a 1930s establishment with simple, comfortable rooms and a dam for swimming. The nearby steam railway is bookable from here. The **Drakensberg Hotel**, Barkly East, ✆ (04542) 277, is gloomy and overpriced, but a convenient place to break the journey if you arrive too late to go up into the mountains proper. It also arranges trout fishing on local farms, with accommodation in cottages.

Franschoek Guest Farm, near Barkly East, ✆ (04542) and ask for 1722, offers great walking, mountain biking and 4x4 routes. Self-catering or B&B.

cheap

There is little cheap accommodation in the Cape Drakensberg. However, Rhodes has a quiet, equipped camp site, or you can camp on just about any farm, with permission. Alternatively, as tourism has dropped off in the area lately, it is always worth bargaining with the hotels, which often have empty rooms.

The Former Ciskei

My heart is far-off between the peaks
Away off where the south wind speaks

Vusumzi's Song, L. T. Manyase

The former 'republic' of Ciskei (re-incorporated into South Africa in April 1994) forms a rough triangle, with the base between the mouths of the Great Fish and the Chalumna Rivers at the coast (about 75km) and the apex in the Stormberg and Winterberg Mountains near Queenstown, about 200km to the north. The tiny regional capital, Bisho (built in 1981 and not worth visiting), lies to the extreme east of the region, within sight of the much larger King William's Town. In the centre rise the beautiful, forested Katberg and Amatola

Mountains, heartland of the Ngqika Xhosas in the 19th century, and the scene of much bitter fighting between Xhosa, British, Boer and Khoi from 1800 to 1870. The central Katberg and Amatola Mountains are still densely forested, while the Winterberg area to the north and much of the Fish River Valley are also fairly wild, and have some excellent private game reserves. The rest of the region is overpopulated, overgrazed and eroded, due to the forced overcrowding resulting from its recent history as a 'homeland'. By contrast, the coastline is beautiful and undeveloped, especially around the Keiskamma and Chalumna River mouths, where long, white sand beaches and coastal bush fall to a sea known to harbour huge, unexploited shoals of fish.

History

Much of the Eastern Cape's violent history was played out in this area. The territory between the Great Fish and Keiskamma Rivers was known through most of the 19th century as the Ceded Territory, referring to a series of treaties made between the British and the Ngqika Xhosa after the first Frontier Wars in the 1790s and early 1800s. In the 1820s the Ngqika were expelled from everywhere in the region, with the exception of the Amatolas, but were given back the territory when the British government realized that the volatile frontier could not absorb a homeless, wandering Xhosa clan. From this time, the area was known to the colonists as 'British Kaffraria'.

The Ngqika became the most militant of the Xhosa, suffering the brunt of colonial mismanagement of the frontier, as first the Dutch and then the British tried to force the chiefs Ngqika, Maqoma and Sandile to answer for the raiding and/or wars of the entire Xhosa nation. The colonists were jealous of the magnificent Amatola country and, having put the Ngqika in an impossible position, applauded as the government launched campaign after campaign against the Ngqika, gradually stripping them of the territory.

However, this was a slow process. The British found campaigning in the Amatolas ineffective and costly; the regular troops were unused to the terrain and were unable to come to grips with their foe, relying on the Khoi to do the bush fighting. By the 1840s the entire region of what became southern and central Ciskei was dotted with a series of forts, centred around the Amatolas, which the British used as bases from which to partition ever-increasing amounts of Ngqika land. Most of the region's larger towns are on the sites of these old forts.

During the 1840s Ciskei was the scene of the final tragedy of the Cape Colony's freeholding Khoi. In 1828 the Cape Governor, Lord Charles Somerset, gave a large group of Khoi their own self-governing colony on well-watered pastureland at the foot of the Katberg, to be administered by the humane but unpopular missionary James Read, who had married a Khoi woman, and was ostracized by most frontier whites. Read had campaigned passionately for the Khoi since his arrival on the frontier in the early 1800s.

But, unfortunately, the land had been confiscated from Ngqika chief Maqoma after yet another war. Over the following two decades the resentful Ngqika raided the settlement at will, while white settlers, outraged that such good land should be given to mere Khoi, clamoured to have the settlement annulled. On top of these difficulties, the Kat River Settlement, as it was known, was required to provide soldiers for the Frontier Wars of the 1830s and '40s; 90 per cent of its males between 16 and 60 were pressed into service as part of the **Cape Corps**, the 'coloured' regiment started by the Dutch in the late 18th century and which went on to fight for the British in the two World Wars. But despite a loyal war record, many influential white settlers suspected that the Kat River Khoi were liable to ally with the Xhosa and turn on the colony, even though this flew in the face of evidence to the contrary: on two occasions, it was the Kat River Khoi who tipped off the British about forthcoming Xhosa hostilities. But the frontier whites insisted that the Kat River land be annexed and sold to the highest bidder.

In the late 1840s, colonial mistrust of the Kat River Khoi became outright persecution. White colonists claimed that many of the settlement's inhabitants were illegal squatters—not proper Khoi, but mixed-race 'coloureds', an indication of how the continual mixing of races in the colony was beginning to undermine the Khoi, marking the start of their final slide from an officially equal race to a disenfranchised group of colonial dependants.

Sir Harry Smith, the egocentric new Cape Governor, who hated the frontier missionaries (especially the liberal James Read), saw Kat River as a chance to undermine them. He sanctioned the removal of the 'squatters' from the settlement, which was carried out in the worst of a severe winter (1849). Huts were burned and families driven into the *veld*. The Kat River Khoi, by now as educated and 'westernized' as any white frontier community, bore this latest humiliation as stoically as ever. But in 1850, when Sir Harry Smith was worsted by a combined force of Ngqika, Gcaleka and Ndlambe warriors in the violent, drawn-out Eighth Frontier War, and called on the Khoi to fight for the British once again, the Khoi's patience finally snapped, and in desperation the young men allied with the Xhosa. For the following three years the joint Khoi/Xhosa force kept the British bogged down in an expensive campaign, but the colonists brought in massive reinforcements and the combined Khoi and Xhosa forces were brutally subdued in 1853. The Kat River Settlement was taken away and its inhabitants, whether they had rebelled or not, reduced to wandering the countryside seeking employment as farm labourers, while their land was bought up by frontier whites.

In the 1860s the Ngqika Xhosa were also expelled once and for all from the Amatolas. Sandile, the last Ngqika chief, led his people back to the mountains for a brief campaign in 1878, but he was killed there, and his people again expelled. Much of the country was then given over to European settlers (predominantly German) and Mfengu from Transkei. Not until the late 20th century, when Ciskei was declared an 'independent' republic (1973), were Xhosa people allowed to move back. As a puppet state, Ciskei's government toed the apartheid government's line and suppressed black political organizations like the ANC, a fact that came to the world's attention when Ciskei troops opened fire on an ANC march from King William's Town (just over the the Ciskei/Cape border) to Bisho, the republic's small capital. The pictures, published around the world, brought home the fact that South Africa's 'homelands' were nothing more than military dictatorships propped up by apartheid.

On the other hand, some Ciskei residents claim that the ANC itself was less than ethical in using violence to force people to join the organization. However, in general, Ciskei suffered less political violence than some of South Africa's other 'homelands', and, even through the troubled build-up to the 1994 elections, remained a tranquil place to travel. Today, although Ciskei (and the other former 'homelands') are back 'inside' South Africa, having been separate for a generation, the place offers an alternative view of South African life to the white-owned areas of the Eastern Cape, and, for both its village life and its superb landscapes, should not be missed.

Xhosa Culture

In his book of South African oral history, Credo Mutwa, a Zulu witch doctor and historian writing in the 1960s, said this of the Xhosa:

The Xhosa are not a tribe, they are a true nation, a group of tribes inhabiting one land and united by a common language... The Xhosa are an ancient people. In Southern Africa they are older than the Zulus.

Certainly the Xhosa are a large, diverse people of several distinct groups, the most prominent today being the Tembu, Ngqika, Gcaleka, Qayi and Mfengu (Fingo). Traditionally, the Gcaleka were the paramount clan, and all deferred to the Gcaleka chief. Having said that, the Gcaleka chief would not interfere directly in the political affairs of other chiefs. In general, authority still rests with chiefs and headmen of inherited lineage, both in the villages and in the bureaucratic and business hierarchy of the towns.

The Xhosa are primarily a cattle-owning people. Cattle equals wealth, and brides must be paid for in cattle, so a rich man can therefore have several wives. In the countryside sheep and goats provide the staple meat; cattle are usually only slaughtered on special occasions.

Rural Xhosa culture, as everywhere in Africa, still revolves around reverence for the ancestors. Although evangelical Christianity has mostly replaced traditional worship, diviners have not lost their function as mediums between the human and the spirit world, from which comes everything that affects human life. Diviners and traditional healers are important members of society and will generally be consulted before a medical doctor.

The most well-known Xhosa spirit is the *tokoloshe*, characterized by a short, sturdy form and an immense phallus that can be thrown over his shoulder when running. The *tokoloshe* is neither good nor bad, but can be enslaved by a witch or wizard and made to act malevolently. Rural people fear him and often stand their beds on bricks, so that the *tokoloshe* can pass underneath.

Water has always held ritual importance for the Xhosa. It was formerly believed that the dead lived at the bottom of rivers and lakes, and there are gentle water-dwelling spirits who look after the drowned. Less benevolent is the Lightning Bird (*Impundulu*). Tall as a man, it can assume any shape, and is traditionally used by witches (rather than diviners; historically, people accused of witchcraft were the only people traditionally executed under the Xhosa's otherwise tolerant law, and always by torture) to perform the most evil deeds. If one among you will not drink beer at a gathering, beware, it is the *Impundulu* in human guise.

Rural beliefs have been eroded among many urban Xhosa, whose involvement in the modern world is replacing tradition. Many of the older generation regret this, fearing a breakdown of moral and social codes. However, even in townships near large cities, you will always spot Xhosa boys painted with white clay. This is evidence of the circumcision rite, perhaps the strongest Xhosa tradition, which has survived everywhere. When boys turn 13 (or when they can spare the time) they are taken in groups by elders to secret camps in the bush and put through rigorous survival tests, culminating in painful, ritual circumcision. The initiates are then daubed in white, the colour of light and goodness, and turn from boys to men. So strong is this tradition that a taunt from Xhosa to Zulu men during their often lethal faction fighting in the townships is 'Uncircumcized Ones', which translates roughly to 'not men'.

Perhaps the strongest facet of Xhosa culture is their lack of xenophobia and nationalism, and their great pragmatism, forged during the endless wars with the British, and subsequent semi-enslavement following their near mass-suicide during the Great Cattle Killing of 1856 (*see* p.359). Although closely rivalled, the Xhosa are arguably the most politically successful black group in South Africa, despite the many petty rivalries between clans.

The Ciskei Coast

The R72 crosses the Great Fish River within sight of its mouth, passes the Fish River Sun Hotel and Casino (with its own swimming beach), and continues across several more estuary mouths to the small settlement of **Wesley** (which has a large arts and crafts store), where the road curves inland. After about 20km, a dirt road (R345) turns sharp south along the Keiskamma estuary to the coastal village of **Hamburg**. A white resort before the inauguration of Ciskei as a 'republic', Hamburg's old hotel and many of the beach houses now lie derelict while cattle graze around them, and traditional huts dot the surrounding hillsides. A tranquil spot, Hamburg is known to fishermen and a few holidaymakers, but is completely undeveloped. A trading store, a kiosk that doubles as a bar after dark, a camp site and some two-roomed guest cottages comprise the facilities. If you do not have fishing tackle, you can borrow or hire a prawning net from the locals (as well as buying their fresh catches). It takes about an hour to learn how to cast the net so that it lands on the water in as near-perfect a circle as you can manage. Cast along the estuary for an hour or two after dark, when the large river prawns are running, and you will catch enough for supper and breakfast.

The **Shipwreck Hiking Trail** runs along the whole Ciskei coast from Great Fish Point to Chalumna Mouth, crossing 14 estuaries, including the wild, forested Mtati and Mgwalana river mouths. The 3-day trail passes several beached wrecks. Day-long sections of it are accessible from where roads meet the coast at the Fish River Sun, Hamburg, Kilwane and Chalumna mouth.

The Fish River Bush

Double Drift Game Reserve, ✆ (0401) 952 115, covers 22,000ha of Fish River mimosa, thorn and euphorbia bush, about 10km north of the small town of **Peddie**. Originally Fort Peddie, this was the site of the Frontier Wars' only massed cavalry charge, during the War of the Axe (the Seventh Frontier War, 1844–46), and the area to which the British moved the Mfengu clan (today's Fingo) in the 1830s, as a reward for fighting with the British against the main body of Xhosa chiefs during Sir Harry Smith's Transkei campaign (*see* p.314).

Double Drift, entered at Breakfast Vlei on the R345, forms part of a massive wild area backing on to the Andries Vosloo Kudu Reserve and Sam Knott Game Reserve on the west (Cape Province) side of the Fish River (*see* p.330). Big game includes black rhino, buffalo, hippo, eland, kudu, bushbuck, blesbok, impala and blue wildebeest.

Facilities include two luxurious game lodges (*see* 'Where to Stay') and a network of game-viewing roads. A hiking trail of 1–3 days (with overnight huts) visits a series of cliff caves along the Fish River. These have good bushman paintings, and evidence of much earlier inhabitants (as early as 20,000 years ago), whose stone tools can be found lying on the cave floors. Two ruined British forts, Fort Wiltshire and Fort Montgomery, both scenes of fighting in the 1830s and '40s, lie in the bush, and can be reached on foot.

The Katberg Mountains

The Katberg is best reached by the R67 from Fort Beaufort, just over the Cape border to the southwest, or from Whittlesea and Queenstown in the north. The massive, almost sheer, forested upland is accessible via two nature reserves: Mpofu, to the south, bordering the Cape, and the Katberg and Readsdale Forests, a few kilometres further north.

Mpofu, ✆ (0401) 952 115, 12,000ha of rolling grassland and forest in the foothills of the Katberg, supports a lot of game—blue and black wildebeest, red hartebeest, eland, bushbuck and duiker abound. Leopard, caracal, bushpig, grysbok and blue duiker tend to be more shy and keep to the forest. There is a horseback trail and hiking (the reserve is linked to the Katberg Hiking Trail), and the lowland section of the reserve has game-viewing roads and a lodge (Mpofu Lodge). The upland section also has a lodge (Ntloni Lodge) and a hiking hut. The horseback trail camp is in the west of the reserve, on the banks of the Blinkwater River.

The **Katberg and Readsdale Forests** are in the high Katberg, a massive amphitheatre giving fabulous views over the Eastern Cape and southern Ciskei. With clear mountain streams, waterfalls, ferns, huge yellowwood trees and clean, cool air, this is heaven after the heat of the lowlands. The two forests (accessible from Katberg and Buxton Forest Stations on the R67, a bad dirt road) have 1–4 hour hiking trails, as well as the 2-day **Katberg Trail** that links the forests with Mpofu Reserve. Green louries, samango and vervet monkeys, baboon and bushbuck are the most usually spotted game, and the lack of regular visitors makes it one of the best places to see the shy bushpig by day. Leopard and caracal hunt by night.

Just below the Katberg Forest is the **Katberg Protea Hotel** (also on the R67), a fairly luxurious establishment that offers horseback trails up into the mountains (*see* 'Activities'). The lowlands at the foot of the Katberg were the site of the ill-fated Kat River Settlement, home of the Cape's last freeholding Khoi in the 1840s. At **Seymour**, on the R67 south of the Katberg, one of the British forts survives intact—the ghostly **Eland's Post**, built in 1846, and beseiged by the Kat River Khoi in 1850, which is open to visitors.

The Amatolas

The most bitterly contested territory of the long Frontier Wars is now one of the Eastern Cape's most tranquil areas. More extensive than the Katberg, the Amatolas consist of dense forest, mountain pasture, clear streams, waterfalls and some of the country's cleanest air. The 6-day **Amatola Hiking Trail** (*see* below), reputedly South Africa's hardest, winds through the wilder portions of the range.

Amatola Forest Reserve, ✆ (0401) 91131/2/3, covers a vast area of mountain north of the town of Keiskammashoek, with three access points along the R352 gravel road: the Cata, Dontsa and Zingcuka Forest Stations. The game is shy, but bushbuck, baboon, samango and vervet monkey, bushpig and rock dassie are common. There is good bird life, including green lourie, the rare, brightly coloured narina trogon, crowned eagle, sunbirds and sugarbirds. At night you might be woken by the scream of a tree dassie. The Amatola Hiking Trail, all six days of it, passes through the Amatola Forest Reserve into the lower reserve of **Pirie Forest** (no office or phone), reached by travelling 13km north of King William's Town along the R30, then turning north on to the gravel road to Maden Dam and Trout Hatchery. Do not turn into the hatchery but keep going on the rough road, and you will reach the forest entrance. As well as access to the Amatola Trail, Pirie Forest has several walking trails. The most interesting leads 7km up through the forest to cliffs where Chief Sandile, the last Ngqika Xhosa chief to fight the British, made his stand in the Ninth, and last, Frontier War (1877–8), after which the Xhosa of the Ciskei territory were stripped of their independence.

The Pirie Forest does not receive a lot of visitors, and so the forest tends to crowd densely over the trails. Watch out for large, three-dimensional spider's webs at face-level: these are the webs of golden orb spiders, a large arachnid that won't bite if you blunder head-first into its home, but may freak you out by scuttling across your face. Green louries, samango and vervet monkeys, bushbuck, bushpig and duiker are all common.

Alice is a large town in the Tyumie Valley below the Amatolas (on the R63), now housing Fort Hare University (*see* **History**, p.42). Its handsome Victorian streets, well-kept houses, neat park and bookshops contrast sharply with the usual straggle of hut, house and garden that make up most Ciskei towns. The campus itself has a superb collection of black artists (*see* **People and Culture**, 'Art and Architecture'). The surrounding Tyumie Valley was the scene of fierce conflict between settler and Xhosa in the 1840s and '50s, when the British settled ex-soldiers on one side of the valley, and allowed the Xhosa to herd on the other. The settlers had the provocative habit of impounding any Xhosa cattle that 'trespassed' on to the wrong side of the valley, despite the fact that neither group used fences. The Ngqika Xhosa's mounting resentment against this and other provocations within their own territory helped to spark the disastrous last Frontier Wars of the 1850s and 1870s. Today's Alice and Tyumie Valley are more peaceful, though the student bars in town can get rowdy in the evening, and it is best to visit them by invitation.

Hogsback, a village in the Amatolas north of Alice along the R345 is, strictly speaking, in Cape Province, but only just, and is most easily reached via Ciskei. Hogsback is one of South Africa's loveliest spots. Around the village stretch high pastures and forest through which a series of walking trails lead to waterfalls, some of them quite large. Most spectacular is the Madonna and Child Falls, reached by a trail leaving the road on the south end of the village. Hogsback gets its name from the high, rocky ridge that runs above the village (also accessible by walking trail), and resembles the spine bristles of a bushpig.

The village itself is very quiet, strung out along about 3km of gravel road, the forest hiding most of the buildings. However, there are two old country hotels and several more moderate places to stay, as well as a forest camp site. Along the road, young Xhosa men sell animals fashioned from unfired red clay, usually horses, bushbuck or bushpigs. Some of these are very beautiful, and it is worth stopping when they hail you to see what they have.

Reckoned as one of the least developed of South Africa's mountain tourist spots, Hogsback is worth taking time over. Walk or ride the forest trails, drink in the fresh scents, and take tea on the sunny lawns of the old hotels.

Those interested in Xhosa history will be tempted to drive south of Hogsback to **Sandile's Grave**, via a signposted detour down a long, straight dirt road (used by forestry trucks) north of the R346 from King William's Town to Stutterheim. Sandile lies in a field under an ornate tomb surmounted by a bust, having fallen here after being driven from the caves of the Pirie Forest in the Ninth Frontier War. Two British troopers he killed at this last stand are buried next to him.

The Winterberg

The high, wide-horizoned plateau between the Stormberg and Winterberg ranges comprises northern Ciskei. In the western section **Tsolwana Game Reserve**, ✆ (04582) 5402, is a high, wild grassland stretching towards the Karoo. Rock-strewn, and overshadowed by the Winterberg Mountains, Tsolwana is home to large herds of antelope, zebra and wildebeest. It also harbours white rhino (more than 30 breeding wild in the reserve) and giraffe.

Visitors from Europe might be surprised to see fallow deer wandering the reserve. They are there as trophies for hunters; Tsolwana is one of the few game reserves open to sport hunting, ploughing the money back into the reserve and the local communities, from whom the land is rented, as a way to prevent poaching. Its policy seems to be working: Ciskei is extremely poor and one rhino horn represents a huge sum to any prospective poacher, yet the rhino flourish unharmed and the reserve is popular locally, even though its 17,000ha would normally be used for grazing.

A 3-day hiking trail winds through the reserve, bringing the walker very close to game—in the case of the rhino sometimes uncomfortably close (although white rhino are not irascible and are unlikely to charge). There are also horses for hire, game-viewing roads, and a small shop selling game curios, camera film, food, etc. Accommodation comprises two comfortable safari lodges and two bush camps.

Whittlesea, a small market town on the R67 to Queenstown, is the nearest point to Tsolwana (about 20km) for buying supplies and petrol. At weekends there is an open street market, and, in the lively, friendly atmosphere, a new face will be hailed and joked about loudly. Hang on to your wallet if the market is crowded. **Shiloh Mission**, near Whittlesea, is a Moravian mission built in 1828 and still active, with a fine, stuccoed church and a working water-mill. The Moravian missionaries were less active in frontier politics, and less censorious of Xhosa nudity and 'feckless' pastoralism than some of the more meddling, pompous English missionaries.

Activities

Hiking amongst game or in mountain forests is undoubtably Ciskei's most attractive feature. This can be done at **Double Drift, Tsolwana** and **Mpofu** Game Reserves, each reserve offering trails of between 1 hour and 2–3 days. Hiking in mountain forests can be done at **Hogsback** (several hikes of 1–4 hours). In the **Amatola Mountain Forest** (hikes from 1 hour–6 days), **Pirie Forest** (hikes from 1 hour–6 days), **Mpofu** (hikes of 1 hour–2 days) and in the **Katberg** and **Readsdale** Forests (hikes of 1 hour–2 days). For details of the above reserves, see individual listings. There's also a general info line for these and other Ciskei trails, ✆ (0431) 22 571.

Riding: The Xhosa are a horse-owning people, and tourists to Ciskei will see many people going about their everyday business in the saddle. For tourists, **Mpofu** and **Tsolwana** Game Reserves both offer riding amongst herds of game. The **Katberg Protea Hotel**, at Balfour, also offers horses for trails into the Katberg Forest.

Swimming: Ciskei's coast does not have many safe beaches. Exceptions are found at the **Fish River Sun**, which has its own beach, at the **Mpekweni Sun Marine Resort**, just a few kilometres to the east, and **Kiwane**, the next coastal village east of Hamburg, which has a lagoon. Elsewhere, fooling around in the shallows is fine, but avoid river mouths when the tide is going out (ask locals if you are unsure of the tide), and never swim far out, as there are cross-currents and sharks.

Game-viewing: Double Drift Game Reserve has some large game—black rhino, buffalo, hippo and most of the large antelope species. **Tsolwana Game Reserve** has white rhino, giraffe and most large antelope species. **Mpofu Game Reserve** has mainly large antelope. All the reserves have hiking trails and, in the case of Mpofu and Tsolwana, riding trails.

Where to Stay and Eating Out

expensive

King's Lodge, ✆ (045) 962 1024, is a wooden hotel just off the main street in Hogsback, with quiet gardens, a trout pool by the entrance, and Cape country cuisine (the excellent lamb is taken from local sweet-grass Amatola farms). The rooms are done up in imitation Victorian style, and are somewhere between very comfortable and luxurious. The **Katberg Protea Hotel**, ✆ (040494) 31 151/2, at the foot of the Katberg, between Balfour and the Katberg State Forest, is a large, neo-colonial affair set in parkland bordered by forest. The interior is a little bland, as with all the Protea hotels, but the surroundings are idyllic: green lawns, crowding evergreen woods, and the peaks of the Katberg, a vast amphitheatre, towering above. It has a pool and hiking/riding facilities.

Imvubu and Mbabala Lodges, at Double Drift Game Reserve, ✆ (0401) 952 115, are a collection of four cottages on the Fish River, overlooking a hippo pool, and an old Victorian farmstead in the heart of the bush. Both lodges are self-catering, but staffed. **Ntloni Lodge**, in Mpofu Game Reserve, ✆ (0401 952 115, is modern, panelled in yellowwood, and is within walking distance of some bushman paintings below the Katberg Mountains. Also self-catering and fully staffed. **Lilyfontein Lodge**, in Tsolwana Game Reserve, ✆ (0401) 952 115, is a late 19th-century Afrikaner homestead. Quite grand, the house is surrounded by a veranda overlooking Ntabethemba Mountain, a massif cut off from the main Winterberg range. Tsolwana has two smaller lodges: **Indwe Lodge** and **Otterford Lodge**. Indwe is also a late 19th-century gabled farmstead, next to the Tsolwana offices and reception, while Otterford is on the banks of the Swart Kei River. All three can be self-catering or full board by request.

moderate

Hogsback Mountain Lodge, on Main Street, ✆ (045) 962 1005, comprises several thatched self-catering rondavels looking out from the forest to the Tyumie Valley below the Amatolas. Also in Hogsback, on the main road through town, is the **Hogsback Inn**, ✆ (045) 962 1006.

Double Drift Hiking Lodge, in Double Drift Game Reserve, ✆ (0401) 952 115, is a bush camp on the Fish River, surrounded by dense euphorbia bush, and providing basic, self-catering accommodation. **Mpofu Hiking Trail Camp**, ✆ (0401) 952 115, a 10-bed dormitory-style refuge hut with water, wood and cooking utensils, sits below the Katberg Mountains in Mpofu Game Reserve. **Fundani Trail Camp** and **Pumlani Trail Camp**, both in Tsolwana Game Reserve, ✆ (0401) 952 115, are also dormitory-style refuge huts with basic self-catering facilities (including a bucket-shower heated by a wood stove), surrounded by large herds of grazing game.

On the coast, at Hamburg, the **Hamburg Hotel**, ✆ (0405) 881 061, offers clean and comfy rooms in one of the most relaxed resort towns in the whole of South Africa.

cheap

Hogsback has two backpacker lodges: **Amatola Backpackers**, ✆ (045) 962 0159, and **Away With the Fairies**, ✆ (045) 962 1031.

Hamburg has a great backpacker lodge, **Oyster Lodge,** ✆ (0405) 881 020, on the Ciskei coast, which is incredibly good value. Apart from dorms, doubles and camping, they offer a chance to catch the big cob and kingclip that teem in the river mouth. They'll pick you up from East London if you ring from there.

The Border Region

The Border region is a narrow corridor running between the former Ciskei and Transkei. A green land of sheep farms, forestry and cattle pastures, its central section is mountainous—the Amatolas—while the south gives way to a coastline of green, rounded hills and wide estuary mouths known as the Cape Wild Coast, a wistful appellation for this more developed extension of the more spectacular Transkei Wild Coast, further east. The N6 runs through the region, from Queenstown in the north to East London in the south.

History

Until the 1850s the Border Region was the home of the Gqunkhwebe clan of the Xhosa people, whose chief, Pato, led them there after being ejected from the Ciskei coast by the

British in the early 1820s. Pato then steered an awkward course with the colonists—sometimes fighting them, sometimes remaining neutral—in the series of Frontier Wars between 1824 and 1856.

When Sir Harry Smith invaded the area in the 1830s, he set up a military village, King William's Town, and a supply port, East London, in Pato's country, which he claimed (without orders from Britain) as British territory and named Queen Adelaide's Land. Smith was sent to India for his rash antics, and the territory was abandoned by the British for a while. However, in 1847 Smith returned to South Africa as Governor, to 'save' the frontier after the Xhosa re-invasion of the Eastern Cape during the War of the Axe (see p.314), and King William's Town was re-occupied. The name of the region was then changed to Victoria East, after the young English Queen. Once the war was over, Smith used the settlement as his private court. Seated on a throne, he repeatedly called in the various Xhosa chiefs to swear him fealty, to the point of kissing his boots under threat of bayonetting. He even forced the powerful warrior-chief Maqoma (see 'Frontier Wars', p.314) to kneel in front of an audience of thousands, placed his boot on the fighter's neck and publicly called him a dog.

But these theatrics did not impress the Xhosa, who again fought Smith in 1850, after he had sent a patrol into the Amatolas to depose Sandile, chief of the Ngqika Xhosa. Maqoma and Sandile persuaded most of the frontier chiefs to join in this war (which lasted until 1853), and, although Pato kept his Xhosa neutral, Chief Siyolo, of the neighbouring Ndlambe clan, laid siege to King William's Town and blockaded the roads in and out so that Smith could not reach his troops, nor supply them from East London.

This war, bloodier in terms of British and colonial losses, and costlier than any frontier war before it, dragged on for three years. Smith's consistent failure to beat the Xhosa decisively ended his military career. He and the arrogant, ineffectual Henry Somerset (the son of Lord Charles Somerset and the frontier's military commander for almost 30 years) were recalled, to be replaced by Henry Cathcart, who methodically drove off the Xhosa cattle, burned their crops and imprisoned their women (who tilled the land and supplied the warriors in the bush) until the chiefs, already exhausted by the long war, capitulated. At this point the Ngqika clan were forcibly removed from the Amatolas to a small reserve in present-day Border Country, which created serious overcrowding. Lung sickness hit the Xhosa cattle in 1854, and this coincided with the suicidal Great Cattle Killing of 1856, when, in despair, most of the Xhosa clans, including the Ngqika, destroyed their herds and grain in the belief that this would summon their ancestors and drive the hated British into the sea.

After the nation had reduced itself to starvation, Sir George Grey, Cape Governor at the time, treated the Xhosa chiefs as criminals. Among those he brought to 'trial' (on the shaky charge of inciting their people to a desperation that would force them to invade the Cape Colony and attack farms) were Pato and Siyolo of the Border Country, and Maqoma of the Ngqika. All three were sent to Robben Island, the bleak penal colony off Cape Town.

With the chiefs out of the way, Governor Grey planned to turn the Border Country and neighbouring regions into a 'chequer-board' of black and white farmers living in harmony. For this he wanted British immigrants similar to those brought out to Albany Region near Grahamstown in 1820. Instead he got Germans, mostly a rough crew of bachelor soldiers from a volunteer regiment that had fought as part of the British army in the Crimea. After a feckless few years this rowdy lot eventually settled down, capitalizing on the cheap labour of

Xhosa rendered dependent on the settlers for employment after the loss of their herds, land and crops. Today, many Border Country farmers still bear German names.

The area's tradition of Xhosa resistance continued through the apartheid years, King William's Town producing perhaps the best-known martyr of them all, Steve Biko—who died in police detention in September 1977, after which his body was brought back to King William's Town for burial. In the years leading up to the 1994 interim government, the region's proximity to the 'homelands' of Ciskei and Transkei made it subject to occasional political strife, evident in the APLA (Azanian People's Liberation Army—the terrorist wing of the PAC) attacks on white restaurants in Queenstown and King William's Town in 1992, and some isolated killing of white farmers. But for the most part the area's rural hinterland remains quiet, a region of tranquil farms that carry no outward sign of the bitter struggles that once raged across their green acres.

Queenstown

This northern region of the Border Country has little to offer the tourist, except the N6 highway leading to the Cape Drakensberg and the Free State, and the wild Stormberg Mountains. Queenstown, which lies at the foot of the Stormberg, is a large regional centre, useful for stocking up and resting, but with little to see. Dubbed the 'Rose Capital' of South Africa, for the summertime blooms in its parks (though Bloemfontein also makes this claim), Queenstown was proclaimed in 1847 by Sir Harry Smith, flush with his victory over the Xhosa chiefs during the War of the Axe. Originally a military village, Queenstown was one of the few on the eastern frontier never to be attacked. The town settled into prosperity early, and since the 1860s has held an agricultural show that is still one of the country's largest.

It is worth strolling along the two marked hiking trails at the **Berry Reservoir**, on Milner Street, which wind through a large garden of flowering aloes, all identified. The **Collector's Museum**, 4 Reservoir Street (*open Mon–Fri 9–5*), is an excellent monument to one man's quiet eccentricity. The private home of a Mr Rex Abbott, it exhibits his vast collections of telephones, dolls, car badges, and old kitchen implements, all labelled with any appropriate anecdotes. The garden is a collection too—of exotic cacti and indigenous Karoo succulents. The car badge collection claims to be the biggest in the world. The **Frontier Musuem**, on Shepstone Street (*open Mon–Fri 8.30–12.45 and 2–4.45*), is more conservative—the usual monument to the hardships of pioneer life. The museum has even constructed a rough-and-ready frontier cottage. The Frontier Wars are given several rooms of paintings and regimental regalia. The accompanying labels tell the colonists' version of events, rather than that of the Xhosa and Khoi. The **Old Market Business Plaza**, to the west side of the **Hexagon Park**, on Cathcart Street (the town's main drag), is a redeveloped but handsome market building (built in the 1850s), whose inside has been partitioned into shops and craft workshops.

Around Queenstown

In the **Lawrence De Lange Game Reserve**, numerous plains game species (including kudu, black wildebeest, zebra, ostrich, blesbok and springbok) wander the hillside among the flowering aloes for which the reserve is known. The best time to visit is in winter, when the *Aloe ferox*, which flowers a vivid red, covers the hillside in bright colour. There is no accommodation, but hikers are allowed to pitch tents.

The **Koos Ras Game Reserve** is about 40km north of town along the N6, then 10km west on the R56 towards Sterkstroom. A small reserve, it has hiking trails through transitional grassland/karoo scrub terrain. Kudu, blesbok, eland, impala, black wildebeest, zebra and springbok are common. **Carnarvon Estate** is a family-owned farm 50km north of Queenstown along the N6, and 8km east towards the village of Haseleton. The farm incorporates a large private wetland reserve, with two hiking trails and two lodges. The reserve has springbok, waterbuck, reedbuck, lechwe (introduced from Botswana), steenbok, black eagle and ostrich, as well as waterfowl, particularly fish eagle, snipe, various duck species, heron and egrets. Blue cranes sometimes stop here on their migratory flights.

Where to Stay

expensive

Carnarvon Estate, on the road from Queenstown to Sterkstroom, ✆ (04592) 3311/3320, offers full board in an old homestead at the foot of the Stormberg. There is hiking, riding and game-viewing for guests. Expect to be pampered, especially with the food; game and Karoo mutton are the speciality. **Eagle's Ridge Mountain Inn**, ✆ (0433) 31200, by the Kologha State Forest, west of Stutterheim, is an old-fashioned country hotel complete with a library of old novels in the lounge, horses to ride, forest walks and a tennis court. The hotel itself is not particularly attractive, but the surroundings are very lovely, being at the forested foot of the Amatolas. The rooms are pretty standard: clean, neat and en suite without any special luxury.

moderate

Aloe Grove Guest Farm, ✆ (0451) 5910, 17km from Queenstown along the Dordrecht road, is a Victorian farmstead set in mountain country. There are rondavels, or a double room in the farmhouse, with breakfast (and lunch and dinner by request). Facilities include a pool, good bird life and mountain walks. **Bradford Guest Lodge**, ✆ (0451) 3313, is 18km from Queenstown towards Tarkastad, in another farmhouse offering full board in airy, comfortable rooms with a farm to wander. Good home cooking. Fishing and watersports can be arranged, as well as daycare for children.

In Queenstown itself try: **Carthew's Corner**, ✆ (0451) 4112; **Longview Lodge B&B**, ✆ (0451) 82 967; **Shaw's**, ✆ (0451) 3993; **Siesta B&B**, ✆ (0451) 2337.

cheap

Koos Ras Nature Reserve, ✆ (04592) 8, on the R345 near Sterkstroom north of Queenstown, offers chalets and camping.

Eating Out

The **Grand Hotel**, Queenstown, ✆ (0451) 3017/8, has a restaurant serving big juicy steaks and seafood amid a strange mixture of plastic chairs and wood-panelled walls. **Hotel Bagatelle**, just north of Stutterheim, ✆ (0436) 31220, is a country restaurant offering game, some Cape dishes and the usual steaks in an 'olde worlde' atmosphere, with much dark wood and a blazing log fire in winter. King William's Town lacks good independent restaurants, and the only eating out to be had is either in the town hotels, which offer the standard *à la carte* fare, or at the chain restaurants, **Spur** and **Mike's Kitchen**.

The Border Country Amatolas

Cathcart, a village off the N6 some 55km south of Queenstown, is one of the jumping-off points for the Amatolas. The village is just a small farming centre, however, in the mountains nearby is **Benghoil**, a guest farm offering horse trails and hikes (*see* 'Activities', p.356).

Stutterheim, a 19th-century German town, is another 48km south along the N6. Useful as an entry point to the Amatolas, the nearest slopes are about 15km west of town at the **Kologha State Forest**, which has a short walking trail following a series of waterfalls through the woods. There is a camp site just outside the gates to the reserve. Following the R346 southwest of Stutterheim, the road re-enters Ciskei and the **Pirie Forest** (part of the Amatola Hiking Trail), passing Sandile's grave (*see* p.344).

King William's Town is 50km southwest of Stutterheim on the R346. 'King' is a strange town. Founded in war by Sir Harry Smith in the 1830s, abandoned, then re-occupied after the War of the Axe in 1847, it has always been something of a hot-bed of Xhosa/settler tension, hiding under the guise of a quiet regional town. Steve Biko was born and buried here. In **Bisho**, the hurriedly built capital of Ciskei (1981) that sits on the opposite hill, former Ciskei's then president Oupa Xhosa ordered his troops to fire on ANC supporters during a march in 1991, killing several and injuring many. The following year, APLA blew up the Spur restaurant in King William's Town, killing two whites. But a sense of exterior calm is maintained by the handsome façades of its older buildings, and its quiet, tree-lined residential streets.

The **Kaffrarian Museum**, on Main Street (*open Mon–Fri 9–12.45 and 2–5*), is one of the few museums in South Africa to depict history from a non-colonial viewpoint. It is housed in two adjacent buildings: the newer section has a Xhosa history put together by Xhosa historians, dealing plainly with Britain's role in shattering the Xhosa culture during the endless Frontier Wars. But the account is not completely partisan; the section on modern Ciskei and Transkei is frank about the factional in-fighting that has plagued black politics throughout this century, and tells how traditional culture, particularly folk medicine, has survived the breakdown of most of the old traditions. Xhosa mythology and art are well represented.

The main building houses a very good collection of stuffed South African mammals. If you are still unsure of the differences between the numerous small antelope species, or want to see just how many rodents inhabit the *veld*, this is the museum for you. Also displayed is Huberta the Hippo, who wandered down the coast from St Lucia in Zululand to the Border Region between 1928 and 1931 (a distance of more than 1000km) until a local farmer shot her, and the museum stuffed her. With Huberta are the press cuttings that charted her progress; she was a national personality until her demise, being the only hippo to venture into the Eastern Cape for about 50 years. Today, hippo have been reintroduced in some game reserves. The museum also has a history of the Cape Mounted Rifles, better known as the Cape Corps, a Khoi cavalry regiment founded in the early 1800s. Frontier commanders relied on the Cape Corps to do the bulk of the fighting during the Frontier Wars, yet treated them as second-class citizens and exhibited obvious distrust of them. Some units did finally rebel in exasperation, and fought with the Xhosa in the Eighth Frontier War (1850–53), but the regiment was kept on and was later sent to Europe to fight in both World Wars. They acquitted themselves heroically, but little was said of it at the time, the South African establishment being ever-uneasy of praising 'coloureds'.

The **Missionary Museum**, on Barkly Street (*open Mon–Fri 9–5*), is a must for any serious student of South African history. More than the colonial governments and even the *trek-boers*, it was the early 19th-century missionaries from Moravia, London and Glasgow who opened up the interior to colonial expansion. Frequently at odds with the military governments, the missionaries began as a humanistic bunch, unwilling to break down indigenous traditions such as nudity and polygamy, concentrating instead on the 'soul'. Stephanus Van der Kemp and his assistant, James Read, who in the early 1800s became the Eastern Cape's first missionaries (first to the Khoi and then to the Xhosa), were particularly high-profile advocates of this approach and did their best to stop the white settlers from abusing the indigenous people. This made them very unpopular with the colonists. Van der Kemp died in 1812, but James Read continued his liberalist methods and, by the 1830s, the frontier settlers were demanding a more Europeanist type of missionary, who equated the material trappings of 'civilization' (i.e. clothes, working for money, becoming British subjects) with salvation. The frontier was duly evangelized by a number of incredibly narrow-minded, reactionary men who did much to provoke the frayed patience of the Xhosa. However, these missionaries unwittingly trained the first generations of black activists (who began to campaign as early as the 1870s), by pioneering black education, and opening a path for the slow journey from conquered subjects to citizens. The museum gives a more colonial view of the missionaries' work, but there are plans to change this, and the present exhibition at least provides an accurate chronology.

Where to Stay

There is a range of moderately priced accommodation in the area. If you need to spend a night in King William's Town, there are the standard chain hotels along the main drag. For B&B, however, try **Grosvenor Guest House**, ℰ (0433) 33 107, or the **Grosvenor Lodge Hotel**, ℰ (0433) 21 440.

Otherwise, Stutterheim has some good guest farms and B&Bs: **Amoglen**, ℰ (0436) 32 452; **Rogues Roost**, ℰ (0436) 32 535; **Waterfall Farm**, ℰ (0436) 31 532.

In Cathcart, try the **Glenfinlas B&B**, ℰ (045) 633 1727.

East London

Getting There

By bus: TransLux, ℰ (0431) 442 333, connect between here and Port Elizabeth, Durban (via Umtata) and Gauteng. They pick up and leave from the train station on Station Road, parallel with, and two blocks east of, Oxford Street, the city's main drag. **Greyhound** are more problematic. For some reason they insist on stopping at/leaving from a Shell station (Shell Auto Care) in Amalinda, a few kms out of town, which necessitates an R30 taxi ride. And they only do the Port Elizabeth–Durban route via East London and Umtata. A better bet is **InterCape**, ✆ (0431) 533 184, or **MiniLux**, ✆ (0431) 413 107, who also do the coast route, and use the train station. Backpackers should use the **Baz Bus**, ✆ (021) 439 2323, *see* **Travel**, p.9.

By train: East London sits on the Port Elizabeth–Jo'burg route, connected by a train service called the **Amatola**, ✆ (0431) 442 719.

Tourist Information

East London Publicity Association, 35 Argyle Street, ✆ (0431) 26 015.

This port, on the N2 at the mouth of the Buffalo River, was founded by Harry Smith in the 1830s to supply his military headquarters at King William's Town. Now a small city with a still-active dock, East London is used by most travellers as a jumping-off point for the Cape Wild Coast and Transkei.

The small town centre is quite handsome (a lot of imposing Victorian buildings have survived), but it is rather unexciting, despite its bustle. The main thoroughfare is Oxford Street, which runs north–south to the docks. East London has a beach and a seafront: but the latter was, alas, re-developed in the 1960s, and is now a series of concrete block buildings with no real charm, despite having lively bars. In short, East London is a town to pass through quickly.

However, there are some points of interest. The **East London Museum**, on Oxford Street (*open Mon–Fri 9.30–5, Sat 9.30–12, Sun 11–4*), has the stuffed body of the first coelacanth to be found. A prehistoric fish species has survived in South African waters since the Mezoic Period, 250 million million years ago; this modern specimen was netted by an East London trawler in the 1960s. The museum also has a dodo's egg from Mauritius, apparently the only known surviving egg in the world.

The **Gately Museum**, on Queen Street (*open weekends only, 3–5*), was the house of East London's first mayor, John Gately. The period furnishings are intact. The **Anne Bryant Gallery**, off Oxford Street between St Mark's Road and St Luke's Road (*open Mon–Fri 9–5, Sat 9.30–12*), has some good Pierneff landscapes and some mediocre sporting sculpture. About 13km east of town on the Maclean Town Road is the **Calgary Museum** (*open Weds–Sun 9–4*), which contains a collection of old horse-drawn vehicles. The **Dog Box**, on Oxford Street, is a strange place. Ostensibly a pet shop, many black East Londoners buy live poultry here—the shop is alive with the birds and their chicks. Run by an energetic, elderly woman from Sussex, whose prize-winning Alsatian dog is memorialized in a large colour photo above the counter, the Dog Box is not something you would expect from such a staid town. Look for the Victorian building with painted cartoon dogs on the front.

The **Old Lock Street Gaol**, on Fleet Street (in fact one of the old garrison forts, and later South Africa's first women's prison), has been turned into a small complex of shops and cafés. All the old buildings remain, while some of the gaol's original features have been preserved, including the hanging chamber.

Orient Beach and Eastern Beach, next to the town, are safe for swimming, have good rock-pool life and are excellent places from which to see dolphins, whole schools of which sometimes appear in the surf.

expensive

East London has the standard chain hotels, the most popular being the **King David Hotel**, on Inverleith Terrace, ✆ 23 174. **Le Petit**, 54 Beach Road, ✆ 353 685/6, Nahoon (a suburb of East London), is rather self-consciously upmarket with expensive chintz decor, but nonetheless serves very good classical French dishes. The service is very formal and correct. **Bellami's**, 18 Marine Terrace, ✆ 432 145, offers nouvelle cuisine without being overly pretentious (and the helpings are a bit larger than the average nouvelle restaurant). The dining room is rather stark but the service is friendly and the atmosphere relaxed. The fish dishes are the best. Superb seafood can be had at the **Sunset Restaurant**, ✆ 474 821, in the Blue Lagoon Timeshare flats on Beacon Bay, a few kilometres from town.

Other hotels in this price range are: **The Dolphin**, ✆ 351 435; **The Esplanade Hotel**, ✆ 22 518—with good ocean views; **The Garden Court**, ✆ 27 260 (now owned by Holiday Inn); the **Majestic**, ✆ 437 477; the **Osner Hotel**, ✆ 433 433. All offer luxury but tend to be a little bland.

moderate

If you're looking for B&B, try **Marianne's Bed and Breakfast**, out at Beacon Bay, ✆ 472 760; **Seagull's Guest Lodge**, 34 Bonanza Street, ✆ 21 049, out in the suburb of Quigney; **St Andrew's Lodge**, ✆ 435 131; **The Loerie Hide**, ✆ 353 206; **Wetmore's Pad**, ✆ 51 606.

The **Tug and Ferry**, ✆ 431 188, on Latimer's Landing, in the old harbour, serves a mixture of seafood, steaks and pasta to a predominantly young clientele. Also down on Latimer's Landing is **Hunter's Jetty**, ✆ 438 410, a grill which offers you a choice of skewered, seasoned meat which is then cooked at your table. **Casbah**, in the King David Hotel, is fairly expensive, and serves an *à la carte* menu of French dishes, seafood and steaks. **Tropics**, at the Osner Hotel, on the Esplanade, is more fun, and specializes in stir-fry dishes. The **Prawn Inn**, on Clifford St, ✆ 24 253, is a good seafood joint with the standard nautical bits and bobs on the walls, offering fresh line-fish and shellfish caught that morning. **Finnegan's**, 40 Terminus St, ✆ 25 585, is a decent restaurant serving steaks, seafood, good burgers and the odd French dish. A bit bland inside, but good value for money.

cheap

The **Sugarshack Backpackers** ✆ 28 240, is on Eastern Beach. On the town's actual beach front is the **Blooming Buffalo Backpackers**, ✆ 439 157. Also try **East London Backpackers**, ✆ 23 423.

The **Spud Rock Café**, 21 Devereux St, ✆ 57 298, does baked potatoes and kebabs. Some of the seafood fillings are really delicious. Bring your own booze. **Platform One**, ✆ 420 185, is a bar in one of the ugly modern buildings on the Esplanade, serving bar meals. Surfers and business people gather here in the evening. The bar is nothing special, but the window tables look out over the ocean. **Santa Monica** is a cheap seafood, steak and fried chicken place on the Esplanade (another ugly building). As the name suggests, it caters for surfers, with big music video screens and young beach folk drinking beer. There is a camp site just outside the gates to the **Kologha State Forest.**

cafés

East London has a couple of continental coffee houses. **Café Wien**, in the Patcyn Centre, Frere Road, does home-baked pastries and really good coffee, while **Stephanie's Coffee Shop**, on St Luke's Road, offers the more standard toasted sandwiches and hot drinks.

Nightlife

East London has a few clubs, all of which play a standard mix of oldie rock and Top 40. If you want to dance, try **Numbers Nightclub**, close to the Osner Hotel (mostly students and yuppies), or **Numbers Disco**, in the Quigley Centre on the Esplanade. The **Beach Hotel**, 12 Kirkpatrick Street, hosts a 'Weekend Rave' in its Seaview Bar. Surfers hang out here.

Lively bars are: **Buccanneer's**, **Santa Monica** and **Platform One** on the Esplanade, and the **Rose and Crown**, in the Patcyn Centre, Frere Road, a straightforward pub.

For live music, try **Jekyll & Hyde**, in the Lock Street Gaol. Every April the town hosts a rocking **Reggae Festival**.

Around East London

Mpongo Park, a game reserve set in rolling grassland along the Pongo River, some 29km from East London, has some big game—elephant, white rhino and giraffe—as well as the usual complement of large antelope species. At the park office is a small animal orphanage for creatures that have been injured or abandoned. Visitors are sometimes allowed into the pens with a staff member, and even to handle the animals. Mpongo has a **camp site**.

Bridle Drift Nature Reserve is set around a dam about 10km west of town along the R346. There are only walking trails, and you cannot drive inside the reserve. You are unlikely to spot any game, but the bird life is prolific; fish eagles in particular are often seen. **Gonubie Nature Reserve** is a tiny (8ha) piece of wetland next to the holiday resort and beach of Gonubie, a short drive east of East London along the N2. Crowned cranes nest here (as well as a host of other birds) and there are observation platforms built into the *vlei*. Of further interest is a small indigenous herb garden, called the Witchdoctor's Garden, from which local Xhosa herbalists and diviners gather their stock. Some of the plants are labelled, and their medicinal properties listed.

The Cape Wild Coast

Between East London and Transkei is the stretch of coastline known as the Cape Wild Coast. Neither as wild nor as beautiful as the Transkei Wild Coast, the Cape section is mainly composed of small resorts clustered around old-fashioned hotels, reached from the N2 by dirt roads through the bush. However, if you know where to go, this coastline has some lovely, unspoilt bits, listed below.

Bosbokstrand Nature Reserve is about 40km east of East London along the N2, then a few kilometres south on the gravel road to Haga-Haga, a small beach resort with a very ugly hotel. Set along the coast west of the resort, Bosbokstrand comprises forest, beach and estuary. Bushbuck, eland, blesbok and impala wander the reserve, and even browse along the beach. There is safe swimming, a camp site, rondavels and a shop for general supplies.

Cape Henderson Nature Reserve sits immediately next to Bosbokstrand, by Haga-Haga. Also composed of coastal forest and beach, the reserve is good for spotting green lourie and sunbirds. There are a few shy bushbuck and duiker; vervet monkeys live in the trees.

Morgan's Bay, on the coast about 90km east of East London (follow the N2 for 66km, then turn south on the gravel R349 to Kei Mouth), is a small resort village comprising a hotel, a few houses and little else. Set beneath great cliffs, Morgan's Bay is undoubtedly the most attractive resort near East London. From the hotel, several good walks (east to Kei Mouth or west to a wild lagoon) lead along beaches known for their rich shell deposits.

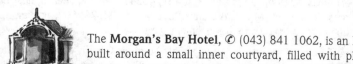

Kei Mouth, a slightly larger resort village 10km east of Morgan's Bay, looks across the Kei estuary to Transkei. The best way to visit is to stroll about an hour along the beach from Morgan's Bay. The estuary mouth itself is very wide, and a fabulous view of it can be had from atop a small wooded hill in the centre of the village, which has a marked footpath leading to the summit. East of here, the real Wild Coast begins. Kei Mouth has some shops, a bank (*open Tues and Thurs only*) and a petrol station. Its hotel is more modern than, but not as attractive as, the one at Morgan's Bay.

Ocean View Guest Farm and Nature Reserve, ✆ (04372) 2603, in the bush along the R349 to Morgan's Bay and Kei Mouth, is a working farm, but with a large stretch of forest that is great for bird-watching. Crowned and long-crested eagles (two rare species) breed here, as do massive ground hornbills—the rottweilers of the bird kingdom—and elegant crowned and blue cranes. There are also bushbuck, duiker and samango monkey. The forest is cut through with walking trails and there are bird-watching hides (*see* below).

Where to Stay

expensive

The **Morgan's Bay Hotel**, ✆ (043) 841 1062, is an Edwardian hotel built around a small inner courtyard, filled with plants and caged parrots, and overlooking the sea. It has a good pub, fresh seafood in the restaurant, fishing tackle for hire, and a free pick-up from East London. The rooms are not fancy, but are comfortable, with en suite bathrooms; most have a sea view.

moderate

Buccaneer's Retreat, ✆ (0431) 383 012, in Cintsa, 35km east of East London, is a group of 8 small self-contained cottages overlooking a freshwater lagoon and the sea with their own stretch of private beach, safe for swimming. Birds flit among the coastal bush separating the cottages. It is very tranquil; guests can cook for themselves or eat in a central dining house, and the limited number of cottages makes for a limited number of people. Fishing and watersports can be arranged. **Crawford's Cintsa Beach**, ✆ (0431) 385 000, on the north bank of the Cintsa River mouth, across from Buccaneer's Retreat, is slightly more expensive. Crawford's has some 30 white-washed, thatched cottages surrounding a large central house set in coastal bush, with a restaurant (mostly seafood) and good views over the ocean. In summer you eat on a terrace. There is a bar, sauna, jacuzzi and private beach.

cheap

Buccaneer's Backpackers, ✆ (0431) 383 012, right on the beach at Cintsa Beach, has cheap rondavels and dorms, as well as free use of surfboards, canoes and boogie boards. Further east, the **Kei Mouth Backpackers**, ✆ (083) 701 2106, offers a similar service.

Ocean View Guest Farm and Game Reserve is on the R349 to Haga-Haga and Morgan's Bay, about 75km from East London. The farm and forest reserve have self-contained chalets, as well as a small camp site with an ablution block. The air is full of the incessant chatter of wood hoepoes and the booming of louries. Excellent value, and a beautiful place to stay. **Bosbokstrand Nature Reserve**, ✆ (04372) 4512, next to Haga-Haga, has chalets that, if split between two or more, fall within the cheap price range, as well as a **camp site**.

Activities

Walking and Hiking: The Border Region has several good trails. The **Lawrence De Lange Nature Reserve** has overnight trails (hikers must bring a tent and a camping stove). **Carnarvon Estate** also has an overnight trail, with two camping huts. Both are good for game-spotting. Day-hikes can be found in the **Lawrence De Lange Reserve**, the **Kologha State Forest** (forest and waterfalls) and **Bridle Drift, Bosbokstrand, Cape Henderson** and **Ocean View** reserves.

Riding: **Benghoil Horse Safaris**, ✆ (04562) 2203, in the mountains above Cathcart, offers trails from a couple of hours to several days through wild country rich in bird life, exotic plants—such as cycads—and antelope, to caverns rich in bushman paintings. **Welcome Stables**, ✆ (0461) 462511, at Igoda Beach, near East London, offers beach rides. **Mpongo Game Reserve**, ✆ (04326) 669, also arranges game-spotting horse trails by prior arrangement.

Swimming: Safe beaches can be found at East London (**Orient Beach, Nahoon Beach** and **Kidd's Beach**) and at many places up the coast between East London and Transkei. The most attractive of these are **Gonubie** (10km east along the N2), **Buccaneer's Retreat** (35km east along the N2), **Bosbokstrand** near Haga-Haga (72km east along the N2) and **Morgan's Bay** (90km east along the N2).

Fishing: If you'd like to try your hand at marlin and shark, or the smaller kabbeljou, snoek, grunter and kob, ring **Deep Sea Fishing**, © (0431) 25 151.

Transkei

There is a world of roving grass
White-faced huts looking down on paths and cattle...
Beyond and beyond, afloat
Topple the blue peaks of the Drakensberg

The White-Faced Huts, H. F. Sampson

East of East London and the Cape Wild Coast begins the great sweep of upland pasture, mountain and wild sub-tropical coastline of Transkei, heartland of the Xhosa people. The N2 highway winds across the hills and valleys of central Transkei, linking the Cape Province with Natal. In between is Africa. Transkei has few modern towns, despite running its own civil service from the small capital, Umtata. Here traditional Xhosa life goes on in a way that has largely disappeared inside the borders of Cape Province. Xhosa herdboys and horsemen use the grass verge as their own turf road, and cattle and goats graze alongside the highway, making fast driving extremely dangerous. Round huts, often brightly painted, dot the green, rounded hills.

Away from the highway, life is slow and superstition and folklore strong. Spirits and ancestors are very much present in the minds of rural Transkeians. Life is still lived around the cattle kraal, and wealth is still calculated in head of cattle. Traditional dress has largely disappeared (except among the long-braided, enigmatic diviners that exist in every community), but the tenor of rural life has changed little.

The traveller's main reason for visiting Transkei is the **Wild Coast**, over 300km of verdant, sometimes forested downs fronting white sand beaches so unspoilt that shoals of fish can be seen swimming in the surf. Great estuary mouths and freshwater lagoons cut across the beaches every 20km or so, along whose mangroved banks live small communities of fishermen. The Wild Coast has a few quiet resorts, and a hiking trail running along its entire length that is ranked as one of the best in southern Africa.

History

In the early 19th century, the Xhosa clans living in Transkei (i.e. east of the Kei River) were the Gcaleka, paramount clan of the Xhosas, and their satellite clans, the Mfengu and Mpondo. Protected from the struggles of the Eastern Cape frontier by geographical distance, they were left pretty well undisturbed by colonists (with the exception of missionaries and the odd emissary from the Cape Governor) until 1835, when Sir Harry Smith rashly decided to invade the Transkei.

The immediate results of this invasion were tragic, and the long-term effects disastrous for the whole Xhosa nation. Sir Harry Smith had been bogged down, campaigning inconclusively against the Ngqika Xhosas near the Fish River (see 'History', p.313), and only in exasperation turned his attention to the Gcaleka, paramount clan of the Xhosa, mistakenly believing that he could demand compensation from Hintsa for cattle stolen from colonists by the Ngqika, despite the fact that Hintsa was not involved in any border raiding, living over 200km east of any white farmer, and that the Ngqika acted independently of any direction from Hintsa. Moreover, Smith demanded that Hintsa order the frontier Xhosa to cease warring with the British, even though, again, he was not involved in the war and had no direct influence over the frontier chiefs. Weak though his reasoning was, Smith marched into Transkei, demanded a vast amount of cattle, and when this was only tokenly met, took Hintsa prisoner, making him promise to stop the Ngqika from continuing the war. Hintsa, seeing the impossibility of his position, tried to escape but was pulled from his horse by Sir Harry Smith, then shot in cold blood and his ears cut off as trophies.

The outrage and insult was indescribable. To the Xhosa, a chief and his property were inviolate and, until Hintsa's murder, most colonists had respected this. It was now clear that no chief could trust the British, whose arrogance was seen to be lethal. Hintsa's murder did not stop the war. The Ngqika only ceased hostilities later in the year, after both they and the British had been ground down into stalemate. But the Xhosa's cease-fire was voluntary, and there was no surrender.

Transkei then remained untouched by the colonists (again, except for missionary activity) for over a decade. However, the British invited the 16,000-strong Mfengu (Fingo) clan, then living in Transkei, to settle in the new province of British Kaffraria (modern Ciskei) on land confiscated from the frontier Xhosa clans. The Mfengu were not proper Xhosas, but a refugee tribe that had fled west from Natal during Shaka Zulu's wars of the 1820s. The Gcaleka had allowed them to settle in Transkei, but treated them as second-class citizens. The Mfengu were therefore very open to British influence and, when the chance came to move out of Transkei onto land of their own, they readily accepted, giving the colonists both Xhosa allies in time of war, and a buffer zone between the colony and the Transkei in times of peace.

Transkei remained peaceful through the Frontier Wars of the 1840s, but in 1850 Sir Harry Smith (now Cape Governor) again invaded. But this time the Gcaleka, under Sarili, Hintsa's son, were ready. They joined the general war west of the Kei, then retreated back to the Transkei and led the British columns a merry dance in the region's northern mountains. Driving their cattle into safe mountain hideaways, the Gcaleka threw boulders down on the British, and harried them with ambushes, always remaining one step ahead of the pursuit. The British gave up and withdrew in 1851, to concentrate on fighting the Ngqika and Ndlambe clans further west.

However, by 1853 the tables had turned. The British had forced the Ngqika and Ndlambe to surrender by burning their crops and imprisoning the women, who kept their men in the field supplied with food (a ruthless tactic that was later to win the Anglo-Boer War for the British, *see* **History**). By the end of the war (1853) the Xhosa clans west of the Kei had lost their land, and the Gcaleka found themselves isolated, the last pocket of Xhosa resistance on the eastern frontier.

The Great Cattle Killing

Sarili seems to have known that the days of his Gcaleka independence were numbered, and in his desperate search for a solution, he was perhaps susceptible to irrational influence. Certainly, through the mid 1850s, which were marked by drought, famine and low morale caused by the loss of the Eighth Frontier War, he and his people were slipping towards despair. But in 1856 came the event which caused the collapse of the entire Xhosa nation. A young woman called Nongqawuse, niece of a diviner living near the Qolora River mouth (just east of the Kei), claimed that strange voices had spoken to her from one of the river pools, telling her that if the Xhosas would destroy all their grain and kill all their cattle, the ancestors would rise, bringing new herds and filling the granaries, and sweep the white man into the sea. A few months later another adolescent seer made similar claims, and soon news of the prophecies spread across the entire Xhosa nation.

The Xhosa chiefs had heard about Britain's war in the Crimea, and of her heavy losses there, and fostered a naïve, desperate hope that the British South Africans might be defeated by Russians invading in ships, with whom the Xhosa could ally. This, combined with the millenarian claim of the young woman and her diviner uncle, seem to have convinced Sarili, who after some initial scepticism began to slaughter his own herds and sent word to all other chiefs to do the same by 11 August 1856.

The order met with various reactions from the Xhosa chiefs in Transkei and on the frontier, and caused much strife between believers and unbelievers. Still, vast amounts of cattle were killed, and granaries destroyed. When the ancestors failed to rise on the appointed day, the failure was attributed to the disobedience of unbelieving chiefs. A second date was set for February 1857.

The reactions of white frontier colonists ranged from horror to glee. The Governor, Sir George Grey, admitted that this was a chance for the British to settle the Xhosa once and for all without spending a single penny, while their inevitable self-imposed destitution would reduce them to dependence on white farmers for employment. He made no move to stop the killing.

By the end of February many frontier and Transkei Xhosa were already starving. By July thousands had died, including Nongqawuse's uncle, and Sarili renounced his belief. In just under a year and a half, the Xhosa had lost everything. Many streamed into the towns on the frontier looking for food. It was common to see Xhosa dead in the streets. Cannibalism broke out in the more remote districts, and those Xhosa who had not destroyed their grain and cattle found themselves under attack from those who had.

Some British missionaries set up famine relief centres, but Grey shut them down. Nongqawuse was taken away for questioning (and for her own safety). Sir George Grey set up a series of courts to try the Xhosa chiefs who had taken part in the cattle killing on loose charges of inciting their people to war through putting them in such desperate straits, and sent them to Robben Island. Sarili remained free but, despite his pleas for food for his people, was warned that the British government now regarded him as hostile and that he would be arrested at the slightest provocation.

There is still confusion as to why the Great Cattle Killing happened. Governor Grey asserted that Sarili saw this as a chance to force the Xhosa to band together and fight a decisive war against the British to take back their confiscated lands. Others maintain that his belief was sincere, and that the movement was an attempt to unify the nation to a cohesive unit that could properly resist white incursions. In his chapter on the Cattle Killing in the *New Illustrated History of South Africa* (Human & Rousseau, Cape Town, 1986), the historian John Benyon suggests that the killing was a premeditated political strategy on the part of Sarili: 'Instead of victory in war, as in 1847, the old Xhosa order in 1856–7 aimed at victory through reconciliation, and this resulted in the so called "Great Cattle Killing". Still other historians believe that the situation was manipulated by wealthy settlers and the British government. The only thing that is certain is the extent of tragedy.

The Transkei was declared a British magistracy and opened to colonization, and the destitute Transkei Xhosa provided a ready market for white traders and livestock speculators, and towns grew up around the mission stations at Butterworth, Umtata, and Port St Johns, as well as around the larger trading posts of Flagstaff and Willowvale. As the price of wool rose steadily through the 1880s Transkeians showed a remarkable resilience; by concentrating on sheep-farming, they were soon prospering again, albeit as British dependants.

The government became alarmed, seeing the unexpected Xhosa prosperity as a threat to the cheap labour pool on which the Cape Colony depended, especially for the newly booming mines up at Kimberley. In an attempt to force the Transkei Xhosa to seek employment with whites, legislation was passed in 1887 to curb their voting franchise, and to make 'squatting' (i.e. occupation of non-privately owned land, such as village common land) an offence.

But by now, many mission-educated Xhosa were beginning to enter the professional classes in the Eastern Cape, and resistance to government interference was strong. Individual Xhosa farmers resisted by refusing to have their land valued to see if their possessions qualified them for the vote, or as freeholders of their acreages. But through the early 1900s increasing pressure from white farmers and industrialists caused more and more repressive legislation to be passed, including the infamous Native Land Act of 1913 which set aside just 13 per cent of the new South African Republic for black Africans, dispossessing hundreds of thousands of people. The Transkei Xhosa found themselves pushed on to smaller and smaller parcels of land, with chiefs being gradually stripped of their power. Severe droughts through the 1920s, coupled with cattle sickness and locust plagues, reduced them to desperation again.

By the 1920s political campaigning by Xhosa leaders began to have violent repercussions. White Transkei magistrates jailed one Wellington Buthelezi, a Natal-born black campaigner active in Transkei (no relative of today's famous Zulu leader of the same name), whose urges to the rural population to resist colonial government were so successful that taxes had become almost impossible to collect. However, good land was now too scarce to support significant populations, and more and more Transkei Xhosa drifted to the mines. The government's attempts to make the place into a cheap labour pool were succeeding.

By the time the Nationalists took power in 1948 and introduced apartheid, Transkei had firmly established its present status as the power-base of black action among the military wings of the ANC and PAC. After the Sharpeville riots of 1960 eastern Transkei erupted into violence, and a state of emergency was declared. Although many of the young ANC activists at the time were Transkei-born (including Nelson Mandela), the ANC was not very active in Transkei. However, the PAC's military wing, *Poqo*, largely based in the Transkei (*see* **History**), favoured direct attacks on whites. Police stations in the Cape were targeted, but also white civilians and, in 1963, the first of many murders of whites in Transkei occurred at Mbashe Bridge, where a group of people, including women and children, were attacked and killed. Arrests followed, but a precedent had been set that still makes Transkei a potentially dangerous area for whites.

In 1976 Transkei was declared an independent state, along with several other South African black 'homelands', in a move both to ensure the region's export of cheap labour to the cities and mines (by making Transkeians foreigners, the government would have no obligations to provide services, while setting favourable labour prices in their own territories) and to curb Xhosa militarism by setting up puppet rulers from the existing hierarchy of chiefs. The plan backfired. While the cheap labour pool was ensured, Transkeian activists had, with the removal of South African police and army, a freer base from which to act. In the 1980s Bantu Holomisa, the Transkei's military commander, began to take an increasingly confrontational stand against South Africa. By the early 1990s attacks on whites within Transkei by APLA (the Azanian People's Liberation Army, as the terrorist wing of the PAC was then called) had become commonplace, and fewer and fewer whites dared venture there. Meanwhile, South Africa's recession caused thousands of Transkei Xhosa men to lose their jobs in the mines and to drift home penniless and landless, a ready pool of disaffected youth for the political organizations to draw on.

While the Transkei government denied any encouragement of terrorist groups, most South Africans believe that Transkei remained the base of APLA, whose 1993 'one settler, one bullet' slogan made travelling there very hazardous. Many Transkei Xhosa, unable to make a living in the Eastern Cape, have drifted to the cities, particularly Cape Town, to look for work, living in squatter camps. Transkei was re-absorbed into South Africa in 1994, but the region, though outwardly calm in the countryside, is still one of South Africa's most volatile.

Safety

The political climate in Transkei has calmed down considerably since 1993, but many travellers are shy of the region, and even the largely peaceful Wild Coast—for a long time an established playground for travellers—now receives few visitors, leaving the small resorts that used to flourish there in financial trouble. However, for the adventurous, the tourist infrastructure still exists and confidence is returning among travellers. It is worth seeing the Transkei, and particularly the heavenly Wild Coast, if at all possible.

The bottom line is: avoid the cities, where mugging is frequent (theft is general throughout the region), and get as much local information as possible from the hotels and hostels within Transkei before going in. One of the best ways to get around safely is to arrange a Xhosa guide through one of the Transkei local government offices in South Africa (they have one in most cities), usually at little or no cost.

When travelling in Transkei, always carry your passport, particularly if driving. Police checkpoints are common, and cars with South African licence plates will almost always be stopped. Usually the police will take a cursory look at your passport and wave you on, but it is important to have it to hand.

Inland Transkei

The N2 highway runs through central Transkei, a rolling country of rounded, grass-covered hills, plateaux and sudden uplands, vivid green in summer, pink and golden-yellow in winter. Along the northwest horizon marches the distant blue line of the Transkei Drakensberg, a region inaccessible to the traveller who does not speak Xhosa or have a guide and a horse to get about on.

The majority of Transkei's population lives in this central zone, and the region's only large towns lie along the route.

Butterworth has grown from the original mission station (1827) to a reasonably sized market town. It was near here that the faithful Xhosa gathered to await their ancestors after the Great Cattle Killing in 1856. Today Butterworth is a compact, lively place of shabby old buildings and raw, new industrial structures. The University of Transkei has a campus here, but the town has little for the traveller, except petrol stations and shops to stock up at before heading down to the southern Wild Coast. Bear in mind that wandering the side streets can be dangerous here, especially after dark.

However, a short drive from town are the spectacular **Bawa Falls** and the **Butterworth River Cascades**. Tradition has it that one section of the falls was used up to the mid 19th century as a place of execution for people who had been 'smelled out' (found to be witches), the only capital crime among the Xhosa, who almost never executed people—even murder and rape were punished by fines.

Umtata, the capital of Transkei, is roughly in the geographical centre of the region. Founded by the British in the 1860s, it marks the boundary between the Mpondo and Tembu Xhosa clans, today's dominant clans. A bustling, rather unfriendly town (especially after dark), Umtata must be visited to collect permits for the Wild Coast Hiking Trail from the Transkei Department of Agriculture and Forestry. Umtata also has such essentials as mechanics and tyre shops for those whose vehicles have suffered on the rough roads to and from the coast.

There is no question that Umtata is a rough town, and that anti-white feeling is strong. Avoid the taxi-ranks, particularly at rush hour when there is a large crowd. These are classic mugging spots and you can expect no help from bystanders, and seldom even from policemen. The same goes for bars after dark. By night always park your car in hotel car parks and stow your belongings in your room. Obviously, do not walk around with cameras and jewellery.

If you want to explore Umtata, however, there are some handicraft workshops worth visiting. The **Wonk'umntu Handicraft Centre** is about 6–7km west of town, on the Butterworth road. There are also two good pottery centres: **Izwezi** and **Izandla**, again, both out of town. For information on visiting these, and also **Nelson Mandela's Childhood Home**, in the village of Qunu, about 35km from the city, talk to the **Tourist Office**, on the first floor, corner of York and Victoria Streets, ✆ (0471) 23 766.

Libode, off the N2, on the R61 to Port St Johns, is very small and unremarkable except for its position near a high mountain called Executioner's Rock, a lone massif that juts unmistakably from the surrounding landscape. Like the Executioner's Falls near Butterworth, this was a place where witches were hurled into oblivion in olden times.

Despite its wonderful name, **Lusikisiki** is not much more than the usual collection of falling-down colonial buildings and assorted shacks, with a petrol station and a general trading store. The old hotel has a functioning bar that used to be a well-known stopping point for fishermen on their way through to the coast. But, since the recent troubles, the atmosphere has changed somewhat, and few travellers stop there now. Some interesting graffiti adorns the walls of the police station: rather than the usual 'One Settler, One Bullet' slogan seen elsewhere, Lusikisiki's youth appeal to the police to 'Stop Killing Us', giving an insight into the Transkei's own internal problems.

Lusikisiki is the town from which to approach the northern Wild Coast spots such as Embotyi and Mkambati. From Lusikisiki the road becomes really terrible: drive very cautiously unless you are in a truck, and always have a couple of spare tyres.

Umtata ✆ (0471–)

Where to Stay

expensive

The **Umtata Protea**, 36 Sutherland St, ✆ 311 751, is expensive and new, and has the town's safest car park. All the rooms are done up in tasteless comfort (bright blue curtains and bed spreads) with TV, en suite bathrooms, fridge bars, etc. The hotel bar is used as a general meeting place for businessmen and, like the restaurant, it is open to non-residents. The **Umtata Holiday Inn**, ✆ 370 181, on the N2 west of town, is much the same as the above, only bigger, with a tennis court and swimming pool.

moderate

If there's space, try and get in at **Charlet's Place**, 55 Alexandra Road, ✆ 311 751. It's a safe, clean, comfortable guest house offering moderately expensive B&B.

Much cheaper is the **Sutherland Arms Hotel**, ✆ 312 281, just round the corner from the Umtata Protea—run-down, but safe for white travellers, though things can get pretty rowdy in the bar (itself barred off from the main hotel) which the owners recommend you do not use. There is safe parking. Very basic rooms, sometimes clean, sometimes not. Breakfast is optional: a grim serving of porridge and toast in a grey-carpeted room without windows; better to eat out at one of the many take-aways in the town centre. Round the corner and slightly more expensive, though also a bit run-down, is the **Royal Hotel**, ✆ 22 231, some of whose rooms are en suite. The **Grosvenor Hotel**, on Sutherland and Madeira Streets, ✆ 312 118, has an old-fashioned feel, with rather formal service. Or try the **Transkei Hotel**, on Elliot Street, ✆ 24 445, or the **Imperial**, ✆ 311 675. All the above offer B&B, with dinner as an option.

There is no safe cheap accommodation in Umtata. The best bet is to share a room between several people in one of the moderately priced hotels. Most of the hotels are amenable to this, owing to Transkei's recent fall-off in tourism.

Umtata ✆ (0471–)   ***Eating Out***

Umtata is not known for its restaurants. Most of the hotels have *à la carte* eateries, varying in price according to the standard of the hotel. The **Grosvenor Hotel** serves reasonable food in a dining room that has changed little since colonial times, and is something of an island of calm in the chaotic town centre. A recent influx of ex-pats since the 1994 elections has resulted in a few non-hotel eateries opening up. Try **Prim's**, Metropolitan Place, at the corner of Leeds and Craister Streets, or **La Piazza**, in the newish Fort Gale shopping centre, a few miles from the town centre. Cheap eating is available at the take-away places which can be found on any street.

The Wild Coast

Only superlatives spring to mind when trying to describe the Wild Coast. The green hills of central Transkei fall steeply to the Indian Ocean, their seaward slopes often covered with the dense sub-tropical forest that used to cover much of Transkei. The human population then thins out, reduced to a few small villages among the trees, on the cliff-tops or at the wide estuary mouths. Antelope, monkeys and exotic birds live in the trees, and fish jump in the mangrove-fringed rivers and swim in clearly visible silver shoals just off the endless, empty beaches.

Living off fish and shellfish is a relatively new experience for the Xhosa of the Wild Coast. Even 50 years ago the sea was considered unclean. Tradition has it that once a year a chosen woman from coastal villages would ceremoniously cleanse herself in the surf, thus cleansing the menstrual juices of all the women of the village. As a result, fish and shellfish were taboo. The taboo has faded now, and with good reason. The pure, unpolluted waters of the Wild Coast support vast beds of shellfish that can be cut from the rocks of any cove. The density of estuarine and marine fish is so great that anglers from all over South Africa flock there. For the traveller, a few rand exchanged with any Xhosa fisherman or woman can buy large amounts of fresh mussels, oysters, crayfish, prawns, and a huge range of fish. It is worth remembering to take lemon, butter and garlic with you.

Flora and Fauna

The Wild Coast has several game reserves through which the Wild Coast Hiking Trail passes. Most harbour antelope such as eland, kudu, blesbok, bushbuck, and duiker, and Dwesa Game Reserve has larger animals such as buffalo, crocodile and wildebeest. Bird life is abundant, with louries, trogons, sunbirds and a wide variety of raptors providing the most spectacular sights.

Much of the coast is covered with evergreen, sub-tropical hardwood forest of great beauty, mostly composed of yellowwood, milkwood, stinkwood, hardpear, assegai and the other South African hardwoods. Some species, such as the Pondoland coconut palm, are found only in Transkei on the coastline around Port St Johns. More intriguing are the night-flowering creepers. It's worth walking in the forest after dark to sea these large, enigmatic flowers hanging from the trees. Shaped like trumpets of white petals, the ghostly blooms are pollinated by moths, and close their buds at dawn.

Getting There

By car: There is no road running along the coast, but various dirt roads connect points of the coast with the N2 highway, approximately 70km inland. These are often in appalling condition and it is advisable to carry two spare tyres. All of the Transkei's nature reserves are on the Wild Coast, as are its resort hotels, which occupy isolated spots at various river mouths.

The coast has one largeish town, Port St Johns, in the northern stretch. Reckoned by most travellers who have been there to be the mellowest town in South Africa, many people arrive at Port St Johns for a few days and stay for weeks, months, or sometimes even settle there; various artists and craftspeople from South Africa have also found the cheap living, gentle climate and sheer beauty of Port St Johns addictive enough to stay.

By bus: **Greyhound**, **TransState** and **TransLux** all stop at Umtata (Greyhound and TransState drop off at the Shell UltraCity outside town, TransLux at the old train station) , as does the **Baz Bus** (at the Steers restaurant in the town centre). Wherever you get dropped off, make your way to the Steers, then take a minibus taxi to either Port St Johns or Coffee Bay, where you will find backpacker lodges.

The Wild Coast Hiking Trail

Without doubt, the best way to see the Wild Coast is to walk the Wild Coast Hiking Trail, or at least a section of it. The trail runs the full length of the coast and takes 25 days to complete. But shorter sections, even of just one day, can be walked. Accommodation is in rondavels set at roughly 20km intervals along the coast. The most popular sections are the five days between Port St Johns and Coffee Bay (which can involve swimming two estuary mouths at low tide, with packs floated across in inflated plastic bags) and the two-day cliffside walk through Mkambati Game Reserve, where waterfalls plummet over the cliffs into the sea.

Unfortunately, permits issued from Umtata have to be purchased before starting the trail, and shown to the custodians of each rondavel where you stop for the night. These can be bought from the Department of Forestry and Agriculture in Transkei, either direct from the office or by post, if you have a month to spare.

For more information on the trail, ring the Nature Conservation Division of the Agriculture and Forestry Department, ✆ (0471) 312 711. The office is on the 3rd Floor, Botha Sigcau Building—the multi-storey building on Leeds Street—but don't expect much in the way of service. If you want results, you have to show up and hassle the staff.

Once again, a word of warning on personal safety. The Coast should not be hiked alone or even in couples. Groups are best. Expect attempts at theft from rondavels (which do not lock), no matter how isolated they seem. Some places are known for trouble; several groups of hikers have been attacked at night at Mpande rondavel (between Port St Johns and Coffee Bay). The best way to ensure personal safety is to request a guide from the Transkei Department of Forestry and Agriculture when applying for a permit (you will have to pick up the guide from Umtata when you collect your permit), or to hire a reliable guide at Port St Johns (*see* below).

swimming

Away from the hotels, the Wild Coast beaches are remote, so do not swim far out. There are sharks and treacherous currents out there. Within the surf, one is generally safe. Avoid river mouths when the tides are changing or ebbing.

Villages and Reserves along the Coast

Qolora Mouth is the southernmost point of the Wild Coast accessible by road, and has two large, old-fashioned hotels, Trennery's and Seagull's, which are comfortable and safe. A beached ship, the *Jacaranda*, a Portuguese vessel that foundered here in 1971, is a beautiful hour's walk north along the beach. Near Qolora Mouth is the river pool where, in 1856, the young prophetesss Nongqawuse claimed to have spoken with the ancestors prior to the Great Cattle Killing (*see* 'Transkei History', p.359).

Wavecrest, at the Nxaxo (pronounce each x as a tongue click) River mouth, is a hotel/resort about 10km up the coast from Qolora Mouth. There are forest hiking trails (look out for narina trogons), water-skiing and the usual boundless white sand beaches.

Mazeppa Bay is the next point north accessible by road. The beaches here are better for swimming than those at Qolora Mouth and the fishing is famed. Ask the manager at the large Mazeppa Bay Hotel about hiring tackle for barracuda, kob and hammerhead shark. Bushbuck and duiker lurk in the coastal forest, and wood hoepoes chatter incessantly.

Qora Mouth, on the coast south of Willowvale, has a less fancy hotel called the Kob Inn, with safe bathing and good fishing. The superbly named pignose grunter (a large, heavy fish that actually grunts when landed) runs in shoals near Qora Mouth in winter (July and August). Inland from Qora Mouth the land is hilly and cut with deep kloofs through whose dense forest wind a series of hiking trails.

Dwesa Nature Reserve, accessible from Nqabara, north of Qora Mouth, is a large stretch of coastal forest still populated by large game. Buffalo, eland, red hartebeest, blesbok, warthog, wildbeest and kudu live among the trees, while crocodile bask on the mangroved mudbanks of the Bashee River, which runs at the northern end of the reserve. This is not a river to swim in. Bird life includes green lourie, narina trogon, fish eagle and mangrove king-fisher. The Wild Coast Trail passes through. Be careful of buffalo when walking about. Bear in mind that no fuel is available at the reserve.

Cwebe Nature Reserve, on the north side of the Bashee River from Dwesa, is accessible via the Haven, which is linked to Elliotdale (also called Xora) by a gravel road. Unlike Dwesa,

Cwebe has no big game, though there are crocodiles. Smaller game, such as bushbuck and duiker, are common. Listen for tree dassies (which scream at night) and samango monkey (which call with a loud 'Ak' sound). Waterfalls run through the kloofs towards a large freshwater lagoon where you may spot otters if you are quiet. The bird life is the same as in Dwesa. Inside Cwebe is The Haven, a hotel with the feel of a small frontier settlement, surrounded by virgin bush.

Hole in the Wall, a huge rock arch standing in the sea north of Cwebe (accessible from Coffee Bay), appears on the cover of most brochures promoting the region. The arch is much larger than the photographs suggest, the top being a plateau about the size of a football pitch. The noise the sea makes as it crashes through the gap has given Hole in the Wall a place in Transkei mythology as a home of angry spirits.

About 10km north of Hole in the Wall is the tiny settlement of **Coffee Bay**. The surrounding geography is dramatic: mountain forest and high cliffs fall to a narrow bay and river mouth, with the usual vast sweep of golden beach, coastal bush and aquamarine surf. Coffee Bay is one of the most favoured tourist spots on the Wild Coast.

Hluleka Nature Reserve, north of Coffee Bay and accessible by dirt road from Libode inland via the village of Notintsila, is a small reserve of high coastal hills concentrated around the Hluleka River mouth. Forest and grassland cover the hills, which are grazed by zebra, eland, blesbok and duiker. Louries, narina trogon, wood hoepoe and sunbirds are common sights. The reserve has chalet accommodation, which must be booked in advance, but no fuel. There are walking trails (again, the Wild Coast Hiking Trail passes through), and fishing is permitted, but bring your own tackle.

Umngazi River is a small resort of thatched bungalows set around a main restaurant and overlooking a wide river mouth. There is good walking down to a mangrove forest and along the river to deserted cliffs, and small, hidden coves. Fishing tackle can be hired.

Port St Johns is the Wild Coast's only town of any size. Connected with the Transkei capital, Umtata, by the tarred R61, the town got its name from a ship wrecked just off the bay. Port St Johns sits at the mouth of the Umzimvubu River, beneath towering, forested mountains, where lie two nature reserves, the **Mount Thesiger Nature Reserve**, west of town, and the **Silaka Nature Reserve**, south of town, where begins the Port St Johns–Coffee Bay stretch of the Wild Coast Hiking Trail. On the road into town children sell large bags of avocado, banana, guava and mango for next to nothing.

There is a fixed community of white South Africans living in Port St Johns, many of them artists and craftspeople who sell their work in Cape Town and Johannesburg. It is not hard to see why they have settled here: the atmosphere is relaxed to near inertia, and the town itself is gentle, decaying and lively. Many of its 19th-century colonial buildings have fallen down, or been burned out and left, the vegetation gradually reclaiming them. Travellers often find it hard to leave Port St Johns, and locals call this sudden languor 'Pondo fever'.

If you want to hike along the coast from Port St Johns, reliable guides can be arranged through a man called Kirk, an Australian who runs the Backpackers Hostel in Port St Johns, and who is now something of a public figure there.

Embotyi (pronounced Emboyki) is a quiet spot on a river mouth on the coast north of Port St Johns. Access is via the inland town of Lusikisiki (a truly awful road in its last stretch) or via the R61 from Umtata (turn right over the bridge as you approach Port St Johns). From its very small resort of wooden bungalows, forest walks lead to various mountain views and waterfalls. The resort also has horses, and offers guided rides to a grassy plain where wildebeest graze.

Port Grosvenor, a tiny place north of Embotyi (also accessible from Lusikisiki via a bad dirt road), gets its name from a ship that went down off the coast near here in 1782. The event is remembered because its survivors were succoured and absorbed by the coastal Mpondo people. Travellers visiting the area in the early 1800s encountered white women living as Mpondo, who had been little girls when their ship was wrecked. Oddly enough, Port Grosvenor was the scene of an earlier, similar shipwreck in the 1550s, when a Portuguese ship went down: her crew were also helped in their distress by the Mpondo. However, the Portugese decided to try and walk over 1000km north to Delogoa Bay (modern Maputo) in Mozambique, then a Portuguese trading station. Out of an original party of almost 500, only 25 made it through the foetid, tropical journey.

Mkambati Nature Reserve marks the final wild access point to the Wild Coast before Transkei ends and Natal begins. In the early part of this century Mkambati used to be, of all things, a leper colony, but there is no trace of such tragedy today. The forest is more noticeably tangled and jungle-like than further south, as Mkambati is close to the more tropical Natal coast. The grasslands of the reserve support large herds of eland, wildebeest, hartebeest, blesbok, gemsbok and reedbuck. There are horses for rent, trails to walk and wild beaches to swim from.

Most spectacular of all, however, are the **Horseshoe Falls** which plunge down a series of cascades and finally over a cliff directly into the sea. Access from the N2 is via a dirt road through the town of Holy Cross.

The **Wild Coast Sun**, the final northern point of the Wild Coast, comes as a brutal shock to anyone who has travelled up the coast through Transkei. The quiet African pace and beauty is abruptly changed by this brash, crass, overpriced casino of the most noisy, tasteless, glitzy variety. Unless you have an irresistible urge to gamble, it is best avoided.

Where to Stay

The hotels are listed in order, south to north. Bear in mind that due to the fall-off in tourism in Transkei, most hotels are open to bargaining. Although individual phone numbers are listed below, you can also make reservations through a central phone number in Umtata: **Wild Coast Central Reservations**, ✆ (0471) 23 766.

expensive

Trennery's, ✆ (0474) 4102, is an old-fashioned colonial hotel at Qolora Mouth, whose thatched cottages have picture windows overlooking the Indian Ocean. A short walk takes you down to the beach. There is a shipwreck to visit, tennis courts, windsurfing, fishing tackle for hire, a good bar and a better seafood restaurant. **Seagull's**, ✆ (0474) 3287/3283, is on the other side of the bay. Not quite as attractive as Trennery's, but closer to the beach. The facilities are much the same, plus canoeing, horseriding, a waterfall walk and snorkelling/scuba diving. Accommodation is in large double rooms, rather than separate cottages.

Wavecrest at Nxaxo River Mouth, ✆ (0474) 3273, offers luxurious rondavels with some good forest hiking, bird-watching, water-skiing, a bar and seafood restaurant. It also has its own airstrip. **Mazeppa Bay** resort/hotel, ✆ (0474) 3287 or (0431) 420 382, is surrounded by thick coastal bush. Sub-tropical flowers such as hibiscus and bougainvillea are in abundance. Thatched cottages surround a central lodge. Activities include scuba diving, snorkelling, safe swimming, tennis and snooker. Perhaps the biggest attraction is the hotel's own island, linked to the mainland by a chain-bridge. Here, there are forest trails and a shore-line where dolphins play. Traditional Xhosa dancing is often arranged at night, and, though one can feel a little uncomfortable being performed for, it is a compelling, beautiful sight.

The **Kob Inn**, ✆ (0474) 4421, is smaller and more remote than the other hotels on this list, which, although seldom full, are nonetheless small settlements in themselves. Once again there are thatched bungalows to sleep in, fishing tackle and scuba equipment for hire, and water-skiing, canoeing and windsurfing are offered. Below the Inn are magical rock pools full of brightly coloured life. It has a bar and seafood restaurant, though your can cut your own mussels from the rocks and dive for crayfish, if you know how.

The **Haven**, ✆ (0474) 620 247, a large resort set in the bush of Cwebe Nature Reserve, has some of the best day-hikes for bird- and game-spotting in Transkei. The Haven has less to offer from the swimming and watersports point of view, but has beaches within walking distance through the bush. Of particular interest are boat trips among the crocodile-infested mangroves of the Bashee River.

Hole in the Wall Holiday Village, ✆ (0475) 442 002, a 2km walk from the famous rock arch, has thatched cottages in landscaped gardens around a central lodge, with horses, forest and beach hiking, water-skiing and fishing.

The **Ocean View Hotel**, ✆ (0471) 25 344, near the tiny settlement of Coffee Bay, occupies a promontory between two rivers. Excellent shellfish-gathering, fishing for kob and grunter, and beach hiking are the main attractions. **Umngazi River**

Bungalows, ✆ (0471) 22 370, for Umngazi Mouth, are set in forest fronting the Umngazi estuary. The thatched bugalows and central lodge sit under palms and trailing hibscus. Windsurfing, water-skiing, tennis and snooker are on offer, as well as the usual bush and beach hiking.

Embotyi River Bungalows, ✆ (0471) 25 654, break the thatched cottage tradition and house their guests in log cabins with verandahs. There are good walks to waterfalls, and horses to ride. Bear in mind that the last section of road from Lusikisiki to Embotyi is very bad.

Mkambati Lodge (no telephone), in Mkambati Game Reserve, is a handsome 1920s sandstone building (the house in which the governors of the old leper colony lived) overlooking a deserted cove and river mouth inside the game-rich reserve. The rooms of the lodge have been comfortably done up in semi-period fashion, and there is a large staff to pamper you. Mkambati has horses, game-viewing, and one of Africa's most unusual waterfalls (off a cliff into the sea). Mkambati has a variety of accommodation, from basic self-contained rondavels to the lodge, where servants and full board are offered. Mkambati is not a reserve where accommodation must be booked in advance.

moderate–cheap

Hluleka, Dwesa and Silaka Nature Reserves all have moderately priced chalet accommodation, booked through the Department of Agriculture and Forestry in Umtata, ✆ (0471) 249 111. There are ablution blocks and cooking facilities, but take your own food. **Mkambati Nature Reserve** has moderate and cheap chalets and rondavels (*see* above), with ablution blocks, cooking facilities and a restaurant.

Port St Johns has a great B&B—**Second Beach Lodge,** ✆ (0475) 441 171.

The Wild Coast also has several backpackers' lodges, connected with the rest of the country via the Baz Bus (*see* p.xxx). At Port St Johns there is the excellent **Port St Johns Backpackers,** ✆ (0475) 441 057, in the centre of town. A pleasant walk southward is **Second Beach Backpackers'** (no phone). About 5km north of town is **The Pont,** ✆ (0475) 441 324.

Coffee Bay also has backpacker lodges (again, with Baz Bus transportation in and out): **Coffee Bay Backpackers,** ✆ (0471) 370 335, and **Woodhouse,** ✆ (083) 300 1711, are opposite each other by the river. A little further away is the more popular **White Clay,** ✆ (0475) 442 004, which does pick-ups from Coffee Bay Backpackers.

Wild Coast Hiking Trail rondavels are found every 20km or so along the Wild Coast. Again, they must be booked from Umtata. Reaching them entails a day's or half-day's walk, but the hikes are beautiful, and, if taken at a leisurely pace (particularly in summer), not over-tiring. Firewood and cooking pots are provided. Local fishermen and shellfish gatherers usually come by to sell you your supper very cheaply. Avoid the rondavels at Mpande between Port St Johns and Coffee Bay, where several travellers have been attacked.

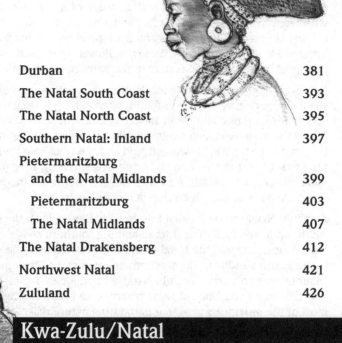

Kwa-Zulu/Natal

Everything grows immediately, and just as immediately stands still.
Time and the climate both combine to growth and growth's suspension.

Riotous Assembly, Tom Sharpe, talking about Natal

For most South Africans, who live in landscapes that are dry and brown for
at least half the year, KwaZulu-Natal provides verdant relief from the
seasonal droughts of their own region. Much of KwaZulu-Natal is blessed
with South Africa's highest rainfall, and a warm, often humid climate that
plants like; green rounded hills and flat-topped mountains fall through
forested kloofs to a sub-tropical coast of flowering trees; KwaZulu-Natal's
perennial mantle of green is dear to the parched South African heart.

However, like most romantic ideals, this one of all-year green does not
stand close scrutiny. True, the foetid, often stifling KwaZulu-Natal coast
gets year-round rain and never loses its luxuriant, sensual verdure, but
inland the scenery changes colour with the season. During the dry winter
the grasses turn pink, brown and gold and the trees lose their leaves. But
the forests never shrivel and the many rivers, though they may slow to
mere trickles, seldom fail. And with the summer rains, the whole province
turns a vivid, startling green that out-emeralds Ireland.

KwaZulu-Natal can be divided into roughly five regions: the well-settled
south, up to and including Durban and the southern coast;
Pietermaritzburg and the Natal Midlands, whose temperate upland
pastures rise steadily to the western mountains; the Drakensberg
Mountains; northwest KwaZulu-Natal, a high, lonely region of mountain
foothills, space and isolated game reserves; and Zululand, which includes
most of the province's big-game harbouring nature reserves, and the wild,
tropical northern coast.

Natalians used to mean the southern part of the province (i.e. not
including Zululand) when they talked of Natal. They can't really do that
now that the province has been renamed to incorporate KwaZulu, but
confusion remains because the coastline north and south of Durban is
universally referred to as the North and South Coasts: the South Coast
stretching to the Cape border, and the North Coast to the Tugela River
mouth. North of this 'North Coast' lies the majority of the KwaZulu-Natal
province's coastline, but this is referred to as the Zululand or Tsongaland
coast. Confused? Don't be—avoid the official North and South Coasts
entirely—their resorts are brash and have long been a haven for crowds of
Gauteng holiday-makers. Head straight for the Zululand/Tsongaland coast
instead, where the wild beaches and forest are largely intact.

KwaZulu-Natal is South Africa's second smallest province (after Gauteng)
yet vast areas of it, particularly in the Drakensberg and northern Zululand,
are sparsely settled, even though, agriculturally, Natal is a land of plenty.

Sugar cane fields cover the hills just inland from the coast, while the good pasture land of the Midlands supports rich cattle ranches and racehorse studs. Sorghum, millet and maize are intensively cultivated and forestry has come to most of the higher uplands of the central region. But for all this, each region has large swathes of wild country, often protected by giant nature reserves and supporting healthy game populations.

Natal's human landscape is not so diverse. With the exception of the Tsonga in the far north, the Hlubi in the Drakensberg and some Xhosa near the border with Eastern Cape, almost the entire black population is Zulu. Up until the 1830s, the population was divided into scores of separate clans, all of whom were gradually transfromed into the Zulu nation during the conquests of Shaka, the first Zulu king, and his half-brother Dingane. The result is the country's largest single black language group, and the one that has inherited the most militaristic identity, still theoretically subject to a single monarch.

As for whites, Natal was mostly settled by the British in the mid-to-late 19th century, so Natalian whites are predominantly English-speaking. However many Voortrekkers settled here during the Great Trek of 1836, and again during the 1880s and '90s, making the white population of the northwest part of the province staunchly Afrikaans.

Natal also has a large Asian population, mostly the descendants of Indians brought over in vast numbers in the 1860s and '70s to cut the new sugar cane fields (plus a smaller population of 'free' Indians who came over as traders). This community of agricultural labourers slowly worked its way out of pauperdom (with no help from Briton or Boer), and Durban now claims to have the highest concentration of Indian residents outside India. Mosques and Hindu temples abound in the city, and the spice markets and bazaars can make you feel that you have misplaced continents.

Climate

KwaZulu-Natal is wet in summer and dry in winter, except on the near-tropical coast, where it rains year-round. Coastal summers are humid and breathless (Durban in summer is unbearable for those not used to it), and winters are warm with mercifully cool nights. Just inland the terrain rises from the cane fields to bushveld, also hell's hot (a South African phrase) and humid in summer, but warm and dry in winter, with bitter nights. The Natal Midlands are temperate, with warm to hot summers, and cold winters with regular frost and occasional snow. The Drakensberg gets very cold in winter, with a sustained (if thin) coating of snow up high. Zululand verges from the sub-tropical to the tropical (up near the border with Mozambique). Depending on altitude, the climate can be steamy or temperate. Some of the inland valleys can also be surprisingly arid, where a freak of geography causes the rain to pass over one place and fall on another. North-west KwaZulu-Natal is green and hot in summer (though not humid), and brown and dry in winter.

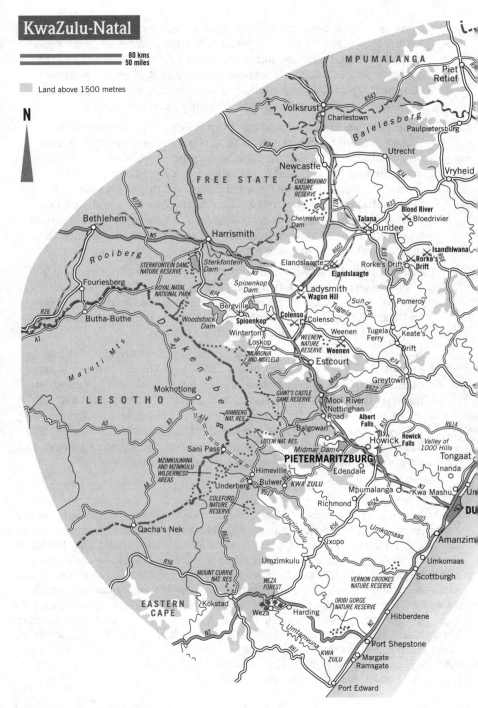

KwaZulu-Natal

| | | 80 kms |
| | | 50 miles |

Land above 1500 metres

N

MPUMALANGA

Piet Retief

R543

Volksrust

Charlestown

Balelesberg

Paulpietersburg

Utrecht

Newcastle

Vryheid

FREE STATE

CHELMSFORD NATURE RESERVE

R34

N3

R720

Chelmsford Dam

Talana

Blood River
Bloedrivier

Bethlehem

Harrismith

Dundee

R602

R33

Isandhlwana

N5

Rooiberg

STERKFONTEIN DAM NATURE RESERVE

Sterkfontein Dam

Elandslaagte

Rorke's Drift

Rorke's Drift

Fouriesberg

ROYAL NATAL NATIONAL PARK

N3

Spioenkop Dam

Elandslaagte

R74

Bergville

Ladysmith
Wagon Hill

Sundays

Pomeroy

R26

Butha-Buthe

Woodstock Dam

Spioenkop Dam

Colenso

Colenso

Tugela

A1

Winterton

Loskop

WEENEN NATURE RESERVE

Weenen

Tugela Ferry

Keate's

Maluti Mts

Drakensberg

MLABONJA AND MDELELO

Weenen

Drift

Estcourt

R74

Mokhotlong

GIANT'S CASTLE GAME RESERVE

Mooi

Greytown

R622

LESOTHO

A3

A3

A14

KAMBERG NAT. RES.

Mooi River
Nottingham Road

Albert Falls

R33

R614

Balgowan

Howick
Falls

Howick

Howick Falls

Valley of 1000 Hills

Tongaat

LOTENI NAT. RES.

Sani Pass

Midmar Dam

PIETERMARITZBURG

Inanda

MZIMKULWANA AND MZIMKULU WILDERNESS AREAS

Himeville

Edendale

A4

Underberg

Bulwer

KWAZULU

Mpumalanga

N3

Kwa Mashu

Un

COLEFORD NATURE RESERVE

R617

Richmond

R624

R603

DU

Qacha's Nek

Umzimkulu

R56

Umkomaas

Ixopo

Amanzim

R56

Umzimkulu

Umkomaas

R617

MOUNT CURRIE NAT. RES.

WEZA FOREST

VERNON CROOKES NATURE RESERVE

Scottburgh

EASTERN CAPE

Kokstad

Weza

Harding

ORIBI GORGE NATURE RESERVE

Hibberdene

N2

Umtamvuna

KWAZULU

Port Shepstone

R61

Margate
Ramsgate

Port Edward

Map labels:

Big Bend

SWAZILAND

Ingwavuma

ITALA NATURE RESERVE

Pongola

ouwsberg

R69

Pongola

Ubombo Mountains

MOZAMBIQUE
NDUMO GAME RESERVE

Kosi Bay
KOSI BAY NATURE RESERVE

TEMBE ELEPHANT RESERVE

4x4

Lake Sibaya

PONGOLAPOORT NAT. RES.

Pongolapoort Dam

Jozini

Mkuze

LAKE SIBAYA NATURE RESERVE

Sodwana Bay

MKUZI GAME RESERVE

601

NTENDEKA WILDERNESS

R618

Nongoma

Black

PHINDA RESOURCE RESERVE

THE GREATER ST. LUCIA WETLAND PARK

HLUHLUWE GAME RESERVE

Lake St. Lucia

Ulundi

UMFOLOZI GAME RES.

Dingane's Kraal

Ulundi

R34

White Umfolozi

Piet Retief's Grave

CAPE VIDAL STATE FOREST

Mtubatuba

St Lucia

Melmoth

Shaka's Kraal

DUKUDUKU STATE FOREST

Cetshwayo's Grave

Empangeni

ENTUMENI STATE FOREST

Eshowe

Richards Bay

Tugela

Gingindlovu

Stanger

Indian Ocean

Salt Rock
Shaka's Rock
Ballito

nga

AN

Flora and Fauna

KwaZulu-Natal is home to the **Big Five**: elephant, rhino (both black and white), lion, leopard and buffalo—found mostly in the great game reserves of central Zululand. The northern rivers still abound with hippo and crocodile. Large herds of antelope, zebra, wildebeest and other plains game are common to most nature reserves, of whatever size, though the largest densities are, again, found in central and northern Zululand.

Natal also has some of South Africa's rarer **mammals**. Most spectacular of these is the large nyala antelope, a close relative of the kudu but even more striking, with finer horns, a dark brown striped coat (in the male, females are chestnut and striped) and a long beard and neck ruff. The smaller oribi, a shy, short-horned little antelope, is also found in KwaZulu-Natal, along with the tiny, forest-dwelling red duiker, usually glimpsed as a disappearing red blur. Bushbabies are common up north, around Kosi Bay, where their chilling yell (loud for so minute an animal) often wakes campers at night. The near-extinct black rhino is more common than in the other South African provinces. KwaZulu-Natal's **birds** are colourful and diverse. Bright, jewel-like sunbirds, parrots, rollers, twin spots, nicators, louries and trogons, bee-eaters and a host of other species flit among the trees, with the general rule that the further north you go, the more colourful the birds become. Hadeda ibis are everywhere, as are the large raptors, especially in the windblown, silent heights of the Drakensberg (good for black and booted eagle, jackal buzzard, lammergeier vulture and bald ibis, as well as sugar-birds and other smaller beauties). In the dense coastal forests live the more exotic-looking crowned, snake and long-crested eagles. KwaZulu-Natal has some avian oddities, among them the Pel's fishing owl, which snatches fish from estuary marshes, and the palm nut vulture of Kosi Bay, which eats the fruit of the raffia palm.

Reptiles abound, particularly snakes. Although you have to be very unlucky to be bitten, be aware of mambas, boomslangs and other nasties when climbing trees or striking off into dense bush. In the Drakensberg, keep an eye out for berg and puff adders. Having said this, most of Natal's reptiles are harmless—there are hundreds of lizards, from the tiniest bright-coloured skinks to the leguaans (or rock monitors) that can grow to a metre long. On the sands of the Tsongaland beaches, sea-turtles crawl ashore to lay their eggs.

If one had to be re-incarnated as a **plant**, KwaZulu-Natal would be the place to come back to. There is an exuberance to the plant-life that is astonishing for those used to a temperate climate. Entire trees that flower pink and white, creepers that grow wooden spikes ten centimetres long, wild fig trees the size of buildings (especially dense in Mkuzi Game Reserve) and a host of exotic species run riot here. The Drakensberg has subtler wonders, particularly its small wild orchids, the lilies that grow by the mountain streams, and the protea woodlands of its lower slopes.

Natal has some superb **forests**, from the coastal jungles to the wider-spaced hardwood forests of central Zululand, where yellowwood, stinkwood and assegai thrive. Around Sibaya in the far north is a dense, cathedral-like, and largely uncharted thorn and wild fig forest. However, large areas of KwaZulu-Natal are simply bushveld and aloe scrub, and oddly enough it is these, rather than the more spectacularly vegetated zones, that support the most wildlife species.

History

KwaZulu-Natal's well-watered, fertile land was the undisputed hunting ground of San (bushman) clans until cattle-herding, Bantu-speaking clans began moving in from the north during the first few centuries AD. The San were gradually pushed towards the Drakensberg (where they remained until the 19th century). The Nguni-speakers were undisputed masters of the region when the first Portuguese mariners passed the Natal coast in the 15th century.

It was the Portuguese who gave the land its present name. In 1497 the explorer Vasco da Gama rounded the Cape and, after landing around present day Mossel Bay in the Garden Route, kept sailing east. On Christmas Day, 1497, he sighted the bay which he took to be the estuary of a great river which he named *Rio do Natal*—Christmas River. Da Gama did not land, however, but sailed on to Mozambique and the East African coast.

There were then few European landfalls on the KwaZulu-Natal coast over almost two hundred years; despite the presence of a good natural harbour where Durban now stands, the Portuguese lacked the resources to develop anything permanent there. Those Portuguese crews shipwrecked on the coast reported maltreatment at the hands of the Natal Nguni. However, such tales may have been propaganda; the crew of two English ships, *The Good Hope* and the *Bonaventino*, wrecked on the south coast of Natal in 1685, set up camp on the Bluff overlooking the bay of present-day Durban, and found conditions so good that many elected to stay on after help arrived. Other shipwrecked sailors later joined them, and established a small village. The Englishmen joined forces with the crew of a Dutch ship—the *Stavenisse*—that had also been wrecked nearby. The combined crews managed to build a makeshift boat capable of handling the coastal waters, and sailed back to Cape Town (an impressive feat) having been amply provisioned by the local Natalians.

Their favourable reports made to the Dutch East India Company officials in Cape Town, of Natal's fertile country, friendly inhabitants, and abundance of game (particularly elephants for ivory), persuaded the Company to acquire the little post as a provisioning point. They sent a ship called the *Noord* to the Bay of Natal with an official aboard who duly negotiated a land grant from the local chief. Following the tradition of South African coastal shipping, the *Noord* was wrecked on its return, and only a few survivors returned to Cape Town. The document was received, then forgotten, and, fortunately for the indigenous inhabitants of the Bay of Natal, no colonial office or settlement was established there.

But by about 1750 this bay was well-known to ships from all over Europe, and various temporary settlements of shipwrecked sailors (particularly English, for some reason) seem to have thrived on the Bluff, so that the site acquired the nicknames among Dutch sailors of *Engeleche logie* (English village). It also became famous for a great underwater sand bar that made the bay unsafe for large ships, and its commercial potential continued to be ignored by the Dutch and after them (in the early 1800s) by the British.

In fact, by the 1800s, the reports of sailors' villages die off—perhaps because at this time there began a wave of political and social upheavals that were to disrupt Natal's peaceful existence. Several dominant clans had emerged from the mass of small chiefdoms in the region, gaining sufficient power to maintain standing armies of warriors (known as *amabutho*) used to mount large-scale raids on their neighbours. Many historians now believe that these clans rose to prominence by establishing control over the inland trade routes—for ivory to the Dutch and British in the Eastern Cape, and a small trickle of slaves to Delagoa Bay (modern Maputo) in Portuguese Mozambique—that had grown up through the 18th century. By the early 1800s, two clans, the Mthethwa and the Ndwandwe, had become dominant north of the Tugela River. Around 1810, contemporary reports tell of heavy warfare between the two.

It seems that the stronger clan were the Mthethwa, led by one Dingiswayo. Colonial histories relate that he was a violent man who seized power from his father after acquiring a horse and gun from a luckless white traveller, whom he had murdered. However, this is now being denied as myth—certainly Dingiswayo was a charismatic figure who organized his army, by whatever means, into a number of highly disciplined regiments, each of which could act independently. One of his generals was a young man called **Shaka**, the illegitimate son of a chief of the then unimportant Zulu clan, an offshoot of the Mthethwa. Again, tradition has it that in 1818, Dingiswayo awarded Shaka with the Zulu chieftaincy in reward for his continual success in battle. (*See* **Zululand** 'History', p.429.)

With the Zulu section of Dingiswayo's army now at his disposal, Shaka seems to have hatched plans for creating his own state. He allowed Dingiswayo to be killed by the Ndwandwe and then took control of the Mthethwa army, defeating the Ndwandwe in turn in 1819. Pressing his advantage, Shaka then took his forces north and successfully attacked the Zwide clan, who blocked the trade route from modern Zululand to Mozambique. By 1820, there was no group in the area powerful enough to challenge Shaka. He began exacting tribute from every chiefdom and homestead, and sent raiding parties as far as Pondoland to the south and Swaziland to the north.

The southward raids caused havoc among the clans around the Bay of Natal. The site had not been forgotten by South Africa's trading community; in 1824 two English naval officers,

Francis Farewell and Henry Fynn, decided to try their luck at trading with the new Zulu empire. Trade and control of its revenues had been at the root of the original power struggle in Natal, and Shaka received the Englishmen well, granting them the Bay of Natal as a neutral trading post, to be called Port Natal. The two men hoisted the Union Jack over the settlement (rather cheekily, as the land had been granted to them, not King George IV) and opened for business. They were soon joined by other traders, and a small, independent-minded community formed, supplemented by waves of refugees from the various Zulu wars.

The traders prospered, but their accounts of Natal under Shaka dwell on mass executions and general blood-letting. Many historians now suggest that this was mere propaganda designed to convince the Cape authorities to extend military protection to Port Natal. Others say that this propaganda was never circulated by the traders at all, but by later colonial agents seeking to justify their gradual annexation of the Zulu kingdom. Whichever you believe, it seems likely that Shaka's rule was a violent one, whether or not he was the absolute monster that many suggest.

For the traders life was certainly a continual process of adapting to the volatile nature of the Zulu state. They weathered several alarms after Shaka was murdered by his half-brother Dingane in 1828. Dingane sent troops into southern Natal to put down local tribes, and once to attack the traders themselves, suspecting them of plotting his deposition. Forced to flee overland towards British Pondoland in the south, some of the traders were overtaken and killed. Realizing how much he depended on the Port Natal trade, Dingane hurriedly recalled his troops, apologized to the traders and persuaded them to return to Port Natal, but he had convinced them that they needed protection.

The British were initially unwilling to interfere with Natal, being already bogged down in a series of expensive, inconclusive wars against the Xhosa in the Eastern Cape. However, history was on the traders' side—in 1837 a large Voortrekker wagon train arrived in Natal, seeking to found a free republic away from British rule. Wherever the Voortrekkers went, British authority was soon to follow, intent on thwarting any rival colonies to the Cape.

Dingane, too, became concerned about this sudden white presence in his country. In 1838 the Boer leader, Piet Retief, and his party were massacred while visiting Dingane's kraal to negotiate for a land grant, and Dingane's troops wiped out the two northernmost Voortrekker parties. Rightly suspecting that the traders and the Boers might be in cahoots over plotting to take over Natal, Dingane then sent a Zulu regiment to attack Port Natal but the traders took refuge in a ship. Inland the Voortrekkers rallied and, later in 1838, beat the Zulu army decisively at Blood River in northwest Natal without losing a single Boer life. Dingane retired north of the Tugela to lick his wounds and think.

Meanwhile, a British force had landed at Port Natal, with orders unclear as to whether to proceed against the Zulus, the Voortrekkers, or simply to establish Port Natal as British territory. They stayed a year, annoying the Voortrekkers by negotiating with Dingane for areas of Natal that the Boers now considered theirs by right of conquest. In retaliation, the Voortrekkers approached Mpande, a brother of Dingane, and offered to help him seize the throne. Greatly pleased, Mpande promised the Boers most of southern Natal in anticipation of victory, while Dingane, unaware of any treachery, granted the same land to the British. The plot was revealed after a few weeks, and Dingane ceased all negotiations, calling out his army against his brother and the Boers. The British, deciding that this was all too complicated and potentially expensive, retired to Port Natal, and then left for Britain, having achieved nothing.

The Voortrekker Boers, under Andries Pretorius, rejoiced, and declared the Republic of Natal. The traders at Port Natal had to pretend to be pleased, as Mpande and the Boers drove Dingane far north to the Lebombo Mountains on the Mozambique border, where he was killed, probably by the Swazis, whom he had continually raided during his reign. He was buried near present-day Mkuzi Game Reserve.

However, life soon became complicated for the new Boer republic. Nguni clans like the Hlubi, who had fled southern Natal during Shaka and Dingane's ferocious raiding campaigns, began flooding back—and the Boers were at a loss where to put them. Then, in 1841, they made a blunder that would eventually cost them their hard-won land. They raided Pondoland, to 'punish' a chief who had accused a Boer party of cattle theft. Pondoland was British territory. In 1842 a British force was despatched against the Boers but lost, with heavy casualties, and had to hole up at Port Natal. The Boers laid siege, but a British trader named Dick King managed to ride through the Boer lines and galloped all the way through Transkei to Grahamstown in the Eastern Cape in just 10 days (a distance of over 1200km), where he alerted the British governor, Sir Benjamin D'Urban. A ship of reinforcements was sent, and the siege raised by bombardment. Natal became British territory (1843) and Port Natal was renamed Durban, after the Cape governor that had sent the troops.

The Boers then founded their own town, Pietermaritzburg, in the Drakensberg foothills, about 100km northwest of Durban, naming it after Retief and Maritz, who had been killed by Dingane in 1838. But the old Boer desire to get away from the hated *Engelssman* reasserted itself, and gradually the Boers trekked away north, to the Transvaal, abandoning the land they had shed so much blood to win, and nursing their resentment of the British.

For the next three decades, the Zulu king Mpande remained friendly and open to trade in the north, giving the Zulus their first (and last) period of tranquil prosperity. Southern Natal continued to fill up with returning Nguni clans as well as with several thousand Griqua from north of the Orange River, who settled around modern-day Kokstad (*see* p.398). In addition, about 5000 English settlers were brought out between 1849 and 1852 to open the Natal Midlands for farming. Through the 1860s sugar cane plantations (worked by poor Indian labourers imported on 10 year contracts) began to creep up the coast. By the early 1870s, southern Natal was 'full', and both the settlers and the Natal government began looking covetously towards Zululand to the north. By 1879 Britain had found enough justification for sending troops in to Zululand. (For the full Zulu War history, *see* pp.428–31.)

The Zulu War did not go well for the British straight away, and a series of initial reverses culminated in the massacre of almost 1000 British and Native auxiliaries at Isandhlwana. However, despite an offer from Cetshwayo for peace (he must have realized that his victory would bring down the full wrath of the British), the war dragged on and Chelmsford finally caught the Zulu army in the open at Ulundi and destroyed it with cavalry and cannon.

Fragmented by the British, Zululand plunged into a savage civil war and, in 1887, the Natal settlers' long-awaited annexation of Zululand came, with speculators allowed to buy up land at knock-down prices.

Natal saw war again in 1899 when the Boers made the Tugela River their line against the invading British forces in the first months of the Anglo-Boer War (1899–1902). The British lost thousands of men before dislodging the Boers and pushing them back into the Transvaal. Since then, KwaZulu-Natal has remained one of South Africa's most prosperous regions— sufficiently so for its local leaders to threaten secession from the union on more than one occasion. The Zulu nation, despite its incessant and violent internal wranglings (*see* above), has survived as the largest and most nationalistic black group in South Africa. In the 1970s, under apartheid, large tracts of Zululand and Natal (60 per cent of the entire province), were designated part of the 'self-governing tribal homeland of Kwa-Zulu', which has done much to promote Zulu nationalism (for better or worse). Since the 1994 elections, Buthelezi, leader of the Inkatha Freedom Party (IFP), has been absorbed into the national government as the Minister of Home Affairs, and the IFP still has the majority of electoral support. The province's new Premier, Frank Mdlalose, is IFP, as are most members of the local government. Unless the ANC's local support grows at a faster rate than at present, Natal looks set to become the seat of official opposition to the ANC in the next decades.

Getting To and Around Natal

By car: Most of the province's roads are accessible by ordinary car.

By bus: Buses from Durban and Pietermaritzburg connect with most of the regional centres, from which local tour companies (contacted through local tourist offices) can take you into game reserves or into rural Kwa-Zulu if you have no private transport. The Drakensberg are easier to reach by bus than the game reserves. The larger towns of the foothills (Kokstad, Underberg, Winterton and Bergville) are all reachable by bus from Durban and Pietermaritzburg, and local lifts to camp sites and trail-heads in the mountains can be arranged through the tourist offices or hotels and garages. The trick is to ask first, rather than to hitch. One or two Drakensberg hideaways even arrange their own pick-up and return transport to Durban.

By train: Trains are limited in KwaZulu-Natal. The one main line goes due north from Durban, through the province's least interesting bushveld country, to Gauteng. A steam train, the **Banana Express,** runs from Port Shepstone in the south, through to Paddock, at the entrance to the spectacular Oribi Gorge Nature Reserve (*see* 'South Coast'). Other than this, trains run from Durban up to Richard's Bay and the north coast, and through central Zululand, but the few remaining services are erratic, chaotic and very slow, owing to massive cut-backs in the national rail system. You may wait a week for a train.

By black taxi: Of course, there are always black taxis, which connect every town in KwaZulu-Natal with the outside world. But these do have a propensity for crashing, and, depending on the political situation, the sections of former Kwa-Zulu they travel through are not always safe.

Southern Natal is the most populated part of the province, with most of the population centred around Durban or strung along the coastal towns, which merge into each other along the N2 highway. Inland, however, the country gets hilly, empties, and reveals some surprises for the traveller with enough time to explore.

Durban

Durban is the third largest city in South Africa, and the country's sea, surf and kitsch capital. The hideous concrete hotels fronting its four beaches (known as the Golden Mile), the beaches themselves, and the bars and nightclubs between hotels and beach, are crammed with beautiful-bodied surfheads, beach bums, sunburnt holiday makers from the high veld (known as 'Vaalies' by the Durbanites), bikini-clad beauties, beer-drinkers and pot-smokers. Of course, however kitsch and shallow this may be, it is also great fun, and one cannot help feeling that other South Africans, who may sneer at the brash city, secretly envy Durban its relaxed, unashamed hedonism.

Of course, that is only one side of Durban. The city is also the Asian capital of South Africa: mosques and bazaars take up whole blocks of the compact city centre. These, combined with the tropical heat of the place (insupportable in summer) and the luxuriant vegetation, create a genuine feeling of exoticism. But do not be fooled into thinking that Durban is not an African town. Despite the predominantly white beach culture and the Asian flavour of the city centre, Durban belongs to the Zulu. The townships surrounding central Durban stretch for almost twenty miles, and the highways pass some of the worst poverty in southern Africa. Behind the orderly Indian Bazaar on Victoria Street sprawls a huge African market where you can buy anything from groceries to (illegal) guns, spare parts for cars, animal parts for witch-craft, medicinal herbs, electronics, clothes, beads, baskets, you name it. Traditionally, blacks have been kept out of Durban's city centre, but that is changing, and the place is beginning to have a much more African feel.

History

Durban acquired its name in 1843 when Port Natal was renamed after Sir Benjamin D'Urban, the Cape Governor who had ordered the British annexation of Natal.

Through the 19th century Durban prospered, even though the port was slow to develop owing to a large sand bar cutting across the entrance of the Bay of Natal. Not everyone had faith in the town's future: the indefatigable British writer and traveller Anthony Trollope, who visited the city in the early 1870s, speculated that the Durban businessmen would eventually lose their shirts because of the sand bar. At a dinner given in his honour, when one of the guests light-heartedly toasted the bar, Trollope reported that he had his eyes vehemently damned by his fellow diners. The battle against the bar was eventually won in the 1900s and, since then, Durban has thrived as South Africa's largest port after Cape Town. Whether the city's 20th-century economy has grown more from cargo or from the thousands of Transvaal holiday-makers who, since the 1930s, have turned the city's beachfront into a gigantic playground is any one's guess.

Despite the city's light-hearted reputation, 20th-century Durban has seen some major events—such as the founding of the Phoenix Peace Commune by Gandhi in 1903. However, against the usual South African tradition, violent political events have never been a great feature of Durban's life. Even during the widespread rioting in 1993, in the long build-up to the 1994 election, Durban got off more lightly than the other South African cities, including Cape Town.

Today, this apolitical feeling continues—and most western travellers fall headlong into the beach-culture for which the city is justly famed. The only real observable difference to the place has been the long-overdue integration of its beaches. And perhaps this is the way it ought to be—too often in this over-politicized country, you find yourself judging the worth of towns and cities by their history of political struggle, regardless of the suffering it has caused on all sides, instead of concentrating on lighter aspects. Give in to Durban's seductive pleasures and relax.

Durban ✆ (031–)

Getting Around

by bus

Buses connect the city centre with the beachfront and the residential neighbourhoods to the west and north. The **Mynah Minibus** links the beachfront with the city centre, and is the best for visitors. It stops outside the 320 West St Building, ✆ 307 3503. Fares are still generally under R5 for anywhere inside the city centre.

by black taxi

These are useful in the city centre, but are not too safe outside this area, as the townships can be rough for travellers, even if just passing through. Black taxis are usually more expensive than buses, about R1 for a ride anywhere in the city centre, but the service is much faster.

by taxi

For late-night travel, take a taxi. These have to be picked up from the taxi ranks in West Street (central Durban's main drag), or (safer) you can phone for one by looking in the *Yellow Pages*.

car hire

Durban has all the big names, but the best deals are local. Try Forest Drive Rent-a-Car, ✆ 562 8433, Windemere, ✆ 230 339, or Maharani Car Hire, ✆ 337 0211.

long distance train and bus

Durban Railway Station is on Umgeni Road (the R102) at the west end of the city centre, for regular services north to the Free State and Gauteng and local services up and down the coast. Durban bus station is also here: services include **Greyhound**, ✆ 309 7850, for Jo'burg, Bloemfontein and Port Elizabeth; **TransLux** and **Transtate**, ✆ 361 7461, or 8333 after office hours, for all major cities and points in between; **Eagle Liners**, ✆ 507 6363 and **Golden Wheels**, ✆ 292 894, for Jo'burg only; **Interport**, ✆ (0351) 91791/4, for Richard's Bay and Zululand.

Durban ✆ (031–)   *Tourist Information*

Publicity Association: Tourism Durban, ✆ 304 4934, has its main office at 160 Pine Street and also has an office on the beachfront, opposite the Beachfront Hotel at Shop 6, Ocean Sports Centre, ✆ 332 2595 (*open Mon–Fri 8–4.30, Sat 8.30–12.30*).

Hospital: The Addington Hospital, on South Beach Avenue (facing the beachfront), ✆ 333 211, is a public hospital. The private Entabeni Hospital, 148 South Ridge Road, Berea, ✆ 811 344, also takes outpatients but is quite expensive.

Emergency ambulances: ✆ 309 1404.

Post office: The main post office is on the corner of Gardiner and West Streets in the old town centre, ✆ 305 7521.

Durban's Golden Mile

Durban's brazen, rather than golden, monument to kitsch gets its name from the sands of its four beaches. The whole beachfront has been pedestrianized, with a few large car parks at various points along the 'mile' (in fact it runs for almost 6km). The best access from town is by the Mynah minibus. Durban's young social life is most active here; the beachfront bars are lively and busy by day as well as night. Apart from the beaches (which have clean, safe swimming with large breakers for body-surfing), the Golden Mile's day-time attractions are magnificently kitsch:

Seaworld (*open daily 9–9*), with its performing dolphins and seals, is the largest attraction along the Golden Mile (where it meets West Street). It also has an aquarium complete with sharks, turtles and other Indian Ocean exotica. Shark-feeding Mon, Wed and Fri.

Snake Park (*open 9–4*), on the Snell Parade, North Beach, has all the poisonous slitherers plus crocs, giant tortoises, leguaans and other toothy reptiles.

Minitown (*open Tues–Sat 9.30–8.30, Sun 9.30–5.30*), also on the Snell Parade, is exactly what it says: a miniature town complete with cars, planes and other machines. For fun, try the mini drive-in the evenings.

Funworld is an all-day amusement park on the beachfront in front of the Marine Parade Highway Inn. The dodgems are good, and there is an overhead cable-way, like a seated ski-lift, that takes one aimlessly from one end of the beach to the other.

The Little Top is a miniature red and white striped theatre tent on South Beach. Puppet shows for kids are the usual fare, with the occasional concert.

On Gillespie Street, just behind the beachfront, is **The Wheel,** a much publicized shopping mall that has been done up to look like a ship inside, with a working ferris wheel over the entrance. This is expensive schmaltz of the highest order. Tens of millions have been invested to encourage the public to part with their money.

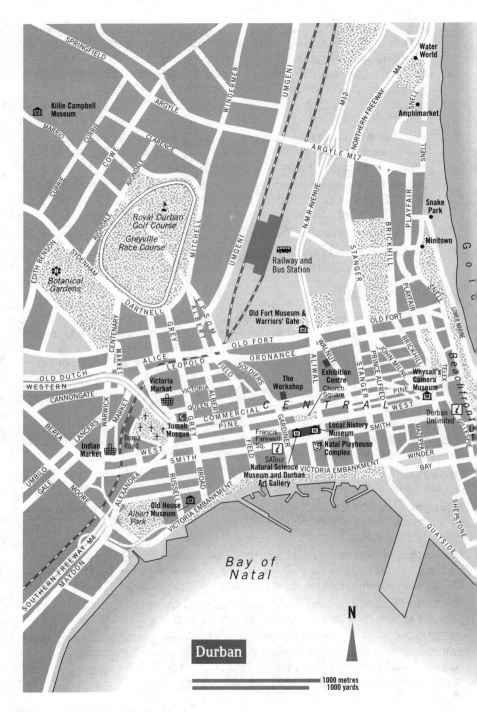

Durban

N

1000 metres
1000 yards

Water Wonderland (*open daily 9–5*), between Snell Parade and the North Coast Highway, is for those tired of the ocean. The place has all kinds of water chutes and artificial rapids to scream your way down.

The fabulously dressed **Ricksha** drivers you see plying for trade up and down the beachfront have been a feature of Durban since the 1890s. The rickshas have the stigma of political incorrectness attached to them, despite the fact that their drivers rely on them for a living, so they may disappear from the beachfront soon. This is a classic Third World Catch 22 situation: the clash between what is acceptable to the western eye and what is economic. The sight of the sweating, puffing ricksha drivers ferrying indolent whites about might offend you, but then if you take a ride yourself, you will at least contribute something other than moral support to the people who labour to keep Durban's tourist industry going.

Durban City Centre

Like all of South Africa's city centres, the compact downtown area of Durban is laid out along a grid. The business centre, which begins immediately behind the beachfront, is not terribly interesting by day, but has many lively bars and clubs to enjoy at night. The most interesting part of Durban is around Grey, Victoria, Russell and Queen Streets, which comprise **Oriental Durban**.

Durban's massive Indian population originates mostly from southern India, but several cultures and languages are represented, as are both Hinduism and Islam. The most easily recognizable landmark of Oriental Durban is the handsome **Grey Street (Jumah) Mosque**, ✆ 304 4858, the largest in the southern hemisphere, but the hub of Oriental Durban's town life is the **Victoria Street Market**. This is a modern, functional building (the old Victorian one burned down about 10 years ago) mostly filled with spice and herb sellers, butchers and fishmongers. Latterly, the market has taken on an African flavour too; of particular interest are the *muti* (medicine) sellers, who sell various herbs, charms, bones, skins and other, weirder animal bits and pieces to diviners and traditional healers.

Durban's downtown Asian culture is mostly Moslem. Hindu Durban lies in the old Indian townships north of town. Most interesting of these is the **Phoenix Park Settlement**, which is where, in 1903, Mahatma Gandhi set up his retreat centre. It was from here that the moral support was drawn for the Indians' anti-Pass Law demonstrations of 1913 (*see* 'History'). Unfortunately, Phoenix has had to be abandoned due to the growth of the Kwa Mashu squatter camp next door. The residents of Kwa Mashu have already destroyed much of the old settlement, and it has become a shanty town. Tours of the settlement and surrounding townships can be arranged by calling ✆ 304 8893. Also see the

Indian Durban Cultural & Documentation Centre, ✆ 309 7559 (*open Mon–Fri 7.30–4, after hours on request*) which reflects South African Indian culture from 1860 till today.

Colonial Durban

This is the downtown area immediately surrounding the main square (Church Square) and the ornate, Victorian City Hall.

The **Natural Science Museum** (*open Mon–Sat 8.30–5, Sun 11–5*) occupies the first floor of City Hall. The usual stuffed denizens of the African bush stand frozen behind glass cases, but of particular interest is the skeleton of a dodo (the last one died in 1790). The **Durban Art Gallery,** on the second floor of City Hall, has some surprising European treasures, including several Constables and some of the minor Impressionists. Look out for the Rodin sculptures. There is also a changing exhibition of local art, and it is worth taking pot luck on what's on offer. Some Black artists from the local townships have begun successful careers from exhibitions in Durban's Art Gallery.

The **Local History Museum,** on Aliwal Street (where it joins Church Square), ✆ 300 6212 (*open Mon–Sat 8.30–4, Sun 11–4*), gives a colonial's-eye perspective of the history of Natal, concentrating on the days of Shaka (portraying him only as a bloody tyrant), the Voortrekkers' brief attempt at a republic, and the Zulu Wars. There are some interesting old photographs of early Natal, as well as the usual rooms done up as Victorian houses and pioneers' cottages. The **Campbell Collection & Centre for Oral Studies** (on the corner of Essenwood and Marriott Roads) is an old Victorian house with a large library of Africana. (*Open to the public by prior arrangement only,* ✆ 207 3432.) The **Old House Museum,** (on Andrews Street) is another colonial set-piece (*open Mon–Sat 8.30–4, Sun 11–4*).

The **Old Fort** (*open Tues–Fri 11–3, Sat 10–12, Sun 11–3*) on Old Fort Road comprises the old barracks and chapel of Durban's original British fort (built in 1842) where the Boers of the short-lived Natal Republic besieged the British for almost a year before capitulating, while **Warrior's Gate,** also on Old Fort Road (*same hours*) contains military artefacts. **Kwa-Muhle Museum,** 132 Ordnance Road, ✆ 300 6311, (*open Mon–Sat 8–5, Sun 11–5*) is dedicated to 20th-century African urban life. This was the office of the notorious Department of Native Affairs and now houses exhibitions which show the full barbarism of the apartheid era and the indomitable spirit of those who suffered under it.

For the matelot ashore there is the **Natal Maritime Museum** in Maritime Place, ✆ 300 6320 (*open Mon–Sat 8.30–4.30, Sun 10.30–4.30*), and for the vacationing medic the **Addington Hospital Museum,** ✆ 322 111, at Addington Hospital in Hospital Road (*open Thurs only 9–12*). Two little museums that also deserve a mention are the **Bergtheil Museum,** 16 Queens Avenue, Westville, ✆ 203 7107 (*open Mon–Sat 8–4, Sun 8–12*), which has a collection of German immigrant artefacts, and the **Pinetown Museum,** 6 Compton St (corner of Old Main Rd), Pinetown, ✆ 718 2740 (*open Mon–Fri 9–5, Sat 9–12*), dedicated to the history of Pinetown and its surrounding area.

Finally, for the surf-head, there is the **Surfing Museum,** 120 Lower Marine Rd, Ocean Sports Centre, ✆ (082) 452 1637 (*open daily 10–2*), near the Tourism Durban office on the beach, which has a small display on the history of surfing.

Durban's Parks and Nature Reserves

Central Durban has some very quiet spots of glorious vegetation, both wild and tended, most of which still support small game and good bird-life.

The **Bluff Nature Reserve** on Tara Road, Jacobs (*open 7–4.30*), covers 45ha of The Bluff, the promontory that rises above the Golden Mile. The reserve is thickly wooded, and is still home to some little buck. There are footpaths and bird-watching hides.

The **Botanic Gardens** (*open daily sunrise to sunset*), Sydenham Road, Berea (the residential neighbourhood due west of the city centre), were founded in 1849, and are a formally laid-out haven of ordered quiet and soft colour amid the humid bustle of central Durban. The **Kenneth Stainbank Nature Reserve** (*open daily 6–6*), on Coedmore Road, Yellowwood Park (the neighbourhood behind Berea, reachable by bus) is a large block of coastal forest, surrounded by metropolitan Durban. The reserve is big enough to support some quite large game, notably nyala, zebra, impala, the rare red duiker, reedbuck, impala and bushbuck. Walking trails wind through this lovely green lung of the sweaty city.

Pigeon Valley Nature Reserve, ✆ 334 466 (*open daily 7–4.30*), on King George V Avenue, in the suburb of Bulwer (north Durban), is a clump of unbuilt-on forest that makes a pleasant place to wander. **Beachwood Mangroves Nature Reserve** is just north of Durban proper, off the M4 highway, before the turn-off for Umhlanga. Despite the over-developed nature of the coast near Durban, this sizeable strip of mangrove forest has somehow survived. All the mangrove exotic denizens are there: mudskipper fish that can survive out of water, fiddler crabs with their one outsize claw, and dense bird life. The best way to see the reserve is by guided tour in a boat.

Silverglen Nature Reserve (*open daily sunrise to sunset*), at the Clearwater Dam, Silverglen (a suburb in southwest Durban), unwittingly supplies many of Durban's local herbalists, who poach plants from the reserve. Moves are afoot to stop this plant theft, but you would never know there was anything wrong, the vegetation is so lush. This large chunk of forest has beautiful walking trails and good bird-watching.

Kranzkloof Nature Reserve (*open daily sunrise to sunset*), at the northern side of the suburb of Kloof to the north of the N3, consists of a deep gorge with riverine vegetation, waterfalls and abundant bird life.

Shopping

Durban lacks outdoor activities apart from walking in the nature reserves listed above, and swimming on the Golden Mile beaches. But shopping is a big activity. The **Asian Markets** are a good place to browse. Victoria Street Market, the largest, is probably the most culturally vibrant part of Durban. Other Indian markets can be found on Warwick Avenue and in the old Indian 'townships' of Clairwood and Chatsworth.

The **African Arts Centre** at Tourist Junction, 160 Pine St, 2nd floor, was set up as a race-relations project to bring arts and crafts from the black townships and squatter camps into town. Superb Zulu beadwork, weaving (grass and wool), fabric prints, pottery and sculpture are on sale.

The Workshop, just north of Church Square, is a big mall housed in a large Victorian building that was once the maintenance centre for Natal's railways. The shops are mostly upmarket boutiques, but the place has some pleasant, shaded outdoor cafés in which to escape the heat.

The **flea markets** are more interesting, both for merchandise and atmosphere. Durban has several: **The Amphimarket** (*open Sun*), in the Amphitheatre on the Golden Mile's North Beach, sells jewellery, crafts and clothes.

South Plaza Market (*open Sat and Sun*), in the Durban Exhibition Centre on Aliwal Street, in the city centre, sells less ethnic, more slick goods. Some very good African artefacts and printed cloths can be found, though.

Farepark Market (*open daily 9–5*), on the lawns between Pine and West Streets, is a permanent market housed in log cabins, with crafts people making shoes, fabric prints, jewellery and suchlike. The **Fleamarket** (*open daily, no fixed times*), on top of Durban Station, sells more electronics and modern goods than arts and crafts.

Activities

Township tours: (c/o Tourism Durban). An alternative to beaches, nature reserves and shopping are the guided tours around Durban's black townships and squatter camps. Although there is something distasteful in the idea of a human safari, this is the only really safe way for a tourist to go into the townships. The guiding is done by locals. Despite the violence that Durban's townships are celebrated for, they are vibrant, friendly places if visited by day, and not during times of political strife.

Tours include visits to the remains of Mahatma Gandhi's Phoenix settlement, Kwa-Mashu and Inanda (Durban's largest townships, with visits to the single men's hostels), Richmond Farm and Lindelani.

Tekweni Eco Tours: ✆ (031) 303 1199, 🖂 303 4369, offers a multitude of day trips, trails and tours—enjoy a traditional meal with a Zulu family in the Valley of a Thousand Hills, plunge in to the river rapids, enjoy a beach *braai* or study the history of apartheid via the street markets and temples.

Deep sea diving and fishing: A number of operators give diving courses and take people out to catch the big game fish, like marlin, dorado, kingclip and sharks, that teem in the Indian Ocean.

Andy Cobb, ✆ (031) 964 329, is one of the better known operators, and offers scuba courses from scuba diver to dive-master, and trips to the principal dive venues on the coast; they also have a game park package. **Meridian Dive Centre**, ✆ (031) 524 822, offers dive courses, charters and equipment sales.

Blue Dolphin, ✆ (082) 783 7671, charters water craft and jet skis. Other operators can be contacted through Tourism Durban.

luxury

Durban's Golden Mile has several brash, ugly ★★★★ tower-block hotels. The **Holiday Inn Garden Court**, Snell Parade, ✆ 332 7361, ✆ 337 4058, is the most famous. Two other options are the **Marine Parade Holiday Inn**, 167 Marine Parade, ✆ 373 341, ✆ 337 5929,a close rival, and the ★★★★★**Karos Edward Hotel**, ✆ 337 3681, ✆ 332 1692, also on Marine Parade.

expensive

The **Royal Hotel**, Smith Street, ✆ 304 0331, in the city centre, carries the most cachet of any hotel in town. Like the Mount Nelson in Cape Town, this is a survivor of Victorian colonial days, although fully modernized in the 70s. The rooms are simple, but rather beautiful, with dark mahogany furniture and high ceilings. Back on the beachfront is the ★★★ **Blue Waters** on Snell Parade.

moderate

Braeside Guest House, 206 Chelmsford Road, ✆ 253 115, is a large, white double-storey suburban house, about five minutes' drive from the beachfront, looking out over the ocean, with a pool and a small garden. Rooms are clean and bright, but simply furnished. Smoking is not allowed. Minutes from the city centre, **Stonegarth B&B**, 3 Halford Rd, Berea, ✆ 202 8249, all rooms en suite, has a swimming pool, *braai* area and secure parking. **Garland Place**, 88 Currie Rd, ✆ 202 6345, in the Berea, offers good guest-house accommodation and yacht charters. In the suburb of Morningside, near Berea, is **Foxily B&B**, 71 Silver Avenue, ✆ 777 1405, which offers a large double room in a family house.

Overlooking the bright blue Indian Ocean, about 10 minutes' drive south of the city centre at Brighton Beach is **Beach Getaway B&B**, ✆ 472 486, which has two large rooms. There are a number of city centre holiday apartment blocks which make economic sense if you are in a group and are staying any length of time: try **Coastlands**, ✆ 337 3511 or **Tenby**, ✆ 328 181.

cheap

There is a **Formule 1**, 10 Jelf Taylor Rd, ✆ 301 1551, conveniently placed at the Translux Coach terminus. **Tekweni Backpackers**, 169 9th Avenue, Morningside, ✆ 303 1433, near the Berea neighbourhood, has dormitory and double room accommodation, with shared bathrooms, and a games room (including pool table). You can check in any time of the day or night. To reach it by public transport, take a bus to Mitchell Park Circle or Musgrave Road Circle, and ask from there (it's a short walk). After 9pm take a taxi, or they can arrange a pick up from the station. The **Durban Beach Youth Hostel**, 19 Smith Street, ✆ 324 945, 2 minutes from the Beachfront, has double rooms and dormitory accommodation. **Durban Destinations**, Musgrave, ✆ 207 1769, has a selection of private self-catering garden cottages, flatlets and B&B to suit all requirements.

expensive

La Dolce Vita, Durban Club Place, ✆ 301 8161, is an excellent Italian restaurant situated on the august upper floor of the Durban Club, with a magnificent view over the yacht harbour. Entry is eccentrically through the Durban Club garage. Dress smartly. **Saagries,** on the Beachfront, ✆ 332 7922, is a fine Indian restaurant, modern in décor and informal, which specializes in dishes from southern India.

Api Taki, 320 West Street, ✆ 307 1847, serves Indonesian, Chinese and Polynesian food, all highly spiced (the spices are specially imported from the Far East), served with fresh vegetables picked that day. The food is hot, but not heavy, designed for Durban's humid climate, but is occasionally disappointing. The **Colony,** in the Oceanic Hotel on Sol Harris Cresent, ✆ 368 2780, celebrates the British, rather than the Oriental side of the Empire. Victorian furnishings, excellent game dishes (in season) and seafood.

The **Royal Hotel** on Smith Street, ✆ 304 0331, has two restaurants in Victorian colonial settings: the **Royal Grill,** which serves French cuisine, and the **Ulundi,** which serves a mixture of Indian food, game (in season) and seafood. Both are very formal. **Villa D'Este,** Daventport and Bulwer Rds, ✆ 702 7920, is a small restaurant, set in a courtyard, which serves very tasty pasta and seafood dishes. You can eat well in all the major hotels, especially the **Edward,** ✆ 337 3681.

moderate

O Pescador, on Albany Grove (opposite the Durban Playhouse), ✆ 304 4138, is an informal Portuguese seafood restaurant which is popular with the younger crowd. Take your own wine. **Lord Prawn,** on the second floor at 47 West Street (the beach end), ✆ 337 2928, is very good value, with huge helpings of shellfish and steak (the big swimming prawns are its speciality). Also very popular with the beach crowd. **Trawlers Restaurant,** at the Ocean Terminal, Durban Harbour, ✆ 337 3737, serves simple line fish and shellfish platters amidst standard seafood restaurant décor—ropes, nets and stuffed fish: but the food is as delicious as you would expect from fish caught that day. Two relatively new fish restaurants have opened at the Point and both are worth a visit: the **Famous Fish Company,** ✆ 368 1060, and the **Cafe Fish,** ✆ 305 5062. The **Orient,** 191 Marine Parade, ✆ 337 2083, serves very good Chinese food (the Peking duck is good, but must be ordered in advance) and sharp Malay satays. The chefs are from Hong Kong, and know their business. *Closed Tues.* The most promising Indian restaurants are the **Jaipur Palace,** ✆ 830 287, in Riverside and the **Jewel of India,** ✆ 337 8168, on the beachfront.

cheap

Durban has all the normal fast-food restaurants that you would expect, including the Luso-South African **Nandos.** For the more adventurous there is **Mimmos,** 30 Silverton Rd, Musgrave, ✆ 214 482, or the **Coimbra,** another Portuguese place at the Umbilo Centre, Teignmouth Rd, ✆ 255 447. Also recommended is **Mykonos,**

20a West St, ✆ 223 136, and the **Centrecourt Restaurant and Coffee Shop**, 30 The Pavilion, Westville, ✆ 265 0837. **Spaghetti Junction**, 243 Marine Parade, ✆ 324 913, is a pizza, pasta and seafood place, with a chain-restaurant feel and piped mainstream pop, but the servings are large and the prices lowish. The **Porterhouse**, 66 Gillespie Street (opposite The Wheel), ✆ 368 1821/2, also serves steaks, seafood, pizza and pasta, this time in an attempt at an English pub setting (mock Tudor beams and hunting prints). Good-sized helpings and low prices make up for the interior and the irritating music.

Entertainment

Durban has a symphony orchestra, a theatre company and a ballet/modern dance company. All perform a range of work, from Shakespeare, classical ballet and classical music, to more up-to-the-minute political plays, musicals, experimental dance and modern compositions. Their home is at the **KwaZulu-Natal Playhouse**, on Smith Street, ✆ 304 3631, which has two large auditoriums. Visiting orchestras, theatre and dance companies also play here. The Playhouse was built in the 1920s, in two adjoining buildings, one built in Disneyesque Tudor style, the other resembling a Moorish mansion. Both get away with it, and are excellent examples of successful Art Deco fantasy. Watch the press—particularly the *Natal Witness* and the *Natal Mercury*—for upcoming concerts and shows. The self-explanatory **Durban Arts Lunch Hour Concerts** are held at the City Hall. Call Patrick on ✆ 231 236.

Nightlife

Durban is a pleasure-seeking city, and bars and clubs abound. They mostly come and go with the season, so it is worth asking around when you arrive. Durban has a vibrant music scene, with excellent jive and African jazz bands playing at several venues. There are also supper theatres, for instance, **Sica's Place**, 19 Owen Avenue, Mayville, ✆ 812 768, opposite the Westbridge Tennis Stadium, which regularly presents musicals, opera, drama and comedy and charges about fifty rand (includes a three-course meal). Booking is essential. Slightly dearer is **El Guappo** in Westville at the Blue Heights Centre, ✆ 267 0424. Performances Mon and Wed; Italian food.

Bars: Joe Kool's, on North Beach, is where most people start off the evening if they've been on the beach (though it's just as popular as a daytime bar). Light rock is generally played, and outside and inside tables are crammed with young beach-heads and students, all trying to out-cool each other, However, the place is quite friendly, and useful for finding out what is new on the nightclub circuit. **Bonkers Pub**, on Florida Road, ✆ 303 1146, stays open day and night, and gets quite lively. Also on Florida Road, though more conservative, with a slightly older crowd, is **Trawlers Pub**. The **Rainbow Restaurant**, 23 Stanfield Lane, ✆ 729 161, and the **Moon Hotel**, on South Coast Road, ✆ 465 1711, in the suburb of Clairwood, also host township jive bands. **Bean Bag Bohemia**, 18 Windemere Rd, Greyville, ✆ 309 6019, is one of the best known musical venues on a Sunday night, where there is a round-robin of local musicians who play jazz ranging from ragtime to ambient. There is no cover charge but you are expected to have a meal. **Music on the Deck** at the

Bat Centre, 45 Maritime Place, Small Craft Harbour Esplanade, ✆ 337 8451, is the place to be on Fridays if the weather is fine, to hear good local jazz, much of it township influenced. Ask for Nicolla. Brain-child of saxophonist Mfana Mlabo, **Jubes**, Jubilee Hall, University of Natal, Prince Alice Avenue, Glenmore, ✆ (083) 779 3777, is the cozy hang-out of local jazz enthusiasts at the university; Friday nights feature a band, Saturday is a jam. Base player Smelly hosts popular swing, trad and blues bands at **Smelly's Bar**, 124 Point Rd, ✆ 368 1625. At the other end of the formality spectrum, overlooking the Greyville race track on Mitchell Cresent, Greyville, is **The Horse with No Name**, ✆ 309 6066, which offers jazz, rock and blues on a Sunday. **Funky's** at the Bat Centre, 45 Maritime Place, Small Craft Harbour Esplanade offers live music all week; phone Wendy Wiper on ✆ 368 2029. Funky's also hosts the **Durban Folk Club**. For more details about their schedule ring Fionna on ✆ 773 458. Sessions are held every Monday night at eight o'clock: the first half of the evening is open stage and the second has a performance from a feature artist.

Dance clubs and discos: Durban's clubs are very changeable. However, standard favourites include **Bassline**, on the corner of Gillespie and Rutherford Streets, which plays funk and house on nights when bands are not showcased. The same goes for **Club Zoom**, on Dick King Street. After dark, **Bonkers Pub**, on Florida Road, plays oldies to a drunken crowd.

Cabaret: The **Drostdy-Hof Cellar**, ✆ 304 6713, at the Natal Playhouse, has cabaret acts in a café-type atmosphere (little tables, candles in bottles). Comedy bands play at **Father's Moustache** on North Beach.

Around Durban: The Valley of a Thousand Hills

North of Durban, to the north of the road to Pietermaritzburg, lies a chunk of the former Kwa-Zulu whose landscape ranks among the greatest natural wonders in Africa. The Valley of a Thousand Hills is a vast natural depression formed by the course of the Umgeni River. From the floor of the valley rise a confusing array of flat-topped green hills with traditional Zulu villages clustered at their feet.

Despite the splendour of the scenery, the Valley of a Thousand Hills is little troubled by tourism; there are few good roads through it, and there has been political trouble, particularly around the highest of its hills, the Natal Table Mountain (over 1000m high). This is a shame, because the forests and waterfalls that crown Table Mountain's vast summit used to be accessible to hikers. Indeed, the rest of the valley harbours equally spectacular vegetation, and rural African life far removed from the modern urban scene of nearby Durban.

The ordinary traveller can drive a road that skirts the southern end of the valley, running parallel with the N3 highway. You reach it from the N3 by taking the signpost for the Valley of a Thousand Hills at Hillcrest, just north of Durban. There are several spectacular lookout points over the valley. From the same road, look out for the sign to **Phezulu**, ✆ 777 1000 (*open daily 8.30–5*), a Zulu show-village and rural crafts centre. While the village itself is a contrived tourist attraction, the crafts for sale are some of the best to be found in Zululand, especially the beadwork and baskets, and guided trips further into the valley can be arranged from here. This is especially worth visiting for travellers who have no time to go exploring in Zululand proper.

The developed South Coast stretches from Durban down to Port Edward on the Eastern Cape border, a long string of beach towns and resorts all running into each other. Most of the towns consist of holiday homes which have reduced the coastline to an extended suburb. The first of these beach towns is **Amanzimtoti** (known locally as 'Toti'), about 30km south of Durban. With its good, safe swimming, lively bars and formal Japanese garden on Fynn Road, Amanzimtoti gets very crowded at weekends.

Nearby are a couple of small nature reserves: **Ilanda Wilds** (signposted from the town centre) is a small area of riverine forest containing some short hiking trails; **Umdoni Bird Sanctuary** is another coastal forest reserve, good for viewing river birds, especially herons and kingfishers. Umdoni has a hide and a short walking trail.

Kinsburgh, just south of 'Toti', has a very long beachfront (10km), which has shark nets for safe swimming. **Scottburgh** is more of a town in its own right. Again, there is safe beach bathing, and the usual bars and seafood restaurants overlooking the beachfront, as well as a tidal pool with a big water slide. About 4km north of town is **Croc World**, a typical bit of South Coast kitsch, comprising a mock-up Zulu village (with the obligatory dancers), poisonous snakes and crocodiles.

The **Vernon Crookes Nature Reserve**, inland from Scottburgh, is a natural haven away from the ugly buildings and noisy roads of the coast. The reserve is one of rounded, grassy hills, cut by deep forested kloofs that are full of ticks in summer. Zebra, impala, bushbuck, duiker and blesbok graze the reserve. Visitors can walk at will, or drive the game-viewing roads. There are chalets and a camp site.

Hibberdene is the next town south of Scottburgh, although the 40km of coast in-between is built up. The beaches here are quieter than those further north, largely because Hibberdene is a popular retirement centre. Again, there is safe sea swimming and a tidal pool. **Umzube**, south of Hibberdene, is a much smaller resort clustered around one rather ugly hotel. This bit of coast is better for fishing than for swimming, though safe beaches can be found at **Banana Beach**, a few kilometres to the south. Banana Beach is fairly undeveloped by South Coast standards, with a narrow belt of forest fronting the sea and screening the holiday homes behind.

Port Shepstone, a large, sweaty town at the mouth of the Umzumkulu River, is the gateway to the beautiful inland areas near Harding, Kokstad and Oribi Gorge (*see* p.397). The town itself was developed as a small port in the 19th century, and named after Sir Theophilus Shepstone. Today it is a mixture of holiday resort and industrial centre, with few of the old buildings still standing.

There are some good beaches south of town, however, including **Shelly Beach** (inclined to get crowded with ski-boat enthusiasts at weekends), **St Michael's-on-Sea**, a lagoon resort good for windsurfing, **Uvongo**, a larger resort with a small nature reserve that protects a forested waterfall, and **Margate**, a large, brash beach town and the busiest beach resort south of Scottburgh. Margate is very similar to Durban's Golden Mile in feel. Beach bums and beautiful people flock here, as well as 'Vaalies' on holiday. The beach-side bars are busy, and there is a fun nightlife.

The Monster of Margate

Margate has its own modern legend: in 1921, crowds gathered on the beach to watch two whales fighting with some other giant sea creature, generally described as a huge polar bear, as it seemed to be covered with white fur. After three hours, the whales left, and the creature floated still on the surface. That night it was washed up on the beach between Margate and Ramsgate. Hugh Balance, a resident of Margate, described the creature as '47 feet long, ten feet in breadth and five feet high. At one end it had a trunk about 14 inches long. At the end was a tail two feet thick and ten feet long. This horror was clothed in snow-white hair and seemed to be devoid of blood'.

The creature lay on the beach for ten days while people tried to move it with oxen. Each day the smell rose higher. Scientists were called in to identify it, but a spring tide took the corpse away. Today, most people believe that it was the half-decomposed body of a whale, the white hairs in fact strings of blubber, and the trunk and tail also lumps of blubber detaching themselves from the carcass.

Ramsgate, just south of Margate, is for the rich, with large, private holiday homes, which are particularly grand around **Southbroom**, a beach just to the south of town. The small **Frederika Nature Reserve**, a stretch of surviving coastal forest, makes a pleasant place to wander, and Margate's Main Street has a lively feel, full of the adolescent children of the rich drifting among the curio shops and bars.

Port Edward, the farthest spot south on the South Coast, marks the border with the Eastern Cape. Just across the Umtamvuna River to the south (the official territorial boundary), is the horrible, loud, expensive and rather boring Wild Coast Sun Hotel and Casino. However, Port Edward is one of the more pleasant South Coast towns. It has the usual suburban look, with bars and restaurants behind a safe swimming beach, but the atmosphere is a little more relaxed, less frenetic than at the other towns elsewhere on the coast, where status-symbol cars and clothes and brash displays of wealth are the norm. Perhaps because of its proximity to the Transkei, Port Edward is quieter and less pretentious.

The little town also has a historical incident attached to it. In 1831, all but a few members of the family of Henry Fynn were killed by Dingane's troops at a large, scrub-covered dune south of town, thereafter called **Tragedy Hill**.

Umtamvuna Nature Reserve, a few kilometres inland from Port Edward, is another escape from the extended suburb of the South Coast. The reserve is large (over 3000ha) and follows the deep gorge of the Umtamvuna River. The cliffs, kloof forest and grass-covered heights are home to reedbuck, duiker, bushbuck, baboon and leopard, and the bird life includes crowned eagle and peregrine falcon. Flowering orchids are a feature of the reserve. There are walking trails, but no accommodation. Don't bathe in the river, which is known to carry bilharzia.

The Natal North Coast

This name is misleading, for it refers only to the coast north from Durban to the mouth of the Tugela River, which marks the regional boundary between the old colony of Natal and Zululand. North of here, the much wilder coastline that stretches to the border with Mozambique is known as the Zululand or Tsongaland Coast. This is confusing for travellers, who are not aware that Natal and Zululand are still regarded as separate by most Natalians, even though both regions fall within the Province of KwaZulu-Natal—a typically bewildering legacy of the chopping and changing of boundaries and region names that has been South Africa's lot since the earliest colonial days.

The North Coast immediately north of Durban (along the N2) is as built up as the South Coast, and again, from a traveller's point of view, there is little to see until the Zululand coast north of the Tugela Mouth. However, if only for the purposes of orientation, it is worth knowing the main North Coast resorts.

Umhlanga (pronounced 'Umshlanga') is a large suburb and beach town about 20km north of Durban along the N2. Umhlanga has a safe beach much favoured by surfers and pleasure-seekers from Durban, but otherwise the town is nothing much; a collection of ugly modern buildings with restaurants, bars and shops, surrounded by equally ugly modern apartment blocks. However, it is worth stopping at the **KwaZulu-Natal Sharks Board**, ✆ (031) 561 1001, on Umhlanga Rocks Drive, whose aquarium is stocked with some of the Indian Ocean's fiercest inhabitants: tiger sharks, great whites, hammerheads, blue sharks and others. Shark-feeding: *Tues at 9, Wed at 9, 1 and 2.30, first Sun of each month at 2.30.*

Umdloti (pronounced Umshloti) has a good swimming beach and tidal pool about 5km further north, as does **Ballito**, about 15km north, next to the sugar-processing town of Tongaat. Ballito also has a camp site and small shopping centre among the large, ugly holiday homes crowding the hillsides behind the beach.

Shaka's Rock and **Salt Rock** were secluded until recently, but suburbia has caught up with them. The beaches are safe but have very slippery rocks under the surf, so tread carefully when wading out. The waves are big quite close to shore, though, so body-surfing is good. Both have hotels and camp sites behind the beaches.

Stanger, another sugar town just inland from the coast about 16km north of Salt Rock, marks the end of the North Coast, and the beginning of the interesting coastline. Stanger has a prime place in KwaZulu-Natal's history; it stands where Shaka had his last, and biggest, royal kraal, *Dakuza* (the word means 'labyrinth' and gives some idea of the scale on which Shaka lived). Shaka was killed here, prudently stabbed in the back by his half-brother Dingane in 1828. A small garden marks the spot. Apart from this, there is little in Stanger except for shops and fuel stops for the journey north into Zululand and its wilder shores.

Where to Stay

South Coast

Both coasts are crammed with places to stay. Most are very bland, but here is the pick of the bunch.

expensive

Selborne Sun Intercontinental Lodge & Golf Resort at Pennington (15km south of Scottburgh), ✆ (0323) 757 1811, is a 1930s mock Elizabethan mansion with 7 bedrooms furnished with Victorian antiques. Famous for its beautifully groomed golf course, Selborne also offers tennis courts, pools, walking and fishing, a private beach, a restaurant and beach *braais*.

The **San Lameer Estate Hotel**, ✆ (03931) 30 011, is a luxury hotel in Mediterranean style, set in exotic tropical vegetation, with its own championship golf course and private beach. The **Beach Lodge Hotel** at Margate, ✆ (03931) 20 372, is at the cheaper end of the expensive range, in a modern, Spanish style, set around a pool. The beach is a few minutes' walk away, and all rooms are en suite.

moderate

The **Dumela Holiday Resort** in Margate, ✆ (03931) 73 301/7, has self-contained chalets with central facilities including a pool, sauna and gym. The rooms are clean, neat and comfortable, and the resort is close to the beach.

The **Blue Marlin** at Scottburgh, ✆ (0323) 20 971, is large (92 rooms) and at the expensive end of the moderate range. Rather glitzy and dull, but a good place to meet people, mostly friendly Transvaal families on holiday. All rooms are en suite.

cheap

Umtamvuna Nature Reserve, ✆ (03930) 3283, and **Uvongo Nature Reserve**, ✆ (03931) 51 222, both have self-contained chalets which, if shared by a couple, fall within the cheap range; surrounded by nature rather than suburb, they are far nicer places to stay than almost any other on the South Coast. There are also **camp sites** in both reserves, as well as at Banana Beach, Hibberdene, Margate, Scottburgh, and Port Edward.

There are two budget hostels on the South Coast offering cheap dormitory bunks and double rooms: the **Banana Beach Club Tropicana**, ✆ (039) 681 3547, and the **Margate Youth Hostel**, 2 Bank Street, Margate (no phone).

North Coast

expensive

Shortens Country House near Ballito, ✆ (0322) 71 140/1/2/3, is an Edwardian bungalow with an all-round verandah set in a large, luxurious tropical garden. There's a bar and small restaurant specializing in fresh seafood. Guests sleep in their own garden cottages. **Westbrook Beach Hotel**, at Tongaat Beach, ✆ (0322) 42 021, has 24 rooms and a good seafood restaurant. Otherwise a very ordinary hotel with clean, bright rooms, and a pool.

moderate

Ballito Accommodation, ✆ (03211) 61 525, is self-contained flats overlooking the sea, among the general suburbia on the hillside behind the beach. Unfortunately, you cannot just turn up, but have to book a few days in advance. It is easier to arrange rooms in the **Umdloti Beach Hotel**, about 10km north of Umhlanga, ✆ (0322) 61 525, which is right on the beach and rather bland, but offers good rates and lets you eat as much as you like at breakfast. **Villa Dilla**, Umdloti Beach, ✆ (031) 568 1981, 🖷 568 1737, has self-contained beach cottages which are serviced daily. **Pine Lodge, Salt Rock**, ✆ (031) 7644 739, a fully equipped, self-catering, 2½ bedroom beach house behind Little Maritzburg, has superb sea views and a servant's room and bathroom.

cheap

The Natal North Coast has no cheap accommodation apart from **camp sites**, which can be found at Umhlanga Rocks, Ballito and Blythdale beach in the north, and on the coast east of Stanger.

Southern Natal: Inland

Much of inland southern KwaZulu-Natal is occupied by large chunks of former Kwa-Zulu, which are inaccessible to the traveller. However, the area around Harding and Kokstad (both of which are along the inland section of the N2) is beautiful, and worth exploring if you are passing through.

Oribi Gorge Nature Reserve is signposted from the N2 between the coast and the Eastern Cape, and is the first stop if travelling inland from Port Shepstone. Oribi Gorge follows the deep, deep ravine cut by the Mzimkulwana River through the surrounding uplands. Waterfalls, cliffs, giant boulders, forest and grassland are home to reedbuck, baboon, bushbuck, duiker, dassies and vervet and samango monkeys. Crested and crowned eagles are often sighted perching on the trees of the forested kloofs. Black eagle and jackal buzzard are also sighted frequently. Oddly enough, there are no oribi in Oribi Gorge; presumably someone mistook a duiker, which looks not dissimilar, for the oribi antelope, which occurs further north in Zululand and the Mpumalanga. Leopard hunt the kloofs. The gorge has walking trails, chalets and camping. Do not bathe in the river, which has bilharzia. If staying, try to arrive before 4.30, as the gates sometimes shut at this time.

Harding is a timber town about 42km inland from Oribi Gorge along the N2, and is indistinguishable from many such small country towns scattered throughout the country.

However, west of town (along the N2 towards Kokstad) is the beautiful **Weza Forest,** a dense hardwood forest with walking trails through fantastic vegetation. One extraordinary tree found here is the knobwood, whose trunk is covered with blunt spikes. Look out for bushbuck, and crested and crowned eagles. The trailheads begin at the Weza Motel, which sits by the N2, about 10km northwest of Harding.

Kokstad lies just below the foothills of the mighty Drakensberg, whose southern section rises along the skyline west of town. Despite being one of Natal's backwaters, Kokstad has a sad, epic story.

History

Kokstad was founded in 1861, by Adam Kok, a Griqua (mixed Khoi and Boer, what today would be called 'coloured') leader, who trekked away from the Orange River, on the western side of the mountains after large parties of Boer trekkers from the Cape started settling the land traditionally occupied by the Griqua. The Boers renamed the territory the Orange Free State (1854) and established their own republic there. Kok, wisely deciding that his people would have no future living under Boers, appealed to the British Cape Governor for some land under British protection (itself a pretty unsure guarantee). The Governor (Sir George Grey) offered Kok a piece of country called Nomansland, where modern Kokstad now stands.

To get there, Kok had to lead 2000 people and 20,000 cattle right across the jagged, steep mountains of Lesotho and over the precipitous cliffs of the Drakensberg, a journey which took two years. But the fertile land of southern Natal was worth the terrible journey, and only thinly populated by Pondo and Sotho clans. The Griquas erected a turf fort on the slopes of nearby Mount Currie, outspanned their wagons, built a church and set themselves to live in this green, well-watered country. In 1872, Kok moved to the site of present-day Kokstad, setting up an unofficial Griqua republic, far from the grabbing hands of white settlers.

But such good country was coveted by Briton and Boer alike. The Cape Colony annexed it in 1874, calling it East Griqualand (West Griqualand was in TransOrangia, near present-day Kimberley), and Kok was bought off with a magistracy and given a salary. He tried to safe-guard his people as tax-paying British subjects, but he was killed in an accident in 1875. He had decreed that no land should be sold to white settlers, and had also exerted strict control over liquor. But with his death, the community began to fragment. The British began to try paying for Griqua livestock in alcohol, and the local police started to raid Griqua houses, on spurious 'treasonable' suspicions (the Griqua made no secret of their dislike of the British). Thus provoked, rebellion eventually broke out and a Griqua/Pondo force skirmished with British Frontier Police on Mount Currie. They lost. Survivors were imprisoned and sent to Robben Island. Almost all the Griqua had their land confiscated and, within three years, Boer and British settlers owned most of the farmland, bought cheap from the government.

The later 19th century saw the local Griqua decline into alcoholism and despair, as they were forced to beg for work on the farms they had previously owned. But the final chapter in the brief, sad history of East Griqualand came this century. In 1917, a group of Griqua bought wagons and trekked again, this time to the Karoo, but their attempt to form a village failed, due to lack of all-year water, and most returned. Then again in 1928, a group walked and rode in donkey carts to Plettenberg Bay, on the temperate southern Cape Coast, where a few still survive among the farm worker families. As always in South Africa's history, those of Khoi descent had been dispossessed.

Today's Kokstad hardly matches its epic history. It is a quiet, rather handsome Edwardian town surrounded by rich farmlands. Worth visiting nearby is **Mount Currie Nature Reserve**, a large chunk of isolated mountain east of town, where the first Griqua pioneers made their ill-fated skirmish against the British Frontier Police. Today there is a dam with a camp site, with footpaths over the grassy spurs. Look out for grey rhebok, and mountain reedbuck. Springbok, blesbok, reedbuck, duiker and bushbuck also graze the hills.

Where to Stay

Kokstad has three rather grim and over-priced town hotels. Instead try the moderately priced **Ingeli Forest Lodge**, ✆ (039) 433 1175, which is surrounded by the Ingeli Forest and Nature Reserve and offers mountain-biking, riding and hiking trails.

Cheap accommodation can be found at **Oribi Gorge Nature Reserve**, ✆ (0331) 471 91, which has self-contained chalets and camp sites, and **Mount Currie Nature Reserve**, which has a camp site only. No need to book. The gates for both reserves close at 6.

Pietermaritzburg and the Natal Midlands

Free of mosquitoes, the air invigorating, the streams clear of bilharzia... the bushmen, when they found this highland, must have thought of themselves as having passed through the gates of heaven.

Natal and the Zulu Country, T.V. Bulpin

KwaZulu-Natal's provincial capital is a small city of handsome brick and wrought-iron Victorian buildings lying at the foot of a high escarpment, about 100km north of Durban. Pietermaritzburg ('Maritzburg for short) is often referred to as 'sleepy hollow' by Durbanites. But sleepy 'Maritzburg is not. The large University of KwaZulu-Natal on the city's southern fringe, coupled with a vibrant mix of Zulu, Indians and mostly English-speaking white, give 'Maritzburg a street life and nightlife unusual for a regional South African city. The compact Victorian city centre has an air of civic grace of which its people are rightly proud, and its surrounding old neighbourhoods have largely escaped the terrible 'town improvement' that erased so much of South Africa's best colonial architecture in the 1960s and '70s.

This grace does not extend to the surrounding townships of Edendale and Sweetwaters, which have suffered much inter-clan and political fighting among the inhabitants. However, their geographical distance from the town centre means that the traveller to 'Maritzburg will neither see nor experience this side of the Natal Midlands.

History

Pietermaritzburg's Victorian exterior and English-speaking business life belie its origins. The well-watered site below the first escarpment of the Drakensberg foothills was settled by the

Voortrekkers on land then controlled by the Zulu king Dingane, following the hard-fought war of 1838 between Dingane and the Voortrekkers (see pp.378–9), after which the Boers declared the whole region of southern Natal their own Republic of Natal. They erected a small stone church (the Church of the Vow) in the bowl under the escarpment of the Drakensberg foothills as a thanksgiving for the victory, and around the church grew the new capital—Pietermaritzburg—named for the Voortrekker leaders Piet Retief and Gert Maritz. But 'Maritzburg was a Boer capital for only three years. In 1842, the Republic was annexed by the British, after a three-year campaign, and in early 1843, after much shuffling of papers between Cape Town and London, the Union Jack was hoisted over the little Voortrekker town, the new administrative centre for the new British colony of Natal.

'Maritzburg and the Midlands suffered a depopulation immediately after the annexation. Between 1843 and 1849 most of the Boers trekked away north, unwilling to live under British rule. However, they were replaced by thousands of people who had fled Natal during the Zulu raids of Shaka and Dingane and who, now that the Zulus had been pushed out of southern Natal, were returning. These clans sought, if not to have their original homelands back, at least a livelihood with the settlers. Martin West and Theophilus Shepstone, appointed to govern the new territory, were alarmed at the departure of the Boers, and now had to find a way of accommodating the returning clans without allowing them to occupy the prime land, reserved for future colonists. West and Shepstone placed the returnees in 'locations' along the Tugela River border with Zululand and the Drakensberg mountains, there to act as buffer zones between Natal, the Zulus and the new Boer republics of the Orange Free State and Transvaal, which lay beyond the Drakensberg.

However, the problem of the Natal's now empty Midlands still had to be addressed. Benjamin Pine (who succeeded West in 1849) and Shepstone hit on the idea of filling Natal with settlers imported from Britain, as had been attempted in the Eastern Cape in 1820. That venture had failed, owing to continual wars with the Xhosa people (whose land the settlers had been given) and seasonal droughts. But Natal, being peaceful, well-watered and now full of refugees ready to be put to work on white farms, was surely a different matter. Between 1849 and 1858, thousands of British settlers, mostly from northern England, arrived in Durban, made the 100km journey up to 'Maritzburg and its surrounding farmlands by ox-wagon, and took over plots of prime land granted to them by the British Colonial Office.

But, like most colonial stratagems, this one proved to be full of holes. The plentiful labour that Pine and Shepstone had counted on was not forthcoming. The returned Hlubi and other clans had established a prosperous subsistence agriculture in the 'locations' during the few brief years they had been there, and saw no reason to come on to the white farms. Through the 1860s Pine and Shepstone struggled to force them into employment, introducing hut taxes, marriage taxes, and even forbidding the men to appear on the streets of 'Maritzburg without trousers on, all of which required money, which in turn could only be earned through working on settler farms. These ploys were only partially successful. Through the 1850s, the settler farms struggled, while the Hlubi and others earned money to pay the taxes by producing cash crops and livestock which they sold to the very settlers that the government wished to work for! The resentful settlers pressurized the government into taking action against the Hlubi (see 'Drakensberg History') who were gradually forced into servitude on the farms by a steady increase of punitive laws and taxes. Their labour brought a long-awaited prosperity to the Midlands. From the 1860s 'Maritzburg flourished as a trading station en route to the southeast African interior, where ivory hunters, cattle dealers and general goods merchants would gather to trade in the town's market square.

As befitted the administrative capital of a British colony, some fine new buildings were built in 'Maritzburg, among them the Cathedral of St Peter (now merely St Peter's Church). Once the British had installed John Colenso as bishop it seemed that 'Maritzburg had everything a colonial capital needed. But here again things did not go quite as the Natal government intended them. Bishop Colenso was, unusually for the period, an arch-humanitarian and defender of black rights. He recognized the government's measures as pure tyranny, and began saying so from the pulpit.

Despite censure from most 'Maritzburgers, and even being locked out of the cathedral by his own dean, Colenso found enough liberal government supporters in Natal and London to retain his position into the 1870s. His countless acts of individual humanity to black labourers who came to him needing legal and medical help earned him the Zulu nickname of *Sobantu* ('father'). In the 1870s the English writer Anthony Trollope heard him preach, and wrote that the visit 'allowed me to come into contact with that clear intellect, the gift of which has always been allowed to him. He is still bishop of Natal and will probably remain so until he dies'. 'Maritzburg's civic authorities have done little to preserve Colenso's memory, but his name lives on in the town of Colenso, northeast of 'Maritzburg on the Tugela River. The Zulu War of 1879 only served to further enrich 'Maritzburg's tradesmen, who supplied the British army and, some historians claim, also sold guns to the Zulu. Similarly, the Second Anglo-Boer did not touch 'Maritzburg; although the Boers invaded Natal in 1899, they drew their battle line at the Tugela River northeast of the city, and again, its inhabitants and local farmers made money from supplying the huge British army that trundled up from Durban.

'Maritzburg's 20th-century life has been remarkable mainly for its upholding of British colonial institutions, such as the Victoria Club, and nearby Michaelhouse, a prestigious private school modelled on Eton. Hereford and dairy cattle farms and thoroughbred horse studs thrive in the Midlands. Trout fishing, bird shooting, and even a pack of foxhounds, provide the recreation of many wealthy English-speaking 'Maritzburgers, and the city's annual Royal Agricultural Show provides a spectacle reminiscent of an English county gathering.

However, this picture of tranquil colonial privilege is all veneer. Much of 'Maritzburg's commercial life is dominated by Indians, who arrived as paupered indentured labourers in the 1860s, and have slowly clawed their way to prosperity, despite active white legislation aimed at hampering their prosperity from the early 1900s until the demise of apartheid in 1994 (*see* **History**). The northeast part of town is almost entirely dominated by Indian businesses and Indian suburbs, a quarter disparagingly referred to as 'Coolietown' by many whites. 'Maritzburg's black townships (the largest being Edendale to the west) suffered appalling black to black violence during the 1980s and early 1990s, with the Inkatha Freedom Party (IFP) and ANC supporters waging a war that has claimed more lives than in any other part of the country. The violence has put many of the townships' businessmen out of operation, and whole tracts of the townships have been reduced to wastelands.

What is extraordinary is that these conflicts have stayed almost entirely within the Zulu community, hardly touching 'Maritzburg's centre. Only on two occasions, both in 1993, did mass political action spill out of the townships. The first was when the ANC youth sacked the city centre after the South African Communist Party (SACP) chief, Chris Hani, was assassinated by a white supremacist (*see* **History**, p.48), the second when the IFP marched with their 'cultural weapons' of assegais and knobkerries, although no fighting occurred until the demonstrators returned to the townships, 10 minutes' drive away from the city centre. Central 'Maritzburg is thus something of an ivory tower. Although the town's crime has become worse over the last few years, as unemployment has risen dramatically in the townships, the city centre remains one of the safest of any South African city, and walking at night around the bars and music clubs clustered around Church and Commercial Streets (almost all patronized by English-speaking whites) is safe enough, although the local tourist office does advise caution.

Getting To and Around 'Maritzburg and the Midlands

By road: 'Maritzburg is connected with Jo'burg by the N3 and by the parallel R74, which used to be the main road north. The R56 runs southwest towards southern Natal and the Eastern Cape, while the R33 heads northeast into Zululand.

By bus: TransLux, InterCape and **Greyhound** all run luxury long distance services between Durban and Jo'burg via 'Maritzburg, as well as services to and from Bloemfontein. **Transtate, Golden Wheels** and **Eagle Liners** offer the same route but for less. Travellers from the Cape should take a Greyhound, TransLux or InterCape bus up the N2 to Durban, and transfer to a 'Maritzburg bus from there.

Transtate run several local daily services between Durban and 'Maritzburg, and also connect both cities with Umtata Eastern Cape, Maseru in Lesotho (via the Eastern Free State Highlands) and Welkom in the Free State, as well as up into Zululand. A local minibus service runs to Underberg and Himeville at the foot of the southern Drakensberg (*see* below). Transtate buses pick up and set down opposite the railway station on Church Street in 'Maritzburg. Eagle Liner buses stop at the municipal bus depot on Havelock Street, just off western Longmarket Street near the railway station (be careful here at night). All others stop on eastern Longmarket Street near the junction with Commercial Road. For information and bookings for Greyhound, TransLux, Golden Wheels, InterCape and the minibus to Underberg call ✆ (0331) 423 026, for information on Transtate, ✆ Durban (031) 361 8333, and for Eagle Liners, ✆ (031) 507 6363.

By rail: 'Maritzburg's railway station, ✆ (0331) 958 2272, was where Gandhi was thrown off the train for occupying a whites-only first class carriage. Today, the sleepy Victorian edifice runs limited services—once a week to Cape Town via Durban or Bloemfontein, and daily to Jo'burg via the northern Natal and Free State towns. There is also an infrequent run to Kokstad at the foot of the southern Drakensberg.

By black taxi: The black taxi rank is at the Havelock Street bus depot. The taxis pass through and stop in the townships around 'Maritzburg, which are known to be violent. Take a bus or train out to the countryside and then switch to black taxi.

Tourist Information

Pietermaritzburg Tourist Association, corner of Commercial Road and Longmarket Street, ✆ (0331) 451 348.

Running east–west through the centre of town is the pedestrianized section of **Church Street**, a parade of Victorian and modern shop fronts between **Commercial Road** (and the huge, clock-towered, red brick Victorian town hall) and **Chapel Street** (and the Church of St Peter). Church Street's pedestrian section is the main shopping area, surrounded by a network of narrow lanes with some of the best Victorian colonial architecture in Africa: the courtyards, bridges between buildings, and stucco mouldings (usually of elephants, a motif that occurs on many of 'Maritzburg's older buildings) are designed in an understated mock-Italianate style. There are some interesting bars, cafés and nightclubs, and, just off **Theatre Lane**, is a fine arcade housing a huge second-hand bookshop, where collectable books can be found at prices way below those in Britain or North America.

On **Longmarket Street**, parallel with and south of Church Street, is the huge **Central Post Office**, a massive grey stone edifice, and the **Victoria Club** (men only), which can be visited (by men and women) if you ask the doorman. The club's fusty old rooms, smelling of leather armchairs and pipe tobacco, hung with trophy heads and lined with Victorian first editions, exudes an atmosphere of outdated privilege. The **Tatham Art Gallery**, on the corner of Commercial Road and Longmarket (*open Mon–Sat 9–4.30*), was once the Supreme Court. Today it houses a surprising collection of work by 19th- and 20th-century European Impressionists and Modernists, including Renoir, Degas, Sisley, Chagall, Picasso and Henry Moore. The **Natal Museum**, on Loop Street (*open Mon–Sat 9–4.30*) (parallel with Longmarket, one block south), has a stuffed wildlife collection typical of South Africa's provincial museums, as well as local geology and fossil history, an introduction to Zulu life, culture and beliefs, and a history of the Zulu Wars presented from a colonial perspective. This latter exhibit is being changed and the ethnology displays should become less biased.

Such British colonial emphasis in architecture and museums makes one forget that 'Maritzburg was founded by Boers trying to escape British rule. But on **Lower Church Street** (east of the pedestrianized section and opposite the modern, red-brick local government buildings), stands the **Church of the Vow**, a modest whitewash-and-thatch affair. The 16 December, the Day of the Vow (or the day of Blood River, *see* p.378), was instituted as a public holiday by the Afrikaner government in 1948, but has now been abolished—or rather replaced—by a new public holiday known as the Day of Reconciliation, which is aimed at erasing the Afrikaner nationalist stigma attached to the Day of the Vow.

Today the church houses a small **museum** (*open Mon–Sat 9–5*). Exhibits include Piet Retief's diary, found on his unburied body two years after his murder (though its authenticity is disputed by historians). A welcome note of humour has crept into this rather solemn museum, despite the Church's central place in Boer tradition: on display is a mannequin of an enormously fat and ungainly Boer in stereotypical wide-awake hat and bandoliers.

The stone **Voortrekker House**, on Boom Street, north and east of Church Street (*open Mon–Fri 9.30–4.30, Sat 10–12.45*), is another survivor of Boer 'Maritzburg. Built in the early 1840s, the rooms are sparsely decorated in pioneer style, with saddles, skins, uncomfortable-looking beds and lithographs of stern, bearded Church elders. By contrast, the **Macrorie House Museum**, on the corner of Loop and Pine Streets (*open Tues–Thurs 9–4.30, Sun 10–12.15*), celebrates British Victoriana with period clothes and furniture.

Two other 'Maritzburg buildings open to the public are the small ornate **Hindu Temple** on the east end of Longmarket Street (part of the Indian quarter of town unvisited by most Western travellers), and the **KwaZulu-Natal Archive** on Pietermaritz Street (*open Mon–Fri 9–5*), whose huge collection of Africana books and old documents are open to both researchers and those just wanting to browse.

Pietermaritzburg's Parks and Nature Reserves

'Maritzburg has some superb parks, some of which connect with the indigenous forests on the escarpment northwest of town, which provide showcases for the spectacular vegetation that thrives in Natal.

For peace and quiet, the **Botanical Gardens**, out of the town centre on Church Street (*open sunrise to sunset all week*), are hard to beat. Take a reflective wander across the wide lawns beneath stands of huge exotic trees. A bridge crosses the small ornamental lake, and leads to a footpath up into the forest of the escarpment.

Alexandra Park, just south of the town centre (reached via Park Drive from Loop Street), has a wide open section of lawns along the small Umsunduzi River (locally known as the 'Duzi'), at the east end of which is a flea market every Sunday, around the Victorian pavilion and bandstand. It also has a superb formal rock garden and trellis walk lined with indigenous flowering aloes.

The city's loveliest park is **Queen Elizabeth Park** (*open Mon–Sat 6–6*), about 6km outside 'Maritzburg (drive north up the Howick Road towards Hilton, and look out for the signpost). Sitting halfway up the escarpment, the park overlooks the 'Maritzburg bowl, and on a clear day you can see as far as the Valley of a Thousand Hills. The Natal Parks Board has its headquarters here (including a small natural history museum and curio shop), and has stocked the park with antelope and zebra, which wander freely among the large trees. A specially constructed *boma* houses two white rhino, which can be observed from a wooden viewing platform. You can also get very close to antelope—particularly the delicate, soft-eyed impala and white-blazed, snorting blesbok—and walking one of the woodland trails can bring you face to face with a bushbuck for a split second before it crashes off into the undergrowth.

Ferncliffe Forest (*open daily sunrise to sunset*) also rewards anyone willing to drive halfway up the escarpment west of Queen Elizabeth Park (follow Town Bush Road up past Grey's Hospital for about 4km, then turn right on to a bad dirt road at the Waterworks). Ferncliffe's woodland is all indigenous (unlike the massed pine and eucalyptus plantations that occupy much of the escarpment slopes) and full of natural wonders: creepers with wooden spikes 10cm long, luxuriant wild flowers and small waterfalls. Rock dassies, bushbuck and duiker may be encountered on the short walking trail that leads up to a rock with sweeping views out over the city.

Pietermaritzburg ℭ (0331–)

The more interesting accommodation is out in the countryside of the Natal Midlands (*see* pp.410–11) and Zululand (*see* pp.440–42). However, there are a few good, expensive hotels in 'Maritzburg itself. The **Imperial Hotel**, on Loop Street, ✆ 426 551, is an early Art Deco building with 50 en suite rooms, unfortunately not decorated in Art Deco style.

The **Karos Capital Towers**, on Commercial Street, ✆ 942 761, is an ugly modern tower block (one of the few in 'Maritzburg), with over 100 en suite rooms decorated in typical expensive chain hotel style with simple, suburban furnishings. The **City Royal Hotel**, towards the station on upper Loop Street, ✆ 947 072, is a Victorian building, unfortunately much modernized inside. Next door, in the old stable, is the **Stables Night Club**—very popular with students and teenagers.

moderate

Heritage House B&B, 45 Miller St, ✆ 45 7321, is comfortable, inexpensive and central. **Campecina**, 39 Windemere Rd, ✆ 426 564, offers B&B or self catering. **1 Pape Rd B&B**, off Armstrong Drive, ✆ 420 797, has 2 double rooms in a large, pleasant house.

cheap

Sunduzi Backpackers, call Brian or Trish on ✆ 940 072.

Eating Out

expensive

 Two of the best thought-of restaurants in the area are the **Crossways Country Inn**, on the Old Main Road, ✆ 433 267, and **Game Valley**, ✆ (033) 569 0011, out at Karkloof to the north of the city.

Despite its Mediterranean leanings, **Els Amics**, on Longmarket Street, ✆ 456 524, in a Victorian house with a faintly colonial feel, has a bistro-style menu—generally Mediterranean, mostly poultry and fish—with good wines and excellent service. Much more formal is the **Oak Room** in the Imperial Hotel, also on Loop Street. In season, the game dishes are superb, especially francolin and venison (usually reedbuck from the Natal Midlands), and the fresh trout with almonds is available all year.

moderate

The **Plaka Taverna**, ✆ 947 727, an informal Greek restaurant on upper Church Street towards the station, is favoured by the younger crowd. The falafel and kebabs are very good value. Upstairs is a small concert hall where local folk bands play regularly. Take your own wine.

Another good-value Greek restaurant is the strangely named **McDaniel's Greek Taverna**, in the small arcade of shops called the Joshua Doore Centre, off Commercial Road, south of Longmarket Street, ✆ 423 923. The menu offers an even stranger mix, with spicy oriental dishes competing with Greek, and not a word to explain why the restaurant has a Scottish name. However, the food and the prices are good, and McDaniel's is popular with the city's students.

Da Vinci's, on Commercial Road, north of Church Street, ✆ 456 632, is also a regular student hang-out, and it gets very crowded at weekends. The food is nothing special—good, filling traditional pasta and pizza—but the atmosphere can be festive.

Bimbos Fun Food, on Chapel Street, stays open until about 2am, sometimes longer, and is very much a late-night stop for the city's young pleasure-seekers. It serves mostly burgers and chips, but also does good bunny chow (curry in a loaf of bread). Piped rock and cartoon murals. No need to book. For light lunches, try the **Botanical Gardens Tea Rooms** on Mayor's Walk (*open 10–4*), opposite the ornamental lake, which serves toasted sandwiches and other simple fare, in a lovely setting.

'Maritzburg is full of good take-away places, but the best is the **Upper Crust** on Longmarket Street, opposite the black taxi ranks. Italian-run, the place bakes its own pasties and pies, which can be bought hot from the oven. It has a special meaning for the author, who took shelter here during the riots following Chris Hani's assassination, when the ANC youth sacked Longmarket and Chapel Streets.

Bars and Clubs

For a town of its size, 'Maritzburg is surprisingly well stocked with bars and clubs, and there is a lively local music scene.

Drifters, on Theatre Lane (off the pedestrianized bit of Church Street) is a small live music bar (usually two guitars and an appreciative, drunken crowd) that rocks after midnight. The regulars are friendly, and it is a good place to meet people. There is a small courtyard with outside tables if you need to come up for air. **Take Five** is a larger bar/club down an alley between the pedestrianized bit of Church Street and Timber Street. Local rock bands play at weekends, when the place gets packed to the gills with students. There's a large balcony to drink on and enjoy the summer nights (and a small cover charge).

Stables, next door to the Royal Hotel on Loop Street, plays house and techno. This place gets packed at weekends, but is rather dead during the week. The crowd, though young, tends to be a little conservative.

Sax, on Commercial Road, is the hang-out for 'Maritzburg's Afrikaans youth (a minority in this English-speaking town) and has a reputation for vulgar, raucous fun. On a busy night, Sax's dance floor is packed, with much hard drinking (there is often a special on sambuka or tequila) and occasional fights taking place on the periphery. If you keep a low profile in this shameless pick-up joint, it can provide a classic view of the Great South African 'Jol' (pronounced 'jawl'), which means a huge, drunken blow-out. The most spectacular example is on Miss Wet T-Shirt nights (*usually Wed*), notorious in 'Maritzburg, when most of the city's young Afrikaans policemen, with their regulation clipped moustaches and bulging jacket pocket concealing guns, gather to get furiously drunk. They can barely be contained by the MC, who encourages the girls to behave as outrageously as possible while the plastered mob howls and bays for more. Amazingly, these nights attract as many female as male spectators, and contestants seem very easy to find.

Upstairs at the Plaka, above the Plaka Taverna on upper Church Street, is more relaxed, a folk music club (*usually Thurs, but check the posters around town, or ask at other bars*) that often has very good musicians playing.

The Natal Midlands

Travel up the escarpment north or east of 'Maritzburg and you enter the Natal Midlands. Wide sweeps of high, green downland grazed by sleek cattle and thoroughbred horses create a landscape more European than African. Many farms have planted European trees, and in some places even hedgerows. Clear trout streams wind through the cattle pastures and in April the country lanes are lined with clouds of pink and white cosmos flowers.

Riding, walking and trout fishing are the best way to see the country, although the local villages have also co-operated to form the Midlands Meander, a driving route which takes in tourist attractions over the whole region. The route offers a structure for those wanting to explore by car and some of its stopping points are definitely worth visiting (*see* below).

The most extensive and beautiful area lies west of the N3 to the Drakensberg, a country of steep hills, sometimes rugged and strewn with boulders, sometimes covered with gentle grassland that seems to have been smoothed by hand. This area has few villages and some lovely, isolated nature reserves, and always the dim blue line of the Drakensberg marching along the western horizon. Northeast of the N3, around Greytown, the Midlands landscape alternates between upland pasture and forest, and lowland bushveld along the Tugela River, which marks the border with Zululand.

The Central Midlands

The area from Pietermaritzburg to Mooi River is the most developed part of the Natal Midlands. The area's small towns and villages set up the **Midlands Meander**, which allows travellers (with their own vehicle) to visit various craft studios, riding stables, restaurants, small hiking trails, farms, studs and galleries of local artists. A Midlands Meander map is available from the Pietermaritzburg Tourist Association and at the principal Midlands villages of Nottingham Road, Mooi River, Greytown and Howick.

Howick is the first Midlands town north of 'Maritzburg, a small agricultural centre that grew up in the 19th century around a ford in the Umgeni River. This ford is dangerously close to the 100m Howick Falls, which have claimed the lives of scores of people, both in accidents and suicide. The falls can still be visited, but there is little else to explore in the town except a small museum of Victorian farm life (*open Mon–Sat 9.30–4.30*). The Howick Hotel, built in 1873, only a few hundred metres from the falls, makes a good place have a drink before moving on. Many of the falls' victims were swept away by the Umgeni's fast current as they staggered back across the ford after a heavy night at the Howick Hotel.

About 7km west of Howick (signposted from the N3) is **Midmar Dam**, a resort popular with local fishermen and watersports enthusiasts. There is a rather lame theme village supposedly recreating Zulu, British and Indian pioneer life. Both should be avoided, especially at week-ends, unless you are keen to waterski—you can sometimes beg a go from one of the many boats. But surrounding the dam is a nature reserve that is worth visiting midweek; it is stocked with white rhino and various antelope species. Horses are hired out, and the dam is safe to swim in. Midmar also has chalets and a camp site, and makes a good place to break a journey north/south along the N3.

Less heavily touristed is the **Umgeni Valley Nature Reserve**, a few kilometres east of Howick along the Karkloof road, which follows the Umgeni River and has cool walking trails through riverine forest. The reserve is great on a hot day, as its stretch of river is safe for swimming and game (giraffe, nyala, kudu, eland, reedbuck and bushbuck) is plentiful. The reserve's Information Centre has some good educational displays concerning Natal's wildlife and habitat conservation.

The mixed woodland and grass-covered downs of the **Game Valley Private Nature Reserve** contains a large buffalo herd and some of the rarer antelope, such as roan and sable. White rhino wander the valley, as well as the more common game species such as zebra, kudu, nyala, reedbuck, bushbuck, duiker and warthog. Guided bush walks and game drives are offered. It lies just below the impressive **Karkloof Falls**, and has a forest trail right up to their large pool, where you can bathe. The Falls are best viewed from Game Valley, but are also accessible from the Karkloof Road out of Howick; look for signs to the right down a minor road that winds through forestry plantations. There is a picnic site, but limited exploring. Game Valley also has isolated bush camps by water-holes (*see* 'Where to Stay').

The next town north is **Nottingham Road**. The N3 goes there, but the parallel R74, the old main road north, is much prettier. Thoroughbred studs abound, as do country hotels—two of which, **Granny Mouse's**, and **Fern Hill**, rank among South Africa's best (*see* 'Where to Stay'). Nottingham Road itself has little except for its old coaching inn, which does good Sunday lunches. From Nottingham Road, you can make a loop back to 'Maritzburg through rolling countryside (covered in pink and white cosmos flowers in summer) via the tiny hamlet of **Fort Nottingham**, which has one of the best points of the Midlands Meander—a restaurant set among trees called **Café Le Fort** (*see* 'Eating Out'). A dirt road heads southwest from Fort Nottingham back to 'Maritzburg via the village of **Dargle**. This route passes through deep Midlands country, similar to the more remote western Midlands. For those without time to explore, the road to Dargle gives a good idea of its high, empty downland, forest kloofs, fresh air and silence. At Dargle, you hit the main R617 road which leads back to the N3 at Howick.

West to the Drakensberg Foothills

West from Nottingham Road winds one of the loveliest roads in South Africa, the road to the **Little Berg**, the first heights below the main Drakensberg. The road leads through progressively higher uplands, cut through by bright streams. Occasionally a track leads off to a distant farm, but otherwise the landscape is unpopulated and always there is the great blue wall of the Drakensberg up ahead. **Kamberg Nature Reserve** lies at the end of the road, under the Little Berg. The infant Mooi River passes through, and you can fish for trout in its narrow course or wander the trail along its banks. Look out for kingfishers and reedbuck. Another trail leads up to a sandstone outcrop called Gladstone's Nose, where some good bushman paintings of eland hunting can be found. Eland still graze the reserve's higher slopes, and bushbuck, hunted by lynx and leopard, inhabit the wooded kloofs.

Also in the Drakensberg foothills is **Loteni Nature Reserve**, to the south of Kamberg. Access is by dirt road via the hamlet of Lower Loteni. Trout fishing is allowed here, and there is a 12km hiking trail, as well as horses for hire. Even more isolated than Kamberg, Loteni is sometimes cut off during the summer rains, when the dirt roads can become liquid mud. The game includes leopard, reedbuck, grey rhebok, eland, bushbuck, duiker and oribi. Look out for black eagles.

South of Loteni are two villages, **Himeville** and **Underberg**, both reached from 'Maritzburg via the main R617 road through Bulwer. The two settlements are just 6km apart and lie under Sani Pass, the one point of road access (only in a 4x4) over the Drakensberg between KwaZulu-Natal and Lesotho. Himeville has a hotel with a good pub, and a small nature reserve around a dam, with boats for hire and trout fishing available. Waterfowl such as Egyptian geese and black duck congregate here.

Underberg is a little bigger, with a bank and supermarket. South of Underberg, along the R617, is the **Coleford Nature Reserve**, also known for trout fishing, walking and riding. There are cottages set among the grassland and hills where black wildebeest, blesbok and reedbuck graze. East of Underberg (on R617) is the **Swamp Nature Reserve**, set around a wetland known for rare birds such as the wattled crane. Reedbuck live in the marshes, and the swamp has a walking trail, but no accommodation.

Underberg is also known for its annual folk/rock bash, the **Splashy Fen Music Festival**, which attracts South Africa's best musicians, black and white, for a Woodstock-style weekend of music, peace, love and *dagga* (marijuana), although LSD has become popular over the last few years. The festival is one of the few occasions where you stand a chance of socializing across the (now unspoken) South African race barrier, and some of the music is very fine indeed. Splashy Fen is usually held in May, but the Pietermaritzburg Tourist Association will know the exact dates.

Between Pietermaritzburg and Zululand

The northeastern stretch of the Midlands, which borders Zululand, centres around **Greytown**, a prosperous country town surrounded by forested hills and reached by the R33 from 'Maritzburg. On the way is the **Albert Falls Nature Reserve**. Like Howick, the Albert Falls are on the Umgeni River. A variety of plains game grazes the reserve, including blesbok, zebra, red hartebeest, bushbuck, duiker, reedbuck and oribi. Walking trails cut through the bush. However, Albert Falls is over-popular with 'Maritzburgers at weekends; those seeking solitude would do better to go on to Greytown, then take the mountainous R74 via Madden to **Weenen**.

Weenen ('the place of weeping') marks the turning point between the high downland of the Midlands and the harsher thornveld of Zululand, although the village itself sits in a green, fertile bowl of intensive farmland on the Little Tugela River. It was here that, in 1838, Dingane's *impis* massacred 500 Boer women and children, shortly after Piet Retief had been killed in Dingane's kraal while negotiating for a grant for the Boers to settle in Natal. The massacre has become an integral part of Afrikaner mythology, and was often cited as a warning against power-sharing with blacks during the apartheid years.

Weenen Nature Reserve, to the north of the quiet village, is very beautiful. A mixture of grassland, thornveld and high hills, it harbours a healthy white rhino population, as well as eland, kudu, reedbuck, duiker, giraffe and a few shy, rarely seen black rhino. There are also buffalo (but very few), ostrich and the little steenbok. The reserve has three good walking trails, one of which has spectacular views out over the Little Tugela Valley from a high escarpment. There are also bird-watching hides; blue cranes often come down to the water holes, whose reeds are home to bright yellow and red bishop birds.

Plans are afoot to declare the vast farming district around Weenen a biosphere, which will mean taking the land out of farming and putting it back under game. This would result in one of the largest game reserves in the country, big enough for elephant and lion to range. So it is worth visiting Weenen to see how the plan has advanced, and what new game species have been introduced.

Activities

Walking: Almost all the nature reserves of the Natal Midlands run good one day-trails (*see* above).

Riding: Good hill riding, with occasional sightings of antelope, can be arranged at **Ishashi Trails**, ✆ (033) 234 4319. **The Saddle & Trout Farm**, near Mooi River, ✆ (0333) 32 758, has an equestrian centre for serious riders who want to brush up their technique. You can also hire horses at Loteni and Midmar Dam nature reserves.

Trout Fishing: The Natal Midlands were first stocked with trout in the 1870s. Since then they have established themselves as one of the southern hemisphere's best fly-fishing regions. Fishing is allowed in Kamberg, Himeville and Loteni nature reserves, as well as at some of the larger country hotels listed below, and tackle can be hired from **The Fisherman's Hut**, Nottingham Road, ✆ (0333) 36 151. Alternatively there is **Trout & About**, ✆ (033) 701 1642, which also organizes fishing trips.

Where to Stay

expensive

Granny Mouse's Country House, ✆ (033) 234 4071, ✉ 234 4429, at Balgowan, on the R74 just south of Nottingham Road, is an old thatched building set on a rise above the Lion's River. Despite the name, the hotel is superb and does not accept children under twelve. Most rooms have their own balcony and fireplace, and there is trout fishing, a pool and lovely walking along the river.

Fern Hill Hotel, ✆ (0332) 305 071, just north of Midmar on the R74, is an old colonial trading post with 19 en suite rooms and a formal garden. Riding, swimming and tennis are available. **Game Valley Lodge**, ✆ (033) 569 0011, in the valley below Karkloof Falls, is a private game reserve with individual bush camps set by waterholes, where you can watch buffalo come down to drink without seeing or hearing another human. The game drives and walking/swimming around Karkloof Falls are recommended.

Old Halliwell Country Inn, ✆ (0332) 302 602/573, ✉ 303 430, near the hamlet of Curry's Post (east of Mooi River along the R114), is another Victorian house converted into a small hotel, with 12 rooms in imitation Victorian style. A veranda runs around the building giving views out over the Karkloof Valley. Log fires in winter make this a cosy place. The cooking is good—all vegetables, milk, eggs and most of the meat come from the farm next door. **Troutbrook Farm**, ✆ (011) 477 4131, offers luxury accommodation either in the main house or a cottage, with 3½kms of river frontage, hiking and of course, fishing. **Rawdon's Hotel**, ✆ (0333) 360 44, a charming country hotel in the Drakensberg foothills, has rooms, cottages and suites overlooking a lake. **Mulberry Hill Guest House**, ✆ (0332) 305 921, ✉ (0331) 304 424, has luxury en suite rooms with walking, fishing, riding, bird-watching and biking on the Midlands Meander. **Millgate Cottage**, 5km south of Michaelhouse School, just off the R103, ✆ (033) 2344 230, has luxury en suite B&B accommodation, with views over the Balgowan Valley and acclaimed glass studio in the grounds.

moderate

The **Nottingham Road Hotel**, ✆ (0333) 36151, a substantial Victorian building, was established in 1854 as a coaching inn. It is popular as a Sunday lunch spot with weekenders from Durban and 'Maritzburg. Hunting prints and chintz make up the decor, and the pub is lively. **Hawklee Country House**, ✆ (0333) 36 008, offers B&B in the tiny hamlet of Fort Nottingham, near Nottingham Road. The thatched house has riding, fishing, cycling and walking for its guests, as well as a scaled down model railway. The **Happy Hill Guest House**, ✆ (0333) 36 008/209, at Balgowan, south along the R74 from Nottingham Road, is a clean and bright whitewashed house offering B&B, with pleasant gardens to wander in. **Gowan Valley**, Balgowan, ✆ (033) 234 4413, has B&B accommodation on a dairy farm. **Cranford Country House**, ✆ (0332) 304 308, ✉ 305 510, has comfortable en suite accommodation and good food. Children very welcome.

cheap

Loteni Nature Reserve, **Midmar Dam** and **Albert Falls Public Resort** all have self-catering chalets and cottages that fall into the cheap category if shared, and into the bottom end of the moderate range if taken alone. There are also campsites with ablution blocks at the above reserves and at **Weenen Nature Reserve**. **Kamberg Nature Reserve** is divided into two sections: the main area has a group of thatched chalets and a camp site, but ask for the stone cottage, which overlooks its own valley in the southern, more isolated part of the reserve. **Freelands**, ✆ (033) 234 4126, has B&B in a 2-bedroom cottage (sleeps 4), with packed lunches on request. **Wozane Fly Fishing Cottage**, ✆ (011) 789 8355, sleeps 6, with fishing in the Mooi River.

Eating Out

expensive

Granny Mouse's (*see* above), serves country dishes to residents and non-residents. Try the fresh river trout cooked in herbs. All dishes come with home-baked bread, and meals are served in a Laura Ashley-style dining room. **Fern Hill** (*see* above), offers similar fare—fresh trout is again a speciality, and also game. Meals are served in a roomy Victorian dining room with a polished wooden floor.

The Natal Midlands' best restaurant must be **Café Le Fort**, © (0333) 336 354, a small cottage restaurant in Fort Nottingham hamlet, serving genuine *provençal* food with imported French wines. Moroccan and Corsican dishes are also on the menu, and the restaurant holds theme evenings when the entire menu is changed to suit a Pagnol story (entire menus are invented around books such as *La gloire de mon père* and *Le château de ma mère*), or to celebrate Napoleon's birthday. Delicious local cheeses and home-baked bread add to the fun. For such a good restaurant, prices are very reasonable (at the expensive end of the moderate range), but booking is essential. The **Nottingham Road Hotel** (*see* above), serves substantial, well-cooked meat-and-two veg dishes. Again, the trout is good—always fresh, and served with lemon and garlic.

The Natal Drakensberg

Khalamba—the Barrier of Spears
The old Nguni name for the Natal Drakensberg

The highest range of South Africa's Great Escarpment curves eastwards from Lesotho into Natal in a giant buttress whose cliffs fall sheer to the bare green foothills of the Natal Midlands. From a distance, only the highest ridge (which tops 10,000ft) is visible, a thin blue line suspended above the western horizon and hung with shifting cloud.

The 'Berg, as most South Africans refer to the range, is the country's most popular wild hiking area, and with good reason. Their scale is dwarfing. At some points, river gorges fall over a thousand feet away from the trail, while above soar cliffs of equal height. There is a crystal quality to the air (locals call it 'champagne air') that leaves you light-headed and exhilarated. Waterfalls and cold streams cascade down hidden forest kloofs to wild, open plateaux of montane grassland grazed by small herds of shy antelope. Balancing rocks and jagged, tooth-like columns hundreds of metres high jut from the great massifs of the square-topped basalt peaks. The landscape is fabulous in the true sense of the word, its quality reflected in the names of the best-known landmarks: Giant's Castle, Giant's Cup, Cathedral Peak, the Sentinel and the huge Amphitheatre. The mountains have a central place in both black and San (bushman) myth. The author J. R.R. Tolkien, who was born in South Africa, is said to have found the inspiration for his imaginary world of Middle Earth in the Drakensberg ('Dragon-stone') landscapes.

Climate

Because of the abrupt rise in altitude, the lower Drakensberg slopes have a much more temperate climate than the hot Natal plain below. Midday temperatures in the green, rainy summer can be blisteringly hot, but evenings are always cool and even summer nights get cold. Winter nights are bitter and usually frosty. Above the 2000m line, extremes of temperature occur year-round. Violent rainstorms can blow in at any time, and in winter snowfalls are common.

Flora and Fauna

Eland, blesbok, mountain reedbuck, grey rhebok, klipspringer, and sometimes black wildebeest, are often seen skittering across steep slopes away from the hiker. Secretive bushbuck inhabit the forest kloofs. Leopard, caracal and serval cat live in the more remote caves and rock overhangs. Dassies leave great heaps of droppings anywhere there is a cluster of boulders large enough to support a colony. The sharp bark of baboons, echoing along the cliffs of a deep gorge, is a familiar sound to anyone who has walked in the 'Berg. Black, martial, crowned eagles, buzzards, ibis and the smaller falcons cruise the heights, while sugarbirds and sunbirds flit among the wildflowers of the lower slopes. Hikers should watch out for plump berg adders sunning themselves on the trails. Lizards by the thousand bask on the rocks and paths.

Most of the Drakensberg is dressed in a smooth coat of montane fynbos (heath) and grassland, brilliant green in summer and pinkish gold in winter. Protea woodland—groups of strange, gnarled, flowering trees that grow to stunted, crazy shapes, as if frozen in mid-dance—is common at low altitude. In the forest kloofs, hardwood trees such as yellowwood and assegai cover the steep slopes. Delicate wildflowers, purple orchids and ericas dot the fynbos grasslands in spring and summer.

History

The sandstone caves and overhangs of the 'Berg often have galleries of bushman rock paintings, many of which can be reached via the 'Berg's hundreds of walking trails. Traditional San hunting and ritual pictures sometimes alternate with scenes from the white settler invasion, such as ox-wagons and horsemen with guns; the San had inhabited the Drakensberg since being driven there by black African pastoralists around the 14th century. Eventually it was this range that provided the South African San with their last mountain stronghold, before being wiped out by both white settlers and black tribesmen in the mid-19th-century, neither of whom would tolerate the San's practice of hunting cattle when there was insufficient game. Today, the S n survive only in the Kalahari, 1000km to the northwest.

During the rise of the Zulu empire through the 1820s and '30s, various Nguni tribes from Natal fled into the Drakensberg to escape the *impis* of Shaka and his brother (and successor) Dingane. Some, like the Hlubi and Ngwane, crossed the mountains and dispersed onto the highveld beyond, either raiding other tribes or being assimilated by them. Some smaller refugee clans, like the Bele, stayed in the Drakensberg and turned to cannibalism as game became too scarce, the climate too harsh and the time too chaotic to allow for settled farming. Some cannibal caves can be explored along a few of the 'Berg's many hiking trails. The Bele and other cannibal clans represented such a danger to travellers and clans living at the foot of the mountains that first Zulu and Sotho war parties and then white settlers began hunting them out. By 1850 the cannibal bands had disappeared from the Natal Drakensberg, though a few held out in the wild uplands of Lesotho for another decade.

The last of the San hunters were finally exterminated by farmers and by Hlubi tribesmen returned from exile in the 1860s, after Natal became a British colony and the Zulu were confined to the country north of the Tugela River. The Hlubi were settled in 'native locations' in the Drakensberg foothills and in pockets further into Natal. Taking advantage of the plentiful water and temperate climate, they soon became prosperous farmers, and by 1870 were supplying the new colonial towns at the foot of the 'Berg (such as Estcourt, Winterton and Bergville) with meat and vegetables. The Hlubi's prosperity began to excite the envy of Natal's white settlers, who were often struggling, being little experienced in African farming.

After the 1871 Kimberley diamond boom, mineworking recruitment agents travelled all over South Africa looking for labourers, and many young Hlubi men left their 'locations', and went to Kimberley to work for a year, returning with the statutory pay-off of a small lump sum and a gun, while the Hlubi women continued to produce crops for the local farmers' markets. By now, both the local settlers and the Natal government were uneasy at the thought of a prospering nation of armed natives sitting in the mountain foothills. The assumption was that the Hlubi might one day decide to join forces with their old enemies the Zulus and attack the white settlers, though there was absolutely no evidence to support this.

In 1873, John Macfarlane, the magistrate of Estcourt, demanded that all firearms in the Hlubi 'location' be brought into town to be registered. The Hlubi, under their chief Langalibalele, guessed that this was simply a ploy to confiscate their guns. So the old chief ignored the order. Macfarlane then persuaded Theophilus Shepstone, then the Secretary for Native Affairs and later the Governor, to summon Langalibalele to Pietermaritzburg to explain his non-compliance with the order.

The young Hlubi men forced their old chief to stay at home, in case the British arrested him in Pietermaritzburg. Macfarlane sent officials with a second and a third summons. The young Hlubi men, by now confused and suspicious, searched the envoys, kept them under guard, and ejected them from the 'location' next day. Macfarlane saw this as his opportunity for action, and demanded to know if the Natal government meant to tolerate such high-handedness from its black subjects. His strategy worked: a force of over 10,000 regulars and native levies were sent to arrest Langalibalele, to confiscate his land and cattle, and to disperse the Hlubi among other 'locations'.

The Hlubi warriors got wind of the force and fled into the mountains. An advance troop of soldiers under Major Anthony Durnford (later to be killed by the Zulus at Isandhlwana in 1879) was sent to block off the Bushman's River Pass, in the vast present-day Giant's Castle

Nature Reserve. They were too late to stop Langalibalele but were in time to confront a mass of armed Hlubi warriors. Most of Durnford's troops fled, but the major and a few volunteers vainly attempted to block the pass. All but Durnford were killed.

In retaliation, British troops annexed the Hlubi's main location, drove off some 15,000 head of cattle, kidnapped the women and children, and gave them as virtual slaves to surrounding farmers. So too the land. Unable to survive in the harsh uplands, Langalibalele and his men surrendered. The old chief was sent to Robben Island for a year and the clan dispersed.

However, the Natal government did not get away scot-free. Native sympathizers, among them the influential bishop of Natal, John Colenso, caused an outcry in the British press about barbarous colonial tyranny, and Benjamin Pine, the Natal governor who had sanctioned the use of force in the Langalibalele affair, was recalled. The British Colonial Office sent orders to restore the Hlubi land and cattle, but these were quietly ignored. The Hlubi returned to the Drakensberg foothills, where some remain today, but their prosperity had been broken.

Despite its history, the Drakensberg have been among the least politically eventful areas of South Africa through the 20th century. Apart from the villages and resorts that line its feet, and the transitory Sotho, Zulu and Hlubi people crossing the mountains, like most of South Africa's ranges, the 'Berg are all-but uninhabited. Only the town of Estcourt, 30km east of the range and now the site of a large Nestlé factory, and the Kwa-Zulu 'location' near Loskop, have seen any real unrest during the struggle against apartheid. Today, the Drakensberg continues to be South Africa's most peaceful region, a place where the conflicts and problems of the country can be forgotten, and where the traveller can look down from the heights and simply feel exhilarated by being on the roof of Southern Africa.

Hiking in the Drakensberg

The 'Berg has so many different hiking and climbing routes that they warrant a book of their own. The most authoritative guide available is Jaynee Levy's superb *Guide to Walks and Hikes in Southern Africa*, which deals with the scores of individual trails in the 'Berg, as well as in other areas of South Africa. Here, there is only room to outline the main trails. Some of these are well hiked and can become quite crowded, especially in Giant's Castle Nature Reserve and Royal Natal National Park. But there is a wealth of remoter trails, particularly in the Mzimkulwana Wilderness Area of the southern 'Berg, and the Mkhomazi and Mzumkulu Wilderness Areas of the central 'Berg. On these you may not meet another soul.

Safety on the Trail

The Drakensberg Mountains should be treated with particular respect on account of their sudden changes of weather. Mist and low cloud are particular hazards. It is imperative that you stick to the marked trail; the 'Berg's uplands are vast and many hikers who wander off-track get lost, sometimes with fatal consequences.

If camping or sleeping in caves (rather than in overnight hiking huts) do be aware that Sotho and Zulu tribesmen do sometimes pass through the area, so do not leave tempting hiking and camping equipment lying around, and always remember to greet whoever you meet confidently and with friendship, as the mountain people can be touchy and have had experience with frightened travellers being apparently rude by ignoring their greetings. Learning the Sotho and Zulu forms of greeting is a good idea (*see* **Language**, p.624).

The Three Drakensberg Regions

The Drakensberg is usually divided into three sections, southern, central and northern, for easier orientation. The signposts from the N3 highway use this system, and this guide will follow the same pattern.

The Southern Drakensberg

The southern section of the Natal Drakensberg runs from the southern Natal border north to Sani Pass, near Underberg. Most of this area is protected by the vast **Mzimkulwana and Mzimkulu Wilderness Areas**, and includes the high mountains visible from the towns of Underberg, Cedarville and Kokstad. Hiking trails through the valleys and lower passes can be easily reached from two resort hotels, the **Bushman's Nek Hotel** and the **Drakensberg Garden**. Both hotels also hire horses for guided rides of up to four hours.

One of the best things about this massive block of wilderness is that no vehicles are allowed, except near the hotels. Hikers who penetrate deep into the wilds can stay in designated caves (marked on the trail maps available from the hotels). From Bushman's Nek, there is a superb two-day walk up to the Selabethebe National Park in Lesotho, with overnight huts along the way.

Up on the highlands, the cold streams tumble, and a mixture of grassland, montane fynbos and kloof forest supports a healthy population of eland, mountain reedbuck, klipspringer and bushbuck. Baboon are plentiful on the steeper slopes, as are dassies. Predators include leopard, lynx, black and crested eagle and jackal buzzard. Lammergeier (bearded vulture) and bald ibis (which has iridescent green feathers) are rarer sights.

Sani Pass, just north of Mzimkulwana Wilderness Area, is the one road directly linking Kwa Zulu-Natal and Lesotho (a second road, via Qacha's Nek in the south, passes through Transkei). It's a rough road, only accessible for 4x4s, but a steady stream of traders from Lesotho come regularly down the pass to buy supplies for their mountain stores. Hitching a ride up Sani Pass is easy; the best point to pick up lifts being about 15km along the dirt road to the pass from the village of Himeville at **Sani Lodge**, the last point accessible by ordinary vehicle (*see* 'Where to Stay'). A number of very beautiful trails begin and end at Sani Lodge, some of which lead to superb bushman paintings, or to natural swimming pools of crystal spring water. It is best to spend a couple of days there so as to try at least two of the trails, each of which takes about half a day to walk. Eland and reedbuck are common, and hikers often have the trails to themselves. Those without transport can pick up a minibus service to/from Sani Lodge from either Durban or 'Maritzburg, ✆ (033) 701 1017. If you intend to travel up Sani Pass you will need your passport to cross the Lesotho border, which is halfway up. At the top is a small lodge, a hiking hut (a three-day trail leaves from Sani Top) and horses for hire.

The southernmost reserve in the 'Berg is **Garden Castle**, ✆ (033) 701 1571, where you can spend the night in caves, or stay at the camp site. From here you can hike to see rock art. A little further north towards the Sani Pass, **Cobham Nature Reserve**, ✆ (033) 702 0831, has an open camp site with huts, and a cottage which sleeps 7. There are also opportunities to camp in the wilderness, and good trout fishing. **Loteni**, ✆ (033) 702 0540, also has good fishing, plus scenic walks and climbs, and the Settlers' Homestead Museum.

The Central Drakensberg

Giant's Castle Game Reserve is a huge protected area (about 35,000ha) of mountain north of Sani Pass, accessible from Estcourt on the N3 or Winterton on the R74. The reserve is named after the central massif that dominates the mountain horizon—at 3314m it is one of the higher peaks in the 'Berg—which is said to look like a sleeping giant. The Little Tugela River rises in these mountains and cascades down to the plain below, eventually joining the mighty Tugela River, whose waters marked the old border between Natal and Zululand. Giant's Castle has three camps, with self-catering cottages or camp sites available. The largest is **Main Camp**, whose entrance, called **Witteberg Gate**, is accessible from the town of Winterton on the R74. Petrol is available here. **Injasuthi Camp**, the second largest, is also accessible from Winterton along the Cathkin Peak road, and **Hillside Camp**, the smallest, is reached via Loskop. Be aware that Loskop is a volatile area, and that the road can be dangerous at times of political unrest.

Due north of Giant's Castle Nature Reserve and Sani Pass is the combined **Mlabonja and Mdelelo Wilderness Area**, a great sweep of wild mountain reached via the R600 from Winterton (on the R74) or from Estcourt, on the N3, via the Loskop road. The famous **Cathedral Peak** is here, a 3004m massif resembling a Gothic cathedral with twin towers. **Cathkin Peak** (3181m), famous among climbers, is also found here, as is **Champagne Castle** (3377m), which was christened by two British officers who climbed it just after the Second Anglo-Boer War (1902), having towed a champagne picnic along with them. God knows how—it's a gruelling 2-day walk to the top. The foot of this wilderness area has more resorts and hotels than the Southern 'Berg—mainly along the road from Winterton—but the mountains themselves are as wild as anywhere else in the range. The principal points of access are from **Champagne Castle Hotel** or the adjacent **Monk's Cowl Camp Site** (*see* 'Where to Stay'). The walking is spectacular. In the northern section of Mlabonja Wilderness Area is **Ndedema Gorge** (also called Rainbow Gorge). A particularly beautiful hiking trail leads along the river bed of the Ndadema (a tributary of the Tugela), between great rock walls that eventually become so narrow that they have caught a great boulder in mid-fall. Standing beneath this rock offers one of the classic photo-opportunities in the 'Berg.

The Northern Drakensberg

The Northern 'Berg is the most spectacularly scenic part of the range. The highest accessible point, **Mont aux Sources** (3282m), juts from the rampart of a 3000m cliff wall called the **Amphitheatre**, where the Tugela River rises.

Royal Natal National Park and the smaller, adjoining **Rugged Glen Nature Reserve** (accessible from Bergville via the R74) are the best points from which to explore the mountains around, whether on foot or horseback (*see* 'Activities' below). With its protea woodland, fast-running streams, waterfalls and flat-topped heights, Royal Natal is picture-postcard Drakensberg scenery. Hiking trails snake through the mountains, and, while walking, you may meet Zulu women cutting reed grass for basket-making, as they have done since before the park existed.

Fauna in the park includes mountain reedbuck, bushbuck in the forested kloofs (often seen by the camp site at first light), grey rhebok, klipspringer, duiker and baboon. Leopard hunt the more remote areas.

Qwa Qwa, just east of Royal Natal, was South Africa's smallest 'homeland'. It covers only about 60,000ha, half of which has been set aside as a conservation area between Mont Aux Sources and the Maluti Mountains in Lesotho. Apart from providing quicker access to Mont Aux Sources than the hike from Royal Natal, the reserve has a 3-day hiking trail, a small hotel, **Witsieshoek Mountain Resort**, and a camp site. Much of the reserve is over 3000m, so be aware of the altitude and expect sudden changes of weather. Access is via the R74 from Bergville to the R712 to Phuthaditjaba (pronounced 'put-a-ditch-arba'), the tiny, scrubby Qwa-Qwa former capital, from where the Witsieshoek Mountain Resort is sign-posted, 30km down a good dirt road.

Activities

Walking and hiking: NB: Before setting off on any Drakensberg hike, make sure that you have a waterproof, map and some warm clothing, no matter how sunny it is. Weather can change quickly, dragging the temperature down. If hiking above 2000m, carry a full pack with survival gear such as a bivvy bag, food, compass etc.

The **Main Camp** at Giant's Castle is the access point for several walks and hikes. The most popular is up to Giant's Castle itself, a 2-day journey to and from a refuge hut at the foot of the cliffs that make up the final massif. Once there, hikers can continue north/south along a contour path for several days, sleeping in overnight huts (maps from the camp office). Anyone attempting the high paths *must* inform the camp office, which involves giving details of your leaving time and expected return time. You need warm clothing for the higher hikes. A gentler walk leads from the camp to a cave of bushman paintings that has been declared a museum of rock art, so dense and varied are the pictures. Guided tours leave about three times daily, but you can go up independently. The Main Camp also offers guided walking overnight trails (from September to May only), and bird-watching from hides (particularly good for lammergeier vulture). Injasuthi Camp has more walking trails (short day walks or access to the longer, high hikes). Black wildebeest, blesbok, oribi, duiker, red harte-beest and grey rhebok may be seen nearby, and are often encountered on trail.

The **Mlabonja and Mdelelo Wilderness Area** has 12 marked trails leading up through waterfall and forest to the high plateaux. As well as eland, mountain reed-buck and baboon, look out for the elegant, straight-horned grey rhebok in the kloofs. It is worth taking a tent for the overnight trails, although some of them do have designated caves for sleeping.

The best walk in the **Royal Natal National Park** is the 2-day hike up Mont Aux Sources (one day in, one day out, with an overnight hut at the top). Start early to ensure you have plenty of time to scale the chain ladders that make up the final 200m or so to the summit. Another much shorter walk is up to the Mudslide, also reached by a chain-ladder, at the top of which is a hidden waterfall that plunges 200ft over a cliff. Maps for all the park's hikes can be had from the main office.

Qwa Qwa has a 3-day trail with overnight huts. Much of the reserve is over 3000m, so be aware of the altitude and expect sudden changes of weather. Access is via the R74 from Bergville to the R712 to Phuthaditjaba.

Riding: Horses are available at any of the resort hotels listed below, all of which rent by the hour, as do the stables at Rugged Glen Nature Reserve, which adjoins the Royal Natal National Park. Hillside Camp, in Giant's Castle Nature Reserve, runs 3-day horse trails into the 'Berg between September and March. These have to be booked in advance via the Natal Parks Board in Pietermaritzburg, ✆ (0331) 471 981.

Fishing: Injasuthi Camp has trout fishing in the Little Tugela River, but you need to bring your own tackle.

Where to Stay

expensive

The **Drakensberg Gardens Golf & Leisure Resort**, near Underberg in the southern 'Berg, ✆ (033) 701 1355, is one of the old-fashioned family hotels that one finds throughout the 'Berg. There are 80 rooms, horses, tennis courts, a pool, a restaurant and bar. Hikes and short walks lead off into the mountains from the hotel (open to non-residents too).

Further north, near Winterton, the **Champagne Castle Hotel**, ✆ (036) 468 1306, is an old-fashioned gem with 49 en suite rooms set in a park of fragrant pines, looking out on the Champagne Castle massif. Again, there are horses, tennis, walking and hiking trails, and a feeling of being back in the 1930s. The **Cathedral Peak Hotel**, ✆ (036) 488 1888, also reached from Winterton, is from the same era, with similar facilities of riding, hiking, tennis and clean air.

For solitude, try **Giant's Lodge** in Giant's Castle Nature Reserve, ✆ (0331) 471 981, a self-catering lodge let to individual parties. It has 7 en suite rooms, and, although you bring your own food, a cook and domestic servants are provided. The Lodge is set into the hillside like a luxurious bunker, hidden by turf, yet with spectacular views out over this central section of the high 'Berg. **Tendele Lodge** in the Royal Natal National Park, ✆ (0331) 471 981, is also turfed over, though not built completely into the hillside. The three en suite bedrooms look out to the Amphitheatre and Mont aux Sources. Again, bring your own food, but there is a resident cook.

The **Royal Natal National Park Hotel**, ✆ (036) 438 6200, is another old-fashioned family hotel. Set under the requisite tall trees, with the requisite riding stables (for guests only), tennis courts, pool and bowling green, the hotel has 49 en suite rooms. Bushbuck can often be seen stealing across its lawns in the early morning. The hotel makes a convenient place to have a drink or a meal if you are staying in the adjacent Parks Board chalets or camp site. North of Royal Natal, along the R74 is **Little Switzerland**, ✆ (036) 438 6220, a small private resort of thatched cottages around a central lodge. The place sleeps 50, and has some superb hiking trails into the 'Berg, a trout stream (tackle available), and guaranteed peace.

Bonny Glen B&B, ✆ (036) 488 1222, is a beautiful stone-built dairy farm in the Drakensberg foothills near Winterton (on the D187, north of the R600). It makes a good base for walking in the Champagne Castle area which is a short (20 minutes) drive away.

Further north is **Sandford Park Lodge**, ✆ (036) 448 1001, a late 19th-century thatched bungalow set in woodland near Bergville with a pool, restaurant and bar. **Uitzicht Holiday Farm**, ✆ (036) 488 1492, on the west side of the R74 south of Winterton, has a self-catering cottage that sleeps 8, with walking, swimming, fishing (tackle available) and canoeing on the Little Tugela River.

Near Underberg is the **Bushman's Nek Hotel**, ✆ (033) 701 1460, in the foothills of the 'Berg, with a great view of the peaks. There are self-catering chalets and meals on request.

Strathmore Cottage, Himeville, next to Cobham Reserve, ✆ (033) 702 0821, has 4 fully equipped comfortable rooms next to a dam, with fly fishing on offer. **Hopewell Cottage**, Underberg, ✆ (033) 701 1944, is a thatched cottage which sleeps 8, situated on a 2ha dam 7km from the Umzimkulu river, with canoeing, bird-watching and trout-fishing.

Natal Parks Board cottages and chalets are found in all the reserves and adjacent state forests listed above. There is seldom any need to book unless you intend to be there during school holidays (particularly over Christmas), when it is advisable to book accommodation at the Natal Parks Board in Pietermaritzburg, ✆ (0331) 471 981. All cottages and chalets are self-catering only.

Sani Lodge, in the southern 'Berg, ✆ (033702) 0330, is the last point accessible by ordinary car on the Sani Pass road from Himeville. One of the cheapest and best-value places to stay in South Africa, Sani Lodge used to be an old trading store, and has a choice of dormitory bunks or double-bed rondavels painted with traditional designs. Russell, the owner, is a mine of local information and can advise on where to walk, where to see bushman paintings, where to organize riding or mountain biking; he also makes superb fudge and chocolate cake. Guests gather round a roaring log fire in the evenings.

The Lodge arranges pick-ups and drop-offs from Durban or Pietermaritzburg for travellers with no transport; call them for the timetable. Guests range from backpackers to local Sotho and Zulu traders journeying up and down Sani Pass. You can often hitch a ride up the pass with them. Take your own food, and be prepared for a long-drop toilet.

Natal Parks Board camp sites offer a cheap way to explore the Drakensberg nature reserves. All of the reserves listed above have camp sites with ablution blocks. A separate Parks Board camp site can be found at Monk's Cowl, further along the road from Champagne Castle Hotel. All Parks Board camp sites are at the trailheads for day and overnight (or longer) marked hiking trails.

'Why,' said I, 'Mrs Joubert, do you accompany the General on all his campaigns?'

'Oh yes,' said she. 'Piet [Joubert] couldn't get along without me... I have been with him in every battle since Majuba Hill. I shall continue following him around until one or the other of us is killed.'

'Yes,' said the General. 'I try to keep Mother [Mrs Joubert] at home, but it is useless to try.'

American journalist interviewing General Joubert (commander-in-chief of the Boer forces 1899–1900) after the battle of Elandslaagte (from *Thank God We Kept the Flag Flying*—a history of the siege of Ladysmith by Kenneth Griffith).

Between the Drakensberg, Zululand and the Transvaal border is an obscure strip of Natal that few travellers visit. True, Northwest Natal's principal towns—Ladysmith, Dundee, Glencoe, Newcastle, Utrecht and Vryheid—are all rather ugly, small semi-industrial towns with little architecture to speak of, but the countryside, a beautiful upland of Drakensberg foothills, high grassland, forestry plantations and game reserves, has a lonely, exhilarating sense of space and freedom. Big game still thrives in the superb Itala Game Reserve (one of the largest in the province), and the region's many mountains (in fact, eastern foothills of the Drakensberg) offer some of South Africa's least explored hiking trails.

Unusually for the province, Northwest Natal's white population is historically staunchly Afrikaans, and even declared itself a republic in 1884, a move which was supported by the British colonial government, in recognition of the local Boers' support during the Zulu War of the 1870s.

Battlefields are two-a-penny in Northwest Natal—one of the most fought-over regions of South Africa. Since the first recorded encounter, when Dingane's Zulu *impis* hurled themselves to disaster against the *laagered* wagons and disciplined musketry of Andries Pretorius' Voortrekkers at Blood River in 1838, this part of Natal has witnessed several heavy engagements of the Zulu War of 1879 and many of the pitched battles from the opening months of the Second Anglo-Boer War of 1899, including the bloody British defeat of Spioenkop.

Getting There

By road: Most people enter the area via the north/south N3 highway from Harrismith, Estcourt or Colenso. A more interesting way in is via northern Zululand along the R68 between Empangeni and Vryheid, through high downland, forest and battlefields. Travellers from the Transvaal should head southeast over the Balelesberg via the N11 or R33.

By bus: TransLux, Greyhound and Transtate run buses from Durban and Pietermaritzburg to Newcastle, Dundee, Vryheid, Glencoe and Utrecht. The number varies from town to town, and can be found in the *Yellow Pages*.

By rail: Daily services between Jo'burg and Durban stop at Harrismith and Estcourt. From Harrismith, infrequent local services connect with the area's main towns. In general it is more convenient to take a bus.

Tour groups: Several small tour companies offer trips to the smaller towns, nature reserves and battlefields. Contact them through the towns' Publicity Offices.

Itala Game Reserve

The Itala, reached via the R69 between Vryheid and the N2, is all that survives of the once huge Pongola Game Reserve, declared by Jan Smuts in the 1900s, but subsequently opened up for farmland. This huge bowl beneath an upland amphitheatre remained wild, and was finally declared a park in 1973. Crocodiles still swim in the Itala stretch of the Pongola River, and elephant browse the riverine forest. The reserve is known for its large white rhino population, while the denser bush harbours a few shy black rhino, cheetah and leopard as well as spotted and brown hyena. Most of the bushveld antelope species occur, as well as klipspringer on the cliffs of the amphitheatre and the rare red duiker near the river. Wildebeest, tsessebe, zebra and giraffe are common, as are baboons and vervet monkeys. Caracal lynx and honey badger may be seen in the evening. The reserve runs excellent guided walks from an hour to five days in length (*see* 'Activities').

Vryheid

Tourist Information

Vryheid Tourist Information, Corner of Mark and High Streets, ✆ (0381) 812 133.

Vryheid itself is not an attractive town, but is a useful stopping point for petrol and supplies if heading to or from Itala or up into the Transvaal and Swaziland. Since its five-year stint as capital of the Boer Republic of Vryheid (1884–9), the town has settled into an ugly, though prosperous, minor industrial town. However, of interest to shoppers is the **Knabbelhuisie Craft Centre** on President Street, where Zulu crafts and Boer biscuits, pastries and preserves are sold. There is a small nature reserve on the hills north of town where zebra and various antelope species graze. You can walk where you please, but there is no accommodation.

Natal Spa, a small hot springs resort set in the hills just north of Vryheid, has two outdoor pools of about 40°C, horses, tennis and squash courts, a bar and restaurant and moderate to expensively priced accommodation. It is a bit staid, being mostly used by local Afrikaans farmers and their families, but is a good place for a relaxing plunge before driving on to a game reserve or guest farm.

Blood River, the famous Boer/Zulu battlefield, lies just south of the R33 between Vryheid and Dundee. A life-size bronze wagon *laager* marks the site (*see* 'Natal History').

Dundee

Dundee itself is even less attractive than Vryheid, but its position on the R33 makes it unavoidable if heading down towards Ladysmith and the northern Drakensberg. Southwest of Dundee is the **Elandslaagte battlefield**, where, in 1899, the British invaders won a hard-fought battle—losing many men to sniper fire, but finally pushing the Boers out of their position with artillery bombardment and cavalry charges. **Talana battlefield** also lies near Dundee, on the R68 to Melmoth. It was here, also in 1899, that the British broke through a strong Boer trench and artillery defence—again incurring heavy losses—only to get bogged down by guerilla fighting around Ladysmith until 1900, when the unwieldy British columns finally lumbered north into the Transvaal.

Ladysmith

Tourist Information

Ladysmith Publicity Office, Murchison Street, ℗ (0361) 22 992.

Ladysmith is a large agricultural town of interest mainly for its role in the Anglo-Boer War, when it suffered a four-month siege that resulted in several bloody battles as the lumbering British columns tried and repeatedly failed to relieve the town. There is a small museum dedicated to the siege next door to the Publicity Office (*open Mon–Fri 8–4, Sat 8–1*).

The Siege of Ladysmith lasted 115 days, from October 1899 to February 1900 and was a classic example of the Boers' lack of experience with conventional warfare. Like the war's other two sieges of British garrisons, Kimberley and Mafeking, Ladysmith was of little strategic value. The Boers were right to try and take the town, lying as it did behind their defensive line at the Tugela River, but the artillery and manpower invested could have been better expended against the main British invasion force south of the Tugela. As it was, that front held for almost a year, and breaking through it cost thousands of British lives. However, once the line had broken, the Boers abandoned most of their heavy artillery and took to the bush where, although they held out for a further two years, they could never win any decisive action, and the British victory, if slow in coming, was assured. The siege was of immense propaganda value, romanticized by Victorian Britain as an example of British fortitude in the face of overwhelming odds. But, as so often with colonial history, the real victims were the Zulu and Hlubi who acted as messengers and skirmishers for the British (many of whom died) and who bore the brunt of the food and water shortages.

Southwest of Ladysmith on the R74 to Colenso is **Spioenkop**, a classic South African kopje where, on 24 January 1900, three hundred British troops on their way to break the siege of Ladysmith died in their trenches at the hands of Boer sharpshooters on higher ground. Instead of charging, the soldiers were ordered to wait it out, and finally, when so many had been killed as to make an assault impracticable, to retire. A waste of life in true colonial style. Many of the British defending Spioenkop that day were members of the Kings Liverpool Regiment, and the main stand at Liverpool United Football Club's newly built Anfield stadium was endowed with the name in honour of the dead. Known ever since as 'The Kop', the old terrace has witnessed some of the greatest moments in British football. But it is unlikely that many of the fans who crowd into the Kop every Saturday remember the 300 men who died, crouched and thirsty in the South African heat.

Today, the site of the battlefield has been absorbed into a game park and water-sports resort—**Spioenkop Dam and Nature Reserve**, ℗ (0368) 78. The dam (on the Tugela River) gets crowded at weekends, but the reserve is worth visiting for its white rhino and larger antelope, walking trail and horses. Guided tours of the battlefield are available. Accommodation is available in self-contained chalets or a camp site (with ablution block).

Northeast of Ladysmith lie **Newcastle**, a bleak coal-mining centre, and **Utrecht**, a small country town close to the high Balalesberg Mountains.

The Lion Cubs, the Minister and the English Adventurer

An old frontiersman and hunter called Loxton (great great great-uncle of the author) retired to Utrecht in the early 1900s with his wife and two playful lion cubs, Saul and Deborah. When the cubs were half-grown, old man Loxton was visited by an English adventurer, Major Tudor Trevor. Trevor was sitting on Loxton's veranda, when he saw the town's Dutch Reform Church minister walking by. Deborah saw him too, slipped through the garden hedge and followed him. The minister, hearing breathing, turned, saw the young lion and set off up the street, yelling. Deborah loped after him and, with an easy swing of her paw lopped off first one coat tail, then the other. The minister redoubled his pace, just as Saul jumped out of the hedge in front of him and roared. The minister fainted, and Saul sat on top of him, licking his face. Trevor ran to the rescue, kicking Saul, who snarled and tore off a chunk of trouser-leg with a cuff of his paw. It was old Mrs Loxton who saved the situation by driving the young lions off with a *sjambok* while Trevor and the minister fled to the house. Next day the outraged minister brought a law-suit. Loxton was ordered to destroy the lions, but he and Trevor smuggled them out of town by night, back to the Zululand bushveld, where they set them free.

Utrecht was the headquarters of the British army for a while during the 1879 Zulu War, when Lord Chelmsford was commander-in-chief. The **Chelmsford Nature Reserve,** southwest of town on the N11, carries his name. Another reserve set round a large dam, Chelmsford is known for wildfowl, particularly spurwing and Egyptian geese, which congregate here in large numbers. Nomadic blue cranes often visit the dam on their journeys to and from accross southern Africa. Avoid the reserve at weekends, when large numbers of water-skiers from Newcastle and Utrecht come out to play; on weekdays you are likely to have the veld to yourself. The walking trails may lead you past white rhino, hartebeest, zebra, blesbok and the smaller antelope (duiker and steenbok) which graze the fringes of the dam.

Ncandu Waterfall, on the dirt road to Muller's Pass (on the border with Mpumalanga), is a beautiful place to walk in the lower slopes of the Balalesberg mountains, an offshoot spur of the high Drakensberg foothills. Horses can also be hired from here.

Along the N11, north of the range, are the sites of two fairly minor skirmishes of the Second Anglo-Boer War: **Laingsnek** and **Ingogo** (near Volksrust). **Majuba Hill,** the site of the only battle of the First Anglo-Boer War of 1881 (a major humiliation for the British), is also alongside the N11 just north of the Laings Nek Pass. Majuba Hill is open to the public (i.e. there is a small admission charge) and visitors are given a small booklet to take around a self-guided trail, the gist of which is how foolish the British General Colley was to allow his 400 troops to be driven from the hill and out of the Transvaal by just 150 Boers.

No visitor to Northwest Natal should leave without taking at least a day-hike into the wild **Balelesberg,** which rise in a blue wall northwest of Utrecht and Newcastle. This range is one of the least visited in Natal and its trails are uncrowded. Day and overnight hikes wind through several parts of the range among trails of waterfalls, protea woods, cycads, secret gorges, baboons, eagles, small antelope, but above all, silence and clean air.

Activities

Walking and hiking: Itala Game Reserve, ✆ (0331) 471 961, runs four 1-day trails from March to September, all following circles leading back to the same bush camp, so there is no carrying of heavy packs except for the hike between the camp and the park office. Sightings of large game are guaranteed. **Spioenkop** and **Chelmsford** reserves both have self-guided trails with good chances of seeing game. The seldom-visited **Balelesberg Mountains**, ✆ (0433) 3041, have a series of 2-day trails (accommodation in huts with mattresses, firewood, water and toilet).

Battlefield tours: Majuba Hill has a self-guided walk, as do most of the battlefield sites listed above. **Fugitive's Drift Lodge** and **Babanango Lodge** offer qualified guides (with transport) for the local Zulu War sites and the Boer War ones further afield (*see* p.441). If you want to follow the battlefields independently, pick up the detailed map of all the sites from the Publicity Offices in the province's main towns.

Spa and hot mineral pools: Thangami Safari Spa, Black Umfolozi Valley, ✆ (03824) 793/780, ✉ 850, is situated in the bush, with indoor and outdoor pools. Accommodation is either self-catering or B&B, and, after a relaxing soak, you can go on game drives or 4x4 trails, or go river-rafting, riding or bird-watching.

Where to Stay

expensive

Ntshondwe Lodge, ✆ (0331) 471 981/963, is a thatched brick house inside Itala Game Reserve, with 6 en suite rooms looking out over forested and boulder-strewn slopes grazed by a variety of game. You have to take your own food, but there is a cook. The lodge also has a sun-deck and pool. Less remote is **Magdelena Game Ranch**, ✆ (0386) 71 865, in the uplands near Vryheid, which has a small lodge overlooking a waterfall, as well as a self-contained cottage, a pool, walking, riding, and various species of antelope (including nyala, bushbuck and blesbok) roaming its open hills.

moderate

Itala Game Reserve, ✆ (0388) 75 105, has a variety of self-catering chalets and cottages. It is worth spending at least two nights here to make sure of seeing game in the reserve's thick bush. These are seldom full, and most visitors simply turn up. There is also Natal Parks Board accommodation at Spioenkop Dam and at Chelmsford Nature Reserve.

Elandslaagte, ✆ (036) 211 878, a farm cottage in the Biggarsberg Mountains, overlooking a 250ha dam, offers self-catering accommodation for 6–8 people (serviced daily). It is a good base for fishing, water sports, walking, mountain biking, and riding. **Balele Mountain Lodge**, Utrecht, ✆/✉ (017) 730 0418, is a good stopping-off point mid-way between Durban and Jo'burg. It has 5 chalets with open log fires and a grass caravan park, with 1- or 2-day hiking trails, riding and trout fishing

The **Penny Farthing**, ✆ (0346421) 925, is a country guesthouse in the heart of the Natal battlefields near Dundee on the R33 to Helpmakaar. The chintzy late 19th-century farmhouse has been in the same family for 150 years. There are antelope on the farm, and walking, fishing, and guided battlefield tours are on offer. The farm also has a set of caves that were inhabited by Bele cannibals during the Mfecane upheavals of the 1830s.

Mambasa Hutted Camp & Bonny Glen Cottages, ✆ (036) 488 1313, is on the banks of the Tugela River, down a 2km farm track off the R600 between Spioenkop and Winterton. The traditional Zulu grass dome huts have permanent beds, cooking and ablution facilities, and bushveld all around. The camp is managed by an old Zulu man, and there is none of the irritating 'theme park' Zulu culture that so often accompanies this sort of place—local Zulu families go about their daily business regardless of tourists. The camp has two walking trails up into the surrounding wooded hills. Take your own food.

Chichester Bush Camp, ✆ (03841) 41146, 45km east of Itala on the R69, has a basic bush camp (with a hot shower), with hiking trails through bushveld inhabited by a healthy antelope population (nyala, kudu, bushbuck, etc.). Take your own food.

Chelmsford Nature Reserve and **Spioenkop Nature Reserve** both have camp sites. The **Balelesberg Hiking Trail Huts** are all 1-day's walk into the Balelesbergs, cost little, and have water, toilets and firewood, but you must bring your own food.

Zululand

> *Command the warring king*
> *to lay aside his deathful lance awhile*
> *and seek his consort of the shining smile*
> *and with her fight and win a sweeter war*
> *where shield is kiss and assegai desire*
>
> *Indaba My Children*, Credo Mutwa

Until 1994, most of the land from the Tugela River north to the border with Mozambique was administered by Kwa-Zulu, one of the 'tribal homelands' invented by the Nationalist Party in the 1970s. Kwa-Zulu was divided into scores of fragmented chunks, some large, some tiny. Although now no longer 'separate', when driving through Zululand you cannot fail to notice the ever alternating difference between land owned by white farmers and land belonging to the Zulu villages of what was the Kwa-Zulu 'homeland', creating sharp contrasts in an already spectacular landscape.

Zululand is divided into three main chunks: the inland section, the coast and Tsongaland. The inland section houses the massive **Umfolozi** and **Hluhluwe Game Reserves** (home to the Big Five), and among its high hills and valleys traditional Zulu life continues more or less as it always has. To the east, the foetid and sub-tropical coast is dominated by the massive lake complex of **Lake St Lucia**, one of the largest wetlands in Southern Africa. Tsongaland sits north of the main coast, in a rough square formed by the Mkuze River, the Lebombo Mountains, the Mozambique border, and coastline even wilder than around St Lucia. Remote from the rest of the country, most of Tsongaland is dense sand forest shared by cattle and game. It too has large game reserves, and a tropical coast whose few accessible points, such as **Kosi Bay** and **Lake Sibaya**, are unspoilt. The Tsonga still consider themselves a separate people, though most speak Zulu and are administered by Kwa-Zulu.

Visitors to Zululand should try to allow a week at the very least in order to have a look at all three regions, as the distances between those places open to travellers can be great, and the country itself is very beguiling, both for its beauty and for the friendliness of its people. Despite the Zulu reputation for inter-clan violence, fighting is usually contained within groups that have a specific quarrel with each other, and travellers are generally treated with much warmth and respect, particularly in Tsongaland, which is only nominally part of Zululand and largely apolitical.

Visitors should be aware that Zululand is malarial.

Flora and Fauna

Zululand's inland section is mostly savannah and bushveld, with a wet, humid summer, and warm, dry winter that becomes parched just before the first rains. The Big Five abound in the large Umfolozi and Hluhluwe Game Reserves, which used to be the Zulu kings' hunting ground in the 19th century. Rarities such as wild dog, spotted hyena and brown hyena also occur, as do most of the antelope and grazing species, which roam in large herds through all the inland reserves. Some of the upland areas have large stretches of temperate hardwood forest, supporting small numbers of shyer game.

The coast is mostly forested with dense, sub-tropical growth. Some big game, such as buffalo, rhino and leopard, still thrives there, as well as plentiful antelope. Hippo and crocodile are found in most of the lakes and rivers. Wild fig trees and wild fruits such as the monkey orange and marula tree feed a host of colourful songbirds, while forest raptors such as fish and crowned eagle are common.

The dense forest of Tsongaland is still home to elephant, most of which now inhabit the new Tembe Game Reserve. At Ndumo Game Reserve, rhino, hippo and crocodile make up the bigger game, and at Kosi Bay and Lake Sibaya, sea turtles crawl on to the beaches to lay their eggs on summer nights. The coast has some rare birds (Pel's fishing owl and the vegetarian palm nut vulture), while inland Tsongaland has spectacular bird life, especially at Ndumo, where rollers, nicators, bee-eaters and sunbirds attract bird-watchers from around the world.

The Zulu People

Much has been written of the Zulu people. Their military tradition and apparent national solidarity have held a fascination for academics, historians, and the generally curious public throughout the world, and their fiercely independent character has changed little over the years, becoming if anything more consolidated under South Africa's oppressive white regime. Today, despite, a recent rise in ANC support within Zululand, the reigning monarch (King Goodwill X) and the local chiefs still inspire great respect and obedience through much of Zululand—evident even among those living away from Zululand in the big cities, where support of the Inkatha Freedom Party (IFP), the Zulu political party under the leadership of Dr Mangosotho Buthelezi, is almost as strong as within Zululand itself.

Most rural families still live in the traditional round, woven-grass huts or, in drier areas, clay rondavels. Cattle represent wealth and are given as payment (*lobola*) for a bride. Although clinics now operate throughout Zululand, *sangomas*, or witch doctors, still tend to the medical and spiritual needs of most rural Zulus, and it is not uncommon to see their distinctive braids and inflated animal bladders (a sign of office) even in the larger towns.

Having said this, the Zulu are anything but 'backward' (although there are people in some of the remoter parts of Zululand who have never seen a white person), despite their tragic tendency to inter-clan feuding which today manifests itself most violently in the bloody clashes between ANC and IFP in the townships around Durban and Pietermaritzburg. Under Mangosotho Buthelezi, Kwa-Zulu has been welded into what is probably the most powerful single ethnic minority in South Africa.

History

Until about 1820 the Zulu were an insignificant clan in a larger mosaic of cattle-herding Nguni-speaking peoples who, through the 18th century, had traded ivory and slaves with the Dutch and English at Port Natal (modern Durban) and the Portuguese and English at Delogoa Bay (modern Maputo). Amongst these clans the Ndwandwe and the Mthethwa (*see* 'KwaZulu-Natal History') competed for dominance, organizing their young men into permanent regiments (known as *amabutho*) and raiding, first within present-day Zululand, then further afield. By plundering smaller clans the Mthethwa and Ndwandwe could provide supplies for their warriors while at the same time augmenting their number with captives. By 1800 the two clans were intermittently at war, with most young men of the small Zulu clan levied to fight for the Mthethwa, under chief Dingiswayo.

Chief of the Zulu at this time was Sezangakhona who, in his youth, had made pregnant a girl from the neighbouring Langeni clan—an unhappy accident; Nguni youths and maidens were encouraged in non-penetrative sex-play before marriage, involving friction between the girl's legs, but to impregnate a girl before marriage was to strip her of status, cutting the bride-price, and bringing scandal to her clan. The girl's name was Nandi, meaning 'sweet'. According to the oral tradition, Nandi began to swell a few months after her encounter with Sezangakhona. An accusation of paternity was sent but the Zulus denied it, claiming that the swelling was caused by a parasite, called *ishaka*. But a child was born and, with ironic jest, Nandi called him Shaka. Mother and baby were dumped at the Zulu capital, where Nandi was given a menial domestic position, while still kept as a concubine by Sezangakhona.

The various accounts of Shaka's childhood all agree that he was persecuted by the Zulus. In his book *Chaka* (an alternative spelling of the name), Thomas Mofolo, himself a Zulu, relates how the young Shaka was victimized, even in his sleep:

> *Twice or three times, Chaka had his hands tied right there in the young people's hut, and was made to sleep outside near the door tied up like that, so that the hyena should see him as soon as it came. This would be done when a hyena was seen near the village, and it was expected that it would catch some people after dark. But on those occasions, the hyena would feast on goats and leave the people alone. Chaka's growing-up was truly painful.*

Shaka and Nandi were finally banished from the Zulu village after Shaka was accused of allowing a sheep to die while in his care. They went back to the Langeni clan. But again,

Shaka was persecuted. After some years, when Shaka was in his late teens, a severe drought forced mother and son to forage abroad again, and they eventually wandered to the main village of the Mthethwa clan.

Shaka joined the most junior *amabutho* and proved an heroic and ferocious fighter on Chief Dingiswayo's raiding campaigns. Tradition has it that he invented a short stabbing spear for personal use in combat against champions of opposing clans, which was later adopted by the whole Mthethwa army. (The spear made battles bloodier, more hand-to-hand and more decisive; larger numbers of the enemy could be killed than by the traditional light throwing spear.) Dingiswayo rapidly promoted the young fighter, and Shaka took advantage of his growing influence to perfect a new fighting strategy, known as the 'horns of the bull', in which the enemy was attacked in a pincer movement, surrounded and destroyed.

In 1818 Shaka (now an *induna*, or general) learnt of his father's death, and Dingiswayo gave him permission to claim the Zulu chieftaincy. Shaka duly killed his rivals and assumed both the chieftaincy and command of the Zulu and Langeni regiments of the Mthethwa army. Shaka reorganized the men into four regiments divided by age. The youngest were to remain bachelors until they had proved themselves on campaign, the incentive of acquiring a wife making them fight harder. After marriage they would join a veteran's regiment of experienced warriors who, as they aged, would move to the two older regiments, to provide back up and carry out specialized tasks. In this way no able-bodied man, young or old, would ever be out of the army. Shaka now made his own bid for power.

From this point on Shaka never let up campaigning, as far afield as modern Natal, Transkei, Swaziland and even Mpumalanga and Northern Province, hundreds of miles to the north. The Zulus became the dominant clan, absorbing the Mthethwa. Shaka's incessant wars caused many small clans to flee Natal into Transkei or over the Drakensberg to the highveld, both areas that were undergoing their own political upheavals at the time (*see* 'Ndebele' and **Lesotho** 'History'). Some of these refugee clans, like the Bele, were so reduced by this cycle of warfare and famine that they turned to cannibalism; others, like the Ngwane and Mfengu, were merely absorbed into other, larger clans (*see* 'Transkei' and **Swaziland** 'History'), while still others, like the Hlubi, managed to dodge the disturbances and return to Natal long after Shaka's death (*see* 'Drakensberg History'). The whole process, with its parallel upheavals on the highveld, became known to historians as the *Mfecane* (the Zulu word for 'crushing') and caused widespread dislocation of the peoples of southern Natal—the reason why the Voortrekkers of the 1830s claimed to have found large tracts of it apparently empty.

Shaka built himself two great capitals: the first, *Bulawayo* ('place of killing'), was just east of the modern town of Empangeni. After a few years, he moved to the Natal North Coast, building *Dakuza* ('labyrinth') near the modern town of Stanger. Traditional histories depict Shaka as a bloody tyrant; mass executions, the impaling of defeated warriors and 'smellings-out' (execution for witchcraft) have been cited as regular atrocities. But recent historical opinion tends to dismiss this as fiction. Shaka was clearly an able ruler who united the fragments of Natal's Nguni clans, organized his army into mining for iron ore and reopened the trading station at Port Natal (abandoned during the Mthethwa/Ndwandwe wars) through the maverick British traders Henry Fynn and James King.

Shaka was eventually assassinated by two of his half-brothers, one of whom, Dingane, took the Zulu throne. Dingane carried on raiding campaigns but pursued a placatory foreign policy with the British in Pondoland, and communicated with Cape Town via the traders at Port Natal. The resulting white interest in his domain was to prove to be Dingane's downfall. The Boers then controlled Natal until the British annexed it in 1842 after a two-year campaign (see pp.xxx). The Zulus had lost half their kingdom, but under their new king, the peace-loving Mpande, there was no further trouble with the white settlers for over 30 years.

However, in the 1870s, the Natal authorities determined to force an annexation of Zululand. Mpande had died, and his son and successor, Cetshwayo, made no attempt to disguise his dislike of the British (though he saw them as a lesser evil than the Boers). He tolerated, but longed to cleanse his country of, the missionaries that Mpande had allowed to settle, rightly thinking that the new religion eroded Zulu culture and belittled the people by criticizing their customs and forcing them to wear cheap European clothes. Cetshwayo was restrained by his advisors (including an English adventurer called John Dunn) and he continually asserted to the Natal authorities that he had no wish for war or quarrel with the British.

But nobody could prevent Cetshwayo from raiding the non-Zulu clans placed by the British along his southern border and by the early 1870s he had accumulated an unfair record of 'hostile' action against these British subjects. Nevertheless, despite the Natal authorities' avid desire for war, the British government only agreed to send troops in 1878, after being persuaded by colonial administrators such as Sir Bartle Frere and Theophilus Shepstone that an annexation of Zululand would both secure Natal from a 'native' threat and move British troops closer to the coveted Boer South African Republic (SAR) of the Transvaal. Troops were moved to the Zululand frontier in October 1878 and Cetshwayo was presented with a trumped-up 'Ultimatum' demanding that (among other impossible things) the entire Zulu army be disbanded within 20 days. This Cetshwayo could not do, with hostile neighbours to the north and west, and even had he been willing, the time given was insufficient. British troops crossed the Tugela and the Anglo-Zulu War had begun (see 'History', pp.376–80).

The Zulu War

The invasion of Zululand cost the British dear. The British general, Lord Chelmsford, vastly underestimated Cetshwayo's military might and, for the first few months, the Zulu won every engagement. The British failures culminated in the historic defeat of 22 January 1879, when Chelmsford and his adjutant, Colonel Glyn, rode out with a column of several thousand to scout enemy positions, leaving about 1500 British and 'native' auxiliaries encamped in the open under a lone hill called **Isandhlwana**. Unbeknownst to Chelmsford, on the previous day over 20,000 Zulu had quietly moved into position just to the north, and were watching every British move. Once Chelmsford and his troops had ridden out of sight, a small Zulu force ranged itself on the ridge above the British camp. A company despatched to drive off these Zulu discovered the huge army behind the ridge. For the Zulus, attack was now imperative and, as the British scouts galloped back, the officer-in-charge, Colonel Pulleine, saw the *impis* massing on the ridge. He and his second-in-command, Colonel Durnford, organized the troops and repelled this first attack but, with no palisades or entrenchments, the camp was hopelessly vulnerable. In mid-afternoon the entire Zulu army poured over the ridge and engulfed the camp in the classic 'horns of the bull' pincer movement. Despite organized fire the British were overwhelmed and only a few managed to escape the slaughter, galloping full tilt for the British military hospital at Rorke's Drift, just over the Natal border 10km to the south. Cetshwayo had instructed his army not to go across into Natal but 4000 Zulu troops disobeyed, pursuing the British and attacking Rorke's Drift. The 150 or so defenders, many of them badly wounded, managed to repulse the now tired warriors with sustained rifle fire and the *impis* retired, having lost about 500 men.

Isandhlwana claimed the lives of over 1200 British and auxiliary troops, including commanding officers, with roughly the same number of Zulu fallen. The largest single military defeat of the British colonial forces (excluding the battles of the Indian Mutiny), Isandhlwana and Rorke's Drift have inspired two feature films—*Zulu Dawn* and *Zulu*—both of which give romanticized but reasonably accurate accounts of the slaughters.

It took the British some months to turn the tide, leaving the main army holed up in the Norwegian mission station near the modern town of Eshowe, while the Zulus laid siege from the surrounding forest. Massive reinforcements were brought up from the Cape, but unfortunately for Chelmsford, the embarrassment of the Isandhlwana defeat was compounded by the later loss of the young Louis Napoleon—the French Prince Imperial, heir to the throne, and great-nephew of the great Bonaparte himself—who blundered into a Zulu ambush with his escort while on his way to join the army at Eshowe. Young Louis was officially under the protection of the British Crown and his death ensured both Chelmsford's full military disgrace and a full deployment of modern military technology against Cetshwayo.

The main Zulu army was finally caught in the open at Cetshwayo's capital of Ulundi (the regional capital of modern Zululand) and Lord Chelmsford, now under the shadow of a shameful recall, unleashed a merciless artillery barrage. Cetshwayo was deposed and Zululand's most powerful chiefs put on the British Government payroll, relying on the divide-and-rule principle to keep the Zulus down. The policy worked too well—Zululand promptly sank into a series of civil wars (which continued even after Cetshwayo was reinstated in 1883) from which the region has never fully recovered: many say that the endless clan warfare still afflicting the Zulu nation has its roots in this time.

The Zulus staged a last, ill-fated rising in 1906 (although, oddly enough, the main area was south of the Tugela and not in Zululand proper), which was put down with brutal reprisals. The various white governments consistently failed to lure Zulu men to Natal to work; they understandably scorned to labour on farms (regarded as women's work), and took off in force to work in the Transvaal gold mines through the early 20th century, establishing a Zulu majority among mineworkers on the Reef that persists today.

Even under apartheid, Zululand cut a largely independent path. The largest noticeable change in the region has been the passing of direct political power from the monarchy, under King Goodwill X, to the chiefs, under Mangosotho Buthelezi, leader of the Inkatha Freedom Party (IFP). Meanwhile, the ANC has claimed many Zulu converts in southern Natal, exacerbating the traditional feuding with clashes between IFP and ANC supporters. This may creep into the Zulu heartland before long. But feuding and abrupt power shifts have always been a feature of Zulu political life and have yet to diminish the nation's overall cohesion.

The Zulu Heartland: Battlefields and Villages

The most scenic way into Zululand is the R33 from Pietermaritzburg, via Greytown. This is an area known for clan fighting (read the Msinga chapter of *My Traitor's Heart* by Rian Malan—*see* 'Further Reading'), but the traveller need not worry. High mountain, arid, aloe-covered slopes, spectacular patterns of soil erosion from overgrazing, and thick thornveld characterize this southern region of inland Zululand, which begins at **Keate's Drift** on the Mooi River, about 30km north of Greytown. Keate's Drift is little more than a single-lane bridge across the river, plus a few shacks and a permanent market where Zulu women sell fruit, vegetables and cloths, and some of the best beadwork and pottery you can buy in South Africa. You will be expected to bargain. Here and at Tugela Ferry, another single-lane bridge and market 15km north on the Tugela River, visitors should see Zulu women wearing the traditional headdress or *isicolo*, a large, fan-like affair with a beaded browband. Some young women still go bare-breasted (indicating that they are unmarried), though this is becoming less common. Remember to ask before photographing anyone, and you will normally be expected to pay R2 to R5 for the privilege.

Pomeroy, a small town 25km to the north, is little more than a dusty street of falling-down houses and an old fort left from the Zulu War. However on Thursdays there is another regional market here that is known for pottery. After Pomeroy, the road leads through the small farming hamlet of Helpmekaar where you can turn east on a dirt road to **Rorke's Drift**, the second of the Zulu War battlefields. This is now a museum (*open daily 9–5*), with the story of the battle told from both perspectives.

Northeast of Rorke's Drift, via the same dirt road back to the tarred R68 then along another dirt road, is the battlefield of **Isandhlwana**, scene of a disastrous British defeat. In an attempt to offset the disaster, the Victorians celebrated (and romanticized) the deaths of Lieutenants N. Coghill and T. Melville, two officers killed trying to carry the colours of the 24th Regiment to safety across the Buffalo River, at a place now called Fugitive's Drift. Scattered all over the landscape are hundreds of white-painted cairns marking the exact spots where men fell and where they lay unburied for several months.

From near Isandhlwana a dirt road leads 110km south through hilly country of Zulu villages and past a high mountain overlooking the small town of **Kranskop**. Zulu tradition has it that a siren living on the mountain lured travellers into a cave with her song, never to let them out again. The mountain dominates the Tugela Gorge, which in summer is a thundering torrent with some of the world's best white-water rafting. Southeast of the Zulu War battlefields is the old heart of Zululand, where the kings Shaka, Dingane and Cetshwayo had their main royal kraals, and where the graves of Piet Retief and some of his party may be found.

To reach them from Isandhlwana head southeast along the R68 through mixed hill, grassland and thornveld, to the site of **Dingane's kraal**, the site where he ordered the killings of the Voortrekker leaders Gert Maritz and Piet Reitief (and their party) in 1838 (*see* p.378).

From Dingane's kraal, the R68 leads southeast to the little trading village of **Melmoth**, from which you can either go north on the R34 and R66 (past the R66 turnoff to pass Retief's grave, which is marked on the road maps) to **Ulundi**, or head southeast towards Empangeni and the coast (*see* below). Ulundi is where the British destroyed Cetshwayo's Zulu army with artillery, and has lately been developed into a small town housing the administrative offices for Kwa-Zulu. At **Ondini**, just east of Ulundi, is a reconstruction of King Cetshwayo's kraal and a Zulu cultural museum with Zulu-designed displays (*open Mon–Fri 9.30–5*).

Southeast through forest from Melmoth, the road forks again. The south fork leads past Shaka's first great capital, **Bulawayo**, now a short distance from a small Zulu theme village and hotel called **Shakaland**. Despite the terrible name, it is a good place to stop for a drink and look around. The site of the film set for the visually spectacular but historically dubious TV series *Shaka Zulu*, the place looks out over the wide Tugela Valley and there are 'witch doctors' and people in traditional dress. Although the recreation is shamelessly artificial, and not as culturally accurate as the Zulu museum of Ondini, the place is nonetheless very attractive, and provides employment for many people in the area.

Continue along the R68, and you come to **Eshowe**, where Cetshwayo established his first capital (1860) and where the British army was besieged by the Zulus after the defeat at Isandhlwana in 1879. Sitting on a high ridge, Eshowe is pleasantly temperate after the heat of much of Zululand, and it has a remarkable feature—a forest in the middle of town. **Dhlinza State Forest** is an indigenous hardwood stand of about 220ha, harbouring bushbuck, bushpig, duiker, monkeys and a variety of birds. There are two shady walking trails under the great, silent trees. **Entumeni Nature Reserve**, a forest surrounded by sugar-cane fields, lies about 15km from town on a dirt road. It too has great hardwood trees harbouring game. At 400ha it is twice the size of Dhlinza.

These reserves are all that survive of a much larger forest that once covered the whole surrounding area, but was felled in the late 19th century to make way for sugar-cane fields. It was in these forests that the Zulus hid while besieging the fortified Norwegian mission station at Eshowe. **Eshowe Fort** is now a museum (*open Mon–Sat 9–4.30*). interesting for the story of John Dunn, an English privateer who established himself as an advisor to Cetshwayo before the war (*see* 'Zululand History'). He quickly changed sides once British troops invaded and was later re-instated by the British as one of the 13 chiefs left to govern (or rather feud over) Zululand after Cetshwayo's deposition.

East of Eshowe, before reaching the Zululand coast via the large agricultural town of Empangeni, the R68 leads past **Ocean View Game Park**, a private park of only 50ha where reedbuck, kudu, impala, wildebeest and other antelope graze. There are guided walks around, offering good opportunities for photographing animals that are very used to people. The park has no accommodation.

Inland Zululand: The Umfolozi and Hluhluwe Game Reserves

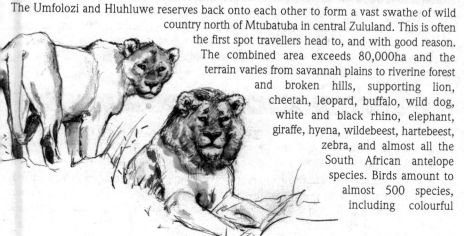

The Umfolozi and Hluhluwe reserves back onto each other to form a vast swathe of wild country north of Mtubatuba in central Zululand. This is often the first spot travellers head to, and with good reason. The combined area exceeds 80,000ha and the terrain varies from savannah plains to riverine forest and broken hills, supporting lion, cheetah, leopard, buffalo, wild dog, white and black rhino, elephant, giraffe, hyena, wildebeest, hartebeest, zebra, and almost all the South African antelope species. Birds amount to almost 500 species, including colourful trogons, louries, sunbirds, hornbills and some of the more spectacular raptors, such as bataleur eagle and chanting goshawk, as well as vultures. Both reserves were proclaimed in 1897 to protect what had once been the hunting preserves of the Zulu kings, and into which white ivory-hunters poured after the Zulu War.

Umfolozi has a **five day guided bush hiking trail** into deep wild country, one of the best bush experiences available in South Africa. Otherwise there are game viewing roads. Umfolozi and Hluhluwe are popular, so it is important to book if you want to stay overnight (*see* 'Where to Stay'). Also, be aware that both reserves' rivers carry bilharzia.

Ubizane Game Ranch is a private reserve about 7km northeast of Hluhluwe (accessible from the N2). Apart from white rhino, this bushveld reserve mostly harbours antelope (though leopard and hyena pass through). However, there are walking trails and horses to ride.

Mkuzi Game Reserve lies in the far north of Zululand, where it borders Tsongaland. The Lebombo Mountain escarpment rises above the small town of Mkuze, dominating the 35,000ha reserve. A particularly prominent lofty white cliff—*Tshaneni*, or Ghost Mountain—was the burial place of the Ndwandwe chiefs before they were absorbed into the Zulu tribe in the mid-19th century. The mountain is said to be haunted, and strange lights are sometimes seen on it. The reserve is about 10km down a roughish dirt road from Mkuze. Famous for its large rhino population (both black and white), Mkuzi also harbours hippo and crocodile, giraffe, zebra, blue wildebeest and almost all the South African antelope. Nyala are particularly common. Much of the reserve is thick bush, with many light-coloured fever trees, but there is also a large forest of wild fig trees—spectacular things the size of small buildings. There are also bird-watching hides—the reserve surrounds the Mkuze River and a large lake, and waterfowl are much in evidence, including Egyptian geese, pelican, gallinules (like colourful moorhens) and jacanas (also like colourful moorhens), a variety of herons, fish eagles, bright red bishop birds and storks. Among a number of wilderness trails is a five-day guided hike that takes you very close to rhino.

Ntendeka Wilderness Area is west of Mkuze, on the R618 to Vryheid. This forest (about 5000ha) of dense, subtropical hardwoods, giant ferns and trees in excess of 30m makes a surreal backdrop. There are walking trails and it is worth doing at least two of the day-hikes through this fabulous forest. It was here that Cetshwayo hid from the British after his defeat at Ulundi, and it is easy to see why. Not only is the forest dense, but there are steep ravines and cliffs pockmarked with caves and hidden by hanging forest. Bushbuck, duiker, bushpig, leopard and baboon live in here, as do some of the more spectacular forest birds, like trogons, the rare purple-crested lourie and iridescent sunbirds, which look like winged jewels. Monkeys and baboons live among the cliffs.

The Zululand Coast

North from the village of Tugela Mouth to Sodwana Bay (where the Tsongaland Coast begins) is a protected strip of wild, tropical beach, coastal jungle and freshwater lake systems, accessible by several large nature reserves.

The **Harold Johnson Nature Reserve**, on the south bank of the Tugela estuary, is a good place to break the journey if heading north on the N2. This riverine forest reserve is small but has lovely walking trails. One, the 2km **Rituals and Remedy Trail**, passes some 30 numbered trees and bushes; an accompanying handbook details the medicinal and ritual uses of each plant. The reserve also has the Ultimatum Tree, a huge fig under which (in 1879) the Natal authorities informed Cetshwayo of their intention to launch the Zulu War, unless he allowed them to annexe his kingdom as a British territory. Impala, bushbuck, bushpig, duiker and vervet monkey live in the reserve.

Umlalazi Nature Reserve, on the other side of the Tugela mouth from Stanger and the Harold Johnson Reserve, marks the first point accessible to visitors on the southern Zululand coast. There are walking trails through mangrove swamp and coastal forest, and rowing boats for hire. However, be wary of crocodiles near the banks and do not swim, even near the mouth, where there are sometimes sharks. Umlalazi is peaceful in the week, but tends to be invaded by Durban fishermen and water-skiers at weekends. There are log cabins hidden in the bush and a small camp site.

Empangeni and **Richards Bay** are two large towns between Tugela Mouth and St Lucia. Richards Bay, an industrial port, is strangely out of place on this wild coastline and rather depressing to visit. Empangeni is further inland and, as the N2 cuts through its suburbs, is a good place to stock up with petrol and supplies before heading north. The town is a regional shopping and administrative centre for eastern Zululand, composed mainly of modern, ugly buildings. However, south of town at **Gigindlovu** there is a quiet beach and superb hotel converted from a 19th-century sugar baron's mansion. It was at Gingindlovu that the Zulus staged their only serious attempt to stop the second invasion force that was sent into Zululand to relieve Lord Chelmsford's beleaguered army after Isandhlwana.

North of Empangeni there is also a pleasant private reserve, **Nyala Game Ranch**, a permanent bushveld camp with walking trails through bush populated mostly by antelope. The ranch is also open to day visitors.

Dukuduku State Forest sits astride the road between Mtubatuba and St Lucia. The protected area is about 6000ha of jungle-like forest, most of which is impenetrable, but there is a short walking trail from the picnic site (signposted from the road). Dukuduku is home to bushbuck, bushpig, leopard, red and common duiker, and the gaboon viper, a highly venomous snake usually found in Central Africa. The gaboon viper scents warm-blooded creatures and camouflages itself into the leaf-mould of the forest floor, so tread carefully.

St Lucia Nature Reserve, a lake system east of Dukuduku, is one of the largest wetlands in southern Africa. Lake St Lucia alone covers almost 13,000ha, including the protected

strip of forest and beach around it. Also part of the reserve are the coastal forests running for about 30km up the coast from where the lake meets the sea. Crocodile and hippo cruise through the entire lake system and there is plentiful game in the forests around. St Lucia is a sub-tropical wilderness of great beauty, and no trip to Zululand is complete without a visit.

However, of the several ways into St Lucia, avoid the main entrance in the south (east of Dukuduku and Mtubatuba). The Natal Parks Board has allowed a small, glitzy holiday resort to grow up around this entrance, complete with a massive camp site stuffed with Transvaal holiday makers whose greatest love is to drive their 4x4s aimlessly up and down the beach all day. Speed-boats are also popular; in the evenings, when the mullet are running in the lake mouth, people drive up and down at speed, making the fish jump from the water in their hundreds, while someone on deck swings a bat at them. Even the huge crocodiles at the lake mouth retreat to the banks while this goes on.

If you have to go in at the south end, head straight past the camp site up the coast for about 20km to **Cape Vidal**. This much quieter stretch of wild beach and jungle has a small fresh-water lake—Lake Bangazi—and an offshore marine reserve of coral reef teeming with tropical sea fish, which provides outstanding snorkelling. Cape Vidal's 12,000ha forest has frequent clearings where antelope, black rhino, kudu and buffalo roam. Reedbuck occur in great density, and there are a few hippo in the marshes. Cape Vidal has log cabins, chalets and a camp site. Trails in the forest include the five-day guided Mkizi Trail from Cape Vidal to St Lucia and back.

St Lucia has two other camps further north, reached from the N2. **Charters Creek** and **Fanies Island** both have a few cottages and a small camp site. The former has a fine view over the lake and a recently opened bar. Be careful of hippo wandering among the tents at night and crocs on the lakeshore. However, there are safe walking trails, and you can gener-ally hitch a ride on someone's fishing boat and explore the lake from the water. A three-hour boat trip leaves from the main camp every day at noon. It is common sense not to swim anywhere at St Lucia, except on marked beaches. The lake has plentiful hippo and croc, and sometimes sharks near the mouth. Also, the St Lucia wetlands are an ideal breeding ground for mosquitoes, so do not go near unless you have been taking malaria tablets for at least three days prior to arrival.

False Bay Nature Reserve is a separate reserve around the northwest corner of Lake St Lucia and accessible from the N2. Among the great walking here is an overnight trail, a 7km walk and a 10km walk through forest and lakeshore meadow. The reserve has the rare suni antelope—smaller even than the red duiker or grysbok—as well as zebra, nyala, waterbuck, reedbuck, bushbuck and duiker. Fish eagles are common on the lake.

Phinda Private Nature Reserve is a large private game reserve north of St Lucia, just inland from the coast (signposted from the N2), covering a vast area of coastal forest, grass-land and swamp. Home to big game, including lions, Phinda does not take day visitors and is very expensive to stay in, modelled on the luxury private reserves bordering the Kruger National Park in Mpumalanga. However, the wilderness area is extremely beautiful, and its sub-tropical forests and grasslands are grazed by large herds of game. Apart from lions, big predators—such as leopard and cheetah—inhabit the Phinda bush, and the reserve made itself famous in 1992 by losing one of its guests to a lion that wandered into the luxury camp.

However, since then, fences have been erected and the camp is now 100 per cent safe. Game drives and guided walking trails with an armed game scout are features of the reserve, and the accommodation is truly luxurious (*see* 'Where to Stay'). If you have the money, Phinda is one of the most rewarding pieces of wild Zululand that you can visit.

Sodwana Bay is the next accessible point up the Zululand coast, and marks the border between Zululand and Tsongaland. Despite its relative remoteness (from the N2, you have to drive for two hours down a long dirt road through dense sand forest), Sodwana Bay has, sadly, become much like the southern end of St Lucia—a beach playground for 4x4 drivers causing much noise and rutting the sand. The vast camp site has 600 stands. In holiday seasons, this is packed, and the beach is too noisy and crowded to bear. In general it is better to head further north to Kosi Bay Nature Reserve—which is more remote and lacks the crowds (*see* below). However, out of season, during the week, Sodwana can be very quiet, and reverts to being a sub-tropical paradise. There is a coral reef offshore, and a diving school can take you out there to swim among the brightly coloured fish and coral (*see* 'Activities'). Sodwana has a state forest attached, with some short walking trails. Bushbuck, red duiker, suni antelope, reedbuck, bushpig and steenbok live under the trees. The rare Tsongaland red squirrel is another inhabitant, but is unlikely to be seen. Sodwana Bay has petrol, a permanent Zulu craft market, a shop, log cabins and a private lodge for those who want to be pampered, as well as an enormous camp site.

Tsongaland (Northern Zululand)

The man who does not travel will marry his own sister.

Tsonga Proverb

This area of dense forest, between the Lebombo Mountains in the west, the Indian Ocean in the east and the Mozambique border in the north, is the far northeast of Zululand and of the KwaZulu-Natal province. The few accessible points are all nature reserves. Although it was conquered by the Zulus in the 19th century, and long administered by the Kwa-Zulu government, the Tsonga people of Zululand have only been semi-absorbed into Zulu culture and retain both their own language and a more relaxed attitude to life—the clan fighting and militarism of the Zulu heartland is almost unknown in Tsongaland. The one tarred road through the territory (from Jozini in the Lebombos to Kosi Bay) passes hundreds of villages, and cattle on the road are a problem—almost all settlement is along the forest fringe next to the road. Unless you have a 4x4 you have to use this road, but it does provide access to three of Tsongaland's four superb nature reserves.

Ndumo, the first, lies between the road and the Mozambique border, 80km from Jozini. The last 14km stretch is sand road and can be heavy going, so go in low gear, but not too slow. Ndumo's 10,000ha is mostly acacia forest with fever trees and wild fig. Black and white rhino, hippo, crocodile, nyala, bushbuck, suni and impala are the most common animals, but Ndumo is known for its birds. Broad-billed rollers, Pel's fishing owl, parrots, and some of the colourful tropical species such as nicators and twin spots, are just a few. There are guided game walks, game-viewing roads and bird-watching hides at the many pans where the birds tend to gather.

Tembe Elephant Reserve, 30km further down the tar road to Kosi Bay, was set up in the late 1980s to protect one of the last herds of wild Tsongaland elephant, which used to roam freely through the surrounding sand forest of Tsongaland and Mozambique, but which were poached almost to extinction in the 1980s.

Because of this, Tembe's elephants were more aggressive than usual, and the park was initially tentative about allowing the public in, which they only did in 1993. The elephant now seem to behave themselves with the tourists, although their shyness, combined with the thick forest, can make them difficult to spot.

Apart from the elephants, Tembe has much the same game species as Ndumo, as well as leopard, but lacks the variety of birdlife. There is currently no accommodation on offer, but plans were afoot to build a camp, which might open any day now. Either ask at the gate or telephone the Kwa-Zulu Parks Board in Ulundi ✆ (0020) and ask for Sihangwana 3, or call the Natal Parks Board in Pietermaritzburg, ✆ (0331) 428 101.

Kosi Bay Nature Reserve is the last stop before the Indian Ocean. The tar gives way to sand about 13km from Kosi Bay. The road forks about 9km along, and as the signposts are regularly stolen, bear in mind that the left hand track is only good for 4x4s.

Kosi Bay is not a bay at all, but a series of freshwater lakes surrounded by coastal jungle and open to the sea only at a small mouth where there is a coral reef. The jungle is very beautiful—wild fig trees, monkey orange, and clearings of close-cropped greensward grazed at night by hippos. There is a 22km guided day hike on very flat terrain from the camp site at Third Lake down to the Fourth Lake, where a forest of raffia palms makes a natural pillared hall reminiscent of the Moorish Alhambra mosque at Granada in Spain.

This forest is home to the palm nut vulture, a rare creature that feeds on raffia palm nuts. Pel's fishing owl is another resident, as are crocodiles and hippos in the lakes, and bushbuck, duiker, bushpig and samango monkey in the jungle. There is also a short trail near the camp site and a three-day guided trail around the whole lake system (bookable in advance). Kosi Bay teems with fish and fishermen and it is worth hitching a ride with a fishing boat out to First Lake to see the wicker fish-traps still worked by the local Tsonga people, and to have a go on their rods. A boat is the easiest way to reach the mouth (otherwise a hot 15km walk from the camp site) where there is superb snorkelling on the reef.

Lake Sibaya is an even larger freshwater lake system on the coast between Sodwana Bay and Kosi Bay (the largest freshwater lake in South Africa). Accessible only by 4x4, Sibaya is very wild and seldom crowded. Boats are hired out, and there are walking trails, bird-watching hides and fishing with a permit. Hippo and crocodile abound in the lakes, but otherwise there is little large game. Reedbuck are plentiful, but the real attractions are the dense and varied bird population and the peace and quiet.

Shopping

Zululand is famous for its beadwork jewellery, its pottery, basketwork and coloured cloths. The best places to buy from locals are at the markets at Keate's Drift and Tugela Ferry, Ulundi, Sodwana Bay and sometimes at Mtubatuba. There is also a large Zulu-run curio shop just before Shakaland just off the road between Eshowe and Empangeni (signposted) that sells Zulu crafts.

Activities

Game viewing: This is the primary tourist activity in Zululand (*see* above for nature reserves, their game and facilities, also 'Where to Stay'). Only Umfolozi, Hluhluwe and Phinda have big predators, however. Rhino are found in most reserves, but are densest at Mkuzi. Elephant are also found at Tembe in the north. There are a number of tour operators if you require them.

Walking: All the above listed reserves have one-day walking trails. Overnight wilderness trails (March to November only) are found at Umfolozi (3 days among big game including lion, cheetah, leopard, buffalo and elephant), St Lucia (2 days—you'll see a lot of hippo), Mkuze (3 days, good for rhino, nyala and birds), Ndumo (2 days, superb for birds and plains game), and Kosi Bay (3 days through jungle, good for birds and hippo). To book for Umfolozi and Ndumo contact the **Natal Parks Board**, ✆ (0331) 471 981, or ✆ (035) 591 0032, and for Mkuze, ✆ (035) 573 1120. For Tembe and Kosi Bay, ✆ (0331) 946 696/7/8/9. The five-day guided Mkuze Trail leads from Cape Vidal to St Lucia and back.

Riding: The foetid coast is not kind to horses, but in the bushveld at **Ubizane Game Ranch**, ✆ (03562) 1020, between the N3 and Hluhluwe Game Reserve, horses can be hired for rides out to view wildlife. **Nyala Game Ranch**, north of Empangeni, ✆ (0351) 928 185, also has game-viewing rides. Longer riding trips of up to five days are available in the hills of Qwibi, near Melmoth, through **Jacana Trails**, ✆ Pretoria (012) 346 3550/1/2.

Scuba diving: For those without their own equipment, there is a diving school at Sodwana Bay which offers trips on the reef for experienced divers and courses for beginners. Courses last about 4 days and start at around R900, including accommodation, instruction and all equipment. For details of this and other dive operators contact the **Zululand Tourist Association**, Suite 2, Tawny Terrace, Kruger Rand, Richard's Bay, ✆ (0351) 41 404.

Fishing: Zululand's coast and lakes are full of exotic and big game fish. You can either hitch a ride on a boat, and use someone else's tackle, or contact one of the commercial operators such as **Le Jon**, ✆ (035) 590 1259, **Adcan Marine**, ✆ (0351) 533 419, **Zululand Fisheries**, ✆ (0351) 987 739, **Len**, ✆ (0351) 987 485, or **Danie**, ✆ (035) 590 1199.

Canoeing and white water rafting: In summer, the Tugela Gorge in central Zululand becomes a roaring torrent. Rafting and canoeing trips are arranged through

Kwa-Zukela River Adventures in Johannesburg, ✆ (011) 463 3167/8 or ✆ 706 1079/80, **Sunwal Ventures** in Durban, ✆ (031) 561 4429, or **Felix Unite** in Durban, ✆ (031) 304 6806.

Tour groups: Most Zululand reserves are inaccessible without your own transport. **Essenes Safaris,** ✆ (0351) 924 114 and **Coastal & Bush Tours,** ✆ (0351) 923 971/925 692, Zululand, offer reasonably priced tours into the Zululand reserves. You could also try **Crackerjack,** ✆ (0351) 753 2417, who specialize in overseas visitors, particularly from Germany.

Battlefields and historical sites: Guides can be hired locally for detailed tours of Isandhlwana, Rorke's Drift and the other Natal/Zululand battlefields.

The centenary commemoration of the Anglo-Boer War of 1899–1902 will begin with an exhibition and demonstration of militaria in Durban on 17th October 1999 and finish with a function on 31st May 2002 in Pinetown commemorating the closure of the concentration camp there. There will be 16 other functions between these two which should be a bonanza for battlefield buffs. Details are included in a publication by the provincial government called *The Battlefield Route, KwaZulu-Natal*, which takes the visitor round the sites of conflict in this beautiful and blood-stained province; first to the battlefields of the Great Trek, 1836–1852, then the Anglo–Zulu War of 1879, then the First Anglo-Boer War of 1880–1881, the Second Anglo-Boer War of 1899–1902 and finally the Bambatha Rebellion of 1906. This publication is available from most tourist offices in the province.

Where to Stay

Most visitors to Zululand stay in Parks Board accommodation in the reserves they visit. The majority offer moderately priced accommodation in chalets or cabins (mostly self-catering, although a few of the larger reserves have restaurants) and a cheaper camp site. The exceptions are the **Umfolozi** and **Hluhluwe** reserves, which have luxury lodges and no camping facilities. **Ubizane Game Ranch** has a choice of moderate self-catering or expensive accommodation, but no camp site. The **Harold Johnson Nature Reserve** and the **Ntendeka Wilderness Area** both have camp sites only. **Tembe Elephant Reserve** and **Ndumo** have cottages but no camping.

Some reserves—like Umfolozi, Hluhluwe and Mkuzi—get booked up well in advance, but there are usually cancellations, so it is always worth just turning up. **Kosi Bay Nature Reserve** has a camp site and several beautiful wooden chalets half-hidden in the forest near Third Lake. These must be booked in advance through the Kwa-Zulu or Natal Parks Boards (*see* below), as the reserve is popular and the number of people allowed in at any time deliberately limited.

Lala Lapa, Kosi Bay, ✆ (035) 592 0201, has overnight accommodation and a caravan park with full catering bar and 5 star ablution block. **Kosi Bay Lodge**, 500m from Lake Nhlange, ✆ (031) 864 172, ✆ 266 9118 (or ✆ (011) 789 9336/9342, ✆ 781 0968), offers comfortable full board or self-catering lodges, a restaurant, swimming pool, pub and viewing deck with 4x4 excursions, boating, fishing, snorkelling, bird-watching, walking trails and evening turtle walks in season (Nov–Feb). You can arrange for a boat to pick you up when you confirm your booking. **Camp Abandon**, Lake Sibaya, ✆ (031) 765 7087, ✉ 765 6618, *islrock@iafrica.com* is a self-catering camp on the shores of the lake, which is fully equipped and serviced (including hot water) and sleeps 10. There is abundant wildlife, canoeing and hiking through the woods on the shoreline, and access to the Tembe Elephant Reserve and coral coast.

NB Plans are afoot to bring all the Kwa-Zulu parks under the administration of the Natal Parks Board in Pietermaritzburg, ✆ (0331) 946 696/7/8/9), but this may take some time to effect and until that happens Tembe Elephant Reserve, Kosi Bay Nature Reserve, Ndumo and Lake Sibaya should all be booked through the Kwa-Zulu Parks Board in Ulundi, ✆ (0020) and ask for Sihangwana 3.

However, if you want to break the journey elsewhere, or stay on a private game ranch, here are some pointers:

expensive

Mine Own Estate, at Gigindlovu, on the coast between Tugela Mouth and Richards Bay, ✆ (0353) 301 262, is a beautiful sugar estate mansion built in 1927 and similar to a Southern United States plantation manor: white stucco, tall pillars and a convincing neo-Georgian front. The sugar estate still functions. The owner will play the piano in the living room if you ask. The house has extensive tropical gardens, a pool and a tennis court.

Fugitive's Drift Lodge, at Rorke's Drift, ✆ (034621) 843, stands on the Buffalo river, overlooking the ford where the fleeing survivors of Isandhlwana crossed. The small late-Victorian house has 6 simple, clean, airy rooms lit by gas lamps rather than electricity. The owner is a registered guide to the Zulu War battlefields and has a fund of anecdotes.

Babanango Valley Lodge, ✆ (034) 642 1843, is a 1930s farmstead in the Nsubeni River Valley in northern Zululand, off the R68 northwest of Melmoth, with pleasant rooms, delicious home cooking and a pool. The surrounding valley bushveld and hill woodland is open to walking with good birdlife. At the cheaper end of the expensive range, and a convenient place to break a journey across north Zululand (the owner is also a registered guide).

Shakaland, ✆ (035) 460 0912 912, the reconstructed Zulu kraal (the remains of a film-set) lying west of the Eshowe–Empangeni road, is owned by the Protea hotel chain. Accommodation is in large, traditionally-built Zulu grass huts with very comfortable beds and bathrooms, beautifully constructed and fun to stay in.

Phinda Resource Reserve, ✆ (011) 784 7667, lies inland from St Lucia, south of Mkuze. Famous for its luxurious cottages, rich food (much venison on the menu) and big predators, Phinda is at the highest end of the expensive range. If you can afford it, the game viewing is excellent.

Sodwana Bay Lodge at Sodwana Bay, ✆ (031) 571 0095, organizes diving and game fishing in luxurious log cabins overlooking Lake Shabize, just inland from the bay. Seafood beach *braais* at night are a speciality.

Ndumo Wilderness Camp in Ndumo Game Reserve, Tsongaland, ✆ Jo'burg (011) 884 1458, is a luxury tented camp on the Banzi Pan, a good site for bird-watching and regularly visited by game that comes down to drink in the evenings. By night, hippos graze nearby. **Rocktail Bay Lodge & Hotel Resort**, ✆ Jo'burg (011) 884 1458, is off the dirt road (for 4x4's only, or arrange to be picked up) between Sodwana Bay and Lake Sibaya. Accommodation is in 'Robinson Crusoe' style chalets in the trees. Facilities include a wild beach, reef snorkelling, forest walking and trips to Lake Sibaya.

moderate

Sungulwane Game Lodge at Bayala, near Mkuze, ✆ (035) 562 0420, has private rondavels around a pool. Venison *braais* are a speciality, and there is walking in the surrounding private game farm, as well as trips to Mkuzi and Hluhluwe.

Nyala Game Ranch, north of Empangeni, ✆ (0351) 924 095/24 543, also has rondavels, walking and riding trails into the bush and *braais* of culled game.

Eating Out

 There are few restaurants in Zululand, apart from in town hotels or in the expensive accommodation listed above, most of which are too remote to visit for just a meal and so cater for guests only. The exception is the small town that has grown around the southern end of Lake St Lucia, which has some small, moderately priced restaurants:

The **Tropicana** on Main Street, St Lucia, serves Italian and Portuguese seafood fresh from the ocean, as well as standard pasta and pizza dishes. Rather tasteless and plasticky inside, but very good food.

Street Pizza on McKenzie Street, St Lucia, makes good pizzas in a wood-burning oven. The dining room is unpretentious, with checked table-cloths and candles.

The **Captain's Cabin**, also on Main Street, St Lucia, serves standard seafood at moderate prices. Very fresh fish and shellfish make up for the nautical decor of nets and stuffed fish.

Lesotho

On the navel of the Boer's domain...
stands an antheap, an eye-catching target,
a goad to the white one slackened in plenty
where he sits like a king down on the plains...

Lesotho, B. Makalo Khaketla's epic poem

The mountain kingdom of Lesotho (pronounced Le-soo-too) sits high above the surrounding plains of South Africa, remote from its great neighbour in altitude, if not in actual distance. From a small, well-populated, arable Lowland plateau—where lies the capital, Maseru—rears the vaster Highland region, whose treeless moors, deep-cut with narrow gorges, culminate in peaks exceeding 3000m. From these spring a host of infant rivers, including the great Orange, which flows away west 1000 miles to the distant Atlantic.

Travellers wise enough to journey into the Highlands find themselves in a world of horsemen, whose sure-footed ponies dance along the rugged trails like goats, their riders wrapped tight in coloured blankets, sitting with the careless ease that comes of a lifetime in the saddle. Lonely villages of stone and thatch sit perched on hillside spurs. The herdboys carry long sticks, hollowed through the middle, which serve as flute or staff or club as need demands. Fierce heat at midday drops to freezing cold by dusk, and the morning frost burns from the thatch in spiral plumes of steam. Lesotho carves its memories deep—of waterfalls and torrents, distant cow-bells and narrow valleys planted with meagre crops, of eagles hunting silent along the cliffs, of high, clean air and the drifting scent of woodsmoke, and the sky framed ahead between the twin crescents of your pony's ears.

Climate

The Lowlands have a hot, rainy summer, and a warm, dry winter, but Lesotho's Highlands are subject to extremes of temperature all year round. Rain falls most heavily in summer, usually in the afternoons. Daytime temperatures can be very high, but fall fast when the sun goes down. Winter days are warm with occasional rain and snow, but the temperature drops well below freezing at nights. Waterproofs and good sleeping bags will be required for hiking or horse trekking. Summer rain and winter snow can make some roads impassable, so try to get local information on the state of the roads before you go, particularly to the Highlands.

Flora and Fauna

Despite the wild landscape, Lesotho's game has been largely hunted out, with the exception of the grey rhebok, which, for some reason, is considered inedible. At Sehlabethebe National Park in the southeast Highlands, however, eland, mountain reedbuck, duiker, caracal and leopard still thrive. Bird life is abundant, especially large raptors, which prey on young sheep and goats. Tawny eagles and lammergeier vultures are not uncommon sights in the mountains. The rare bald ibis is also widespread in the narrow river valleys.

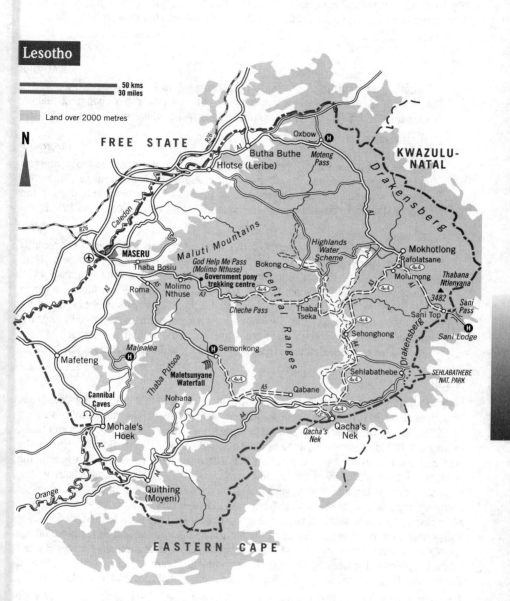

Lesotho

50 kms
30 miles

Land over 2000 metres

N

FREE STATE

R26

A1

Oxbow [H]

Butha Buthe *Moteng*
Pass
Hlotse (Leribe)

**KWAZULU-
NATAL**

Drakensberg

Caledon

R26

A1

MASERU

Thaba Bosiu

God Help Me Pass
(Molimo Nthuse)
Government pony
trekking centre

Maluti Mountains

Highlands
Water
Scheme

Bokong

Mokhotlong
Rafolatsane
[4x4]
Molumong
A3
[4x4]
**Thabana
Ntlenyana**
▲

A2

Roma

Molimo
Nthuse

A3

[4x4]

Cheche Pass

Central Ranges

Thaba
Tseka

[4x4]

3482

*Sani
Pass*

Sani Top

Drakensberg

[4x4]

Sehonghong

[H]
Sani Lodge

Mafeteng

Malealea
[H]

[H] Semonkong

Thaba Putsoa

Maletsunyane
Waterfall

Nohana

[4x4]

A5

Qabane

A5

[4x4]

Sehlabathebe
[4x4]

SEHLABATHEBE
NAT. PARK

Cannibal
Caves

Mohale's
Hoek

A2

M1

Qacha's
Nek

Qacha's
Nek

Orange

Quithing
(Moyeni)

EASTERN CAPE

445

As for flora, Lesotho has few trees, except along rivers and the Lowland roads. Most of the Highlands are covered in high grassland that is vivid green in summer and golden in winter. This barren beauty is not unlike Scotland or the Welsh uplands, but on a far larger scale.

Practical A–Z

currency

Lesotho's own currency, the **maloti**, exchanges 1 to 1 with the rand. Rands are accepted everywhere in Lesotho, but you will often be given change in maloti. Maloti will not be accepted in South Africa, so spend whatever you have before re-crossing the border to South Africa.

language

Sesotho, part of the Sotho/Tswana language group, is the national language, and it is useful to learn the formal greetings and their responses (*see* **Language**). However, Lesotho was long a British protectorate and English is widely spoken, even in the remote Highlands. Lesotho's education system is closely modelled on the British.

safety

Owing to its independent status, Lesotho never suffered apartheid, and until recently had been spared the political violence of South Africa, despite failed coups in 1993 and 1994. At the time of going to press political unrest has erupted (*see* p.449); check on the situation before you go. The Highlands and rural Lowlands are generally safe for travellers, despite the occasional theft. Travellers might be asked for money by strangers, but this is seldom aggressive and a smiling 'no' usually ends the matter. Maseru has some violent crime and mugging, though not as much as most South African cities. Best not to go alone after dark, although the city is safe by day.

History

Lesotho's history is a remarkable tale of independence sustained in the face of appalling odds, largely because of the tireless energy and statesmanship of the kingdom's founder, Moshoeshoe, Mosheshwe or Moshesh (depending on which of the many sources you read). In the early 1820s Moshoeshoe, a minor chief of a Sotho-speaking clan, fled the chaos of the wars raging across the highveld at that time (*see* **History**), and moved his villagers from the plains to the broken country of the Lesotho Lowlands. With a good eye for a defensive spot, he first chose an isolated, flat-topped mountain near modern Butha Buthe, but, after narrowly repulsing a fierce attack from the neighbouring Tlokwa (a Tswana clan), Moshoeshoe moved to another, larger mountain overlooking the long, fertile Caledon River Valley near modern Maseru. He named the natural fortress Thaba Bosiu ('the mountain of the night'). From there he defended his flocks and people against successive waves of other migrating peoples displaced by the aggressive raiding armies of the Zulu, Ndebele, Rolong Tswana and Pedi, who were ravaging the whole eastern half of modern South Africa.

Among the refugee tribes that unsuccessfully attempted Thaba Bosiu in the early days were the Ngwane, Hlubi, and various Tswana clans, all reduced to raiding since the loss of their land. The Sotho chief fought off all advances, gradually attracting a following of warriors who became part of his own BaSotho army. At a time when no part of the highveld or mountains was safe from marauders of some sort, and some tribes, like the Bele from Natal, were reduced to becoming cannibals, Thaba Bosiu was a sanctuary.

By 1830 his people numbered around 5000, enough for him to raise an army and begin annexing large areas of the fertile Lesotho Lowlands from the Ngwane, who had settled there after trying to take Thaba Bosiu. Moshoeshoe's warriors won a series of decisive victories that pushed them north towards modern-day Swaziland, where they still live. Following these successes, refugees poured into Moshoeshoe's enlarged kingdom. By 1840 he was king of about 40,000 people, all calling themselves BaSotho.

As his power base grew, Moshoeshoe found himself having to fight off hostile groups intent on rustling his ever-growing herds and settling the good arable land around the Caledon River that he had taken from the Ngwane. Large armed and mounted war parties of Griqua and Koranna attacked from the west during the 1830s. Moshoeshoe also had to repel raids from various Tswana clans, such as the Rolong in the northwest and the Ndebele in the east.

Moshoeshoe managed to trade for guns with the Voortrekkers, who arrived in the region around 1836, and again managed to beat off his attackers, allying with the powerful Taung Tswana who had occupied the country directly north of Thaba Bosiu. Finally able to keep marauders at bay, the BaSotho began producing grain on their fertile river valley. With grain in short supply on the highveld, the Taung/BaSotho state acquired a powerful trading influence, and the surrounding states became increasingly dependent on Basutoland for food.

The early 1840s saw several attempts by Boer settlers to invade Moshoeshoe's kingdom, and some applied for client status as a pretext for settling the fertile lowlands. Moshoeshoe accepted them at first, but, as more and more clustered into the kindgdom, he became alarmed, fearing they would eventually usurp him.

Fortunately for Moshoeshoe, the British Cape authorities were also unwilling to have a Voortrekker republic in the volatile western highveld; it was too close to the Orange River, the Cape Colony's northern boundary, for comfort. In 1843 Moshoeshoe appealed to Sir George Napier, the Cape's High Commissioner, for help. Napier helped set up two treaties, one ensuring Basutoland's boundary with its Tswana neighbours (1843) and one giving the Boer settlers a deadline by which they had to leave (1845).

The Boers and the Tswana ignored the order, and Moshoeshoe appealed to the Cape again—this time to Sir Harry Smith, the new Governor and High Commissioner. Smith, a military man rather than a statesman (his troops knew him as 'Hurry-along-wackalong-smite'), had, as a general during the Sixth Frontier War, murdered the Gcalaka Xhosa chief Hintsa and illegally annexed large areas of Xhosa land (see **Eastern Cape**, 'History').

With his usual arrogance, Smith imagined he could settle the highveld conflicts, and in 1848 asked Moshoeshoe to allow his country to become a British protectorate, with British arms to stave off the Boers and anyone else who might intrude. Moshoeshoe accepted this nominal loss of independence and Smith, against his promise, annexed Basutoland and all the country around it as imperial domain. Smith then bullied the British government into accepting the new territory, which he called the Orange River Sovereignty (ORS).

The Boers deeply resented the British annexation of the surrounding territory and blamed Moshoeshoe for inviting the British in. They duly invaded late in 1847. Moshoeshoe called on Smith, who sent a force which drove them away. Smith himself now started showing interest in settling Basutoland. British land speculators began to appear along the Orange and Caledon River Valley, and approached Moshoeshoe about selling parts of his kingdom, which, they reminded him, was now British territory anyway. Realizing that Smith had tricked him, Moshoeshoe drove the speculators away. Smith promptly sent two armies north. But here Moshoeshoe showed his teeth, defeating both British forces in 1851.

Moshoeshoe knew to expect further trouble from the British, and that it might yet cost him the kingdom. Another force invaded his land in 1852, under the new Governor, Sir George Cathcart, and again, Moshoeshoe's large, well-disciplined BaSotho and Taung army drove them away. But the BaSotho king then displayed his masterful statesmanship with a placatory letter to Cathcart, asking to be considered an ally, rather than an enemy of the British. Cathcart was already looking for an excuse to wash his hands of the troublesome kingdom, and this allowed him to do so without losing face. Cathcart 'pacified' the region, re-arranged the boundaries (allowing the Boers to take some of Moshoeshoe's best arable land) and left. The old king kept quiet and let the land go in return for his assured independence.

Moshoeshoe was now almost 70 years old, but still there was no rest for him. With the British withdrawal came a renewed Boer threat. The infant Orange Free State now lay just over his western border. Fortunately, the BaSotho had bought thousands of guns from the Pedi tribe, who had passed through Moshoeshoe's kingdom in the late 1840s. The Free State Boers attacked in 1858 and were driven off. Moshoeshoe again appealed to the British, who did little but growl at the Free State Boers, and in 1865 the Boers attacked again in greater numbers, calling thousands of freebooting Afrikaners and British up from the Cape Colony with a promise of rich pickings. The British at the Cape sat by. In desperation, Moshoeshoe appealed to the new colony of Natal for protection, even offering his kingdom for annexation. Meanwhile the Transvaal Boers, under Paul Kruger, joined the invaders, and the combined army plundered the Lowlands at will. But Moshoeshoe's own army, which matched the Boers in numbers, horses and guns, and trained through the incessant warfare of the previous 30 years, won several battles and kept the Boers from Thaba Bosiu. The Cape Governor finally intervened in 1868 and declared Basutoland to be British territory.

The British allowed the Orange Free State to keep almost all of Moshoeshoe's good arable land, and the BaSotho began to settle in the harsh Highlands, cultivating the river valleys as best they could, but never managing to achieve the prosperity that their lowland grainlands had given them.

Moshoeshoe died in 1870 at Thaba Bosiu, unconquered, aged 84. Basutoland was never invaded by British settlers, and the Boer threat was permanently removed. Peace reigned until 1879 when the British, following their massive defeat by the Zulus in the same year, decided that all their black subjects should be prevented from carrying guns. The BaSotho were indignant, as they relied on their guns for defence. Rebellion broke out, and a few whites were killed. A British force engaged the rebels at Mafeteng in western Basutoland with little result, and a truce was declared. The BaSotho were now only to register their guns, but most refused. The Cape government had spent £3 million for nothing, and appealed to London to take Basutoland directly under Crown rule, which happened in 1884.

Basutoland quietened. The BaSotho remained neutral during the Anglo-Boer War, and voted to retain its Crown status when the Union of South Africa was declared in 1910. The territory escaped apartheid, gaining its independence from Britain in 1966 at a time when blacks over the border in South Africa were being oppressed as never before. Lesotho declared itself a constitutional monarchy, with the present King Moshoeshoe II as head of state. Democracy lasted until 1986, when Major General Lekhanya staged a military coup. He was thrown out in 1991, and Lesotho was run democratically again by Prime Minister Ntsu Mokhele. The King has kept his throne throughout. Brief fighting broke out between rival factions of the army in January 1994, but soon died down. As we go to press, opposition supporters' smouldering disaffection has developed into more widespread violence, with South African and Botswanan troops sent in to assist the Lesotho army.

BaSotho Culture

The BaSotho people have a mode of dress that is markedly different from South Africa's other nations. The three most obvious characteristics that set them apart are their brightly coloured, patterned blankets, worn like togas, their conical straw hats (though these are seen less and less) and their horses. The BaSotho are a passionate horse people, relying on their mounts to take them across the difficult terrain of the Highlands. They have even evolved their own breed, the BaSotho Pony, from mixing Javanese ponies, brought out by the British in the 1900s, with English thoroughbreds and the Boer horses of Dutch descent. These sturdy, elegant beasts are trained to a high standard, and most BaSotho men own several. English thoroughbreds are also kept, even in remote mountain villages, for running at monthly horse races that are a central part of Lesotho's social life.

After horses, the BaSotho value livestock above all. Cattle (and horses) represent wealth. Goats are kept for slaughter, and angora goats and merino sheep provide most of the rural cash income from their mohair and wool. These flocks are tended by young shepherd boys in their early teens, who are sent into the hills for a few years before returning to their villages as men to be given land of their own. Shepherd boys live an isolated and independent existence on the highest ridges in summer. Left alone for long periods, their great sport is to rustle each other's flocks, which often ends in fighting and, occasionally, death. If you hike or ride in the Highlands, you will often come across these boys, usually accompanied by a large dog or pack of dogs, playing music on long sticks hollowed out to make a rudimentary flute (held sideways from the mouth while playing) that also double as a weapon and walking stick.

Despite great military prowess in the 19th century, the BaSotho have not fostered an overtly aggressive warrior cult. Being a mountain people, who have never lost their independence, they are proud and hospitable, and visitors are treated with great courtesy. Villages consist of a number of stone family homesteads clustered around cattle kraals. Village headmen control the land around, and allot grazing and arable acreages as they see fit. However, headmen must refer to the village council for all decisions, and the process is very formally democratic.

Most young BaSotho men go away to find work in the Rand gold fields for a few years after serving their time as shepherds, and it is generally women who work in the fields. However, recent lay-offs at the South African mines have forced many young men to return home and unemployment is becoming a problem. Overpopulation has also hit the Lowlands, where soil erosion from overgrazing is common. Even the Highlands are more populated than before. It remains to be seen whether this can be curtailed.

BaSotho education tends to be of a high standard, with most children being taught English at primary school, most of which are attached to numerous mission stations scattered throughout the country. Cambridge 'O' and 'A' levels are taught at secondary school, but mostly it is girls who take these, as the boys have usually been sent into the hills by then. Lesotho has a university of international standing, at Roma, in the Lowlands.

Look out for a white flag flying from a pole outside huts; this means that *joala*, or sorghum beer, is being sold. Green and red flags mean meat and vegetables.

Getting There and Around

You must have a passport to enter Lesotho. All visitors technically require a visa (with the exception of South African, British, Danish and Israeli passport holders), but this is generally not enforced; presenting your passport at a border post should get you a stamp allowing a stay of two weeks or a month.

by car

Most of Lesotho's entry points are in the Lowland region bordering the Free State. All Lowland entry points give access to the A1 and A2 highways, which connect with Maseru and the main Lowlands towns, which in turn give access to the Highlands. There are only two road entry points in the Highlands: Sani Pass, from Natal (*see* p.416), and Qacha's Nek, via the Transkei. Both require a 4x4. Of the two, Sani Pass is the safest and most travelled, and has a lodge at the top. Qacha's Nek involves travelling a short distance through the Transkei, which can be dangerous for white travellers.

Most of Lesotho's roads are accessible by car, although in the Highlands progress will be slow. Those roads accessible by 4x4 only are Sani Pass, the Makunyapane–Sehonghong road and the Sehonghong–Sehlabathebe road.

by bus

Transtate run buses to Maseru from Jo'burg only. Buses from Jo'burg, © (011) 773 600, leave 3 times per week. **Sani Pass Carriers**, © (033) 710 1017, run small buses from Durban and Pietermaritzburg to Sani Lodge, © (033) 722 1330, on Sani Pass, from where you can hitch a ride or arrange a lift into Lesotho, to Sani Top and Mokhotlong. The journey takes about four hours from Durban.

Lesotho has a good bus system between the major towns, including the Lowland towns along the A1 and A2 and the Highland towns of Semonkong, Thaba Tseka, Molimo Nthuse and Mokhotlong. The **Maseru Bus Station** is on Main Road South.

by air

Lesotho Airways, © (09266) 324 500, flies from Jo'burg to Maseru.

by rail

There is no rail link from South Africa to Lesotho.

hitch-hiking

Once on the Highland roads hitch-hiking is easy and fairly safe. You may be asked to pay a small fee towards petrol.

Horse is the most widespread form of transport in the Highlands. The BaSotho have evolved their own breed of mountain pony and an entire culture around it. Trekking can be arranged from just about any lodge, and through the government's own pony-breeding centre, on God-Help-Me Pass (*see* 'Activities').

A very good guide book, the *Backpacker's Guide to Lesotho*, written and published by Russell Suchet of Sani Lodge, ✆ (033) 722 1330 (on the Natal side of Sani Pass), has the most up-to-date details on public transport (internal and external), where to stay and hiking routes—the author has spent years travelling the country. Published in booklet form, the guide is handy to carry but is not yet widely available, though some South African backpackers' hostels now carry it. Give the author a ring at the above number to find out where you can pick it up.

Maseru

Because of the political unrest at the time of going to press, you may need to check the current situation before relying on the following information.

Tourist Information

Lower Kingsway, opposite the BaSotho Hat, ✆ (09266) 312 896. Do not park your car out front. You will return to find it badly washed, with a young man demanding an exorbitant sum. You will probably have to pay him something to go away.

The capital is a large, bustling, lively town strung out along a central road called the Kingsway. Owing to its easy accessibilty by road from South Africa and its tourist information centre, Maseru is the point from which most travellers begin their exploration of Lesotho. The town started life in 1869 as a British administration post, built to keep watch on Thaba Bosiu, Moshoeshoe's mountain fortress and capital, which lay just to the east.

Opposite the tourist information is the **BaSotho Hat**, a large craft shop that sells the best of the regional crafts, in particular woven rugs and clothes, pottery and jewellery, and books on BaSotho culture by Sotho authors. The shop, built in a round, and crowned with a thatched roof that resembles a hat (hence its name), is unmistakable, and a good rendezvous point. Next to the BaSotho Hat is a small shopping centre with fast food joints, banks and most of the South African chain stores—a good place to get supplies. West along Kingsway on the same side of the road is the **Post Office** (although you may want to wait to post letters from South Africa, which is quicker) and an open fruit and vegetable market with very good produce at cheap prices. Hold on to your wallet. Opposite the market on Kingsway is a café and restaurant called **L'Auberge**, run by Germans. This is another convenient spot for meeting that incidentally serves really good coffee and food in a very continental atmo-sphere. Go in at lunchtime and you will meet young Westerners working in Lesotho, and thereby tap into the local information network.

The Department of Land, Surveys and Physical Planning on Lerothili Road (take the third left off Kingsway after the Post Office, then left again and immediately right) sells very good hiking and road maps with the relief clearly marked. The bus station and taxi-rank are on the west end of Kingsway, near the large, Art Deco, Roman Catholic cathedral. The bus station is generally safe, but it is better to be in a group.

expensive

More expensive are the **Maseru Sun** and **Lesotho Sun**. Like all the Sun hotels, they are modern, ugly, bland and overpriced, but offer great comfort. The Maseru Sun, ✆ 312 434, is on the road that runs north from the BaSotho Hat. The Lesotho Sun, ✆ 313 111, is set in 100 acres of park on a hilltop at the west end of town.

moderate

Maseru has two comfortable, moderately priced hotels. The **Victoria**, ✆ 312 922, on Kingsway, has a swimming pool, bar, restaurant and a disco that can be quite lively at weekends. The **Lakeside**, off the Main North Road, ✆ 313 646, is smaller, but also has a swimming pool and a restaurant. Both hotels have safe parking.

The **Lancer's Inn Hotel**, ✆ 312 114, on Kingsway, near the Post Office, has long been the place for non-tourists to stay. The bar is usually full of businessmen, both BaSotho and South African, and you can meet interesting characters here. The rooms are fairly standard, and all en suite.

cheap

The **Anglican Training Centre**, ✆ 322 046, off Assisi Road (take the third left off Kingsway after the Post Office, then first right, first left, and left again onto Assisi Road, and look for the sign), offers accommodation in shared rooms. Meals can be arranged and the place is spick and span, but you must turn up before about 7pm to get a room.

The **Lesotho Work Camps Association**, ✆ 314 862, is behind the cathedral. Go west on Kingsway to the cathedral, then turn on to the Main North Road until you reach a dirt road that is also a taxi-rank. The Association is down this track. Dormitory accommodation and a small kitchen are available, but be aware that this area can be rough.

Apart from the hotels, which generally serve reasonable *à la carte* fare, Maseru's restaurants are basically fast food places you will find in the shopping centres along Kingsway. However, an exception is **L'Auberge**, on Kingsway, opposite the street market and west of the Post Office, which is a good, moderately priced German-run restaurant serving really good French and German dishes and game (in season). There is a formal dining room or, alternatively, a café for light meals or snacks. No need to book.

Also worth trying is the Italian fare at **Boccacio**, on Bowker Road, off Kingsway, and the **Chinese Garden**, on Orpen Road.

Nightlife

Maseru has several discos along Kingsway that can be fun at weekends, although you will mostly hear Western Top 40 and very little African jive. The **Crossroads disco** at the Victoria Hotel and the Lancer's Inn are safe for foreigners, but are known pick-up joints.

South of Maseru

The A2 west of Maseru provides several jumping-off points for the western Highlands, including the A3 to the Government Pony Trekking Centre at God-Help-Me Pass, and the A5 to the lodges of the Thaba Putsoa Mountains.

The first major town along the A2 is **Mafeteng**, some 80km south of Maseru. Although Mafeteng is a large town by Lesotho standards, it consists of little bar a few shops for stocking up on supplies and petrol.

From Mafeteng, the A2 curves south, around the Thaba Putsoa range to **Mohale's Hoek**, another jumping-off point for the Thaba Putsoa lodges, and a rest stop for those on the way round to Qacha's Nek and Sehlabethebe National Park. Signposted from the A2 between Mafeteng and Mohale's Hoek are a set of **Cannibal Caves**. There is little to see, but it sends a shiver down the spine to think that just over 100 years ago you may have been caught and eaten when travelling along this road.

East of Maseru

If you are going to spend more than a day in the Lowlands, you must visit **Thaba Bosiu**, the old mountain stronghold of King Moshoeshoe. This natural fortress repelled Boer, Zulu, British, Ka Ngwane, Koranna and Ndebele attacks. It is now a sort of open-air archaeological site, with the remains of some of the fortifications and village still there, along with the great King Moshoeshoe's grave. There is now an information centre at the base of the mountain, where you pay a small entrance fee, and are given a map and an official guide. It's an interesting day out, and a crucial excursion if you are at all interested in how the BaSotho nation came into being.

North of Maseru

The A1 is the main road north, leading eventually to the Maluti Mountains, their lodges, and the remote town of Mokhotlong, deep in the Highlands. On the way, there is one other access point to the mountains: a tarred road leading up to the Lesotho Highlands Water Scheme, but this is a there-and-back road providing no access to the Highlands.

There are several large towns on the A1 north of Maseru. The first is **Hlotse**, also known as Leribe, which is famous for weaving and knitwear, and has two craft centres where you can buy straight from the workshops: the **Leribe Craft Centre**, which sells rugs, table-cloths and shawls beautifully made by disabled women, and **Lesotho Knits**, which sells wool and angora sweaters, both signposted from the A1.

About 30km north of Hlotse is Butha Buthe, the only town in Lesotho with a reputation for unfriendliness. Whether this is true or not, there is little reason to stop at this small industrial centre, except perhaps for **Lesotho Handknits**, signposted from the A1, which has very good sweaters and scarves in angora and wool.

North of Butha Buthe, the A1 curves west into the Malutis and soon becomes a tortuous climb up the Moteng Pass to Oxbow and the northern Highlands. This pass is demanding on petrol, so fill up at Butha Buthe beforehand.

moderate

Riverside Lodge, ✆ (5191) 2681/3173, just outside Maseru, provides a good alternative to staying in the city. The lodge has comfortable thatched rondavels set under large trees, with blesbok grazing nearby, a pool, a good restaurant and a large garden. The **Hotel Mount Maluti**, at Mohale's Hoek, ✆ (09266) 785 224, is at the opposite end of the Lowlands from the Maluti Mountains. But never mind. This fine (though quite expensive) country hotel, set in gardens, offers hikes and pony treks into the nearby Thaba Putsoa range. The quiet **Trading Post Guest House**, at Roma, southeast of Maseru on the A5 to Semonkong, ✆ (09266) 340 202/267, has bedrooms in the old house, or self-contained rondavels. The management can also arrange riding. The old sandstone **Leribe Hotel**, ✆ (09266) 400 362, in the hills just west of Hlotse (Leribe,) on the A1 north of Maseru, makes a good rest stop on the way to the northern Highlands. Wisteria climbs around the veranda, there is a tea-garden, and the hotel sits under large trees. Also at the expensive end of the moderate scale. Up at Butha Buthe, stay at the **Crocodile Inn**, on Reserve Road, ✆ 460 223.

Near Thaba Bosiu is the small **Melesi Lodge**, ✆ 357 215—clean and comfortable, with a decent restaurant attached.

cheap

The **Farmer's Training Centre**, at Mohale's Hoek, offers dormitory accommodation for travellers heading south towards Qacha's Nek. **Ha Thabo Ramakatane**, a hostel run by one Mr Ramakatane, in a village called **Ha Sechele** about 4km from Butha Buthe, is one of the best places to stay in the Lowlands. With its gas lighting, water from an outside pump, and friendly villagers, it makes a good introduction to Lesotho village life. Ask for directions in Butha Buthe. The last section of road to the hostel is very rough, so drive slowly, or walk.

The Lesotho Highlands

The Lesotho Highlands, the roof of southern Africa, are the real reason for coming here. The rugged mountain country is divided into three main areas: the Thaba Putsoa Mountains to the south, the Central Ranges, and the Maluti Mountains in the north, all of which converge at the Drakensberg escarpment on the border with Natal. Most of this paradise of high moorland, deep-cut river valleys, soaring peaks and remote villages is inaccessible to vehicles, and the BaSotho horse culture is at its strongest. Blanketed horsemen riding through the wild country between stone villages give the landscape a medieval feel.

The few towns have a frontier feel, owing to their remoteness. Most visitors ride in over the mountains, rather than by car or truck, and horses tied up outside shops and bars are the norm. Do remember that even vehicles are likely to be very slow on the rocky Highlands roads, so short geographical distances can take many hours.

The Lesotho Highlands are one of the few trekking areas in southern Africa where drinking water is not a problem. As long as there is no human settlement immediately upstream, then

water from the mountain streams is not only drinkable, but is probably among the cleanest water in the world. However, it is still advisable to take purification tablets, in case you have no choice but to take water from a stream near a village.

Thaba Putsoa Mountains

The southern end of the Highlands is reached via the A2 and A5, and is best explored from the two lodges at the villages of **Malealea** and **Semonkong** (*see* 'Where to Stay'). Semonkong is the more remote, taking four hours up and over a series of spectacular passes along the A5 (mostly dirt road) from Maseru via Roma. The lodge sits in a narrow valley, at the end of a small farming village. Nearby is a deep gorge into which plunges a mighty waterfall of over 200m. This, apparently, is the highest set of falls in southern Africa, although there is some confusion over whether this means the highest in altitude or in the length of the fall. Either would seem to be plausible.

Horse races are held on the mountain plateau above the lodge on the first weekend of every month. These are great fiestas, with thoroughbred horses being ridden for days over the mountains to be raced, dressed in expensive travelling blankets and leg bandages. The young male jockeys risk life and limb to bring their horses in first. A lot of money changes hands at these events, and they offer a glimpse of the Highlands' robust social life.

The Central Highlands

The Central Highlands are reached via the A3 from Maseru, which becomes dirt after Molimo Nthuse (God-Help-Me Pass), and can only be driven by ordinary car as far as Cheche Pass, 20km further on. However, most visitors will only be going as far as the **BaSotho Pony Project**, or Government Pony Trekking Centre, at God-Help-Me Pass.

The BaSotho Pony Project

This is Lesotho's most widely used pony trekking centre. It was designed by, and is still run by, Irish consultants brought in by the government to monitor the breeding of high-class

BaSotho ponies. It is worth asking to see some of their impressive stallions, which are used to compete in endurance competitions as well as for breeding.

Treks of one to five days are offered very cheaply—far cheaper than at any of the lodges. Having said that, the standard of pony is much lower here than at the lodges, which hire the best of the local horses. But for inexperienced riders who would nevertheless like to see Lesotho from the saddle, these quiet, rather underfed government horses are ideal. If you can ride, these beasts will prove better trained than they appear and it is worth asking your guide to show you the special BaSotho tricks that put the horses through their paces. The routes taken by these treks are beautiful indeed, following rivers along precipitate hillsides, over incredibly steep passes, stopping at waterfalls, and sometimes finding level tracks where you can canter. You will often be passed by BaSotho horsemen, or even whole families on the move, and shy shepherd boys playing their home-made pipes are a common sight. Eagles and vultures cruise the heights. Be prepared to spend about six hours a day in the saddle.

The centre provides a guide and pack mule, but you must supply food and sleeping bags. You will be expected to tip the guide afterwards, usually about R10 per rider. On the overnight trails you will be required to pay an extra R7 per night for accommodation in huts in the remote villages. Treks are supposed to be booked a month in advance, but in fact, just turning up is almost always enough to book a trek of several days, usually beginning the day after your arrival. This is just as well, as the telephone to the centre does not work. To pass the time between booking your trek and setting off, you can either camp at the centre or stay at the hotel just down the pass towards Maseru. This hotel is expensive, but it lacks custom and the price can sometimes be negotiated.

The Maluti Mountains

An interesting route into the Malutis is along the A1 to Butha Buthe and then up the incredibly steep Moteng Pass to **New Oxbow Lodge**, where the tarred road ends. This is more upmarket than the other Highlands lodges, though the rates are still moderate. Oxbow is one of the few places in southern Africa's mountains that receives enough snow for skiing, and the lodge has a ski-lift in the mountains behind, which is usually open between June and July—but whose future is uncertain as the lodge has reported a decline in the numbers of skiers coming in. Oxbow also offers the usual Highlands activities of guided hiking, pony trekking and trout fishing. From Oxbow there is almost no settlement for about 100km (or five hours of driving or bus ride) until the remote town of **Mokhotlong**. Do not attempt this drive after dark, as the road can be treacherous in places, and allow plenty of daylight before starting the journey from Oxbow. Until the 1950s no vehicles could reach Mokhotlong, and even now the road on from there to Sani Top, on the Drakensberg Escarpment, can only be driven in a very tough 4x4. Up here, the horse is king.

The Highlands Water Project

From Leribe (Hlotse) a tar road now climbs up into what used to be one of the remotest parts of the Malutis—the village of Katse, where the massive dam built by the Highlands Water project can be seen. Katse has an information office, ✆ 314 324, and a small lodge—**Katse Lodge**, ✆ 910 202. If you only have time for a quick look at the Highlands, this makes a great day-trip. Otherwise I would be inclined to give it a miss—a dam is a dam after all—and head into the mountains on foot or pony from the Basotho Pony Project or Semonkong and Malealea Lodges.

The Drakensberg Escarpment

This, the western edge of Lesotho and the country's highest point, can only be reached by ordinary car at **Sehlabethebe National Park**, ✆ 323 600, near Qacha's Nek on the A4. All other roads require a 4x4. Sehlabethebe is one of the only areas of Lesotho that still harbours a healthy game population. Eland, grey rhebok and mountain reedbuck graze the mountainsides among flowering aloes and forested kloofs. Eagles and vultures, bald ibis and sugarbirds are common. Sehlabethebe has several hiking trails, including a 2-day trail out of the park, over the escarpment to Bushman's Nek in Natal. North along the escarpment from Sehlabethebe is **Sani Top**, sitting at the head of Sani Pass, the only direct road access from Lesotho to Natal, which also requires a 4x4, good legs or a quadruped.

South along the escarpment from Sehlabethebe is **Qacha's Nek**, accessible by ordinary vehicle (you have to pass through Qacha's Nek to reach Sehlebethebe), and with road access to Natal via a short stretch of Transkei. This has been said to be dangerous for private vehicles (although the author could find no evidence of any attacks on the Transkei side), but South African backpackers recommend it as a safe route to travel by black taxi from Lesotho into South Africa. On the tarred section of the A4 between Qacha's Nek and Mohale's Hoek is the town of **Quthing** (also known as Moyeni), a good place to break a journey.

Where to Stay and Eating Out

Readers should note that the telephone numbers in this section, if local—and not to booking offices in South Africa—may not work, as Highlanders often steal the copper wire of the phone lines. Don't worry; the lodges are rarely full and expect visitors just to turn up.

expensive

The **New Oxbow Lodge**, ✆ (051) 922 247, at the end of the tarred road over Moteng Pass, can arrange riding, hiking, trout fishing, and (in season) skiing. **Semonkong Lodge**, ✆ (051) 933 3106, is one of Lesotho's best. Friendly, informal, tranquil and well run, it lies next to Semongkong, a remote village in the Thaba Putsoa Mountains, near the highest waterfall in southern Africa. The lodge can arrange hiking and trout fishing, and every month there are horse races on the plateau above. Attached to the lodge is a pub where visitors can drink and chat to local BaSotho, who tether their horses outside. The bar gets very lively, and most of the drinkers must trust to their mounts to take them safely home.

Malealea Lodge, ✆ (051) 447 3200, is an old trading post in a small oak forest at the foot of the Thaba Putsoa, which dreams away on the close horizon in a sheer wall of orange and gold. So beautiful is this view that the last ridge on the road into Malealea is known as the Gates of Paradise. Malealea can arrange just about anything from pony trekking on good BaSotho ponies to hiking (with pack donkeys) and 4x4 expeditions, all guided, for between an hour and 6 days.

moderate

The three lodges above all have more moderate accommodation. The **New Oxbow Lodge** does B&B, while **Semonkong** and **Malealea** both have self-catering rondavels. **Sehlabethebe Lodge**, in Sehlabethebe National Park, offers very comfortable self-catering accommodation, but must be booked at the office at the park's entrance. The **Mokhotlong Hotel**, ✆ 920 330, in Mokhotlong, and the **Orange River Hotel**, ✆ 750 252, in Quthing, make good rest stops when driving to Sani Pass and Sehlabethebe respectively. Both have modest, comfortable rooms with shared bathrooms. The gloomy **Nthatuoa Hotel**, ✆ 950 260, in Qacha's Nek, has a few en suite rooms. All three have à la carte restaurants and bars.

There is now a good lodge just down the pass from the Basotho Pony Project: **Molimo N'thuse Lodge**, ✆ 370 211.

cheap

Semongkong Lodge and **Malealea Lodge** both have cheap dormitory and rondavel accommodation for backpackers, with bedding available. **Molumong Lodge** (not as you might expect in nearby Molumong village, but in Rafalotsane village, 15km down the Thaba Tseka road) has similar accommodation but you must provide a sleeping bag and food. The **Farmer Training Centre**, in Mokhotlong itself, offers shared rooms with bedding. Take your own food. **Quthing Merino Stud Farm** has clean, self-catering double rooms on a farm 3km from the town (signposted from the road between Qacha's Nek and Mohale's Hoek). Selhabethebe Lodge has a cheap bunkhouse, and visitors can camp in the mountains. If you arrive late and need to stay overnight before entering the park, the **Range Management Centre**, in nearby Sehlabethebe village, has dormitory accommodation in a clean hostel. Bring your own sleeping bag. It can be worth spending a couple of days here, as there are good walks to local bushman paintings.

Sani Top's **Mountaineer's Chalet** overlooks the magnificent pass and has self-catering accommodation in dormitories and cheap double rooms, with bedding provided. At the foot of Sani Pass, on the Natal side, is **Sani Lodge**, ✆ (033) 701 1466, a very cheap, very good-value self-catering lodge with either dormitory accommodation or double beds in rondavels, in an old trading post that also has access to hiking trails and horses.

We learned to ride, shoot and swim almost as soon as we could walk

Deneys Reitz describing his Free State childhood
in his Boer War memoir, *Commando*

The Free State, forming a rough oval on its side, plumb in the middle of South Africa, is the province least visited by tourists. Even many South Africans avoid it unless to drive between Gauteng and the Cape, and certainly its central flat farmlands, northern industrial towns and old-fashioned rural Boer culture are not to everyone's taste. However, the Free State has landscapes that are among the most beautiful in South Africa, as well as several game reserves of great size, some of which support big game, and in which you can walk at will. The mountainous grasslands of the Eastern Highlands, where the Free State borders Lesotho, are heavenly beautiful, blessedly free from tourists, cut through with hiking and riding trails, and small, secluded country inns.

History

The Orange Free State was proclaimed in 1854 by Boers who had gone north with the Great Trek of 1836 to look for settlement away from British rule. The empty highveld grassland, temperate climate, fertile soil and plentiful game made the area highly attractive. Moreover, large tracts of the country (though by no means all) had been temporarily abandoned by fleeing tribes during upheavals that followed the rise of the Zulu empire of the 1820s and the Ndebele and Tswana ravaging of the highveld in the 1830s (a process generally known as the *Mfecane*—see **History**). Despite this, the Boers still found plenty of resistance to their settlement from groups living in the area: the BaSotho, under King Moshoeshoe in the east, the Rolong, and Taung Tswana in the drier west, and the Griqua, or free bands of Dutch-speaking 'coloureds', who had migrated into the southern area, near the Orange River, in the late 18th century, to escape the racism of the Cape Colony.

With their firearms, horses and wagons (which could be laagered into a makeshift fort), the Voortrekkers set out to break the Ndebele power in the highveld, inflicting a crippling defeat on them at Vegkop, in the northeast of the region, in 1836, having been sheltered and provisioned by the Rolong Tswana's chief, Moroka. After Vegkop, there was little to challenge Boer supremacy, and in 1854 the region's Voortrekkers proclaimed the Orange Free State on the central plains around their small capital of Bloemfontein, a settlement that had existed since at least the 1830s. And although the region came under a nominal British sovereignty between 1848 and 1854, the area soon established itself as a Boer heartland.

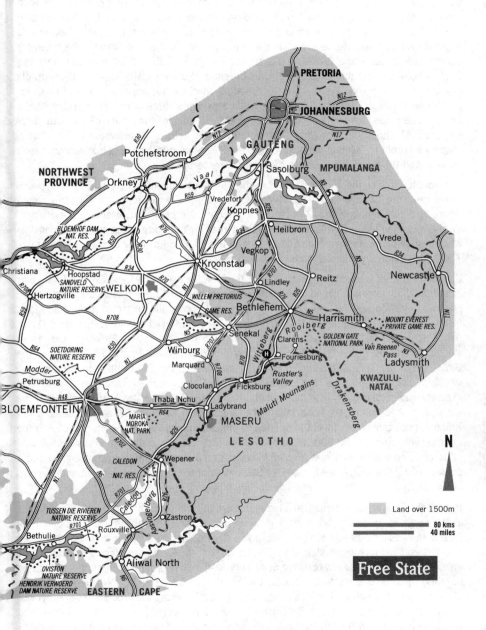

PRETORIA

JOHANNESBURG

GAUTENG

Potchefstroom

NORTHWEST
PROVINCE
Orkney

Sasolburg

MPUMALANGA

Vaal

Vredefort

Koppies

Heilbron

Vrede

BLOEMHOF DAM
NAT. RES.

Vegkop

Christiana

Hoopstad

Kroonstad

Reitz

Newcastle

SANDVELD
NATURE RESERVE

WELKOM

Lindley

Hertzogville

WILLEM PRETORIUS
GAME RES.

Bethlehem

Harrismith

MOUNT EVEREST
PRIVATE GAME RES.

R708

SOETDORING
NATURE RESERVE

Winburg

Senekal

Rooiberg

Clarens

GOLDEN GATE
NATIONAL PARK

Van Reenen
Pass

Witteberg

Modder

Marquard

Fouriesburg

Ladysmith

Petrusburg

Clocolan

*Rustler's
Valley*

KWAZULU-
NATAL

Thaba Nchu

Ficksburg

Maluti Mountains

BLOEMFONTEIN

Ladybrand

MARIA
MOROKA
NAT. PARK

MASERU

Drakensberg

CALEDON
NAT. RES.

Wepener

LESOTHO

N

TUSSEN DIE RIVIEREN
NATURE RESERVE

Caledon

Aasvogelberg

Zastron

Bethulie

Rouxville

Land over 1500m

OVISTON
NATURE RESERVE

Aliwal North

80 kms
40 miles

HENDRIK VERWOERD
DAM NATURE RESERVE

EASTERN CAPE

Free State

461

Ever hungry for more territory, these Afrikaans-speaking settlers soon began to look with envy at the fertile lands around King Moshoeshoe's mountain fortress at Thaba Bosiu near the Caledon river, at the eastern end of the Free State, in modern Lesotho. Moshoeshoe resisted several Boer attempts to dislodge him, even when the Free Staters advertised for adventurers in the Cape Province and attacked with a combined force of *burghers* and English colonists. Unable to get rid of Moshoeshoe, the Free State *burghers* then simply began settling in his valleys west of the Caledon. Moshoeshoe appealed to the British for protection (even though the British army had also made three attempts at taking Thaba Bosiu). The Cape Government agreed the present border of the eastern Free State after declaring Moshoeshoe's kingdom (modern Lesotho) a British protectorate. The fertile country west of the Caledon was awarded to the Free State *burghers*, much to Moshoeshoe's chagrin, and the Free State's eastern highlands were secured.

But trouble came to the western border in the 1870s after diamonds were found on several farms near the Orange and Vaal Rivers, followed by a large deposit on a farm called Vooruitzicht near present-day Kimberley. The Free State president, Brand, a Boer expansionist, who had led a *Kommando* during the Great Trek and organized the attacks against Moshoeshoe in the eastern Free State, claimed the diamond-bearing land for his republic. The British, naturally, did the same.

But the land itself was officially outside both the Free State and the Cape Colony, being part of a British protectorate called West Griqualand, whose Griqua ('coloured') people were governed by Nicolaas Waterboer, a fighter who had successfully protected his people's land from white settlement for over 20 years. Waterboer employed a land agent called David Arnot, to represent his claim to the diamond land at Cape Town. President Brand, on studying the maps, insisted that the deposits lay clearly within the Orange Free State. But the British surveyor, G. Gilfillan, fiddled with the name of the ranges of hills near the deposits, swapping one name for another, so that the Cape Colony was stretched east by the few kilometres necessary to enclose the diamond-rich farms. This knocked Waterboer out of the game, as he had neither the financial nor the military back-up to challenge the decision. But Brand did not give up, and went to London to protest. Britain dug in its heels and offered the Orange Free State £900,000 in compensation if it let the claims go. President Brand reluctantly complied, and was given 37 well-watered farms, a lump sum of £4000 and a pension of £500 a year. The Orange Free State was not to benefit from the diamond diggings at Kimberley.

Instead the little republic remained a loose-knit agricultural community of giant sheep farms, as the *burghers* gradually shot out the game in most areas of the plains and intimidated the local Sotho and Tswana-speaking clans into working on the farms. Blacks were not permitted to own land, and many drifted west to look for work at the Kimberley diggings. Nonetheless, enough remained for the Orange Free State to prosper slowly. Britain's attention was focused on the larger Boer state to the north, the South African Republic (Northern Province, Gauteng and Mpumalanga), which it occupied in 1877, leaving the Free State be. However, when Paul Kruger ousted the British during the First Anglo-Boer war (1880–81), and proclaimed the South African Republic independent again, the two states drew much closer together, despite the fact that the Free State lost even more of its African labour to its northern neighbour when the Rand gold fields began to flourish in the 1890s.

When the Second Anglo-Boer war broke out in 1899 the Orange Free State allied with the South African Republic and sent more than 20,000 men to war against the British. *Kommandos* from the Free State laid siege to Kimberley, Mafeking and Colesberg and the Stormberg mountains in the Cape, while the combined main army under General Joubert occupied Natal east of the Free State border. Things went well for the Boers during the first year of war, but the British broke through Joubert's line in 1890, after the British General Roberts was sent out to replace General Buller. More than 60,000 British troops invaded the Free State, forcing the besiegers to withdraw.

The Orange Free State *Kommandos*, under General De Wet, could not stop the British from taking Bloemfontein, which opened up the road and rail route for the British to invade the South African Republic. Pretoria and Johannesburg were occupied, and the two Boer republics became effectively British territory.

However, the *Kommandos* then split up into a mass of highly effective guerilla bands and dispersed over the Free State and the South African Republic, while large, unwieldy British columns lumbered after them, unable to bring the Boers to direct battle. General De Wet's Free State *Kommandos* managed to cut the British supply lines to the Cape, and the Boers decided to fight on until a foreign power could be persuaded to intervene against the British. This was not altogether unrealistic, as Britain was receiving much censure in Europe for making war on colonial whites. Free State *Kommandos* began to raid far into the Cape Colony and occupied several towns in the Karoo, such as Calvinia and Kuruman during 1900–1901, living off the veld, raiding African homesteads and farms, and getting help from Cape Afrikaner sympathizers.

The British, under Field Marshal Kitchener, responded by systematically burning the farms of the Free State and the South African Republic, and removing the women and children who had remained behind when their men had gone to fight in the *Kommandos*; this destroyed the Boers' supply base. The woman and children were put into 'concentration' camps, the first of their kind, where tens of thousands died from disease and malnutrition, creating a Boer hatred of the British that is still felt to this day.

African farming communities were also uprooted and put in camps, to prevent the Boers from surviving by raiding African villages and homesteads. Many thousands of Africans thus imprisoned also died. Bloemfontein had two of the largest such camps. The British then criss-crossed the Free State and the South African Republic with long barbed wire fences to impede the *Kommandos*' mobility, and set up a system of blockhouse forts across the Cape Colony to monitor movement in the more fertile districts, especially where there were large Afrikaner populations who might assist the fighters. Anyone found doing so was hanged.

Still, De Wet, commanding the Free State *Kommandos*, fought on with some success, capturing enough British rations and ammunition to keep his men in the field. However an increasing number of the smaller *Kommandos* were captured, some of whom were recruited by the British to fight the *Kommandos* at their own game. They were known as *hensoppers*, or 'hands-uppers'. This discouraged the fighting Boers. Meanwhile, huge British columns began to sweep tracts of country between one barbed wire fence and another, forcing the *Kommandos* into a continual retreat. The British began to recruit regiments from African clans who had scores to settle with the Boers. Zulu and Tswana forces became active on the fringes of the Free State, while others helped the British in the South African Republic.

The Boer generals capitulated in 1902, though the Free State *Kommandos*, still under General De Wet, wanted to continue. After the war, the Free State crawled slowly to its feet as the surviving Boers returned to their burned farms and tried to get back their African labour force. The Transvaal immediately began to prosper once the gold mines re-opened, and Johannesburg and Pretoria quickly became as cosmopolitan as they had been before the war. Meanwhile, after the Union of South Africa in 1910, the Orange Free State became the centre of the growing Boer nationalist movement. The Nationalist Party was formed in Bloemfontein in 1914.

Gold and platinum were discovered in the northern Orange Free State around the modern town of Welkom in the 1920s and '30s, and the Free State began to share in the country's mineral wealth. During the Second World War, this new prosperity, combined with undiminished Boer nationalism, made Bloemfontein one of the hot-beds of the *Broederbond* ('brotherhood'), a secret society of Boer industrialists and wealthy landowners that had been founded back in 1918. Sworn to oust the British through the National Party, and to remove voting rights from the Free State's more numerous black population, the *Broederbond* soon spread across the nation. Eventually, the society managed to permeate all levels of the country's administrative, judicial and industrial institutions, in a successful attempt to make the South African establishment more Boer than British.

Once the National Party came to power in 1948, these objectives became possible. The Orange Free State and Transvaal became South Africa's political power centres, particularly after the opening of the northern Free State's gold fields in the 1950s, augmenting the more established gold fields of the Transvaal.

During the apartheid years from 1948 to 1990, the Free State resisted sanctions through its synthetic petrol-producing plant at Sasolburg on the Transvaal border. However, today most of the Free State is still farmland and mountain, and many white South Africans regard the Free Staters as yokels. The Free State's image may change dramatically in the future, as the province's black majority (of mostly South Sotho and Tswana) now control local government, despite the region's entrenched Boer nationalism. So far, the sleepy, agricultural Free State has adapted peacefully.

The Eastern Highlands

This region of the Free State, where it borders Lesotho, should not be missed. High grasslands roll beneath table-like *mesas*; sandstone outcroppings jut from the soil almost anywhere you look, and the air here has a quality of raw health that makes you almost light-headed. The area's national parks and nature reserves (and many of the farms) still support large game populations, and offer hiking and riding through the wild hills and tended valleys, whose orchards and poplar-fringed fields make stark contrast with the hills behind. Bushman paintings can be found in almost any range of hills, whose sandstone overhangs and caves provided sanctuary for these hunter-gatherers until the early 19th century.

In spring the valleys are white with cherry blossom; in summer, when most of the rain falls, the country shines a vivid green. In the drier, cold winter (snow is not uncommon on the hills) the region turns a deep gold, tinged with red as the grasses die. Along the eastern horizon (in Lesotho) marches the long, blue line of the Malutis, southern Africa's highest mountains. Relatively few tourists reach the Free State's Eastern Highlands, and you may well see no one else if exploring on foot or horseback; the region is a convenient jumping-off point for Lesotho. Even the towns are pretty, generally composed of handsome single-storey 19th-century sandstone buildings, clustered around a central square.

Getting There

By car: The R26 runs through all the towns along the border with Lesotho and can be picked up from the N5 at Bethlehem in the north or from Rouxville on the N6 in the south. The R708 via Marquard connects the Eastern Highlands with the N1 highway at Winburg, just north of Bloemfontein.

By bus: Twice weekly Transtate services run along the R26 towns (Fouriesburg, Ficksburg, Clocolan and Ladybrand) to/from Jo'burg. Unfortunately, bus services to/from Bloemfontein are non-existent, unless you take a Greyhound out to Senekal or Bethlehem and pick up a Transtate service from there (alternatively, hitch or take a black taxi). Call Rennies Travel in Bloemfontein for details, ✆ (051) 430 2361.

Golden Gate National Park

This mountain reserve is at the northernmost point of the Eastern Highlands, where the Drakensberg and Maluti foothills meet, just below the tiny mountain 'homeland' of Qwa-Qwa (now reabsorbed into South Africa, but still marked on the road signs).

Golden Gate is named after two massive sandstone outcroppings which command the northern entrance to a spectacular valley that links the Free State with Qwa-Qwa. A tarred road runs along this main valley, and a graded dirt road leads up the slopes on the border with Qwa-Qwa, but otherwise the 12,000ha upland park is an unbroken swathe of unspoilt montane grassland, grazed by eland, black wildebeest, red hartebeest, blesbok and springbok.

Alongside these live smaller groups of zebra and smaller antelope such as mountain reedbuck, grey rhebok, klipspringer and oribi. Eagles and vultures are not as common here as in some of the other mountain reserves, but jackal buzzard are well in evidence, and the many sandstone cliffs and overhangs are home to thousands of doves. Dassies thrive here and feed a sizeable but nocturnal population of caracal and a few shy leopard. You can explore the park via numerous day walks, an overnight trail (with a refuge hut supplied with firewood and water), and guided horse trails from one to three hours, and a limited network of game roads near the main valley.

To reach the park follow either the R712 from Clarens in the Free State, or the R74 from Bergville in Natal. Watch out for the signs to the park from either road. Trails can be booked on arrival or in advance via the National Parks Board in Pretoria ✆ (012) 343 1991.

The Heart of the Eastern Highlands: The Rooiberg and Witteberg

Clarens, nearest town to the Golden Gate National Park, lies on the R711 at the foot of the Rooiberg, ('red mountains', named for the golden russet colour of their winter grasslands). This tiny, picturesque sandstone town has been occupied by many of the foreign workers contracted to manage the building of the Lesotho Highland Water Scheme, a massive set of dams currently in construction just over the border. As a result, this little town has a good restaurant in the main square, called the **Guinea Feather**, and some good craft shops of local Sotho and Tswana artefacts. About 10km east of town, on the road to Golden Gate, is **Bokpoort Farm**, which offers 1- to 4-day guided horse trails and hikes into the Rooiberg.

South and then west along the R26, which follows the Lesotho border, is **Fouriesburg**, slightly larger than Clarens. The 19th-century **Fouriesburg Country Inn** (*see* 'Where to Stay'), is a good place to break a journey or to visit in the evening. Otherwise it is worth wandering Fouriesburg's few streets; the trading stores are old-fashioned, with dark wooden counters and the stock piled up on old panelled shelves. There is usually a craft shop/café selling Sotho handiwork, Boer breads and pastries and serving tea and coffee were opening. South of Fouriesburg, the R26 winds to Ficksburg through a wide valley between the low Witteberg (meaning 'white mountains', because of their winter snows) and the Caledon River that borders Lesotho. About 20km out of Fouriesburg is a sign for **Rustler's Valley**, one of the most beautiful and unusual places to stay in South Africa.

Rustler's Valley (*see* 'Where to Stay') is a large, well-watered private farm and guesthouse commanding a whole valley of the Witteberg foothills. Perhaps because of the hills, which rise on three sides of the valley, hiding it from the rest of the world, the farm has developed with an individualism seldom encountered in South Africa. From the original farmhouse, Frik, the owner, has built a series of beautiful, highly individual buildings that blend with, rather than jar against, the landscape. The farm has accommodation for all budgets, and a very good restaurant and bar with a rather hippyish atmosphere. The farm still produces vegetables, and horses graze the wide pastures. Blesbok wander at will, and in the bush-covered slopes of the Witteberg there are caracal and a few nomadic leopard, as well as 14 species of antelope, wildebeest, zebra, black rhino and a number of raptors.

As a polo player, Frik keeps good horses: the adjoining estate offers polo and it is pure heaven to take off into the surrounding country on one of his throroughbreds. Hiking at Rustler's Valley is also excellent; there are short walks to rock formations and caves (including what purports to be a cannibal cave) and a two-day hike around the entire valley that involves sleeping in a sandstone overhang.

Once a year, at Easter, the tranquillity of Rustler's Valley is broken by a three-day music festival—one of only a handful in the whole country—which attracts some of South Africa's best musicians. South Africa's hippy/bohemian culture comes out to play, and it would be hard to find a better setting for a party.

Ficksburg, south of Rustler's Valley, is a very handsome little town surrounded by cherry orchards, which in spring (Sept–Oct) fill the air with a rich scent of blossom. The town itself has little for the tourist besides rural atmosphere, sandstone buildings and shops and petrol for supplies. But every spring there is a Cherry Festival, and the whole town parties. It is a moveable feast, but Rustler's Valley should know the date.

The R26 then cuts west to the town of **Clocolan**, another 19th-century sandstone farming town set under the Witteberg. There is a very good weaving centre in town, **Lethoteng Weavers** on First Street, which employs local Sotho and Tswana women on a profit-share basis, producing rugs, hangings, sweaters and cardigans from local wool and mohair. Outside Clocolan is a private game farm, **Ikebana** (*see* 'Where to Stay'), with hiking and riding trails into the Witteberg.

North of Clocolan, the R708 winds for about 35km through empty hill country to **Marquard**, a village at the western end of the Witteberg. Several good hiking and riding trails lead into the mountains from local farms, which offer B&B, refuge huts, or cave over-hangs to stay in. South of Clocolan, the R26 continues to **Ladybrand**, the closest South African town to Maseru, capital of Lesotho. Ladybrand is larger than the other Eastern Highlands towns, but has little beyond the basic amenities; most tourists just pass through on their way to Maseru.

West of Ladybrand is a section of what was Bophuthatswana, whose small central town, **Thaba Nchu** (pronounced Tha Banchu), forms an unexpected island of ugly glitz in this otherwise beautiful region. Thaba Nchu has a casino: Bophuthatswana was exempt from South Africa's prudish anti-gambling laws, and capitalized on this lucrative income. A holiday park sits next to the casino which, unless you have an irresistible urge to gamble, is best avoided. However, its present-day ugliness belies Thaba Nchu's history—during the 1830s, the flat-topped mountain above the resort (after which the place is named), was a stronghold of the Rolong clan of the Tswana, who sheltered the Vootrekkers, under Andries Potgieter, in 1836. Thaba Nchu gave the Voortrekkers a secure base from which to challenge the powerful Ndebele people, breaking their monopoly of power on the highveld at the battle of Vegkop later that year (*see* 'Ndebele History' pp.542–3).

The vulgarity of Thaba Nchu is made up for by the nearby **Maria Moroka National Park**, © (051) 873 2427, which covers a great swathe of classic Eastern Highlands hill country. The beautiful park supports a lot of game; mostly eland, zebra, red harte-beest, black wildebeest, blesbok and springbok, as well as some of the smaller antelope. Twitchers flock here to see the rare blue korhaan—a miniature bustard—and raptors such as black and martial eagle. There are game-viewing roads, and walking trails that can take you very close to game. Unfortunately there is no accommodation except for the casino hotel at Thaba Nchu (*see* above phone number); it is best to visit early in the morning and drive back to Ladybrand (about 50km) in the evening, rather than stay in Thaba Nchu.

Where to Stay

Golden Gate National Park offers a range of accommodation. The expensive rooms are in the large **Brandwag Lodge**, and include full board in very comfortable rooms overlooking the Golden Gate rocks. The self-contained rondavels are moderately priced, and there is cheap camping with ablutions. To book, telephone the National Parks Board in Pretoria, ✆ (012) 343 1991. Except for at the height of the summer holidays, it is usually safe just to turn up, as the accommodation is seldom full. **Rustler's Valley**, ✆ (05193) 33 939, is one of the country's most unusual and imaginative places to stay and caters for all budgets. Hiking and riding are offered, and the food is almost all home-produced and very well cooked. The bohemian atmosphere of the place, coupled with its quiet beauty, makes it hard to leave.

expensive

Oaklands Country Manor, ✆ (058) 671 0067, sits in oak woodland atop the Van Reenen Pass where the Eastern Highlands flatten into a plateau overlooking the province of Natal. The old colonial house has simple, comfortable rooms and offers riding, shooting, bass fishing, walking and a superb view down over Natal. The country cooking is hearty and excellent. **Mount Everest Private Game Reserve**, ✆ (05861) 21 816, near Harrismith, is spread over three entire mountains. The game, which includes white rhino, walks freely among the guest rondavels. There are several hiking trails and horses for hire, and guests can fish for bass or trout. **Ikebana**, ✆ (05194) 30 516, a private game reserve south of Clocolan on the R26, is at the moderate end of the expensive scale. Its thatched chalets and rondavels surround a central lodge. Full board or B&B is offered. Hiking and riding among the game can be arranged. **Rebellie Game Farm**, ✆/✉ (058) 256 1152, surrounded by mountains and overlooking the Malutis, is a fully equipped luxurious lodge, with abundant game, bird-watching, scenic mountain trails, and hunting in season. Helicopter transport from Gauteng can be arranged.

moderate

The **Fouriesburg Country Inn**, ✆ (058)223 0207, occupies the oldest house in town, decorated in period and owned by a Swiss family. The food is good and guests are invited to make their own selection from the excellent wine cellar. **Kiara Lodge**, ✆ (058) 256 1324, is on the edge of the Golden Gate National Park, nicely situated short of the park entrance, and is developed around a 19th-century farm house. **Franshoek Mountain Lodge & Polo School**, ✆ (05192) 2828/3938, at the foot of the Witteberg, offers B&B in a secluded sandstone farmhouse. The farm has a 22km hiking trail during which you overnight in a large cave at the head of a beautiful gorge. Bass fishing, riding and swimming in the dam are offered. **Cranberry Cottage**, ✆ (05191) 2290, in the centre of Ladybrand, has 4 double rooms in an old sandstone townhouse, renovated in Victorian style, and home-cooking.

Bokpoort Farm, ✆ (058) 256 1181, about 17km east of Clarens on the road to Golden Gate, offers comfortable B&B or self-contained backpackers accommodation in an old farmhouse close to the **De Ark Game Reserve** and the **Rebellie Game Park**. **Hoekfontein Guest Farm**, ✆ (05192) 3915, offers cheap accommodation in a camp at the foot of the Malutis, signposted from the R26 between Ficksburg and Fouriesburg, with 3 rondavels and 6 thatched chalets. Venison *braais* are available, and there is riding and hiking. The game is mostly antelope, but there are hippo in the dam. **Die Ou Stal B&B**, Zastron, ✆ (051) 673 1268/1369, a comfortable cottage overlooking the Malutis, is the ideal overnight stop between the north and south on the Highland Route. Evening meals on request. **Riebeeck Country Guesthouse**, a beautiful farmhouse and haven in the Eastern Freestate Highlands, with bird-watching and mountain biking, has one self-catering rondavel and 3 en suite rooms. Meals available on request. Booking essential. **Zevenfontein Country House**, ✆ (05192) 3778, just 3 hours from Gauteng, has B&B in sandstone cottages, with walking, bird-watching, mountain biking, horse riding and *à la carte* meals.

A cheap option in Ladybrand is the **Ladybrand My Housy B&B**, 17a Prinsloo Street, ✆ (05191) 410 010, ✉ 2777, *myhousy@lesoff.co.za*. The **Liliehoek Resort**, ✆ (05191) 40 267, in the wheat and sunflower fields east of Ladybrand, is very good value, with 14 comfortable thatched rondavels, and even cheaper camp sites with ablutions, in a landscaped setting among trees and giant sandstone boulders. Hikes of an hour to 3 days can be made from here, with overnight huts in the surrounding hills. All accommodation is self-contained, and there is a large swimming pool.

The Southeastern Highlands

South of Ladybrand and Thaba Nchu, the R26 follows the western bulge of Lesotho's border to the small town of Wepener, about 20km east of which is the **Caledon Nature Reserve**, which surrounds a large dam on the Caledon River. Here the high grasslands of the Eastern Highlands merge with Eastern Karoo veld, offering a mixed landscape of thornbush, high grassland and riverine hardwood forest. Game thrives here, notably black wildebeest, reedbuck, springbuck and blesbok. Bird watchers come here for the waterfowl, particularly the handsome black stork. There are no marked trails, but there is nothing to stop you walking at will. Unfortunately, there is no accommodation (though if you camped quietly, no one would notice), so it is better to visit in the morning and continue south to **Zastron**, a little town at the foot of the **Aasvogelberg** (meaning 'vulture mountains'). Zastron has a little hotel, and there are marked trails into the mountains from here, where vultures still breed.

The Devil's Pipe

Zastron is famous for a set of legends concerning one of its first white inhabitants, Renier Du Wenaar, who lived to be over 100 years old, as his gravestone in the old churchyard testifies. The stories of Du Wenaar and his faithful Khoi servant, Boesman, are numerous, and most seem to have originated from the old man himself, but the most famous (told and beautifully illustrated in Alice Miller's *Myths and Legends of Southern Africa*, T.V. Bulpin Press, 1979) warrants retelling here. In the middle of the rocky outcrop that forms the summit of the Aasvogelberg is a round hole resembling an eye, apparently the result of one of Du Wenaar's exploits. One day he and Boesman were walking near the mountain when they noticed the devil—cloven hoofs, horns and all—sitting amongst a large troupe of baboons. The devil wished Du Wenaar good morning and, pointing to his large, old-fashioned musket, asked what the funny-looking object was. Du Wenaar resented the devil poking fun at his ancient gun and answered that it was his pipe, which, owing to its size, had to be smoked out of doors, as the smell irritated his wife.

The devil laughed, saying, 'So let's smoke. Light it up.' Du Wenaar loaded the musket and told the devil to put it to his mouth and draw, while he struck a light from the flint. The devil sucked at the barrel as De Wenaar lit the fuse; the gun went off with an almighty bang, blowing the devil's head clean off and straight through the Aasvogelberg. 'Hell!' came a faint voice from the other side of the mountain, 'That's strong tobacco!' The body sprang up and ran off stumbling over the mountain. Du Wenaar and Boesman laughed until they cried.

Zastron has hardly grown since Du Wenaar blew the devil's head off, but there is a marked hiking trail up into the Aasvogelberg where you can inspect the hole from the foot of the outcropping. However, as a qualification to Du Wenaar's claim, different versions of the story crop up in other locations in South Africa, the closest one being told in the eastern Karoo, near the town of Graaf Reinet— except that there it is a Khoi hunter and his old flintlock who are the heroes. Perhaps old Du Wenaar heard the story from his Khoi servant Boesman. Either way, the devil seems to have lost a lot of heads in South Africa.

Tourist Information

Caledon Publicity Association ✆ (051) 583 1920.

Activities

Hiking: All the guest farms listed offer hiking trails of between 1 hour to 2 days. The longer **Brandwater Trail**, ✆ (058) 2223 0050, covers 5 days (with a shorter, 2-day option) in the Witteberg, with accommodation in sandstone caves and overhangs. The trail starts from the Meiringskloof Nature Reserve, just outside Fouriesburg.

Canoeing: Quaggafontein, ✆ (05542) 3212, offers canoeing in the Orange River.

Where to Stay

There are few places to stay in the southeast Highlands. Visitors to the Aasvogelberg and the Caledon Nature Reserve could try **Quaggafontein**, ✆ (05542) 3212, near Zastron. This self-catering farm has a beautiful wrought-iron veranda, a log fire and candlelight only. Canoeing can be arranged in the nearby Orange River, and there are some short hikes.

Also recommended by travellers is the **Tienfontein Guestfarm**, ✆ (05542) 2931, and the nearby, **Champagne Holiday Farm** ✆ (05542) ask for 2730, which offers great home-cooking, riding, walking and hikes into the mountains. If the above are full, try the **Maluti Hotel** in Zastron, ✆ (051) 673 1657, which, despite being rather ugly, offers comfortable, moderately priced accommodation with breakfast and good traditional Boer dishes like Karoo mutton, in the small restaurant. The bar is touchingly twee—done up to resemble the front of an old Frontier hotel. You could also try the **Vogelensang** in Zastron, ✆ (05542) ask for 3412.

The Southwestern Free State: The Karoo Fringe

Southwest of the Eastern Highlands, around the grasslands bordering the wide Orange River, the Free State widens into great plains which are dry for most of the year, but receive sufficient rainfall to keep the land grass-covered and to support a variety of game. Around the huge **Hendrik Verwoerd Dam** on the Orange River are three large nature reserves. **Oviston Nature Reserve** sits on the Cape Province side of the river, where the Great Karoo begins (*see* 'Bo Karoo', p.278). The two reserves on the Free State side are slightly lusher: the **Hendrik Verwoerdt Dam Nature Reserve**, which fronts the dam's shoreline, is mainly flat with sparse game populations, but bordering this is **Tussen Die Rivieren Nature Reserve**, also known as Tussen Die Rivieren Game Farm.

This vast sweep of country, surrounding the convergence of the Orange and the Caledon Rivers (the name means 'between the rivers'), is one of South Africa's best-kept secrets. The grassland, scrub, riverine woodland and broken hills support a huge game population, and there are several hiking trails that take you past or through great herds of animals. White rhino, eland, gemsbok, kudu, zebra, black and blue wildebeest, blesbok, springbok, impala, reedbuck, steenbok and red hartebeest are all common and, because of the mixed terrain, the bird-life is varied and prolific. Small predators such as caracal, bat-eared fox and jackal occur throughout the reserve, and there are a few shy hyena. The rare, nocturnal aardwolf, a large hyena-like dog that eats termites, is common. The 3 one-day hikes are worth walking, as they take you very close to the game, in an ever-changing terrain. The reserve is only 50km from Aliwal North and the N6, so makes a convenient side-trip for anyone travelling to the Cape Drakensberg or into the Eastern Cape.

Where to Stay

Tussen Die Riveieren, ✆ (051762) 2803, has moderately priced, comfortable self-contained cottages, and very cheap hiking shelters (with very hard floors!) whose only mod cons are ablution facilities and firepits.

Bloemfontein

The Free State's capital and largest town is situated on a plain beneath a line of broken hills. Bloemfontein's modern tower blocks are incongruous against the surrounding landscape—the result of the Free State's mineral wealth coming into its own in the 1960s and '70s. Bloemfontein is an ugly town, and not one to stay in.

by air

SAA, ✆ (051) 331482, and **Airlink**, ✆ (051) 33 3255, fly to Bloemfontein Airport from Jo'burg and Port Elizabeth. SAA also fly from Cape Town, Durban, East London, Kimberley and Upington.

by car

Bloemfontein sits astride the N1 highway, roughly two-thirds of the way from Cape Town to Jo'burg. The N5 highway links Bloemfontein with Natal via Bethlehem and Harrismith. The N6 highway heads south to Port Elizabeth, while the R64 connects the city with Kimberley and the Northern Cape.

by coach

Greyhound (book through Rennies Travel, ✆ (051) 430 2361), **TransLux** and **Transtate**, ✆ 408 3242, all run services from Bloemfontein to the country's major centres, while the city's limited Transtate services connect with several smaller regional centres in the Free State (useful for getting to/from the Eastern Highlands towns) and Lesotho.

Greyhound Buses pick up and set down from Shell Ultra-City pit stop on the Bultfontein Road, about 4 inconvenient kilometres north of the city centre, necessitating a taxi for journeys to and from Bloemfontein itself. TransLux pick up and set down from Cricket Street in the city centre. Transtate uses the Railway Station on Maitland Street, close to the city centre.

by rail

Bloemfontein Station, on Maitland Street, ✆ (051) 408 2407, runs daily services to Cape Town, Kimberley and Jo'burg, and weekly services to Durban, Port Elizabeth, Queenstown and East London. Less frequent services run south to Mossel Bay via Outdtshoorn and George on the Garden Route.

History

The well-watered site was probably named by Jan Bloem, a Griqua leader who lived here before the Voortrekkers settled it in the early 1840s and built a tiny capital for their nascent Orange Free State. Life continued peaceably for the Bloemfontein Boers until the Second Anglo-Boer War (1899–1902). When the British invaded Bloemfontein in 1900 they used the town as a centre of British operations, chasing down the elusive Boer guerilla *Kommandos* dispersed across the veld. However, the Free State's military commander, General Christian de Wet, was so effective in disrupting the British army's communications between the Cape and the Transvaal that the invaders were forced to retaliate strongly. Farms were attacked; Boer women and children and thousands of Africans were interned in two 'concentration camps' in Bloemfontein (*see* p.463). By 1902, most of the internees of the two huge Bloemfontein camps, both black and white, had died.

However after the Boer War the town seems to have recovered quickly. Money from the Rand gold fields found its way into Bloemfontein as thousands of people travelled through on the way to and from the mines and the Cape. When the Nationalist Party was formed in

Bloemfontein in 1914, the town's wealthy businessmen began organizing themselves into a secret Nationalist brotherhood (*broederbond*) with a view to ousting the British and taking the voting franchise away from the Free State's black majority.

During the later years of apartheid, although the northern Free State industrial towns of Welkom and Sasolburg saw a lot of trouble, Bloemfontein remained largely untouched by the political violence. Despite the town's hitherto rabidly right-wing stance, day-to-day life was more relaxed than in the mining towns; Bloemfontein, lacking mines, has always been an administrative rather than political centre. Since the fall of apartheid, and the accession of the ANC, Bloemfontein has continued to grow and prosper quietly. Whether the country's new administration will shake the Free State capital's solid calm remains to be seen.

Tourist Information

Hoffman Square, ✆ (051) 405 8490. Another knowledgeable source is Bloem Tours, on the corner of Zastron and De Villiers Streets, ✆ (051) 430 2184.

Old Bloemfontein

The compact old town centre, which radiates outward from **Hoffman Square**, still contains several handsome buildings amongst the post-war concrete ugliness. These are all to be found within a couple of minutes walk from the junction of Aliwal and Henry Streets. The **Old Raadsal** on St George's Street (*open Mon–Fri 10.15–3, Sat and Sun 2–5*), an adobe and thatch cottage with a beaten dung floor, dates from the 1840s, and is all that remains of Bloemfontein's frontier past. The building served various public functions simultaneously; the headquarters of the army and civil service, town hall, school, church and dance-hall. However, Bloemfontein prospered sufficiently fast for this building soon to prove too small for the centre of the republic's government. Three more *raadsals* were constructed, each larger than the one before. The first two still survive as national monuments, while the third now houses a literary museum (*see* below) and the **Fourth Raadsal** (built 1893), an imposing structure, still operates as a government building (*open by arrangement, ✆ (051) 447 8899*). This marble and stained-glass edifice, also on St George's Street, is as solid and substantial as any British colonial public building of the same period.

As if conscious of this, Bloemfontein's few British settlers built a large **Anglican cathedral** on the same street between 1850 and 1890, and embellished it after the British invasion of 1900. On nearby Brand Street (named after President Brand, who tried to claim the Kimberley diamond area for the Free State in the 1870s) is the **Old Presidency** (*open Tues–Fri 10–12 and 1–4, Sat and Sun 2–5*), home to the three Free State presidents from 1885 until the British invasion. A simple, handsome building, it is now a concert hall housing a small collection of early presidential paraphernalia such as documents pertaining to the province's original land grants and some old clothes.

Also on Brand Street is the **National Afrikaans Literary Museum** (*open Mon–Fri 8–12 and 1–4, Sat and Sun 9–12*). The wealth of poetry and fiction written in Afrikaans is unknown to many foreign readers (*see* **People and Culture**), though they may well have unwittingly read some in translation. Original manuscripts by such novelists and poets as Chris Barnardt and Eugene Marais are housed here. It is worth reading some of Marais' work; writing around the turn-of-the-century, he became famous for his semi-mystical books of natural history—on the lives of termites (*The Soul of the White Ant*) and baboons, whom he referred to as 'Twilight People'. Original manuscripts by contemporary Afrikaans writers can also be looked at, and there is a a brief chronology of 19th- and 20th-century Afrikaans literature (some liberal, some pro-apartheid) and its central place in South African society.

The **National Museum**, on Aliwal Street (*open Mon–Sat 8–4, Sun 1–6*) is a small and rather dull museum of local natural history, with rows of old stuffed animals and shelves of minerals and fossils. The **Freshford House Museum**, on Kellner Street (*open Mon–Fri 10–1, Sat 2–5*) is a preserved Victorian townhouse. On McDonald Street, at the south end of the city centre is **Hertzog House**, the home of the Boer General and later prime Minister Barry Hertzog. Famous as the founder of the Afrikaans-supporting, right-wing National Party in 1914, Barry Hertzog was one of the most vociferous voices in the country's early 20th-century politics for taking away the black and 'coloured' franchise. He became Prime Minister in 1929, and again (with Jan Smuts) in 1934, but resigned over Smuts' decision to aid the British war effort. In 1940, the reactionary old Hertzog was pushed out of his own party and he retired from public life. But his championing of the poor white cause, by urging continued legislation against non-whites, made him something of a hero in Afrikaner history.

However, as is so often the case with these old presidents' houses-cum-museums (there are several such in South Africa), there is little in the collection of memorabilia and furniture that gives clues to the personality of the man himself, nor to the turbulent events of his time. But students of white/black history may be able to extract anecdotes about the man from the museum's curator.

A reminder of the hard fighting that marked the Free State's early history is the **Queen's Fort** on Church Street (*open Mon–Fri 9–4*), built in 1848 to protect the Voortrekker town from BaSotho raids—most of which, it must be said, were provoked by the *burghers* (*see* **Lesotho** 'History'). On Monument Street, the **Military Museum** (*open Mon–Fri 8–4.30, Sat 9–5, Sun 2–5*) deals with the military history of the Orange Free State and Transvaal from an exclusively Boer viewpoint. On view are photographs of stern, starving Boer fighters from the second Anglo-Boer War, the prison camps of the period, the slightly better-fed fighters of the earlier 'native' wars and first skirmishes against the British, as well as weapons and brief personal histories of the military commanders involved in these wars.

Next door to the museum is the **National Women's Memorial & War Museum**, commemorating the 26,000 Boer women and children who died in British 'concentration' camps between 1899 and 1902. The ashes of Emily Hobhouse, an Englishwoman who campaigned for better treatment for the internees, are buried under the monument. The many thousands of Africans who also died in such camps are not remembered here.

Bloemfontein's Parks

Bloemfontein's rose gardens and parks, public and private, are undoubtedly the ugly city's most attractive feature. The biggest rose garden is in **King's Park**, just west of the town centre (reached by Henry or St Andrew's Street). The park has a small zoo and a boating lake, incongruously named Loch Logan. The largest park, **Naval Hill**, which covers several hundred hectares, sits above the old town centre. At the top is a small theatre. About 200ha of this form the **Franklin Game Reserve**, where antelope such as eland, red hartebeest, blesbok and springbok graze. You can wander the reserve from sunrise to sunset every day. At the bottom of the hill is **Hamilton Park**, a formal garden famous for its Orchid House, a giant conservatory through which flows and artificial stream. **Signal Hill** is a smaller park on the opposite (westward) hill from Naval Hill. Less formally laid-out than Naval Hill, this is fine to wander by day, but is best avoided at night.

About 11km northwest of the town centre, adjoining the N1, is the **National Botanical Garden**. Laid out below a large dolerite outcrop, the garden is small, covering only 45ha. However the displays of indigenous vegetation vary greatly and give the impression of a much larger area. There is a small hardwood forest of widely spaced trees, a section of formalized Karoo veld with flowering thorn trees and aloes, and open grassland. The place has been carefully prepared, with an eye for beauty, and the effect is marred only by the roar of traffic from the N1.

Bloemfontein ✆ (051–)   **Where to Stay**

expensive

Bloemfontein has the usual expensive chain hotels, but nothing else of any interest within the price range. The **Bloemfontein Hotel**, ✆ 430 1911, is on East Burger Street, the **Holiday Inn Garden Court**, ✆ 447 0310, is on Union Avenue and the Protea-owned **Halevy House**, ✆ 448 027, is on the corner of Charles and Magraaf Streets. Better, and almost as well-equipped, are Bloemfontein's B&Bs (*see* below).

moderate

The **Waverley Gasthuis B&B**, on Peter Crescent in Waverley, ✆ 312 622, is a pleasant 1930s colonial house set in a large garden. A choice of B&B or full board is offered in 3 very comfortable en suite rooms. **Dagbreek B&B**, ✆ 332 947, a large, modern suburban house built in neoclassical style at the north end of Bloemfontein, about 7km from the N1, has a small restaurant and pool, as well as a garden. **Unitas Herberg**, on Logemanstraat, ✆ 522 6874/5/6, is in the west end of the city, near the university. The rooms are simple, clean and comfortable, and there is a small restaurant. There are many B&Bs in and around the city. You might try the **Hobbit House**, ✆ 447 0663 (J.R.R. Tolkien's father was a bank manager in Bloemfontein).

If you are simply breaking a cross-country journey and don't need to be in the town centre, then about 40km south of Bloemfontein is a very pleasant farmhouse, **Die Oude Kraal Country Lodge**, ✆ (05215) 636/733, which offers a few en suite rooms on a working farm. The house is set in gardens, and has a small pub attached where the locals drink. The home-cooking, especially the mutton and home-made breads, is superb, and guests can wander the farm.

cheap

Bloemfontein has some good-value cheap accommodation. Try **Die Herberg**, on Barnes Street, ✆ 430 7500, just north of the city centre. Not to be confused with the Unitas Herberg (*see* above), this one has 48 en suite rooms, which, if shared, fall into the cheap price range. The **Roberta Guest House**, ✆ 448 3601, has 52 en suite rooms, but is about 3km south of the city centre (catch a no.11 bus from Hoffman

Square). Again, if you share a room (some rooms have four beds), you can bring the price down quite considerably. Both the above hotels can provide breakfast for an extra charge, and the Roberta has a cheapish *à la carte* restaurant. There is also a **Formule 1**, ✆ 446 8630, which, if not particularly charming, is always clean, predictable and very good value, especially with three sharing. **Bloemfontein**, 9km from the N1 bypass on the Jagersfontein Road, ✆/✉ 441 8861 (evenings), is a self-catering cottage with 2 bedrooms (6 single beds), bathroom, kitchen/lounge, TV and telephone, for just R50 per person.

There are at least two backpackers' choices: **Naval Hill Youth Hostel**, ✆ 430 7962, and **Taffy's Backpackers**, ✆ (436 4533).

Bloemfontein ✆ *(051–)*

Eating Out

expensive

Blomfontein's restaurant scene has taken a bit of a battering during the recent recession but the main hotels have good restaurants. Also try, but you have to book, the **Beef Baron**, in Second Avenue, ✆ 447 4290, and **La Fontana** in First.

moderate–cheap

New York Restaurant, in Greyvenstein St, ✆ 447 7279, is popular locally, as is the **Victorian Express**, at the Duplessis Centre in Langenhoven Park on the R64, ✆ 451 1440. A cheaper, Italian restaurant, **Schillaci's Trattoria**, on Zastron Road, ✆ 447 3829, is great in summer as it has outdoor tables. But the best value food in town is probably **St Mary's Kitchen**, on the corner of Fichardt Street and Charles Street, a very cheap place used by black workers. Traditional African food like mealie-pap with beans (very filling and keeps you regular) or deep-fried junk food predominates. You can eat there or take away. The pub-grub Keg chain is represented by the **Keg & Goose**, ✆ 430 0820, and the South African–Portuguese fast food chain by the omnipresent **Nando's**, ✆ 73 502

Nightlife and Entertainment

Despite its stolidly provincial feel, Bloemfontein has a good theatre, and regular classical concerts and ballet/modern dance at the **Sand Du Plessis Theatre** on Markgraff Street, ✆ 447 7771. Bloemfontein cannot compare to other South African cities for nightlife. Clubs come and go each year, but two stalwarts are **Arthur's Club** and **Simply Red**, both on St Andrew's Street, and both of which cater for live blues and local reggae, with the occasional visit by a township band. The crowd is not heavy at these clubs, but the drinking can be.

The Northern and Central Free State

Many South Africans denigrate the wide, level plateau of flat farmlands that make up the central and northern Free State. Certainly, the countryside is unspectacular, but the skies are big and the muted ochres and browns of the highveld grassland have a quiet beauty.

Soetdoring Nature Reserve is on the R64, about 70km north of Bleomfontein, and surrounds the Krugerdrif dam on the Modder River. The R64 connects Bloemfontein with Kimberley, and the reserve makes a good place to break the journey and stretch your legs. The riverine woodland, thorn scrub and grassland support zebra, blue and black wildebeest, blesbok, springbok and duiker, and there are plans to re-introduce more species. The dam is home to large flocks of waterfowl, particularly spurwing and Egyptian geese. Look out for secretary birds in the grasslands. Unfortunately, there is no accommodation.

Further into the highveld, about 40km north along the N1 from the town of **Winburg,** is the **Willem Pretorius Game Reserve**, a large reserve surrounding a large dam. Large game, such as buffalo, white rhino, giraffe, eland and kudu, and most of the medium and small antelope species thrive here. The reserve is a good place to stop if driving north to the Northern Province, and there are chalets and a camp site, as well as boating on the dam. A small restaurant, shop and petrol station complete the facilities. Waterfowl thrive here, and fish eagles are a common sight over the water. Large raptors, such as martial eagles, chanting goshawk and secretary birds, are common in the thornbush of the main reserve.

Further north, towards the Vaal River begin the ugly Free State mining fields. This area, which surrounds the hideous industrial towns of Welkom, Orkney, Kroonstad and Sasolburg, should certainly be avoided. However, in the dry west of the region, where it borders the Northwest Province, are two large nature reserves surrounding a massive dam; the **Bloemhof Dam Nature Reserve** and the **Sandveld Nature Reserve** (✆ (053453) 1706 for both), both west of Welkom along the R34, or the N12 between Johannesburg and Kimberley. Both reserves are largely thornveld, with many tall, yellow-flowering camel-thorn trees and grassland, and support large numbers of giraffe, eland, red hartebeest, blue wildebeest, gemsbok and smaller buck such as duiker and steenbok. The dam supports great flocks of ducks and geese, and blue cranes and white storks are regular visitors. Vultures, small hawks, sociable weaver birds (which build vast nests housing whole flocks) and hornbills are common sights. There are hiking trails and both reserves have basic accommodation: camping with an ablution block.

Further north, where the farmlands meet the fringe of the industrialized Vaal Triangle, is a place that historians will find interesting— **Vegkop Battlefield**. Set just outside the small village of Vegkop, reached by dirt road from the town of **Heilbron**, on the R34 between Kroonstad and the N3 highway, Vegkop is the site where the Voortrekkers repulsed a massive Ndebele attack with devastating musket fire in 1836. The ferocity of the Ndebele's attack convinced the Voortrekkers that they must break the power of Mzilikazi, the Ndebele chief and the most powerful warlord on the highveld.

The defeat forced Mzilikazi and his people to move *en masse* the following year into modern Zimbabwe where most of their descendants still live today (*see* 'Ndebele History'). Today, like so many of South Africa's great battlefields, there is little on the lonely site of Vegkop to suggest the great event that took place there, but the high, lonely landscape has great presence and the battlefield makes a good detour if travelling through the northern Free State to the Northern Province.

Where to Stay

moderate

Should you find yourself having to overnight in the northern Free State, there are plenty of small hotels and guest houses in and around Kroonstad, Welkom and Frankfort. Between Koppies and Kroonstad is the **Sonnebloem Guest House**, ✆ (05672) and ask for 5112, and 30km north of Kroonstad (5 km off the N1) is **Verblyden Guest Farm**, ✆ (90562) 24031. Welkom boasts two substantial hotels, the **Welkom Hotel**, ✆ (057) 51 411, and the **Welcome Inn**, (057) 357 3361. Frankfort offers the centrally situated **Lodge 1896**, ✆ (0588) 31 080. Good parks board accommodation at all three budgets can be found at the **Willem Pretorius Game Reserve** near Winburg, ✆ (05777) 4003, though to stay cheaply you will have to camp.

In the great, flat farmlands of the central Free State, travellers can find a variety of moderately priced accommodation. The town of Bethlehem, on the N5 connecting Bloemfontein with the Rooiberg in the Eastern Highlands, has the **Fisant Gasthuis**, ✆ (058) 303 7144, a sandstone suburban house, very twee, but comfortable inside and offering B&B. **Lindley**, northwest of Bethlehem on the R76, has the **Vaalhoek Guest Farm**, ✆ (05612) 1512, an old farmhouse providing B&B, riding and farm walks. **Senekal**, on the N5 between Bloemfontein and Bethlehem, has **Arcadia**, ✆ (05848) 2867, a neo-Cape Dutch farm offering B&B, riding, walks, and a pool.

Swaziland

The Ox rushes out wild. The young men must catch it and with bare hands pummel and drag it back into the sanctuary.

A History of Swaziland, Dr J. S. M. Matseluba

Tucked between Mpumalanga, KwaZulu-Natal and neighbouring Mozambique, the Kingdom of Swaziland has never been a part of South Africa. The country is small enough to drive across in a day, but there is within this area a great variety of landscape: from high, cool mountains to sub-tropical lowveld, temperate grasslands and montane forests. The area around the capital, Mbabane, is westernized, but in the rural areas traditional life goes on as ever, and there are large stretches of very wild country, designated as nature reserves, supporting big game.

Swaziland has a modest but healthy economy—based primarily on sugar and forestry—and the country moves to its own, relaxed rhythm, regardless of any troubles in neighbouring South Africa. This difference is noticeable as soon as you cross the border. People smile more and the slight tension that you have become used to in South Africa miraculously lifts. Most visitors to Swaziland remark on this fact, and many lament that they did not allow enough time to explore the little country properly.

Travellers should note that Swaziland is malarial.

Climate

The uplands of western and central Swaziland have a generally temperate climate of hot, rainy summers and warm, dry winters. The mountains can be cold at any time of year, especially at night. Eastern Swaziland is lowveld, and has a sub-tropical climate of humid, blisteringly hot summers and a dry 'winter', where mid-afternoon temperatures can still be very high indeed.

Flora and Fauna

Despite Swaziland's small size and comparatively large population, the country has a very successful conservation policy, and big game flourishes in the several large reserves which comprise most of the country's diverse habitats and landscapes. This success is largely due to the efforts of a man called Ted Reilly, who pioneered the country's first game reserves in the 1960s. The King of Swaziland has also been instrumental in financing and promoting nature conservation, so that Swaziland's natural resources are among the best managed in southern Africa. Elephant and rhino have been re-introduced to Mkhaya, in the lowveld, as have some of the rarer antelope, such as sable and roan. Leopard still inhabit the mountain reserves and remoter reaches, and lion have been re-introduced to Hlane. Plains game species are common in all the reserves, and in Mkhaya and Mlilwane hippo and croc can still be found.

Swaziland's flora varies greatly, due to the different altitudes and their corresponding climates. Hardwood forest and grassy downland dominate the western uplands, while bushveld, with sub-tropical riverine woodland, cover the low-lying east. The Lebombo Mountains, bordering Mozambique, are also forested, and giant wild fig trees are a common sight throughout the country, especially along riverbanks.

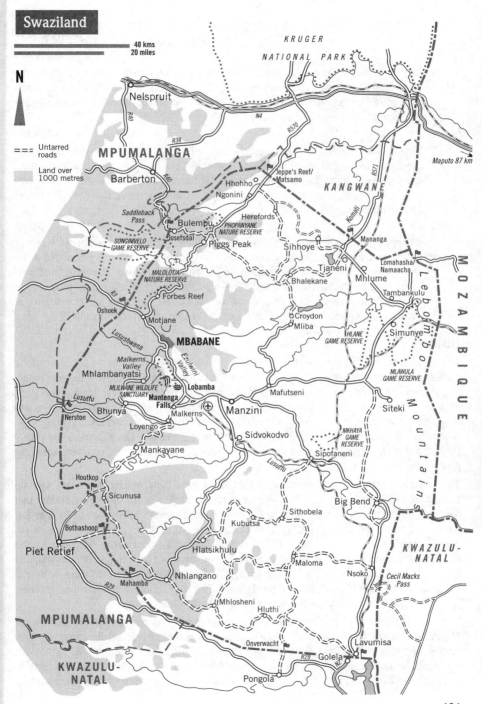

Swaziland

40 kms
20 miles

N

=== Untarred roads

Land over 1000 metres

KRUGER NATIONAL PARK

Nelspruit

MPUMALANGA

Barberton

N4

R40

R38

R40

R570

R571

Maputo 87 km

Jeppe's Reef/ Matsamo

Hhohho

Ngonini

KANGWANE

Herefords

PHOPANYANE NATURE RESERVE

Saddleback Pass

Bulempu

Josefsdal

SONGIMVELO GAME RESERVE

Piggs Peak

Sihhoye

Komati

Mananga

Lomahasha/ Namaacha

MALOLOTJA NATURE RESERVE

Forbes Reef

Bhalekane

Tjaneni

Mhlume

Tambankulu

Oshoek

R2

Motjane

Croydon

Mliba

HLANE GAME RESERVE

Simunye

Lusushwana

MBABANE

L e b o m b o

M O Z A M B I Q U E

Malkerns Valley

Mhlambanyatsi

MLILWANE WILDLIFE SANCTUARY

Ezulwini Valley

Lobamba

Mantenga Falls

MLAWULA GAME RESERVE

Lusutfu

Bhunya

Nerston

Malkerns

Mafutseni

Manzini

Siteki

M o u n t a i n

Loyengo

Sidvokodvo

MKHAYA GAME RESERVE

Mankayane

Lusutfu

Sipofaneni

Houtkop

Sicunusa

Big Bend

Bothashoop

Sithobela

KWAZULU-NATAL

Piet Retief

Kubutsa

Hlatsikhulu

Maloma

Nsoko

Cecil Macks Pass

Nhlangano

R29

Mahamba

Mhlosheni

Hluthi

MPUMALANGA

KWAZULU-NATAL

Onverwacht

Lavumisa

R29

Golela

N2

Pongola

481

currency

Swaziland has its own currency, the **elilangeni**, which exchanges 1 to 1 with the rand. Rands are accepted everywhere in Swaziland, but you will often be given change in Swazi currency. This is not accepted in South Africa, so spend all your *elilangeni* before leaving Swaziland.

language

Siswati is the Swazi language, but the visitor will seldom need to use even the simple greetings, as English is spoken almost everywhere; the Swazi education system emphasizes learning English, and, even in the countryside, most people learn it very young. However, a few greetings and phrases are always useful, if only for politeness (*see* **Language**, p.624).

safety

Swaziland is one of the safest places in southern Africa. Despite sporadic recent strikes and student political action, racial and political strife have not affected the country on anything like the same scale as South Africa. Most crimes against travellers involve simple thieving and the occasional mugging after dark in the large towns, though this is still rare. However, it is best to avoid the side-streets of Mbabane and Manzini at night, unless there are two or more of you.

History

Swaziland is known to have been inhabited for over 100,000 years. In the 1960s some of the earliest *Homo sapiens* remains ever found were excavated from the eastern Lebombo range, and from a site known as Castle Cavern in the western mountains near Malolotja Nature Reserve, where evidence was found of mining activity dating back 30,000 years. By the late Stone Age, it seems that the majority of the country was inhabited by San (bushman) groups, whose paintings can still be seen in some of the mountain caves. The San were eventually pushed out of the region by the southward migrations of large numbers of Nguni-speaking peoples between the 12th and 14th centuries.

The Swazi as a composite nation only appeared in the early 19th century, when the Ngwane tribe, displaced by the emerging Zulu empire in Natal, was led north by its paramount chief Sobhuza into modern Swaziland and the Eastern Transvaal. In the 1820s the southern end of Swaziland was overrun by repeated Zulu raids, as Shaka sent his *impis* to ravage neighbouring lands. The Swazi, under King Mswati, Sobhuza's successor, retreated to the mountains in the north of the country. Some of their number migrated up to modern-day Malawi to become, in time, the Maseko tribe, whilst those that stayed held their own until the death of the Zulu king Dingane in the 1850s, when they re-settled the southern reaches. By 1860 Mswati had re-established his people over their former range.

Now it was the turn of the Voortrekkers to make incursions into this fertile land. After Mswati's death in 1868 the Swazi were unable to prevent the Boers from annexing their land as part of the short-lived South African Republic (SAR). And when, in 1877, the SAR was taken under British control, the new King Mbandzeni was similarly powerless. Britain returned Swaziland to independence in 1881, but did nothing to stop whites from settling where they wished. As most of the country was, and still is, owned by the king, this undermined the monarchy's prestige, and Swazi culture seemed threatened with fragmentation.

In 1889 Mbandzeni died, leaving his queen and infant son to deal with the increasing white settlement. The SAR resumed government of Swaziland in 1895, but Mbandzeni's surviving queen, Libotsibeni, set out to get the land back, actively encouraging young Swazi men to go to the booming Transvaal gold reefs to make money with which to buy land back from the white settlers. Libotsibeni was helped in her quest by the Anglo-Boer War, which forced the Boers to withdraw from Swaziland, to be replaced in 1903 by a loose British administration. Her strategy of buying land went unopposed by the British Special Commissioners appointed to govern the country and, by 1921, when her son Sobhuza II acceded to the throne, Swaziland was largely owned by the Swazi, with title deeds that would stand up before a British court.

Sobhuza continued to work quietly towards independence, absorbing British institutions into the traditional Swazi government of absolute monarchy. In 1960 he proposed the forming of a Legislative Council, based on European law, and a National Council, based on Swazi culture, to work side by side—a sort of double house similar to Westminster, with the monarch as head of state. The King also held the right of veto, but political parties were allowed. When elections were eventually held in 1964 and 1967, the National Movement (called Mbokovdo), a party that preached independence, won both.

When independence followed in 1968 Swaziland slipped into it with few of the problems that have beset other southern African countries shrugging off colonial rule. This is partly because the clan in power represents almost all the country's inhabitants—unlike most African countries, where independence has often been followed by wars to establish which of several clans should take power.

Some claim that this lack of social strife has been no more than subservience to monarchical rule, but it is hard to contest the apparent good reasoning behind many of the monarch's decisions, and the people's apparent satisfaction with them. For example, King Sobhuza and the two councils adopted a strictly non-racist policy for their legislature in the 1960s, re-wrote the British-proposed national constitution in 1973, making it conform to Swazi culture, and formed a parliament. Nature conservation, progressive agriculture, water conservation and forestry were all promoted, and today Swaziland's natural resources are among the best-administered in Africa.

This rational approach has continued under King Mswati III (acceded 1986), who has tolerated political parties opposed to the monarchy, even though they are officially illegal. He continues to maintain rule with a comparatively light hand, despite his immense power in terms of Swaziland's natural wealth, almost all of which is owned by the Crown. As a result the monarchy continues to be popular with the majority of Swazis, though there is a growing anti-monarchist movement that may yet emerge into a fully fledged opposition.

Swazi Culture

Swaziland is one of the few African countries that seem to have successfully married Western culture with their own. Despite its westernized towns, rural life in Swaziland is, like most southern African cultures, based around cattle, a patriarchal system of headmen and elders, and ancestor worship (mixed now with evangelical Christianity). However, the most striking aspect of Swazi culture is the absolute power that still rests with the monarchy. Not only does the Swazi king still directly control the government and economy, but the nation still swears him fealty every year at a great festival known as the *Ncwala*, a moveable feast which usually occurs at the end of December or beginning of January, when the rainy season is in full swing. The *Ncwala*, or 'First Fruit' ceremony, is a combination of harvest festival and symbolic renewal of the monarchy and Swazi nation presided over by the King. The *Ncwala* lasts for four days, but its preparation time is in fact, much longer, as holy water must first be gathered from the sea at Maputo in Mozambique, and from the Crocodile River in Mpumalanga. A large number of chosen youths then spend three days building a royal kraal from acacia branches—which must not wilt or die after being cut from the tree, as this is taken to mean that the youth in question is impure (having seduced a married woman or impregnated a virgin, both crimes in Swazi culture). On the third day a young bull is released among the youths who must attack, fell and kill it using only their fists. On the fourth day, the King eats the first fruits of the new harvest in front of his youths, the hut of acacia branches and the King's bedding and household items are burned, and the King dances before his people. Great fires are built on the surrounding hills—offerings to the rain gods—and, amid feasts and general dancing, the new year can then begin. The *Ncwala* always takes place at the Royal Kraal at Lobamba in the Ezulwini Valley. Spectators are allowed at some parts of the ceremony, but photographs are forbidden.

Another annual ceremony is the *Umhlanga*, or Reed Dance (held in August or September), a week-long festival to initiate unmarried maidens into womanhood and eligibility for marriage. Again, a large number of the nation's young unmarried women gather at the Royal Kraal, and the ceremony is presided over by the Queen Mother. The *Umhlanga* used to double as a sort of human livestock show of potential wives for the King. Young women related to the royal family are particularly in evidence, and are identified by the purple lourie feathers they wear in their hair. Spectators of the *Umhlanga* are free to take photographs.

Swaziland also has its own traditional popular culture in the form of a dance known as *sibhaca*, which has evolved into something of a national sport. Teams of young men, often from schools and colleges, compete at traditional ceremonies and agricultural shows all over Swaziland, with an annual championship at the Manzini Trade Fair, every August or September. The Swazi Sun Hotel, in the Ezulwini Valley, near the capital, Mbabane, maintains two teams of *sibhaca* dancers, and displays are put on twice a week (*see* below). *Sibhaca* dancing is a thrilling sight: the troupe provides a rhythmic backdrop for each member in turn to come forward and perform a fast, high-kicking solo, before returning to the troupe as another takes his place without a break in the rhythm. One white Swazilander I spoke to dismissed the dancing as 'all for the tourists', but that hardly seemed to dim the enjoyment of either the dancers or the audience.

Like many other Nguni-speaking cultures in and around the Transvaal, Swaziland has a strong tradition of rural occultism. The government even has a national school to train *inyangas* (diviners—usually male) and *sangomas* (herbalists and healers—usually female) at Siteki, in the far east of the country, under the Lebombo Mountains, and travellers can visit the school by prior arrangement through Swazi Tourism in Mbabane (*see* below). However, not all of Swaziland's traditional *inyanga* and *sangoma* culture is so high-profile, and some aspects are downright morbid. The most extreme evidence of this darker side are '*muti*' murders—ritual murders to acquire human body parts for magical purposes. As recently as the 1980s, several cases of *muti* murder came to light, usually of children. Most people who have lived in Swaziland for any length of time will have a story of brushing with the occult, in however intangible a form, but they tend to over-emphasize this side of Swaziland's strong spiritualist culture, and it has never reached the epidemic proportions said to have occurred in Venda and Lebowa further north.

Getting There and Around

All visitors must have a valid passport to enter Swaziland, and visas are issued gratis at the border posts. Drivers will be expected to pay a small charge for road tax.

by air

Royal Swazi Airlines run daily flights to Mbabane from Jo'burg and Durban, as well as from Harare in Zimbabwe, Gaberone in Botswana, Lusaka in Zambia and Maputo in Mozambique.

by car

Of the four main entry points into Swaziland, Oshoek, Mahamba and Lavumisa are open 7am–10pm. Josefsdal and the several minor entry posts are generally open 8–4. The most direct way in from Jo'burg is via the N4 to Carolina, then the R38, R451 and R39 to Mbabane, through Oshoek, the largest and busiest of the border posts. In the north, Jeppe's Reef (called Matsamo in Swaziland) is reached by the R570 which connects with the N4 just south of the Kruger National Park. Mahamba entry point is along the R29 from Piet Retief. There are two entry points from Natal: Lavumisa, at the very end of the N2, and another from northern Zululand via the Cecil Macks Pass over the Lebombo Mountains. This is rough, and not always passable for ordinary vehicles. The most picturesque route is the dirt R40 over the Saddleback Pass to Josefsdal, winding up through forest and grassland and with breathtaking views out over the Transvaal and the large Songimvelo Game Reserve.

Swaziland has good roads; even the gravel roads are generally in good condition and do not require a 4x4. Mbabane and Manzini are connected by the Ezulwini Valley Road, along which most of the country's traffic goes. There is one border post with Mozambique, at Namaacha in the east of the country, an easy 85km drive to Maputo. Visas must be bought from the Mozambiquan embassy in Mbabane before leaving Swaziland. These take about a week to process (you need two photos) and cost around R40.

by bus

Transstate, ✆ (011) 773 6002, a sub-company of TransLux, runs buses to and from Jo'burg and Manzini, Swaziland's second city, via Piet Retief and Mbabane. Transstate buses also run between Durban and Pongola. If you get off at the little town of Golela, it is an easy taxi-ride or hitch across the border at Lavumisa. Both bus services run several times per week.

Swaziland has a good, if irregular, internal bus network between the main towns. Buses are cheap, but slow.

Swaziland is also on the **Baz Bus** route, ✆ (021) 439 23231.

There is no passenger rail link with South Africa, nor within Swaziland itself.

by taxi

Black taxis are quicker and more frequent than buses and cost a little more, but have a high accident rate. Ordinary taxi firms within Mbabane are: **City Taxis**, ✆ (268) 43 084, and **Mbabane Taxis**, ✆ (268) 45 707.

hitch-hiking

Swaziland is one of the best areas of southern Africa for hitching. Drivers are generally not afraid to pick up hitchers, even after dark. However, some mountain roads see little traffic, and hitchers may experience long waits. As anywhere, women should think twice about hitching alone.

by tour group

Swaziland has two good local tour companies, both whom know the country intimately, and both of whom also offer forays into neighbouring Zululand and Mpumalanga. **Umhlanga Tours**, ✆ (268) 61 431, are based in the Royal Swazi Sun, Ezulwini Valley. **Swazi Trails**, ✆ (268) 62 180, run trails all over the country from Sondzela Lodge, in Mlilwane Game Reserve, in the Ezulwini Valley.

Mbabane

✆ *(268–)*, ✆ *(09268–) from South Africa*   **Tourist Information**

The **tourist office**, Swazi Plaza, ✆ 42 531 or 44 556, is at the south end of Mbabane on the road parallel to and west of Western Distributor Road.

The **post office** is on Warmer Street, which connects with the south end of Allister Miller. You can make international calls from here.

Mbabane, capital city of Swaziland, lies at the north end of the Ezulwini Valley, the traditional seat of the Swazi Royal Family since the mid 18th century. Although a pleasant town, Mbabane has little in its tiny centre to interest the traveller, beyond shopping for supplies before heading off to the nature reserves, or visiting the restaurants and/or nightclubs. There are no museums or indeed any specific tourist facilities in Mbabane, except for the **Tourist Office** in the brand new Swazi Plaza, which sits opposite The Mall, just out of the town centre. The Tourist Office has detailed information on nature reserves, hikes, traditional Swazi activities etc. It is also worth going to one of the hotel bars at night, as people are very approachable, and you can tap into the local information network with ease.

Swaziland did not change its street and town names after independence, and the main street is still called **Allister Miller** after the first European to be born here. Most of the banks, shops and take-away places are found here. For those shopping for authentic Swazi crafts, the **Mbabane Market** is worth a morning visit. Prices are cheaper than in South Africa. Head for the Jabula Inn on Allister Miller, and cross over to Msunduza Street.

The **Mozambiquan Embassy**, ✆ 43 700 (*open Mon–Fri 9–1*), is useful for buying visas for Mozambique at far cheaper rates than in South Africa. The embassy is on a dirt road reached from the town centre by following the Manzini road to the sign for the Mountain Inn, turning left, left and left again. Visas take about a week. Spend no more than a night in Mbabane, as Swaziland's real pleasures lie further afield.

© (268–), ©(09268–) from South Africa

Where to Stay

expensive

Just south of town, overlooking the Ezulwini Valley, are the **Swazi Inn**, © 42 235, and the **Mountain Inn**, © 42 781. The Swazi Inn is posh and rather formal, mostly filled with wealthy South African tourists, while the Mountain Inn seems to attract more business travellers, and can be good for bar-room conversation. Both offer clean, comfortable rooms with private bathrooms, decent restaurants, a pool and gardens. Both are only moderately expensive.

moderate

City Inn, on Allister Miller Street, © 42 406, is a good spot for meeting locals and finding out about nightlife. Also try the **Taverna Hotel**, © 42 341, on Gilfillan St.

cheap

The Chillage, on the corner of Gilson Road and Nicholson Crescent, © 48 342, is a backpackers' on the Baz Bus Route, offering dorms, doubles and camping.

Hill Street Lodge, on Hill Street, © 46 342, is in a residential district west of the town centre. There are pleasant, comfortable rooms with shared bathrooms.

Dirt-cheap accommodation can be found at two hostels, the **Thokose Centre**, on Mhlanhla Road (parallel with Allister Miller Street and reached from there via Walker Street), © 46 681, and the **Youth Centre**, on Isomi Street, at the far south-eastern end of town, © 42176. Both require a short taxi ride, and offer clean, safe accommodation. Ring first to make sure there is space. If these are full, try the even cheaper **Sebenda Institute**, on Sitwanshini Street (currently no telephone).

© (268–), ©(09268–) from South Africa

Eating Out

expensive

Most of the area's good expensive restaurants are out in the Ezulwini Valley. The **Swazi Inn** © 42 235, and the **Mountain Inn**, © 42 781, have good à la carte restaurants offering a standard range of dishes. More popular with the locals is the **Hwa Li** Chinese restaurant on the corner of Walker Street and Tin Street, in Mbabane, which serves really good Chinese food.

moderate and cheap

Oddly enough, Mbabane has an interesting range of cheaper restaurants. **Maxim's** serves reasonably priced steaks, pizzas and pasta (at indoor and outdoor tables) in a friendly atmosphere. Locals often eat here before going to the nightclub attached to the hotel of the same name.

The **Indinglizi Gallery and Restaurant**, on Johnstone Street, © 42 613, serves wholefood breakfast and lunch only, in a friendly, bohemian atmosphere. (Inside and outside tables.) Local Swazi artists and craftspeople exhibit here regularly. **Marco's Trattoria**, on Allister Miller, ✆ 45 029, serves good, cheap Italian food with a choice of tables inside or on a balcony.

The oddly named **Mediterranean Restaurant**, ✆ 43 212, also on Allister Miller, is an Indian restaurant serving reasonable southern Indian food at very low prices. Good Portuguese food is offered at **Lorenço Marques**, ✆ 43 097, again on Allister Miller, with the standard spicy chicken peri-peri and fried seafood dishes predominating. In The Mall, opposite the Swazi Plaza, is the **Casserole**, ✆ 46 425, which serves decent German and French dishes. Cheapest of all is the **Copacabana**, on the corner of Warmer and Allister Miller Streets, run by Mozambiquan Portuguese, serving basic but very tasty food.

Nightlife

Mbabane has a few lively clubs, some of which have live music. **Maxim's** is one of the most popular, with a disco through the week and live acts at weekends. Smaller nightclubs come and go and it is worth asking locals in the bars. About 15km out of town, on the Ezulwini Valley Road, is the **Why Not? Disco**, in the Happy Valley Motel, an unashamed pick-up joint that is light-hearted and fun. Bands from Jo'burg are sometimes booked to play here, and these can range from township jive, to hard rock, to easy listening.

The Ezulwini Valley

Between Mbabane and Manzini runs Swaziland's vibrant Royal Valley, site of the Royal Palace. Traffic streams continually between the hotels, restaurants, camp sites, curio shops, health spas and craft workshops that crowd along the road. Yet despite such densely packed human activity the valley is still green and beautiful and you do not have to venture far into the hills on either side of the road before finding yourself again surrounded by traditional rural land or wild country.

It only takes about half an hour to drive the valley, so it is worth cruising along once just to take it all in. By picking up one of the many locals who hitch regularly along between the two towns, you will have access to any local information you need.

In the centre of the valley is **Lobamba**, the large, modern royal palace for the King and his household, and the **National Museum**. Both are signposted from the main road, opposite the entrance sign for the Mlilwane Wildlife Sanctuary. Lobamba is not open to visitors, and photographs are prohibited. However, it is here that the *Ncwala* and *Umhlalanga* dances are held, and on the latter occasion tourists can enter the Royal Kraal in front of the palace and take as many photos of the dancers as they wish. The National Museum has a good, concise display explaining Swazi customs, both royal and commoner, Swazi ritual and belief, and some history.

Further up the road from here are the **Mantenga Falls**, an impressive set of large cascades. Sadly, this is one of Swaziland's few tourist spots to have a reputation for danger; people have been attacked here. So be vigilant and visit in a group if possible. The road up to the Falls is badly maintained and can be difficult to negotiate in an ordinary car.

Off the main road, opposite the turn-off to Lobamba, is **Mlilwane Wildlife Sanctuary**. This large stretch of grassland, forest and mountainside was the first of Swaziland's wildlife refuges to be pioneered by Ted Reilly, the man behind most of the country's nature conservation programmes. Mlilwane used to be his family's massive estate, and Reilly donated it to the country for the preservation of wildlife back in the 1960s.

Despite being so close to the busy Ezulwini Valley the reserve is quiet and wild, and is home to white rhino, buffalo, giraffe, impala, zebra, blue wildebeest, eland, waterbuck, duiker and mountain reedbuck. There are a few shy leopard and spotted hyena. Warthog are so common that one family has become semi-tame and has taken up residence outside the reserve's office, shop and picnic area, which overlooks a hippo pool. There are crocodiles in the lakes further into the reserve.

Mlilwane has excellent **hiking, mountain biking** and **horse trails** among the game. There is self-catering accommodation in cottages, a backpackers' hostel, and a camp site. Prices range from cheap to moderate. Tame blue cranes wander between the cottages.

The Ezulwini Valley is a good place to buy Swazi jewellery, wool and mohair clothing, printed cloths, baskets and carvings. There are several shops along the main road all selling work by locals, and run by locals. **Siswati Crafts**, on the east side of the main road just north of the turn-offs to Lobamba and Mlilwane, is a good place to start; its range is wide and its prices are very low compared to the more upmarket craft shops in Mbabane, while its goods are as authentic as those in the Mbabane and Manzini markets. Also well worth visiting is the **Mantenga Craft Centre**.

The **Swazi Spa Health and Beauty Studio** is a real gem. On the west side of the road north of the two Sun hotels, it offers a very reasonably priced sauna, qualified masseurs and other treats, but its real attraction is the large outdoor mineral bath: a pool fed by a mineral spring that bubbles out at about 40°C. It has an awful name—the Cuddle Puddle—but anyone can swim there for about R2 (buy your ticket at the entrance). It is a good place to meet locals, especially in the evenings when people go there for a relaxing dip after work. There are changing rooms and a safe place to leave clothes and valuables.

℡ (268–), ℡(09268–) from South Africa   ***Activities***

Walking, mountain biking and hiking: Mlilwane Wildlife Sanctuary, ℡ 61 591–3, or ℡ 61 165, has self-guided walking trails through montane forest and upland grassveld. Trails are from 1 to 3 hours, and the game/bird spotting is good.

Riding: Mlilwane offers guided riding trails through its lowland grassland, taking the rider quite close to game. Trails last about an hour. **High Hopes Riding Stables**, ℡ 84 364, at the far southern end of the valley, just before the town of Manzini (look out for the signpost on the western side of the road), has very good horses for trail rides into the surrounding mountains, and lessons in dressage and jumping by well-qualified, friendly staff. All riding levels can be catered for.

There is a lot of riding in the Ezulwini Valley. If High Hopes can't accommodate you, try **Ezulwini Stables**, ℡ 61 001, **Hanlana Stables**, ℡ 24 109 or **Nyanza Stables**, ℡ 83 090.

expensive

Swaziland's most expensive hotels are on the valley's main road: the **Royal Swazi Sun**, ℘ 61 001, the **Ezulwini Sun**, and the **Lugongo Sun**, both ℘ 61 201, all offer the usual bland 5 star Sun luxury, but have bars and restaurants that are convenient to visit after a dip in the Swazi Spa's mineral pool. All hotels have casinos.

moderate

Mlilwane Wildlife Sanctuary, ℘ 44 541, has clean, neat self-catering accommodation in huts, and a cheaper camp site with ablution blocks. All overlook a hippo pool, and tame warthogs root around between the buildings. If you do not have a car, hitch or take a bus or taxi to the Mlilwane signpost on the valley's main road, then walk the 10 minutes to the park entrance from where the ranger will arrange transport into the reserve.

The **Mantenga Falls Lodge**, ℘ 61 049, is a small hotel, just east of the National Museum on the road to the Mantenga Waterfall. The rooms are cosy, and the food very good. The **Happy Valley Motel**, ℘ 61 061, on the main road, is a notorious pick-up joint and prostitutes' hang-out. The **Why Not? Disco** attached is, for this reason, extremely popular. You will hear so much about this place, and it should be visited. You are likely to be approached in the bar by any number of prostitutes, some heart-breakingly beautiful. The rooms are clean and some have separate bathrooms.

The **Mgenule Hotel**, ℘ 61 041, is cheaper, and very close to Mbabane, with clean, unpretentious rooms, a pool and (of all things) an Indian restaurant, while **Smoky Mountain Village**, ℘ 61 291, has a group of attractive, self-contained A-frame log cabins set well back from the road.

cheap

Sonzela Lodge, ℘ 61 165, is a backpackers' set inside Mlilwane Wildlife Sanctuary. From here you can hike, ride or mountain bike among the game, as well as arrange white-water rafting trips down the Usutu River in the Swazi lowveld. The Baz Bus stops at Sondzela. If arriving independently, make sure you do so before 5.30pm, when the sanctuary shuts its gates for the night. It's a great place, with dorms, doubles and camping.

Another backpacker lodge in the Valley is **Khayaletfu**, ℘ 87 225, signposted from the main Mbabane–Manzini road. They are also on the Baz Bus. If you arrive too late to make it to Sondzela, this is a good fall-back. They also run trips into Mlilwane, to Mkhaya Game Reserve and Hlane National Park, in the lowveld, and up to the Khomati Valley, near Piggs Peak. Rafting on the Usutu River can also be arrranged, as can paragliding, near Piggs Peak, at Malolotja Nature Reserve.

Jimmy's Bar and Paradise Caravan Park, ℘ 84 935, is 7km north of Manzini on the main road, and offers very cheap camping, or a bed in a caravan. **Timbali Caravan Park**, ℘ 61 156, has a variety of accommodation, from camp sites with ablution blocks to self-contained chalets that are cheap if shared.

All the hotels in the valley have reasonable restaurants priced according to their level of accommodation. However, it is worth visiting the moderately priced **First Horse Restaurant**, ☎ 61 137, and **Yen Saan**, ☎ 61 051/2, both in the same enclave of shops signposted west of the main valley road near Mbabane. The First Horse is an Indian restaurant with a very colonial feel that serves excellent curries. The Yen Saan offers good Chinese food in an informal atmosphere, and is popular with Mbabane's younger crowd. Also moderate is the **Calabash**, ☎ 61 187, at Timbali Caravan Park, and which, despite its African name, serves German and Austrian food.

Manzini

At the southern end of the Ezulwini Valley, Manzini is Swaziland's commercial hub, and is slightly larger than Mbabane. Newly built industrial complexes surround the old centre that, in 1890, was the Boer capital of the region. When the British took over, they moved the capital to Mbabane for its cooler climate (Mbabane sits higher than Manzini). Today Manzini is known as the only seriously rough town in the country, though only at night.

However, Manzini does have a daily **Craft Market**, on Mnlakuvne Street, one block south of Ngwane, the main road. Country people travel for miles to sell their wares, some of which are very beautiful indeed. Apart from this, there are banks, shops and some restaurants, but Manzini is not recommended as a place to stay; visit the craft market on your way through.

☎ *(268–), ☎(09268–) from South Africa*   ***Where to Stay and Eating Out***

The Ezulwini Valley's accommodation is conveniently close to Manzini, but if you do have to stay in town the **New George Hotel**, on Ngwane Street, ☎ 52 061, offers fairly expensive accommodation in a bland, uninteresting modern complex. More moderately priced are the **Prince Velebantfu Hotel**, at the Mbabane end of the Ngwane Road, on the south side of town, ☎ 46 465, and the **Mozambique Motel**, on the corner of Meintjies Street and Mahleko Street, ☎ 52 489 or 52 586, one block north of Ngwane. The bars of both hotels are patronized by locals, and both have safe parking.

Gil Vicente's Restaurant, on Mahleko Street, ☎ 53 871, one block north of Ngwane, offers Portuguese Mozambiquan dishes such as chicken peri-peri and spiced seafood at good prices. No need to book.

The Malkerns Valley

Just southwest of the Ezulwini Valley runs the Malkerns Valley, a more rural area of stock farms, orchards and forest, all quite beautifully landscaped under the western mountains. The valley is not long, but it has one small town, **Mhlambanyatsi**, an old-fashioned farming settlement with three very good small hotels and restaurants (*see* below). All can arrange **hiking** and **riding** through the valley and into the mountains, and sometimes **trout fishing**. One of the most tranquil areas of rural southern Africa, the Malkerns Valley hotels are favourites among Swazilanders from the city, and driving out to Mhlambanyatsi for Sunday lunch has become something of a tradition.

Mhlambanyatsi has three charming country hotels with walks and rides up into the farmlands. **Meikles Mount**, ✆ 74 110, has a moderately priced, self-contained cottage, with walking, riding and trout fishing, at the foot of a forested mountainside. The **Forester's Arms Hotel**, ✆ 74 177, is more expensive, and justly famous for its food, particularly the hearty Sunday lunches of roast beef and Yorkshire pud. **Malandela's**, ✆ 83 115, is a restaurant offering quite expensive country cooking in a farmhouse in the centre of the valley, with lovely walking on the farm.

Northwest Swaziland: the Mountain Country

North of Mbabane the landscape changes dramatically, rising to high mountains and huge sweeps of empty country. On the road to the small town of Piggs Peak is the fabulously beautiful **Malolotja Nature Reserve**, ✆ 61 171, a huge chunk of open upland cut by deep, forested valleys where cold, clear streams run, and game abounds. Malolotja is a paradise for the hiker: a series of trails winds through the 18,000 acre reserve. On these you are unlikely to meet any other humans, but zebra, warthog, vervet monkey, baboon, grey rhebok, reedbuck, oribi, klipspringer, blesbok, hartebeest, blue and black wildebeest and duiker can be encountered at any time. There are marked camping spots under trees, and you can walk for up to four days without exhausting the trails. Leopard, lynx and jackal thrive in the reserve, as do a host of birds, from the large raptors such as black and crowned eagle, to small sugarbirds. Blue cranes breed here, and the large Stanley's bustard is a regular sight. Protea forests, similar to those found in the Drakensberg, crowd close to the streams. Rare cycads—prehistoric giant tree-ferns—dot the grasslands.

For those who do not want to hike overnight, there are chalets and camp sites with an ablution block near the park. But the really beautiful country begins about two hours' walk from here. If you are planning to make a hiking trip at some time during your holiday, this should be high on your list. Trails must be booked in advance and you must have your own tent and stove, as fires are not allowed. The water from the mountain streams is safe to drink. The mountains in Malolotja are high; two of the peaks exceed 1800m, and the area is known to archaeologists for its relics of early man found in the Lion's Cave, where people were mining over 43,000 years ago. Bear in mind that this reserve can be very cold at night, and remember to take a waterproof in case of sudden weather changes.

Further along the road from Malolotja, after Piggs Peak, the country becomes forested. Most is commercial, but a hidden stretch of magical indigenous forest lies along the 3km-long Phopanyane Waterfall, inside the **Phopanyane Nature Reserve**, ✆ 71 319 (also *see* **Mpumalanga**, p.574). Look out for the signposted turning after the sign for the Piggs Peak Hotel. This leads about 10km down a forestry road to another sign for the reserve entrance, a further 2km down a steep hill. Phopanyane is friendly, relaxed and one of the loveliest places to stay in southern Africa. Although you can enter as a day visitor, the place is so beautiful that a stay of at least one night is recommended. The reserve is run privately by Rod de Vletter, who was born and brought up in Swaziland, and has been closely involved in education and nature conservation for the past 20 years. Phopanyane has been lovingly created by him; there are trails through the hardwood forest and bushveld on both sides of the falls, wildflowers grow in abundance, and there are landscaped gardens. Bushbuck and duiker are abundant, and the reserve is a good place to spot the colourful narina trogon, as well as green and (if you are very lucky) the rare purple-crested lourie. Phopanyane should not be missed.

℗ *(268–)*, ℗*(09268–) from South Africa*   **Where to Stay and Eating Out**

Phopanyane Nature Reserve, ℗ 71 319, has three luxurious cottages and comfortable safari tents (fully equipped with electricity and water) hidden in the forest close to the Phopanyane Falls. There is a choice of self-catering, half or full board, but the small restaurant and bar is very good, serving light to full meals with an emphasis on tasty wholefood, served with home-grown vegetables and home-cooked breads. Teas with home-baked cakes are also a speciality.

Malolotja Nature Reserve, ℗ 61 171, offers moderate to cheap self-catering accommodation in comfortable log cabins, as well as camping.

The **Piggs Peak Protea**, ℗ 71 104, towards the northern border, about 5km further up the road from Phopanyane, is a glitzy casino hotel full of noisy fruit machines and a few gaming tables, and expensive, rather bland rooms. While the hotel is comfortable enough, it should only be used if the above two places are fully booked.

Eastern Swaziland: the Lowveld

The hot, subtropical eastern Lowlands are a world apart from the temperate hills of western Swaziland. Along the main road from Manzini to the sugar-cane processing town of **Big Bend**, the altitude falls dramatically and the temperature rises by the minute. Bushveld replaces the grassy plains, interspersed with vast sugar-cane growing estates. Despite its name, Big Bend is no more than a mill surrounded by houses for the plant workers, with a couple of small hotels. It is for the lowveld's superb stretches of wild country that travellers visit the area, particularly its three game reserves, Mkhaya, Hlane and Mlawula.

Mkhaya Game Reserve, ℗ 44 541, 55km along the road from Manzini to Big Bend, is a centre for breeding rare African species. *Mkhaya* is the Swazi name for the weird, spike-trunked knob-thorn tree, which thrives here. Bookings must be made in advance, whether for overnight stays or for a day visit, as only very small parties are allowed in. Accommodation is in a luxurious tented camp in a riverine fig forest. Mkhaya is known for rhino—both black and white—and harbours such rare antelope species as roan, sable and tsessebe. There is a small elephant herd, and buffalo are common. Crocodile and hippo swim in the pools. Zebra, giraffe and other plains game are prolific. There are leopard and hyena. The game drives at Mkhaya are particularly good for getting you close to game, sometimes uncomfortably so, and there are guided walks in the evening. The catering is of the highest standard, despite the kitchen being in the deep bush. No vehicles other than those belonging to the reserve are allowed in Mkhaya, and visitors must leave their cars at the entrance lodge, from which one of the reserve's open-top Land-Rovers will take them to the bush camp, and out into the veld for a game drive. Those staying overnight can also take a guided game-walk morning or evening.

Mkhaya also offers **white-water rafting** trips in the Bulungu Gorge nearby, an experience rated by white-water enthusiasts as one of the best south of the Zambezi. These are also bookable in advance. Trips run year-round and include abseiling down into the gorge. They can be booked through **Sondzela Lodge**, ✆ 61 165, the backpackers' lodge in Mlilwane Wildlife Sanctuary.

All in all, Mkhaya, although not cheap, and despite the fact that it has no big cats as yet, offers a similar quality of safari to the very expensive private game reserves of Mpumalanga, at far cheaper rates.

Hlane Game Reserve, ✆ 44 541, about 100km north of Big Bend, is cheaper than Mkhaya. This large reserve of classic bushveld country supports elephant, white rhino, giraffe, zebra, kudu and most plains game. Cheetah have been re-introduced and there are lion. Spotted hyena and leopard are present, but shy. The lakes have a few hippo. Formerly a royal hunting reserve, Hlane was donated by King Sobhuza II in 1967. There is a network of game-viewing roads, and guided early-morning walks. Accommodation is in self-catering chalets and there is a camp site with ablution blocks. Elephant and rhino often visit the camp's water-hole, and semi-tame ostriches wander about, sometimes unnervingly close. Be aware that Hlane has no shops or fuel. Gates are open sunrise to sunset.

Mlawula Game Reserve, ✆ 61 151 or 61 178/9, lies just east of Hlane, in the foothills of the Lebombo Mountains bordering Mozambique. The two reserves are linked via a good tar road straddled by the small town of Simunye, where all supplies can be bought, and which has a bank and a post office. The reserve is seldom visited, and worth going to just for its seclusion. Accommodation is in two camp sites with very basic ablution blocks, which are often left unattended. Walking trails run thoughout the reserve, which supports mostly antelope and zebra though there are (shy) spotted hyena and

leopard, and hippo and crocodile in the Mbuluzi River, which runs along the northern boundary. At the camp site by the railway crossing the reserve you can arrange game drives and guided walks to a 'vulture restaurant'—a baited rock where you can watch the scavengers jostle over carrion. Like Malolotja Nature Reserve, the mountains at Mlawula have yielded some important archaeological finds—human remains dating back to about 110,000 years ago, among the earliest human remains found anywhere in the world. Although not quite so primitive now, Mlawula still lacks fuel and supplies, so stock up before you go.

Siteki is a tiny town at the far eastern end of the country, set under the Lebombos, and connected with Manzini by a good, tarred road. Although the town is so small, it is known for its *Inyanga* and *Sangoma* **School**, which is run by the government to train traditional doctors and diviners (over 80 per cent of Swazilanders regularly consult the holders of both offices). The school is a fascinating mix of spiritualism, botany and natural science, all held in a strangely ordered, institutional framework. A visit here is imperative if you are in the area. Visits to the school must be arranged in advance, either through the Siteki Hotel, ✆ 34 126, or Swazi Tourism in Mbabane, ✆ 44 556.

Outside Siteki is the appropiately named **Muti-Muti Nature Reserve**, run by Eco-Africa Safaris at Phopanyane, ✆ 71 319. The word *muti* is generally used for both folk-medicine and magic in South Africa, and the reserve's proximity to Siteki's *Inyanga* and *Sangoma* School only partly explains the name. Within the reserve grow a variety of herbs and roots used by *sangomas* for part of their work, and the Eco-Africa guides who take you into the reserve can point out many of them, and know their remedial and ritual uses. Muti-Muti covers an extensive wild area of differing landscapes, including hardwood forest, savannah, rocky hills and cliffs. Over 200 bird species have been recorded. (*This reserve is temporarily closed to tourists. Check whether it has re-opened when you get to Swaziland.*)

✆ (268–), ✆(09268–) from South Africa   **Activities**

Hiking: Day and overnight trails (without overnight huts) can be found at **Mlawula Game Reserve**, ✆ 61 151 or 61 178/9. The trails wind through dense bush, well populated with game, and climb up into the Lebombos. Otherwise, if you get detailed maps from Swazi Tourism in Mbabane, ✆ 44 556, you can hike from village to village in the lowveld, and either camp by permission, or rent a hut for the night at each village you arrive in. Guided game walks are offered in **Hlane Game Reserve**, ✆ 44 541, with a good chance of seeing elephant or rhino, and short evening walks are part of the package at **Mkhaya Game Reserve**, ✆ 44 541.

Canoeing and White-water rafting: Mkhaya Game Reserve organizes trips down the Bulungu Gorge all year round. Choose between regular 8-man rafts or a wilder ride in a 2-man inflatable. You can also abseil. Book via Sondzela, ✆ 61 165.

✆ (268–), ✆(09268–) from South Africa   **Where to Stay and Eating Out**

expensive

Mkhaya Game Reserve, ✆ 44 541, offers a luxurious tented camp with first-class chefs and a bar, set under the giant trees of a wild fig forest. You have to book at least a day in advance, however, and leave your car at the reserve's gate (there is safe parking here), before being taken in by an open Land-Rover.

moderate

Hlane Game Reserve, ☎ 44 541, offers self-contained stone cottages in its main camp, which overlooks a waterhole where elephant and rhino gather in the evenings, while the **Siteki Hotel**, ☎ 34 126, offers more standard accommodation in an old-fashioned family-run hotel with an *à la carte* restaurant and bar. The **Bend Inn**, and the **Riverside Motel**, ☎ 36 012, both offer good, clean rooms, some en suite, with a bar and restaurant. Of the two, the Riverside Motel is the more popular with locals, who use the bar as a pub, and discos are occasionally held here.

cheap

Mlawula and **Hlane** Game Reserves both have camp sites with ablution facilities, and Hlane's cottages, if divided between two or more people, fall into the cheap category. Accommodation in both reserves is self-catering only.

The Grand Valley and Usutu Forest

From Manzini south to the little town of Hlatikulu runs the Mkhondvo River, whose valley (known as the **Grand Valley**) is forested, with an overhanging mountain. This route is accessible via a good tarred road connecting Manzini with the southwestern border post of Mahamba and the town of Piet Retief over the border.

The Grand Valley serves as more of a scenic drive than a place to be explored in depth, unless you speak Siswati, or have a Swazi guide who can take you into the villages. You can make it a round trip by heading south past **Hlastikulu** for about 6km, then turning off onto the good dirt road heading north to **Mankayane**, which also passes through some very spectacular country. From here continue north to **Loyengo**, where you meet the tarred road. Head west through the little town of **Bhunya** and look out for the signs for the massive **Usutu Forest**, whose 65,000ha of plantation and indigenous trees hide a wealth of interesting things, such as bushman paintings, forest trails and waterfalls. The signposted road takes you to the forest station, from where maps can be obtained, but it is easier to take a guide, as getting lost in the forest is easy.

From Usutu, head back to Bhunya, where the tarred road forks, and take the north road to Mhlambanyatsi and the Malkerns Valley. You can either stay here (*see* above) or make the short trip back northeast to Mbabane.

Activities

Hiking: The Usutu Forest has a good network of day trails, some of which follow the course of the fast-flowing Lusutfu River, while others head off to caves with bushman paintings. Follow the signs to the forest station, or organize a guide by asking around locally; if this doesn't work try through a tour operator, but it's rather pot luck.

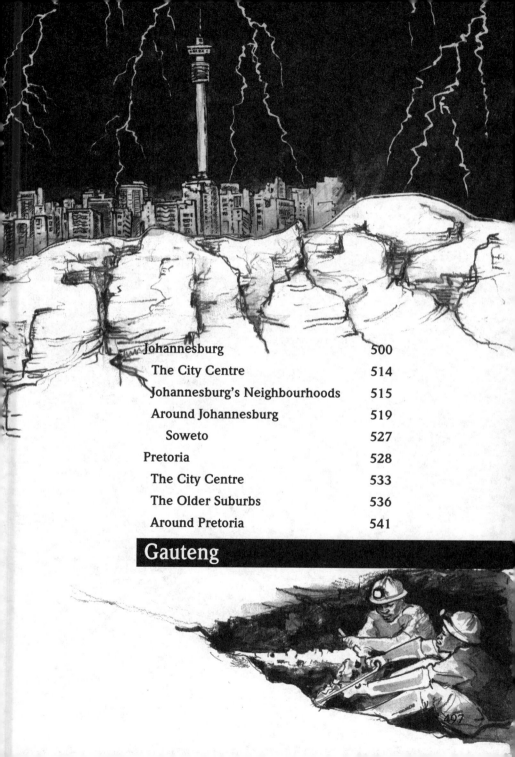

Gauteng

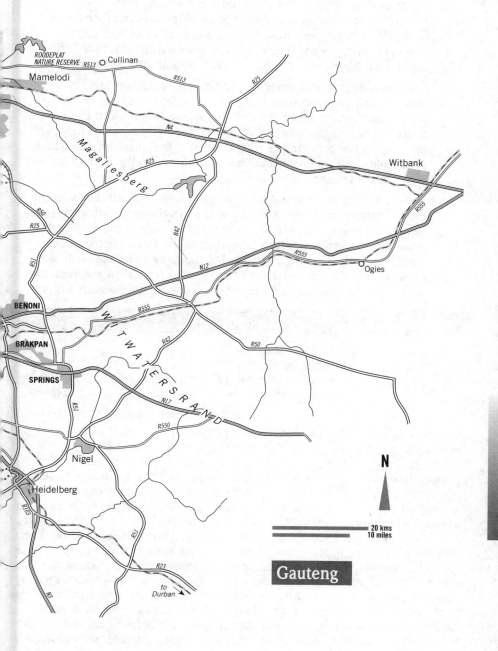

ROODEPLAT
NATURE RESERVE   R513 ○ Cullinan

Mamelodi

R513

R25

Magaliesberg

N4

R25

R50

R25

R51

R42

Witbank

R555

R555

N12

Ogies

BENONI

R555

Witwatersrand

BRAKPAN

R42

R50

SPRINGS

R51

N17

R550

R51

Nigel

Heidelberg

R103

R51

N3

R23

to
Durban

N

20 kms
10 miles

Gauteng

Gauteng—the Sotho for 'Place of Gold'—is the name of the area comprising Pretoria, Johannesburg and the Witwatersrand (previously called PWV). After much prevarication, and a choice of over a dozen possible names, the province was finally given a name that reflects the region's black majority—for the first time in South Africa's history.

Founded after the 1994 elections, the new province takes in what is generally known as the 'Vaal Triangle', that is Johannesburg, and its surrounding industrial belt (which stretches south to the Vaal River—hence the name); the 'Rand' or Witwatersrand ('White-water's Ridge'), the range of low hills running west and east of Johannesburg where most of the goldmines are found; and the South African capital of Pretoria, which lies 60km north of Witwatersrand.

The vibrant city of Johannesburg, quiet, handsome Pretoria, and some of the surrounding country—in particular the Magaliesberg Mountains—are definitely worth seeing, and, if you have time to take in one of the subterranean mine tours, a half-day's immersion in the fiercely hot, cramped tunnels amid the clanging of drills, a full kilometre under the earth, will explain better than any book the savage energy, frustration and quest for money that has dominated South Africa's turbulent 20th-century history.

Johannesburg

One of the men points for him
—Johannesburg umfundisi
...His heart beats like that of a child. There is nothing to do or think to stop it. Tixo, watch over me, he says to himself. Tixo, watch over me.

Cry the Beloved Country, Alan Paton

Johannesburg, Jo'burg, Joeys or Egoli (meaning City of Gold in the African lingua of the mine) is Africa's most aggressively Westernized city, and one of its most vibrant. There is nothing in the mix of late 19th- and early 20th-century buildings dwarfed by post-war concrete and glass skyscrapers to remind you that you are in Africa. But despite the physical ugliness of much of its downtown area , and the fact that most South Africans run it down, *and* the fact that it can be dangerous, Johannesburg should not be missed, if only for a weekend. Some of its suburbs are very pretty, with wide tree-lined streets, cafés and bars. And almost all aspects of South African culture can be found here in the people drawn to the city for work, creating an atmosphere of intense human activity. Anything happening in South Africa in terms of art, culture, music, drama, literature, happens in Johannesburg first, or at least finds its outlet to the public through the great city. Since geographically the city has nothing else to distract its inhabitants—no beach, no mountain, few parks, not even a river—Johannesburg's entertainment and nightlife are what people live for. Music, especially, thrives here as nowhere else in South Africa, and, except for the city centre, which becomes something of a combat zone after dark, it is only at night that Johannesburg really comes alive.

Like Cape Town three hundred years before, Johannesburg suffered an artificially accelerated evolution from a confused mixture of race and culture. But while Cape Town's origins lie in its strategic importance for Europe's empire-builders, Johannesburg is the result of private enterprise, and its history is only loosely connected with Europe. The city evolved from the pursuit of fortune, pure and simple, and was never intended to be a defensive or administrative centre. Perhaps because of this lack of pretence to anything but the quest for money, Johannesburg is somehow freer than other South African cities, a place of greater possibility, where all the elements of South African culture—urban black, traditional black, urban Afrikaner, rural Afrikaner, 'coloured', English, Indian, Chinese, bohemian, reactionary—all come together, however uneasily, to form a society based entirely around the individual endeavour, in whatever sphere.

Contrasting with Johannesburg's white suburbs is the huge 'township' (almost a city in its own right) of Soweto, which lies just southwest of Johannesburg, and houses most of the city's black workers. Soweto, created in the 1950s, is not an African name, but merely an abbreviation for 'southwestern townships', and, although grindingly poor in some districts, it shares Johannesburg's quest for money; most people live in Soweto not by choice, but because they were banned (until 1990) from living in Johannesburg itself, which was reserved for whites only. Since the breakdown of apartheid, many Sowetans who have the money have moved into Johannesburg, especially the Jeppestown, Hillbrow, and Bezuidenhout Valley areas. But for most blacks on the Witwatersrand Soweto is the cultural centre, the place from which the most effective anti-apartheid resistance was organized, and, despite frequent police raids, a place where life could be lived away from the eyes of white authority. Unfortunately however, Soweto, and Johannesburg's other large 'townships' of Alexandria (east of the city) and Katlehong, have suffered from intense violence since the mid-1980s. Factions within the PAC (*see* p.508), ANC and IFP (the latter mostly composed of Zulu migrant workers living in hostels) fought out their political differences, leaving an uncounted death-toll behind them. Organized crime has also flourished during the recent chaos in the Witwatersrand townships, and wars between rival black taxi companies and general lawlessness and violence have also claimed hundreds of lives. The result is that Soweto and the other townships are largely out of bounds for the visitor, unless travelling with a group of locals or on one of the organized tours during a period of political stability.

This is a shame, as much of the Johannesburg area's best music and culture is therefore inaccessible. Whether Soweto will become reasonably safe for travellers under the new ANC government remains to be seen.

In short, Johannesburg has the best and the worst of human South Africa openly on view; all its conflict and creativity, poverty and obscene wealth, open-mindedness and reaction, race hatred and racial mixing, violence and indolent tranquillity, all thrown together in one confused mass driven by money with all the human energy that goes into its pursuit.

History

Before White Settlement

The highveld, South Africa's treeless, high grassland plateau, was populated between the 4th and 12th centuries AD by groups of semi-nomadic Bantu-speaking cattle herders (the

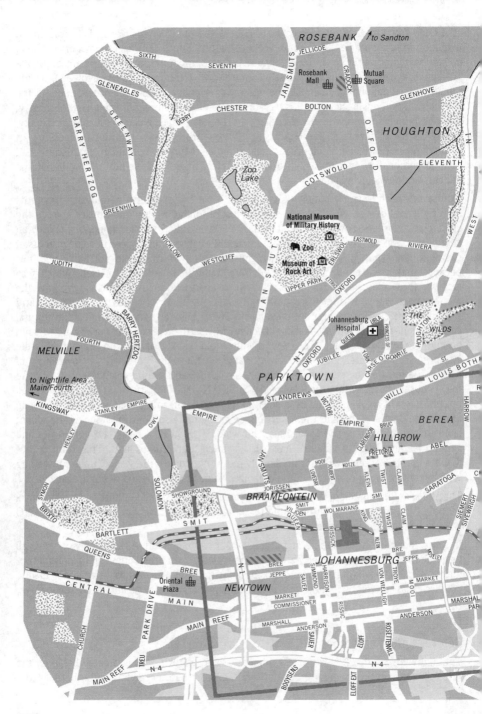

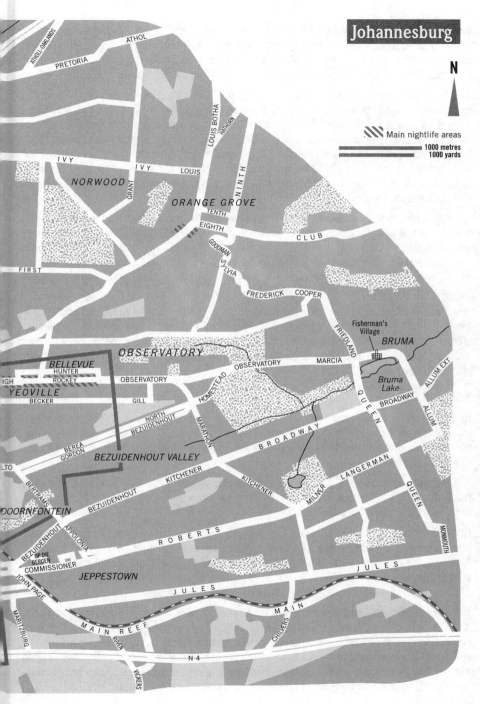

ancestors of today's Tswana and Sotho people), some of whom lived a pastoral life, wandering with the seasonal grazing, some of whom built permanent stone villages, tilled the soil and worked with iron. Wildlife wandered at will, clustering around the region's perennial streams, that incised the flat landscape with narrow ravines.

This timeless cycle was suddenly devastated in the 1800s, when an abrupt series of political upheavals plunged the highveld into warfare and chaos. Modern historians claim that the wars were caused by clans fighting to control ivory- and slave-trading routes that had become established across the eastern side of South Africa in the late 18th century with the arrival of European traders at Port Natal, the Cape and Delagoa Bay. Powerful clans in the highveld included the Taung, Rolong, Tlokwa and Thlaping (all Tswana-speaking), and these began to fight amongst themselves, creating standing armies and raiding each other incessantly for livestock and captives.

In 1820 a renegade clan called the Ndebele (meaning 'fleeing ones') arrived in the highveld from the south under their king, Mzilikazi, who had been a general of Shaka, the Zulu king, whose empire was expanding in Natal (*see* **Natal** 'History'). The Ndebele carved out their own highveld kingdom, destroying some of the Tswana groups, and by the mid-1830s parts of the highveld had been depopulated—although the Tswana clans were still active, they had lost their dominance to the Ndebele.

However, the bulk of the Ndebele soon moved on to the Orange Free State where, after a heavy defeat by Boer settlers at Vegkop, they pushed north into modern-day Zimbabwe. However, a group of Ndebele-speaking people (earlier Nguni immigrants to the area who had adopted the language and, to some extent, the culture of Mzilikazi's raiders) remained, and remain to this day.

SAR and Gold

Into this confused picture stumbled the Voortrekkers in 1836. After being worsted by Ndebele attacks, they allied with local Tswana clans and, having pushed the Ndebele north, they settled in the Witwatersrand in the 1840s as part of their new South African Republic (SAR).

A few towns were founded, including the ramshackle village of Pretoria (which later became the SAR's capital), but as recently as 100 years ago the area where Johannesburg sprawls today was still open grassland.

In 1886 the area's fortunes changed abruptly. An Australian prospector, George Harrison, discovered signs of gold-bearing rock on the Witwatersrand. He purchased a claim from the SAR, but was not impressed with the quality of the ore he found, and left for the gold rush already happening in the Eastern Transvaal. But other prospectors began trickling in, and by 1888 several hundred were scratching away on the Witwatersrand.

More gold was found, and in what promised to be vast reefs, but it was of low quality, and lay in seams too deep for individual miners to reach. To be profitable, the reefs would have to be mined on an industrial scale by a large company with plenty of capital. President Kruger and the SAR government, determined to establish control over the new diggings but lacking the vast funds needed to exploit them, courted the diamond magnates of Kimberley, offering concessions to whoever had sufficient finance to establish large-scale mines.

Meanwhile, in 1886–7, the SAR laid out four small tented villages, selling plots to all-comers at exorbitant rates. Dubbed 'Johannesburg', possibly after Johannes Rissik, the surveyor, or after Paul Kruger, whose first name was also Johannes, within a month the makeshift town was full of speculators intent on the coming boom. Concessions were granted to several mining companies, but the chief investor was Cecil Rhodes' De Beers Diamond Company, which opened its Witwatersrand office under the name of Consolidated Goldfields.

The one obstacle facing the mining companies was labour. Because the gold ore was of low quality, and the capital investment enormous, only the cheapest possible labour could be employed. Except where specialized machine skills were necessary, white labour was thus out of the question. The mine bosses knew that rural blacks could be persuaded to work for very low wages—as at Kimberley—but the proposed Witwatersrand project would need far more labourers than Kimberley ever had, more even than were available within the whole SAR. Recruiting officers were sent all over South Africa to persuade rural black men to come and work on 'the Rand', as the area was already known, attracting them with lies about high wages and good living conditions. In fact, the only housing was in primitive compounds near the mines, to which the workers were not allowed to bring their families.

City of Sin

Johannesburg grew up a violent, hard-drinking town servicing tens of thousands of black labourers, skilled white machine-operators (mostly imported from Britain) and entrepreneurs. Within three years it was the largest city in South Africa. With so few available females, prostitution soon became the most lucrative industry after mining, and pimps began sending scouts to Europe, tempting working class girls to come to Johannesburg with paid passage and a promise of domestic work, then keeping them as virtual slaves in the brothels that sprang up all over town. By the early 1890s a few genteel suburbs, like Parktown and Houghton, had appeared for mining magnates and their families, but the great, squalid city remained an anarchic place governed by money, greed and raw energy.

Paul Kruger and his government were appalled at the city of sin they had helped create. But their mining dividends soon became so large that, although laws were passed to try to curb prostitution and liquor manufacturing, little was done to temper the vice of the brash new city. However, Kruger was shrewd enough to see a potential political threat in the growing fortunes of the *uitlanders* (foreigners) of Johannesburg; the mining bosses, in particular, were known to be very pro-British. Kruger instituted a blanket policy to protect his government: no *uitlander*, whether magnate, technician, pimp, or whore, was to be granted citizenship of the SAR. And without citizenship, the *uitlanders* could have no vote.

This soon caused great dissent, as the magnates and miners knew that they were fuelling the SAR's now burgeoning economy. Throughout the 1890s Johannesburg's press called on both the Cape and the British government to persuade Kruger to grant them the franchise, by force of arms if necessary. The mining magnates, or 'Randlords', also took up the cause; Cecil Rhodes, of the De Beers Company, was now South Africa's richest man, and, from 1890, managed to get himself elected Prime Minister of the Cape Colony. From Cape Town, he began secret negotiations with the British government to provoke a war with the SAR. In 1895 Rhodes financed an attempted *coup d'état* on Pretoria. But the raiding party, under one Dr Jameson, was caught by Kruger's *Kommandos* and promptly thrown in jail.

Strife and Strikes

Such was probably Rhodes' intention; the Jameson Raid excited much ridicule and censure from the European powers, and inspired calls in the British press for the army to redress the embarrassment. As much from this pressure as from a desire to grab the gold mines, Britain officially took up the 'plight' of Johannesburg's *uitlanders* in 1896 and began moving towards a serious attempt at annexing the gold-rich SAR. The Second Anglo-Boer War was declared in 1899 (*see* **History**). Johannesburg fell silent as the *uitlanders* fled south of the SAR. The British army occupied Johannesburg in 1900, and the city remained unusually quiet until the Boer surrender of 1902, when business opened again with renewed vigour.

By 1904 the shallowest gold reefs had been exhausted. Deeper seams would have to be tapped. But working at deeper levels meant increased costs for the companies and terrible conditions for the black miners. To make sinking the shafts profitable, the mine bosses brought over thousands of Chinese labourers on three-year contracts at pitiful wages. Strikes were attempted by black and white miners alike, but were quickly put down. The Chinese stayed from 1907 to 1910, and were repatriated, having sunk the shafts much deeper; the miners had no choice but to go back to work under worse conditions.

But the Rand's political problems were just beginning. From 1911 the government, pressurized by newly formed white trade unions, passed laws reserving unskilled mine labour for blacks and skilled jobs for whites. This displeased the mining companies, who knew they could reduce costs by training blacks for skilled work at low wages. For quite different reasons, the job colour bar also displeased the Rand's growing numbers of poor whites, as it excluded them from the unskilled labour market. Finally, it displeased black workers because it denied them any possibilty of an increase in wages. The only group whose future had been secured for the better were the skilled white mineworkers, but even they were unhappy—with the deep working conditions—and began to demand better wages and more flexibility from the mine bosses.

In 1913 some 19,000 white workers went on strike over the sacking of five men who disputed their working hours. Every mine was shut down, riots broke out in Johannesburg, and troops were sent in. Alarmed, the government reinstated the five men who had been fired, but passed the Riotous Assemblies bill, which empowered them to use force to stop any meeting that threatened public order. However, between 1914 and 1920, taking advantage of the government's need for increased production to pay for its war effort, strikes and fighting between white mineworkers and police became a regular feature of life in the Witwatersrand, and the mining companies were forced to grant several pay rises.

The success of white strikes inspired the Rand's black workers to organize their own industrial action. In 1918 Johannesburg's 'bucket boys' (human night soil collectors) went on strike over low pay and poor conditions, and the revolt spread to the mines where tens of thousands of workers also went on strike. Despite being brutally put down, the black strikes caused the mining companies more worry than the white strikes, as the whole industry ultimately relied on black labour. The Randlords told the government that the job colour bar would have to go if gold mining was to be ensured for the future.

This incensed the skilled white workers. In 1922 a general strike was called, with 24,000 white workers in the Witwatersrand downing tools and taking over the city. Prime Minister Smuts sent in the army and airforce, and more than 200 people were killed in street battles before the miners went back to work. However, Smuts took the lesson to heart—South Africa's skilled whites represented the bulk of the voting public. Despite the mining companies' protests, the job colour bar remained in place.

The Townships

Meanwhile, the government decided that the best way to control the Rand's black workers would be to physically contain them. From 1923 to 1927 a series of laws were passed confining blacks to specially demarcated residential areas. By the mid-1930s several 'townships' had been built where modern Soweto sprawls today, but the law was too much for Johannesburg's local government to cope with, and urban black culture began to flourish in the city, particularly in Sophiatown, just west of the central business district. Literature, dance and jazz (known collectively as *Kwela* culture) thrived in Sophiatown between the 1930s and '50s, and was strong enough to launch some international careers, notably those of saxophonist Dollar Brand and singer Miriam Makeba.

The *Kwela* movement did much for black morale in Johannesburg—reflected in the appearance of the first black trade unions. The Council for Non-European Trade Unions (CNETU) was founded in 1936, changing its name to the African Mineworkers' Union (AMU) in 1941. From 1939, the Rand's black workers profited from the government's distraction by the war effort. By 1943 the AMU had grown to 25,000 members and had won several campaigns for wage increases. A series of successful bus boycotts brought commuter fares down, and blacks began to alleviate the severe overcrowding of the new townships and Sophiatown by setting up squatter camps, in direct defiance of the segregation laws. The South African Communist Party (SACP) also became multi-racial during the late 1930s, and this, combined with the growing powerbase of the ANC, made it look as though Johannesburg's blacks might at last gain some real political prestige.

Apartheid

But once the Second World War was over, Smuts' government decided that the Rand's blacks had gone far enough. In 1946, when 60,000 AMU members went on strike over pay and working conditions, the police were sent in with guns. Over two days, twelve miners were killed and more than 1000 injured. But Smuts was perceived by many South African whites as having allowed too many concessions. In 1948 the Afrikaner-led, ultra right-wing National Party won a general election and promised the systematic and strict enforcement of total colour segregation—in short, apartheid—and the advances made by Johannesburg's blacks were quickly reversed.

In 1950 the SACP was outlawed, and the ANC came under strict surveillance. In 1952 the government announced that the hated pass books, which black mine workers had been forced to carry to qualify for work, were to be carried by all blacks at all times. Not being able to produce the book would mean jail, and probably a beating. Thousands of ANC supporters across the country were arrested for flouting the new law. However, this confirmed the determination of the ANC's members to resist. In 1953, in Kliptown, just outside Johannesburg, the organization drafted a 10-clause **Freedom Charter**, which aimed to introduce non-racism at all levels of life, and started to lobby parliament to have it accepted. Forty-one years on, the Charter has finally become ANC government policy, but in 1953 the Afrikaner government was in no mood for such concessions. Instead, legislation was passed to make squatting illegal, giving local authorities the right to use force for eviction. Next, the Rand's mission schools, where the black intelligentsia that had led the pre-War movements had been educated, were shut down, and blacks were barred from the major universities. Johannesburg's University of the Witwatersrand staged a massive protest, and the ANC tried to set up independent schools in Johannesburg, but money for this had run out by 1956. Black children were to be educated only as the government thought fit. Finally, prime minister D. F. Malan ordered the forced removal of Sophiatown's residents to the newly constructed township of Soweto in 1955. Armed police arrived with bulldozers, and in less than a week Sophiatown, the heart of urban black South Africa, had ceased to be.

Having razed the Rand's centre of black resistance, the government turned its attention to the resistance organizations themselves. In December 1956 police arrested about 500 people, black and white, on charges of treason. A series of mass trials (known as the Treason Trials) were held in Johannesburg's Old Drill Hall from 1957 to 1961. Most defendants were eventually acquitted, but the protracted hearings and detention of ANC and SACP members did considerable damage. Resistance merely went underground: in 1959 several ANC leaders met in Soweto and formed the more militant Pan African Congress, or PAC, pledging to fight apartheid step by step, starting with the Pass Laws.

On March 21 the PAC spearheaded a call for all African men in the Rand to throw away their pass books, and present themselves for arrest. It was an inspired idea: the Rand's industry came to a sudden halt as tens of thousands of black men assembled at police stations in the townships around Johannesburg. The police were baffled, and their jails could not cope with the numbers. But the plan went awry; at **Sharpeville**, south of Johannesburg, the police, scared by the size of the (unarmed) crowd around them, opened fire without orders. Some 69 protesters were killed and 180 wounded.

Rather than prosecute the murderous policemen, the government took advantage of Sharpeville to call a State of Emergency, ban the ANC and PAC and arrest their leaders. The response of both organizations was to form military wings and set up training camps abroad. But in 1963 a young lawyer named Nelson Mandela, head of the ANC's armed wing Umkhonto we Sizwe (MK), and several colleagues arrested at Rivonia near Johannesburg were charged with plotting terrorism and given life sentences. In July 1964 a bomb exploded at Johannesburg's railway station, injuring 23 people. The saboteur, a white schoolteacher named John Harris, was arrested in Roodepoort in western Johannesburg. The MK was implicated and John Harris was hanged.

Education and Violence

The resistance movement in the Rand's townships was silenced for over ten years after the Rivonia Trial. But resentment still smouldered, particularly amongst Soweto's school-children, who saw their parents cowed, and themselves moulded by apartheid through compulsory learning of the government's language—Afrikaans. In June 1976 students of Meadowlands Tswana School and Marius Isaacson High School in Soweto vandalized their school buildings and had minor clashes with local police. Students from all over Soweto planned a mass rally at Orlando Sports Stadium. Hundreds marched; local police fired tear gas canisters, and the schoolchildren replied with a hail of stones. The police opened fire. General rioting ensued, and sporadic clashes with police and schoolchildren continued through the next two years, in which several hundred schoolchildren and others died. The government closed most of Soweto's schools and a whole generation of Witwatersrand blacks lost their formal education, a legacy that the present government has now inherited in the form of an unemployable, disaffected and increasingly criminal youth.

Through the late 1970s and '80s the region became increasingly violent. Unfortunately, most incidents of mass violence came from the increasingly factionalized black political parties and degenerated into horrific ethnic fighting, under the banner of the parties themselves or in the form of irrational violence. Many people suspect the government's security forces of incitement, especially for the waves of attacks on black workers travelling on local commuter trains, which became endemic in the late 1980s, yet seemed inexplicable at the time. The townships' *tsotsis*, or criminal youth, had a field day, and crime became rampant, even in Johannesburg's city centre, which became a no-go zone after dark.

But, despite high crime rates, Johannesburg's city centre and white suburbs saw almost no political violence until early in 1994, when IFP and ANC supporters clashed in central Johannesburg, leaving scores of bodies in their wake. However, this has been the one exception; since the 1994 elections, violence across the whole region has declined remarkably (with the exception of Katlehong). Many of the imbalances and wrongs of apartheid have yet to be redressed, and crime still runs high, but Johannesburg itself is one of the few places in South Africa where the races mix, at all levels of life, as a matter of course—especially in the yuppie/bohemian suburbs of Yeoville and Berea. Houses in the inner neighbourhoods are increasingly being bought by black families—especially east of the city centre in Jeppestown, the Bezuidenhout Valley, and Hillbrow.

In the one, brief century since its birth, Johannesburg has been the dynamo for almost all the events in the country's turbulent political history. The hope is that, after such a difficult childhood, the city will mature into a more mellow centre for South Africa's urban culture, and grow away from its cycle of violence; but meantime there is still no more exciting city in the whole of South Africa.

Johannesburg ✆ *(011–)* **Getting to and from Johannesburg**

by air

Johannesburg International Airport, ✆ 356 1111 or ✆ 975 9963 for flight details, receives daily flights from Britain and Europe, and domestic flights. The airport is about 25km northeast of the town centre along the R21 highway towards Pretoria. Impala Buses connect the airport with Jo'burg's Airport Terminal in the Rotunda Bus Station, whence buses can be taken to all of South Africa's main towns and cities (*see* 'Getting Around: by bus'). **Lanseria Airport**, ✆ 659 2750 for flight details, the other domestic terminal, runs no shuttle service to or from the city centre, but most charter companies throw in transport to or from Lanseria as part of the flight package.

by car

Jo'burg is linked to the Northern Province, Free State and Cape Town (via the Karoo) by the N1 highway, to Mpumalanga and Mozambique via the N4, to Durban, Natal and the northeastern Free State by the N3, and to the Northern Cape via the N12.

Long-distance buses run from the **Rotunda Bus Station**, on the corner of Rissik and Wolmarans streets, at the western end of the city centre, and the adjacent **Train Station**—there is safe walking between the two. Bus services connecting Jo'burg with most of the country's major towns and points in between include: **Greyhound** ✆ 830 1400, **Transtate**, ✆ 774 7449, and **TransLux**, ✆ 774 3313, for both, and **Intercape** ✆ 333 5231. These are the main services for long-distance bus journeys. Unfortunately, the Rotunda has no central information line.

For backpackers, the **Baz Bus**, Cape Town, ✆ (021) 439 2323, offers door-to-door service between Gauteng and the Cape, KwaZulu-Natal and Swaziland.

The train station also has offices and departure/arrivals for several bus services connecting Jo'burg with other parts of Africa. Buses to Zimbabwe, Botswana, Mozambique and Malawi (as well as Swaziland and Lesotho) are now run on a daily basis. For Mozambique (Maputo) try **Panthera Azul**, ✆ 337 7409. For Harare and Masvingo try **Silverbird**, ✆ 337 7215.

by rail

Jo'burg's central railway station entrance is on Wolmarans Street (information ✆ 773 2944). Trains leave daily for Cape Town, via Bloemfontein and Kimberley (a 24-hour trip), for Durban Sun–Fri 12.30pm, and for East London/Port Elizabeth Tues, Thurs and Sun. The Blue Train (*see* **Travel**, p.7) can also be booked from here. Suburban trains out to Pretoria run from here about every half-hour, and are much used by commuters. In the late 1980s and early '90s random attacks became common on these services, as well as on the lines connecting Jo'burg with the townships, but armed guards now patrol the trains, and they are safe to travel.

hitch-hiking

A way to get around the problem of hitching out of Jo'burg's dangerous inner-city freeways, is to dial **Share-A-Lift**, ✆ 444 1559. While this is not completely free, you will only be asked to share minimal petrol costs, and, provided you have a few days to wait for a lift to come through (they go to most areas and cities), this is undoubtedly the cheapest way to travel safely. Also ask at the backpacker hostels for the door-to-door minibus taxis that operate between Jo'burg and just about everywhere else in the country. These cost a little more than the regular minibus taxis but save you the danger of going down to the city's taxi ranks.

Johannesburg ✆ *(011–)*

Getting Around

by bus

Buses to and from the airport run every half-hour between 5am and 10pm connecting Johannesburg International Airport with the Rotunda in the centre of town (25–35mins). From the Rotunda, always take a taxi to the place you intend to stay. Don't wander out on to the street with your bags. You'll get mugged.

For services in town, Jo'burg's central buses run from Eloff Street in the city centre to all neighbourhoods (information: ✆ 838 2125) about once every 15 minutes. However, if you have just arrived in the city and have a backpack full of your belongings, then take a taxi to your accommodation. Walk out of the train or bus station with a backpack on and you're begging to be mugged. The same applies to standing at a bus stop with obviously stealable stuff.

Weekend services to most neighbourhoods can be picked up from Vanderbijl Square, on the corner of Rissik and Main Streets. Weekday and (infrequent) weekend services shut down after 8.30pm, but after dark it is *always* better to take a taxi, as the city centre becomes highly unsafe, especially if you are carrying baggage.

by taxi

You cannot hail a taxi in Jo'burg. Either ring for one, or take one from a taxi rank. These can be found at the Rotunda Bus Station and outside the Carlton Centre on Commissioner Street. Telephoning is much easier, and you can get a price before you travel. Try **Rose's Taxis**, ✆ 725 3333; **City Taxis**, ✆ 336 5213, or **Maxi Taxi**, ✆ 648 1212.

by black taxi

These pick up from bus stops along all the main routes and go out to most neighbourhoods. Fares average around 1–2 Rand. However, as ever, these minibuses have a high accident rate and mugging is not unknown.

car hire

As well as the standard, overpriced car hire firms, there are some good local deals: **U-Drive**, ✆ 331 3735; **Tempest**, ✆ 397 5402; **Dolphin**, ✆ 394 6605; **Imperial**, ✆ (0800) 131 000; **Alisa's**, ✆ (0800) 21 515; or **Tony's Car Hire**, ✆ 393 1895.

by tour group

This can be a good way to get your bearings safely in Jo'burg and the townships. Try **African Impressions**, ✆ 609 5867, or **Backpackers Budget Safaris**, ✆ 788 5182.

Johannesburg ✆ *(011–)*   **Tourist Information**

There are Publicity Associations at the airport, at the Rotunda Bus Station, and in the city centre's North State Building, on the corner of Market and Kruis Streets, ✆ 336 4961.

After dark, you must always, always, always take a taxi to wherever you are going, unless it's just across the street.

Johannesburg ✆ *(011–)*   **Useful Addresses and Numbers**

GPO: On Jeppe Street, between Von Brandis and the Smal Street Mall. *Open Mon–Fri 8–4.30, Sat 8–12.*

Medical emergencies: Ambulance, ✆ 403 4227. **General Hospital**, ✆ 488 4911. *Open 24hrs.* **Yeoville Medical Centre**, Rockey Street. *Open till 9pm.*

Police (Flying Squad), ✆ 10111.

Travel Agents: SA Students Travel Association, ✆ 716 3045; **Rennies Travel**, ✆ 331 5898—branches in most of the northern suburbs.

Money: Amex, ✆ 339 5954—branches in most of the northern suburbs. **Thomas Cook** is handled by Rennies Travel.

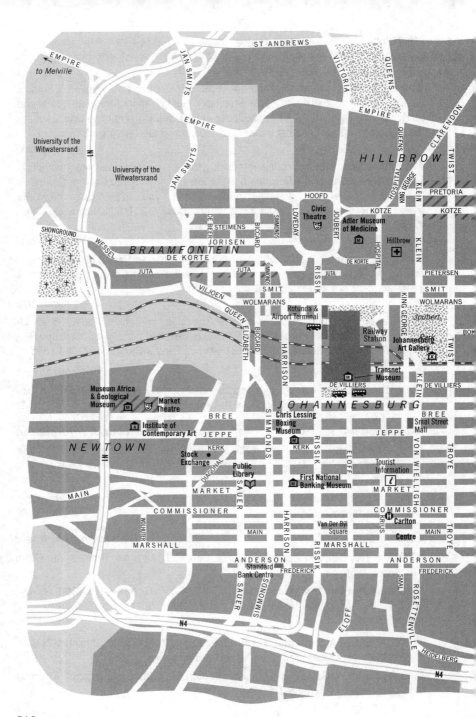

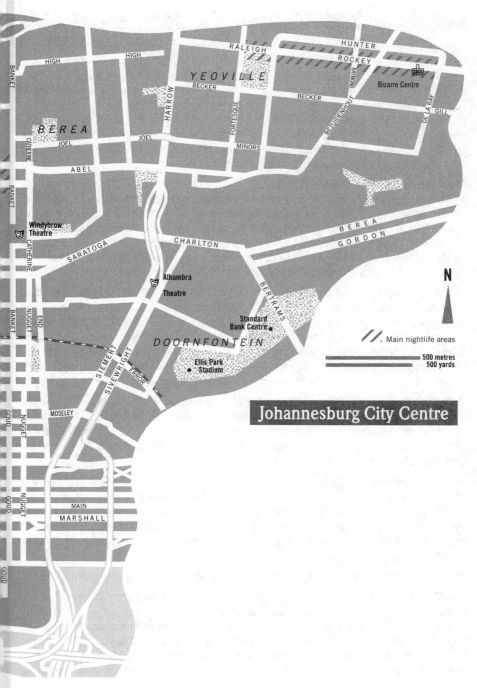

Johannesburg City Centre

Downtown Jo'burg has little to interest the traveller except for its transport centres, a few museums, plush shopping centres, and the chance of being mugged. The most central zone—called the CBD (central business district)—becomes a deserted and dangerous urban ghetto after dark. Even by day, an obvious foreigner is likely to become a target for crime. If you are going to explore downtown Jo'burg, only do so during office hours, decide where you are going, and walk purposefully. On no account wander around with a backpack, jewellery, camera, etc.—and no expensive running shoes or designer gear either. When arriving at the bus or train station, take a taxi to your destination, even if it is a rip-off, and stow your belongings safely before walking the streets.

Museum Africa, on the corner of Wolhunter and Bree streets, ℗ 833 5624 (*open Tues–Sat 9–5*), is one of South Africa's most comprehensive cultural museums. The emphasis is on African art and craft from all over the continent, including colonial exhibits, displays of ethnic life and belief, and exhibits dedicated to modern Africa and its international culture. The museum hosts regular exhibitions specializing in groups of artists and specific crafts. On the fourth floor is an excellent photography museum whose displays include a photographic history of Sophiatown and Soweto. Telephone first to find out what's on.

The older **Geological Museum** used to be on Market Street, but is now housed in Museum Africa. It has a breakdown of South Africa's astonishing mineral wealth and varied geological make-up. Apart from the inevitable diamonds and gold nuggets, the museum has a history of the mining industry that brought about the country's present wealth. The **Public Library**, on Market Street, houses the renowned Harold Strange Library of African Studies, the Michaelis Art Library and a Music Library, as well as such useful things as nationwide Yellow Pages, and national and international newspapers and magazines.

Railway enthusiasts will enjoy the **Transnet Museum** (*open Mon–Fri 7.30–3.45*), in the old main hall of Jo'burg's central railway station. The entrance is on De Villiers Street. Old steam locomotives dominate the displays, but there are also boats, cars and wagons, as well as a small gallery of paintings by Pierneef, one of South Africa's best-known landscape-painters, active at the turn of the century.

The **Johannesburg Art Gallery** (*open Tues–Sun 10–5*), founded in 1910, is at the edge of the infamous Joubert Park, on King George Street. It houses a general collection of old and contemporary South African art, combined with some international works, old and new, of varying quality. There are early 20th-century works by the better-known South African artists, such as Pierneef and Irma Stern, combined with modern township art. Next door is a shop selling African handcrafts.

Please be warned, however, that Joubert Park is one of the surest mugging spots in the city.

The **Carlton Centre**, which occupies almost the whole block between Commissioner and Main Streets, is central Jo'burg's principal landmark, and houses a massive shopping centre which, above its plush shops, has a revolving tower, the **Carlton Panorama**, on the 50th floor. There is a small charge payable before entering the lift that takes you up. From here, the view out over the wide, flat Witwatersrand is unparalleled. The mines, mine dumps, 'townships', and the great sprawl of Jo'burg itself (which now stretches almost all the way to

Pretoria) are all laid out before you, giving you a sense of the sheer scale of the place, and of the human energy that has gone into creating it in such a short time.

The **Standard Bank Centre**, on Frederick Street, ✆ 636 4231 (*open Mon–Fri 8.30–4.30, Sat 8–12.30*), has a gallery that hosts exhibitions of contemporary South African and foreign art, as well as concerts and lectures. Selected works from the Grahamstown Festival usually go on show here.

Shoppers usually flock to the **Smal Street Mall**, linking Bree and Jeppe streets, near their intersection with Von Wielligh Street. This is a pedestrian strip fronted by small but smart shops, with a few outdoor cafés. Worth looking into is the **Operation Hunger Craft Shop**, which sells very good work from all over Africa at far cheaper prices than the Smal Street address would imply. Continue west along Jeppe Street for about nine blocks, and you come to **Diagonal Street**. This used to be one of the most dangerous areas of Jo'burg (and still is after dark), but, by day, its old function as the city's financial centre has re-established itself. The old colonial-style shops have now become rather smart, and, apart from a monstrous skyscraper, the street has a pleasant, old-world feel. Also on Diagonal Street is the magnificent old **Stock Exchange** (*guided tours Mon–Fri 11 and 2*). Tours are quite fun, and the guides have several good anecdotes about the early Randlords and the almost obscene size of some of the deals they struck when the gold reefs first boomed in the 1900s. The Stock Exchange also made the news in 1991, when PAC terrorists planted a bomb there that killed several stockbrokers and money dealers.

Diagonal Street makes a good place from which to walk to the Market Theatre complex in Newtown (*see* below) or to Doornfontein, just north-east of the city centre. This is both the university and the theatre district. Its **Alhambra Theatre**, on Sivewright Street, is the city's most handsome, a turn-of-the-century building with many late-Victorian and Art Nouveau elements. Now a national monument, it still stages large productions (*see* 'Entertainment').

Downtown Jo'burg has three small, specialist museums, including the **Chris Lessing Boxing Museum** (*open Mon–Fri 8–1 and 2–4.30*), on the corner of Kerk and Harrison streets, and the **First National Banking Museum**, on Market Street (*open Mon–Fri 9–4*), which offers a dry history of banking and money-making in South Africa since the early days of 17th-century Cape Town, through the diamond and gold booms, to the uncertain present.

Johannesburg's Neighbourhoods

Most of the city's life goes on in the neighbourhoods immediately surrounding downtown, including most accommodation, points of interest, entertainment, nightlife and restaurants. For this reason, it is as well to acquaint yourself with the city's geography before arriving.

Yeoville, Rosebank and **Melville** are the three liveliest suburbs, with the most enjoyable streetlife. They all have galleries, restaurants, bars and music venues, particularly Rockey Street, on the Yeoville/Berea border. **Hillbrow**, which used to be safe, has now become dangerous by night (and increasingly by day as well), but is still known for the cabaret clubs established there in the late 1950s. **Braamfontein** houses the University of the Witwatersrand (known as 'Wits'), South Africa's most prestigious university after Cape Town, and is a theatre and nightclub distict by night. Just west of the city centre is **Newtown**, which has a lively precinct around the old town market that now includes a large theatre, flea market, galleries and restaurants. East of the city centre is the man-made **Bruma Lake**, on whose southern shore lies the 'largest flea market in southern Africa'. North of Yeoville is the yuppie area of **Orange Grove**, which also has good bars, and north of here, start the rich residential neighbourhoods known collectively as The Northern Suburbs, including **Houghton** and **Parktown**, where the first Randlords built their mansions, **Rosebank**, known for upmarket galleries and restaurants and a growing back-packer scene, and **Sandton**, known for wealth, pure and simple.

Newtown

This area, just to the west of the city centre, is reached by Bree and Jeppe Streets. The **Market Theatre**, and its surrounding restaurants and bars, are the main attraction, and the area is lively (and safe) by night. By day, the **Market Galleries** are worth checking out. These are in what is known as the Market Precinct, or AngloVaal Mall, which runs in front of the large theatre entrance. Contemporary art is displayed, mostly painting, sculpture and prints. The **Thupelo Art Gallery** is in the basement underneath the precinct, and displays township art and pottery. The **Institute of Contemporary Art**, near the flea market on Jeppe Street, claims to 'bridge the gap between academic and commercial galleries'. Its displays tend to the avant-garde. The **Newtown Galleries** occupy an old warehouse at the corner of Bree and Wolhuter streets, also by the flea market, and sell modern art, jewellery, and other crafts.

If your head is reeling from too much art, visit Newtown on Saturday for the **flea market** (*open 9–4*), one of the city's best, selling everything from antiques to T-shirts, puppets, rugs and shoes. The **mineral market**, on Bree Street, sells semi-precious southern-African gems (mounted and unmounted) all through the week. Another market, but of totally different character, is the **Oriental Plaza** off the west end of Park Road, an Indian Bazaar selling spices, foods and general goods. You will be expected to haggle.

Braamfontein

This is the northwest part of downtown. The vast central campus of the **University of the Witwatersrand** is here, on Jan Smuts Boulevard, as is the large **Civic Theatre** (opposite the **Civic Centre**), which shows both mainstream and fringe productions. On the corner of Hospital and Stiemens streets is the **Adler Museum of Medicine** (*open Mon–Fri 9–4*), which, apart from displaying implements and histories (the world's first heart transplant was performed in South Africa), also has a herbarium, with the medicinal properties of each plant explained, and a *sangoma's* (witch-doctor's) hut. These attractions aside, Braamfontein is best visited at night for its plentiful theatre, live music and nightclub scene.

Yeoville and Bellevue

These two neighbourhoods, just northeast of the city centre, comprise one of Jo'burg's liveliest areas—though they suffered during the 1990s from a huge rise in crime and have only just become usable again. Be careful, though, and don't wander off the main drag (Rockey Street) after dark. Linked by one long road, called Raleigh Street at the west end of Yeoville, and becoming **Rockey Street** at the beginning of Bellevue, this part of town has some of the liveliest bars, cafés, nightlife and music. Almost all the places worth visiting are on Raleigh and Rockey Streets. The residential avenues leading off are home to a large concentration of Jo'burg's bohemians, and, increasingly, to many black families. Don't go wandering off on to these streets until you have thoroughly sussed out the area.

The best way to take it in is to walk, by day or night, from the first few blocks of Rockey steadily west on to Raleigh Street, until you reach the sign telling you that you are entering the Berea neighbourhood (approximately 3km). Listings of the cafés, bars, restaurants and music venues appear below. Suffice to say here that, by day the long strip includes a regular flea market, outside terraces to drink on (the most popular being **Rockerfellas Jazz Bar** and the **Bar Pita** on lower Rockey Street), and a mixed crowd of black and white trendies, students, and others. By night it is just as busy, but with people moving between restaurants, bars and clubs.

The Yeoville end is smarter and fairly yuppified, with cafés being the main attraction. The Rockey Street end is (appropriately) more rocking—a mix of hippies, metalheads, funk, techno and jazz fans, and young people just hanging out. Most of the bars and music venues are down here. There are also some interesting shops, including second-hand bookshops, and jewellery and clothing shops, some of which are clustered together just off Rockey Street, in a little enclave called the **Bizarre Centre**. Set out and explore. The tension so pervasive in many parts of Jo'burg is happily absent here. Upstairs at the **Tandoor** on lower Rockey Street, just by the entrance to the Bizarre Centre, there is one of the few bars in Jo'burg where whites can drink comfortably in a predominantly black bar.

Hillbrow

This used to be Jo'burg's number one area for nightlife. Situated on the hill just north of downtown, and recognizable from afar for its tall radio tower, Hillbrow is undergoing rapid change. Its original inhabitants, mostly poor Afrikaners, were later joined by European immigrants, who in turn gave way to blacks moving into the city from the townships. This should be a positive change to an already cosmopolitan district, but so far the inevitable tensions resulting from a mix of these groups has made Hillbrow unsafe for tourists, especially by night. However, the jazz and cabaret clubs, for which Hillbrow became famous in the 1960s and '70s, still thrive, and it is worth checking them out—only be sure to take a taxi both to and from the venue. You can wander the two main strips by day—there are some good record shops—but still stay out of the side streets. Also worth a visit, the **Windybrow Theatre**, a whimsical 1920s mock-Tudor building, has several stages (*see* 'Entertainment').

Melville

This suburb, west of the city centre (reached via the R55, Empire Street) has become what Yeoville used to be—a safe play area for Jo'burg's young bohemians—you can walk around here at night very safely if you stick to the main drags (Main Street, 7th Street and 4th Avenue). Melville is now Jo'burg's best area for live music, as well as good bars, restaurants and cafés. Melville also has good moderate and cheap accommodation, and makes a good place to stay if you have a car and don't have to rely on buses from the city centre. However, the backpacker lodges have yet to move in here as they have in Yeoville, Rosebank and the Bez Valley/Observatory area (between Yeoville and Bruma Lake). So the atmosphere is still authentically South African—if predominantly white.

Bruma Lake

Bruma Lake has what claims to be the largest covered flea market in southern Africa at the weekend—you can buy just about anything here, but the emphasis is on jewellery and crafts. Look out for the traders from Zaire, who sell incredible masks, palm-leaf mats, carvings, printed cloths and other artefacts. They will expect you to bargain. If you speak French to them, the prices may drop considerably.

The market sits by a large man-made lake. On the opposite bank to the market, and linked to it by a footbridge, is a development called **Fisherman's Village**, a series of cafés, bars and restaurants designed to resemble a Mediterranean village. This sounds ghastly, but it is one of the few such enterprises in South Africa that actually seems to have worked—if only for weekend pleasure-seeking—a combination of the dry, sunny light, and the crowd. Bruma Lake is great fun to visit at the weekend, but is rather dead through the week.

Orange Grove

This is another yuppie/bohemian area about 2km northeast of Yeoville and Rockey Street. It is mainly composed of houses, but its commercial strip, Louis Botha Avenue, has a very good bar that should not be missed, the **Radium Bar**, which has not changed since the 1940s. On the contrary, the Portuguese-run bar still attracts the same mixed crowd of professionals, drinkers and young pleasure-seekers. The place gets very busy most nights, and it is a good place to meet people and get local information. There are also good night clubs here.

The Northern Suburbs

This is where the money is. The real money, that is. **Houghton** and **Parktown**, the oldest of the northern suburbs (just north-west of the city centre), were built at the end of the 19th century by the Randlords, or mining magnates, who moved their operations from Kimberley to Jo'burg when gold began to pay better than diamonds. Their mansions are mostly still private houses. Tours into some of them can be arranged via **Parktown Heritage**, © 482 3349 (*mornings only*). The tour guides dress in period costume and are ready with anecdotes about the rich eccentrics who built the mansions. Some of them are worth seeing for the gardens alone.

Trendier than Parktown is **Rosebank**, with many upmarket art galleries, restaurants and a repertory cinema along its main strip, Oxford Road. Some of the galleries showcase the most fashionable artists, both black and white. Over the last few years many of the former residents of Yeoville (those who could afford to take a loss on their houses) moved up to Rosebank—which is a lot safer. There is also a thriving backpacker scene, with many bars and restaurants centring around the main Rosebank Shopping Mall. However, Africa is catching up. Now the once squeaky-clean streets have hundreds of craft vendors from all over the continent offering their wares. There are also beggars, and the odd quiet mugging. But mostly the influx of blacks has been positive—offering some of the best craft shopping in Jo'burg at cheap prices. Just don't flaunt wads of cash as you buy from the different stalls.

Sandton, the next suburb north, is the wealthiest of all. Sandton housewives are the butt of many Jo'burg jokes, for example:

> Q. *'How many Sandton housewives does it take to change a lightbulb?'*
> A. *'Mah dear, we have people to take care of those sorts of things.'*

Behind their giant, security-fenced walls, the vast homes rival those of Beverly Hills in opulence and ostentation. Other than that the area is dead, except for the massive **Sandton Centre**, a vast, shopping centre on several floors that sells only the most expensive of everything, and where the traveller can observe the housewives in question at play. For all its status as a monument to money, the Sandton Centre does have one or two very good shops, particularly those selling Africana. The **Totem** shop (shop U17, in particular, sells very beautiful artefacts from West Africa, some antique, some modern, at prices that, owing to the favourable exchange rate, most travellers can afford.

Around Johannesburg

North of the city, although development stretches along the M1 highway almost as far as Pretoria, there are still some large stretches of open countryside, reached by the R511 and R512 roads north of Randburg and Sandton. This is predominantly horse country, and several riding stables operate in the area (*see* p.545). The most interesting from a traveller's point of view is the **Lippizaner Riding School**, an imitation of the Spanish Riding School, in Vienna. Displays of highly skilled classical dressage are given, just as in Vienna, on white Lippizaner stallions whose riders wear 18th-century costume. Founded by an Austrian emigré in the 1960s, Jo'burg's Lippizaner Riding School is an incongruous thing to find in the bare highveld grassland that stretches around the great city. The school is reached via the R55 from Sandton (about 15km) and is signposted from the road.

South of the city, along the N3 highway towards the Free State and Natal, then along the R550, following the signposts, is the **Suikerbosrand Nature Reserve**. This is a large, unspoilt area of highveld (almost 14,000ha), with mixed woodland, some marsh, and even one or two pockets of fynbos heath, which is usually found only in the Cape. The reserve's empty silence is a blessed relief after Jo'burg, and makes a superb escape for anyone working in the city, or simply staying there for a few days. Game includes eland, kudu, red hartebeest, black wildebeest, zebra, reedbuck, duiker, oribi and steenbok. A few shy cheetah and brown hyena also inhabit the reserve.

Suikerbosrand has several hiking trails, from one hour to six days in length, with overnight huts supplied with firewood and water. There are also three camp sites, with ablution facilities and communal kitchens. Hiking trails of more than one day must be booked in advance, ✆ (0151) 2181/2/3.

Even further south is **Parys**, on the Vaal River. This is a good venue for **white water rafting**. Many of the backpacker lodges in Jo'burg organise trips out to here, as well as to participate in other adrenalin sports in the Gauteng area

Gold Reef City

This theme park (comprising a reconstructed pioneer town and funfair) lies just southwest of the city centre along the M2 highway. A squeaky-clean re-creation of Jo'burg during its early prospecting days of the 1880s, the place exists for tourists to spend their money. But a visit can be fun: of particular note are the **Gumboot Dancers** (*performances daily 1 and 2*), performing African dances originated by the first of the migrant workers to come to Egoli (the city of gold) in the 1890s. Their loose-fitting rubber boots, part of the standard uniform issued to mineworkers on arrival at the Reef, are incorporated into the dance by slapping and stamping to create a rhythm.

Most of Gold Reef City's rebuilt houses now host small museums of early Jo'burg life, and there are bars and restaurants staffed by people in Edwardian costume. The highlight of the place is an old mine shaft, down which you can ride in an old elevator. The adjoining funfair complex has some good rides, such as the water-ride 'Thunder Mountain' and the 'Runaway Train'. An imitation Victorian funfair, a farmyard, Zulu village and the over-promisingly named 'Night-time Action Bar' are among the other attractions. For those who like theme parks, there is also an expensive hotel.

The ticket you buy at the gate entitles you to all buildings and rides. For information on shows, and buses out to Gold Reef City, call ✆ 496 1600.

Zoo Lake

Jo'burg's zoo is worth visiting for the museums attached to it, rather than for the animals, which are better seen in the wild. Zoo Lake (the zoo sits next to a large, man-made lake) is about 15km north of the city centre via the R24, or the number 27 Bus to Parkhurst. Inside the zoo is the superb **Museum of Rock Art** (*open daily 10–1 and 2–4*), which features reproductions of South Africa's best rock paintings and engravings by San (bushman) artists (at least the best ones that are known about). The art displayed varies in antiquity from thousands of years ago to just the last century (South Africa's last San rock artist was shot in the Drakensberg Mountains in the 1850s). Some of the later paintings, which depict settlers' ox-wagons and men on horseback, are of particular interest.

Next door to the zoo is the **National Museum of Military History** (*open Mon–Sat 9–4.30*). This deals with the South African army's 20th-century campaigns (with the exception of Boer and British army weaponry, uniforms and photographs from the Second Anglo-Boer War, 1899–1902).

The Gold Mines

There are no working mines immediately around the city centre, but tours out to mines on the Reef can be arranged via the Publicity Association or the Chamber of Mines, ✆ 498 7100. Tours leave from the Carlton Hotel and are often booked up in advance, especially at weekends, so try for a midweek slot if possible. Although quite expensive, usually between R170 and R250 per person, tours last for almost a full day, include all transport and sometimes lunch, and are very interesting. Some take you down more than a kilometre below ground, into the surreal, stiflingly hot world of South Africa's underground industry. The sweating workers, incessant noise and weird, high-tech machinery seem oddly out of keeping with Africa, and provide some insight into the hell lived by those who have made the country rich. Spare a thought for what conditions must have been like in the early days. You will be very glad to get above ground again at the end of the day.

Shopping

There are **flea markets**, selling both African and European crafts, at the Market Theatre Complex, Newtown (*weekends*), at Bruma Lake, in the Bez Valley (*Wed, Fri, Sat and Sun*), at the Randburg Waterfront (*Tues–Sun*), and on the rooftop of the Rosebank Mall (*most days*).

Galleries and Studios

Apart from the main galleries listed above, Jo'burg has a host of small commercial galleries selling work by South Africa's contemporary artists, and more general arte-facts. The **Apple Gallery**, 33 High Street, in Berea, sells African and eastern work, and **Congo Joe's Artworks**, 13a Raymond Street, which crosses Rockey Street, in Yeoville, sells European hippy-style crafts. In Rosebank, the **Jacana Gallery**, on Cradock Street, specializes in township art and crafts, and the **Everard Read Gallery**, 6 Jellicoe Avenue, is a prestigious gallery dealing in modern South African work. The **Alternatives Gallery**, on the lower level of Rosebank Mall, Oxford Road, sells ceramics and furniture, as well as paintings, as does the **Marialuisa Marino Gallery**, in shop W16, Mutual Square. Sandton also has some prestigious galleries, notably the **Goodman Gallery**, 3b Hyde Square, Hyde Park, the **Natalie Knight Gallery**, 8 Lower Mall, Hyde Park, (both contemporary art), and the **Mordechei Brodie Gallery of African Magic** (folk and totemic art).

The **Johannesburg Studio Route** opens the studios of several working South African artists on the first Sunday of every month. A map with information on each studio is available from the Jo'burg Publicity Association. **Operation Hunger**, on Smal Street, has a craft shop selling superb work, from both South African and other countries, at cheaper prices than at the more chi-chi galleries.

Johannesburg ✆ (011–)   **Other Attractions**

Since Mandela's release from jail something of a cult has, understandably, grown up around the man. Experience it at the **Madiba Freedom Museum**, ✆ 970 1355, out at the Erikson Diamond Centre, in the suburb of Kempton Park—halfway to Pretoria. A taxi there from town costs R100 or so.

Colonial historians will prefer the **Johannesburg Fort**, on Kotze Street, in Hillbrow, built in the 1890s. As a measure of how rowdy this city has been since its founding, the fort was used as a police/military base from which to control the miners way back in the 1880s and '90s. After that it became a prison. The security forces under the apartheid regimes tortured dissidents here. To arrange a visit, call one of the publicity offices. Don't just wander there—it's in a very dangerous area.

The **Randburg Waterfront** is fast taking over from what Sandton used to be—a completely safe, moneyed enclave for whites and blacks at the top of Jo'burg society. Randburg is a suburb north of Sandton, and it's quite an expensive taxi ride there from, say, the Bez valley or Yeoville (around R150). There's a flea market, a whole bunch of shops selling all sorts of expensive rubbish, and some good restaurants. But it's safe, and a genuine slice of Jo'burg nonetheless. The entrance is on Republic Road; call ✆ 789 5052 for more details.

Johannesburg ✆ (011–)

expensive

 Jo'burg has many large, bland expensive chains, such as Sun, Holiday Inn and Protea. Of these, the best are the luxury ultra-modern **Sandton Sun and Towers**, on the corner of Alice and 5th Streets, ✆ 780 5000, the **Carlton Hotel**, on Main Street, in the city centre, ✆ 331 8911, and the **Garden Court Holiday Inn**, on Smal Street, in the city centre, ✆ 297 011. Also worth trying for standard expensive fare are the **Aloe Ridge Hotel**, on Muldersdrift Road, in the suburb of Honeydew, ✆ 659 0605, and the **Devonshire Hotel**, in Braamfontein, ✆ 339 5611. Up in Bryanston (adjacent to Sandton) is the **Curzon Manor**, ✆ 463 7404, which is not ridiculously expensive and comes recommended by many travellers.

However, more interesting places to stay within this price range include: **Joel House**, 61 Joel Road, Berea, ✆ 642 4426, an Edwardian townhouse still furnished with period antiques, with 5 en suite bedrooms (some with fireplaces). Again, it's not too expensive, and there's a choice of B&B or full board. Take a taxi to and from, however, as Berea is close to the city centre and can attract crime. The **Rosebank Hotel**, ✆ 447 2700, at the corner of Tyrwhitt and Sturdee Avenues, is in the safe neighbourhood of Rosebank—handy for shops and restaurants.

Further out, in Sandton, is the stylish **Cullinan Hotel**, ✆ 884 8544, on Katherine Street. The **Parktonian**, ✆ 403 5740, on De Korte Street, in the historic suburb of Parktown, is also recommended.

moderate

At the top end of the scale, the **Jacaranda Guest House**, on Cedar Avenue, in the suburb of Fourways, ✆ 708 1542, is popular with mid-budget travellers for its family run B&B set in beautiful gardens. In Bryanston, a suburb adjacent to Sandton, there's **Maple House**, 298 Main Road, ✆ 706 3553, **Curzon Manor**, ✆ 463 7404, and **Inyoni Guest House**, ✆ 883 1977.

Melville is always a lovely place to stay—safe walking, cafés, shops and eateries. **Chez Simone B&B**, 9 Seventh Avenue, ✆ 726 2926, is right in the heart of the action. Rosebank, another good area for wandering about in, has **Granny's House**, 40 Haswell Street, Oaklands, ✆ 728 2879.

In Parkview there's **Abigail's B&B**, and **Gull Cottage**, which occupies a cottage in an artist's garden. Both are cosy and low-key. There's a joint phone number, ✆ 646 4071, for contact details and addresses.

In Observatory, which is poised midway between Yeoville and Bruma Lake, there's a great B&B: **Rambling Gardens**, 28 Gill Street, ✆ 648 6287, a pleasant old colonial house in its own grounds.

More central is **Irene's Guest House**, in Catalina Gardens, off Hatfield Road in Berea, ✆ 402 9622. You might also try these three in Berea: the **Chelsea Guest House**, on the corner of Katherine and Soper Roads, ✆ 642 4541; the **Coronia**, on O'Reilly Road, ✆ 643 7011; and the **Sands Guest House**, on the corner of O'Reilly and Fife, ✆ 642 7211.

Given the recent rise in tourism to South Africa, a number of new guest houses and B&Bs are sure to open—especially in the safe, and relatively central, suburbs of Rosebank, Hyde Park, and Melville. Contact the **B&B Association**, ✆ 482 2206/7.

cheap

Jo'burg has seen a similar 1990s boom in backpackers' hostels to Cape Town. This is a good thing. Competition has lifted an already fairly high standard and, apart from dorms and double accommodation, most hostels now offer really good travel information for budget travellers going round South Africa and the surrounding countries.

To stay in the heart of big, bad downtown, but in safety, try the **Central Hostel**, 4 Fife Avenue, Berea, ✆ 643 1412. It's near everything, including the red light district, and the owners can organize safe forays into the netherworld of downtown and Hillbrow, for those feeling adventurous.

If you want to stay in funky (though also dodgy) Yeoville, there are various choices. **Rockey Street Backpackers'**, 34 Regent Street, ✆ 648 8786, is actually round the corner from Rockey Street. They can sort you out with trips to Mpumalanga and Kruger, plus car rental and airport runs. Other good choices in Yeoville are: **The Pink House**, on Becker Street, ✆ 487 1991, which also offers safe camping, the **Explorers**, a mile or so down Innes Road from Rockey Street towards the suburb of Observatory, ✆ 648 7138, and **Backpacker's Underground**, 20 Harley Street, ✆ 648 6132. They also offer camping. In Observatory itself is **Brown Sugar**, 75 Observatory Avenue, ✆ 648 7397.

The Bezuidenhout Valley (Bez Valley) is halfway between the city centre and Bruma and has two choices: **Backpacker's Castle**, a large Victorian house on 1st Street, ✆ 614 2555, is usually friendly and lively, with dorms, double rooms and a bar. (But be warned, the atmosphere can be a little eccentric, following the unpredictable character of the owner, who has been known to physically attack people he doesn't like.) And there's **Egoli**, 109 Third Street. (If you can stay at one of the hostels in Yeoville or the northern suburbs, they might be a safer bet.)

Parktown has the **Zoo Lodge**, 232a Jan Smuts Avenue, ✆ 788 3292, which has a great garden. A little further north, in Hyde Park (handy for Rosebank), is **The Backpacker's Ritz**, on North Street, ✆ 327 0229—a place with truly excellent security. You can also camp in the big garden.

Out at Bruma Lake is **Bruma Lodge**, 42 Hans Pirow Road, ✆ 615 1092, which operates free airport and city pick-ups.

There is now a growing crop of backpacker hostels in the farther-flung suburbs verging on the country. These are great if you have a car and have already explored the city. The largest, on a sizeable holding of land, is the **Ranch Hostel**, ✆ 708 1344, out at Witkoppen, north of the city. It's like staying at a country resort—only cheaper. There's a tennis court, jacuzzi and pool, you can ride horses nearby, and you can camp. To get there, go to Fourways Mall and ring for the exact directions or a pick-up.

The **Woodpecker Inn**, out at Bapsfontein, ✆ 964 2593, is another ranch-style set-up. The main house has a thatched roof, which adds charm. Similar again is **Happy Valley**, on Nayuki Road, in Sunninghill Park, ✆ 807 0972.

Johannesburg ✆ *(011–)*

Eating Out

expensive

Leipoldt's, on Juta Street, in Braamfontein, ✆ 339 2765, is named after the South African poet, doctor and gourmet C. Louis Leipoldt, whose books on Cape cuisine, written in the 1920s, are famous in South Africa (*see* **People and Culture**, 'Cape Cuisine'). Moderately expensive, it serves some of the best traditional Cape recipes, such as *bredies*, *sosaties* and *bobotie*, and also specializes in game (through the winter) including buffalo fillets (surprisingly tender) and crocodile's tail, whose delicate meat is reminiscent of crayfish. Unmissable.

Harridan's, at the Market Theatre, Bree Street, Newtown, ✆ 883 6729, serves French and spicy Cape dishes in an informal atmosphere. **Gramadoela's**, also at the Market Theatre, ✆ 838 6960, serves Cape, Ethiopian and southern African specialities (including fried mopane worms and black tripe) in a recreated Cape Dutch interior. Also try **Anton van Wouw**, 111 Sivewright Street, Doornfontein, whose Cape cuisine almost matches Leipoldt's. Also in the city centre, try the **Taj Palace**, 21 Bree Street (corner of Mint Street), ✆ 836 4925, for good north Indian fare.

There are any number of good expensive restaurants in the Sandton Centre, in the Northern Suburbs. But rather exceptional is **La Margaux**, in a neo-Georgian house, on Rivonia Road, ✆ 884 4597, which serves traditional *cordon bleu*. Of note are the frog's legs in a Pernod and mushroom sauce. Equally good is **Isle de France**, 26 Cranemere Centre, 227 Main Road, Bryanston, ✆ 706 2837. The chef here belongs to the celebrated order: *chef cuisinier de France*.

For sushi, head for **Daruma**, ✆ 880 2548, way out in the suburb of Melrose North.

moderate

Melville has any number of good, moderately priced restaurants. **Question Mark Bistro**, 85 4th Avenue, ✆ 726 3930, and **Sam's Cafe**, on 7th Street, ✆ 726 8142, both serve great Mediterranean dishes. **Horatio's**, ✆ 726 2890, is good for seafood, and **Koala Blue**, on 4th Avenue and Seventh Streets, a Thai (not Aussie, as one might expect), is recommended by locals and travellers alike.

Widgeon's Bistro, 60 Tyrone Road, in Parkview, ✆ 486 2053, has some really good pasta/seafood combos.

Yeoville also has several very good, moderately priced restarants. **La Lanterna** (also known as Mama's Place), 2 Rockey Street, ✆ 648 6287, serves good Italian pasta and seafood in a superbly tasteless dining room.

In Rosebank, try **O Fado**, 291 Jan Smuts Avenue, ✆ 880 4410, a Mozambiquan Portuguese place, or **Paros Taverna**, upstairs in the Rosebank Mall, on Oxford Road, ✆ 788 6211. Also in Rosebank, is **Tivoli**, on Mutual Square, off Cradock Avenue, ✆ 788 1718, a good-value pizzeria and Italian restaurant, which makes pizzas up in a proper fire oven.

Linger Longer, on Wierda Street, in Sandton, ✆ 884 0465, is a bit pricier, and serves mostly French dishes. Also up north is the great Punjabi Restuarant, **Shamiyana**, at 71 Corlett Drive, ✆ 786 8810.

cheap

Rockey Street in Yeoville has a good selection of cheap eateries. The **Bar Pita** serves Middle-Eastern food (*shwarmas* and *falafels*) in a hippy/rock 'n' roll atmosphere. No need to book; take your own wine.

Melville also has plenty of choice, and walking around here is safer. If you like Indian, though, head straight to **Sahib**, on 4th Avenue, ✆ 482 6670. The **Full Stop Cafe**, on Seventh Street, also does good cheap light meals.

In Parkview, **Franco's Trattoria**, 54 Tyrone Avenue (in the Parkview Centre), ✆ 646 5449, serves really good pizza and pasta at low prices. In the town centre, **Leipoldt's** (*see* above for details) now serves a great value all-you-can-eat Cape cuisine buffet, featuring game meats like kudu and zebra. There's also a well-kept secret right downtown: **Chon Hing**, 26 Alexander Street. Take a taxi to and from the door though, especially in the evening.

Bars and Cafés

In Yeoville, **Rockerfella's**, on Rockey Street, is an open-air bar and café that often has live jazz/fusion, and where a lot of beautiful people hang out, as well as oddities such as the very well-behaved Jo'burg Hell's Angels. The **Bar Pita**, opposite Rockerfella's, has a lively bar, next door to its restaurant, that plays good rock and reggae, and is a good place to meet people and get information on Jo'burg's nightlife. Upstairs at the **Tandoor**, also on Rockey Street, is a roof garden patronized by up-and-coming young black businessmen. It's okay to be white and be there.

In Melville, the **Roxy Rhythm Bar**, on Main Street, has drinking and good live music, as does the **Bassline**, on Seventh Street. If, however, it's an outdoor coffee/drink/light meal you want (in other words, a good place to people-watch) head for the **Full Stop Cafe**, on Seventh Street, ✆ 726 3801. More ordinary cafés are **Hard Times**, 63a 4th Avenue, and the neighbouring **Rat** and **Ant** cafés on Seventh Street.

The **Radium Bar**, on Louis Botha Avenue, in Orange Grove, is Portuguese-run and has not been redecorated since the early '40s. It gets very busy, but is a good place to meet people among a mixed crowd of yuppies, drunks and young partygoers.

Theatre and cabaret are long-established Jo'burg traditions. For listings, look in the entertainment section of the *Weekly Mail & Guardian*. Larger productions, both mainstream and fringe, can be found in Newtown, Braamfontein and the city centre. The **Market Theatre Complex**, ✆ 832 1641, is in Newtown, on the corner of Bree and Wolhunter Streets. The **Civic Centre**, Braamfontein, ✆ 403 3408, carries the largest-scale productions, while, nearby, the **Alexander Theatre**, on the corner of Stiemans and De Beers streets, ✆ 339 3461, stages more fringe productions, and acts from the townships. In the northeast city centre, the **Alhambra Theatre**, on Sivewright Avenue, ✆ 402 7726, is one of the city's oldest and specializes in dance. In Hillbrow, the **Windybrow Theatre**, on the corner of Nugget and Pietersen Streets, ✆ 720 7009, stages small, often very good productions from the best of the fringe, but don't ever walk here after dark—always take a cab to and from the place.

Jo'burg is known for cabaret, sometimes risqué, sometimes comedy, sometimes song and dance, generally political. Venues change a lot. Hillbrow used to be the centre of it all until it just became too damn dangerous. Check the listings in the *Weekly Mail & Guardian* entertainment section, or the 'Tonight' section of the *Johannesburg Star* to see what's on.

Nightlife

For dance clubs, try **Sub Zero** or **Le Club**, both on Market Street. They play housy, hip-hop-y techno-y stuff, as does **ESP**, 90 End Street. If you like jungle and drum n' bass, go to the jungle night (*Wed*) at Hunter's Pub, on the corner of Conrad Drive and Hillcrest, in the suburb of Blaigowrie. A mixture of dance, hip-hop and trippy, housy funk can be had at **Club 206**, 206 Louis Botha Avenue, in Orange Grove.

More underground clubs are **Club Crave**, at the corner of Plein and Claim Streets, ✆ 483 1349. There's also a kind of shebeen/beat bar called the **Drum Café**, in Greenside, on the corner of Gleneagle and Greenfields Roads. To dance to African sounds with Africans (many of them young guys on the make from West Africa—so single females should be careful) there's **La Rumba**, in the Orchidea Hotel, 90 De Korte Street, downtown. Check out the current safety of this place via the Jo'burg backpacker hostel managers. **Raves** are held every weekend out at Fourways Mall, 194 Witkoppen Road. The DJ outfit that puts them on is called **Synergy**.

In recent years a new form of black music, called **kwaito**, has come out of Jo'burg. It's a kind of dreamy, dancy hip-hop sung in Zulu, Xhosa and Sotho/Tswana. The sound is great, both to listen and dance to. Clubs that specialize in kwaito are **Flava** and **Piccadilly Café**, both on Rockey Street. The kwaito scene is one of the few in South Africa that allows any real ease of social access between young whites and blacks. The scene is too consciously mellow to attract much violence.

If your scene is more singer/songwriters and good live bands try **Wings**, on Ameshof Street, Braamfontein, the **Roxy Rhythm Bar**, on Main Street, Melville, the **Bassline**, on Seventh Street, Melville and **The Doors**, 161 Marshall Street, downtown (also a rock/goth dance club). Look out for flyers and posters as to which bands are playing in these clubs. Don't miss the Honeymoon Suites if they're in town.

Folk nights and Irish *ceilis* are held at **TJ's Folk Club**, the Chambery Hotel, 363 Main Avenue, Ferndale, Randburg. A more central folk club (also has Latin) is **Jargonelle's**, on Caroline Avenue, Brixton, ✆ 837 3770.

For jazz, **Kippie's**, in the Market Theatre Complex, must rank as one of the best-known and oldest jazz clubs in the world. A more recent rival is **Mojo's**, on Louis Botha Avenue, Orange Grove—on the same street **Club 206** also features occasional jazz acts on its non-dance nights. There's also the **Shebeen**, in Rosebank Mall—but the future of this venue currently looks a bit shaky, so check to see if it's still going.

There is a thriving **gay scene** in Jo'burg for both men and women. Try **Krypton**, in Rosebank, ✆ 788 4708, **Champions**, in Braamfontein, and Yeoville's **Champs Elysées**. Listings and addresses of all the current clubs can be found in two magazines: *Exit* and *Outright*.

If you want to check out the seamier side of Jo'burg—and it's there all right—there's the downtown red light district, which gets going around Jeppestown after dark. Hillbrow is also a good place to find trouble, drugs and sex for sale, especially the **Brazil Bar**, on the Hillbrow/Berea border, the **Red Lion**, on Kotze Street and the **Summit Club**, at the corner of Pretoria and Claim streets. A little more upmarket—though still pretty dodgy—is **Base**, on the corner of Twist and Kotze streets. *Be warned: only venture into these places with a regular who will protect you should things get nasty. Otherwise, leave well, well alone. No matter how hard you are, Jo'burg is harder—these places see some of the worst of it. You can easily get killed in a Hillbrow bar or street fight.*

It also goes without saying that, after dark, you must always, always, always take a taxi to wherever you are going, unless it's just across the street.

Soweto

The South Western Townships (Soweto is an abbreviation), sit southwest of Jo'burg along the N1 highway. Home to over two million people, Soweto is the powerhouse from which the Witwatersrand's mines, service industries and general labour are drawn. Of course, Soweto is not the only large 'township' in the region, but it has become the cultural heartland of the black Witwatersrand, and was the centre for most of the resistance to apartheid from the 1950s to the 1990s. Few other 'townships' comprise such a cultural cross-section as Soweto:

most of South Africa's black ethnic groups can be found here, there are areas of great wealth, with huge mansions, areas of grinding poverty and tin shacks, and large neighbourhoods of ordinary houses. In fact, to call Soweto a 'township' is to mis-name it—Soweto is more of a city in its own right, even though it is hardly 40 years old (*see* 'Johannesburg History').

Unfortunately, in recent years, Soweto has become a no-go area for casual visits by whites, whether South African or foreign travellers. There are two reasons for this: the first is crime. Soweto is generally very poor, despite its few rich neighbourhoods, and unemployment is high. A white skin represents money to many 'township' residents, and Soweto has a high enough crime rate in its own right; simply wandering in is to tempt fate too hard. The second reason is race hatred. Many of Soweto's residents have good cause to dislike white people, and have been subject to the humiliations of apartheid for most of their lives. Although most residents of Soweto are not prone to race hatred, there is a strong enough minority of people, especially male youth, who are.

However, it must be said that this has come rather recently; in the late 1970s and early '80s Soweto's jazz clubs and bars were reasonably safe for whites, and there was greater movement between Jo'burg and Soweto. With the change of government, this may yet happen again, and it is worth asking around in Jo'burg for the latest word as to whether there are any clubs in Soweto now open to all comers.

For the time being, you can see Soweto can only do so safely by taking a guided tour. The Johannesburg Publicity Association has details of the tour companies which leave from outside the Carlton Hotel, on Commissioner Street in Jo'burg city centre, most weekday mornings. Tours usually last for about half a day, and some include tea in private homes, as well as visits to the houses of such celebrities as Nelson Mandela, Winnie Mandela, Desmond Tutu, etc. Recommended tour companies are: **Mars Maximum**, ✆ 933 4177, **Abantu**, ✆ 648 7066, and **Face to Face**, ✆ 331 6109. Expect to pay R150 or so per head.

Pretoria

The Volksraad decided to establish in the centre of the territory a new village to be called Pretoria after the late commandant... at the base of a range of mountains which, owing to a petty chief named Magali having been found at its western extremity... has since been called the Magaliesberg.

History of the Boers in South Africa 1887, George McCall Theal

The staid older sister city of noisy Johannesburg sits on the highveld 65km to the north, marking the gateway to the Northern Province. Although handsome, especially in its leafy suburbs, Pretoria is rather dull and conservative. As the country's seat of government, the small city centre is rather sober and business-like, lacking the vibrancy and street culture of neighbouring Johannesburg. Wide streets lined with great jacaranda trees that become clouds of purple blossom in October, a measured pace of life, and (apart from the semi-industrial suburb called Pretoria North) a general prosperity among the white inhabitants give the impression of a large regional town rather than a city.

Pretoria is also much safer than Johannesburg, and is a pleasant place to pass a couple of days on the way north or south. There are also some surprisingly wild and rugged landscapes and reserves within reach.

History

Named after Andries Pretorius, the Voortrekker leader who defeated the Zulus at Blood River in Natal (*see* **Natal** 'History'), Pretoria was founded on the banks of the Apies River in 1853. It was the second capital of the infant South African Republic (or SAR, one of three statelets founded by the Voortrekkers in the Transvaal—*see* **History**), the first having been Potchefstroom in the Western Transvaal. After 1860 Pretoria became the general capital of all three Transvaal states when they united to form the greater South African Republic. Before the Voortrekkers arrived, the fertile, well-watered grasslands around Pretoria had been farmed by Sotho/Tswana groups whose communities had suffered depredations by the warlike Ndebele who had migrated from Natal in the 1820s. Under the leadership of their king, Mzilikazi, the Ndebele had established dominance over most of the highveld through the 1830s, before finally being pushed up into modern Zimbabwe (*see* **Northwest Province** 'History'). The temporary depopulation caused by the Ndebele/Tswana/Sotho fighting resulted in the myth, propagated by colonial historians, that the Transvaal and Orange Free States were 'empty' when the Voortrekkers arrived.

But if the *burghers* of the new SAR manged to subdue the Ndebele, their own society was riven by family feud and petty rivalry. Even after unification in 1860 leaders of the different Transvaal regions spent most of their time squabbling over the constitution and how the new republic should be run. The first president, Marthinius Pretorius, was unable to raise the necessary revenue to run any kind of administration, and Pretoria was not much more than a show-capital with little real authority. This suited most of the Boers around Pretoria who, through the 1850s and '60s, took advantage of returning populations of Sotho, Kgatla, and other clans, who had been driven from the area by the Ndebele and were now drifting back to their former homes. Many local Boer farmers pressed these people into servitude, and even went on kidnapping raids to neighbouring areas to bring back children to work on their farms (a practice that later became common throughout the SAR).

With such help the Boers could run cattle and plant maize over huge tracts of land, as well as freely butchering the local game, especially elephants, whose hides and ivory they sold to agents from the Cape and Natal. By the late 1860s a few individuals had amassed large personal fortunes. Some used their connections to buy land from government officials at low prices, among them Paul Kruger and Piet Joubert—later to lead the SAR to war against the British—who soon had more money than the SAR's creaking government. By 1870 most of the good land in the SAR was in the hands of a select group of Boers, while the rest of the country sunk steadily into poverty. A measure of the republic's disastrous early economy was the failure of its paper money, issued in 1866 by President Pretorius. Not a single *burgher*—not even government officials—would accept it.

The rich Boers (who bought and sold in English pounds) began selling off farms to incoming European settlers at great profit, which incensed the smaller farmers. They felt (quite rightly) that the government was hand-in-glove with the larger landowners, and there was talk of rebellion. This became real during the late 1860s, and Pretoria itself was besieged by angry *burghers*. Pretorius managed to calm them, and persuaded them to return to their farms without reprisal (not that there was a regular army to carry out such tasks). However, an impoverished class of landless Boers, or *bywoners*, was emerging, which was to haunt South Africa into the following century.

The foreign (usually British) settlers were quick to take advantage of the corrupt republic. One Alexander McCorkindale set up the first commercial bank in Pretoria, and started several mining, immigration and farming companies. In return for organizing a loan of £250,000 for Pretorius' government, he secured 200 farms for himself.

Britain, taking advantage of the region's instability, sent troops into the eastern region, supposedly to subdue the Pedi (whom the Boers had been unable to subjugate), regardless of the fact that the SAR government had not asked for British assistance. Then gold was found in the Transvaal Drakensberg and in 1877 Britain, correctly judging that the republic could offer no concerted resistance, occupied Pretoria, and the SAR was declared British territory. Only *after* taking the SAR did the British put down the Pedi, using Swazi mercenaries.

The republic's new president, Thomas Burgers, had power politely wrested from his hands, and the SAR seemed destined to become another British colony. However, faced with the presence of the hated British (from whose authority they had trekked away in the first place) the SAR's squabbling *burghers* finally put aside their internal wranglings and organized resistance. Such was the chaotic nature of the SAR that it took four years for this to have any concrete result, but, through the late 1870s, Paul Kruger (who had himself profited from the lucrative sale of land to foreigners that had led to the British annexation) quietly began to organize armed *kommandos* in the Pretoria district and along the SAR's border with Natal. The British were too busy transforming Pretoria into a proper regional capital, regularizing the SAR's tax system and erecting public buildings, to take much notice. They expected little resistance, as the invasion had gone off with hardly a shot fired, and the Boers were generally regarded as too fragmented and short-sighted to come together and fight. But the British were very wrong. In 1881 the small British garrisons of the SAR were attacked. Paul Kruger declared the First Boer War, and defeated the British main force at the battle of Majuba, on the Natal border. The British were forced to retreat, highly embarrassed, and, lacking the resources to re-occupy the SAR, they restored the republic's full independence in 1884.

Paul Kruger assumed the presidency and set out to unify the disparate republic, and to prevent it from relapsing into the bankruptcy, corruption and disharmony that had allowed his own rise to prominence. His principal policy was to seal off the SAR from outsiders, or at least to contain them in some way and keep the government strictly Boer. In the early 1880s large reefs of gold were found near Barberton in the east, and prospectors and speculators poured in uncontrolled, with little of the revenue going to government. When gold was discovered on the Witwatersrand south of Pretoria in 1886, Kruger and his government determined to secure the wealth for the SAR by controlling the number of foreigners coming into the goldfields.

They sent Johannes Rissik down to the newly discovered mines, who laid out plots for four tent villages, which were then sold at great profit to Boer and foreign speculators. Next they invited the Randlords of Kimberley to develop the reefs under direct government control.

The project worked up to a point: Kruger managed to control the number of mining magnates, and the hitherto empty coffers of the SAR began to fill. But it was impossible to curb the influx of foreigners. Within three years Johannesburg exceeded any other South African town in size, and became a seething pit of prostitution, gambling and hooch rackets, as the miners, starved of women and flush with money, turned the new city into one of 'unbridled squalor'.

For all their previous corrupt financial practices, Kruger and his ministers looked at their self-created Sodom with pious horror. From their moral eyrie at Pretoria they decided that, as long as these *uitlanders* (foreigners) could be kept as temporary residents, then the SAR would not come to too much moral harm. They refused to grant any foreigner the vote, or citizenship of the SAR.

There was an outcry from Johannesburg, and the Randlords, in particular Cecil Rhodes, began to stir up support in the Cape and British press for the *uitlander* cause, with the tacit support of the British government. Neither side was prepared to back down and, in 1899, the SAR and Britain entered the Second Anglo-Boer War (1899–1902) (*see* 'Johannesburg History', p.506).

After the initial Boer successes of 1899, the British invaded the Orange Free State and SAR, and occupied Pretoria in 1900, formally dissolving the Republic and renaming it the Transvaal—a British colony. Kruger went into exile, and the war dragged on until 1902, when the Boer generals finally surrendered at the Treaty of Vereeniging.

Between 1903 and 1910 Pretoria dropped from the centre of the political stage, as Milner and his British administrators set about running South Africa (at this stage still divided into four separate colonies; the Cape, Natal, Orange Free State and Transvaal). But, after Britain decided to unify the colonies and grant them independence as the new Union of South Africa (1910), Pretoria was made the new country's administrative capital. In 1913 the elegant Union Buildings were built on the hill overlooking the city centre, and Pretoria began its 20th-century job as South Africa's quiet capital.

Quiet is the word; for all the controversy and violence that has marked South Africa's 20th-century history, Pretoria itself remained largely aloof from the political events inspired by the presidents who governed from here. Although the ANC bombed the city centre in 1983 (killing 19 people), and several (largely peaceful) mass demonstrations went through the city centre in 1993/4, the political strife of neighbouring Johannesburg and the Vaal triangle towns hardly disturbed the calm surface of day-to-day white life in Pretoria, which, as the seat of government, was a heavily protected bastion of apartheid. Despite many pessimistic predictions, this unruffled surface has continued since the government change-over of 1994.

Pretoria © (012–)

Getting There

by air

Pretoria is serviced by Johannesburg International Airport, about 50km south along the R21. Airport buses pick up and set down at the **Tourist Rendezvous Centre**, on the corner of Vermeulen and Prinsloo Streets in the city centre, © (012) 323 3222, or © 313 7694. Services run every hour from 7am–7pm daily.

by road

Pretoria is on the N1 about 65km north of Jo'burg. The N4 connects Pretoria with Mpumalanga, and the Northern Province is reached by a series of minor tarred roads.

by bus

Long distance buses run between Pretoria and most of the country's main centres, setting down and picking up at the **railway station**. Call **Greyhound**, © 328 4040, **InterCape**, © 328 4599, or **TransLux**, © 315 2111, for details.

The **Baz Bus**, Cape Town, ✆ (021) 439 2323, also serves the Pretoria hostels.

For **airport buses**, call Pretoria Airport Shuttle, ✆ (012) 323 1222. They pick up and drop off at the Tourist Rendezvous roughly every 40-45 minutes. Journey takes about an hour.

by train

Pretoria is linked to Jo'burg, and from there to most of South Africa's larger towns. The Blue Train (see **Travel**) starts and finishes its Cape–Transvaal route at Pretoria. For timetables and fares from Pretoria to Jo'burg call, ✆ 315 2007; for long-distance journeys call ✆ 315 2401.

Pretoria ✆ (012–)   **Getting Around**

Pretoria's city centre is only about 1km by 2km and walking is often the quickest way to get around, especially in the busy middle of the day when it gets so choked with traffic that driving and parking can be a real problem. The best place to park is around Struben and Bloed streets in the northern city centre.

By bus: Buses for the suburbs leave from Church Square. The routes are advertised at bus stops, or call ✆ 313 0839.

By train: Commuter services to some of the more remote suburbs between Pretoria and Jo'burg (such as Irene and Verwoerdburg) leave every half hour from the 19th-century railway station, on the corner of Kruger and Scheiding Streets, ✆ 315 2007.

By black taxi: As in all South African cities, these provide quick transport along the bus routes, but have a worrying accident record. However, within the city and inner suburbs such accidents are rare: most occur along the M1 (N1) highway.

By taxi: Pretoria's taxis must either be called via the *Yellow Pages* or picked up from a taxi rank; you cannot hail them on the street. Taxi ranks can be found at the corner of Vermeulen and Andries streets, and at the corner of Church and Van der Walt streets. A recommended taxi firm is **Rixi**, ✆ 325 8072/3.

Pretoria ✆ (012–)   **Tourist Information**

Pretoria Publicity Association, The Information Bureau, Ground Floor, Sammy Marks Centre, ✆ 323 1222, or ✆ 313 7694.

Pretoria ✆ (012–)   **Useful Addresses and Numbers**

GPO: corner Pretorius and Van der Walt Streets. *Open Mon–Fri 8–4.30, Sat 8–12.*

Travel Agencies: Rennies Travel, ✆ 325 3800, has several branches around town.

Money: Amex, in the Tramshed Shopping Complex, corner of Van der Walt and Schoemaan streets, ✆ 322 2620. **Thomas Cook** is handled by Rennies Travel.

Police: ✆ 10 111.

Ambulance: ✆ 326 0111.

Embassies: Australia, ✆ 342 3740; **Britain**, ✆ 343 3121; **Canada**, ✆ 342 6923; **Mozambique**, ✆ 343 7840; **USA**, ✆ 342 1048 (*see* **Practical A–Z** for addresses).

Pretoria's small city centre is very busy by day, and all but deserted at night. **Church Square**, a small park around a large statue of Paul Kruger, is more or less the geographical centre. The city's buses terminate here, among some of the city's oldest buildings, including the main post office. On crisp winter mornings those waiting for buses sun themselves around the high wall of the south side of the square. In the afternoon city workers eat their lunch on the lawns. Anywhere in the city centre is within ten minute's walk of Church Square, including most of the city's museums.

The **Pierneef Museum,** on Vermeulen Street (*open Mon–Fri 8–4*), has an extensive collection of works by this well-known South African landscape painter from the 1900s. His paintings of the Namib are particularly dramatic, and all the works manage to capture something of the deep, indefinable calm that seems to hang over African landscapes. The **Transport Museum** (*open Mon–Sat 8–4*), one block north on Struben Street, displays old wagons, cars and photographs. Also on Struben, about two blocks further east, is the small **Jansen Collection of Africana** (*open Mon–Fri 8–4*), which displays mostly Cape furniture and silver.

The more interesting **National Cultural History Museum** (*open Mon–Fri 8–4*), on Boon Street, near the zoo, covers both black and white interests with a collection that includes exhibits as diverse as Cape Dutch furniture and San (bushman) rock engravings. Particularly good are the scenes of African life painted by a nun, Sister Vorster—a remarkable woman and artist. Born in 1887, the daughter of a Dutch Reformed Dominee, as a child she would slip out at night to join the servants round their fires, for which her father beat her. Married at 17, to a husband who also beat her for her independent mind, she had 2 children before leaving, training as a nurse and working with the coloureds of District 6 during the great flu epidemic of 1918. Seeing native farmworkers' children making clay oxen, she began, at the age of 40, to model African figures—many of them portrait busts of African rural workers. Unable to make a living out of sculpture, she returned to nursing, and took to drink, but kept modelling until her death in 1945. It's really worth stopping to look at her work.

South of Church Square, on the corner of Paul Kruger and Skinner streets, is the **South African Museum of Science and Technology** (*open Mon–Fri 8–4, Sun 2–5*), which has standard educational displays explaining the workings of various machines.

The **Transvaal Museum of Natural History**, on Paul Kruger Street (*open Mon–Sat 9–5, Sun 11–5*), is one of the best in South Africa. Apart from the usual displays of stuffed fauna, there is an emphasis on early man, including some of the fossil remains found in Mpumalanga dating back roughly one million years. African hunting cultures are presented clearly with the help of video, and there is a superb collection of South African birds. Map buffs will enjoy the attached **Museum of Geographical Survey** (*open Mon–Sat 9–5, Sun 11–5*), a smaller affair which shows what a huge task the mapping of South Africa has been. There is also an extensive collection of rock and semi-precious stones.

Burgers Park, two blocks southeast on Andries Street, is a formal, square set of lawns and large shade trees covering several hectares. In the centre is an exotic hot house (which seems odd for Africa, but Pretoria winter nights can be very cold), with a luxuriant garden of

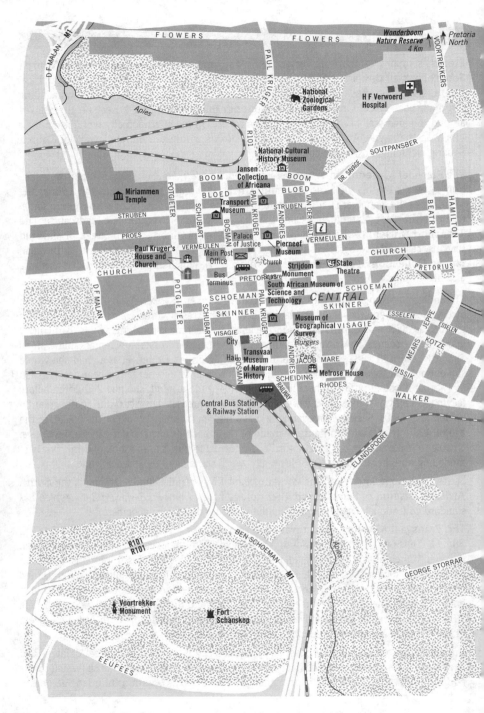

FLOWERS   FLOWERS

Wonderboom
Nature Reserve
4 Km

Pretoria
North

D·F·MALAN·M1

PAUL KRUGER

VOORTREKKERS

Apies

National
Zoological
Gardens

H F Verwoerd
Hospital

R101

SOUTPANSBER

National Cultural
History Museum

DR. SAVAGE

BOOM   BOOM

Jansen
Collection
of Africana

Miriammen
Temple

BLOED   BLOED

BEATRIX

HAMILTON

POTGIETER

SCHUBART

Transport
Museum

PAUL KRUGER

STRUBEN

ANDRIES

VAN DER WALT

STRUBEN

PROES

BOSMAN

VERMEULEN

Palace
of Justice

Pierneef
Museum

VERMEULEN

CHURCH

PRETORIUS

Paul Kruger's
House and
Church

Main Post
Office

Church

Strijdom
Monument

State
Theatre

CHURCH

CHURCH

Bus
Terminus

PRETORIUS

South African Museum of
Science and
Technology

CENTRAL

SCHOEMAN

D F MALAN

POTGIETER

SCHUBART

SCHOEMAN

PAUL KRUGER

SKINNER   SKINNER

ESSELEN

ESSELEN

Museum of
Geographical
Survey

VISAGIE

MEARS

JEPPE

KOTZE

VISAGIE

City
Hall

ANDRIES

Burgers
Park

MARE

RISSIK

BOSMAN

Transvaal
Museum
of Natural
History

JACOB

SCHEIDING

Melrose House

RHODES

WALKER

RAILWAY

Central Bus Station
& Railway Station

ELANDSPOORT

BEN SCHOEMAN

R101
R101

M1

Apies

GEORGE STORRAR

Voortrekker
Monument

Fort
Schanskop

EEUFEES

534

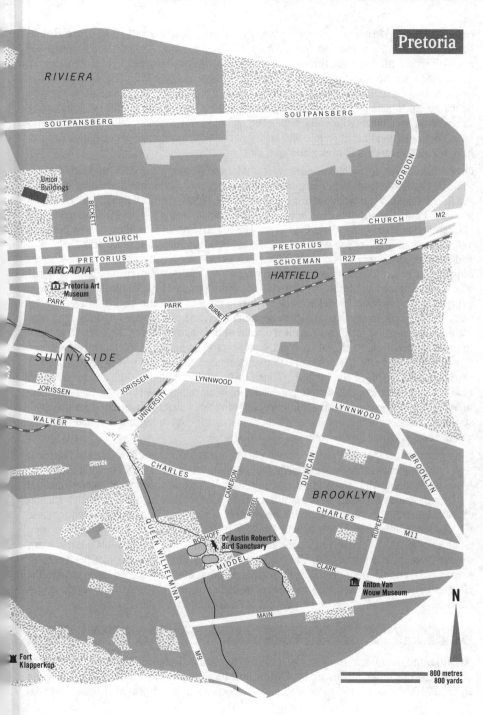

RIVIERA

SOUTPANSBERG

SOUTPANSBERG

GORDON

Union
Buildings

BECKETT

CHURCH

CHURCH

M2

PRETORIUS

PRETORIUS

R27

ARCADIA

SCHOEMAN

R27

Pretoria Art
Museum

HATFIELD

PARK

PARK

BURNETT

SUNNYSIDE

LYNNWOOD

JORISSEN

JORISSEN

LYNNWOOD

UNIVERSITY

WALKER

CHARLES

BROOKLYN

CAMERON

DUNCAN

QUEEN WILHELMINA

BOSHOFF

RIDDEL

Dr Austin Robert's
Bird Sanctuary

BROOKLYN

CHARLES

RUPERT

M11

MIDDEL

CLARK

Anton Van
Wouw Museum

N

Fort
Klapperkop

MAIN

M9

800 metres
800 yards

tropical plants. On Rissik Street, which runs by the south side of the park, is **Melrose House** (*open Tues, Wed, Fri and Sat 10–5, Thurs 10–8, Sun 12–5, closed Mon*), a Victorian mansion where the Boer and British generals met to sign the Treaty of Vereeniging in May 1902, following the Boers' surrender at the end of the Anglo-Boer War. There is little in the house to suggest such momentous events, although there is one room full of artefacts made by the Boer prisoners of war who were sent to St Helena between 1899 and 1902, including ships carved from bone (with every piece of equipment made to scale), religious pictures and tools. Works of great beauty and detail testify to the enforced leisure of camp life. You can have tea on the veranda of Melrose House, looking out over the lawns.

On Bosman Street, a few blocks northwest of Melrose House, is the old **City Hall**, a handsome piece of overblown Victoriana, overlooking statues of Andries and Marthinus Pretorius, the Boer father and son who founded the town in the 1850s. Of more direct historical significance is **Paul Kruger's House** (*open Mon–Sat 8.30–4, Sun 11–4*) at the western end of Church Street, lived in by 'Oom Paul' from 1884–1901. As an indication of how personal and classless (as long as you were white) the old Boer republics were, it is true that 'Oom Paul' used to sit outside his house on days when he was not busy in any of the government offices, and would converse with anyone who so wished. Apart from the usual personal effects, photographs and furniture, there is a display of presents from European governments expressing their support for the Boer cause during the war with the British. Kruger did not want presents, but foreign troops. These he did not get, and the exhibits of handsome silverware and other trifles make a poignant reminder of the impossibility of the Boers' resistance to British imperialism. At the far west of the city centre, on Seventh Street, just below Boom Street, is one of Pretoria's few attractions not related to Boer or British nostalgia—the **Miriammen Temple**, a Hindu temple (*open daily, all day*). Built in 1905, and hence as old as anything in Pretoria, this temple is devoted to, of all things, the Hindu goddess of infectious diseases. Its exotic, perfumed interior, full of votive images, is a far cry from the staid, stately atmosphere of most of Pretoria's monuments and museums, and is worth visiting if you have time, if only for the contrast.

Just north of the town centre, fronting Boom and Paul Kruger Streets, are the **National Zoological Gardens** (*open daily 8–5*). Although it is far more interesting to observe game in the wild (and Pretoria is within reach of several good game reserves) it is still worth visiting if you are seriously interested in wildlife. Rare indigenous species, such as giant eland, cheetah and aardwolf, have been raised here, some for re-introduction to the wild. Other rare African species, such as the scimitar-horned oryx (which has been all but shot to extinction in its natural ranges of North Africa and Arabia), Hartmann's mountain zebra and pigmy hippo, as well as completely foreign rarities like the Brazilian maned wolf, and Chinese Pere David's deer, are bred at the zoo's special game farm in the Northern Province. The zoo has examples of all its rare species on show. Many of the enclosures can be viewed from above by a special cable-car.

The Older Suburbs

Arcadia, the oldest suburb, is just east of the city centre. Here, on the hilltop park at the eastern end of Church Street, are the **Union Buildings**, South Africa's official seat of power since 1910. Among the most successful neoclassical buildings of British imperial architecture, they were designed by Sir Herbert Baker, who was responsible for many of South Africa's turn-of-the-century public buildings. Built from red sandstone, the Union Buildings have an Italianate feel, and surround a long ornamental lake with good views out over the city. Unfortunately, visitors are not allowed inside. Also in Arcadia, on Schoeman Street, is the **Pretoria Art Museum** (*open Mon–Sat 10–4.30*) whose small collection of South African art, by such painters as Pierneef and Frans Oerder, and a few old Dutch Masters (Van Dyck, Frans Hals) are worth a visit on the way down from the Union Buildings.

If you follow Church Street a few kilometres out towards Bronkhorstspruit, it will bring you to the fascinating **Sammy Marks Museum** (*open Tues–Fri 9–4, weekends 10–9*), the home of perhaps the biggest South African mining magnate after Cecil Rhodes (they were contemporaries). It was Sammy Mark's Cullinan Mine, just north of here, that in 1905 produced the famous Cullinan Diamond, presented to England's own fat king Teddy (Edward VII) by the Transvaal Government as a kind of post Boer-War olive branch. The mansion is still stuffed with all kinds of costly Victoriana, and is well worth a visit.

Sunnyside, the first suburb southeast of the city centre, is something of a centre for nightlife, with a large, multi-storey shopping centre housing a variety of bars and restaurants. Most of Pretoria's nightlife goes on here. East of Sunnyside, along Walker Street (which becomes Charles Street as you leave the area), is Brooklyn, a handsome suburb of late 19th- and early 20th-century houses, where many of Pretoria's wealthy professionals live. There is a small museum at 299 Clark Street (*open Mon–Fri 9–4.30*), once the home of sculptor **Anton Van Wouw**, whose massive bronze statue of Paul Kruger frowns down on Pretoria's Church Square. Inside the house are various smaller works, mostly in bronze.

South of town two old hilltop forts overlook the city, **Fort Klapperkop** and **Fort Schanskop** (*open Mon–Sat 10–4*). Both these late 19th-century fortifications house small military museums devoted to the Second Anglo-Boer War and the South African soldiers who fought in the Second World War desert campaigns. Nearby is the massive, rather grim **Voortrekker Monument** (*open daily 8–5*) which, like the two forts, is clearly signposted from the R28 south of the city centre. The square stone 1940s edifice, built to commemorate the Great Trek of 1838, is surrounded by giant stone wagons, representing the *laagers* used by the Voortrekkers as a fortress from which to mow down the attacking Zulu at Blood River.

The monument is ponderous but full of solemn presence, like a Boer farmer's beard. If the outside is a little like a giant stone fridge, guarded by the statue of a gaunt, fierce Boer woman shaking her fist at the unknown, the inside is rather beautiful—a vast, airy vault with a neoclassical frieze depicting the Great Trek. Although similar in style, the various panels could have been carved by different artists. The uniformity of expression, features and clothing produces a slightly comic effect, especially in the faces of the Boer heroes—Piet Retief, Louis Trichardt and Andries Pretorius—who are almost indistinguishable from one another. Most interesting is the battle scene between the Voortrekkers and the Xhosa, which shows Xhosa warriors mounted on oxen trained to charge, surround and maul the enemy, a tactic learned from the Khoi. Riding oxen, for racing or warfare, died out in the Eastern Cape by the late 1870s, after the Frontier Wars (*see* **Eastern Cape** 'History'), and today the practice is preserved only in ancient cave paintings or in works of art such as this frieze.

The top of the monument is open to the sky, and has been designed so that at noon on 16 December—the Day of the Covenant, a public holiday commemorating the Voortrekkers' defeat of the Zulu at Blood River—a ray of sunlight falls on to the long stone slab in the centre of the the the building, lighting up the carved words: 'Ons Vir Jou, Suid Afrika' (We are yours, South Africa).

For some years, at an accompanying semi-religious ceremony, thanks were given to God for delivering the Voortrekkers from the threat of massacre by the Zulu, and for the foundation of the modern Boer society—a neat illustration of how deeply entwined are the Boer political and religious creeds. Since April 1994 the Day of the Covenant has been abolished, but the public holiday has been kept under a new name, the 'Day of Conciliation' (*see* p.378).

Two galleries run around the top of the monument. One inside is terrifyingly vertiginous, as it seems to bend downward towards the parapet and the floor 100ft below. An outside gallery gives excellent views out over the city and over to the lovely Magaliesberg Mountains. Inside the main hall is a small gift shop which sells among its range of souvenirs what must be one of the most prized items of South African kitsch—scale-model candles in the form of the Voortrekker Monument.

Pretoria ✆ (012–)

Where to Stay

expensive

Pretoria has no lack of expensive chain hotels, but **La Maison**, ✆ 434 003, is without doubt the best (and not too expensive). Set in the suburb of Hatfield, near most of Pretoria's foreign embassies and consulates, La Maison offers B&B and en suite bedrooms in an opulent Victorian white-stuccoed mansion, with beautiful gardens and a pool.

Orange Court Lodge, in the city centre, on the corner of Vermeulen and Hamilton Streets, ✆ 326 6346, is an old Victorian stone hotel with dark-stained beamed ceilings, fireplaces and a large garden. Self-catering only, and reasonably priced.

Die Werf, ✆ 991 1809, in Lynnwood, at the far eastern edge of Pretoria, is a charming Cape Dutch country house, with private verandahs opening from simple, rustic bedrooms and superb Boer country cooking. Such delights as pumpkin fritters, turmeric rice, Karoo lamb and *bobotie* are served in the little restaurant.

Also try **Meintjieskop Guesthouse**, 145 Eastwood Road, Arcadia, ✆ 433 711, and the classic **Victoria Hotel**, where Schnieding and Kruger streets meet, ✆ 323 6052.

moderate

That's It, 5 Brecher Street, in Sunnyside, ✆ 344 3404, is a great B&B. **Battiss Guest House**, 92 20th Street, in the suburb of Menlyn Park, ✆ 467 318, a 1930s family house, used to be the home of Walter Batiss, a moderately well-known South African artist, some of whose paintings are still in the house. The two en suite rooms open on to courtyards. **59 Brooks Street**, in Brooklyn, ✆ 436 834, is a larger, Victorian manor house built in a mixed classical-Gothic style, complete with a little turret. **The Malvern Guest House**, 575 Schoeman Street, in Arcadia, ✆ 341 7212, is an oldish suburban house offering clean, comfortable rooms and B&B near the city centre. **Greenwoods Guest House**, ✆ 348 7929, and **Dunkelly**, ✆ 667 1207, in the pleasant village of Irene, south of Pretoria, are also recommended.

If you cannot find room at these places, also try the following B&Bs in and around Pretoria: **Lady Godiva Guest House**, 16 Godiva Street, Valhalla, ✆ 715 729; **Jane-Anne's Junction**, 175 Rubinda Street, Murrayfield, ✆ 833 535; **El Nise Guest House**, near the university, ✆ 465 694; **Swaeltjie Gastehuis**, ✆ 811 0394; **Ted's Place**, ✆ 807 2803, and **Clydesdale Cottage**, ✆ 344 2988.

Finally, if all else fails, ring the **Pretoria B&B Association**, ✆ (011) 482 2206/7, or **Jacana**, ✆ (012) 346 3550.

cheap

Pretoria Backpackers, 34 Bourke Street, Sunnyside, ✆ 343 9754, will pick you up from anywhere in town. They also run trips out to Sun City, Soweto, Pilanesberg and the Ndebele Village. **Word of Mouth Backpackers**, 145 Berea Street, Muckleneuk, at the corner of Mears Street, ✆ 341 9661, organize trips into the Kruger and Magaliesberg. Newer than the above is **Mazuri Backpackers**, 503 Reitz Street, in Sunnyside, ✆ 343 7782.

Pretoria ✆ (012–)   *Eating Out*

expensive

The **Theatre Restaurant**, in the State Theatre, on Church Street, ✆ 322 4147, serves very good Italian and more simple traditional food. It is modern, unpretentious, popular and usually lively. **La Madeleine**, 258 Esselen Street, Sunnyside, ✆ 446 076, offers fine Belgian cooking and a low-key feel. Go for the mussels. Out in Arcadia, try **Gerard Moerdyke**, 752 Park Street, ✆ 344 4856, which serves some of the best South African cuisine in the republic. Game is the speciality.

moderate

La Perla, on Skinner Street, downtown, ✆ 322 2759, is a good place to kick off an evening in the city centre, although it's fairly expensive. They specialize in fish. Really good value are the huge Italian plates at **Pavarotti's**, in the Sammy Marks Centre, near the Tourist Rendezvous. If you don't have a gargantuan appetite, try the **Victoria Hotel**, on the corner of Schneiding and Kruger streets, ✆ 323 6052.

Sunnyside has some great moderately priced restaurants. Go Russian at the **Magic Samovar**, 115 Gerard Moerdyke Street, ✆ 341 9500. The restaurant often has Ukranian folk groups to liven things up. On the same street is a great value Mediterranean place called **Sirocco**, ✆ 341 3785.

cheap

Apart from take-aways, it is hard to find cheap food in the city centre. However, **Pinocchio's**, a Portuguese restaurant on Paul Kruger Street, serves very good value set menus specializing in seafood (try the calamari) and spicy chicken. No need to book. A cheap chain restaurant, **Nando's**, in the Tramshed Centre on Schoeman Street, serves an excellent chicken and chips. Also good value is the **Buffet De l'Opera**, on Church Street, near the theatre.

More variety can be found on Esselen Street in Sunnyside, which has a wealth of good, cheap restaurants. The stuffed vine leaves and fish dishes at **Santorini's**, ✆ 448 045, are worth leaving the city centre for, as are the stuffed pancakes a few doors down at the appropriately named **Fillings For Pancakes**, ✆ 343 1683, which sometimes features live jazz. Good pasta and pizza can be found at **Giovanni's**, ✆ 341 0689/0846, and light meals (breakfast and lunch only) at the **Grapevine Café**. In Hatfield, you might try the American burger joints **Ed's Easy Diner** and the **Hard Rock Café**, on Park Street. On Burnett Street, in the centre of Hatfield, is **Bachini's**, a small Italian restaurant. No need to book for any of the three.

Entertainment

The **State Theatre Complex**, on Church Street, ✆ 322 1665, stages large- and small-scale productions of drama, ballet, modern dance and music in its five theatres. For movie-going, the **Tramshed**, a converted railway terminus on Schoeman Street, has a good cinema that screens non-mainstream movies. For more Hollywood-style films, the **Sterland Centre**, on Beatrix Street, has two cinemas, and, of all things, an ice-rink. Cabaret acts and avant-garde/fringe companies perform at the **Teaterhuis**, on Gerard Moerdyke Street, in Sunnyside, and at the **Basement Theatre**, below Café Riche, in Church Square, ✆ 328 3173.

Nightlife

In comparison with wild Jo'burg, staid Pretoria's nightlife is not exactly humming, despite the city's two universities. However, Pretoria has a few places that can offer something more than just Top 40 music and 'smart casual' punters. **Crossroads Blues Bar**, upstairs in the Tramshed, on Schoeman Street, ✆ 322 3263, is a late-night bar that plays a good mix of rock, reggae and soul for a mix of professionals, students and pleasure seekers. Arrrive after work. Later in the evening live bands play. If you want a good dance club, try **Subway**, on Beatrix Street, Arcadia, or the **Viper Room**, on Esselen Street. If you like reggae, head for **Things and Themes** in Hatfield. Rockers will enjoy **Upstairs At Morgan's**, also in Hatfield.

The **gay** scene is represented by **Incognito**, in the Belgrave Hotel, 22 Railway Street, and nearby **Steamer's**, which is close to the main railway station.

Again, Jo'burg dominates the area's music scene, but live blues can generally be found at the **Crossroads Bar**. Other places for live music are: **Tequila Sunrise** (often has reggae acts) and **Café Galeria**, on Esselen Street, in Sunnyside. There's a bar on Beatrix Road in Arcadia, called **Oscars**, which also has bands from time to time. If you want to hear jazz or township beat, you have to head for the townships. As everywhere in South Africa, you should not do this alone. Talk it through with one of the backpacker lodge managers and see what can be arranged.

Around Pretoria

South of Pretoria, on the M1 and on the commuter line, is the old village of **Irene**, now fast becoming a suburb of Pretoria. Irene was built on a massive dairy farming estate, most of which still stretches south of the suburb. The tree-shaded lanes, meadows, irrigated pastures and woodlands of the still-active **Irene Farm** make a welcome change from the city and give an idea of what the Witwatersrand looked like before creeping urbanization.

Also in Irene is Prime Minister Jan Smuts' house, **Doornkloof Farm** (*open Mon–Fri 10–5*), a ramshackle tin affair which contains most of its original furniture, his photographs and letters, and his pressed and documented collection of African herbs. Smuts achieved international fame for leading South Africa into the Second World War, but his contribution to South African history, both good and bad, lasted from 1900 to 1948, and included the Second Anglo-Boer War, the 1920s' violent industrial unrest, and the 1930s' power struggle between imperial government and Afrikaner nationalism (*see* **History** and 'Johannesburg History'). The house seems to embody Pretoria's dull but safe tranquility. Next to the house is a tea-room and camp site.

A little further south is the **Van Riebeeck Nature Reserve**, reached by the same road from Irene to Doornkloof, but a little further east. This extensive wild area surrounds a dam, and has a network of hiking trails up to two hours in length. Expect to see eland, zebra, oribi and duiker. There is no accommodation.

Wonderboom Nature Reserve, on Voortrekker Road, on the outskirts of Pretoria's northern suburbs, was founded to protect a huge wild fig tree, the *Wonderboom* ('wonder tree'). The size of a small building, this magnificent tree is over 1000 years old and 23m high. It was a traditional meeting-place for Ndebele chiefs, and later for Voortrekkers and settlers, who left messages for each other here. The spreading branches cover a huge area, and some have even grown back into the soil to form underground runners which have re-emerged as separate trees around the old parent, creating a wood. The effect is magical: the twisted, randomly spiralling, smooth branches, and the massive bulk of the main tree, provide welcome shade from the harsh Transvaal sun. Today, the reserve covers about 90ha, run through with self-guided walking trails.

Roodeplat Nature Reserve surrounds a dam only 16km northeast of the city along the R512 to Cullinan. It can be crowded at weekends, but mid-week there are few visitors. From the walking trails and game-viewing roads you are likely to spot antelope such as sable, kudu, waterbuck, blue wildebeest, red hartebeest, impala, steenbok and duiker. Zebra are also common. The water is safe for swimming, and there is a small camp site with ablution blocks. About 100km northeast of Pretoria is the small former 'homeland' of **Kwa-Ndebele**. Now officially re-absorbed into South Africa, the area is still markedly undeveloped compared to the surrounding countryside, and is still marked as separate on most road maps.

Kwa-Ndebele

Ndebele History and People

The Ndebele of this area are often thought to be the descendants of a renegade Zulu regiment that fled their homeland in the 1820s under their general Mzilikazi, an opportunist who saw a chance to carve out his own kingdom amid the upheavals of the *Mfecane*. But this is only partly true. It seems that, despite the common name and language, today's Transvaal Ndebele are in fact descended from a much earlier Nguni immigration, who adopted Ndebele ways during that tribe's occupation of the area, but who did not subsequently move on with Mzilikazi to the Orange Free State, and from there to modern-day Zimbabwe, but stayed put.

Whatever the true descent of this Transvaal clan, it is worth knowing something bout the more general history of the Ndebele. Having been trained in the Zulu fighting tactic known as known as the 'horns of the bull', the itinerant Ndebele would defeat each new tribe they came to conquer by encircling their flanks while attacking on a full front, then close in for a general slaughter with short, stabbing spears, whose blades were wide to inflict maximum damage. Through the late 1820s and '30s, the Ndebele raided and conquered the Sotho-Tswana clans living in the highveld, being repulsed only by the BaSotho (*see* Lesotho). The Ndebele settled in the Western Transvaal and absorbed the women of conquered clans into their own. Their numbers grew rapidly and, by 1835, Ndebele raiding parties were penetrating far west to the Griqua territory near the Orange River in modern Bushmanland, and to Swaziland and Venda in the northeast Transvaal.

Mzilikazi was as much statesman as warlord, and he established diplomatic relations with Robert Moffat and John Campbell, British missionaries of Griqualand. With his clan's mastery of the highveld undisputed, Mzilikazi might have looked forward to the dubious benefits of becoming a British protectorate and keeping a measure of independence as white settlement penetrated the highveld in the 1830s.

But the first white settlers to arrive in his territory *en masse* were the Voortrekkers, in 1836. Armed with muskets, and supported by Griqua and some Tswana auxilliaries, the Boers set about enslaving the Ndebele. After initial skirmishes, Mzilikazi wiped out three Voortrekker parties, then attacked the main Voortrekker *laager* at Vegkop late in 1836. Mzilikazi's frontal tactics failed against the Voortrekker's massed musketry, and he lost thousands of warriors in one fell swoop. Mzilikazi withdrew to the Northern Transvaal, pursued by a Voortrekker, Griqua and Rolong Tswana force, who again defeated the Ndebele at Mosega in 1837. Mzilikazi escaped with most of his people and livestock, but ran into another combined force under Andries Pretorius near modern-day Pretoria, and suffered a heavier defeat.

In one year the Ndebele had been reduced from one of the most powerful clans in the Transvaal to its weakest. Mzilikazi bowed to the inevitable and took his remaining regiments over the Limpopo River into modern-day Zimbabwe, where he subdued the Shona people and established a dominance that passed to his son Lobengula and lasted until the British invaded the territory in the 1890s. Now known as the Matabele, Mzilikazi's clan are modern Zimbabwe's second largest nation; a few isolated groups still live in South Africa.

After Mzilikazi went north the Boers experienced little resistance to their new dominance of the highveld, and the Voortrekker leaders, Andries Pretorius and Hermanus Potgieter, began to found more permanent towns. However, black military endeavour had not been totally crushed. In 1854 a large Sotho band under chief Makapan went to war with the highveld Voortrekkers and were defeated near modern Potgietersrus, but succeeded in killing a large number of Boers, including Hermanus Potgieter himself. Determined to put an end to the troublesome Makapan, the Boers pushed the chief and his people into a set of deep caves (the Makapansgat, where fossil hominid remains were found in the 20th century) and laid siege until all the Sotho had died from hunger, thirst or disease. (*see* **Northern Province**).

Kwa-Ndebele Today

However, the creation of modern Kwa-Ndebele was due to modern Afrikaner rather than to Ndebele history. The former 'homeland' was declared in 1981, the last to be created by the Nationalist government in their attempt to re-settle South Africa's blacks in their own 'independent' areas. Ndebele people were uprooted from their homes and forcibly moved to the present site, an arbitrary location supposed to represent the Ndebele's 'original' range.

Now that the former 'homeland' has been re-absorbed into South Africa, these people face a long fight to reclaim the properties from which they were moved, and which were confiscated from them when the 'homeland' was created.

Like most former 'homelands', Kwa-Ndebele is poor, overcrowded and overgrazed, with a growing rural population struggling to exist on too little land, and with most of its young men seeking work in Jo'burg. However, many traditions survive, in particular the painting of huts in beautiful, exact geometric designs, a series of polygons filled in with vibrant colours. And the Ndebele maidens' practice of wearing beaded neck rings that gradually elongate the neck can still be seen in places. The former 'homeland' draws some income from the **Ndebele Show Village**, where tourists can watch Ndebele customs at work; from dancing and 'witchdoctor' ritual, to the more every-day grinding of millet and maize, and preparing food. Crafts, such as bead-work and woven rugs, might be on sale. Although the whole concept of such show villages, let alone tribal 'homelands', is a legacy of apartheid, places such as this are as close as many

tourists have time to get to traditional African culture. Bear in mind, too, that visitors inject much-needed money into the local, struggling economy. The village is near **Hammanskraal**, about 80km northeast of Pretoria on an unnumbered road between Pretoria and Marble Hall, south of the Rust De Winter Nature Reserve.

Rust De Winter Nature Reserve is about 65km north along the N1 from Pretoria, at the gateway to the bushveld zone of the Northern Province. At weekends it is packed out by water-skiers and fishermen from Pretoria, but it can make a convenient rest-stop on a long drive along the N1. Bird watchers will enjoy the waterfowl species, such as black duck, Egyptian goose, and white stork. There is unlimited walking along the dam's shore, but remember that there are crocodile and bilharzia in the water, so don't paddle. Accommodation is in a camp site only, and you must get there before 6pm.

The Magaliesberg Mountains

The Magaliesberg range runs west of Pretoria. Although most of the area belongs to private farms, the hills are surprisingly wild and open to hikers. Two reserves, **Rustenburg Nature Reserve** (about 100km west of Pretoria along the R27 at the western end of the range) and **Mountain Sanctuary Park** (45km west of Pretoria along the R27, then 30km along the R512 after the junction at the Haartebeespoort Dam) provide immediate access to the Magaliesberg; to get into the rest of the range requires arrangement in advance via the National Hiking Way Board in Jo'burg, ✆ (011) 886 6524.

Rustenburg, the larger of the two, has interesting rock formations and strangely mixed vegetation, comprising woodland, marshland (whose reedbanks look a shimmering blue when seen from a distance), dry aloe hillsides and thornveld. There are even pockets of fynbos, which is rare outside the Cape, over 1000km away. There is a 2-day trail with overnight huts or a 3-hour self-guided trail, along which hikers can expect to see waterbuck, kudu, red haartebeest, klipspringer, duiker and, if lucky, the rare sable antelope. Raptors are common, in particular black and martial eagles and Cape vultures, and the views from the Magaliesberg out to the north are lovely. A few shy leopard and caracal hunt in the hills, and brown hyena are present, but the visitor is unlikely to see these. Apart from hiking huts, accommodation is a camp site with ablution blocks.

Mountain Sanctuary Park also has self-guided walks and a variety of plains game, such as zebra, kudu and reedbuck. Again, there are long views out over the Transvaal plains, and accommodation is in chalets or a camp site with ablution blocks.

About 100km due north of Pretoria, a section of what used to be the Bophuthatswana 'homeland' (accessible along the trunk road to Mapobane via the town of Brits), is the superb **Borakalalo National Park**, which stretches over 14,000ha of bushveld, riverine woodland, dry forested kloofs and grassland. It harbours white rhino, giraffe and most large antelope, including sable, kudu, tsessebe, gemsbok, waterbuck and eland. The reserve has excellent guided hiking and riding trails into the bush, from which game spotting is almost inevitable. Accommodation is self-catering in permanent safari tents.

Visitors should be aware that the Klipvoor Dam, which the park surrounds, carries bilharzia, so do not swim there.

Walking and hiking: Short, self-guided day-trails can be found at **Wonderboom Nature Reserve, Roodeplaat Dam Nature Reserve, Rust De Winter Dam Nature Reserve**, close to Pretoria, and at **Rustenburg Nature Reserve** and **Mountain Sanctuary Park**, in the Magaliesberg. **Borakalalo National Park** also has self-guided trails, but visitors should stay overnight in the permanent tented camp, as the distances to and from the park are long, and driving at night in the former Bophuthatswana is not recommended, owing to the amount of stray stock on the roads. Directions for all the parks and reserves are given above.

Hikes of more than a day can be found at **Rustenburg Nature Reserve**, ✆ (01421) 31 051 (a 2-day trail with overnight hut, bookable in advance), and in the main **Magaliesberg** chain, with accommodation in tents and caves, bookable in advance from the National Hiking Way Board in Jo'burg, ✆ (011) 886 6524.

Also try **Eagle Cove Hiking Trails**, ✆ (0142) 750 102—private trails on which you are unlikely to meet anyone else.

Many lodges and guest farms have hiking trails for their guests.

Guided game-spotting hikes can be arranged at **Borakalalo National Park**, ✆ (00200) and ask for Jericho 0264.

Riding: Roberts Farm Horse Trails, ✆ (0142) 773 332, offers day and overnight rides on good horses through some of the emptier stretches of mountain. **Africa Horse Safaris**, ✆ (011) 465 9168, offer trails in a small private reserve called Motsetse, about 45 minutes drive from both Jo'burg and Pretoria.

Abseiling, rock climbing and rap jumping: Trips in the Magaliesberg are run by a company in Jo'burg. Ring Vincent on, ✆ (011) 902 4652. (Rap jumping is abseiling face-first.)

Paragliding: Courses and experienced flights are run by the South African Hang-Gliding and Paragliding Association, ✆ (011) 825 55429, in the Magaliesberg and various other sites in the Transvaal.

Where to Stay

expensive

Mount Grace Country House, ✆ (011) 880 1675, is a luxurious thatched hotel, at the foot of the Magaliesberg, just west of the town of Magaliesberg, on the R24. Accommodation is in individual stone cottages with gardens, a pool, a tennis court and walking trails into the surrounding hills. Classical music concerts are held once a month in a small theatre attached to the hotel.

Valley Lodge, ✆ (0142) 771 301, is a Victorian country house set in a nature reserve on the banks of the Magalies River, just a few miles from Mount Grace. The bedrooms have four-poster beds and, in some cases, views of the river. Boating and fishing can be arranged. There is a large pool, three tennis courts and a series of walking trails. Also try **Celtis Lodge**, ✆ (0142) 773 952, a stone guest house on a private farm at the foot of the hills.

moderate–cheap

Bardenview Mountain Lodge, ✆ (0142) 92 204, backs on to the Rustenburg Nature Reserve. Not far away, **Out of Africa Guest House**, ✆ (0142) 771 126, is a cosy thatched affair that does not allow kids. **Bergbrieds Lodge**, ✆ (0142) 771 217, has small chalets with open log fires in winter, hiking trails and good bird-watching. Also near Rustenburg is **Vorster's Folly**, ✆ (0142) 771 553, a small B&B overlooking the Magalies River Valley.

Further out into the country are **Seven Hills Guest Farm**, ✆ (0205) 51 181, and **Mountain Sanctuary Park**, ✆ (014222) 1430, also at the southern foot of the Magaliesberg, which has comfortable self-catering chalets, a camp site, walking trails (with plentiful wildlife) and swimming.

Camp sites can be found at **Rustenburg Nature Reserve**, ✆ (01421) 31 050. Those prepared to hike for a few hours can stay in one of the overnight refuge huts further into the mountains. **Rust De Winter Dam Nature Reserve**, ✆ (0121712) 2422, 85km north of Pretoria via the N1, also has a camp site with ablution blocks, as does **Roodeplaat Dam Nature Reserve**, ✆ (012) 808 1164, about 45km northeast of Pretoria along the N1 and R513.

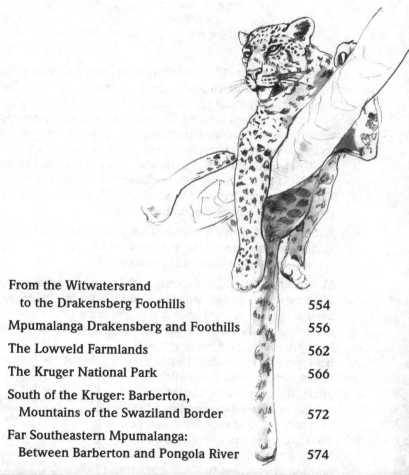

Mpumalanga

On a morning in mid-May I saw the Bushveld for the first time. My car breasted the last turn of a mountain pass. The air was startlingly clear; a beryl sky overhead...straggling mimosa trees in the foreground, multiplied by thousands in the middle distance—sandstone, or more likely dolomite, tors at infrequent intervals...patches of grass in-between—the dust raised by a herd of zebra or wildebeest to the right—and the road winding through the scrub to be lost very soon in that impenetrable secondary forest.

Bushveld Doctor, Louis Leipoldt

About 200km east of Johannesburg the highveld grasslands begin to flow into broken hills which soar sharply into the mountains of the high Mpumalanga Drakensberg. In an abrupt change from flat grasslands of the highveld, you climb amid forest, mist and great empty sweeps of mountain, cut through with fast-flowing rivers. And then the landscape changes again: east of the Drakensberg the altitude drops severely and the lowveld, a great expanse of bushveld, stretches away to the low Lebombo Mountains on the border with Mozambique. Most of this is wild country. The easternmost strip is dominated by the Kruger National Park which, to give an idea of scale, is larger than Israel.

With these contrasts Mpumalanga has a huge variety of vegetation and animal life and is one of the few regions where big game is in general abundance, albeit within fixed reserves.

Many South African game-spotters holiday in Mpumalanga and there are some overdeveloped spots to be avoided. However, the region is large enough to make solitude easy to find. For those wanting to see game there is a confusing variety of private and state-owned reserves. In general, the large private reserves, most of which border the Kruger National Park, offer luxury and big game at extortionate prices, but on a limited budget you can see the same game by spending a few days in the Kruger itself. To make the choices clearer, the following section breaks down the parks and reserves in terms of price and game.

Mpumalanga's contrasts extend to its people. The region is inhabited by Boer, Swazi, Pedi, and a few British South Africans. The Boers of the region have a reputation for a hard-line right-wing attitude, but the reality is the usual paradoxical hotch-potch of prejudice and liberalism that characterizes

GAME AND NATURE RESERVES

1   HANS MERENSKY NATURE RESERVE
2   CYCAD NATURE RESERVE
3   TSHUKUDU GAME LODGE
4   KLASERIE PRIVATE NATURE RESERVE
5   INGWELALA
6   UMBABAT GAME RESERVE
7   THORNYBUSH GAME LODGE
8   TIMBAVATI PRIVATE NATURE RESERVE
9   BLYDE RIVER CANYON NATURE RESERVE
10 MANYELETI GAME RESERVE
11 INYATI
12 SABI-SAND GAME RESERVE
13 LONDOLOZI GAME RESERVE
14 MALA MALA GAME RESERVE
15 SABI-SABI GAME RESERVE
16 OHRIGSTADT DAM NATURE RESERVE
17 MOUNT SHEBA NATURE RESERVE
18 MTHETHOMUSHA GAME RESERVE
19 MAHUSHE SHONGWE GAME RESERVE
20 SONGIMVELO GAME RESERVE
21 EBENEZER DAM NATURE RESERVE
22 WOLKBERG WILDERNESS AREA
23 LEKGALMEETSE NATURE RESERVE

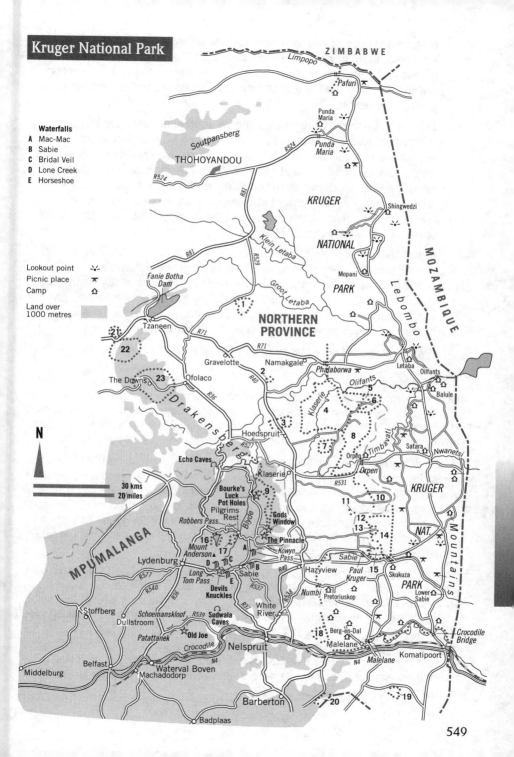

Kruger National Park

Waterfalls
A Mac-Mac
B Sabie
C Bridal Veil
D Lone Creek
E Horseshoe

Lookout point
Picnic place
Camp

Land over
1000 metres

N

30 kms
20 miles

farming communities all over South Africa. What is true is that, under apartheid, more black people were forced into 'homelands' here than almost anywhere else in the country. The former 'homelands' of Lebowa, Gazankulu and KaNgwane were fragmented into sections of varying sizes all over the region.

Driving through the Mpumalanga means continually entering and leaving stretches of former 'homeland', usually marked by a sudden overcrowding of people and cattle after hours of driving through an emptier landscape of huge white-owned cattle and game ranches. Life in these former 'homelands' varies from the westernized to the traditionally rural, or completely wild, and parks in the former homelands are often cheaper alternatives to the expensive private game reserves of the 'white-owned' lowveld, or the tourist mecca of the Kruger National Park.

Mpumalanga has some of South Africa's best hiking—in the Drakensberg and surrounding forests and foothills is some of South Africa's most spectacular mountain walking. In the lowveld are some of the best game trails. In particular, the Kruger National Park has some heartstoppingly exciting trails where walkers sleep in bush camps and are guided by armed rangers to within close range of elephant, buffalo and lion.

Travellers should note that parts of Mpumalanga are malarial.

History

Before the Voortrekkers arrived in the Mpumalanga (formerly Eastern Transvaal) in the early 1840s, the area was inhabited by various Nguni and North Sotho groups (today represented by the Swazi and Pedi) and isolated Tsonga communities, all three of whom had contributed to driving off the original San (bushman) hunter/gatherers early in the Middle Ages.

The early Boer settlers had a difficult time; although the temperate mountain regions had good grazing and were not densely inhabited, the lowveld was well populated by people hostile to white settlement. The Boers fought unsuccessfully with the most powerful clan, the Pedi, and in 1845 negotiated land with them on which to build a small town, Ohrigstad. As far as the Pedi were concerned, they were only tolerating the Boers, and for some time the settlers' small Ohrigstad Republic was kept from expanding by malaria, tropical fevers, seasonal drought and abundant wild predators.

Boers from the neighbouring South African Republic (or SAR, the first of the three Boer Transvaal republics, the others being Ohrigstad and Zoutpansberg in the north) made repeated raids into the Eastern Transvaal, hunting for ivory and looking for good land, most of which had already been claimed. Having been repeatedly repulsed from the land in the north of the region by the warlike Pedi, the Boers turned their attention to the Swazi in the southeast, who had been ground down by Zulu raids sent north by Shaka and Dingane during the 1820s and '30s (*see* **KwaZulu-Natal** 'History'), and were just beginning to re-establish themselves over their former wide range, despite sporadic raids by the new Zulu king, Mpande.

In 1847 the Lydenburg and SAR Boers offered to end the Zulu raids for good, in return for cattle and land grants. The Swazi King Mswati rashly opened up his territory (modern Swaziland) for Boer hunters and granted his allies all the land between the Crocodile and Oliphants rivers, almost the entire eastern lowveld. But, though groups of Swazis lived in the area, most of it was Pedi territory and it was not really his to give away. The Boers turned a blind eye to this, drove Mpande's marauding Zulus south and began settling the lowveld wherever there was water enough for cattle.

Ohrigstad was proving an unhealthy capital for the now large republic, owing to its heavy subtropical climate and propensity for malaria. In 1850 the Boers again courted Pedi anger by establishing a new town further north, at a higher, more temperate altitude. Lydenburg is still a regional centre for the Mpumalanga Drakensberg.

After 1860, when Lydenburg became part of the SAR (*see* **Gauteng** 'History'), more settlers began arriving in the Eastern Transvaal, and the Pedi, unwilling to lose more land, began to raid white farms, confining settlers to the area around Lydenburg and Swaziland. They further strengthened their position by sending thousands of young men to work on farms in the Cape and Natal and spending the money they sent home on guns.

Frustrated, the Boers began seizing more Swazi territory. King Mswati appealed to the British Natal Native Administrator, Theophilus Shepstone, for British protection. Shepstone, a passionate believer in the Anglicization of all South Africa, agreed. Nevertheless, over the following twenty years the Boers moved aggressively into Swazi territory, settling where they liked, while Mswati looked on anxiously. It could only be a matter of time before British troops arrived in the Eastern Transvaal.

In 1870, following the discovery of diamonds in Kimberley, over 1000 miles west in Griqualand, the Pedi offered their services as labourers and began to make money and buy arms. Soon afterwards, gold was discovered in the Drakensberg just east of Lydenburg. Although the deposits were patchy and alluvial, with no large underground seams, the mountains were soon crowded with adventurers from all over the world.

At the small town of Barberton a stock exchange was opened, and small mining towns, such as Pilgrim's Rest, Sabie and White River, began cropping up around the diggings. The resident Boers looked on with some disquiet as the profits from the gold went, not into the state coffers or to local *burghers*, but to the few miners who struck it rich, and the merchants, dealers, gold-buyers, black labourers, liquor-sellers, prostitutes and thieves who flocked to the mountain towns.

The discovery of gold refocused unwelcome British attention on the area. In 1877 Shepstone persuaded the Colonial Secretary Lord Carnarvon to annexe the SAR, take advantage of the gold finds and bring the errant Transvaal Boers back under British rule. The British also sought to contain the Pedi, who were gaining in power to such an extent that farmers in the northern area of the Eastern Transvaal were paying taxes to them rather than to Pretoria.

While the British prepared for invasion, the Boers took an unsuccessful swing at the Pedi in 1876. The following year, British troops entered the SAR, ran up the Union Jack at Pretoria and sent an expedition against the Pedi, partly as a gesture towards the Boers, partly to crush the tribe and thereby ensure a future cheap labour pool.

During the British occupation, the gold diggings in the Eastern Transvaal gradually wound down and the Boers took over the territory of the conquered Pedi. Swaziland remained a British Protectorate and no more settlers were allowed in. From 1882 until the outbreak of the Second Anglo-Boer War in 1899 the Eastern Transvaal was systematically opened up for cattle ranching. However, the obstacles that had confronted the first settlers—tropical disease, drought and wild animals—remained, preventing rapacious settlement and preserving the vast expanses of wilderness for which the region is renowned.

The Eastern Transvaal saw little action during the Second Anglo-Boer War (1899–1902), except for some brief fighting around Pilgrim's Rest, which earned one mountain pass the name of Long Tom Pass after the huge naval guns that the Boers hauled up there to take pot shots at the advancing British. Hunting and farming became the region's main industries and during the early 20th century the Eastern Transvaal settled down into a backwater. There were a few farm strikes by black workers during the 1920s, but these were ineffectual, being so isolated from the black political centres of the Witwatersrand and Eastern Cape.

Through the Second World War and the subsequent apartheid years, the Eastern Transvaal developed along two parallel paths, one positive, one negative in the extreme.

The positive movement was that of nature conservation. The Kruger National Park, established in 1898 by Paul Kruger himself (following the pleas of a now forgotten land surveyor and conservationist called Charles Marais), continued to be protected as a showcase for African conservation. During the 1970s and '80s, when massive poaching operations almost wiped out elephant and rhino populations in Africa, the Kruger and its surrounding reserves brought in some of the first shoot-to-kill anti-poaching patrols, and the park is now a major breeding centre for repopulating reserves elsewhere in Africa with rare species. For example, the black rhino, threatened with extinction outside South Africa, has retained a sufficient gene pool in the Kruger to make this the only African country where it is increasing its range.

But the Mpumalanga reserves did not escape poaching. Today there are almost no large tuskers left and evidence has come to light suggesting that high-ranking South African army officers may have been behind some of the intensive 1980s poaching raids (as has proved to have been the case in Namibia). A full inquiry has yet to be brought, if it ever will; the new South Africa has more pressing problems to deal with than tracking down ex-poachers.

Another negative side of Mpumalanga's recent history was the forced removal of tens of thousands of blacks into 'homelands' in an attempt to strip local Tsonga, Pedi and Swazi of their South African citizenship. These puppet states of Lebowa (for the Pedi), Gazankulu (for the Tsonga) and KaNgwane (for the Swazi) suffered all the usual poverty and lack of opportunity of South Africa's 'bantustans'. Self-governing rather than officially independent, Lebowa, Gazankulu and KaNgwane's 'governments' (of South African-paid local chiefs elevated to ministers) have been accused of human rights abuses; for example, mass graves found in Lebowa in 1986 contained the bodies of people who had protested against the rule of the 'homeland's' prime minister, Cedric Pathadi. However, as with the poaching in the Kruger, it seems unlikely that any inquiry will be made into these allegations as the 'homelands' have been re-absorbed back into South Africa since 1994, and the new government now faces problems of a more national scale.

The re-absorption of KaNgwane, Gazankulu and Lebowa may bring its own problems, as overpopulation and depleted land resources threaten to spill a huge, unemployable rural population out of confinement and into the pristine veld. To contain this, while at the same time reversing the wrongs of apartheid and continuing the area's excellent record of nature conservation, is the task facing the Mpumalanga's new provincial government into the next century. Already some progress has been made as parts of the Kruger National Park have been returned to their former owners; not for resettlement, but to be a source of income to them, rather than to central government.

Getting There

By car: From Jo'burg and Pretoria the N4 heads east to Mpumalanga's border with Mozambique at Komatipoort, at the southeast corner of Kruger. From Swaziland the R40 from Bulembu to Barberton, the R570 from Ngonini to the N4, and the R571 from Tjaneni to Komatipoort, all provide access. From Natal, the N11 from Ladysmith to Ermelo joins the R542 which leads straight to Barberton and Nelspruit.

By bus: Greyhound, ✆ (011) 333 2136, **Transtate** and **TransLux**, ✆ (011) 774 3333 for both, all run regular bus services from Jo'burg to Nelspruit and Tzaneen, jumping off points for the southern and northern sections of Mpumalanga respectively. The same companies also run buses to Komatipoort, convenient for the southern end of the Kruger National Park.

By air: Comair, ✆ (011) 973 2911, runs regular flights from Jo'burg International Airport, outside Jo'burg, to Skukuza in the Kruger National Park. Either pick up local car hire (Comair will arrange this) or arrange a pick-up if you are staying in some of the private reserves. Most private reserves have their own landing-strips and you can arrange flights when booking.

By rail: The **Komaati Express** runs daily from Jo'burg to Komatipoort (and vice versa) via Nelspruit, call Jo'burg railway station ✆ (011) 773 2131.

(✆ 013–)   ***Getting Around***

By car: This is by far the best way, as entry to the game reserves is almost impossible without a vehicle. The cheapest option is to hire from one of the private car hire companies listed in the Jo'burg section of this guide.

By bus: Transtate run services between most of the smaller towns from Nelspruit and Tzaneen.

If you are without a vehicle and cannot afford a safari company, the **Kruger Backpackers and Adventure Centre**, ✆ 737 7224, in Hazyview, near the Kruger's Numbi Gate, runs a private bus service from Jo'burg and will drive you into the park more cheaply than you can find elsewhere.

By black taxi: All the region's towns and most of the villages can be reached by black taxi. These are safer here than in cities, but they do have a worrying safety record. They are cheap, but use them at your own risk.

By tour group: Lawson's, ✆ 755 2147, offer specialized wildlife and birdwatching trips into the lowveld from Nelspruit, as do **Green Rhino**, ✆ 751 1952. You could also try **Lowveld Environmental Services**, ✆ 744 7636, or **Trackers**, ✆ 235 2121. More expensive is **Ingwe Safaris**, ✆ 752 2447, which offers both

Mpumalanga and KwaZulu-Natal packages. If there are no vacancies call the **Johannesburg Metropolitan Tourist Association,** ✆ (011) 336 4961, or the **Mpumalanga Tourism Authority,** ✆ 752 7001, for other companies.

From the Witwatersrand to the Drakensberg Foothills

The drive east along the N4 highway from Johannesburg runs through the high, flat golden grasslands of the Witwatersrand plateau. For the first 150km the highveld pasture is dominated by mine towers, chimneys and other industrial sights, until the highway clears the pungent coal mining town of Witbank. If you are not in a hurry it is worth driving into Mpumalanga through the highveld farm country, along the R25, R555, R540 or R36, all of which head northeast from the N4. Away from the highway, the scenery has a wide, empty splendour, without the strip developments that beset big roads. Great, empty horizons—with perhaps an isolated farmhouse surrounded by dark gum trees—stretch away on every side. The roads run straight as arrows and you can drive for miles without seeing another car; the sense of isolation up here on the highveld can be exhilarating.

Along the R35, in the farming country north of **Middelburg,** is **Loskop Dam Nature Reserve,** ✆ (01202) 3075/6, which has an adjacent resort (*see* Where to Stay). The reserve is mostly grassland and has a high density of game, including white rhino, buffalo, sable antelope, eland, kudu, nyala and a host of other antelope species. Waterfowl cluster around the dam's shoreline. But be careful walking close to the water; crocs lurk on the banks, and the shallows carry bilharzia. Leopard, brown hyena and jackal are quite common here, but are very shy and mainly nocturnal. A walking trail and a few roads run through the reserve. The accommodation in self-catering chalets or a camp site is often full at weekends, but deserted in the week.

A few kilometres south of Loskop along the R35 is the smaller **Botshabelo Nature Reserve,** ✆ (013) 243 1319/5020, which covers a narrow river valley. Again, game is plentiful, mainly zebra, wildebeest, eland and the smaller antelope. The Oliphants River, which runs through the reserve, has a rare species of cycad growing on its banks. Walking trails and game-viewing roads wind through most of the reserve and there is an **Ndebele Village,** with geometrically painted houses, at the edge of the reserve, which welcomes visitors. Accommodation ranges from B&B in an old farmhouse, to a cheap hostel with dormitory bunks. Still further south along the R35, just 15km from Middelburg, is a sign for **Slaghoek,** ✆ (013) 249 7206, a farm with thatched huts offering self-catering accommodation and three hiking trails into the surrounding hills.

North of the small towns of **Machasdorp,** about 100km east of Middelburg, is the lovely **Schoemanskloof,** a narrow farming valley with low mountains falling to the swiftly-flowing Crocodile River (which no longer harbours crocodiles). The R539 exits from the N4 between Machasdorp and Waterval–Boven, runs along the valley and rejoins the N4 about 45km west of Nelspruit.

Orchards, pastures and small wheatfields adjoin the road, giving the countryside an almost European look, especially where lines of poplars have been planted as windbreaks and, in autumn, when the wheat is cut by hand and laid in stooks on the stubble. Tributary streams fall from the bare uplands above the river, and several walking trails run up into the hills from a country inn halfway along the valley called **Old Joe's Kaia** (*see* 'Where to Stay'). 'Old Joe' is a rock formation, just west of the inn, resembling a gnarled old man. The altitude drops steadily from west to east along Schoemanskloof, and marks a gradual transition from highveld to lowveld. At the far eastern end of the valley the Crocodile River drops falls into a large cascade known as the **Montrose Falls**. These are signposted from the R539, and are reached by a short walking trail.

(✆ 013–)   *Activities*

Walking and hiking: The **Cycad Trails**, ✆ 282 6101, near Middelburg, offer a choice of 4 trails. The 7km Cycad Tarenaal Trail runs between the huts and the Oliphants river. Cycad (Cycad)Trail (about 14km) winds in a circle from the huts, taking in river scenery and cycad vegetation. The Cycad Suikerbos Trail (12km) and Cycad Bobbejaan (21km) follow the Oliphants River through cliffs and narrow ravines. Accommodation is provided. Trails of more than one day can be found at Elandskrans Holiday Resort, ✆ 262 176. The 2-day **Elandskrans Trail** follows a set of waterfalls along the Eland's River valley and has overnight huts supplied with firewood and water. The trail leads from the Elandskrans Holiday Resort to the small village of Waterval–Boven.

Trout fishing: The development of trout fishing over the last few years on the Mpumalanga escarpment has been impressive. **Critchley Hackle Lodge**, ✆ 254 0145, and **Walkersons's County Manor**, ✆ 254 0246, near Dullstroom on the R540 between the N4 (Belfast Exit) and Lydenburg. Also at Dullstroom is **Trout Royalty**, ✆ 254 0822, 10km to the east of the town on the Kruisfontein road, and **Trout Valley**, ✆ 254 0491, 2½km east of it on the R540 to Lydenburg. 10km from Belfast on the R33 towrds Stoffberg is the **Cosy Valley Hide Away**, ✆ 253 1087, and in Belfast itself, **Woody's Place**, 101 Kerk St. There are many more, and the **Mpumalanga Tourism Authority**, ✆ 55 1988/9, has a full list.

(✆ 013–)   *Where to Stay*

expensive

Old Joe's Kaia, ✆ 223 764/8, at the Nelspruit end of Schoemanskloof, fronts the Crocodile River and offers accommodation in private log cabins secluded in indigenous bush around a 19th-century coaching inn. Walking trails and trout fishing can be arranged. **Critchley Hackle Lodge**, ✆ 254 0145, outside Dullstroom, is said to offer the best trout fishing in Mpumalanga. Built of stone in the 1920s, the lodge resembles, of all things, an English country church. There are 23 rooms, lake and stream fishing, tennis courts, indoor and outdoor pools, walking trails, a golf course and a sauna.

Walkerson's, ✆ 254 0246, is another lodge, also near Dullstroom (12km along the road to Lydenburg), with a small nature reserve harbouring antelope stretching away from it, and trout fishing offered in the estate's lakes. Furnished with antiques, it is a little pretentious but very comfortable, and the surrounding scenery is beautiful.

Bergwaters Lodge, ℂ 257 0104, is signposted north from the N4 near Waterval–Boven. This small, intimate country inn sits in the Eland's River valley, amid a variety of hardwood and bushveld vegetation with 11 rooms, a bar, a pool and a tennis and squash court. Trout fishing can be arranged.

moderate

The **Wayside Inn** at Waterval–Boven, ℂ 262 425, is an old coaching inn (built in 1879) next to a house lived in by Paul Kruger. A little adjoining cemetery contains the graves of British soldiers killed during the Second Anglo-Boer War. The large, comfortable en suite double rooms are good value for money. **Die Gashuis**, ℂ 243 2262, offers country cottage-style self-catering units at a sensible rate and special rates for dinner, bed & breakfast. **Elandskrans Holiday Resort**, just north of Waterval–Boven, ℂ 262 176, offers self-catering thatched cottages with shared kitchen and *braai* facilities. Bring a sleeping bag. Four secluded hiking trails follow the Elands River valley through natural bushveld and woodland.

cheap

Loskop Dam Nature Reserve, ℂ (01202) 3075/6, along the R35 north of Middelburg, has self-catering chalets with bathrooms, and a camp site with shared ablutions and kitchen. There is superb walking, with rare species such as white rhino and sable antelope roaming free in the bush. **Botshabelo**, ℂ 243 1319, offers B&B in an old farmhouse, and very cheap dormitories. Apart from walking trails with game, its Ndebele show village and restored mission station are fun to explore.

Mpumalanga Drakensberg and Foothills

The Mpumalanga Drakensberg run south to north in a narrow 200km chain from White River and Lydenburg to Tzaneen. The most populated section is the southern end, between Sabie, White River and Pilgrim's Rest; north of here the range is split by the spectacular **Blyde River Canyon**, one of South Africa's principal natural marvels, then gives way to a further 100km of all but uninhabited mountain accessible only on foot. **Lydenburg**, the westernmost town of the Drakensberg foothills, is reached from the N4 via the R540 and Dullstroom, a very pretty drive through steadily rising farm and forest. Established in 1850 as the centre of its own republic, Lydenburg was in fact the second Voortrekker town to be founded in the Eastern Transvaal, the first, Ohrigstad, on the nearby lowveld, having been abandoned after a few years because of its feverish climate. It was from Lydenburg that the early Eastern Transvaal Boers launched their wars against the Pedi and Swazi, as well as their massive ivory-hunting expeditions in what is now the Kruger National Park. The town was incorporated into the South African Republic in 1866, becoming the prosperous little farming town of today. Some interesting old buildings remain, their style resembling that of late Cape Dutch vernacular. These include the original **Voortrekker School** (built in 1851), a long, low building with whitewashed mud walls and a thatched roof, the **Voortrekker Church** (1852) and **Kruithuis** (old powder magazine, built later in 1889). Most of the town's few streets have surviving 19th-century houses, and its tranquil air gives it a feel of the past.

East of Lydenburg, the R37 leads up into some of the most spectacular scenery in the country, entering the Drakensberg via the steep **Long Tom Pass**, with splendid views out over the highveld and along the Drakensberg escarpment.

At the foot of the pass, about 3km east of town along the R37, is the **Gustav Klingbiel Nature Reserve**. Clinging to the slopes of Mount Anderson, the first tall peak east of Lydenburg, this reserve harbours antelope such as eland, mountain reedbuck, bushbuck and duiker, but is best known for the late Iron Age walled villages found here, archaeological discoveries which suggest how settled Bantu-speaking culture had become over the centuries leading up to the wars and upheavals that had raged across the highveld in the early 19th-century. Three walking trails lead to the sites (and also to some old Boer War trenches), and up into the hills. There is accommodation in a trail hut, supplied with firewood and water.

On the eastern side of the Pass, linked to the Old Lydenburg Road by a short trail from the signposted car park, the **Bridal Veil Falls** are surrounded by dense yellowwood and assegai bush, but litter and graffiti mar this lovely and secluded spot. The 13km circular **Lourie Nature Walk** makes its way through the mountain grassland and forest near the falls.

Sabie is a pleasant, prosperous rural town which grew up around the forestry industry pioneered in Mpumalanga back in the 1900s. It is the beginning of the **Fanie Botha Hiking Trail** and the main tourist centre for the region. The excellent **Sabie Tourism Association** on Ford Street, ✆ (013) 764 3492, has information covering all of Mpumalanga. True to South African tradition, Sabie has a small museum dedicated to its local industry. The **Forestry Museum,** on Ford Street (*open Mon–Fri 8–4.30 and Sat 8–1*), charts the history of South Africa's timber trade and has a section on the conservation of indigenous forests and the ecology of the exotic eucalyptus and pine plantations that cover vast stretches of South Africa's mountains. If you find yourself looking for a restaurant on a Sunday, don't despair: **The Huntsman's Pub and Restaurant** is open, serving reasonable food.

The **Lone Creek Falls Trail**, an undemanding walking trail through the mountain plantations near the town, is signposted 13km west of town along the Old Lydenburg Road. The falls themselves plunge 70m into a narrow kloof filled with dense indigenous montane forest.

About 12km north of Sabie, along the R532, are the **Mac Mac Pools**, a set of natural rock pools below a large waterfall. Swimming here is heaven: the clear water is pure, free from bilharzia, and surrounded by forest. Little rustic changing rooms have even been provided, and the surrounding glades are now popular picnic spots. Anyone sweating through a hot mountain drive should cool off here. A short trail, the **Secretary Bird Walk**, winds through grassveld and scattered indigenous trees to the Mac Mac Falls.

The R532 then climbs higher over the **Mac Mac Pass** to an intersection with the narrow R533. A right turn (east) leads to the small village of **Graskop**, beyond which the road drops sharply down into the lowveld. Graskop has recently developed from being a forestry village to quite a little tourist hub, with a couple of hotels and a number of self-catering chalets, art galleries, shops, restaurants and specialist food shops. It also has a retail outlet for the region's only silk farm, **Tsinini.** The farm itself is off the Nelspruit–Hoedspruit road; there are guided tours and an entry fee. Call Sandra, ✆ (083) 700 6281, or Ronel, ✆ (083) 3765 033.

A left turn (west) leads through mountain heathland to the tiny, perfectly preserved 19th-century mining village of **Pilgrim's Rest**, founded in 1873. The village's small stream and surrounding mountains were once the scene of a frenzied gold rush. A few fortunes were made, but by the 1920s most of the gold was gone. One mine stayed open until the early 1970s, but by then Pilgrim's Rest (named in hopeful expectation of wealth) had settled into a comfortable farming village.

Pilgrim's Rest (Publicity Office, ☏ 768 1060) was bought up by the Transvaal provincial government in 1974 for conservation as a living museum. It markets itself accordingly; its narrow street, lined by a single, long row of handsome late 19th-century tin houses, is now mostly given over to curio shops selling olde worlde mock Victoriana. However, some of the residents are genuine locals, and the new lick of paint that undoubtedly did not grace the tin houses in pioneer days in no way detracts from their charm. The setting is magnificent, with solemn, mist-shrouded heights looming above the valley. The original **Royal Hotel**, one of the few double-storey tin houses in the village, has been restored to its original order, an old mine at the western end of the village is open to visitors, and panning for gold (a few alluvial deposits still remain) is demonstrated by actors in period costume.

Most interesting of Pilgrim's Rest's museums is the **Town Museum**, which gives a photographic history of the town and its eccentric characters. The **Miner's House**, a rough-and-ready recreation of the basic life of pioneer diggers, and the **Old Bank Museum** complete the Victorian picture. (*All open daily 9–12.45 and 1.45–4.15.*) The **Diggings Museum** offers a tour with gold-panning demonstration (*daily at 10, 11, 12, 2 and 3*), as does the **Alanglade House Museum** (*daily 11 and 2*), with refreshments thrown in.

After a couple of hours, the rather forced period atmosphere of Pilgrim's Rest begins to pall. However, a short drive of about 2.5km southwest along the R533 leads to the beautiful **Mount Sheba Nature Reserve**, a small conservation area protecting a stretch of indigenous temperate montane rainforest. Yellowwood and stinkwood, ironwood, mountain cedar (one of the only conifers to occur naturally in Africa) and a bewildering variety of other hardwood species occur, some enormous, some mere saplings. Bushbuck, red duiker, samango and vervet monkeys inhabit the lush undergrowth. Gentle walking trails snake through the forest, but there is no Parks Board accommodation, only the rather expensive **Mount Sheba Hotel**, just outside (*see* 'Where to Stay'). To continue west is to drop steeply back down to the highveld. However, turn back along the R533, back through Pilgrim's Rest to Graskop, and then turn north along the R532, staying on the central mountain spine. A few kilometres north of Graskop a looped detour leads to the area's best known geological features, **Pinnacle Rock** and **God's Window**.

Pinnacle Rock juts like a stone finger from a steep forested mountainside that drops suddenly away for hundreds of metres to the eastward expanse of the sub-tropical lowveld. God's Window, about 3km north of Pinnacle Rock, affords the same view, but through a cleft in the mountain wall. North of God's Window the loop detour rejoins the R532, which itself continues almost due north, past two sets of waterfalls, the **Lisbon Falls** and **Berlin Falls**. Both are signposted from the road. The Lisbon Falls pour over a horseshoe-shaped cliff into the forest below, and can be reached by a short walking trail from the car park. Berlin Falls are bigger, plummeting 80m into a deep pool surrounded by broken rock. A wooden viewing deck has been built above them to give a safe view of the vertiginous drop.

Blyde River Canyon

The R532 continues north along the westward escarpment of one of Africa's most spectacular geographical splendours, the breathtaking Blyde River Canyon, now a protected nature reserve. The sheer, jagged cliffs rise over 2000m on either side of the river to form strange, rounded columns of rock clothed in hanging vegetation and cut through with spectacular waterfalls. Because of the dramatic changes in altitude, the 35km canyon contains indigenous hardwood forest, patches of rainforest, protea woodlands, grassland and heath, interspersed with arid stretches of bare rock and scrub similar to the vegetation of the Karoo.

Archaeologists have found human remains here dating back to the early Stone Age, and from the density of San (bushman) paintings in the riverside caves it seems that the canyon was one of their principal hunting grounds until the Voortrekkers hunted them out in the mid-19th century. Certainly, the plentiful water and varied vegetation supported large concentrations of game, and even today mountain reedbuck, grey rhebok, klipspringer, bushbuck and oribi are plentiful enough to feed a large (but shy) leopard, serval and caracal lynx population. Baboons shout from the cliffsides, and the forests echo to the sharp 'yack' of samango monkeys, the low booming of louries and, at night, the eerie scream of bushbabies. Vervet monkeys live in the riverine woodland, and hippo and crocodile still inhabit the deep pools of the Blyde River's dammed sections. Black and martial eagles cruise along the cliff faces, hunting for dassies.

Temperatures vary greatly in the canyon. The floor becomes unbearably hot on summer afternoons, but the whole reserve can be bitterly cold at night, and in winter the upper slopes are often gripped by frost. Summer rainstorms can turn the canyon floor into a careering torrent, and swathe the upper cliffs in dangerously thick mist.

The Blyde River Canyon has several hiking trails running through it, all scenically spectacular, and varying in length from an hour to five days. Overnight huts with water and firewood are provided about every 15km. At the north end of the canyon is an access road to the irritatingly overdeveloped **Aventura Blydepoort Resort**. The only access down into the canyon from the resort is on foot; if you want to enter the canyon by car, you must drive around the head of the nature reserve, over the Abel Erasmus Pass, turn east off the R527 and south on the R531 (which drops down to the lowveld), from where a signposted road leads into **Swadini Resort**, which sits in the valley underneath the peaks of Swadini, Marieskop and the humped, free-standing massifs known as the Three Rondavels. An information office and a very small network of game-viewing roads surround the camp. Both resorts get very crowded at weekends and public holidays, but the main expanse of the canyon is accessible only via the hiking trails and there are usually few people down there.

About halfway down the canyon are an intriguing set of perfectly round holes set in the rock of the riverbank, known as the **Bourke's Luck Potholes**. The holes, some of which are sunk several metres into the rock, look as though they must be man-made; but are in fact the result of flood whirlpools made where the Treur and Blyde rivers meet.

The naming of these two rivers is attached to a poignant story. In 1844 a party of voortrekkers under Andries Potgieter set out from the highveld to reach Delagoa Bay (Maputo). Bearing in mind the fate of Louis Trichardt twelve years earlier—his party had been decimated by malaria—Potgieter left the wagons and families camped on the escarpment while his group made a dash across the fever country on horseback. A date was agreed for the base camp to be abandoned if the party did not return. When the date came and passed the families sadly departed, naming the adjacent river, Treur, *Sorrow*. A few days later Potgieter and his men, mission at the coast accomplished, caught them up as they were fording another river. They called it Blyde, *Joy*.

Two days' hike south of Bourke's Luck, the canyon carves its way to the foot of the mountains below God's Window. There are several excellent sets of San (bushman) rock paintings accessible from the hiking trail here.

The Echo Caves and Around

About 10km west of the Blyde River Canyon, just north of the junction of the R532 and R527, is a smaller, more secretive natural wonder, the **Echo Caves** (*open daily 8–5, tours every half-hour*). Only part of this massive cave system is open to the public: the closed section, called Cannibal Caves, apparently harbours a bat population of millions. Whether cannibals did inhabit the caves—which is not unlikely, as the Natal Drakensberg certainly harboured cannibals in the 1830s (*see* **Natal** Drakensberg 'History')—groups of bushmen definitely lived here until the mid-19th century. Many of the chamber walls are adorned with their totemic pictures of animals, men and spirits, and it is here that archaeologists have found human remains dating back to the middle Stone Age.

The Echo Caves derive their name from the stalagmites in one of the largest chambers—100m long and over 50m high—which, if tapped with a piece of metal, will echo the sound back louder. Outside the public entrance to the caves is the **Museum of Man** (*open Mon–Sat 8–5*), in which the larger Stone Age remains and artefacts are displayed, along with reproductions of some of the cave paintings.

North of the Echo Caves, the Drakensberg chain swings northwest into a wild stretch inaccessible by road. The R532 twists down the northern face of the range to the lowveld via the Abel Erasmus Pass, a descent so difficult that a tunnel has been constructed over part of it, which unfortunately obliterates the view.

On the foothills west of the Blyde River, in a section of the former Lebowa 'homeland', is the massive **Lekgalameetse Nature Reserve**, ✆ (015) 230 215, reached from the R36 via the Ofcolaco road (signposted from the R36), and then along two short gravel roads. Lekgalameetse's 20,000ha comprise a mixture of indigenous forest and grassland inhabited by small herds of mountain reedbuck, lone bushbuck, duiker, leopard and caracal. Baboons and samango monkeys may appear suddenly on the forest trails. The region is lushly green, benefiting from a high local rainfall, and seldom has more than a few visitors at any one time.

The section of the Mpumalanga Drakensberg furthest to the north is protected by the vast **Wolkberg Wilderness Area**, reached from Tzaneen (*see* **Northern Province**).

Less rugged but still very beautiful is the small **Ebenezer Dam Nature Reserve**, reached from the R36 near Tzaneen via the R528. Tall forest plantations provide shaded walks along the dam's shoreline where waterfowl breed in sizeable numbers, although you are unlikely to see any game. The reserve has a small camp site with ablutions.

Activities

Walking and hiking: The only true way to explore the **Blyde River Canyon** is on foot, hiking from hut to hut. Several hikes of 1–5 days can be booked, with cheap overnight huts, firewood and water provided. The 5-day **Fanie Botha Trail**, from Ceylon State Forest Station on Long Tom Pass to God's Window, is not a circular trail, but there are two circular options (3 days each), bringing the hiker back to the Station. Overnight trails are provided. Two 5-day trails with shorter options run from **Mac Mac Forest Station**. Again, cheap overnight huts with firewood and water are provided. These all give access to the most beautiful and secluded parts of the Mpumalanga Drakensberg. **Lekgalameetse Nature Reserve**, in Northern Province, west of the Blyde River Canyon, has 2- and 3-day trails, with overnight huts, through some superb indigenous forest. The **Wolkburg Wilderness Area**, south of Tzaneen, has a network of hikes ranging all over the wild northern Drakensberg. For booking all hiking trails contact **Safcol**, ✆ (013) 764 1058. Gentle forest walks of up to 4 hours can be found at Mac Mac Falls, Forest Falls and Bridal Veil Falls near Sabie, and the Blyde River Canyon has some short, circular walking trails in the bush near the two resorts at the northern end. Lekgalameetse Nature Reserve has some short forest walks.

Game-viewing: All the Drakensberg nature reserves listed above harbour game, usually antelope, shy leopard and primates. Blyde River Canyon has the largest density of antelope, as well as hippo and croc in the wider river pools, and large raptors on the heights. Leopard, serval and caracal are present, but seldom show themselves, preferring to hunt the wooded kloofs by night.

Trout-fishing: Stretches of streams can be booked and tackle hired via the **Sabie Tourism Association**, on Ford Street, Sabie, ✆ (013) 764 3492.

Canoeing and rafting: Sabie river day trips are offered by **Adventure Seekers**, ✆ (083) 804 5115; ask for Andrew or Lisa.

(✆ 013–)

Where to Stay

expensive

The original two-storey corrugated iron building of the **Royal Hotel**, Pilgrim's Rest, ✆ 768 1100, has been refurnished with period antiques, and is comparatively far more expensive now than it would have been in mining days. However, it is handsome and historically important, the food is good (trout and game are specialities), and its 19th-century ambience is genuine. There are 8 en suite rooms, a bar and restaurant.

The **Mount Sheba Hotel**, ✆ 768 1241, next to the Mount Sheba Nature Reserve, is grand but rather impersonal. The dining room has a stone fireplace and beamed ceiling, and guests stay in individual stone and thatch cottages, each with their own log fire. A swimming pool, tennis and squash courts complete the facilities. **Misty Mountain**, ✆ 764 3377, ✆ 764 1482, is a 280ha National Heritage Site on Long Tom Pass, with chalets, log fires, fishing, bird-watching, a pub and a restaurant. **Pilgrim's Rest Luxury Tents**, ✆/✆ 768 1367, offer accommodation in safari-style tents with views over the Blyde River, 70km from Kruger, access to hiking trails etc.

moderate

At the expensive end of the range, **The Inn on Robber's Pass**, ✆/✆ (013) 768 1491, has outstanding cuisine, as well as nature trails, fishing, riding, bird-watching, and golf nearby. **Log Cabin Village**, ✆ 767 1974, in Graskop, has very comfortable self-catering chalets in the village and a host with a specialist knowledge of the surrounding area. **Fern Tree Park**, ✆ 764 2215, near Sabie, has a collection of self-contained cottages nestling in hills near town. There is a pool, several hiking trails into the surrounding forest and trout fishing. The **Lisbon Hideaway**, ✆ 767 1851, in the mountains near Graskop, offers self-catering in old stone mining cottages overlooking the Lisbon River. Nearby **Summit Lodge**, ✆ 767 1895, offers thatched rondavels offering full board, half board, or B&B, set in gardens with a pool.

Kloofsig Cottages, ✆ 767 1489, along the R533 (Kowyn's Pass) east of Graskop, are very comfortable self-catering thatched cottages for up to 5 people. The Fanie Botha Hiking Trail and two shorter trails, the Hadeda Trail and Treefern Trail, are accessible from here. The **Wayfarers B&B**, 92 Malieveld Street, Sabie, ✆ 764 1500, has two en suite bedrooms. **Die Stoep Guest House**, Lydenburg, ✆ (013) 233b 078, a fully equipped guest house 6km from Lydenburg on the Ohrigstad Road, has easy access to Pilgrim's Rest, Graskop and Kruger. B&B, *braai* facilities and dinner on request. **Trackers**, ✆ (015) 795 5033, a private game reserve and wildlife education centre just outside the eastern entrance to the Blyde River Canyon, is signposted from the dirt road heading north from the canyon's access road. Trackers offers chalet and lodge accommodation and a very cheap camp site. Canoeing, hiking, climbing, game-viewing and hunting can be arranged, as well as cheap trips into Kruger. **Aventura Blydepoort Resort**, ✆ 769 8005, is a collection of self-contained cottages and a camp site, complete with a supermarket, restaurant, garage and small airstrip. The smaller **Swadini Resort**, ✆ 795 5141, is at the top of the Blyde River Canyon Nature Reserve. Both have stunning settings under the great rock massifs, but have been over-developed South African style, with all the necessary amenities plus plastic tack rudely shoved into pristine wilderness. Luxury self-catering lodges are also available at **Crystal Springs Mountain Lodge**, ✆ 768 1153, near Pilgrim's Rest, which also offers game drives, tennis, squash, hiking and trout fishing.

cheap

Jock of the Bushveld Hostel, on Main Street, Sabie, ✆ 764 2178, has dormitory accommodation and cheap double rooms. **Themeda Hill Mountain Rest Camp** near Pilgrim's Rest, ✆ 768 1352, is a quiet mountain retreat of four thatched rondavels (self-catering only) reached via the Robber's Pass Road, then signposted off down a rough forest road (4.5km). **Lekgalameetse Nature Reserve**, ✆ (015) 230 215, west of the R36 (in Northern Province), has self-contained cottages and chalets surrounded by forest. Camping is also allowed, and ablutions are provided.

The Lowveld Farmlands

East of the Drakensberg the land drops away sharply to a low, flat plain of sub-tropical bushveld and savannah stretching east to Mozambique. Blisteringly hot and humid in the rainy summer, warm and dry in the 'winter', or cooler season, the lowveld is mostly given over to game farming and nature reserves, and is South Africa's best region for viewing big game. The far eastern section, which runs along the Lebombo mountains, is occupied by the massive Kruger National Park. Backing on to the western boundary of the Kruger are a number of private game reserves (*see* Kruger National Park).

South of the Kruger is a prosperous arable farming area, and the towns of White River and **Nelspruit**, the regional capital. Nelspruit is modern, having been given a concrete and glass facelift in the 1970s, and has banks, garages, tyre dealerships and supermarkets—useful for people driving to and from the bushveld. Nelspruit also has some private safari companies which take people into the game reserves (*see* 'Activities'). If heading east to Maputo in Mozambique, it is also wise to stock up here on food and possibly a spare tyre or two.

Signposted from the town centre is the elegant, ordered **Lowveld National Botanic Garden**, which covers about 150ha along the banks of the Crocodile River. Small belts of forest, marsh, aloe and voluptuous sub-tropical flowers are linked by a short walking trail. This is a good place for birdlife, particularly the iridescent sunbirds and exotic species such as the paradise flycatcher and lilac-breasted roller.

About 26km west of Nelspruit are the **Sudwala Caves**. Travel along the N4 to the Sabie road, then look out for the signposts. These claim to be the oldest caves, in geological terms, in the world. Certainly, they are known to be 200 million years old. Late Stone Age remains have also been found here. However, the caves are best known for having been a hide-out for dissident Swazi factions during the civil wars that split the nation in the early 19th century. From 1815 to 1840 it was used as a fortress, sometimes housing up to 3000 people and 500 cattle. During the Anglo-Boer War (1899–1902), the Boers used the caves as an ammunition store for their Long Tom cannon shells (*see* 'Long Tom Pass' above), and their deep, resonant chambers were the inspiration for the caverns in the popular Edwardian adventure stories by H. Rider Haggard, *King Solomon's Mines* and *She*.

About 20km north of Nelspruit is **White River**, a forestry town that marks a convenient gateway to the southern lowveld game reserves. The town started life as a British colonial enclave around the turn of the century, but over the past 30 years has become almost completely Afrikaans, to the point that on most maps its name now appears as 'Witrivier'. The tiny town has changed little since the colonial era, and produces an enormous percentage of all the fruit and vegetables consumed in Gauteng.

Around White River are several lodges set in their own estates, which offer safaris into the game reserves for people without their own transport (*see* 'Where to Stay'). However the cost is usually high, and it is probably more economic to hire a vehicle in Johannesburg or Nelspruit. About 150km east of Nelspruit, at a low pass in the Lebombo Mountains, is **Komaatipoort**, a small town with a caravan and camping site, supermarkets and a garage. The bank is only open on Mondays, Wednesdays and Fridays.

'Mad' Mostyn Owen

There is an amusing story attached to Komatipoort, concerning an English eccentric called Mostyn Owen, or 'Mad Owen', a cashiered officer who lived in the district in the 1870s. Stories about him abound, but this is the best. Riding to the hotel at Komatipoort from the Mozambique side one night, Owen's horse was attacked by a crocodile as he forded the Komati River. Owen beat the reptile off with his stirrup-iron, rode into town and strode into the hotel, roaring for a gun with which to shoot the offending croc. A German tailor staying at the hotel offered to lend him one, and followed Owen to the ford. Once there, Owen said, 'Now I'm going to stand in the middle of the ford, and when the crocodile comes for me, I want you to shoot him.'

The German protested; he was not a good shot, the night was dark, and he ran the risk, not only of missing, but of hitting Owen.

'All right,' said Owen. 'You go into the river and I'll shoot.'

Owen bullied the unfortunate tailor into the water. Out swam the crocodile, and Owen shot with deadly accuracy. The tailor was relieved, but soon after the incident went completely bald.

Further south, near the border with Swaziland, rise cool mountains, an offshoot of the Drakensberg chain. At their foot is Barberton, the site of South Africa's second gold rush in the 1870s and the gateway to the hiker's paradise of the mountains behind.

The lowveld's former 'homelands', KaNgwane, Lebowa and Gazankulu, though generally overcrowded, have some very good game reserves. The best are: **Songimvelo Nature Reserve**, in the section of former KaNgwane bordering western Swaziland, which protects a huge sweep of pristine uplands in the mountains south of Barberton inhabited by most of the original game; **Mthethomusha Game Reserve**, at the southeast corner of the Kruger Park; and **Manyeleti**, a large bushveld reserve with big game in the section of Gazankulu bordering the western Kruger Park. These reserves are particularly rewarding to visit as few tourists know of them. (*See* 'Kruger National Park'.)

(℃ 013–)

Activities

Safaris: *See* pp.553–4 'Getting around by tour group', or try **Hamba Kahle Tours**, ℃ 741 1618, **Maruba Safaris**, ℃ (082) 965 7958, **Lowveld Environmental Services**, ℃ 744 7063, **Solitaire Tours and Safaris**, ℃ 752 4527, **Vula Tours**, ℃ 741 2238, **Lowveld Tours**, ℃ 752 6108, or **Lion Tours**, ℃ 737 7332. Cheaper still are tours and minibus safaris organized by the **Hazyview Youth Hostel**.

Riding: Sabie Horse Trails, ℃ 764 1655, offers a range of rides from one hour to two days, all accompanied by a guide knowledgeable about the local fauna and flora, forestry and history of the area. **Kaapschehoop Horse Trails**, ℃ 734 4995, offers much the same and also has a guest-house and camping facilities. There are many more operators in the area offering riding so it is probably just as well to talk to the tourist office in the district you are interested in.

Walking: The Lowveld National Botanic Garden, signposted from Nelspruit's town centre, is a large landscaped park on the banks of the Crocodile River. A gentle walking trail of about 2km winds through the varied displays of lowveld vegetation.

(℃ 013–)

Where to Stay

expensive

Frangipani Lodge, ℃ 751 3224, is a newly built mock-period lodge on a working farm between Nelspruit and White River (reached via the R40 then left at the Heidelberg traffic light). The lodge has a veranda-cum-sitting room, and serves lavish meals. Its five en suite rooms are charming in a twee, enthusiastic way.

Near White River, 6km along the Plaston Road, is **Kirby Country Lodge**, ✆ 751 2645, which has private cottages set among gardens. The food is prepared with home-grown vegetables and herbs. The White River flows through the woods adjoining the gardens, and a thatched great hall doubles as a sitting and dining room. Also near White River, along the road to Hazyview, the luxurious **Hulala Lakeside Lodge**, ✆ 764 1893, ✉ 764 1864, sits on the wooded spur of a man-made lake, offering very comfortable rooms overlooking the water, where ospreys and fish eagles snatch their prey. Sailing, canoeing and fishing are also available.

The ★★★★ **Pine Lake Sun**, ✆ 751 5036, is on the main Hazyview road and offers all the facilities of this up-market chain. Similar in rating is the **Cybele Forest Lodge**, ✆ 764 1823, on the R40 between White River and Hazyview. The suites have private swimming pools, and no children under ten are allowed, which probably defines it quite well. Less exclusive is the **Hotel Promenade**,✆ 753 3000, in the centre of Nelspruit and under the same management as the Royal in Pilgrim's Rest, a modern hotel adjacent to the town's principal shopping mall.

moderate

Riverside Cottages, on the banks of the Sabie River near Hazyview, ✆ 737 8143, offer stone-and-thatched comfort (self-catering) in 14 old farm cottages with a pool, fishing rights (tackle is sometimes available) and private walking trails. **Shandon Lodge**, ✆ 744 9934, on Saturn Street, Nelspruit, is a large, handsome colonial bungalow with a big veranda overlooking the town. The 4 mock-period en suite bedrooms each have their own veranda. The **Townhouse**, 5 Ferreira Street, Nelspruit, ✆ 752 7006, is another handsome colonial suburban house, beautifully decorated with good modern art.

Hazyview luxury B&B, Kiepersol, ✆ (013) 737 8415, ✉ 737 8497, has a fully self-contained 2-bed float on a subtropical fruit farm. No children under 16. **Aan de Vliet Guest Lodge**, ✆ (013) 737 8154/5, ✉ 737 8156, in the Hazyview valley on the banks fo the Sabie River, is ideal for day trips to Kruger and elsewhere, and has a restaurant, swimming pool, hiking trail, tennis, and self-catering rondavels.

cheap

Shingalana Guest House, Hazyview, near God's Window, ✆/✉ (013) 737 7045, offers luxurious B&B accommodation at reasonable prices, with bathrooms en suite. **Hazyview Youth Hostel** offers cheap dormitory accommodation near the Orpen Gate to the Kruge. Nelspruit has a **Formule 1**, ✆ 741 4490, on the corner of the N4 and the Kaapsehoop road, on the western edge of town.

Likusasa Country Lodge, near White River, ✆ (013) 750 0963, @ 750 0782, has fully equipped self-catering apartments and luxury thatched cottages with B&B. There are swimming pools and a children's playground, a restaurant, volleyball court, walking trails, bird-watching and a small shop, plus magnificent views. Nelspruit, Komaatipoort and White River all have camp sites. Otherwise, the nearest cheap accommodation is at the Jock of the Bushveld Hostel, Sabie (*see* above), or at the camp sites inside the Kruger National Park. For more budget accommodation contact Hazyview Tourism Association, ✆ 737 7414).

It is worth mentioning that most of the Kruger National Park and the game-viewing in the Hoedspruit–Klaserie area are in fact in the Northern Province not in Mpumalanga. They are included in this chapter because the lowveld and the escarpment belong to the same part of a travel itinerary, and the provincial borders are a bit of a technicality.

Travellers should note that Kruger National Park is malarial.

History

Larger than any other reserve in South Africa, and one of the largest on the African continent, the Kruger covers a staggering 19,445 square kilometres, bigger than Israel or Wales. It was founded in 1898 by Paul Kruger, president of the South African Republic, after urgent prompting by one of his land surveyors, Charles Marais. The reserve was first known as the Sabie Game Reserve. Like many other leading Boers of the time, Kruger had made his early fortune through intensive ivory hunting in Mpumalanga and Northern Province, but both he and Marais had the foresight to see that unless game was actively conserved it would be wiped out in little more than a generation, as was to happen in the Cape during the late 19th century. At the time the reserve was declared, freebooting professional hunters still operated in the area. The best account of this dangerous life is told in the beautifully illustrated book, *Jock of the Bushveld* (*see* **Further Reading**), by Sir Percy Fitzpatrick, who hunted in the area during the 1880s while a transport rider to the local gold fields. He subsequently became one of the magnates of the Witwatersrand and, in wealth and old age, wrote the book, which is about his dog, at the behest of, among others, Rudyard Kipling. (What is not so well known is that it was Fitzpatrick who, having lost a son on the western front in 1917, suggested that a two-minute silence be observed in tribute to those who died for their country, an event that has become an annual custom in Britain).

The reserve was re-ratified when the British took over the region in 1902, following the Second Anglo-Boer War, and founded another great reserve next to Sabie—the Shingwedzi Game Reserve. These were later combined to form the present Kruger Park. From 1903 the ranger appointed to look after the enormous territory, Major James Stevenson-Hamilton, found the area largely denuded of game through poaching, and immediately established the system of armed patrols that is common practice in most of Southern Africa's game reserves today. This obviously made him unpopular with the lowveld Boers, who still regarded the area as their own hunting ground for hides and ivory, and the local Africans, who killed for meat. A mixture of tough tactics combined with employing local people in the park gradually helped to alleviate the poaching, the park being seen as a source of employment for local blacks. White farmers stopped shooting the game once fences were erected and their crops were no longer in danger from marauding antelope, nor their lives from elephant and lion.

During his 44 years in the Kruger (he retired in 1946), Stevenson-Hamilton managed to re-establish the huge game populations that the Kruger harbours today, and left a legacy of commitment to effective conservation that subsequent governments have retained.

Today's National Park is 350km long and about 65km wide, stretching from the Crocodile River near Komatipoort right up to South Africa's northern border with Zimbabwe. The eastern boundary is marked by the Lebombo Mountains, which form the Mpumalanga's border with Mozambique, and there is talk of South Africa and Mozambique co-operating to extend the protected area far into Mozambique, to the east of the Lebombos, and bringing it on to the borders of Zimbabwe's Gona-re Zhou National Park, which would make it the largest game reserve in Africa. But as yet, Mozambique lacks funds to implement the project.

Flora and Fauna

The Kruger National Park is mostly flat bushveld and savannah, with pockets of marula and wild fig woodland, and large areas of widely spaced mopane forest. Several perennial rivers—the Crocodile, Oliphants, Sabie, Timbavati, Letaba, Luvuvhu and Shingwedzi—flow through the park. Game is plentiful. There are large numbers of elephant, black and white rhino, lion, leopard, cheetah, wild dog, hyena, buffalo, and almost all native antelope species from the rare sable and roan to the tiny suni, with herds of impala appearing around almost every bend in the road. Blue wildebeest and tsessebe, zebra, warthog, bushpig, and the nocturnal rarities such as bushbabies, aardwark, aardwolf, genet and civet inhabit the bush, as do large troops of baboons and vervet monkeys, while hippo and crocodile rule the rivers.

The Kruger's range of bird life is enormous; especially common are the exotic blue and crowned crane, rollers, trogons, storks (including black and marabou), bee-eaters, sunbirds, drongos, grey louries (known as 'go-away birds' because of their weird call), and, of course, ostrich. Raptors such as bataleur, martial, black and fish eagles, the pale chanting goshawk and Cape vulture are also regular sights. A host of rarer species, many of them spectacular, also inhabit the park and you should not go in without a field guide.

Getting There

The southern section of the Kruger has several entrancs: **Phalaborwa**, reached from Tzaneen via the R71; **Orpen**, signposted from the R40 from Klaserie; **Paul Kruger**, reached via the R536 from the R40 via Hazyview; **Numbi**, reached via the R538 from Nelspruit; **Malelane** and **Crocodile**, both reached via the N4 east of Nelspruit.

Getting Around

By car: Unless you have booked one of the superb guided hiking trails, you are confined to your car except within camps and at some picnic sites. So you may as well hire a comfortable vehicle with plenty of room, as you will be stuck in it for hours as you drive around the bushveld roads. If you can afford it, hire a bakkie (pick-up), minibus or 4x4, as the raised chassis will afford much better game viewing than an ordinary car, which is too low to see over the first line of bush. For this reason, it can be worth going in with a tour company (*see* 'Getting Around Mpumalanga').

Please be aware that you should not drive faster than 50kph.

On foot: This is by far the best way to see both the game and the bushveld country. There are several 1–5 day **guided walking trails**, taking small groups far off the roads to special camps. Armed rangers accompany the groups as close as possible to big game such as lion, elephant and buffalo. The trails are often booked up as much as a year in advance, but it is possible to get a cancellation, which you can book in advance from abroad, via the National Parks Board in Pretoria, ✆ (012) 343 1991.

Bush Camps

The Kruger has a variety of bush camps. The main one, Skukuza, is the size of a small town, complete with an airstrip, bank, post office, petrol station, supermarket, car hire, police station, doctor, library, large restaurant and school for the children of the park's rangers. The majority are smaller, although still well provided with amenities, while some of the more expensive camps are no more than a cluster of cabins built on stilts. Each camp has its own specialities and local game. There is accommodation to suit all budgets (*see* 'Where to Stay'). A good general rule is to book well in advance (throughout the year) through the National Parks Board, ✆ (012) 343 1991, and to avoid weekends or holidays if possible. All camps close their gates overnight (*c. 5.30–6.30pm*); the times are posted on the gates. If you're staying in the park and you're caught on the roads after the advertised time you will be picked up by rangers and tersely escorted in; if you don't have overnight accommodation and fail to leave when the gates close you'll receive a heavy fine.

Where to Stay

private camps (expensive)

Boulders Camp has room for just 12 people in thatched log cabins built on stilts that the animals pass underneath. Book through the Letaba Camp, 50km east of the Phalaborwa Gate. The cabins have solar-powered electricity and are self-catering only. **Roodewal** and **Nwanetsi** take 19 and 16 people respectively. Accessible from the Orpen Gate, they are booked through Satara and Olifants Camps. Further south is **Jock of the Bushveld Camp**, also self-catering, which also takes 12 people. Bookings are made from Berg-En-Dal Camp, near Malelane Gate in the far south of the park. **Malelane** also has a small private camp of small cottages, bookable from Berg-En-Dal Camp.

general camps (moderate–cheap)

The general camps all have cottages and chalets with their own kitchens and bathrooms, and cheaper camping. All have *braaiing* facilities. **Oliphants Camp**, east of the Phalaborwa Gate, sits on a high bluff overlooking the Oliphants River. Game viewing is good from here, particularly in the evening, and the camp has a shop, restaurant, petrol station and small museum. The small **Orpen Camp** is more intimate, with a petrol station and shop, but no restaurant. Even smaller is one of the quietest public camps in the park, **Balule Camp**, on the Oliphants River near Letaba Camp, with only a few rondavels. East of the Paul Kruger Gate, **Lower Sabie Camp** is popular for the large concentrations of game in the vicinity, and has a shop, restaurant and petrol station. **Crocodile Bridge Camp** lies on the banks of the Crocodile

River in the far southeast of the park. Just 20 chalets and a small shop make this a pleasant place to stay, although it is some way from other points of the park.

Those wishing for greater privacy should try and book into the very small **Talamati Camp** near Orpen Gate, **Mbyamiti Camp**, on the banks of the Crocodile River in the far south, **Sirheni**, in the west, on the banks of the Nwawitsonto River, between the Orpen and Paul Kruger Gates. Travellers should book these camps at the nearest entrance gate, and remember to bring their own food. Three new, small camps have opened far inside the park— **Jakkalbessie, Shimaweni, Mopani** and **Bateleur.** All have self-contained cottages with their own bathrooms. **Letaba Camp** is a large, well-landscaped camp on the Great Letaba River east of Phalaborwa Gate, with a large restaurant, shop, petrol station and garage. **Satara Camp**, east of the Orpen Gate, is set in flat country, and game-viewing from here is not good, but this is one of the largest camps, popular with tour groups from Jo'burg, and a good place for young people to meet. It has 2 restaurants, a shop, petrol station, laundry, information centre and garage.

Berg-En-Dal Camp, near the Malelane Gate in the far south of the park, is more attractively landscaped than the other big camps, with the cottages spaced out under large shady trees. It has a pool, restaurant, shop, petrol station and laundry. **Skukuza Camp,** by the Paul Kruger Gate, is the largest in the park and a convenient place to stop, but it gives little sense of being in the bush. However, it does overlook a hippo pool on the Sabie River. **Pretoriuskop and Shingwedzi**, further inside the park, have accommodation in self-contained cottages and chalets, bungalows with shared bathrooms, and camping, as well as a restaurant and shop. **Maroela Camp**, just east of the Orpen Gate, is the cheapest camp, open to campers only. It has a full range of facilities, including a shop, petrol station, restaurant and laundry.

The Private Game Reserves

Tacked on to the western border of the Kruger are a number of private, rather exclusive, game reserves, also harbouring big game. These offer a more intimate look at the bush than is possible in the Kruger (unless you are on one of the National Park's Wilderness Trails). Open-top Land Rovers allow you to breathe the open air of the bushveld and add a frisson of excitement when approaching a potentially dangerous animal, such as a lion or elephant. Some of the private reserves also offer walking trails similar to those of the Kruger. The bush camps of the private reserves tend to be beautifully laid out, small, and strictly limited in the number of guests allowed at a time, so there is no risk of competing with other vehicles for a sight of game. Most specialize in certain kinds of game, particularly dangerous game, and make a point of bringing their guests as close as possible.

A drawback to the private reserves is the cost, which ranges from the ludicrously expensive to the merely expensive. Hospitality tends to be lavish and the prices include all game drives, food (and sometimes drinks), and facilities such as special hides for photographing animals. But these reserves are generally beyond the reach of anyone travelling on a low budget.

Purist wildlife enthusiasts may also not wish to visit the private reserves, as many conservationists accuse their management of creating false environments out of the need to assure sightings of the 'Big Five'. Practices such as baiting and shining permanent night-time spotlights so as to sight shy species like leopard are commonplace, and opinion is divided as to whether this seriously upsets the natural order of the bushveld. However, tourism is a way of ensuring the wildlife's future (as well as that of its fragile habitat). Make up your own mind.

Johannesburg ✆ (011–)

Where to Stay

very expensive

Sabi Sand, ✆ 483 3939, is the largest private reserve, a 60,000ha block of bushveld just north of the Paul Kruger Gate (along the R536 from Sabie). It is split into three separate reserves, each offering slightly different game specialities. **Sabi Sabi**, the best known and most expensive and luxurious, has the Big Five and is famous for a huge bull elephant called Mandleve, one of the last real tuskers (they reach almost to the ground) left unpoached on the entire continent. **Inyati**, smaller than Sabi Sabi, is known for night drives, and the night-time spotlights near the camp that attract shy animals, such as leopard, to a baited tree. **Ulusaba**, built on a rock outcrop, is surrounded by wild fig forest, and has commanding views of the *veld*. Slightly cheaper than Sabi Sand's other two reserves, Ulusaba specializes in straightforward safaris looking for the Big Five. **Mala Mala**, ✆ 789 2677, is next to Sabi Sand, and is reached by the same road. It is only half the size, but its game concentration is high, and you can more or less guarantee seeing the Big Five. Again, the bush camps are luxuriously appointed, the food lavish, and the prices very high.

Londolozi, ✆ 784 6832, adjoins both Sabi Sand and Mala Mala, and is also a luxury reserve with high prices. Although most big game species are present, it is famous for its leopards. Guided walks into the bush are a speciality. **Umlani Bushcamp** at **Timbavati**, ✆ (012) 329 3765, is reached via the R53 to the Orpen Gate of the Kruger. Also at Timbavati are **Motswari** and **M'Bali**, ✆ 463 1990, the former offering luxury chalets and the latter a luxury camp; ranger-escorted walks, game and night drives are offered at both. Timbavati has long been known for its white lions, a pride that lack certain pigment in their coats but are not albinos. Thrilling game drives take you to within feet of these unique animals, without the security of metal and glass between you. The lions are accustomed to people and there have been no attacks. There are night-time hides from which you can watch lions feeding. The reserve also has particularly large herds of both elephant and buffalo.

Thornybush Game Reserve, ✆ 883 7918/9, near Hoedspruit on the R40 between Nelspruit and Tzaneen, borders Timbavati. Once again, it is a luxurious lodge and the Big Five are the main attractions, with guided game walks available. **Sandringham Private Nature Reserve**, ✆/⊕ (015) 793 2449, stretching across 5000ha on the border of Kruger, has a lodge on the banks of the Timbavati River and four stone and thatch chalets with en suite facilities, plus pool, day and night drives and dinner under the stars. **Ngala Game Reserve**, ✆ 803 8421/8616, ⊕ 803 1810/1898, was donated in trust to the World Wide Fund for Nature, and its philosophy concentrates on conservation and sustainability. Accommodation is in 20 luxury chalets, with superb food, trees hanging with orchids, a swimming pool over-looking a water hole, and game walks and drives with experienced rangers.

expensive

Klaserie, a huge reserve (60,000ha) just northwest of Timbavati, is signposted south of Hoedspruit. Klaserie has no specific game speciality, but the Big Five are all present. **Buffalo Lodge**, ✆ 792 5197, in the north, offers luxury accommodation for a limit of 12 people, a pool and all the facilities of a private game lodge, such as the attention of qualified rangers on game drives. There are a number of operators in the district, one of the best known of which is **Kapama Game Reserve**, ✆ (012) 804 1711. Accommodation is in large safari tents and lodges. There are guided game walks during the day and game drives at night. In Kapama is the **Hoedspruit Research and Breeding Centre for Endangered Species**, ✆ (015) 793 1633, (no need to book unless you are in parties of more than 10), on the road between Klaserie and Hoedspruit (*open Mon–Sat 8–4*). It is currently famous for its **Cheetah Project**. Cheetah, which now face extinction in many parts of Africa, are bred here for release into the wild. The very rare, dark-spotted king cheetah, a larger sub-species of the endangered cat, has also been successfully bred. A visit entails handling tame cheetahs (which enjoy being stroked and tickled and purr like a motor-bike engine) and a film on the research and work of the project. **Tshukudu Bush Camp**, ✆ (015) 793 1885, is a family-run reserve without the sometimes oppressive VIP treatment that the more expensive reserves cultivate. It has the Big Five, but is particularly known for rhino (black and white), and for its animal orphanage, where guests feed baby elephant and lion (which wander about the lodge).

moderate

Manyeleti Game Reserve, near the Orpen Gate of the Kruger Park, is signposted from the R536. Run by the provincial government, it lacks the luxury of the above reserves, but the thick, unspoilt bushveld seldom has more than a few tourists at a time and provides a peaceful alternative to the crowded Kruger National Park, at budget prices. There is a small bush camp of self-contained rondavels, a shop, petrol station, restaurant and bar, and the Big Five. Also near the Kruger (at the southwest corner) is **Mthethomusha Game Reserve**, which has all of the Big Five except for lion. Administered by the Mpumalanga Parks Board, Mthethomusha has a luxurious lodge, **Bongani**, and the local Swazi people have a share in its profits. You have to book via the Mpumalanga Parks Board in Nelspruit, ✆ (013) 759 4000, to arrange to be met at the gate by a Parks Board vehicle—no private cars are allowed in the park. **Nyaleti River Lodge**, ✆ (011) 792 9359, is in The Klaserie Nature Reserve and provides comfortable self-catering lodges over-looking the Klaserie River.

The small colonial town of **Barberton** lies at the foot of high, temperate mountains similar in appearance and vegetation to the Drakensberg. Barberton has a special place in South African history as the site of the country's second gold rush, but today there are only one or two national monuments to interest the visitor. The mountain country behind is empty and wild and has some of the province's best hiking, as well as a game-rich nature reserve.

History

Barberton sprang into existence in the early 1880s as a gold-buying and mining centre. The extensive gold finds in the Eastern Transvaal Drakensberg during the 1870s had sent prospectors hunting through the region's mountains for the elusive metal. The first strike in Barberton (named after one Graham Barber, one of the area's earliest successful prospectors) was made in 1883 by a Frenchman named Auguste Robert. Unlike the Drakensberg finds, those around Barberton were mostly in undergound reefs, rather than alluvial deposits, and so promised greater fortunes. One reef, on the Sheba claim, gave up 50,000 ounces of gold in its first 11,000 tons of ore, making it the richest gold mine in the world at that time. Within weeks of the find, a corrugated iron and tent village called Eureka City had emerged near the site of the present town. Within a few months permament buildings were going up, some of them grand, like the elegant Stock Exchange, which still stands as testimony to the riches that the surrounding mountains yielded up. However, it soon became clear that only a few of the reefs ran deep enough to provide long-term yields, and after 1886 most of the prospectors moved north to try their luck on the Witwatersrand.

Barberton soon settled into a small, prosperous regional town with a mostly English-speaking population, owing to the large numbers of British prospectors that were attracted to the original Eureka City in the late 19th century. Today, the town still has some working gold mines nearby, and is connected by a cable-way to the asbestos-mining town of Bulembu in Swaziland. The cableway does not take passengers, which is sad, as the views would be magnificent; one unfortunate man tried it a few years ago, but got on too late in the day and was still sitting in the cable-car when the cableway shut down for the night. Owing to the high altitude, he froze to death.

Tourist Information

Barberton Publicity Bureau, Main Street, Barberton, © (013) 712 2121 ext 242.

The Town

The **Barberton Museum** on Pilgrim Street (*open Mon–Sun 9–4*), has a good local history of the mining days, with old photographs of characters such as Cockney Liz, a barmaid at the Phoenix Hotel (which still exists) who 'used to put herself up for sale every night and was hopelessly immoral', but who nonetheless would have no bad language in her bar, and who later joined the Salvation Army. The more sedate side of Barberton's early days is preserved in the **Bellhaven House Museum** (*open Mon–Fri 10–3.30*), a late Victorian set-piece. Having experienced such a rapid gold boom, Barberton even sported a **Stock Exchange** during the late 1880s and '90s, and the elegant Cape Dutch-style façade (built 1887) has been preserved. Other surviving historic buildings include the **Masonic Lodge**, the old

Globe Tavern, which saw more than its share of riots and brawls during the rush, and the Victorian houses of **Stopfoth** (*open Mon–Fri, tours 10, 11, 12, 2, and 3*), and **Fernlea** (*Mon–Fri 9–12.30 and 1.30–4*), both of which now contain the usual collection of old town Victoriana. There is also a monument to the Staffordshire bull terrier Jock, the hero of the South African colonial classic, *Jock of the Bushveld*—see **Further Reading**. Indeed, in Mpumalanga you cannot escape the omnipresent Jock. Apart from the *Jock of the Bushveld Hostel* and *Lodge*, there are eponymous trails, drives, shops, an appreciation society and even a golf competition.

In Barberton's central park is a **giant fig tree** under which Paul Kruger is supposed to have set up a court to settle cases between miners, on one of his rare visits to the town—as a rule the old Boer president did not like the *uitlanders* that invaded his republic to make money from its minerals, despite the revenues they generated.

Just outside town, on the R38, is the **Barberton Nature Reserve**, which covers a large section of the mountain foothills near town; there is no accommodation, but visitors can walk at will. The hills are mostly grassland, but forested kloofs with fast-flowing streams cut through them. There is little game apart from some shy duiker, baboon, vervet monkeys, and dassies. However, to the south, Barberton borders the enormous (56,000ha) **Songimvelo Nature Reserve**, ✆ (017) 883 6800, which stretches over the foothills and into the high mountains separating Barberton from Swaziland. White rhino, giraffe, zebra, kudu, bushbuck, reedbuck, and the smaller antelope live here, while hippo wallow in the bilharzia-laden Komati River, which cuts through the reserve.

Songimvelo has a network of beautiful hiking trails through its mixed grassland, heath and woodland, some of which climb up to almost 2000m. The reserve is reached by the R40 from Barberton to Bulembu in Swaziland, with its entrance just before the apex of the Saddleback Pass.

Two other hiking trails into the mountains, the **Pioneer Trail** and **Gold Nugget Trail**, are both 2-day hikes with overnight huts. To book call ✆ (013) 712 2121. The flora is particularly good, with forest, grassland and wildflowers such as the large, red Barberton Daisy. The trails pass some of the old mine shafts and hikers may enter them, but to go in farther than about 20m is dangerous. The trails begin at the **Dias Reef Base Camp**, about 2km out of town along Crown Street.

(✆ 013–)

Where to Stay

expensive–moderate

The luxurious safari lodge at **Songimvelo Nature Reserve** is very expensive, ✆ (017) 883 800. Expect to be waited on hand and foot in a superb mountain setting. The surrounding reserve teems with game, and there are guided hikes of one hour to several days, guided riding trails (for guests only) and game drives in the reserve's open-topped vehicles. Drive up the road to Saddleback Pass and Swaziland for about half an hour and look out for the sign (which points to the south).

Just inside the moderate category is the **Phoenix Hotel** on Pilgrim Street, ✆ 712 4211, one of early Barberton's liveliest liquor joints, which has sadly lost both its outrageousness and the original décor. 14km out on the Kaapmuinden Road is the **Diggers Retreat**, ✆ 719 9681, which is the only other hotel in the immediate area. However, if you are not in a hurry, it is worth crossing the mountains behind Barberton via the R40, which heads over Saddleback Pass into Swaziland. After about 30km on the Swaziland side is the delightful **Phopanyane Lodge and Nature Reserve**, ✆ (09268) 71319, reached via the little towns of Bulembu and Pigg's Peak. Phopanyane, set in forest by a long set of waterfalls, has expensive cottages and moderately priced safari tents hidden from each other under trees, as well as a small, very good restaurant. Remember to set off before 3pm, as the border post east of Saddleback Pass closes at 4.30pm. See Northwest Swaziland for details of Phophanyane. There are a number of B&Bs, for example, **Kloof House**, 1 Kloof St, ✆ 712 1268, and (surprise surprise) **Jock's Place**, 2 Retief St, ✆ 712 4650.

cheap

Self-catering chalets and camp sites with ablutions can be found at the **Barberton Caravan Park** in the middle of town, ✆ (013) 712 23323, and at the **Dias Reef Camp Site**, about 2km from town along Crown Street. A few hours' hike from Dias Camp, along the Pioneer Hiking Trail, is an overnight hut with water and firewood. 10 km out on the Nelspruit Road are the **Jock of the Bushveld** self-catering cottages, ✆ (013) 712 4002.

Far Southeastern Mpumalanga: Between Barberton and Pongola River

If driving down to central Swaziland or northern Zululand from Johannesburg, you will pass through this vast, high, landscape of golden grasslands, dotted with huge blocks of forestry. Although it is mostly composed of large private cattle and timber farms and small farming towns, there are one or two stops worth making.

About 50km southwest of Barberton is the small but overdeveloped town of **Badplaas**, which has a mineral spa—unfortunately built into a frightful leisure complex during the 1970s. However, just north of town on the R38, the **Badplaas Nature Reserve** has walking and riding trails through a stretch of rolling hill country where large antelope graze. There are moderately priced self-contained chalets and a camp site with ablutions. The R541 leads from Badplaas straight into the Swazi capital Mbabane, about 75km to the east, so the reserve makes a good place to break a journey to Swaziland.

Further south, near the town of Ermelo, on the R29 between the N11 and Piet Retief, is the **Ermelo Game Park**, a small reserve surrounding two dams, harbouring large antelope and large populations of waterfowl. A camp site and some self-catering chalets make this a convenient spot to break a long drive. About 50km further along the R29 towards Piet Retief is **Jericho Dam Nature Reserve**, a larger reserve with little game but very good bird life; blue, crowned and wattled cranes in particular have made the dam a regular stop on their ceaseless foraging flights, perhaps because of its isolation. There is a camp site.

From Jericho Dam, the R29 leads on to Piet Retief, from where you can either head east into southern Swaziland, or south on the R33 to northern KwaZulu-Natal.

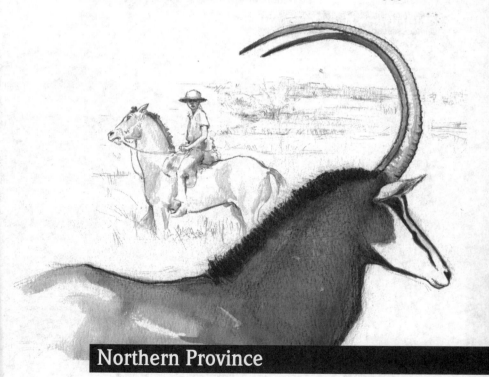

Northern Province

Animal, and bird and beast revealed
The secret of the wilderness that guides
All rebel creatures, singular or spurned
Along safe trails to water-holes and hides

The Lowveld, Charles Eglington

From Pretoria north to the Zimbabwe border, the Northern Province becomes progressively wilder and more open. Game abounds, and in the region's more northerly reaches hunting ranches have almost entirely replaced stock farms. The landscape consists mainly of flat plains, from which rise three mountain ranges: the baobab-covered Soutpansberg in the far north, Waterberg in the west and Strydpoortberg in the Drakensberg foothills of the east. These heights, green from year-round rains, provide

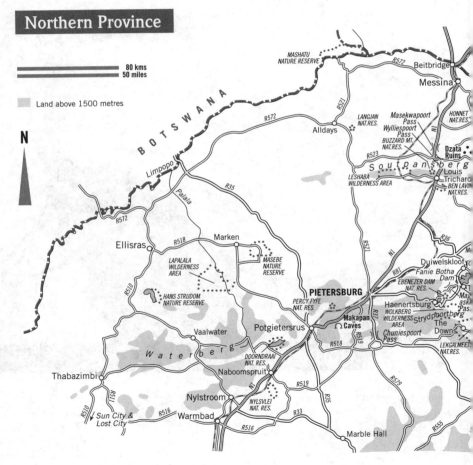

Northern Province

80 kms
50 miles

Land above 1500 metres

cool relief from the relentless heat of the plains. From the high montane forests and waterfalls you can gaze down at the flat bushveld far below and feel yourself a world away from the drought and dust of Africa.

The Northern Province has few towns of any size except Pietersburg, Potgietersrus, Louis Trichardt and Messina, all of which are strung out along the 600km section of N1 highway that links Pretoria and Johannesburg with Zimbabwe. Of little interest in themselves, these towns provide access to the region's mountain hiking trails and many game reserves, such as the northern Kruger National Park, the beautiful Lapalala Wilderness Area, and the Leshaba Wilderness.

Under apartheid, vast areas of this former Northern Transvaal were set aside as the 'tribal homelands' of Lebowa, Gazankulu and Venda. Although now officially back in the union, these areas still retain a very different look and feel to the other 'white' areas of the Northern Province, with traditional villages and communal systems of land ownership creating a more obviously African landscape. Most road and tourism maps still show the old 'homeland' borders.

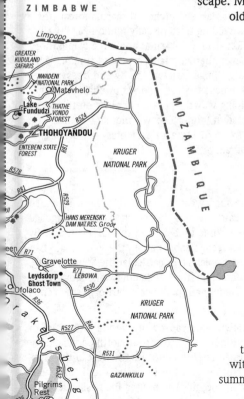

Of the three, Venda, stretching north from the Soutpansberg to the Limpopo, is the most unmodernized, a remote territory whose natural landscape has not been obliterated by over-population or over-grazing. In some areas of rural Venda, the people live side by side with game, providing a glimpse of South African life before colonial days.

Travellers should note that parts of the Northern Province are malarial.

Climate

Like all eastern parts of South Africa, the Northern Province has a summer rainy season and a dry winter. The low-lying bushveld plains seldom become cold, except on winter nights, and summer days are blisteringly hot. However, up in the mountains a more temperate mini-climate prevails, with rain occurring all year (though mostly in summer) and occasional frosts on winter nights.

Flora and Fauna

The 'Big Five'—lion, leopard, buffalo, elephant and both rhino species—are common in the Kruger National Park, as are large herds of antelope, zebra and wildebeest. Big game such as white rhino, giraffe, buffalo, roan and sable antelope occur in the Waterberg region, especially the Lapalala Wilderness Area, and to the north in the Leshaba Wilderness and Nwanedi National Park in former Venda. In the Soutpansberg and Drakensberg forest reserves leopard, caracal lynx, bushbuck, the rare red duiker and samango monkey thrive, but are shy and tend to stay hidden. Crocodile and hippo can be found in the rivers of the Kruger and Waterberg, as well as in the Limpopo, and the region has numerous smaller reserves, most of which support large numbers of indigenous antelope. Game also lives wild on farms, many of which have harnessed the wildlife commercially, becoming game farms and hunting ranches. This is particularly so north of the Soutpansberg, where most of the large game species can be found.

The birdlife on the plains is colourful and diverse; lilac-breasted rollers and bee-eaters are a common sight on the telephone wires along the roads. Bateleur eagles, Cape vultures, pale chanting goshawks, hornbills and other birds associated with the lowveld wilderness are common. Black eagle, green lourie and narina trogon inhabit the mountain forests.

The common thorn tree is not alone on the plains: large stretches of marula forest (their berries a favourite food of elephants), spectacular wild fig trees (usually found near dry river beds), huge baobabs (in the northernmost section around Messina) and large camel-thorn trees (in the west, near Botswana) provide an ever-changing landscape and support large numbers of browsing animals. In the Soutpansberg a huge variety of hardwood trees such as assegai, hard pear, yellowwood and lemonwood (whose fresh scent drifts through the higher reaches of the forest) line the middle slopes, giving way to spectacular aloes on the rocky summits, while in the Drakensberg foothills of eastern former Lebowa and near Tzaneen are rare stretches of cycad forest (giant, prehistoric tree-ferns), creating a fantasy landscape that local tribesmen still believe is ruled by a mythical rain queen.

History

The original San (bushman) inhabitants were pushed west from their Northern Province hunting grounds by the southward migration of cattle-owning tribes, who spoke a language similar to that of the Shona in modern Zimbabwe, some time around the 12th century. By the 16th century these people had emerged into a recognizable nation, the Venda, and had established themselves in the region's northernmost uplands, in particular the Soutpansberg. Made prosperous by perennial springs and year-round rain, the Venda built walled towns and established an empire that spread over much of the modern province's territory (*see* 'Venda History' p.594).

However, in the late 17th century, prolonged civil wars caused the Venda monarchy to collapse. A loose confederation of chiefdoms continued to thrive in the fortified villages of the northern uplands but, from the late 17th and early 18th centuries, the rest of the territory came under the sway of two other powerful people, the Pedi and the Swazi, who established strongholds in the northern Drakensberg foothills and hunted the bushveld of the Northern Province's hot central plain.

Although these clans fought periodic raiding wars with each other, the territorial balance of power remained stable until the 1820s, when large Zulu raiding parties from present KwaZulu-Natal began to ravage the north. The Swazi bore the brunt of these depredations and retreated into the most remote mountain valleys of their territory (see **Swaziland** 'History'), while the Pedi and Venda managed to beat off the raiders and continue as normal in the years between raids. A Nguni people—the generic name for the language group which includes the Zulu, Swazi and Xhosa—called Ndebele did settle on the central plain. In the 1820s a more bellicose Nguni renegade clan, also known as Ndebele, arrived from what is now Zululand, and adopted a predatory existence until finally expelled by the Boers.

These Ndebele confined the Venda, Pedi and Swazi to the uplands and began to raid the cattle-rich highveld, while keeping large villages around the modern towns of Potgietersrus and Pietersburg. So when the Voortrekkers appeared on the scene in the late 1830s the territory was already war-like. The first party, under Louis Trichardt, passed through peacefully en route for Mozambique but, in 1840, a second wave, under Andries Potgieter, arrived.

Potgieter's Voortrekkers had come up though the Ndebele country of the Western Transvaal, and had fought Mzilikazi's warriors every step of the way. Although the new Voortrekkers settled at various points along the modern Great North Road (the N1 highway), and founded the Zoutpansberg Republic near the site of the modern town of Louis Trichardt (1848), their aggressive policies of raiding black villages for children to work as farm labourers, and their wholesale slaughter of the local game, especially elephant, won them few friends. War with the Ndebele continued until the 1850s when the last powerful chief in the area was finally besieged with his people in a set of caves near Potgietersrus, and there starved to death (see 'Potgietersrus'), but the Pedi and Venda remained hostile and, despite frequent Boer and Swazi raids, never lost hold of their territories for more than temporary periods of time.

From 1860, the Zoutpansberg republic amalgamated with the Transvaal's two other Boer republics to form the South African Republic (SAR). Although the SAR had to eschew slavery in order to be recognized by the British Cape Colony, the system of kidnapping for forced labour continued to flourish under the innocuous title of 'indentured labour'. Not only the Pedi, Venda and Swazi suffered, but also the Tsonga from the lowveld of neighbouring Mozambique. But the tide was turning against the Northern Transvaal Boers. By the early 1860s, the region's elephant herds were almost destroyed, and the Zoutpansberg ivory hunters realized that they would have to go east into Mozambique if they wanted to keep their livelihoods. Unwilling to enter that country's fever-ridden lowlands, they taught their 'indentured labourers' to shoot, and sent them into the bush instead, under the supervision of loyal foremen. This was a tactical error; no sooner had the African hunters been armed, than most absconded for the homelands from which they had been snatched as children.

The Tsonga then began demanding payment from the Boers for hunting rights, a tactic which soon caught on with other tribes. Boer rule was further undermined by the Tsonga and Pedi discovering lucrative labour markets away from the harsh Boers, who paid badly and flogged often: by the 1860s these young Tsonga and Pedi were travelling to Natal (and a few years later, to Kimberley), from which they returned with both guns and money.

In 1867 the Northern Transvaal Boers attempted to reassert their dominance by attacking the Venda. But the *kommando* (led by Paul Kruger, the future president of the SAR) was beaten off.

The Boers, now embroiled in a little civil war of their own, abandoned Schoemansdal and retreated south to Pietersburg, then as now the region's largest town, and concentrated on farming the Waterberg and the lush Drakensberg foothills, and attacking the Swazi and Pedi. However, the chaotic nature of events in the SAR was attracting British attention. The Swazi invited the British authorities in Natal to mediate in border disputes with the Boers and the Pedi (*see* **Swaziland** and **Mpumalanga** 'History'). Pretending that it was necessary to ensure the Swaziland boundary, Britain sent a force against the Pedi, subdued them, and turned their attention on the Boers. For a few years, they deliberated on whether or not to invade the republic. After gold was found in the Northern Transvaal Drakensberg, the matter was settled. In 1877, British forces invaded the SAR and formally annexed it for the Crown.

Although the Boers did manage to eject the invaders in 1881, they could not re-establish their dominance in the Northern Transvaal away from the central plain. In the late 1890s, both the Venda and the Pedi launched large attacks on Boer settlements near their borders. The Boers retaliated by sending a commando under Joubert against the Venda, this time successfully. Mpephu, their chief, fled across the Zambezi and did not return until the British annexed the Transvaal in 1902. The town of Louis Trichardt was founded under the lee of the Soutpansberg, being named after the old Voortrekker whose grandson led the *kommando's* artillery. The following year saw the outbreak of the Second Anglo-Boer War of 1899. All *kommandos* were sent on active service against the British in Natal, leaving the Northern Transvaal tribes in peace.

After the war ended in 1902, the territory came back under British rule and steps were taken to open it up. The fertile country around Tzaneen was slowly opened up, while coal and iron ore mines were opened up in the northeast, and cattle-ranching began to creep north towards the Soutpansberg. The Venda were ordered to burn their unregistered rifles, but the law proved impossible to enforce, and the remote Venda country remained more or less independent, with only visiting British administrators and missionaries to represent colonial rule. Venda chiefs were put on the Government payroll as magistrates, a practice that persisted until the 1950s. Meanwhile, at the southern foot of the Soutpansberg, the new town of Louis Trichardt, built about 20km east of the ruins of Schoemansdal, developed its farming and forestry interests, eating up large chunks of former Venda territory and bringing white settlement back to the far north.

Similarly, the farming centres of Pietersburg and Tzaneen prospered. From the 1950s and '60s many northern ranchers changed from cattle- to game-ranching; cattle were vulnerable to disease and drought, whereas the bushveld could support dense game populations which were disease and drought resistant. The potential revenue from hunting, hides and meat made it more profitable to put the land back under indigenous wildlife. The resulting widespread game-ranching has helped to keep much of the region's habitat intact.

However, a far less positive trend from the 1950s–70s was the creation of the region's three tribal 'homelands' of Lebowa (1972) for the Pedi, Gazankulu (1973) for the Tsonga, and Venda (1979). Thousands of people were forcibly moved to these infertile, rocky areas, losing both land and livestock, which was never compensated for. Severe overgrazing and overcrowding of this desert land soon forced many to seek work in South Africa, either in the cities, where they had to live without their families, or in the farms and towns bordering the 'homelands', which necessitated long and expensive travelling to low-paid jobs. The rulers of these 'states' were usually drawn from the tribe's nobility, but were no longer accountable to the tribe and could be easily bought off by the South African government.

Lebowa and Gazankulu opted for self-government within South Africa, but Venda chose to be a separate country. This nominal 'independence' was never recognized internationally, and served only to strip the residents of their South African citizenship, while still retaining them as cheap labour for the country's industries. However, Venda, perhaps because of its traditional seclusion from the rest of the country and largely unbroken history of self-government, seems to have suffered less than other 'homelands' from overcrowding and the drift to the cities. Water is plentiful and irrigation fairly simple to arrange, so the problems of over-grazing and erosion have largely been avoided.

Today, the Northern Province remains somewhat isolated from the rest of the country, politically more peaceful, with most of its wild land still intact. The 'homelands' have been re-incorporated into South Africa, which will probably result in more development of the tribal areas. This is likely to be agricultural, rather than industrial, with an emphasis on game farming and eco-tourism.

✆ (015–)   **Getting There and Around**

By car: The most direct route to Northern Province is via the N1 from Pretoria and Jo'burg, which heads straight through the centre of the region to Messina and the Zimbabwean border. A more beautiful drive is from Mpumalanga, up the R40 from the Mpumalanga Drakensberg to Tzaneen, or from the west, along the R510 and R572 through the empty sandveld region bordering Botswana, and the rolling Waterberg. The region is largely remote and not well served by public transport, making a car the simplest way to get around.

Car hire: Cheap car hire can be found in Jo'burg (*see* 'Getting Around'), or otherwise try **Avis**, ✆ 288 0169, **Budget**, ✆ 288 0169, **Imperial**, ✆ 288 0097, or **Ultra City**, ✆ 293 7228.

By bus: Greyhound, ✆ (011) 333 2136, and **TransLux** and **Transtate**, ✆ (011) 774 3333, buses from Jo'burg travel up the N1 and stop at all the main towns. Some continue on into Zimbabwe.

Hitch-hiking: Pick-ups to get into the wild areas can be arranged through private game reserves, or you can hitch to hiking trail-heads. The N1 carries a lot of long-distance traffic, while off the main roads it is easy to get lifts from local traffic. Hitching inside former 'homelands' is problematic, and the traffic intermittent.

By rail: Potgietersrus, Pietersburg, Louis Trichardt and Messina are all linked by rail to Jo'burg and Pretoria, with daily services, ✆ (011) 773 2131.

Black taxis: These provide a convenient way into the former 'homelands' for those without a car or the money to use a tour company. However, while the people are generally unthreatening, the vehicles have a bad safety record and travellers use them at their own risk.

Tour companies: Several private companies offer tours to private or public game reserves in the Northern Transvaal. **Clive Walker Trails**, ✆ (011) 453 7645/6, offers expensive but superb guided walks through the big game areas, with transport to and from Jo'burg. **Dubel African Travel**, ✆ 297 3899, operates in the far north, as does **Omnica Travel**, ✆ 291 2702, and **SA Tours and Bookings**, ✆ 297 3937. **North Link Tours**, ✆ 219 13101, offers direct transport to towns and reserves. In Tzaneen are **Letaba Active Tours**, ✆ 307 3538/32551.

The Waterberg and the Tuli Block

The Waterberg is a wild corner of South Africa. The quickest route is 100km along the N1 north from Pretoria to the overdeveloped spa town of **Warmbad** (an unpleasant resort around a mineral pool), or the small agricultural town of **Nylstroom**, from which the R516 or R517 lead into the Waterberg. A slower, more interesting drive is up the R511 or R510 through the former Bophuthatswana to the small town of **Thabazimbi** at its west end.

Whichever route you take, the first place to head for is the superb **Lapalala Wilderness Area**, ✆ (011) 453 7645, signposted from the dirt road connecting the R517 and R518 west of Warmbad and Nylstroom. Lapalala occupies a vast stretch of high hills covered with bush and hardwood forest, above the crocodile-infested Palala river. Walking trails lead to close encounters with white (and occasionally black) rhino, kudu, roan and sable antelope, zebra and blue wildebeest. Shy leopard hunt in the cliff caves above the river. Guided canoe trips along the Palala River lead to crocodile-free pools with safe swimming. Be aware that you must have fuel and supplies before you go in. Lapalala has several self-catering bushcamps with ablution and cooking facilities.

Adjoining Lapalala is an even larger private reserve, **Touchstone Game Ranch**, ✆ (014) 765 0203, which harbours even larger game, such as elephant, buffalo and giraffe, as well as the wildlife species of Lapalala. More expensive than Lapalala, Touchstone offers superb horse trails of up to ten days, game drives and guided walks. Access is along the R517, 60km west of Nylstroom to the village of Vaalwater, then 45km north to Melkrivier. Touchstone's signpost is on the south side of the road a few kilometres east of Marken, which lies about 38km northwest on the R518.

It is worth visiting the small town of **Thabazimbi** (on the R510 at the western edge of the Waterberg), the centre of the local game farming and hunting industry. The town holds an annual Game Festival, which includes a game auction, where private game reserves buy stock. There are many such auctions in the Province, but this is one of the few open to the public. Most of the game is sold in absentia, then tranquillized and collected from its vendor, but some of the smaller antelope species arrive in the auction ring. It is strange to see wild creatures such as impala in these surroundings. If the idea of treating wildlife commercially repels you, rest assured that every care is taken to ensure the animals' safety and comfort. Game farming lies at the heart of South Africa's highly successful game conservation programme, and even the large National Parks sell surplus animals. This not only helps to pay for habitat maintenance, it also saves having to cull excess beasts from land that can only support a certain number of each species. The Game Festival and auction is a movable feast; **Thabatoer**, ✆ (014773) 22 590, will know the dates.

The land around Thabazimbi is taken up with cattle farms and two small mines (gold and platinum), but wild country soon takes over. South of Thabazimbi, on the far southwest edge of the Waterberg region, is the **Ben Alberts Nature Reserve**, ✆ (014773) 79 670, signposted west from the R510 south of town. A small protected area within a greater wild region, this reserve is good for budget travellers, with a secluded, cheap camp site. There are no marked walking trails but there is nothing to stop you wandering the bush or driving the dirt roads in search of white rhino, eland, kudu, giraffe, red hartebeest and other browsers. Also on the southern edge of the Waterberg, just northeast of Thabazimbi, is **Kransberg National Park**, a 27,000ha wilderness area which, except for a walking trail up to a famous vulture colony, has not been open to tourists. The National Parks Board, ✆ (012) 343 1991, will have the latest details. **Mabula Game Lodge**, ✆ (014734) 616/717, is signposted north from the R516 between Thabazimbi and Warmbad. There are guided walks and drives in open-top vehicles among elephant, white rhino and buffalo.

Also at the eastern end of the Waterberg, close to the N1 near Potgietersrus, is **Doorndraai Nature Reserve**, ✆ (015423) 629, an area of bushveld around a large dam. Like most dam reserves, Doorndraai gets crowded with weekend water-skiers and windsurfers but is quiet during the week. Walking trails lead into wooded kloofs where waterfalls tumble down from the Waterberg foothills. Sable antelope and the equally rare tsessebe breed here. Impala, reedbuck, zebra, giraffe and some smaller species are also common. Look out for fish eagles on the dam's wooded shore.

Also on the eastern fringe of the region, just outside Naboomspruit, is the **Nylsvlei Nature Reserve**, ✆ (014) 743 1074, a large wetland supporting a huge variety of birds, including goliath heron, black stork, fish eagle and jacana. The rare roan antelope, waterbuck, kudu, impala, tsessebe and a few giraffe graze the lush water meadows. There is a camp site, but the reserve is so fragile that only 30 people at a time are allowed in, so be sure to book.

North of the Waterberg the landscape flattens out into dense thornveld used for cattle and game ranching. About 50km south of the area's main town, **Ellisras**, is the **D'Nyala Nature Reserve**, ✆ (014) 763 5148, signposted east of the R517. The rolling foothill terrain is home to mostly antelope, and the rare roan antelope breeds here. There are crocodiles and bilharzia in the dam, so swimming is discouraged, at least from the banks. This does not stop local farmers bringing their noisy fishing and water skiing boats here in the belief that there are no crocs in the centre of the dam, and you are less likely to contract bilharzia in deep water. So avoid the dam at weekends or public holidays. The **Langjan Nature Reserve**, ✆ (015) 516 0040 (Soutpansberg Marketing & Tourism), near Vivo, comprises sandy, Kalahari-type scrub, shaded at intervals by large camel-thorn trees, and patches of lowveld woodland, such as marula and fever trees, near the dry river beds. The reserve is good for birds; look out for bateleur and tawny eagle, kori bustard, ground hornbill and the small barred warbler. Mammals are plentiful, particularly gemsbok (the reserve was set up in the 1930s to protect the Province's last wild herd, though the species now flourishes throughout the province). Giraffe, kudu, eland, red hartebeest and blue wildebeest are also common. At dusk, you should see jackal and bat-eared fox. Leopard and caracal lynx come out after dark. Walking trails have been laid out from the central camp of rondavels.

West of Langjan, across the Limpopo in Botswana, lies the **Tuli Block**. Game from this wild region migrates on to the South African side quite regularly. The larger antelope are common migrants, but even elephant sometimes wander across. If you are in the area, it is well worth making a short side trip into the Tuli Block to **Mashatu Private Game Reserve** (cross the border at Pontdrif on the R521, northwest of Alldays, and look out for the signpost). Mashatu occupies a vast (90,000ha) plateau above the meeting of the Sashe and Limpopo Rivers. Staying there is not cheap, but Mashatu offers some of the best game-hiking in Southern Africa including a 4- or 5-day trail that specializes in guiding walkers close to elephant, staying always downwind of them, but with much holding of breath and creeping about so as to remain unseen by the great beasts.

Activities

Game-viewing: All the reserves listed above harbour game, in some cases big game such as elephant, white and black rhino, and buffalo.

Walking and hiking: The Waterberg and Tuli offer some of the most rewarding hiking in southern Africa because of the opportunities of getting close to game. Guided trails of 1–5 days can be arranged at **Lapalala Wilderness Area**, **Touchstone Game Ranch** and **Mabula Private Game Reserve**, in the Waterberg region. Further north, in the Tuli block of Botswana just over the border, the vast **Mashatu Private Game Reserve** has a 4- or 5-day elephant trail that must be booked through **Clive Walker Safaris** in Jo'burg, ✆ (011) 453 7645/6.

Gentler walks with a good chance of seeing game (mostly antelope) can be found at **Doorndraai Nature Reserve** and at the **Ben Alberts Nature Reserve**.

Riding: The Waterberg is one of the best places for riders to experience wild bush and big game in South Africa. **Equus Trails**, based at the Touchstone Game Ranch, have superbly schooled horses that are a joy to ride. The game is less disturbed by horses than humans and you can get much closer. Trips of 1–10 days are offered, with camping in the bush. Book either in Jo'burg, ✆ (011) 788 3923, or through the Touchstone Game Ranch.

Where to Stay

expensive

In the Waterberg, **Touchstone Game Ranch**, ✆ (014) 765 0230, the **Lapalala Wilderness Area**, ✆ Jo'burg (011) 453 7645, and **Mabula Game Lodge**, ✆ (014734) 616/717, offer luxurious accommodation. Lapalala has a tented camp, Touchstone private rondavels, and Mabula a comfortable lodge. Lapalala is self-catering, except by prior arrangement, but Touchstone and Mabula offer full board.

Welgevonden, ✆ (0147) 552 ask for 661, is a smaller private reserve, also in the Waterberg, with three bush camps and the option of self-catering or full board. Walking and Land Rover safaris are offered. Nearby is **Kolobe Lodge**, ✆ Jo'burg (011) 453 7645/6/7, which has four thatched rondavels. Again, guided game walks are a feature, and on some you can visit rock overhangs painted with bushman art. At the cheaper end of the expensive scale, **Shangri-La**, ✆ (01531) 2071/71153/ 3188, offers full board in thatched rondavels. Access is via the N1 to Pietersburg, then 10km west along the Kranskop road.

Further north, in the Tuli Block in Botswana, **Mashatu Private Game Lodge** has luxurious bush camps in a vast area of primeval wilderness, with guided hikes and game drives on offer.

moderate

Langjan Nature Reserve, ✆ (015) 593 0126, has a camp of moderately priced self-contained thatched rondavels. In the Waterberg, **Mabula Farm**, ✆ (014734) 717, near Mabula Game Reserve, is a comfortable self-catering farmhouse on the edge of thick woodland. There are walking trails, and fishing can be arranged. **Aventura Warmbad**, ✆ (014) 736 2200, is the resort near the hot springs in this small town just off the N1. Pietersburg has plenty of overnight accommodation including two ★★★ hotels, the **Holiday Inn Garden Court**, ✆ (0152) 291 2030, and the more individual **Ranch Hotel**, ✆ (0152) 293 7180, 24km to the south on the N1. You might also try **Col-John**, overnight accommodation, ✆ (0152) 295 9430/1/2/3.

cheap

Rietbokspruit Farm Cottages, ✆ (014) 743 2525, are self-contained cottages looking out on to open bush. Prices are very low for the comfort provided, and Rietbokspruit offers one of the best value-for-money deals in the Transvaal. **Ben Alberts Nature Reserve**, ✆ (014773) 21 509, southwest of Thabazimbi, has a cheap, secluded camp site with ablution blocks. Visitors can walk in the reserve, which also has game-viewing roads. **Doorndraai Nature Reserve**, ✆ (015423) 629, southwest of Potgietersrus, has a camp site, as does **Nylsvlei Nature Reserve**, ✆ (014) 743 1074, but, owing to the fragile ecosystem of the marsh it protects, the reserve limits the number of visitors. Booking is advised.

The Drakensberg Foothills and the Lowveld

East of Pietersburg the long, hot plain of central Northern Province rises in a series of rounded hills where high summer rainfall produces a landscape of lush, sub-tropical vegetation a world away from the harsh bushveld country around Pietersburg. In the dim distance rise the north most peaks of the Drakensberg mountains. The still, foetid air of the plains becomes cooler as the road climbs between high hills. Tea plantations, orchards and groves of almond and macadamia nut trees announce the quiet country town of **Tzaneen**.

Tzaneen

Tourist Information

Tzaneen Tourism Centre, Danie Joubert St, ✆ (015) 307 1294, is the local booking office for all tourist accommodation.

Tzaneen was a tiny pioneer settlement until the 1920s, but experienced a modest boom when the hills around were laid over to tea- and fruit-growing by the mostly English-speaking settlers. A medical research centre was set up here that managed to eliminate malaria from much of the region. Today's Tzaneen has the usual 'improved' ugliness of so many South African regional towns, but a few elegant colonial buildings survive, and the surrounding landscape is so gentle that it is impossible not to be charmed by the place.

Around Tzaneen

West of Tzaneen is one of the region's best scenic drives, through the twisting mountainside of **Magoebaskloof**, whose forested slopes give way to the lowland orchard country at the village of **Haernertsburg**. One of the larger fruit farms, **Cheerio Halt**, is signposted off the R71 towards Haernertsburg. Visitors are welcome, whether to pick their own cherries or to wander in the orchards, which are a delight in the spring. An entrance fee is charged.

Despite its beauty, Magoebaskloof is named after a tragedy; the name Mgoeba is a corruption of Makgoba—after chief Makgoba, who ruled the local Pedi clan in the 1860s and '70s and was a fierce resistor of white rule. He fought numerous raiding wars with the local Boers, who eventually decided to eliminate him after he refused to pay the hut tax to the SAR. In the early 1870s, Makgoba and his followers were hunted to this wild pass and eventually killed by Swazi mercenaries hired by the Boers.

The Letaba river plunges down the steep kloof, forming a man-made lake just west of Hearnetsburg, the Ebenezer Dam, whose quiet waters are fringed with tall plantations of pine and eucalyptus. The **Ebenezer Dam Nature Reserve**, ✆ (015) 276 234, is crowded with water sports enthusiasts at weekends, but is a contemplative place through the week. Egyptian geese, storks, herons, blacksmith plovers and other waterfowl feed in the shallows. The reserve has a small camp site. To the south rise the Strydpoortberg, and behind them the northern tip of the Mpumalanga Drakensberg. This wild mountain interior can be reached via the **Wolkberg Wilderness Area** (*see* **Mpumalanga**), by following the R71 from Tzaneen to the junction with the R529 and looking out for the signs for the New Agatha Forest Station, ✆ (015) 276 1303.

Grootbosch Nature Reserve, west of the Ebenezer Dam along the R71, is accessed from the De Hoek Forest Station. This area of Drakensberg foothills and forestry plantation is crossed by the **Magoebaskloof Hiking Trail** (*book through Tzaneen Tourism Centre*), which is divided into 3-day and 2-day sections. A hiking hut is provided at the forest station, but thereafter, hikers must pitch tent at designated spots. The Grootbosch section of the trail passes through the largest indigenous forest in the Province and passes several waterfalls. One of these, the **Debengeni Falls**, can be visited by car, as can part of the forest, via the **Woodbush Forest Drive**, details from Tzaneen Tourism Centre.

North of Tzaneen, the R36 leads past the **Fanie Botha Dam Nature Reserve**, known for its coarse angling, over the **Duiwelskloof** pass, on the far side of which is a village of the same name. Another lush area of high rainfall, the Duiwelskloof has several forest hiking trails leading to waterfalls; information from the Duiwelskloof Publicity Office, Botha Street, ✆ (015) 309 92461.

From Duiwelskloof, the R36 leads north to a signpost for the **Modjadji Cycad Forest** in Lebowa. This strange reserve, filled with thousands of giant cycads (prehistoric tree ferns) is considered sacred by the Lobedu, a clan affiliated to the Venda, and is the traditional home of the **Rain Queen**, a mythical hereditary title held by a real-life woman who lives in seclusion in a royal homestead near the forest. H. Rider Haggard's classic Edwardian adventure story *She* was based on the legend of the local Balobedu people who fled from tribal wars in the Eastern Highlands of Zimbabwe during the 19th century with their queen, who held the power of rain-making. The Rain Queen does exist, having now been absorbed into Pedi culture, and even today she is credited by many to have the power of rain-making. During the region's occasional droughts many farmers, both black and white, have been known to seek her intercession with the rain spirits. You can walk in the forest, but there is no accommodation. Walkers are likely to see nyala crashing into cover, and antelope such as bushbuck and waterbuck are common, while impala browse at the forest fringe.

If you go back to the R71 from Modjadji, and continue east of Tzaneen, towards Phalaborwa, the **Hans Merensky Nature Reserve**, ✆ (015) 386 8763/4, is in the hills at the southern tip of a great chunk of Lebowa and Gazankulu. The entrance to the reserve has unfortunately been developed by the company responsible for overpriced and ugly holiday resorts all over the Northern Province. But the reserve itself is wild and beautiful and worth visiting for its 3-day **Giraffe Trail** and its two half-day walks. The plentiful game includes giraffe, sable antelope, blue wildebeest and other antelope. In the Letaba River and the dam itself, crocodile and hippo are common. The terrain varies between lowveld mopane woodland, riverine forest along the Letaba, grassland and bushveld.

Apart from hiking, access to the reserve is only allowed in a resort bus, to prevent over-crowding with cars. A rather kitsch touch is a Tsonga show village where tourists can watch traditional practices like maize-meal grinding and dancing.

Continue further east along the R71, and you come to the small village of **Gravelotte**, near which is a huge baobab tree that once served as an open-air store and bar for the gold miners from the ghost town of **Leydsdorp**, about 12km east. The town's brief 1890 gold rush collapsed after the opening of the main Witwatersrand gold reefs in the 1890s. Leydsdorp itself is a detour; its abandoned buildings are well preserved and some are being restored.

For a beautiful mountain drive, follow the R36 south to **Ofolaco**, and then the dirt road west into the mountains through the little settlement of **The Downs**. This leads into the spectacular **M'Thalepsi Valley** of indigenous forest and traditional kraals. Much of this area lies within former Lebowa, and the huge **Lekgalameetse Nature Reserve**, ✆ (051) 383 0015, which has chalets, provides a chance to walk in the beautiful hills. The forest and grassland supports mountain wildlife such as leopard, caracal, bushbuck, duiker, reedbuck, klip-springer, baboon and both monkey species. There is a variety of accommodation.

West of Lekgalameetse the road eventually joins the tarred R37 at Zeekoegat and heads west and north to Pietersburg; from here the R71 leads back over Magoebaskloof to Tzaneen. Those without time to make the round trip should turn around about 15km after The Downs and head back to Ofolalo.

East of Gravelotte, the R71 continues to the Phalaborwa Gate into the northern Kruger National Park.

Activities

Walking and Hiking: Pleasant day-walks can be found at the Ebenezer Dam Nature Reserve, the Fanie Botha Dam Nature Reserve, Grootbosch Nature Reserve, Duiwelskloof, the Hans Merensky Dam Nature Reserve, at New Agatha Forest Station, the Lekgalameetse Nature Reserve and the Modjaji Forest Reserve in Lebowa. Hikes of more than one day are the Magoebaskloof Trail (2 or 3 days) at Grootbosch, the 3-day Giraffe Trail at the Hans Merensky Dam Nature Reserve (with overnight huts equipped with firewood, cooking utensils and a shower), the 2-day Leopard Trail at Duiewlskloof, the 2-day Lekgalameetse Nature Reserve, and in the Wolkberg Wilderness Area (up to 5 days). *See* above for details, except Wolkberg *see* **Mpumalanga**.

Fishing: Coarse fishing for South African species such as black bass, kurper and yellowfish can be arranged at the dams around Tzaneen, particularly Fanie Botha Dam Nature Reserve. Tzaneen Tourism Centre has the details.

Shopping

Wheelbarrow Farm Stall, ✆ (015) 305, on the R71 sells local Pedi and Tsonga crafts, including wood-carving and woven rugs, Boer pastries and fruit preserves, and curios such as skins and semi-precious stones. Local information can also be gathered here. The **Sasikele Carpet Factory**, on George Valley Pass on the R528, sells beautifully woven carpets made from karakul sheep wool (a breed imported from Mesopotamia for their resistance to dry climates and extremes of temperature).

Where to Stay

expensive

Mid Creek Ranch, ✆ (015) 383 0214, 40km south of Tzaneen on the R36, is signposted from the Luxembourg turn-off near Ofolaco. The old colonial country house has a beautiful veranda overlooking the Ngwatsbitsi River. Furnished with colonial antiques, the house sits amongst some of the Province's loveliest farmland, and hiking in The Downs can be organized. Accommodation is in six self-contained suites. The **Coach House**, ✆ (015) 307 3641, ✆ 307 1466, is in the small village of Agatha at the foot of the Wolkberg mountains. A coaching inn during the 19th century, it has 45 airy rooms and good cuisine, with views out over the hills and log fires in winter. Trails have been marked out in the surrounding woodlands, and the garden has good bird life.

Harmony Game Farm, ✆ Jo'burg (011) 783 4870, near Mica, along the R71 and R40 from Tzaneen, is a private lowveld game reserve. The Blyde and Oliphants Rivers meet here, so hippo and crocodile are plentiful, as are giraffe, kudu, blue wildebeest, zebra and other plains game. Predators include resident spotted hyena and occasional leopard and wild dog, which wander across from the nearby Kruger National Park. Game walks and mountain bike trails are offered, as well as day trips to other reserves. Accommodation is in five comfortable en suite rooms around a huge central living room. **Magoebaskloof Hotel**, ✆ (0152) 276 4276, is at the top of the Groot Letaba valley on the R71, and has magnificent views.

moderate

Glensheil Country Lodge, ✆ (015) 276 4335, 8km from Tzaneen on the Wolkberg road, offers self-contained chalets in an eccentric, ramshackle private theme park whose oddities include a castle made of bottles, a Buddhist garden, a Polynesian Village (don't ask why), a restaurant, pool and jacuzzi. Day visitors are welcomed at a small charge. **The Chalets**, ✆ (015276) 4264, signposted from the R71 between Magoebaskloof and Haernertsberg, is quieter. Built of dark wood and in Swiss style, the chalets do not look out of place in the surrounding hilly country. Fishing, hiking and boating can be arranged, and there is a pool to cool off in. **Magoebaskloof Lodge**, ✆ (0152) 305 3147, offers self-contained rondavels in a hillside spur on the R71 between Haernertsburg and Tzaneen. Again, fishing and hiking can be arranged, and there is a pool.

cheap

The **Lekgalameetse Nature Reserve**, ✆ (015) 383 0015, has very low-priced, comfortable rondavels and a camp site. **Grootbosch Nature Reserve**, ✆ (015) 305 3203, has a hiking hut with a shower, firewood and all cooking utensils, bookable in advance. Take your own bedding. The **Ebenezer Dam Nature Reserve**, ✆ (015) 276 2341, has a camp site, as does the **Fanie Botha Dam and Nature Reserve**, ✆ (015) 305 3019. Both have ablution blocks and are quiet during the week. Bird-watching for waterfowl is good at both dams. There are a good number of other hotels and B&Bs in the district, among them **Maxim's Guest House**, ✆ (0152) 307 4209, just outside Tzaneen on the R71 going towards Magoebaskloof.

Gazankulu

Proclaimed a 'homeland' in 1973, but officially re-absorbed into South Africa in 1994, most of Gazankulu lies in a long strip along the western border of the Kruger National Park. Gazankulu is home to predominantly Tsonga people.

Most tourists drive through Gazankulu at speed on their way to the Kruger but, although it lacks any tourist infrastructure, the area is rewarding to explore. Here, traditional Tsonga rural life takes its leisurely course, with a mixture of cattle-herding and market-gardening providing the staple livelihood. The numerous fruit and vegetable markets lining the road testify to the Tsongas' skill at raising crops, and it is worth stopping, not only to buy, but to chat with the women selling their wares, particularly if you know a little Afrikaans, the area's *lingua franca*. Traditional crafts, such as basket-weaving, beadwork and rug-weaving can usually be bought at roadside kraals.

Although heavily populated along the main R71, large tracts of Gazankulu are wild, inaccessible by car, and home to large wildlife populations. One such area south of the R71 has been designated as **Manyeleti Game Reserve**, where visitors can see elephant, white rhino, lion, cheetah, leopard, spotted hyena, buffalo and all the attendant lowveld game species (*see* **Mpumalanga**).

Potgietersrus, Pietersburg and Louis Trichardt

The long, straight N1 highway, and the north/south passenger railway that run up the Northern Province's central plain travels through the region's least spectacular country, but must be travelled to reach the wild sections. Its three large towns, of Potgietersrus, Pietersburg and Louis Trichardt, along the highway in the hot central plain, are of interest only as supply stops and jumping-off points for the nearby mountain ranges, game reserves and tribal areas.

Potgietersrus

Tourist Information

Information available on ✆ (154) 491 2244.

Potgietersrus takes its name from the Voortrekker leader Piet Potgieter, who, with Andries Pretorius, settled the local territory in the late 1830s. The Boer farms needed more labour and began raiding the kraals of local Ndebele and Sotho clans, snatching children for 'indentured labour'. Hermanus Potgieter, a cousin of Piet's, was responsible for most of these raids.

The Ndebele had ceased to be a military power in the highveld by this time, having moved north away from the Voortrekkers, under Mzilikazi, to modern Zimbabwe. But the Sotho, under chief Makapan, retaliated in 1854, attacking Boer farms and finally killing over 40 Boer men from a *kommando* sent out to punish them. Hermanus Potgieter was among the dead. Piet Potgieter and Andries Pretorius, worried at this sudden show of teeth, and by the fact that the Sotho had begun acquiring firearms, gathered a large *commando* of over 100 Boers and 300 Kgatla warriors (a local clan hired with a promise of a share in the spoils) and attacked Makapan. But he and his people had fled to a set of caves nearby. The Boers and their allies laid siege. After a few skirmishes, during one of which Piet Potgieter was shot dead, the Boers realized the whole clan would eventually perish for want of food and water. Many women and children surrendered, consigning themselves to life as virtual slaves on Boer farms, but after a month the Boer *commando* entered the cave and found the rest of the Sotho dead. The region was now open for unchallenged Boer settlement.

Potgietersrus remains a quiet country town, although its primary economy today comes from the ceaseless traffic travelling between Zimbabwe and South Africa.

Should you find yourself with time in Potgietersrus, the **Arend Dieperink Museum** (*open Mon–Sat 9–4*), on Voortrekker Road, has an interesting record of early Transvaal life, including pioneer tools, guns, clothes and furniture and some photographs from the late 1800s. Just north of town is the **Potgietersrus Nature Reserve and Game Breeding Centre**, a reserve belonging to the National Zoological Gardens in Pretoria and devoted to breeding rare species, including cheetah, black and white rhino and the West African pygmy hippo. Plains antelope wander free around the breeding centre and there is also a small camp site. The larger **Percy Fyfe Nature Reserve**, about 30km north of town (look for signposts on the west side of the N1), is also devoted to rare species, specifically roan and sable antelope and tsessebe (also known as topi, which is endangered in Southern Africa, but common in East Africa). Visitors can walk in the reserve's bush and rocky outcrops. Again, there is a small camp site with ablution blocks.

Tourist Information
Pietersberg Marketing Company, corner of Vorster and Landdros Mare Streets, ✆ (015) 290 2010.

Pietersburg, the largest town in the Northern Province, is the region's administrative centre. It is convenient for both the Waterberg and Tzaneen, but the town is unattractive—mostly modern, hot and noisy, with through traffic that has to fight its way across town before rejoining the N1.

A large park, the **Civic Centre,** has been laid out around an ornamental lake in the city centre, a good place to stop if you need a break from driving. At the south end a large conservatory of exotic plants and a little restaurant (Mike's Kitchen) overlook the lake. On Vorster Street, just off Civic Centre Park, is the **The Pietersberg Museum,** better known as the **Irish House,** (*open Mon–Fri 8–4, Sat 9–12, Sun 3–5*), a collection of Victorian houses in what was a vast late 19th-century trading store. Nearby, a small photographic history of the town is housed in the **Hugh Exton Photographic Museum** (*open Mon–Sat 9–4*), which occupies an old Dutch Reformed Church. On the northern edge of town is the **Exhibition of Historic Memorabilia** (*open Mon–Fri 9–4.30*). This collection of agricultural and industrial machinery, such as tractors, ploughs, a steam engine and a gold-ore crusher, are only really of interest to the specialist. Of more interest to the visitor is the **Bakone Malapa Open Air Museum,** 9km down the Chuniesport road, with displays of traditional Sotho living, culture, arts and crafts. There is also an **Art Museum** in the Danie Hough Culture Centre; for details of this or any of the other museums call ✆ (015) 290 2183.

Despite the rather unimaginative name, Pietersburg's small **Municipal Game Reserve,** about 5km south of town along the Molepo road, has a pleasant walking trail leading through bush and grassland where white rhino and large antelope, such as gemsbok, eland and blesbok, graze. Red hartebeest and zebra are also present, and there is accommodation in self-contained chalets and a camp site with ablution blocks.

Tourist Information
Soutpansberg Marketing & Tourism, ✆ (015) 516 0040.

The last of the main towns on the highway north, Louis Trichardt, like Potgietersrus and Pietersburg, is mainly of interest for its surrounding country, in this case the magnificent Soutpansberg mountains and Venda country, a corner of Southern Africa steeped in living folklore that provides the traveller with a rare glimpse of old Africa. It is also the birth place of one of Africa's most famous civilizations. On a hill in the Vembe Nature Reserve, about 100km west of Messina, is **Mapungubwe,** an Iron Age site famous for its gold artefacts. The ruins of this stone town pre-date those of Great Zimbabwe (after which Zimbabwe is named) and so this is the first of the Iron Age centres of the Zimbabwe Culture, which, at its height, was represented from Botswana to the Indian Ocean. There are also newer settlements of this culture in the Northern Province; Machema Ruins, near Waterpoort, Dzata Ruins near

Thohoyandou and Thulamela Ruins in the Kruger National Park, all dating from the 13th to 16th centuries. Unfortunately the Vembe Nature Reserve is under army control and permission from them has to be sought to visit.

Originally called Zoutpansberg, a town was founded in 1848 by Andries Potgieter, Piet's father, as the capital of a small republic, also called Zoutpansberg. In 1854, the name was changed to Schoemansdal by Stephanus Schoeman, Andries Potgieter's son-in-law. But, as if in punishment for this hubris and for the shameless trade in black slaves that Schoeman allowed to flourish in the town, Schoemansdal was burned to the ground in 1867 after its burghers, under a young man called Paul Kruger, invaded the Venda country to the north of the Soutpansberg mountains with a combined force of Boer, Pedi and Swazi fighters. The Venda beat back the motley army and, after the Boers had abandoned it, razed the town. The site then lay abandoned for a generation. In 1898 the Boer general Joubert re-invaded and drove the Venda king Mphephu over the Limpopo into Zimbabwe. But, again, this Boer incursion was short-lived. Two years later, during the Anglo-Boer War, British troops annexed the Transvaal, and the Venda returned to take up their old territory once again. Nothing remains today except for an archaeological site and an interesting site museum some 20km from Louis Trichardt on the Vivo road (R522). However, the town revived in the early 1900s, when the British made it a magistracy. Despite this British influence, the town became a firmly Boer enclave, servicing the local cattle- and nut-farmers and trading with the Venda, whose territory comes almost to the town limits.

The violence of Gauteng's recent history has hardly touched the north, and Louis Trichardt saw little unrest, even through the height of apartheid. This is probably in part due to the fact that the black population, the Venda, have traditionally been less oppressed than most of South Africa's other black tribes, and have held themselves rather aloof from the country as a whole. In the last 20 years, commercial forestry has extended the wooded regions of the Soutpansberg that rise north of the town. The setting is now one of bushveld giving way abruptly to plantations of pine and eucalyptus, and it is from the forest stations north of town that most travellers begin their exploration of the more interesting indigenous forests of the wild Soutpansberg.

The Soutpansberg

On the first slopes of the Soutpansberg foothills, the marula, thorn and mopane woodland of the bushveld begins to give way to the aloe scrub and hardwood trees of the mountain vegetation. This transitional zone is protected in the **Ben Lavin Nature Reserve**, ✆ (015) 516 45345, southeast of Louis Trichardt. Visitors can walk several trails and stand a good chance of encountering giraffe, tsessebe, sable antelope, kudu, nyala, waterbuck, wildebeest and a variety of smaller antelope. Birdwatching is good here; rollers, louries (especially cheeky grey louries that scavenge in the camp), crowned eagle and bishop birds (in the vleis) are worth looking out for. There are rondavels, permanent tents and a camp site with ablution blocks.

North of town begin the Soutpansberg proper, which run east/west for 150km, linking Venda and the Northern Province and marking the last range of uplands before the Limpopo River and the border with Zimbabwe.

The name, which means 'Salt Pan Mountains', could not be less appropriate for this landscape of fresh water, moist forest and fern. The lower slopes are mostly covered in plantations of eucalyptus and pine, but above about 600m this gives way to an indigenous hardwood forest. The air becomes fresh and clear after the heat of the plains, and the lemonwood trees, a species unique to the Soutpansberg, emit a fresh scent of citrus that carries on the breeze. On the peaks above the forest, spectacular aloes cluster on rock outcrops whose caves and buttresses are home to leopard and caracal.

The N1 highway crosses the range north of Louis Trichardt via the low Wylliespoort Pass, on either side of which is a tamed upland landscape of orchards and soft fruit plantations. Apart from this small corridor the range is wild, and the quiet hiker can expect to surprise bushbuck, baboon and the rare red duiker.

Much of the Soutpansberg lies in former Venda and, although the range is sacred, much of it is open to hikers, with marked trails and overnight huts provided (*see* 'Venda'). Two good hiking trails leave from a point about 3km from the centre of Louis Trichardt (ask Soutpansberg Marketing). One, the 2-day **Hanglip Trail** (with huts, water and firewood provided) can be divided into two sections of one day each. The 4-day **Entebeni Trail** makes a circle around the whole area of indigenous forest. There are also trails further east into the Venda part of the range, and follow the much longer **Mabudashungo Hiking Trail** (*see* 'Venda').

Activities

Walking and hiking: All the reserves and state forests listed above have marked walking and hiking trails, with overnight huts where necessary. Short walking trails can be found at the Percy Fyfe Nature Reserve, the Potgietersrus Nature Reserve, the Pietersburg Game Reserve, the Ben Lavin Nature Reserve, and in Hanglip State Forest near Louis Trichardt. All but the Hanglip trail offer good game-viewing possibilities.

Longer hikes through the southern Soutpansberg can be made from Hanglip Forest Station and Entabeni State Forest, near Louis Trichardt. To book the trails and overnight huts, call **Safcol Eco-tourism**, ✆ (013) 764 1058.

(✆ 015–)

Where to Stay

expensive

There is a dearth of good expensive accommodation unless you detour off into the Waterberg, Tzaneen, or far northern areas. One exception, **Shi-awela Safaris**, ✆ 516 1220, at the foot of the Soutpansberg near Louis Trichardt, has 4 en suite painted rondavels in a private game reserve. Guided hiking, climbing and bush drives are offered. Also worth trying are the **Ingwe Ranch Hotel**, ✆ 517 7087, and **Mountain View Hotel**, ✆ 517 7031, both up on the Wylliespoort Pass on the N1 north of Louis Trichardt. The hotels are not special, but their situation up in the cool woodlands and their views south over the bushveld plains are superb. At the foot of the range on the southern side is also the comfortable **Cloud's End Hotel**, ✆ 517 70231, which offers day hikes as well as the usual facilities.

moderate

Ben Lavin Nature Reserve, ✆ 513 834, just south of Louis Trichardt, has self-contained rondavels, permanent safari tents (with bedding) and a camp site. The bushveld setting at the foot of the Soutpansberg is particularly beautiful and the wildlife plentiful. Further south, the **Pietersburg Nature Reserve**, ✆ 2193 1114, has self-contained chalets. **Buzzard Mountain Retreat**, ✆ 514 196, sits atop the Soutpansberg north of Louis Trichardt and offers secluded self-catering stone cottages or log cabins with sweeping views out over the forests. Recommended for those in search of solitude. Well-marked trails wind off into the mountains. Just south of Louis Trichardt is the **Adam's Apple Hotel**, ✆ 516 4187, conveniently on the main road for the north-south traveller.

cheap

The **Ben Lavin Nature Reserve** and **Percy Fyfe Nature Reserve** both have camp sites with ablution blocks. No need to book.

Venda

Proclaimed 'independent' in 1979, now officially re-absorbed into South Africa, Venda is one of the least 'westernized' corners of the country.

Although it is perfectly possible to tour Venda alone, it is far more rewarding to arrange a local guide through **Venda Tourism** in Thohoyandou, ✆ (0159) 41577. In this way, the country's extraordinary web of myth and legend will be opened up to you, particularly the local legends attached to Venda's many sacred sights. Without a guide, you may find it difficult to gain access to sacred areas, and having someone able to interpret from VaVenda, the local language, will enable you to talk to people and to see Venda life at close quarters.

History

By the 16th century, the Venda kings had built a great walled city at Dzata, in the centre of the range, from where, tradition has it, trade in ivory and slaves with both the Arabs (who wandered deep into southern Africa during the 16th century) and the Portuguese seems to have flourished. Modern historians, however, mostly dismiss this as sheer fantasy.

What is more certain is that a series of civil wars among the Venda nobility in the 17th and early 18th centuries century eventually caused the monarchy to collapse, and the country to fragment into a loose federation of chiefdoms. Dzata was abandoned some time after 1740, but smaller fortified villages sprang up all over the country, and the Venda remained militarily powerful. In their remote mountain corner, they were hardly touched by the depredations of the great northward Zulu raids of the 1820s and '30s (*see* **History**).

Into this self-contained world wandered Conraad De Buys in 1820. Described by contemporary writers as a physical giant, with immense charisma and political ability, De Buys had lived in the court of Ngqika, one of the Xhosa's most powerful chiefs, had been his advisor against the British, and had even had an affair with Ngqika's mother, who was reputed to be the power behind the throne (*see* **Eastern Cape** 'History'). But De Buys had been chased from the Xhosa country by the British after stirring up a joint Boer/Xhosa rebellion. By the time he arrived among the Venda, he had amassed his own clan of African wives and children, and the Venda allowed him to settle. His village, called Mara, remained the home of his descendants (known as the 'Buysvolk') long after Conraad himself had died. However, Buys did not make a huge impact on the Venda people, who only tolerated the presence of his clan as long as they did not interfere with matters of state. His descendants still live in **Buysdorp** on the R522, west of Louis Trichardt.

The next Boer settlers did not appear until 1836, when Louis Trichardt and his Voortrekkers stumbled into the region. Trichardt got on well with the Venda, and his men helped the Venda paramount chief, Ramabulana, to regain his ascendancy over the other clans. Trichardt moved on to Mozambique (where he and his party died of fever), but other groups trickled in over the next few years, each intent on annexing the Venda territory. In 1839, an invading Swazi army was beaten off, then an invading Pedi army, as well as a regiment of Zulus under general Manukosi. Meanwhile, civil war in Mozambique resulted in large numbers of Tsonga refugees wandering into Venda. These were allowed to stay, and formed a buffer zone between the Venda and the Pedi and Swazi to the south.

1839 saw the arrival of the next batch of Voortrekkers under Andries Potgieter, who carved out the small Zoutpansberg republic south of the Soutpansberg mountains. Although they did not risk an invasion of Venda for 30 years, these Boers soon made themselves unpopular, hunting the local elephant herds almost to extinction and kidnapping and selling Venda, Tsonga and Pedi children. Finally, following the 1860 amalgamation of all the Transvaal Voortrekker republics into one South African Republic (SAR), the burghers of Schoemansdal (as Zoutpansberg was now called) finally decided to invade. A huge *kommando* of Boer, Pedi and Swazi soldiers, led by Paul Kruger (the future president of the SAR) crossed the Soutpansberg, only to be chased back to Schoemansdal. This, coming on top of a mini civil war between the Afrikaners, was too much for the burgers of Schoemansdal and they decamped, taking what they could with them. The gleeful Venda burned the rest.

Despite this interference from the white man, the Venda tolerated missionaries, the first of whom had drifted into the country during the 1860s. From about 1872 there was something of a rush for the Vendas' souls, with Dutch Reformed, Swiss and German missions setting up one after the other. These survived the unrest that accompanied the great drought of 1881, which caused famine and civil war all across the Venda country. During this time, a warlord called Makhado emerged as a binding force in the country, subduing the fragmenting clans one by one. It was just as well; by the 1880s, the Boers of the SAR were again looking covetously at Venda.

Makhado upheld the borders of Venda country until his death in 1897. The Boers saw this as their chance to re-invade. Continued droughts had resulted in a spate of cross-border cattle raids from Venda into the SAR, and this provided sufficient justification for annexing the kingdom, whose throne had just been filled by the inexperienced young king Mphephu.

A large Boer force, under Piet Joubert, the commander who later became famous for inflicting a series of humiliating defeats on the British, entered Venda, and forced Mphephu to flee across the Limpopo to Zimbabwe. The base camp for Joubert's commando was laid out as a town, and named after the old Voortrekker Louis Trichardt, whose grandson served in the campaign. But the outbreak of the Second Anglo-Boer War in 1899 saved the Venda from proper annexation, as Joubert and his troops were recalled to fight the British in Natal, and Mphephu returned and took back his throne.

In 1902, Venda came under British rule, and the new government, uncomfortable at having such a powerful African kingdom within its boundaries, ordered the Venda to burn all their unregistered firearms. But this was largely avoided, and the Venda wisely kept the peace, giving the British no reason to send troops into the country. Through the first half of the 20th century, white settlement remained confined to missionaries. Rather than spend money on expensive resident administrators, the British decided to exploit the already able system of tribal government, appointing the various Venda chiefs as magistrates. This lasted until the 1950s, and, even under the new Boer apartheid government, partial self-government was allowed in the Venda, largely because of its isolation from the rest of South Africa.

In 1969 Venda's self-government was recognized in Pretoria, and in 1973 it was declared a 'homeland', opting for full 'independence' from South Africa in 1979 (as did Ciskei and Transkei in the Eastern Cape). Since then, some attempts have been made at establishing modern industry in Venda, notably with the building of the new capital of Thohoyandou, a hideous eyesore of raw concrete built with South African money. Outside the capital, Venda's rural life has remained largely unchanged, with chiefs governing through a democratic council of tribal elders. However, since the abolition of apartheid, evidence has come to light of government abuse in Venda, in particular of an increase in ritual murder. It appears that government officials, paid from Pretoria and therefore no longer feeling accountable to the nation, secretly sanctioned the gathering of human body parts to make *muti* (medicine) for their own political advancement (*see* 'Venda Culture').

Despite this, the Venda remains a safe place for those not involved in the region's internal political struggles. Although relatively prosperous, it is also one of the few places that visitors can see traditional tribal life without having to trek into inaccessible areas.

Venda Culture

Certain aspects of Venda culture, such as building in stone and styles of wood-carving, bear closer resemblance to Zimbabwean and Malawian culture than to South African. The language, VaVenda, also has its roots north of the country and bears little resemblance to the Northern Sotho and Tsonga languages common in the rest of the Northern Province.

But everyday life in Venda is very similar to other traditional areas of South Africa. Local government is run along the traditional system, with a chief who has nominal control over clan land and resources, but must consult with a council of elders before making any decision that affects the group. To avoid autocratic rule these councils, which happen every two years or so, are compulsory. Failure to attend is punishable by fines.

The rural Venda count their wealth in head of cattle. Their lifestyle is still largely agricultural, with male and female roles clearly defined; men tend the livestock, plough the soil, build and thatch huts and sow crops, while women look after all other phases of crop-raising, which involves most of the hard labour, as well as taking care of all domestic duties. Polygamy is still widespread in the countryside, with a division of agricultural and domestic work among the women. Because of the relative prosperity of Venda's farmlands, fewer men leave to work in the mines than in other tribal areas, and traditional life has held together in Venda as a result.

Ritual and belief in the spirit world are still very much a part of rural Vendan life. The 'homelands' forests, lakes and perennial rivers have traditionally been regarded as the homes of spirits that are constantly in need of appeasing. Lake Fundudzi, in the centre of the region and one of the largest natural lakes in South Africa, is still a sacred site—visitors can only approach its shoreline with permission from the lake's priestess. Formed a few hundred years ago by a massive landslide, Fundudzi is the home of the Python God, a central figure of the old Vendan pantheon, after Raluvhimba, the Supreme Being, who is detached from both the human and the spiritual sphere.

The Python God

The Python God is responsible for the rains and rivers, and is attended by strange beings called *Dituwane*, humanistic creatures with one eye, one arm and one leg. It is said that to see one is to die; fortunately they are so shy as to remain hidden if at all possible, although one legend has it that a party of Boers raiding Venda in the 19th century were driven off by *Dituwane*, after watering their horses at a sacred pool.

The Python God of Lake Fundudzi is still honoured with a gift of beer poured into the lake once a year, and in the Python Dance, the most famous part of Venda's intricate web of ritual. Also known as the *Domba*, this is performed by Venda's maiden girls as the final stage of their initiation into womanhood, preparatory to being made available for marriage. The young women, naked but for a short beaded skirt, form up in single file and dance solemnly in winding lines, like a snake. The *Domba* can last all night, and its observance is important for securing good rains for the coming year.

Another figure of Venda myth is Sankhabi, a mischievous bird-like spirit who travels between the spirit and human world. A series of moral tales surround Sankhabi, usually involving punishment of human folly or disrespect for the gods and ancestors. Like most South African tribal cultures, ancestors are central to Venda life, and are the spiritual mediums through which men must deal with the world.

A more sinister side of Venda culture involves witchcraft and ritual murder. Human body parts are used to prepare special *mutis* or medicines, usually for battle or political intrigue.

Muti murder, usually of children, has been relatively common in South Africa's most traditional areas, but in Venda it appears to have reached epidemic proportions during the 1980s and early '90s. Many Venda blame this on a breakdown in traditional tribal values among government officials aiming to advance their careers, and businessmen wanting to ensure success. This typically South African mix of ancient medical and modern political practice is by no means unique to Venda, but the concentration of incidents here in the last 10 years has been abnormal. A Vendan journalist, Risimathi Mathunzi, stated in a 1991 article in the independent socio-political *Cross Times*:

> The people involved in government today are the people who have the businesses and they, the very people who are supposed to be protecting us, are killing us for muti.

In the same article a nurse from a rural clinic commented on a local girl who had been murdered:

> We heard that her boyfriend picked her up one evening around six. He took her for love, but they went past where they were initially going, off into the woods. Then a group of men came out. Her father was one of them, he was living away from the family. They start cutting you while you are still alive. And they cut the girl at the wrist, the elbow and shoulder. And she said, 'Please let me go, I won't say anything.' But they finished it.

In 1991 Edwin Ritchken, a researcher in rural politics at the University of Witwatersrand, and Eddie Kock, a journalist for the *Weekly Mail*, published an article in the *Cross Times* in which they alleged a spate of *muti* murders between 1986 and 1990, implicating cabinet ministers. They reported that a mass stay-away from work in 1988, which resulted in the enforced resignation of the Vendan Minister of Justice, was organized in protest against the ritual killings.

A further problem of these murders are the counter-murders of those accused of being witches, of which 70 were reported in the first six months of 1994 in the Northern Transvaal (*SA Times* June 1994). But despite this side of Venda culture, travellers need not fear *muti*, which is a practice kept firmly inside the local community. Visitors are too far removed from Vendan culture to have any relevance to or involvement in such practices.

The Country

Tourist Information

Venda Tourism, Thohoyandou, ✆ (0159) 41577.

Visitors should avoid Venda's ugly new capital, **Thohoyandou**, named after a legendary 18th-century chief who is said to have unified the kingdom briefly during its period of civil war. An unpleasant mix of concrete buildings, industrial sites and dust that was quickly erected in 1980, Thohoyandou's main attraction is its brash yet bland Sun Hotel and casino—a standard feature of the 'homelands', where gambling is permitted. Better simply to visit the **Tourist Office** in the Venda Development Corporation building just north of the main through road, arrange your guide and get out as quickly as possible into the farmlands, forests and mountains. Before going, however, visit the **Ditike Craft Centre**, whose woven textiles, wooden carvings and clay pots are among the best available in Venda. South of

Thohoyandou, the **Venda Soutpansberg** can be explored by means of the 4-day **Mabudashango Trail**.

West of the capital are **Lake Fundudzi** and the surrounding **Thathe Vondo Sacred Forest**, both of which lie at the heart of Venda mythology. The forest can be walked via marked trails, and hikers can gaze down on the lake from the surrounding hills. Formed by a landslide that dammed the Mutale River several hundred years ago, Fundudzi's waters must never be mixed with that of other rivers, for fear of angering the Python God. Even the shores are sacred, as these are thought to be the gardens of the dead ancestors of the VaVenda, whose ashes used to be ceremonially scattered over the water in times past.

Like the Soutpansberg's woodlands, the Thathe Vondo Forest is a dark green world of waterfalls, cool forest, giant ferns and mountain streams. Venda tradition has it that it is guarded by a deity called Nethane, who is half-lion, half-man, and who sleeps in caves under the ground. Certain parts of the forest are out-of-bounds to visitors, as it is thought that their footsteps might disturb his sleep. The existing trails lead through some superb hardwood and cycad stands, to the Mahovhovho and Mutale waterfalls. The forest is one of the few places in southern Africa that is known for mushrooms—in this case giant ones (known as *mwimbi*) which are regarded as the food of Nethane, and so are not eaten by the Venda.

Southeast of Thohoyandou, at the foot of the Soutpansberg, are **Lwamondo Kop** and the nearby **Mpophulo Cycad Reserve**. Lwamondo is famous for its sacred baboons, whose barking used to warn the Lwamondo clan of the approach of strangers, and thus kept the stronghold (there is a ruined stone fort at the top) safe through the endless petty clan wars fought by the VaVenda until the 19th century. About 25km west along the foot of the Soutpansberg are the **Tshatshingo Potholes**, deep river pools that until the 1900s served as places of execution for those accused of witchcraft.

Game is plentiful in the east of Venda, near the Kruger National Park, but the 'homeland's' only official game reserve is the **Nwanedi National Park**, a mixed terrain of acacia-covered Soutpansberg foothills, and mopane and marula lowveld woodland. White rhino, kudu, eland and a number of antelope roam free, while lion and cheetah can be viewed in enclosures. It seems a pity that the predators should be cooped up, but at least their absence from the main park allows visitors to walk safely along a number of marked trails as well as driving the game-viewing roads.

It is worth visiting Nwanedi for the walking, but anyone who really wants to see the Big Five in the wild should drive east to the new **Makuya Nature Reserve**, hard by the Piaffer Gate of the Kruger National Park (near the town of Maces), where the pristine wilderness has been preserved and the big game roams at will between Makuya and the Kruger. Accommodation within Makuya must be booked through Venda Tourism. Venda also has some hot mineral springs. Two are accessible via small resorts—**Sagola Spa** and **Mphephu Hot Springs**. Sagola, in the north of the country, is set among huge baobab trees, one of which, the **Big Tree**, is reached by a short dirt road from the resort, and is reckoned to be over 3000 years old. Mphephu is west of Thohoyandou and can be visited just for the day. Accommodation for both is bookable through Venda Tourism.

Finally, if you want to see the *Domba* dance, you need to travel between September and December, and contact Venda Tourism who will organize transport out to the village where it is happening. Thrown in as part of the outing is generally a trip to the village of **Mutale**, just north of the capital, where the sacred drums made to accompany the *Domba* are made. If you ask, the guide will then take you to see a local diviner. This is no piece of tourist kitsch, but the real thing, and if you have questions about the future to ask, you might find them being answered with uncomfortable accuracy. Several travellers have reported Venda diviners' predictions coming to pass after their visit.

Activities

Walking and hiking: Day hikes can be found at Nwanedi National Park, the Thathe Vondo Forest and in the Soutpansberg foothills. The 4-day Mabudashango Trail, ✆ (013) 764 1058 (Safcol), follows a wide circle through the Soutpansberg forests and upland meadows. Huts with firewood and water are provided. There are several pleasant day-walks in the Mpophulo Cycad Reserve, and in Nwanedi National Park.

Where to Stay

expensive

The overpriced **Venda Sun**, ✆ (0159) 824 600, in the new capital of Thohoyandou, should only be a last resort. Its tasteless, suburban interior is indistinguishable from any chain hotel anywhere. However, its casino, while brash, attracts interestingly dubious 'businessmen' and other characters passing through.

moderate–cheap

The **Nwanedi National Park**, ✆ (015) 539 723, offers a range of accommodation in central Venda's baobab country. Luxurious rooms in a central lodge fall within the top end of the moderate range, while the self-contained rondavels and camp site with ablution blocks are much cheaper. **Mphephu Resort**, ✆ (01595) 30049, offers self-contained chalets, as does **Acacia Park**, ✆ (0159) 22506/23095, in central Thohoyandou. The **Sagola Spa**, in the far north of Venda, and Mphephu Resort in the west (booked through Venda Tourism) offer slightly more expensive accommodation around their hot mineral springs.

Messina and the Baobab Plains

North of the Soutpansberg the country becomes drier, harsher and wilder; the landscape of mopane woodland, thorn and strange rock formations is dominated by the massive, bulbous, utterly African bulk of baobab trees, which jut from the bush every few hundred metres.

The only town to speak of in this area is **Messina**, which sits in the bushveld 16km south of the border with Zimbabwe. The country around is hardly even farmed; about 30 years ago, most of the cattle ranchers in the area realized it would be more profitable to reintroduce indigenous game and sell hunting licences, meat and hides, rather than steers, which tended to sicken in the sub-tropical heat. As a result, the wild landscape is little changed. A few of these game ranches run guided walks and photo safaris for guests and day visitors, offering a variety of habitat and game types. **Greater Kuduland Safaris**, ✆ (015539) 720, signposted from the R525 southeast of Messina, comprises typical mopane woodland populated by zebra, giraffe and the larger antelope. **Sheldrake Game Ranch,** ✆ (015) 534 2714, in the north near the junction of the Sand and Limpopo Rivers, overlooks the wide Voorburg Dam, and has buffalo and rhino as well as plains game.

Medike Mountain Reserve, ✆ (015) 516 0481, and **George's Place,** ✆ (015) 575 1441, in the Sand River gorge, in the northern foothills of the Soutpansberg, have shyer game such as leopard, bushbuck and klipspringer, and walking trails through the beautiful Sand River Gorge—where thin belts of hardwood forest, aloe and wild herbs fringe the water margins, and the mountains rise sheer on all sides. Bushman paintings are also a feature.

If you are driving along the R525 towards the Greater Kuduland Safari ranch, it is worth stopping in at **Aventura Tshipise,** a hot springs resort with a large nature reserve at its back, ✆ (015) 534 3235. Unfortunately an ugly supermarket, bad restaurant and camp site full of 'Vaalies' in camper vans has been built near the entrance, but if you ignore the small complex of buildings it is bliss to relax in the naturally heated water after a long, dusty drive. The resort's adjacent nature reserve has walking trails into the surrounding bush, which comprises the lower northern foothills of the Soutpansberg, and supports a healthy population of antelope, zebra, wildebeest and giraffe.

The town of **Messina** is a regular stop for truck drivers going between South Africa and the great African interior, and backpackers congregate here in search of long-distance lifts, giving the small town a quietly cosmopolitan feel. It is the only place in the Northern Province with hostel accommodation specifically aimed at backpackers (*see* 'Where to Stay'), and the bar in the town hotel is lively with people passing through.

Just south of town, between the R525 and N1, is the excellent **Messina Nature Reserve,** ✆ (015) 534 3235, a large protected area with a high density of enormous baobab trees, some of which are reckoned to be as much as 4000 years old. Unless you see them just after the summer rains, baobabs are usually leafless and seem to support little life.

However, they do produce a large, gourd-like fruit, known as monkey bread, and if you are lucky enough to see them in the short bushveld spring

(September), their strange, stunted upper branches (ludicrously out of proportion to the great bulk of their trunks—like the arms on a *Tyrannosaurus rex*) can be gay with white blossom.

The mopane woodland between the vast baobabs supports a large population of the more spectacular antelope (sable, nyala and kudu) as well as the inevitable impala and other small buck. Giraffe, wildebeest and zebra congregate in the open glades. Leopard and cheetah hunt in the reserve, but are seldom seen by visitors, unless you phone the ranger in advance and ask to be taken to a known lair, which he may or may not do, depending on his mood.

Game-viewing roads criss-cross the reserve, but it is better to walk one of the trails, and stand underneath the baobabs, getting an idea of their outsize scale. The woodland fronting the Sand River, the southeast boundary of the reserve, is particularly good for birdlife. Look out for rollers flitting between the trees, and bee-eaters nesting in holes in the river bank.

Activities

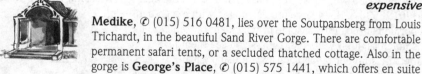

Marked nature trails have been laid out among the giant baobab trees, weird rock formations and plentiful game of **Messina Nature Reserve**. **Medike Lodge**, in the beautiful Sand River Gorge, has walking trails leading along the river to bushman paintings. Longer hikes (up to 5 days) can be booked at **Greater Kuduland Safaris** and **Sheldrake Game Ranch**. These are guided, owing to the presence of buffalo, and must be booked in advance. Short day trails can be found in the mopane woodland of the nature reserve adjoining the **Aventura Tshipise**.

Where to Stay

expensive

Medike, ✆ (015) 516 0481, lies over the Soutpansberg from Louis Trichardt, in the beautiful Sand River Gorge. There are comfortable permanent safari tents, or a secluded thatched cottage. Also in the gorge is **George's Place**, ✆ (015) 575 1441, which offers en suite rooms in a lodge, or a more private log cabin. Only 6 guests at a time are allowed, so there are no crowds. Guided bush walks along the river allow a good chance of sighting game.

Sheldrake Game Lodge, ✆ (015) 534 2714, is a private reserve and working game ranch overlooking the Voorburg Dam, which sells hunting licences to cull a percentage of its game every year. It also sells the meat and hides, and organizes photo safaris. There are 3 lodges (each with a pool), white rhino, most of the large antelope species, and good fishing in the dam (tackle can be provided).

moderate

Greater Kuduland Game Lodges, along the R525 southeast of Messina, ✆ (015539) 720, has a luxurious hutted camp and two more moderately priced bush camps in the mopane and baobab country just north of the Soutpansberg foothills.

cheap

Messina Backpackers, 11 Cheynes Street, Messina, ✆ (01553) 40 160, offers very cheap double rooms and dormitory accommodation, a kitchen and sitting room.

Northwest Province

We were sitting in Jurie Steyn's voorkamer at Drogevlei, waiting for the government lorry from Bekkersdal to bring us our letters and empty milk-cans. Jurie Steyn's voorkamer had served as the Drogevlei post office for some years, and Jurie Steyn was postmaster. His complaint was that the post office didn't pay. It didn't pay him, he said, to be called away from his lands every time somebody came in for a penny stamp. What was more, Gysbert van Tonder could walk right into his voorkamer whenever he liked, without knocking. Gysbert was Jurie Steyn's neighbour, and Jurie had naturally not been on friendly terms with him since the time that Gysbert van Tonder got a justice of the peace and a land-surveyor and a policeman riding a skimmel horse to explain to Jurie Steyn on what side of the vlei the boundary fence ran.

The Budget, Herman Charles Bosman

A dusty, remote territory of dry grassland and thornveld, the Northwest Province, formerly the Western Transvaal, is mostly 'platteland'—flat farming country—whose immense mealie and cattle 'camps' stretch to a distant horizon. To the north is the dry wilderness of Central Botswana, to the west the Kalahari, to the south the parched Karoo, and to the east the brown highveld of Gauteng.

There are few nature reserves or national parks, yet the region has a feeling of wildness, of remoteness, that impresses how independent of man the landscape is, though cattle farmers have denuded it of game and, in places, the country has been grazed raw. There is a great and silent beauty here, especially at evening, when the dying light turns the grassland a soft grey-blue, like a dove's plumage, and the heart sighs with pleasure at the sheer space.

The Northwest Province's white population is largely Afrikaans-speaking, although most have some English which can be haltingly started up, like an old, rusty car, if need be. As with the Karoo and the Free State, the traveller who makes it to the Northwest Province has penetrated the heartland of Afrikanerdom, and the dry, flat heat of the place offers clues to understanding the dour character of many of the Afrikaners themselves. The black population is mostly Tswana-speaking, and until 1994 large sections of the province were administered by the nominally independent former 'homeland' of Bophuthatswana, to which many Tswana people were forcibly removed during the 1970s.

Most tourists know of Bophuthatswana through the casinos of Sun City in Northwest Province's eastern corner, and indeed, from a traveller's point of view, the former 'homeland' has little to offer besides a tapestry of overgrazing and overcrowding on semi-desert scrub. However, the region's only significant game reserves, the Pilanesberg National Park and Madikwe Game Reserve, lie within the former Bophuthatswana, and offer a glimpse

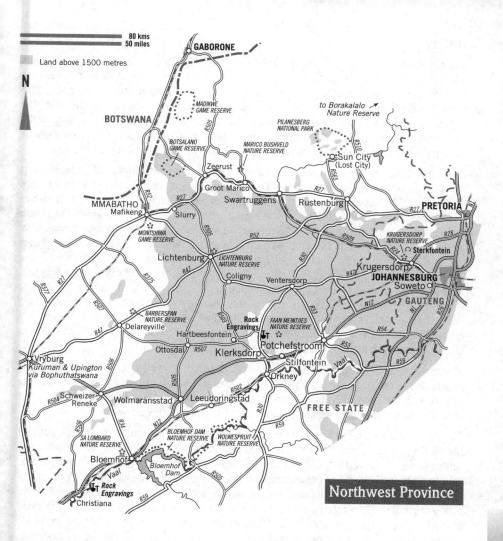

of wild Africa, including the 'Big Five' game species. Those who go further into the former 'homeland' are usually only crossing the region at speed on their way to the national parks of the Northern Cape. But should you be passing through, take a little time to savour the open emptiness away from the main roads, and lose yourself for a while either in the big game parks or in the dusty, eroded donkey- and goat-grazed waste of the former Bophuthatswana, or the grass-covered emptiness of the white farmlands, your eyes fixed on the far, flat horizon beyond the steering wheel, your mind numb from the heat and space of the endless land around you.

History

The Northwest Province has been inhabited by hominids since fossil times, proved by the excavation of the remains of a pre-human creature called *Australopithicus* from caves near Sterkfontein. But while this lends credibility to the common anthropological theory of Africa as the 'cradle of mankind', the Sterkfontein discovery sheds little light on who inhabited the region through the millennia preceding our own. All that is known for sure is that, until the early Middle Ages, it was the hunting ground of numerous San hunter-gatherers whose paintings have been found in caves and rock overhangs throughout the province.

It is not known exactly when the first Nguni settlers came to this area, but archaeologists think that a complex relationship between them and the hunter-gatherers was in existence well over 1000 years ago. However, the San seem to have been pushed west to the Kalahari and Bushmanland around AD 1000 by the Nguni, who appear to have developed a high Iron Age culture around this time. As usual there is no recorded history of this early period, only an inherited oral tradition, but archaeologists have found evidence of large settled villages whose inhabitants were skilled in metal-working and animal husbandry. This presumably was the forerunner of the region's present Tswana culture, the main difference being that settlements seem to have been more fragmented in the early period, whereas by the 1800s, when the first white travellers visited the area, the Tswana were living in larger, more centralized groups, or kingdoms, whose leaders ruled after the style of monarchs—with a court of ministers and loyal chiefs to rule the more distant territories. The most powerful of these Tswana clans were the Tlhaping, Taung, Rolong and Tlokwa.

Modern historians believe that this Tswana centralization was part of a more general picture of upheaval among the clans of the highveld clans and Natal, caused by increased trading activity with the Dutch, British and Portuguese. Those clans that became wealthy established standing armies, and began to mount large-scale raids on their neighbours.

The clan whose expansion was best documented was the Zulu of Natal, under Shaka, during the 1820s (*see* 'Zululand History'). An offshoot of this clan, the Ndebele, raided north and settled in the Northwest Province around this time, seizing territory from the Tswana clans. Into this arena of Ndebele/Tswana conflict blundered the Voortrekker Boers, during the Great Trek of 1836–8. Alternately trading, allying and fighting with the various Tswana clans, the Boers concentrated on pushing out the Ndebele, who had become the most powerful clan in the highveld. Pitched battles were fought, notably at Vegkop in 1836, where 400 Ndebele were killed in under an hour by musket-fire from a *laager* of wagons. With the help of the Tlokwa and Rolong Tswana, and with Griqua and Koranna fighters from Bushmanland, the Boers managed to push the Ndebele north through the Marico district and into the Northern Province. By 1838 the Ndebele had gone north to modern-day Zimbabwe.

The Boers, with the aid of their firepower, began to establish towns in what was to become the Western Transvaal (and across the entire highveld), and to subdue the Tswana chiefdoms. Despite increased centralizing of power among these groups, the Tswana were still too fragmented to offer concerted resistance to Boer settlement, and allowed themselves to be played off against each other. By 1838 the Boers had succeeded in establishing a small town at Potchefstroom which, in 1841, became the first capital of the South African Republic (SAR), under the presidency of the trek leader Andries Hendrik Potgieter.

The infant republic's first task was to eliminate the Ndebele, who posed too powerful and organized a threat to the Boers' colonial ambition. Throughout the 1840s and '50s Potgieter and the Boers of the other Transvaal republics of Lydenburg and Soutpansberg, along with considerable Tswana and Griqua help, managed to push most off the Ndebele north of the Limpopo into modern Zimbabwe.

The *burghers* of the new Republic soon found that, although technically masters of large areas of the Transvaal, they were too few to establish and maintain agricultural colonies, and began trying to coerce the local Tswana into working on Boer farms. This was not easily done and, by the late 1860s, raiding parties of Boers were snatching children from Tswana villages and homesteads to work as 'indentured labour'—virtual slaves.

In 1860 the three Transvaal republics decided to amalgamate, keeping the name South African Republic (SAR), but moving the capital north to Pretoria, a convenient midway point, and the Western Transvaal settled into a peaceful agrarian life (albeit a white-dominated one) that was barely ruffled by the British occupation of the SAR from 1877–84, or by the gold boom on the Witwatersrand in the 1880s, despite the migration of thousands of young Tswana men to the mines. But conflict returned to the Western Transvaal in 1900, the second year of the Anglo-Boer War, when the British re-occupied the SAR, and the Boer *Kommandos* retreated to the more remote regions of the Transvaal and Orange Free State, leading the unwieldy British columns a dance across the endless veld until the final surrender in 1902. The Western Transvaal was the operational centre for the Boer general Koos de la Rey, whose effective use of trench warfare around the Modder River area checked the British advance for months, and bought time for the Boer besiegers of the garrison in Mafeking (modern-day Mafikeng) on the border of West Griqualand, then a British protectorate.

The siege of Mafeking—like those of Ladysmith and Kimberley—was a waste of time for the Boers, as none of these towns were of particular strategic importance. The Mafeking garrison, under Lord Baden-Powell, was held up by the British press as a model of stiff-upper-lipped endurance, but in fact seems to have suffered little; most of the fighting (and starving) was done by the Rolong Tswana living on the outskirts of town, who hoped that a proven loyalty to the British would rid them of Boer (and other white) oppression. Their ordeal was chronicled by one Sol Plaatje (*see* p.615).

General de la Rey was a 'bitterender', as those who kept guerilla fighting until the end of the war were called. Following the Boer surrender of 1902, the Western Transvaal and de la Rey remained strongly anti-British, holding to their isolationist stance even after the ex-Boer generals Louis Botha and Jan Smuts assumed the leadership of the new Union of South Africa in 1910. When Botha agreed to send South African troops to France in 1914 (he had little choice—the new Union was still a British Dominion), de la Rey snapped, and called the Western Transvaal to arms again with the intention of leading a full-scale insurrection against Pretoria. But, by a weird twist of fortune, he was shot dead in his car before the rebellion could even get off the ground, after running an army roadblock. Without its charismatic leader, the revolt petered out a few weeks later.

From that point on the Western Transvaal became a rural Boer backwater, staunchly nationalist, but politically inactive compared to the other areas of the Transvaal, perhaps owing to its remoteness. Through the troubled 1930s, when black political organizations and trade unions first began to campaign effectively on the nearby Witwatersrand, through the Second

World War and the years of apartheid, the Western Transvaal, while always a stronghold of Afrikaner nationalist support, remained politically inactive, having no large industrial centres or cities—traditionally the centres of political activity.

Not until the creation of the black 'homelands' (or *bantustans*) in the 1970s did the Western Transvaal see direct political action—this time the forced eviction of tens of thousands of Tswana, Ndebele and other black people from landholding in areas that had been designated 'white'. Large areas of the poorest land were declared part of the 'republic' of Bophuthatswana, and the majority of the region's blacks were moved there, or to other parts of the Transvaal.

As the prospect of a final dismantling of apartheid became a reality in the late 1980s, many fearful Western Transvaalers found a political voice in support of the ultra-right wing AWB under Eugene Terr'Blanche, and the region became a core of white resistance. Yet, having pledged to mount a concerted fight against black government, the AWB remained largely inactive through the early 1990s, beyond some tragic, random killings and pre-election bombings that failed to impede to any great extent the country's progress towards democracy. In fact, the Western Transvaal was, ironically, the scene of a major humiliation for the far right just before the 1994 elections, when an AWB *Kommando* drove into the former Bophuthatswana to put down demonstrations against its corrupt regime.

However, the regime in question had not called in the AWB, nor had Pretoria asked them to intervene. The organization was acting on its own initiative, to make a public show of upholding the Pretoria-backed Bophuthatswana government. The *Kommando* found itself quickly isolated amid an angry mob and a hostile Bophuthatswana police force and was chased out of the 'homeland'. On its way out, three AWB men in a car opened fire on the crowd, and had their fire promptly returned by the police. The driver was hit and the car swerved from the road and stopped. The three occupants were then shot dead by a Bophuthatswana policeman, while pleading for their lives. The horrific event was captured by a freelance journalist and published around the world. As a grim sequel to the event, the journalist, Kevin Carter, shot himself two weeks after the pictures were published.

Bophuthatswana, like all South Africa's 'homelands', has now officially ceased to exist. Perhaps the razing of the random borders will allow some inter-racial harmony into this stratified land, as well as some wealth sharing between the two communities.

Getting There

By car: From Jo'burg and the Witwatersrand the most travelled route is through dead flat country to Vryburg via the N14. A more interesting way in is via the R24 or R27 from Pretoria, which run along the south and north foot of the Magaliesberg. From the south, take the N12 up from Kimberley or the R700 from Bloemfontein, via the Bloemhof Dam Nature Reserve. From the west follow the N14.

By bus: Inter-Cape, TransLux, Transtate and Greyhound all run services along the N12 and N14, stopping at the towns along the way. There are also bus services from Jo'burg to Gaborone in Botswana, via the Marico District. If coming from the east, call Jo'burg or Pretoria's Publicity Offices for fares and times. From the south, telephone the Kimberley Publicity Office.

By rail: Services run between Kimberley and Jo'burg most days along the Vaal River, taking in the main towns, and a daily service runs through the Marico district on the way between Jo'burg and Gaborone.

The Marico District

> *No (Oom Schalk Lourens said) you don't get flowers in the Groot Marico. It is not a bad district for mealies, and I once grew quite good onions in a small garden I made next to the dam. But what you can really call flowers are rare things here. Perhaps it's the heat. Or the drought.*
>
> From the short story *Willem Prinsloo's Peach Brandy*
> by Herman Charles Bosman

This deeply rural corner of the Northwest Province is only 100km from Johannesburg. Travellers on their way through to Gaborone in Botswana have to cross the Marico via the towns of Krugersdorp and Zeerust, a landscape of wide, yellow hills, sheep and mealie fields, and lonely farmhouses shaded by dark green eucalyptus trees, that was made famous in the short stories of Afrikaner writer Herman Charles Bosman in the 1920s. The stories are narrated by Schalk Lourens, a wily, compassionate, humorous old Boer with a love of the land, its people—black, white and *rooinek*—and its occult soul. Among the best are *The Witchdoctor*, in which a bullying Boer farmer is stripped of his power by a witch-doctor, and *Funeral Earth*, in which a group of Boers returned from the Anglo-Boer War learn from their old enemies, the local Tswana clan, how much better it is to farm than to fight.

Krugersdorp's heart is in the Marico, even though, since the recent boundary changes, the town is officially in Gauteng. At the far eastern end of the Marico, it is reckoned by many to be the most staunchly Afrikaans enclave in the country, partly because of its name, which celebrates 'Oom' Paul Kruger, the Transvaal president who went to war against Britain in 1899. In fact it is mainly a dormitory suburb for those working in the western Witwatersrand area, and so is hardly a Boer (i.e farmer's) town. However, English is not the first language of most of the residents, and the town does serve as a transitional point between the cosmopolitan Witwatersrand and the conservative Western Transvaal.

Apart from its **Railway Society Museum** (*open Mon–Fri 7.30–1 and 2–5, weekends 8–1 and 2–5*), whose old rolling stock is a delight for steam buffs, Krugersdorp is not a town that caters for tourism. However, just west of town along the R24 is the **Krugersdorp Game Reserve**, a tract of bushveld country harbouring most plains antelope, including the rare sable and roan antelopes. Two streams which run through the reserve have guided walking trails to follow along their banks. Look out for waterbuck and fish eagle. Separate enclosures for lion, white rhino and buffalo can be seen near the reserve's entrance.

North of town towards the Magaliesberg are the spectacular **Sterkfontein Caves** (*open daily 9–5*), famous among anthropologists the world over for their fossils of pre-human primates. It was here in 1896 that Dr Robert Broom, excavator of several caves in the Transvaal, found the fossil skull of a humanoid creature known as *Australopithecus africanus*. The skull, over 1,000,000 years old, is thought to have belonged to an ancestor of *Homo erectus*, which preceded *Homo sapiens*. There have been several such finds in the

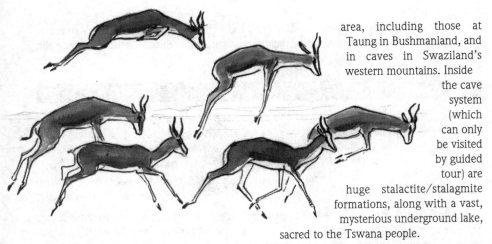

area, including those at Taung in Bushmanland, and in caves in Swaziland's western mountains. Inside the cave system (which can only be visited by guided tour) are huge stalactite/stalagmite formations, along with a vast, mysterious underground lake, sacred to the Tswana people.

While waiting for a tour, drop into the small **Robert Broom Museum**, next to the cave entrance, where a speculative history of the local humanoids shares space with other fossil finds from the area.

West of Krugersdorp you enter the Marico proper, around the appropriately named town of **Groot Marico**, a back-country farm town as sleepy today as it was when Bosman wrote about it in the 1920s. The Marico's largest town is **Zeerust**, an outwardly conservative place that hosts an annual *mampoer* festival—a mad binge of hard spirit drinking. *Mampoer* is a locally (and legally) brewed hooch, similar to peach schnapps, that removes your head after a few glasses and replaces it with a turnip. The festival is a moveable feast, but the **Willem Prinsloo Agricultural Museum**, ✆ (01213) 44171, will know the dates. Apart from this annual binge, Zeerust is a straight-down-the-line Boer farming town. However, it connects Johannesburg with the nearest Botswana border crossing and also lies astride the road to Mmabatho, a gambling town and capital of the former Bophuthatswana, reached via the excellently named village of Slurry.

South of Zeerust is **Lichtenburg**, a larger, richer farming town set in a greener landscape. The **Lichtenburg Town Museum**, on De La Rey Square (*open Tues–Fri 10–12 and 1–5, Sat 10–1*), is a must for Boer War enthusiasts, as it has a collection of artefacts belonging to the 'bitter-end' Boer General Koos de la Rey, whose trench warfare against the British at Modder River was so effective that the British themselves adopted it for use in the First World War. Also housed in the museum is a small collection of early paintings and sketches of the Transvaal.

Northeast of town and signposted from the R52 is the **Lichtenburg Game Breeding Farm**, covering a 6000ha stretch of typical bushveld and home to a number of large antelope species. Lichtenburg is also a game-breeding station for the National Zoological Gardens in Pretoria, and its rare species include pygmy hippo (from West Africa), sable and roan antelope, and cheetah (in an enclosed area).

Southwest of Lichtenburg along the R47, just north of the town of Delareyville, is an extraordinary wetland—the last thing you would expect to find in the dry grasslands of the Western Transvaal. **Barberspan Nature Reserve** comprises a freshwater lake and surrounding marsh that is home to thousands of waterbirds. Large numbers of flamingoes can usually be seen feeding in the shallows, while storks, ibis, egrets, herons, Egyptian geese, black ducks and a host of other species thrive on the lake's plentiful fish and can be observed from a wooden hide.

Activities

Hiking: Both Krugersdorp **(move to Gautent?)** and Lichtenburg Nature Reserves have short hiking trails with game viewing opportunities.

Where to Stay

moderate–cheap

Krugersdorp Game Reserve, ✆ (011) 660 1076, has some self-contained rondavels and also a restaurant. **Lichtenburg Game Breeding farm,** ✆ (0144) 22818, has a camp site, as does **Barberspan Nature Reserve,** ✆ (053) 948 1854. Barberspan is popular, especially at weekends, and it is advisable to book.

Potchefstroom and Southwest to the Vaal

'Potch' is the oldest European town in the Transvaal and the original capital of the South African Republic (SAR), founded by the Voortrekker leader Hendrik Potgieter in 1838. The town's capital status was removed to Pretoria in 1860 after which Potchefstroom became what it is now, a conservative Afrikaans-speaking university town—the Potchefstroom University for Christian National Education.

Despite its age and although not unattractive, Potch has little beyond some good Victorian buildings to distinguish it from many other Western Province towns. It also seems to lack the slightly frivolous atmosphere of a university town—perhaps because the university is a Christian organization and tends to attract a more serious breed of student—whatever the reason, the *joie de vivre* one expects from a university town is not in evidence.

The **Potchefstroom Museum** (*open Mon–Fri 8.30–4.30*) is understandably dedicated to the Voortrekkers. The highlight is one of the wagons used in the *laager* at Blood River, the Boer victory over Zulu *impis* in 1842. Two of the original buildings open to the public are the **Old Fort** (*open Mon–Fri 8.30–4.30*), on the Klerksdorp road opposite the railway station, and the **Powder Magazine** (*open Mon–Fri 8.30–1 and 2–4.30*), also on the Klerksdorp road, in Potch's small industrial area . The Boer general Cronje besieged a small British force in the Old Fort for three months during the First Anglo-Boer War (1880–1), forcing them to surrender and abandon the post. However, Cronje is not well remembered in Boer History, having earned the unfortunate distinction of being the first Boer general to surrender during the Second Anglo-Boer War (1899–1902) after being heavily shelled by British artillery at the battle of Paardeberg (1900).

Dating from 1868 is **President Pretorius' House** on Van Der Hoff Road (*open Mon–Fri 10–1 and 2–5, Sat 9–12.45, Sun 2.30–5*), the residence of the SAR's second president. The interior has been restored and decorated with his paintings and personal effects and the outbuildings, including an old smithy, set up as a display of early farm life. The **Totius**

Museum (*open Mon–Fri 10–1 and 2–5, Sat 9–12.45, Sun 2.30–5*) is a lovely red-roofed Victorian bungalow, set in spacious gardens, once the home of the late-19th century writer J. D. Du Toit, a leading light in the Afrikaans language movement, whose writings are somewhat religious and sombre. However, the museum is one of the few in the country that charges no admission, and this alone marks it out as special.

In keeping with the town's generally pious atmosphere is the **Hervormde Kerk** (built in 1866, but substantially added to since then) opposite the town hall, the oldest surviving church north of the Vaal River.

Southwest of Potch, along the N12, you pass through the small industrial town of **Klerksdorp**. Apart from its one street of surviving old buildings, **Hendrik Potgieter Road**, the town itself is not much to look at, although its **Town Museum**, on the corner of Lombaard and Margeretha Prinsloo Streets (*open Mon–Fri 10–1 and 2–5, Sat 9.30–12.30, Sun 2–5*), occupies the original gaol and powder magazine (built 1891) and now houses some interesting early man tools found in the area.

The curators can arrange for you to visit a hill 18km north of town along the R30 on a farm called **Bosworth**, which has some very ancient bushman rock engravings, whose occult, animalistic designs seem to have had some ritual purpose, and it is easy to let the imagination go on this lonely rise. Easier to understand are the old gold diggings at **Goudkoppie** (meaning 'gold hill'), on the Silfontein road, where abandoned mine shafts from the 1880s are still to be found, as is some graffiti engraved by British soldiers in the Second Anglo-Boer War (1899–1902).

At the **Faan Meintjies Nature Reserve**, signposted from the R30 north of town, white rhino are the main attraction, with large antelope (including sable), giraffe and black wildebeest as the supporting acts. The reserve has no accommodation.

From Klerksdorp, the N12 crosses the flat grasslands to the small, dusty town of **Wolmaransstad**. In the 1870s and '80s this was a cosmopolitan resting-point midway between the minefields of Kimberley and the Witwatersrand. Today there is nothing to suggest this: the only attractions are the **Makwassie Conservation Area**, 10km east of town, and the old homestead and hotel, **Lindbergh Lodge**.

The Makwassie Conservation area covers several thousand hectares of bush, but has only recently been formed and has no tourist facilities as yet. However, plans are afoot for major game restocking. Ask at the Town Clerk's Office, ☎ (018) 462 3919, for the current situation. Lindbergh Lodge on the other hand is a vast private estate and game reserve, well-stocked with indigenous game, open to residents of the hotel only (*see* 'Where to Stay').

Two reserves front the northern bank of the Vaal River south of Wolmaranastad. **Wolwespruit Nature Reserve**, is close to the small town of Leeudoringstad on the R504. Covering about 2500ha, the reserve supports large antelope, zebra, red hartebeest and wildebeest, and has some short walking trails through riverine woodland. Adjoining Wolwespruit to the west is the much larger **Bloemhof Dam Nature Reserve**, which covers 14,000ha and supports much the same game species as Wolwespruit, only in larger numbers. It is also home to white rhino. The bird life is very good, especially after rains, with a variety of waterfowl contrasting with grassveld species such as korhaans (miniature bustards), weavers and secretary birds. Telephone before arrival (*see* 'Where to Stay').

Away from the river, about 14km east of the small *dorp* of Bloemhof, is the **S. A. Lombard Nature Reserve**, ✆ (01802) 31 705. This is a 4000ha block of grass and thornveld used as a breeding station for highveld game. Telephone first; there is no accommodation.

Southwest of Bloemhof along the N12 (also signposted as the R29), is the riverside town of **Christiana**. Site of yet another short-lived diamond rush in the 1870s, Christiana enjoyed a brief Edwardian boom before lapsing into its present torpor. However, because of its proximity to the river, Christiana retains a pleasant old-world charm sadly lacking in many dusty Western Province towns. This makes a good point to break the journey with a stroll along the tree-lined riverbank. Just outside town to the northeast is a less attractive mineral spa with the standard over-priced, rather ugly resort built around it. However, the warm waters (around 40°C) are soothing, and the outdoor pool provides cool relief from the effects of a hot car.

The resort has a small (2300ha) game reserve attached to it, where you can walk among large and small antelope (including gemsbok and eland), wildebeest and zebra. Less visited are the **prehistoric rock engravings**, estimated to be tens of thousands of years old, on the Stowlands-on-Vaal farm 6km south of town towards Hertzogville. A short walking trail from the farmhouse leads to the site. For directions, ring the Town Clerk's Office.

Activities

Walking: Only Wolwespruit and Bloemhof Nature Reserves offer walking trails, as well as the short one to the bushman rock engravings at Stowlands-on-Vaal near Christiana. Otherwise there are no marked long-distance hiking trails in the region.

Riding: Lindbergh Lodge hires schooled horses to residents (and to non-residents if arranged in advance) for rides through wild grassland rich in game.

Fishing: The Vaal River teems with indigenous species such as yellow-fish, mud-fish and barbel. To hire tackle, call the Town Clerk's Office, ✆ (0534) 2206/7/8.

Where to Stay

expensive

Lindbergh Lodge, ✆ (018) 22041, has its original Victorian thatched lodge, with a log fire and ancestral portraits in the grand dining room. There are just five rooms. Black wildebeest, sable antelope, giraffe, zebra, gemsbok and other game species wander the reserve. Hiking and riding are offered, and balloon rides over the veld—an unforgettable, silent hour of bliss in the African sky. If you can afford it, Lindbergh is one of the best places to stay in the area.

moderate

The **Rob Ferreira Nature Reserve**, just east of Christiana in the far southwest, has a small, ugly resort tacked onto it, run by the Transvaal company Overvaal Resorts. However, the reserve itself, which fronts the Vaal river, is beautiful, and its self-contained chalets moderately priced. There is a shop and fuel. Access is via the R29.

Bloemhof Dam Nature Reserve, ✆ (01802) 22041/2, has a camp site with ablution blocks overlooking the Vaal River (access via the R29 or R34). Also on the Vaal is the **Wolwespruit Nature Reserve**, ✆ (01813) 2026, whose large camp site is popular with fishermen. **Boskop Dam Nature Reserve**, ✆ (018) 298 1337, has a camp site overlooking the dam. Boskop is north of Potchefstroom along the R501.

The Former Bophuthatswana

Fragile and fairy-like was Menyenyane, the little Tswana girl, so named for the dainty, soft short veld grasses that danced their delicate white flowers up and down in the breeze.

From *Bantu Folk-tales of Southern Africa*
(Timmins, Cape Town, 1974), Elizabeth Mattanyane

Bophuthatswana was only created as an 'independent homeland' in 1977 as part of the grand plan of the apartheid government to contain all South Africa's blacks within reserves. Many Tswana people were forced to move thousands of kilometres to their new 'homeland', leaving behind property and jobs. 'Bop' was not even a cohesive space, but was confusingly fragmented into seven different chunks, of which the largest and most commercially viable fall within the Northwest Province.

The puppet state of Bophuthatswana grew rich from the gambling revenues of Sun City and the fortunate discovery of platinum; the capital, Mmabatho, is a kitsch monument to Bophuthatswana's financial success. But only the government leaders and bureaucrats have seen any of this money. The majority of the population remained grindingly poor, living in crowded, semi-urban conditions around the few towns that dot the huge swathes of dry, barren grassveld. However, in parts, the wild veld has been preserved, and game conservation thrives as a secondary means of culling money from the tourist industry. **Pilanesberg National Park**, near Sun City, now ranks as one of South Africa's best large game reserves.

Tswana History

Bantu-speaking groups, the ancestors of the modern Tswana people, have been present in the region for at least 1000 years. A cattle-owning people, the Tswana's oral tradition is thought to date from around the 12th century. Skilled smiths, their iron tools and weapons established them as powerful warrior-traders when first African, then Portuguese, then Dutch trade routes began to penetrate the area from the 15th to the 18th centuries. The principal Tswana clans—the Rolong, Tlokwa, Thlaping and Taung—fought periodically among themselves, but more often with their Sotho-speaking neighbours and with the Griqua and Kora raiders who rode in from the dry country around the Orange River in the early 1800s. In the 1820s the Tswana found themselves fighting for dominance with the mighty Ndebele nation, who took advantage of the Tswana's settled lifestyle to raid for slaves and cattle.

By the time the Voortrekkers arrived in the Northwest Province in 1836, the Ndebele were the most powerful force in the area. Longing to be rid of the Ndebele menace, the Rolong and Taung allied with the Voortrekkers and together defeated the Ndebele at Vegkop in the Western Transvaal. But it was a Pyrrhic victory for the Tswana—no sooner had the Voortrekkers ejected the Ndebele than they set about enslaving the Tswana, denying them the right to hold their own land and forcing them to work as farm labourers, or tenant farmers at best.

For a powerful nation, who had dominated the region since before the 12th century, this was a bitter pill. But the military superiority of the Boers was hard to challenge. At the outbreak of the Anglo-Boer War in 1899 the Tswana allied with the British where possible. The British garrison then resident at Mafeking (modern Mafikeng) was besieged by a strong Boer force, and the Tswana, particularly the Rolong, turned out to help. Among them was a young Rolong man called **Sol T. Plaatje**, whose mission education and gift for languages had earned him a job as translator in Mafeking's magistrate court. His account of the siege, *Sol T. Plaatje's Diary*, is one of the important early texts describing the realities of black life in the colonial era. He makes light of Rolong suffering during the siege—by shelling, skirmishing and starvation—but points an unerring and dispassionate finger at the British commander Lord Baden-Powell, of Boy Scout fame. Baden-Powell promised to give back Rolong land after the War in return for their loyal service, while at the same time denying them food in favour of the town's white residents, and using them as messengers with no thought for those who fell into Boer hands. When the siege was raised in May 1900, Baden-Powell conveniently forgot the Rolong and let them suffer at the hands of vengeful Boers.

Plaatje's Mafeking experience left him with no illusions about the realities of white rule, whether Boer or British. He became a lawyer and used the position to become one of the country's first national campaigners for black rights. He is best remembered for his work as a founding member of the South African Native National Congress (SANNC), which later became the ANC. He was one of the most vocal opponents of the Natives' Land Act of 1912, a bill that proposed the eviction of black 'squatters' (i.e the dependants of black farm workers) from white farms. Plaatje claimed that this was tantamount to imposing slavery on these dependants by forcing them to labour for no wages if they wanted to avoid eviction. Plaatje and other SANNC members also led two delegations to London, in 1913 and 1919, to appeal for a complete rethink of colonial policy towards blacks. Both delegations were unsuccessful, but that did not stop Plaatje from campaigning at home until his death in 1932, during which time he devoted his scant hours of leisure to translating works of English literature into Tswana, including Shakespeare plays.

Later activists have accused him of not being sufficiently militant, but for the time Plaatje's achievements were extraordinary. Not only did he manage to persuade Cape Town and Johannesburg publishers to back his work, but he was one of the first black political activists to attain real credibility in the eyes of the colonial authorities and the British government, which in turn did much to establish the black freedom struggle as a worthwhile cause both in South Africa and abroad.

However, for the majority of Tswana people, the 20th century presented a choice between rural poverty or migrant work in the mines. The permanent water sites in their region of the Transvaal were almost all white-occupied by the 1930s and they were unable to support the livestock that had made them rich in earlier times. By 1950 the Tswana had become one of South Africa's poorest groups, a state that the National Party aimed to perpetuate when they declared the seven regions of Bophuthatswana in 1977. The government set up by Pretoria to administer the fragmented 'homeland', some of whose territories were isolated from each other by as much as 300km, did not reflect any real support from the Tswana people as a whole, and the rulers could only stay in power as long as they co-operated exactly with Pretoria's guidelines.

The plan backfired; Bop's government managed to assert some financial, if not political independence from Pretoria after platinum was found in the 'homeland'. By law, the Bop government could legally keep the mining revenues for this mineral for its own coffers, not South Africa's. Capitalizing on this good fortune, the new Tswana government took advantage of being technically exempt from South Africa's strictly Calvinist anti-gambling laws to open a huge casino at Sun City. The idea of 'homeland' casinos soon took off, but Sun City, and its new addition the Lost City, remain one of South Africa's biggest money-spinning operations; with their gambling and mining revenues, the Tswana look set to become a major influence on South African politics now that Bop is fully reabsorbed back into the Republic of South Africa.

Sun City and the Lost City

Situated in the western chunk of the two bits of 'Bop' northwest of Pretoria, Sun City and the Lost City comprise a vast pleasure-house of conspicuous consumption, known to most westerners as the place where a few foreign pop acts, such as Elton John, Queen and Black Sabbath, played in defiance of the 1980s sanctions (remember 'I Ain't Going To Play Sun City', a song that came out in 1986). Sun City is an interesting example of the South African contrast between rich and poor; the gaming rooms and one-armed-bandits operate night and day, while outside the perimeter fence many local Tswana live in terrible poverty. And it is not only the white and the wealthy that come to gamble. A common sight on the gaming machines is a poor black gambler throwing hard-earned money into the great Moloch with the fixed intensity of one who cannot afford to lose.

Sun City itself has now been upstaged by the even larger Lost City—an unimaginably expensive complex that claims to recreate the atmosphere of *King Solomon's Mines*, H. Rider Haggard's turn-of-the-century novel based in Southern Africa. Of course it does nothing of the kind, except perhaps to suggest how the book's heroes might have spent their money when they got home. However, the buildings, covered in intricate carving, wood inlay and mosaic, are truly beautiful, and transcend the Grand Kitsch of their design (see 'Where to Stay'). Suffice to say here that if money is of no object, then a ridiculously expensive night spent at the Lost City should definitely be included in your itinerary. But if your budget is lower, avoid the blander Sun City—go in for a day, lose some money, and then head out for the nearby **Pilanesberg National Park,** ✆ (01465) 55351.

Founded amid hushed-up controversy in 1979 (many Tswana people had to be forcibly removed from the site to make way for the park), today's Pilanesberg is one of the best accessible wild areas in the Transvaal, stretching over more than 50,000ha of bushveld. As well as the Big Five there are cheetah, spotted and brown hyena, hippo and croc, and most of the antelope and plains game species. The bird-watching is very rewarding, with large raptors such as bateleur and booted eagle, secretary birds, Cape vulture and smaller species such as sunbirds, grey louries, korhraans, bee-eaters and rollers. Guided game hikes with armed rangers are one of the main attractions. These are similar to those in the Kruger National Park, except they do not need to be booked so far in advance. There is a variety of accommodation to suit all budgets.

The Western Transvaal section of Bophuthatswana has two lesser-known game areas: **Madikwe Game Reserve** is new, covering a huge area north of Mmabatho, on the Botswana border, and is home to the 'Big Five'—almost all its animals were transported from the Kruger National Park in a massive trans-location known as 'Operation Phoenix'—but the reserve is only for those with big budgets (*see* 'Where to Stay').

Borakalalo Nature Reserve lies about 175km west of Pilanesberg and Sun City, north of the capital Mmabatho and its dirt-poor satellite of shanties, thin donkeys and thinner people. **Botsalano Game Reserve**, by contrast, stretches over 6000ha of lovely hill country of grassland and wooded kloofs. White rhino, giraffe, sable and waterbuck antelope, wildebeest and zebra are all common, as are the smaller antelope species. Again, there are guided hikes into the bush and a variety of accommodation.

Lotlamoreng Cultural Reserve (known as Montshiwa), is far less wild, covering approximately 200ha on the banks of the Lotlamoreng Dam south of Mafikeng. Although officially known as a nature reserve, it supports little game bar waterbirds on the dam's shoreline. Instead, the area has been divided into several African show villages supposed to demonstrate the traditional life of South Africa's main black cultures.

The Tswana, Zulu, Ndebele, Pedi, Xhosa, Sotho, and Venda villages are manned by local Tswana in traditional gear. While obviously aimed at tourists, Montshiwa is interesting both because it occupies the site of an old mission station (which is still standing), and for its sheer incongruity with the nearby squatter camps of Mafikeng and Mmabatho. Lotlamoreng has no accommodation.

Far to the south (about 150km,) along the R47 via the town of Vryburg, is the **Taung Heritage Site**, a small set of caves from which some of the earliest-known pre-human anthropoid fossil remains ever found by archaeologists were excavated earlier this century. Like the fossil remains found at Sterkfontein, these belong to the hominid primate *Australopithecus africanus*, one of the 'immediate' (in evolutionary terms) precursors of ourselves. There is a small museum on the site, and a history of both the archaeologists and the early pre-men. There is no accommodation, but nearby is the Taung Sun Hotel.

Activities

Gambling: Sun City and the Lost City have gaming tables and one-armed bandits you can play 24 hours a day for an entry fee of about R40, 30 of which is refunded in tokens to be used for gambling/purchases in the complex. Do not expect the same perks that go with the big casinos in the USA, such as free food and booze. Sun City and the Lost City are strictly here to take your money, and nothing is free.

Hiking: To soothe the inevitable financial loss, book a guided game walk at Pilanesberg National Park, © (01465) 56135, or Borakalalo National Park, © (011) 465 5423. Hiking huts and food are provided.

expensive

The Palace of the Lost City, ✆ (014657) 73 195, is probably the most luxurious (and the most hyped) hotel in South Africa, and certainly the most interesting of the Sun chain. For once a corporate hotel chain has managed to produce something extraordinary: nothing has been stinted; the marble is real, inlays are of carefully selected hardwoods, and the sculptures, from the life-sized elephant in the entrance hall to the carved wooden foliage in the bedrooms, have been skilfully produced. The effect is of a set from one of Cecil B. de Mille's 1930s Hollywood epics. If only it had been built out in the bush instead of attaching it to the car parks, golf courses and tacky Vegas-style nightlife of Sun City, the Palace would truly be a marvel.

The **Sun Cascades Hotel**, ✆ (01465) 71 268, with indoor fountains, the **Sun City Hotel**, a bland, uninteresting lump of concrete rising from irrigated lawns, and the **Cabanas**, a smaller place set in beautiful gardens, and which for some reason has its own crocodile park, offer plush comfort, but with nothing like the style of the Palace. However, the tariffs are slightly lower and for those intent on gambling it hardly matters what the bedrooms are like, for the casinos stay open all night.

For all of Sun City's hotels, you can book through a central reservation telephone number, ✆ (011) 780 7800.

In the **Pilanesberg National Park**, ✆ (01465) 56 135/57 624–7, three luxurious private lodges offer lavish hospitality and guided game drives. Both have swimming pools and are within reach of Sun City. Pilanesberg also has several luxury tented camps which offer a more tranquil experience of the bush. The new **Madikwe Game Reserve**, north of Mmabatho, also has luxury lodges. Book through Pilanesberg .

The **Taung Sun**, hard by the Taung Heritage Site, ✆ (01405) 41820, offers the usual expensive/bland luxuries of the Sun chain.

moderate and cheap

Pilanesberg National Park, ✆ (01465) 56 135/57 624–7, has two camps at the upper end of the moderate price range, a basic camp site and some shared log cabins that just fall within the cheap range. At **Borakalalo National Park**, ✆ (011) 465 5423, (Golden Leopard Central Reservations) there is a permanent tented camp with ablution blocks and cooking facilities, and a cheaper camp site. At Madikwe there are the **Tau Game Lodge**, ✆ (140) 672030, the **Madikwe River Lodge**, (14778) 891/2 and the more modest **Wonderboom Guest House**, ✆ (1466) 55960/3.

Afrikaans

A Note on Pronunciation

'ou' (as in 'Oupa') is pronounced 'oh'; 'oo' (as in 'kloof') is pronounced 'oo-a'; 'w' is always pronounced as an English 'v', while the Afrikaans 'v' is always pronounced as an English 'f'. If a 'j' is used in a word's spelling (as in 'kopje') it is almost always silent, unless it links two distinct syllables, when it becomes an English 'y', for example 'bobbejaan' (meaning baboon) is pronounced 'bob-e-yarn'; an 'a' is usually pronounced as a long 'ar' (as in Sara); a 'y' used as a vowel (as in 'Strydpoortberg') is pronounced as a long 'a' (as in 'hay'); if a word ends in 'dt', you only pronounce the 't'; a 'tj' or 'ty' (as in Embotyi), is usually pronounced as an English 'k', and the preceding 'o' sounds more like 'oy' as in 'boy'.

An irritating habit among South Africans can be that they begin every sentence with 'No'. This does not mean that they are disagreeing with you. Using the the word is merely a formalized slang method for starting a sentence that is completely neutral, and developed from the Afrikaans *ja-nee* ('yes/no')—a traditionally equivocal way of expressing one's objectivity before expressing an opinion.

Herdboys in Bushman shelter in Lesotho

Language

Afrikaans Basics

yes	*ja*
no	*nee*
Good morning	*goeie More*
Good afternoon	*goeie Middag*
Good evening/night	*goeienag*
please	*asseblief*
thank you	*dankie*
nice, lovely,	*lekker*
very	*baie*
where?	*waar?*
what?	*wat?*
how?	*hoe?*
when?	*waneer?*
to know	*ken*
far	*ver*
and	*en*
from	*van*
to speak	*praat*
Sir	*Meneer*
Madam (also wife)	*Vrou*
I, myself	*Ek*
You	*Jou*
grandfather	*oupa* (often a term of address for an old man)
grandmother	*ouma*
uncle	*oom* (polite term of address for an older man)
left	*links*
right	*regs*
room	*kamer*
information	*inligting*
house	*huis*
shop	*winkel*
town	*stad/dorp*
office	*kantoor*
chemist	*apteek*
station	*stasie*
meat	*vleis*
potatoes	*aartappels*
cheese	*kaas*
tree	*boom*
thorn	*doorn, or doring*
a small stream	*spruit (*pronounced 'sprate')
game reserve	*wildtuin*
beach	*strand*

antelope	*bok*
little antelope	*bokkie* (term of endearment)
pig	*vark*
horse	*perd*
sheep	*skaap*
dog	*hond*
cow	*koei*
lion	*leeu*
leopard	*luiperd*
impala	*rooibok*
rhino	*rhenoster*
zebra	*quagga*
elephant	*olifant*
cheetah	*jagtluiperd*
warthog	*vlakvaark*
vulture	*asvoel*
hippo	*seekoei*
snake	*slang*
spitting cobra	*rinkhals*

Numbers

one	*een*
two	*twee*
three	*drie*
four	*vier*
five	*vyf*
six	*ses*
seven	*sewe*
eight	*ag*
nine	*nege*
ten	*tien*
twenty	*twintig*
thirty	*dertig*
forty	*veertig*
fifty	*vyftig*
hundred	*honderd*

Some Useful Afrikaans Phrases

What is your name?	*Wat is jou naam?*
How much?	*Hoeveel?*
Where is there a filling station?	*waar is daar 'n petrol stasie?*
How far is it to …?	*Hoe ver na?*
I cannot speak Afrikaans	*Ek kan nie Afrikaans praat nie*

English South Africanisms (mostly from Afrikaans words)

Ag Shame	expression of sympathy, 'oh what a pity'
Bakkie	a pick-up truck
blikkiesdorp	mega-hicksville
Boet/ie	little brother
bokdrolletjie	(pronounced 'bok-drollocky'), a ball of antelope dung— amazingly, a term of endearment between lovers
braai or *braaivleis*	barbecue
Brou	brother, as in 'listen my brother'
bundu	bush, as in 'he lives in the bush'
buttons	mandrax (a powerful narcotic)
Café	a grocery store or mini market, almost never a place to have coffee
camp	a fenced field
China	Mate (cockney rhyming slang, brought over by the sailors)
dagga	marijuana
dop	a drink
dorp	a small country town—hicksville
drift	a river ford or crossing of a dry river-bed
vrot	disgusting or rotting, as in 'my mozzie bites went vrot'
fully	absolutely
Howzit?	How d'you do?
Izit?	'oh really?'(polite, not ironic, said very often)
just now, or *now-now*	sometime in the indefinite future
jol	(pronounced 'jawl'), party
kloof	narrow, steep valley
koppie	hill
kraal	livestock pen
Location	a more acceptable word for a black township
Mealie	maize, corn-on-the cob
moere	to kill (usually to beat-up)
moffie	homosexual (derogatory)
meisie	(pronounced 'maisy'), miss, specifically, a young Afrikaans woman
Ou or *Outjie*	a bloke
overseas	abroad
Poort	mountain pass
poytjie	(pronounced 'poyky'), iron pot/a dish slow-cooked in an iron pot
Robots	traffic lights
sif	horrible
sis	'ugh'
stompie	cigarette butts
Takkies	gym shoes or trainers
tikkiedraai	a country dance

toyi-toyi dance seen	(pronounced 'toy-toy'), the distinctive running warrior during black political demonstrations
Tsotsi	black gangsters
voetsek	bugger off (this is the polite interpretation!)
veld	wild land
verlep	tired, worn out
vetkoek	little dough cakes
vlei	marsh or swamp, even if dried-out
zol	(pronounced 'zawl'), marijuana

Xhosa

Note that an 'X' is pronounced as a click.

hello	*molo*
How are you?	*usaphila?*
I am fine, how are you?	*ndisaphila, uphila njani?*
yes	*yebo*
no	*xha*
Where?	*phi?*
Over there	*phaya*
Your cattle are beautiful	*Zintle iinkomo zakho*
sir	*umhlekazi*
madam	*inkhosikazi*
woman	*umfazi*
person	*umntu*
father	*bawo* (polite term of address for an older man)
circumcised boy	*umkhwetha* (in white clay during the initiation rites)
village	*umzi*
hut	*in-dlu*
cattle kraal	*ubuhlanti*
water	*amazi*
ox	*inkabi*
cow	*inkomo*
horse	*ihashe*
dog	*inja*
lion	*ngonyama*
leopard	*ngwe*
jackal	*mpungutye*
rhino	*nkhombe*
wildebeest	*ingu*
giraffe	*indlulamthi*
car	*imoto*
water	*amazi*
the sea	*lwandle*

Johannesburg	*Rawuti*
Cape Town	*Kapa*
Port Elizabeth	*Bhayi*
Grahamstown	*Rini*
East London	*Monti*
Queenstown	*Khomani*

Zulu

Note that although spellings vary the Zulu greetings are also applicable to Siswati.

Hello	*sawubona* (meaning 'I see you')
I'm fine, how are you?	*siyaphila* or *lungili, unjani?* (short for *injani gama lakho*)
We're fine	*iyaphila nathi*
Where are you going?	*uyaphi?*
yes	*yebo*
no	*cha*
Is it far?	*kulude yini?*
lion	*ibhubesi*
leopard	*ingwe*
rhino (white)	*umkhombe*
rhino (black)	*ubhejane*
elephant	*indlovhu*
buffalo	*inyathe*
hippo	*imvubu*
crocodile	*ingwenya*
duiker	*impunze*
red duiker	*umsumpe*
fish eagle	*inkwazi*
green lourie	*igwalagwala*

South Sotho

(or Sesotho, as spoken in Lesotho by the BaSotho)

Hello father (greeting a man)	*lumela ntate*
Hello mother (greeting a woman)	*lumela 'me*
How are you?	*o phela joang?*
I am well	*ke phela hantle*
mountain	*thaba*
water	*meetse*
flock of sheep	*maku*
wild land	*lesoka*

1–3 million years ago	*Australopithecus africanus* present in South Africa (finds at Sterkfontein and Taung caves in Northwest Province).
90,000–1 million years ago	*Homo erectus* present in South Africa (finds at Makapansgat caves in Northwest Province).
30,000 years ago	*Homo sapiens* (possibly San culture) present in South Africa (rock engravings found near the Vaal River in Northwest Province).
2500 years ago	San tribes in Botswana began learning pastoralism from black African tribes, and this practice appeared in the Northern Cape, marking the beginning of Khoi culture.
1300–2000 years ago	Iron-using black peoples first appeared in Northwest Province (possible ancestors of the modern Tswana people).
1415	Portuguese sack the Moorish city of Ceuta in northwest Africa (near modern Tangier) and begin exploring south along Africa's west coast.
1488	Bartholomeu Dias rounds the Cape and enters Mossel Bay.
1490	Dias names the Cape of Good Hope.
1498	Vasco da Gama rounds the Cape, barters with and fires a cannon at the Khoi at Mossel Bay, then sails on to the East Indies.
1590–1650	English and Dutch sailors begin rounding the Cape and trading with the Khoi on their routes east.
1647	Dutch ship *Haarlem* wrecked off Table Bay. Crew survive by trading and hunting.
1652	Dutch East India Company founds relief station at Table Bay. Jan Van Riebeeck sent out with 100 colonists. Cape Town established.
1660s	Dutch settlement expands into today's Winelands and West Coast.
1688	Huguenot settlers arrive from France. Beginning of SA wine cultivation. Beginnings of Cape Khoi resistance to white settlement.

Chronology

1690s	Emergence of the *trekboer* class, who penetrate Namaqualand, the Karoo and modern Garden Route.
1713	Smallpox epidemic devastates Cape Khoi—end of organized Cape Khoi resistance, beginning of their assimilation as a labour class.
1743	Swellendam district established in Overberg.
1750s	*Trekboers* establish farms in Eastern Cape west of Fish River.
1770s	First clashes with Xhosa and *trekboers.* Major civil wars among Xhosa east of Fish River.
1795	Britain annexes the Cape Colony for the first time
1803	Britain gives the Cape back to Holland. First Griqua settlements in Northern Cape.
1806	Britain re-occupies Cape. Wars between the African clans in Natal.
1812	Fourth Frontier War of British against Xhosa under John Graham.
1815	Shaka becomes chief of Zulu and begins wars of conquest against other Natal clans, pushing some on to the highveld.
1819	Fifth Frontier War: Ndlambe Xhosa unsuccessfully attack Grahamstown.
1820	Arrival of British settlers in Algoa Bay—Port Elizabeth founded. Emergence of BaSotho leader Moshoeshoe, whose fortress at Thaba Bosiu near modern Maseru protects his people from wars on the highveld. British traders granted concession at Port Natal by Shaka.
1828	Kat River Colony for Eastern Cape Khoi founded on Ngqika Xhosa land. Shaka assassinated by his brother Dingane.
1830–2	Ndebele establish political mastery over highveld clans, except BaSotho.
1834–5	Ngqika Xhosa invade Cape Colony—Sixth Frontier War. British General Sir Harry Smith murders paramount Xhosa chief Hintsa and illegally annexes land between Keiskamma and Kei Rivers for Britain.
1836	Great Trek starts. Voortekkers under Andries Potgieter defeat Ndebele at Vegkop.
1845	Potgieter founds Ohrigstad (later Lydenburg republic) in Eastern Transvaal after treaty with the Pedi people.
1846	Seventh Frontier War (War of the Axe) between Ngqika Xhosa and British. London Missionary Society sends young Xhosa man Tiyo Soga to Britain for education (graduates from Edinburgh University 10 years later). Boers settle in Swaziland.
1838	Breakaway group of Voortrekkers arrive in Natal under Piet Retief. All but wiped out by Dingane, they rally to defeat the Zulu army at Blood River and drive Dingane north of the Tugela, founding the short-lived Boer republic of Natal.

1839	Natal Boers assist Dingane's brother Mpande to usurp Zulu throne.
1843	Britain annexes Natal from Boers.
1848	Natal Boers trek north to highveld. Potgieter founds a new republic of Zoutpansberg at edge of Venda country. Zoutpansberg Boers begin slave raids against peoples of the Transvaal.
1850–53	Eighth Frontier War between Xhosa and British. Kat River Khoi join Xhosa, both suffer loss of independence in aftermath. Moshoeshoe prevents Boers from annexing his BaSotho kingdom and sues for peace with British crown.
	Last San rock artist killed in Natal Drakensberg.
1854	Orange Free State proclaimed.
1856–7	Great Cattle killing among Xhosa. Tens of thousands starve.
1860	The three Boer republics in the Transvaal amalgamate to become the South African Republic (SAR). First Indian labourers arrive in Natal to cut the new sugar-cane plantations of the coast.
1865	Moshoeshoe fights off the Orange Free State Boers.
1867	Hopetown diamond found near Vaal River. Venda sack Schoemansdal and Boers driven from far Northern Transvaal for a generation.
1871	Kimberley diamond strike made. Britain annexes Griqualand West. Start of migrant labour tradition as black Africans travel to Kimberley to work the claims.
1877–8	Britain annexes SAR and defeats the Pedi nation in Eastern Transvaal. Ninth and last Frontier War ends Xhosa military resistance.
1879	Anglo-Zulu War. Britain annexes Zululand and imprisons Cetshwayo, the Zulu king.
1880–1	De Beers mining company founded in Kimberley by Cecil Rhodes. SAR Boers eject British occupation troops at battle of Majuba, beginning and ending the short-lived first Anglo–Boer War. Gun War in BaSotholand (modern Lesotho) lost by British. Xhosa intellectual leader J. T. Jabavu founds the first African language newspaper.
1884	BaSotholand becomes a British protectorate.
1886	Gold deposits found in the Witwatersrand. Johannesburg founded.
1890	De Beers company gains control of all Kimberley diamond mines. Cecil Rhodes becomes Cape Colony's Prime Minister.
1893	Gandhi arrives in Durban.
1894	*Uitlander* cause taken up by Johannesburg, Cape Press and London.
1895	Jameson Raid against Paul Kruger's government fails.
1899	Outbreak of Second Anglo-Boer War. Venda and Kgatla people of Northern Transvaal defeat Boers and drive them from Soutpansberg and northern lowveld.

1902	Boers surrender at Pretoria. End of Second Anglo-Boer War. Transvaal and Orange Free State recognized as British territory.
1903–7	South Africa's gold output exceeds 30 per cent of world total. Gandhi begins self-help project for poor Indians outside Durban.
1908	Gandhi organizes passive resistance campaign in protest at Indians being made to carry pass books.
1910	Union of South Africa created as a British Dominion. Ex-Boer general Louis Botha becomes its first Prime Minister.
1911	Laws passed to prevent blacks from holding skilled jobs in the mines.
1912	South African National Native Congress (SANNC) formed (the forerunner of the ANC).
1913	Over 20,000 white mineworkers strike in protest against mining companies' threat to overturn skilled labour colour bar. Natives Land Act passed, preventing blacks from becoming large landowners.
1914	South Africa enters the First World War. More mass strikes in Witwatersrand among white workers put down using 70,000 troops. National Party formed in Bloemfontein. Gandhi returns to India.
1916	Battle of Delville Wood in France, tens of thousands of South African troops killed. J. T. Jabavu founds first black university at Fort Hare.
1918	First World War ends. First strike by Africans—Johannesburg's 'bucket boys' (night-soil removers) negotiate a small wage increase. Underground right-wing *Afrikaner broederbond* founded.
1919	Jan Smuts becomes Prime Minister. First black trade union founded.
1920	70,000 blacks in the Witwatersrand strike over wage increases. Protests against Pass Laws across the Transvaal. Put down by police.
1922	General Strike of white workers over threatened mine closures and lifting of the skilled job colour bar brings the whole Witwatersrand to a halt. The army is sent in and over 200 strikers are killed.
1923	SANNC becomes the African National Congress (ANC).
1927	Compulsory racial segregation in cities.
1929	National Party leader Barry Hertzog wins general election.
1934	Hertzog and Smuts form joint United South National Party government—too liberal for hardline Afrikaners, who break away under D. F. Malan to form new National Party (NP).
1936	Cape black Africans lose their franchise.
1939	Outbreak of Second World War. Hertzog resigns, Smuts becomes Prime Minister. Many right-wing Boers oppose British war effort.
1940–6	Blacks in the Witwatersrand organize a series of successful bus boycotts, pay strikes and squatter camp movements. Soon after the armistice, a black mineworkers' strike is broken by police.

1948	Right-wing, Afrikaner-led National Party wins general election. Era of official apartheid begins.
1949	Mixed marriages made illegal.
1950	Group Areas Act passed: blacks no longer to live in 'white' areas but in separate 'locations' (townships).
1952	Reference books (new pass books) to be carried by all non-whites.
1953	Education Act passed; blacks denied access to white universities.
1955	Sophiatown in Johannesburg razed. Black residents forcibly removed to new township of Soweto.
1956	Cape 'coloureds' disenfranchised. Government crackdown on all 'subversive' groups (including ANC and South African Communist Party) leads to mass 'Treason Trials' which last until 1960, effectively immoblizing resistance leadership.
1959	PAC formed.
1960	PAC leads massive anti-reference book protests in Witwatersrand. During demonstrations at Sharpeville, police open fire on unarmed protesters, killing over 200. Government declares State of Emergency and bans ANC and PAC, whose leaders go into exile and form armed wings. Nelson Mandela becomes head of MK, military wing of the ANC and goes to Ethiopia for training.
1962–3	Mandela returns to South Africa and is arrested. MK leadership arrested at Rivonia near Johannesburg. Government witch-hunt nets most ANC and PAC leaders, who are imprisoned (including Mandela). Beginning of 'Silent Decade' for South African resistance to white rule.
1966	District Six in Cape Town razed. 'Coloured' inhabitants forcibly removed to new township of Mitchell's Plain on Cape Flats.
1969	Start of Steve Biko's 'Black Consciousness' movement.
1974	South African troops sent into Angola to destabilize revolutionary government there. Namibia occupied.
1976	Soweto uprising of black schoolchildren protests the forced learning of Afrikaans. Pitched battles with police and army. Government begins 'Tribal Homelands' policy to form 11 'bantustans' (lasts until 1981). Tens of thousands of blacks across the country forcibly removed from their farms and resettled in the 'homelands', losing their property.
1977	Steve Biko dies while in police detention in Port Elizabeth.
1982–3	Mass factional violence in Soweto, between supporters of PAC and Biko's 'Black Consciousness', continuing throughout 1980s.
1984	United Democratic Front (UDF) formed as an above-ground wing of banned ANC.

1985	National Union of Mineworkers (a black union) founded. Township violence intensifies. Government calls State of Emergency. Anyone suspected of subversive activity detained without trial, including many white UDF members.
1986	International Sanctions hit South African economy. Half-hearted reforms made by apartheid government include abolition of Pass Laws.
1988	F. W. de Klerk becomes Prime Minister. Pledges further reforms. Far-right breaks away to form Conservative Party. Militant Afrikaner military wing, the AWB, formed.
1990	Nelson Mandela freed from 27 years' detention.
1990–3	F. W. de Klerk pledges commitment to a democratic government. Political vigilante forces claim thousands of lives in townships and mineworkers' hostels—many people suspect involvement of government security forces (referred to as 'Third Force'). Political battling between ANC and Zulu-based Inkatha Freedom Party (IFP) reaches fever pitch in Natal Midlands. AWB pledge to go to war against any black-led government. Massive private disinvestment of whites as those who can leave the country, leave.
1994	Democratic elections held with almost no violence. IFP decides to support the elections at the last minute. ANC voted in by huge majority. 'Homelands' abolished and re-absorbed into South Africa. MK absorbed into South African army. Nelson Mandela becomes state president.

History/Early Accounts

Portuguese Voyages, Everyman Library, 1960. Contains the journal of Vasco da Gama, who rounded the Cape and bartered with the Khoi people in 1497/8.

South African Journal 1834–1836, by Andrew Smith, edited by W.F. Lye, published for the South African Museum by A. A. Balkema, 1975. An epic, if understated, eye-witness journal from one of the first English-speakers to penetrate the highveld regions. Smith met and talked with such legendary figures as Moshoeshoe, Mzilikazi, Waterboer.

Baines' Journal of Residence in Africa 1842–1853, Van Riebeeck Society, 1964. Pictures and travelling diary by a remarkable adventurer who witnessed the last Frontier Wars of the Eastern Cape.

Travels in South Africa, by Anthony Trollope (written (1877), Allan Sutton, 1987. An objective travelogue dealing with social, political, geographical and economic issues in late 19th-century South Africa, humorously written, with a great eye for landscape and blessedly free from colonial racism.

The Shaping of South African Society 1652–1820, edited by R. Elphick and H. Giliomme. Clear commentary on the early white settlers and their effect on the Cape Khoi, San and Xhosa peoples.

A History of Natal, University of Natal Press, Brookes and Webb, 1965. A straightforward, if rather colonial, account from the 1490s onwards.

Thank God We Kept the Flag Flying, Heinemann, 1974. An irreverent, deadly accurate look at the Siege of Ladysmith in 1900.

The Boer War Diary of Sol. T. Plaatje, Sphere Books, 1976. An in-depth eye-witness account of the siege of Mafeking during the Second Anglo–Boer War (1899–1902). A dispassionate tale of British arrogance and double-dealing.

To the Bitter End, by Emmanuel Lee, Penguin, 1985. Informative pictorial history of the Second Anglo-Boer War.

The Boer War, by Thomas Packenham, Abacus, 1979. Solid and informative.

The Scramble for Africa, by Thomas Packenham, Abacus, 1991. Puts the 19th-century colonial confusion into its European perspective.

The Old Transvaal 1834–1899, by Cartwright and Cowan, Purnall, 1978. Good photographic record, including the early towns and main personalities, both black and white.

Reader's Digest History of South Africa—the Real Story, edited by Dougie Oakes and Chris Saunders PhD (Cape Town). A superbly readable, comprehensive history from the earliest pre-human remains to 1990, with chapters by various academic experts.

A New Illustrated History of South Africa, edited by Trewella Cameron and S. B. Spies, Human and Rousseau, 1991.Very useful for those interested in the fate of the Cape Khoi.

Further Reading

George Grey and the Xhosa, by G. Weldon, Heinemann-Centaur, 1993, a well-researched school text on the Xhosa people before, during and after the Frontier Wars, and the colonial policies affecting them.

People and Power, by Andrew Proctor, Academic Books (Harare), 1994. A good, straight-forward account of the complex political and social upheavals that have shaped South Africa. Particularly good for understanding the rise of the Zulu empire.

Frontiers, by Noel Mostert, Pimlico Press, 1991. The history of the Xhosa people and the tragedy of the Frontier Wars; South African history traced with academic precision, and a master's pen, from prehistory to the present. An impassioned account, beautifully written.

Black Consciousness in South Africa, by Steve Biko, Vintage Books, 1979. The last writings before his death.

Wildlife and Natural History

Field Guide to the Mammals of Southern Africa, by Chris and Tilde Stuart, New Holland, 1992. Detailed treatment of characteristics and behaviour from the largest to the smallest. Good photographic identification guide. Handbook size.

Field Guide to the Snakes of Southern Africa, by Bill Branch, New Holland, 1993. Same format as above. Handbook size.

Field Guide to the Butterflies of Southern Africa, by Ivor Migdoll, New Holland, 1993. If you intend spending time in the southern Cape forests, pack this book. Handbook size.

Roberts Birds of Southern Africa, by Gordon Maclean. The well-acknowledged twitcher's bible. Recommended by the Ornithological Society of Southern Africa. A large handbook.

The Plains of the Camdeboo, by Eve Palmer, Collins, 1966—a beautifully written account of the natural history of the Eastern Karoo's rich semi-desert environment, centred around a farm near Graaff-Reinet. Fauna from fossils to *trekbokke* to the recolonization of the farm-lands by wild animals. Entomologists and botanists will also find much here.

The Soul of the White Ant, and *My Friends the Baboons*, by Eugene Marais. Beautifully if a little whimsically written in the 1930s by the poet, natural historian (and opium addict). For a sense of South Africa's fierce but gentle natural rhythms they are hard to beat.

Veld Plants of Southern Africa, by Hobson, Jessop, Ginn and Kelly, Macmillan, 1975. Everything you need to know, including medicinal/other uses. Coffee table size.

Field Guide to the Trees of Southern Africa, by Eve Palmer, Collins, 1977. Handbook size.

Landscapes and Geography

A Guide to the Rocks and Minerals and Gems of Southern Africa, by E. K. Macintosh, Struik, 1976. Good colour pictures.

Land of Beauty and Splendour, by T. V. Bulpin, Reader's Digest, 1976. Despite the corny title, a photographic coffee table book that does justice to the southern African landscape.

The National Parks of Southern Africa, by Gordon and Bannister, New Holland, 1992. Spectacular photographic record of the landscape, flora and fauna of most of the country's national parks (the latest ones, such as the Richtersveld and Vaalbos, are sadly absent) with an informative text. Coffee table size.

The Living Deserts of Southern Africa, by Barry Lovegrove, Fernwood Press, 1993. A beautiful book, with a rare focus on the Namaqualand and Karoo semi-deserts, as well as the better-known Kalahari and Namib. Coffee table size.

The Mountains of Southern Africa, by Briston and Ward, Struik, 1988. Not all the ranges are treated, but geological histories are accurate and photographs good. Coffee table size.

This is South Africa, by Peter Borchett, New Holland, 1993. Despite the twee title, a good general introduction to the people, landscapes and wildlife. Coffee table size.

Culture, Myth and Legend

Myths and Legends of Southern Africa, Penny Miller, T. V. Bulpin Publications, 1979. A beautifully illustrated (by the author) guide to the rich mythology of the sub-continent, from Cape Malay and Afrikaans legends to Swazi, Zulu, Xhosa, Sotho, Venda and even up to the Herero of Namibia and the Mashona of Zimbabwe. Pure delight.

The Lost World of the Kalahari, by Laurens Van der Post, Penguin, 1962. A moving account of the San people's besieged primeval culture.

Nisa, by Marjorie Shostak, Earthscan Publications Ltd, 1990. A laudably straightforward record of the life-story of a San woman of the Kalahari, from childhood, through adolescence and sexual exploration to motherhood and maturity.

The White-Faced Huts, H. F. Sampson, 1979. Cases of witchcraft killings in the Transkei 1930–55 by an advocate of the supreme court. A strange read.

The Griquas of Griqualand, by S. J. Halford, Juta and Co. Ltd., a dispassionate, colonial account of the people of TransOrangia's wild past.

White Tribe Dreaming, by Marq De Villiers, Macmillan Canada, 1987. A look at the Afrikaner myth of might and right.

Soweto, by Peter Magubane, Struik, 1990. Everything from coal merchants and football teams to glue sniffing by one of South Africa's best photographers. Coffee table size

Dorps, by Roger Ballen, Clifton Publications, 1986. Photographs of modern poor white life in the *platteland* towns. Coffee table size.

Language

Lumko—Self-Instruction Course in Xhosa, Rhodes University Press, 1969. An all-purpose primer with some useful phrases.

A Southern Sotho/English Dictionary, by P. A. Paroz, Morija Sesotho, 1950.

Handbook of the Northern Sotho Language, J. C. Van Schaik, 1969.

Tsonga Proverbs, Junod and Jaques, Central Mission Press, 1957. A sensitive collection of wise (and often humorous) sayings from the Tsonga people in both Tsonga and English.

Transvaal Ndebele Texts, N. J. Warmelo, 1930. Poems in Ndebele and translation.

Zulu Proverbs, by C. L. S. Nyembezi, Witswatersrand University Press, 1954. Also much poetry here, with the Zulu texts translated and explained.

A Grammar of Afrikaans, by Bruce C. Donaldson, Mouton and Greyer, 1980.

Art and Architecture

Major Rock Paintings of Southern Africa, edited by Tim Maggs, Indiana University Press, 1979. Superb pictures and interpretative text as well as where to find the featured pictures.

Rock Engravings of Southern Africa, by Thomas A. Dowson, Witwatersrand University Press, 1992. Similar to the above, plus some good sections on mythology.

South African Graphic Art and its Techniques, by F. L. Alexander, 1974. Colonial to township art; all the big names plus some you've never heard of. Good reproductions.

The Life and Sculptures of Sister Joe Vorster, by Naka Pitman, Hugh Keartland Publishing 1976. Remarkable photographic record of the artist's life-like sculptures of San people, some of which can be found in the Pretoria National Cultural History Museum.

The South African Mural, by Changuion and Mathews, Struik, 1989. Mostly South Sotho and Ndebele house painting, with a good interpretative text.

The African Dream—the art of John Muafengo, by Orde Levinson (foreword by Nelson Mandela, Thames and Hudson, 1992. Mostly lino cuts by the well-known township artist, depicting scenes from rural life and wilderness to the spirit world and township life.

Cape Wine Homesteads, Hoefsloot and Parma, A. D. Donker, 1980. All you need to know about Cape Dutch styles.

Historical Buildings in South Africa, by Desiree Picton-Seymour, Struik, 1988. Cape Dutch to Art Deco, plus where to find the best buildings.

Food and Wine

Leipoldt's Cape Cookery, by C. Louis Leipoldt, W. J. Flesch and Partners, 1976. Brief, but an acknowledged masterpiece on Cape Cuisine and *veldkos* by the famous poet, doctor and gourmet (who died in 1947 and is buried on the Pakhuis Pass in the Cape's Cedarberg Mountains). Recipes from ultra-traditional *boboties* to lion steak and tortoise in jelly.

Food from the Veld, by Fox and Young, Delta Books, 1982. The complete veldkos.

The South Africa Wine Buyer's Guide, by Dave Hughes, Struik Timmins, 1993. Essential handbook for those really interested in what is produced where.

South African Literature, Prose

A Century of South African Short Stories, Marquard Ed., A.D. Donker, 1978. All the big names and some of the little ones.

The Story of an African Farm, by Olive Schreiner, Penguin London, 1981. First published in 1883, an authentic, if overly tortured tale of life and love on an isolated white farm in the arid, Biblical landscape of the Great Karoo.

Mafeking Road, by Herman Charles Bosman, Human and Rousseau. Short stories by the Afrikaans writer dealing with Boer life in the Western Transvaal.

From the Pit of Hell to the Spring of Life, by Daniel Kunene, Ravan Press, 1986. Stories of apartheid in the mid 1960s and '70s seen through the black middle-class eye.

A Walk in the Night, by Alex La Guma, Heinemann, 1967. An exceptional picture of poor 'coloured' life in Cape Town—a culture that usually goes unseen by white tourists, yet is responsible for Cape Town's whole atmosphere of fatalistic *joie de vivre.*

The Lying Days, by Nadine Gordimer, Penguin, 1980. Her first novel, set in the early 1950s in bohemian Johannesburg. Written before Sharpeville, this was one of the first books to set out the injustices of apartheid,

A Dry White Season, by Andre Brink, W. H. Allen, 1969. A young Afrikaner tries to investigate the circumstances of a black friend's death while in police detention, and finds himself in the dark, confused world of Soweto at the height of apartheid oppression.

Cry the Beloved Country, by Alan Paton, Scribner and Sons, 1948. Written the year the first apartheid government came to power—the story of a Zulu minister from Natal coming to Johannesburg to look for his lost son.

I Write What I Like, by Steve Biko, Penguin, 1988. A burningly perceptive look at black endeavour and white obstruction by the man who gave his life for his beliefs.

Waiting For the Barbarians, by J. M. Coetzee, Penguin, 1988. Allegorical tale of the impending end of apartheid written as if on an imperial outpost of the ancient world.

All One Horse, by Breyton Breytonbach, Faber and Faber, 1990. Surreal stories by the man regarded by many as South Africa's best white writer.

You Can't Get Lost in Cape Town, by Zoe Wicomb, Virago, 1987. A 'coloured' girl student from Namaqualand's tragic involvement with a white boyfriend.

My Traitor's Heart, by Rian Malan, Bodley Head, 1990. Powerfully written, nothing in here is fiction. Those who wish to understand modern South Africa must read this book.

Last Days in Cloud Cuckooland, by Graham Boynton, Random House, 1997. Journalistic vignettes charting the recent upheaval in the lives of white South Africans.

South African Literature, Poetry

The Penguin Book of South African Verse, edited by Jack Cope and Uys Krige, Penguin, 1968. From early San and Khoi songs, to 19th-century Zulu, Sotho and Xhosa praise poems, to more contemporary black and white poetry.

Lithoko—Sotho Praise Poems, by Damane and Saunders, Clarendon Press, 1974. Stirring warrior poems from the old oral tradition.

Musho!, Zulu Popular Praises, by Gunner and Gwala, Michigan University Press, 1991. More stirring stuff.

South Africa in Poetry, edited by Johan Wyk and Pieter Conradie, Owen Burgess Publishing, 1988. Comprehensive anthology from prehistoric oral traditions to the present.

Black Mamba Rising, an anthology, Worker Resistance and Culture Publications, University of Natal, for Cosatu Workers' Cultural Local, 1986. South African worker poets in struggle. Powerful, bitter poems of black humiliation and anger under apartheid.

Prey, by Dennis Brutus, published in the anthology *Voices of 20th-Century Africa*, Faber and Faber, 1988, is more considered. A 'coloured' English teacher born in Zimbabwe, Brutus was interned, shot and beaten, but survived to write some superb poetry

Travel Literature, Narrative

Jock of the Bushveld, by Sir Percy Fitzpatrick, Longmann Green, 1909. A beautifully illustrated account of the life of a freebooting hunter in the lowvveld of the late 19th century.

Forty Years in Africa, by Major Tudor Trevor, Hurst and Blackett, 1932. A very colonial view, but engagingly written and providing an eye-witness account of the adventurous life of a young Englishman on the Transvaal frontier back in the 'earlies'.

Bushveld Doctor, by the doctor, poet and gourmet C. Louis Leipoldt, Lowry, 1989. Written in 1989, this is Leipoldt's account of his time as inspector of schools in the Eastern Transvaal lowveld in the 1920s and '30s. Combines an unromantic journal of the poverty and sickliness of the lowveld Afrikaner families of the time with chapters on birds, beasts and magic. A must for travellers in Mpumalanga.

The Electronic Elephant, by Dan Jacobson, Hamish Hamilton, 1994. Engaging look at the dry regions of Northern Cape and Northwest Province in footsteps of early missionaries.

Travel Literature, Practical

Discovering Southern Africa, by T. V. Bulpin, T. V. Bulpin Publications, 1992. An entertaining, informative introduction to almost every town and region in the sub-continent No places to stay or eat, but excellent background information. Large handbook size.

Field Guide to the National Parks and Nature Reserves of Southern Africa, by Chris and Tilde Stuart, Struik, 1993. Useful list of every single protected wildlife area, with maps, access information, fauna and some flora, hiking trails, accommodation. Handbook size.

Mike Lundy's Best Walks in the Cape Peninsula, Struik, 1991. Superb, detailed information on foot forays in the mountains and on the beaches. Small handbook.

Day Walks in and around Cape Town, by Tim Anderson, Struik, 1990. Well laid out and informative set of walks in old Cape Town and the Winelands. Small handbook size.

The Complete Guide to Walks and Trails in Southern Africa, by Jaynee Levy, Struik, 1993. A must for anyone who wants to get out into the *veld*, the trails for foot, horse and canoe are described in detail. Heavy for a backpack, but worth consulting before setting off.

A Backer's Guide to Lesotho, by Russell Suchet, Sani Lodge Publications, 1993. An in-depth and sensitive guide for the budget traveller and hiker—the author has spent many years travelling the 'kingdom of the clouds'. Small handbook size.

The Swaziland Jumbo Guide, by Hazel Hussey, Hussey and Co. Publications, 1992. A good all-round guide to what's available at all budgets, with some very well informed cultural background. Handbook size.

A Guide to the Guest Farms and Country Lodges of Southern Africa, Struik, 1994. Very useful for mid-budget travellers. Covers all areas.

Page numbers in **bold** indicate main references. Page numbers in *italics* refer to maps. There is a separate wildlife index at the end of the main index, p.652.

Index

Port Nolloth 285–6
Port St Johns 367–8
Port Shepstone 393
Portuguese 35–6
Potberg Mountain 208
Potchefstroom 611–12
Potgieters, Andries 559
Potgietersrus 590
practical A–Z **12–32**
Prentjiesberg Hiking Trail 336
Pretoria 528–41, *534–5*
    city centre 533, 536
    eating out 539–40
    entertainment 540
    getting around 532
    getting there 531–2
    history 529–31
    music 541
    nightlife 540
    suburbs 536–8
    tourist information 532
    where to stay 538–9
Pretorius, Andries 379, 529
Pretorius, Marthinius 529
Prince Albert 270
Prince Alfred's Pass 256
Pringle, Thomas 332
Prinsloo, Jan 257–8
private game reserves 31
pronunciation 619
prose 104–6
Protea Heights Nature Reserve 169
Provincial Parks 23
public holidays 24
Python God 597
Qacha's Nek 457
Qolora Mouth 366
Qora Mouth 366
Queenstown 348–50
Quthing 457
Qwa Qwa 418
Rain Queen 587
Ramsgate 394
Ramskop Nature reserve 220
Read, James 338, 351
Readsdale Forest 342
religion 85–6
reptiles **65–6**, 376
Retief, Piet 183, 378, 409

Rex, George 234–5
Rharabe 309, 312
Rhebokskloof winery 176
Rhodes 335
Rhodes, Cecil **40–1**, 294, 505, 31
    house (Groot Schuur) 97–8, 138
    Rhodes Cottage (Muizenberg) 142
Richards Bay 435
Richtersveld National Park 286–7
riding 27
Riebeek Kasteel 226
Riebeek West 225–6
Rietfontein 302
Riversdale 231
Roaring Sands 297
Robben Island 136, **149**
Robberg Nature Reserve 239
Robertson **192**, 195
Rocher Pan Nature Reserve 215
rock art 98–9, 335, 342
Roggeveldberg Mountains 267
Rolfontein Nature Reserve 278
rondavels 98
Roodeplat Nature Reserve 541–2
Rorke's Drift 430–1, 432
Royal Natal National Park 417
Rugged Glen Nature Reserve 417–18
Rust De Winter Nature Reserve 544
Rust-en-Vrede Waterfall 253
Rustenberg winery 169
Rustenburg Nature Reserve 544
Rustler's Valley 466–7
S.A. Lombard Nature Reserve 613
Sabie 557
SACP (South African Communist Party) 43, 402
Sadawa 188
Safari Ostrich Show Farm 252–3
safaris 3, 28
safety 24–5
    Cape Town 127
    Drakensberg 415–16
    Lesotho 446
    Swaziland 482
    Transkei 361–2, 366

Sagola Spa 599
St Helena Bay 214
St Lucia Nature Reserve 435–6
St Michael's-on-Sea 393
Saldanha Bay 210, **213–14**, 217
Salem 329
Salt Rock 395
Sam Knott Reserve 330
San 34, 35, **88**
    Drakensberg 413–14
    Northern Cape 289
    Northern Province 578
    poetry 101
    rock art 98–9, 335, 342
    spirituality 108
    Western Cape 117, 197
    Western Karoo 266
Sandile's Grave 344
Sandveld Nature Reserve 477
Sandy Bay 147
sangomas 107
Sani Pass 416
Sani Top 457
Sao Ganzalo 239
SAR (South African Republic) 40, 504–5, 529–31, 579, 607
Sardinia Bay 324
Sarili 359–60
Scarborough 148
Schoemanskloof 554
Schreiner, Olive 104
Scottburgh 393
scuba diving 29
Sea Point 146
Seal Island 136, 233
Second World War 120
Secretary Bird Walk 557
Sedgefield 234
Sehlabethebe National Park 457
self catering holidays 4–5
self-drive safaris 3
Semonkong 455
Sendelingsdrift 286
Settler Country 324–32
    activities 331
    where to stay 331–2
Seymour 342
Shaka 377, 378, **428–9**
Shakaland 432–3
Shaka's Rock 395

Wildlife Index

Picture Credits

All photographs used to illustrate the cover and the Wildlife chapter of this guide are © South African Tourism Board except for the following, which are © **Bruce Coleman Collection:**

Caracal, *p.59*, Steven C. Kaufman

Black-backed Jackal, *p.61*, HPH Photography

Hyrax, *p.63*, Peter Evans

Eland, *p.67*, Dr Eckart Pott

Roan, *p.68*, Rod Williams

Blesbok, *p.70*, HPH Photography, Heinrich v.d. Berg

Oribi, *p.70*, Johnny Johnson

Klipspringer, *p.70*, Theo Allofs

Steenbok, *p.71*, Werner Layer

Sacred Ibis, *p.74*, Trevor Barrett

Saddlebill Stork, *p.74*, Tero Niemi

Cattle Egret, *p.75*, HPH Photography

Hornbill, *p.75*, HPH Photography, Heinrich v.d. Berg

Whydah, *p.76*, Gunter Ziesler

Hoepoe, *p.76*, N.G. Blake

Crowned Crane, *p.77*, HPH Photography

Bishop Bird, *p.77*, HPH Photography, Philip van den Berg

Little Bee-eater, *p.78*, HPH Photography, Heinrich v.d. Berg

Grey Lourie, *p.78*, Werner Layer

Southern Right Whale, *p.79*, Jeff Foott Productions

Cape Fur Seal, *p.79*, HPH Photography

Great White Shark, *p.80*, Carl Roessler

Also Available from Cadogan Guides...

Country Guides

Antarctica
Belize
The Caribbean and Bahamas
Central Asia
China: The Silk Routes
Egypt
France: Southwest France;
    Dordogne, Lot & Bordeaux
France: Southwest France;
    Gascony & the Pyrenees
France: Brittany
France: The South of France
France: The Loire
Germany
Germany: Bavaria
Greece: The Greek Islands
Guatemala
India
India: South India
India: Goa
Ireland
Ireland: Southwest Ireland
Ireland: Northern Ireland

Italy
Italy: The Bay of Naples and
    Southern Italy
Italy: Lombardy, Milan and the
    Italian Lakes
Italy: Tuscany and Umbria
Italy: Three Cities—Rome, Florence
    and Venice
Japan
The Yucatán and Southern Mexico
Morocco
Portugal
Portugal: The Algarve
Scotland
Scotland's Highlands and Islands
Spain
Spain: Southern Spain
Spain: Northern Spain
Syria & Lebanon
Tunisia
Turkey
Zimbabwe, Botswana and Namibia

City Guides

Amsterdam
Brussels, Bruges, Ghent & Antwerp
Florence, Siena, Pisa & Lucca
London
Manhattan

Moscow & St Petersburg
Paris
Prague
Rome

Island Guides

The Caribbean: NE Caribbean;
   The Leeward Islands
The Caribbean: SE Caribbean;
   The Windward Islands
The Caribbean: Jamaica
Crete
Cyprus

Malta
Mykonos, Santorini & the Cyclades
Rhodes & the Dodecanese
Corfu & the Ionian Islands
Madeira & Porto Santo
Sicily

Lazy Days

Lazy Days Out across the Channel
Lazy Days Out in Tuscany
Lazy Days Out in Provence
Lazy Days Out in Andalucía

Lazy Days Out in the Loire
Lazy Days Out in the Dordogne & Lot

Plus...

Southern Africa on the Wild Side
Healthy Travel: Bugs, Bites & Bowels
Travel by Cargo Ship
Henry Kelly in the West of Ireland
London Markets
Mars
Hell